★★★★★★★★★★★★★

The Folklore of American Holidays

★★★★★★★★★★★★★

SECOND EDITION

The Folklore of American Holidays

SECOND EDITION

A Compilation of More Than 500 Beliefs, Legends,
Superstitions, Proverbs, Riddles, Poems, Songs, Dances,
Games, Plays, Pageants, Fairs, Foods, and Processions Associated
with Over 120 American Calendar Customs and Festivals

Hennig Cohen and Tristram Potter Coffin, Editors

Gale Research Inc. • DETROIT • LONDON

Permission to reprint copyrighted material has been kindly granted
by the following publications, organizations, and individuals:

*American Anthropologist, American Quarterly, American Speech, Atlanta Journal-Constitu-
tion, Baltimore Sun, Boston Globe, Charlotte Observer, Chicago Tribune, Classic, Detroit Free
Press, Detroit News, El Palacio, Ethnicity, The Horse Digest, Inside, Jewish Exponent, Journal
of American Folklore, Journal of the West, Kentucky Folklore Record, Louisville Journal-
Courier and Times, Mississippi Folklore Register, New Mexico Folklore Record, New York
Folklore Quarterly, New York Times, New Yorker, Orlando Sentinel, Pennsylvania Dutchman,
Pennsylvania Folklife, Philadelphia Bulletin, Philadelphia Inquirer, Play as Context, Provi-
dence Journal-Bulletin, Smithsonian, Southwest Journal of Anthropology, Tennessee Folklore
Society Bulletin, Tradition, Travel & Leisure, Travel-Holiday, Traveler, Utah Historical
Quarterly, Village Voice, Washington Post, Western Folklore, Wilmington News-Journal*

Texas Folklore Society, Wayne State University Folklore Archive

Diane Ackerman, Leland Agan, Janice Beran, Edwin Buxbaum, Linda Dégh,
Shifra Epstein, Richard Feinberg, Father Felician, John A. Gutowski,
Colleen Hayes, Bronius Juodelis, William Kenney, Constance Poten,
Ruth Rubin, Benson Schambelan, Lucien K. Truscott, IV, Evon Z. Vogt, Marta Weigle

Please refer to the *Source* and *Source and Comment* sections for
complete references to reprinted material.

Cover photograph by Arthur Chartow

The paper used in this publication meets the minimum requirements
of American National Standard for Information Sciences—Permanence
Paper for Printed Library Materials, ANSI Z39.48-1984. ∞™

Library of Congress Cataloging-in-Publication Data

The Folklore of American holidays / Hennig Cohen
and Tristram Potter Coffin, editors. — 2nd ed.

    p.   cm.
    "A Compilation of more than 500 beliefs, legends,
superstitions, proverbs, riddles, poems, songs, dances,
games, plays, pageants, fairs, foods, and processions
associated with over 120 American calendar customs
and festivals."
    Includes index.
    ISBN 0-8103-7602-4 ; $85.00
    1. Holidays—United States.   2. Folklore—Unit-
ed States. 3. Festivals—United States.   4. United
States—Social life and customs.   I. Cohen, Hennig.   II. Coffin, Tristram Potter, 1922–
    GT4803.F65   1991
    394.2'6973—dc20   91-14994
                            CIP

Printed in the United States of America.

Published simultaneously in the United Kingdom
by Gale Research International Limited
(An affiliated company of Gale Research Inc.)

Contents

The Folklore of American Holidays

Indexes

Preface

The Folklore of American Holidays presents the folklore associated with calendar customs and festivals that have become an integral part of the social habits of Americans in general, as well as regional, occupational, or ethnic groups in particular. While some holidays have arisen from ancient practices, others are fresh attempts to celebrate neglected festivals or, in some cases, the results of political or ethnic groups wishing to strengthen their sense of identity. Still other holidays have been created by the passage of laws. The traditional lore surrounding a given holiday, regardless of its origin, comprises the heart of this book.

Scope

The Folklore of American Holidays contains over 525 items of folklore associated with more than 120 American holidays and festivals. This reference source is designed to meet the information needs of a wide variety of users—librarians, historians, scholars, researchers, students, general readers—by providing in one convenient location a listing of American holidays and the lore and legend associated with them. Holidays included in *The Folklore of American Holidays* range from well-known religious and secular holidays, such as Christmas and Independence Day, to more obscure celebrations like Tater Day. The equally diverse items of folklore following each holiday vividly illustrate the rich body of history behind these special celebrations, thus providing a ready source of information for researchers seeking facts, librarians fielding questions, pageant chairpersons looking for inspiration, or general readers simply satisfying their curiosity.

Two questions were used to decide a holiday's suitability for inclusion: "Would this festival continue to be celebrated if there were no legal or commercial reason to celebrate it? Is the event creating, or has it in the past created, its own set of traditions, with associated legends, anecdotes, superstitions, foods, and the like?" If the answer was "yes" to either or both questions, the editors included the festival and associated folklore in *The Folklore of American Holidays.*

The Folklore of American Holidays reflects the ever-evolving culture of America from colonial times to the present. Oral traditions brought from already-established cultures in the Old World to America evolved as immigrants intermingled their traditions and developed new ones. With the changes in immigration patterns, American culture—and thus its folklore—changed as well. Therefore, alongside the Irish St. Patrick's Day Parade and Italian St. Anthony's Festa, readers will find the Puerto Rican San Juan Day and Vietnamese Tet. Some holidays and types of folklore may be more extensively treated than others simply due to the limitations of available published material. But *The Folklore of American Holidays* aims to capture the spirit and richness of American festivals and represent the vast range of associated lore: legends, beliefs, proverbs, superstitions, charms, sayings, songs, recipes, processions, parades, pageants, fairs, food, games, gifts, dances, contests, poems, riddles, music, plays.

Compilation Methods

The items of folklore in this book have been selected by the editors from a wide range of published sources and unpublished collections, including scholarly journals in the areas of folklore and local history, doctoral dissertations, public and private archives, private collections, and even newspapers, magazines, souvenir programs, and publicity materials. Without the numerous scholars, collectors, and reporters who located, investigated, and documented the American holidays and their lore included in these sources, compiling this book would not have been possible. Complete information concerning the festivals and folklore, circumstances of collection, and informants appears in the "Source" and "Source and Comment" sections along with full bibliographic information on published sources.

Format

Chronologically arranged according to the Gregorian calendar, *The Folklore of American Holidays* begins with New Year's Day, January 1, and concludes with the Twelve Days of Christmas, a period which not only returns to but also overlaps with the Gregorian New Year. Each holiday's name is followed by its date or inclusive time frame. Since some festivals are moveable both in relation to the Gregorian calendar and to their own calendars (Chinese, Jewish, lunar, or other), these idiosyncrasies are noted. A description of the holiday's origins, historical background, and general characteristics is provided, and associated items of folklore follow in subgroupings. The "Source" and "Source and Comment" sections give full bibliographic information and also include the following when available:

names of collectors, informants, or translators; place and date of collection; cross-references to related holidays and items of folklore within this book; and commentary, observations, analogues, and additional information from the editors on the particular custom or associated lore.

Indexes

To best serve the needs of users by providing quick and easy access to entries in a variety of ways, *The Folklore of American Holidays* contains five different indexes.

Subject Index—Includes all holiday entries, which are indicated in boldface type for quick reference (e.g., All Saints' Day, Chinese New Year); general subject categories (e.g., Animals, Food, Music); and references to more specific topics or entries (e.g., Apple games, Bicycle races).

Ethnic and Geographic Index—Contains a listing of ethnic groups (e.g., Blacks) and geographic locations (e.g., Dublin) and directs the user to folklore collected from or associated with these groups and locations.

Collectors, Informants, and Translators Index—Cites those individuals who have located, investigated, and reported on the calendar customs and festivals included in this volume. Within the text, these individuals are cited in the "Source" and "Source and Comment" sections.

Song Titles and First Significant Lines Index—Lists the titles of all songs discussed in the text as well as the first significant lines of untitled songs or of songs not best known by their titles. In addition, those songs with musical scores included in the text are indicated with an asterisk (*).

Motifs and Tale Types Index—Indicates references made within the "Source" and "Source and Comment" sections to motifs listed by Stith Thompson in his *Motif-Index of Folk Literature,* and to tale types listed by Antti Aarne and Stith Thompson in their *The Types of the Folktale.*

Acknowledgments

The editors are indebted to the collectors, reporters, and others mentioned in the "Source" and "Source and Comment" sections who have located and described the material included in *The Folklore of American Holidays.* In particular, we would like to thank the following people for their invaluable assistance: Leland Agan, Peter Bartis, Nancy Cheng, Leonard P. Deleanis, Patricia C. Fry, Morton H. Fry, Henry Glassie, Kenneth S. Goldstein, Albert Harkness, Jr., Theodore Holmberg, Ruth Kelly, Peter Koelle, Michael Licht, Adolph Matz, Teresa Pyott, James W. Renny, Reverend H. Seki, Reg Slater, Patty Stout, William Strachan, Joanne Takagi, Betty Takagi, Priscilla C. Whitford, and Don Yoder. We are also grateful to the staffs of the Brown University Library, University of Pennsylvania Library, and University of Rhode Island Library for making their resources available to us. But most of all we owe a debt to our research assistant, Steve Stuemfle, who worked long, hard, and careful hours for us.

Suggestions are Welcome

The editors welcome the comments and suggestions of readers to expand the coverage and enhance the usefulness of future editions of this work.

Introduction

Agricultural Communities and the Seasonal Cycle

Once a community gives up hunting and food gathering and settles down more permanently to plant crops and to live in villages, the changing seasons assume deeper magic and religious significance. Winter, spring, summer, fall—want, promise, fulfillment, harvest—the cycle recurs year after year, generation after generation. With a limited understanding of the ways of nature, agricultural peoples may see the weakening of the sun in winter, the death of vegetation, and the barren landscape as phenomena that threaten to last forever. Only with the help of prayer, sacrifice, and sympathetic magic will spring return with its green fertility and will survival be possible. By the same token, the flowering of the crops, the reproduction of the women and animals, and the eventual harvest seem almost too wonderful to be true. Each part of the cycle of the year is delicate, crucial, and sacred. It is only natural that the religions of farming peoples center about these changing seasons and those rites that insure the successful completion of each cycle.

The phenomenon of the seasons is almost always embodied in a god-force which is born each year, grows strong, weakens, and dies, only to be replaced by a new god-force. The sun, with its daily rising and setting, its seasonal strengthening and decline, is usually the symbol or the embodiment of this power. The sun fertilizes the earth, their mutual role in producing food seen as parallel to the roles of the male animal and the male human in relation to their female counterparts. Plants that retain their green in the barren months of winter (holly, ivy, mistletoe) suggest that this reproductive god-force is not dead, but simply absent, able to return (if it will) in spring. Liquors and hallucinogens, made from plants and fruits harvested from the summer just past, assure that the force of one year is transferred to the next. A desire to cleanse whatever has been evil in the old seasons is present. The new year, especially as it is born, must be freed from the curses of the past, and purges, noise to scare evil spirits, or frivolities to mask the seriousness of the situation are felt to help.

It is from such beliefs and customs that many of the basic equations of the seasonal rites develop: that the sun is male and equivalent to a bull, perhaps, or to a god in the shape of a man like Apollo; that the earth is feminine, personified by a mother figure like Hertha; that evergreens are sacred; that liquor is crucial to religion; that a scapegoat (sometimes in the form of the old sun-king himself) must be driven from the group annually as a means of purging sin.

It also follows that a typical calendar of an agricultural people would begin with a celebration not unlike the one practiced in the mid-nineteenth century by some Missouri and Pennsylvania German groups which featured feasting, drinking, rioting, and noisemaking (especially music and the shooting of guns). In the spring they would hold another festival, heralding the first appearance of the crops and the birth of animals and children. At this time they would bless the livestock, worship phallic symbols such as the maypole, and hunt for and decorate eggs. Midsummer rites, such as those connected with Marie Laveau and voodoo ritual in New Orleans, glorified the full growth of the fruit of the crops and often included bonfires, a symbol of the full-burning sun. Here, as in other celebrations, dancing, sexual license, feasting, and drinking were common. Finally, the agricultural year closed with harvest celebrations at the time when the crops were gathered and the animals were recalled from the fields. These were feasts of thanksgiving during which surplus food was consumed and animals that could not be kept for the winter were slaughtered. At this time, one offered thanks for the richness of the year past and prepared himself for the long, hard winter ahead.

The Development of Formal Calendars

Because the cycles of the seasons were so important to early man and because he studied them so closely, it was not long before he devised a means to calculate and record their passage. Thus, formal calendars were developed by most peoples as they began to advance technologically. From the basic unit of the day (measured from dawn to dawn, from midnight to midnight, from sunset to sunset), formal calendars evolved. Days were grouped so as to correspond with the cycles of the moon (months). Later, shorter groupings of four, six, seven, or ten days were used to establish periods between market days. Our seven-day week was originally Hebraic and was adapted by the Roman world and subsequently the Christian during the first century B.C.

The grouping of days by the cycles of the moon appealed because it approximated closely the menstrual cycle of women, but it was not fully suitable for determining the seasons of the year, whether they were divided into two (wet and dry), into three (flood, seeding, harvest), or into four. Seasons of the year depend on the sun. As the sun's varying positions result in a year of approximately 365 days and as the lunar month is 29½ days, the two systems are never fully compatible. Even early civilizations recognized this, and the history of the calendar is a search for means of harmonizing the lunar and solar calculations, the seasons, and the established holidays.

We do not know when the first calendar came into use, but we can say that all known communities have had at least the rudiments of a calendar. Everywhere man has noticed the changing seasons; the movements of the sun, moon, and stars; and the migration patterns of animals, if only because they are crucial to his survival. Where these matters have been recorded, a certain level of social organization with an accompanying system of number, measurement, and script or protoscript must be present. Moreover, the calendar implies the sort of awareness by man of his environment that is associated with deities, rituals, and social organization. The resemblance of calendars across the world also suggests a similarity in the development of mankind's patterns of culture, the general similarity of instincts and mental processes creating general resemblances of behavior and institutions. For while some calendars have been carried from one society to another along trade and migration routes, it is difficult to account in this fashion for similarities between pre-Columbian American Indian calendars like the Mayan and ancient Mediterranean calendars like the Egyptian.

The Chinese Lunar Calendar

In this book the lunar calendar is well illustrated by the old Chinese calendar, which was discarded by the Chinese Republic in 1912 in favor of the solar Gregorian calendar borrowed from the West. Chinese native festivals are still celebrated according to the old calendar, even in New World cities like New York and San Francisco. In the Chinese lunar calendar, the first day of the year comes with the first new moon after the sun has entered Aquarius, a date which falls between January 21 and February 19. There are twelve months or moons, designated simply as First, Second, and so forth. Each month, which lasts 29½ days, begins with the new moon. As needed, an intercalary month is added to make the lunar and the solar years correspond. This additional month is inserted at varying intervals, often at the beginning of the year, but it does not affect the month in which a given festival is normally held, because festivals continue to be celebrated in their regular lunar months. The calendar fits nicely with the four seasons, allowing three months for each, with the Ninth Day of the Ninth Month, the autumn equinox, and the Fifth Day of the Fifth Month, the summer solstice, assuming particular importance as agricultural dates. There are also two complex methods of identifying the years: one based upon the reigns of emperors; the other involving combinations of characters. The years are given twelve popular names. Nineteen ninety-one is, for example, the Year of the Sheep. The sheep is followed in sequence by the monkey, cock, dog, boar, rat, ox, tiger, hare, dragon, serpent, and horse, until the sheep is reached again and the pattern recurs.

The Solar Gregorian Calendar

The solar Gregorian calendar is now universally used by all Christian nations, as well as many others, and probably will soon be the only calendar by which the business of the world is conducted. It was introduced by Pope Gregory in a papal bull dated March 1, 1582, to replace the Julian calendar, devised under the auspices of Julius Caesar, which had been in use since 46 B.C. In the Julian calendar, which was also solar, the year was too long, and every 128 years the error added up to a full day. By the sixteenth century the Julian calendar was no longer in harmony with the agricultural practices of the time, and the farmers who were planting and reaping in accordance with the holy and feast days of the church found nature and the church out of step. By 1582 the calendar was ten days off, an error which Gregory corrected by changing the date of October 5 to October 15. The change, which was required in all Roman Catholic countries, was ignored in Protestant Britain and subsequently in the British colonies. It was not until 1752 that the English-speaking countries adopted the Gregorian calendar. By then, the discrepancy between the two systems was eleven days. Moreover, the Eastern church did not accept the Gregorian calendar as official until 1923, by which time there was a thirteen-day discrepancy. The result has been that many festivals celebrated by the common folk, who are often ignorant of or indifferent to official calendars, appear idiosyncratic in their dating.

Establishing Festival Dates

Any point in the lunar or solar year may be used as the starting point for the annual round of agricultural and sacred rites. The Gregorian calendar begins just after the winter solstice, the Chinese about three to seven weeks later; the Julian calendar begins on March 1, the Jewish close to the autumn equinox. Of course, the solstices and the equinoxes are natural beginning points, but a major festival such as the Christian Easter may be even more important in establishing certain related festival dates.

Easter is a lunar date set in the midst of a solar calendar year and is reckoned as the first Sunday following the first full moon that falls on or after the vernal equinox, March 21. If the full moon falls on a Sunday, Easter is celebrated one week later. Once set, the date of Easter, which always falls between March 22 and April 25, determines the dating of Shrove Tuesday, Ash Wednesday, and Lent; Palm Sunday, Maundy Thursday, Good Friday, and Holy Saturday; as well as Ascension Day (forty days after Easter), Whitsunday (the seventh Sunday after Easter), and Corpus Christi (the following Thursday).

Thus, it is important to know that while the Western church establishes Easter from the Gregorian calendar, the Eastern church, even after adopting the Western system, continues to establish Easter by means of the Julian calendar. The result is serious differences in the dates of Easter and many moveable feasts among the Western Christians and the Albanians, Greeks, Bulgarians, Russians, Syrians, and others within the Eastern church. Nor is there any consistency among the various Eastern churches. For instance, the Greeks use the Julian calendar only for Easter and associated dates, while the Russians use the Julian calendar for all festivals.

Before 325 A.D., some of the Christians celebrated Easter at the same time as the Jews celebrated Passover, and, of course, the Jews were using their own calendar. The Jewish calendar is primarily lunar, numbering the years from what their historians believed to be the "birth of the world" on October 7, 3760 B.C. Nineteen ninety-one is, for instance, the equivalent of 5761. To adjust the lunar month of 29½ days, the Jewish calendar alternates twelve months of 29 and 30 days. The calendar also introduces leap years and an extra month seven times in every nineteen years in order to regulate it. As we have noted, the Jewish calendar begins in late September or in October, and each day in the calendar begins the night before in keeping with the Biblical concept that the night precedes the day.

The Pagan Influence on Christian Holidays

The variety of calendars ranges greatly, from the Armenian, Hindu, and Persian calendars of today to the Babylonian, Egyptian, Aztec, and Incan calendars of the past. The dates of folk festivals are not always adjusted to meet the changes of place, religion, and computation that go with calendar adaptations and revisions. As a result, one finds what appear to be inconsistencies and confusions in the dates of folk holidays. Furthermore, a large amount of overlapping has occurred in the various festivals as people have migrated, acculturated, and changed religions. Each society had its own day or period during which it conducted its particular rites, often employing remarkably similar mimes, processions, feasts, orgies, sacrifices, and such. For each, the time chosen was dependent on many factors: geography, climate, local traditions, chance. Moreover, as Roman Catholicism spread, it became the policy of the church not only to establish new holidays, but to convert pagan holidays into Christian ones rather than suppress local celebrations.

This practice accounts for the large number of saints' days included in this book, for, in fact, their chance for survival has been enhanced by the pagan element they contain. Thus, Midsummer's Day and St. John's Day are made to coincide; the Easter season has become both a celebration of Christ's death and a fertility rite; and Christmas has assumed many of the characteristics of the Teutonic and Roman New Year's festivals. The use of Assumption Day as a thanksgiving day by the Florida Poles or of St. Barbara's Day as a day to test wheat in France are good cases in point. What's more, as pagan festivals center on the struggle between warm light in the form of the summer sun and cold darkness in the form of winter sterility, it was relatively easy for the church to introduce the struggle between God (as light) and the devil (as darkness) into the ceremonies, a point well illustrated by the Old Nick and his Hobby Horse selection in this volume and by St. Lucy's Day.

Climate, of course, was a major influence in determining the character of holidays. The weather in England on St. John's Day is much warmer than the weather in Sweden on the same date. It is no accident, therefore, that the Anglo-American St. John's Day features the midsummer solstice rites, while the Swedish celebration on the same date is centered on spring and the first flow of the sap. Whitsunday, forty days after Easter, is for England a rough equivalent to St. John's Day in Sweden.

Many communities also repeat their celebrations, sometimes in different and less intense forms. E.K. Chambers once wrote that "the Christmas celebration is spread over half the winter calendar." The statement is true, for as Christianity moved north from Italy to Scandinavia, the repetitive pagan festivals were adapted and refocussed on a whole sequence of saints' days. Thus, All Hallows (November 1), St. Martin's (November 11), St. Barbara's (December 4), St. Nicholas' (December 6), St. Lucy's (December 13), Christmas itself (December 25), St. Stephen's (December 26), New Year's (January 1), Epiphany or Old Christmas (January 6), and Plough Monday (mid-January) cover much the same ground and repeat many of the same customs. The Anglo-American Whitsunday and May Day also have striking similarities to the Anglo-American Easter, although the religious emphasis is greater at Easter. And Plough Monday and St. Distaff's Day are parodies of the more serious New Year's observances, their mumming recalling that done at Halloween, Christmas, Boxing Day, the New Year, and Mardi Gras.

Some days, such as St. Nicholas', celebrate the season just past as well as the season yet to come. On the one hand the feasting and thanksgiving associated with December 6 is a vestige of the fall roundup of cattle and the storage of winter provisions. On the other hand, it is similar to Christmas and other midwinter rites in that gifts are exchanged, evil purged, and resolutions for the next year made. A study of St. Nicholas' Day as it is celebrated across Europe shows it related to calendar events occurring as early as the English Lammis Day (August 1) and Polish Assumption Day (August 15), and to events as late as Plough Monday, which may not come until the second week of January.

Partly because of this association of pagan celebration with church holidays, many rituals and customs have survived into modern times, long after their original symbolism and purpose have been forgotten by all but the scholars. Few girls dancing about a maypole on an American college campus are aware that they are paying tribute to the reproductive powers of the phallus; few people having a drink at a Christmas party in the factory believe that they are to be transformed by the power of the liquor just as the barren landscape is to be transformed by returning spring; few people think the horns and bells and shouting on New Year's Eve are for the purpose of frightening whatever evil spirits are abroad. Yet year after year Americans and Western Europeans perform such rituals by rote.

Perhaps nowhere is this juxtaposition and the church's role in it better shown than in the fusion of the Roman custom of gift-giving at the midwinter Kalends with Santa Claus and Kris Kringle. Santa, who is actually St. Nicholas (Sanct Herr 'Claus), was a legendary saint who supposedly saved three impoverished virgins from prostitution by throwing money down the smoke-hole of their cottage and into their stockings drying by the fire. St. Nicholas mingled with pagan gift-givers and judges of behavior such as Befana and Knecht Ruprecht and developed into an elf with a fur-trimmed cardinal robe or suit who gives presents to the good and whips the bad. This confusion was further complicated by his association with the tradition that the shepherds took gifts to the newborn Christ, so that the Christ-Child (Christ Kindl or Kris Kringle) actually became the gift-giver and a figure identical to Nicholas. Furthermore, when one realizes that sometimes, as in North Carolina, St. Nicholas and Old Nick (the devil) became confused, one gets an idea of how difficult a festival's history may become.

The Durability of Folk Festivals

Folk festivals, because they are so durable, commonly preserve much lore that would otherwise vanish. Often we find what was once a religious festival surviving as a secular drama, dance, or game as has *La Pastoría* or the Plough Monday drama. Greek dramas, the great plays of Aeschylus, Sophocles, and Euripides, evolved from old Dionysian rites and were still performed in Athens in the fifth century B.C. as a part of a quasi-religious service. Robin Hood plays and St. George plays, performed into the twentieth century, retained elements common to the May Day vegetation ceremonies of medieval England. The Mexican dances in which Moors oppose Christians are survivals of ancient European fertility rites enacted as sexual confrontations and once mimed as part of the New Year rituals. Even American square dancing can be traced directly to similar rites. Bullfights are modern elaborations of the ritual killings of the male fertility symbol, the bull, perhaps as part of the festival involving the death of the king of the old year. Soccer (English football) and American football are disciplined forms of ancient rivalries between villages once involving a struggle for the possession of a skull or inflated animal bladder. In fact, some scholars (surely with too much enthusiasm) have seen all narrative art, from myths to short stories and comic strips, as having evolved from ritual and the miming which results from it.

Customs, Calendar Customs, and Festivals

Scholars have also caviled over the distinctions between a custom, a calendar custom, and a festival. Generally, they agree that a *custom* is a traditional practice (for instance, sending a Welcome Wagon to greet new neighbors or tossing the coxswain into the water after winning a boat race) that has become ingrained in a society through some combination of habit and community pressure. If a custom is observed on a certain date each year (for instance, the sending of valentines on February 14 or "trick or treat" on October 31), then it is called a *calendar custom*. If, however, a calendar custom is celebrated by a whole or nearly a whole community at once, with various members playing different roles, and with features such as mumming, processions, bonfires, traditional food, and the like, it is called a *festival*. A festival, then, is a fully elaborated calendar custom.

In this book, we do not concern ourselves with the distinctions between calendar customs and festivals. Scholars themselves have difficulty in knowing where to draw the lines. April Fools' Day is clearly a calendar custom. But is May Day, which is far more elaborately observed, a festival? And what about Halloween with its mumming? Or New Year's Day with its parades, parties, and football games? In this book we treat the two categories together, assuming that if the traditional practice occurs regularly year after year among a significant group of people and is celebrated with some degree of formality, it may be called a festival.

Genuine, Revived, and Fabricated Folk Festivals

Nonetheless, we are obligated to distinguish clearly between a genuine folk festival, a revival of a genuine folk festival, and a fabricated or artificially invented festival: between, say, May Day, Ground Hog Day, and Mother's Day. At first thought, it may seem odd, but a revival of a folk festival or a fabricated festival is usually celebrated with far greater enthusiasm and more care than a genuine folk festival. There is a certain stolidity and absence of stir connected with a rite that one has grown up with and perpetuates year after year for no other reason than that it has always been done. Perhaps the easiest way for twentieth-century Americans to understand this perfunctory attitude toward traditional ritual is to think of New Year's Eve, which most of us celebrate by going to a party that drags its way toward a midnight of false hilarity or by staying home before the television in order to toast twelve o'clock with mediocre champagne. There is certainly a different temper to that celebration than there is to the frenzy that accompanies the preparation of a band or a float for the Philadelphia Mummer's Parade or the Pasadena Tournament of Roses the next morning. Halloween mumming and much of Christmas and Easter are also treated quite routinely by many Americans. One can say, almost for certain, that if there is a doggedness, rather than a fervor, associated with a ritual, then that ritual is traditional in the fullest sense.

The May Day customs of various communities of rural blacks and whites in the American South illustrate this attitude. The farmers, hanging the long-necked gourds between their legs, sowing turnip seed, and chanting as they walk across their fields; the little black girls dancing about an imaginary maypole; the children who are barefoot for the first time on May Day; and the blacks who go to the well and, reflecting the sun's rays into the water, predict the future are all undertaking the rites of an authentic folk festival quite exactly. Their observances are disjointed, somewhat whimsically performed, practiced only here and there. They are quite different from such carefully prepared revivals as a May Day celebration on a college campus.

Although many college May celebrations have become traditional as far as one particular campus community is concerned, none of them go directly back to authentic folk celebrations or religious adaptations of such. Most have, however, reinstituted many of the traditional symbols, even if the meaning of those symbols is vaguely understood. College May Days are usually highly organized, featuring a processional of coeds dressed in white or pastels and carrying spring flowers. One, perhaps the prettiest or most talented, is chosen as queen, and she may well have a court of runners-up. Hoop races, dancing on the green, band music, and the decoration of a pole erected for the occasion are common. Sometimes, one of the more dramatically inclined students or faculty members plays the role of Father May, possibly even dressing in Elizabethan style and reciting an appropriate poem. Awards may be announced and an honor roll read. At one Eastern women's college, Bryn Mawr, each senior is awakened by her "little sister" with a May Day morning kiss. The local fireman's band is hired to play music. This same college used to celebrate a "Grand" or "Big" May Day every fourth year. During Grand May Day, plays, masques, recitals, and circuslike acts were added to the usual May Day races and dances. These were activities with no roots or connections whatsoever with the sort of May Days the Southern blacks and whites know. Excessive cost and preparation went into Grand May Day, which became too expensive and time-consuming and was dropped in 1936, although partially performed in 1978. It was an excellent example of a revival: self-conscious, exhilarated, planned.

Of course, the longer a revival survives, the more it tends to take on the atmosphere of a truly traditional festival, and in time it may even assume a casualness that makes it indistinguishable from the genuine. This statement probably could not be made concerning a completely artificial festival such as May Day in the Soviet Union. Almost always promoted by governmental or commercial forces, this sort of celebration is carried through with an efficiency, organization, and purposefulness never seen at the folk level and unlikely in revivals. All is in step. The display of troops, planes, guns, tanks, industrial might, and physical fitness which once attended Soviet May Day was carefully calculated to show the world what the Soviet Union is capable of. There is little tradition behind such displays and still less choice or informality open to the participants. One newsman describing the 1984 Soviet May Day wrote as follows in the *Providence* (Rhode Island) *Journal* of May 3rd: "The Moscow celebration appeared as trite and contrived as usual. Selected workers were shepherded in to act as spectators. Live cheering (on cue) was supplemented by tape-recorded voices. Pictures of Konstantin U. Chernenko, new leader of the Soviets, were everywhere. And never was heard a discouraging word." The result was, to be sure, a magnificent tribute to the aims of the Communist state; but with the weakening of the central government which began in the early 1990s, the Soviet May Day celebration described above will surely disappear, although the traditional elements of May Day, which lie beneath the surface, will probably remain. Even at the height of Soviet influence, the May Day parades in Hungary, for instance, retained a nationalistic coloration and celebrated the return of spring, with family picnics in the park behind the parade route and May Day posters more likely to display spring flowers than military might.

Obviously, artificially created, highly commercialized festivals such as the Tournament of Roses (or the equivalent orange, azalea, cotton extravaganzas) have no more connection with pagan agricultural rites or Roman Catholic saints' days than does Soviet May Day. The fact that the Tournament of Roses, which began in 1890, comes on New Year's Day, features a football game, a parade of flowers, and the crowning of a queen might cause one to think that it is still preserving the old mimic contest, the interrelationship of floral and female fertility, and the god-in-human-form worship so common to the ancient celebrations of the changing year. However, these connections are more accidental than traditional, introduced into the Pasadena and similar festivals because championship football is a great drawing card for tourists, because the local Chamber of Commerce advertises warm weather and flowers to colder areas, and because a parade is a showcase for Hollywood and television stars and starlets.

This is not to say that there are no folk festivals emerging in America today. Just as the revival may eventually take on the casualness that makes it hard to distinguish from the genuine, so a commercially or politically sponsored occasion may in time become fully traditional. The Kentucky Derby with its juleps, parties, and post parade, the Darlington "500" Stock Car Race with its growing superstitions and tales, as well as the Boston Marathon, the Army-Navy football game, the many state fairs, and the various jazz and music festivals all are close to being events which might be called "folk festivals." They are certainly modern variations of races, games, dances, fairs, and musical performances which have come and gone throughout the traditions of various cultures, and much lore has grown up about them.

Perhaps the American holiday Thanksgiving demonstrates best how difficult it is to distinguish between the genuine, the revived, the artificial, and the emerging elements in modern festivals. Rooted in the fall and prewinter agricultural rites associated with bringing in the crops and slaughtering the surplus stock, Thanksgiving still features indulgence and merrymaking and is related to the many harvest home festivals described in this book. However, Americans have made it their own holiday, a major event which recalls the first thanksgiving of the Pilgrims on the shores of the New World at the start of America's history. It even retains the simple religious atmosphere which was so important to those settlers. Forgotten is the fact that the Pilgrim thanksgiving was a one-time affair to celebrate a particularly good harvest, forgotten is the fact that Thanksgiving as a regular, national event didn't begin till the middle of the nineteenth century, forgotten is the fact that it is now a legal holiday, proclaimed and fixed by our presidents, which has no specific, ongoing folk tradition behind it. Today it is characterized by "PR hype," football games, commercial parades, and television programs. Moreover, for many merchants it marks the opening of the Christmas shopping season. And yet, most of us do accept our Thanksgiving with a stolidity and casualness which makes one believe that it is, for whatever reasons, becoming a folk event in the fullest sense of the word, powerful enough to absorb similar festivals brought here by ethnic groups like the Poles and the Czechs and powerful enough to be observed by Puerto Ricans and Vietnamese who knew nothing about it till they came to America.

However, although a national holiday like Thanksgiving may absorb and make insignificant local and ethnic celebrations, many local events which parallel major national holidays are still flourishing. Memorial or Decoration Day, like Thanksgiving, is a proclaimed, legal holiday set on May 30 (in most states) to honor the war dead. It is a means by which our government has nationalized the old custom of decorating and cleaning graves, which was customarily undertaken during the late spring and midsummer, particularly in the rural South. Perhaps because the proclaimed holiday is not personal and intimate enough, many communities still do things the old way, celebrating Memorial Day to honor the nation's heroes, celebrating their own decoration day to honor those dearer and closer to them. Local attitudes cannot be legislated easily.

Selection of Festivals and Holiday Lore

So, when all is said and done, the key word is "tradition." Whether the festival has arisen from ancient practices, is a fresh attempt to celebrate an older festival which has been disregarded for a time, or has been artificially created by the passage of a law, a Chamber of Commerce decision, or a political or ethnic group that wishes to strengthen its sense of identity, the editors have included it in this book only if we have been able to see it as an integral part of the social habits of Americans at large or of a regional, occupational, or ethnic group within the nation. The questions asked were: "Would this calendar custom or festival continue to be celebrated if there were no legal or commercial reason to celebrate it?" and "Is the event creating or did it at some time in the past create its own set of traditions, with associated legends, anecdotes, superstitions, food and the like?" If the answer is "yes" to either or both, the festival and the associated materials were included.

So we have felt free to include the Bryn Mawr College May Day, the Kentucky Derby, and the Darlington "500" along with Memorial Day and Thanksgiving, because we have seen the elements of a genuine traditionalism emerging in them. However, there are exceptions. Labor Day, even though it has spawned its share of annual beauty contests, strawberry fests, and county fairs, really has few folk ties at all. Only where an established folk tradition, like the West Warwick, Rhode Island, Portuguese *festa* has attached itself to Labor Day does the celebration qualify for inclusion in the book.

Certainly the fact that the editors of this collection have selected their material from scholarly journals primarily in the areas of folklore and local history, from doctoral dissertations, from public and private archives, and from a few private collections has assisted greatly in deciding what passes muster. But we have ranged more widely also, from time to time selecting a description of a festival or an example of holiday lore from newspapers, magazines, and even programs, where considerations other than scholarship are the criteria for publication. However, we felt this necessary, not just to show that festivals are adapted to modern life (like the "take-out Passover food" selection in this book), but also to emphasize those revivals and fabricated festivals which are reestablishing or creating traditions of their own (like the Keeneland horse sales or the Pancake Day Race of Liberal, Kansas). As the editors of *Western Folklore* have shown us over the years with their section on "Folklore in the News," there is a great deal of genuine folklore reported in the press, especially in the local publications.

Of course, we are fully aware that newspapers, magazines, and programs are not as reliable a source of folkloristic materials as scholarly journals, archives, or even private collections, where the persons who assemble and discuss the lore usually have had the benefit of formal academic training in what defines traditional matters. And we are also aware that the newspapers, magazines, and programs feel no particular obligation to distinguish between the genuine, the revival, and the fabricated festival, often being more enthusiastic about describing a summer Tuna Derby or ten-year old Heritage Festival, which is a simple sports event or carnival, than they are in reporting a Belsnickel or May Day rite, which has a tradition reaching toward antiquity. After all, newspapers, magazines, and programs are dedicated to describing events of public interest. Still, we do feel confident that the materials included in this anthology which we have taken from these sources are part of an American tradition stretching back to colonial times. We are confident that what we have assembled is not only a guide to folk festival matter brought from already-established cultures in the Old World, but even more significantly a guide to folk festival matter which has been evolving and developing in this polyglot nation from a juxtaposition of those Old World traditions and a new context of locality, mass culture, and commercialization.

Ethnic Roots of American Festivals

For American culture is anything but static. Even the flow of immigrants into the land is forever changing. In a feature article in the *Providence* (Rhode Island) *Journal* of March 24, 1980, Richard Polenberg made the following remarks:

> . . . On the eve of World War II, more than one in four Americans was a first- or second-generation immigrant. Ethnic culture, European in linguistic origin, Roman Catholic and Jewish in religion, flourished in such cities as New York and Boston. In the last 15 years, the sources of immigration have shifted from Europe to Asia and Latin America.

> Today, the United States receives fewer immigrants from Italy and Greece combined than from India alone, fewer from West Germany than Thailand, fewer from Ireland than from Egypt. Spanish is the most commonly used foreign language, and there are more homes in which Chinese, Japanese, Korean and Filipino is spoken than homes in which people ordinarily use Italian.

This book, like the sources from which it was drawn, reflects these changes. Thus, alongside the Irish St. Patrick's Day Parade or the Italian St. Anthony's festa, we have the Vietnamese Tet and the Puerto Rican San Juan Day. The book also reflects the firmly established, confident ethnicism of some of the groups which have been in this country now for 100 years or more. Not only have the Rhode Island Portuguese picked an utterly American date, Labor Day, for their *festa,* but an African group has selected Christmas as a time for preserving black customs in a new land. And Italians, finding that Columbus Day has been made a national holiday, have chosen to celebrate it as an ethnic holiday as well, while the Norwegians have responded by creating a Leif Ericson Day. It takes ethnic groups a number of generations and some intermarrying to lose their identity. In the meantime, the old festivals are revitalized and new ones are created.

Many of the older festivals brought to the New World have not survived. Guy Fawkes Day is not celebrated by Americans of English stock any more, its political message and relevance obscured. It has given way to newer events like "Return Day" in Delaware and "Lantern Night at Bryn Mawr College," which have contemporary appeal. Local events with local heroes (like Captain Brady Day, rattlesnake round-ups, and Turtle Day) seem more pertinent than a long-forgotten gunpowder plot to blow up the British Parliament. Nonetheless, people don't, as we have seen, discard the old easily, and they often feel the urge to reinstitute a festival that has died out. Guy Fawkes Day may have vanished from the American scene forever, but one can't be sure. Such unlikely affairs as medieval jousting tournaments were brought back during the flush of Sir Walter Scott romanticism which swept the South in the nineteenth century. And if the elaborate tournaments described in this book have never fully established themselves, other revivals of lagging folk festivals, many sponsored by city governments, have grown and grown, even to the point of getting out of control. The Philadelphia Mummers Parade, New Orleans' Mardi Gras, often the scene of crime and riot, and New York's St. Patrick's Day Parade, recently used as a propaganda vehicle for Irish nationalists and for advocacy of the rights of homosexuals and the handicapped, are cases in point.

The sources from which revivals and new festivals can come are myriad. There is really no limit in a country as large and diverse as this, unless it be the warning in the Shakespearian aphorism: "If all the year were playing holidays, To sport would be as tedious as to work."

Festivals, whether genuine, revived, or artificial, do take on characteristics which reflect their ethnic roots, the time of year in which they occur, and the saints' days associated with them. Thanksgiving is predictably characterized by food and drink; Mardi Gras by miming, costumes, and music; May Day by maidens, flowers, and planting customs; and the Fourth of July by outdoor events, noise, and parades. Sometimes, one holiday will even encourage one of its major characteristics in another. American Jews, influenced by the lavish gift-giving of Christmas, have increased the amount of gift-giving at Hanukkah. Nor is it unusual for two or more holidays to share beliefs or customs. The idea that if it rains on St. Swithin's Day it will rain for forty days and nights is also common to St. Médard's Day, Ascension Day, and Whitsuntide. The variety of lore associated with American festivals is vast indeed.

In this book, partly because we are dependent upon the collectors and reporters of the various festivals, certain holidays and certain examples of the lore associated with them are more fully represented than others. There are, for example, Thanksgiving football games, May Day breakfasts, and gift-giving at St. Lucy's. We have included no material about these. To cover everything would have been well beyond the scope of this work. Thus, we are not in a position to claim that our selections are fully representative of either the holidays or the groups that celebrate them. But we do feel that the book does catch the full spirit of the festivals in America and is representative of the range of the lore that is associated with them: the legends, beliefs, proverbs, charms, sayings, songs, recipes, processions, and the like that are to be found. If some groups are more frequently included than others, similar logic applies. Some (like the blacks, the Pennsylvania Dutch, the Italian-Americans) have been more steadily collected than others (like the Islamic cults or the Japanese-Americans). And some have remained more traditional than others, acculturating more slowly. Even if the book does reflect these differences, the editors feel the whole to be most representative.

Beginning the New Year and Dating Holidays

As mentioned earlier in this Introduction, many points in the lunar or solar year might be, in fact have been, used to begin the annual round of agricultural and sacred rites. Thus, the editors have had to ask themselves: "Precisely when does the New Year begin? Where should this volume start?" Is it when the death of winter is succeeded by the birth of spring? Or is it after the harvest, when the growing season is over and the fields lie fallow and asleep? In either case, ancient farming peoples patterned their calendars after the changes on the face of the land. Their wise men also watched the sky and observed that the seasons of the earth were matched by the seasons of the heavens. The priest-astronomers of the Babylonians and Druids and Aztecs learned how to measure out the year by the course of the stars. Yet here, too, was a question of where to begin. Did the new year commence with the longest day, at midsummer, when the sun showed its might in the firmament, or the shortest, when it was at the depth of its decline but at the point that it would start once more its upward arc? Or with the vernal equinox? There was still another way of ordering time and of indicating the place of its annual beginning. This was the chronicle of the experience of man himself, his history. Time began with the creation of the world, and the new year marked its anniversary; or the new year commemorated the birthday of a messiah, king, or culture hero or the revelation of a prophet. Whether the new year is determined by the cycle of the agricultural season, the circular path of heavenly bodies, or the turning wheel of history; whether it is the new year of aboriginal Americans or recent immigrants from Southeast Asia, any collection of festival folklore makes two things clear: mankind has had many new years, and these various and almost arbitrary points on the calendar encompass both end and beginning.

As our starting point we have simply chosen the New Year's Day of the Gregorian calendar, January 1, and let the natural flow of holiday lore structure the contents, concluding with the Twelve Days of Christmas, which not only return to but overlap the Gregorian New Year. The result is a cycle, never-ending, and it is as such a circle the book should be viewed. We have also used the Gregorian calendar as a basic means of dating holidays, even though these days may be set according to the Chinese, Jewish, or other calendars. In 1991, for instance, Purim was celebrated February 28 and Passover March 29 according to Gregorian dating. They, along with Rosh Hashanah, Hanukkah, and the like are given their places in the book accordingly. The same is true for the Chinese festivals. By Gregorian reckoning, Rosh Hashanah, the Jewish New Year, occurred September 24 in 1987; the Chinese New Year occurred January 30 in 1987. Rosh Hashanah appears late in our anthology; the Chinese New Year close to, but not at, the beginning of the book. The Islamic New Year, which moves backwards through the whole cycle of the Gregorian calendar year by year, could have been placed anywhere. It seemed appropriate to put it close to the Gregorian New Year, but there is little logical reason for this decision.

Moreover, many of the festivals are moveable, moveable both in their relationship to the Gregorian calendar and to their own calendars. (We designate as "moveable" only the latter.) Easter, for instance, moves according to a fixed pattern within the Gregorian calendar, as do all the days dependent on it. Labor Day (the first Monday in September) and Thanksgiving (the last Thursday in November) also move, but are predictable. On the other hand, a rattlesnake round-up or a graveyard decoration outing may be as casually dated as "late winter or early spring" or "a week-day in July or August." The Senecan Green Corn festival is merely "called" when the tribal leader decides the crop has reached the proper stage of ripeness. Other dates, like Passover or the Chinese New Year, are fixed within the Jewish or Chinese calendars, but move within the Gregorian. This is also true of the Iroquois White Dog Feast which comes after the first new moon in what we call January. Other days, like Thanksgiving (once the last, now the fourth Thursday in November), have been changed over the years by legal decree. Recent federal regulations have also rescheduled old holidays like Columbus Day (once October 12) to the second Monday in October and Washington's Birthday (once February 22) to the third Monday in February. Thus, holidays and festivals which were formerly fixed have become moveable. There are even examples such as the one in Honolulu in 1978 where city officials urged parents to keep their children home on Halloween because of the heavy rains, saying a "make-up Halloween" would be declared when the weather cleared.

In Conclusion

There may be a conclusion with a wider application to be drawn from this rainy Halloween in Honolulu: festivals are remarkably flexible and this flexibility makes for their remarkable ability to survive. Pagans and popes and public officials, even the power of nature herself, may alter and shape them. They may erode, revive, merge, flourish, decline, sink almost into oblivion; and, if the rain is heavy, it may even be necessary to issue a local rain check. But the danger of a festival's being washed completely away by the floods of time is not as great as one might expect. Besides, if old ways and holidays are swept off, new ones are forever appearing on the scene.

This book suggests in its range and diversity the durability of holiday lore, especially its power of survival through adaptation to new environments and its capacity for being put to new uses.

Hennig Cohen
Tristram Potter Coffin

Abbreviations

The following abbreviations are used in the *Source* and *Source and Comment* sections
for publications that are cited frequently

Baughman   Baughman, Ernest W. *A Type and Motif-Index of the Folktales of England and North America.* Indiana University Folklore Series, 20. The Hauge: Mouton & Co., 1966.

Folklore in America   Coffin, Tristram Potter, and Hennig Cohen. *Folklore in America.* Garden City, N.Y.: Doubleday Anchor, 1966.

Folklore from the Working Folk of America   Coffin, Tristram Potter, and Henning Cohen. *Folklore from the Working Folk of America.* Garden City, N.Y.: Doubleday Anchor, 1973.

Motif   Thompson, Stith. *Motif-Index of Folk Literature.* 6 vols. Bloomington, Ind.: Indiana University Press, 1955.

The Parade of Heroes   Coffin, Tristram Potter, and Hennig Cohen. *The Parade of Heroes.* Garden City, N.Y.: Doubleday Anchor, 1978.

Tale Type   Aarne, Antti, and Stith Thompson. *The Types of the Folktale.* 2d. ed. Folklore Fellows Communications No. 184. Helsinki: Academia Scientiarum Fennica, 1961.

★★★★★★★★★★★★★

The Folklore of American Holidays

★★★★★★★★★★★★★

SECOND EDITION

New Year's Day
January 1

New Year's festivals once included rites which were supposed to ward off the barrenness of winter and insure the return of spring with its fertility. In pre-Christian times among certain peoples, these midwinter rites included the actual or symbolic killing of the king of the old year and the welcoming of a new king. Sometimes a sacred animal was sacrificed, to be replaced by a new one; sometimes a scapegoat, upon whom the sins of the tribe were visited, was driven out to wander or die. New Year's in America, which occurs at the midpoint of the Twelve Days of Christmas and aside from Christmas itself is the most festive celebration of this joyous season, brings to the Christ-Mass many pagan vestiges: the veneration of evergreens, the burning of the yule log and the kindling of new fires, indulgence in sexual license and intoxicating drink, processions of mummers and maskers, ritualistic combat between opposing parties, and the pledging of good resolves in order to redeem the bad behavior of the past.

Rivers Stop Flowing on New Year's Eve

At twelve o'clock on New Year's Eve [according to Armenian-American storytellers] all rivers and springs stop flowing for five minutes. If one should go to a spring when it starts again he would find gold dust pouring from it for a moment or two. There was once a woman who went for a pitcher of water just at this time. On coming to the light the water looked dirty, and without thinking what was the matter she threw it out. Next morning she found a little gold in the bottom of the pitcher.

Source

Journal of American Folklore, XII (1899), 99. Selected from among "Items of Armenian Folk-lore Collected in Boston" by G. D. Edwards. He made use of translators during the collecting and observes that "customs are changing in Armenia as well as among Armenians coming to America."

* * *

Mourning the Old Year

Up to the year 1900 it was customary in Kau district for every Hawaiian to wear black on the last day of the year as a sign of mourning for the year just ending. Feasts were held all over the district and guests came on foot and on horseback and went from one feast to another bent on pleasure. At midnight each household held a family feast and everybody changed into a white dress to welcome the New Year. Feasts were held on this day also and the day was given up to sports and dancing. I have never heard of the "mourning" for the old year and welcoming of the new in this way in any other district, but in Hilo, in Honolulu, on Kauai I have seen *luau* ("feasts") held at midnight

between the old and new years and this idea of a midnight *luau* is still clung to.

Source and Comment

California Folklore Quarterly, II (1943), 213. Kawena Pukui recalls games and amusements from her Hawaiian childhood. Notes are provided by Martha Beckwith who writes: "She was brought up by her Hawaiian grandmother, a remarkable old lady who, although the family fortunes had become much impaired, saw to it that the child, born as she was of high chief ancestry, was brought up as far as possible according to the old taboos due her rank." Kawena Pukui compiled her recollections about 1930, "in middle life."

Laments are chanted in certain European communities at harvest time, the end of the agricultural year. Their purpose is to mourn the death of the vegetation and thus to appease the crop spirits so that a new crop will grow in the coming year.

* * *

Greeting the New Year

Our German forefathers had a custom of saluting the incoming New Year. They exchanged visits of greeting on the night wherein the Old Year ended, and the New Year began. Parties would be formed, to deliver these greetings to the families in the neighborhood. An hour before midnight their calls began, and were continued till towards morning. Usually a few guns were taken along to fire the salutes. Musicians, if any such were in the neighborhood, took their flutes and violins along, to accompany the New Year's hymn, sung before the door. One of the party committed and delivered the address (*Spruch*). This usually consisted of a New Year's hymn, to which a few original sentences were added, to suit the occasion. Sometimes the custom led to scenes of rioting and drunkenness, disgraceful to the neighborhood, and through an imprudent use of firearms, disastrous to the guilty parties.

A venerable friend informs us, that fifty years ago he occasionally helped to salute his neighbors with a New Year's greeting. In the dead of night they quietly approached a home. After each had gently taken his place before the chamber window, where the parents slept, the spokesman, with a solemn voice, recited the beautiful New Year's hymn:

> Nun lasst uns gehn und treten
> Mit Singen und mit Beten
> Zum Herrn, der unserm Leben
> Bis hieher Kraft gegeben.
> Wir gehn dahin und wandern
> Von einem Jahr zum andern;
> Wir leben und godeihen,
> Vom alten zu dem neuen.
> Durch so viel Angst und Plagen,
> Durch Zittern und durch Zagen,
> Durch Krieg und grosse Schrecken,
> Die alle Welt bedecken.

> Now let us go
> Singing and praying
> To the Lord, who up to now
> Has given power to our lives.
> We walk along and wander
> From one year to the other,
> We live and grow
> From the old (year) to the new,
> Through so much anguish and torment,
> In fear and trembling,
> Through war and great terrors
> Which cover the entire world.

At the close of the hymn the speaker continued:

> Damit will ich mein Wunsch beschliessen
> Und euch das Neue Jahr anschiessen.
> Wann es euch aber sollt verdriessen,
> So müsst ihr's sagen, ehe wir schiessen,—
> Indem wir hören kein Verdruss,
> So sollt ihr hören unsern Schuss.

> With this I want to close my wish
> And shoot in the New Year for you.
> But if it should annoy you
> Just say so before we shoot—
> Since we hear no complaint,
> You shall hear our shot.

And then a dozen guns were pointed skyward. The leader's command, "ready," "aim," "fire," was followed by an ill-concerted discharge of arms. For in those peaceful days, the country had no well-drilled warriors yet. Noise enough the firing made, which brought all the children out of bed in one leap. The horses and cattle in the stables sprang to their feet, and the frightened poultry on their roost set up a great cackling.

By this time the door was opened, and the greeters invited to enter. Hard cider, cakes, pies and all manner of delicacies were set before them. After singing a few more hymns, they proceeded on their mirthful tour....

A few lines, we remember of the *Spruch* [speech] in the neighborhood of our boyhood home:

> Ein glück-seliges Neues Jahr,
> Eine Brathwurst wie ein Ofen-rohr,
> Ein Kuchen wie ein Scheuer Thor

> A happy New Year,
> A Sausage as (big as) a stovepipe,
> A cake as (big as) a barn door.

Source and Comment

Pennsylvania Dutchman, V (January 1, 1954), 3. Reprinted from "New Year's Eve" by B. Bausman, which first appeared in *The Guardian,* Philadelphia, January 1868. It comments that the "custom has well nigh become extinct." Cf. "Christmas Shooters," p. 448 and for the origin and the relationship of Christmas and New Year's, see Walter L. Robbin, *Journal of American Folklore,* 1973, 48-52. Translation by Don Yoder.

The "hymn" is not really a hymn but a chant, and it is in High German and not Pennsylvania Dutch. The custom of wishing-in and shooting-in the New Year was known in German settlements from Pennsylvania to the Carolinas. According to a feature story by Bob Baker written for the *Los Angeles Times,* reprinted in the *Philadelphia Inquirer* of December 31, 1987, New Year's shooting "From the rural community of Cherryville, N. C., to the Southern California shores" has resulted in "injury and even death." A Los Angeles detective, who went to investigate a burglary, found that the lady of the house owned a new handgun. She explained to him that she never used it except "New Year's Eve, when it's legal to do it."

* * *

Letting Out the Old

On New Year's Eves, the mother would go to the front door and open it wide, go to the back door and open that wide, and stand for a moment honoring the biting chill that invariably swept through the house.

"Letting out the old," she would say, "letting in the new."

These days, we open the front door on New Year's Eve, and we even take the trouble to open the back. Only to breathe the night air. Nothing more.

Source

Philadelphia Inquirer, January 2, 1984. From a daily column, "The Scene," by Walter F. Naedele. He remembers this family custom from the 1940s and sees it as illustrative of the "blend of the religious and the superstitious" in "the [Bridgeport, Connecticut] home where we grew up." His mother, of Irish-Catholic and French-Canadian descent, was born in New Haven.

Ring in the New

At one time, New Year's Eve [in Maryland] was a favorite occasion for private "masquerade parties," at which all the guests were masked and remained so until the clock struck twelve, when the masks were removed and the identity of the guests revealed. At the present time [c. 1925] a large proportion of the community may be found on the stroke of twelve engaged in silent prayer within the various churches, for "watch meetin's," originally confined to one or two sects, are now held in churches of various denominations. Among the Negroes, attending "watch meeting" is a universal custom, and is looked upon as part of one's religious duty. The custom of ushering in the New Year by the ringing of bells and chimes and the blowing of whistles from factories and steamboats has recently been introduced into the cities and towns of the state. This begins as the town clock strikes twelve, and lasts five minutes. In some of the smaller towns, the tolling of the bells announces the death of the Old Year before the new one is rung in. During the "ringing in," those who have remained at home exchange greetings, while from room to room where sleepers are aroused, may be heard the calls "Happy New Year!" "Happy New Year!" "Same to you!" "I said it first!" There is always an effort to give the greeting before the person addressed can do so. Among those who take no part in any general celebration, as the Old Year dies and the New Year comes some may say:

> "Ring out the old,
> Ring in the new,"
> "Ring out the false,
> Ring in the true."

Source

Memoirs of the American Folklore Society, XVIII (1925), 111-12. "Folk-Lore from Maryland," collected by Annie W. Whitney and Caroline C. Bullock. Data on sources incomplete.

* * *

Graffiti on New Year's Eve

On New Year's Eve there is a church service and the [Cape Verde] children are kept in church until one A.M. Then the children go forth, and mark in chalk on every house:

> *Bons Dias*
> *Bon Ans*
> *Boas Feste*
> *An'* [1918.]
>
> Good Day
> Good Year
> Good Holiday
> Year [1918]

Source

Journal of American Folklore, XXXIV (1921), 106. Collected by Elsie Clews Parsons "from Portuguese Negroes from the Cape Verde Island living in Rhode Island and Massachusetts."

Calendar Confetti

What appeared to be confetti [in the San Francisco business district] is actually yesterday's dumping of calendar pages from office windows, a New Year's tradition downtown.

Source

San Francisco Chronicle, December 29, 1979. From a caption accompanying a photograph.

* * *

New Year's Eve at Times Square

New Year's Eve is a precise ritual for Tama Starr. At 5:30 p.m., she will climb on to the roof of One Times Square at the south end of the famous intersection of Broadway and Seventh Avenue [New York].

She will be wearing three wristwatches: two digital and one Mickey Mouse. At 7, 9 and 11 p.m., Starr will tune in a shortwave radio for the correct time from WWV, the broadcast station for the National Bureau of Standards, in Fort Collins, Colo.

Then, at *precisely* 11:59.00 p.m., and unbeknown to hundreds of thousands of revelers, Starr will let the fun begin.

On her signal, a crew of workers will use a pulley to lower a glowing six-foot apple 70 feet in a New Year's Eve's tradition with which her family's business, the Artkraft Strauss Sign Corp., has been entrusted for the last 80 years.

"For me, New Year's Eve is a cross between a very moving, religious ritual and being present at the fall of Saigon. You're really in the eye of a hurricane with excruciating boredom and mind-numbing tension," Starr said.

Adding to the tension this year is a special attraction: When the ball hits bottom after 60 seconds, it will shimmer with a strobe light and spinning mirrors to mark the "leap second," an extra second added to 1987 to correct for the slightly slowing rotation of the earth.

Tama Starr has her grandfather to thank for her role on New Year's Eve. The late Jacob Starr, a Russian immigrant who took a job as a metalworker and signmaker after arriving in New York, built the first ball for New Year's Eve in 1907, after the city outlawed fireworks for the celebration.

He later earned the title "The Lamplighter of Broadway" by making theater marquees and neon signs.

Source

Philadelphia Inquirer, December 31, 1987. By staff writer Jennifer Lin.

Philadelphia Mummers Parade

[It is 1966.] The sound comes before the sight—*Oh, Dem Golden Slippers,* barely heard, then swelling as thousands of banjos and glockenspiels feed out of the narrow lively streets into Broad Street. They come out of the heart of Philadelphia, these unique "Shooters" in their stunning and incongruous magnificence, and the rest of Philadelphia—at least a million and a quarter people—stand to watch them: a Viking carrying a hundred square feet of costume, a Fancy Captain with a train a block long, uncountable clowns in indescribable array, a myriad of musicians—the work of a year expended on one day of glory.

The splendor of the past is lightened by the satire of the president: "General Charles de Gaulle" rests on the seventh day of his labors of creation; "Mary Poppins" drifts above a seamier city than London; "Prince Philip" and "Princess Margaret" mumm out the fate of modern monarchs; oil lamps are offered neighbors to the north, New York, in case of subsequent power failures; a Hegeman Bandsman walks in space; American soldiers in Vietnam were warmed by the burning of draft-card burners; the "Great Society" is lampooned by the lesser one. The dead year is held up to a fun house wavy mirror, and its events are put in their proper significance of insignificance.

Inconspicuously rebellious, a few blackface clowns do their strut in defiance of minority groups, majority groups, and the mayor; the other clowns bow (as Mummers, with their curious bent-knee dance, can so easily do) to the latest idiocy decreed by the authorities, and put aside the burnt cork (forbidden by decree) for gold makeup—gold to daub the faces of willing and eager girls along the way and thus to lay the letter and the spirit of a past prohibition. Black for gold, gold for black; a golden lining for the blackface controversy of the past, and "Golden Slippers" yet once more in the streets of Philadelphia....

[By the 1960s the Philadelphia Mummers were represented by three groups of marchers: the Comic Clubs, the Fancy Clubs, and the String Bands.]

The earliest of all the Mummer clubs anyone can remember is the Chain Gang, which was believed to have been organized about 1840. A Comic Club as we know it today, this group organized and took a name with the expressed purpose of parading over New Year's Eve and the next day. Nothing else is known of this, our first organized club.

Shortly after the organization of the Chain Gang, some members of the Shiffler Hose Company, also known as Santa Anna's Cavalry, made the rounds in South Philadelphia on New Year's Eve and New Year's day in costumes. They wore simple costumes, and uncomplicated makeup.

In the years immediately preceding the Civil War, the residents of Southeast Philadelphia paraded on a fairly regular basis over the New Years' endings. This era has become known as the lampblack period, because the marchers used a combination of lard and lampblack to disguise themselves. Wearing this disguise, and generally, jackets turned inside out or women's clothes, etc., they would roam the area of Smoky Hollow, Stone-house Lane, Prospect Bank, Martin's Village and other sections east of League Island, in the southeastern portion of Philadelphia. The paraders quite often carried stockings filled with flour with which they would sock unwary pedestrians.

These neighborhood excursions were discontinued for five years during the Civil War. At the war's end, many clubs were organized. Among them were: the Bright Star, Morning Star, Golden Crown, and Silver Crown. Some of these clubs were short-lived, by 1882-83 the Morning Star had already disbanded. These clubs were all Fancy, though they were not yet so classified....

One of the first Comic Clubs organized was the Cold Water, which first went out in 1884. This club had a notable reputation for many years, and won many prizes. In 1900 it changed its name to Forty Sevens, and continued to make the folks on the sidelines laugh. This club soon after the turn of the century disbanded, and its members joined other clubs. Many of these old Comic Clubs had picturesque names, there were: the Hardly Ables, the Dill Pickles, the Red Onions, the Dark Lanterns, Mixed Pickles, Energetic Hoboes, and the Blue Ribbons. Later, as we shall see, the clubs were named after prominent Philadelphians.

It is difficult to separate Comic from Fancy Clubs in these early days; some clubs started as Comic and ended Fancy....

When the winds blow cold up Broad Street, the longest straightest street in the world, and the coldest when the breezes blow, the Mummers suffer intensely. The great street forms a kind of wind tunnel which throws the capes of the Fancies around as if they were sailboats on a pond. Stately and serene in fair weather, the capes become menacing burdens in foul.

This was not always so, for the early Parades were relatively small affairs. The Shooters kept close to home, and usually wore simple costumes, the kind that could be whipped up in a hurry. Clowns, Indians and Devils were much in evidence. A favorite costume was a greatcoat turned inside out. This continued until after the Civil War when the Shooters east of Broad Street, in 1875, organized the Golden Crown Club. Then on the west side of Broad Street a rival sprung up, the Silver Crown Club. Founded in 1875 the Silver Crown lasted longer than any of the other fancy clubs, marching into the thirties. It was these two clubs which brought in the Fancy Dress idea.

Following the fashion set by the "Crown" clubs, in the early eighties the following Fancy Clubs were organized: William Banner, George A. Baird, Independents, Thomas Clements, Sr., and Thomas Clements, Jr. These clubs were loosely organized, and many soon dropped out, but not without making contributions to the tradition of the Parade. For example let's take the Independents and their founder Samuel Coett. When the Independents took to the street, the costumes of the paraders were quite simple, there were none of the flaring headpieces, the widespread collars, and the flowing capes. The idea for these was conceived by Mr. Coett, assisted by his wife, daughter, and son-in-law Billy Walton. Billy Bushmeier took out the cape designed by Mr. Coett in 1880, and this was the first cape requiring page boys.

This was a period of great rivalry, and the beginning of prizes for the best paraders. This money was given by local merchants; cakes and other food items were also presented to the marchers. The Thomas Clements, Sr. Club won the first cash prize in Mummer history in 1888; this prize was presented at the McGowan Political Club. As the prizes grew in number, the rivalry grew. A custom grew up of the winners serenading the losers with a funeral march, or some similar piece. This solicitude on the part of the winners for the losers often resulted in fierce fights. During this period the Baseler Club and the Clements, Sr. Club staged a fight that resulted in a riot call.

The String Bands were not on hand to welcome in the twentieth century, but they missed it by only one year. The late Bart McHugh and the late Abe Einstein suggested to John F. Towers that he lead his band in the Parade. Here is Mr. Towers' story as printed in The Mummers Magazine of 1948; pages unnumbered.

"Birth of the String Bands"

(As told by Jack Towers, one of the four who originated the String Bands)

In the fall of 1898, I was employed in one of the leading department stores in Philadelphia. Just as with the young men of today, we would meet at noon hour and discuss different topics.

One day the subject of music was mentioned. A chap by the name of John Wygand said that he played 'banjo' and he with three others would play against any four string instrument players at any time. It just so happened that I played 'flute' with three others who played 'banjo,' 'mandolin,' and 'guitar.' His challenge was accepted and we arranged to have a 'contest' to see who were the better players.

We met the following week and after tuning up, I started to play a number that the three boys whom I had with me were familiar with. The other four, instead of waiting to play their number, immediately started to play with us. That was the

start and the end of the 'contest.' We became so interested that we played the rest of the evening together and arranged to meet every week. From time to time, new boys came to rehearsals and before the following New Year's Day, we had about 30 pieces, all string except the flute.

After two years, we were asked by Bart McHugh, who was then an entertainment promoter and who was interested in the Mummers' Parade, to go in the Parade as a novelty. We agreed.

Then came the problem of costume. We decided on a black face minstrel outfit. The entire cost was not as expensive as one string band captain's suit today. After three years, another string band was formed, 'The Oakey.' From time to time others followed.

The competition was of such a friendly nature that harmony prevailed both in music and spirit and while other instruments had been added—the sax, accordion, bass, etc.—to lend volume, yet the string instruments predominated as of today.

This is a brief outline of how the string bands came into being. I do not want to take all the credit to myself, but being the only surviving member of the organizers, I wish to share it with my departed friends, John Wygand, William Siebert, and Louis Samuels, whose memory I cherish.

Source

Charles E. Welch, Jr., "The Philadelphia Mummers Parade: A Study in History, Folklore, and Popular Tradition," Ph.D. Dissertation, University of Pennsylvania, 1968, 12-13, 61-62, 75-76, 87-88.

* * *

Philadelphia Mummers Parade
The Parade's Golden Sunrise New Year's Association

It was chilly inside the former slaughterhouse, but John Lucas was mopping his brow.

"Nerves," he said. "I get morning sickness, afternoon sickness, all kinds of uptight sickness. But once we move out for the parade, I'm fine."

Lucas, 47, is captain of the Golden Sunrise New Year's Association. Tomorrow [January 1, 1981], barring weather that is less than clement, he will lead about 300 club members up Broad Street in the Fancy Division of the 1981 Mummers Parade.

But yesterday was Lucas's last full day to inspect personnel and equipment because this morning, at 7:45, there begins the 24-hour countdown for the parade.

In the former slaughterhouse at 230 Greenwich St. in South Philadelphia, the Golden Sunrise's clubhouse since 1974, Lucas was busier than a behind-schedule beaver. He moved from costume to costume, checking them out with the people who will wear them. Then he turned to the "captain's suit" that will be his attire.

Calling Lucas's costume a suit is like calling a deep-sea diver's outfit a bikini. The outfit, titled "Oriental Fantasy," is 15 feet high. Dominated by a pagoda-like structure on top, it is 35 feet long, including a huge plastic dragon that stretches like a pre-inflation dollar and weighs about 800 pounds.

The part with the pagoda rolls on wheels, with two muscular aides, stationed inside, providing the foot power. Two other men are at the front and back of the dragon for propulsion purposes.

The suit's colors are predominantly red, orange and gold. "I feel," Lucas said, "as though I'm surrounded by flames."

What is rocking Lucas's dreamboat is the long-range forecast for New Year's Day issued at 5 p.m. yesterday by Gordon Tait, the forecaster for the National Weather Service.

"We are looking for increasing cloudiness Wednesday, with snow likely Wednesday night," Tait said. "On New Year's Day, we look for a possible snowfall of one to three inches."

"If snow falls on the plastic dragon, or on a lot of other items that are far from weatherproof, we're in big trouble," Lucas said . . . .

The Golden Sunrise Club, which finished third in the Fancy Division in last January's parade (it last won in 1978), will put close to $100,000 worth of costumes on the street. It also will feature several family combinations, including three generations of Doyles.

There will be Bill Doyle, 63, a machinist foreman, who will participate in his 55th parade as a king clown, which means he will be wearing a weighty costume. There will be Bill Doyle, Jr., 36, a warehouse worker for Acme, who will be a king jockey. He will wear a costume featuring a large figure of the Statue of Liberty.

And there will be Michael Doyle, 4, the junior Bill's son, who will wear a pot of gold outfit in the end-of-the-rainbow tableau in the parade . . . .

Keeping busy throughout the day was Palma Lucas, the captain's wife, who did just about everything from stapling costumes to making sandwiches. She maintained her cool all the way.

"And why not?" she said. "The day after the parade, the sun is going to rise, no matter what."

Source

Philadelphia Inquirer, December 31, 1980. Report on preparing for the Mummers Parade by staff writer Edgar Williams.

Philadelphia Mummers Parade
The Parade and Television

Tomorrow [January 1, 1987], weather permitting, about 20,000 Philadelphia Mummers arrayed in sequins and spangles or clothed in outrageous outfits that satirize the issues of the day will strut up Broad Street in the 88th consecutive Mummers Parade.

Ordinary Philadelphians by the thousands have been doing this every year since 1901, cheerfully enduring a 2 ½-mile march from South Philadelphia to City Hall, often in bone-chilling weather.

It's a raucous and noisy ritual whose original purpose was to frighten away any evil spirits who might be lurking around, planning to stir up trouble in the new year.

Over time, though, the Mummers Parade has gotten bigger, longer, louder and glitzier. In recent years, performances have incorporated high-kicking chorus girls and complicated mechanical devices, and the parade has acquired a sheen suggestive of a Broadway musical or a Las Vegas revue.

For as primitive as its roots are—and some trace the origins of the Mummers Parade all the way back to the worship of Momus, the ancient Greek god of mimicry—the modern-day festival, with its increasingly brilliant costumes and polished choreography, is also very much a child of television.

"The era of television, and especially color television, has drawn a lot more viewers. In order to attract attention to themselves, the groups, especially the string bands and fancy divisions, have had to come up with more and more elaborate presentations," said parade coordinator George V. Karalius.

Attracting attention to themselves is, after all, the major consideration for parade participants, who compete for prizes in four divisions: comic clubs, fancy clubs, string bands and brigades.

"They all want to win first prize, which is the name of the game," said Norma Gwynn, executive director of the Mummers Museum, the official repository of Mummer lore at Two Street and Washington Avenue. "They all want to be number one."

Even before television, the Mummers were extremely competitive, said Karalius, a deputy recreation commissioner for the city. "There are records of brawls between clubs in the 1920s and 1930s."

But television stations, by contracting for the right to broadcast the annual event, added to the competition. By pouring more money into club coffers, television has made it possible for clubs to purchase increasing quantities of feathers, sequins and spangles with which to bedeck their members, and to hire more and more professional help.

KYW-TV (Channel 3) owns exclusive rights to televise the parade, with coverage beginning at 8 a.m. and lasting until the last Mummer passes the reviewing stand 12 hours or more later.

While millions are expected to view the parade in the comfort of their living rooms, up to a million Philadelphians and visitors have lined the streets in years past to observe the festival up close.

Gwynn noted that when the Mummer tradition began, "it was a homey-type celebration, where people visited from house to house. Then it evolved into a neighborhood ritual, and then a citywide celebration, and with each evolution it became a bit more elaborate."

Source

Philadelphia Inquirer, December 31, 1987. From an article headlined "Broad St. strut grows glitzier each year" by staff writer Beth Gillin.

*   *   *

Springtime Mummers Parade

They marched on the wrong day—the 98th day of the year, not the first. And they marched the wrong way—south on Broad Street [Philadelphia], not City Hall-bound.

But the thousands of screaming, cheering and clapping spectators who packed stoops, windowsills and sidewalks along 18 blocks of Broad Street yesterday [April 8, 1989] didn't seem to mind. The Mummers were back, and they weren't in buses.

"January first was the worst," said Sylvia Romano of the 1600 block of South Broad Street, remembering the drenching rains of New Year's Day, the traditional day for the Mummers Parade. The rain that day drove many of the string band performers—and their elaborate costumes of feather and satin—to the safety of buses.

But there was no need for artificial shelter in yesterday's brisk, refreshing breeze and squinting sunshine.

"C'mon, drill for us," Romano screamed at the penguin who led the Quaker City String Band. The band strutted its considerable stuff, to Romano's shrieking delight. "This more than makes up for" the aborted New Year's Day parade, she said.

The shindig yesterday was a stripped-down version of the usual affair: just 23 string bands in a 3 ½-hour parade. There were no fancy brigades, comics, judges or prizes. And fewer people than usual....

A spectator could enjoy all the wonderful sounds of a Mummers Parade. Whistles and glockenspiels and cornets and banjos. Children shrieking. Pretzel vendors hawking.

The soft hum of a Cadillac convertible idling. The muted roar of a subway running underneath Broad Street....

Donna Murareesku, a member of the Duffy String Band, said she was pleased to have a second chance after the New Year's Day debacle. "You could hear the people screaming," she recalled yesterday, " 'Get off the bus and march! Be a string band!' They were throwing tomatoes and bottles. What a mess. Today, people were happy that we were out."

But Murareesku found it strange to be marching down Broad Street in spring, not winter, and going southbound, not northbound. "It was awkward, 'cause you kept looking for City Hall and not seeing it. You kept wondering how many more blocks you had to go."

She was talking at the finishing point of the parade, at Marconi Plaza at Broad Street and Oregon Avenue, several blocks north of Veterans' Stadium.

Several hours earlier, at the parade's starting line, Frank Foidl, music director of the Polish-American String Band, said he felt he was making history. He's been a Mummer for 35 years, and he's never marched on Broad Street on a day other than Jan. 1.

"Lots of other streets on lots of other days, but the Mummers Parade *is* Broad Street and it *is* New Year's Day. This is nice," Foidl said of the spring air and the festive surroundings. "Nice for the marchers and nice for the people, but it's not the same thing."...

*   *   *

[Nonetheless,] some radicals even suggested that Mummers Parades should regularly be held in the spring rather than Jan. 1.

"They ought to always have it in April," said Andrea Wasser, a Fairmount resident whose daughter Molly, 1, was just a little frightened at seeing her first Mummers Parade yesterday.

"It's beautiful. The sun is shining on the sequins and feathers and everything," said South Philadelphia resident Yolanda Ciarrocchi. "Today was the right day."

Donna Howard, 33, of Holmes, bragged that her family had been "the best crowd and the loudest crowd" at Broad and Mifflin Streets since she was 2 years old.

But was an April Mummers Parade really the same?

"We had the same spirit [as on New Year's Day]. We had a good time," she said. "It was beautiful today, it was exceptional, it was really nice.... We had good weather, nobody got wet."

Howard and others who had attended the Jan. 1 parade said they were willing to forgive the city for the New Year's Day fiasco, when the snow and rain ruined costumes and forced many parade participants to ride buses—past vocally disappointed onlookers—up Broad Street to Walnut Street, where they resumed marching.

Source

Philadelphia Inquirer, April 9, 1989. A composite of two articles, by staff writers Michael Bamberger and Mark Fazlollah.

* * *

Fantasticals

Fantasticals, or fantastics, were grotesquely clad men—young men usually—who paraded the streets on horseback, in wagons and sleighs or on foot in a noisy fashion on certain festival days, primarily on New Year's morning....

My attention was first called to fantasticals about six years ago, when I was collecting lore in the area of the Moonshine church in Lebanon County (north of Indiantown Gap) [Pennsylvania]. Old-timers there told me it used to be a custom for young men to disguise themselves, mask and all, on New Year's Day and visit the one-room schools of the neighborhood, principally to frighten the innocent youngsters....

How old the custom is and whence its origin are both unknown quantities as of now. The name fantasticals or fantastics itself strongly suggests British Isle roots. The earliest evidence for fantastical parades in the area under study is for the year 1829. On New Year's Day of this year a group of Schuylkill Countians participated in a fantastical parade in neighboring Berks County. One of the participants, Solomon Berwin, in 1895, described their experiences as follows: "About three o'clock on the morning of January 1 [1829] we had visited thirty-seven different farm houses and traveled at least ten miles. We then all struck for Shartlesville and thence the entire party proceeded to Rehrersburg, where a parade was to be held at eight o'clock. We Schuylkill Countians took our teams and loaded on as many of the rest as could get on. We could not drive fast on account of our heavy load, so it was almost daylight by the time we reached Rehrersburg. Here everybody was already astir. A number of teams that were to enter the procession arrived some time before our party. By eight o'clock at least thirty large teams were in line, about half of which were composed of six and eight horses. The drivers were dressed in all sorts of fantastic costumes. Several large hay wagons loaded with young women dressed in the most ludicrous manner possible, were mixed in with the sleighs. The teams were followed by about seventy men on foot each of whom carried a gun. On account of the horses the shooting was postponed until after the parade, but then there was a series of reports that could be heard for miles."

Source and Comment

Pennsylvania Folklife, IX (Winter 1957-58), 28-29. Alfred L. Shoemaker studied the custom of "fantastical parades" mainly in eastern and central Pennsylvania. His sources were "diaries, newspapers of the area, and field work." Cf. "Cajun Country Mardi Gras," p. 92

In the Pennsylvania Dutch country, "fantasticals" also paraded on "Second Christmas," the Feast of Epiphany, and they sometimes formed part of the processions on Washington's Birthday, July 4th, and "Battalion Day," Whitmonday, the day set aside for mustering the militia. Their processions and antics survive in the "comic divisions" of the Philadelphia Mummers parade on New Year's Day.

* * *

La Guiannée

The walls of once-powerful Fort de Chartres have crumbled and the mighty Mississippi River has changed its course, but the centuries-old French New Year's tradition of *La Guiannée* lives on in this southern Illinois town.

Liberally translated as "mistletoe of the New Year," the singing and drinking fest today will continue as one of the oldest folk traditions still observed in this country.

The tradition reminds the 650 inhabitants of this 260-year-old community, nestled under the cliffs overlooking the Mississippi, of an era when nearby Fort de Chartres was the strongest French colonial strong-hold in North America.

The fest starts as soon as the 6:30 A.M. Mass ends at St. Joseph's Catholic Church. Revelers don costumes, many made from cornhusks, and begin a door-to-door trek to sing traditional French songs.

Townspeople who want to be serenaded telephone ahead to schedule the singers, who now travel by bus. In years past, everyone walked.

Fort de Chartres will be the second stop this year, and that stop will be "the only real chance the public will have to see the singers," said Steve Anderson, a site interpreter.

The fort will be illuminated with torches and candles and the singers will see a roaring fire in the hearth and a long oak table laden with cold meats, cookies and mulled cider, Anderson said.

At private homes, they will be tempted with whiskey, wine or homemade cherry brandy, a return to the custom in which mummers performed for alms or refreshments.

Source

Philadelphia Inquirer, January 1, 1982. An Associated Press feature by J. L. Schmidt, filed from Prairie du Rocher, Illinois. Cf. "Cajun Country Mardi Gras," p. 92.

First Night Revels in Boston

With organizers promising the celebration would be bigger and better than ever, an estimated 600,000 revelers jammed Boston's chilly streets yesterday to bid farewell to 1987 and usher in 1988 at the city's 12th annual First Night extravaganza.

Turning Boston into a stage, more than 1,000 artists and performers entertained children and adults at 58 indoor and outdoor sites. More than 200 events were featured, including opera, dance, storytelling, juggling, ice sculptures, face-painting and laser shows.

The lively sounds of jazz and the pungent smells of spicy sausages and salty pretzels filled the 34-degree air.

As night came, dozens of vendors swarmed onto Boylston Street hawking gaudy masks, colorful balloons, party hats, favors and horns. "So far so good," reported vendor Mary Salvadore. "Little by little, they are selling."

Although the day's events officially began in the early afternoon, most people agreed that First Night didn't really get into gear until the sun went down and the parade began. And it didn't end until midnight, with the three-minute fireworks display over Boston Harbor.

As the parade kickoff drew near, hordes of party-goers squeezed onto the streets and sidewalks near the Prudential Center, many admiring the colorful lights of the giant Christmas tree in front of the building.

For the 60 minutes the parade lasted, Boylston Street resembled Times Square on New Year's Eve as people stood shoulder-to-shoulder, sporting garish costumes, many singing and yelling. The blaring sounds of party horns competed with the shouts of vendors trying to attract customers.

First Night organizers had encouraged people to wear costumes, have their faces painted and don masks to break down the barrier between performer and audience.

Forming on Boylston Street in front of the Prudential Center shortly after 5:30 p.m., the nearly quarter-mile procession with its several thousand marchers captured the eclectic essence of First Night.

A convoy of police cruisers led the way, slowly inching through a gauntlet of party-goers squeezing in from both sides of the street. Following Mayor Flynn and his family was a Father Time figure dressed in white and carrying three doves in a wooden cage.

The colorful column cut a swath through Boston from the Back Bay to the Boston Common. Among other things, it featured a giant inflated spider, skeletons atop stilts, Chinese dancers, unicyclists and the Geometric Progressions marching band.

Many of the marchers wore oversized heads, arms and hands, adding a touch of Mardis Gras to the scene.

An 8-foot-tall ice sculpture with the dates 1987 and 1988 carved in it sat atop a trailer. As the parade streamed down Boylston Street, a sculptor slowly picked away at 1987 and by the time the procession reached the Common, the old year had disappeared....

The start of a New Year has traditionally been a time for people to make resolutions. In response, First Night organizers crafted a 25-foot "Resolution Tree" out of pine. With holes drilled into the tree, passersby could jot down resolutions on green and white silken leaves and stick them in the slots.

"I wished for good things for ourselves and for the birds and the animals," said Al Haskell of Cohasset.

"I resolved never to make another resolution," said Carolyn Menan of Quincy.

Jackie Dawson, making her way through the slush-filled Common with her children, Christopher, 10, and Kimberly, 9, lauded an operatic rendition of Little Red Riding Hood performed at the Tremont Temple Baptist Church.

"It's a great opportunity for the kids to see plenty of things that they normally would not get to see all at once," Dawson said of the day's festivities.

Source

Boston Globe, January 1, 1988. By staff writers and Diego Ribadeneira, Alexander Reid. Cf. "The John Kuner Ceremony," p. 445.

* * *

Tournament of Roses

When Dr. Charles Frederick Holder suggested sponsorship of a midwinter community festival to Pasadena's [California] Valley Hunt Club in 1889, he must have faced a ready audience. Not only did the community need a day of pleasure—Pasadena had just come through the most devastating real estate crash it would probably ever experience—but it wanted to show the rest of the nation its utopian climate, which produced roses and oranges in the middle of winter.

At the suggestion of Dr. Frances F. Rowland, the event was patterned after a festival of roses in Europe. The Valley Hunt Club adopted the plan and, on January 1, 1890, held a community parade and picnic with prizes for the most beautifully-flowered buggies and tally-hos. Awards were also given to the best horsemen and winners of various games and sports.

By 1895 the parade had become so large and complex that the Pasadena Tournament of Roses Association was formed to administer it. The last straw for the Valley Hunt Club may have come when the 1895 parade had to be run through a week's accumulation of rainwater and mud (it has rained on New Year's Day festivities in Pasadena only seven times since 1890: in 1899, 1906, 1910, 1916, 1922, 1934, and 1955).

The new association's first 10 years saw the parade grow and change tremendously. The first reporters sent from major eastern newspapers in 1898 only hinted at the nearly worldwide media coverage the parade would eventually receive. Other harbingers of change came with the first cars allowed in the parade (1901), the first intersectional football game (1902), and the first Rose Queen (1905).

The introduction of the automobile caused quite a stir. Cars were relegated to the end of the 1901 parade so that the horses wouldn't be frightened, but had to move to the front when the slow pace of the parade caused their engines to overheat. The machines made their mark though, and by 1920 virtually all parade floats were motorized.

The first football game in 1902 was equally tentative. Michigan smashed Stanford 49-0 in Tournament Park before a crowd of 8,000. Football wasn't again attempted until 1916, when Washington State proved the competence of West Coast teams with a 14-0 victory over Brown.

The coronation of Hallie Woods as first Rose Queen (1905) had equal impact. Tournament directors experimented with the idea of parade royalty on and off in the following years, even selecting a Rose Queen and King in 1913 and 1914. Finally, in 1930, Queen Holly Halstead became the first in an unbroken chain of Rose Queens that continues to the present.

The Rose Parade today is a colorful melange of roughly 60 floats, 24 bands and 250 equestrians.... The 60 Rose Parade floats are entered by cities, states, countries, corporations, and many other types of organizations. Most of them are built by professional contractors in the Pasadena area, though some entrants build their own. All floats in the parade are completely covered with fresh flowers, seeds, leaves, and other natural materials. In judging for the top prizewinners, exceptional use of roses counts heavily in a participant's favor. There are 17 major parade prizes.

With a curbside audience of more than a million people and a post parade viewing audience of perhaps 250,000, Rose Parade floats set the standards for quality throughout the industry.

In the same way, the Rose Bowl Game is recognized as the granddaddy game; the one some 14 other post-season bowl games have patterned themselves after, though none has met with equal success. The Rose Bowl formula is really very simple: it brings together the best college football teams of the Big Ten and Pacific-8 conferences. This arrangement has endured since 1947, and has resulted in sellout Rose Bowl crowds nearly every year since then. The

record attendance of 106,869 was set at the 1973 Rose Bowl classic, when USC defeated Ohio State 42-17.

Source

Pasadena Tournament of Roses: Tradition on Parade, 1980, 1-2. From mimeographed publicity material supplied in 1982 by the Tournament of Roses Association, 391 South Orange Grove Boulevard, Pasadena, California 91105. The Pacific-8 is now the Pacific-10.

* * *

Tournament of Roses
Sports and Games: A Rose Bowl Tradition

Afternoon sports were the climax to New Year's Day in Pasadena, 1890, as Don Arturo Bandini, a member of the prominent Early California family, signaled the start of the first event—the 100 yard dash.

H.R. Hertel, who became Association President ten years later, was second in the one mile run. Following were horse races, pony races, burro races, and bronco riding. Bandini proved to be an expert at the Tourney of Rings, also called tilting of the rings [cf. "Jousting Tournaments," p. 265]. A tug of war team from Duarte out pulled a Pasadena team and the members of the winning unit each received a manicure set.

Bicycle races were held from 1895 through 1898 at a track on North Lincoln Avenue. In the 1899 procession, there was a very hardy soul by the name of G.A.W. Haas, who pedaled his way the length of the procession in his finest hour. It was a very easy effort for him—rain or no rain. He had become something of a celebrity after riding the same bicycle from New York to Pasadena. He also wore the same outfit that clothed him as he cycled the entire way across the United States.

Polo was introduced in 1901 as a team from Riverside defeated Santa Barbara 4-1. A crowd of 5,000 witnessed the exciting contest.

The first intersectional college football game was played in Tournament Park on the afternoon of January 1, 1902, between Michigan and Stanford after the stalwarts of both elevens had ridden in the parade.

Tournament officials turned thumbs down on football in 1903 and decided on staging another polo match. Only 2,000 persons watched the event. Inspired by the recently published book, "Ben Hur" by Lew Wallace, C.D. Daggett, Tournament President, suggested the staging of chariot races.

In 1913 there was an ostrich race, a race between an elephant and a camel, and a race between an American cowboy, cowgirl, Mexican, and an Indian. In 1914 and 1915 chariot races were held, interspersed with track events.

In 1916 the directorate scheduled a game between Brown and Washington State, reinstating football and launching a series that remains unbroken today. The Rose Bowl is the grandfather game. There were just 1,000 seats at Tournament Park during the first game. The seating capacity was enlarged two-and-one-half times in 1904. During the chariot race era, the capacity was expanded to 20,000 by 1912. Five years later another 5,000 seats were added.

Economics of chariot racing and the unending rise in the popularity of college football brought about a day of decision for the Tournament officials. Chariot racing was given back to the Romans. Football was to be featured in Pasadena on New Year's Day.

Football's most talked about play occurred in the 1929 game when Roy Riegels, Cal center, scooped up a Georgia Tech fumble and raced toward the wrong goal, being tackled by his team-mate, Quarterback Benny Lom. Also, on a quick kick, the ball went flat and Georgia Tech took the contest 8-7.

Source

Pasadena Tournament of Roses: Tradition on Parade, 1980, 1-2. From mimeographed publicity material supplied in 1982 by the Tournament of Roses Association, 391 South Orange Grove Boulevard, Pasadena, California 91105.

* * *

Tournament of Roses
Rose Bowl Scoreboard Shenanigans

It was late in the third quarter of the Rose Bowl game Monday [January 2, 1984] when officials, watching the scoreboard, began to have a sinking sensation. The computer-controlled board had taken on a life of its own.

"We knew we were being intruded upon. And we knew it must be Caltech," said Terry Belanger, who runs the Rose Bowl for the City of Pasadena.

First, the scoreboard's operators heard a curious static. Then strange messages began appearing on it. Continuing a tradition of sophisticated shenanigans, students from the California Institute of Technology had once again engineered a prank of impressive proportions:

Two seniors, Ted Williams and Dan Kegel—displaying computer wizardry that even IBM would cherish—took control of the Rose Bowl scoreboard and, among other things, changed the names of the competing teams—UCLA and the University of Illinois—to Caltech and its chief academic rival, Massachusetts Institute of Technology (MIT).

And Kegel is going to get academic credit for his role in the scoreboard switcheroo.

With more than nine minutes to go in the game, frustrated officials, unable to stop the pranksters, shut down the scoreboard. As the game ran down, spectators had no idea how much time was left.

For at least one person, the blackout was a relief. "The highlight of the game came for me when the scoreboard went out," said University of Illinois coach Mike White, whose team lost, 45-9.

Dennis Meredith, director of Caltech's news bureau, said yesterday that "people are pleased here. Caltech is proud of its prowess in these kinds of things. The prank was clever and elegantly wrought. Second, it was harmless. And finally, it had an element of humor that everyone could enjoy."

Meredith said that Kegel, 21, from Seattle, told a faculty member in electrical engineering about his plans to override a computer-run scoreboard and received the professor's approval. Kegel did not tell the faculty member until Sunday that it would be the Rose Bowl scoreboard, Meredith said.

"I think Kegel applied for six credits, but I think he'll get nine," Meredith said.

Williams said yesterday that he and others at the Pasadena school talked in late 1982 about what they could do to "make Caltech better known." In 1961, Caltech students subverted the half-time card show at the Rose Bowl game by counterfeiting the written instructions to fans in the stadium and then distributing 2,232 phony instruction sheets. So, instead of University of Washington students spelling out WASHINGTON at halftime, they unknowingly flashed NOTGNIHSAW and CALTECH to a national TV audience.

Wanting to strike at the Rose Bowl again, Williams, Kegel and others decided to try to gain control of the scoreboard.

"We did a little espionage in the next few months to figure out how the scoreboard works." Williams said yesterday....

Williams said that last week "we snuck in" and planted a computer the size of a small radio in the Rose Bowl stadium. Then on Monday, with their backpacks laden with binoculars, another computer and a radio control, they perched on a hill of the San Gabriel Mountains about two miles away. They could see the scoreboard. Confederates brought a television set and a radio.

They were ready. In the first quarter, they tested their system by inserting periods after the letters in UCLA on the scoreboard. They kept the periods there for 30 seconds. It worked.

But there was one problem: No one noticed. There was no reaction among the more than 100,000 in the stands. And the television announcers said nothing.

In the second quarter, the pranksters put DEI on the scoreboard, a piece of arcane Caltech graffiti that has also found its way onto the Voyager spacecraft which, at the moment, is hurtling its way out of our solar system.

Still nothing.

GO CIT! drew no response. Nor did a matrix picture of a beaver, the school's emblem. At that point, Kegel and Williams decided that the 30-second messages were not doing the job.

"We were pretty depressed that no one was noticing our stuff," Williams said. "We decided to be more obvious."

So, in the fourth quarter, with the score 38-9, the teams suddenly changed to Caltech and MIT on the scoreboard. And this time, instead of stopping after 30 seconds, Kegel and Williams kept control. And this time, the television announcers noticed....

Meredith said the campus was buzzing yesterday and that he had received calls from former students congratulating the school on keeping the prankster tradition alive.

Kegel said there had also been a very special call.

"It was from the two guys who set up the 1961 Rose Bowl stunt. They called to congratulate us. But they wanted to know why it had taken 23 years."

Source

Philadelphia Inquirer, January 4, 1984. By staff writer Murray Dubin, reporting from Pasadena, California.

* * *

Kissing Day

When missionaries began to work among the Minnesota Indians, particularly among the Chippewa of the North, they found that the natives made much of New Year's Day. They celebrated the holiday, which they called "Kissing day," after the manner of the French-Canadian traders and voyagers. The puritanical religious leaders often were obliged, much against their wishes, to observe the day in the native manner. William T. Boutwell, who went to Leech Lake in 1833, found that the Indians there were in the habit of visiting the resident trader on January 1 to receive presents, "when all, male and female, old and young, must give and receive a kiss, a cake, or something else." They seemed to expect similar treatment from Boutwell, for on the first day of 1834 they caused the pious missionary considerable annoyance by appearing at his cabin at breakfast time. He relates the story as follows:

> Open came our door, and in came 5 or 6 women and as many children. An old squaw, with clean face, for once, came up and saluted me with, "*bon jour,*" giving her hand at the same time, which I received, returning her compliment, "*bon jour.*"

But this was not all. She had been too long among Canadians not to learn some of their New Year Customs. She approached—approached so near, to give and receive a kiss, that I was obliged to give her a slip, and dodge! This vexed the old lady and provoked her to say, that I thought her too dirty. But pleased, or displeased, I was determined to give no countenance to a custom which I hated more than dirt.

At Red Lake twelve years later a band of missionaries planned a New Year's celebration which seemed to please the natives, who "honored" them "with a salute of two guns." The missionaries at this place recognized the Indian custom and took part in the celebration. According to Lucy M. Lewis, the wife of one of the missionaries, all the mission workers gathered at early dawn at the house of their leader, "the most convenient place to meet the Indians who assemble to give the greeting and receive a cake or two & a draught of sweetened water. It is the custom through the country to make calls & receive cakes." But instead of offering kisses, these Indians sang a "New Year's hymn learned in school for the occasion." The Red Lake missionaries marked New Year's Eve by assembling the pupils of the mission school and giving them presents. In 1845 the gifts consisted of flannel shirts for the boys and "short gowns" for the girls. The Indian children "came with cleaner faces & hands than usual," writes Mrs. Lewis, "as a little soap had previously been distributed."

Source

Minnesota History, XVI (1935), 375-76. Holiday customs on the Minnesota frontier during the nineteenth century are described by Bertha L. Heilbron. She quotes the manuscript Boutwell Diary, January 1, 1834, and correspondence in the Minnesota Historical Society collections.

* * *

New Year's on a Louisiana Plantation

New Year's Day on the plantations was an occasion of great merriment and pleasure for the slaves. Its observance gave rise to scenes so characteristic of old times that I shall endeavor to describe them.

At daylight, on the 1st of January, the rejoicing began on the plantation; everything was in an uproar, and all the negroes, old and young, were running about, shaking hands and exchanging wishes for the new year. The servants employed at the house came to awaken the master and mistress and the children. The nurses came to our beds to present their *souhaits* [wishes]. To the boys it was always, "*Mo souhaité ké vou bon garçon, fe plein l'argent é ké vou bienhéreux*" ["My wish is that you are a good boy, that you lot of money and that you have good luck"]; to the girls, "*Mo souhaité ké vou bon fïe, ké vou gagnin ein mari riche é plein piti*" ["My wish is that you are a good girl, that you marry a husband rich and kind"].

Even the very old and infirm, who had not left the hospital for months, came to the house with the rest of *l'atelier* [hands] for their gifts. These they were sure to get, each person receiving a piece of an ox killed expressly for them, several pounds of flour, and a new tin pan and spoon. The men received, besides, a new jean or cottonade suit of clothes, and the women a dress and a most gaudy headkerchief or *tignon,* the redder the better. Each woman that had had a child during the year received two dresses instead of one. After the *souhaits* were presented to the masters, and the gifts were made, the dancing and singing began. The scene was indeed striking, interesting, and weird. Two or three hundred men and women were there in front of the house, wild with joy and most boisterous, although always respectful.

Their musical instruments were, first, a barrel with one end covered with an ox-hide,—this was the drum; then two sticks and the jawbone of a mule, with the teeth still on it,—this was the violin. The principal musician bestrode the barrel and began to beat on the hide, singing as loud as he could. He beat with his hands, with his feet, and sometimes, when quite carried away by his enthusiasm, with his head also. The second musician took the sticks and beat on the wood of the barrel, while the third made a dreadful music by rattling the teeth of the jawbone with a stick. Five or six men stood around the musicians and sang without stopping. All this produced a most strange and savage music, but, withal, not disagreeable, as the negroes have a very good ear for music, and keep a pleasant rhythm in their songs. These dancing-songs generally consisted of one phrase, repeated for hours on the same air.

In the dance called *carabiné* [vigorous, spicy], and which was quite graceful, the man took his *danseuse* by the hand, and made her turn around very rapidly for more than an hour, the woman waving a red handkerchief over her head, and every one singing,—

> "*Madame Gobar, en sortant di bal,*
> *Madame Gobar, tiyon li tombé.*"

> ["Madame Gobar, leaving the dance,
> Madame Gobar, the little one, she fell."]

The other dance, called *pile Chactas* [Choctaw post], was not as graceful as the *carabiné,* but was more strange. The woman had to dance almost without moving her feet. It was the man who did all the work: turning around her, kneeling down, making the most grotesque and extraordinary faces, writhing like a serpent, while the woman was almost immovable. After a little while, however, she began to get excited, and untying her neckerchief, she waved it around gracefully, and finally ended by wiping off the perspiration from the face of her *danseur,* and also from the faces of the musicians who played the barrel and the jawbone, an act which must have been gratefully received by those sweltering individuals.

The ball, for such it was, lasted for several hours, and was a great amusement to us children. It must have been less entertaining to our parents, but they never interfered, as they considered that, by a well-established custom, New Year's Day was one of mirth and pleasure for the childlike slaves.

Source

Journal of American Folklore, I (1888), 136-37. From an essay on "Customs and Superstitions in Louisiana" by Alcée Fortier, historian and folklorist, at Tulane University, New Orleans.

* * *

New Year's Calling

New Year's calling was a pleasant custom of the late nineteenth and early twentieth centuries. On New Year's Day all doors were open to the young men of the city [New York]. There were no fixed invitations. The callers wandered from home to home—tenement or brownstone front—whether they had ever before visited in this place or that. The one requirement for entry was a calling card. On this point the girls of the household were insistent. A desire for cards prompted all preparations. No matter how divergently one might talk about the custom, say in terms of girls meeting eligible boys or parents renewing old friendships, the cards none-the-less underlay the whole business. In quality and quantity, they, to the female mind, meant social success or failure.

For this reason each young man sought a type face compatible with his personality and a quality cardboard distinguished to the touch. All during December local printers were kept busy duplicating the samples in their show windows, conservative and bearing austere block letters on a white background, cards printed in crimson capitals filigreed with gold, novelty cards to which a small mug bearing the caller's nicknames was attached by a red or green ribbon, cards that stood up by themselves or that glittered open under the springy thrust of an accordion fold.

On New Year's Day, the caller appeared at the door, probably in the old Scotch tradition of "first-foot," and was welcomed by the head of the house—usually Father in his smoking jacket. Then surrounded by girls, the young man was led to a cut glass bowl at a table in the hallway. Here he drew from his vest pocket a leather or silver case pranked with delicate designs, opened it, and tossed a card into the twinkling bowl.

With such importance placed on these tokens, no wonder consternation and fretting prevailed if the first arrivals, as so often happened, were delayed. Horsecars and buggies moved slowly when snow was copious and backs of animals steam under fallen flakes. But eventually, through the wintry day in sleighs of jingling bells or on foot, ankledeep in drifts, with scarves blowing back over shoulders, hats awry, the callers came. Sometimes they came in groups, a little tipsy and singing as they came....

On the sideboard in the parlor the callers found decanters surrounded by plates of sugared *pfefferneusse,* spicy and hard as stones. Across the room, sarsaparilla, creamy and effervescent, splashed into stoneware mugs, and on the table glimmered many-tiered cakes, covered with glazed fruits or lush with different colored icings....

Under mistletoe and jaded boughs of Christmas, the first day of the new year was celebrated to its end. The hostesses insisted that "tomorrow will be Ladies' Day," but few really intended to go calling next morning. Ladies' Day was more of a threat than a custom.

Source and Comment

New York Folklore Quarterly, XVI (1960), 295-97. Alonzo Gibbs describes, in general terms, the New Year's custom of "calling" in New York. The time is not specified but is presumably the latter part of the nineteenth century.

The popular *Hill's Manual of Social and Business Forms* (... edition [of] 1880) has an extensive section on the etiquette of the New Year's "call":

> Of late years it had become fashionable, for ladies in many cities and villages, to announce in the newspapers the fact of their intention to receive calls upon New Year's Day, which practice is excellent, as it enables gentlemen to know positively who will be prepared to receive them on that occasion; ...

> Upon calling, the gentlemen are invited to remove overcoat and hat, which invitation is accepted unless it is the design to make the call very brief.... Gloves are sometimes retained upon the hand during the call, but this is optional. Cards are sent up, and the gentlemen are ushered into the reception room. The call should not exceed ten or fifteen minutes, unless the callers are few and it should be mutually agreeable to prolong the stay....

> The two or three days succeeding the New Year's are ladies days for calling, upon which occasion they pass the compliments of the season, comment upon the incidents connected with the festivities of the holiday, the number of calls made, and the new faces that made their appearance among the visitors. It is customary upon this occasion of ladies meeting, to offer refreshments and to enjoy the intimacy of a friendly visit. This fashion of observing New Year's Day is often the means of commencing pleasant friendships which may continue through life.

New Year's Calling in Early Wisconsin

In frontier Wisconsin the New Year was made welcome with the ever popular ball. Barely had the participants recovered from their Christmas revelry when they made ready for the New Year day visitors. Making a round of calls on that day was a recognized social practice, noticeably participated in by the men of the community. Convention required the serving of refreshments by the 'at home' hostesses. In Milwaukee 'the first day of New Year [1851] ... was enjoyed, apparently, by all concerned. The Ladies were "at home" to receive visitors and had no lack of calls thro' day and evening. The pleasant weather and capital sleighing did much to make the day pass off agreeably.' January 1, 1857, 'the streets were alive with people enjoying the holiday, there were numbers of sleighs filled with gentlemen paying the annual visit of congratulation.' There was less calling in 1859 though New Year's eve was one of general hilarity: 'There was considerable jollity about our city, Friday night, and a very general seeing of "the Old Year out and the New Year in." There were four, or five Balls, during the evening.... The "calling" was not general, though quite a number of gentlemen went the rounds....'

A Madison journalist in 1857 says of this holiday: 'The day passed off very pleasantly. The social custom of calling was quite generally observed. The day was an admirable one for the purpose, the sleighing capital, and the streets in good condition for pedestrians.' He informs the public of an accident to mar the day's pleasures. A large sleigh containing people from Lake Side watercure overturned on the corner of Washington avenue, near the Episcopal church, but no one was severely injured.

Source

Wisconsin Magazine of History, XXII (June 1939). From "Social Life in Wisconsin" by Lillian Krueger, which deals with the territorial period through the mid-1860s. Footnotes credit Milwaukee and Madison newspapers of the 1850s as a major source. Cf. "Greeting the New Year," p. 1, and "New Year's Calling," p. 13.

* * *

New Year's Dance

New Year's was celebrated [by Polish families in New York Mills, New York] with a dance held in a large hall, decorated with fruit hanging from the walls. While the couples were dancing, the lights went out, and attempts were made to steal the fruit before the lights came on again. At the dance were "policemen" to catch the thieves, and a "judge" to fine them a coin or two. (My mother remembers going to dances like these when she was young, but they are no longer [in 1968] held.)

Source

New York Folklore Quarterly, XXIV (1968), 302–303. From "Polish Customs in New York Mills, N.Y.," by Robert Maziarz. See "Polish

Christmas Eve Supper," p. 440, and note, p. 441, for background and information.

* * *

Japanese New Year

In contrast to the elaborate manner in which New Year is welcomed in Japan, the same holiday as celebrated by Japanese in America [c. 1934] is quite simple. In chatting with members of the older generation, there was disclosed the interesting fact that, graphically illustrated, there has been a distinct curve in the degree of observance of Japanese New Year. Though exact dates and figures cannot be given without more extensive research, the following observations, though they indicate only roughly the trends that have taken place, are nevertheless revelatory.

For about ten years after the 1890s—which may be considered the beginning of extensive Japanese settlement in Alameda County [California]—the Japanese holidays, not even expecting the all-important New Year, were scarcely observed. Not only the scarcity of Japanese people at that time, but also the lack of appropriate paraphernalia for celebrating the holidays and the fact that these pioneers were too busily occupied in the task of colonization, account for this seeming absence of feeling for the festivals of their mother country. However, from about 1900 and for some twenty years after, a renewed interest in their national holidays developed, literally flared up.

A rather large Japanese community, added to greater leisure after the first years of hard work and the opening of stores handling merchandise from Japan, encouraged the Japanese people to satisfy their instinctive wish to celebrate the festivals of their home country. According to one of the older members of the Japanese community in Oakland [California], until about the year 1906 approximately one-tenth of the Japanese kept strict observance of the New Year spirit in the Japanese style by arranging the triple-tree decoration ... just outside their doors. He added that though this custom was not preserved in private homes after 1906, proprietors of large Japanese concerns, particularly in San Francisco, elaborately bedecked their store-fronts with pine, bamboo, and plum tree branches until as late as 1920.

Another new feature of the New Year celebration was the setting out of the American and Japanese flags, a practice retained by three-fourths of the Japanese people in America until about the year 1917. Since that date, flags have not been prominently displayed outside the houses, except in front of large stores or, less conspicuously, inside the homes. The year 1917 also seems to mark the decline of the observance of the custom of making New Year calls, a proceeding which up to that time the Japanese had followed almost one hundred percent. Furthermore, only until about 1917 or 1918 did the Japanese girls spend part of New Year's day playing battledore and shuttlecock, whereas *karuta*—a Japanese card game—and *sugoroku* (backgammon) parties were popular even as late as 1928 and 1929. The custom of exchanging New Year gifts has been steadily fading out among the Japanese in America, giving way to the more universal Christmas presents.

The one feature of the New Year celebration which has been preserved even to this day, at least within the family, is the provision and consumption of some of the special New Year foods and the drinking of wine. Many members of the older generation chuckled when asked whether they were forced to give up their custom of imbibing *sake* during the period of prohibition. A very great minority of them, even to this day, spend some days before New Year's Day pounding out rice into *mochi* .... [Characteristic New Year's food, rice dumpling, steamed and pounded.] The bright red lobster—supposed to be a symbol of old age on account of its crooked back—which is a feature of the outdoor decoration in Japan, has been given a less conspicuous place. Nevertheless, it still adorns the interior of many homes....

Yet it is to be doubted whether here in America, even at the time of the fullest and most elaborate New Year celebrations, the holidays lasted more than a day, for economic exigencies demanded resumption of business as soon as possible. The one clear cut manifestation of the holiday spirit even today is the three-day period of non-publication observed by all the Japanese newspapers, a luxury indulged in on no other occasion. As a whole, therefore, New Year's as celebrated by the Japanese in America has lost that air of relaxation and carefree rejoicing so easily submitted to and so contagious during the New Year holidays in Japan.

A questioning of the members of the younger generation of Japanese in America brought to light also the fact that they are slowly but surely discarding Japanese traditions of the New Year celebration. The custom of giving the house a thorough cleaning, for instance, as well as that of remaining at home on December 31st to welcome the New Year, are both disappearing. Boisterous hilarity with confetti, bells, horns, and so forth, and going to New Year's Eve dancing parties and midnight-shows seem to be more to the taste of the younger Japanese. Today, there still exists an unresolved conflict between the parents' desire to have the entire family home on New Year's Eve, and the children's desire to celebrate it in the American style. This circumstance accounts, in part, for the relatively poor attendance at dances given on that evening.

With the passing of the years, however, there is an indication that the younger folk will do as they please, and that their elders will have to resign themselves, as best they can, to the influence of American modes and manners on their children. Whether or not they go out on New Year's

Eve, it is true that today the younger generation no longer spend New Year's Eve playing Japanese cards and backgammon, nor do they indulge in the simple pastimes of spinning tops, flying kites, and playing battledore and shuttlecock.

As to the matter of food, it is to be expected that in families in which the parents are of the first generation, the special preparation and partaking of Japanese foods will continue.

Source and Comment

Southwestern Journal of Anthropology, II (1946), 166–68. Collected and reported by "Miss N.I.," a researcher for Paul Radin, who edited her material, as part of a study he directed in 1934 of "customs and beliefs of the Oriental minorities in the San Francisco Bay area."

In Japan Shōgatsu, or New Year's, is probably the gayest and most significant celebration of a national culture unusually rich in festivals. Preparations begin during the last week of December and the festive season continues until the middle of January. (Japan now uses the solar calendar.) It is an occasion for settling accounts, giving presents, having reunions of family and friends, and eating holiday dishes. Some of them require elaborate preparations and are designed to appeal to the eye as well as the mouth. Although Japanese-Americans note the passing of traditional practices, within the family circles many of them, especially food traditions, survive.

* * *

Japanese New Year

Japanese Food for New Year's

Prior to World War II, I can remember the call for community Japanese males, both *issei* (first generation) and *nisei* (second generation) in Seattle, Washington, to participate in the making of *mochi* [rice cakes, made from cooked rice pounded into a sticky paste in wooden mortars]. The rice-pounding was usually done on the weekend before New Years. It was a communal social event where there was much merry-making as each took turn pounding the rice. Each family had already ordered the quantity of *mochi* they desired, so they had a general idea of how much was necessary. For several days, my sisters and I helped mother prepare special foods. The central item would be broiled red snapper or sea bream, called *tai*.... It would be broiled whole, and it was important to skewer it carefully so that it appeared to be in motion. Sometimes they would improvise by tying the head and tail to shape it.

A great variety of *sushi* [rice cooked in wine vinegar and spices topped with various kinds of seafood, sometimes uncooked, or combinations of specially cooked vegetables] are prepared. Analogous to the foods associated with our Easter celebration, many foods such as eggs, fingerlings of the sardine family, cod roe, bamboo shoots and beans— indicating new life and new beginnings—were prepared and arranged in the *jubako* [a lacquered box with four tiers, beautifully arranged, the first tier with sweet foods, the second broiled foods, the third boiled, and the fourth raw fish and vegetables].

Early on the New Year's morning the soup, *ozoni* [rice cake soup] was made. It consists of stock made variously in the different provinces in Japan, a few pieces of green vegetables about one and a half inches in size, slices of carrots which have been decoratively cut, dried mushrooms and *mochi* which has been toasted on a wire rack over an open flame. Other dishes such as *kombu* [kelp] and *umani,* a dish consisting of meat and vegetables with a soy sauce-sugar flavoring, were also served. The entrance would be decorated with a branch of pine and plums to assure longevity, and on the hall table two rice cakes of different sizes would be placed on top of each other, with a tangerine above.

My father would leave the house around 6:30 A.M. on New Year's Day to make calls on friends, relatives and business associates. He chose this early hour because it was traditional to visit and eat and drink at each home, but to avoid over-eating and drinking, he would leave his calling card on the doorsteps of as many as possible before the families had arisen. He would be gone all day, and I remember that he would sometimes be drunk by the time he came home in the evening.

The rest of us arose a few hours later. We would post ourselves in the living room to invite the callers in for food and *toso-sake* [sweet sake spiced with medicinal herbs to encourage longevity]. The traditional greeting, "*Shinen omedeto gozaimasu,*" was exchanged, which is equivalent to "Happy Year." The visits were usually brief, 15-30 minutes, as they also had other calls to make.

In the evening we would play *karuta,* a Japanese card game. The caller would say the beginning of a poem on the subject of love and the object would be to find the matching half of the poem as quickly as possible. Shuttlecock was also played. My father is tone deaf, and he would make us laugh uproariously by exaggeratedly singing songs off key.

This type of New Year's celebration has greatly diminished since World War II. Many first generation Japanese are now deceased, and the second generation are involving themselves less and less with feast making, probably due to the great effort required and the dearth of some of the foods. I note the use of more and more instant foods and canned goods among the recent Japanese immigrants, and I am told they now use electric *mochi* makers. My sister who still resides in Seattle said that many of the *niseis* visit on New Year's Day but are now served a combination of traditional Japanese New Year's foods with a greater concentration of American foods served buffet style. As for the third generation, I do not know any who follow the Japanese New Year's traditions although I must confess that our contacts with those of Japanese heritage are minimal.

My husband, who is also a *nisei* but was born and reared on the East Coast, specifically, New York and New Jersey, also remembers the special New Year's foods and the social calls from a few Japanese friends. He is a gourmet and a gourmand and has made it a point to make certain that we have these special foods on New Year's. In lieu of preparing them, we have gone to those Japanese restaurants in New York City that serve these items and dined out about three days successively. At one time, there were quite a few restaurants, namely *Miyako, Nippon, Suehiro, Aki,* etc., that offered these dishes, but they are dwindled to a very few. This is probably due to the labor involved, and many Japanese prefer to cook at home for the holidays. The consumption of *ozoni* and *mochi* persists today. The *mochi* can be bought at the Japanese food stores in New York City either fresh or frozen.

The practice of closing businesses at this time of year still exists in New York. All Japanese business firms are closed for about three to five days. Many of the Japanese restaurants are closed on New Year's Day here, and some a few days additionally.

Ozoni

2   chicken breasts, skinned and boned (Pork slices may be substituted.)
3   dried Japanese mushrooms
¼- pound leaf spinach
12 pieces of *mochi* (rice cakes)
6   cups *dashi*
     salt
     pepper
     soy sauce
6   pieces lemon rind

Soak dried mushrooms in boiling hot water about twenty minutes, drain, cut off stem, and cut into about six pieces.

Boil six cups of water and add three packets of instant *dashi-no-moto* to make soup base. Salt, pepper, and soy sauce may be added to taste. Add mushrooms and chicken breasts and boil six minutes, longer if pork is substituted. Pork must be fully cooked.

Meanwhile, peel carrots, slice crosswise, and cut into flower petal shapes. Add to soup and cook until tender.

Wash spinach leaves and boil in small amount of water, cooking until barely tender, but still green.

Toast cubed *mochi* on wire rack over open burner flame, turning frequently until lightly browned and puffy.

Slice lemon rind into thin slivers, to represent pine needles, an evergreen symbolizing long life.

Serve soup in bowls and place chicken or pork pieces, mushrooms, carrots, spinach leaf, lemon slice, and two pieces of *mochi* into each bowl, arranging it so that it is appealing to the eye.

Tai

Gut and scale a whole red snapper, leaving intact the tail, head, and fins. Skewer fish with long, thin bamboo sticks or use a string or thread and tie it around the tail, pulling string taut and tying it around the head. This is to shape the fish so that it appears to be swimming.

Sprinkle with coarse salt and broil until done.

Arrange cooked fish on platter with green pine branch and lemon slices.

Serve with dip of soy sauce mixed with lemon juice.

Turnip and Carrot Salad

3   turnips
1   carrot
6   teaspoons cider vinegar or rice wine vinegar
1   teaspoon *mirin* or light white wine
     salt
1   teaspoon sugar

Wash turnips and slice crosswise into one-quarter inch slices. Then slice again lengthwise into thin slices.

Peel carrot and slice similarly.

Place vegetables into dish and sprinkle with salt. Squeeze slices to remove moisture, and let stand for about thirty minutes.

Add vinegar, sugar, and *mirin,* mix well, and let stand for another thirty minutes.

Source

University of Pennsylvania Folklore Archives, unclassified, 1980. The recollections of traditional New Year's customs and foodways, and the recipes were obtained in 1978 by Joanne Takagi, of Albertson, New York, a student at the University of Pennsylvania, from her mother, Betty Y. Takagi, born in Seattle, Washington, in 1923. Cf. "New Year's Calling,' p. 13.

*   *   *

Mother Lavender's New Year's Dinner

Every year in Utica [New York], on New Year's Day, needy individuals are fed at a "Mother Lavender Dinner." In 1950, 375 persons ate food donated by dealers and individuals; some of it was purchased with money contributed towards the dinner. 175 basket-dinners were distributed to families. This annual project perpetuates a tradition established by Mrs. Elizabeth Lavender, a slave-born evangelist who during her lifetime daily denied herself in order to aid the poor and hungry seeking her aid. If ever the Church had an unknown Saint, this woman is that one.

A *Utica Daily Press* editorial at the time of "Mother Lavender's" death in 1928 characterized her as "a link with the Nation's past" because she had actually experienced the transition from slavery to freedom. "The fact that she made herself a helpful factor in the community is a great tribute to her native ability.... And the lot in life of slaves who were taught nothing except the job they were expected to do, and sometimes were fed from troughs, like animals, seems an unbelievable memory. But she knew all about it and for more than fifty years has been able to tell what has transpired."

Lizzie Lavender, known as Sister or Mother Lavender during her lifetime, was born in Georgia about 1841. She was a slave and one of nine children. Her first master was John McLewis, who raised cotton, rice and yellow pine. The child's first work was picking cotton. When she was seven, her mother and nine children—six boys and three girls—were put up at the auction block and sold, but they all went in different directions. When the mother herself was sold, there was but one more child of the family remaining to be disposed of. He was a boy two years old; and while the mother was almost heartbroken at the thought of leaving him, the little fellow sat playing in the grass, not realizing what had happened. Lizzie was sold for $700 to George Hicks, who took her to Watertown, South Carolina. Here she worked as a house slave. Her new owner raised corn, rice, cotton, timber. Lizzie was taught to weave the homespun material worn by the slaves. She was expected to weave twenty-two yards a day and generally did.

The second time Lizzie was sold, she brought $1000. She received no education but was brought up as a field hand. She was a woman of strong build with heavy arms and shoulders, and could do any amount of work and swing an axe like a man. The Negroes were at times fed out of a trough in which was placed hominy covered with lobbered [clabbered] milk. Toward the close of the war, her master told the people in charge of the house to take good care of it, as he and his wife were going to the city. They would return as soon as possible, they could not tell just when; but in the meantime they cautioned the Negroes to look after things and not let the Lincoln soldiers get them. As the master and mistress did not return in a day or two, the slaves down at the quarters heard of their prolonged absence, came up to the great house, and took possession.

There was not a white face left on the place, and many of the field hands got their first peep at the interior of the great house. Lizzie, who had never worn anything but homespun, determined to be dressed up like a lady for once in her life. She put on one of the best dresses her mistress had, and a very fine hat and silk mantilla, but she found it impossible to put on gloves and shoes. She was dressed in costly and elegant material, but her hands and feet were, as usual, bare. While she was enjoying finery for a brief hour, the "Lincoln soldiers" came along and captured the place. Most of the slaves were very much frightened, for they had been told pretty bad stories of what these soldiers would do. But the soldiers only laughed at their fears and especially at the predicament in which Lizzie found herself.

This ended their period of bondage. Lizzie remembered that she was then twenty-four years old. She had no other knowledge of her birthdate.

After the war Lizzie Lavender remained in the South some time, working on a plantation, but like most of the other ex-slaves she had a desire to be where all were said to be treated as equals, and so she came first to New York and then to Albany. In the Capital city she lived for sometime supporting herself by doing laundry and other housework....

Mother Lavender came to Utica in 1883 as a member of a choir of Negro "jubilee singers" who were traveling with Andrew Dixon, Negro revivalist of that time. Later she returned to Utica to lecture in the Old Opera House on slave life. Then there was a camp meeting near Utica about the year 1892, and Mrs. Lavender came there to participate. The late Edward Curran, who was Charity Commissioner, advised her that this was a good field for her, and she decided to remain. She gave a lecture describing slavery which at once attracted attention. A number of churches opened their doors to her, and she became quite popular for a time....

She was best known to the public for her annual dinners on behalf of poor in the city. These, it is remembered, were generally given "on Thanksgiving or New Year's Day ... most of the material (would be) in shape of contributions from storekeepers and housekeepers. At these dinners she fed hundreds." In making preparations, she would send out notices that she "would greatly appreciate any contributions of money or food to enable her once more to greet the stranger within her gates in the name of the Master."

Mother Lavender was active until her death in 1928. Having always denied herself, she died a pauper. She never owned a home but rented. Mrs. Freeman said that her grandmother never refused anyone who came to her for aid. Mother Lavender had rented the empty house next door to where she was living (630 Broad Street). She wanted to be able to house more of the needy. The place was so damp that she caught a chill. She worked all that New Year's Day on the dinner. She became ill with the dropsy. It was the first time that Mrs. Freeman had known her to be sick; she had been able to get around well for an old lady who was all of ninety. The first Mrs. Crouse helped her during her illness, bringing linen and flowers to her every day. Mrs. Freeman told me her grandmother had a peculiar way about her. She would always pray that she might outlive her children and see them buried. She did.

Source and Comment

New York Folklore Quarterly, VIII (1952), 283–86, 289. From "Mother Lavender and Her Holiday Dinners" by James P. Francis. His main source was Mother Lavender's granddaughter, Mrs. Ruth Lavender Freeman of Utica, New York. He also consulted the Utica

Observer Dispatch, September 8, 1928, and the *Utica Daily Press,* September 10, 1928.

The continuation of the dinners appears to be as much veneration of "an unknown Saint" as a significant local charity. Cf. the mixed motives evident in "Mama D. on St. Joseph's Day," p. 133.

* * *

What to Eat on New Year's Day

Georgia

To have good luck all the year, eat a piece of boil [sic] meat on the first day of January.

Source

Journal of American Folklore, XII (1899), 265. Collected by Ronald Steiner at Grovetown, Columbia County, Georgia. The informant was not given.

* * *

Tennessee

We always ate hog jowl and blackeyed peas on New Year's Day for good luck. Many people say you should put a dime in the peas, but we never did that .... My oldest brother had a cook who truly believed that it was bad luck for a woman to come to your house first on New Year's Day. So she always had the hired man go to the house and go into every room before she would cook breakfast. That meant late breakfast on New Year's Day.

Source

Tennessee Folklore Society Bulletin, XX (September 1954), 54. From a selection of "superstitions at home" contributed by Mrs. Marion T. Faye of St. Bethlehem, Tennessee, who grew up on a farm.

* * *

North Carolina

On New Year's Day cook something that swells for a prosperous year. Eat turnip greens, hog jowls, blackeyed peas, and peaches on New Year's day to bring health and wealth during the year.

Hog jaws, cabbage, and blackeyed peas for New Year's dinner will bring luck.

Eat collard greens at New Year's to have paper money all the year. Cook blackeyed peas and hog head on New Year's Day and have plenty to eat all year.

Rice and peas on New Year's Day bring good luck.

Money cooked in blackeyed peas on New Year's means you will have money all year.

Source

Southern Folklore Quarterly, XXVI (1962), 210-11. Collected by Joseph D. Clark from first-year students in English at North Carolina State College, Raleigh in 1955-56 and 1960-61, "who came from many counties of the state."

Pennsylvania Dutch

Eat sauerkraut on New Year's Day to keep well the rest of the year.

If people eat sauerkraut on New Year's Day they become rich.

A common explanation as to why Pennsylvanians today eat turkey on Christmas and pork (with sauerkraut) on New Year's Day is that pork symbolizes the "forward look" of the turn of the year. A fowl scratches backward—a pig roots forward ....

There are a few references to sauerkraut at New Year's from the 19th Century. They would appear to be associated with the Christmas-New Year's custom of feasting on sauerkraut. One of the earliest of these references comes from Norristown, where sauerkraut was featured on New Year's Day, 1861: "Saur Kraut lunches were the order of the day at the different lager beer saloons" (Norristown *National Defender,* January 1, 1861).

In the 20th century, it is a widespread custom. In Central Pennsylvania the custom is so common that pork and sauerkraut advertisements appear in the commercial columns of the newspapers throughout the dying days of December. One such ad, from the *Altoona Mirror* of December 27, 1960, emanating from Pielmelet's Market, Corner 1st Ave. and 15th St., urges readers to "Follow the Tradition for New Year's Day," by serving "Sauerkraut and Pork," and adds the bid for confidence "We make our own Kraut." On December 29, 1960, The "Endress Market" advertised "Sauerkraut: Our Own Make! It's Truly Delicious! Serve it for Your New Year's Dinner." In the same issue of the *Mirror,* the "Sanitary Market" informs the readers that "Blocher's Fresh Dressed Pork will guarantee the success of your New Year's dinner," while "Honsaker Bros." advertises "Pork for New Year—Spare ribs, loin and ham cuts, shoulder cuts, tenderloin, sausage." It was obvious that Altoona was preparing for New Year's in the (more or less) traditional Dutch fashion.

Source

Pennsylvania Dutchman, XII (Summer 1961), 62. From an article on sauerkraut by Don Yoder. The first saying is from Mrs. Lilly Hyle of Rexmont, Pennsylvania; and the second from J. S. Greiner of Elizabethtown, Pennsylvania.

* * *

New York German

[It was believed ca. 1940] in the old German section of Buffalo [New York] that if you kept cabbage or herring in the house on New Year's Eve, you will have money all year ... if you *eat* a piece of herring at the stroke of midnight, you will be *lucky* all year.

Source

New York Folklore Quarterly, XI (1955), 258. Collected by Alice P. Whitaker from Mrs. Matilda Popp, age fifty, and Lilian Wind, "about fifty," both of whom learned them from their German parents.

* * *

Japanese-American

Eat blackeyed peas on New Year's to bring happiness and health throughout the year. (Practiced by families in the United States and Japan.)

For New Year's, lobster represents good health and happiness. If in preparing it, the lobster is dropped or the feelers broken, a new lobster should be fixed. The feelers should also be as symmetrical as possible. (Observed by Japanese families.)

You eat *mochi* (rice cakes).

You must not eat lotus roots.

Source

Journal of American Folklore, LXII (1949), 298. From unnamed persons of Japanese descent living in the Los Angeles area, collected by Fumi Kawamoto. She states that many folk beliefs "have been perpetuated into the third generation living on without significant change" but among them are "numerous items that seem to have been borrowed from American folklore." Miss F. Kawamoto is the informant for the first eating belief and Miss A. Kajioka for the second. The last two customs were collected by Gwladys F. Hughes at Waialua sugar plantation, Oahu, Hawaii. Informants for both beliefs were schoolgirls of Japanese origin.

* * *

New Year's Beliefs

Tennessee

If you wash your clothes on New Year's Day, you will wash someone out of your family.

If a woman comes to see you on New Year's Day, the chickens will all be pullets; if a man comes, they will all be roosters.

On New Year's night, place a gold band in a glass of water, go into a dark cellar, and see your husband's picture in the bottom of the glass.

Source

Tennessee Folklore Society Bulletin, X (December 1944), 4 and II (October 1936), 12. The first two beliefs from a collection by Ruth W. O'Dell of Newport, Tennessee; the third collected in "Middle Tennessee" by Neal Frazier.

* * *

The Alleghanies

If a girl wishes to know whether her future husband will be a stranger or from the vicinity, she can find out by going alone and after night on New Year's Eve, standing silently by a peach-tree and shaking its stem. Should a dog bark, her suitor comes from a distance, but if a cock crows his home is near.

Source

Journal of American Folklore, VII (1894), 108. Collected by J. Hampden Porter from "mountain whites . . . in remoter parts of the Alleghanies between southwestern Georgia and the Pennsylvania line."

The Ozarks

Always make sure the salt-shaker is full on New Year's Day, and you will prosper throughout the year.

Source

Journal of American Folklore, XLVI (1933), 17. From a collection of mountain white superstitions recorded by Vance Randolph.

* * *

Creole Louisiana

If you sew on New Year's Day, you will sew a shroud before the year is out.

Always wear something new on New Year's Day for good luck during the year.

Source

Journal of American Folklore, XL (1927), 190. Collected by Hilda Roberts in Iberia Parish, southwestern Louisiana.

* * *

Illinois

If you cry on New Year's Day, you will be sorry throughout the year.

What you do the first hour of the New Year will be what you do most of the year.

Animals kneel at midnight on New Year's Eve.

Source

Journal of American Folklore, LXIII (1950), 314-15. Collected by Lelah Allison from southeastern Illinois.

* * *

North Carolina

Whatever you do on New Year's Day, you'll do the rest of the year.

Don't do anything on New Year's that you don't wish to do all year.

Source

Southern Folklore Quarterly, XXVI (1962), 211. From a collection of superstitions made by Joseph D. Clark in 1955-56. His informants were students of North Carolina State College, Raleigh.

* * *

Hawaii

Don't sweep the house during the day.

Don't sweep the house during the evening.

Girls must not go out early in the morning of New Year's Day.

Men do most of the work on New Year's Eve.

Bad luck comes if a girl is your first visitor: good luck, if a man comes first.

Luck will go away if you open the front door.

Source

Journal of American Folklore, LXII (1949), 296, 298. Collected by Gwladys F. Hughes at Waialua sugar plantation, thirty-four miles from Honolulu in 1946-47. Informants were children of Japanese ancestry, many of whom "speak broken English." Yet most of these items are well known on the mainland, especially to those of Anglo-Saxon origin.

* * *

New Year's Weather Forecasts

South Carolina

A dark New Year is a sign of a good fruit year.

Source

Southern Folklore Quarterly, XII (1948), 282. Collected by Margaret M. Bryant in Edgefield County, South Carolina.

* * *

Tennessee

The way the wind blows on January 1, it will not be out of that direction for more than forty-eight hours, for forty days.

Since the first twelve days of the year predicted the months of the year, Mother always wrote a description of them on her calendar.

Source

Tennessee Folklore Society Bulletin, XXIV (June 1958), 67 and XX (September 1954), 54. the first weather sign collected by Mary E. Miller in Dickinson County, Tennessee; the second by Mrs. Marion T. Page of St. Bethlehem, Tennessee, whose mother was born in Mississippi.

* * *

Illinois

Mrs. Rhoda Smith of Wayne County, Illinois, had a method of telling weather conditions for the coming of each new year, and she often spread the news to her neighbors so that they might know what to expect and plan their garden and field planting accordingly.

On each New Year's day she took twelve onions and removed their tops; she placed them in a row and sprinkled salt on each and let them stand for a few days. The first onion represented January, the second, February, etc. If an onion soaked in the salt, the month represented by the onion would be wet, if not, dry.

Source

Journal of American Folklore, LXI (1948), 69. Collected by Lelah Allison in southeastern Illinois, but also known to Polish-Americans in New York. See *New York Folklore Society Quarterly,* XXIV (1968), 305.

* * *

Printer's Boy Verses for the New Year

The New Year's Greeting of the Printer's Boy dates back to at least 1720 in Pennsylvania.... These verses were a recounting of the major political and military events of the preceding year and as such are valuable records of what was considered important or noteworthy to those contemporaneous with the events. They reflected the political and social bias of the publisher who printed them. The purpose of their distribution is disclosed at the end of these pieces in a few lines, some more subtle than others, soliciting a monetary token of gratitude for service rendered. [The example which follows was published as a broadside titled "The Yearly-Verses Of the Printer's BOY, who carries the *Pennsylvania Gazette* to the CUSTOMERS." It is dated January 1, 1746.]

Since 'tis a Custom ev'ry Year,
When it begins, for to appear
In an emphatick Rhimish Mode,
To greet you at your own Abode,
Relating to you Things again
Which now are past; in humble Strain,
Wishing you all a happy Year,
With Peace, and plenty of good Cheer; ...
May good Fires warm your Room;
Inviting Summer back to come.

But you've enough of home Affairs;
I must proceed to horrid War,
And trace the Deeds of *Cumberland,*
Prince *Charles,* and all that have Command
In Honour's Cause; and had I Skill
To write as well as I have Will,
I'd Sing of the *Sardinian* King,
And not forget one single Thing, ...

I'd sing of Battles, and of Sieges,
Of *Fontenoy,* and taking *Bruges.*
With *English,* and the Frenchmen
dead: ...
How bravely they sustain'd the Fire;
And *French* did beat, and then retire?...

And since the *Chevalier,* and Friends
Unto his Cause, have got their Ends
So far, as to Invade our Isle,
(Our Mother Country) and beguile
Some of th'unthinking *Highlanders;*
Which have commenced horrid Wars:
But may kind Heav'n befriend our Cause,
Keep us from under *Popish* Laws;
And may the next News that we hear,

Be Fatal to the *Chevalier,*
And send him packing with *Monsieur.*

And not forgetting *Cape-Breton*:
By *Boston* Men, what Wonders done:
How Gen'ral *Pepperell* led their Bands,
And *Louisbourg* fell in their Hands:
How *Warren* brave, from Westward came,
To save the sinking British Name;
And let their Enemies to see,
Britains are Rulers on the Sea: ...

How many of the *India* Fleet
Fell in our Hands, worth Wealth so great,
Would but surprize you, could I count,
And tell you but the just Amount.

Such Things are these (altho' too high
For me to soar, for me to fly)
I fain would sing, could I aspire;
Or had I but a Poet's Fire.

But now I should conclude my Song,
And not delay the Time too long:

Hoping you will not think it strange,
That something's wanting in Exchange.
Kind SIRS:—I do not name the Sum:
But WHAT YOU PLEASE; and I'll be gone.

Source and Comment

Keystone Folklore Quarterly, IX (1964), 68, 70. Harold Krelove published eighteenth-century examples of broadsides in the collection of the Historical Society of Pennsylvania with a head note in which he observes that "Modern newspapers still print year-end verses," and newspapers often provide the carrier "with a simple greeting card which serves as an advertisement and a gentle reminder that now is the time for a little extra over the normal payment...."

The main events mentioned include the Jacobite rising of 1745 which ended with the defeat of Prince Charles Edward Stuart, *"Chevalier,"* by the Duke of Cumberland at Culloden Moor in April 1746; the victory of Marshal Saxe at Fontenoy, Belgium, over the British and their allies in the War of the Austrian Succession; and the capture of the French fortress of Louisbourg on Cape Breton Island, Nova Scotia, by a largely American force under William Pepperell and Sir Peter Warren.

Islamic New Year

Retrograde in regard to the Gregorian Calendar

According to the Qur'ān, Allah created the universe with an exact number of days, months, and years so mankind might be able to calculate time conveniently. However, because the Muslim calendar is totally lunar, and is not adjusted to the sun, it moves backwards through the years, making a complete retrograde cycle about once every thirty-two and a half years. Practical-minded farmers who wish to know when to plant their crops use the sun as a guide. The Islamic New Year is a religious event, occurring on the first day of the first lunar month, Muhàrràm, with prayers for peace and prosperity, but its secular traditions include the exchange of good wishes and coins, which are supposed to bring good luck.

Islamic New Year in South Carolina

South Carolina Muslims will join others of their faith around the world today in marking their New Year—the opening of the Islamic year of 1401 H.

The H refers to the *Hejira,* or flight of the Prophet Muhammed from captivity in Mecca to the Holy City of Medina.

In the Carolinas there are estimated to be more than 3,000 members of the Islamic faith—coming from such countries as Saudi Arabia, Pakistan, Jordan, India, Iran, Iraq, Nigeria, Kuwait, the United Emirates, Egypt and Libya.

Members of the Muslim Students Association at the University of South Carolina will gather for a New Year's observance of the founding of their religion at 1 P.M. today [November 7, 1980] in Room 303 at the Russell House. Ibrahim Benomran, president of the students who represent a number of different Muslim countries in the Middle East, will speak.

The program will also celebrate the opening of the month of Muharram, the first month of the year and regarded as a holy month of peace and prayer.

Source

The (Columbia, South Carolina) *State,* November 7, 1980. News item by Barbara H. Stoops, "Religious Editor." The holiday moves in a retrogressive cycle, falling on a different date each year until the cycle is completed. In 1980, the New Year began on November 9, according to the Gregorian calendar. For the next three years it fell in October, and by the year 2006 will have moved backward to the month of January.

Emancipation Day

January 1

There have been a number of Emancipation or "freedom" celebrations. The first was held on January 1, 1808, to commemorate the legal termination of the importation of slaves into the United States. Regional celebrations have also taken place honoring various military proclamations such as that of General David Hunter, Commander of the Department of the South, who on May 9, 1862, freed the slaves in South Carolina, Georgia, and Florida, and General Gordon Granger who issued an order freeing the Texas slaves on June 19, 1985. And there were smaller celebrations of a more obscure origin that are less easily explained but apparently recall that date on which slaves in a particular locality learned that they were free at last.

President Lincoln issued a formal Emancipation Proclamation on January 1, 1863, after a preliminary announcement on the previous September 22. The latter date was celebrated also, but it is on the anniversary of Lincoln's official proclamation that the most important observances take place, in part because January 1 is both a traditional and legal holiday. One of their notable features is the reading of his proclamation, often in a rhythmic, dramatic style that elevates the language of a government document to the level of folk poetry.

Emancipation Day, Sacred and Profane

There has never been a day in Afro-American history equal to January 1, 1863.... Free blacks and white abolitionists gathered in churches across the Northeast, anxiously awaiting the dawn ... and its statement of freedom. In northern cities like Boston and New York, racially mixed congregations spent the last night of 1862 singing and praying for freedom in special Emancipation-watch night services.... Soon after midnight their prayers were answered when a copy of President Lincoln's Emancipation Proclamation was read to them just moments after it arrived over the telegraph wire. After the reading of this document, there was much applause and speechmaking in praise of President Lincoln for having the courage to issue such a statement and of the eternal God for giving him the wisdom to see that it must be done....

[I]ndicative of the sacredness of the celebrations is the serious attitude that most celebrants bring to it. In *Army Life in a Black Regiment,* Thomas Wentworth Higginson noted this serious mood in his account of the January 1 celebration he attended in South Carolina in 1863:

> The multitude were chiefly colored women, with gay handkerchiefs on their heads, and a sprinkling of men, with that peculiarly respectable look which these people always have on Sundays and holidays.

Mingo Scott used the term "intellectual" to describe the ambiance of January 1 celebrations:

> It's more on the basis of an intellectual celebration. There you come with the reading of the Emancipation Proclamation, speeches are made, appropriate music and then some of the most outstanding speakers among black people come and they are very prepared.

But there were some lighter, secular aspects of the celebration. Perhaps the most spectacular is the parade. In 1973, for example, parades were held in Charleston, South Carolina, and Phenix City, Alabama. Both affairs were modest .... The Charleston, South Carolina, parade had less than a hundred marchers. In its ranks were a uniformed scout troop, about five motorcycles, two cars decorated with crepe-paper streamers and placards on the doors. The procession was led by a motorcycle policeman and the American flag was carried by the scout troop.

Mrs. J.C. Cook, the wife of a local Baptist preacher, described the Phenix City, Alabama, parade in the following conversation:

> Now yesterday they formed their parade in the yard of the Mount Zion Baptist Church and marched from North Phenix City to Phillips Temple. There were quite a few men in the march. I know most all of the men, but I can't recall right

now. One is the president of the Association, the Betterment Association of Russell County. They had cars that were decorated and the Mount Olive School band led the parade. They gave music right out of Fort Mitchell School. That parade began some few years back. I can't recall now, just how far back that's been.

This parade was routed through the black community and appears to be similar in size to the 1890 January 1 parade witnessed by Clara Neale, a ninety-year-old, retired schoolteacher, in rural South Carolina. She recalled past celebrations as days where there was "music and different people spoke . . . and the band. Now the music that they had was [her voice is muffled here]. And the speaking, different people spoke. And some who had horses and mules and things dressed them up and paraded around."

Many of the celebrations in such smaller communities as Fitzgerald, Georgia; Phenix City, Alabama; and Hopkins, South Carolina, included meals after the noon program. Leila Blakey tells how it was done in Monticello, Georgia: "Well . . . it was . . . I guess you couldn't say it was spread on the ground. This was January 1 and you know winter time. And in Monticello we had winter. So they had this long table all set up where you could go around and just pick up what you wanted, that type of thing."

In Hopkins, South Carolina, a meal was also served after the Emancipation Program, but unlike this free meal at Monticello, Georgia, the celebrants had to pay for the food. Wilemenia Crelow, a retired South Carolina schoolteacher, remembers:

> They'd kill a big hog and sell barbecue. You could get a 25 cents sandwich and a 50 cents plate. [With] lemonade and cokes [to] drink. [But] this wouldn't necessarily be at the church. Barbecues wouldn't be at the church. That would be at another meeting place, at the school house or something, or someplace like that. See, we would have this service at the church. Then we leave there and go on to the school house or some other community house and have barbecues.

The Nashville, Tennessee, celebration also has had after-program dinners, but not on an annual basis. (Mingo Scott notes that the January celebration in this city is sometimes "concluded or climaxed with a banquet.")

The most important part of the celebration is the program that comes after the parade and before the eating. This program has evolved over the years into a highly ritualized religious service. Original chance actions, such as the reading of the Emancipation Proclamation, have become essential segments of the service, as has the singing of James Weldon Johnson's song "Lift Every Voice and Sing." And always at the center has been the spoken word—the major address or sermon to be given on that

day. These three parts of the program form the tripod foundation on which all else done in that one-and-a-half-to two-hour service is based. The opening paragraph of a 1941 Atlanta *Daily World* editorial underscores this fact:

> And they came here: it was January first, the official celebration day of the Emancipation. From the little country schoolhouse to the large city metropolitan churches they gathered and sang "Lift Every Voice and Sing," listened to the reading of the Emancipation Proclamation and the fine phrased eulogy from the great spokesman.

And the following statement by the Reverend Kelly Miller Smith, pastor of the First Baptist church in Nashville, Tennessee, and a former speaker at past January 1 celebrations, further confirms this cultural fact: "Well, in Nashville here, prior to last year it was an observance which was on or about January 1, which included a major address, always the singing of 'Lift Every Voice and Sing,' always the reading of the Emancipation Proclamation. Those were the must items, the must ingredients in the observance."

Tradition has fashioned a ritualistic order in which the Emancipation Proclamation is always read before the major address is given. However, such a fixed place has not yet been accorded the song "Lift Every Voice and Sing." For example, in 1973 it served to open the celebration in Columbus, Georgia, but closed the celebrations in Atlanta, Georgia, and Indianapolis, Indiana. In both programs it was sung just prior to the benediction, and on the Indianapolis program it was called the "Closing Hymn of Challenge." In all cases, the address climaxes the celebration and comes very late in the program. As the Reverend William Holmes Borders, the pastor of the historic Wheat Street Baptist church in Atlanta, Georgia, and a past speaker at numerous May 5, August 1, and January 1 Emancipation celebrations, has commented: "the addresses which I have made have always been last, the climax of the whole thing, the program."

The majority of these celebrations has some sort of printed program. In 1973, as a case in point, the programs of Atlanta, Georgia, and Indianapolis, Indiana, were mimeographed, while the programs of Phenix City, Alabama, and Columbus, Georgia, were printed. This latter program was printed in black ink on pages of folded 8 ½- by 11-inch gold paper. The order of service for this noon program was as follows:

Negro National Hymn ...."Lift Every Voice"
Prayer ....Rev. E. Adams, Jr.
Selection ....New Providence Church Choir
Scripture ....Rev. H.L. Gladney
Selection ....Mount Pilgrim Church Choir
Welcome ....Mrs. Rosie Walker
Selection ....New Providence Church Choir
Emancipation
    Proclamation ....Mrs. Ethlyn Kirby

Instrumental
Solo ....Dr. D.C. Grant
Introduction of
Speaker ....Dr. W.B. Howell, President
Speaker ....Dr. George B. Thomas,
Instructor, Interdenomi-
national Theological Center,
Atlanta, Georgia
Selection ....Mount Pilgrim Church Choir
Emphasis "Urban
League" ....Rev. J. H. Flakes

Offering and Church
Donations ....Finance Committee in charge
Selection ....New Providence Church Choir
Remarks ....Rev. J. H. Johnson, Vice
President
Benediction .... Speaker

There is an important cultural aesthetic beneath this formal program. In the 110-year history of the Emancipation celebration, Afro-Americans have come to attach different values and standards to the three foundation pillars of this celebration. For example, the reading of the Emancipation Proclamation has evolved over the years from a straightforward news report to a highly developed genre of oral narration within Afro-American culture. Tradition has also dictated that the reader of this precious document must be young, preferably in his or her late teens or early twenties and preferably female, though young men have been selected with some success....

Mrs. Ethlyn Kirby gave a brilliant artistic rendition of the Emancipation Proclamation during the 1977 Columbus, Georgia, celebration. After the congregation sang "We Shall Overcome," she slowly rose from her seat, dramatically walked to the lectern, mesmerized the congregation as she flattened out the text of her presentation and began to speak in a dramatic tone and cadence reminiscent of the black preacher.

KIRBY: America, I saw you grow. I saw your rocks and rills, thy woods and temple hills. America, I saw your military forces on land and sea ... Alabama ... Arkansas ... Florida ... Georgia ... Mississippi, North Carolina, South Carolina, Louisiana, and Virginia ... I saw you.
I saw you ignore the warning of God and Lincoln's Preliminary Proclamation....

CONG: Yes.

KIRBY: I can hear you America. I can hear you at the Emancipation Proclamation. January 1, one thousand eight hundred and sixty three issued by the president of the United States containing among other things the following: "To whit I, Abraham

Lincoln, President of the United States, by virtue of the power in me vested as commander in chief of the army and navy of the United States, order and declare that all persons held as slaves within said designated states and parts of states are and henceforth forward shall be free...."

CONG: Amen.

KIRBY: "And that the executive government of the United States including the military and naval authorities thereof will recognize and maintain the freedom of said persons."

CONG: Amen.

KIRBY: "And I hereby enjoin upon the people so declared to be free to abstain from all violence unless in self defense."

CONG: Amen.

KIRBY: "And I recommend to them that in all cases when allowed they labor faithfully for reasonable wages."

CONG: Amen.

KIRBY: "And I further declare and make known that such persons of suitable condition will be received into the armed service of the United States to garrison forts, positions, stations and other places and to man vessels of all sorts and said service. And upon this act, sincerely believe to be an act of justice warranted by the Constitution of where military necessity I envoke the considerate judgment of mankind and the gracious favor of almighty God."

CONG: Amen.

KIRBY: "And testimony of where of I have here unto set my name and caused the seal of the United States to be affixed. Done at the city of Washington, this first day of January in the year of our Lord, one thousand eight hundred and sixty-three, and of the independence of the United States, the eighty-seventh, by the President, Abraham Lincoln."
America ... I saw you.

CONG: Amen.

KIRBY: I saw you at the Emancipation Proclamation.

CONG: Yes, yes.

KIRBY: I heard Abe Lincoln, Booker T. Washington, Langston Hughes, Malcolm X, John Kennedy and M. L. King....

CONG: Amen.

KIRBY: America, America, God shed his grace on thee. And crowned thy good with brotherhood from sea to shining sea.

CONG: Amen! Amen! (Loud hand clapping)

Source

Prospects: An Annual of American Cultural Studies, IV (1979), 331-32, 335-41. William H. Wiggins, Jr., a folklorist and historian, discusses the origin of Emancipation Day and its ritualistic celebration. Cf. "Juneteenth," p. 243.

Old Christmas, the Epiphany Season, and Twelfth Night

January 4-8

January 6, the twelfth night after Christmas, is the present date of the Feast of the Epiphany. According to the Gospels, on this date the Magi or Three Kings venerated the Infant Jesus. Literally, the word " Epiphany" means "manifestation," and in addition to this first manifestation of Christ, two others are commemorated—the baptism in the Jordan River, and the transformation of water into wine at the marriage feast in Cana, Christ's first miracle. The Eastern Church emphasizes the journey of the Three Kings to Bethlehem, eventually reserving the eighth day of the Epiphany season to honor the baptism. In England and America, the change from the Julian to the Gregorian calendar in 1752 eliminated eleven days from the year; this and the fact that the Nativity was a moveable feast in the Western Church until the designation of December 25 as Christmas, has created much confusion. "Old Christmas" on January 6, prior to the acceptance of the calendar reform, is not altogether forgotten, though it has been generally superseded by "New Christmas" on December 25. Furthermore, in some places various dates from January 4 through January 8 are observed as "Old Christmas." Twelfth Night, the eve of the Feast of Epiphany, is an occasion for merrymaking. It marks the end of Christmastide and the beginning of the carnival season, which reaches its climax with Mardi Gras. According to the reckoning of the Julian Calendar, it falls on the same day as "Old Christmas." This coincidence compounds the confusion.

Old Christmas Frights

Near the village of Darden [North Carolina], to the southwest of Jamesville and within and about the areas which comprise Free Union, Tar Kiln Ridge, and Wolfpit Branch in eastern Martin County, rare and quaint Old Christmas customs have survived perhaps two centuries or more among a group of tradition-wise people. Here, too, the observance has gone virtually unnoticed by even the closest neighbors.

These people quote their foreparents as saying that they are descended from Tuscarora Indians and free people of color who for many generations worked the pine barrens lying southward from the Roanoke River to the dismal swamps, for tar and turpentine. They tilled small farms, hunted the wilds, and fished the streams. Descendants live to this day on land never owned by the white man.

Here as elsewhere Christmas is observed in the modern manner with the coming of Saint Nick, or Santa Claus, as the chief event. Nevertheless, Old Christmas remains little changed from an older time. On the night of January 4, two legendary frights shrouded in mystery pass from home to home as constantly and indefatigably as they did when great ghostly pine barrens stretched mile after mile southward from the Roanoke River. The two frights are stern and rugged disciplinarians traveling with the magic of witches and demons upon their mission to make wayward children behave. Like evil spirits, their work must be completed before the break of day on January 5, for by then they must have retired to the place from which they came, a mysterious faraway place which lies somewhere miles and miles beyond the inhospitable Western Dismal Swamp of Martin and Beaufort counties.

One Old Christmas fright is Old Nick; and it is little wonder that the rugged old people of the pine barrens gave him one of the popular names for the Devil. He is part man and part beast, having a man's body and "bullish head and horns." In these parts about two centuries ago, the Devil took the form of a large black goat while meeting with the witches at remote places in the forest. Old Nick's head and body are covered with long hair, bringing to mind the greatly feared Flying Head, a legendary Tuscarora Indian fright who brought suffering and death to people.

Even so, Old Nick is said to be the father of Santa Claus, who as Saint Nick in some lost time past brought the new Christmas which today's children enjoy.

Were it not for the old people, the young would not have learned how Old Nick looks. For those children who dare to peep, he brings along salt and pepper to dash into their eyes. Some say that he keeps Old Christmas undefiled by witches. When he finds an old hag out of her skin, he sprinkles her skin with salt and pepper so that she cannot get back in. Where he finds a naughty child, he leaves a bundle of switches at the hearth place, enough to last the parents throughout a year. The child who continues wayward is assured a visit from an even sterner fright when Old Christmas Eve night returns again.

The second fright is the Hobby Horse. He must have come from eighteenth-century England to the coastal plains of North Carolina along with the first settlers and the blood witch, the vampire witch, the banshee, and other frights.

In legend, the Hobby Horse, feared by man and demons alike, thunders unseen across the sky, heard by some and unheard by others....

If a child was very bad, Old Nick would leave him for the Hobby Horse to take and ride off. A long time ago, many children were taken away to a land of no return. This region lay southwest of Wolfpit Branch, across the dark pine barrens and then far beyond the inhospitable eight-mile-wide Western Dismal Swamp. No child taken there has been able to find his way back to Free Union.

A much gentler Hobby Horse than the legendary one now comes to Free Union each Old Christmas Eve. This has been so during the memory of Mrs. L.J. Gordon, now 71....

The men of the neighborhood dress in a cloth costume and play the Hobby Horse. For several years 65-year-old Chulch Whitaker and 56-year-old Wheeler Smith have been the Horse. Smith, who has fashioned the costume in recent years, says, "We give him a long head and long ears."

The two men set out early on Old Christmas Eve night so that they can complete their rounds before it is time for the children to be in bed. Meanwhile, parents warn their children that this is the night of the Hobby Horse and that they may be carried away.

When the Horse approaches a dwelling, Whitaker and Smith "make a big fuss, stomp our feet, and slam things around" to alert the children and to get them excited. Then they fling a door open and stomp into the room where parents have assembled their breathless youngsters. Whitaker, serving as the head, inquires after bad children, but no bad child is to be found. Soon the Horse is on his way to another house, leaving each child some small gift and a warning he'll be back again on next Old Christmas Eve night.

Source

North Carolina Folklore Journal, XIX (1971), 146-49. Collected and described by F. Roy Johnson in an article entitled "Survivals of

Christmas." His informants, natives of Martin County region, were L. J. Gordon, R.F.D. No. 1, Jamesville; William J. Barber, Roper; and Wheeler Smith and Chulch Whitaker, R.F.D. No. 1, Jamesville. For parallels and background, see "A Visit from El Agüelo," p. 437 and note, also p. 437.

The Cherry-Tree Carol

Among ... additions to the list of American versions of British ballads is "The Cherry-Tree".... This [variant of the] quaint and beautiful carol was found ... in the mountain region of Kentucky....

1. When Joseph was an old man,
   An old man was he,
   He married Virgin Mary,
   The Queen of Galilee.

2. As Joseph and Mary
   Were walking one day:
   "Here are apples, here are cherries
   Enough to behold."

3. Then Mary spoke to Joseph
   So meek and so mild:
   "Joseph, gather me some cherries,
   For I am with child."

4. Then Joseph flew in anger,
   In anger flew he:
   "Let the father of the baby
   Gather cherries for thee."

5. Then Jesus spoke a few words,
   A few words spoke he:
   "Let my mother have some cherries;
   Bow low down, cherry-tree."

6. The cherry-tree bowed low down,
   Bowed low down to the ground,
   And Mary gathered cherries
   While Joseph stood around.

7. Then Joseph took Mary
   All on his right knee:
   "O, what have I done?
   Lord have mercy on me!"

8. Then Joseph took Mary all,
   All on his left knee:
   "O, tell me, little baby,
   When thy birthday will be."

9. "On the sixth day of January
   My birthday will be,

When the stars in the elements
Shall tremble with glee."

Source and Comment

Journal of American Folklore, XXIX (1916), 293-45, 417. Collected by Josephine McGill from Will Wooten who learned it from his grandmother who was from North Carolina. She "died about thirty years ago at a very advanced age." The reference in stanza 9 to "the sixth day of January" evidences the continued celebration of Old Christmas.

The British ballad, "The Cherry-Tree Carol" (#54 in Francis James Child's *The English and Scottish Popular Ballads,* 5 Vols., Boston, 1882-98), is well known on both sides of the Atlantic. The variant presented here was collected near Hindman, Knott County, Kentucky. The text derives from an apocryphal story in the Pseudo-Matthew Gospel. The earliest English versions appear in fifteenth-century mystery plays, where, as here and other English versions, the cherry tree figures. In some Continental versions the date tree, which has the authority of the Apocrypha, is preserved. Others substitute an apple tree.

* * *

Little Christmas

January sixth, or the Feast of the Three Kings, is called Little Christmas [by Polish-American children]. The priest came to the homes and wrote the initials of the three kings (Kaspar, Melchior, and Balthasar) above the door, with crosses between them:

K+M+B 1968

He then sprinkled incense on the stoves, which were wood burning, and soon the whole house smelled like the church on holy days. In addition, the family was to have holy water, blessed candles, and palms in the house. These protected the house from damage and brought good luck to the inhabitants. Children unable to remember the names of the three kings called them:

> Kaspar: *Kapusta*: Cabbage
> Melchior: *Marhaf*: Carrots
> Balthasar: *Buroki*: Beets

(In the small town of New York Mills [New York], where my grandparents settled, the priest used to come to the houses; today little packets containing incense and chalk may be picked up in church.)

Source

New York Folklore Quarterly, XXIV (1968), 303. Reported by Robert Maziarz. See "Polish Christmas Eve Supper," p. 440, and note, p. 441, for background and informants.

* * *

Kings' Day and the Kings' Cake

Kings' Day [in New Orleans] is the beginning of a series of parties which are climaxed by Mardi Gras. The party itself can take any form, either children or adults, but usually a mixed group of men and women or boys and girls. It may be a dance, cocktail party or card party.

The one common factor is the existence of the King Cake. This is an oval shaped ring gaudily decorated with colored sugar. Baked into the cake is either a bean or doll. When refreshments are served each person takes a piece of cake. Whoever gets the token will be the king or queen of the next successive party which would take place one week later. If the party is made up of married couples and the man gets the token, his wife will be queen and acts as hostess for the next party. If the party is a group of unmarried people, the man who receives the token chooses his queen. When it is the woman who gets the token, she will choose her king. The queen is hostess, the party being held in her home, and the king will pay the bill.

It is usually the same group of people who continue throughout the series of parties. The persons who have been king or queen do not take a piece of cake until the token has been found. This relieves the possibility of giving more than one party in the series. The final party which would take place the week preceding Mardi Gras is traditionally a masquerade.

Source and Comment

Wayne State University Folklore Archive, 1961. Collected by Marvy Evelyn Hill, a student of folklore at Wayne State University in 1961. Her informant, Mrs. Hazel Heine, age 55, of New Orleans, Louisiana, explained that the "religious significance" of Kings' Day is "the commemoration of the visit of the three Kings to the Infant Jesus."

On Kings' Day or Epiphany, the twelfth day after Christmas, the Three Kings from the East presented their gifts to the Infant Jesus. The anniversary was once observed with revels and merrymaking, probably through the influence of the Roman festival of Saturnalia, which was notorious for its license and disorder. At the French court during the Christmas holidays, a Lord of Misrule called "King of the Bean" was allowed to govern for a day provided he found a bean baked into the "Cake of Kings." Sir James Frazer in *The Golden Bough* explains that "the King of the Bean on Twelfth Night and the medieval Bishop of Fools, Abbot of Unreason, or Lord of Misrule are figures of the same sort. . . ."

Twelfth Night is the eve of Twelfth Day. Shakespeare's comedy, *Twelfth Night,* was first performed to celebrate this festive season. Its sub-title *What You Will* captures the spirit of the holiday.

* * *

The Latino Nativity

Donned in robes of bed sheets and satin, the three Magi braved the lashing winds and traversed the icy streets yesterday, bearing gifts to sleeping toddlers inside Camden's [New Jersey] Centro Comunal Borincano.

Children rubbed their eyes as the three kings and their entourage of carolers with Puerto Rican straw hats crowded the day-care center at 617 N. Second St., singing softly in Spanish until all the children awoke:

"The Magi that arrived in Bethlehem announced the arrival of the Messiah and we, with happiness also announce it today. From a faraway land we came to see you, the Orient star serves as our guide."

Just as centuries ago the three wise men brought gifts of gold, frankincense and myrrh to the humble stable where the infant Jesus lay, yesterday the three kings sojourned through Camden, offering gifts to children at day-care centers and to Mayor Randy Primas and stopping at various community centers and churches.

Three Kings Day, or the Epiphany, is a popular Yuletide celebration in Puerto Rico and much of Latin America. It is known as the Latino Nativity because it was once the day when everyone exchanged gifts, rather than on Dec. 25.

Yesterday [January 6], El Dia de los Tres Reyes Magos was the first time the day was celebrated as an official school holiday in Camden.

"Just as the Magi came to the barrio where Christ was, we come to you Camden. This is our present to you," said Juan Ramon Dones, director of El Museo del Pueblo, which sponsored the event.

Three Kings Day is the most important Yuletide feast in Puerto Rico, where children leave hay in shoe boxes for the Magi's camels. The three kings, in return, leave gifts under the children's beds as they sojourn East, following the shining star. Children often leave their shoes outside their rooms so the Magi know which rooms are the children's.

Throughout the day, parents tell their children that they must be good or the Magi will not pass by their bedrooms.

On Jan. 5, the celebrations begin at midnight with twilight *parrandas* or parties that travel from house to house as revelers sing and dance. At each house, the hosts are expected to supply food and drink and then join the revelers as they descend upon another home.

On Jan. 6, all stores and government offices are closed, and the festivities continue each night until eight days later, Jan. 13.

Although Santa Claus has begun to replace the Magi as the prime gift-giver in Puerto Rico, the Three Kings celebration is still kept alive by the *jibaro,* Puerto Rico's hillbilly and folk hero.

And, besides being observed as a religious holiday, the Three Kings celebration has become cherished folklore to Puerto Ricans living in the continental United States who fear that their culture is becoming diluted with American customs.

"It is symbolic biblically and culturally," said Dones, whose cultural museum has traditionally celebrated the feast each year. "When Puerto Rican children begin to understand Three Kings Day, we will recapture what it is to be Puerto Rican, what we have lost. If the Puerto Rican cannot respect his values, he cannot respect other cultures' values."

El Museo del Pueblo, a Puerto Rican cultural museum at 218 Vine St., and George Rivera, an aide to Primas, organized the Magi's sojourn yesterday, when 500 gifts were distributed.

The procession first descended upon City Hall, where two children dressed as Mary and Joseph in sandals and robes made from bed sheets led the singing parade to Primas' office. Behind the children were the three wise men, Balthazar, Melchior and Gaspar, bearing incense, a wooden treasure box with pennies inside and a white glass vase. Beside the Magi was a 6-year-old boy dressed as a *jibaro* and wearing a *pava,* a hat made from palm.

"Happy, I come from the mountains .... How happy is my hut, and for my friends I bring them flowers from my best rose bush," sang the procession of about 20 carolers.

The carolers presented Primas with Puerto Rican eggnog made with coconut milk and rum and rice pudding, two traditional Yuletide dishes.

"It makes me feel good to see that you have not forgotten your culture, and, in fact, you are bringing it with you," Primas told the group. "That is the only thing that we have as a people."

Much like in the traditional *parrandas,* the Epiphany parade stopped in various community centers singing and asking to be admitted and fed. The procession also stopped at the home of Rosa Santiago, a community activist who has cancer.

Jose Perez, 16, a shortstop for Audubon High School who is being scouted by major league baseball teams, was dressed as Gaspar, wearing a Vandyke beard fashioned from his grandmother's wig. Perez, who has played that role for the last three years, said Three Kings Day is the Yuletide celebration that means the most to him.

"I think it is really Christmas because Christ didn't receive gifts until Jan. 6, when the three kings brought him gifts," he said.

Elsa Colon, 57, of Mount Ephraim, who was one of the carolers, recalled when she was a little girl in Puerto Rico and the *parrandas* would go from town to town.

"It was a time when the children lived the moment; it was a time when the children wondered if they would *ever see*" the Magi, Colon said. "It was a time of innocence."

Source

Philadelphia Inquirer, January 7, 1988. By staff writer Patrisia Gonzales.

Kings' Day at Santo Domingo Pueblo

Upon arrival at the Pueblo of Santo Domingo [New Mexico], about 2 P.M., [January 6, 1940] we found the celebration of Kings' Day, or Reyes Day, already in progress. A crowd of several hundred celebrants was gathered in front of a house which proved to be that of the newly appointed governor of the pueblo. A chorus of singers was in the house, and the crowd was waiting their reappearance. Later, it was learned that the chorus had entered this home and that of the newly appointed lieutenant governor. Homes of other new officers and those of people having the name of Rey or Reyes, whose day was being celebrated were visited but not entered.

After a few minutes the chorus emerged; they were dressed as French chefs. (In 1939, the chorus had been dressed as Chinese.) There were twenty-seven in the group, mostly younger men. The face of each was painted with pink clay and adorned with some form of false mustache. White aprons and chef's caps were made from flour sacks. The chorus formed an arc facing the doorway as they sang. Three men stood in front of the others, also facing the door. In front of all stood the leader who wore a very heavy, dark beard and mustache, a black sheepskin wig or hat, and an olive-drab smock. One chorus member carried a small, two-headed drum.

After several songs by the chorus, the house occupants threw presents from the roof to the crowd. Then the chorus, followed by the crowd, moved to another house where more songs were sung and presents were again thrown from the roof. The crowd was composed almost entirely of Santo Domingo residents as neighboring pueblos were holding their own celebrations that day. Some Spanish-Americans and a few Anglos were present. We were told that there were about sixty-five houses at which celebrations occurred, of which we watched the proceedings at about thirty-five. The ceremonies had begun shortly before noon and continued until about five o'clock that evening. At that time the people returned home to eat and rest for the dancing which began soon after six o'clock and continued until well after midnight.

Presents distributed from the housetops included the following items: cigarettes, Bull Durham and papers, candy bars, stick candy, candy suckers, packages of hard candy, gum, tin trays, pails, wash tubs, biscuit tins, dippers, pans, flour sifters, egg beaters, oranges, apples, grapefruit, glass bowls, 50 lb. sacks of flour, loaves of bread (mostly of native baking), cans of sardines, canned fruits and vegetables, 10'-12' halter ropes, rolls of linoleum, cooking utensils, cookies, wafers, crackers, crackerjack, yards of cloth, handkerchiefs, and head scarves.

Ready-made cigarettes and the tin ware seemed most popular. Everything was received enthusiastically, however, and the people throwing the presents were constantly urged by members of the crowd to throw an object in their direction. The crowd remained jovial throughout the day. Non-Indians were treated hospitably, and no objection was raised to their scrambling for presents. Occasionally, struggles for presents became quite spirited, but the losers usually shifted their attention quickly to the next offerings with a minimum of animosity.

Many presents were thrown toward the chorus; a few were purposely directed toward friends or relatives, especially women and small children. For the most part, however, presents were thrown at random.

Singing by the chorus included native songs and also adaptations of such pieces as "*La Varsuviana*," and other Spanish songs. While singing, the chorus members usually remained motionless although there were some of the hand and arm gestures commonly seen in Pueblo Indian dance choruses.

The atmosphere of the entire afternoon was one of gaiety and good-naturedness which are not always present at Santo Domingo ceremonies, at least when non-Indian visitors are concerned. The same gaiety and hospitality characterized the events of the evening.

After eating supper in one of the homes, the woman guided us to a neighboring house where dancing was to occur. After a futile wait, a small boy was directed to escort us to another home where a group of dancers was known to be. During the evening, seven groups were observed, several of them in a number of different homes. . . .

For each of the seven groups of dancers there was an older man, only one of whom appeared to have donned any special dress for the occasion. This one person had put on his best clothing, dressing very much like the chorus members for a Feast Day dance; the others appeared in their daily work clothes. In each group, this leader was clearly in charge, entering the house first, leading the dancers from the house at the end, and making the decision as to whether encores were deserved and, if so, how many.

On the average, there were a half dozen in each chorus, including one drummer. Three groups performed without a chorus or drum: these were primarily clown groups. In one or two choruses, the members wore red velvet shirts, false mustaches, and sunglasses, in imitation of the Navajo. In several houses, these chorus members also danced. The seven dance groups were as follows:

First Group: Nine dancers. There were three men on each side of a woman (actually a male impersonator) in a line with two leaders in front of them. The woman wore a yellow Navajo skirt. The six men in the line had their thighs painted white, bells at their knees, and knee-length black stockings and high, dark brown moccasins. The two men in front wore regular long pants of white cotton. All had on dark colored, velvet shirts, and wore many strings of turquoise, coral, and other beads. They wore a silver bow-guard on the left wrist, concho belts, and kilts of various sorts, saddle blankets. Saltillo serapes, but not one of the usual Hopi dance kilts. In their right hands, the men in the line carried black gourd rattles and in their left, fan-like objects of sticks and ribbons. A pendant foxskin hung from the belt in back. At the neck of this foxskin there was a glass or metal disk from which long ribbons hung. One of the leaders carried a rattle and sprigs of Douglas fir; the other carried a rattle and a foxskin. The men's hair was not flowing but confined under a large headdress of feathers (most of these were turkey but one or two men had eagle feather headdresses) and ribbons. This headdress was arranged as a fan, three or four feet wide, the outer edge of which had four ribbons, two in front and two in back, which hung down on either side to the dancer's waist. A few men had a scarf around their head. Face painting consisted of a black and red smudge across the cheeks and nasal bridge, and the lower jaw was painted white. In the back of the headdress, concealing the ties, there was a cluster of turkey breast feathers.

Second Group: Nine dancers. This group was almost identical with the first.

Third Group: Nine dancers. This group also had a line of seven dancers with two leaders in front. However, there were three female impersonators, arranged alternately with the four men of the line. Except for small tassels of down on each feather tip of the headdresses, these were essentially the same in costume and behavior as the first two groups.

Fourth Group: Six dancers. However, the chorus with this group included seven singers, five of whom also drummed. This was perhaps the most spectacular group, the increased size of the chorus and greater volume of the singing and drumming supplementing the more active type of dancing which was a modification of the so-called "Comanche War Dance."

The bodies of three dancers had been completely blackened. Beaded moccasins, white breechcloths, bow-guards on the left wrists, straps of several sleigh bells from the waist down the outside of each leg to the ankle, headdress, short spears in the right hand, and a small round shield in their left hands completed the costumes. The headdress appeared based on a sort of winter cap, or helmet, with flaps coming over the ears and fastening under the chin. This was dark brown, and there was a roach attached to it from front to back. Two large eagle tail feathers were attached to the roach, and at the nape of the neck were two smaller eagle feathers.

The other three dancers had large eagle feather headdresses, based on a similar arrangement although composed of many eagle feathers in a line from front to back along the roach. Two had the left side of their bodies painted green, with the other side unpainted. All of the face was green. The third dancer wore trunks and a vest of bright yellow. All three had the straps of sleigh bells as noted for the first three. The second three also wore bustles of eagle feathers fastened just above the buttocks and consisting of a semi-circle of feathers which flapped loosely with the dancers' movements. In the center of this bustle was a glass or piece of tinsel with many bright ribbons attached. On each side of this bustle, a single eagle wing feather, tipped with a purple plume, reached straight up to the dancers' shoulders.

Fifth Group: Five dancers. This group consisted of five men dressed as Negresses and was accompanied by neither chorus nor drum. All wore sunglasses. The performance of this group lacked the routine of the already described groups, each performance being largely improvised as it proceeded. However, the songs, mostly parodies, and comic dialogue were apparently well done as the group's efforts were received enthusiastically by all.

Sixth Group: Four dancers. This was another group of clowns, all wearing blackened sheepskin wigs. Again there was no chorus nor drum. Other items of costuming included ordinary European clothing, one or two straw or felt hats, false beards and mustaches, and blackened faces. The acts consisted primarily of song parodies and comic dialogues, partly Keresan, partly Spanish, and some in English. Again, their antics were received with great bursts of laughter from the entire crowd.

Seventh Group: Seven dancers. The costumes of this group were very similar to the other clown groups. They included sheepskin wigs, false beards and mustaches, blackened upper faces, and ordinary street clothing, except for moccasins. The middle man of the line wore a sun helmet instead of the sheepskin wig. Each wig had a bare portion over the forehead on which there was painted a yellow, or red, cross. One dancer had a New York World's Fair pennant stitched across the front of his sweatshirt; another had the words, "Ouch, Papa, Push More," stitched across his. Again, there was no chorus nor drum; their slow, jovial actions, songs, and jokes were an obvious adaptation of the minstrel show.

As noted, the chorus in the afternoon had frequently rendered "*La Varsuviana*," and other familiar Spanish songs. In the evening, these and many others were used by all three clown groups to the great delight of everyone. Some of the songs used, most often as parodies, included: "Reuben, Reuben," "She'll be Comin' 'Round the Mountain," "The Old Grey Mare," "Joy to the World," "I Wish I Were Single Again," "*Frère Jacque*," and "This is the Way We—." This last selection included "iron our clothes," "wash our hands," "comb our hair," "march to school," and other activities associated with Indian Boarding School routine. The songs were all well received, and several Indians were openly interested in our understanding and appreciating the satire.

At almost every home the host asked for more numbers and sometimes received as many as half a dozen encores. As the group finally departed, the woman of the house gave a present of food to one of the attendants accompanying each group. This was native bread, pieces of uncooked meat, or a dish of stew. These were taken to some central place where they were kept for the group's feast after the night's festivities had ended. Presents were given at every house.

Source

El Palacio, LVIII (1951), 398-400, 402-05. Charles H. Lange, at the time an anthropologist at the University of Texas, describes ceremonies at Santo Domingo, a Keresan pueblo on the Rio Grande in northwestern New Mexico, which he observed on January 6, 1940. For another example of present throwing, see "Mardi Gras," p. 84.

* * *

Puerto Rican Fire Festival

Different saints are specially cultivated at different places—as San Sebastian in Caguas and San Carlos in Aguadilla, while *Candelaria* is celebrated especially at Mayaguez [Puerto Rico]. This is connected with the beginning of the sugar cane crop, which has superseded coffee as the principal product. The *fiesta* consists in burning the waste of the plant, and these fires can be seen far and wide the day after "Three Kings' Day," the English Twelfth Night. Then gifts for children are placed under the pillows, in little boxes of straw for the camels of the Wise Men. There is in fact a holiday season from Christmas, which is especially the American celebration, to January 6th, which is the Puerto Rican.

Source

Folklore, XXXVIII (1927), 64. Collected by Peter J. Hamilton of San Juan, Puerto Rico. Informants not supplied. "*Candelaria*" literally means "Candlemas" but candles here, like burning the sugarcane stalks, appear to be a vestige of midwinter fire festivals, as is the custom of "Burning the Greens," which follows below.

* * *

Burning the Greens at Old Christmas

In the evening [in Sussex County, Delaware] the last rite in the Old Christmas celebration takes place—the burning of the Christmas greens. This formally ends the Christmas season. Strangely enough, a good many people, either knowingly or unknowingly, carry out this old tradition, for they keep the holly, mistletoe, and evergreens used as decorations at Christmas until January 6 and then burn them in a huge bonfire.

Source

Delaware Folklore Bulletin, III (1952), 11. Reported by Ruthanna Hindes. See note on the "Puerto Rican Fire Festival," above.

* * *

A Religious Old Christmas

In Hertford County [North Carolina], descendants of Sallie Lewis, an unlettered "Christian Meherrin Indian woman" who was bonded with a free man of color midway the nineteenth century, have banned the secular from Old Christmas in quest of a more nearly perfect religious observance.

Sallie lived "four or five miles in the woods" from the Hertford County seat at Winton. She ignored the December 25 holiday but sought to make January 5 a day of "natural enjoyment," says the Rev. R. R. Lewis of Winton, a great-great-grandson.

To this day neither Santa Claus nor any other mythical being visits the children on Old Christmas Eve night. Instead family and friends join in the giving of gifts.

On January 5 all work is laid aside, and at dinner family and friends sit down to a table spread with large dishes of greens, "symbols of money and vigorous health." The day coincides approximately with the time when Sallie's Iroquoian foreparents gave oblations to give strength and vigor to the new life that spring would bring. Morning and afternoon thanks in prayer and thoughts are given "in double portion." Each prayer intones, "Lord lead us from death into life and from darkness into light."

Source

North Carolina Folklore, XIX (1971), 145-46. From an article on "Survivals of Old Christmas" by F. Roy Johnson. His informant was the Rev. R. R. Lewis of Winton, North Carolina.

* * *

Praise Day

"Ol' Christmas," twelve days after Christmas, "Praise Day," is or was treated (the custom is passing) like Sunday; people would do no work. That night the domestic animals go down on their knees, and "Praise Day breaks [dawns] twice." Chickens come down from their roost; "it gets dark again, and dey have to go back—I seed it." Rosemary and poke [pokeweed] "put out—I seed it."

Source

Journal of American Folklore, XXXII (1919), 393. Collected by Elsie Clews Parsons in 1919 from members of the Lockley family who lived on the Lumbee River near Wagram, Scotland County, North Carolina. They were a racially mixed family, now usually termed Lumbee Indians, and were tenant farmers. "Cattle Kneeling at Midnight" is Motif B 251.1.2.3.

Keeping Old Christmas

"Nex' Friday will be Ol' Christmas," said Henry Stockton, a Negro of about forty, before whose fireplace I was at the time sitting. "My gran'mammy used to take a piece of coal an' mark up here each day after Christmas for twelve days," and he pointed to the whitewashed lintel of the fireplace.

By him and by many others, old and young, white and colored, I was told that on Old Christmas "day broke twice," that the Poke (*Phytolacca americana* L.) stalks and the hopvines put up early in the morning to go back again when the sun is well up; and that before "sun-up," or more commonly at midnight, the beasts, the cows, and the horses fell on their knees to pray. "We had an' ol' horse called Nellie," said one girl, "an' one year Popper took us out to see her at midnight. She was sure lyin' down." ...

On Old Christmas even to-day the older people will not work. One old colored woman had a story of how one year in her youth her mother had forgotten about the day, and was spinning. Her mother's sister came in, and exclaimed about it. "But it's not Ol' Christmas," said her mother. "Yes, 'tis. I know it is Ol' Christmas, because I saw the hopvines up." Apart from not working on the day, there seems to be no other way of celebrating.

Source

Journal of American Folklore, XXX (1917), 208. Collected by Elsie Clews Parsons in Guilford County, North Carolina. See "Praise Day," p. 33. "Cattle Kneeling at Midnight" is Motif B 251.1.2.3.

* * *

Animals on Old Christmas

Although Christmas is celebrated in the usual way throughout the three counties of Delaware, in Sussex, the southernmost county, January 6 is also celebrated, ... on the night of January 5th ... many strange things are said to take place. It is said that on the stroke of midnight all the cattle and all the sheep on the farms will kneel for a few minutes, as a sign of their adoration of the Child in the Manger in Bethlehem, and then all will rise simultaneously. It is also said that on this evening the animals of the farm form a perfect circle with all the male animals in the center and the females around the edge, the significance, perhaps, being the love and protection of Mary for her Child.

On this unusual night, not only the animals are aware of the miracle of long ago, but also the fowl of the farms. It is said that at midnight the oldest gander of a flock of geese will let out a shrill cry, and that the roosters have been known to crow from sundown until midnight.

At this season of peace and good will, there is good will even among wild animals, which depart from their usual habits. On this night the foxes bark to each other, and the fox hounds disobey the law of nature and refuse to trail the scent of a fox during the season of Old Christmas. No one has seen these things happen, but many people of Sussex County will assure you that they do occur.

Source

Delaware Folklore Bulletin, III (1952), 10. Reported by Ruthanna Hindes. Informants not given. "Cattle Kneeling at Midnight" is Motif B 251.1.2.3.

* * *

A Skeptic on Old Christmas Eve

Many of the old settlers believe that the cattle all kneel down and bellow at midnight on January 5th—the eve of "old Christmas"—in honor of the birth of Jesus, and there are men still living in the Ozarks who swear that they have actually witnessed this strange ceremony. A neighbor tells me that when he was a boy he watched repeatedly to see his father's oxen kneel, but was always disappointed. His parents told him, however, that the presence of a human observer broke the spell—that the cattle must always salute the Savior in private. "But I jus' drawed a idy right thar," he added thoughtfully, "thet they war'nt nothin' to hit, nohow."

Source

Journal of American Folklore, XL (1927), 93. Told by Vance Randolph. "Cattle Kneeling at Midnight" is Motif B 251.1.2.3.

* * *

A Cow's Prayer on Old Christmas

A man went out on Ol' Chris'mas and saw the cow prayin'. the man said the cow got down on her knees. He said that when the cow got up, he said to her, "What was you prayin'?" The cow replied, "I was prayin' to get strong enough to haul lumber to build your coffin with." The man went to runnin'.

Source

Southern Folklore Quarterly, XII (1948), 199. Collected by Margaret M. Bryant from Dicie Smith, of Trenton, Edgefield County, South Carolina in 1945, but originally told to her by Dicie Smith "as she worked about the house when I was a child." "Cattle Kneeling at Midnight" is Motif B 251.1.2.3.

* * *

New Year's Bread

For families who observe their religious holidays by the Julian calendar, today [January 6] is Christmas. For others it is Twelfth Night, a dozen days after Christmas and the official finale to the holiday season. For the Jack Demetris family, all members of St. Luke Greek Orthodox Church in Broomall [Pennsylvania], it is the feast of the Epiphany, a happy celebration honoring the Magi or wise men who came from the East bearing precious gifts for the Christ child.

Grandmother Pauline Doukakis was born in Smyrna, Turkey, 87 years ago and her energetic presence in the holiday kitchen ensures keeping the old traditions. Let daughter Dolly Demetris bake her own high, handsome bread for the day; Grandmother has her own special *Vasilopita* (New Year's Bread). Both versions hold a wrapped coin and finding the coin in one's slice ensures good fortune for the year ahead. But while Dolly's *Vasilopita* is undecorated, Grandmother's has a design in its center made by pressing a special wooden mold (given her by her mother) into the dough before baking.

The bread is an essential element of the meal; other foods and traditions are somewhat more flexible. Take the pomegranate, for example. An old custom was for the first male visitor of the day to throw the fruit in the vestibule and when the red seeds spattered widely, it would mean widespread happiness for the house. The way Mrs. Demetris sees it, a pomegranate can still bring luck if it's neatly displayed on the holiday dinner table rather than on the walls of the family's lovely St. Davids [Pennsylvania] home.

Vasilopita or New Year's Bread

1 cup butter
6 eggs, separated
2 cups sugar
1 cup milk
1 teaspoon baking powder
2 tablespoons brandy
1 teaspoon baking soda
   Juice of half a lemon
4 cups flour

Beat butter until creamy, then beat in egg yolks, sugar and milk until well blended. Add baking powder dissolved with brandy and soda dissolved with lemon juice. Add flour, then add stiffly beaten egg whites.

Wrap a coin in foil, add to batter and pour batter in a buttered 12-inch round cake pan or 11-by-13-inch pan. Bake at 350 degrees for 45 minutes to one hour or until cake tester comes out dry.

Source

Philadelphia Inquirer, January 6, 1982. By Elaine Tait, food columnist. The recipe is from Dolly Demetris.

*   *   *

Epiphany Celebration of the Sponge Fishermen

The Epiphany celebration involves the entire town for about three days. The town is decorated with banners and signs that are sold by the Epiphany committee and the receipts are used for the expenses of the Epiphany day celebration. Thousands upon thousands of tourists, both Greek and American, come from all parts of the United States to witness the celebration and events connected with it. There is a gala atmosphere in the city. After an elaborate church service which includes the "blessing of the waters" by a very high ranking church official, usually the Archbishop of North and South America, there is a parade from the church to the Spring Bayou where the "recovery of the cross from the waters" takes place. The parade lasts perhaps an hour or more, and during this time, all of the shops in the city close. There are costumed paraders from the Greek groups in the neighboring towns of Clearwater, Tampa and St. Petersburg, and several bands, including high school bands, are in the procession. Crowds line the streets and the edge of the water around famous Spring Bayou. The governor of the state usually attends the ceremonies as do many other state officials, senators, and civil representatives from many Florida cities. The high officials of the Greek AHEPA [fraternal club] are always there.

It is only in the last few years [c. 1965] that Tarpon Springs had been named the "focal point" of the Epiphany celebration by the Archdiocese of North and South America. It has always been the mecca of the older Greeks from all parts of the United States when they wanted a place to retire.

The climax of the morning's ceremony comes when the golden cross is thrown into the water and then is retrieved by one of many young men who have signed up for the privilege of diving for the cross. The lucky one who recovers the cross from the water, receives a blessing from the archbishop and is supposed to have good luck for a year. This good luck also extends to his family. In the afternoon, many hundreds go to the sponge exchange where a Greek dinner is served, and there is Greek *bouzouki* music and Greek dancing. This is called a *glendi* and it is an annual affair looked forward to by young and old. The large enclosure of the sponge exchange seems to be appropriate for this very Greek celebration. In the evening and on the following day, dances are given by various Greek groups.

Although many thousands come to the celebration, most do not stay longer than one day. Although the merchants claim that the visitors to Tarpon Springs do not buy very much, the restaurants, camera shops, motels and the hotel do excellent business. This is the one day of the year when the Greek group is completely in charge of all attractions in the city. Americans accept this and seem to take some pride in the fame which the city has acquired because of this ceremony. When the only notice about Tarpon Springs in guide books is about the Epiphany day celebration, these same people are not so pleased. There seems to be an unexpressed pleasure among the Greeks that for at least one day in the year, the Greek group is dominant again as it was during the affluent years of the sponge fishing industry.

Source

"*The Greek-American Group of Tarpon Springs, Florida,*" Ph.D. dissertation, University of Pennsylvania, 1967, 342-44. Described and discussed by Edwin Clarence Buxbaum. His anthropological study centers on "ethnic identification and acculturation," especially the interaction between the Greek-Americans and the community at large. Cf. "Feast of Lights," below.

* * *

Blessing the Waters on Epiphany

The Epiphany Day ceremonies [at Tarpon Springs, Florida] commemorating the baptism of Christ begin with a formal religious service, during which the water in the church is made holy through special prayers and rituals. Following this mass, a lengthy and colorful procession ... makes its way to the Spring Bayou. Crowds of local citizens and tourists line the streets and encircle the bayou to witness the proceedings. The priests read the story of Christ's baptism from the New Testament. At the stroke of noon, a white dove—symbolic of the Holy Ghost as he appeared on the day that Christ was immersed in the waters of the Jordan—is released. The archbishop then throws a gold cross into the bayou; and when it strikes the water, it is believed that the sea has become holy once again.

Source and Comment

"*Greek-American Folk Beliefs and Narratives: Survivals and Living Tradition,*" Ph.D. dissertation, Indiana University, 1964, 69. Observed and described by Robert A. Georges.

In the Eastern Church the Feast of the Epiphany commemorates concurrently several apparitions of Christ's divinity—the baptism or spiritual birth, the physical birth, the star of the Magi, and the miracles of Cana and feeding the multitudes. For this reason, the holiday sometimes has a plural designation, Feast of the Epiphanies. An earlier emphasis on the celebration of Christ's baptism has been retained while the Western Church observance centers on the three kings. In the Eastern Church Epiphany is the traditional time for baptism.

* * *

An Epiphany Superstition

The [Tarpon Springs] fishermen are afraid even to leave port [in the New Year] before Epiphany lest disaster befall them.

Source and Comment

Southern Folklore Quarterly, VII (1943), 105. Reported by J. Frederick Doering. He cites *The Epiphany Day Book,* Tarpon Springs, 1937 edited by George Anastassiou.

Robert Georges explains in his dissertation, "Greek-American Folk Beliefs and Narratives," 68-69, cited above, that spongers consider it unsafe to sail on waters that have not been blessed, and hence do not

leave port from the end of December until January 6 when the blessing for the ensuing year takes place.

* * *

Epiphany Sunday: Icy Waters

The Greek Orthodox ritual of Epiphany Sunday was observed yesterday [January 11, 1981] on the Delaware River at the foot of Race Street [in Philadelphia]. The Rev. Constantinos Pappas offered prayers, and a Police Department launch aided in the recovery of a cross tossed into the icy river to bless the waters in commemoration of the baptism of Jesus.... The cross floated on the Delaware as Gus Rapits of Upper Darby [Pennsylvania] swam out to get it. Cross recovered, the ritual is completed.

Source

Philadelphia Inquirer, January 12, 1981. Captions to photographs of a swimmer recovering a cross cast into the frigid Delaware River as a police launch stands by to assist.

* * *

Feast of Lights

The ninth annual Feast of Lights, a rite of the Greek Catholic Orthodox Church commemorating the baptism of Christ by John in the River Jordan, was observed yesterday [January 10, 1960] at Rainbow Pier, Long Beach [California]. Due to the inclement weather and the condition of the sea, the yearly ceremony was altered on the advice of the Long Beach lifeguards. Bishop Demetrios, spiritual leader of the church for twelve western states, did not put out to sea in a fishing boat and no diving to retrieve the symbolic cross was permitted. The Greek prelate and five priests were driven to the outermost point of the pier where the church leader hurled the gilded wooden cross into the water in keeping with the centuries-steeped pageantry. A large crowd watched while Angelo Kouropis, 34, of 361 19th Street, San Pedro, entered his small blue boat to search for the cross which he found floating about one-quarter mile east of where it was tossed in. Kouropis passed the cross up from his boat to waiting hands and it was returned to Bishop Demetrios.

Source and Comment

Los Angeles *Times,* January 11, 1960. Reprinted by Mimi Char as an example of "Folklore in the News" in *Western Folklore,* XIX (1960), 135-36. Cf. "Epiphany Celebration of the Sponge Fishermen," p. 35; "Blessing the Waters on Epiphany," above, and "Retrieving the Cross: Combining Church Festivals," p. 337.

The Feast of Lights is also known as the Day of Lights and the Feast of the Jordan because Christ, upon baptism in the River Jordan, is said to have been illuminated by divine light.

Serbian Christmas in a Mining Camp

The house of Pete and Milka Loverich was warm from more than the flame on the hearth and the glass in the hand when Dr. Paul Snelgrove Richards first paid his friends a Christmas visit. That snowy day in 1923 he called on nine different families at Highland Boy, a Utah mining camp in the right-hand fork of Bingham Canyon. As in the other homes of the settlement of between 3,000 and 4,000 people, at the Loveriches he was greeted with the joyous expression, "*Mir Boze, Kristos se Rodi!*"

Pete slapped his new friend on the back and gave him a kiss on both cheeks.

Young Milka, Sophie, and the boys in the family echoed their parents' greeting in English, "God's peace, Christ is born!"

The whole large dining room of people, miners who were boarding at this house and some of their friends from other homes, spoke up, offering the traditional greeting. "You honor us," said one. Another man gave the doctor a friendly slap. Genuine hospitality would be extended to everyone who entered this door during the three days of the festivities.

Some of the women were dressed in their native costumes. And as it slowly burned, the large end of the *Badnyak*, the sacred log—an oak in Serbia, a juniper in Highland Boy—scented the room. Mrs. Loverich passed Dr. Paul the wine, bobbing an old-world curtsy as she held the tray. He reached for a glass of red wine. She deftly turned and with a smile indicated the choicer but also homemade white beverage.

Like Christmas bells the doctor's characteristic laugh rang through the room. He smelled the bouquet. For the first time he toasted these patients, these friends, at the beginning of the three-day festival. On the last Christmas before his death [in 1958], he again toasted those who were still living but now in young Milka's home. She was then Mrs. George Smilanich, a widow, with some of her children quite grown. Her parents no longer kept the boardinghouse. Like young Milka's husband, they too had gone. In 1958 Dr. Paul's face was as white as the snow through which he had ridden horseback to the feast in 1923. Yet, as with all but very few Christmases after that first year, nothing could have kept him from his friends.

Lost for a moment in the crowd while all were still toasting each other on this January 7th, 1923, he noticed the Serbs lifting the glass to the Austrians, and the other way about. Having already visited many homes this day, he realized that the Austrians—who, as a nation, were strictly Roman Catholic—had joined the Serbs in observing the day set aside for the Nativity according to the Gregorian Calendar. In their religion the Serbs at the camp were Eastern Orthodox. The doctor fell in with the spirit and atmosphere, but he could hardly believe the pattern of these toasts. Two men known to be fiercely at odds were raising the glass to each other. He looked, he gulped and cracked a joke hardly fit for a nun but which was undoubtedly aimed at cementing still further this amazing act of friendship.

As the day passed he learned that this offering was no more than typical. All enmity was now banished from the homes. The doctor may have recalled the tree which he had placed at the door of the building down the canyon, which housed both hospital and medical clinic. The tree still stood on the porch in the center of the town of Bingham, glittering with tinsel and colored baubles. His new friends, the miners and their families, had been so impressed by this first public display for Christmas in Bingham that several of them immediately urged Dr. Paul to attend their January 7th celebration.

"You would honor us," said a man with a crushed finger.

"We would like to have you come, Doc," said his wife. "Please, do."

At the Loveriches, as an undertone to the merriment, Dr. Paul studied the spirit which seemed so very different from the Christmas rites among his own beloved people. He watched, he waited, he had to understand the nature of this distinction.

With another ringing laugh, he accepted a second glass of wine. Once more he toasted both men, the Austrian and the Serb. He toasted this house. The boarders stood around. They had all chipped in for the feast; they were now ready to receive their reward. The ruddy faces reflected the light from the embers of the log. Everyone was keen for the meal. The actual preparations had begun months ago, in late September and early October, with the vintage of the grapes imported to Bingham, almost by the carload. Each year it was the same. The day that the children showed up on the schoolgrounds with their feet stained purple, the whole town knew they had been crushing the fruit in the great vats at Highland Boy.

The immediate beginning of the feast had occurred with the roasting of the suckling pig in the dooryard of the boardinghouse, only yesterday. The tantalizing odor of the meat had risen with the steam. As it wafted down canyon, up the hill trailed the youngsters. Nearing the spit, they broke into a lively gait, tramping down the snow, rushing forward with great chunks of bread in their hands. Breathlessly, each waited his turn to scoop up some of the drippings from the pan beneath the spit. With this act, Christmas had really begun for the camp. Pete Loverich had never turned down a single youngster. Though their mischief could at times rise to the sky, at this moment the kids were his gang. The meat would taste all the better at the table because they would have had their taste of the drippings.

Milka, Pete's wife, had commenced her preparations at sink, stove, and counter weeks ago. A great storeroom ran directly into the mountain, connected with the kitchen by a narrow passage. This underground cooler, or "refrigerator," had been heaped with smoked hams and other meats, such as beef, bologna, sausage; with salted fish, pickled cucumbers, and preserved fruits; with cheeses, butter, and large pans of *sarma*; almost anything one could put away ahead of time.

At each place at the long table, to be occupied mostly by men and served by women, a soup plate now stood waiting. Once the guests were seated, Milka brought in a huge tureen of her delicious broth. It was simply floating with homemade noodles, cut as fine as the blades of rosemary she had dropped into the pot. Here she had also simmered the tender part of a head of cabbage. At the same time she had parboiled some outside leaves for the *sarma*. Sniffing the aromatic odor, Dr. Paul, as guest of honor, was the first to pass his dish forward.

After the soup the cold meats were served, and now came the *sarma*, piping hot. For this typically Eastern dish, Milka had held on the palm of her left hand, one at a time, the parboiled leaves. With exactly the right turn, she had folded in the edges of the cabbage leaf around a tablespoonful of wonderfully seasoned, ground pork. After filling several large pans with the meatballs, she put them aside in the underground room. The *sarma* now came to the table straight from the oven. What a tantalizing note it added to the cold meats and the sauerkraut, and even to the pickles, preserves, and fancy breads that Milka had made! One of these was the *pevitza*, mixed with honey and crushed walnuts.

Still no man's appetite was dimmed. The real highlight of the feast was yet to come. Milka, followed by the girls with dishes of hot vegetables, brought from the huge iron stove the suckling pig. She placed the great platter, smoking hot, before her husband. Cheers and sighs went up from the men. Pete took his sharp knife and severed the head. He arranged it upright on a special plate. Before transferring the plate to the center of the table he removed the apple that was resting on the top of a glass of red wine. He sipped the wine and offered the glass to Dr. Paul, who also took one sip and then asked the blessing of the Lord upon this house and all the friends therein. Pete placed the glass in the mouth of the pig as the symbol of the Serbian Boar's Head and the blood of Christ. Near the center of the table a can tied with a small bow of ribbon held a cluster of sprouted wheat which Milka had planted on December 19th, St. Nicholas' Day. Its fresh and charming green complemented the ceremonial wine as the sign of the resurrection after the Cross.

When the meat was served, the guests fell to, singing their praises and again cracking their jokes. The laughter rang

from end to end of the table. Milka, the daughter, clapped her hands when Dr. Paul found a coin in his piece of the round flat loaves baked for the occasion. The children had washed and polished several pieces of money until they shone brighter than any little old bauble on a fir tree. The mother had hidden them in the dough as a token of the giving of one's means as well as his heart.

Finally, with appetites still quite competent, the guests were ready for the dessert. Over a rich dough, beaten, kneaded and rolled thin upon a cloth that covered the top of the kitchen table, Milka, the mother, had spread a bounteous layer of freshly sliced apples. After sprinkling them with cinnamon and other spices, she picked up the corner of the cloth to roll the strudel. As the concoction took shape, she peeled the cloth away and then folded the roll, tripling it from end to end so that it just fit into her largest roasting pan. At the table she cut the strudel crosswise and served it hot with another taste of wine.

Source and Comment

Utah Historical Quarterly, XXXIII (1965), 316-19, 321. By Claire Noall, based on the manuscript "Memoirs of Dr. Paul Snelgrove Richards," company physician to the United States Mining, Smelting, and Refining Company of Bingham, Utah, for thirty-five years, and on family notes and interviews. She reports that "Highland Boy is a ghost town." The Western Church celebrates St. Nicholas' Day on December 6. See p. 426.

* * *

Kifle: Serbian Christmas Pastry

"*Kifle*," or "the Belgrade Cookie," is a Serbian Christmas pastry that was supposed to have originated in Belgrade, Yugoslavia. This cookie was known only in "the city," where, according to the informant, the cooking was always "more refined." ... "*Kifle*" is traditionally served during the Serbian Christmas season which, because of its doctrine of going by the "old calendar," is celebrated on and around January 7th. According to the informant, "Don't plan anything the day you make these." In fact, it is usually made in two parts, each taking up a good part of a single morning.

Kifle Recipe

The Filling
1   8 oz. can shelled, rolled or ground walnuts
2   tablespoons butter
¼   cup milk
1   egg, beaten well
⅓   rounded cup sugar
¼   teaspoon salt

Melt butter, milk, egg, sugar and salt over low heat. Then add walnuts and cook slowly for about ten minutes. Taste for sweetness. Add more milk and sugar if necessary. (Makes about 85 cookies)

Dough

Cream with hands:

½ pound soft butter
2 tablespoons sugar
⅓ teaspoon salt
1 cake yeast, broken in pieces
2 egg yolks
½ cup sour cream

After thoroughly creamed, add in three parts:
3¼ cups flour (Measure before sifting. Sift 3 times, mixing well after each addition with hands.)

Chill and divide into two parts. Roll out one part dough quite thin and cut in squares. Lay filling (about one teaspoon) diagonally, and then roll up. Then bend. Bake at 325 degrees for 15 to 20 minutes, until lightly browned (on an ungreased cookie sheet). Then roll in powdered sugar. Dough and filling can be made a day in advance—store in refrigerator.

"Revision: Helpful Hints"

Divide dough into four parts—filling too.
Roll each part into a 9″ by 21″ rectangle.
Cut into 3" squares (21 squares).
Make filling one day, cookies the next.
Chill one hour.
Add little or no flour to board.
Bake 15 minutes—let cool about 15 minutes before rolling in powdered sugar.

Source

Arizona Friends of Folklore, III (1973), 39-40. Collected by Craig Soland from Mrs. W. A. Soland, who learned to make *kifle* from her mother, Mrs. Louis Varda, who learned it from Dorothy Madelyn, originally from Belgrade, Yugoslavia.

* * *

A Plough Monday Play

Soldier:

> In comes I, the cruising [recruiting] soldier,
> With orders from the Queen
> To list all you fellows
> That follows horse and plough.

Tom (the farmer's boy):

> In comes Tom, the farmer's boy,
> Don't you see my whip in hand?
> To my plough I do attend.
> 'Tis Plough Monday makes me bold,
> I hope you won't be offended.

Old Jane (carrying a baby):

> In comes I, Old Jane,
> With my neck as long as a crane,
> Long time I've sought thee, Tom,

> And now I've found thee,
> Pray, Tommy, take thy child.

Tom:

> It's not mine and I won't have it.

Old Jane:

> Look at its eyes, nose, cheek, and chin.
> It's a picture of you as ever did grin.
> Take it home and feed it.

Tom:

> Go away home,
> I'll see you in hell fire.

St. George:

> In comes I, St. George,
> In my hand I carry a club.
> What old woman can sass me?

Old Jane:

> I can.
> My head it is of brass,
> My body it is of steel.
> Nobody can't make me feel nothing.

St. George:

> If your head is made of brass,
> And your body's made of steel,
> I can make you feel.
> (He knocks Old Jane down to the floor.)

Tom:

> What have you done?
> Killed the best woman
> Under the sun.
> Two pounds for a doctor.

St. George:

> Ten pounds to stay away.

Tom:

> He must come in a case like this.

Doctor:

> Hold my horse by the tail, boy. He's only a donkey. Give him a good feed of water and a bucket of ashes to drink. In comes I, a doctor good to stop the blood.

Tom:

> Be you a doctor?

Doctor:

> Yes, I am a doctor.

Tom:

> What ailments can you cure?

Doctor:

> Just what my pill pleases. I goes about for the good of the country. I'd sooner kill than cure. I cured my own wife of rheumatism in all four of her elbows, and I'll cure this woman if she ain't too far gone. Hold my bottle till I feel her pulse.
> (He feels of the woman's belly.)

Tom:

Is that where the pulse do lie?

Doctor:

Yes, it lies in the strongest part of the body.
She's not dead; she's only in a trance. She's
swallowed a horse and cart, and can't pass off
the wheels. These are virgin pills. Take one
tonight and two tomorrow, and rub your belly
with the bottle next day. Jump up Jane, and
we'll have a dance.
(Jane gets up and they dance around a spell.)

Soldier:

Come my lads, it's time for listing,
Listing do not be afraid,
You shall have your fill of liquor.
[Several lines missing.]
Tell me, who is this pretty maid?

Lady:

In comes I, a lady fair,
My fortune in my charms.
It's true I've turned away
Out of my true-love's arms.
Oh, he did marry me,
As all do understand,
And then he listed for a soldier
In a far and distant land.

Soldier:

Madam, I've got gold and silver,
Madam, I've got house and land,
Madam, I've got golden treasure,
All at your command.

Lady:

What care I for your gold and silver?
What care I for your house and land?
What care I for your golden treasure?
All I want is a nice young man.

Tom:

Here am I all brisk and spry,
And I'm hungry as well as dry.

Old Jane:

Here am I, Old Jane,
With my neck as long as a crane.
Once I wore a wig behind
And a wig before,
Now I'm a poor widow.

Tom:

I'm the nice young man you want, miss.

Soldier:

Madam, I've got gold and silver,
Madam, I've got house and land,
Madam, I've got golden treasure,
All at your command.

[Section missing]

Last song (to be sung by all the actors):

Uncle Joe's version:

We are not the London actors
That act upon the stage.
We are the country plough boys
That work for little wage.
Good master and good mistress,
Just think of us poor boys
That plough through mud and mire.
We'd thank you, dear master,
For a pitcher of your best beer.

Aunt Mary's version:

Good master and good mistress,
As you sit by your fire,
Remember us poor plough boys
That plough amongst the mire.
The mud it is so nasty,
The water is not clear.
We'd thank you for to give us
A drink to give us cheer.

Source and Comment

Journal of American Folklore, LI (1938), 18-21. Marie Campbell
collected fragments of folk plays from the Kentucky mountains in the
1930s. Her informants for the Plough Monday play were "Uncle Joe
and Aunt Mary," described as "very old people" who "did not
remember that the play had been 'acted out' within their lifetimes of
over seventy years. They said nobody else knew the play, and they
argued over the way the speeches should be worded. There are
portions they could not remember at all." In her Ph.D. dissertation,
Mummers Plays in the Americas," New York University, 1976, Alice
I. Richardson describes the Campbell text as "an attempt to simulate
the normal mutations of folk tradition" and compares it with British
prototypes. Cf. "St. George's Play," p. 380, and for additional
examples of mumming and begging, see "Cajun Country Mardi
Gras," p. 83 and note.

The Soldier's lines beginning "Madam, I've got gold and silver," in
Campbell's text, are often found in an Anglo-American song titled
"The Quaker's Wooing" or "Madam, I Have Come A-Courtin'" and a
related song, "No, Sir, No."

In England, the Christmas holiday season ended on Twelfth Day,
humorously called St. Distaff's Day, because women were supposed to
return to their spinning wheels and other daily tasks. Men, however,
were not expected to go back to the plough until the following
Monday. On the preceding Sunday their ploughs were blessed to
assure good crops. The next day the ploughmen dragged them from
house to house and asked for food, drink, and "plough money." If no
such treat were forthcoming, like Halloween pranksters they ploughed
some obviously inappropriate piece of land as a trick. A traditional
part of this Christmas mummery was the performance of short plays,
especially the St. George folkplay, of which the Plough Monday play is
a comic variation. St. George plays usually consist of a sequence of
stock characters who introduce themselves, a fight in which St.
George is killed, his miraculous revival by a comic doctor, and
requests for gifts by the actors.

Battle of New Orleans
January 8

General Andrew Jackson, with a motley army made up of militiamen, sailors, and pirates fighting from behind barricades, stopped an assault on New Orleans by eight thousand British veterans of the Napoleonic wars on January 8, 1815. The British suffered some two thousand casualties while the Americans had only eight killed and thirteen wounded. The victory made Jackson a national hero, and before the Civil War its anniversary was widely celebrated.

The Ursulines Pray for Victory

When the Ursuline nuns came to New Orleans in 1727, they brought with them a small statue of the Blessed Mother.

On a number of occasions the Ursulines, at the request of the inhabitants of New Orleans, prayed to the Blessed Mother to intercede for them. The occasions were the yellow fever epidemics, a fire which almost destroyed the city and other similar tragedies.

During the war of 1812 it seemed inevitable that the city would be destroyed in the battle with the English. Again the people went to the Ursulines and requested the prayers of the nuns on behalf of their city. The only salvation for the city had to be an immediate answer to the prayers.

The nuns prayed to the Blessed Mother under the title of Our Lady of Prompt Succor and promised that if the city be saved they would have sung a Pontifical High Mass and *Te Deum.*

The Battle occurred on January 8, 1815, and the Americans were victorious. Since this day the Ursulines and all those connected with them have kept the promise.

On the morning of January 8, the Archbishop of New Orleans celebrates a Pontifical High Mass followed by the *Te Deum.* The eight days preceding are dedicated to a novena in honor of Our Lady of Prompt Succor, the climax of which is the High Mass and *Te Deum.* This mass takes place at the National Shrine of Our Lady of Prompt Succor which is in conjunction with the convent and girls' school which the Ursulines have maintained since their arrival in New Orleans.

Source

Wayne State University Folklore Archive, 1961. Collected by Marvy Evelyn Hill, a student of folklore at Wayne State University, in 1961. Her source was Joy M. Haine, age 34, of New Orleans, Louisiana, a graduate of the Ursuline College and former teacher in the Ursuline Academy. For mention of another celebration of this victory, see "First Thanksgiving in Illinois," p. 411.

Carberry Day

Every Friday the 13th

Professor Josiah Stinkney Carberry, whose exploits are celebrated on Carberry Day, is an academic joke, a hoax that has become a tradition at Brown University, Providence, Rhode Island. He exists only in the imagination of the Brown faculty, students, and alumni though his fame extends afar. In the course of his fictional life, he has acquired an eccentric family and traveled widely and with notable rapidity on various research projects: "One day Carberry will be translating inscriptions in Cambodia's Angkor Wat. The next day he will be in Mozambique studying the habits of the Zambesi River shrimp."

Professor Carberry

Carberry was born in 1929. One of the young faculty members at Brown, seeing the glass cover of an official bulletin board unlocked, put up this notice:

"On Thursday evening at 8 o'clock in Sayles Hall, J. S. Carberry will give a lecture on 'Archaic Greek Architectural Revetments in Connection with Ionian Phonology.'"

Shortly thereafter, Ben C. Clough happened by. This professor of Latin, now retired, spotted the notice as a hoax. But instead of taking it down, he printed the word "not" between "will" and "give."

Somehow this bit of whimsy caught the imagination of a coterie of the more youthful faculty members. Treatises under Carberry's name began appearing in scholarly journals, such as the *Classical Weekly*. By an exchange of telegrams, letters and postcards, the group not only kept the professor alive but gave him a confused wife, Laura, and two odd but literary daughters, Lois and Patricia.

From the farthest corners of the globe came news of the professor's esoteric research missions, together with a steady flow of innovative ideas. On Cape Cod he devised steel sails for boats. Amid the blue grass of Kentucky, he developed chlorophilly for horses. From Zurich came his proposal for a rotatable laboratory for conducting revolutionary experiments.

In recent years the university has enshrined the professor as a continuing legend. Archives at the John Hay Library preserve letters, cards, clippings—accounts of his exploits as they occur.

On June 6, 1966, Brown gave Carberry a bona fide MA degree. (It was awarded in absentia. The professor was, of course, traveling at the time.) And the university has designated every Friday the 13th, no matter in what month it occurs, as Carberry Day.

On those occasions, small brown jugs, set conspicuously about the campus, serve as repositories for students' and teachers' gifts of small change. This money goes into a university sanctioned book fund that Professor Carberry asked be established "in memory of my future late wife, Laura."

Source and Comment

Chicago Daily News, September 21, 1974. From a feature story with the headline, "Prof. Carberry, Paul Bunyan of the high road," by Ernest Dickinson. Clippings and mimeographed "Background information on Josiah Stinkney Carberry, Professor of Psycho-Ceramics" supplied by the Brown University News Bureau. A brief item in the *New York Times* on January 14, 1981, notes that the "annual Friday-the-13th tribute" to Carberry "again took place yesterday" and explains that his specialty, "psycho-ceramics," means "cracked pots."

Iroquois White Dog Feast

First Quarter Moon in January

The sacrifice of the white dog or dogs at the new year ceremonies of the Iroquois tribes was dedicated to Teharonhiawagon, the Master of Life. He was believed to have revealed through his dreams that a sacrificial victim and an offering of tobacco were necessary to insure the return of spring and the rebirth of all life on earth, and thus to thwart the Gods of Winter and Famine. Joshua Clark, who described the ritual in 1849, compared the white dogs to the biblical scapegoat "laden with the sins of the nation" (*Onondaga*, p. 59). The ceremony was performed in each longhouse or assembly hall of the various tribes. The sacrificed animals were usually eaten. Fires, dances, games, and other new year ceremonies accompanied the sacrifice. The festival lasts for a number of days, constituting the major mid-winter rite.

White Dog Feast at the Onondaga Reservation

This religious festival is usually 'called' during the first quarter of the moon in the month of January [1888]. It may be held on various days during that period, its special beginning being named by the sachems of each nation, and continues for six successive days, including in its various ceremonies nearly all the features of the Iroquois religion. In accordance with olden customs such feast was "called" last week by the Onondagas on their reservation near Syracuse [New York]....

On the first day of the 'new year jubilee' a white dog is selected and strangled. It must be, by the law, 'spotless and free from all blemish;' they are careful not to shed its blood nor break its bones. It is decorated with ribbons and red paint, and ornamented with feathers, and the very pious, who are taught that with each gift to the sacrifice a blessing is bestowed, hang upon its body trinkets and beads of wampum. Thus decorated, it is fixed to a cross-pole and suspended by the neck about eight feet from the ground. There it hangs until the fifth day, when it is taken down and carried by 'faith keepers' to the council-house, and laid out upon a bench, while the fire of the altar is kindling, while a priest, making speeches over it, relates the antiquity of this institution of their fathers, and its importance and solemnity, finally enjoining the people to direct their thoughts to the Great Spirit, concluding with a prayer of thanks that the lives of so many have been spared through another year. On this occasion, at 'noon by the sun,' twelve young warriors who were stationed at the northern corner of the council-house, firing their rifles, announced the procession as formed. Headed by four 'faith keepers,' who bore the sacrifice, and who were followed by the priests and matrons, and the old and young people, the procession slowly moved toward the main council-house, under which

the remains of the celebrated prophet Ga-ne-o-di-yo (Handsome Lake) are buried. Passing through the building from the western to the eastern door outward, and around the council-house, reentering it at the eastern door, they laid the sacrifice on the altar; and, as the flames surrounded it, a basket containing tobacco was thrown on the fire, its smoke rising as incense, as the priest, in a loud voice invoking the Great Spirit, chanted as follows: 'Hail, hail, hail! Thou who has created all things, who ruleth all things, and who givest laws to thy creatures, listen to our words. We now obey thy commands. That which thou hast made is returning unto thee. It is rising to thee and carrying to thee our words, which are faithful and true.'

This was followed by the 'great thanking address' (given by the priest and people).... This concluded the religious rite, after which the people dispersed in various directions, to reassemble in the afternoon, attending the exciting and peculiarly Indian 'snow snake' game. The fifth being a day devoted to religion, there were no dances. The 'great f[e]ather dance,' a religious one, was given the next afternoon, followed by the 'trotting,' 'berry,' 'fish,' and 'raccoon' dances. Previous to the sacrifice the 'cousin clans' were divided: the Wolf, Turtle, Snipe, and Bear sat in the new council-house; the Deer, Beaver, Eel, and Hawk were in the old council-house, from whence the procession formed. Sachem Ha-yu-wan-es (Daniel Lafort, Wolf), Oh-yah-do-ja-neh (Thomas Webster, Snipe), hereditary keeper of the wampum belts, were masters of the religious ceremonies in which about two hundred Indians participated.

Source and Comment

Journal of American Folklore, I (1888), 83-85. Reprinted from an article by Harriet Maxwell Converse, an adoptive member of the Seneca tribe, in the Elmira (New York) *Telegram*, January 29, 1888.

In the "snow snake game" a stick carved in the shape of a snake was thrown on the ice in a contest for distance. A detailed description of this festival, including an explanation of its timing and purpose, is provided by F. W. Hodge, *Handbook of the American Indians,* II (1912), 939-44. W. M. Beauchamp reports on the decline of the ritual: " . . . no dog has been burned at Onondaga for two years past. I asked Chief Lafort why this happened, and he said the sacred breed of dogs had run out. Other Indians, however, think this is but an excuse for discontinuing the sacrifice, which had lost its solemnity. Forty years ago the Onondagas burned two white dogs on an altar pile; then but one; then it was dropped into a stove, and now the white dog seems to have finally disappeared." See *Journal of American Folklore,* I (1888), 195.

* * *

White Dog Feast

Games at the White Dog Feast

Some Iroquois games have a high antiquity, having survived the test of time. Two forms of the game of white and black still exist, and there are frequent allusions to one of these in the Jesuit Relations, where it is termed that of the plate or dish. It excited the highest interest; for though it was of the simplest nature, nation played against nation, and village against village. From the floor to the ridgepole of the cabin the eager spectators looked at the two players, showing their sympathy by their cries.

Two forms of this simple game of chance remain, and perhaps there were never more than these. Father Bruyas alluded to one of them in his Mohawk lexicon of radical words, speaking of it as the game in which the women scatter fruit stones with the hand. This distinction of throwing remains, although disks of bone or horn are now used instead of the stones of fruit. L. H. Morgan described this as the game of deer buttons, called *Gus-ga-e-sá-ta* by the Senecas. They used eight circular buttons of deer horn, about an inch in diameter, and blackened on one side. These are about an eighth of an inch in thickness, and bevelled to the edge. He said: "This was strictly a fireside game, although it was sometimes introduced as an amusement at the season of religious councils, the people dividing into tribes as usual, and betting upon the result." In public two played it at a time, with a succession of players. In private two or more played it on a blanket, on which they sat and threw. His counting differs at first sight from that which I received, but amounts to the same thing. Beans were used for the pool, and Morgan said that six white or black drew two, seven drew four, and all white or black drew twenty. Less than six drew nothing, and the other player had his throw until he lost in turn.

Among the Onondagas now eight bones or stones are used, black on one side and white on the other. They term the game *Ta-you-nyun-wát-hah,* or Finger Shaker, and from one hundred to three hundred beans from the pool, as may be agreed. With them it is also a household game.

In playing this the pieces are raised in the hand and scattered, the desired result being indifferently white or black. Essentially, the counting does not differ from that given by Morgan. Two white or two black will have six of one color, and these count two beans, called *O-yú-ah,* or the Bird. The player proceeds until he loses, when his opponent takes his turn. Seven white or black gain four beans, called *O-néo-sah,* or Pumpkin. All white or all black gain twenty, called *O-hén-tah,* or a Field. These are all that draw anything, and we may indifferently say with the Onondagas, two white or black for the first, or six with the Senecas. The game is played singly or by partners, and there is no limit to the number. Usually there are three or four players.

In counting the gains there is a kind of ascending reduction; for as two birds make one pumpkin, only one bird can appear in the result. First come the twenties, then the fours, then the twos, which can occur but once. Thus we may say for twenty, *Jo-han-tó-tah,* you have one field, or more as the case may be. In the fours we can only say, *Ki-yae-ne-you-sáh-ka,* you have four pumpkins, for five would make a field. For two beans there is the simple announcement of *O-yú-ah,* Bird. There is often great excitement over this game.

The game of peach stones, much more commonly used and important, has a more public character, although I have played it in an Indian parlor. In early days the stones of the wild plum were used, but now six peach stones are ground down to an elliptic flattened form, the opposite sides being black or white. This is the great game known as that of the dish nearly three centuries ago. The wooden bowl which I used was eleven inches across the top and three inches deep, handsomely carved out of a hard knot. A beautiful small bowl which I saw elsewhere may have been used by children.

The six stones are placed in *Kah-óon-wah,* the bowl, and thence the Onondagas term the game *Ta-yune-oo-wáh-es,* throwing the bowl to each other as they take it in turn. In public playing two players are on their knees at a time, holding the bowl between them. When I played, simply to learn the game, we sat in chairs, the bowl being on another chair between us. Beans are commonly used for counters, but we had plum stones. Many rules are settled according to agreement, but the pumpkin is left out, and the stones usually count five for a bird and six for a field. All white or all black is the highest throw, and five or six are the only winning points. In early days it would seem that all white or all black alone counted. The bowl is simply struck on the floor; and although the game is said to be sometimes intensely exciting, the scientific spirit restrained my enthusiasm. I was not playing for beans, but for information.

This ancient game is used at the New Year's or White Dog Feast among the Onondagas yet. Clan plays against clan, the Long House against the Short House, and, to foretell the harvest, the women play against the men. If the men win, the ears of corn will be long, like them; but if the women gain the game, they will be short, basing the results on the common proportion of the sexes.

Source and Comment

Journal of American Folklore, IX (1896), 269-70. From a paper on "Iroquois Games" by W. M. Beauchamp read at the annual reading of the American Association for the Advancement of Science in 1896.

A similar description of a "dice game" played with bone disks or peach or plum pits, which are tossed in a wooden bowl or basket, is in F. W. Hodge, *Handbook of American Indians,* I (1912), 484. For a "game of peach stones," see "Seneca Green Corn Dance," p.340. Universally, games played on certain holidays often serve the double purpose of adding to the jollity of the occasion while implying the importance of the force of fortune. The Jewish festival, Hanukkah, celebrating the rededication of the temple at Jerusalem after the victory of the Maccabees over King Antiochus of Syria, features the spinning of a *dreydl* or top with four sides, each of which is marked to indicate whether the player wins or loses from a store of nuts and candy. The Japanese traditionally play card games and dice games on New Year's Day. During New Year's White Dog Feast, a gambling game is an exciting but at the same time serious part of the festivities. Clan plays against clan, and the women, who live in the "Long House" and in the matrilineal Iroquois society have a powerful role, play the unmarried men. The results of the game predict the quality of the corn crop.

Chinese New Year
January 21-February 19

New Year's is the principal holiday of the Chinese calendar and one which has attracted public attention in the United States for the pageantry of its Golden Dragon Parade. The date is determined by a lunar calendar, with solar adjustments so that holidays recur in a pattern of seasonal regularity. The holiday begins with the first new moon after the sun enters the sign of Aquarius. The years are named for a sequence of twelve symbolic animals—rat, ox, tiger, hare, dragon, serpent, horse, ram, monkey, rooster, dog, and boar. Festivities extend over several days, the first day being essentially a family celebration. Homage is paid to ancestors at household shrines, and visits are exchanged among relatives and intimates. To avoid bad luck, impeccable behavior is insisted upon. The climax of the holiday period is the Dragon Parade, a gala event in the Chinatowns of many American cities. The Dragon is thought to dispel evil spirits, a process aided by firecrackers, drums, and gongs.

Observing Chinese New Year

Chinese New Year's Day occurs between January 20 and February 19, and begins properly at midnight on New Year's Eve. Certain ancient customs are still observed, such as the mothers' admonishing their children to avoid the use of all vulgar words, or words which may be interpreted as bad. Persons who are financially in debt try their best to repay their debtors before the old year dies, but if they are unable to do so they are no longer morally obligated to do away with their lives, as ancient custom once dictated.

All the meeting halls and headquarters of [San Francisco] Chinatown's fraternal, district, clan, trade guild, and other associations are brilliantly lighted at the time the New Year dawns. This is one custom observed in all Chinatowns. In recent years the practice of hoisting the national flag of China was added, as a gesture of nation-consciousness, a spirit which was lacking among most California Chinese up to fifteen years ago [c. 1932].

At least twenty-four hours before the advent of the New Year, the floors of all mercantile houses, association buildings, and private homes are swept, cleaned, and washed thoroughly, and they must not be swept again until the New Year's celebration is over. This follows the ancient practice of symbolically avoiding misfortune, since the sweeping of floors in this period means the sweeping away of all good luck for the new year.

The shooting of firecrackers—to call the attention of the gods and scare away malignant devils at the same time—is, of course, a *sine qua non* of any Chinese New Year's celebration, past or present. The firecrackers start exploding promptly at midnight, if permission from the local police authorities has been obtained.

But the most important custom which heralds the beginning of the new year is a gastronomic one. It is the eating of *lohan chai,* a vegetarian dish adapted for common use from a recipe of Chinese adherents of Buddhism. *Chai* denotes a vegetarian meal, whereas *lohan* is the Buddhist term for 'saints' as it pertains to Chinese Buddhism.

Another meatless dish eaten in the first twenty-four hours of the New Year is *yu sang,* which means 'raw fish.' That is, the basic ingredient of this repast is raw fish which has been skinned, boned, and neatly sliced into thin strips. It is then made palatable and delicious by mixing it, salad-fashion, with chopped green onions, peanut oil, ground roasted peanuts, lemon juice, sesame seeds, chopped raw ginger, Chinese parsley, soy sauce, sliced turnips, and crisp fried-rice noodles. This Cantonese epicure's delight is eaten along with bowls of steaming rice gruel called *congee.*

Sweets eaten at the New Year's celebrations include homemade steamed and fried pastries; "thousand-layer" sweet cake—a symbol of longevity—and deep-fried sweetmeats flaked with sesame seeds, and other pastries made from rice flour. The recipes for all these are traditional, handed down orally from one generation to another.

Fruits for this festive season are the orange and tangerine—because their skins are red, the color of good luck; preserved lichee nuts (actually a fruit and not a nut); and sugar cane. Candies include candied melon, sugared plums, lotus seeds, melon seeds, preserved sugared ginger, lotus roots, and a variety of sweets made from Chinese fruits.

Flowers which are highly prized for this holiday are the plum blossom, pussy willow, azalea, peony, and the traditional water lily or narcissus.

For those who still adhere to the ancient religious rites at least one visit must be made to a public temple in the week of the New Year, to make sacrificial offerings and to propitiate the gods. This is usually attended to by the womenfolk and the smaller children. In San Francisco's Chinatown, at this writing, there are still three public temples where New Year sacrifices may be made: the T'ien Hou temple on Waverly Place, the Kong Chow temple on Pine Street, and the Lit Sing Kung temple on Spofford Alley. The deities which the California Chinese favor are Kwan Ti (God of War), Kwan Yin (Goddess of Mercy), and Hou Wang (Duke Hou). It is interesting to note that of these three gods two were actual historical personages: Kwan Ti was the famous General Kwan Yu of the Three Kingdoms period in the second century of this era, and Duke Hou, a Cantonese, was a benevolent magistrate in Canton's Chungshan (formerly Heungshan) district some centuries ago. After his death and during a plague Hou appeared in a dream to a farmer and gave him a remedy to alleviate a scourge. The remedy worked, and in time the folk imagination deified him as a god. Only the Goddess of Mercy has no real earthly beginning, since her origin stemmed directly from the Buddhist religion. Chinese popular religion has attributed her origin to a sainted Chinese woman, but this is a myth, conjured up to make Kwan Yin more acceptable to the masses.

Since there is no congregational worship in popular Chinese religion, the faithful may go to the temple at any time of the day they please and perform the ceremonies of burning incense and paper money, offering wine and meat to their favorite gods, and reciting the proper incantations. Those who still maintain ancestral shrines in their own homes light incense sticks and red candles in front of the spirit tablets. The proper amount of food and wine is also placed there.

The colorful lion dance, of course, is also an integral part of the New Year's festivities. The lion, Buddhist symbol of courage, majesty, and constancy, is also a harbinger of good luck, and so he is enticed to dance and prance before every door. In San Francisco's Chinatown in the early days, the temples—and there were over half a dozen then—used to sponsor the lion dance through the streets and alleys of the quarter, and the plentiful silver collected went into the coffers of the temple keepers. Sometimes the august Chinese Six Companies took the privilege and hired local operatic actors and acrobats to perform the intricate but conventionalized dancing of the ceremonial lion. Today, by community consent, the community-sponsored Chinese Hospital holds the lion dances during the New Year. The money, wrapped in lettuce leaves, is collected from persons before whose doorways or shops the lion prances and roars, to the accompaniment of beating drums, clashing cymbals, and exploding firecrackers, and goes into the general fund of the hospital for charity cases. Thus an old Chinese New Year's ritual is well adjusted to modern needs.

On the social side a "must" on every family's calendar between the first and third day of the New Year is the paying of social calls to the homes of relatives and friends. On these visits tea (sweetened by Chinese red dates), red melon seeds, and sweetmeats are ceremoniously offered to each guest. The sweets repose usually on a traditional octagonal black-and-red lacquered tray, which takes its shape from the eight-sided *pa kua* used in Chinese divination. Taking several pieces of sweets from the tray, the visitor, if an adult, places a folded red-paper package containing silver on the center compartment of the tray. This package, called *lay shee* (good-luck piece), is also given by adults, especially the married ones, to all unmarried children and babies. The giving of *lay shee* at New Year's is one of the oldest, most universal, and unchanged customs of the Chinese people, and symbolizes the giving and receiving of good luck. Notice how the color of red permeates this portion of the New Year custom—the red date in the tea, red melon seeds, the red tray, and red *lay shee* packages.

Since, except for the catering trade, everyone stops working during the New Year's celebration, there must necessarily be social festivities and recreation for the celebrants to while away the three to five days of this period. Home and restaurant banquets are continually given at noon, evening, and midnight. Where women and children are not present, these banquets are occasions for drinking bouts accompanied by the game of finger guessing. All night mah-jongg sessions are held in homes, bachelor quarters, and family tong headquarters. The less energetic usually attend the Mandarin theater to view special Cantonese operas, or go to the Grandview and Great China theaters on Jackson Street to see Cantonese-language moving pictures, either locally made or imported from Hongkong. And each afternoon everybody can follow the lion-dance troupe as it dances up and down every Chinatown street, or shoot firecrackers during the hours allowed by the police.

On the third day of the New Year, if a family has decided that a three-day celebration is sufficient, the ceremony of "opening the year" (*hoi nien*) is performed. This, however, is more or less a duplication of the rituals attending the first day. A visit may be paid to a temple, where more incense sticks, candles, and paper money are offered to the gods. There is a final big dinner, either at home or in a restaurant, and the shooting of the last rounds of firecrackers. And if the New Year's social calls have not yet been completed the last must be paid on this day.

In this manner the three days of this festival pass quickly enough, and another Chinese year begins.

Source

Western Folklore, VII (1948), 243-46. William Hoy provides "outline descriptions" and notes on significant details "where the significance is a matter of established tradition...." He "participated in ... California Chinese native festivals in San Francisco's Chinatown" for "more than a decade." He also observed celebrations of the Chinese New Year in more than a dozen California cities and mainland China in 1944-46, with which "in essentials they remain the same." Cf. the American tradition of "New Year's Calling," p. 13; mumming and parading, p. 4; eating traditional food, pp. 16, 17, 19; and not sweeping the houses, p. 20.

* * *

Chinese New Year

Chinese New Year's Tragedy

It was in this manner that my friend Jung, the son of my Uncle Quan, met his death, a death which started its fatal course on the seventh day of the Chinese New Year, the Birthday of Men. And although Jung did not die till the tenth day of the New Year, the Birthday of the Robber, all his relatives and friends ascribed his death to what occurred on that fateful Birthday of Men.

It all happened like this. My Aunt Quan was one of the most superstitious women in town and during the New Year's celebration she was doubly so, being very particular about our manners, our duties, our speech, and the correctness of our behavior.

Jung, her eldest son, was, on the contrary, very modern in speech and manner, and he scorned the strange customs and observances of the old mother country.

I remember very well how, one day, when I was out in the street playing with him, he said to me, "Ming, I wish my mother was like yours. Your mother does not have small feet and she does not dress herself up in the old Chinese clothes. My mother is so old-fashioned that sometimes I feel ashamed of her."

And Jung's face took on a disgruntled and hurt expression.

"You mustn't speak like that about your mother," I told Jung. "After all, she came from China, and you were born here in America."

"I know," Jung said, "but your mother came from China. Look how much she has changed."

"I guess your mother is a little slow in adopting western customs," I said to Jung.

Jung was twelve years old then and I was eleven. Many times he and I talked about China and how, perhaps, we would some day go back to the old country together to visit our native land about which we had heard so much.

My Aunt Quan had two children, both boys. They were so different that no one would have ever known they were brothers. In looks, in speech, in the way they acted, they were miles apart.

Aunt Quan used to say to mother, "Although Jung is always quarreling with me, nevertheless I like him better than Hoi. Hoi is so much afraid of people. He will never get anywhere in the world like that."

My mother would then say, "But Hoi is small. When he grows up he will lose his fear of people. All small boys are like that. When my Ming was small, he was just like your Hoi."

My Aunt Quan and my mother were very close friends, almost as good friends as were Jung and I.

Jung died on the Birthday of the Robber. It was a tragic year and it all started because of Aunt Quan's superstitious beliefs. Perhaps that is not true but, somehow, I still cannot shake that idea from my mind.

I remember everything connected with that celebration very well, every single day of that New Year, and especially that seventh day when Jung came into our house and precipitated the event that was to foreshadow his death, so at least, according to my Aunt Quan.

It was on the New Year's eve that Jung took me into his bedroom, a very small room near the end of the house, and showed me the red papers on the walls.

"This is what I mean," he began, his face pained at all the bother that accompanied the New Year, "all this fuss and nuisance. Every single year my mother puts those mottoes in my room, a small orange under my bed and a dime wrapped in red paper under my pillow. I'm too big for that sort of thing. Your mother doesn't do that to you, does she?" Jung suddenly demanded.

I answered, "No, not any more."

Jung felt ashamed suddenly, looking around the room, feeling thoroughly uncomfortable.

"I used to like the New Year," he explained, "but now everything seems to be the same year after year. I wouldn't mind it if I didn't have to do all these various things. And my mother is so particular about everything. Why, last year she locked me up in my room because I happened to say something that wasn't the proper thing to say."

I looked at Jung. He was in tears.

"I guess your mother is a little particular, Jung," I told him.

Then we went out of the room, and into the kitchen to watch Aunt Quan prepare the *jide* [traditional New Year's dish] for the night.

Aunt Quan was busily engaged in the kitchen, her hair falling down in uneven streaks across her brown face, her apron loosely tied on her thin body.

"Well, Ming," she said, lighting the gas with a match, "why aren't you home helping your mother to prepare for the New Year?"

"Mother isn't planning anything elaborate this year," I told her.

Aunt Quan said, "Your mother is getting just a little too modern now. But she has always been like that ever since I can remember."

Aunt Quan moved across the kitchen with her quick steps, carrying bowls of water and fancy Chinese foods to the stove.

"Why don't you stay for the midnight *jide*," she suggested. "Your uncle can take you home tonight."

"I'll have to phone mother," I said.

I went outside the hallway and phoned my mother.

"Mother says that I can stay," I told my Aunt Quan as I came into the kitchen again.

"Fine," Aunt Quan said. "You and Jung can help me decorate the tables tonight, and help me fold the *lay shee* [traditional gift for children]."

And then she went about her duties of preparing the special dinner for that night.

When Aunt Quan finished her work she came out of the kitchen tired, the perspiration streaming down her face.

Aunt Quan cleared the parlor table, put on a new oilcloth with red flowers painted on it, and arranged three cups of wine, three cups of rice and three pairs of chopsticks. She took a large coffee can filled with sawdust, and in it she put three large red wax candles, and what we call "long life" punks. Then she went quickly into the kitchen and came out with a large steaming hot chicken which she put in the middle of the table. Then she took up some golden papers, trimmed with designs and lit them with the flame of the good luck candle.

I stood near the corner of the room watching my Aunt Quan with eager eyes. I remember my mother doing the same thing many years before.

Jung, too, watched but with an uninterested expression. He had seen her do it many times and it was tiresome to have to see it again.

Aunt Quan twirled the burning papers around the room, and then gently let them down in a pan on the floor. She watched the papers burn slowly and darken into ashes. "Hoi," she called out, "Hoi, come here!"

Hoi, all dressed up in his new clothes, came rushing into the room. Then Aunt Quan made Hoi bow his head in front of the table while she murmured something that I could not hear.

Seeing this, Jung went outside. I followed him.

"She can't make me do that," he told me.

"It does look kind of strange," I told him.

"I guess my mother never will change," he said sadly, looking away into the distance.

Aunt Quan's voice called out, "Jung, Ming, come in and help me with the tables."

Jung and I got up and went into the house. Aunt Quan was putting black and red melon seeds in delicate Chinese bowls. Hoi was filling the other dishes with melon, candy and lichee nuts. Aunt Quan handed me the filled dishes.

"Arrange them neatly on the table," she told me.

The double layer Chinese lilies were already on the table, stately and really magnificent in their queer but fascinating Chinese bowls.

"We have the double layer kind, too," I said to my Aunt Quan.

"Ah, yes," she said, "they are the good luck kind."

Uncle Quan came home just then and he greeted me with, "Well, well, Ming, you are here. Why are you not home helping your mother?"

"She can manage alone," I answered, "and I'm staying for the midnight *jide*."

"Your aunt makes the best *jide* in the world," Uncle Quan said.

Aunt Quan was sitting at the table folding small pieces of red paper and wrapping up quarters and fifty cent pieces in them.

"You must come with your mother tomorrow, and I'll give you one of these *lay shee*," Aunt Quan told me.

Later that evening Uncle Quan came out of his room with a whole stack of red papers, and he wrote many good luck mottoes on them about prosperity, good fortune, and greetings for the New Year.

He pasted two or three of them in each room.

I noticed that the windows and floors had been cleaned the day before. I also knew that my Aunt Quan would lock up her brooms and dustpans this evening before she went to bed. She did it every year and she would not take them out until after the Birthday of Men.

I remember once asking Aunt Quan why she did it.

She answered, "New Year is a time of good fortune. All the dirt and things that have accumulated on the floors are signs of money and fortune. One must not sweep up money."

Midnight was drawing near and the rice and *jide* were about ready to be served.

Aunt Quan was talking to her children, "I want both of you to call everyone by their right names tomorrow. Tomorrow is the New Year, and you must be polite. When anyone comes, you must serve tea and be sure to offer it with both hands. You must pass the sweet melon candy and the black and red melon seeds. When you give them to the guests, remember to say, 'Won't you gather some gold dust?' To the men you must pass cigars and cigarettes. When you offer tea, also offer the slices of thin coconut candy for the guests to sweeten the tea. And also wear your new clothes."

Jung listened to all this in a sort of dreamy disgust.

"And, remember, no fighting tomorrow," Uncle Quan put in.

Midnight was approaching rapidly. Aunt Quan set the kitchen table, arranging the bowls and chopsticks. The odor of cooked food filled the kitchen air. I felt very hungry. At exactly midnight Aunt Quan called us in and we seated ourselves at the table while she brought forth the *jide*. There were bamboo shoots, bean sprouts, dried bean cakes, black silky delicacies and many other ingredients all cooked in one tempting mixture. We all had a big bowl of rice as well.

"Do you eat *jide* with your family?" my Aunt Quan demanded of me.

"We have that tomorrow morning," I told my aunt.

We ate in silence.

After we had eaten my Uncle Quan took me home.

"Come tomorrow," he said in parting.

"I will, Uncle Quan," I said. I entered into the darkened house and went to bed.

Then the first day of the New Year arrived, the Birthday of the Chicken. I remember that it dawned dark and gray, and that heavy rain clouds clustered in the distance, threatening to rain on this first day of the celebration. I remember that I woke up weary and completely tired, having gone to bed late the night before, after twelve. The sky was gray and dreary exactly as it had been year after year. Somehow the first day of the New Year is always dark and solemn.

I came downstairs all dressed up in my new clothes. Mother was wearing her long silk robe, her face all powdered and rouged with fresh colors. She looked much younger, the new clothes and makeup making her much more beautiful than usual.

"Happy New Year, mother," I greeted her.

Mother took out a fifty cent piece, wrapped in red paper, and handed it to me.

"And here's one from your father," she said, handing me another one.

"Thanks, mother," I said.

On the table there were two bowls of oranges, arranged in a very neat design. And also there were two dishes of melon seed. We had nothing elaborate like my Aunt Quan.

Mother said to me, "Be ready to go over to Aunt Quan's soon. Don't soil your clothes with the firecrackers."

I went out into the street and opened the package of Wong Kong Hing firecrackers, lit a punk, and then shot them off complete in one chain. Mother watched me from the window, smiling.

At noon mother took me over to Aunt Quan's house, telling me on the way, "Be careful of your behavior and your manners. You know how particular your aunt is."

Jung was out in the street with Hoi, and both of them were wearing their new clothes, looking very clean and neat.

Jung greeted me and said to mother, "May luck and fortune be with you." Mother smiled a big smile and handed a *lay shee* to Jung and another one to Hoi.

Aunt Quan was all dressed up that morning. She was wearing her long earrings, and golden bracelets gleamed on her slender arms. Her hair was smoothly oiled with wax and her brown face was white and pinkish in color. Like mother, she looked much younger than usual that day.

Aunt Quan and mother exchanged greetings and my Aunt Quan invited us to go into the living room where Jung offered mother tea and melon seeds. Aunt Quan and mother talked about lottery tickets and everything pertaining to the good and the fortunate. Uncle Quan talked about riches, money, and in the end he said to mother, "May you have lots of good fortune in the coming year." And mother said politely, "And you, too."

Early that morning Aunt Quan had prepared some *gin dur,* Chinese dough cakes, and she brought them out, nice and brown and very good to eat.

I went out into the street with Jung and Hoi. Each of us had three packages of firecrackers, a package of Wong Kong Hing, and two packages of Silver Flashlight crackers.

"You know, Ming," Jung said, "I remember how I used to collect all my *lay shee* and put them into a tin box. Now it doesn't seem to be fun any more. I guess I am too big for that sort of thing."

Hoi interrupted and said, "I have already received about ten *lay shee* today."

We shot firecrackers all along the street, and they made a lot of noise and disturbance.

Mother was about to go home. She said, "Ming, go wash your hands."

The firecrackers' powder had smudged my hands black and mother did not want me to soil my new outfit.

Before mother left she said to my Aunt Quan, "Be sure to come over tonight. I am going to make *gin dur* and *woo tow go* for the guests."

My Aunt Quan said, "I shall be over at seven."

Then my mother and I went home.

When we reached home I saw that one of mother's friends had come and he was munching melon seeds and talking to father about business for the past year. He stood up and smiled a big smile when he saw mother. He dipped his hands into his pocket and pulled out a fifty-cent piece that was not wrapped in red paper, for he was quite modern and so did not wrap his money in red paper. I thanked him and offered him cigars and cigarettes.

"Why, Ming is a big boy now," he said to mother.

"He is twelve, just as big as your Wei Mon," mother said.

"My Wei Mon is thirteen according to Chinese age," he said.

Father told me, "Go play some good music, 'The Big Open Door' now."

The loud music echoed through the house.

"Don't play any sad or melancholy music today," mother told me, "Your father does not like it."

All day long guests came and went and in the evening I found that I had received quite a lot of money, about four dollars. Mother told me to save it and put it in the bank after the New Year.

In the evening Aunt Quan, Uncle Quan, Jung and Hoi came over. Jung was very moody and unhappy.

He said, "All day long I have been offering tea and melon seeds to guests. This new suit of clothes is just killing me. I hate to wear it." Jung was unhappy, feeling uncomfortable and lost in his clothes.

I asked Jung, "How much have you collected already?"

He said, very disinterestedly, "I don't know. I don't count it any more."

I leaned close to Jung and said in a very soft voice, "I opened my *lay shee* and I counted them."

"Hoi received more than I did," Jung told me.

As evening drew on, more guests came until the house was filled and echoed and reëchoed with greetings and talk of the New Year. We children walked together watching everything and everybody. Hoi stayed near his mother, waiting for the other people to give him money.

Mother was very busy in the kitchen preparing the dinner. The odor of cooked food was very tempting.

Soon we had dinner. I helped mother to prepare the long table, adding three extra boards to it. Then mother took out the new white tablecloth and covered the table with it. Tonight she brought out the ivory chopsticks, instead of the bamboo ones. Bottles of Ng Kai Pay wine stood at each corner of the table. The women, all very young and beautiful that night, sat together on one side, and the men sat on the other side of the table. We children squeezed in wherever we could.

First the men drank whisky in their little green wine glasses, picking up little pieces of the delicacies that went with the wine.

Father poured out the Ng Kai Pay, filling up the cups as soon as they were empty. The women were a little bold that night, drinking homemade rice wine. Mother's face suddenly grew red after she had drunk one small cup of wine. But father kept drinking and drinking, and there was no change in the color of his face.

There were roast chicken, mushrooms cooked with abalone sauce, ducks, bird's-nest soup, roast pork and many varieties of fancy foods. Jung sat in his place, eating very little, waiting impatiently to get home. Hoi sat near his mother, eating whatever his mother picked for him with her chopsticks.

The party was dominated by the gayest of spirits.

Mother said, "May all you women have many children in the coming year." All the women smiled, and Lum Shee answered, "You are young, but we are old. Just let me have some luck, that is all I desire. Not children."

Mother said to Lum Shee, "You are still young, it is I who am old." And all the other women broke into hearty laughter. The bottles of Ng Kai Pay became empty. The men and women were a little drunk, it appeared. One of the men began to play a game called Chi Mew.

Father, too, was a little affected by the strong wine.

Mother told me to go over to the food store and bring back some brown sugar. She melted that in boiling water and told father to drink it. He was much better after that.

The women put on aprons to protect their long gowns and went into the kitchen to make *gin dur*.

51

Mother was busily cutting up sweet melon and coconut candy, cutting the small candy with quick movements of her hands.

My Aunt Quan was boiling oil on the stove, taking great care to keep us children away.

"Go outside, all of you," she said to us, "we will call you when the dough cakes are ready." Another woman was roasting peanuts near the stove. An old woman whose face was all in wrinkles was putting candy and coconut into a small round piece of dough, and she rolled it tightly with her hands. The dough became round like a ball. Quickly she sprinkled some seeds on the table and rolled the dough cakes over them, the small seeds sticking to the dough like glue. Lum Shee was mixing the dough with her bare hands. She poured melted brown sugar into the dough, squeezing and pounding it with the strong movements of her hands.

The oil was now boiling on the stove. My Aunt Quan was an expert *gin dur* maker. Mother let her do everything. Aunt Quan was very superstitious and she insisted that the dough cakes for the first day of the New Year should be nice and beautiful.

My Aunt Quan dropped the dough cakes into the oil one by one, squeezing and pounding them down with a long flat spoon which she was holding in her hands. The other women crowded around and exclaimed, "My, but they are beautiful." And Aunt Quan was proud, for she loved to have people praise her cooking.

The men sat in the living room, munching melon seeds and listening to the photograph records, talking about everything they could think of.

Mother brought the cooked dough cakes out into the room when they were finished. Jung ate the sweetened kind, but I preferred the salted kind. That evening I received many more quarters but I was so tired that I decided to count them the next morning.

Before Jung went home, he said to me, "Are you going to school tomorrow?"

"I think so," I told him, "there is no use of being absent tomorrow."

"Hoi is going to stay home for another day," Jung said.

"You come and call me in the morning," I told Jung.

The guests all left late that night, thanking mother for the nice party and the very pleasant evening.

I went to bed, tired and yet happy, for I had received quite a lot of money.

And that second day of the New Year, in the year when Jung passed away, that, too, still remains clear in my memory. I remember everything that happened.

The night had passed, and the Birthday of the Dog, the second day of the New Year, came rushing in gray and dark; but no rain.

The day was as dreary and dull as the first day. I still wore my new suit and shoes and the small sailor cap which I admired very much. Jung came and called me in the early morning and we went to school. When I came back mother told me that she was taking me to a party in one of the biggest restaurants in Chinatown.

Now the second day of the New Year is one on which great and elaborate parties are given, both the restaurants and the homes are decorated and everyone is full of the gay and carefree spirit of the New Year.

My Aunt Quan was going to the same party. Mother and I were going, since father had to stay home and take care of the small baby.

Aunt Quan came in her bright red new car. Hoi was with her. Jung was missing. I asked Hoi, "Is Jung not going, too?"

Hoi said, "He said a bad word today and mother locked him up in his room."

I knew that if Jung did say anything not quite proper Aunt Quan would surely punish him severely. She was a little more liberal with Hoi.

The bright lights of the restaurant glittered in the streets, red, blue, yellow, and white. Men and women, dressed up in their best new suits, new long robes, were evident everywhere. I climbed the long steps up to the big room where the party was to be held, and the murmurings and noise of the great crowd sounded like the rising and falling of the great sea waves, pounding against the shore.

The big room was illuminated with many bright lights and the tables were arranged in regular party fashion. Some young boys and girls were passing melon seeds and tea to the guests. Mother dropped a *lay shee* into a box, as was the custom.

The party was to start at seven, but it really commenced at eight. The guests arrived one after another, until the place was crowded with men and women, all eager to start the party.

Mother and I sat at the same table with Aunt Quan and Hoi. One dish followed the other. The men drank Ng Kai Pay wine by the cupfuls, talking and laughing with loud, strident voices.

I thought about Jung all the time. I knew how miserable he was, locked up in his room, rebelling against his mother, as he had always done in the past.

At ten the guests began to leave. My Aunt Quan got many paper boxes together and collected the leftovers to take home for the next day. My mother helped my aunt and my aunt gave mother two boxes of leftovers.

And thus the second day of the New Year passed away....

Then came the dawn of the third day, the Birthday of the Pig.

I saw Jung at school that day and he was mad at what Aunt Quan had done to him the day before.

"My mother is so old-fashioned," he commenced irritably. "She locked me in yesterday because I called Hoi a fool. It's all so foolish and silly. I know your mother wouldn't do it to you if you did that."

I thought awhile and I knew that what Jung said was the truth.

"Mother and I are going over to see the fortunetelling woman tonight," I told Jung, "and your mother has handed your name in on a piece of red paper."

Jung scowled, his face took on a hateful look.

"She does it every year," he said slowly, "and I don't see any good in it at all." He turned away, and started for home. I followed after him.

"My mother does it every year, too," I said to Jung.

Jung didn't feel like talking so I left him alone and went home.

That evening about six, mother called me, "Ming, Ming, get ready," her voice echoed through the house.

"I'm ready," I called back.

My mother came down, her bright robe showing her up to best advantage.

Putting on her new fur coat, she said quickly, "Come, we must go see the Goon Yum Goddess."

I remember going the year before to an old dirty woman living in dark rooms. She made lots of money with her mysterious ways of telling fortunes and mother went there every year; sometimes my Aunt Quan went there, too.

Mother and I stopped in front of a large dark house, the windows were covered with heavy films of dust, through which could be seen dirty curtains now blackened from time and grime.

Mother pressed a very small bell. Soon I heard the shuffling of feet and the door was opened. We entered a small hallway and proceeded up a dark stairway. Mother and I went up very slowly so as not to fall down. The old fear that I always felt in going there seized me again and I held mother's hands tight, frightened lest I be lost in this drab and utterly mysterious house of the fortuneteller.

After reaching the top of the stairs we had to go down another long hallway, to the very end door and then to the room occupied by the old woman with the dirty white hair. I saw a small idol, crudely colored with now faded paint, resting on a small box near her doorway. The god had an ugly expression on his face and a small glass of oil was slowly burning in a steady flame in front of him. All around this god there were spread red papers on which were written many Chinese characters in gold and black letters.

All of the darkened doors looked the same. Mother knocked on the very end door. An old fat woman came out, her hair white, yet black from dirt and she smiled at mother.

She opened the door wide for both of us, and said in her dry voice, "Happy New Year."

Mother took the red paper from out of her pocket, handed it to the old woman, and remarked, "Let us hope that all of us will have good fortune for the coming year."

I looked around the room. Nothing had been changed. Everything was exactly as if it had not been touched since the year before and the year before that. The same old bed stood near the corner, the same old red tablecloth and the same box of worn-out bamboo slits.

The old woman picked up the box of bamboo and began shaking it up and down with easy, graceful movements, chanting the name of one of our family in that voice of hers which always managed to frighten me, somehow. She shook the box of bamboo slits until one slit fell down on the table. Then she put the number right next to the name she was chanting out loud.

The monotonous chanting, combined with the dim gaslight of the room, gave a peculiar and spooky feeling to the whole ceremony. Mother watched everything with eager eyes for she was so interested in whether our fortunes were to be good or bad that she did not have time to notice the uncanny characteristics of the whole room.

This chanting went on for many minutes; the longer it lasted, the more I began to get frightened. But the end came at last. I felt strangely glad when the old woman finished. She handed the red paper back to mother.

"Thank you so much," mother said gratefully, taking out a dollar and handing it over to the old woman.

The old woman smiled and acknowledged the money with thanks.

Then my mother and I left that terribly dreary place.

"We have to get a book for tomorrow," mother said, "to find out about the different numbers."

It was late at night when we got home and mother decided that tomorrow we would call Aunt Quan over and discuss the numbers. I was already imagining how Jung would feel when I told him. I knew that Jung did not believe in such things.

The very next day, the Birthday of the Lamb, I told Jung. He was not surprised, just answering, "I knew it all the time. Mother does the same thing every year."

"So does my mother," I told him.

"Well, I guess Chinese women are like that," he remarked.

That very evening Aunt Quan and her whole family came over to our house. We found that it was not necessary to buy a book at all, for Aunt Quan knew a man who had memorized the one hundred rules of the fortunetelling book. He was a genial looking man, short and fat, who talked with a very feminine voice, manipulating his hands unconsciously while he talked and making amusing gestures with them.

He told each number for ten cents apiece, explaining the origin, the meaning and the good and the bad of each one.

Jung sat there, sullen and moody, paying no attention to all that was said. However, the rest of us took the occasion lightly, joking and laughing as something amusing turned up.

When the man came to Hoi's number he said, "This is the best one of all. Everything that this person does and thinks will be successful in the end. In luck, in health, in fortune, in everything—success in every endeavor."

Aunt Quan's face beamed with a wide smile, for she believed implicitly in these numbers. Jung sneered, although I was the only one who noticed it.

The man read on, explaining in detail everything connected with that particular number. Soon he came to Jung's number and he became solemn and said, his tone of voice changed, "This is the first sad note."

Aunt Quan's face clouded over with worry.

The man continued, "This says that Jung must be very careful of his health during the coming year. His health is threatened by dark shadows."

All of us sat there staring with wide open eyes. Jung was calm. Aunt Quan was actually frightened.

Later that evening Jung took me aside and said, "Ming, you just watch; nothing is going to happen to me. If my health does get bad it is not because of these numbers, but because it has just come about naturally. You know, all of these sayings seem pure nonsense to me." He cared little about what happened to him.

That evening my Aunt Quan lost her spirit of gay and carefree joyousness. What the man had said about Jung worried her greatly. She was quiet, glancing repeatedly at Jung, fearing that something terrible was to happen soon.

Uncle Quan was not much worried about these things. He was not as superstitious as Aunt Quan, for he had dropped many of his old beliefs after he came to this country, which was fifteen years ago.

Late in the evening mother and Aunt Quan, Uncle Quan and another man played mah-jongg until midnight. Aunt Quan was so worried about Jung that her mind was not on the game. She lost over a thousand points in the two rounds of mah-jongg.

I counted my money that night, and I had received a total of almost thirteen dollars in *lay shee*.

When Jung went home he said to me again, "Nothing is going to happen to me; just you watch."

The fifth day of the New Year, the Birthday of the Cow, came and went without any undue excitement. However, that day some guests came to visit my mother. I received some more money. The Chinese lilies had blossomed into flowers. Mother was glad, for she was afraid that the bulbs might not sprout flowers and that was a very bad sign.

"I think all the flowers will be open by the Birthday of Men," mother said to father late that evening.

"This year we have good bulbs," father said. I happened to think of Jung that night and was a little bit worried myself, somehow. Would something really happen to him as the man said? I had thought of the matter a long while after he went home the day before. I remembered clearly about a certain man who had his fortune told. He was to come into great fortune. It came true. Then there was the story of another man who was to suffer from very bad luck, that he would never have a chance to go back to his homeland. However, in spite of the prediction, he did go back and returned bringing a lot of money. Thus worrying and thinking of Jung, I fell asleep to await the coming of the next day, the Birthday of the Horse.

The next day I saw Jung again at school.

He laughed, "Well, so far nothing has happened to me. I told you nothing was going to happen to me."

I did not tell Jung that I was worried about him.

I said to Jung, "Some of the flowers have already bloomed in our house."

Jung answered, "Mother was talking about the flowers this morning. She was afraid that they might bloom too late. She thinks that it is a sign of bad luck if the flowers do not bloom before the seventh day of the New Year."

When I went home that evening I told mother what Jung told me. She looked rather puzzled, then said, "Your Aunt Quan is a very superstitious person. She is always worrying. If her flowers do not bloom she will think she is going to have a very bad year ahead of her, a year of misfortune, sadness and sorrow."

And yet it was in that year that Jung passed away.

Then the tragic Birthday of Men dawned, the day that Jung came into our house and did something that clearly foreshadowed his death, at least, according to my Aunt Quan. Not only that. Aunt Quan's Chinese lilies failed to bloom on the seventh day of the New Year. The bulbs sprouted forth, but only long green leaves came out, the flowers were lost inside the leaves and failed completely to emerge.

I woke up quite early that morning for it was the last legal day to shoot firecrackers and I wanted to take advantage of every spare moment. I came downstairs and saw mother opening the brown pudding with a long sharp knife. The brown pudding had hardened like brown cement and mother was having a hard time struggling through it.

I asked mother, "When are we going to eat it?"

Mother said, "I'm going to fry it in the afternoon when your Aunt Quan comes over."

Mother cut the pudding into thin brown slices, putting them in neat piles on a flat white plate.

There was a big dish of raw fish, cut in small pieces, on the table. Carrots, sliced in very thin pieces, were on the same dish. Inside a brown paper bag I saw some fried objects.

"Are these fish to be eaten raw?" I asked mother.

"Of course," mother said. "It is the custom to eat raw fish on the seventh day of the New Year.

Mother was stirring a big bowl of boiling broth. She opened the big bowl, and the escaping steam filled the air with its delicious aroma. Mother stirred the broth with a long spoon.

"For those who can not eat the fish raw, we have this hot, boiling broth." I remember that I liked this broth very much, and every single year I poured it over the raw fish, and found the taste very delicious.

In the afternoon my Aunt Quan, Uncle Quan, Jung, and Hoi came over. Hoi was still wearing his new costume, but Jung had changed into a less conspicuous one.

Father mixed the raw fish with the carrots, and sprinkled some small seeds over them. The fish appeared red and raw. They looked indigestible to me. Mother brought the hot broth over and she served it to the children and Aunt Quan.

I could hear the firecrackers exploding all along Chinatown and the loud noises kept up a continuous rhythm like the flow of a machine gun. When this rhythm was broken by a moment of silence, the city seemed quiet and strange until the noise began again. So it was all through the day.

Jung and I decided to go down to the important shops and watch the people shoot off firecrackers. We stopped in front of one of the more prosperous stores in Chinatown where the firecrackers had been exploding for over a full hour. And still the men were shooting them off, having the time of their lives. The men lined up close to the store, each with a burning punk in his hands, and thick stacks of firecrackers near him. The whole street was lined with burnt papers, red, green and white. The smell of powder burnt into the nostrils of everyone, making their throats thirsty and dry.

Jung and I watched for over an hour, and when we left the men were still shooting them. My ears began to ring from having been so close to the noise and explosion.

When I got home, my father gave Jung and me some packages of lady fingers, small Chinese firecrackers which had to be shot off in a whole chain or else they would not explode at all.

Jung tried to separate his firecrackers into single ones.

I said, "They will not explode well unless you shoot them off in a whole chain."

Jung answered, "This way it will last longer." And he separated his firecrackers into single ones.

But I was right. And Jung gave up in the end.

It was late afternoon when we heard the prolonged sound of gongs and Chinese music. I knew that the good luck dragon was coming. Mother hurriedly prepared to receive the dragon. She went to the kitchen and got out a fresh lettuce, and tied it to a long string.

Father hung the lettuce up near the top of the outside door. He wrapped up a dollar bill and tied that to the lettuce. Down the street the Dragon parade slowly made its way, stopping at every store or house that had a lettuce hung up in front of it. Jung and I went down the street, running so as not to miss anything. The dragon was a huge one, with bright colors. The head shone as it caught the reflection of the sun, and gleamed in all its splendor, the bright red and green tail moving now in this, now in that, direction as the men manipulated the head in rhythmic movements.

The moving dragon, followed by a group of musicians, stopped in front of our house. My Aunt Quan was looking out of the window, her bright new clothes glittering in the sun. Father shot a package of firecrackers, and the dragon danced an intricate dance. Then it bowed three times before the door of our house, deep, placid bows. After that the musicians played a noisy Chinese tune, the cymbals and gongs melting together in a melodious harmony. The man under the dragon head moved it with great skill, while the man who held the long silk tail of the dragon fanned the tail up and down, swinging it in accord with the movements of the head.

Father shot off one package of firecrackers after another. A man was stationed there to sweep the exploding firecrackers onto the sidewalk so that they would not interfere with the dancing of the dragon. The dragon's mouth was wide open, and the man under the dragon chewed off the lettuce, money and all with one bold sweep. Then the dragon made three bows of thanks and continued on its goodwill tour of the different homes and stores.

Father continued shooting packages of firecrackers.

A man approached and gave two red cards of thanks to mother, and mother said to Aunt Quan, "The goodluck dragon has visited our house, and now we must have luck for the coming year."

Aunt Quan answered, "If I didn't live so far away from the main town here, I would hang up a lettuce and some money to chase away the evil that may be in my house."

Aunt Quan was staying for dinner that night, and she helped mother to prepare a large and elaborate meal.

That evening I said to Jung, "New Year is almost over, I suppose you must be glad of it."

"Yes, I'm glad," Jung answered, while munching away on black melon seeds. "Didn't I tell you that nothing was going to happen to me? I knew that all this talk was just pure nonsense. I think it is a waste of money to spend it on such foolish things as fortunetelling and other such beliefs."

He got up quickly then and went over toward the table to get some more melon seeds. Jung was not very tall, and he had to reach up high to get them. Suddenly I heard a loud noise of dishes being broken, and when I turned around there was Jung gathering up the broken pieces of glassware. A sudden fear leapt into his eyes and his face was red with shame. My Aunt Quan came running out of the kitchen, her hands holding a long sharp knife with which she was cutting meat, when she heard the noise. She saw Jung on the floor picking up the broken dishes with his hands.

"You'll cut your hand," mother said, "Ming, go into the kitchen and get the broom, and sweep it up."

Jung did not look at Aunt Quan and Aunt Quan did not say anything, so impressed was she with what had happened. Jung said in an almost crying voice, his face full of shame and humiliation, "I didn't mean it. It just happened." Then he broke into audible crying. Aunt Quan took him home immediately.

"He's always getting into trouble," my Aunt Quan told mother, "and that this should happen on the seventh day! It is a bad sign." Aunt Quan's face wore a worried expression and she seemed suddenly to have become an old woman.

Then she said to mother in a very strange and quiet voice, so that no one else could hear it, "This very morning I broke an electric-light globe. My bulbs did not blossom into flowers. Now Jung has broken your dishes on the Birthday of Men. These are all bad omens."

When Aunt Quan left, mother, too, was worried. And although she was not superstitious, she couldn't help feeling depressed and sad. That evening she said to father, "I wonder if what the man said about Jung's health will come true or not."

Father said, "Let us hope for the best."

Now the New Year was officially over. There were three more days but they were of no importance. Yet to us and to my Aunt Quan, they were the most trying days of the year for on one of them my friend Jung passed away.

On the Birthday of the Wheat, Jung became sick, a slight and unimportant illness it was at the beginning. That day I went to see Jung. He was in bright spirits, still insisting that nothing was going to happen to him.

He said, looking straight at me, "I know what my mother is thinking now. She is going to blame all this on what I did at your house yesterday and what the old man told her about my number." Jung was cheerful, although his face was white and pale. I knew that many people got sick during the New Year because of the oil and rich foods they ate. And undoubtedly, I thought, Jung was sick because of that.

To comfort Jung I told him, "You will get well soon. I know that all those foolish beliefs have nothing to do with your illness. I will come and see you tomorrow."

Yet, somehow, I felt worried when I left him.

My mother asked me how Jung was, when I reached home.

"He is just a little sick," I told mother.

Mother went over that night to visit Jung. Try as she would, she couldn't get rid of the feeling that somehow Jung's sickness had been brought about by what had happened the day before.

Aunt Quan was greatly worried.

"We are going to have a bad year," Aunt Quan told mother that night. "Everything seems to be against us this year."

Mother told Aunt Quan not to worry and that everything would come out for the best in the end.

Then came the Birthday of the Soldier. I went over that morning to see Jung. His condition had become worse, and he had a bad fever. Jung was asleep when I arrived at Aunt Quan's house so I did not have a chance to talk to him that day.

The doctor was just coming out from Jung's room.

He said quite solemnly, "His heart is very weak. It is best to send him over to the hospital for a few days and as soon as possible. His condition is quite bad now."

I told Aunt Quan what the doctor said but there was no need for, from her face, I knew that she understood exactly what it was. Aunt Quan did not want to do it. She said, "Jung is such a strong boy. He will get well soon."

The doctor went away, shaking his head slightly.

Late that afternoon Jung complained that he had a sore throat. His voice was low and dry. The doctor had told Aunt Quan that Jung had diphtheria and that his heart was very weak. But Aunt Quan was determined to consult a pulse-reading doctor first.

It was late that night, almost ten o'clock, when Aunt Quan telephoned to mother. She was excited, talking quickly and loud. Mother told me to phone the doctor to come over to Jung's house. I did that. When I reached Aunt Quan's house with my mother, the doctor was already there. Jung moved uncomfortably, writhing in his bed. Aunt Quan was sobbing softly. She was afraid.

The doctor said, "This boy must be sent to the hospital immediately." Aunt Quan did not know what to do. Mother tried to make Aunt Quan see it the doctor's way, but even in this hour of supreme tragedy Aunt Quan was very stubborn.

The doctor said to me before he left, "That boy will die unless he is given the greatest of care." I told that to mother when I got home. Mother said, "One can never tell about this sort of thing. It all depends. But your Aunt Quan should have let Jung go to the hospital."

That night I dreamt about Jung and that he had died in his home. I was afraid, but I did not tell mother about my dream.

The Birthday of the Robber dawned, the day that my friend Jung died. It was quite early in the morning when the telephone rang out through the house. Mother got up quickly, and she knew that in this early hour there must be something unusual. She was right. Aunt Quan was sobbing over the telephone.

Mother hung up quickly. She came rushing into my room, holding a small glass. She wanted some urine to save Jung.

Jung was acting so strangely and queerly that Aunt Quan was afraid. Mother took the filled glass, and told me to telephone the doctor to go over to Jung's house.

Mother hired a taxi and rushed over to save Jung with the urine. Aunt Quan poured it down Jung's throat. He choked; then he died. My Aunt Quan cried. Jung was now as white as a corpse. But Aunt Quan did not believe Jung was dead.

She yelled out loudly, frantically, "Get him over to the emergency hospital. He must be saved!" Jung was already dead, but Uncle Quan and my father took him over to the emergency hospital.

Jung had died long before he reached there. When Uncle Quan heard that Jung was really dead, he slumped down on the floor, cold and white. He had fainted. Father took the dead body back to the house. Aunt Quan lost control of herself completely, weeping and moaning loudly. I became frightened. I had never seen a big person crying before. Mother wiped her eyes. Uncle Quan and father sat very quiet, each unable to say anything.

The doctor arrived. There was nothing that he could do. He went back to his office. I went back home, the memory of Jung's white body still lingering in my mind. I could not believe that Jung was dead. A few days ago I was laughing and talking with him. We shot firecrackers together. Now he no longer moved; he was dead. And suddenly I burst into tears, crying for my friend Jung. He was the best friend that I ever had, and now I would see him no more.

The next day I brought some flowers to Aunt Quan. Her face was full of lines and her eyes were red with weeping. Aunt Quan gave me a dime wrapped with a piece of brown sugar. Then I came home.

The New Year was over and the tragic death of Jung threw us all into a sad and unhappy state. How many times in the days that followed I heard Aunt Quan telling the old folks that Jung's death was inevitable! Jung simply had drawn a bad number, she said, and the flowers had not bloomed on that seventh day. Jung broke dishes on the Birthday of Men, and she broke an electric-light globe. "How could all this be coincidence?" she asked.

And the very old folks, who were ready for the grave, nodded their heads and agreed. . . .

Source and Comment

California Folklore Quarterly, I (1942), 337-57. By Jon Lee. In a preliminary note the editors explain: "This account of the customs and superstitions of the Chinese New Year was written by a young Chinese for Paul Radin [the anthropologist], who has been engaged in collecting folklore of the various cultures of California." They state that Lee's narrative "is an authentic description of the beliefs and practices current among the Chinese residents of San Francisco Bay area." For factual explanations of most Chinese terms and customs, see "Chinese New Year," p. 46.

Year of the Horse

The ferocious gold, green and pink Komada Dragon may have been an unnecessary precaution at yesterday's [February 13, 1978] Chinese New Year's Parade.

Though the huge creature was belligerently swinging its tail, snapping its jaws and flashing its red eyes to scare off evil spirits for the coming year, the parade's organizers were expressing nothing but optimism for the year 4676, the Year of the Horse, which officially began last Tuesday.

"It will be a very good year," promised John Ton, the young, stylishly dressed coordinator of the parade sponsored by the Chinese Benevolent Association and the Philadelphia Chinatown Development Corp.

"The horse means power, strength, love, success and women," Tom said. "The way I interpret it, it means a lot of luck at the race track."

Last year—the Year of the Snake—not even a dragon could help. "The snake is such a bad year, we didn't even have a parade," sighed Cecilia Moy Yep, the other coordinator of the parade, who said she was laid off from her job last year.

Despite the year's hopeful portents, the traditional Chinese warders-off of evil—the clanging symbols, exploding firecrackers, the dragon and several lions—made their way along Race Street yesterday in Philadelphia's Chinatown.

They were joined by a not-so-traditional Chinatown drum and bugle corps, the police and firemen's band, a float carrying Miss Chinatown (Helen Louie) and various other misses, and city dignitaries riding electric golf carts.

Leading this group was Fire Commissioner Joseph Rizzo, whose department forgets its firecracker regulations for the parade.

"Firecrackers? What firecrackers?" he asked over the crackle of dozens of explosions, when asked about the rules.

"The bands, the beauty queens, they are Americanization," said Richard Den, Secretary of the Benevolent Association, who remembers the New Year's parades of his native province of Hunan, on the Chinese mainland. There, he said, business leaders marched with representatives of each district and each surname—the Lees, Lings and Wongs and so on.

Bringing up the rear at yesterday's parade was Miss Future Chinatown, eight-year-old Susie Wong, who rode on a cart with her father.

Asked what year it was, the Americanized Miss Future Chinatown answered, "1978."

Source and Comment

Philadelphia Inquirer, February 13, 1978. From a news item by Julia Cass, staff writer. Traditional features such as the firecrackers and the "several lions" are explained by William Hoy, p. 43.

The association of each new year, in many oriental cultures, with a symbolic animal is at least two thousand years old. But more recent and American elements such as the drum and bugle corps and "Miss Future Chinatown" are emerging traditions. Somewhere between is the association of the new "Year of the Horse" with good luck at the race track and the old "Year of the Snake or Serpent" with a layoff from a job. Names have always exerted their magic.

* * *

Year of the Monkey

Greetings of "*kung hay fat choy,*" the Cantonese expression of good fortune competed with a volley of firecrackers yesterday [February 16, 1980] as thousands of people jammed the narrow streets of [New York's] Chinatown to usher in the Chinese lunar year 4678, the year of the monkey.

Eight teams of youths accompanied lion dancers through the streets, striking gongs and drums to chase away evil spirits from local shops. At the culmination of each dance, the lion would snatch a red envelope and a chunk of lettuce strung on a pink cord in front of each shop.

"We bring the stores luck," explained Stanley Leung, a member of the team that danced along Bowery Street. After a 15-minute dance, the lion would grip the envelope between its teeth and dash off with a small sum of "lucky money," the team's reward for saving the proprietor from demons.

Dragons also dizzily wended their way along Mott Street, with young people holding the colorful bodies high above their heads on gold posts. Red, yellow and silver flags accompanied the processions that moved along Pell and Bayard Streets.

The monkey, one of 12 animals that cyclically rule the lunar calendar for a year, represents craft, charm and intelligence. The humorous creature is supposed to portend 12 months of improved communication between the peoples of the world.

The Chinese also draw upon the Western depiction of the monkey as representing the absence of evil, since it hears none, sees none and speaks none. Yesterday, those who defied the rain and snow to celebrate the new year behaved like the traditional triumvirate of monkeys, covering ears, eyes and mouths to shut out the deafening pops, bright white flashes and smoke of the firecrackers.

"This isn't the time to worry about catching a cold," said Raymond To, who had brought his five children from South Orange, N.J., to see the processions. "I want my children to know what the Chinese costumes and traditions are about—the American New Year is never as exciting as this."

People nestled in doorways and sought refuge from wet weather beneath awnings and umbrellas, but few complaints were heard. Paul Ling, a 31-year-old who came to the United States from Hong Kong 19 years ago, spoke for many when he said: "I wouldn't miss the Chinese New Year for anything. It really makes me feel like I'm back home."

Friday night, the eve of the new year, many Chinese families gathered for the traditional reunion dinner, at which seemingly endless platters of pork, chicken, beef and vegetables were served. The dishes also included "*yu*" (fish). Most of the new year's dishes have names that contain a special greeting, and the word for fish closely resembles "*yao yu*," the word for abundance.

Source

New York Times, February 17, 1980. By Jill Smolowe, staff writer. Cf. "Chinese New Year," p. 46 for firecrackers, food, and dragons.

* * *

Sweets for the Year of the Dragon

"Usually the Chinese would celebrate the New Year for five days. During that time, there would be no work. They would concentrate on eating, playing games and gambling. At least that's the way it used to be at the turn of the century," said Fu Shen Chang, a chef born and trained in Beijing....

"During the New Year period, it is winter in northern China, and people there gather together in the evening, play games and eat sweets or snacks. And this is one of them," said Chang as he started to shape bean-paste centers for sweet rice dumplings....

The task of making these holiday snacks, in the old days, would have fallen to the Chinese wife or grandmother. She would have made the bean paste from scratch, soaking the beans, removing the skins, grinding the paste, blending in the sugar. Now, however, at Asian markets the sweet red-bean paste comes canned and ready to use.

"Or some people will use peanut butter," said the younger Chang. He runs the restaurant Ming Dynasty, 622 S. Second St., at which the senior Chang is executive chef. The *Tong Yuen* or New Year's Dumplings will be included in the eight-course New Year's banquets that the restaurant has scheduled on Monday evenings into March.

The round shape of the dumplings offers a symbolic hope for a well-rounded New Year. They typically are served, too, at the Lantern Festival, which marks the end of the official New Year's celebration. This occurs on the 15th day of the first lunar month.

With either filling ingredient, the dumplings are a change for the American palate. The glutinous rice-flour coating is a bit gummy after the traditional boiling. To get around this, chef Chang offers the option of deep-frying, which gives a firmer texture and more familiar feel to the sweet.

Just as the recipes are being Westernized, so, too, is the holiday itself.

Traditionally, everything must be cleaned and put in order before the New Year. And for the first month, it is the habit to wear new clothing. When you meet someone on the street, it is customary to clasp hands and wish each other luck in the New Year.

"And they don't do it these days anymore," says Chang, "but traditionally on the fifth night of the New Year celebration, the younger generation is supposed to thank the older generation, within the family, by bowing to the ground as in prayer."

Though officially 15 days long, the public or business celebration has been steadily shortened. Even in Taiwan, the work holiday has been cut to just the first three days of the New Year, says Chang. But for a few days afterward, banquets and parties are given by business owners for their employees.

"During those banquets," says Chang, "you usually have a chicken dish, and it is tradition that whoever the chicken head points to is being laid off work and won't be around that next year."

And what if the full staff is going to stay? Then the chicken head is directed at the owner.

Particularly among farm families and in northern China, where the New Year period and icy cold winters coincide, it is traditional to gather together in the evening to play games and eat sweets or snacks. Tong Yuen is one of those sweets. Although originally associated with the New Year's celebration, the sweet is eaten now throughout the year, says Chang.

Hung Tong Tong Yuen (Red-Bean New Year's Dumplings)

1½ teaspoons black sesame seeds
1   can (18 ounces) sweet red bean paste
1   tablespoon sesame or other oil
2   cups rice flour, approximately
    Water

Heat dry wok or skillet over medium flame. Add black sesame seeds, and cook, stirring, for about one minute or until aroma is released. Remove. Let cool. Using straight roller or mortar and pestle, grind dry seeds to a powder. Combine sesame with bean paste, blending thoroughly.

Moisten palm with oil and roll small amounts of bean paste into balls one-half inch to three-quarters inch in diameter. Place on plate or waxed paper that has been lightly oiled.

Pour flour into large mixing bowl. Drop the balls, six at a time, into flour.

Remove and place coated balls in strainer. Ideally, the strainer should be the flat ladle type to allow for separation of dumplings. Dip dumplings into water in second mixing bowl, holding them under water for just a few seconds to wet the rice flour. Remove and drain. Drop wet dumplings back into flour. Shake or stir to coat again. Repeat wetting and coating procedure five times. After final coating with rice flour, set dumplings aside, or refrigerate for at least two hours to allow moisture in the coating to even out. When set, the coating will have a matte finish and be very smooth.

To cook dumplings, bring water to low boil in wok or large saucepan. Cook dumplings, a few at a time so as not to crowd, a few minutes until coating is translucent. Serve in bowl with some of the cooking liquid. The water may be sweetened as desired with sugar or honey. Makes about 36 dumplings, enough for 12 to 18 servings.

Note: As an alternative cooking method, the dumplings may be deep-fried in oil heated to 325 degrees. The oil is purposely kept at a lower temperature than for normal frying because hot oil will make the dumplings puff up and pop open, releasing bits of the filling into the oil. Fry gently until dumplings are golden.

Some Chinese cooks substitute peanut butter sweetened with brown sugar and flavored with ground sesame for the traditional sweet red-bean paste in the recipe above.

In Fujian, an eastern province of China, the cooked dumplings are frequently sprinkled with or rolled in sesame seeds, ground peanuts and sugar.

Source

Philadelphia Inquirer, February 17, 1988. By Marilynn Marter, staff writer.

Fortune Cookies for the Year of the Rooster

If you would like to usher in the Chinese New Year with fortune cookies this year [1981, the Year of the Rooster], you can improve on both the cookies and the fortunes by making your own. Unlike their store-bought counterparts, homemade fortune cookies have a buttery taste and melt-in-your-mouth texture. And they can be filled with bits of your own cleverness or personal wishes rather than factory wit. . . .

3	egg whites
⅔	cup sugar
⅛	teaspoon salt
¼	teaspoon vanilla
½	cup melted butter
2	tablespoons strong tea
1	cup flour

Prepare fortunes, fold and set aside.

In a medium bowl, combine egg whites, sugar, salt and vanilla. Stir in melted butter and tea. Mix well. Stir in flour until batter is smooth. Chill batter at least 30 minutes.

For each cookie, place a rounded teaspoonful of batter on a greased baking sheet. With the back of a spoon, spread out batter to form a thin circle about 3 inches in diameter. Bake no more than 2 or 3 cookies at one time, because they must be folded before they begin to cool and harden.

Bake in a preheated 350-degree oven for 3 to 5 minutes or until edges of cookies are brown. Remove baking sheet from oven and carefully remove one cookie with a spatula. Lay cookie flat on a clean plate and place a fortune on top. Working quickly, fold the cookie in half to form a semicircle and enclose the fortune. Lay the semicircle across the rim of a glass and press the folded edge against the glass, half inside and half outside. The curved edge should be left to flare out, to give the cookie its characteristic "nurse's cap" shape. Set completed cookie in the well of a muffin tin to hold the shape while it cools. Repeat procedure with subsequent cookies.

Note: As cookies must be shaped when hot, handle with care. Makes 45.

Source

Washington Post, February 5, 1981. By Ruth Glick for the "Food Section" during the Chinese New Year period.

How Not to Begin the New Year

Gambling charges pending against 103 men who were arrested in eight Chinese social clubs Feb. 6 [1981] yesterday were placed on file by Chief Justice Harry Elam in Boston Municipal Court.

By placing the complaints on file, Elam has ended any prosecution of the defendants, which results in no criminal record of the charge. However, the individual complaints can be reviewed if any of the defendants is arrested again.

Elam ordered police to return approximately $30,000 which was seized in the early morning raids in the basement clubs on Tyler, Beach and Oxford streets.

The judge also criticized "police officials" for being "insensitive" by scheduling the raids on the Chinese New Year, noting, however, that he was not "condoning gambling.". . .

At the time of the raids, Chinatown civic leaders criticized police because of the timing of the raids.

A Chinatown merchant who asked not to be identified explained the significance of the holiday, the first day of the "Year of the Rooster."

"Chinese people are very superstitious, and the celebration of this day was important for the rest of the year. That's why everyone smiles and wishes their friends a happy new year. It sets the tone for the coming year," he said.

"For the people who were arrested—they didn't want to go to the police station—the year is spoiled for them."

Source

Boston Globe, February 21, 1981. News report by a staff writer. For other examples of gambling on the New Year, see note on "Games at the White Dog Feast," p. 44.

Tet

January 21-February 19

Tet, a seven-day festival, is an abbreviation for "*Tet Nguyen-Dan*," a Vietnamese phrase meaning "first day." It celebrates both the beginning of a new year and of spring. In keeping with the Chinese belief (and for that matter, certain American folk beliefs as well), it is important that only good things occur during Tet, for the year will proceed as it begins. It is a time for family reunions and feasting. Old debts are cleared, houses repainted, and new clothes bought. During this festival a household spirit, also known as "Tet," is said to travel to the abode of the Jade Emperor and report on the affairs of the family. For this reason a preliminary ceremony is held to send him off in a good mood. While he is gone, a tree made of bamboo and red paper is erected in order to ward off evil spirits, and sacrifices are made to deceased members of the family.

Vietnamese Tet Comes to America

Several hundred Vietnamese refugees and their friends gathered in Queens [New York] yesterday [February 19, 1977] to hold a celebration for Tet, which, while it offered a showcase for the gay dances and fireworks that normally adorn the New Year holiday, also represented a deliberate effort to help buttress a flagging sense of community and pride.

There was merriment enough as befits a proper welcoming of the Year of the Serpent, but organizers spoke of a more sober purpose that was reflected in some of the dances and songs.

The festivities were held at the Catholic Preparatory Seminary, at 56-25 92d Street in the Elmhurst section.

As a half-dozen young girls in the background performed a dance to "Song of the West," alluding to their new life, Le Thanh Hoang Dan, a leading organizer of refugees here, said cooperation had been sought from various local Vietnamese organizations to join in a single celebration, in what for most of them was their second new year in this country. The primary goal, he said, was to raise money to be distributed by the Red Cross to help other Vietnamese refugees now scattered in Thailand, Malaysia, Hong Kong, and other parts of Southeast Asia.

The $500 that was expected to be raised, according to Mr. Dan, a City University doctoral student, would be more symbolic than anything else—a gesture intended to demonstrate that these earlier refugees, most of them intellectuals and professionals who fled in 1975—had not forgotten countrymen who remained when Vietnam went under Communist control....

"We are trying to feel proud of our community. It's not that we haven't wanted to help before, but we are poor," Mr. Dan said. A former lecturer on the philosophy of education at the University of Saigon, he works at a bakery, in this country he said. His wife, My Chau, is a bank teller.

Huong Marra, a self-described housewife who lives with her husband, an engineer, in Huntington, L.I., looked away from the folk dancing to say that Tet in this country was treated "as a Memorial Day, to think about our country."

Source and Comment

New York Times, February 20, 1977. News items by Judith Cummings, staff writer.

This celebration of Tet, the Vietnamese New Year, is not simply an instance of recent immigrants observing a traditional holiday in their adopted homeland. Because of the circumstances of their emigration, it conveys their psychological, political, and social needs with unusual immediacy. As these are satisfied, Tet celebrations may well become, like those for the Chinese New Year in San Francisco and New York, a time of feasting, relaxation, an expression of pride in cultural origin, and a part of the diversity of the American scene.

Tu B'Shevat
(January-February)

Tu B'Shevat, the New Year of the Trees, is the fifteenth day of the Jewish month Shevat. Originally, it had no religious significance, with no celebration or liturgical observation, though the day was used to reckon tithes on fruit. In medieval times the custom of eating fruits associated with the Holy Land arose as a means of recalling the Jewish homeland. Then, in the 17th century a special ceremonial, inspired by the verse "For man is like the tree of the field," was developed mostly by the kabbalists. Today, in the State of Israel, Tu B'Shevat has become an arbor day for tree-planting by children. Because of this, the day is being popularized across the world.

The New Year of the Trees

On Tuesday night, as the 15th day of the Hebrew month of Shevat unfolds, Jews will take note of Tu B'Shevat—an ancient minor holiday that may one day become a major Jewish festival celebrating the natural world.

Also known as Rosh Hashanah L'eilanot, the New Year of the Trees, Tu B'Shevat has its roots in the ancient custom of reckoning the age of a tree in order to tithe its fruits.

The observance is mentioned in the Talmud, but not in the Torah.

Observing that most of Israel's rainfall occurs before the 15th day of Shevat, Rabbi Hillel ruled that the age of a tree would be counted from that day. Thus, whatever fruits the tree yielded after that day would be tithed as fruits of the new year.

Knowing the age of a tree is also important in order to fulfill the halachic [Religious law] injunction against eating the fruit of a tree less than four years old.

The *Encyclopaedia Judaica* notes that it was traditional among the Ashkenazic communities in Europe to observe Tu B'Shevat by eating 15 different kinds of fruit, with special preference given to fruits grown in Eretz Yisrael.

To Sephardic Jews, the encyclopedia reports, the New Year of the Trees took on a greater significance. During the 16th century, the kaballists of Safed expanded the Sephardic liturgy and customs for the festival and devised a special order of service for the day—a Tu B'Shevat seder [Ritual Meal].

To Dr. Arthur Green, president of the Reconstructionist Rabbinical College in Wyncote [Pa.], the kaballists' centuries-old order of service can serve as a model for modern times. In his view, Tu B'Shevat is an ancient holiday with a modern message: Care about, preserve and protect the natural environment. . . .

It is also a new age in human history, Green said—an age in which the very existence of the earth is threatened by nuclear weapons and assaults on the environment.

"I think this means something for us as Jews," he said. "We who have been victims of destruction have to bear an extra sensitivity."

Tu B'Shevat, if observed as a major Jewish holiday, can foster such sensitivity, he said. A Tu B'Shevat seder, he said, is "a time of education, of reflection, of celebrating the divine within creation and realizing that creation remains fragile and we have to protect it."

Source

Jewish Exponent, January 29, 1988. From an article by Marilyn S. Lieberstein, staff writer.

* * *

Tu B'Shevat

Children Plant New Year Trees

"Does anyone know what bark is?" the young woman asked.

Several small hands darted up, fingers stretching urgently.

"It's the tree's skin," a little girl answered in a near whisper, though with evident pride.

She was one of 15 children—kindergarteners, first-, second- and third-graders from Congregation Or Ami—who participated Sunday in the annual Tu B'Shevat celebration at the Morris Arboretum of the University of Pennsylvania in Chestnut Hill.

The Tu B'Shevat program, held in the arboretum's Widener Education Center, was begun eight years ago at the suggestion of volunteer guides Gerry Schneeberg and Beverly Miller, who wished to broaden the facility's outreach to children during a season when most people would rather stay indoors.

The celebration, which, in the words of Education Intern Catherine Maxwell, strives to introduce the children to "all the ways we use trees and all the ways trees help us," has three parts.

First the children watched a film, donated by the Central Agency for Jewish Education, which depicts the founding, 10 years ago, of Israel's Jewish Children's Forest.

The worldwide project was a cooperative effort by the Jewish National Fund, Israel's president, prime minister and the Ministry of Education. The goal was to create a bond between Israeli children and Jewish children in the Diaspora every Tu B'Shevat.

Each Israeli child would plant two trees, one for himself and one for his pen pal in the Diaspora. A third tree would be planted in honor of a child who perished in the Holocaust.

In a pre-screening introduction, Phyllis McGusty of the arboretum spoke of Tu B'Shevat—the New Year of the Trees—and its importance to Israel's ecological system.

"Israel knows that it has to plant trees to replenish all the forests and groves that have been destroyed over the years," McGusty said. "Without trees, there's a lot of erosion. The soil dries out, the winds blow the soil away and there's lots of decay. So we plant trees to renew the landscape."

Source

Jewish Exponent, February 5, 1988. By Robert Leiter, staff writer.

Candlemas or Groundhog Day
February 2

In the Eastern Church, Candlemas celebrates the Presentation of Christ in the Temple; in the Western, the Purification of Mary. The blessing of the candles, for which this day is named, did not enter the ceremony until the eleventh century. In Europe, Candlemas was combined with pagan candlelight processions to purify and invigorate the fields before the planting season, for light was associated with the sun's power and with fertility and darkness with sterility. In Mexico, Candlemas coincides with the Aztec New Year.

On Candlemas, the woodchuck is said to emerge from his hibernation in order to look for his shadow. If he sees it, he will return to his burrow for six more weeks. If he doesn't, he knows spring will arrive soon. The belief is related to the association of Candlemas with the sowing of the crops, sunny weather foreboding harsh days and so poor planting. In Germany, the badger, and in England and France the bear, had analogous roles as weather prognosticators.

An Early Groundhog

Of course everybody knows that February 2 is groundhog day. If the *dox* (the dialect word for groundhog) sees its shadow on this day, the belief is that six weeks of bad weather will follow; if the day is cloudy, however, the weather will be mild and moderate from then to spring.

The earliest reference we have to groundhog day at the Folklore Center is an entry in James L. Morris' diary under the date of Feb. 4, 1841. A storekeeper at Morgantown, Berks County [Pennsylvania], Morris wrote: "Last Tuesday, the 2nd inst., was Candlemas day, the day on which, according to the Germans, the Groundhog peeps out of his winter quarters and if he sees his shadow he pops back for another six weeks nap, but if the day be cloudy he remains out, as the weather is to be moderate."

Source

Pennsylvania Dutchman, V (February 1, 1954), 11. The reference is reprinted by Alfred L. Shoemaker from the files of the Pennsylvania Dutch Folklore Center, Franklin and Marshall College.

* * *

More Recent Groundhogs

Punxsutawney Phil

Once again tomorrow [February 2] in a small town in north-central Pennsylvania [Punxsutawney], a four-legged oracle will predict when spring will come.

The famous forecaster is Punxsutawney Phil, the legendary groundhog said by believers to be nearly a century old and an infallible prognosticator of winter's end.

On Groundhog Day, according to the German folklore of this region, groundhogs, also known as woodchucks, emerge from their underground hibernation. If they see their shadows, the legend says, they scamper back into their burrows and winter continues for six weeks. If they do not, spring is just around the corner.

It is not clear just how Phil acquired his special status as spokesman for his species, but Punxsutawnians insist that their groundhog is the "seer of seers."

Perhaps accuracy has something to do with it.

"In 92 years of Punxsutawney Phil's emergence, he has never, never, never been wrong," says Charles M. Erhard Jr., president of the Punxsutawney Groundhog Club.

There was a miscue once, Erhard admits, but it wasn't Phil's fault.

"One year the weather was so terrible on Groundhog Day that Phil sent a message out that any durn fool would know enough not to go outside," he recalled.

"So since there wouldn't have been any shadow, we predicted an early spring. The worst part of winter followed, which just goes to show that when humans get involved, they can't get it right, but Phil never misses."

This town has a heavy stake in Phil's reputation, and the annual prediction is made amid great pomp and circumstance, ending with the trek up Gobbler's Knob to Phil's heated bunker to get The Word.

Erhard, clad in tails and striped pants, will lead the pilgrimage, rap with a special acacia wood cane at the stone facade of the burrow, speak intimately with Phil in "groundhog language" and translate for the assembled multitude.

Phil actually lives most of the year with his mate in a nearby park and must be installed at Gobbler's Knob in advance of the big event.

Animal authorities say woodchucks generally hibernate until March, and Phil is not always happy to have his sleep disturbed.

"A few years back, one of the inner circle had his finger bitten, and it gave us a scare," Erhard recalled. "But so far I've been on friendly terms with him."

Source and Comment

Philadelphia Inquirer, February 1, 1978. The article on Punxsutawney Phil, unsigned, was distributed to member newspapers of the Associated Press.

Like the return of the migrating swallows to San Juan Capistrano in California (see pp. 133, 134), a natural occurrence first accumulates a body of folk traditions and then attracts public attention through the mass media, providing an opportunity for various promotional enterprises—in the name of folklore, good clean fun, and local boosters.

* * *

Pothole Pete

New York City's official groundhog-designate is hereby christened Pothole Pete.

The name for the still-hibernating critter was suggested by seven of the well over 50 entrants in *The News* groundhog-naming contest. The first two suggesters of Pothole Pete, whose entries arrived on the same day, were declared winners.

Kimberly Wilkes of the Bronx and Tom Bishop of Cornwall, N.Y. are the winners. Jerry Curran of Manhattan, Fred Brunner of Glendale, Queens, Russell Reed of Allentown, Pa., Virginia Ekerman of Cambria Heights, Queens, and Robert Thillet of Rego Park, Queens, are the runners-up.

Kimberly, a quiet, shy-sounding 8 year-old who said she loves animals, explained that she had made a long list of names, and finally narrowed them down to the three she submitted: Pothole Pete, Subway Sam and Apple Head.

Tom also submitted two names in addition to Pothole Pete: Apple Andy and Manhattan Mergatroid.

The reason for the contest—and the groundhog—was the fact that New York City found itself in the embarrassing position of being without a resident groundhog for Groundhog Day early this month. So *The News,* in the finest tradition of civic responsibility, bought one for the city.

At the moment, Pothole Pete is still hibernating in his box at the Space Wild Animal Farm in Beemerville, N.J. As soon as he comes to and finishes his spring cleaning— about May 1—Fred Space will make delivery. We'll turn Pete over to the city's Parks Department so he can be installed in a new cage at Flushing Meadow-Corona Park Zoo in Queens.

We'll invite Kimberly and Tom to attend the official adoption ceremony, and at that time we'll present them with their surprise awards.

Source

New York *Daily News,* February 13, 1978. By Donald Singleton, a staff writer.

* * *

Chipper and Sunshine

Officials of the Brookfield (Ill.) Zoo are resorting to the inducements of food and sex, so determined are they to give Groundhog Day visitors a glimpse of Chipper, a groundhog with a bad attitude who spent the past three Groundhog Days inside of his hollow log. Today, Chipper is to be reunited with Sunshine, a 2-year-old female groundhog separated from him since November. Sunshine will be taken to the mouth of the log to see if she can entice Chipper to come out. In case that fails, there will also be a "Welcome to Spring" cake on hand for Chipper, concocted of his favorite foods—carrots, honey and oats.

Source

Boston Globe, February 2, 1981. The attempt to seduce Chipper is reported in a column headed "Names and Faces."

* * *

From Bear to Groundhog

To the folk-lorist there are few pleasures which excel that of the discovery of a familiar superstition parading in ancient garb. Such was the writer's fortune, upon reading a discussion which took place before the *Société Préhistorique Française* in January of 1917. There M. Catelan records,—

"On running through the numerous calendars that were given me for the *Capo d' Anno,* we noted that our *Studio* calendar bore for the 1st of February the fête of the Holy Bear (*Saint Ours*).

"Now, there is an alpine Provençal proverb which says, '*Si, pour le Chandeleur, l'Ours sorte de sa tannière et voit son ombre, il rentre et de quarante jours ne sorte plus.*' ['If, on

Candlemas, the Bear comes out of his den and sees his shadow, he returns for forty days more.']

"We have thought to interest our colleagues by calling attention to this date of the 1st of February and that of the 2d of February (*le Chandeleur*), both of which treat of the bear, and at the same time are brought into relation with the sun. In any case, we have brought a stone, perhaps useful, to the temple which is being rebuilt."

When and how this Provençal bear migrated to the New World may never be known; but there would seem to be no possible doubt of its identity with the American groundhog, which, on the 2d of February, annually casts its shadow across the pages of our daily press.

Source

Journal of American Folklore, XXXII (1919), 521. From a discussion of "The Groundhog Myth and Its Origins" by H. Newell Wardle.

* * *

From Bear to Groundhog

Bear Dance

In the fall the snow comes, and the bear has a wickiup in a hole. He stays there all winter, perhaps six moons. In the spring the snow goes, and he comes out. The bear dances up to a big tree on his hind feet. He dances up and back, back and forth, and sings, "Um, um, um, um!" He makes a path up to the tree, embraces it, and goes back again, singing "Um, um, um!" He dances very much, all the time.

Now Indians do it, and call it the "Bear Dance." It happens in the spring, and they do not dance in the winter. The bear understands the Bear Dance.

Source and Comment

Journal of American Folklore, XXIII (1910), 363. Collected by J. Alden Mason "during the summer of 1909 from the Uintah Utes at White Rocks, Utah. The informant, Snake John, was an old White River Ute, reputed to have been the leader of the Meeker Massacre, 1879. His mother was a Shoshone."

The Bear Dance is a ritual of regeneration, depicting the awakening of the bear from his winter sleep. It is associated with the coming of spring. Among the Utes it is mainly a social event. The Blackfeet, Crow and Kutenai traditionally perform the dance when the bear emerges from hibernation.

* * *

Candlemas Weather Rhymes

As far as the sun shines out on Candlemas Day
So far will snow blow in before May.
As far as the snow blows in on Candlemas Day,
So far will the sun shine out before May.

Source

Memoirs of the American Folklore Society, XVIII (1925), 114. "Folk-Lore from Maryland," collected by Annie W. Whitney and Caroline C. Bullock, who do not supply the name of the informant.

If Candlemas is fair and clear,
There'll be two winters in the year.

Source

Pennsylvania Dutchman, V (February 1, 1954), 11. Reported by Alfred E. Shoemaker, who learned it from a "former student" who collected it "from Abram Hess of the New Holland section" of the Pennsylvania Dutch country

* * *

If the sun shines on Candlemas Day,
Half the fuel and half the hay.

Source and Comment

Journal of American Folklore, XLVIII (1935), 195. From a collection of "Weather Sayings from Maryland" by Milton Whitney of the Maryland Agricultural College. This last rhyme apparently combines a weather saying with the proverbial notion that a provident farmer will have an ample supply of fodder in February. Cf.: "A good farmer will have half his corn and half his hay left on Candlemas day," reported from rural Connecticut in *Journal of American Folklore*, XLV (1932), 501. Also cf. "Candlemas Spinning," below.

* * *

Candlemas Spinning

The German-language almanacs used to call groundhog day "*Lichtmess*" or "Candlemas" in English. Willis D. Faust of Bernville R.D. [Pennsylvania] remembers hearing old people say on this day:

> *Lichtmess,*
> *Schpinn fergess,*
> *Holb fooder gfress.*

(At Candlemas forget spinning; half of the cattle's provender is eaten.)

In an old, but undated, clipping at the Berks County Historical Society an 80-year-old woman, a native of Berks County, reminisced: "In the small towns the girls and women used to form spinning parties of 10 or 15 persons, but each brought their spinning. We all tried to finish our spinning by *Lichtmess*."

Source

Pennsylvania Dutchman, V (February 1, 1954), 11. Reported by Alfred L. Shoemaker from the Pennsylvania Dutch country.

* * *

Christmas Wreaths after Candlemas

It is an old superstition [in Delaware] that all Christmas wreaths and evergreens must be taken away before Candlemas, or there will be a goblin for each leaf.

> For look how many leaves there be
> Neglected there (maids, trust to me);
> So many goblins you shall see.

Source

Journal of American Folklore, V (1892), 243. Contributed by Mrs. S. D. Derrickson of Wilmington, Delaware. No further information supplied. Cf. "Burning the Greens at Old Christmas, p. 33.

St. Blaise's or Blase's Day
February 3

St Blasius was beheaded on February 3, A.D. 316 during the persecutions of Diocletian. As he was being led to the place of execution, he miraculously cured a child suffering from a throat infection.

Blessing Throats on St. Blaise's Day

Throats are blessed on St. Blaise's Day in almost every [Buffalo, New York Roman] Catholic parish....

Source

Indiana Folklore, IX (1976), 167. Collected by Lydia Marie Fish. For her source, see note on St. Joseph's Day Feast, p. 132.

[Near] Bethlehem, Pa., [in early February], the Rev. Clarence Kelly ... in a tiny rural chapel ... celebrated Mass and performed the blessings of the throat, a ceremony marking the Feast of St. Blaise.

Source

Philadelphia Inquirer, February 11, 1981. From background material by staff writer Linda Loyd on a "conservative Roman Catholic priest" and his "traditionalist flock."

Powamû Festival
February 3

From the earth, which had always existed, the Hopi Indian Sky Father, represented by a hawk or eagle, and the Earth Mother, represented by a spider, generated the human race and a number of marvelous animals.

Man emerged from beneath this earth through an opening, and upon his death is supposed to return to the underworld. The Sky Father, who is also known as the Sun God and by other names as well, symbolizes the male generative force. His arrival, in a personified form, and his departure, are occasions for two major Hopi festivals, which take place at the Walpi Pueblo, Arizona.

The Arrival of the Hopi Sky-god

Hopi Indians personate in their worship the spirit ancients of their clans, by masked men wearing totemic designs characteristic of those clans. They also represent them by graven images and figures with like symbolism. The spirits of the ancients, their personations by men, the festivals in which these personators appear, and their representation by images and figures, are called Katcinas. The power which is personated objectively, or that which we call the spirit, is the magic potentiality conceived of as an anima or invisible aerial or breath body....

In certain elaborate festivals these Indians also personate other beings besides clan-ancients, prominent among which may be mentioned the Sky-god. It is the author's purpose, in this article, to consider at length the objective symbolism and acts of this personator in certain festivals. The distinction between the terms, Sky-god and Sun-god, is verbal, not real, for the sun is the shield or mask, a visible symbol of the magic power of the Sky-god conceived of as an anthropomorphic being. Both these names are used interchangeably in the following pages....

In order to obtain a clear idea of the nature of Sky-god personations among the Hopi let us first describe those of the so-called Katcina clan, to be followed by a consideration of the modifications which appear among other clans.

The two most important festivals of this clan at Walpi [northeast Arizona] celebrate the advent and exit of personations of its clan-ancients. In one, the arrival, and in the other, their departure, are represented by men who personate these beings. They are supposed to enter the pueblo in February, an event dramatized in the festival called Powamû; to leave the pueblo, or go home, in July, and the representation of that event is called the Niman. In the intervening months the clan ancients are supposed to remain in the village or its neighborhood, publicly appearing from time to time in the pueblo in masked dances lasting a single day.

While these dramatizations of advent and departure are festivals of one clan, the actors are not restricted to this clan. Several others combine with it and personate their ancients, so that it has come about that while in the main these two great festivals are controlled by one clan, whose chief is chief of the festivals, fragments of dramatizations by other clans survive in them, and personations of many clan ancients unconnected with the leading clan likewise appear. With all these additions, however, the main events are distinctly those of one clan or group of clans.

When the advent and departure of the ancients are dramatized a being is personated who leads them into the pueblo, and another who conducts them from it to their home, the underworld. The former leader represents the Sky-god as a Sun-god; the latter the same god, ruler of the realm of the dead, and god of germs.

The Sun-god of the Katcina clans, the advent of whom is celebrated at the Powamû festival, is generally called Ahüla, the returning one, although sometimes called the "Old-Man-Sun."

The author witnessed the public dramatization of the return of this god on the morning of February 3d, the opening day of the festival, at Walpi, in 1900. As this dramatization is a type of other presentations a somewhat detailed description of his dress and symbolism, with an account of the acts performed, is appended. Like most dramatizations the ceremony has two parts, a secret and a public exhibition....

The man wears a mask which has a circular or disk form, with periphery bounded by a plaited corn-husk in which are inserted eagle-wing feathers, and a fringe of red horsehair representing sun's rays. The upper part of the face is divided into two quadrants, one of which is yellow; the other green, both decorated with black crosses. The middle is occupied by a triangular figure, and the chin, here hidden by a foxskin, tied about the neck, is black in color. A curved beak projects from one angle of the triangular symbol in the middle of the face.

The clothing consists of two white cotton ceremonial kilts, one tied over the shoulder, and the other around the loins. The leggings are made of an open mesh cloth with a fringe of shell tinklers tied down the side. In his right hand this figure carries a staff, to one end of which two feathers are tied, while midway in its length are attached a small crook, feathers, and an ear of corn. Among many objects carried in the left hand may be mentioned sprouts of beans, a slat of wood, a bag of sacred meal, and stringed feathers; the uses of these will be referred to in an account of the acts of this personage. The most characteristic symbolism, as is always the case, is shown on the face-shield or mask, which resembles somewhat that of the conventional Hopi Sun-disk.

A man who personated the Sun-god donned this characteristic mask and dressed near the sun shrine at Walla, northeast of the pueblos, and after certain preliminaries at this shrine, led by the Katcina chief, proceeded up the trail to the pueblos, first Hano, from which he proceeded to Sichomovi and Walpi, visiting the kivas and houses of all the principal chiefs in these three villages. The acts at each house are substantially identical, so that one description may serve for all....

As the personator of the Sun-god walked through the pueblos he imitated the gait and general manner of an old man, using a staff for support as he proceeded from one room to another, and performed the following rites at each kiva. Having approached the hatchway of one of these rooms he leaned down, and drew a vertical mark with sacred-meal on the inside of the entrance, opposite the ladder. Turning to the east he made solemn inclinations of his body, bending backward and bowing forward, uttering at the same time a low, falsetto growl. He then turned to the kiva entrance and made similar obeisances, calling in the same voice; two or three of the principal men responded by coming up the kiva ladder, each bearing a handful of prayer-meal, and a feather-string which he placed in the hand of the Sun-god, at the same time saying a low, inaudible prayer.

At the houses of the chiefs the personator performed similar acts having the same import. Advancing to the doorway, he rubbed a handful of meal on the house wall, at the left of the doorway, making a vertical mark about the height of his chest. He then turned to face the rising sun, and made six silent inclinations of his body, uttering the falsetto calls, holding his staff before him at arm's length. Turning again to the doorway he bowed his body four times, and made the same calls.

The chief man or woman emerged from the house and placed in the hand of the personator a handful of prayer-meal and stringed-feather, saying at the same time a low prayer. In return for which the Sun-god handed him a few bean sprouts.

All the prayer offerings which the Sun-god had received in this circuit of the towns were later deposited in a sun-shrine, and the personator returned to the kiva, where he disrobed; the mask was carried to the house of the Katcina chief in whose custody it is kept, and to whom it is said to belong.

The above actions admit of the following explanations: The personator of the Sun-god enters the pueblos from the east at or near sunrise, receiving at each house the prayers of the inmates symbolized by the meal which each chief places in his hand, receiving in return sprouted beans symbolically representing the gifts for which they pray. The inclinations and obeisances with the accompanying calls may be theoretically interpreted as signs to his beneficent followers, the clan-ancients, and the bows to the doorways, gestures indicating the houses that he wishes them to enter, bringing blessing. The whole performance is a "prayer by signatures," or a pantomimic representation in which the desires of the Hopi are expressed by symbols and symbolic actions. The priests ask the Sky-god to aid them, and he answers in a symbolic way for himself and his followers, the ancients of clans.

The representation of the departure of the clan-ancients is not less dramatic than that of their advent; in it they are conducted or led away by a personage with symbols which are characteristic of another god.

Source

Journal of American Folklore, XV (1902), 14-19. From an anthropological report by J. Walter Fewkes.

The Gasparilla Pirate Festival
February 9

During the period of Mardi Gras celebrations in other cities along the Gulf Coast, Tampa, Florida, civic leaders, probably inspired by the "krewes" or men's clubs, began in 1904 to sponsor a parade of ships and a mock pirate invasion. This invasion from the sea and other festivities now attract almost a million participants annually and have given rise to a few genuine folktales as well.

The Pirate Who Became a Civic Legend

A curious quirk of his, this, that the bloodthirsty [José] Gaspar—who was accustomed to refer to himself as "Gasparilla"—should now be installed as a sort of civic patron rogue of the Florida West Coast. In Tampa his carnival time each February sets the populace to dancing in the streets and shouting his name.

Time has pretty well bleached out the memories of his sins. Tampans like to think of Gaspar as a hearty old swashbuckler, with courtly manners and possibly—just possibly—prankish habits; but never as a man to scuttle a ship or slit your throat.

In good truth, little enough is known of the worthy fellow, save that while a lieutenant in the Royal Spanish Navy he led a mutiny in 1783 aboard the Spanish sloop-of-war, the *Florida Blanca,* seized command of the vessel, and set sail for the Florida straits. Preying on the shipping of all nations, his freebooting exploits quickly established his status as one of the dreaded "Brethren of the Coast."

Research in the archives of the Spanish Navy at Madrid some years ago resulted in the discovery of Gasparilla's own diary of his first twelve years as a pirate. This remarkable fragment had fallen into Madrid's hands in 1795. In it Gasparilla boasted thirty-six ships captured and burned, their crews given the option of joining his ranks or walking the plank. Captive ladies were disposed of according to the fancy of the moment. How many other ships fell prey to Gaspar in later years is unknown. His buried treasure is still being sought by treasure hunters along the Florida coast.

The sea-rover's luck ran out in 1814 when he and his buccaneer band, emerging from their safe rendezvous in the shelter of an island in Charlotte Harbor south of Tampa—now the site of Boca Grande, near Punta Gorda—made their fatal mistake. About to pounce on a lone brig, apparently a merchantman, Gasparilla saw to his consternation the Stars and Stripes break out at the masthead, and discovered that his proposed victim was a Navy warship, the U.S.S. *Enterprise,* Lieutenant Kearney commanding. The battle was joined, and in a few minutes Gasparilla's flagship, the *Gasparilla II,* was a burning shambles. A few of the crew escaped in a long boat. Gasparilla did not wait for the *Enterprise*'s boarding party. Wrapping a heavy chain around his waist and neck, he leaped into the sea, in a final gesture of defiance. A surviving dozen of his crew were taken to New Orleans and eleven of them hanged. The cabin boy got ten years in federal prison.

Old Gaspar himself almost touched modern times. In Tampa in 1904, when Ye Mystic Krewe of Gasparilla was formed, there were men living who had known men who had actually known Gasparilla.

Source

Descriptive brochure, Greater Tampa Chamber of Commerce. Unsigned and undated, this brochure was written for the information of tourists.

* * *

The Pirate Who Became a Civic Legend
José Gasparilla's Party

It is said that this famous Corsair made one particularly profitable raid down the Spanish Main. He determined then to return to one of his favorite retreats, the environs of Tampa Bay. Here he held a celebration which is famous for its splendor. Determined to impress people with his power, the pirate's train outshone that of any European monarch of his day. After the festivities, José returned to his predatory raids on merchantmen plying the waters of the Spanish Main.

Source

Southern Folklore Quarterly, II (1938), 218. From a collection of "fragments of folklore" made by J. Frederick Doering. His informant was Mrs. Frederick Webster, "a visitor to Tampa, Florida."

The Pirate Who Became a Civic Legend

Gasparilla's Golden Woman

The best story I know about the Gasparilla Festival concerns the competition among the floats of the Tampa elite in the parade. The story goes that a beautiful Cuban woman who worked in a Tampa cigar factory around 1930 allowed her nearly naked body to be covered with gold paint to win a prize, and she died a couple of days later, leaving her family without her income and in debt because the cigar factory would not even pay for funeral expenses.

Source

Collection of J. Russell Reaver. Collected by J. Russell Reaver, a professor of English and Folklore at Florida State University. He notes a printed version in Stetson Kennedy, *Palmetto Country,* New York, 1942, 314.

St. Valentine's Day
February 14

This day is dedicated to lovers who, according to custom, express their affection for each other through messages and gifts. Originally the choice of a lover was made by lot or by rhyming and riddling, and it was part of spring rituals during which unmarried couples were paired before their participation in orgiastic ceremonies. Such pairing might prove to be permanent, but that was not its initial purpose. Later, in some places on this holiday, the first persons of opposite sex to see each other by chance became valentines, thus encouraging a sportive and intimate relationship. Today cards and candy and affectionate rhymes are sent to one's valentine, sometimes anonymously and sometimes not.

St. Valentine's is a day in honor of two Christian martyrs of the same name who were persecuted under the Roman Emperor Claudius II (A.D. 214–270) and who were buried on the Flaminiian Way on the same day. A church was built over their graves in the fourth century. Since the Middle Ages the day has been dedicated to romantic love, probably because it is the date on which the birds are supposed to start spring mating.

Scholars have thus related the customs of choosing a Valentine's Day sweetheart to a primitive game symbolizing the selection process and mating season of birds in the spring. In any event, birds, love birds particularly, are associated with Valentine's Day.

Valentine's Day in the Classified Ads

74

J.R. HATCHER
You have been—you are; I hope you will be for the next 17 yrs. & more, not the best—but the most wonderful thing that has happened to me. Forever yours, Gloria.

♥

Janet & Chuck

Just to let you know we love you and miss you. But Rochester ain't all that far away. Happy Valentine's Day.
The Gang

GLADY
I LOVE YOU ALWAYS
ADRIAN

GOD'S "LOVE GIFT"
to YOU!

ST. JOHN 3:16

♥

POOPSIE
YOU ARE MY LIFE!
WOOPSIE

TO MY HONEY, MIKE R.

Always and Forever,
Each moment with you,
Is just like a dream to me,
That somehow came true.
All My LOVE,
Your Sweetheart,
Kissing Babbles

To Kevin, the love of my life.
My lover, best friend, & Valentine
You mean the world to me
From your one and only bride to be
Sherri

♥

MARY
LOVES
MICK

♥

MARGARET McKEE
MOTHER of 10
GRANDMOTHER of 52
GREATGRANDMOTHER of 14
HAPPY VALENTINE'S DAY
From "THE WHOLE GANG"

♥

MARK
HAPPY VALENTINE'S DAY
WITH LOVE, BARB

Source

Philadelphia Inquirer, February 14, 1980, and February 14, 1984. Gleanings from the classified advertising section, a recent medium for an old custom.

* * *

Valentine's Day in the Classified Ads
Valentine Ads from A to Z

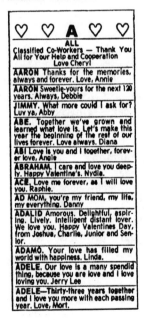

♥ ♥ **A** ♥ ♥
ALL
Classified Co-Workers — Thank You
All for Your Help and Cooperation
Love Cheryl

AARON Thanks for the memories, always and forever. Love, Annie

AARON Sweetie-yours for the next 120 years. Always, Debbie

JIMMY. What more could I ask for? Luv ya, Abby

ABE. Together we've grown and learned what love is. Let's make this year the beginning of the rest of our lives forever. Love always. Diana

ABI Love is you and I together, forever love, Angie

ABRAHAM. I care and love you deeply. Happy Valentine's. Nydia.

ACE. Love me forever, as I will love you. Raphie.

AD MOM, you're my friend, my life, my everything. Danny

ADALID Amorous. Delightful, aspiring. Lively. Intelligent distant lover. We love you. Happy Valentines Day, from Joshua, Charlie, Junior and Senior.

ADAMO. Your love has filled my world with happiness. Linda.

ADELE. Our love is a many spendid thing, because you are love and I love loving you. Jerry Lee

ADELE—Thirty-three years together and I love you more with each passing year. Love, Mort.

...to...

♥ ♥ **Z** ♥ ♥
ZELDA may the love I have for you grow eternally for I cherish you with each passing day. You make my life complete love Ed.

ZETRA. As we begin year nine, you're still my Valentine

ZINGIE. Get well. I love you so much. Love Maria.

ZINNO. Happy Valentines Day, one more time sweety. Love Denise.

ZIVARGO Our Love is eternal your "A" Number one friend.

Source

New York *Daily News,* February 14, 1981.

* * *

Valentine's Day in the Classified Ads
Valentine Letter Ads

"Jumbo"—
Our dreams will have come true when I'm sharing my life with you! Happy Valentine's Day.

Love, "Teets"

Danny—
The best father and husband. Your love puts us at the top of the world.

Always,
Leslie, Adam and Andrew

Wayne—
To my loving, caring, sexy husband. I love you, hon. You're my Valentine.

Jane

Steve—
My Valentine is on a rig, he travels near and far. When my Valentine returns, I thank my lucky star.

We love you
Joyce Brandi

Michael—
The seed was planted and the flower has blossomed into something strong and beautiful. This flower will keep growing inside of me because I love you more and more every day! Happy Valentine's Day.

Love, Monique

Happy Valentine's Day to one big male chauvinist—but I wouldn't trade you for anyone else.

Love, Nancy

Source

The Narragansett (Rhode Island) *Times,* February 8, 1984. Cf. "May Day Maybe Letter," p. 195.

Old-fashioned Valentines

Fifty years ago [1875 in Maryland] St. Valentine's day was a general occasion for sending really handsome, and sometimes anonymous, gifts of jewelry; these were enclosed within elaborately fashioned valentines, and sent by the lover to his sweetheart, or by friend to friend. Comic valentines became more and more popular and the sentimental kind were less used. At present [1925] children are the chief devotees of the valentine.

Source

Memoirs of the American Folklore Society, XVIII (1925), 115. "Folk-Lore from Maryland," collected by Annie W. Whitney and Caroline C. Bullock, who do not supply informants.

* * *

Antique Valentines

If Nancy Fletcher sends you a valentine, she may very well include a note asking you to send it back.

The director of public information at Mount Holyoke College has hundreds of valentines, some dating from as far back as 1848—most from a collection of antique valentines given to her when she was 10 by Marion Winslow Emerson, a distant cousin who was a founder of the Valentine Collectors of America.

Except for one—an elaborately framed shadow box with an intricate 1876 valentine depicting the four seasons that her mother kept in the family room of their Connecticut home—the valentines languished in the family attic for nearly 20 years. Fletcher didn't open the boxes until 1977, when a New Britain, Conn., museum whose officials had heard about the collection from a relative asked if she would display it.

In her attic she discovered valentines large and small, frilly and simple, sentimental and saucy. "It was like moving into another world," she said.

At first, Fletcher said, she thought valentines were frivolous. But she has come to realize, she said, that they "have to do with people and relationships. They chronicle how people relate. They are the expression of what love is, so they end up being central to life."...

Fletcher's oldest valentine, the 1848 specimen, is a beauty once sent to Elizabeth Rockefeller, a cousin of tycoon John D. Rockefeller. Some in the collection were made by Esther Howland, a graduate of Mount Holyoke who in 1848 became the first maker of valentine cards in the United States....

Turn-of-the-century valentines often were hinged so they would stand up, and many incorporate two to seven layers of flowery detail, Fletcher said. She has valentines that open like fans, others bordered in silk fringe, many with movable parts—such as the cherubic girl of the 1930s whose eyes move when a tab is pulled.

Source

Boston Globe, February 14, 1989. By special writer Jean Caldwell.

* * *

Prince Charming's Valentine Gift

To **Alice Leitner,** her fiance is "my Prince Charming."

Her Valentine present was a box wrapped in pink and fuchsia fabric.

When she opened the box in a parking stall Friday she found a $65,000, silver 560 SL Mercedes–Benz convertible coupe.

"He always does very romantic surprises," she said. "If I come home (from a trip) he'll always have 10 dozen roses for me. Once he gave me a ring with dolphins on it."

Source

Providence Sunday Journal, February 14, 1988. From a series of features compiled from wire reports in the "People" section.

* * *

Gingerbread Valentines

In Victorian times lovers declared their affections in a veritable froth of words, songs, pictures and foods [such as] gingerbread "life cakes" in the shape of hearts....

2½ cups unsifted flour
2 teaspoons cinnamon
1½ teaspoons ginger
½ teaspoon ground cloves
¼ teaspoon salt
½ cup margarine
½ cup packed dark brown sugar
⅓ cup dark corn syrup
1 large egg

In large bowl, sift together flour, cinnamon, ginger, cloves and salt.

Blend together margarine and brown sugar until smooth. Add corn syrup and egg; beat well. Add dry ingredients, about one-third at a time, mixing until smooth after each addition. Chill dough one hour.

Roll out half of dough on lightly floured surface to one-quarter-inch thickness. (Reserve other half for decorations or for a second batch of cookies.) Using heart-shaped cookie cutter, press out cookie shapes or use knife to cut around a pattern. Place hearts on cookie sheet. Decorate as desired. Bake at 350 degrees for 15 to 20 minutes until golden. Remove and place on wire racks to cool. Store in covered container. Makes about eight 4½-inch cookies.

Source

Philadelphia Inquirer, February 11, 1981. From an unsigned collection of recipes for "valentine cookies in the Victorian style" printed in the "Food" section of the newspaper prior to the holiday.

* * *

St. Valentine's Day Planting Signs

A real old-time hill man [sows] lettuce on St. Valentine's Day. Otto Ernest Rayburn tells me that once, when Valentine's Day fell on Sunday, his neighbors at Kingston, Ark., got up before daylight to plant their lettuce, so as not to be seen violating the sabbath!

Source

Journal of American Folklore, XLVI (1933), 14. From a description of "odd beliefs connected with agriculture" collected by Vance Randolph in the Ozarks.

* * *

Plant English peas (garden peas) on St. Valentine's Day.

Source

Tennessee Folklore Society Bulletin, XXXI (September, 1965), 63. Collected by Gordon Wilson of Western Kentucky State College in the "Mammoth Cave country."

* * *

Sow seed in the garden on February 14.

Source

Southern Folklore Quarterly, XII (1948), 282. Collected by Margaret M. Bryant in Edgefield County, South Carolina.

* * *

St. Valentine's Weather

Nearly all Ozark people say that the 14th of February, and not the 2nd [Candlemas], is the real Ground Hog Day, and are firmly convinced that if it is cloudy and cold on the 14th there will be six more weeks of winter weather.

Source

Journal of American Folklore, XL (1927), 87. Collected in the Ozark region of Missouri by Vance Randolph from unnamed informants. See p. 65 for Candlemas and its associations with weather forecasting.

* * *

A Pound Supper on Valentine's Day

On February the fourteenth, that was in eighteen, eighty six, February the fourteenth ... I stopped at my uncle's, who lived very close to us, an' they had a, what they called a Valentine drawing, but it was a, what they call a poun' supper. Ev'r boy brought a, a pound of sumpthing in f'r supper. An' then they took the girls' names ... put ... each girl's name on a strip of paper, 'n' put it 'n a hat, an'-uh th' fellas, th' men drew th' names out, an'-uh he, he carried th' uh girl whose name he drew, to uh the dining room to ... supper that night. 'N' (chuckles) I don't remember whether I, I wadn' but fourteen years ol', 'n' I don't suppose I, but I did join in th' play party, I remember that, an' an' I think they turned it into a dance maybe, also (chuckles), because I know there were some fiddlers there an' they played the fiddle, an' I think they must've danced some.

Source and Comment

Tennessee Folklore Society Bulletin, XXXIV (September, 1968), 81. An excerpt from a taped interview conducted in 1967 by Kay L. Cothran, then a student at Georgia State College. Her informant was George W. Mitchell, age 96, of Thomaston, Upson County, Georgia. He was formerly a country school teacher. She attempted "a literal, semi-phonetic rendition" of his speech. A "play party" is a song game substituted for dancing where dancing was banned for religious reasons.

* * *

Judge Goodheart Plays Cupid

There was really nothing unusual about Courtroom 1105 yesterday afternoon [February 14, 1988] unless you count the four-piece band stationed next to the jurors' box and the fact that it was Sunday.

Then again, maybe the throng of reporters and camera crews that jammed the inside of the courtroom was just a little strange. And, perhaps, it seemed odd that all of those going before the presiding judge came in pairs—usually a man dressed in a handsome suit with a carnation pinned to his lapel accompanied by a woman wearing a beautiful dress and holding a bouquet.

OK. So the scene may have seemed out of the ordinary, but it wasn't necessarily uncommon.

For the last 12 years, Common Pleas Court Judge Bernard J. Goodheart, a King Cupid if you will, has joined in matrimony hundreds of lovesick couples wanting to wed on this most cherished of days—St. Valentine's Day.

Yesterday was no different. More than 30 couples wanting to tie the knot came to Goodheart's courtroom on the 11th floor of the East Penn Square Building in Center City [Philadelphia] to do just that.

The first couple was joined in holy matrimony at 11:45 a.m. and the long assembly line of lovers didn't end until about 2:30 p.m., when the last couple kissed and marched arm in arm from the courtroom.

It was definitely a day to remember, and Goodheart didn't let any couple walk away from his bench without dispensing a few words of wisdom.

"You are each separate individuals. You were each raised in different homes with different families and different values. So don't try to impose yourself on one another because nobody likes to be told what to do," the judge would say over and over again throughout the day to the parade of brides and grooms.

Afterward, Goodheart would stick a small, bright red Valentine heart on each of their marriage certificates and bid them farewell. As the couples would make their way to the elevators, the band would strike up such tunes as "Love Is a Many Splendored Thing," "All the Things You Are," "Make Someone Happy" and "My Funny Valentine".

The band, the Reading Terminals, included city Housing Director Edward A. Schwartz on keyboards, Common Pleas Court Judge Richard B. Klein on drums, architect Herman DeJong on bass and surgeon David Reiter on guitar. The group has played previously for Goodheart on Valentine's Day.

"By doing 30 some weddings in a day, we fill out our quota for the entire year," said Schwartz, the band-leader.

The music and Goodheart's words of wisdom provided just the right touch to make the ceremony special for everybody.

"We didn't want to have a big church wedding," said Isabella O'Brien, 46, who had just married Dominic Pugliese, 29. The couple, who live in the Tacony section of Philadelphia, had been dating for six years and decided to make it official.

The bride wore a laced white blouse with hot-red slacks, while the groom wore his "Pat Boone outfit"—a red sweater with lily-white slacks and a pair of spotless, white leisure shoes. The couple looked more dressed for a Valentine's Day party than for a wedding.

When asked why they chose Valentine's Day to wed, Pugliese simply replied: "Why not? This is the best day of the year to get married."

Source

Philadelphia Inquirer, February 15, 1988. From an article by staff writer Sergio R. Bustos.

* * *

Judge Goodheart Reties the Knot

It's been a Valentine's Day tradition for 14 years now with Judge Bernard J. Goodheart, and yesterday [February 14, 1990] he again lived up to his name, joining couples in matrimony in his Common Pleas courtroom on the 11th floor of the East Penn Square Building [Philadelphia]. Among those enlisting his services on Cupid's day were Frank and Jeanne Matise of South Philadelphia, who were retying the knot after divorcing in 1986.

Source

Caption for a photo feature in the *Philadelphia Inquirer*, February 15, 1990.

Valentine's Day Massacre and Its Ghosts

Sixty years ago today [February 14, 1989], machine-gun fire echoed from a garage in a Near North Side neighborhood [of Chicago] and seven members of George "Bugs" Moran's gang fell dead.

The St. Valentine's Day Massacre was the Prohibition era's goriest crime and the beginning of the end of gangster rule.

Now Prohibition is dead and the garage is gone, but the memories live on for some Chicago residents who vividly recall when "gangland graduated from murder to massacre," as news accounts of the day put it.

A home for the elderly borders the site, and residents say their parking lot is on the very spot where the seven fell. Some residents believe the gangsters' ghosts still walk.

"I'd be sitting on my reclining chair and hear things moving around … knives and forks clanging together…. I'd hear someone go out the door," said Madeline Bushbaum, 84, who lived in the neighborhood at the time of the massacre.

"We always figured it was the dead ones looking for the ones that killed 'em," said Bushbaum, a resident of the Lincoln Park Senior Center who has moved out of the room closest to the murder site. "I don't hear 'em anymore, but several people moved out of the building because they said they were disturbed."

At the time of the massacre, "Scarface" Al Capone, leader of Near South Side bootlegging operations, wanted Moran's territory up north.

On the morning of Feb. 14, 1929, four men—two wearing police uniforms—raided Moran's garage headquarters. They lined the men up against the wall as if for a routine frisk for weapons, and instead riddled their bodies with a hail of gunfire that almost severed limbs of some of the victims.

Bushbaum, then a 24-year-old evening telephone operator, was playing pool with the guys in the back room of Drake Braithwaite undertakers, about three blocks from the scene, where she worked from time to time.

"While we were playing, the garage door flew open and there were the coppers and the paddy wagon," she recalled.

"They brought in two bodies on two slabs and just slid 'em off on the floor and said, 'We gotta go back, we got five more dead out there!'…

Moran, who was not at his headquarters that day, later told police: "Only the Capone gang kills like that."

Authorities never proved a Capone connection, and the massacre still is listed in police files as "murder by persons unknown."

Source

Philadelphia Inquirer, February 14, 1989. By Sheri Prasso of the Associated Press.

* * *

Safe Sex for Valentine's Day

America flirted with Valentine's Day this year with traditional weddings, flowers and a not-so-traditional barrage of warnings about AIDS and safe sex.

In the nation's capital, a florist capitalized on the acquired immune deficiency syndrome epidemic with the "Safe Sex Bouquet," a dozen roses spiced with baby's breath and a dozen condoms.

And some 10,000 Valentine cards containing condoms were distributed at bars across Connecticut to mark "National Condom Week."

On the business side, a survey of New York state florists shows the average price for a Valentine's Day gift of a dozen long-stemmed roses was $59.25—$17 more than three weeks ago.

Source

Providence Sunday Journal, February 14, 1988. From a series of features compiled from wire reports in the "People" section.

College Students Flunk on Origins of Valentine's Day

If all goes as planned, Valentine's Day will be celebrated this coming Sunday. Some may be excited. Some may be depressed. How many know why we are celebrating in the first place? Where did this ambiguous holiday come from?

"Either from the French or the English," offered a pensive sophomore, "the French I think." Right hemisphere, wrong answer.

"I'd guess Italy," stated one junior, placing us on the right track.

A senior, scratching his head thoughtfully tried, "I used to know the story. Something to do with a guy named Valentino, I forget his first name." We are getting close.

"Probably has something to do with the Middle Ages," guessed another junior. He guessed correctly, but not completely.

"It's on the 14th. I have no clue where it came from," said one senior, obviously not losing sleep over his lack of historical knowledge.

Source

The Good 5¢ Cigar, February 12, 1988. Students at the University of Rhode Island were interviewed by Angela Boffi, Assistant News Editor of the university daily.

Paul Bunyan Ball
Mid-February

The legendary Paul Bunyan is largely the creation of an advertising man, W. B. Laughead, who fleshed out a few lumbermen's jokes and allusions into full-blown tall tales and published them for promotional reasons in a trade journal. Even though by birth Bunyan might not be an entirely legitimate folk hero, he is certainly one of the most popular, endearing himself to lumberjacks, chambers of commerce, and generations of children. For forestry students in a state famous for its logging industry, he is accepted as a kind of secular patron saint.

Paul Bunyan College "Formal"

Old Paul, Paul Bunyan, the patron saint of all lumberjacks, who, according to legend, had an irreconcilable aversion to the society of women, might not have looked with favor on the "formal" dance staged in his honor by the Michigan Foresters, Friday, November 20, [1943], in the Michigan Union Ballroom. But, Old Paul, being a true American, would probably have consented wholeheartedly to the dance had he known that one couple received a grand prize of two United States War Bonds.

But if he had been here to object, he would have found himself a minority of one, for everybody who could get a ticket was on hand when Bill Sawyer's orchestra swung into the first number and the "would-be-lumberjacks" began dancing. Paul Bunyan and Babe, his great blue ox, attended the dance in person and both stood silently at one end of the ballroom, towering above the surrounding pines. Paul's huge ax hung directly above the band stand. Carefree informality prevailed throughout the entire evening.

This was not the first Paul Bunyan "Formal." 1938 saw the beginning of this campus favorite. It started as a barn dance at the Saline Valley Farms with only a small group of Foresters attending. The following year the real Paul Bunyan "Formal" was started....

Informality prevailed unanimously at the dance. Nearly every person wore a plaid shirt, and levis were far more common than pants. Girls wore slacks or old skirts; one lumber jill even came attired in a skirt made of burlap. Bill Sawyer gladly agreed to dress the entire orchestra just as informally as the dancers so that none of the Paul Bunyan atmosphere would be lost.

From 9 'til 12, dancers swayed gayly to fox trots and waltzes, jitterbugged, and had a grand la conga line. Everyone left the ballroom feeling that it had been an evening well spent. Praises for the dance were many. Bill

Sawyer, who leads the campus' most popular band, said, "The Paul Bunyan 'Formal' is the most popular dance of the year."

After a lapse of ten years SNR [School of Natural Resources, University of Michigan] students this winter [February 16, 1979] revived an old School tradition, the Paul Bunyan Ball. The Natural Resources Club and the committee in charge did such a good job that its success rivaled that of any of its predecessors.

Led by "Bull of the Woods" Doug Boor and an active committee, the old format of the ball was thoroughly researched and in many cases followed. The affair was held in the Michigan Union Ballroom with an adjacent room for a cider bar and School displays.

The ballroom, decorated with Douglas fir trimmings (*Pseudotsuga menziesii* to the initiated) from Stinchfield Woods, held a massive sculpture of Paul Bunyan built from the ground up. Local merchants and restaurants contributed so many prizes, through committee urging, that contests were held throughout the evening to give them away. Very popular was a continuous Jack-and-Jill sawing event.

The main program was square dancing. The beginners were given a short instructional period before a full-size country band appeared on the scene. A jug band supplied intermission entertainment with conventional dancing at the evening's end.

Source and Comment

Michigan Forester Yearbook, 1943, 19, 21; *School of Natural Resources News,* University of Michigan, 1979, 4.

Clippings and background information supplied by John Carow, Professor Emeritus, School of Natural Resources, University of Michigan, who writes: "For the last two years we have not tried any so-called round dancing. It has been all square dancing.... As in earlier years there are a lot of displays and activities going on in other rooms besides the dance floor and we have had an ongoing sawing contest with male and female partners at one end of the dance floor that has attracted up to 100 pairs of sawyers... My experience has shown that there is a revival of some of the old-time college traditions such as dancing and fraternity living, so that I look for a long continued success of this school's Paul Bunyan Ball."

For additional background and tales of Paul Bunyan, including an account of a "Paul Bunyan Winter Carnival" formerly held at Bemidji, Minnesota, see *Parade of Heroes,* 485-97.

Leap Year Day

February 29

The Earth takes five hours and forty-eight minutes longer than 365 days to complete its cycle of the sun. Consequently, "leap days" have been incorporated into the Gregorian calendar to accommodate this discrepancy. Such intercalary days are added once every four years at the end of February, and they have evoked superstition, humor and confusion in popular tradition. February 29 is also known as "Ladies' Day," because of the tradition that women are free to propose marriage on that day, and as "St. Oswald's Day" after a tenth-century archbishop of York who died on February 29, 992.

Leap Day

Well, it has happened again. The Earth has circled four times around the sun, astronomers have designated this a leap year and anxious bachelors won't answer their telephones until midnight.

It's Leap Year Day—the one day in four years when, by ancient custom, shy women may propose marriage. For women who have been wanting to pop The Big Question to the dawdling men of theirs—or who simply want to ask that hunk in algebra class out for a milkshake—now's the time....

But sometime back in the Middle Ages women indeed acquired the "privilege" of proposing marriage during a leap year. In 1288 the Scottish Parliament even codified the tradition with a law that read: "For [each] year known as lepe yeare, any maiden ladye of both highe and lowe estait shall hae liberte to bespeke ye man she like." If he refused to make her his wife, he was fined one pound, "except ... he can make it appear that he is betrothed to another woman."...

Since leap year is the result of man's efforts to adjust the calendar to the movements of the sun, it is not surprising that it is known in folklore as a disruption of the natural order.

Source

Philadelphia Inquirer, February 29, 1984. From a feature article by David O'Reilly, staff writer.

Job's Birthday

February 30

Job, whose story is told in the Old Testament, lived in the land of Uz. A God-fearing man, he was rich and happy. However, Satan claimed that Job loved God only because God had been good to him. So God decided to test Job. He saw to it that Job's cattle were stolen, his servants and possessions destroyed, and his children killed. Although his wife urged him to think of God as evil and although he himself had doubts, he remained faithful, repenting his doubts and gaining God's forgiveness. God rewarded him for his faith in the end, and Job lived happily for many years after his misfortunes. The Book of Job is considered one of the literary masterpieces of the Bible.

Job's Birthday Prayer

Negroes [in Maryland c. 1925] say that Job's birthday was February 30th, but that his sufferings were so great, he prayed to have that date blotted out of the calendar, and his prayer was answered.

"Let the day perish wherein I was born.... Let it not be joined until the days of the year; let it not come into the number of the months." (Job 3:3 & 6)

Source

Memoirs of the American Folklore Society, XVIII (1925), 115. "Folk-Lore from Maryland," collected by Annie W. Whitney and Caroline C. Bullock. Data on informants incomplete. Cf. Motif A 1161 on losing days in February.

Shrove Tuesday or Mardi Gras
Moveable: February-March

Shrove Tuesday immediately precedes Ash Wednesday and is the last day before Lent. Also called *Fastnacht* (German: Eve of Fast), *Mardi Gras* (French: Fat Tuesday), and Carnival, it has been noted for the elaborate mumming parades and boisterous parties that characterize its celebration in New Orleans, Trinidad, France and Italy. The name comes from the custom of "shriving" or purification through confessing one's sins prior to Lent. The holiday is related to the coming of a New Year. In England, while football games were played on Shrove Tuesday, ritualistic contests embodying the conflict between winter and summer, darkness and light, death and rebirth. Traditional food for this holiday includes thick soups of pig's feet, beans, peas, and pancakes. In fact "Pancake Day" is another name for Shrove Tuesday. Carnival season begins on Twelfth Night and ends at midnight on Mardi Gras.

Mardi Gras: New Orleans

Around 1820 a group of Creole youths, returning to New Orleans from Paris, decided to liven things up in the continental style with masked processions of substantial size. They appeared in the streets in every variety of costume while women leaned over galleries to throw roses and bonbons.

In 1857, the date usually given as the beginning of the Mardi Gras, a new organization was formed. It was to present a parade with floats and torchlights. The organization called itself "The Mystick Krewe of Comus," and it put on a parade of two floats—one carrying a king, the other showing Satan in a blazing hell. Since that time only major conflicts have interfered, the Spanish American War not having been considered "major."

Mardi Gras owes its present day exuberance to a twenty-two year old Russian Grand Duke, who was present only by chance. In 1872 Alexis Alexandrovich Romanov, brother to the Tsar's heir apparent, was in America traveling. While in New York he became enamoured of an actress, Lydia Thompson, who was then appearing in "Bluebeard." As she sang the song "If Ever I Cease to Love," Alexis found himself completely lost to her charms. He trailed her on a tour south, and caught up with her in New Orleans. It was almost Mardi Gras and when the local inhabitants discovered a real Grand Duke was to be among them, they sat up and took notice. A new Carnival krewe was being planned and the project was elaborated.

A new king was named—Rex, Lord of Misrule. An official holiday was announced and street maskers were bidden to form a united procession. Carnival colors were chosen—

purple, green, and gold. At the City Hall a thronelike chair was erected for Alexis.

Alexis arrived on the scene and the parade ensued. Since all the bands knew of his great liking for the song "If Ever I Cease to Love," band after band played it. The song has remained an integral part of Mardi Gras.

Alexis Alexandrovich had helped to fix the pattern that Mardi Gras would thenceforth follow: official holiday, Rex, and "If Ever I Cease to Love" as its song.

At the present time the number of krewes had increased to encompass nearly every conceivable group of people, from common work interests to nationality groups. The krewe captain is unpaid for his labor but wields vast influence. One of his major responsibilities is the preparation of the krewe's annual parade. Work begins for the next year at the close of the current season. The captain also chooses the king for the krewe. It must be a person of some wealth for he must provide his own costume, jeweled train, and accessories, give suppers and parties, buy presents for the queen and her maids, meet a hundred obligations.

The men rather than the women rule around the Mardi Gras time. The question of who shall be chosen queen for each of the older krewes—Comus, Rex, Twelfth Night, Atlanteans, and a few others is a seriously important issue.

To be queen of one of these older krewes a girl must usually belong to the well-defined group of the season's debutantes. A man may be quite old to be king, but a girl must be chosen at the debutante stage and this leads to acute tension.

The choice of queen is governed by a number of factors: family traditions, general social standing, wealth, business affiliations, and political obligations. When a candidate's mother has been a queen it is understood that the daughter will reign in her turn. The same girl may be queen twice, or even (though rarely) three times, or she may be queen at one ball and maid at others.

Christmas is the momentous day when the news is brought (or isn't). A male friend calls with a box of roses and a scroll that bids the girl to the court.

The persons to be invited to the ball given by a particular krewe can pose a serious problem. Committees work for weeks to pass on lists sent in by krewe members, each of them being allowed a limited number of invitations. The chairman of the committee often wishes he had not been granted the honor for he has to watch women cry, has alienated friends and has made permanent enemies.

At last comes the night of the parade. The warehouses, called "dens," near South Claiborne Avenue and Calliope Street, begin to fill with members arriving to don costumes and mount floats on which each has been assigned a specific position. According to the rules no one under the influence of liquor may ride. A generous buffet supper is provided for the participants.

Bands blare along the route and slowly floats move along, their path being cleared by policemen on horses and motorcycles. As each float passes, its maskers reach into bags holding the throw-outs: beads, whistles, and other trinkets for the crowd. "Throw me something!" "Gimme something, mister!" are the cries heard as the floats move by.

The parade route leads up St. Charles Avenue to Washington or Louisiana Avenue, then down the other side of St. Charles Avenue to Canal Street and along it or into the French Quarter for its destination, the Municipal Auditorium at Beauregard Square. Here the audience moves through closely guarded doors for the approaching ball. Each person must show an invitation in his own name to be admitted.

A visitor will not see a ball unless he is a relative or good friend of a member of the organization. Certain celebrities have had arrangements made and two of the krewes, Rex and Hermes, have invitations available for out-of-towners. However, these are in considerable demand.

Inside the auditorium the participants are dividing off. An invitation entitles a guest merely to look on from a seat upstairs. But various women have received call-outs, permitting them to sit below and be called forth for dances with members of the masked krewe. Each member is allowed a limited number of call-out cards and, understandably, they are major prizes. At the beginning of each dance committee members go about calling the names and finding the faces that match them.

On the dance floor the lady pretends that she does not recognize her partner. She always receives a favor, some handsome trinket of durable value. Some gifts have been silver cigaret urns, dresser sets and silver card trays. These are engraved with the crest of the krewe and the year of the ball.

Always there is the more public part of the Carnival. The week before Mardi Gras parades multiply. Thursday and Friday two major organizations, Momus and Hermes, have night marches which all the city comes out to see. On Saturday there is a child king of the Krewe of Nor with a line of princes riding Shetland ponies, floats with older boys to pull them, and a queen awaiting His Majesty. Older monarchs stop at City Hall to toast first the Mayor, and then at one of the social clubs to toast the queen. Nor does much the same with hot chocolate or lemonade in place of champagne.

On Sunday a comparatively new organization, Venus, reverses the order: ladies wearing masks pick the king and dukes, whose names are given out while the ladies' identities supposedly remain secret. Sunday also sees Alla, King of Algiers, chugging down the river with a procession of tugs and ferries. Monday night Proteus of the Sea has his march through the streets.

Tuesday morning—Mardi Gras itself—finds the children up soon after dawn scrambling into their costumes and trying to hurry up the elders. On the streets trucks are being loaded with masked youths. Along St. Charles Avenue for 35 blocks the banquette or sidewalks are filling with early arrivals, for it is here that they will see the main parade.

The first king on the scene is Zulu from Africa. His every act is a satire on self-conscious whites and their pretensions. He wears a rabbit skin and a grass skirt. He generally arrives on the float snorting audibly. His floats are decorated with moth eaten palm trees. His knights strut in the guise of medicine men and black face Keystone cops. Zulu does not salute the Mayor, but stops to toast bars which in return give him bottles of free stuff. He visits the Japanese Tea Room in the heart of the Negro section, and his queen awaits him at the Geddes and Moss Funeral Home. Zulu has a route which is seldom followed and he may be found all day rambling through the town.

About eleven A.M. Rex, chosen by the captain of the krewe, rides out with a procession of pastel floats. Mardi Gras has reached fever pitch and one finds people dressed in all manner of costumes.

The last parade of the year, Comus, takes place in the evening of Mardi Gras. The parade passes along Orleans Street toward the auditorium. Comus prepares to alight for his own tableaux and ball. Near midnight Rex, the other king, leaves with his court to go and salute Comus, the older monarch. Following a grand march, with a promenade of the two courts, there is a supper and officially Mardi Gras ends.

Source

Wayne State University Archive, 1961. Prepared in 1961 as a research report by Marvy Evelyn Hill for a course in folklore at Wayne State University. Her informants were Mrs. R. L. Sherwood, age 55, and Mrs. M. Lemarie, age 60, both of New Orleans French background, and she cites Harnett T. Kane's *Queen New Orleans,* New York, 1949, for supportive information.

* * *

Mardi Gras

Mardi Gras Words

The Mardi Gras season in New Orleans has assumed tremendous local importance both socially and commercially, and the nature of this celebration and the traditions which surround it have given rise to a limited number of vocabulary items which fulfill its peculiar needs. 'Carnival,' to distinguish between Mardi Gras day itself and the entire period between Twelfth Night and Lent, is observed by a series of balls and parades presented by a variety of organizations which represent almost every national and social group in the city. Frequently clubs which were formed for social, fraternal, educational, or religious purposes merely assume a different name and present their balls and parades, but the majority of carnival clubs exist for the sole purpose of celebrating this holiday. The names of these organizations fail to reflect to any extent the religious origin of the festival or the Creole background of a large segment of the local population. They do, however, reveal certain patterns, the origin of which may be traced to the manner in which Mardi Gras was first observed in New Orleans.

Although the custom of masquerading on Mardi Gras was popular in New Orleans as early as the 1830s the first formal masked parade did not take place until 1857. It was presented by an organization which called itself 'The Mistick Krewe of Comus,' and it was modeled upon a club which existed in Mobile, Alabama, for the purpose of sponsoring an annual Mardi Gras parade and ball. The 'theme' or motif which the New Orleans group selected for their parade and ball was Milton's *Paradise Lost.* Apparently the name of the organization was suggested by Milton's mask, 'Comus,' and the line from 'L'Allegro' in which the poet calls upon Mirth to 'admit me of thy crew.' However, the origin of the name of this and many other carnival organizations is uncertain because of the strict secrecy which surrounds their membership and the significance of their ceremonials.

With the passage of the years, the parades and balls have become highly formalized. The usual parade consists of some fifteen or twenty floats illustrating a particular theme, interspersed with bands and the mounted royalty of the carnival club. The parade is followed by a ball which also conforms to a traditional pattern. It begins with a series of 'tableaux' and the presentation of the queen and her court. Special dances reserved for members of the club and their partners follow. Afterward there is general dancing.

The following is a list of words and phrases associated with the Mardi Gras parades and balls in New Orleans:

Call out: One of several dances reserved for the masked members of the carnival organization and their partners; an invitation to participate in such a dance.

Call out boxes: A previously designated section of the ballroom in which guests of the club who are to participate in call outs are seated.

Call out favor: A souvenir gift presented by a member of the carnival organization to his partner following each call out.

Captain: The master of ceremonies and general manager of a carnival ball and parade. He is a permanent official in contrast to the king, queen, dukes, and maids who are selected annually.

Carnival court: The masked members of a carnival organization other than the king and dukes.

Carnival throw: A trinket thrown by a masker on a float to spectators at a parade. Usually pl.

Cast, to be: To be selected to participate in one of the tableaux presented at the ball or to ride on a float during the parade.

Den: The warehouse in which a carnival organization makes or stores its floats; the clubroom of the carnival organization.

Duke: An official of the carnival organization subordinate to the king.

Edicts: A series of published communications supposedly emanating from Arabia which reveal the progress of 'Rex,' Lord of Misrule, toward New Orleans. They are printed in the local newspapers for several days preceding Mardi Gras.

Go-between: One of several officials at a ball who announce the names of guests who are to participate in call outs and who escort them to the dance floor.

Krewe: Originally part of the name of the first carnival club but now a generic term for any carnival organization.

Mardygraw: A costume worn on Mardi Gras; a masker (used mainly by children).

Masker: A person who wears a costume on Mardi Gras.

Maskers' dance: A dance at a ball limited to masked members of the carnival organization.

Mister throw me something: The traditional catch phrase of spectators at a parade requesting carnival throws from the maskers on floats.

Proclamation: Same as *edict.*

Property wagon: A truck which follows the parades, containing equipment for emergency purposes.

Royal host: The king and dukes of a carnival organization, especially of 'Rex.'

Tableaux: An entertainment presented at the beginning of a ball consisting of a series of skits, scenes, or dances at which usually the queen and her maids are introduced; also, formerly, the scenes presented on parade wagons.

Theme: The motif, often from literature of history, of the costumes and design of the floats of a carnival organization at a parade and ball.

Throw outs: Same as *carnival throws.*

Truck rides: Trucks which follow the 'Rex' parade, decorated by private groups. They are organized into two processions known as the 'Krewe of Orleanians' and the 'Krewe of Crescent City.'

'The Mystick Krewe of Comus' remained the sole carnival organization until 1872 when two additional groups made their appearance, 'The Knights of Momus' and 'Rex.' The former was organized upon the pattern of 'Comus,' but the latter grew out of a movement to form a parade of all 'promiscuous maskers,' costumed individuals who were not members of a krewe, in honor of Grand Duke Alexis of Russia who was then visiting New Orleans. In 1882 a fourth carnival organization, the 'Krewe of Proteus,' was established. The selection of names derived from classical mythology and literature by the older krewes exerted a strong influence upon dozens of subsequent carnival organizations. Thus in a compilation of the names of these groups, those derived from Greek and Latin sources form the largest single category.

Another factor which seems to have reinforced the trend toward the use of names from classical sources was the themes of the early parades. In 1858 'Comus' presented a parade entitled 'Mythology.' It was followed by 'Homer's Iliad' in 1872 and 'The Metamorphoses of Ovid' in 1878. 'Rex' depicted 'The Gods of Greece' in 1878, 'Momus' gave 'Popular Myths' in 1881, and 'Proteus' presented 'The Aeneid' in 1884. It is difficult to explain why the classics rather than some other source provided names for carnival organizations and themes for parades, but it is not surprising that they did in a city which named streets for the nine Muses and has a suburb known as 'Elysian Fields.'

The largest group of krewes with names of Greek origin are those named after individual mythological figures. Examples are Adonis, Apollo, Eros, Hera, Hermes, Iris, Nereus, and Prometheus. Another group was named after Grecian cities, races, and geographical areas. Examples include the Achaeans, Athenians, Corinthians, and Dorians. Krewes were also named after Orpheus and Eurydice, and Naiads, and the Argonauts. Only one personage from Greek history, Pericles, provided the name for a krewe. Among the figures from Latin mythology who provided names for krewes are Consus, Diana, Fortuna, Janus, Jupiter, and Venus.

A second category of carnival clubs chose names of actual or apparent Arabic or Near Eastern origin. This choice can also be traced to influences in the early history of the krewes. The first appearance of 'Rex' was heralded by a series of 'edicts' and 'proclamations' colored by pseudo-Arabic terms and titles, and ostensibly emanating from Arabia. They caught the popular fancy, and the custom of issuing 'edicts' couched in simulated Arabic terms has persisted to the present day. The 'Rex' parade was headed by a mounted escort disguised as Arabs, who created something of a sensation at the time.

Arabic themes for parades and balls were also utilized at an early date. 'Rex' presented 'The Arabian Nights' in 1881, 'Proteus' gave 'A Dream of Egypt' in 1882, and 'Momus' depicted 'The Moors in Spain' in 1883. The original purpose of the selection of Arabic and Near Eastern themes, guises, and language was probably to create an air of the mysterious and the exotic.

Examples of names inspired by this trend are the krewes of 'Alhambra,' 'Moslem,' 'Omarez,' and 'The Caliphs of Cairo.' An interesting manifestation of the Arabic influence are the krewes of 'Alla,' 'Grela,' and 'Jeffla.' Though a conscious effort seems to have been made to produce an Arabic effect, these names were actually formed by taking the first syllable of the suburb in which the members of the krewes live (Algiers, Gretna, and Jefferson, respectively) and combining it with the standard abbreviation for *Louisiana.*

Several minor patterns in the names of krewes may be observed. The desire for the occult and the unusual appears to have inspired certain carnival clubs to choose names based upon the mythology and religion of the nonclassical world. Examples of this influence are the krewes of 'Mithras,' 'Osiris,' 'Thoth,' and 'Druid.' Some alliterative names exist, such as 'The Bards of Bohemia' and 'The Prophets of Persia.' Other carnival clubs selected names which combine significant initials. 'Caysee,' the carnival organization of a local chapter of the 'Knights of Columbus,' is a case in point. A small number of krewes reveal a surprising lack of imagination in their choice of a name. For example, the krewes of 'Carrollton' and 'Mid-City' are made up of men who live in those particular sections of New Orleans, and the krewe of 'Krauss' consists of employees of a department store of that name. With the exception of Shakespeare, who inspired the names of the 'Falstaffians,' 'Titanians,' and 'Elves of Oberon,' there are no examples derived from nonclassical literature. The name of only one krewe, 'Alexis,' honoring the grand duke who visited New Orleans in 1872, can be traced to a historical personage of the modern period. The source of the name of 'Zulu,' a Negro carnival organization, is obvious. . . .

The following is a list of New Orleans carnival organizations from the earliest period of their history to the present day. . . . The letter b following the name of a krewe signifies that it presented a ball during the 1950 season, and the letter p signifies that it presented a parade. Krewes without such letters following were either inactive during that season or no longer exist. In the list given below, where the names of krewes consist of one word only it can be assumed that their full name is preceded by the phrase 'Krewe of——.' Names of more than one word which do not include this phrase are given in full.

Achaeans b	Harlequins b
Adonis b p	Hera b
Alexis	Hypatians b
Alhambra b	Independent Order of the
Alla b p	Moon
Alpheus	Ir b
Alpoem	Iridis
Amphectyon	Iris b
Aparomest	Janus b
Apollo	Jefferson City Carnival
Argonauts	Club b
Athenians b	Jeffla b p
Atlantians b	Jupiter b
Arabi Carnival and Athletic	Knights of Hermes b p
Club b p	Knights of Momus b p
Babylon b p	Krauss b
Bacchus b	Laurent b
Bards of Bohemia b	Les Danseurs b
Caliphs of Cairo b	Les Marionettes b
Caronis b	Les Pierrettes
Carrollton b p	Maria b
Carthage b	Masque b
Caysee b p	Melson
Chief Choctaw b p	Mid-City b p
Children's Carnival Club b	Mistick Krewe of Comus b p
Consus	Mithras b
Corinthians b	Mittins b
Crescent City p	Mokana b
Cynthius b p	Moslem b
Diana b	Musica b
Dorians b	Mysterieuses
Druids	Mystery b
Eirene b	Mystic Club b
Eleanians b	Mystick Merrie Bellions
Electra b	Naiads b
Elves of Oberon b	Neobians b
Eros b	Nereus b
Eurydice b	Nippon
Falstaffians	Noblads
Fantasy b	Nor b
Fenasci b p	Nuss b
Fortuna b	Okeanos b p
Grela b p	Olympians b

Omardz b	Rex b p
Omarez	Sonians b
Orion	Spilka b
Orleanians	Theron b
Orpheus b	Thirdists
Osiris b	Thoth b p
Pandora b	Titanians
Pericles b	Twelfth Night Revelers b
Ploger b	Venus b p
Prometheus b	Virgilians b
Prophets of Persia b p	Yami
Proteus b p	Zulu b p
Raggio b	

In addition to the krewes there are in New Orleans a number of marching clubs organized for the purpose of participating in the Mardi Gras parades. The first of these was the 'Phorty Phunny Phellows' which followed the 'Rex' parade of 1878 but no longer exists. The oldest marching club still functioning [in 1950] is the 'Jefferson City Buzzards,' founded in 1890. In contrast to the more or less unorganized groups which appear sporadically and sponsor truck rides, the marching clubs are highly organized and actually march in the parades. Their costumes, like those of 'Zulu,' frequently tend toward the extravagant, the satiric, and the ridiculous. The names of the marching clubs are often alliterative and usually indicate the part of the city in which the members reside.

The following is a partial list of New Orleans Mardi Gras marching clubs:

Bourbon Street Bounders	Jolly Boys and Girls
Eleanore [street] Club	Gentilly [suburb] Gents
Garden District Carnival	Phorty Phunny Phellows
Club	Royal Street Revelers
Gay Fourteen	Royal Street Rounders
Jefferson City Buzzards	

Source

American Speech, XXVI (1951), 110-15. Collected and discussed by Hennig Cohen from printed sources, 1857-1950, including newspaper files, city histories, guidebooks, and Mardi Gras programs and memorabilia in the Tulane University library.

* * *

Mardi Gras

An 1890s Parade in New Orleans

While Evie and I were helping the younger boys put on the red devil Mardi Gras suits we had made them, adjusting the stick-up horns and the long tails stuffed with cotton, we lectured, "Now don't take candy from maskers, or cookies either. They might be poisoned. Don't go anywhere with anybody you don't know even if they are wearing girls' pink dominos and bells and curly wigs. They might be toughs out to steal you, or kidnappers wanting to hold you for ransom." I was too old to mask, I thought. We told Angy, who wore a crepe-paper dress, that she must stay near home and not talk to maskers. Soon groups of maskers began strolling along the banquette [sidewalk]. The boys and Angy ran out yelling, "Moddy Graw, chickle-a-paw, catch me behind the street caw."

The maskers chased them into the yard and down the alley, tapping them lightly with their canes. . . . But the great day did seem tame. . . especially since we had not been given an invitation to ride down the river on a launch to meet King Rex (the Lord of Misrule) the day before and to accompany him to the city where he would receive from the Mayor the great key to New Orleans and thus take possession. It was worth going to the parade just to see some of our mean and unattractive neighborhood boys, who had joined the Washington Artillery, in neat uniforms and white gloves. Some rode on heavy cannons, arms folded, eyes staring at the horses' tails. Their self-importance and exaggerated dignity looked so silly that we girls had a bad case of giggles while they passed. They pretended not to see us. . . .

The city had done everything possible to make the celebration alluring, hoping that thousands would lose their fear and flock in to help relieve the financial distress of the Queen of the Gulf. Mama and Evie had volunteered to help serve lunch in a store building on Canal Street, the proceeds to be used for tuning the church organ. Mrs. Lever, a neighbor, did not want to see the parade so she stayed with the two youngest children while Papa took the rest of us to the big show.

We found a place that was not crowded in front of a large house on Saint Charles Avenue. I stood on the edge of the banquette beside two Negro women and kept an eye on Bub and Roy who had pushed into the street in front of the crowd.

We had not been waiting long when mounted policemen began clearing the way for the parade, ramming their horses into the crowd, pushing them back to the banquette. The boys fled in terror to grab hold of Papa's pants' legs when a big black horse, teeth bared, eyes fiery, almost trampled them with his steel-shod hooves. They did not recover from their terror until a huge float came along bearing the great Rex beef. The red steer calmly chewed his cud and gazed into space. He was so fat that there was hardly room on the float for the make-believe butchers who danced around him with knives and cleavers poised threateningly.

The front gallery of the house near which we stood was packed with richly dressed people—satins and velvets, expensive furs, the bouncing long plumes on picture hats, the dazzle of diamond rings and breast pins in the morning sun. Someone mentioned that the principal of a popular business college lived there.

The float, bearing the gorgeous King of the Carnival, stopped in front of us. Rex rose from his lofty golden chair and bowed low to the ladies on the gallery behind us, his hand on his heart. They laughed happily, waved handkerchiefs, and threw kisses. A Negro man in full evening dress came out of the gate bearing a bucket full of ice in which several bottles reposed. A ladder was placed against the

float. The old servant climbed it, handed the king a silver goblet, uncorked a bottle with a loud pop, and poured the sizzling liquid into the goblet, holding the bottle with a napkin that looked alarmingly white against his black hand. The King drank to everyone on the gallery, kissing the rim of his goblet and extending it toward each lady. When he had drunk all he wanted, he sat down again and handed the Negro a fist full of jewelry—broaches, bracelets, strings of pearls—and indicated with his scepter the lady he wished to receive the gift.

A chilly wind was blowing, and the other men on the float had to dance vigorously in their gauzy butterfly costumes to keep warm. It was hard for us to realize that the dainty masked creatures, the fairies, the dragon flies, were staid businessmen of the city, bankers, lawyers, merchants, politicians—men with wives and children, probably grandchildren.

Finally the ladder was taken away, and the white-swathed Negro men who walked beside the plumed white-shrouded horses gave each a jerk. Rex's float began to move, the King waving his scepter to the crowd and throwing strings of beads and shiny jewelry, for which the crowd scrambled boisterously. Rex looked right at me and threw a diamond necklace that looked real, but a big Negro woman pushed me aside and caught it. I wanted to fight about it, but Papa pulled me away.

I watched one splendid float after another go by, each seeming more gorgeous than its predecessor. Could the night parades be any more magical than this dazzling shine and color? I had always thought they were, with their flaring rows of jets held up by Negroes lighting the floats, and the green and red torches sending a fairyland glow on the dancers and the dragons, the jewels and the satins of the whimsically designed floats, pulled along by ghost horses shrouded in white with only their eyes showing through the tape-bound holes.

The bands kept up their drumming, people waved handkerchiefs, and children and Negroes laughed and shouted at the antics of bands of comic maskers riding in decrepit wagons or threading through the crowds on the banquette. As one float approached, someone near me remarked that it took a whole year to design and build a Mardi Gras pageant, but in every parade I had always found one float so breathtaking that I was sure just the planning of it must have taken ages.

Suddenly the strains of "If Ever I Cease to Love" sprang like zigzag lightning from the thunder clouds of drumming. A float was passing, so ethereal and lovely that it seemed to lift me away from the crowd, to thrill me almost to unconsciousness and waft me away in a state of suspension among the stars of the universe which the float revealed. I gasped, "I've got to see it again," and started down the street; but, held back by the pushing crowd, I could not catch up.

The boys begged Papa to take us to Canal Street. "I wanta see that big beef cow," said Roy. "I wanta be there when the butchers bang down with the cleavers." Explanations that he would not see the butchers kill the steer did no good, but Papa took us to Canal Street anyway. With hundreds of others we rushed to a line of waiting street cars and pushed and squirmed until we were on the back platform of one of them. Someone snatched the tail from Bub's red devil suit, and Angy's pink domino was torn and her mask knocked off. With maskers hanging onto the back of the car we proceeded so slowly that the parade almost caught up with us on its trip down the other side of Saint Charles Avenue.

We found a place to stand on the neutral ground [traffic island] opposite the Boston Club just as the policemen on their charging horses began pushing the frightened people back. The club had built a well-propped balcony over the banquette. It jutted out from its second story, the rows of tiered seats, reaching to the edge of the street. It was packed with richly dressed people, and in the front row sat the beautiful Queen of the Carnival and her attendants. Evie had said she was sure the lovely creature was the older sister of one of her school friends whom she sometimes visited.

The boys again exclaimed over the monster steer chewing his cud so calmly amid the excitement. The King's float stopped just in front of the Queen. His high throne was on a level with her seat so that he could toast her, drinking from a golden goblet, and present her with gorgeous jewels on a white velvet pillow. There was much bowing and waving and presenting of jewel boxes and other gifts before in a flurry of throwing kisses the float moved on.

Accompanying many of the floats were courtiers or attendants on horseback. Masked and gaily dressed, they rode spirited steeds trained to dance to the lively music. They were costumed like rich lords and nobles of the long ago. Following all that magnificence and dignity, came the riff-raff parade: masked roisterers drinking from bottles, turning somersaults and doing monkey-shines, riding mules decked with frying pans and pots; burros bucking their riders off joyfully; droves of maskers, some riding in old wagons playing banjos and beating pans; carts drawn by billy goats that chased children—all doing their best to make the watchers double up with laughing.

I felt sad as I watched those marvelous floats disappear and pass out of my life forever. . . . Those amazing floats were what I would always remember. I decided that if I ever got to heaven and someone there asked me what reward I wanted, I'd tell him, "Just let all the Mardi Gras parades I've ever seen come back, and let me sit quietly and watch them moving through some uncrowded street."

Source

Louisiana History, VI (1965), 196-202. From a series of "New Orleans Scenes" remembered by Marion Sherrard Oneal, who was born in the 1880s in Alabama and shortly thereafter moved to New Orleans.

* * *

Mardi Gras

Mardi Gras Indians

It's 7:00 A.M. on Mardi Gras morning, and already a crowd is beginning to gather outside the H & R Bar, on Dryades Street in uptown New Orleans. The H & R is home base for the Wild Magnolias, one of about twenty tribes of Mardi Gras Indians who parade throughout the neighborhoods of Black New Orleans on Mardi Gras day. Nearby, another crowd has gathered outside the house of Bo Dollis, Big Chief of the Wild Magnolias, who has not yet appeared in all his regal splendor. Other members of the tribe are present however, strutting and prancing and having their picture taken with the family in their "new suits." There are perhaps twenty members of the tribe, each in a different, but equally impressive, costume. A jam begins in the middle of the street with one of the Indians leading off with *Big Chief Died on the Battlefront.* A crowd gathers around the singer and begins to beat out the rhythm on tambourines, beer cans, pots, and adjacent automobiles. A car full of revelers headed for the "other Mardi Gras" downtown pulls into the street, tries to get through the crowd, and finally turns off the motor in disgust. He knows he's in Indian territory on Mardi Gras and will proceed when they're ready to move and not before. Shortly, however, there's a commotion outside the Big Chief's house as he emerges, resplendent in a magnificent array of orange and yellow ostrich plumes, ready to lead his tribe through the streets in search of a confrontation with some of the downtown tribes. Suddenly, a parade seems to form, as the Wild Magnolias begin moving down the street. Spy Boys and Flag Boys out front are followed by the Wild Man, the Trail Chiefs, the Queen and her attendants, then finally the Big Chief, Bo Dollis, who sings to an intricate accompaniment:

Chief: The Indians are coming.
Response: Two-way pa-ka-way.
Chief: The Indians are coming.
Response: Two-way pa-ka-way.
The Big Chief is coming.
The Wild Magnolias are coming. . .

As the Indians move off down the street, the whole crowd begins moving with them, singing and dancing along with the music. Unlike most other parades, there is little or no distinction here between the marchers and the crowd, or second line, as they are known locally, other than the costumes. Mardi Gras is the Indians' day in their community and everyone turns out to admire them and join the celebrating.

The parade goes on for seven or eight hours, covering several miles, weaving throughout the neighborhoods' streets, with frequent stops at local taverns to wet throats along the way and occasional run-ins with other tribes, replete with elaborate ritual. Eventually, the parade ends up back at the H & R where the Indians shed their suits and party till the wee hours.

No one is quite sure how or when the Mardi Gras Indians got their start. An educated guess seems to be about 1880, since by the turn of the century there were numerous tribes going through the Black district on Mardi Gras day. At that time, the more prominent chiefs of the tribes were feared and respected members of their community; violence was not uncommon when uptown and downtown tribes met each other in the streets, and the best-known chiefs were those who had killed or maimed the most enemies. Early costumes were not nearly as elaborate as today's are. Standard materials for decoration were bottle caps, glass, and colored egg shells....

Usually, four or five months of rehearsal are involved in preparing for the masking on Mardi Gras. Every Sunday, from October until Mardi Gras, a tribe will assemble in its home bar to practice the songs and dances they will later perform in costume. One corner of the room is reserved for the musicians who play drums, tambourines, rattles, and just about anything else that produces a percussive sound, including beer bottles, cans, spoons, and the juke box. On the dance floor, intensity builds as the songs progress, some lasting as long as half an hour at a stretch. Members of a tribe always gather at the same bar, although the Big Chiefs may go visiting within the uptown or downtown tribes, occasionally even visiting a rival group.

Since WWII, there has been steady movement away from violence and towards elaborate costuming as the competitive criterion among the Indians. Every year, each tribe makes new costumes according to a set color scheme, kept secret as long as possible. The suits are worn on Mardi Gras day, St. Joseph's Day, and then dismantled. Only the elaborate beadwork pictures or patches are left intact to be included in future costumes. In the last few years a few of the Indian tribes have also worn their suits to appear at festivals including the New Orleans Jazz and Heritage Festival and the National Folk Festival. Crowns and suits are designed and made by the men who wear them, and are decorated with beaded pictures of Indian heroes, wild animals, birds, flowers, and geometric designs. Glass beads are used as well as sequins, velvet, rhinestones, maribou, lace, and ribbon. The crowns are elaborately decorated and topped with voluminous ostrich plumes costing $75 a pound. When finished, the average costume will represent an investment of over $1000 and could weigh upwards of 100 pounds.

The influence and significance of the costuming and ritual is as obscure as the origins of the Indians themselves. Personally, I feel the tradition is much closer to the *Carnival* costumes and celebrations of the West Indies and Latin America than it is an attempt to mimic the American Indian of the Old West. The Indies were closely allied to New Orleans during the slave trade of the 18th and 19th centuries. Oddly enough, the most striking parallel in costuming traditions in the United States would probably be the Philadelphia Mummers, also neighborhood social clubs, which parade in that city each New Year's Day.

The structure of each tribe is rigidly fixed by tradition. There are from twenty-six to thirty members in each of about twenty tribes at present, with such exotic names as the Wild Magnolias, the Golden Eagles, the Yellow Pocahontas, the Wild Tchoupitoulas, and the Wild Squatoolas. They are strictly divided into uptown and downtown tribes, with Canal Street being the historic line of demarcation. To join a tribe, a man must know the songs, dances, and rituals, and be willing to commit himself to practice sessions and to the considerable investment in a suit. There are three Spy Boys, three Flag Boys, a Wild Man, a First, Second, and Third Trail Chief, in addition to the Big Chief himself. The Spy Boys spot oncoming tribes and signal danger. The messages are conveyed from first to third in each rank until they reach the Big Chief, who gives the signal either to stop and make way for the other tribe or to continue. If he decides to continue, the chief will lift his war lance over his head to signal a mock "war," which consists of the rival chiefs singing and dancing about their respective greatness and prowess in a face-to-face confrontation. The object of all this is to get the other chief to "humbah" or bow down and let the other pass. This rarely happens any more, as one or the other manages to yield the right-of-way without losing face.

The music and songs of Mardi Gras Indians deserve an article all by themselves.... All the songs are in the traditional African call and response pattern, with what seems to be Caribbean influence. They are passed on by oral tradition, and are topical songs for and about Indians. Many of them are used for specific purposes, such as *The Big Chief is Coming,* used to call members of the tribe together and present them to the public; *Get the Hell Out of the Way,* used to clear the streets in crowded situations; and *Big Chief Want Fire Water,* used when the chief is in need of libation after marching with the burden of his oppressive outfit. Most of the songs are common to all tribes, with a few having been made up by and reserved for the chief who composed them. Strange words whose significance is known only to Indians are not uncommon, such as "two-way, pa-ka-way" quoted earlier. There are numerous theories as to the origins of these phrases, including corruption of Louisiana Indian, African, or

Creole languages, but there is little evidence to support any of these theories.

One final word about the Indians as they relate to the New Orleans social structure and Mardi Gras in particular. They are an important part of the Black community, known and admired throughout the many neighborhoods they come from. For the most part they belong to the lower economic strata. They have never had any desire for their Mardi Gras celebration to be associated with the more famous affair taking place a few blocks away. More affluent Blacks have formed their own krewes, such as the Zulus, and in recent years a few of the liberal krewes have accepted Blacks as members. But the Mardi Gras Indians are the glittering jewels of their own people.

Source

Tradition, XVII (Winter 1978), 2. Based on the observation and investigation of Andy Wallace, a folklorist and performer.

* * *

BBC Televises Mardi Gras

The British infatuation with jazz has spilled over into Mardi Gras this year with a BBC extravaganza—four hours of live, prime-time televised Carnival debauchery to be shown worldwide on Feb. 16, Fat Tuesday.

"It's got to be one of the longest live productions BBC has ever done," said Jim Gabour, a local film maker who is coordinating the mammoth electronic feed that will ship the height of pre-Lenten madness into the homes of 400 million viewers around the globe.

More than a year's preparation has gone into the New Orleans segment, which will trade off live broadcasts with carnival celebrations in Trinidad and in Rio de Janeiro, Brazil....

Gabour said the telecast, which was turned down by U.S. affiliates because it would interrupt profitable afternoon soap operas, will be shown live that night in Britain, Europe, Africa and some parts of the Western Hemisphere.

The climax of Dionysian abandon preceding the 40-day austerity of Lent also is available for broadcast in the Soviet Union, with shortened, delayed versions scheduled for airing in Japan and Australia, Gabour said.

Source

Providence Sunday Journal, February 14, 1988. From an article in the "People" section.

* * *

Mardi Gras

Cajun Country Mardi Gras

If you want to see what old-style Cajun Mardi Gras is all about, you should go to the area around Praire Mamou or Eunice [Louisiana], right in the heart of what is called Cajun country, an area a hundred miles or so square extending from the Atchafalaya Basin to the Texas border down to the Gulf. There are perhaps a dozen towns in the area that still *courir le mardi gras* (run the Mardi Gras), with Mamou's being the biggest and best known. It features an all day street celebration with continuous live music to coincide with the traditional festivities described below. The following account is based on attendance at the Mamou, L'Anse Megre, and Eunice Mardi Gras runnings.

About 6:00 A.M., the Mardi Gras revelers start gathering at a central meeting place in their neighborhood to prepare for the day's excursion. At the Mardi Gras I've attended, several hundred people have participated. Of this group perhaps forty or fifty formed the hard core, mounted on horseback and wearing homemade costumes and masks, with some in blackface, others dressed as women or clowns. These were followed by a couple of flatbed trucks full of maskers, a truckload of musicians, then wives and families following in cars. To this day only males actively ride out on Mardi Gras, though women may tag along behind.

After an hour or so of milling around eating hot *boudin* (sausage), getting primed on beer and "trop d'antifreeze," the procession moves out and begins making the rounds of all the farms and houses in the neighborhood, led by a captain and three assistants on horseback. The captain is always a respected member of the community, someone who's capable of keeping his troup in order as the rowdiness progresses. At each house the captain, who is never masked, and who alone drinks no alcoholic beverages during the ride, dismounts, goes up to the master and mistress of the house, and asks if they will receive *les Mardi Gras* (the maskers). If the answer is "*Ouais*" (yes), as it always is, then the maskers come into the yard, clown around, and sing a haunting modal melody that is, as far as I know, unique in contemporary Cajun music.

There are minor variations in text from singer to singer, but the melody always seems to be the same....

Of course, the entire song is no longer sung at each house; instead the captain usually asks for a gift for the group. The household then obliges by offering food, usually a sack of rice, a few feet of sausage, or a chicken on the hoof, tossed in the air. Several frantic minutes ensue while some more-or-less inebriated maskers chase the fowl around the yard, finally capturing and dispatching it by whirling it over their heads with a shout of triumph—*oh, ye yie!* Once dispatched, the offering is sent back to the gathering place to become part of the evening's gumbo.

The procession continues on for several hours, sometimes covering thirty or forty miles. Between stops, the revelers consume plenty of cold beer, hot *boudin,* and dozens of boiled eggs. In Mamou, the entire procession then parades down the main street of town, where several thousand folks are gathered for the festivities, and a riotous street dance ensues.

Around five, everyone adjourns a few blocks away to the spot where a huge gumbo is being prepared from the day's catch, and the last big feast before the Lenten fast commences. Gumbo is a Cajun stew, consisting of a base of *roux* (flour browned in oil) added to a stock of water laced with onions, garlic, scallions, parsley, salt, and pepper, in which pieces of meat, poultry, or seafood are cooked. The gumbo is served over rice. Mardi Gras gumbo is traditionally a chicken gumbo. After supper comes the *bal Masque* or dance party, the final fling until Easter lifts the Lenten restrictions. By midnight, everyone has retired to their homes for some much-needed rest.

Source and Comment

Tradition, XVII (Winter 1978), 1. Andy Wallace also gives a composite description of Mardi Gras customs in the Cajun country based on his observations within recent years. Among other processions and requests for gifts are New Year's "shooters," p. 2; printer's boys, p. 21; Plough Monday mummers, p. 39; and the John Kuner Ceremony, p. 445.

* * *

Carnival in Galveston

In the old days the celebration of Mardi Gras in Galveston [Texas] took place on an extended scale, and during the 1870s the street pageants at night, as well as the tableaux and balls, were both gorgeous and brilliant, attracting thousands of visitors to the city from the interior. Before these annual demonstrations were abandoned they were the event of the year, but the financial burdens resulting from their elaborate portrayal became too heavy for the exchequer of the majority of the residents of Galveston upon whom devolved the duty of meeting them, and the custom finally fell into disuse. In this sketch it is proposed to allude briefly to some of the principal demonstrations of this character in the city, the themes portrayed and the principal persons engaged in presenting them. The first celebration took place in 1867, when a dramatic entertainment and masked ball took place in the old Turner Hall on Avenue I, near Center street now occupied by the marble works of Charles S. Ott. The dramatic entertainment was a scene from "King Henry IV," where Alvan Reed, a Justice of the Peace, who weighed 350 pounds, essayed the character of Falstaff, without padding. One of the local papers remarked that "he was certainly without padding but not without pudding, and certainly cut it fat enough." Justice Reed in his day was a noted local character and was termed by the reporters of the epoch "a prodigious judicial hogshead."...

The first time Mardi Gras was celebrated to any great extent was in 1871, when there were two night parades by separate organizations, one known as the "K.O.M." and the other as the "Knights of Myth." The former had a [procession] representing the following themes:

1. Punch and Votaries.
2. Ancient France.
3. Crusades.
4. Peter the Great and His Friends.
5. China.

After traversing the principal streets the procession entered Turner Hall, where a number of tableaux were presented, followed by "a grand ball."

The second procession, under the auspices of the "Knights of Myth," was composed of four cars, headed by a transparency bearing the legend, "Organized January, 1871," and represented:

1. Knights of Myth.
2. Pokehontas.
3. Bismarck's Grand Band.
4. Scalawag's Enemies.

This procession, after covering its route, entered the Casino Hall.... Many of the visitors from the interior were present and paid their attention to a huge bowl of champagne punch, into which some practical joker had poured a vial of croton oil. The result can better be imagined than described....

During the early '80s the custom of celebrating Mardi Gras by a grand street pageant was abandoned, the expense bearing too heavily upon those upon whom the greater portion of the burden fell. One of the last displays was by illuminated cars which traversed the principal lines of the electric roads, shortly after the installation of that system which supplanted the old "hay burners," as the mules, long the motive power, were popularly termed. The large cotton sheds, which were numerous in the old days, were used for shelter in the preparing of the illuminated floats, and there was no little degree of skill displayed in fitting them up.

Source and Comment

Galveston Daily News, August 11, 1907. "Written Especially for the News" by Ben C. Stuart, a local historian.

The carnival season and Mardi Gras, celebrated in Gulf Coast communities for generations, have always combined elements of Christian piety, folklore, social pretension, commercialism, and the capacity to adapt to the times. In Galveston, Texas, Mardi Gras pageants and processions were first dominated by community leaders, but when they could no longer bear the expense, ordinary people, in the best folk tradition, continued to hold "impromptu parades" and street revels. Then businessmen took over again, sponsoring "cotton carnivals" and reviving Mardi Gras as a civic and social festival. Meanwhile, there was a locally hallowed spring rite, "Splash Day," which signaled the opening of the beaches, and incidentally, a profitable tourist season. It eventually superseded Mardi Gras, but after one riotous celebration, it was transformed into a "shrimp festival" which features an ecumenical blessing bestowed upon the fishing fleet. It is usually held in April, but like Easter is a moveable feast.

Carnival in Galveston
Street Maskers and Cotton Carnivals

While lack of money forced the discontinuance of the mammoth parades in the late 80s, the Mardi Gras spirit was carried on by a secret organization known as the F.F.F. or Forty Funny Fellows.

This group specialized in staging impromptu parades which were participated in by thousands of maskers who filled the streets during the gala season.

Following the year 1900 the Mardi Gras events were discontinued for several years. The celebrations were gradually revived, but not on an extensive scale, backed by a strong organization, until about 1914.

In the period from 1910 to 1914 there were impromptu parades. Some fun-loving citizen or a small group would hire a band which would march around the streets. Groups of revelers in fancy costume would join in.

In 1910 the Galveston Business League announced that a plan would be worked out for Mardi Gras celebrations on an extensive scale, but records indicate this idea was not carried out to any great extent. It is believed that in this period the old cotton carnivals overshadowed attempts to put the Mardi Gras celebrations back into the picture in a big way.

In 1914, however, the old K.K.K. or Kotton Karnival Kids took over the Mardi Gras events. The name was originated by Ed Kauffman, state senator at that time from this district and secretary of the Galveston Business League.

Source

Galveston Tribune, January 30, 1932. Unsigned background article published in the magazine section "While officials of the Boosters Club are making last-minute preparations for the staging of the 1932 Mardi Gras events...."

* * *

Carnival in Galveston
King Frivolous

Mardi Gras, as it is staged in Galveston today [1924], had its premiere Feb. 19 and 20, 1917, when R. M. Tevis was crowned as King Frivolous I at the city auditorium.

The king and his two pages, E. R. Cheeseborough Jr. and R. Starloy Tevis, arrived on the launch Colonel of the United States engineering department on the morning of Feb. 19. Then followed the parade to the city hall, where the king was presented with the key to the city by Judge Lewis Fisher, then mayor. The king then went into seclusion.

The parade that night of sixteen floats, the first given as a part of Mardi Gras, depicted characters of the comic sheets.

The first children's party was held between Twenty-third and Twenty-fifth streets on Avenue J, with Miles Kirk Burton and Miss Alice Mamie Cavin as prince and princess of the affair. Dances of different kinds had been arranged and prizes were given for the best costumes in the various divisions.

The ball that night was a thing of splendor, and revealed Frank C. Briggs as the queen. Rear Admiral A. W. Grant of the United States navy was made an honorary member of the organization. The grand march that year passed in front of the royal party, instead of being led by them, as is the custom now.

The U. S. S. Columbia was in port for the celebration, and the members of her crew, along with soldiers stationed at Fort Crockett, took part in the parade.

Source

Galveston Daily News, February 23, 1924. From a daily series of historical background stories preceding the carnival season. The dynasty established by King Frivolous I reigned until well into the 1930s.

* * *

Carnival in Galveston
Splash Days and Bathing Beauties

There will be quite a bit of difference between the scantily clad bathing beauties adorning the beaches these Splash Days, May 2-6 [1957], and those well-covered ones who appear in the first bathing revue here thirty-seven years ago.

Bathing beauties paraded in revue on Galveston beaches for the first time Sunday, May 23, 1920....

The summer season in Galveston was ushered in about Easter time with Splash Day and was formally opened with the Bathing Girl Revue, an event given countrywide attention. The revue was conceded to be the "most artistic and spectacular display of feminine beauty seen anywhere in the country." It became a Galveston institution which many cities later adopted.

In 1926 the revue went even further than usual and became an international pageant held in May. Plans were made to change and improve the methods of presenting the beauties by the sponsors, the Galveston Beach Association, Chamber of Commerce and Merchants Association.

A tremendous publicity campaign began to attract the interest of the nation to Galveston and its beauty show and beaches. Managing Director Willett L. Roe put wheels in motion for the campaign.

A card printed in six colors of oils, showing a bathing beauty riding an aquaplane, and with inserts of beauties from Mexico and Canada, was one of the advertising methods adopted. These cards were sent to city ticket offices of every railroad running into Galveston. The railroads cooperated in every way possible.

Trailers showing scenes of former revues, both in motion picture and slide form, were sent to more than 100 theaters. And a newspaper advertising campaign was carried on in every major city in the Southwest....

It was assured that women of high moral standing as well as physical attraction would be present by a rule making it necessary for all contestants to be elected by contests conducted in home cities and sponsored by the chamber of commerce or other reliable agency.

Willett Roe announced that this contest was the "first beauty contest ever staged with an International feature" and "the first contest where the four essentials of beauty of face, grace, perfection of figure and personal charm will be considered equally by the judges."

The old Venus De Milo standards of judging were to be discarded in favor of modern standards. Ned Wayburn, then famous Broadway theatrical man and Ziegfeld follies producer, assured this when he accepted the chairmanship of the board of judges for the first international pageant.

The 40 cities, Mexico and Canada sent entries from large contests conducted in their areas. Their candidates were introduced to the pageant committee by telegrams and letters saying they were sending "sure winners who had captivated their city or nation."

And the entries were sent to Galveston in high style.

The Omaha Daily News, in connection with the trip to Galveston of Miss Omaha, arranged a "sunny South Special" to run over the Missouri Pacific Lines with stops in Hot Springs National Park, New Orleans, and other points of interest. A fare of $49.95 for the 2950 mile round-trip was charged. All along the route the special picked up entries and parties from other cities.

Miss New Orleans was sent in a special train with a large illuminated picture of her on glass displayed on the observation platform. Huge banners on each side of the cars announced the purpose of the trip and the name of the beauty inside....

The pageant, witnessed by 150,000, was climaxed with the elaborate coronation of Miss Universe, chosen after a final judging of the girls in evening gowns and bathing suits.

The first Miss Universe, Miss Catherine Moylan, Miss Dallas, received the grand prize of $2000 in gold and a "beautiful and valuable plaque suitably inscribed."

Source

Galveston Tribune, April 25, 1957. Feature story by Ann Abshier, staff writer.

Carnival in Galveston
Blessing the Galveston Shrimp Fleet

Galveston's first "Blessing of the Shrimp Fleet" as a Splash Days event Saturday seemed to have won the hearts and captured the imagination of hundreds of spectators.

Clergymen of three faiths blessed 65 shrimping boats in Galveston Ship Channel at Pier 20 in a two-hour ceremony.

The Rev. Lionel T. DeForrest, rector, Grace Episcopal church; the Rev. A. Daregas, pastor of the Assumption of the Virgin Mary Greek Orthodox church, and the Rev. Walter Montondon, assistant pastor of St. Mary's Cathedral, each blessed the gaily decorated vessels in the language of the respective churches—English, Greek and Latin.

The three clergymen, wearing vestments identified with the respective churches, were accompanied by acolytes carrying flags, crosses, candles, fans and other symbols of the churches....

The U.S. Coast Guard directed traffic in the channel as the shrimp boats formed a graceful and colorful aquatic procession as they passed before the clergymen to be blessed.

Source

Galveston Daily News, April 29, 1962. By staff writer Kitty Kendall.

* * *

Carnival in Galveston
Parade of the Shrimp Boats

The blessing of the fleet is carried out in both a serious and festive manner. Commercial and private boat owners and their immediate relatives hold strongly to the religious significance of the blessing. But they also take an active part in competition for the most elaborately decorated boat.

Preparations for the event begin weeks in advance when boat crews and family members secretly plan and produce the decorative themes for their crafts. Not until the morning of the blessing are the boats' full dress unveiled. It is only then that the pre-made adornments are brought from under wraps at home and taken down to the pier and lashed onto the boats.

Drab commercial vessels are transformed within hours into vibrantly colorful and fanciful arks done up in crepe paper, banners, flags, balloons and theme stylizations. Private yachts, sailboats, motorboats and inshore trawlers become floating mirages of colors and patterns.

Most vessels taking part in the competition are decorated to themes which are made known to judges only on the morning that the blessing is to take place. The procession this year [1973] featured nearly 60 vessels, about half of which were dressed up to such diverse themes as: "Alice in Wonderland," "Traveling Texas," and "Texas: Industrial Giant."

Many of the undecorated commercial boats had steamed into the channel in time only to receive the blessing and steer back out into the Gulf to resume fishing.

Each entry in the parade is given a Saint Christopher's Medal which is blessed to ensure safe passage. The blessing of the fleet usually begins in midafternoon. As the parade fleet begins to circle into position in the lower channel basin, the water is ablaze with rippling reflections cast from the gaudily rigged vessels. The crew and passengers aboard each boat shout and clap as they are applauded by the crowd ashore.

Then, on cue, they steam around and form a line down the channel. Each craft passes beside a barge upon whose upper deck stands a row of priests and altar boys who cast holy water in the direction of the boats and offer the awaited blessing.

"My Boat is so Small and the Seas are so Vast," reads the hastily drawn inscription painted along the gunnel of a dirty, wood hull shrimper, just arrived for the procession.

Source

Texas Highways, July 1973, 28. From an article by Bob Parvin on the "two-week Shrimp Festival held in late April" in Galveston. The magazine is designed to promote tourism.

* * *

Pennsylvania Dutch Shrove Tuesday Lore

Fasnacht—the dialect word for Shrove Tuesday—and Christmas have one thing in common in the Dutch country: they are the two days in the year when the kiddies get up unusually early. On Christmas it is to see what the *grischtkindel* [Christ-child] has brought; on *fasnacht* morning the children get up early because the last one out of bed becomes the *fasnacht* and is teased unmercifully all day long, not only by the members of his family but by his schoolmates as well.

In the past few years I have collected several variants to the name *fasnacht*—all of them in the York-Adams County area, however. Dr. Colsin R. Shelly tells me the last one out of bed in his family on Shrove Tuesday was called the old cluck and the first one the little *peepie.* Mrs. Anna Trimmer, who grew up in the Dover section, says she used to hear the word *faws-gloock.*

Mrs. William E. Werner of Jefferson, who is in her 80s, told me some months ago that the last one up was *die faws* [Fasnacht] and the first one *die alt asch* [the old ash]. Mrs. Harry Senft of the same place says in their family the first one up was called *der gansert* [the gander]. And Mrs. Willis

Burns also of Jefferson relates how her mother came to her rescue when her brother teased her overmuch. Her mother told her to call him, the first riser on Shrove Tuesday morning, *der schpeel-loombasoockler* [the dishrag sucker].

As on the other religious holidays in the Dutch country, there is a work taboo on Shrove Tuesday. William Reinert of near Fredericksville, Berks County, tells me if you sew on *Fasnacht* you will sew up the hens' cloacae and prevent them from laying eggs. Victor C. Dieffenbach of Bethel used to hear the old-timers say if a woman sewed on Shrove Tuesday the snakes would come in her house in spring and summer.

The most welcome thing about Shrove Tuesday was the special kind of doughnut, called a *fasnacht,* which was baked only at this time of year. It has a shape all its own, rectangular with a slit in the middle. To the traditionalist, the shape of the *fasnacht* is more important than the age-old debate in Dutch country: raised versus unraised dough for the *fasnacht-koocha* [cake].

Of course, *fasnachts,* like all other cakes in the Dutch country, must be dunked to be good. In Lancaster and Lebanon Counties—our saffron belt—they are dunked in saffron tea. Mrs. J. R. Cresswell of Morgantown, West Virginia, wrote us at the Folklore Center some years ago, "The most delightful use we put saffron to was on Shrove Tuesday when we put it in tea. For supper on that day we always had *fasnachts*—big, rectangular ones, with lots of air holes inside them. You split the *fasnacht,* filled the holes up with molasses and then dunked them in the saffron tea. The only time I get really homesick to be back on the farm is on Shrove Tuesday evening."

Saffron tea may be all right for someone who has his roots in the western section of our Dutchland. As for me, there is nothing that can compare with good old blue balsam tea. Naturally, the *fasnachts* must be dripping molasses before they are really dunkable.

In some of our Dutch families the first *fasnachts* that were baked were always fed to the chickens. Mrs. John Beaver of Kratzerville, Snyder County, tells me the old-timers used to lay a *blucks-line* [plow line] in a circle and then they crumbled the first three *fasnachts* in it for the chickens. The folk-belief was that if one did this the hawks would not fetch the chickens or chicks in spring. Mrs. Amelia Hildenbrand of the Mount Carmel area of Northampton County says her mother cut up the first three *fasnachts* for the chickens because she believed this would make them lay more eggs.

Then, in fine, there was the custom of barring out the teacher on Shrove Tuesday. (In most areas of the Dutch country barring-out-day was always on Christmas.) J. Steffy of near Red Run, Lancaster County, told me recently that when he attended the White Hollow school between

Red Run [*Die Roat Koo* or the Red Cow in Dutch] and Terre Hill they locked out the teacher John Mentzer on Shrove Tuesday afternoon. That was about the year 1888 says Steffy.

Source

Pennsylvania Dutchman, V (February 1, 1954), 3. Collected by Alfred J. Shoemaker, a Pennsylvania Dutchman himself, who cites his sources in the text. Literally, *Fasnacht* or *Fasenacht* (Pennsylvania Dutch) and *Fastnacht* (German) mean "fast night."

* * *

Pennsylvania Dutch Shrove Tuesday Lore
Genuine Fasenacht Kuche

The shape of the *fasenacht kuche* [cake] has nothing at all to do in determining whether the product is genuine or not. The determining factor is whether or not it is baked with yeast. If it is baked with yeast it is just an ordinary doughnut, regardless of whether it is round, square, triangular, or whatever the shape may be. The hole in the center is also immaterial. That is merely put there to insure thoroughness in baking.

A genuine *fasenacht kuche* is made WITHOUT yeast. This is important. Shrove Tuesday is a religious holiday and the absence of yeast was considered very important by our ancestors. Another thing, *fasenacht kuche* are baked only once a year—on Shrove Tuesday or on the Monday before. The important thing is that they be eaten on Shrove Tuesday, although a sufficient quantity is generally baked to last the rest of the week, providing the family appetite is not too large. Anything baked with raised dough is NOT a *fasenacht kuche* regardless of when it is baked or how it is shaped.

For future reference, I am giving you herewith a recipe for genuine *fasenacht kuche:*

> ¾ cup of thick sour cream
> ¾ cup of thick sour milk
> ¼ cup of sugar
> 1 egg
> 1½ teaspoonful baking soda

> Stiffen with enough flour to roll. Roll about ¼ inch thick and cut into desired shape and size—two-inch squares are preferable. Fry in deep fat. The amount of sugar may be made larger, but this is not necessary if eaten in the approved manner.

To eat, split the *kuche* in half and fill the inside with *gwidde hunnich* (quince jam). To use anything as ordinary as common as molasses on a genuine *fasenacht kuche* is an abomination. In the absence of *gwidde hunnich,* crab apple jelly may be substituted, but in our house we always have the foresight to have on hand at least one jar of *gwidde hunnich* just for this occasion.

This recipe has been used in our family, to my own knowledge, for four generations, and tradition says it was brought from Europe. Surely there must be Berks County homes where it is still used. My mother's family (Metzger) originated in Maxatawny, and old Mrs. Miller (wife of Dr. A. S. Miller) in whose kitchen I was privileged to eat *fasenacht kuche* many years ago, came from Albany in Berks County. My wife's family, which originated in Maidencreek and Richmond townships, were not acquainted with the recipe, but I have introduced it and anyone coming to our house on Shrove Tuesday will find the genuine product.

Source

Pennsylvania Dutchman, V (February 1, 1954), 3. By Raymond E. Hollenbach of Saegersville, Pennsylvania, in the Dutch Country. First published in 1948 in the *Reading* (Pennsylvania) *Eagle.*

* * *

Pennsylvania Dutch Shrove Tuesday Lore
Last One out of Bed on Shrove Tuesday

Just a word about the last one out of bed, or the last one to arrive at school, during the *Fasenacht* season. On Shrove Tuesday the last one out of bed, or at school, was *die fasenacht*. Similarly, on Ash Wednesday that person was *der eschepudl,* and on the Thursday morning following, *der siwweschlaefer*. In industrious Pennsylvania Dutch families, where late rising was considered almost a crime, there was of course some opprobriumn attached to these names. However, since the last one out of bed was often the youngest member of the family, I am wondering if in the original custom the use of these names was not merely a gentle reproach and that they were used with a genuine feeling of affection.

Source and Comment

Pennsylvania Dutchman, V (February 1, 1954), 3. A Shrove Tuesday sleepyhead was called "*Fasenacht*" for the doughnutlike cake prepared for this holiday. On Ash Wednesday the nickname was "Ashpuddle," meaning covered with ashes, a name by which Cinderella was also known. On Holy Thursday the late sleeper was called "Seven Sleeper," a reference to the Christian legend of the Seven Sleepers of Ephesus. To escape persecution they hid in a cave where they slept soundly for two hundred and thirty years. Motif D 1960.1 and Type 776.

* * *

Pennsylvania Dutch Shrove Tuesday Lore
Shrove Tuesday Dance

Dances were held on Shrove Tuesday [in the Pennsylvania Dutch country] "for a good yield of flax for that year," or, in other words, the host's crop of flax would be tall in proportion to the height to which the dancers raised their feet from the floor.

Source

Journal of American Folklore, II (1889), 25. Collected by W. J. Hoffman. Informant not given.

* * *

Vastenavond

On the evening before the beginning of the Lenten Season, the Dutch people celebrate *Vastenavond* (Fast Evening). It is more a Catholic holiday, but the Protestant people have their fun too. Some people start as early as Monday and from then until Ash Wednesday everyone makes merry with eating, drinking, playing cards, etc. 'Pannekoeken' (pancakes) are the most popular food and *Oliebollen* are also in great demand....

Oliebollen

They are made of a bread dough and then fried in deep fat. The recipe is as follows (Translated from the Dutch by my mother):

400	gr.	flour
30	gr.	yeast
		About 4/10 qt. luke warm milk
200	gr.	currants, raisins, and citron
15	gr.	orange peel
		Some lemon juice and peel
3		sour apples
2		eggs
		Pinch of salt
		Wesson or Mazola Oil

Add to the flour enough lukewarm milk to form a soft dough. Beat until smooth. Add the rest of the milk and well-washed currants, raisins, citron, sour apples (in pieces), orange peel, and, if desired, the lemon juice and lemon peel. Mix the yeast with a little warm milk and sugar ahead of time, and let it stand in a warm place. Add this to the batter, and let this dough rise in a warm place for 45 minutes. During this time, heat the Wesson Oil or Mazola Oil in an iron pot, until a blue smoke is given off. Drop by small amounts some dough into the hot fat, and bake the bollen until they are light brown and well done, about 5 to 7 minutes. Test them with a fork or a knitting needle. They are done if the implement comes out dry. Drain the bollen on brown wrapping paper. Sprinkle them with powdered sugar when they are dry.

P.S. When baking them, watch that the oil doesn't get too hot or they will burn....

My father sang for me this rather silly, yet charming Vastenavond song.

> *Vrouw t'is Vaste-avond,*
> *Ho man ho.*
> *Hier's een stoel en daar een stoel,*
> *Op elke stoel een kussen.*

> *Vrouwtje, houw je kinnebak toe*
> *Of 'k sla er een pannekoek tusschen.*
> *Tusschen je neus en tusschen je kin*
> *Kan nog wel een pannelkoek in.*
> *Rommelpottery, Rommelpottery,*
> *Geef m' een cent, dan ga 'k voorby.*
> *Rommelpottery, Rommelpottery,*
> *Geef m' een cent, dan go 'k voorby.*

Wife, this is the eve of the fasting season,
Ho man, ho!
Here's a chair and there's a chair,
On each chair there's a pillow.
Little wife, keep your mouth shut
Or I'll throw a pancake into it.
Between your nose and chin
There is room for another pancake.
Rommelpottery, Rommelpottery.
Give me a penny, and I'll go further.
Rommelpottery, Rommelpottery,
Give me a penny, and I'll go further.

At the "Rommelpottery," the singer tries to make a lot of noise, resembling the sound made when one bangs on a flower pot. Then, upon being paid the bonus of one penny, he continues his song. The song is gay and represents the generally happy spirit of the occasion.

Source and Comment

New York Folklore Quarterly, X (1954), 246-47, 255-56. Louise van Nederynen Atteridg writes on "Dutch Lore in Holland and at Castleton, NY." Her sources include her father, who came to Castleton in 1908, her mother, who came to the United States in 1924, and other relatives and neighbors of Dutch birth. She states that "until about 1930 the family spoke Dutch exclusively at home."

The refrain to the *Vastenavond* song, "*Rommelpottery, Rommelpottery,*" refers to a "Rommelpot," a Dutch or Flemish friction drum often played by children in holiday processions and frolics. It was made by tying an animal membrane over a household pot and vibrated by rubbing or by a stick which pierced the membrane.

* * *

International Pancake Race

What a footrace! The annual Shrove Tuesday race between housewives of Liberal [Kansas], and those of Olney, England. They dash 415 yards through the main streets of the two towns, and winners' times are clocked with stopwatches, then compared by Trans-Atlantic telephone to determine the International Pancake Racing Champion.

This has gone on since 1950. R. J. Leete, then president of the Liberal Jaycees, saw a picture in *Time* magazine of women racing in Olney. For over 500 years it had been the custom to race to the church when the shriving bell rang. The story goes it all started when a housewife was using up cooking fats (forbidden during Lent) to bake pancakes on Shrove Tuesday. When the bell tolled calling all to the shriving service, in her haste she forgot to remove her apron, and ran to the church with skillet still in hand. Her neighbors, not to be outdone, got into the act the next year, and carried their skillets to church, so it became a contest to see who could reach the church steps first and collect a kiss from the bell-ringer. He gave the greeting, "The Peace of the Lord be always with you," so the prize became the "Kiss of Peace," still bestowed in both the Liberal and Olney races.

Leete cabled Ronald Collins, then Vicar of Olney and manager of the race there, and challenged the English to the first race. They readily accepted and it has grown into an internationally known event.

The score now [in 1978] stands at 15-11, in favor of Liberal. The 25th anniversary race was run for goodwill only, and the score did not count. The race is run according to Olney rules. The course is laid out in an "S" shape. In Olney the race starts at the village well, at the sound of a centuries-old bell. Over cobblestone streets, it goes past thatched roof cottages and the Old Bull Inn. In Liberal, a pistol shot signals the start, and we run over brick and asphalt streets.

Traditional garb is housedresses, aprons, and headscarves (the head coverings necessary for the church ceremony following the race in England). Three local wins disqualify a winner. A pancake dropped during the race does not disqualify, but the racer loses valuable time in retrieving it. The pancake must be flipped when the race starts and again after the runner crosses the finish line, to show she still has the pancake. Racers must be at least 16 years old and a resident of their respective towns. The only time this rule was set aside was in 1974 when Mrs. Leete was invited to run in the Olney race after Liberal had sent the Leetes to England as its representatives.

[In 1985 Sally Swallow of Olney won the race, finishing the course in sixty-four seconds, but Liberal still leads the series.]

Source and Comment

International Pancake Day Program, Liberal, Kansas, February 7, 1978. Virginia Leete, publicity committee, of International Pancake Day of Liberal, Inc., wrote a "History of Pancake Day" for the official program of the "29th Annual Event" from which this description is taken.

Featured events include pancake-eating contest; amateur talent competition; Shriving Worship Service; Trans-Atlantic Telephone Call with Olney, England; parade. Cf. "Bastille Day Wine Glass Race," pp. 276.

* * *

International Pancake Race
A Recent Pancake Race

Louise Fitzgerald, 17, of Olney, England, flipped her pancake and took off running yesterday [March 6, 1984] while Mona Canaday, an aerobics instructor in Liberal, Kan., did the same thing.

When it was over, the British had defeated the Americans by two seconds in the 415-yard race. Miss Fitzgerald's winning time was 1 minute, 4.1 seconds....

It's a bizarre race because contestants must flip pancakes while running....

The series now stands at 19-15 in favor of Liberal.

Source

Philadelphia Inquirer, March 7, 1984. From a regular column, "The Scene."

* * *

International Pancake Race
Pancake Race Superstitions

Listed below are a few superstitions that have sprung up [in Liberal] around the race:

It is considered good luck to carry a past winner's skillet in the race. Also to wear a past winner's apron.

One year, the stack of pancakes marking the starting point of the race, were stolen. This was considered a bad omen. The stack of pancakes (concrete) were later returned.

Although the women practice running 415 yards, it is considered bad luck to run the official race course during these practice sessions.

It is against the rules for entrants to run the official race course any time after midnight the day of the International Pancake Race.

All entrants have strong feelings about the traditional blessing bestowed on the winner of the race. This blessing, "The Peace of the Lord be alway (spelling correct) with you," is given by, in England, the Verger or Bell Ringer, in Liberal, the British Consul representing England in this area.

Source

Letter to T. P. C. dated November 10, 1978, from Leland Agan, Pancake Day Chairman for 1979.

* * *

Paczki Day

The day before Ash Wednesday is called [in Polish] *Paczki* day. *Paczki* are jellybuns. This is a day of feasting and merrymaking. (We still [in 1968] have jellybuns on the Tuesday before Ash Wednesday in our family.)

Source

New York Folklore Quarterly, XXIV (1968), 303. Reported from New York Mills, New York, by Robert Maziarz, whose grandparents were born in Poland.

Pancakes and Chickens

No pancakes on pancake day, means no luck with chickens.

As a love-charm, throw a bit of pancake on pancake day to a rooster. If he eats it without calling the hens, you will remain single; if he calls them, you will marry.

Source

Journal of American Folklore, XI (1898), 11. From a "Collection of Maryland Folk-lore" made by Mrs. Waller R. Bullock of Baltimore. Information and date not given. Cf. "Pennsylvania Dutch Shrove Tuesday Lore," p. 97.

Shrove Cakes, Pancakes, Cross-buns

Shrove cakes on Shrove Tuesday, pancakes on Ash Wednesday, cross-buns at Easter, bring good luck. The first should be round and have a hole in the centre. If the grease used in frying them be preserved and applied to the axles of wagons in which the harvest is hauled home, mice will not eat the grain. One cross-bun must be kept during the year if the good influence is to be continued.

Source

Journal of American Folklore, VII (1894), 112. Collected by J. Hampden Porter from unspecified "mountain whites" in the Allegheny mountains.

Ash Wednesday

February-March

In the Western Church, Lent, the forty days preceding Easter, begins on Ash Wednesday. It is a period of fasting in preparation for Easter Sunday, the date of Christ's Resurrection, and the forty days are said to represent the length of Christ's fast in the wilderness after His baptism. On Ash Wednesday, Roman Catholics and many Protestants are marked on the forehead with a cross. The priest makes this mark with ashes from burned palm leaves used in the Palm Sunday service of the previous year. The ashes are a symbol of repentance, originating in the penance of "sackcloth and ashes" invoked by the Old Testament prophets.

Ashes on Ash Wednesday

This is a very sacred day to the people of southeastern Pennsylvania. They have carried this Christian tradition down through the ages. Ash Wednesday is a day of fasting and repentance. The usage of this day is geographical. Mrs. Sarah Weaver, of Strausstown, states that it was the unwritten law to sprinkle ashes on the cattle and poultry on this day to rid them of all lice. She also said that they did not observe it as a holiday, but that her parents and grandparents did. Mrs. Lillian Hollenbach, of Shartlesville, affirmed that it is the custom still at their home that the last one out of bed must empty out the ashes. They also scattered some of the ashes on the cattle and poultry and said the following proverb, "*lice geweg wie die Leute von die Kirche weg.*" ["Lice, go away! Go like people leaving church."] They observed this day as any other day.

Mrs. Sallie Adams of Shoemakersville, said that it was the custom on this day that the last one out of bed was the "*Eshepuddle*" and he had to empty out the ashes. She also asserted that at her parents' home they always spread ashes on the cattle and poultry to rid them of lice. Mrs. Diana Dreibelbis, of Shoemakersville, told me that it was also the tradition at their place that the last one out of bed was the "*Eshepuddle*" and he had to carry out the ashes. She also affirmed that her father was a staunch believer in "straying" ashes over the cattle and poultry to rid them of lice.

Source and Comment

Pennsylvania Dutchman, II (April 1, 1951), 3. Collected by Don F. Geschwindt for a "report on the festival days of the people of Southeast Pennsylvania" for a folklore course at Franklin and Marshall College in 1950. His informants were "farmers and their wives." For exterminating bugs in Maryland with Ash Wednesday ashes, see also *Memoirs of the American Folklore Society,* XVIII (1925), 115; and Motif F 981.5.

"Great Fast"

Prior to Easter there is a seven weeks of self-denial, and, in a measure, fasting. Before the fasttime begins there is a week given up to feasting, dancing, and frivolity. The period of fasting has become personified, until they imagine that a spirit oversees its observance. The name of the spirit is "Great Fast." The seven weeks' fast begins at midnight, and on the evening previous they talk of Great Fast being over behind the mountain. At twilight they say: "Now he is on top of the mountain." A little later, when it is dark, they will say: "Now he is in the valley." Still later: "He is leaving the valley." Thus they go on speaking of him as drawing nearer and nearer, until they will finally say: "He is now on the housetop waiting to come down." At midnight he comes down the chimney, and sits in the fireplace. He goes to everything in the room and smells of it, to the cooking vessels, etc.; and even smells of the mouths of those who are asleep, to see if they have been eating butter, grease, or any other forbidden article of food. In preparation for this scrutinizing investigation, on this night after supper it is customary to scour all the dishes with ashes. Everything must be clean. Some people will even wash their mouths with ashes. After his examination, Great Fast goes back and takes his seat in the chimney, where he sits for forty days in order to watch the people, and to be sure that they do not do any of the things forbidden for that period. However, though he sees everything, he cannot be seen himself. He is invisible.

My informant tells me that when he was a child he awoke one morning while it was still twilight and was frightened to see something black in the fireplace. He asked his mother what it was. She replied that it was Great Fast, and told him to cover up his head while she drove the spirit away. He did so, and on being told a little later to uncover his head, he was unable to see anything out of the ordinary. Later years, however, revealed the fact that it was a kettle he had seen, and that on covering up his head, his mother had carried it out of the room.

Source

Journal of American Folklore, XII (1899), 106. Collected by G. D. Edwards in Boston, Massachusetts, from an informant of Armenian descent.

* * *

The Meaning of Ashes Today

Millions of Americans who normally give little public sign of religious allegiance will walk around today with one smudged on the forehead.

On this as on every Ash Wednesday, Roman Catholic priests and many Episcopal and Lutheran clergy will be making a cross-shaped mark of ash on the foreheads of parishioners. The traditional words of the ritual, which begins the 40-day penitential season of Lent, remind the believer that "you are dust and unto dust you will return."

That smudge of ash, like the yarmulke of an Orthodox Jew, might appear to run against the widespread notion that religion is a strictly private affair in the United States. And such a tangible reminder of mortality may seem out of keeping with a culture reputed to be relentlessly cheerful.

But there is no doubt about the ritual's popularity. Downtown churches in most major cities will find Catholics waiting in long lines before, during and after work to receive ashes.

It is "a statement in a secular world," says Daniel P. Mulhollan, who works at the Library of Congress as a specialist in American government and plans to receive ashes. "It's a leveler, a reminder that we are all going to die," he observed. . . .

The Rev. Roberto Gonzalez, pastor of Holy Cross parish in the southeast Bronx, agreed that the ashes reminded believers of mortality and ultimate reliance on God.

"In a deep and unspeakable way, that mystery is made visible through the ashes," Father Gonzalez said. . . . "It's our best moment as Catholics," said the 52-year-old [Brian Brown, publicity manager for Time magazine]. "We gave up all the spookiness—Latin, incense. This is our last vestige of Catholic culture."

In the late 60's, Mr. Brown concedes, "I decided ashes were part of the past." But then he adds. "Now I've reached an age when I consider myself part of the past."

In recent years, he continues, "I go to the oldest priest at St. Patrick's Cathedral and get the biggest smudge possible so I can walk around the office to remind the yuppies here that the kingdom is not of this earth," adding with finality, "My whole idea is to scare the hell out of the yuppies."

Source

New York Times, February 17, 1988. From an article by Peter Steinfels.

Purim

February-March

Purim is a feast day celebrated on the fourteenth day of Adar, the sixth month of the Jewish calendar. It commemorates the escape of the Persian Jews from a massacre planned by Haman, minister of the King, Ahasuerus, through the intercession of Esther, the queen. This story is recounted in the Old Testament Book of Esther. Haman's anger had been provoked by a Jewish leader, Mordecai, who, for religious reasons, refused to bow in homage to him. Haman persuaded the king that the Jews were disobedient and seditious, and obtained a decree permitting their destruction. Lots were cast to determine when this should take place. Unknown to the king or Haman, Esther was the cousin of Mordecai, and she revealed Haman's machinations and Mordecai's past services to Ahasuerus. The king could not legally alter his decree, but he granted the Jews the right to defend themselves, thus forestalling an attack, and had Haman hanged. Purim, also called the Feast of Lots, is characterized by frivolity—feasting, dancing, masquerade, playacting based on the story of Esther saving her people from Haman, and in more recent times, beauty contests for the selection of a "Queen Esther" who reigns over this Jewish carnival.

A Purim Reading

The stage is set for the happiest holiday of the Jewish year—Purim 5748 [1988]. The characters assemble in the wings, awaiting their entrances: the powerful King Ahasuerus, the beautiful Queen Esther, the righteous Mordecai, the evil Haman.

The scene is Persia, the time some 2,000 years ago. The curtain will go up on Purim as the sun goes down Wednesday, ushering in the 14th day of the month of Adar. The drama of the deliverance of the Jews will unfold as the script—the scroll of Esther, known as the Megillah—is unrolled.

Let the play begin!

Ahasuerus has just banished his queen, Vashti, for refusing to dance before his assembled guests at a seven-day revel in the city of Shushan.

A search begins to find the most beautiful woman in the land to become Ahasuerus' new bride and queen. The king chooses Esther, unaware that she is a Jew and the cousin of his court Jew, Mordecai.

At the same time, Ahasuerus elevates his court adviser, Haman, to the position of vizier, chief among all the king's men. The vicious vizier immediately decrees that all men bow down to him.

The righteous Mordecai refuses. Enraged, Haman vows to destroy the Jewish people. He whispers into the king's ear: "There is a certain people scattered abroad and dispersed among the peoples.... Their laws are different from those of other people, they do not obey the king's law and the king should not tolerate them."

The king listens to Haman's malicious words and agrees to permit the destruction of the Jews. Haman casts lots, known as *purim*, to set the day of destruction. The chosen day is to be the 13th day of the month of Adar.

When Mordecai learns of Haman's evil intentions, he goes to his cousin Esther and appeals to her to come to the aid of their people.

Knowing that she risks death, Esther goes unsummoned to the king and requests that he and Haman come to a banquet in their honor.

Unable to sleep that night, Ahasuerus calls for his scribes and asks them to read to him from the history of his reign. As the scribes read, the king discovers that Mordecai once saved his life by foiling an assassination plot. But the court Jew has never been rewarded.

Ahasuerus sends for Haman and asks his advice: "What should be done for a man whom the king wishes to honor?"

Thinking that he himself is the man to be honored, Haman replies, "Such a one should be dressed in royal garb and led in a procession throughout the streets of Shushan, while a servant of the king walks beside him, crying, 'So it is that the king treats a man to whom honor is due!'"

The next evening, Ahasuerus and Haman attend the queen's banquet. As the feast is served, Esther points an accusing finger at Haman. Haman's plan to destroy the Jews, she tells the king, would mean the destruction of *her* people and the people of Mordecai.

Holding onto his three-cornered hat, Haman flees the banquet hall.

Later that night, Haman appears in Esther's chambers and throws himself at her feet, begging for mercy. But just at that moment, Ahasuerus bursts into the room and finds Haman alone with the queen in her chambers—an outrage punishable by death.

Haman and his 10 sons are hanged from the very gallows that the evil vizier had constructed to take the life of Mordecai. It's curtains for Haman as the curtain comes down on this ancient tale of deceit, deliverance and triumph over evil.

This is the whole Megillah, and it is considered a mitzvah [good deed] to hear every word of it. Everyone is called upon to hear the reading of the scroll of Esther—women and children as well as men.

It is a reading marked by revelry, for as the story is read, the assembled children traditionally hiss and boo and twirl their noisy groggers [rattles] every time they hear the name of the evil Haman.

It is also considered a mitzvah to partake of the joy of Purim—the feasting, drinking, noisemaking, parades and masquerades.

As it is written in the book of Esther, "The Jews of the villages that lived in unwalled towns made the 14th of the month of Adar a day of gladness and feasting, a holiday and an occasion for sending gifts to one another."

The Purim feast, *seudat Purim,* is a feast of victory over evil, as the merrymakers eat *hamantashen,* or Haman's hats: three-cornered pastries filled with sweet prunes or poppy seeds.

The customs of Purim include *shalach manot,* the exchange of small gifts of food, and *matanot l'evyonim,* the gift of charity to the poor.

It is also customary to celebrate Purim with carnivals, games and costume parades of pint-sized Esthers, Mordecais, Ahasueruses and deliciously evil Hamans.

On Purim, Jews are encouraged to get literally drunk with the joys of deliverance. One is instructed to drink wine until incapable of distinguishing between blessing Mordecai and cursing Haman.

This tradition is the source of the name given to the Israeli Purim celebration—*ad lo yadah,* until you do not know.

Let the play begin!

Source

Jewish Exponent, February 26, 1988. An article by staff writer Marilyn S. Lieberstein.

* * *

Purim Recipes

Hamantashen (*Haman's Pockets*)

1½ cups boiling hot water
¾ cup milk
1 tsp. salt
2½ cups flour
¼ lb. poppyseeds
2 tsps. baking powder
2 eggs
¼ lb. melted butter
1¼ cup sugar
½ cup of seeded raisins

Scald the poppyseeds with boiling water and let stand until the seeds sink to the bottom of the bowl. Pour off the water and let poppyseeds drain in a fine strainer until all the water has dripped off. Then grind with the finest knife or food chopper. Fold in an egg, and work in ¾ cup sugar until mixture is well-balanced. Add raisins if desired.

Mix egg, milk, butter, salt, flour, ½ cup sugar and baking powder thoroughly and knead well. Roll out the dough ¼-inch thick and cut into four-inch circles with a cutter or glass. Then put a tablespoon of the poppyseed mixture in the center of each circle. Draw up three sides, and pinch in for sides of triangle. Place on greased pan and bake in medium oven until brown. Recipe makes twelve good-sized *hamantashen.*

Kichlach (*Poppyseed Cookies*)

1 cup sugar
1 cup salad oil
4 eggs
4 cups sifted flour
3 tsps. baking powder
½ tsp. salt
½ cup lukewarm water
¾ cup poppyseeds

Cream sugar and shortening. Add one egg at a time, beating or stirring well after each addition. Sift dry ingredients, adding poppyseeds. Combine both mixtures, adding a little of the water to form a stiff dough. Roll out on a lightly floured board—¼-inch thickness. Cut with a cutter into 2½-inch triangles. Brush cookies with an egg yolk diluted with a tablespoon of water. Sprinkle the cookies with a mixture of poppyseeds and sugar after arranging the cookies on a greased cookie sheet. Bake at 350°F. for 12 to 15 minutes.

Source

Purim: A Workbook and Guide, Jewish Community Center of Detroit, undated, 11. Traditional recipes from a mimeographed booklet on the history and lore associated with Purim for the use of the Detroit, Michigan, Jewish community.

* * *

More Purim Recipes

Anna Goldberg has requested Purim recipes for traditional hamantashen and kreplach. It is also customary to eat cooked beans in remembrance of Queen Esther's diet while she lived at King Ahasuerus' court.

Pareve Hamantashen

3   eggs
1   c. sugar
1   c. oil
1   navel orange, juice and rind, ground
1   lemon, juice only
4   cs. flour
2   tsps. baking powder
1   tsp. salt

Mix in order given. Chill.

Roll out in small amounts on well-floured board. Cut in 2- or 3-inch rounds. Fill rounds of dough with about ½ tablespoon of filling.

Shape dough into triangle. Pinch openings together.

Bake on a greased cookie sheet at 375° for 30 minutes or until browned. Yields 40.

Pareve Filling
for Hamantashen

3   cs. prune or apricot lekvar or a combination of
    both
1   c. seedless dark raisins or currants
1   c. walnuts, coarsely chopped
grated rind of 1 orange
1   apple, unpeeled and grated (optional)

Combine filling ingredients.

Kreplach

Dough:

2   cs. flour
2   eggs
1   tbsp. water
½   tsp. salt

Place unsifted flour on a board and make a well in the center. Drop in eggs, water and salt. Work into flour with one hand and knead until smooth and elastic.

Roll out and stretch dough as thin as possible. Cut into 3-inch squares and place a tablespoon of filling on each.

Fold dough over into a triangle. Press edges together with a little water. Pinch together two points. Drop in boiling

salted water. Cook for 20 minutes or until kreplach rise to the top. Drain.

Cheese-filled kreplach can be fried and served with sour cream. Meat-filled kreplach go well in chicken soup. Makes about 24, depending on how thinly dough is rolled.

Cheese Filling

1   c. dry cottage cheese
1   egg
½   tsp. salt
    dash pepper
2   tbsps. fine bread crumbs

Blend together with a fork and place on dough.

Meat Filling

1   tbsp. oil
½   lb. ground beef
½   c. minced onion
¾   tsp. salt
¼   tsp. pepper

Heat oil in a skillet; add meat and onion and cook for 10 minutes, stirring frequently. Add salt and pepper. Cool before placing on squares of dough.

Tomatoed Lima Beans

1   c. dried lima beans or 2 cs. canned
2½   cs. water
2   tbsps. margarine
4   tbsps. minced onion
3   tbsps. chopped celery
1   tbsp. minced dill or parsley (optional)
½   c. tomato sauce
     salt, pepper to taste
¼   c. cold water

Wash dried beans, cover with cold water and soak overnight. Cook in 2 ½ cups water until tender (about 1 hour) and drain. If using canned beans, simply drain.

Saute onion and celery in margarine until tender. Add remaining ingredients, mix well and heat through. Serves 4.

Source

The first two recipes are from *Purim: A Workbook and Guide,* Jewish Community Center of Detroit, undated, p. 11. Additional recipes are from the *Jewish Exponent,* February 26, 1988, from a food column, "Fannie's Favorites," by Fannie Fertik.

* * *

A Purim Tour

On Sunday [February 27, 1983] Hasidic families in Brooklyn's Crown Heights [New York] section will open their homes to visitors who want to share with them the joys of the Jewish festival of Purim. The excursion, sponsored by the 92nd Street Y, will provide a rare glimpse into the way

Hasidic Jews live, worship and celebrate. Visitors will share a festive family meal, look in on a Hasidic synagogue, view a parade of costumed youngsters and they may join in singing and dancing in the streets. With Purim falling on a Sunday this year, the Crown Heights tour is but one of an unusually large number of holiday celebrations. . . .

The start, at 2 P.M. , is from a Lubavitcher girls school, with the reading of the Purim story from the hand-lettered parchment scroll known as the *megillah.* The reading will be followed by a walking tour of the neighborhood, where some of the *megillah's* principal characters may be encountered.

Purim is a time to dress up and parade through the streets. In Hasidic communities, where sexual stereotyping is alive and well, every girl wants to be the beautiful Queen Esther. . . .

Visitors will stop at the area's major attractions, including a Jewish art gallery and the *mikvah* (ritual bath), and at bakeries, where there will be trays and trays of fresh *hamantashen,* the three-cornered pastry with prune or mohnseed filling. But visitors are urged not to eat too much along the way because at 5:30 the tour breaks up into smaller groups for holiday dinner at private homes.

"It is a chance to see Hasidic life beyond the black garb," said Batia Plotch, organizer of the Y's walking-tour series. "They are normal people, with warm and open homes."

Visitors are asked to respect Hasidic tradition. Women should not wear pants and men should wear yarmulkes, which will be available.

The Purim meal is often a boisterous occasion that includes an extended family of neighbors, friends from out of town and distant relatives. The meal is inevitably interrupted by a Purim tradition known as *m'sloach manot,* in which families send one another baskets of fruit and wine. Young Hamans and Esthers often make the deliveries.

When the meal ends, at about 9, those on the Y tour and their host families will walk to the main headquarters of the Lubavitcher movement, at 770 Eastern Parkway for the major event of the day. It is the *"rebbe's fabrengen,"* a celebration at which the chief Lubavitcher rabbi, Menachem M. Schneerson, presides and addresses his followers. The speech is in Yiddish, but headsets for simultaneous translation are available.

Source and Comment

New York Times, February 25, 1983. Selected from an account by staff reporter Ari L. Goldman of forthcoming Purim celebrations in New York and New Jersey sponsored by Jewish religious, cultural, social, and labor organizations. The Purim observance usually begins with the reading of "the *Megillah*" or Book of Esther, a parchment scroll often kept in a handsomely ornamented case.

Purim Riddle

Fun vanen veys men az Akhashveresh hot gegesn on netiles-yadayim?

Vayl er hot gezogt tsu zayn vayb "Vash-ti," un er hot zikh not gegvolt vashn.

How is it known that Ahasuerus ate without ritually washing his hands?

Because he said to his wife "Vashti" (Yiddish: you wash), and he did not want to wash himself.

Source and Comment

Jewish Folklore and Ethnology Newsletter, February 1978, 3. Reprinted from M. Sharkanski, *A shpitsl fun a purimshpiler* (New York), 1899.

Queen Vashti was dismissed by King Ahasuerus for disobedience and succeeded by Esther. In Jewish practice, handwashing often precedes religious rituals.

* * *

Purim Street Theater

On the morning of Purim, 13th Avenue [Brooklyn], the main artery of Boro Park, is transformed into the stage of a carnival where Bobover, like many other Jews, become both performers and audience in a festive event. The stores are crowded with last-minute shoppers eager to buy all the necessary items for their festival meal before the closing of the shops in early afternoon. By noon young children and even *yeshiva* [religious school] students, as well as occasional adults dressed in traditional and modern costumes, intermingle with each other in the streets. There are modern-day Hamans in Arab dress, young Mordechais and Esthers dressed in contemporary bridal gowns. Some children wear purely fanciful costumes directly or indirectly relating to the specific or general themes of Purim. Animals, soldiers, policemen and clowns and even figures from American history, such as Washington and Lincoln, are all impersonated. Nor is it considered offensive to mimic the most venerated citizens of the community, the hasidic *rebes* (pl. *rebe*) [rabbis], something which small children with long false beards and brocaded *bakeshes* [long ceremonial coat] who smoke cigarettes and assume a hunch-backed posture successfully do.

Many car owners attach loudspeakers on the top of their cars and when driving play Jewish music through them. Others will even have an animal or puppet clown sitting on the top of the car.

Semi-spontaneous street "happenings," which deliver a political message or serve as part of a charity drive have since 1977 become a part of the morning celebration in Boro Park. In 1977, the Jewish Defense League voiced its opposition to [President] Ford's Middle East policy by burning [Secretary of State] Kissinger in effigy. The following is a description of the event.

Several days before Purim, posters were displayed on 13th Avenue, inviting Jews to come on Purim to the corner of 13th Avenue and 48th Street where Ford and Kissinger would address them in person. Purim morning was rainy as it often is. Cars with loudspeakers invited everyone to come at noon to meet Kissinger and Ford. The gathering crowd included a T.V. camera crew and journalists with cameras, mostly Jews but also non-Jews. A young man wearing a blue Israeli Kibbutz hat, khaki shirt and trousers and a *kafiyyeh* (Arabic: a shawl) around his neck asked everyone to be patient since Ford and Kissinger would be somewhat late because of the rain. Suddenly a car stopped at the corner and a child-sized puppet of Kissinger but with a full-sized caricature of his face was put on the pavement. A huge poster was also displayed. On it was drawn a caricature of the late King Faisal of Saudi Arabia (with a white *kafiyyeh* covering his head, but showing his face) and of President Sadat of Egypt (holding a pipe). The caption in large English letters read, "Who is the Real Sucker?" The young man with the Israeli hat started shouting, "Ford, go home!!!" and a few other young men (apparently from the same group) held a poster that read, "I am a Zionist," and began to shout "Ford, go home!!!" The leader, the man with the Israeli hat, told the cameraman to come closer to the puppet and a small poster with a picture of Ford and the words "Ford, go home!!!" was fastened to the Kissinger effigy. Meanwhile more people were gathering, many costumed as Arabs, Israelis and American soldiers. They surrounded the puppet, some also shouted, "Ford, go home!!!" while others just stared. It was impossible to distinguish between the members of the demonstrating group and the bystanders, who celebrated Purim in costume. During the entire event several members of the group distributed flyers saying "Ford and Kissinger Must Go" as well as booklets containing pictures and accusations against their policy towards Israel. Then the young man poured benzene on the puppet, which was wrapped in a red kerchief. When the young man had difficulty starting the fire because the puppet was wet due to the rain, the puppet was wrapped in newspaper on which more benzene was poured, and it began to burn. The T.V. cameramen took several close-up pictures of the burning in effigy and then disappeared. The leader and his men extinguished the fire, distributed more of their flyers, got into the car and drove off towards the main street. Many people remained on the corner, enthusiastically discussing whether or not Ford was good for the Jews and Israel.

Meanwhile, on 13th Avenue a limousine stopped, from which two men got out, one wearing a rubber mask of Ford and the other a mask of Kissinger. They walked several blocks, shaking hands with the passers-by. After several blocks they reentered the limousine and disappeared.

The entire event was sponsored by the Jewish Defense League, but on the materials they gave out during the "happening," they referred to themselves as AJAF (American Jews Against Ford). The event took place under police protection and with a permit from the police.

Source and Comment

Shifra Epstein, "The Celebration of a Contemporary Purim in the Bobover Hasidic Community," Ph.D. Dissertation, University of Texas, 1979, 139-42. The Bobover Hasidic sect originated in Galicia, southern Poland, some 150 years ago. Its founder was Hayyim Halberstamm (1793-1876), and its present leader is his direct descendant. The sect found refuge in the United States and established an Hasidic center in Boro Park, Brooklyn, New York. Today it consists of about 2,000 families in the United States and a large community in Israel. Extremely orthodox, members of the community have little contact with the contemporary world. They do not attend the theatre, movies, or secular concerts and for this reason, their traditional Purim plays and carnival masking are a peculiar mixture of the past and present.

* * *

The Purim *Shpil* of Abraham and Isaac

Purim, a Jewish holiday celebrated usually at the end of February or the beginning of March, is the day Jews recall their threatened destruction by the Persian king Ahashverus and his vizier, Haman, and their deliverance from their fate by Mordecai and Esther. Purim shares several features of festival behavior with non-Jewish carnivals, including feasting, folk drama, masquerading, carousing, jesting, and burlesque.

The origin of the Purim play dates back to the buffooneries and the dramatizations of the ninth and tenth centuries. In the Jewish communities of Germany, for example, Purim plays were known to have been performed in the fifteenth century, although the oldest unpublished text we have is from the end of the seventeenth century. The central figures of the early Purim plays were biblical heroes from the story of Esther. Non-biblical themes were also incorporated into the Purim plays and emphasized ethics and religious behavior similar to the religious play of the medieval church. The motif of the sacrifice of Isaac has become a fertile device for the inculcation of Jewish religious and ethical values. Thus, for example, the motif is part of the Rosh ha-Shanah [New Year] Service as well as the subject of many hymns and legends.

The Bobover Hassidic community, where the folk drama described below was performed, is one of the few ultraorthodox communities which continue this tradition. The Purim play celebrates the community's role as cultural connoisseur of Jewish tradition, by always depicting themes from the Bible or other Jewish sources and by exhibiting its members' abilities to generate artistic creativity despite their almost total lack of exposure to such experiences.

The play is in a Yiddish dialect, popularly known as "Polish Yiddish" and with many Hebrew verses and words, pronounced with Ashkenazic accents. All the members of the cast are male students, teachers and workers in their Rabbinical School.

The Bobover Hassidic community originated in Galicia [southern Poland] more than one hundred and fifty years ago. The current *rebe* [the Hassidic leader] of the community, Shlomo Halberstam, is a direct descendant of Hayyim Halberstamm (1793-1876), the originator of the sect. After the Second World War, Shlomo found refuge in the United States, where he established a Hassidic center in Borough Park, Brooklyn, New York. Today, the sect is made up of more than 2,000 families in the United States and Canada. Most are in New York City and in a large community in Israel. The sect has very little cultural or social contact with the outside world. Following their interpretation of Jewish tradition, members do not attend movies, theater, or secular concerts.

Before the *Shpil*

The Purim *shpil* [play] is performed on Purim night approximately at midnight, but the preparations of the scenery start as early as 5 P.M. It takes place in the *besmedresh* [a house of study and a synagogue] on a small stage on the left side of the ark. The stage, approximately eight feet wide and five feet long, is brought from outside the *besmedresh* (see the sketch p. 116). The rehearsals begin not more than two weeks before Purim in the *yeshive* [rabbinical school] dining room. Mimeographed sheets are distributed to the prospective actors, a cast of no more than five, almost all veterans of earlier plays. Some actors go back twelve years to when the Bobover lived in Crown Heights, Brooklyn. On the mimeographed sheets the different roles are written, as well as the melodies which the roles require. The Purim *shpil* as performed is a genre of cantorial opera. Almost the entire play is sung.

The performance is entirely the responsibility of the *yeshive* students, and the theatrical setting has been, for the last several years, the domain of a *yeshive* student who is famous in the community for his artistic abilities. Some of the arrangements for the play take place in the *besmedresh* on the afternoon of the performance itself while the regular activities are going on. Thus, sometime after five o'clock when some people are praying the Evening Service and others are studying in the main *besmedresh,* lights are hooked up to the ceiling. The colors are blue, red, and white. A movable curtain is hung on poles and several backdrops are rolled up to the ceiling to be rolled down during the play.

Several hours before the Purim *shpil* a few women come to the women's section in order to reserve a place for themselves. Men do not come as early as women to reserve a place, since the men's section affords many more viewing places, but women are restricted to a special section which provides only a limited view, and no seats. Around midnight, when the *besmedresh* starts to fill, a group of people, not dressed like the Hassidim, but in business suits and wearing hats, arrive with musical instruments. This is the famous *Neginah* orchestra, a very popular wedding orchestra which plays for both Hassidic and non-Hassidic weddings in New York. They traditionally come to play before the performance of the Bobover Purim *shpil* and the Bobover are very proud that they do not charge them for this service. They are seated close to the ark and play, for more than half an hour, songs from the Bobover repertoire for Purim. There is no dancing while they play. Meanwhile the main *besmedresh* fills especially with people in Hassidic dress, but also others, including some in business suits and hats, and also young people in jeans and knitted skullcaps.

The *rebe* arrives with several men sometime after the orchestra. He is brought to a table close to the main area of the performance. One of the *rebe*'s relatives tells one of the orchestra members to stop playing and the *rebe* then leads semi-liturgical songs, first from the Bobover repertoire for the Day of Atonement and later from the regular repertoire. This part lasts close to half an hour. Then the *Neginah* orchestra plays several other tunes.

A tall man in Hassidic clothing, including a *shtrayml* [fur-edged hat] stands in front of the closed curtain and thanks the people who prepared the evening, Purim 5736 [1976], but without mentioning any name in particular. Several men in the *besmedresh* applaud, the only such ovation during the entire play. Using a microphone, which will later be passed to the actors, he asks the permission of the *rebe* to perform what he calls "a very old play," not stating its name.

The Performance

At 1:20 A.M. , the play (a prologue and six scenes) begins. An actor comes from behind the curtain. His long white robe is adorned with two wide black stripes on each side of the front, has long flowing sleeves, and has a white sash. He wears a Russian-style white curly lamb hat. Later he will be recognized as Abraham, the protagonist of the play. His introductory words have an ethical emphasis. He addresses the audience (singing solo, accompanied by violin and accordion). He sings of them, honoring them as pious men, Hassidim, teachers and Halakhic [religious law] experts, who have come to hear the righteous words, the secret words both clever and wise, of those who are always ready to execute God's command. (This part is entirely in Hebrew, in Ashkenazic pronunciation.) Then, singing again, as he puts it, "several words about the purpose of the play which is to put lots of emotion into the *Sacrifice of Isaac*," he introduces the first scene.

While the introductory tune is played, the curtain is opened and the paper backdrop is rolled down. It depicts hills covered with brown rocks. On the left side is a huge tree with a wide, green trunk. In front, in the center of the stage, is a small "house," a box approximately two yards wide and one yard high with dark brown paper glued on it to resemble stone. A blue painted entrance rectangle completes the house.

From behind the backdrop two men emerge; one, in a contemporary short suit and a knitted hat, is Eliezer. The other wears striped dark blue and gray pajamas, padded to make him appear extremely fat, and has a belt over his wide waist. He also wears a black-and-white-striped *kafiya* [an Arabic shawl] on his head. He is bare-foot. Like Eliezer he has a bushy beard but black, not red like Eliezer's. He asks Eliezer if he recognizes him and declares in Hebrew, accented according to Israeli practice, "I am Ishmael, I am an Arab." While Ishmael is introducing himself, Arabic music is played on a tape recorder behind the curtain and Ishmael dances a gross belly dance. The audience is very responsive to his act, many laughing aloud. Then the music stops and he comes close to Eliezer, complaining to him that his father likes to study but he would rather go hunting. He tells Eliezer a story about his adventures as a hunter: "I am a hero," says he. "Several months ago in the forest I saw a huge lion, but did not run away from him, but rather came closer and closer to him until I could see his eyes. When a smart-aleck asks me why I did not knock off the lion's head, I answer that his head was cut off already." People laugh again. He continues with a story about Abraham's strange customs. "This year he bought *matses* [unleavened bread eaten during Passover] from the *yeshive* bakery and they were so hard they were impossible to eat." The audience laughs. Eliezer stands frozen and unresponsive and Ishmael starts to perform his "belly dancing" movements, holding the microphone, singing, "I am of ancient origin" and that he will soon get an inheritance which will bring lots of pleasure; "everything," he sings, "will be mine. Oxen and fields, gold and silver, diamonds and brilliants of a thousand carats . . . and white horses with golden wagons . . . I will soon be very successful and I will have everything . . . well-fed kosher pigs (the audience laughs) . . . I will live like a count because I am the only heir." Eliezer is now somewhat relaxed, and he sings, "I do not have to worry. You can speak as long as you wish. Do not tell me stories that you will get the inheritance." Here Ishmael interrupts him, teasing him while touching him, saying: "No, you will not get it." Eliezer continues, "By what right do you deserve the inheritance? You are a savage." Ishmael at this point tells Eliezer that his father is coming. Both of them disappear. Abraham comes to center stage holding the microphone close to his mouth, and sings a moving monologue to God, almost crying, telling God that all his riches are nothing to him as long as he does not have a well-behaved son. Ishmael is not a good child, and

so he and Sara do not have a child to pray for them when they die. He begs God, to whom he had devoted all his life, to fulfill his request. When he finishes his solo, several women in the women's section are holding handkerchiefs in their hands and wiping their eyes. Then from the ceiling (from a tape recorder), a "Heavenly Voice" speaks to Abraham in a cantillated melody, announcing to Abraham that his prayer had been accepted and that his people will be the chosen one of God. Abraham responds with a song of gratitude and with a moral injunction, "Trust in God." (The melody is a very popular melody from the Bobover repertoire—a composition by the *rebe*: "From the Diaspora I will gather you.") When the curtain is closed everyone joins in the singing while clapping hands, to the accompaniment of the accordion and violin.

The second scene has the same backdrop as the first, but a table and chair replace the rustic house. The curtain opens to reveal Isaac, dressed as a little Hassidic man. He sits and reads in the special intonation reserved for it, a passage from an open *Talmud* [compilation of law, with commentary]. His body sways back and forth. Ishmael comes in with a huge bow and arrow and starts laughing at him. Isaac tells him to leave him alone and to let him study. Ishmael says to him, "If you want to study, study—if you want, go on as you wish." He imitates the boy's movements. The audience enjoys it and laughs, because his movements are indelicate due to the cushion inside his clothing. Then Ishmael says to Isaac: "Leave the *Talmud* and come to me. I like to talk to you." Isaac comes closer and Ishmael sings a joyful song on how to use the bow and suggests that he learn how to hunt. Ishmael gives Isaac the bow and arrow and Isaac directs it towards him. Ishmael, worried, cries: "No! No!" The audience laughs. While Isaac holds the bow and arrow a man dressed as Sara enters. Sara wears a yellow gown, a kerchief which covers her hair, and men's shoes, and her beard has been knotted up. Her hands hold the ends of the kerchief to hide the beard. When she asks Isaac where he got the bow and arrow, she speaks in falsetto. When Isaac answers that Ishmael gave it to him, she asks him to come closer to her. Then Abraham enters, singing to Isaac, telling him that Ishmael is not a type for him to emulate and that if he associates with Ishmael he will become an Arab. While he sings, Ishmael sits on the chair where Isaac sat before and poses as if he is studying the *Talmud*. Then he stands and does his belly dance. Sara sings to Abraham, telling him that Ishmael has a bad influence on Isaac and might destroy him; therefore he must send Ishmael away. Hagar enters. She is dressed in a woman's dark robe with a kerchief covering her head and beard. Abraham sings that to please Sara, to whom he refers as "strong Sara," he is sending them away. He will give them a piece of bread and some water for the journey. This is their destiny, says he, and he wishes them all the best in the world, as it is written, "and you will go from here to the Paran desert." Hagar then sings that she accepts her destiny. The curtains close.

The third scene takes place in a desert. The drop is painted with Arizona cactuses of various sizes and shapes, as well as some small bushes. Ishmael and his mother are walking on the stage, his arm on her shoulders. They walk back and forth singing together about how miserable they are. Ishmael says to his mother, "We have been wandering here for a long time since Abraham sent us away, but it is not as bad as might be expected. I am an astrologer," continues he, "and can see what this land will look like many years from now. Now maybe there is no water but I can see a kind of *mashke* [intoxicating drink]. One cannot drink it, it smells terrible, for what it can be used I do not know. [The reference is to petroleum.] I can see how many nations will exchange 'greens' [dollars] for 'black' [oil]." The audience laughs again. "An old story," says he, "I do not understand people ... I see there also somebody, he looks like one of Abraham's children ... now I see him clearly ... he is called Hershel Kis-Kis-Kis-singer.... And I see my grandchildren all looking at an Island.... I see all that will happen in the future, and they say that today the world is crazy" (the audience laughs).... "But meanwhile I have nothing."

Then he sits on the floor and cries several times like a baby, "Mother, water." In the background cries of a jackass are heard, accompanied by the playing of an accordion, as well as an imitation of unidentified animal voices. Hagar sings. Her voice, like Sara's, is a male voice. She sits next to Ishmael, putting her arm around his shoulders, and talks about how life was different before Abraham sent them away. Ishmael then sings a happy song about how with his hunting skills and his wealth he is going to take over the world one day. He is going to rob people. The melody is the same as in the prologue and people join in as the curtain closes.

The fourth scene has the same setting as the first one. The "Heavenly Voice" is heard from the tape recorder in the ceiling. A singing dialogue begins when the voice calls for Abraham and Abraham answers, "Here I am." Then the "Heavenly Voice" asks him to sacrifice his son, and Abraham answers that he is ready to obey but asks the "Heavenly Voice" to tell him which one of his sons. The "Heavenly Voice" replies, "Your son whom you love." When Abraham says that he loves them both the voice tells him he means Isaac. Then Abraham talks to himself: "What shall I tell Sara.... I cannot tell her that I am going to sacrifice Isaac to the Father.... I will tell her I need to send Isaac away to study." He calls to Sara and when she arrives he continues to sing, telling her his plan to send Isaac away from home. He then calls for Isaac. Sara puts her arm on Isaac's shoulders, singing to him about how hard her life will be without him. (In the women's section there is crying.)

The fifth scene has a new backdrop, a desert with a valley between a rocky chain of hills. The sky is blue. There are some small bushes. Abraham calls for Ishmael and Eliezer. They appear and he sings that they should prepare themselves for a long journey. As they walk on their way (pacing back and forth on the stage), Isaac and Ishmael carry branches. Abraham stands close to Isaac at the center of the stage and they sing a dialogue, Abraham explaining that God asked him to sacrifice Isaac. Isaac does not complain but later in the song he laments his fate. Abraham starts each stanza affectionately, with the words "*Yitskhokl*" [*Yitskhok*, Hebrew for Isaac; *l*, Yiddish diminutive]. When Isaac sings he does not look directly at Abraham but rather at Abraham's shoulder. During the dialogue Isaac continues to hold the branches. The lights are red and white. Then from behind the curtain comes a man in a long black gabardine robe with flowing sleeves trimmed with two wide red stripes on each side of the front. In his hand he holds a shepherd's crook. He wears a wig of long hair with a bald spot and is hatless. The lights are focussed towards him. Some people in the audience recognizing him, say, "Satan, Satan." He approaches Abraham, who meanwhile has arranged the branches on the floor with Eliezer's help. Satan greets Abraham, asking him what he is doing with branches and his son. Abraham recognizes him, but asks him to identify himself. Satan tries to avoid revealing his identity and asks Abraham if he is the owner of the restaurant in the desert with four entrances and a big shield on which is written, "No Satan is allowed." [The allusion is to Genesis 18:1-9, in which Abraham entertains the angels.] The audience laughs again. Satan continues, "I would like to know when I can have a conversation with you." Abraham shouts, "Go away, leave me alone." Satan responds, "Maybe I can talk to you on the Sabbath, during the Torah readings?" The audience laughs. Abraham sings a duet with Satan. He sings that he is not afraid of Satan. Satan sings that he cannot be got rid of, and that yesterday he heard that Abraham intended to slaughter Isaac. "How can you use your own son as a scapegoat?" he asks. Abraham again asks him to leave, while Satan sings to Isaac, telling him to think about his poor mother and how she will feel when she finds out what has happened to him. The scene ends with Isaac singing a song of support to his father: Abraham should do what God has asked of him.

The sixth scene has the same backdrop as the first. The house is brought back, but this time without the blue door. Abraham lifts Isaac and places him prone on the house, facing the ceiling. Holding the microphone in his hand, Isaac sings a solo in which he asks Abraham to bind him tightly so he will not flinch when he is slaughtered and reminds him to use a kosher [ritually approved] knife. Meanwhile Abraham ties him with a long rope. Isaac continues to sing, asking Abraham to take one of his bones to Sara. When Isaac is completely bound, Abraham takes a huge silver-painted wooden knife, and while the violin plays, he tests the edge of the blade with his fingers. He does so for two or three minutes; Isaac lies still. The audience is very quiet. Then Abraham says: "I am ready to perform the sacrificial duty." Immediately, the "Heavenly Voice" resounds from the ceiling saying, "Don't touch the boy!" It suggests that instead of Isaac a ram be sacrificed. The prompter, who sits on the side, moves a piece of the backdrop and a painted ram is seen. Abraham releases Isaac from his bonds and the "Heavenly Voice" is heard again, praising Abraham for his obedience. Many of the men in the audience join in the singing of the last song. The curtain is closed, people move, but there is no clapping of hands or shouting of "bravo." The time is 3:00 A.M.

Source and Comment

From the Collection of Shifra Epstein (1976). Shifra Epstein describes the background, production, and performance of a Purim play that was presented on March 16, 1976, at the Bobover *Shul,* Forty-eighth Street and Fifteenth Avenue, Boro Park, Brooklyn, New York. Her study of the Purim festival as observed by the Bobover Hassidic community is part of her research as a doctoral candidate in folklore at the University of Texas.

Yiddish terms have been transliterated according to standard YIVO usage and not according to the dialect of the Bobover Hasidim. See *Esther,* III, 1-13 and IX, 24-26 for the biblical origin of Purim. In *The Parade of Heroes,* pp. 107-17.

* * *

Some Purim Parties

Congregation Tifereth Israel of Lower Bucks County, 2909 Bristol Rd., Bensalem, [Pennsylvania] is asking members of the community to help celebrate the Purim holiday at the synagogue at 6:45 P.M. March 19 [1981]. There will be readings from the Book of Esther and a costume party for families with children under 6. At 7:30 P.M. more readings for the rest of the congregation will follow. A Purim carnival is scheduled from noon to 3 P.M. March 15. All families are invited.

Purim (the Feast of Esther) is a day of merrymaking commemorating the part that Esther played in the defeat of the Persian tyrant, Haman, who sought to secure his power by making scapegoats of the Jews. Each year in March, the Book of Esther is read in the synagogue, and gifts are exchanged and distributed to the poor.

The PTA of Congregation Shaare Shamayim, 9768 Verree Rd., will present its annual Purim carnival, beginning at 11 A.M. March 15. The public is invited.

Source

Philadelphia Inquirer, March 7, 1981. From a column of religious news published each Saturday.

Purim Guide

Purim is the joyous festival which marks the miraculous victory of the Jewish people over the wicked Haman, who plotted their annihilation—2344 years ago.

This year Purim begins Monday night, March 20, and continues until Tuesday night, March 21 [1989].

The Lubavitcher Rebbe, Rabbi Menachem M. Schneerson, has appealed to Jews throughout the world to celebrate Purim properly.

ON PURIM ONE SHOULD:

LISTEN TO THE READING OF THE MEGILLAH (Scroll of Esther) on Monday night, and again on Tuesday during the daytime.

SEND GIFTS—MISHLOACH MONOT—OF AT LEAST TWO EDIBLES, such as pastry, fruit, beverages etc., to at least one friend, on Tuesday during the daytime.

GIVE CHARITY—MATONOT LoEVYONIM—to at least two needy people, or put (at least) two coins in a charity box, on Tuesday during the daytime.

RECITE THE 'AL HANISSIM' prayer in the 'Amidah' of the three daily prayers and in Grace After Meals.

EAT A FESTIVE PURIM MEAL, on Tuesday afternoon.

The day before Purim, this year Monday March 20, is the Fast of Esther. It commemorates the day of praying and fasting which the Jews did before their victory.

It is customary to give three half dollars (Machatzit Hashekel) to charity before the afternoon (Minchah) prayer.

The Rebbe called upon Jews to gather in large numbers in the Synagogue for the Purim services and that children be brought along too. The Rebbe asked that the children, girls below 12 and boys below 13 be taught to observe these Purim Mitzvot, but beyond this age everyone is obligated to fulfill them.

The Rebbe also urged that patients in hospitals and nursing homes, and Jewish prison inmates be helped to observe Purim properly.

The Rebbe extended prayerful good wishes to Jews everywhere for a joyous and inspirational Purim.

Source

An advertisement printed in the *New York Times,* March 20, 1989, by Merkos L'inyonei Chinuch, the educational arm of the Lubavitch Movement, a Hassidic sect. Paid for by "a friend of the Lubavitch Movement."

Rattlesnake Hunts

Late Winter/Early Spring

The folklorist who describes the annual snake hunt at Wiggam, Georgia, calls it "a folk custom," and he is certainly correct. To explain its origin he relates a story (fragmentary and undocumented as folktales usually are) about the death of a schoolgirl who was bitten by a rattlesnake. This custom has become almost a ritual, each year commemorating a local tragedy and purging the community of a potential danger. It is also something more: a sport calling for skill and courage, a festival attracting outsiders characterized by "a carnival atmosphere," and a source of social coherence and pride. The same is true of a rattlesnake roundup at Sweetwater, Texas, each year in the second week of March. One also wonders whether these hunts would have survived had there not been professional handlers from commercial snake farms to provide instruction and financial encouragement.

Rattlesnake Roundup at Wiggam

In southwest Georgia lies the sleepy little town of Wiggam. It is approximately ten blocks long and two blocks wide, the largest building in town being the schoolhouse. Excitement rarely touches Wiggam. Life there is normal; the pace is slow.

Three hundred and sixty-two days a year this is an accurate description of Wiggam. The other three days of the year are devoted to the annual Wiggam Rattlesnake Roundup. People travel to Wiggam from as far away as Kansas City to watch and to participate in this event. Even the Associated Press supplies national coverage.

The roundup is held in late winter or in the early spring of each year because the temperature is still fairly cold outside and the rattler, being cold blooded, stays in his hole in a semi-conscious hibernating state. If the hunt were held during a warmer season, considerably more participants would be endangered because of the snake's increased mobility.

The participants, usually long-time friends, walk the fence rows, fields, and forests in search of gopher holes. When they find one of suitable size, they insert a three or four foot piece of garden hose part way into the hole. Next, one of the team pours two or three tablespoons of gasoline into the hose and blows the fumes down through the tube and into the hole. If the team is especially lucky, the fumes will bring out a fairly large rattler, angered by this unwanted inspection. While the rattler is coming out, the team prepares a snake stick or snag loop for him. When the snake emerges, the team hesitates until the snake's head is completely out of the hole. Then the rattler is snagged in the narrow section of his body, just behind the head. The next step, and the most dangerous, is to transfer five to eight feet of supple, writhing death from the hole to a burlap bag. One of the team members holds the sack open while another inserts the snake and capture stick.

The next step is to release the snake in the bag and to withdraw the stick without being bitten or losing the captive snake. If this is the last snake of the day, the team will collect and transport their catch to the schoolyard in the center of town. When the team arrives at the collection point, they will be greeted by a carnival atmosphere. Tents, concession stands, medical exhibits, and the snake cages are spread out across the schoolyard. Pick-up trucks loaded with rattlers are lined up by the cages waiting for their turn to display their snakes. Professional snake handlers are there to receive, sort, and cage the reptiles. Open chicken-wire cages of varying sizes await the snakes. The larger ones are held up to the crowd who express their approval through great cheers.

At this point there are probably fifteen hundred rattlers in the cages with their rattlers all roaring like the sound of a jet engine at full throttle. The cages are open but roped off, so that only the handlers have immediate access to the snakes. The handlers move through the cages, counting, weighing, and sorting out the snakes by size as they are taken off the trucks. These handlers are employed by and furnished to the town by two snake farms, one in Florida, the other in Louisiana. Together with Wiggam these farms sponsor the roundup. The farms also supply two bounties: a one hundred dollar prize for the largest snake captured and a seventy-five dollar reward for the largest number of snakes.

Why does this event take place in Wiggam, and why is the schoolyard the main area of interest? I participated in the 1972 roundup with a knowledgeable friend who now lives in Chattanooga, Tennessee. We talked it over for some months before we actually left. Our reasons for going were not as personal or community minded as those of the local citizens I talked to after the hunt was over.

It seems that about twenty years ago a young schoolgirl, around seven years old, was walking alone in the schoolyard when she was struck by a fairly large rattler. The child died later that day. The story continues that the local parents were ready to lynch the town council if some immediate action was not taken. A group of Wiggam's young men was organized to avenge speedily the young girl's death. The mob went through the town killing a large number of rattlers. They did not, however, kill them all; and, in fact, more rattlers came into town. Threatened by this danger, the young men needed help and asked for it from neighboring towns. They organized a massive five-county hunt co-sponsored by the town and the previously mentioned snake farms. The snake farm handlers, skilled in snake capturing, taught the teams how to catch the snakes without taking too many risks and how to do it quickly and efficiently.

At the present time the surrounding towns are relatively snake free, and the snake population of the local countryside has decreased to safe levels again. It would appear that these hunters have taken the place of the snakes' natural predators to keep the snake population at reasonable levels and are doing quite well. The hunt is an annual affair, and each year it gains more attention and more spectators.

Why the massive local participation? Perhaps the local citizens are trying to do more than just eliminate a few snakes. They are still in some way trying to clear their collective conscience for what they feel was the useless death of a little girl, a tragedy they might have averted through careful pest control. Hence, the Wiggam schoolyard is still used as the collection point for the hunt rather than the larger town square. The scene of the original "crime" becomes the place for its annual punishment.

Source

Mississippi Folklore Register, VIII (1974), 207–09. Described by Douglas S. Button, who also collected a tale to account for its origin and speculates about its function and significance.

* * *

Rattlesnake Round-Up at Sweetwater

This area [Nolan County, Texas], since the days of its earliest pioneers, has been plagued by the harmful and dangerous rattlesnake. Countless numbers of valuable livestock have been killed by the bite of the rattlesnake. Numbers of humans, particularly young children, have been bitten by these snakes, resulting in lost limbs and lost

lives. . . . Since the Round-Up began in 1958, approximately the same number of snakes are captured each year. This shows that while the hunt helps to control the snake population, it is by no means exterminating them.

The snake hunt begins with wide-spread hunting and collection of the poisonous reptile. The captured snakes are brought to our huge Coliseum. The weigh-in operation can be viewed by the public only through heavy screen partitions. The snakes are placed in doubly lined and floored pits for public viewing.

Safety and handling demonstrations come next. False tales and rumors concerning rattlesnakes are discussed and explained by a professional rattlesnake handler, hired for this event. The public then leaves with a respect for the rattler based on understanding rather than fear. He also leaves knowing the proper procedures to follow in case of rattlesnake bite.

The snakes are milked by professional handlers. The venom is made available for public and private research. . . .

Two types of tours are also provided for visitors. The first is a bus tour for interested people and photographers who only wish to see the snakes caught and not to participate in the actual hunt. Another tour is provided for people who wish to hunt with the assistance of experienced hunters. Hunters are also able to hunt on their own on certain specified ranches in the area. All hunters who wish to participate in any of these tours or hunts must register with the Sweetwater Jaycees. The registration fee covers their hunting permit, insurance and hunting instructions. Equipment is available for rent or purchase at the registration table. All captured snakes turned in at the Round-Up become the property of the Sweetwater Jaycees.

A part of the Round-Up each year is the Miss Snake Charmer pageant. Young ladies from the Sweetwater area participate. This contest, held in the 1400 seat capacity Sweetwater High Auditorium, is held on Friday night. A dance is scheduled for Saturday night.

Source

Annual Sweetwater Jaycee Rattlesnake Round-Up, undated. From a mimeographed information sheet supplied by the Chamber of Commerce, Sweetwater, Texas, describing the "World's Largest Rattlesnake Round-Up."

* * *

Rattlesnake Roundup at Sweetwater
What You Need to Know about the Sweetwater Roundup

When and how did the Sweetwater Jaycee Rattlesnake Round-Up get started?

The first Sweetwater Round-Up was held in 1958. Some enterprising young Jaycees thought it would be a good idea to help ranchers rid themselves of some snakes and make some money doing so. That first year, 3,100 pounds of snakes were turned in. The Jaycees made about $500.00. This year is the 21st annual Round-Up.

What is the largest amount of snakes brought in?

In 1960, 8,989 pounds were turned in.

How long do rattlesnakes get to be?

The longest turned in to the Sweetwater Round-Up was 74" and was turned in by Tom Keene and Jay May in 1970. The longest recorded length is 84".

When was the last snake bite victim?

In 1971—three people were bitten during this event.

What does snake meat taste like?

It's finger lickin' chicken/fish taste.

Why isn't the meat poison?

The venom glands are in the head and are not cooked.

How long do you cook the snake?

Deep fry it like chicken for a few minutes.

What does it cost to hunt snakes?

In order to sell rattlesnakes, you must be a registered hunter. The registration fee is $10.00 and includes insurance.

How do you determine when the Round-Up is to be held?

The Sweetwater Jaycee Rattlesnake Round-Up is always held the second week-end of March.

Where is the Sweetwater Rattlesnake Round-Up held?

It is held in the Nolan County Coliseum at Newman Park in Sweetwater, Texas.

Where can I obtain additional information?

You may call or write the Sweetwater Chamber of Commerce: P. O. Box 1148, Sweetwater, Texas 79556; (915) 235-5488.

Source

Sweetwater Jaycee Rattlesnake Round-Up Program for 1979. For another civic festival sponsored by the Jaycees, see "International Pancake Race," p. 98.

St. David's Day

March 1

The patron saint of Wales, St. David, flourished in the latter part of the sixth century. Legend has it that he was of noble family and became a priest, founding a dozen monasteries and many churches, and finally an abbey at Mynyw or Menevia which was his seat as primate of South Wales. In the British colonies of North America, Welsh immigrants observed his day with song and hilarity, as English colonists celebrated St. George's Day; Scots colonists, St. Andrew's Day; and Irish colonists, St. Patrick's Day. An *eisteddfod* is a national festival to encourage music, literature and a patriotic spirit. The word literally means "a session." The custom of holding such bardic sessions is of very ancient origin. In America, *Eisteddfodau* (plural form) came to be ethnic reunions that featured songfests and merrymaking.

Eisteddfod on St. David's Day

I collected these songs and rhymes in October, 1942. They are the folk sayings and songs of my mother's family. My mother is Mrs. A. J. Jones of Knoxville; she was Edith Wynn before her marriage. She was born in Mahoney City, Pennsylvania, in 1879, the third child in a family of twelve. Her parents were both Welsh. Her father, who was the parent from whom she learned most of her songs and sayings, came from Wales when he was sixteen years old, and settled in Mahoney City. In 1883 the Wynn family moved with several other Welsh families to Dowless, Kentucky, and established the mining settlement of East Tennessee. The Welsh culture was kept alive by Eisteddfodau, which were meetings held in a certain settlement to which other Welsh people from the surrounding territory came for the purpose of competitive singing. These festivals were held only on St. David's day, the first of March, and were accompanied with much merriment. It was in the mining camp, East Tennessee, that Edith Wynn learned the Welsh cultural heritage of folklore. The Welsh people with whom she associated there are no longer a group. They have moved to different parts of the country, and their Welsh songs have moved with them....

This song is one with which Mr. Wynn, Edith Wynn's father, entertained the Welsh people at *Eisteddfodau*. He sang it while dressed in a high silk hat, and while twirling a cane, at which he was quite adept. The song was accompanied by dance steps, which carried the rhythm after the lines, "My name is Pat," and "Just look at that."

My Name It Is McCan

Oh, my name it is McCan, McCan, McCan.
I'm a true-born Irish man, oh man, oh man.
I love the O'Conner, O'Conner, O'Conner;
I do upon my honor, honor, honor.

For my name is Pat——
Just think of that——
We'll dance all night 'til broad daylight
And go home with the gils (girls) in the morning.
We'll dance all night 'til broad daylight
And go home with the gils in the morning.

From Wibbleton to Wobbleton

This song was sung by Cap'n Wynn at the *Eisteddfodau*. There was no other verse to the song, but this one verse was sung over and over, each time as if it were going to be a new verse. Perhaps it is a commentary on the Welsh sense of humor, but it is reported that the audience would laugh until they cried as he began each new verse.

From Wibbleton to Wobbleton is eighteen miles
From Wobbleton to Wibbleton is eighteen miles
From Wibbleton to Wobbleton, Wobbleton to
Wibbleton
Wibbleton to Wobbleton is eighteen miles.

Source and Comment

Tennessee Folklore Society Bulletin, IX (December 1943), 1-3, 7. Wynne Jones, while a graduate student at the University of Tennessee, recorded these songs and supplied their background. She knew them from family tradition. They are edited by Edwin C. Kirkland, with tunes transcribed by Dorothy Horne. Cf. "From Wibbleton to Wobbleton" with French-Canadian songs called "rigamaroles" in *Journal of American Folklore,* XXXI (1918), 158–59. See also Thompson Type 2320 and Baughman, Motif Z 80, which cite rounds and formulistic rhymes.

St. David's Day, 1736

On Monday last the Anniversary of the Birth-day of her Majesty our most gracious Queen Caroline (who then entered in the 53d Year of her Age) was celebrated here [in Charlestown, South Carolina] with all the demonstrations of Joy imaginable.... The same Day being St. David's Day, the Welch Club having met at Mr. Woolford's [tavern], caused several Guns to be fired after Sun-set, contrary to an Act of General Assembly ... whereby they incurr'd the Penalty inflicted by the said Law, and upon Information made against them, paid £10 to the Poor.

Source

South Carolina Gazette, March 6, 1736. Supplied by Andy Cohen of Charleston, South Carolina.

Dolls' or Girls' Festival

March 3

Almost a thousand years ago, Lady Murasaki, author of the Japanese classic, *The Tale of Genji,* described doll-playing as an almost ritualistic pastime that employed "diminutive stands, dishes, chopstick rests, etc." This practice evolved into a festive family ceremonial which expresses loyalty to the emperor, visualized in the five-step shelf with the two principal dolls at the top, and the lesser ranks on shelves below. The dolls also serve as models of decorum, their calm smiling demeanor presumably inculcating like qualities in the young girls honored by this festival. The dolls are exhibited for several days, and the festival provides occasions for family reunions and visits to admire them. For the male counterpart, see "Boys' Festival," p. 203.

Dolls' Day

A holiday which is a source of great delight to the girls in Japan is the Dolls' Festival of March 3rd, well-known in American circles. On this day all the Japanese who have daughters set up a little table in the corner of a room on which to display all the dolls owned by the girls in the family. Boxes or boards are arranged in step-formation and covered with a bright red cloth. On the top row are the miniatures of the Emperor and Empress in antique court costume—dolls perfect in every detail of clothes, headgear, hairdress, and accessories—each seated on a lacquered dais. Below them are the ladies-in-waiting; on the next step, the court-musicians, each with his instrument, and so on until as complete a picture as possible is given of court life in the feudal days of Japan. Besides these dolls, there are numerous others of every description, large and small, new and old, and heirlooms which have been preserved from many years past, less aristocratic perhaps but more lovable. Little lanterns, pine trees and branches of cherry blossoms, in addition to tiny house furnishings in silver, lacquer, and porcelain scattered here and there, tend further to enhance the display. A table set in front of all the dolls is heaped with food which might appeal to them and their fostermothers—sweet wine, white wine, candies, cookies, and pretty tricolored diamond-shaped rice cakes.

All the little Japanese girls on this day don their holiday attire and visit their friends' homes to view the doll exhibits. "Oh-ing" and "ah-ing" over the "little babies" is accompanied by much admiring, caressing, and flattering. The dolls are offered hot tea, and various luxurious refreshments are placed before them, and it is only after they are served that the girls themselves join in the party. Besides thus feasting their eyes and palates, Japanese girls are given gifts of dolls by parents, relatives, or friends. These are added to the collection they already possess.

Source

Southwestern Journal of Anthropology, II (1946), 169. Described by "Miss N. I." who, in 1934, collected information on Japanese holidays for a study of customs and beliefs of Oriental minorities living in the San Francisco Bay area. She used "older," Japanese-speaking informants. Her research director and editor was Paul Radin.

Buzzard Day
March 15

The curious fact that a flock of turkey buzzards return annually on March 15 to Hinckley Ridge, near Hinckley, Ohio, has given rise to legend, speculation and a local festival. Turkey buzzards are so called because their featherless red heads resemble those of wild turkeys. The Hinckley Buzzard Day Festival takes place on the first Sunday after March 15. It features a pancake breakfast, the sale of such souvenirs as T-shirts and bumper stickers, and a bird walk to the south end of Hinckley Lake, the favored habitat of the vultures.

The Buzzards of Hinckley

The uncanny clock-like return of 75+ turkey vultures to Hinckley Ridge each March 15 has been the subject of folk legends dating back nearly 150 years.

But few other than local historians paid much attention to the return of these birds—until recently.

That is, 1957, when Robert Bordner, a *Cleveland Press* writer, became interested in a claim by Metroparks patrolman Walter Nawaleniec. He told the reporter that he had personally observed the buzzards' arrival to Hinckley each March 15 for the past 6 years and that his predecessor, the late Charlie Willard, had kept a personal log of their arrival for the past 23 years!

The reporter's interest was aroused. He wrote and printed in the Feb. 15, 1957, issue of the *Cleveland Press,* the longtime legend of the Hinckley Buzzards. He further predicted their return in exactly one month—March 15.

Excitement mounted as the month progressed. Naturalists, ornithologists, reporters repeated and embellished the original story—and suspense mounted.

To make a long story short, March 15 arrived and so did the buzzards—right on schedule. News travelled fast and the weekend brought throngs of media and sightseers from Ohio, Pennsylvania and Indiana.

The township was unprepared for the 9000 plus visitors that flocked to participate in the biggest bird walk in history....

A normally hospitable Hinckley community was dazed by the volume of people and embarrassed to be caught "with its manners down." Plans to prevent such a reoccurrence began almost immediately.

Carl and Catherine Neu, Edward Spatz and other members of the Hinckley Chamber of Commerce teamed up and made arrangements for a pancake breakfast at Brongers Park, the first Sunday of Spring (the first Sunday after March 15). This day was declared "Buzzard Day." ...

Over the years, the fame of the Hinckley Buzzards has spread—today their legendary return rivals stories of the "Swallows of Capistrano!"

As more learn of the buzzards never failing to return to Hinckley, more and more ask—why?

Theories are plentiful.

Some believe that the buzzards were first attracted by the tons and tons of butchered refuse and unwanted game after the "Great Hinckley Varmit Hunt" of December 24, 1818. At that time, 475 men and boys lined up along Hinckley's 25 mile square perimeters and began moving inward, in one of the largest drives in history to rid an area of predatory animals destroying local farm stock.

An old manuscript account by William Cogswell, one of the first white men to set foot in the township around 1810, makes several references to "vultures of the air" at the gallows of the Big Bend in the Rocky River where the Wyandotes had hung an Indian squaw for witchcraft two years earlier.

The finding of this manuscript indicated that the buzzard had made its home in Hinckley before 1810, so the "why Hinckley" question remains a mystery.

Source and Comment

The Buzzards of Hinckley, Ohio, a brochure published by the Hinckley Chamber of Commerce, Inc. Information also supplied by Reg Slater, secretary of the Chamber of Commerce. See "The First Swallows of San Juan Capistrano," p. 133.

Though hardly a folk festival, Clarksville, Missouri, and other small towns in that state have had "Eagle Days" in late December and January since 1978, when bald eagles fly south from Canada and the Great Lakes. They attract ornithologists and wildlife enthusiasts and are encouraged by conservation authorities.

Iowa Girls State Basketball Tournament
Second Week in March

Girls' basketball was introduced to Iowa as part of the movement to involve women in sports and physical education at the turn of the century. Its popularity was so great, especially among the small towns and rural schools, that by 1979, only three Iowa schools failed to field girls' basketball teams. Although almost all the girls' teams in the world now play boys' rules (five players, instead of six, who, not confined to zones, are free to dribble continuously anywhere on the court), about eighty percent of the Iowa schools persist in the old way, featuring a girls' tournament which has a championship series and pageant that generates enough revenue to support many other girls' programs and which has brought national publicity to the state.

The first tournament took place in 1920 and was played on a court with three zones. By 1934, however, the present two-zone court was adopted and the tendency has been to speed up the game since. In nearly a century of existence, girls' six-player basketball has developed from an almost stationary game to one that accentuates fast passes, planned plays, and agile athletes. And if most of the rest of the country looks on six-player basketball as obsolete, Des Moines hotels are booked months in advance of tournament week, radio and television contracts are prized, and the girls' tournament is received with much greater enthusiasm than is the boys' tournament.

Sport as Ritual: The Iowa Girls High School Basketball Tourney

Girls' basketball has been a distinctive enduring sport in Iowa for the past sixty years. Any newcomer to Iowa, particularly to a smaller community, quickly learns that knowledge of six-player basketball is a vital part of the enculturation process. Iowans residing in metropolitan areas who once looked down their noses in disdain upon girls' basketball are just as involved now that their schools are participating.

In 1979 there were 495 high school girls' basketball teams in Iowa. Each team's goal is to represent their high school at the State Tournament which is held each year during the month of March in Des Moines, the capital city. Great honor and prestige attend the "Sweet Sixteen", those sixteen teams who emerge victorious through sectional and district play.

School mates, fans, teachers, families, and patrons support their team throughout the season and nowhere is this more evident than at the State Tournament. The most tourney attendance numbered approximately 90,000; the state population is 2.9 million. In addition, the tournament is broadcast by major radio networks and the last few games are televised. The television contract for this event is the most lucrative of any high school sport in the United States. It enables large numbers of viewers both in and out of state to witness the final games and accompanying pageantry. The governor of the state attends each yearly championship game. It is evident that girls' basketball constitutes a highly significant socio-cultural facet of Iowa life.

Six-player basketball is a particularly Iowa cultural variant, as interesting, unique, and exotic as sporting events in other cultures. This style of basketball has been remarkably constant during the economic depression of the 1930's, throughout the years of the second World War, and despite recent threats of Department of Health, Education, and Welfare legal action under Title IX.

What is it about this event that brings thousands of spectators from both in and out of state; that allows the organizers to spend in excess of $100,000; that supports a well developed program of 17 other sports for high school girls in Iowa? Is it the sport, the highly structured six-player ball, or is it something more integral to the common life style of Iowa communities? I would like to propose that over time the whole tournament has become a bonafide ritual cloaked in the elaborate framework of play....

Analysis brought out the following: 1) Girls' basketball has fulfilled a need for diversion, and has developed school and community identification; 2) through the years six-player ball has become an acceptable vehicle for athleticism among young women because it is distinct from boys' play; and 3) the rituals associated with basketball are a major factor in the continued success of the sport. In the interest of brevity, only the third will be discussed.

As society has become more complex and people's interest more confederated, the rituals associated with girls' basketball have become more efficient, highly organized, and formal. The technological thrust of this era is reflected in the monies spent for various parts of the tournament, the detailed preparations for the printed program, the hiring of the best cameramen of the nation, and of course, the split second timing of the entire extravaganza.

Thus it is that the Iowa girls' basketball tournament attracts more followers, more media attention, and arouses more enthusiasm than the Iowa boys' tourney. As one of the tournament set clean-up crew members noted to a reporter, "The girls have a lot of pageantry, the boys just play basketball."...

Several months prior to the tournament, the male officials of the Iowa Girls' High School Athletic Union (IGHSAU) begin their elaborate preparation for this event. They make all decisions relative to the conduct of the tournament; it is very firmly under their control, and is managed with notable business acumen.

Various practices associated with the tournament resemble [anthropologist Arnold Van] Gennep's classical interpretation of the significance of rites. These rites will be described; the 1) rite of separation, 2) rite of transition, and 3) rite of incorporation (1960:11).

Stage one, the rite of separation, involves pre-tourney activities such as pep rallies wherein players are recognized by their contemporaries, school faculty, and community residents; extensive news coverage with special issues or special sections being devoted to the team; individual and corporate decision making regarding appropriate clothing, jewelry, and good luck items; and development of posters, banners, slogans, and cheers—intended to publicize and encourage players or cast a spell on the opponents. The athletes are then considered fully ready to be released from their home, school, and community. They are commissioned to represent them as well. School authorities actively support and encourage this activity by allotting released time for these activities and by recessing school the day or days of tournament play. The team and sometimes the whole community begin a period of detachment, suspended in time from the ordinary events of life.

Following their detachment or rite of separation from the home environment, the girls enter the period of transition. Within that period ... they are neither part of their home environment as they once were, but at the same time they have not entered the subgroup of the "Sweet Sixteen", the

sixteen teams vying for the championship. Once they have arrived and are ensconced in their Des Moines motel ... they are cut off from normal social contact. From that point they follow specifically prescribed procedures developed by the coaches (almost invariably male) regarding such things as meals, rest, and contacts with males. They ... experience everything together and individual action such as meeting a friend downtown is not permitted.

As the games commence, there are the usual pre-game, half-time, and post-game behaviors. Oftentimes, in addition, the television commentator will interview mothers or grandmothers of current players, thus emphasizing the linear relationship or the passing down of the skill. In addition to the on-court "huddles" there are the traditional cheers and chants, hand slapping, carrying of stuffed toys or other items for good luck, or the wearing of special clothes or jewelry or the use of an item such as a rabbit's foot....

An important figure in all the proceedings throughout the tournament is the "cover girl" or queen, and her presence is especially important on the final evening as she escorts many dignitaries. Preparatory to selection of the cover girl, basketball players have been carefully observed over a period of three years by male officials at games throughout the state. In the fall of the school year, the choice narrows and school academic records and cocurricular activities are investigated. Final selection is made by a committee of males after a careful screening by Wayne Cooley, the executive secretary of the Iowa Girls' High School Athletic Union. The values espoused by the union must be strongly exemplified in this cover girl. As Cooley said, "All the players look at the cover girl and say, 'That's me'." In Cooley's evaluation, she is a role model for younger basketball players....

Prior to the final game all sixteen teams are introduced. They parade in with split second timing onto the floor while the statistics regarding wins and losses are given, and coaches' records likewise given. Players wear corsages donated by loyal fans. One wonders if the corsages are an effective means of reinforcing femininity in the rough and tumble tournament play. The coaches in the 1979 tourney often wore three piece dark suits and a boutonniere as well.

The approximately 300 basketball players remain on the floor as the champions of the 17 other sports representing the 2,400 teams sponsored under the auspices of the athletic union are introduced. These sports include a wide variety from gymnastics to golf and from softball to synchronized swimming. The girls wear their playing uniform and carry the implement they use, such as a tennis racquet or softball bat, and all wear corsages. These approximately 500 girls, representing the thousands of Iowa girls who participate in sports, then leave the floor in an orderly fashion.

Next follows the Salute to America—a slick, professionally directed production. The intention of this is to entertain, but at the same time to foster pride in Iowa, its heritage, and the nation. It is all planned and directed by men, and only high school girls participate.

A jazz band composed of tuxedo clad high school musicians plays "This is My Country". A female soloist joins in and sings the first two stanzas of "My Country, 'Tis of Thee", and "God Bless America".

The salute to honor all the states begins. Twenty-four attractive flagbearers, wearing silver colored sequined leotards and crowns, parade with the flags of the original thirteen colonies as the announcer reminds the audience of the principles upon which the nation was founded, noting special things such as liberty and freedom.

The next group of states is represented by black and white sequined flagbearers, as the announcer talks about the new frontiers and the slow and steady expansion over the mountains into the lands of midwest.

The states south of the Mason-Dixon line are described as being lands of cattle, oil, and cotton, and are represented by white sequined flagbearers and girls, resembling majorettes, who wear Stetson hats and do a snappy drill routine with wooden guns.

The next group represents the midwest neighbors, and is identified as the land of labor. Dancers (Caucasians) in ankle length red and white feather headdresses wearing war paint do a facsimile of an Indian dance while the usual orange sequined flagbearers do their routine of fancy steps.

The Oregon and Mormon Trail states are represented by gold clad sequined girls. Dance hall girls in satin dresses with ostrich feathers in their hair do a discreet can-can.

The Pacific states are represented by white sequined flagbearers. The announcer calls them the treasury of states while the grass-skirted, lei-draped girls do a demure hula.

As the music in the background gradually builds to a crescendo, the emcee intones, "But the place to live and grow is Iowa ... the best in all the land!", the lights are dimmed, the spotlight focuses on the white sequined crowned flagbearer carrying the Iowa flag. At that precise moment all the other flagbearers unfurl their Iowa flags and the band picks up with the "Iowa Corn Song."

The climax of this extravaganza comes as the announcer says, "The spirit of America is the home of the brave and the free. With God's blessings may we continue to grow and prosper." The American flag then takes center stage on the gym floor, flashing lights focus on it and red, white, and blue bunting is unrolled to frame the flag in a large rectangle. Simultaneously, the Iowa flagbearers kneel. The national anthem is played, and the audience joins in

singing. The cameramen frantically run about trying to get the best angle on the flag.

The ceremony concludes with kudos to the band, the pageant participants, and the soloist with the words, "This is just another example of the outstanding talent being developed in the Iowa schools." Tuxedo clad, boutonniere-wearing young men, tall, handsome basketball or volleyball players, are ready at one end of the floor to clean it. At the instruction, "Men, man your brooms", they begin a dignified, cadenced march to the other end of the floor. At the same precise moment, they all make a snappy about face and sweep going back. The rationale for this is that it is important not to take the television cameras or the audience's attention from what is going on down on the floor. The floors needed to be swept, and so they dressed it up. Young men are eager to do it, and as Cooley says, "Every high school girl basketball player thinks, 'He's doing that for me.'"

The pageantry just described was first held at a time when the managership was having difficulty filling the 15,000 seat auditorium. The Parade of Champions ritual was developed as a good show—a clean show that a family would enjoy. Most people who attend the basketball tourney would not consider going to a night club show, but through this ritualized pageant they satisfy the desire for color and spectacle. The scantily clad, yet demure, young women and the tenor of the production do not offend ritual standards of decency and propriety. The fact that it has a patriotic and quasi-religious theme gives it an aura of respectability. Coupled with an athletic event, its credibility is even more firmly established. In the halftime show a major effort is made to tightly control the production, screen everyone who participates, and alter anything that seems risque or improper. For instance, they refrain from using "too high kickers" because that is too risque. They work to get overall thrust of dignity and prestige to the high school girl and give a good show. As Cooley has so often said, "I've had a romance with the Iowa high school girl. I provided things for her, have been jealous for her and protected her interests. She has returned so much."

One might question whether the game is still the main attraction. As Cooley comments, "Americans are still spectators, not competitors; they look for entertainment." He recognized this, correctly assessed public tastes and values, and has fulfilled a need. At the same time, it has been an economic bonanza.

The championship game follows the pageant and careful attention is devoted to it. The usual introductory procedures are followed. Following the introduction of players, coaches, and officials, the game begins. The striking thing about it is that all management, rule-making decisions are made by men.

Halftime ceremonies feature the induction of a few selected outstanding former players into the Iowa Girls' Basketball Hall of Fame. These women participated in years past and are part of a select group currently numbering 128 in 1979. Their basketball achievements are announced as they are escorted to the floor by the cover girl. They are presented large trophies, Victoria awards, as the spotlight focuses on them. Next, one or two outstanding coaches are given the Honor Coach award. The announcer, with total solemnity, intones their various accomplishments as they are likewise awarded trophies.

At the conclusion of the championship game there is the usual reaction of the winners and losers. There is jubilant jumping up and down, hugging and kissing among the players, and the tearful congratulations of the losers. Of course, they are mobbed by fans. Winners are awarded huge trophies and losers small editions. Winners of the free throw championship are introduced and their accomplishments are announced.

Then the decisions of the coaches in selection of the eight member all-tourney team are announced. The players come forward; some of them still wearing their playing uniforms and others in spring dresses or pants. All of them embrace and shed tears. The winning coach is then awarded the traditional red coat which seems very reminiscent of procedures noted by anthropologists among primitive peoples.

This ritual within ritual is another example of the setting apart of the elite players and coach, part of the rite of transition described by van Gennep. Being selected all-tourney is the ultimate of honors bestowed. Although not actually given instruction or initially secretly as in the classic description of transition rites, there is the symbolic setting apart from the rest of the players.

The announcer finishes the long, exhausting, but nevertheless exhilarating evening with the words, "Some of the finest girl basketball players in the United States play here in Iowa."

Following the championship game, the two top teams, their school officials, board of education, parents, brothers and sisters, are all feted at a formal dinner. After the dinner the girls, as Cooley says, "Are returned to their families whom they haven't seen for a week."

These players, as well as those from the other 14 teams are welcomed home with elaborate ceremonies, car caravans, special programs, newspaper and media publicity, and the admiration of adulatory fans. They have completed the last of the three stages of ritual, that of incorporation. They are given new status and are expected to act in certain ways appropriate for one who has achieved status; their rights and duties are rather clearly defined.

For the community, the Iowa Girls' State Basketball Tournament provides an opportunity to reaffirm its purposes, origins, and beliefs. The metamessages of morality, sanctity, and patriotism conveyed through the Salute to America pageant strike a responsive chord. As much, or perhaps more, the rituals associated with the sport allow for expressions of emotions and sentiment, convey enduring messages about the constancy of life despite rapid technological and social changes, and enable reaffirmation of traditional values.

Additionally, the tournament with its ritual, provides entertainment and excitement. It is held every year at the end of a long winter season when life has been drab and difficult. Throughout the regular season, girls' basketball games represent a major portion of people's entertainment and constitute an important activity. Teams serve to unify and develop community solidarity; participation in the state tournament reinforces community pride and allows for more participation and excitement. Because of its collective representation, girls' basketball has captured the serious attention of the communities in which it is played.

Religion in Iowa, in contrast with that of other cultures, traditionally has been somewhat austere and colorless with little emotional display. The pageant, a quality performance, conducted in a solemn manner following commonly accepted standards of decency, utilizes a quasi-religious theme that is welcomed by tournament spectators. Thus, it would seem that the color, the pageantry, and the encouragement of emotion associated with the ritual of the tournament fulfill a need not met by religion.

For the player, participation in the state tournament culminates years of preparation and fulfills a lifetime ambition. Again, the play is important but the ritual associated with the play gives it added meaning. Through the rites of separation, transition, and incorporation, the players achieve prestige and are ascribed new positions in society. They become role models for younger girls, essentially sport idols. They are almost public property for a time; their scope of influence increases, and their power, likewise, increases because of their achievement. This new position brings both joys and problems. They are besieged with autograph requests, are subjects for media coverage, receiving marriage proposals, and less frequently, receive obscene telephone calls.

The various rituals of the Parade of Champions, the Salute to America, and the Hall of Fame Induction were all designed for specific purposes. The expressed purpose is to honor the outstanding abilities of Iowa high school girls, however, the attendant rituals seem to downplay the athletic achievements. It was conveyed by the individual organizing the rituals that these are an important method of increasing tournament revenue. The Parade of Champions is specifically designed to increase attendance. The

Salute to America, although designed to honor the nation's founding fathers, the State of Iowa, and the United States, also attracts lucrative television contracts which in turn allow for more expansion in services to female high school students and, perhaps, increases monies available to the IGHSAU. The Hall of Fame/Honor Coach ceremony was instituted to honor former outstanding players and coaches.

The reciting of the accomplishments of the inductees effectively communicates the impression that despite the fact that six-player ball is still played in Iowa, the players have achieved success both nationally and internationally. This is intended to rebound to the credit of the IGHSAU in promoting six-player ball and ensures the continuance of this unique and, to many, outdated and limiting basketball.

Source and Comment

From an article by Janice A. Beran entitled "The Iowa Girls' High School Basketball Tournament Viewed as an Institutionalized Ritual" published in *Play as Context,* Alyce Taylor, ed., West Point, N.Y., 1979, 149-57. Some of the information obtained June 27, 1978, during an interview with Wayne Cooley, Executive Secretary, Iowa Girls' Athletic Union.

"Old style" girls' basketball as played in Iowa is a game in which the court is equally divided, players are limited to two dribbles, and each team has three forwards and three guards playing at one time. The guards are not allowed to shoot and are limited to playing in the opposing team's forward court. Players do not cross the center line.

The "queen" or "cover girl" of the tournament is selected by male basketball officials who consider ability, behavior, personal appearance, and academics. Moreover, each year four to six women who played during the first state tournament in 1920 or during the six years prior to their nomination are selected to the Iowa Girls' Basketball Hall of Fame.

St. Patrick's Day
March 17

St. Patrick, born near the Severn in Britain probably in A.D. 389, is the patron saint of Ireland. When he was sixteen, he is said to have been stolen from his home by Irish outlaws and sold as a slave. After six years as a slave in Antrim he escaped into Gaul. He returned to Ireland as a bishop in order to convert the land of his captivity to Christianity. He was highly successful, and by the time of his death in 461, Ireland was well on the way to being a Christian nation. He is reputed to have driven all the snakes from Ireland, although biologists have assured us there were none there at the time, and his name is always associated with the shamrock because he was in the habit of using its three leaves to explain the Trinity. Irish-Americans in New York City have made their annual Fifth Avenue Parade on his feast day a major American event.

In Ireland, St. Patrick's Day is a religious day accompanied by church ceremonies, much like Christmas and Easter. The Irish do not drink green beer, wear shamrocks, or march in festive parades except as a means of meeting the expectations of tourists. Nonetheless, the enthusiasm for this ethnic celebration in America has had its effect on the old country. For example, Galway does hold a full-scale parade, even if it is paid for by shopkeepers and local hotel owners.

St. Patrick's Day Parades

Although the St. Patrick's Day parade may be the largest ethnic spectacle in the United States, many Irish-Americans feel ambivalent about it. On the one hand, the green lines painted on the parkways and the green paper hats appear vulgar and trite in contrast to the joyous array of symbols in the Italian *festa* or the Spanish-speaking community's fiesta. What Irish-American does not feel anger at the sight of a donkey cart bearing "The World's Worst Irish Tenor" or a pudgy young woman in a green T-shirt inscribed "Erin Go Bra-less"? How many of us are not weary of hearing the strident sounds of "Sweet Rosie O'Grady" and "When Irish Eyes Are Smiling" lunge out at us from the crowded bars along the parade route? Every year on March 17 I want to swear off clay pipes and blackthorns.

But then I see in my mind's eye my grandfather in top hat and morning suit, adorned with a sash across his chest proclaiming that the Country Galway was his ancestral home. He always marched with a unit of the Ancient Order of Hibernians—like so many other AOH stalwarts who graced the parades in New York and Chicago and San Francisco 30 years ago. In Boston there are still memories of Mayor James Curley riding in the parade in a fur coat, piously shaking hands with priests and nuns along the way; of Grand Marshall Knocko McCormack (brother of former House Speaker John McCormack) heaving his 300 pounds onto a dray horse that hauled the ashcart for the City of Boston; of Up-Up Kelly, a Curley lieutenant, punctuating the mayor's St. Patrick's Day speech by jumping up every minute to applaud Curley's excoriation of the British and urging the audience to do likewise; of thirsty marchers thronging into P. J. Connelly's Bar for a "one and one"—a half-glass of blended whiskey and a dime glass of draft beer for a chaser. In those days the St. Patrick's Day parade had style and verve, and gave you a sense that the Irish had come from the docks and the railroad construction gangs to win a measure of acceptance in America.

In the nineteenth century, the Irish in America had no ambivalence about their enthusiasm for St. Patrick's Day parades. By the late 1840's the annual turnout in New York had dramatically increased with the coming of the Great Famine emigrants. In 1846 the *New York Herald* reported that during the St. Patrick's Day Mass at St. Columba's Church on 25th Street, the Reverend Joseph Burke preached on the life of the saint in the Irish language. The reporter commented: "The oration was all Greek to us; but to judge from the breathless silence which prevailed during its delivery, we saw that the audience was delighted with it." The New York press described the burgeoning parades of the 1850's and 1860's with increased detail. By 1870 the line of march looked like this: a platoon of policemen; the Sixty-Ninth Regiment; the

Legion of St. Patrick; Men of Tipperary; 21 divisions of the Ancient Order of Hibernians; numerous parish benevolent societies and total abstinence units (e.g., "Father Mathew T.A.B. Society No. 2 of New York, 400 men" and "St. Bridget's R.C.T.A.B. Society, 1300 members"). Thirty-thousand men walked in the procession of 1870.

The parades of that day sometimes drew complaints from certain quarters. The *Irish Citizen* protested in 1868 that because so many German bands were hired, there weren't enough Irish airs in the parade:

> We are aware that there are but a few Irish bands in the city, but if those who hire the German bands insisted on having Irish music ... their demands would be attended to. We feel confident that nearly every man in the procession would prefer marching to one of the spirit-stirring airs with which they are familiar in the old land—if only played by a fife and drum—than to have their ears dinned with the *chef d'ouvres* of some foreign composer, which could never awaken a responsive throb in their hearts, or impart a spring to their step.

But generally the Irish-American press praised the manly bearing of the marchers and the enthusiasm of the spectators or pointed out parade highlights. In 1863 the *Metropolitan Record* told of a group of boys, 10 to 16 years old, who in green jackets and black pantaloons carried two banners. One was inscribed "The Temperance Cadets of the Visitation of the Blessed Virgin" and the other read: "All's Right: Dad's Sober." In 1871 the *Irish Citizen* described "a triumphal car" drawn by 10 white horses "covered completely with green drapery, fringed with gold and ornamented with mottoes in gold." Surmounting this car was a huge bust of Daniel O'Connell and seated in front of the bust a certain Mr. McClean, "harp in hand, to represent the Irish minstrel." McClean was described as a man

> who stands six feet four in his stockings and is splendidly proportioned. Flowing white locks fell over his shoulders and on his head was a wreath of oak leaves, with acorns of gold. A long white plaited beard fell down on his breast. He wore a jacket and skirting, with a heavy cloak and drapery of saffron, trimmed with gold and green. About his waist was a red belt with a gold buckle. His tights were of saffron and his sandals scarlet. With golden bracelets, a large Tara brooch, set with jewels, and a small harp, which rested on his knee—his attire was complete.

To the rear of the bust rested in *papier-mache* an ancient Irish wolfhound "as large as a colt," bearing the legend "Gentle When Stroked; Fierce When Provoked." The car was preceded by a six foot seven inch "Irish Chieftain," with "his long-haired, herculean retainers and trumpeters."

Obviously the Irish of that time in America revered symbols with origins in a distinctive, ancient culture.

Source

Ethnicity, II (1975), 244-46. Charles J. O'Fahey's descriptions of St. Patrick's Day parades of the past are from personal recollections and contemporary newspapers which he cites in his study of traditional oratory associated with this celebration.

* * *

St. Patrick's Day Oration

At the conclusion of the St. Patrick's Day parade in New York in 1860, the Reverend D. W. Cahill spoke for two and a half hours to an overflowing crowd at the Academy of Music. His speech was filled with fantasy themes vividly describing British perfidy in Ireland. Referring to the seventeenth century, he said:

> I remember the history of the priests of those days, and when the poor priest, with brogues upon his feet, with his vestments in a bag on his shoulders, went from house to house, and there was five pounds upon his head but no one ever betrayed him. He stole to meet his flock in a lonely valley, and many a day the sun rose on their devotions ... and they celebrated the Mass under the broad canopy of the skies in the sight of God and the angels of heaven.

Cahill told his audience how he often visited in Ireland the ruins of monasteries destroyed by the invader. He declared:

> How often have I stood where the altar was, and at the priest's grave and said, O God, if I could wish to make a speech, this is the place where I would like to stand, on the martyr ashes of the dead ... and say, will you send me up some of the warmth of spirit you had when living, and teach me speak in the defense of my country and religion.

And all this to Irish-Americans who, five or six years earlier, had encountered Know-Nothing hatred of Irish Catholics on the streets of New York.

Cahill, a professor of history in Ireland who had come to New York to help in the Catholic Church's ministry to Irish immigrants, moved his hearers with accounts of his experiences as a priest during the Great Famine. That the priest and his audience—many of them Famine emigrants themselves—were caught up in the painful memories of this disaster is evident in this passage:

> The potato crop failed and that was the heaviest curse—I won't say curse, I will say trial—that ever fell upon Ireland. The churchyards were red and are red yet with the blood of the dead buried without coffins. How can a man paint hell to please the fancy? How can a man describe damnation in pleasing colors to amuse you? How

can a man walk over the graveyards of the uncoffined dead and speak with politeness?

In another part of his speech he described the effects of the Famine in the County Clare:

No one could believe, in going through Clare, the fearful extermination that took place in those days. During the famine fever I saw little children with not a smile on their faces. The little children starving and fever in their house, in place of seeing them playing in the green fields, their father and mother dead, and the little things sat by the walls and crept about without a smile in their faces. Lamentation covered the country like a dark cloud: the churchyards were brimful, and the coffins appeared above the surface.

It was the practice of these Irish-American orators to balance the tales of persecution and suffering with humorous anecdotes and asides. The editor who printed the text of Cahill's address indicated in parentheses many reactions of laughter to the priest's wit and stories. Even when he talked of the Famine emigration, Cahill could be comical:

Many a time I have gone to the custom house in Dublin to see a ship off for America. I recollect on one occasion of seeing on board an old man with a little child on his back. He had a few scattered hairs on his head, and the poor little fellow had hold of his grandfather's coat behind. This poor old fellow was kissing a dog. "What on earth," said I, "is the reason you are kissing the dog?" Not knowing me, he said, "O sir, it's no matter to you what I am doing." I insisted upon knowing the reason, and he explained that, having been driven from his lands by his landlord, he was obliged to go to America, and that his dog "Brady"—who was born on the same day with the child on his back—persisted in following them. At the solicitation of his children, he was going to take the dog along with them; and so they were paying ten shillings for his passage. In the meantime Brady began to bark and I said, "What is the dog barking for?" "O," said the old man, "doesn't he hear us talking of the landlord, sir?"

The Irish detestation of British landlords was proverbial, and in the Ireland of that day even the dogs knew who the enemy was.

Source and Comment

Ethnicity, II (1975), 247-48. The St. Patrick's Day oration by the Reverend D. W. Cahill is cited by Charles J. O'Fahey as typical of a genre popular during the last century. Using Ernest Bormann's definition of "fantasy themes," meaning "a recollection of something that happened to the group in the past or a dream of what the group might do in the future," O'Fahey explains that such orations gave the audience "a sense of participation in a social drama" vital to their self-identification and hence their ability to survive as a group.

Irish Coffee

Irish Coffee was invented either 34 years ago in the Shannon Airport bar in Western Ireland, or 27 years ago at the Buena Vista Cafe, not far from the bottom of the Leavenworth Street cable car line in San Francisco. The weight of evidence lies with Shannon.

The story is that on St. Patrick's Day 1946 a bartender, coming to work at the airport after observing the hallowed eve, poured a shot of whisky into his coffee to ease his post-operative condition. He liked it. He tried it on some of his customers. They liked it. And so on.

Seven years later, Stanley Delaplane, travel writer and columnist with the San Francisco Chronicle, became one of those customers. When he got home he gave the recipe to an accommodating barkeep at the Buena Vista. The Buena Vista started promoting the drink, so successfully that pride and the mists of time wiped out the memory of Delaplane's gift. At any rate, the "B.V." now claims sole authorship and at last report was selling a Buena Vista Irish Coffee Set—stemmed glasses, a recipe and San Francisco's version of the Irish Coffee Story—as well as a rather inferior Irish Coffee.

How is it made? A thousand ways, 998 of which are wrong. The only proper ones are my way and yours. My way is as follows:

The ingredients: boiling water; 5 ounces hot, strong coffee made from fresh ground beans with a drip filter, preferably with untreated spring water; 1 teaspoon brown sugar; 1½ ounces Irish whisky; *softly* whipped cream. Absolutely nothing else.

The proper vessel is a clear stemmed glass of eight-ounce capacity. One with a handle is preferable; it makes holding the hot glass easier and eliminates unsightly smudges.

Put a spoon in the glass to keep it from cracking and carefully fill it halfway with boiling water. Remove the spoon and pour out the water.

Quickly now, pour in the coffee, the fresher and hotter the better. (There is leeway here in the type of coffee. A dark Vienna blend roast is good on very cold days, while the mellower mocha java seems best when the drink is being served in lieu of dessert; any good coffee will do.) Next the brown sugar. While white sugar was in the earliest Irish Coffees, it has been found that brown sugar better augments the burnished, boggy flavor of good Irish barleycorn.

And now the whisky, which brings up another argument: Which whisky? A roving Associated Press correspondent reported some years ago on a serious argument between supporters of Jameson's and James Power's, the "Catholic" whiskies of Dublin, and backers of Bushmill's, the "Protestant" distillation made in Ulster. The question is moot, because all Irish whiskies are now made by Irish

Distillers Ltd., which is partly owned by an American company, Seagrams.

Lastly comes the cream. The Shannon recipe calls for plain, unwhipped cream. This would be all right if we could still find real cream in our markets—the kind that used to pop the cap off the bottle in winter, thick enough to eat with a fork. We can't and so we whip what we have, but lightly. We are looking for a consistency thick enough to float neatly on the coffee, soft enough to let the coffee be quaffed *through* the cream, thus cooling and enriching the hot brew. This can require experimenting; cream so thick that it floats like a wee iceberg away from the lips when a sip is taken, or rides up into your nose, is one of the commonest flaws in Irish Coffee. You have it just right when the first taste leaves you with a thin, evenly distributed, white mustache.

Source and Comment

Philadelphia Inquirer, March 14, 1980. Excerpt from an article by Bill Collins, by-lined as "Inquirer Food Columnist," who observes that "It is meant to end controversies, but is written, with all humble pedantry, in full awareness that it will only start new ones."

Is drinking Irish coffee on St. Patrick's Day a traditional folk custom? Probably not, or at least not in the same way that eating hog jowl and blackeyed peas on New Year's Day is in rural Georgia, Carolina and Tennessee (see p. 14). Irish coffee doesn't go back as far in time, is not as closely linked to the holiday, and is not found in the oral tradition of the folk (as folklorists conservatively define the term) but in the gourmet columns of urban newspapers. But drinking *something* had always been part of St. Patrick's Day custom, and given the power of the press and the fact that its sophisticated readership needs folk tradition too, Irish coffee on St. Patrick's Day might well be on its way toward becoming traditional if it isn't there already.

* * *

Pennsylvania Dutch on St. Patrick's Day

Won do en feerbletterich glay blawd finnscht uff der St. Patrick's Dawg, no husht do glick.

When you find a four-leafed clover on St. Patrick's Day, you'll be lucky.

Do sullsht ken schlonga dote macha uff der St. Patrick's Dawg.

You should kill no snake on St. Patrick's Day.

Source and Comment

Pennsylvania Folklife, XVII (autumn, 1967), 29. From a collection of weather and calendar folklore, *Wedder Tzaicha*, by Victor C. Dieffenbach (1882-1965) made for the Pennsylvania Folklife Society. Dieffenbach lived in Bethel, Berks County, Pennsylvania. Most of these sayings are in his version of the Pennsylvania Dutch dialect. He collated them with lore in other collections of traditional material.

An Orthodox Irishman on St. Patrick's Day

The only Irishman at Yeshiva University, Robert Rhodes, has solved his problem of how to attend the St. Patrick's Day Parade tomorrow without violating the laws of his religion.

Mr. Rhodes, a native of Dublin and a third-year rabbinical student at Yeshiva, lives near the campus on 187th Street. To catch the parade would mean a subway ride downtown. But being Orthodox precludes riding on the Sabbath.

So Mr. Rhodes will stay tonight [March 16, 1984] with friends in the West 70's so he can walk to the parade, which starts at 44th Street and winds up at 86th. He doesn't want to miss it because, he said, "it's just something I've been doing as long as I can remember."

Source

New York Times, March 16, 1984. From a column, "New York Day by Day" written by Susan Heller Anderson and David Bird.

* * *

To Grow Cabbage

To make cabbage seed grow, sow it in your nightclothes on March 17.

Source and Comment

Journal of American Folklore, XI (1898), 11. From a "Collection of Maryland Folk-Lore" made by Mrs. Waller R. Bullock of Baltimore. Informant and date not given. Also reported among Allegheny Mountains whites, *Journal of American Folklore*, VII (1894), 112; and among the Pennsylvania Dutch, *Journal of American Folklore*, I (1888), 130. Cf. "Planting on May Day," p. 191.

There is a trace of pagan fertility rite in this superstition. Through sympathetic magic, the performance of the sexual act will help the cabbage seed to germinate.

* * *

Luck of the Irish

Pennsylvania lottery players, hoping for a little luck of the Irish on St. Patrick's Day, wagered $15,144 on the number 317—combining the third month of the year with the day's date.

Had 317 come up yesterday, the players would have won $7,572,305. But no such luck: the number 999 was drawn. It paid out $689,375, or 66.3 percent of yesterday's [March 17, 1981] sales, according to lottery spokesman Michael Keyser.

Source and Comment

Philadelphia Inquirer, March 18, 1981. An Associated Press story datelined Pittsburgh, Pennsylvania, March 17. Betting hunches are close kin to folk beliefs, among the best known being "the luck of the Irish," especially on St. Patrick's Day.

An Old Irish Neighborhood

"Que buen dia para un desfile!"

In Spanish, Italian, Cambodian, or Gaelic, it all means the same thing: What a day for a parade!

But yesterday's [March 10] St. Patrick's Day Parade through Smith Hill [Providence, R.I.] was as much a celebration of the Irish patron saint as it was a statement of this neighborhood's ethnic and cultural diversity.

Of course this was a day for the Irish. The streets of Smith Hill were filled with a sea of green hats and green banners and politicians wearing green carnations. Mayor Joseph R. Paolino Jr. and his family were there. So was Governor DiPrete.

Where the cool breeze wasn't blowing, plenty of unmistakably Irish, freckled faces basked in the warm sun.

"We're still here. We've still got our St. Patrick's School and our St. Patrick's parish," said Robert Reynolds, standing on his door stoop at 266 Smith St.

Reynolds, who said his grandfather came to this country from County Cavan, stared down at his friends and family, sitting on blankets on the sidewalk in front of him. They were drinking green beer and eating homemade Irish soda bread.

"Smith Hill used to be about 90 percent Irish," Reynolds said. "But if you look around now, you'll see how it has changed. You'll see the people from places like Peru and Colombia and Cambodia and Nicaragua. Their kids are in the parade now, too. That's all part of it. This is like a neighborhood function."

A smiling man stepped out of Reynolds's house. He wore a button on his sweater that said: "You Betcha Culo, I'm Italian."

Down the street, at Walsh's Pub, the last place on Smith Street where you can still buy a pint of Guinness stout on tap, patrons drank beer and munched on corned-beef sandwiches....

"I'm an American Indian," said Walter Proffit, raising his voice to be heard over the sound of a bagpipe band moving past outside. "But I'll bet you I've been to Ireland more times than most American Irish—four times."

As the parade went by, people looked on from their porches, their front steps or an open window.

Next door to Walsh's Pub is the Asian Place, a Laotian restaurant. Inside the little five-table restaurant, two men sitting below a picture of John F. Kennedy ate noodle soup with chopsticks.

Next door to the Asian Place is V. V. Vorasanes Oriental Food Market; next door to that is Albert's Grocery Store for Spanish and American foods; next door to that is the Mikangelo Clothing Shop; next door to that is Dr. F. Mushnick, podiatrist.

But what would a St. Patrick's Day parade be without all the symbols of the things that matter most to the Irish?

Those messages were there, too.

One man, standing on his porch, displayed a large sign which said: "St. Patrick was Pro-Life."

More than a few people wore buttons that said: "26 + 6 = 1," a phrase used to show that if the 26 counties of Ireland merged with the 6 counties of British-ruled Northern Ireland, they would make one Irish nation.

A little blond-haired, freckle-faced girl with a green beret marched with a band and waved to some people sitting on lawn chairs on the sidewalk.

"There she is!" shouted a woman, taking a snapshot. "Hi, honey!"

Source and Comment

Providence Sunday Journal, March 11, 1990. Ethnic holidays, as here, also provide occasions for political expression and solidarity with the country of origin. Cf. "Tet," p. 62.

Everybody Is Irish

When my grandson, Todd, was 6 (he's 12 now), he reported that his teacher had told him that on St. Patrick's Day everybody is Irish. He wanted to know what that meant. It means, I said, that on this day, just about everyone is happy.

"Well," Todd said, "I must be Irish all the time."

Source

Philadelphia Inquirer, March 17, 1990. From a column on regional nostalgia by Edgar Williams, staff writer.

St. Joseph's Day
March 19

Joseph, the husband of the Virgin Mary and foster father of Jesus, was a descendant of David and by trade a carpenter. His flight into Egypt with his family to escape Herod has long been a popular subject in folklore, literature and art. He is often depicted as an old man carrying a staff. Joseph is the patron saint of carpenters and of the Sicilian capital city, Palermo. In addition, undoubtedly because of Jesus' promise to the dying Joseph that he would bless those who aided the wretched, the poor, the widows and orphans, he is also the patron saint of the poor. This last legend, as do so many others concerning Joseph, appears in the *History of Joseph the Carpenter,* a book that was popular in the Eastern Church.

St. Joseph's Day observances in Southern California, Chicago, and Detroit, which emphasize the decorated altar, religious plays, and processions, are close to their Italian origin. In Buffalo and Minneapolis, while retaining their vitality and meaningfulness, they have been adapted to the American scene. The seasonal miracle, when the swallows return to Capistrano, moved from folk belief into the mass media with news stories and the hit song.

St. Joseph's Altar

Among the sundry customs brought to this country by Sicilians, an important place belongs to the colorful and elaborate celebration of Saint Joseph, the patron saint of the poor and of orphans. Preparations for the festivities of the day of "San Giuseppi," March 19, begin many weeks in advance. Everything must be ready by the eve of the preceding day, when scores, if not hundreds, of friends, neighbors, and curiosity seekers, go visiting the houses where "altars" have been prepared in honor of the saint.

Before describing these altars and the ceremony connected with them, a word must be said about the people who set them up. Contrary to the original custom in Sicily, where festivities are held mainly to help the poorest people of the community, here in Southern California, and probably in all other parts of the United States where Sicilians honor Saint Joseph, the altars are prepared in fulfilment of a promise made to the saint in a moment of need. For instance, a middle-aged Sicilian woman told me that about a year ago her small son was taken very ill with pneumonia. Doctors had almost given up all hope of saving him when the mother prayed very fervently and asked Saint Joseph to help her child, promising that, in return, she would set up an altar in his honor. The boy soon recovered, and when the month of March arrived, his mother did not forget her promise to "San Gisippuzzu." Another woman made an altar because Saint Joseph healed her husband who had

been severely hurt in an automobile accident. And in another family, thanks were thus rendered to the good carpenter for curing one of its members from cancer.

These festive altars are usually set up on a large table in the living-room or in the dining-room of the house, and very frequently, especially if prepared by people of means, the table is so large that it occupies almost every square foot of the room. The altar is placed against the wall facing the entrance of the room, and is dominated by a large picture of the Holy Family: Mary, Joseph, and the Infant Jesus. If in the prayers other saints have been invoked besides Saint Joseph, their images—frequently statuettes—are placed at the foot of the altar. In some houses the altar is artistically decorated with beautiful lace-work, and the walls of the room are completely covered by rich and brightly-colored religious tapestries. Especially impressive are the scores and scores of choice edibles which make the table groan under their weight. With the exception of meat—Saint Joseph's day, it will be remembered, falls during Lent—everything imaginable can be found on those tables of plenty. All sorts of fruits, fresh and cooked vegetables, fish dishes decorated in various ways, rice, many kinds of cookies, cakes (some made or stuffed with figs), numberless loaves of bread of different shapes, wines, and the very characteristic roasted chick-peas, almonds, and horse-beans (they taste much better than the name might imply!). In addition, each table must always have a large square cake with "Saint Joseph" written on it. This cake is usually donated by a friend of the family. Another dish that must be on the table is a platter containing a large baked fish beautifully decorated. And then, a maze of flowers; on one table they even had an orchid. This year [c. 1940], since Saint Joseph's day fell just a few days before Easter, I noticed two new items on the table: a little lamb (made with bread-crumb covered with beaten egg white and sprinkled with coconut), and one or more pots of green wheat symbolizing the Resurrection of Christ.

The Play of St. Joseph

At the end of the table facing the altar there are three or more places set for the three members of the Holy Family, and for as many saints as the hostess has decided to have. On the evening of the 18th, the priest visits the various houses where altars have been prepared, and blesses them. Once these tables have been blessed, no food can be touched or taken away from them until after the ceremony which takes place on the following day.

In the morning the children chosen to represent Jesus, Mary and Joseph, and the other saints, go to church to hear mass. Then, a few minutes before noon, either in their best clothes or, if possible, dressed to resemble the holy persons they represent, they walk to the third house from the one where an altar has been prepared. Saint Joseph knocks at the door and asks to be given shelter:

> *Simu tri poviri pillirini*
> *Simu stanchi di caminu*
> *Vulimu 'nu pocu di risettu*
> *E 'nu pocu di ristolu.*
>
> We are three poor pilgrims
> We are tired of walking
> We wish to rest a while
> And we want a little nourishment.

The people of the house have been warned beforehand, and they refuse admittance to the Holy Family:

> *Chista casa nun è locanna*
> *Itevinni a n'autra banna.*
>
> This house is not an inn
> Go elsewhere.

Then they proceed to the next house, and Saint Joseph asks Mary to knock:

> *Tupuliati vui Maria,*
> *Chi forsi vi dunano accansu.*
>
> You knock Mary,
> Perhaps they will heed you.

But the lady of the second house answers with the same words of the lady of the first, and the "saints" continue to the third house, where Mary asks the Infant Jesus to knock:

> *Tupuliati vui Gesù Bamminu.*
> You knock, Infant Jesus.

When the child knocks he says:

> *Simu Gesù*, Maria e Giuseppi.
> We are Jesus, Mary, and Joseph.

and the woman of the house answers:

> *Site vui Giuseppi, e Maria,*
> *Transiti tutti in cumpagnia.*
>
> Is it you, Joseph and Mary,
> Come in, all of you.

The ceremony is practically the same in every house; the words accompanying the ceremony, however, are frequently very different. There probably are as many versions of it as there are localities in Sicily where Saint Joseph's day is commemorated....

Once the Holy Family is within, the master of the house takes from the table some blessed wine and with it washes the right hand of the children representing Jesus, Mary, and Joseph. Then they are seated at the table, and the people who have come to the ceremony and who are very devout Catholics, kiss the right hand of these "saints." Sometimes they also touch their right foot and then kiss their own hand which has thus become blessed. The washing of the hand and the touching of the foot are not always carried out.

After the "saints" are seated, each one of them is served by an appointed person who sees to it that the saint upon whom he is waiting is not served the same food twice. In some families just the host and the hostess wait on the "saints." Everything is served to them on a clean dish. I was told that they must have three mouthfuls of all they are offered. The first course always consists of an artistically decorated orange: something like an orange salad. This is followed by variously prepared fish, fennels, artichokes, sardines, rice, *pasta ca' muddica* (spaghetti with sauce made of breadcrumbs, celery, and grated cheese), fruit, etc., etc. After about three hours, when the "saints" have finished eating, they are given, to take home, a basketful of the food that is left on the table. Then the food is at the disposal of all visitors who are offered also a dish of spaghetti seasoned with *muddica*. One woman informed me that during the afternoon and evening of Saint Joseph's day she served no less than ninety pounds of spaghetti!

On the following morning, whatever food remains must be distributed among friends or preferably among the poor people of the neighborhood.

I asked several women whether in Sicily they prepared such elaborate and costly tables, and they invariably told me that, because of the much lower standard of living, what they or their parents used to do there hardly compares with what they can afford to do here.

The same family does not necessarily set up an altar just once; it depends entirely on the promise made to Saint

Joseph. In one family they have been making altars for over twenty years.

Source and Comment

Southern Folklore Quarterly, IV (1940), 135-39. Charles Speroni describes the observance of St. Joseph's Day "among the Sicilians of Southern California." He does not give specific dates, places or informants, but he provides full background on the Sicilian tradition in his footnotes. He reports "altars" in honor of St. Joseph "prepared by Sicilians" in Milwaukee and New Orleans. For a similar neighborhood procession and drama preceding Christmas, cf. "Room at the Inn," p. 436. See also "Feed Strangers on St. Anthony's Day," p. 236.

* * *

St. Joseph's Procession

The Sicilian celebrations in Detroit honoring St. Joseph were some of the largest and most richly observed, because the religious societies bearing his name were large and prosperous. On the morning of the saint's day, after the mass, the people crowded around the church to see the beginning of the procession. A huge representation of St. Joseph, a stern-faced, white-bearded figure in flowing robes holding a staff all sprouted with sculptured pink roses was carried, on its velvet-draped platform, by about a dozen young men. This was preceded and followed by priests and nuns, children in white strewing flowers, men and women bearing flags and banners in vivid colors, and loud-playing brass bands, the musicians resplendent in bright uniforms and gold braid. As the parade passed along Congress, Fort, and Champlain (now E. Lafayette) streets, the people at the curb flung offerings of money, jewelry, or flowers upon the platform at the feet of the saint, and received the blessings of the priests. It was a scene of exuberance and color incomprehensible to the average detached observer, as it would undoubtedly be to most of the descendants of those who participated so enthusiastically.

St. Joseph's Table

[A] ritual that I remember vividly (with details confirmed by my elders) is that which came later on St. Joseph's day, after the procession had dispersed. This was "*La Tavola di San Guiseppe*" (St. Joseph's Table), a dramatic scene planned and executed with much the same concern and attention (but all in the spirit of religious devotion) as any commercial stage production. In the old country, one of these ceremonial tables was set up in each village, and in Detroit, for many years, the tradition was kept alive by my paternal grandmother. (Later, when other parishes grew up, other women observed it in their communities.)

Grandmother, a very devout woman, lived with her husband and only unmarried child, a son, in a small frame cottage a short distance from the church. From my earliest recollections of her and to the end of her life she had, always, an altar in her bedroom—a small table with a votive candle on a lace cloth, before a statue of Mary holding the infant Jesus, and on the wall a colored picture of the Holy Family in a gold-colored frame which was one of the few articles she had brought with her from Sicily. (This may have been only a print—it has long since disappeared—but it quite possibly was an oil painting, perhaps valuable, for I remember standing on a chair to study the vivid faces of Mary and Joseph and trying to feel the upraised hand of the child. I was fascinated, too, by the earrings, of yellow gold with long jewelled pendants, fastened to the glass, on the ears of Mary. These earrings, obtained at a considerable sacrifice, were an expression of grandmother's gratitude for the safe arrival of her family to their new home, and were the fulfillment of a pledge). She was a sincere believer in vows as a means of obtaining divine favors, and her observation of St. Joseph's Table was one of these. It was because of her youngest son, who was afflicted with an incurable malady, that she had initiated the ceremony, and she continued it, even after his death, for many years.

The celebration required extensive preparations. The whole house, every piece of furniture and bric-a-brac, every window and curtain and doily, must be thoroughly cleaned and renovated with painting, polishing, and scrubbing. Then a table was set up in the front parlor, and on it a starched, elaborately embroidered white linen cloth. As a girl, she had woven this herself, and then devoted countless additional hours embellishing it with intricate cut-work embroidery at a convent school. Statues of saints, large and small—all that she could borrow, besides her own, were arranged on the table with vases of realistic artificial flowers she had fashioned herself. (I remember watching her, as she sat in her Morris chair on a winter afternoon, cutting and manipulating the bits of colored silks and papers and yarns, and marvelling at her skill as a really beautiful flower emerged.) Using the best tableware and chinaware she could obtain, she set three places at the table, which she further decorated with festoons of bright ribbons.

At the Sicilian bakery, Grandmother ordered loaves of crusted, sesame-seed coated bread in various shapes—a long hooked staff or cane, a crown, a small cross, and dozens of little round loaves. For the meal itself she prepared a rich chicken broth with finely cut homemade noodles, which was served with a thick sprinkling of grated Roman cheese. The chicken was combined with various herbs and seasoning for the next course. Also on the menu there might be veal cutlets in a wine sauce, *finocchi* (a kind of celery with a distinctive taste), whole boiled artichokes with lemon juice sauce, *figi d'India* (prickly pears), *lagrime della Madonna* (long waxy white grapes, very large), *gelati* (rich, fruit and nut-filled ice cream), *granata* (fruit ices)—many extravagant delicacies which seldom, if ever, appeared on the family table.

The guests of honor at this feast were chosen with great care and thoughtful consideration. Usually it was the parish priest who recommended them, but friends and neighbors were also consulted. Three people were sought— an elderly man, a girl in her teens, and a small boy not over five or six years old, all of poor but respectable families. After an extensive search, they were carefully selected from many prospects and painstakingly instructed for their roles in the sacred drama.

At noon on March nineteenth Grandmother's front parlor was crowded with people, some of whom overflowed into the other rooms while others looked on from outside. Waiting inside the door stood Grandfather, dressed in his best clothes, a white towel over his arm. Suddenly there was a hush in the expectant hubbub and a knock at the door.

"Who's there?" Grandfather called.

"Three weary travellers," came the answer. "Will you give us lodging?"

Grandfather replied: "No, there is no room."

This dialogue was repeated three times, until finally, the travellers identified themselves as Joseph, Mary, and Jesus. Then, with cries of welcome from all those present, they were escorted to their places at the table. The child was lifted up to stand on his chair, where, with upraised hand, he recited a short prayer of benediction, after which Grandfather, according to Biblical custom, proceeded to wash the feet of the honored guests. For this he used a set of utensils especially reserved for this purpose—a dainty, flower-decorated, white chinaware pitcher and wash basin. (Articles such as these were in general use before indoor plumbing became common, and were found, usually, on the dresser in the bedrooms. The pitcher was large, holding a gallon or more, and the basin deeply rounded. The usual ones were plain white earthenware, but those meant for guests, or for special occasions such as sickness or lying-in after childbirth, were dainty chinaware, with perhaps ornamental handles and hand-painted decorations. Such was the one Grandmother reserved for the St. Joseph ceremony.)

Then came Grandmother, with the first course of a long and sumptuous meal, which she herself served with great solicitude, while the audience watched, urging and cheering the guests. After they had finished a collection was taken which was divided among the three. They were also given the special loaves of bread to take home—the crown for the girl, the staff for the old man, and the cross for the little boy, also as much food as they could carry. Everyone present also received a loaf of the blessed bread and all departed in a glow of religious joy.

As far as I have been able to learn, this ceremonial has not been practiced in Detroit, as here described, for many years. The tradition was carried over from Sicily with the first of the immigrants who came to work and live in this

city and flourished as long as these people or their immediate descendants were alive and there was a localized Sicilian colony.

Source

Wayne State University Folklore Archive, 1953. Collected by Ida M. Santini of Detroit, a student of folklore at Wayne State University, in 1953. Based primarily on personal observation and recollection "confirmed by my elders," in a report titled "The Preservation of St. Joseph's Day and Something about the Sicilian Colony in Detroit."

* * *

St. Joseph's Day Feast

St. Joseph is the patron saint of Buffalo and his day (March 19) is much celebrated, especially in the Italian community. Families who have made vows to the saint often prepare a St. Joseph's table. The women of the family prepare a banquet of Lenten foods (vegetables, pasta, fish, special breads and pastry) and spread it on a large table decorated with a statue of the saint. The parish priest is asked to bless the feast, to which the entire neighborhood may be invited. Sometimes children from the family or from a local orphanage are dressed as the Holy Family and saints and are given the first helping from each dish. These feasts have become so popular that they are now often held in church halls to raise money for the parish. Last spring the mothers of students in the Italian Club at Canisius College in Buffalo prepared an immense St. Joseph's table for over five hundred people. (The feature which most caught my eye on this occasion was the traditional bread, baked in the form of crowns and crosses.)

Source

Indiana Folklore, IX (1976), 166. From a study of "Roman Catholicism as Folk Religion in Buffalo," New York, by Lydia Marie Fish. Based on "information supplied by students, colleagues, and lay and clerical friends in Buffalo over the past eight years."

* * *

Feasting and Sharing

It's a good thing Pietro Camaci has a large family and a lot of faithful friends. Otherwise, who would have helped him cook the 700 pounds of pasta, the thousands of breads and sweets, and the gallons upon gallons of sauce for his St. Joseph's Day feast over the weekend?

With five brothers, two sisters, three daughters, two sons, a wife, uncounted cousins and friends, Camaci had plenty of helpers to call upon in preparing for the extravagant St. Joseph's table he set Friday through Sunday in his Addison home, where about 1,000 people ate Pasta la Palermitanna (cooked with sardines, bread crumbs and tomato-based sauce) and assorted other Sicilian favorites over the three days.

Pietro Camaci left the small Sicilian village of Borgetto for the United States in 1969, carrying with him happy memories of the huge meals his mother used to make for the St. Joseph's Day tables. The food-filled tables are a Sicilian tradition originally meant to help feed the poor and to give thanks to St. Joseph for answering prayers.

Since leaving Sicily, Camaci had missed the holiday, observed each March 19. About a month ago, he said he had a dream in which his mother appeared. "She asked why I didn't do it (hold a feast), and then the next day, she came in my dreams again and asked again why I didn't do it," said Camaci, who took up the challenge.

The masonry contractor, who works for the family-owned Camaci Builders, started by flying to San Pedro, Calif., to buy cases of olives, hundreds of artichokes, more than 100 pounds of sardines and some fruits native to Sicily and also grown in California.

Spaghetti and sauce were cooked in huge vats in a neighbor's garage over the weekend. A local grocer let Camaci use some refrigerator space to store foods. And a cousin who recently arrived from Italy, and is a baker by [trade, provided] sweet breads.

This feast, however, involved more than food. Camaci wanted to duplicate the traditional religious aspects of the day too. He transformed his family room into a church, draping the walls and ceiling in white cloth and building an altar at one end of the room, hiding a fireplace. Pictures of Joseph, Mary, and Jesus, religious statues and candles lined the altar, which had money of all denominations pinned together in strips. The money had been donated by people who had visited over the weekend.

Three walls of the room were lined with tables holding more than 100 plates of fruits, vegetables, cakes and nuts. Much of that food, along with the money, would be given to the three children who were chosen to play Jesus, Mary and Joseph in the traditional play that was acted out Sunday afternoon. In Sicily, poor children are selected to act the roles and take home large portions of food. In this case, the parts were played by a Camaci cousin and two children of Camaci Builders employees.

"People have been kind of stunned when they walk in here," said Vita, Camaci's 23-year-old daughter. "Some have gotten very emotional and cried. They haven't seen this for 30 years, since they left Sicily."

That was the case for Nick and Ninfa Arato of River Grove, who arrived at the Camaci house before the food was served Sunday. "It's very beautiful," said Nick. "Even if I no eat, I want to stay to the end."

"The last time I see something like this was 27 years ago in Italy," said Ninfa. "There's nothing missing. All the traditional foods are here. Really, it's too much. The quantity is too much."

Camaci, who estimates the feast cost him $5,000, advertised on an Italian radio station and relied on word of mouth. The grapevine worked. Everyone eating at the table in the two-car garage and adjoining tent seemed to be speaking Italian, and many greeted one another like long-lost friends.

"Every Italian is like family," said Nick Pistone of Niles, one of several hundred people to dine in the Camaci garage on Sunday. "This isn't just a holy day, it's a family day, and a day to eat. I love to eat. That's why I'm here."

Source

Chicago Tribune, March 19, 1990, by staff writer Jody Temkin. © Copyrighted, Chicago Tribune Co., all rights reserved, used with permission.

* * *

Mama D. on St. Joseph's Day

Her real name is Giovanna D'Agostino and for the last dozen years she and her son, Sam, have run Sammy D's restaurant in Dinkytown, a Minneapolis neighborhood inhabited largely by college students. It is one of the most famous eating places in that city, for several reasons.

The biggest reason is, of course, Mama D.

It was Mama D. who decided to open the restaurant on March 19—St. Joseph's Day—and provide free meals for the poor. In recent years she has been feeding about 2,000 persons on St. Joseph's Day....

And it began with tragedy. Her husband died 12 years ago, the same year she was badly hurt in a car accident that cost son Sam an eye.

"In the hospital, that's when I prayed to St. Joseph for help. That's why I feed the poor on his day. I do it in thanks."

Source

Philadelphia Inquirer, August 17, 1977. Bill Collins, "Food Editor," for the *Philadelphia Inquirer* interviewed Mama D. when she came to Gimbel's department store to promote her cookbook. Cf. "Mother Lavender's New Year's Dinner," p. 17.

* * *

The First Swallows of San Juan Capistrano

[This is] the story of the original invasion of San Juan Capistrano [California] by the swallows as handed down from past generations: An understandably annoyed inn-keeper of the town, weary of the chattering of the hundreds of swallows that swarmed over his property, destroyed the unsightly nests and drove the birds away. As luck would have it, one of the Mission fathers chanced to be standing by. "Come swallows," said the Padre, "Come to the Mission. We will give you shelter. There is room enough for all." Recognizing in the priest a blood brother of the good Saint Francis, all the dispossessed birds took up residence under the eaves of the sacristy of the Mission church.

Source and Comment

San Juan Capistrano Chamber of Commerce, undated. From an unsigned mimeographed tourist information sheet published about 1979 by the Chamber of Commerce which has as its stated purpose, "to preserve the traditions of the Past."

San Juan Capistrano Mission was founded in 1776 by a Spanish Franciscan, Fray Junípero Serra. Cliff swallows are said to return annually on St. Joseph's Day to the mud nests they have built on the mission walls. A sentimental love song, "When the Swallows Come Back to Capistrano," written by Leon René in 1939, and coverage of the swallows' return by the media has popularized what is, to say the least, a miracle of nature. And the city authorities have organized a "Swallow Festival" featuring parade, rodeo, dance, and various contests. The swallows are supposed to depart on October 23, anniversary of the death of St. John Capistran.

Officially the swallows return on March 19, when observances are held at the Mission, but the annual Fiesta de las Golondrinas usually begins several days before and is followed by what is claimed to be "the largest non-automotive parade in the country."

* * *

Swallows of San Juan Capistrano
The Swallows Return

The swallows returned to San Juan Capistrano Mission today—St. Joseph's Day—as they have every year for decades. The main body of the annual flight arrived, as predicted, at 6 A.M. and immediately took over the nests under the eaves of the historic mission. The mission had for days been bustling with advance scouts which arrive yearly in advance of the main flight to rid the nests of intruders who use them during the winter months.

Source

Los Angeles Examiner, March 26, 1956. Filed by the International News Service.

* * *

Ringing church bells signaled the swallows' annual return to the historic Mission San Juan Capistrano today. But few of the 500 tourists who gathered in the courtyard of the 183-year-old adobe mission sighted the birds.

The first swallow was officially sighted by mission personnel at 8:31 A.M., setting off the traditional bell-ringing.

According to legend, the cliff swallows return to the mission every year on March 19, the feast of St. Joseph. They fly 7,000 miles on a seven-week journey from Argentina.

Betty Jo Moak, a 52-year-old telephone supplies attendant, drove 1,200 miles from Midland, Tex., to see the swallows return.

"It's been a childhood dream for me ever since high school, when I heard the song 'When the Swallows Come Back to Capistrano'," she said.

Source

New York Times, March 20, 1980, as filed by the Associated Press.

* * *

The fact of the matter is that the swallows arrive in small groups throughout the month, something that townfolk have long since rationalized by labeling the early arrivals "scouts" for the main group of birds. It's just that no one ever sees the main group. Swallows have, over the years, been sighted returning as early as March 3, and as late as March 22.

"It's not like you can set your watch by them," conceded the Rev. Paul Martin, pastor of the mission, a charming man who harbors no illusions about the phenomenon that puts his parish on the map every spring.

"It would be an overstatement to say this is a miracle. The birds just have some kind of natural instinct, which God gave them, that brings them back."

And each year, fewer and fewer of the cleft-tail birds, called squaretail cliff swallows, come back to the mission, to nest under the eaves of the old stone church. They opt instead for barns, hospitals, freeway overpasses and even a Presbyterian church in Mission Viejo, six miles to the north.

"Maybe they're tired of being Catholic," said Val Goerner, a newcomer to town.

There is another explanation. People may like swallows, but swallows don't much like people, especially people who destroy their habitat.

As the town has grown, the fields and orange groves that once surrounded the mission, providing the swallows with insects to eat and mud with which to build their tiny nests, have given way to shops and houses. Homeowners new to the area have been known to destroy the nests, even though such acts, under town law, are punishable by a $5,000 fine, or a year in jail, or both.

Flocks of swallows may well have once blackened the sky on their arrival as tourists still expect them to do. But in recent years, the number of birds that eventually nest at the mission has dwindled from 2,200 to less than 500....

Even as the number of swallows is dwindling, the hoopla surrounding them keeps expanding.

"Kind of like the Super Bowl," Father Martin said.

This year, as always, the town fathers are sponsoring a week-long Swallows Festival, which features a toddlers' marathon, ugliest pet contest, rodeo, dinner dance and "hoosegow day," on which a "sheriff" and "hanging judge" arrest and jail anyone not dressed as a cowboy or Indian.

The festivities culminate with a two-hour Swallows Day parade, said to be the largest non-motorized parade in the country.

"We get calls from all over," said Doris Lindsey, manager of the chamber of commerce. "The big question people asked was whether the swallows knew it was leap year."

"The birds are a source of hope for so many people," Father Martin said, "in an age that has lost a lot of its sense of romance and lore and just plain niceness. The mission is such a pleasant reminder of the past. I tell people to come here on St. Joseph's Day for the Masses, for the music, for the pleasure of being in a peaceful spot on a spring day. And if you happen to see a swallow, so much the better."

Source and Comment

Philadelphia Inquirer, March 21, 1980. From a report by staff writer Larry Eichel. Annual newspaper stories on the return of the swallows to San Juan Capistrano have come to be almost as traditional as the swallows' return.

Vernal Equinox
On or about March 21

The equinox comes at that time when the sun shines directly on the equator and the length of the day is the same as the length of the night all over the world. The event occurs twice each year, on or about March 21 and on or about September 23. The vernal or spring equinox signals the beginning of nature's renewal in the Northern Hemisphere and thus has long been a significant event for agricultural peoples.

Upright Eggs and the Spring Equinox

Thirty dozen well-trained eggs stood eggs-actly balanced on end for 15 minutes in New York yesterday [March 20, 1984] to announce the arrival of spring.

No kidding.

"They really do stand up on their fat ends and then about 15 minutes later, they all slowly roll off their axes," Terry Savage said.

About 100 people gathered at a city park at 5:25 A.M. to see the balancing act. It's the only time you can get an egg—not to mention 360 of them—to stand upright.

"I don't really remember how all this works, something about the sun crossing the equator and the balance of the season," said Savage, a director of the Lower Manhattan Cultural Council. "But it works. It was terrific."

It was the ancient Chinese who thought up the ritual; folks balanced eggs—the symbol of fertility—at the Spring Equinox for good luck.

Source and Comment

Philadelphia Inquirer, March 21, 1984. From a column, "The Scene" by staff writer Eddie Olsen. Eggs have been associated with divination and fertility since time immemorial. There are literally thousands of superstitions connected to breaking them, puncturing and draining them, burying them, decorating them, reading their shells, and, as here, balancing them. If an egg balances as the day and night balance in length at the equinox, things are in harmony as they should be. Cf. "No Rooz," p. 137.

The *New York Times* on March 21, 1989, had a photograph captioned "Balancing Eggs: A Spring Tradition" taken at the World Trade Center. It shows "participants in a vernal equinox tradition" attempting, often with success, to stand eggs on end. It explains that "Folklore has it that eggs will balance more easily during "equinoxes ... when the forces of the solar system are in special alignment" but adds that not many scientists take this notion seriously.

Persian New Year
March 21

No Rooz and related celebrations of the Persian New Year are pre-Islamic. They are rooted in Zoroastrian tradition and reflect legends to be found in the Persian epic poem, the *Shah nama* or "Book of Kings" by Firdausi. Even more basic is their relationship to the vernal equinox and therefore seasonal regeneration. In preparation, as in the instance of the Jewish Passover and the Seminole Indian Green Corn Busk, also Spring festivals, houses are thoroughly cleansed and useless articles discarded. Traditionally, during the bonfire that precedes New Year's day, members of the family jump over the flames, chanting a rhyme, "My pallor to you, your ruddiness to me," signifying that winter paleness and cold is replaced by spring warmth and health. The holiday season ends with an excursion into the countryside and a picnic, again suggesting nature's annual renewal.

No Rooz

Last week [the week of March 20, 1989] marked *No Rooz,* the ancient Persian New Year, when families gather for a feast celebrated for centuries. A table is decorated with seven platters—apples, greens, candles, eggs, vinegar, sweets and goldfish—each representing one of the seven spiritual forces of the old religion.

In the center is a dish. On the dish, a colored egg.

It is the symbol of new life.

"Everyone watches this egg, and, at one moment, everyone sees the egg turning," said Mahnaz Afkhami, director of the Washington-based Foundation for Iranian Studies. "It is the exact moment the New Year arrives. Everyone sees the egg turn. At least, everyone claims to see it."

The *No Rooz* feast and other traditional events—such as the bonfires of *Chahr Shanbeh Souri* on the Wednesday before New Year, or the spring picnics of *Sizdah Bedar* 13 days after—have adopted a new meaning for Iran's exiles.

"They take them even more seriously now," Afkhami said. "When we were living in Iran, the traditions were becoming out of style. But now it's different, especially since the Islamic regime has banned them. To observe them, on the full scale, is kind of an act of opposition."

[Nasser] Jahanbani agrees: "If we lose our traditions, our history is lost."

Source and Comment

Philadelphia Inquirer, March 27, 1989. From an article on the adaptation of Iranian political exiles by Rick Lyman, staff writer. Informants include Nasser Jahanbani, formerly an admiral in the Iranian Royal Navy, and Ahmad Ashraf, a University of Pennsylvania faculty member. The No Rooz celebration is crucial to Iranian identity, aside from the political and religious persuasion of those who celebrate it, and it is known to have been observed in the United States at least since the beginning of the present century, according to Mary Martin, Coordinator, Middle East Center, University of Pennsylvania. One Persian New Year tradition is the exchange of gifts of eggs. For related traditions involving eggs, see "Vernal Equinox," p. 136, "Good Friday Eggs," p. 155, and "Decorating Eggs," p. 164. Cf. "Halloween Bonfires," p. 381.

Spring Rites of College Students
Various Days in Spring

Rites of Spring are many and diverse on American college campuses. They indicate the end of winter but also the approaching end of the academic year. Final examinations are soon to come, to be followed by graduation—which means the end of collegiate life. So a kind of pre-Lenten carnival spirit prevails. In addition to customs peculiar to individual institutions, such as "Fountain Day" at Clark University or going barefooted on May 1 as was once the practice of students at the University of South Carolina, there is the tradition of students converging at seaside resorts, the most notorious example being the annual "Spring Break" at Fort Lauderdale, Florida, which at its peak in 1985 attracted some 350,000 college students. Student rites of Spring are cyclic events and parallel more ancient seasonal rites, sometimes even incorporating details from them. The importance of water in many of these rites recalls a Polish custom on Easter Monday when young people drench each other, said to be based on a Spring fertility rite.

Spring Spree Day

Clark [University, Worcester, Mass.] students have firmly established the custom of going a-spreeing on some fine spring day. No classes are held on this day, for which varied programs are arranged by Gryphon [honorary society]. A Faculty-Student baseball game is usually the chief event of the morning. The "tapping" of selected Juniors by which they are chosen as members of Gryphon also takes place on that day and a Boheme [student dance] brings a merry end. Attendance throughout the day is well worth while for the possibilities of the occasion are practically limitless.

Source

Clark University Students' Handbook, Vol. 24, 1933-34, p. 14.

* * *

Spring Begins

The tradition of cancelling classes and arranging social activities on a secret date began in 1903, when a spontaneous "spring festival" was organized in conjunction with St. Patrick's Day. In following years it became customary for Gryphon, the senior men's honor society, to proclaim the beginning of spring for Clark students by running through the classrooms and declaring the end of the academic day. If the interruption was not a false alarm (which often occurred), students and faculty alike would put away their books. The faculty then would overlook both the classwork and the exams temporarily cancelled by the diversion and would join students for the day's festivities.

Eventually called Spree Day, this annual rite fostered a particular closeness between faculty and students.

According to ... newspaper accounts, for many years athletic activities like the greased pole climb challenged the Spree Day stamina. Other activities added to the light-hearted atmosphere such as the pie-eating contest, the canoe-jousting matches on University Park Pond, and the pushball contest, in which a giant ball was rolled around the campus green. The famed rope pull, which was originally a fall event, became a Spree Day tradition in 1942. The contest pitted the freshmen against the sophomores at University Park Pond. The students gathered at opposite ends of the pond, while faculty members judged the contest. The first struggle resulted in a victory for the class of '43 over the mud-soaked class of '42.

Source

Press release from the Clark University Office of Communications by Adam Peretz, prepared for the 1988 class reunions.

* * *

From St. Patrick to Spring

New coats of green paint on the Clark college fence and the cross-campus walks, images of dignified members of the faculty strung up on trees, bonfires and scores of other features of St. Patrick's Day at Clark university which for years has been the date of an annual students' strike, all were conspicuous by their absence today. A dignified and profound quiet reigned on the south Main-street campus. Students went to classes as usual and the only remnant of the verdant garnishings of former years was a sprinkling of green neckties.

The time-honored custom of cutting loose has not been abandoned, according to the students, but merely postponed. Plans are already under way for a "regular fracas" next week, probably on Thursday, unless professorial interference necessitates another plan of action. According to undergraduates, the celebration date is changed because its coincidence with St. Patrick's Day has lead to misconceptions on the part of the public as to its purport. "You see some people thought we were making fun of St. Patrick's Day when we were really only cutting loose," was the way one student put it.

There are, however, dark hints of influence brought to bear on the postponement of the event by Dr. Wallace W. Atwood, Clark's new president, who is understood to have consulted with representatives of the students and urged the discontinuation of the horse-play of former years. This the students deny, however, and claim that they voluntarily postponed the date by vote of a mass meeting.

For years Clark students have refused to go to any classes on St. Patrick's Day. Decked in vivid green, they have assembled on the campus and given vent to their spring animal spirits. Last year there was an unpleasant aftermath to the hanging and the subsequent burning of an effigy of one of the professors.

Source

The (Worcester, Massachusetts) *Gazette,* March 17, 1921.

* * *

Fountain Day

Fountain Day has become one of the most popular spring traditions at the [Albany State] University [of New York]. On that special day everyone gathers on the podium to watch as the President of the University presides over the ceremony during which the campus' huge main fountain is turned on for the first time of the year.

Subsequently, hundreds of students celebrate this rite of spring by wading and playing frisbee in the fountain's pool.

Source

Student Handbook, Albany State University of New York, 1989-90.

* * *

Turning on the Fountain

Spring officially arrives at the University at Albany on Monday, April 30, at noon when the campus's huge main fountain at 1400 Washington Ave. is turned on for the first time this year.

This annual rite attracts thousands of students, faculty, staff and alumni and should provide the same excellent photo opportunities it has in the past. President Vincent

O'Leary will give brief remarks just before the fountain goes on.

Source

News release from University Relations Office, State University of New York, Albany, April 27, 1990.

* * *

Spouting Spring

Students at the State University of New York at Albany participate in the annual spring rite of the turning on of the fountain at noon Monday at the Washington Avenue campus.

Source

Caption to a photograph in *The* (Albany, New York) *Times Union,* May 1, 1990.

* * *

Splash Day in Galveston

Galveston had always been known for its April-May celebration which began in 1920 with "Aquatic Day." It was basically a beauty review and "Splash Day," as locals came to know it, served as the Island's official beach opening. The celebration was as much for the locals as for the tourists because every beachfront merchant knew that once Splash Day hit, those tourist dollars were just around the corner. Splash Day really became a big deal after World War II when local entrepreneur Christy Mitchell took over the reins of the tourist-promoting Greater Galveston Beach Association. By the late 50s the opening of beaches or Splash Day had become one of the biggest tourist promotions of the year.

The 1961 Splash Day was no different. A letter was purportedly drafted and widely circulated through "official" channels (the United States Mail). Colleges, Universities, Fraternities, Sororities, Glee Clubs, Pep Squads, Drill Teams, Marching Bands, Beauty Queens, all were told and asked to tell their friends of the upcoming "Meeting of the Collegiate Tribes" on Galveston Island for Spring Break and/or Easter Holidays, depending upon your persuasion. This also happened to coincidentally be the weekend "officially" designated as "Splash Day Weekend" by the powers at hand and also the "official" kick-off of the tourist season. After all, wasn't tourism the name of the game? What does it matter if the kid was spending *his* money or his *daddy's,* it was still *money* and he was spending it *here*! The drawing board began to wobble under the weight of student response. In distributing "The Letter" they had hardly anticipated selling every hotel room on the Island . . . . By midday Friday, the Causeway was a steady stream of incoming cars. At times, the line on the Port Bolivar side of the Ferry looked like it reached High Island. Law enforcement officials were becoming concerned. What are all these kids going to the same place at the same time for? Hotel management was becoming alarmed. Suddenly, a one-hundred-and-thirty-five pound room clerk was faced with a pair of two-hundred-and-ten-pound linebackers from A&M and a brace of two-hundred-and-fifteen-pound offensive tackles from UT, enthusiastically discussing the respective merits of their squads, and he must find a way to diplomatically explain that the hotel has been "over-sold" ... that is to say, more reservations were taken than the available rooms on hand ... How'd we know everybody was gonna show up? The tension builds. The weather doesn't seem to be helping us out much, either.

The air hung heavy and thick enough to cut with a broken beer bottle. The Buccaneer Hotel (present-day site of the Moody House) had no more rooms, but how were they to know that the two pert cheerleaders from Lamar Tech were going to meet the entire S.M.U. swimming team, whose rooms at the Jack Tar (present-day site of the Islander Beach) had been rented to the Baylor Offensive Backfield, and that now, their "double-occupancy" single room was being occupied by no less than (count 'em) nine people? The story was the same up and down the beach front. No room? Double up ... Triple up ... Sextuple up, aha ...

Everyone you talk to has a different story as to who, why, what, when, where and how it all started ... here goes. The traffic light had changed several times at Twenty-third Street (in front of the Buccaneer Hotel) with no progression of traffic. Horns began to honk. Hotel officials were beginning to get hot. All this noise outside, all this noise inside, and besides that, if there's nine people in that room, we ought to be able to charge extra *money*!...

People: in the streets, on the sidewalks, hanging out of hotel windows ... waving at the cars below ... exchanging words with the cars below ... sharing libations with the cars below ... Tossing half-empty quart beer bottles on the cars below ... Bottles? Yes, bottles....The first bottle thrown at the corner of 23rd Street at 11 P.M. was in response to a bottle dropped from a hotel window above ... The fighting began.

The first police call went out at 11:04 P.M. and it was a report of "two boys fighting on the beach in front of the Buccaneer." At 11:12 P.M., a two-man unit was sent to the scene. Fifteen minutes later a call came ... for help ... then help began to call for help ... then more help called for help ... "There's a million crazy drunk college kids out there ... half of 'em the size of Water Buffaloes."

Five hundred students arrested ... that's the figure released to the press at the conclusion of the weekend-long ordeal ... Charges were made for Drunk & Disorderly, Possession of Alcohol by a Minor, Sale of Alcohol to a Minor, Resisting Arrest, False Identification, and Assault on a Police Officer. Assistance had been received from Law Enforcement Agencies within a one-hundred-and-fifty-mile radius. It seemed as though the back of the revolution had been broken by 2 P.M. ... What brought it under control? Was it the combined efforts of City, County and State Police? The appearance of the Fire Truck on the scene? The arrival and omni-presence of Texas Rangers (plural)? None of the above, I'm afraid. If there is to be any one faction that can be attributed to having effectively dealt with the type of rambunction exhibited that Splash Day Weekend, my bet would ride with the amazingly efficient K-9 Corps that was sent by the Houston Police Dept. Certainly, by Saturday, and throughout Sunday you could see officers totin' riot guns, and even Thompson submachine guns, but that didn't seem to present a real threat ... you're not supposed to shoot somebody that doesn't have a gun ... but those dogs ... that was a different story. So still, the legend grows. Some may ask, "What happened to Splash Days?" As one Native Son so aptly put it: "They had it for a couple more years, and then they changed the name to the Blessing of the Fleet, or somethin'."

Source

Galveston County's In Between, February 1979, 38-40, 42. From an unsigned article titled "Whatever happened to ... Splash Day?" in a regional magazine. Cf. "Splash Days and Bathing Beauties," p. 94.

* * *

Who Came to Fort Lauderdale and How Much They Spent

Due to frequent requests for statistical information pertaining to students who come to Fort Lauderdale for spring break, a survey was undertaken this year [1984] to gain information about this important market segment of our tourism industry in Broward County.

(1) Over the period March 9 through April 6, 324 students from 133 different colleges and universities responded to the survey. These schools were located in the following states, Pennsylvania, Georgia, Rhode Island, Ohio, Florida, Massachusetts, Minnesota, New Jersey, New Hampshire, Wisconsin, Virginia, New York, Washington, D.C., Michigan, Connecticut, Tennessee, Maryland, South Carolina, Missouri, Iowa, Alabama, Texas, Indiana, North Carolina, Maine, Kentucky, Vermont, Illinois, Mississippi, Delaware and California. A few schools from the province of Ontario Canada were among those responding in addition to the 32 states listed.

(2) The average age of all respondents was 21. Males accounted for 64.2% of all respondents while females accounted for 35.8%. On the average students were in their junior year ready to graduate in 1985.

(3) 62.7% of all respondents came to Fort Lauderdale by auto or van. The next most popular means of transportation was by scheduled or chartered airline (32.6%). The

least popular transportation selection was by bus or train (4.7%). Of all means of transportation, the average number traveling together as a group was ten.

(4) On the average each respondent spent 7.4 nights in the area. The greatest number of students stayed at hotels or motels (68.1%); friends and relatives occupied second place with 17.6% followed by condo or campground with 12.1%. Other accommodations which consisted of either car or boat was the selection of only 2.2% of the students. Of all types of accommodations selected, the average number of students staying together in the same place was five.

(5) The average daily expenses of all respondents for lodging, food, beverages, entertainment, local transit, taxis and sightseeing was $45.77. Based on an average stay of 7.4 nights, each student spends $338.70 on his or her spring break vacation to Fort Lauderdale. An estimated 300,000 students yields over $100 million in revenue to the Broward economy during spring break.

Source

Memorandum of the Broward County Tourist Development Council, by Bruce H. Laster, research analyst, dated April 17, 1984.

* * *

Breaking the Spring Break Habit

What started out in the '50s as good, scrubbed, all-American fun—spring break in Fort Lauderdale—had, by the mid-1980s, become an annual time of dread for our area's residents, business people and city officials.

This annual rite of passage had sprung from the collegiate swimming forums of the 1930s and was spurred on by the 1960 movie *Where the Boys Are,* which painted Fort Lauderdale's beaches and weather in their rosiest hues, local law enforcement as benevolent but bumbling and populated this enticing canvas with plenty of attractive young people of both sexes, all enjoying themselves away from the cold winter climes.

Who could resist? Fort Lauderdale—willingly or not—quickly became the "spring break capital." By 1985, some 350,000 college students were cramming our area during a spring period that stretched to six weeks and longer, spending some $140 million in the process. At the same time, these crowds were becoming increasingly raucous

and more destructive, packing beaches, overwhelming facilities, causing massive traffic tie ups, and becoming more and more unmanageable.

Fort Lauderdale had gridlock, beachlock and kidlock.

It also had enough: While $140 million generated in six weeks is nothing to sneeze at, untold revenues were being scared off each year by spring break's distinctly negative image—which masked our real visitor attractions and attributes. Hordes of visitors, anxious to avoid "rowdy" Fort Lauderdale, poured into other areas of Florida.

It was at this point that city and county officials made a dramatic and much debated decision—get rid of the students. Move beyond spring break and refocus on a totally new tourism marketing strategy aimed at families and a more upscale market....

Yes, college students still vacation here in the spring—but in greatly diminished and totally manageable numbers. This past spring, we welcomed fewer than 20,000 well behaved college students.

Source

Orlando Sentinel, July 30, 1989. Edited from a special article by Richard D. Weaver, president of the Greater Lauderdale Convention and Visitors Bureau.

* * *

Barefoot Day for Freshmen

In the 1930s and earlier it was a tradition at the University of South Carolina for upperclassmen to go about without shoes on the first day of May, and being conspicuous for their bare feet, they were obvious prey to other forms of hazing and humiliation. It was also a day of pranks and misbehavior, sometimes excessive. I remember engineering students wiring a metal doormat with an electrical charge which shocked freshmen who stepped on it. Something else that got out of hand was pursuing and attempting to kiss the not always willing co-eds. Such excesses about 1939 led to an investigation by the college administration and the suppression of "Barefoot Day."

Source

Told by Thomas H. Walker of Monroe, North Carolina, who graduated from the University of South Carolina in 1941, to H. C., June 15, 1990. Cf. "Barefoot Day," p. 193.

St. Benedict's Day
March 21

Benedict of Nursia who lived from about A.D. 480 to 543, was the founder of monasticism in Western Europe. He established the monastery at Monte Cassino, which became the fountainhead of the Benedictine Order and a great center of piety and scholarship.

Planting Rhyme for St. Benedict's Day

Benedict mocht die tswivvla dick.

If you plant onions on St. Benedict, you may expect a good crop.

Source and Comment

Pennsylvania Dutchman, March 1, V (1954), 9. From an article by Alfred L. Shoemaker, who quotes John Barr Stoudt and Edwin M. Fogel, Pennsylvania Dutch folklorists.

Nothing in the life of St. Benedict suggests that he had anything to do with planting onions. His day, near the vernal equinox, is simply the right time for planting onions in many localities.

Greek Independence Day
March 25

By the beginning of the 15th century the Ottoman Turks had seized control of Greece, which they ruled for approximately four centuries. Then, inspired by the success of the American and French revolutions, the Greeks began a rebellion in 1821 and, with British, French, and eventually Russian aid, became an independent monarchy in 1832.

Greek Independence Day Parade

Konstantine Sioutis, 5, of Upper Darby [Pennsylvania], may have been born in the United States, but he was caught up in the excitement of the Greek Independence Day parade yesterday.

Clutching bright blue-and-white Greek flags tightly in both hands, he waved them happily as the city's Police and Fireman's Band marched down Chestnut Street followed by scores of Greek-Americans dressed in traditional folk costumes.

Konstantine grew tired several blocks east of the staging point at City Hall and had to be carried a few blocks by his father, Paul. But he was revived by the time they reached the speaker's platform at the terminus at Independence Mall and was energetically waving again as the parade wound down.

In all, 31 colorful groups marched, and city police estimated that more than 10,000 observers turned out for the parade commemorating Greece's independence from the Turkish Ottoman Empire on March 25, 1821.

Sponsored by the Philadelphia Federation of American Hellenic Societies, the annual, daylong celebration began with a church service at the St. George Greek Orthodox Cathedral on Eighth Street and concluded with speeches and Greek folk dances in a Greek Freedom Celebration at the Civic Center. Similar celebrations took place in Greek communities across the country....

Peter Psihogios of Havertown, who operates Olympia II Pizza & Restaurant in Center City, emigrated from Greece 19 years ago. He said he attended the event every year "even if it's raining."

Near the speaker's platform at Independence Mall stood another regular, Peter Apostolos of Mount Holly, who was holding three small cloth flags representing Greece, Cyprus and the United States. Born in Greece, he came to the United States in 1920.

Apostolos said he and his wife, Maria, made it to the celebration in Philadelphia every year. Why? "Because it is an ethnic holiday and we are patriotic," he explained. "Why do you celebrate July Fourth?"

Source

Philadelphia Inquirer, March 28, 1988. From an article by staff writer Martha Woodall.

Feast of the Annunciation
March 25

This church festival celebrates the angel Gabriel's announcement to the Virgin Mary that she would be the mother of Jesus, as recorded in Luke I:26:38. It is also known as Lady Day. An important date, in England it once marked the beginning of the calendar year and (with Midsummer Day, Michaelmas, and Christmas) was one of the quarter days and hence a time for the settlement of debts. A vestige of its financial aspect survives in the designation of the last day of March by some business institutions as the end of the fiscal year.

A Celebration of Diversity

The banner was white, and in large, green capital letters it read: "*Caed Mile Failte.*"

A translation from the Gaelic was provided underneath— "A hundred thousand welcomes"—but unlike when the Incarnation of Our Lord Church was founded 90 years ago, many of the parishioners now need the English explanation.

And not all speak that language.

Times have changed at the church at Fifth Street and Lindley Avenue in the Olney section of Philadelphia.

So when Archibishop Anthony J. Bevilacqua celebrated a special multi-cultural Mass for the Feast of the Annunciation yesterday, he was presiding over what parish officials say is almost certainly the most ethnically diverse Roman Catholic parish in Philadelphia.

"I think we're probably the most," said Sister Mary Quinn, principal of the parish school where teachers instruct 588 children of 31 nationalities.

Where once Incarnation served a congregation of Irish immigrants—with some Germans sprinkled in—there is now a mix from virtually every continent.

In the parish hall, the changes are symbolized by the flags flanking the Gaelic banner—flags of Spain, Cuba and Mexico.

And beneath it at 2 p.m. yesterday were eight women in saris performing the Hindu "Folk Dance."

They were preceded by two girls dancing the "Bambuko" from Colombia, and they took the stage after the special Mass in which there were short homilies in English, Spanish, Portuguese, Hmong and Malayalam.

That's the language of Kerala, an Indian state at the southern tip of the subcontinent.

In addition to celebrating the groups' diversity, the church also unites the various groups, Archbishop Bevilacqua told more than 1,000 people attending the Mass. "There are no Americans, there are no Hispanics, there are no Portuguese, there are no Vietnamese," he said. " ... We are all one in Christ Jesus."

This year marks the 90th anniversary of the parish, and yesterday's Mass was a special, annual event in which the church combines the language groups that typically have separate Masses of their own, in their own language.

"On the Feast of the Annunciation ... we come together to worship in the five different languages," said the Rev. John Shelley, the parish pastor. The Mass was followed by a festival with ethnic food and dances.

Figures collected by the archdiocese said there are 1,625 families in the parish, about 800 of them "Anglo," 550 Hispanic, and the remainder black, Indian, Korean, Vietnamese and Portuguese....

One of the goals of the special Mass and the day's celebration was to remind everyone that they are all members of one community. "I hope they come away with an appreciation that we are all one human family," said Sister Barbara O'Neill, the parish's director of religious education.

Source and Comment

Philadelphia Inquirer, March 26, 1990. By Nathan Gorenstein, a staff writer. The parish has adapted to the shift from its original ethnic homogeneity by emphasizing the diversity but spiritual unity of its current membership. That the Feast of the Annunciation celebrates the incarnation of Christ in this way is particularly appropriate to the Church of the Incarnation of Our Lord.

Passover

March-April

The Hebrew word *Pesach* means "pass over" and refers to the eight days beginning on the fifteenth day of Nisan, the seventh month of the lunar year. It alludes to the story in Exodus about the angel of death who killed the first-born children of the Egyptians but "passed over" the houses of the children of Israel which had been marked, by God's command, with the blood of a lamb slaughtered in preparation for their redemption from slavery. On the anniversary of this date, the Israelites were required to slaughter a lamb, and in the days of the temple at Jerusalem, pour its blood on the altar and eat its flesh. Later a ceremonial meal, the *Seder,* assumed ritualistic primacy. During this meal, the *Haggadah,* a book containing the liturgy and the story of deliverance, was read and symbolic food served. This food includes meat of the paschal lamb; *matzo* or unleavened bread, unfermented and sun-baked because of the hasty departure from Egypt; bitter herbs recalling the harsh life of slavery; and wine symbolizing the fruitfulness of the earth. *Seder* means "order" or "narration," and suggests the order of the service and the ordering effect of ceremonially narrating the biblical story through the generations. Passover absorbed an older Semitic festival of spring renewal. Today it is essentially a household holiday—a reaffirmation of familial, religious, historic and seasonal traditions that have continuing significance. It is ongoing also in another sense, for its culmination is seen as the presentation of the Ten Commandments and the Covenant between God and Israel at Mount Sinai. This is celebrated at the festival of Shavout (see p. 224).

Preparing for Passover

A few days before the holiday a transaction is carried out through the Rabbi wherein a sale of a *Chometz*—any matter of leaven which is unfeasible to discard, is made to a non-Jew. This is known as *M'Chiras Chometz,* "sale of the *chometz,*" and is comparable to a contract of bailment in law wherein possession is transferred for a period of time.

Also, in the weeks before the holiday, the community is busy in the collection of *Ma-osChittim*—literally, a measure of grain. Nowadays, monies are collected so that the poor of the community may be supplied with the necessities of Passover.

On the night before Passover a ritual is followed called *B'dikas Chometz*; it is the searching out of any *chometz* that might have been overlooked in the intensive cleaning of the house. To make sure that some *chometz* will be found, it is customary to place crumbs of bread in advance in certain corners of the house. These are collected to be burned the next morning (*bi-ur chometz*) when an Aramaic formula is said renouncing any *chometz* which may have been overlooked.

The morning of the eve of Passover is a fast day for the first born as an expression of thanksgiving for the sparing of the Israelite firstborn. However, to avoid the fast, the last portion, a tractate of the Talmud is studied and finished.

This completion—*Si-yum*—demands a religious feast, and all participants are thereby exempted from fasting.

Source

Passover: A Workbook and Guide, Jewish Community Center of Detroit, 1953. Traditional material on the celebration of this holiday from a mimeographed booklet "assembled" by Max Chomsky, in the archives of YIVO Institute for Jewish Research, New York.

* * *

The Maxwell House Haggadahs

For 56 years, 33 million Maxwell House haggadahs have been distributed free of charge in markets across the United States. They have been mailed (upon request) to American servicemen stationed the world over, and to anyone else who has asked for them.

The haggadahs, which are used to promote Maxwell House coffee, have often become prized family possessions handed down from generation to generation. Early editions, from the 1930s and '40s, are nostalgic reminders of the immigrant experience, when Jews couldn't always afford to buy them.

It was the late Joseph Jacobs, founder of the New York City advertising and marketing firm that bears his name, who dreamed up the concept of the Maxwell House haggadah to use as an advertising promotion. According to Richard Jacobs, current president of the Joseph Jacobs Organization, Inc., his father had a hard sell.

"The executives of General Foods, the non-Jewish company that owned Maxwell House coffee, were quite reluctant, and understandably so, to use a Jewish prayer book written in English and Hebrew to advertise one of their products," says Jacobs.

Joseph Jacobs finally was able to convince General Foods to go ahead with the haggadah project. He pointed to the increased sales of Maxwell House coffee in Jewish neighborhoods during the holiday of Passover, which resulted after Jacobs had suggested that Maxwell House have its coffee certified kosher for Passover in 1923.

"My father was a marketing genius," says Richard Jacobs. "He knew that many Eastern European Jews mistakenly believed that coffee beans were like lima beans and green beans, not 'legal' Passover food," he explains. (Eastern European Jews traditionally do not eat peas or beans during Passover.) "When Maxwell House coffee was certified kosher for Passover by Orthodox rabbis, my father knew that Jews would buy the product during the holiday."

The elder Jacobs' ideas did not stop there. "My father thought that a haggadah compiled by Orthodox rabbis and imprinted with the Maxwell House logo would make coffee a legitimate Passover item—one that would encourage the Jews who used the free haggadahs to buy Maxwell House coffee."

And he was right on the mark. Sales of Maxwell House soared during Passover. The haggadah, imprinted with advertising copy and illustrations of the coffee, was the first of its kind, and a model for similar haggadahs distributed by other food companies.

Except for two years during World War II, when paper was scarce, the booklets have been used as a sales premium every Passover season since 1934. As a result, the Maxwell House haggadah is believed to be the oldest promotional item in continual use in the history of modern advertising.

The haggadah will also be included in an exhibit, "The Making of the American Jewish Home: 1870 to 1950," this fall at the Jewish Museum in New York City. According to Dr. Jenna Weissman Joselit, guest curator of the exhibit, the Maxwell House haggadah has instant recognition and is a "cultural icon and a resonant text imbued with memories of seders past." The exhibit will include a typical 1940s-style seder table, complete with mismatched haggadahs, wine goblets and the glass dishes most Jews of that era used for Passover.

Source and Comment

Inside: The Quarterly of Jewish Life and Style (Spring 1990), 183-84. From an article by Carol Cott Gross entitled "Coffee & Custom."

* * *

Chicken Soup and Matzo Balls

Passover is one of the holidays most closely associated with food. Special preparations must be made for the eight-day observance. Specific dietary laws, different from those of the rest of the year, are followed.

Ideally, sets of dishes, pots and pans and utensils reserved only for Passover should be used. Any food that contains leavening ingredients (such as yeast, baking powder or baking soda) or has been leavened is forbidden. Grain or cereal products as well as derivatives of these foods, such as corn oil or coffee substitutes made from cereals, are not used. Legumes such as peas, beans, corn or rice are not used, although Sephardic communities do permit rice. As a general rule, all processed foods and drinks should be labeled "Kosher for Passover" but any recipe that does not contain the prohibited foods may be used for Passover . . . .

A Seder without chicken soup is almost unthinkable, so we offer a recipe for chicken soup plus a choice of *knaidlach* (matzo balls) to serve along with it.

Chicken Soup

1	chicken, about 4 to 5 pounds, quartered
4	quarts cold water
2	stalks celery with leaves
1	large onion, peeled and quartered
1	parsnip, peeled and cut in chunks
3	carrots, peeled and cut in chunks
1	small white turnip, peeled and cut in chunks
¼	cup fresh dill sprigs
1	tablespoon salt
¼	teaspoon white pepper
	Knaidlach (see recipe)

Place the chicken pieces in a large soup pot with the water. Bring to boil, then allow to simmer over low heat. A scum will rise to the top. Remove with a large metal spoon. Cover and continue simmering for ½ hour. Add the celery, onion, parsnip, carrots, turnip, dill, salt and pepper. Simmer together for 1 ½ to 2 hours longer or until chicken is very tender. Remove chicken and vegetables, and pour soup through a strainer to remove any remaining vegetables and herbs. Cool and refrigerate until fat solidifies on surface and can be easily lifted off. Serve hot with your choice of knaidlach. Garnish with chopped fresh parsley or a sprig of dill. Makes about three quarts, or 10 to 12 servings.

Knaidlach (*Matzo Balls*)

2	tablespoons soft margarine
2	eggs

½ cup matzo meal
½ teaspoon salt
1 tablespoon finely chopped fresh parsley
2 quarts simmering salted water

In a small bowl, whisk the margarine and eggs together with a fork. Stir in the matzo meal, salt and chopped parsley. Mixture will be soft. Refrigerate for 30 minutes. With wet hands, shape into small balls. Drop the balls, one at a time, into the simmering salted water. Cover and continue simmering for 25 to 30 minutes. Remove with a slotted spoon, and drain. Add to hot chicken soup, and serve. Makes about 12 *knaidlach*.

Note: In this recipe, uncooked *knaidlach* may be made ahead and frozen. Thaw and cook as directed.

Source

Philadelphia Inquirer, April 11, 1984. Written for the "Food" section immediately preceding the beginning of Passover week, "Special to *The Inquirer*," by Ethel G. Hofman. The recipes are traditional within her family.

* * *

Matzo Meal Latkes

6 eggs
2 cups milk or water
2 cups matzo meal
1 teaspoon salt
1 teaspoon sugar
  Oil

Beat eggs with milk or water. Add matzo meal and seasonings. Drop into heated oil in large frying pan. Makes about 20 to 25 *latkes*. Serve with applesauce or sour cream.

Source

Philadelphia Inquirer, April 1, 1981. Recipe provided by Judy Fliegelman of Philadelphia, learned from her mother-in-law. She reports that *latkes* made with meal from unleavened *matzo* rather than potatoes, usually the basic ingredient, are suitable for Hanukkah as well as Passover. Cf. "Potato Latkes for Hanukkah," p. 423.

* * *

Tzipe's Passover Borsht

Ah, Vidukle [name of "*shtetle*" or village]: How vividly you stand out in my memory. I would say I spent a happy childhood there. Orke, my brother, although two and-a-half years older than myself, was my bosom companion.

Sometimes, some of the pranks we perpetrated led into situations that we cannot say we are proud of. Let's take the case of Tzipe, the *borsht* woman, as an example: Tzipe furnished the whole "*shtetle*" with delicious *borsht* for "*pesach*" [Passover]. Of course her *borsht* making did not afford her a livelihood, but the money she earned took care of her necessities for this eight-day holiday.

Many women tried to emulate her masterpiece, but none succeeded. Apparently her secret recipe was an extraordinary one. Here is where Orke and I came into the picture. In all our adventures we never acted out of a sense of maliciousness; we certainly did not intend to hurt anyone. But in this case, it did hurt poor Tzipe.

That we, Orke and I, were snoopers, goes without saying. One day we noticed Tzipe putting a large pumpernickel in a big pot. Out of curiosity, more than for any other reason, we propounded the question to some of our acquaintances, why should Tzipe put a large pumpernickel into a pot? What sort of a brew could she expect from cooking that loaf of bread?

What we did not know, and what later came to be known, was that that pumpernickel gave Tzipe's *borsht* that distinctive flavor, that culinary delight it was known for. But the tragic denouement was that when her secret became known, she was no longer the one and only borsht maker for the important holiday of Passover.

Thus, a childish prank, although unwittingly engendered, had an unfavorable result in the fortunes of one of the *shtetle's*" conspicuous matrons.

Source and Comment

Voice, Fall 1980, 9. The *Voice* is a newsletter published by the residents of the York House and distributed to members of the Philadelphia Geriatric Center. Harold J. Kravitz, assistant archivist of the Philadelphia Jewish Archives, which supplied this item, explains that it was edited by Emil Weiss, who solicits such material from his fellow residents. Many of them, like Simon Abelson who tells stories about his childhood in a Russian *shtetle*, have difficulty writing English, and their recollections are recorded by the editor. The humor of the prank appears to be somewhat complicated. Pumpernickel, a sourdough bread made from flour, is not ritually clean for Passover during which only unleavened bread is permissible. Thus, the "secret" of the Passover *borsht*, or beet soup, is indeed "an extraordinary one." Furthermore, once the secret is known, other *borsht* makers prepare soup that is not strictly *kosher*, ritually fit for use during Passover. In losing her monopoly, Tzipe gets what she deserves. Abelson's tale is not simply a nostalgic memory of "a happy childhood" in a Russian village.

* * *

The Ballad of the Four Sons

Said the father to his children
"At the Seder you will dine.
You will eat your fill of matzos
You will drink four cups of wine."

Now this father had no daughters
But his sons they numbered four
One was wise, and one was wicked
One was simple and a bore.

And the fourth was sweet and winsome
He was young and he was small;
While his brothers asked the questions
He could scarcely speak at all.

Said the wise son to his father
"Would you please explain the laws?
Of the customs of the Seder
Will you please explain the cause?"

And the father proudly answered
"As our fathers ate in speed
Ate the Paschal lamb 'ere midnight
And from slavery were freed.

So we follow their example
And 'ere midnight must complete
All the Seder, and we should not
After twelve remain to eat."

Then did sneer the son so wicked,
"What does all this mean to you?"
And his father's voice was bitter
As his grief and anger grew.

"If yourself you don't consider
As a son of Israel,
Then for you this has no meaning
You could be a slave as well."

Then the simple son said simply
"What is this?" and quietly
The good father told his offspring
"We were freed from slavery."

But the youngest son was silent
For he could not ask at all
His bright eyes were wide with wonder
As his father told him all.

Now dear children, heed the lesson
And remember ever more,
What the father told the children
And the sons that numbered four.

Source and Comment

YIVO Institute for Jewish Research Archives, New York. From *Passover,* p. 19, an undated pamphlet issued by the Labor Zionist Organization of America, New York, and affiliated organizations.

The *Haggadah* is a book containing the service read during the ritual of the *Seder,* or Passover meal. Near the beginning of this service is the passage on "The Four Sons," each representing a typical son of Israel, whose questions about the meaning of the ritual justify the explanations and storytelling which follow. The "ballad" is a modern, American song based on the ancient tradition of the four sons and their questions. It is sung to "My Darling Clementine," a song so familiar that it almost has standing as folklore. It was published in 1884, words and music by Percy Montrose. Originally sentimental to the point of being lugubrious, it came to be regarded as comic and the tune used for parodies and spoofs. But here it is once again put to serious purpose. Such are the ways of folklore—and Americanization.

*　*　*

Dayenu

I - lu ho - tsi, ho - tsi - a - nu, ho - tsi - a - nu mi - Mits - ra - yim,

Ho - tsi - a - nu mi - Mits - ra - yim, Da - ye - nu: Da - da - ye - nu,__

da - da - ye - nu,__ da - da - ye - nu, da - ye - nu, da - ye - nu__ ye - nu, da - ye - nu:

Ilu hotsi, hotsianu, hotsianu mi Mitsrayim,
Hotsianu mi Mitsrayim,
Dayenu:

[If he had delivered us from Egypt,
Delivered us from Egypt,
It would have been sufficient:]

Dadayenu,—
Dadayenu,—
Dadayenu
Dayenu, Dayenu

Source and Comment

YIVO Institute for Jewish Research Archives. From *Passover,* p. 48, an undated pamphlet issued by the Labor Zionist Organization of America, New York, and affiliated organizations.

This chant occurs during the reading of the Exodus story which precedes the ritual Passover meal. The phrase *Dayenu* means "It would have been sufficient," and it refers to the "manifold favors" bestowed upon the Children of Israel during their deliverance from Egypt. It is chanted to a traditional tune by the company at the supper table in response to the recitation of these favors by the reader. After each favor is recited, the company sings out, "*Dayenu!*"

*　*　*

One Kid, One Kid

Perhaps the most interesting survival in the Passover ritual is the use of the cumulative chant of the kid.

"One kid, one kid, which my father bought for two zuzim,
　　　One kid, one kid.

And a stick came and beat the kid, which my father bought for two zuzim,
　　　One kid, one kid.

And a fire came and burned the stick, which beat the kid, which my father bought for two zuzim,
　　　One kid, one kid.

And a water came and quenched the fire, which burned the stick, which beat the kid, which my father bought for two zuzim,
　　　One kid, one kid.

And an ox came and drank the water, which quenched the fire, which burned the stick, which beat the kid, which my father bought for two zuzim,
　　　One kid, one kid.

And a butcher came and killed the ox, which drank the water, which quenched the fire, which burned the stick, which beat the kid, which my father bought for two zuzim,
　　　One kid, one kid.

And the angel of death came and killed the butcher, who killed the ox, which drank the water, which quenched the fire, which burned the stick, which beat the kid, which my father bought for two zuzim,

One kid, one kid.

And the Holy One, blessed be He, came and slew the angel of death, who killed the butcher, who slew the ox, which drank the water, which quenched the fire, which burned the stick, which beat the kid, which my father bought for two zuzim,

One kid, one kid."

How this verse crept into a solemn religious ritual, it is hard to say, and it is equally difficult to make conjectures as to its source and date. The words are Aramaic, not Hebrew; and the tune is a peculiar, monotonous chant. It occurs at the very end of the service. Of course, the Jews have given a religious and allegorical significance to this simple song. To some it means a glorification of the power and strength of God, to whom all things must come back for solution. To others the kid represents Israel, whom God the Father saves from all his enemies.

In spite of the spiritual interpretations given to the song, the Chasidim, a sect among the orthodox Jews, exclude it from their service altogether, saying that it is childish and silly. Since this sect is very old and is especially noted for its piety, and because the rhyme is at the very end of the ritual, it is perhaps possible that the song is a later addition. The fact that the name of God is not given, but that he is referred to by one of his attributes,—the Holy One, blessed be He,—is an indication that the chant is of secular origin, since the Jews never use the name of God in non-religious songs or proverbs.

Source and Comment

Journal of American Folklore, XXIX (1916), 416-17. Reported by Leah R. C. Yoffie. She does not give her source but this chant is widely known and usually included in the *Haggadah,* the narrative of the Exodus and associated materials, read at the *Seder,* or Passover supper ceremony.

The cumulative form of this chant is old and has many parallels as a song, rhyme and tale. See, for example, the article by William Wells Newell in *Journal of American Folklore,* XVIII (1905), 33-48. The traditional tune and Yiddish text provided here from *Passover,* p. 46, an undated pamphlet issued by the Labor Zionist Organization of American, New York, and affiliated groups in the archives of YIVO Institute for Jewish Research, New York.

* * *

A Passover Song and a Christmas Carol

The *Ehad Mi Yodea* (*Who Knows One?*) is sung by Jews at their Passover feasts in nearly all parts of the world. There are very few Jews who do not include it among their Passover chants. A few pious sects, like the *Chassidim,* scorn the song as a mere nursery rhyme, but most Passover rituals include it with the "Song of the Kid" at the end of the Passover service.... I give below the Jewish song of *Who Knows One?* and one version which Campbell and Sharp acquired from Miss Dell Westmoreland, White County, Georgia, in 1908....

Jewish Version	The Georgia Version
Who knows one? I know one. One is our God who is in heaven and on earth.	Come and I'll sing you. What will you sing me? I will sing you one. What is your one? One, O one, is God alone, and He shall ever remain so.
Who knows two? I know two. Two are the two tables of the covenant.	Come and I'll sing you, etc. Two are the lily-white babes clothed in darling green, O.
Who knows three, etc. Three are the patriarchs.	Come and I'll sing you, etc. Three of them are strangers.
Four are the matrons (Sarah, Rebecca, Leah, and Rachel).	Four are the Gospel preachers.
Five are the Books of Moses.	Five are the farmers in a boat.
Six are the Books of the Mishna.	Six are the cheerful waiters.
Seven are the days in the week.	Seven are the seven stars fixed in the sky.
Eight days preceding circumcision.	Eight are the great Archangels.
Nine months preceding childbirth.	Nine are the nine that dress so fine.
Ten are the Ten Commandments.	Ten are the Ten Commandments.
Eleven are the eleven stars.	Eleven are the eleven who went to Heaven.
Twelve are the tribes of Israel.	Twelve are the twelve apostles.
Thirteen are the attributes of God.	

Chad Gadya
(*One Kid*)

Source and Comment

Southern Folklore Quarterly, IV (1940), 73-75. Leah R. C. Yoffie compares and comments on a traditional Passover song, reprinted from *Forms of Services for Passover,* New York, 1859, 57, and a carol collected by Olive Campbell and Cecil Sharp which they include in *Folksongs of the Southern Appalachians,* New York, 1917, 300-01. In another article, *Journal of American Folklore,* LXII (1949), 383, Yoffie summarizes the scholarship, cites further parallels, and notes: "On two of the numbers, all variants, both Jewish and Christian agree; *one* refers to the Unity of the Godhead, and *ten* to the Commandments. Practically all the Christian versions go on to the number *twelve* for the Twelve Disciples, while the Hebrew service reads 'the twelve tribes of Israel,' and adds the number *thirteen* for the thirteen attributes of God as expounded by the Jewish philosopher Maimonides." Cf. "The Carol of the Twelve Numbers," p. 458, and other Christmas counting songs, p. 459.

* * *

Games for Passover

The majority of games for *Pesach* [Passover] are played with nuts....

"Passover Polo": A small circle is drawn on the floor. Nuts are thrown into a circle. If an even number go in the circle the player receives from the banker the same amount of nuts plus the original nuts. All nuts falling outside the circle belong to the banker.

"*Pesach* Golf": Various places or holes are marked on the floor. Each player flips the nut with his thumb and forefinger to move it from hole to hole. As in golf, the player who finished the course with the least amount of strokes is the winner.

"Logging Nuts": A line is drawn ten to twenty-five feet away from the players, who stand on a throwing line. Nuts are thrown by the players. The one whose nut is nearest the line wins all the other nuts....

"*Shpitz Tzi Kopp*" (Heads or Tails): The players sit in a row. The person beginning the game approaches the first person in the row, shows him a closed fist in which is found a nut and asks him to guess the position of the nut, whether it is head up or point up, saying "Head or tail?"

Source

Passover: A Workbook and Guide, Jewish Community Center, Detroit, 1953, 10. See note on "Preparing for Passover," above.

* * *

The Pauper and the Pious Jew

This pauper did not have the means to purchase the articles he needed to observe Passover, so he went to a "good Jew" asking that this pious man intercede with God on his behalf. The pauper gave the pious man his last *groschen* and the pious man assured the pauper that God would help him. The pauper waited until two days before Passover. God's help had not arrived. The pauper sold his last goat in order to at least purchase *matzo.* The pious man met him and asked, "Were you able to procure your needs for Passover?" The pauper said, "I sold my last goat in order to do it." The pious man replied, "See, I told you God would provide for you."

Source and Comment

Rubin Autobiography, Jewish Archives of Philadelphia. Harris Rubin was born in 1847 in the Vilkomir district, Kovner province, Russia. This tale is from his manuscript autobiography, p. 81, written in Yiddish at intervals between 1915 and 1919. He was then retired from the dairy business in Philadelphia. The typescript of a translation was deposited by his family in the archive cited above.

* * *

Carry-out for Passover, Yet

There was a time when the Jewish housewife had to put forth titanic energies to produce a massive *seder* meal. After cleaning her home for the springtime festival that features unleavened bread (matzo) she would change dishes, then with only hours to spare, make gefilte fish, matzo ball soup, brisket or chicken, *hareset* (a sweet relish), compote and macaroons. Finally, scrambling to set the table, she would miraculously complete her preparations minutes before the seder meal. Many men and women still work this way.

Even with the assistance of modern mass marketing, food processors, meat grinders and blenders, the job is still an enormous one.

What could be more logical than carry-out food for Passover, which begins Monday night [1980] at sundown?...

Except for the ceremonial seder plate with *hareset,* the typically chopped apple and nut combination, reminding the Jews of the mortar with which they built pyramids in Egypt, caterers will provide entire Passover packages. On extreme urging they will even provide the seder plate.

Locally, for example, David Yegher's Caterers of Silver Spring [Maryland] prepares three types of carry-out dinners. Chicken is $9.50, brisket $11.50 and prime ribs $12.50 per person. The meal includes chopped liver or gefilte fish, matzo ball or vegetable soup, carrot *tzimmes* and potato kugel. Dessert will have to come from elsewhere. Yegher, once a cook at Duke Zeibert's, does not make desserts at Passover. The telephone number is 587-1445.

Schleider and Shabat, Baltimore caterers, are providing Washingtonians with identical Passover packages at $6.50 per person with homemade gefilte fish, horseradish, chicken, soup, matzo balls, roasted stuffed caponette, potato kugel, *tzimmes, knaidlach* and fruit compote. The pick-up place for Schleider's is the parking place of the Jewish Community Center, 6125 Montrose Rd., Rockville [Maryland], on Sunday from 10 A.M. to 2 P.M. and Shabat Shomrei Emunah Congregation, 1132 Arcola Ave., Silver Spring on Sunday from 3 to 5 P.M. Schleider's telephone number is 881-3787, and Shabat is 258-7528.

Both caterers have homemade Passover foods to go, including such items as chopped herring, chopped liver, *kishka* and fruit compote. Shabat is featuring a special potato knish for Passover this year with a potato and matzo meal crust filled with meat.

For those who do not think about ordering in advance, Shalom Market at 2307 University Blvd. in Silver Spring will carry Schleider's matzo rolls, apple *schalet* and potato and noodle kugels. In addition, Shalom will make roast turkey, brisket and rotisserie chicken strictly for Passover.

The other constant on most Washington menus is matzo ball soup. Again, those who do not want to make their own can go to the above-mentioned caterers or even ask Duke Zeibert. He makes at least 300 extra matzo balls for many of Washington's more illustrious seder dinners. Names were not available, as some hostesses would prefer that the accolades stay in the family. Duke used to make his own

gefilte fish at Passover, but feels that it is too expensive today and that the bottled varieties, doctored up, do quite nicely.

Other than the traditional Manischewitz and Barton's macaroons and candies, Four Corners market has brought in a line of European jam and honey cookies made with potato starch from Montreal.

Even Bloomingdale's bakery will be catering to the Passover crowd with daily freshly baked honey cakes, strawberry shortcakes, sponge cakes and coconut and almond macaroons for Passover.

The range of compliance with Orthodox dietary law and customs varies from the kosher-style restaurants and caterers that do not make a pretense of Rabbinic supervision, to caterers who employ rabbis in supervisory rules. The same is true of prepared products. If in doubt of whether the dietary laws are being followed (*kashurt*), consult your local rabbi.

Source

Washington Post, March 27, 1980. Special feature by Joan Nathan.

Easter Week and Easter
Moveable: March 22-April 25

The most important holy day in the Christian calendar, Easter, commemorates the Resurrection of Christ, but its celebration incorporates pre-Christian rites of seasonal regeneration. The Council of Nicea in 325 determined that Easter should be observed on the Sunday after the first full moon on or following the vernal equinox, a range of thirty-five days. This set the date of Lent and determines the dates of Shrove Tuesday and Ash Wednesday; of Palm Sunday and the Holy Week immediately preceding Easter; and Ascension Day, Whitsunday, Corpus Christi Day afterwards.

In many countries Easter is a time of fairs, fiestas, bonfires, promenades, and pilgrimages. The Easter parade and the wearing of bright, new clothes to church exemplify some of these customs. The flowers and eggs associated with Easter are fertility symbols, reflecting ancient spring renewal rites and beliefs that have been absorbed into paschal tradition. The fact that the eggs are brought by a rabbit, another fertility symbol, underscores the pagan elements that remain part of Easter. The rabbit was the escort of the Germanic goddess Ostara who gave her name to a holiday which fell at the time of vernal equinox.

Palm Sunday Palms

The palms blessed on Palm Sunday are placed behind religious pictures and statues in Buffalo [New York] homes, stores and restaurants and are thought to bring good luck.

Source and Comment

Indiana Folklore, IX (1976), 169. Collected by Lydia Marie Fish. For her sources, see note on "St. Joseph's Day Feast," p. 116.

When Christ entered Jerusalem on the Sunday before Easter, He was honored by having palm branches and palm leaves placed in His path. To commemorate this triumphal entry, they are distributed in churches on Palm Sunday, worn on clothing, and kept as emblems of devotion. Holy Week, the last week of Lent, begins on Palm Sunday.

* * *

Greens on Green Thursday

According to Noah Webster, Maundy Thursday is the Thursday before Easter, so called in memory of the new command given at the time of the washing of the disciples' feet by Christ. (John 13: 5, 14, 34.)

Mrs. Lillian Hollenbach, of Shartlesville [Pennsylvania] asserted that if you don't eat anything green on this day, especially dandelion, you won't get rid of your old hair and get new. Mrs. Sallie Adams, of Shoemakersville, said that it was the tradition at their home to eat nine different kinds of "greens." These "greens" usually included dandelion, endive, turnip tops, cabbage, alfalfa, clover, etc. The reason for eating these nine greens was to prevent illness. Mrs. Diana Dreibelbis informed me that they always eat something green on this day, usually dandelion. Mrs. Mabel Miller asserted that they always eat something green on this day. Mrs. Minnerva Seidel stated that she always makes some dandelion for dinner on this day. She also said that they at home always used the eggs that were laid on this day for coloring for Easter; it brought good luck. Mrs. Deborah Geschwindt, of Temple, told me that they always ate something green on this day, usually dandelion. Mr. Henry Stitzel, of Shoemakersville, told me that they too always had something green to eat on this day. Mrs. Myrtle May, whose home county is Northampton, expressed her view by saying that in her home this day was considered a very sacred day. They did not do very much work. This was usually the day for Communion services at their church. Miss Beatrice Weaver, of Northampton County, said that they always had dandelion for dinner on this day. In my own home in Shoemakersville, my mother always makes some dandelion for dinner.

There are other interesting sayings that I have collected which I would like to share and they are: ... eating something green on Maundy Thursday to protect one's health or using an egg laid on Maundy Thursday to reduce hernia, combine in them pagan and Christian elements, for in superstition Maundy Thursday is exceedingly a big day; unless you eat something green on Maundy Thursday, you will get the itch; you will not become lousy if you eat something green on Maundy Thursday, and eat some green vegetable on Maundy Thursday to prevent fever.

Source and Comment

Pennsylvania Dutchman, II (April 1, 1951), 3. From an article by Don F. Geschwindt, "born and reared in Shoemakersville, Berks County, Pennsylvania," written when "a Sophomore at Franklin and Marshall College, Lancaster, Pennsylvania."

Maundy Thursday is known among the Pennsylvania Dutch as "*Green Dunnestag*" and in German as "*Grundonnerstag,*" meaning Green Thursday. In Saxony, green salads are traditionally served on this day. "Maundy" is said to be derived from the Latin *mandatum,* a command, referring to Christ's "new command" to observe the practice of foot washing as a mark of compassion and humility. Other names for this holiday include Holy Thursday, Glory Thursday, and Great Thursday.

* * *

Green Thursday

Feed Chickens on Holy Thursday

If you feed chickens in a coop on Holy Thursday, you will have eggs all year round.

Source

Memoirs of the American Folklore Society, XVIII (1925), 115. "Folk-Lore from Maryland," collected by Annie W. Whitney and Caroline C. Bullock. Specific data on informants not supplied.

* * *

Good Friday Procession of the Virgin of Sorrows

Good Friday is the traditional day of mourning in the Roman Catholic Church. In symbolic recognition of the death of Christ the altar is stripped, candles are extinguished, the host is removed from the altar, the statues are draped, and a purple scrim is hung between the altar and nave of the church, effectively sealing the holy area from view. The church becomes a tomb for the crucified body of Jesus, and the life of the church is considered dead from Good Friday until Easter morning. No liturgical forms can be expressed during this period; mass cannot be said, and benediction may not be given.

The parishioners of the Church of Sacred Hearts and St. Stephen on Hicks Street in Brooklyn turn tradition upside down every Good Friday with the performance of a highly unorthodox ceremony, the Procession of Maria SS Addolorato (the Virgin of Sorrows). St. Steve's (as it is locally known) is situated in the heart of an old Brooklyn-Italian neighborhood, a relatively closed neighborhood in that it is almost exclusively Italian in ethnic composition, the families who live there having remained through generations. Many of the families have immigrated from the same region in Italy (the area surrounding and including Bari in the region of Apulia) and continue to do so. The Procession, in fact, was brought to Brooklyn from the original village parish of Mola di Bari. In recognition of the eternal link between the Italian homeland and the Brooklyn

settlement, the people of Mola di Bari gave the statue of Maria SS Addolorato to St. Steve's some forty years ago. Yet even before the gift statue added spiritual incentive to the procession, the ceremony was held using an American icon.

By 6:30 P.M. the church is filled with parishioners, predominantly women and children. The inside of the church is ablaze with devotional candles and parishioners who are just entering make their way to the front to purchase a load of candles from a man who sells them under the approving image of the Virgin of the Immaculate Conception. With candles in hand, the women push slowly back down the side aisles, greeting neighbors and chatting with friends as they go. At intervals along the way, they suddenly drop on their knees before their favorite saint's statue to offer prayers and a flame of remembrance. By 7:00 P.M. the church is overflowing. The sun has set and the procession must begin. At the back of the church six young men dressed in black tuxedos and wearing white gloves form two lines and begin a solemn march down the center aisle of the church approaching the altar. Between them they carry an ornately carved wooden platform. Simultaneously, the priest enters from the side sacristy (a small room off the altar area), steps in front of the altar and meets the young men as they attain the anterior of the church. Everyone is silent now and all eyes follow the priest and these six sons as they approach the side niche which holds the image of the Virgin of Sorrows. The statue is kept in a glass case in the front of the church at all times, and it is removed only for this procession and the Virgin's feast day in September. Slowly, ever so carefully, they remove the statue and place it on the platform. The statue is remarkably large (approximately five feet) in comparison to all others in the church. She is dressed in fine black lace, with a white ruff around the neck and a heavy black veil just covering the head. A deeply grave and tear-stained dark face stares hypnotically forward. In the left hand a white lace handkerchief is modestly held, but in painful contrast, the heart is noticeably pierced through with a shining silver dagger.

Solemnly the procession leaves the church, everyone silently flowing out row after row behind the image as she is taken to the streets. Four young men conveying tall, gilded torches, surround the Virgin's platform as she emerges from the nave. Outside the church various societies of the parish have taken their places in front of the statue. First in front came the women of the Altar Rosary Society carrying tall, white but unlit candles. In front of them walk the men of the Holy Name bearing a red-stained glass cross electrically lighted, and decorated with the metonymic symbols of the passion (the cock, dice, nails, etc.) Immediately behind the statue marches the church band composed of many tubas, few trombones, at least three snare drums, and one heavy boom drum. The band plays a mournful dirge to accompany the Virgin through the Brooklyn dark. Behind the band walk various school groups including the Girl Scouts and a young girl's group called the Children of Mary. Finally, following them, is the great intermingling procession of parishioners, neighbors, visitors, and occasional strangers, which may amount to as many as 3,000 participants. Old women of the neighborhood dressed in heavy black mourning costume, knotted cords of penance around their waists, take the lead of the slowly moving throng. The procession turns left from the church up Hicks Street and follows a serpentine, circular pattern, which takes in most every street of the parish.

Meanwhile, it must be explained, another procession leaves the church, turning right on Hicks Street, about three minutes before the Virgin of Sorrows is brought out of the sanctuary. This secondary procession, which organizes at the back of the church or across the street at the Virgin of Sorrows Headquarters (an old store where the men of the church meet to make the logistic and physical preparations for the procession) is composed of older and middle-aged men, the elders of the parish. They bear on their shoulders a glass casket in which is laid a life-size figure of the crucified Jesus, draped in pale violet gauze and wearing a bloody crown of thorns. This procession, appreciably smaller, moves in a more limited pattern through the parish. Most crucially, this procession must not cross the procession of the Virgin of Sorrows because the narrative motivation for the ceremony clearly specifies that Mary (the Virgin of Sorrows) is out in the streets looking for her lost son, searching desperately through the neighborhood as any mother would to retrieve a missing child.

As the Virgin of Sorrows winds through the parish, people run from their houses to follow her awhile, or drop to their knees right in front of their homes to offer a prayer and receive a blessing. Unlike processions which accompany *festas* (feast days), offerings of money are not given to the Virgin as she passes. The procession moves along in stop-and-go fashion. Special resting points, which are in effect special points of reference for the members of the community, include another church (The Chapel of St. Francis Cabrini, which is open and brightly lit), a convent, a school, a funeral home and certain street intersections. At these breaks, the honor bearers of the Virgin are relieved by new recruits.

Many women in the neighborhood have made special flower and white light shines in the shape of a cross or circle and cross to greet the Virgin as she passes; these shrines briefly occupy a special place on the front lawn for the three hours of the procession and are then destroyed. Of course, any permanent lawn statuary of the Virgin is specially lighted and decorated with baskets of flowers for the event. White light, symbolic of renewal and purity, is the dominant source of illumination and decoration along the procession route. Although this tradition is dying out, it was once popular to place lamps in front windows and turn them on when the procession passed by, leaving behind a trail of lighted lamps to mark the blessed route.

Most worthy of description are the doorway tableaus created by women of the parish. The women, dressed in black gowns and head veils, stand in the floodlighted doors of their homes next to gigantic (6-8 foot) wooden crosses made for use exclusively on the night of the procession. It is not unusual for a mother and daughter to maintain silent and motionless vigil of this sort lasting the entire period of the procession. The two figures probably represent Mary, the mother of Jesus, and Mary Magdalene, who, according to legend, came to retrieve the body from the cross after the Crucifixion. Often the doors of these houses are draped in black crepe or hung with black banners which emphasize the mournful devotion presented in these doorway spectacles.

Having encircled and crisscrossed the entire parish on her search, the Virgin is once again moving down Hicks Street toward the church. By this time the street is crowded beyond capacity, everyone pressed shoulder to shoulder, straining to see her approach. Heads are stretched out of all the brownstones, meat markets, and *calzone* stands that line the way. Now more slowly, more deliberately she searches. The crowd ripples with anticipation, for in front of the church the secondary procession has already ended. The dead son waits to be found by his mother. She approaches and this is the most significant moment of the entire ceremony: once the two figures are within close range of each other (centered at the footsteps of the church entryway) the men who carry the Virgin stop and raise her as high as they can over the heads of the crowd. Simultaneously the men carrying the casket of Jesus bring it before the Virgin for blessing. Three times they advance to the Virgin and then retreat about ten feet. Immediately after the third round of recognition and blessing the statue of the Virgin is turned backward and triumphantly rushed into the church down the center aisle and placed in front of the altar. The casket of Jesus is brought in behind and placed to the side of the Mother. The church is still blazing with candles but now the altar has been curtained off with a huge purple scrim emblazoned with a white satin cross. Masses of parishioners, both men and women, overfill the church. Briefly, the priest steps out and sermonizes about the sorrow of Mary or the coming joy of Easter but his moment in the affair is quite bathetic and receives merely dutiful respect from the parishioners. The ceremony ended, people move slowly out of the church, some coming forward to kiss the hem of the Virgin's gown. Until the last participant leaves, She stands at the central axis of the church bidding farewell.

Source and Comment

Folklore Papers of the University Folklore Association, Center for Intercultural Studies in Folklore and Enthomusicology, University of Texas, 1980, 2-5. Kay F. Turner describes an Italian Catholic Good Friday procession in an interpretative essay concerned with its historical and symbolic meaning. Her purpose is to point out "certain of the universal, generic meanings of *procession* as a kind of ritual movement." For a Hispanic-American parallel, see "The Encounter of Christ and Mary," p. 143.

For more than seventy years the Catholic parish of St. Stephen in Brooklyn, New York, has held a procession on Good Friday honoring the Virgin of Sorrows. This observance was brought to Brooklyn from Apulia in southern Italy, and is a festival linked with a particular community, Mola di Bari, as, for instance, Naples is associated with the Feast of San Gennaro, its patron saint (see p. 000). The folklorist who describes this ceremony points out that it actually consists of two distinct processions; one centered on an image of Mary and the other of Jesus, and at their conclusion Jesus, in effect, pays homage to His Mother. In fact, one of the unusual features of the ceremony is this emphasis on Mary and the light which surrounds her. "Good Friday is not a time of light, it is a time of darkest darkness, yet the church blazes with candles and the Virgin is often greeted with the turning on of lights in houses wherever she goes."

* * *

Albanian Good Friday

Katherine Costa stood near the top of an aluminum stepladder yesterday, carefully pushing carnations into the latticework of a gilded wooden structure that resembled a vendor's pushcart.

Below, half a dozen women and girls attached red and white flowers to other parts of the structure and wound baby's breath around its legs.

They were decorating a representation of the tomb of Jesus, used yesterday in Good Friday services at St. John Chrysostom Albanian Orthodox Church in Center City [Philadelphia].

Like more than 250 million Eastern Orthodox Christians around the world, the congregation of St. John Chrysostom is observing Good Friday and Easter a month later than Protestants and Roman Catholics this year.

They celebrate Easter tomorrow [April 30, 1989].

The Orthodox churches delayed their celebration to comply with an ancient decree of the Council of Nicaea that Easter not precede Passover.

The Council of Nicaea, which met in 325, declared that Easter is to be celebrated on the Sunday after the first full moon of the spring equinox. But the Council also decreed that Easter should not be celebrated until the Jewish observance of Passover is finished.

The Eastern churches have adhered to the second decree, while the Western churches have not.

Passover began at sundown April 19 and ended at sundown Thursday.

Whatever the date, decorating the tomb of Jesus on the morning of Good Friday is an annual tradition at St. John Chrysostom, which has about 200 parishioners, mostly of Albanian descent, scattered throughout the Philadelphia area.

Some of the women have been coming for years to work on the tomb.

Kiki Notskas, who was born in Albania in 1911, said that she has been coming to help arrange the flowers on the tomb for "maybe 30 years."

Catherine Tolia, who was snipping carnation stems with a pair of scissors, said that she has been helping to decorate the tomb for 19 years.

"I'm the tallest, so I always get the ladder part," said Katherine Costa.

While St. John Chrysostom uses carnations, other churches use roses or orchids or potted plants to decorate the tomb, the women said.

Their handiwork was on view at the front of the church when members of the congregation assembled yesterday afternoon to commemorate the crucifixion of Jesus.

During services on Good Friday afternoon, the Epitaphios, an embroidered picture of Jesus, is placed in the tomb, said the Rev. Dennis Rhodes, pastor of St. John Chrysostom.

A vigil light, hanging down from the wooden structure's dome, is lit.

The Epitaphios is taken out of the tomb during a Good Friday night service, as the congregation sings hymns called the Lamentations, and is carried around the church in procession....

After the service, the flowers are given to parishioners, Father Rhodes said, "as a sign that we receive life from Christ's tomb."

Source

Philadelphia Inquirer, April 29, 1989. By staff writer, Michael D. Schaffer.

* * *

Good Friday

Good Friday Eggs

The ancient Persians, among others, believed that the earth was hatched from a cosmic egg. Perhaps from this lore comes the belief in eggs laid during the Easter season, particularly on Holy Thursday and Good Friday. The Holy Thursday egg, or *antlassei* [German: Holy Thursday Egg], was supposed to stay fresh all year.

According to one lady, a Mrs. Bosworth of Long Beach, Mississippi, the Good Friday egg has even greater power. She says that the yolk of an egg laid on Good Friday will turn into a diamond if it is kept for a hundred years. One such egg she has is more than thirty years old. According to Mrs. Bosworth, eggs laid both before and after Good Friday will rot, but the Good Friday egg, stored alongside it, will not rot. Further, foods prepared with Good Friday eggs will remain fresh longer than those prepared with eggs laid on other days.

Source and Comment

Mississippi Folklore Register, X (1976), 37-38. Reported by Nell Henderson, who was given a Good Friday egg by Mrs. Bosworth, laid in 1973 and at the time of her report still "clear and untainted." For Pennsylvania Dutch beliefs about the special properties of Holy Thursday eggs, see "Greens on Green Thursday," p. 152.

* * *

Good Friday

Hatching Good Friday Eggs

If you set a hen on Good Friday in Maryland, you will have all kinds of speckled chickens.

If you set a hen on Good Friday, every egg will be hatched.

Source

Memoirs of the American Folklore Society, XVIII (1925), 116. "Folk-Lore from Maryland," collected by Annie W. Whitney and Caroline C. Bullock. Informants not given.

* * *

Good Friday

Creole Good Friday Beliefs

There is always rain on that day, for even the heavens weep on the day of the death of Christ.

Go fishing on Good Friday, for fish always bite on that day.

An egg laid on Good Friday will turn to wax if kept until the next Good Friday.

If you dig in the ground on Good Friday you will see blood. (Interpreted by some to mean that you will cut yourself, and by others that the earth is actually bleeding.)

Never dig in the ground planting flowers on Good Friday, for you will see blood before nightfall if you do.

On a picnic on Good Friday someone is always hurt.

Roosters always crow at three o'clock in the afternoon on Good Friday.

Plant parsley on Good Friday and it will not go to seed.

Source and Comment

Creole Good Friday Beliefs, *Journal of American Folklore,* XL (1927), 148, 190-91. Collected by Hilda Roberts in Iberia Parish, southwestern Louisiana. Her collection, she reports, shows white, black and Indian influences "and of the white race there are three dominant nationalities—the French, the Spanish, and the Anglo-Saxon."

Good Friday

Digging Potatoes on Good Friday

On a Good Friday in Louisiana in about 1935 when I was about nine years of age, my father and I were digging potatoes in the patch behind the house. A cry made me look up from where I kneeled in the fresh-turned earth to see our neighbor, Gerard Menard, coming across the rows. He cried out again and gestured and so my father stopped the team, tied the lines around the plow handle and came back a few steps to speak to him.

"Eddie," old Gerard said in French waving his arms once more as he came up to my father. "Don't you know better than to be plowin' on a Good Friday?"

"Why no, Menard," my father answered. "What's the matter, is there something wrong with digging out a few Irish potatoes?"

"*Mais non,* not with that," Gerard Menard said, shaking his thin head, "It's not that but you not suppose to cut the ground on a Good Friday."

"But why not?" my father asked him with some surprise.

"Eddie, don't you know that the blood of the *Bon Dieu,* Jesu Christ, will run out in the rows if you cut open the ground on a Good Friday?"

I don't remember that we stopped digging potatoes that day, but it seems now that my father must have placated the old man in some way.

Source

Tennessee Folklore Society Bulletin, XXXIII (June 1967), 49-50. Recalled by David G. LeDoux of Middle Tennessee State University.

* * *

Good Friday

Planting on Good Friday

Cabbage should be planted on Good Friday, or at apple-blossom time before the sun rises. It should be planted in the new moon or it won't head; it will form a club root and grow up in a straight stalk. No doubt Fred Fryer followed all these precautions the day he lost his watch. It seems that he had been planting cabbage over in Montgomery County [New York]. He looked all over for the watch, but finally allowed that he couldn't find it. In due time the cabbages grew to maturity and were harvested. One day in the winter, Fred's wife sent him down cellar to get a cabbage for salad. He picked out the largest one he could find, brought it up, and started to cut it open. The knife stuck. He cut through from the other side; the cabbage fell open and out dropped the watch. It was good as new and still running, because as the cabbage grew around the stem of the watch, it had kept it wound. It had lost five minutes, though....

Good Friday is the day for planting radishes, lettuce, and tomatoes—also for sweet peas, one of the few garden flowers common in New York State planting lore.

Source

New York Folklore Quarterly, VII (1951), 50. Collected by Edith E. Cutting, who provides a list of informants, "Yorkers," mostly her students and those of Louis C. Jones. She does not supply information about them. For related motifs about lost watches see Motifs X 1755f.

Good Friday

Hanging Things on Hangman's Day

Good Friday is a chosen day for planting everything, but especially beans.

Fridays are good days for planting things that hang down, like beans and grapes, stringing things, because Friday is 'hangman's day.'

Source and Comment

Journal of American Folklore, V (1892), 113. Collected by N. C. Hoke in Lincoln County, North Carolina from an area "settled by Germans ... these people surely the most conservative on Earth."

* * *

Good Friday

Good Friday Cures
Whooping Cough

Won do en kindt noggich in der waitsa huckscht uff der Ker-Freidawg, un doosht no seller waitsa nuch seller dawg in die meel, no doot sell kindt der blow-hooschta net greega.

If you put a child nude in the wheat on Good Friday, and then put that wheat in the mill that very same day, that child will not get the whooping-cough.

Warts

Won epper waurtsa hut, shtay uff moryets uff der Ker-Freidawg un grick en grumbeer, schwetts nix tzu n'iemann, un gay on die shire; schneid die grumbeer darrich, reib sie ivver die waurtsa, un no feeder die grumbeera tzu der coo. Die waurtsa die gaina weck un gaina an der coo era ditts. Wons en grossy grumbeer iss, un mer doot sie ferschneida un no die schticker tsu pawr kee feedra, no iss es net so schlimm.

When anyone has warts, get up in the morning on Good Friday and get a potato, don't speak to anyone, and go to the barn; cut the potato in two, rub it over the wart and then feed the potato to the cow. The warts will go away and go onto the cow's teats. If it is a big potato, and you cut it up and then feed the pieces to several cows, then it's not so bad.

Same as above, only be sure to do it in the dark of the moon.

Almost [the] same as above, only you bury the potato under the eaves; as it rots, the warts disappear.

Rupture

Won epper en bruch (rupture) hut don sull er en wai-chschawlich oye greega os uff der Kerr-Freidawg gelaikt wawr, un no sull er die hout fun sellem oye nemma un ivver sei bruch do, un no die drei graischte nawma—(Fodder, Sohn un der Heilich Geischt) nenna, un der bruch gate weck; in onnera wordta, er hailt tzu.

When anyone has a rupture he should get a soft-shelled egg that was laid on Good Friday, and should take the skin off that egg and put it over his rupture, and name the three greatest names (Father, Son, and Holy Ghost) and the rupture will go away; in other words, it heals up.

Source

Pennsylvania Folklife, XVII (Autumn 1967), 29-30. Collected by Victor C. Dieffenbach. See note on "Pennsylvania Dutch on St. Patrick's Day," p. 127, for details on his collection. Dieffenbach credits the two variants of the wart cure, given in English, to Peter Eisenhauer and Kitty Hertzler but does not supply further information about them. He collected the rupture cure from Henry Yoder of Kutztown, Pennsylvania.

* * *

Blessing Food on Holy Saturday

On Holy Saturday Evening the Slovenes [of Indianapolis, Indiana] go to church with their baskets of food for the priest to bless. The baskets, all covered with their best embroidered towels and linen, contain their favorite Easter food: ham or homemade sausage and the *potica* [filled sweet bread]. The Indianapolis colony depends upon Cleveland butchers to supply this special sausage, a pig's stomach stuffed with meat, something like salami. On Easter Sunday at breakfast this sausage that has been blessed by the priest is broken and passed to each member of the family. Incidentally when a hog is butchered in the late fall, every piece is designated for a certain holiday or gathering, such as, a ham and sausage for Easter, a ham for Christmas, ribs for Ascension Day, another piece for hay-gathering time, and another for the day before Ash Wednesday. This custom is observed in Cleveland today [1947], where there is a very large Yugoslavian community—large enough that Slovenian is taught in their schools.

Source and Comment

Hoosier Folklore, VI (1947), 122. From a "Slovian Folklore in Indianapolis" collected by Margaret Montgomery. In the 1940s some 500 Catholic Slovenes lived in a section of about five square blocks in west Indianapolis. Montgomery's sources included "two young Slovenian housewives," one of them a Mrs. Reinhold. Cf. "Polish-American Easter Food," p. 158.

Polish-American Easter Food

On Holy Saturday [in New York Mills, New York] food is taken to the churches in baskets to be blessed. Foods included are eggs (both colored and hard-boiled which have been peeled), for they are the symbols of life (as Christ came from the tomb alive, life can come from the egg); bread (usually rye and *Babka*), for Christ gave Himself to us as bread; meat (ham and *Kielbasa* or Polish sausage), which signifies the physical Christ, who was not an angel but God-man; horseradish, which represents the bitter sorrows Christ underwent; vinegar, for Christ was given gall to drink; and a lamb (of sugar or butter, decorated with the Polish flag), representing Christ, the Lamb of God who takes away our sins. Eggs were colored with onion skins and decorated with wax, especially in the shape of stars; this kind of egg is called *Pisanki*. On the day after Easter boys would squirt water at the girls through a hollow wooden stick, using a wooden rod. (Today [1968] food is still taken to the church, and it is even possible to have the priest come to your home to bless the food. Decorating eggs with wax is no longer done by the younger people; neither is the day after Easter game used, in which the boys squirt the girls.)

Source

New York Folklore Quarterly, XXIV (1968), 303-04. Reported by Robert Maziarz. See "Polish Christmas Eve Supper," p. 440, and note, p. 441, for background and informants. Also cf. "Paczki Day," p. 99.

* * *

The Woman Who Swallowed the Easter Egg

The day before Easter, the Polish people take a basket of food to church to be blessed.

There was a peasant family who lived in the country and had quite a distance to drive to the church. The father and his children were dressed and ready, but they were still waiting for his wife, who was still dressing. He kept yelling up to her room to hurry. She was dressing as fast as she could. She put on her pearls and her hat, but she was hungry. She took a hard-boiled egg from the basket. Her husband kept yelling louder and louder, so instead of breaking open the egg, she swallowed it whole. The egg caught in her throat and she fell to the floor.

Her husband kept yelling, but after hearing no response, he went up to investigate and found his wife dead. In those days, there were no embalming methods, and the dead were buried quickly in a simple pine box. The husband put his dead wife in the wagon, took her to church, and had her buried.

That evening, he remembered his wife was wearing her expensive pearls. He decided to dig up her grave and take them back. He went to the graveyard, dug up the ground, and opened the casket. He put his knee on her chest and lifted her head to unlock the clasp. Just then his wife woke up. She had swallowed the egg which had been caught in her throat. Her husband was so frightened, his hair turned grey, and he fell down dead.

The lady got up, put him into the coffin and covered up the grave. Then she went home to celebrate Easter with her children.

Source

New York Folklore Quarterly, XXX (1974), 293-94. From "Polish-American Church Legends" collected by Catherine Harris Ainsworth. She got this tale from Mary Anne Jasek, age 18, of Niagara Falls, New York, who heard it the year before from her grandaunt, born in Poland. This story is a variant of Type 990; see Motif K 426.

* * *

Blessing the Animals

A custom dating back to the 13th century was revived here today [Saturday, March 31, 1956] when about 50 children brought their pets to the historic San Gabriel Mission where Father Michael Montoya, CMF, pastor, administered *La Bendicion de Los Animales*—the Blessing of the Animals. Youngsters brought dogs, pigeons, parakeets, turtles, cats and a rooster to receive God's admonition to all creatures to increase and multiply and serve mankind. The colorful procession was the sixth annual revival of the custom sponsored by *Los Compadres de San Gabriel*.

Adding to the color was Clarence Palomares of *Los Compadres* wearing an early California costume and astride a silvermounted horse. Tom Temple, *Los Compadres* president, recalled the "miracle" of three years ago when Mr. Peepers, a duck, received the admonition to multiply. That same night, the duck laid her first egg—to the surprise of her owners who had to decide on a more appropriate name. The blessing of the animals dates back to St. Francis of Assisi. Franciscan padres introduced the custom to California.

Source and Comment

Western Folklore, XV (1956), 204. Newspaper article datelined San Gabriel, California, in the *Los Angeles Times* of April 1, 1956, Easter Day. Collected by Stanley Robé. Cf. "St. Francis of the Pets," p. 359.

"The Blessing of the Animals" is celebrated in California by Mexican-Americans on Holy Saturday. It is probably an adaptation of the Roman custom of blessing animals to encourage their fertility, a rite which took place in early April when homage was paid to Venus, the goddess of love. Among Roman Catholics, animals are also blessed on October 4, feast day of St. Francis of Assisi, famed in legend for his love of animals.

A Cow Led the Holy Saturday Procession

If you are going to be in Los Angeles this Easter, look out for a quaint local custom—the blessing of the animals, in Olvera Street.

This is the street from which Los Angeles originated, now a popular center with Mexican stalls and small shops selling traditional Mexican goods.

It has also, for the last 30 years or so, been the center of a quaint Easter custom.

Animals and pets belonging to the traders of Olvera Street are paraded before an altar to receive the blessing of fertility and health.

Last year [1977] the blessing was bestowed, individually, by Bishop Manuel Moreno, Los Angeles' first Mexican-American bishop, together with the Claretian Fathers from the Old Plaza Church.

The animals are blessed for "providing clothing and companionship and tendering service to the human race since the world began."

Horses, donkeys and chickens have received the blessing, as well as dogs and cats, and the qualification for blessing is obviously only loosely interpreted, for the parade has even included eagles and the odd boa constrictor.

The leader of last year's procession was appropriately a Holstein cow. "Her contribution to mankind has been the greatest," explained Mario Valdez, director of the market.

Source

London, England, *Daily Telegraph*, March 25, 1978. Newspaper feature by Kenneth Murrill published the day before Easter.

* * *

Burning Judas at the End of Lent

Yesterday being the last secular day in Lent, the Catholic Mexicans of this city [Marysville, California] amused themselves by inflicting a sort of martyrdom in effigy upon that wicked old rascal, Judas Iscariot. Their ideas of the Judean costume which ruled in the days of Pontius Pilate are rather crude, for they had poor Iscariot dressed in a very unpretending frock coat and trousers, with a broad-brimmed wool hat. Although hanging ignominiously on an *ex tempore* gallows, the arch traitor had an unlighted cigar in his mouth and appeared to take matters with commendable coolness. A vast crowd of Christians, Pagans, Infidels, and Heretics surrounded the scene of this rather amusing *auto-da-fe*. An orchestra of Mexican musicians occupied the second-story porch of a house that overlooked the deed of martyrdom, and "discoursed most eloquent music" from a harp, violin, and guitar. After hanging for some two or three hours, poor Judas was summarily dealt with by having a lighted match applied to a string of Chinese crackers that ornamented his person, and being charged with various secret packages of gunpowder, he closed his earthly career in some little noise and a great deal of smoke.

Source and Comment

Maryville (California) *News,* April 4, 1958. Transcribed by Henry W. Splitter for *Western Folklore,* VI (1947), 276.

The custom of burning an effigy of Judas during Holy Week, often on the Saturday preceding Easter Sunday, is widespread in Hispanic and Germanic cultures, providing an occasion for elaborate festivities and and merrymaking. The figures are frequently grotesque and satiric. Guy Fawkes' Day, with its bonfires and effigy burning (see p. 386), is an Anglo-Saxon parallel, but such practices today range from the *fallas* or bonfires climaxed by the burning of fantastic figures in Valencia, Spain, on March 19, St. Joseph's Day, to the Dashara festival in New Delhi, India, in late September or October which celebrates the exploits of the god, Rama, by burning a gigantic figure of the demon, Ravana, who had kidnapped his wife. If the tone of the newspaper article describing the Judas-burning seems patronizing, then on the other hand the effigy of Judas mocks the Anglos for whom the journalist wrote it.

* * *

Easter Rock

An Easter rock is one of those [African] rites clothed in Christian symbolism which are not altogether uncommon among Negroes of the South....

Though the Easter Rock itself does not begin until midnight, the "general congregation" begins to assemble between nine and ten o'clock Easter Saturday night. At ten, or thereabouts, a preliminary service, known as "cul'n" (a corruption of *covenant*), begins. Cul'n consists of a series of testimonials of faith in and random requests of the Lord, and lasts about an hour. After each set of two or three testimonials and prayers, the head deacon, who presides until the minister arrives for the sunrise service, declares a brief intermission during which "finances" are [collected].

Cul'n exhausted, the congregation is favored with a program of special events, largely impromptu, by groups of singers representing churches other than the host-church. This program, also interrupted periodically by finances, is stopped shortly before midnight to allow opportunity for arranging the properties required for an Easter rock.

The central aisle of the church is cleared of the movable benches, and a plain long table is set lengthwise down the center of the church, before the pulpit. This table is covered with a spotlessly clean, white cloth. The section of the church to the left or the right of the pulpit is curtained off and used as a repository for the various properties to be employed as the rock progresses. All the kerosene lamps, except one at the rear of the church, are extinguished.

Precisely at midnight, by the deacon's watch, the deacon orders the congregation to "come quiet." Shortly thereafter, the voices of many women and a single man rise in the song, "When the Sancts Go Marchin' In," and a procession moves into the church through a door at the rear.

At the head of the procession is a Negro man carrying what is called "the banner." The banner is a barrel hoop attached to one end of a six-foot stick. The hoop has, stretched across its area in drumhead fashion, a covering of white crepe paper, and to its circumference is attached tasseled crepe of various bright colors. The name of the church is worked into the white drumhead in red or blue.

Two long white strings are attached to the circumference of the banner, one at each end of the horizontal diameter. The loose ends of these are held by the second member of the procession, a woman who is known as the banner-puller.

The banner, according to Tobias and Elizabeth Scott, is in Christian symbolism Christ the Son; but, by construction and by usage, it represents the sun. The man who "totes" the banner and the woman who fills the office of banner-puller apparently have no particular symbolical significance; however, the banner-carrier is usually the song leader and the practice of "banner-pulling" is considered rather an art. The function of the banner-puller is to cause the banner to "rock" in a peculiar rhythmical manner which matches the double-shuffle dance step with which all the members of the procession move forward.

The banner-puller is followed by twelve other women, all dressed in white and each carrying a lighted kerosene lamp. These twelve are the "sancts." By their number they represent the twelve disciples of Christ; but, by their carrying lamps, they represent the wise virgins of the Biblical parable.

Shuffling along to the right of the table and toward the pulpit, always in time with the singing (in which the congregation has now joined), the procession seriously gets down to its principal business—namely, marching around the table again and again. This marching, with occasional intermissions, continues until the preacher is ready to begin the sunrise service, just before dawn.

After the first complete circuit, the sancts deposit their lamps along the center length of the table, without losing step or position in the procession. At this point in the ritual the song changes, and "rocking" begins in earnest. The sancts, no longer hampered by the lamps, begin to shuffle and sway in the manner commonly associated with some phases of the voodoo rites.

This second stage of the ceremony is known as "dressin' de table," and the song with which it is accompanied is, rather appropriately,

> Meet me at de station when dat train come along,
>
> > (Three times.)

'Cause Ah may be blin', and Ah ca' not see.
Meet me at de station when dat train come along,

> (Three times.)

'Cause Ah may be lame, and Ah ca' not walk.
(And so on, through all possible impairments and infirmities.)

As the sancts approach the curtained-off section of the left or the right of the pulpit in their progress around the table, a hand reaches out from behind the curtains and gives to each sanct a large cake, usually angel food or some variation thereof. When all twelve have received cakes and made the circuit of the table with them, the cakes are set down, six upon each side of the table. On the next trip around, each sanct receives from the hand a bottle covered with brightly colored crepe paper; then a glass of "angeliquor" (angelica wine); then a little paper basket containing two or three easter eggs. The cake is a free interpretation of eucharistic bread; the wine is, of course, "the blood of the Savior"; and the bottle contains more of "the blood." The basket of eggs has no especial significance, but it is included to please the children who share the feast. (This again is the interpretation of Tobias and Elizabeth Scott [informants].)

When the table is properly dressed, there is a brief pause for changing banner-carriers—but not banner-pullers, for the original puller retains her office until dawn.

As marching resumes, the song changes to:—

> Choose my seat, set down
> At de table of de Lawd.

(This is the basic stanza, but the song leader alters it according to the various levels of his own spiritual elevation.) Now each sanct, continuing to shuffle the while, looks over the congregation with the object of picking a partner "to set down" with her "at de table of de Lawd." After five or six trips around the table, each sanct has chosen her companion, who shuffles along beside her until she stops at her appointed place at the table. Then the song varies slightly, in words, to:—

> Pull up yo' seat, set down
> At de table of de Lawd.

After two or three repetitions of the stanza in the variation, singing and marching give way to eating and drinking. Though the general congregation are mere spectators, they participate in the supper as actively as they can by means of "hand-outs." ...

With supper ended, rocking is started anew, and with much heightened spirit. Songs which accompany the marching, or shuffling, have no more than a broad general application to the occasion, and their choice or repetition appears to rest solely with the banner-carrier. [Two] of the more popular of the choices follow:—

They Crucified My Lord

Banner-carrier: Dey cru-ci-fied my Lawd.
    Sancts: Dey crowned His haid with thawns,
        On de top of de mountain. (Three times.)
B-c. and sancts: Dey cru-ci-fied my Lawd.

Banner-carrier: Dey cru-ci-fied my Lawd.
    Sancts: Dey nailed His feets and hands,
        On de top of de mountain. (Three times.)
B-c. and sancts: Dey cru-ci-fied my Lawd.

Banner-carrier: Dey cru-ci-fied my Lawd.
    Sancts: Dey staubed Him in de side
        On de top of de mountain (Three times.)
B-c. and sancts: Dey cru-ci-fied my Lawd.

Banner-carrier: Dey cru-ci-fied my Lawd.
    Sancts: De blood come streamin' down,
        From de top of de mountain. (Three
        times.)
B-c. and sancts: When dey cru-ci-fied my Lawd.

Won't You Set Down?

Banner-carrier: O, won't you set down?
    Sancts: Unh, unh, O, no, O Lawd,
        Ah cain' set down,
        'Cause Ah jus' got to He'b'm,
        Got to try on my crown.

Banner-carrier: Now, who dat comin' all dressed in white?
    Sancts: Mus' be de chillun of de Israelite.
    Chorus (sung by the banner-carrier and the
    sancts):
        O, won't you set down?
        Unh, unh, O, no, O Lawd,
        Ah cain' set down,
        'Cause Ah jus' got to He'b'm,
        Got to walk aroun'.
Banner-carrier: Now, who dat comin' all dressed in red?
    Sancts: Mus' be de chillun dat de Moses led.

Chorus

After each song there is an intermission. During these pauses the sancts bolster themselves against spiritual let-downs with frequent cups of angeliquor, and the spectators do not hesitate to follow the sanctified example. . . .

The text of the sunrise sermon, which begins a few minutes before sunrise, is apparently always some variation of one of the Gospels concerning the Resurrection; for example, Luke 24:7, ". . . .the Son of man must be delivered into the hands of sinful men, and be crucified, and the third day rise again."

The exegesis may follow any of several forms; but, as the sun begins to come over the horizon, there usually begins a sort of recitative analysis of the meaning of *Easter,* such as the following:

    Preacher: Where do de sun rise? Do it rise in de
        no'th?

Congregation: Naw, Suh!
    Preacher: Do it rise in de south?
Congregation: Naw, Suh!
    Preacher: Do it rise in de wes'?
Congregation: Naw, Suh!
    Preacher: Den, do it rise in de eas'?
Congregation: Yas, Suh! De sun rise in de eas'.
    Preacher: Why does y'all say de *'eas?*
Congregation: 'Cause dat where de sun rise.
    Preacher: Amen. Now why does us put 'eas' in
        bread?
Congregation: To make it *rise.*
    Preacher: Why does us call it *'eas?*
Congregation: 'Cause it make de bread *rise.*
    Preacher: Now, why does we call dis *Easter?*
Congregation: 'Cause on Easter mo'nin' de Lawd Jesus
        done riz up.
    Preacher: Amen. 'Cause de Lawd Jesus done riz up
        on *Easter*
        mo'nin', *Easter* mean "to rise." Therefo',
        let us all *rise*
        up and go fo'th under de risin' sun on
        Easter mo'nin'.

All rise at the preacher's command, and the procession of sancts re-forms at the table. With one voice the sancts and the congregation break into the "theme song" of the ceremonial:

    O, Easter mo'nin'! Shout for joy!
    O, Easter mo'nin'! Shout for joy!
    O, Easter mo'nin'! Shout for joy!

    Rock li'l chillun! Shout for joy!
    O, you ain' rockin'!
    Shout for joy!

To this accompaniment the procession rocks once around the table and through the back door of the church into the dawn. The members of the congregation attach themselves in single or double file to the sanctified train and likewise shuffle out into the light of the rising sun. The singing and rocking continue until the church is empty. Then the Easter rock is ended.

The name, as the first deacon of the St. John the Baptist Church explains it, is derived from the fact that "every-thing rocks." The sancts rock; the church (always a frame building) rocks; the earth rocks; and the sun rocks. . . .

Source and Comment

Journal of American Folklore, LV (1942), 212-18. Lea and Marianna Seale base their description "upon the writers' observance of its practice on three occasions: twice at the St. John the Baptist Church, at Dunbarton Plantation, near Clayton, Concordia Parish, Louisiana, which adjoins Dunbarton Plantation." Their informants include Tobias and Elizabeth Scott who were not certain of their age but "were children during 'Reb times,' and both have been familiar with the Easter rock since childhood." They provided the interpretation of its symbolism. The explanation of the name was supplied by Deacon Will Stewart, R.F.D., No. 1, Ferriday, Louisiana. Cf. "The Penitentes," p. 168, for a "symbolic re-enactment of *las Tinieblas* 'the earthquakes,' . . . when Christ died."

* * *

Easter

The Sun Dances on Easter Morning

On Easter morning [according to Armenian tradition] the sun dances, and there is no other morning in the year when such is the case. Since they cannot look directly at the sun, they have mirrors into which they look in order to see it dance. It is said, too, that very seldom is there an Easter morning which is not clear.

Source and Comment

Journal of American Folklore, XII (1899), 106. Collected by G. D. Edwards in Boston, Massachusetts, from an informant of Armenian descent. See "Easter Rock," p. 159, for another dancing sun. On Whitsunday in Copenhagen, Denmark, it is the custom to climb Frederikburg Hill at dawn to watch the sunrise and see it "dance." Many churches in the United States conduct Easter "sunrise" services.

* * *

Easter

Easter Eggs

Easter eggs were colored at home [in Maryland] until a few years ago [c. 1920]. They were dyed red, yellow and purple with Brazil wood and logwood and then greased to bring out the color. Alum was also used in the concoction in which they were boiled. Other things used were onion shells, walnut "bulbs," and calico that faded easily. Scratching the eggs was artistic work, and done with a sharp penknife. Hens, roosters on ladders, birds, horses, and cows were favorite designs.

At one time the children in certain parts of the state were not allowed to see the Easter eggs colored; but were obliged to hunt for them Easter morning, when they would find them in nests. Some times they were hidden in the garden; lilac bushes being favorite hiding places.

One old woman in Western Maryland used to color Easter eggs with coffee grounds and these she gave to any who came to her on Easter morning; but some years before she died she had to discontinue this practice because she had such crowds of callers.

In Harford County, the housewife formerly boiled a great basket full of colored Easter eggs, and gave one to every Negro who lived on the place, or who called at Easter. Each member of the family also received one. The basket was then placed on the sideboard so that all who wished might help themselves.

The rabbit was supposed to lay the Easter eggs.

Source

Memoirs of the American Folklore Society, XVIII (1925), 116-117. "Folk-Lore from Maryland," collected by Annie W. Whitney and Caroline C. Bullock. Data on informants incomplete.

* * *

Easter

Picking Eggs at Easter

Picking eggs, though an Easter custom [in Maryland], begins some days before Easter. Two children each hold a hard-boiled egg in the fist so that only the butt shows. They knock one against the other and the egg that breaks is forfeited to the boy who owns the whole one.

For days before Easter, boys call "Hold up!" This is a call to "pick" eggs.

Egg Picking Cry in Baltimore

Who got a - - - igg?
Who got a - - - igg?
Who gotter Guineakee?
Who wanter pickawee?
Oo pick?
Oo pick?
Who gotter aigg?

Source

Memoirs of the American Folklore Society, XVIII (1925), 117. "Folk-Lore from Maryland," collected by Annie W. Whitney and Caroline C. Bullock. Data on informants not supplied. Cf. "Armenian Easter Eggs," p. 163.

* * *

Upper, Upper Egg

Children's call [in Philadelphia] of "Epper, epper, A-a-a-eee!" around Eastertime may be translated to "Upper, upper Egg!" a challenge to come crack eggs.

Source

Philadelphia Inquirer, November 26, 1980, from an article by Harold J. Wiegand, contributing editor, on local speech peculiarities.

* * *

Epper, Epper, Ay-EEE

The Annual Springtime Nicetown Epper Tournament will take place at the Conti house in Blue Bell [Pennsylvania] this year [1990], I have been told by an informed source in the Zeccardi household in Glenside. Those of a certain age who grew up in Nicetown and other Philadelphia neighborhoods may remember the chant, "Epper, Epper, Ay-EEE" which was the challenge offered in the street for any kid who thought he or she had an egg tough enough to meet the Epper test to see whose egg had the hardest shell (hard-boiled need not apply). Many a loser's egg ended up making a "golden splash" on alley walls. Eppering was sort of the same as egg jousting.

Source

Philadelphia Inquirer, April 6, 1990.

Easter

Armenian Easter Egg Game

For three days before Easter the Armenians will gather at a churchyard for the purpose of breaking eggs. Two persons will each take an egg, and one of them will hold his egg stationary while the other strikes it with the point of his egg. If A is holding the stationary egg and B is doing the striking, then, in case A's egg cracks, he turns the other end and lets B strike again. If the other end is cracked, B gets the egg and A must produce another egg to be treated as before and with like possible results. If B's egg cracks, then he turns the other end of the egg and strikes again. If it suffers in like manner, he loses his egg and must supply another, whereupon A does the striking until he forfeits his right by losing an egg. Thus they go on breaking eggs, until oftentimes one couple has broken as many as a hundred. The man with the strongest egg will of course win the most eggs from his opponent. These cracked eggs which he has won he sells at a reduced price. Sometimes a man will pay a dollar for a strong egg before he enters into a contest, if there is evidence to prove that he is really getting a strong one.

Formerly, Easter eggs were always colored red in order to represent the blood of Christ. They are usually colored red now [c. 1899], but are beginning to vary somewhat.

Source

Journal of American Folklore, XII (1899), 106-07. Collected in Boston, Massachusetts, from an informant of Armenian origin by G. D. Edwards as an example of surviving Armenian folklore in the United States.

* * *

Whipping Women for Eggs

Three years ago at Easter time, Sam [Černek] came to visit a Slovak family in Manhattan, and there I met him for the first time. With a willow whip he was to perform the traditional whipping of the women to get painted eggs from them in return. Every year he makes this visit to his numerous friends in New York and the vicinity. "There wouldn't be any Easter without it." Later, however, he told me, referring to the ceremonial whipping, "It is nothing. It is in name only. It is to commemorate that in our country [Slovakia] we used to whip the Christ. It is not real...."

Source and Comment

Journal of American Folklore, LXIX (1957), 275. Described by Svatava Pirkova-Jakobson. Her informant was a native of Vrbovce, a Slovak village on the Moravian border, then living in Heightstown, New Jersey. In *Folklore in America*, p. 216. Whipping the women at Easter recalls the scourging of Christ. However, at the Roman festival of Lupercalia, women were flogged to assure fertility and the egg is a widely known fertility symbol.

Easter

Decorating Eggs: the Moravian Way

In the Triple Cities—Binghamton, Johnson City and Endicott [New York]—many people remember life in former European homes and treasure the traditional customs and designs, making them a part of the American tradition. Among these customs is that of the delicate and painstaking decoration of Easter eggs.

One of the outstanding types of design is that used most often by people of Slovak ancestry, particularly those who came from Moravia. These eggs are dark purple with white designs of birds or flowers. Both color and design have meaning. The traditional purple is almost black. Lighter shades may be used when the dark dye is not available. This purple represents the holiness of the Lenten season, for it is the color of the priests' vestments and the draperies used in the church at that time.

The white, of course, represents the joyous Easter Day. Because the lily of the valley is the national flower, it is one of the most frequently used motifs, though many conventionalized flowers and birds appear, symbolic of spring, of new life, and of love.

In "the old country," on Easter morning, each young man of the community, equipped with a lash braided of eight willow whips, visited the homes of the girls of the village. He tried to arrive before a girl was up in order to whip her from bed—the whipping being symbolic of the lashes received by our Lord before He was crucified—but she was usually ready with gifts to appease him before she received too many blows. These gifts were the Easter eggs, which each girl had carefully decorated, and one or more embroidered handkerchiefs, or for a fiancé, an embroidered shirt. On Easter Monday the girls whipped the boys out of bed and received in return gifts of candy, fruit, kerchiefs, or a gay skirt. They did not receive Easter eggs, for eggs were decorated by women and girls only. Although these customs are not followed closely in the Triple Cities, there are families in which the Easter lashes are still made, and there are women who still decorate Easter eggs with the traditional purple and white designs.

The eggs are boiled hard and, while still hot, are covered with a mixture of shellac, alcohol, and a purple dye that is now difficult to get. (Before World War II, many women had the dye sent to them by relatives in Czechoslovakia.) The dye must be one that will not penetrate the shell, or the clear white design where it is scraped off would be impossible. To give the egg a rich gloss, four or five layers are applied with a cloth dipped in this solution.

When the egg is dry, the designs are outlined on it with a small, three-cornered file. Then with the same file, the dye is carefully scraped off inside the outline to make leaves, shaded petals of flowers, or even words of Easter greeting.

The individual floral or bird designs are often copied from eggs kept from past years; in fact, many are the traditional designs, like those embroidered on kerchiefs or skirts. But the completed designs vary, each person making whatever choice and arrangement of elements which may appeal to him. Naturally, the more delicate and complex the design, the lovelier the egg.

Source

New York Folklore Quarterly XII (1956), 21-23. Edith E. Cutting describes the survival of egg decoration and other Easter customs among residents of Czechoslovakian background in three neighboring south central New York cities. She lists specific informants at the end of her article.

* * *

Easter

Decorating Eggs: the Ukrainian Way

Generations of Ukrainians have also decorated Easter eggs. Indeed, the decoration became such an art that in the Ukraine a woman who was particularly skillful was called a *pysarka* and was asked by people in neighboring villages to decorate special eggs for them. After the colored eggs had been blessed, they were often presented as gifts. One of the hard-boiled eggs was cut into pieces at the beginning of the Easter dinner, and each member of the family ate a portion in token of the end of Lenten fasting. The gaily decorated eggs might also be used in a game as part of the Easter festivities. Young people would try to strike each other's eggs with their own. The owner of the unbroken egg would win the cracked one, thus eliminating from the game those who lost their Easter eggs. Because of the religious significance of the eggs, however, the shells of even the cracked ones were never just dropped on the ground; they were thrown into fire or water.

These Easter eggs are so rare in America that they are not ordinarily either eaten or used in games. Among the Ukrainians in the Triple Cities, though, many people decorate Easter eggs with the traditional designs, for Mrs. Frank Lawryk [of Johnson City, New York], wife of the pastor of St. John's Ukrainian Church, has taught the young people the art of Easter egg decoration. Almost any design may be used; for instance, I have seen a large egg with the picture of the Last Supper done in reverent detail. Most of the designs, however, are geometric, often giving a kaleidoscopic impression because of their brilliant colors and tiny shapes.

These eggs are not cooked because the raw egg shell absorbs the color better than a cooked one. In fact, while a person works on the egg, he holds it with a cloth or tissue so that the oil from his hand will not keep the dye from being absorbed. The egg is not blown out of the shell, either, for a blown egg shell is fragile. In the whole raw egg the albumen eventually dries to the shell, making it stronger.

A batik process is used by the Ukrainians in decorating their Easter eggs. To do this, one holds the egg gently and sketches lightly the main lines of his design. Then he draws on the shell the first lines of the design with a *pysar,* or small, metal-tipped writing tool, dipped in melted beeswax. These lines will be white, the original shell color, when the design is completed, because they are protected by the wax from any dye. When these lines have been completed, the egg is dipped into the lightest vegetable dye, probably yellow. As soon as the egg is dry, the designer covers with wax the parts he wants to stay yellow, and dips the egg into the next darker dye, usually orange or red. This process is continued with each color desired except for a few, like blue or green, which cannot be covered completely with other colors. These, if used, are laid on with a toothpick.

After the design is completed, the egg is held over a candle flame to melt off the wax. Then the egg is shellacked or varnished, and this miniature work of art is complete, ready if carefully handled to brighten Easter for ten or twenty years. Such eggs, or *pysanky,* are presented to friends and relatives on Easter morning with the greeting, "*Krystos voskres* [Christ is risen]" and are received with the reply, "*Voistynu voskres* [He is risen, indeed!]"

Source

New York Folklore Quarterly, XII (1956), 23-24. Specific informants are listed at the end of this article by Edith E. Cutting.

* * *

Easter

Easter Eggs at Tiffany's

Gene Moore is leaning back in his chair this morning in his seventh-floor office at Tiffany & Company dreaming about Easter 1989. "Eggs," he is thinking, as he has every Easter for the 53 years since he began to dress windows in the stores along Fifth Avenue. "What can I do with eggs that I haven't done before?"

Mr. Moore, the dean of display art in American retailing, works a year ahead on his designs for the Tiffany windows, the most expensive display space in the world. "You wouldn't want to think about Easter in November," he said, waving an ever-present cigarette. "I have to be in the mood along with everybody else."

Every year since 1955, he has used eggs to represent the arrival of spring and the joy of Easter. That makes 34 different egg-based displays, so at the moment he is trying to invent new interpretations for this common symbol of creation. He has scrambled them, painted them and strung them into necklaces, some years piling hundreds of them in each window.

Now, at the age of 77, as he approaches the end of his legendary career, he has entered a minimalist phase. This year [1988], in one of Tiffany's five windows, he has suspended a single egg in midair as if by magic and hidden a Tiffany diamond-and-turquoise pin in the clover beneath it.

It is a classic Moore design, the fragile egg ready to drop, the pin camouflaged among the clover and tucked beneath an azalea bush in full bloom. It represents a contrast so full of energy that shoppers cruising past the most important retail corner in the United States pull themselves up short to gaze through the window, then break into a smile as the joke leaps through the glass to grab them....

Source and Comment

New York Times, March 28, 1988. Edited from an article in the "Business Day" section by Albert Scardino.

Gene Moore rose from a $14-a-week prop builder to a top window-display designer for I. Miller, Bergdorf, and Bonwit-Teller, as well as Tiffany's. A Vice-President at Tiffany's, he also designs sets for the Park Taylor Dance Company.

* * *

White House Egg Roll

Bands played and balloons bobbed as **President Bush,** accompanied by his wife, **Barbara,** and six of their 11 grandchildren, blew a whistle yesterday [March 27, 1989] to open the traditional White House Easter egg roll on the South Lawn. About 40,000 youngsters and parents attended. The President hung in for 15 minutes of the four-hour event before slipping back to the Oval Office. Before leaving, he asked one girl if she knew who lived in the White House. "The Easter Bunny," she said. "Who else?" he asked. "I don't know," she said....The American Egg Council gave 5,000 eggs to this year's roll while the White House contributed 23,000 wooden ones as prizes and souvenirs.

Source

Philadelphia Inquirer, March 28, 1989.

* * *

Easter

A Country Egg Hunt

At the White House children roll eggs on the lawn. On Fifth Avenue New Yorkers parade in their spring finery. In Lawton, Oklahoma, the citizens present a passion play; and on Easter Sunday in Stallo, Mississippi, people hunt eggs in a meadow.

Stallo is located on Highway 15 near the northern edge of Neshoba County and is one of the few communities where an egg hunt is still an annual event. Earlier in this century egg hunts were quite common; but with the shift of population from rural to urban areas, egg hunts have, in many rural communities, disappeared.

It is difficult to pinpoint the beginning of a folk activity such as the Stallo egg hunt. One citizen who has lived in Stallo since 1925 says the hunt was not being held when she moved to the community as a bride, but she remembers accompanying her own small children to the event. The hunt seems to have been well-established by the early 1930's, which fact leads to the interesting speculation that perhaps it was an outgrowth of the Great Depression when, although money was scarce, eggs were plentiful, and the people of rural East Mississippi felt a need for an inexpensive diversion.

The Stallo hunt was first sponsored by the two churches in the community and was held for several years in an oak grove behind the Methodist Church. Much of the settlement, including the churches, was then situated near the Gulf, Mobile and Ohio Railroad, some three-fourths of a mile off Highway 15. In 1940 the highway was paved, and many people hesitated to drive their cars on the sometimes muddy and always ill-tended county road, so the egg hunt was moved closer to the "hard road." For three or four years the hunt was held in a grassy plot beside the Snow Family Cemetery, just west of the highway. It was at this time that the hunt lost, for no apparent reason, its connection with the churches. It is still held after the church service in the afternoon (services being moved from morning to afternoon for this one day each year), and the one remaining church is now also located on Highway 15, a mile and a half from its original location. The church, however, makes no pretense of sponsoring the egg hunt, and a majority of the hunters are not members of the local church.

Perhaps the adults hunting eggs (and there are as many adults joining the hunt as there are children) found hunting eggs next to the cemetery fence incongruous, for after only three or four years, the hunt was moved 200 yards east of Highway 15 to a meadow, where it is held today. The meadow provides an ideal setting with gently sloping sides leading down to a flat grassy bottom some 100 yards long. The brown needles under the pines at the top of the slopes, the thick grass in the meadow, and an old fence row on the western edge provide ample hiding places for the more than three hundred eggs hidden each year. The pasture being in use to graze cows, someone with an earthy sense of humor usually hides an egg under a dried disc of cow manure.

The men of the community hide the eggs while the women and children wait at the church or on the porch of Snow's Store. After the hiding is completed and the hunt is in progress, it is not uncommon to see a father who has hidden the eggs helping his children and others who have not been successful in the hunt fill their baskets. In years past, a careful count of the eggs was made; and if all were not found, children and their dogs would spend the next day searching out the missing eggs. Recently, however, an exact count has not been kept.

In earlier years, and in fact until the past eight or ten years, participants in the hunt wore their new "Easter outfits." The dresses of the women and girls were especially important, and their color and pattern were kept secret until Easter day when they were worn to church and afterwards to the egg hunt. A lifetime resident of the community remembers the importance of her Easter outfit. "It was white organdy with many ruffles, and I had new white sandals to match. It had rained the night before, and of course the roads back then were very muddy. I remember walking barefoot and holding my dress up around my thighs. About a hundred yards from the church, I stopped, washed my feet in a rainpuddle, put on my shoes, and entered in style."

Although everyone had eggs during the first years of the hunt, not everyone had the money to buy commercial egg coloring. Some people simply brought eggs undyed; others colored them with bits of crayon; while others boiled their eggs with a scrap of new cloth to receive the benefit of fading. Some hunters also had conventional Easter eggs dyed with "store bought" dye, but there seems to have been no social significance attached to the type of colored eggs a family brought.

One unusual aspect of this particular egg hunt is the hiding of a "Queen's Nest." Traditionally, at egg hunts, the person who finds the most eggs is given a prize. At the Stallo hunt, however, a group of four or six of the brightest eggs are hidden together. The person finding this "nest" receives a small prize, usually candy bars and soda pop from Snow's Store....

Residents agree that during the past forty years the egg hunt has been canceled fewer than five times. Three or four times it poured rain all day, and one Easter afternoon a funeral was held in the Snow Cemetery. Otherwise, not even World War II prevented the egg hunt.

The people of Stallo do not know that by holding an Easter egg hunt each spring they are carrying on a tradition which was begun in Western Europe in the fifteenth century. Neither do they know that the practice of coloring eggs was brought back to England by the Crusaders. They have no concept of the cosmogenic ideas connected with eggs, nor of the fertility powers the ancient Egyptians attributed to eggs in their spring festivals. Many of the residents would not be aware of the tradition of rolling eggs at the White House, but they know that barring torrential rain or community tragedy the Stallo Easter egg hunt will be held on Easter afternoon.

Source

Mississippi Folklore Register, VIII (1974), 183-85. Described by Carol Farish, of Decatur, Mississippi. Sources and informants not cited.

Easter

Why the Cottonwood Trembles

The perpetual movement of the cottonwood-tree was explained by the same narrator as follows:

"Well, chile, yer see dis was what my ole Miss useter tell me. Dem same kind er trees growed in dat garden whar der blessed Lord prayed der night afore he was crucified, an' when Judas cum dar along 'er dem soldiers ter 'tray der Lord an' take him erway ter nail him on der cross, dey done chop down one of dem trees and made der Savior ob der world tote it up ter Calvery. An' dey made der cross outen it, an' dem trees sensed how it was der blessed Lord what was gwine ter suffer an' die on one of 'em, and dey jus tuk ter tremblin' an' shiverin' with fear. An' dey never stop yit, an' never will while one of dem grows, kase dey is der kind er tree what der cross of Calvery were made of."

Source and Comment

Journal of American Folklore, XVIII (1905), 251. Collected by Mrs. M. E. M. Davis of New Orleans, Louisiana. Her "narrator" was "Aunt Cindy, a very old negress, who could remember events that happened some seventy years ago." This is Motif A 2721.2.1.3.

* * *

Easter

Why the Poplar Trembles

Near Marquette, Mich., a mining superintendent, having occasion to lay out a road near a mine, suggested to the foreman, who, like his gang, was Irish, that the men should cut down some neighboring poplar-trees for corduroy. The foreman said that not a man of them could be hired to chop down one of those trees, that the men would as soon think of cutting off their own hands. "Don't you know," said he, "that the Saviour's cross was made of that tree?" and added that you will never see a poplar-tree perfectly still. The idea apparently is that the tree is perpetually agitated or trembling because of the terrible use made of it at Golgotha.

Source

Journal of American Folklore, XIII (1900), 226. Contributed by H. R. Kidder. This is Motif A 2721.2.1.2.

Easter

To Charm an Easter Elf

In the iron-mining towns of northern Minnesota, and the lake country surrounding them, the settlers from Finland and their descendants have kept many old customs. The sauna, the steam-bath built of logs, stands beside the lake shore, the luck-bringing mountain ash tree is planted by the house door. Great gatherings of Finnish people celebrate midsummer with singing and other music, sometimes with dancing and races, and on the rocky homesteads birch branches decorate the place. Folksongs, in great number and variety, are found all over this region: some are very ancient, many beautiful, all have that marked individuality of the Finnish character.

It was while collecting folksongs in this part of northern Minnesota that I heard some of the old charms and incantations once used in Finland to cure injuries, to invoke blessings or curses, or to charm cattle. They were originally used by the professional "*loihtija*" or wise woman, of whom one hears many stories. In this country the charms are remembered as folklore or told to children to amuse them. They are not as commonly known or as plentiful as the folksongs, and they are becoming more rare. . . .

Charms were . . . used by householders to rid the place of unfriendly elves. When they appeared, at Easter time, they could be frightened away by calling out:

> *Hyi, hyi, Hytölään*
> *Hytölän koirat haukku*
> *Piikani, poikani, katsomaan,*
> *Joka ne kaukana tuloo.*

> Hyi, hyi, Hytölä
> The dogs of Hytölä bark.
> My little girl, my little boy,
> Look at them coming from afar.

Elves were not always unfriendly or unwelcome at Easter: on that day, in the country near Oulu [Finland], the friendly household brownies who lived in the hay-barn and had food put out for them by the farm people used to visit the house to wish the master and mistress good fortune. They carried branches of pussy willow with which they lightly struck the couple, calling out:

> *Virpoi, varpoi,*
> *Tuoreeks', terveeks'*
> *Tulevaks' vuodeks'*
> *Kuin monta varpaa,*
> *Niin monta vasikkaa;*
> *Kuin monta oksaa,*
> *Niin monta oritta;*
> *Kuin monta urpaa,*
> *Niin monta uittia.*

> Switch, switch,
> Be fresh and healthy,
> Be well for the coming year.
> As many twigs,
> So many calves.
> As many branches,
> So many colts.
> As many catkins,
> So many lambkins.

Source and Comment

Journal of American Folklore, XLVII (1934), 381, 383. Collected by Marjorie Edgar of Marine on St. Croix, Minnesota. Informants not named. She states that the meaning of the charms "is not always clear to the Finnish-American people who remember them" but they survive "due to a strong oral tradition."

Easter Begins to Look Like Christmas

Is the Easter Bunny becoming another Santa Claus?

While some observers assert that Easter's strong religious tradition keeps it from being transformed into a national folk festival and commercialized in the same way as Christmas, others say that in its secular guise, Easter in recent years has taken on many of its winter counterpart's trappings.

Seen more and more often in front yards, for instance, is the Easter tree or egg tree, usually bare of leaves at this time of year and gaily decorated with colored eggs. This practice is "growing by leaps and bounds," says Jack Santino, professor of popular culture at Bowling Green State University in Ohio and a specialist in folklore. "Special Easter decorations are becoming more prevalent, and we're seeing such things as plastic bunnies on lawns."

The marketing specialists at Hallmark Cards, who closely watch the ways Americans observe holidays to detect new trends, have this season [1990] brought out 229 articles for the Easter market in response to the public's increasing interest in decorating and gift giving. Among them are "trimmers"—plastic eggs, ducks, bunnies and other decorations to be hung on Easter trees and attached to Easter wreaths.

"People today are interested in a fuller holiday experience," said Barbara Miller, marketing media relations coordinator for the Kansas City, Mo.-based company.

"They go to family gatherings, have family dinners, do more things together. It's the baby boomer generation having children. Some have waited, and now that they have children they want to provide them with a full experience, either the kind of Easter they had as children or the kind of holiday they feel their children should enjoy. They want their children to have an Easter they'll remember."

That desire has resulted in a number of growing traditions. Miller says that the Easter wreath is one of them. People usually fashion the wreaths themselves, using grape vines or woven twigs, spray-painted white, or they buy straw wreaths from a florist that they decorate. The wreaths are hung outside on the door or inside over the mantel, or placed flat on the table as a centerpiece, ringed with small candles or with a single large candle stuck in the middle.

Also new is the windsock, adorned with a rabbit design, and hauled up to dance in the wind, heralding the season, Miller says.

Gifts, similar to the items stuffed into Christmas stockings, are tucked into Easter baskets along with jelly beans and chocolate eggs, destined mainly for younger children. Typical gift items include decorated bibs, caps and T-shirts, she adds.

Another growing custom is a direct play off the Santa Claus custom: dressing up as the Easter Bunny to entertain young children. According to Shayna Doll, costume and rental clerk at Party Time, a costume shop in Baltimore, the demand for rabbit outfits has exceeded last year's, and the shop has had to order more of the white, furry suits. The cost is not slight. The suits rent for $50 a day and sell for up to $225. Hotels and shopping malls make up the bulk of the customers.

Santino points out that costumed bunnies now appear more and more frequently at stores and malls.

Despite these changes, some observers believe the religious focus of the holiday remains paramount.

"Easter is still holding tight to tradition," says the Rev. Marion C. Bascom, paster of Douglas Memorial Community Church in Baltimore. "I'm sure it's going to last. There hasn't been the same kind of commercialization as with Christmas."

Santino agrees. "Christmas is both a holiday and a religious holy day," he notes. "Easter is basically a religious day, so there's been less effort made to push it down people's throats."

Indeed, recent Gallup and Roper polls indicate that religion and traditional values are becoming more meaningful to Americans, and Hallmark has found interest in religious cards gaining over the past three years.

But the company also features a "contemporary Christian" card, which depicts a spring scene or motif in soft pastels rather than such traditional symbols as the cross, stained glass window and Bible.

"The contemporary card doesn't highlight Christian symbols as much as it emphasizes shared beliefs," Hallmark's Miller says.

Source

Providence Sunday Journal, April 15, 1990. Reprinted from *The Baltimore Sun,* by Henry Scarupa.

The Penitentes

Self-inflicted punishment and torture as a means of atonement is probably as old as the history of civilization. However, it was not until the early years of the thirteenth century that flagellation as penance became a recognized practice. Under Saint Anthony of Padua, an Italian monk of the Franciscan Order, the lash became an instrument of grace, and for centuries following, solemn processions of flagellants were seen throughout Latin Europe.

Saint Anthony of Padua was dearly beloved as a miracle worker. So pure and humble of heart was he that God bestowed upon him the blessed privilege of holding the Infant Jesus. Hence he is pictured with shaven head, wearing the robes of a Franciscan monk, holding the Infant Jesus in one hand and the Bible in the other. It is not surprising that a religious order, so firmly established in Catholic countries of the Old World was introduced by missionary priests and Spanish colonists into the New World. Nevertheless, it is surprising that nearly four hundred years after the Spanish conquest, flagellation is practiced today by the Penitente Brotherhood in remote mountain villages of New Mexico.

With the conquest also came a lay order, "The Third Order of Saint Francis," and as brought from Spain, the group was a gentleman's society purely for religious study and purification, with flagellation as merely a gesture. In the wills of many Spanish Grandees is expressed the desire to be buried in the brown robes of a Franciscan monk, a privilege granted to lay members of the Third Order.

Colonization in New Mexico spread slowly. Early settlers isolated in high mountain villages and cut off from the outside world intermarried with Indians in neighboring pueblos. Religion took on a mingling of pagan ceremonies with the forms of Christian worship, and the Penitente Brotherhood became the heritage of the masses, with flagellation practiced in stark, bloody reality.

The reasoning of the Penitente is very simple. Christ is Our Saviour and our example. Through His love for us He bore the mortifications, the lashes, curses, and tortures of the Crucifixion; so he too (the Penitente) must atone by means of such punishment, if he is to enjoy the fruits of heaven as promised by the Savior.

The Penitentes have their own meeting house or chapels, called *"moradas."* These small adobes are built to blend into a hillside or in the bend of a lonely canyon, to be unnoticed from the road. If built in a little settlement, they are indistinguishable from the adobe houses about them, although some may have a cross above the door.

The Penitente Brotherhood is active throughout the year. They minister to the sick, help the more unfortunate members farm their land or herd their sheep, and they hold *"velorios,"* or wakes, when a member dies. During the year personal misbehavior or violations of the law by members of the order are brought before a committee dealing with waywardness. . . .

It is during the Lenten season that the Penitentes are most active. Weeks before Lent *"los Hermanos de Luz"* (the Brothers of Light) meet in their little chapels, spending hours in prayer, fasting, and listening to instructions by their elders. Lent is rigidly observed. On Ash Wednesday confessions of sins and flagellation in the seclusion of their moradas signal the beginning of active penance. A *"Cristo,"* or Christ, is chosen by drawing lots with straws, or named by a vision made known to *"el Hermano Mayor* (the Eldest Brother). Often a *Cristo* has been secretly chosen at the August fifteenth meeting.

At this meeting novices are accepted by the order and branded with the Penitente's seal, three slashes cut into the flesh of the back with a sharp flint. Then with a whip, often made of prickly pear or Spanish bayonet (types of cactus) or of rawhide, the novice will receive three lashes on one side the length of his spine and three on the other. He will then ask, "For the love of God, bestow on me the five wounds of Christ," and receive five lashes. Again he will ask, "For the love of God, bestow on me the seven last words," and receive seven lashes. And again he will request forty lashes for the forty days Christ spent in the wilderness. By now his lacerated back will be covered with blood and will be washed with a strong tea of Romero weed, a healing mountain sage. Then the novice will be allowed to go home.

During Holy Week one will see heavy wooden crosses leaning against the *morada* wall or planted upright by the *morada* door. One cold night in March we hid our car in a clump of scrub piñon and with Penitente friends from the mountain village walked up the slope of a lonesome canyon in which a *morada* was hidden. Soon outlined against the frosty, starry heavens was the little mud chapel. Feeble lines of light emanated from the *morada* door and now and then mournful voices accented the mystery of its interior. We were admitted and picked our way through kneeling figures to a mud bench along the wall. As our eyes became accustomed to the dim light we found we were in a fairly large room. A black-draped altar stood at one end and in the rear a door stood open into the secret chamber or discipline room. The earthen floor was packed with kneeling people. Black-shawled women and children knelt or squatted on the left, the men and boys on the right.

On the altar were three objects: a candle, an open Bible, and a crudely carved image of Christ on the cross, gruesome, with human hair, a crown of thorns, and blood-spotted body. On the floor before the altar was a black, wooden candlestick holding thirteen candles. A man with a lighted candle emerged from the back room and came forward to stand by the altar and turn the pages of the Bible. As he turned the pages he chanted a litany in Spanish and the kneeling figures responded in mournful, flowing murmurs.

In a few minutes the chanter at the altar was replaced by another, and he, in turn, by another, reminding me of solemn children playing priest. As one chanter replaced the other, the candles burned lower and lower, until those at the foot of the altar finally flickered and went out—one by one. When at last the candle on the altar, beside the Bible, burned out we were told that all visitors and all women and children must leave. The outside door opened and the chilling frost of a mountain night swept in.

We stepped into the half-moonlight. The silence of ages had settled over the valley and the mountains disdained the folly of men. Snow still lingered under the piñon trees; so we huddled in our sheepskin coats and blankets, in the black shadows of a rocky ledge. After what seemed hours, though I am sure it could not have been more than thirty minutes, the morada door opened and again candle light shone within. A man with a reed fife, or "*pito*," stepped out and sent forth a piteous wail. Dim figures emerged and a procession following "*el pitero*" (the piper) passed not far from where we were hidden. Now several dim lanterns seemed to swing from invisible arms, and in their thin rays we saw the flagellants. Five black-hooded figures, naked to the waist, white cotton drawers rolled to the knees, bare feet stumbling on stones and frozen earth, took a few steps, and then we heard and saw the lash of whips on their bare backs.

Again the five took a few steps and again the slap of whips. Steps and whips, steps and whips—seemed to move in measured rhythm. We knew blood oozed, although we could not see it. Unschooled male voices chanted hymns of penance. The harmonious chords arose like mist through the rugged canyon and somehow conformed to the stark misery of these half-naked, self-made martyrs. The Penitente procession passed and we arose, stiff and cold, and returned to Santa Fe.

Source

New Mexico Folklore Record, XI (1963-64), 18-20. From an article entitled "A Lash for the Grace of God" by Cosette Chavez Lowe. For another observance of the Penitentes see "La Perćingula" p. 307.

Los Hermanos Penitentes, the Penitent Brothers or Penitentes, is a lay religious brotherhood related to the Roman Catholic Church with a membership mainly in northern New Mexico and southern Colorado. Its purposes are spiritual, and its practices emphasize penitence, including flagellation and other mortifications of the flesh, but it is also a charitable association, and an institution which informs the social and political structures of the Mexican-American communities in which it has existed for perhaps one hundred and fifty years. It seems to have grown up in remote villages at a time when members of the church were without the regular services of the priesthood. It is a folk religious sect in the sense that it adapted itself to local circumstances, and for a long time was unsupervised by the Roman Catholic Church. It has tended to be secretive. Religious confraternities for penitential purposes, which practiced corporal penance, were not uncommon in Spanish and Hispanic America in the sixteenth century and thereafter.

* * *

The Penitentes

The Death Cart of the Penitentes

During their Easter procession, the Penitentes of New Mexico and Colorado engage in physical penance including self-flagellation with whips or chains, the dragging of enormous crosses, and the dragging of the *Carreta de la Muerte* (Death Cart). In 1935 the pulling of the *Carreta* was described as follows:

The Penitente dragged the *Carreta de la Muerte* by a horse-hair rope passed over his shoulders and under his armpits. The axles of the cart were stationary and where there was a turn in the path, the entire cart and its inflexible wheels were dragged by main strength.

Riding in the *Carreta* is a figure of Death. In some areas the figure is merely called *La Muerte* (Death); in others it is called *Nuestra Comadre Sebastiana* (Our Comadre Sebastiana) or *Doña Sebastiana*. In the later latter case, Death is treated as a female as often happens in Spain. This may be because *Muerte* is a noun of feminine gender. *Comadre,* in New Mexico as in most other Spanish-Speaking areas, is a term generally used to express kinship between mother and godmother. And the name *Sebastiana* is probably due to a confusion in iconography. That is, the naked Saint Sebastian, riddled with arrows, was confused with the naked skeleton holding a bow and arrow.

Nineteenth-century figures of the *Muerte* that survive fall into two categories: those of the Sangre de Cristo Mountain area of New Mexico, and those of the San Luis Valley of southern Colorado. The *Muerte* from the Sangre de Cristo area is a skeleton, usually about thirty-six inches in height, and is in a sitting or kneeling position holding a bow and arrow. It is carved of wood and usually covered with a light coat of gesso. Generally it is unpainted, although there are a few rare exceptions when a design is placed on the body. When not decorated, the figure is dressed in a black robe with a hood that covers its head.

The Sangre de Cristo *Muerte* generally has large hands and a tiny head, adding to its rather grotesque appearance. Gray and white horsehair is often attached to the crown with animal glue. This is then arranged in such a way as to give the figure the appearance of having a bald spot fringed with hair that forms a braid at the back of the neck. Occasionally eyes of obsidian are added, although the sockets are usually left empty. The mouth of the skeleton is always in a grimace, showing wood or bone teeth. A great deal of attention is paid to the anatomy of the body. The ribs are prominently displayed and the limbs seem to billow at the joints. But the number of ribs is usually inaccurate and the limbs are out of proportion to the rest of the body.

The second type of *Muerte* comes from the San Luis Valley of southern Colorado and is usually dated later than its Sangre de Cristo counterpart. The first Penitentes in the San Luis area migrated from New Mexico in the mid-nineteenth century. The isolation of the area preserved their activities, although the figure of the *Muerte* changed.

The San Luis *Muerte* is a more personalized conception of Death than the Sangre de Cristo figure. Although the same size, the San Luis figure assumes a crouching position in the cart, while holding a bow and arrow. The figure is usually made of wooden blocks which are later covered with outer garments. Only the hands, feet, and head of the figure are carved in any detail. And in the case of the head, only the face is carved; the rest of the block is covered with a hood. Generally the head is large in proportion to the rest of the body. All the extremities are gessoed and then painted with white house paint. The eyes of the figure are painted black and then covered with window glass. The nose is generally quite long and broad, and the mouth is opened showing teeth of bone or wood. The expression of the face is achieved by a hood which, when placed on the head, shades the eyes and gives them a menacing expression. The hood is attached to the brown or black robe covering the figure, the latter cinched at the waist by a rope or chain from which hangs a bunch of keys.

In general, the major difference between the Sangre de Cristo and San Luis *Muertes* is in technology. The Sangre de Cristo figures exhibit a great deal of craftsmanship and care in execution. On the other hand, the San Luis *Muerte* is an example of true expediency in technique with only visible parts of the body executed in any detail. But, notwithstanding these differences in execution, both types of *Muertes* function similarly in the Good Friday processions.

Source and Comment

Journal of American Folklore, LXXXIV (1971), 304-07. From a paper on "The Origin of the Penitente 'Death Cart' " by Louisa R. Stark. Stark traces its origin to religious floats used in Holy Week processions in Spain and Latin America.

* * *

The Penitentes

A Penance

¿ *Penitente pecador,*
Porque te andas azotando?
Por una vaca que robé
Y aqui la ando disquintando.

Penitente sinner,
Why do you go whipping yourself?
For the cow I stole,
And here I go paying for her.

A different version is cited by Rev. Barton:

The general testimony was that the average member is one who is pleased to do up his religion for the year in forty days [of Lent]. The Mexican people sing a mocking little couplet as to the self-inflicted penance:

"Here's for the cow I stole,
And this is for the cow I intend to steal."

Source and Comment

Mary Marta Weigle, "*Los Hermanos Penitentes*: Historical and Ritual Aspects of Folk Religion in Northern New Mexico and Southern Colorado," University of Pennsylvania, Ph.D. Dissertation, 1971,

283-84. The first version of this rhyme is quoted from Charles Lummis' *The Land of Poco Teimpo,* originally published in 1893, which describes Penitente Holy Week rites in 1888 he witnessed. The second quotation is from a pamphlet, undated, by William E. Barton, *The Penitentes of New Mexico.* He describes a Lenten service in the 1890s. Weigle notes that it is well known as a children's rhyme and sees it as a verbal indication of tensions between members and nonmembers of the brotherhood.

* * *

The Penitentes

The Encounter of Christ and Mary

Good Friday in the morning, the call to prayers is sounded from the roof top of the church, not by the sweet tones of the bell, but by a *matraca* [wooden noisemaker] in the hands of the sexton. No bells are heard on this day. It is the day on which our Lord was crucified, and sorrow dominates the scene.

After the prayer service, there is evident a sense of preparation around the church; black-shawled women gather inside the churchyard as if in expectancy of some summons. The sexton atop the church suddenly sounds his rattle. The women flock inside, and taking the figure of the Virgin Mary, one of the most sensitively and beautifully fashioned of New Mexico *santos de bulto* [holy images], place it on a pedestal. The hymn to the Virgin is begun, and the rest of the people fall in line as the image is carried slowly toward the door. Some of the women following behind the image are barefooted and weeping. This procession makes its way across the churchyard, pausing now and then for prayer, after which the singing is resumed. From the direction of the *morada* [chapel or chapter house] a voice is heard intoning, as if reading some very impressive sermon, with the noise of the *matracas* intruding now and then. As the figure of the Virgin with its attendant group of women nears the *Puerta de la Plaza,* the brethren round the corner of the narrow passage way leading into the square, the two groups moving slowly toward each other.

In the fore of the penitent group is a boy, one of the youngest of the brethren, holding in his arms the figure of Christ on the Cross, the blood bespattered image known as *Nuestro Padre* [Our Father] *Jesús.* Behind him are the two singers, but they are silent in this procession. A diminutive figure with misshapen legs, almost dwarflike in his proportions, is reading in a sonorous voice, *La Pasión del Señor* [The Passion of Our Lord]. The reading of this dolorous account of Our Lord's suffering and humiliating path of anguish to the Mount of Calvary has just reached the point where the meeting of Christ and His mother is described, as the two groups meet. Behind the reader follows a blindfolded figure, naked to the waist, who carries a small cross strapped to his shoulders; his outstretched arms are bound tightly to the horizontal pieces of the cross. The women break into soft weeping as they experience the anguish of the mother meeting her son under such sorrowful conditions; they move forward to kiss the feet of the figure on the cross, uttering piteous exclamations of sorrow at such suffering. The penitent with the cross strapped to his back drops to his knees, remaining thus for the rest of the ceremony. The women who have carried the figure of Mary are for the most part members of the order of our Lady of Mount Carmel, to which order belongs the honor of carrying this beloved image of the Virgin on this occasion. The rest of the women are housewives, none of whose family belong to the *Penitente* cult. As the words, '*cara a cara*' [face to face], are sung the figures of Mother and Son are raised so that their cheeks touch and they appear in a sorrowful last embrace.

The women with the brethren are their own wives, mothers, and sisters; many of them are barefoot also. They and the brethren render obeisance to the Virgin, kissing the hem of her gown and prostrating themselves before her. This ceremony is called *El Encuentro* [The Encounter], the meeting of Christ and the Virgin Mary on the Via Dolorosá in Jerusalem [Fourth Station of the Cross]. The reading of the Passion of Our Lord continues as the two groups merge and continue into the church. Here the figure of the crucified Christ is returned to the center of the altar. He is home again.

Source and Comment

Mary Marta Weigle, "*Los Hermanos Penitentes*: Historical and Ritual Aspects of Folk Religion in Northern New Mexico and Southern Colorado," University of Pennsylvania, Ph.D. Dissertation, 1971, 540-41. From Weigle's transcription of the W.P.A. Writers' Project manuscript, "Lent in Córdova." See above. For a similar Italian-American ritual, see "Good Friday Procession of the Virgin of Sorrows," p. 153.

The dramatization of Christ's Passion by means of the processions of the Penitentes includes a reenactment of the meeting of Christ and his Mother on the way to the crucifixion. Usually two processions converge—women carrying an image of the Virgin of the Sorrows and the Penitentes with an image of Christ. The dramatization is accompanied by responsive chanting and reaches its climax when the two images are brought together and the sorrowing mother kisses her son.

* * *

The Penitentes

The Darkness

Las Tinieblas, or Tenebrae, services are always held on Thursday evening. They follow the praying of the rosary conducted by the members. Immediately after the *Rosario* [rosary service], the brothers file out and return to the *morada* [chapel or chapter house]. Those who wish to stay for the Tenebrae await their return. They are very prompt in this second appearance and with them will be many members practicing penance....In some cases, two or three of the penitents will throw themselves face down in front of the door of the church, thus signifying that they wish the people to walk on them as they enter. There is little squeamishness in complying with this request, young and old alike stepping firmly on the bare backs of the prostrate figures. In later years, women wearing high-heeled shoes executed cruel punishment on backs already sore and wounded by the scourge.

When all are inside, the doors are firmly closed. The brethren kneel in front of the altar, inside the rail, except the partly-clothed penitents; these lie prostrate before the altar throughout the ensuing ceremony.

All candles ... are extinguished, leaving only a row of some thirty candles across the front of the altar to light the whole church. There is a subdued sound of shuffling feet and suppressed nervous giggles from the young girls as the villagers kneel in segregated groups on the floor, the women taking most of the space in the center of the floor while the men kneel towards the back of the church and near the side walls. There is an instinctive move towards one's neighbor....

One lone singer from the *morada* takes up his position near one end of the row of candles on the altar and starts a hymn of a peculiarly haunting quality ... As he concludes each verse, he reaches out and pinches a yellow candle flame ... The singer has a carefully shaded lantern under the protecting folds of his coat, so shaded as to throw light only on his song book. Having extinguished the last light, he makes for the low door of the sacristy, which opens off from the altar space to the left. Passing through this door the dim light afforded by his shaded lantern is cut off also, leaving the church in utter and appalling darkness. Suddenly a voice calls out *"Ave María,"* whereupon a deafening tumult breaks out; it is the clapping of hands added to that of the clattering racket of the *matracas* ... in the hands of the brethren. When the noise dies down, some one is heard saying *"Un sudario en el nombre de Dios por l'alma del difunto José"* (a prayer for the repose of the soul of the deceased José——, for the love of God). A subdued murmur is heard as most of the assembly join in a semi-whispered response to the request. Another name is called out, and the request is complied with. Perhaps three or more requests for prayers are called out and complied with when the same voice again calls out *"Ave María,"* and the clapping of hands is resumed with the accompanying sounds as before. As from a great distance, the voice of the lone singer is heard from the sacristy above the tumult of the clapping hands, the *matracas,* and the rattling of heavy chains.

This darkened service continues for nearly an hour, but the time seems longer to eyes that strain to glimpse a ray of light and to ears deafened by the tumult raised to scare away the evil spirits.

Some of the children in the crowd get out of hand, but subside when sternly admonished. The whole service is awe-inspiring, with a touch of the uncanny, and to many it is a great relief when the door of the sacristy opens and the faint light of the lantern signals the end. The brethren form a line and shuffle backward toward the door, with the huddled blood-caked figures in the white drawers in their midst. As they reach the door, they make a genuflection towards the front of the church and pass into the church-yard. Heavy crosses are lifted onto benumbed backs and scourges swing again; the sound of the *pito* [primitive flute], as it grows fainter and fainter, marks the painful progress of bare feet back towards the *morada,* doubtless a welcome abiding place, which the name implies.

Source and Comment

Mary Marta Weigle, *"Los Hermanos Penitentes*: Historical and Ritual Aspects of Folk Religion in Northern New Mexico and Southern Colorado," Ph.D. Dissertation, University of Pennsylvania, 1971, 545-47. Quoted in an appendix to the dissertation. Weigle's source is an undated, anonymous manuscript entitled "Lent in Córdova" [New Mexico], pages 81-84, W.P.A. Project Files, New Mexico State Records Center and Archives, Sante Fe, files as "Social History: Penitentes."

Las Tinieblas—in Latin *Tenebrae,* meaning darkness or Hell—were rites conducted on Holy Thursday, Good Friday and Holy Saturday. From the Middle Ages they took place in darkness. The extinction of a series of candles, except for one, symbolized the burial of Christ. The sole remaining candle suggested the promise of resurrection. the noise and tumult after the candles were put out is said to represent the darkness and the earthquake which, according to the Gospels, occurred when Christ died.

* * *

The Penitentes

The Discipline

The *Morada* [chapel or chapter house] is always outside the village. About half a mile from the *Morada* can be seen a cross. Towards mid-night although there is snow on the ground, and the temperature low, the penitents emerge from the *Morada* for a procession. The brethren of the light wear costumes and chant the rosary; they are accompanied by the brethren of the mask who proceed naked except for white pants, shoe-less and shirtless. Some carry a heavy cross on their shoulders, while others discipline themselves to blood. This discipline lasts during the whole time it is necessary to go from the *Morada* to the so-called Calvary or cross which I mentioned before, and all during the return journey. Each brother is recognized by three scars which are made on the shoulders. These scars consist of three slight vertical cuts which each member receives on the day of entrance to the society. And these three cuts are about four inches long. Every time that a brother disci-plines himself, the scars are opened with a small sharp stone. When the blood begins to flow, the discipline commences; such discipline must intensify the wounds. I assure you that when such a spectacle of fifty, sixty, or two hundred men disciplining themselves is seen for the first time, it is shocking. On returning to the *Morada* the men find prepared for them hot water and something else (I don't know what); they wash themselves, and everything seems over. Sometimes there are brethren of a *Morada* who make a vow to visit one, two, three, or more other *Morada* nearby. And three or four join a brother of light who serves as their companion. Some carry a cross, others discipline themselves; all this goes on for six, or eight miles; they are naked, as I said, wearing only some short pants in the deep of winter. The things they do during Holy Week are incredible. One of these is the crucifixion. A poor brother is tied to a huge cross by his hands and feet; and the cross is then lifted. The brother hangs from it God knows how long. This year, one of these crucified brethren died, I was told, from sheer pain. This happened in a parish seventy miles away from ours [at Conejos, Colorado]. And it is a wonder how these intense colds do not kill off fifty or more every year. On the contrary, only a few take sick; this they ascribe to a special help from heaven. Poor simple people! Some of them count on buying heaven with such indiscretions, and maybe they do, because they do it in good faith. The chiefs do it for political reasons. They use these simple brethren for their votes in the elections.

One more item, and I shall finish. A brother who renders himself unworthy of belonging to the organization is expelled. But before the expulsion, he is obliged to appear at the *Morada* where three horizontal wounds are made over the three vertical wounds in the back, of which I spoke earlier. These horizontal wounds announce that the person who bears them no longer belongs to the organization and has, therefore, no right to enter a *Morada*. We are working, little by little, to destroy these abuses. You can help us with your prayers.

Source and Comment

Colorado Magazine, XXXI (1954), 178-79. Excerpt from a letter from Father Salvatore Persone, first printed in Italian in the *Lettre Edificanti*, 1874-75, of the Neapolitan Province of the Society of Jesus. The translator and editor is E. R. Volmar, S. J.

Father Persone, an Italian Jesuit missionary, was assigned to the parish of Our Lady of Guadalupe at Conejos, Colorado, in 1871, and periodically sent letters and reports to his order. This one was written in August 1874. In it he writes about "the customs of this place."

* * *

The Penitentes

Penitentes Ghost Story

A certain evening during holy week the Penitentes entered the church in Taos [New Mexico] for the purpose of flogging themselves. After flogging themselves in the usual manner, they left the church. As they departed, however, they heard the floggings of a Penitente who seemed to have remained in the church. The elder brother (*hermano mayor*) counted his Penitentes, and no one was missing. To the astonishment of the other Penitentes, the one in the church continued his flagellation, and they decided to return. No one dared to reënter the church, however; and while they disputed in silence and made various conjectures as to what the presence of an unknown Penitente might mean, the floggings became harder and harder. At last one of the Penitentes volunteered to enter alone; but, as he opened the door, he discovered that the one who was scourging himself mercilessly was high above in the choir, and it was necessary to obtain a lighted candle before venturing to ascend to the choir in the darkness. He procured a lighted candle and attempted to ascend. But, lo! he could not, for every time he reached the top of the stairs, the Penitente whom he plainly saw there, flogging himself, would approach and put out his candle. After trying for several times, the brave Penitente gave up the attempt, and all decided to leave the unknown and mysterious stranger alone in the church. As they departed, they saw the mysterious Penitente leave the church and turn in an opposite direction. They again consulted one another, and decided to follow him. They did so; and, since the stranger walked slowly scourging himself continuously and brutally, they were soon at a short distance from him. The majority of the flagellants followed slowly behind; while the brave one, who had previously attempted to ascend to the choir, advanced to the side of the mysterious stranger and walked slowly by him. He did not cease scourging himself, though his body was visibly becoming very weak, and blood was flowing freely from his mutilated back. Thus the whole procession continued in the silence of the night, the stranger leading the Penitentes through abrupt paths and up a steep and high mountain. At last, when all were nearly dead with fatigue, the mysterious Penitente suddenly disappeared, leaving his good companion and the other Penitentes in the greatest consternation. The Penitentes later explained that this was doubtless the soul of a dead Penitente who had not done his duty in life,—a false Penitente,—and God had sent him back to earth to scourge himself properly, before allowing him to enter heaven.

Source

Journal of American Folklore, XXIII (1910), 407-08. Retold by Aurelio M. Espinosa. His source was "my father, who lived in Taos when the tale was current."

* * *

Holy Week Riddle

Santa soy sin ser nacida,
santa sin ser bautizada.
Santa me dice la iglesia,
santa soy santificada.
 Semana Santa.

I am holy without having been born,
Holy without having been baptized.
Holy the church calls me,
I am sanctified as holy.
 Holy Week.

Source

Journal of American Folklore, XXVIII (1915), 333. From a collection of "New Mexican Spanish riddles" made by Aurelio M. Espinosa. Informants not given.

* * *

Holy Week

Children Well-behaved During Holy Week

On the Saturday before Holy Week [in Mesilla, New Mexico], the fathers and mothers of children over ten years old were instructed to tell the children they could not be punished during Holy Week and they asked them to behave themselves. After the last service of Holy Week, all the children would go home with their parents and the father would ask all of them to kneel down with their arms crossed in front of them. Then he would come with a big horse whip and say, "You did this last week," and would give them four or five lashes with the whip until he got through all the children. That was why in those days the children were so well behaved.

Source

New Mexico Folklore Record, V (1950-51), 25. From "Recollections of Early New Mexico" of Teresita Garcia-Fountain, age 88, of Mesilla, New Mexico. Recorded on October 15, 1950, by J. D. Robb. Translated from the Spanish by Joe Salazar.

All Fools' Day

April 1

On this day of license, practical jokes may be played with impunity: sending people on foolish errands, crying wolf, putting salt in the sugar bowl. The custom which is called "hunting the gowk (cuckoo, hence fool)" in Scotland and "*poisson d'avril*" in France may well reflect spring sexual license (for instance, there is the traditional play on the words "cuckoo" and "cuckold") and the efforts to deceive evil spirits which might interfere with fertility at the time when planting and sprouting are occurring. It is also associated with civil and church rebellion such as the Lord of Misrule and Boy Bishop ceremonies.

The origin of the custom is uncertain, but it seems to have come about in France as a result of the change to the Gregorian calendar in 1582 when New Year's was moved from March 25 to January 1. Thus, the first April fools may have been people who failed to make the proper adjustment. In Mexico, where the borrowing of trivial items and the failure to return them is a feature, a similar day is celebrated on December 28, and some countries like Germany and Norway have two such days on the first and last dates in April.

April Fool's Tricks

The first of April has always been celebrated as All Fool's Day.

The April-first greeting of a teacher who taught about 1864 was invariably, "Oh, come out and see the flock of wild geese!"

The little children would catch each other by calling, "Oh, look at that little bird," "It's snowing!" "You have a black mark on your face," etc. Tying a rag on the back of the dress, and pinning a label on the back were popular.

Filling the sugar bowl with salt, stuffing a biscuit with cotton and offering an empty egg shell at breakfast, were good old tricks.

Glueing a penny on the pavement, stuffing an old purse with paper and dropping it, tying handkerchiefs to strings and dropping them, then pulling them back when almost to be picked up were favorite performances. Some sent false orders or April Fool messages through the mails.

Source

Memoirs of the American Folklore Society, XVIII (1925), 119. "Folk-Lore from Maryland," collected by Annie W. Whitney and Caroline C. Bullock. Informants not given.

April Fools

Make up any kind of story such as "Your shoe is untied," and when the person looks, greet him with, "April Fool." If it is a later day, he says,

"Ha, ha. April Fool's gone and past;
You're the biggest fool at last."

Put coffee sacks filled with dirt in the road. Hide and see who picks them up.

Fill a paper sack with manure and set fire to it outside someone's door. Knock. Then watch the person stamp out the fire.

Source

"Folklore from White County, Tennessee," Ph.D. Dissertation, George Peabody College for Teachers, 1969, 194. Collected in 1967-68 by Edwina B. Doran. Her informants were residents or former residents of White County, but she does not always indicate her specific sources.

* * *

April Fool, Go to School

Another good one is to tell a kid in school that the teacher has dismissed the class for an hour. Sometimes it causes the stooge to miss a class. Of course, the teacher is not too hard on the student; he "forgot," is his excuse—when all the time he wanted to miss. This is for the ones that "have lace on their pants."

The rest of the kids live for the next episode. They all assemble off the southwest corner of the school campus at Buchanan. After all the buses have run, and all the other kids arrived, they leave the campus for an all-day hike and picnic. They get the day marked "absent" on the report cards that are sent out every six weeks; however, the teachers expect that all will leave anyway. At lunch time all the kids spread out what they have taken to eat. They make whistles out of hickory sticks. And when they come back to school, they all arrive blowing those whistles. It is a day of good times in and around Buchanan, Tennessee.

Source

Tennessee Folklore Society Bulletin, XIX (September 1953), 61. Remembered from childhood in Buchanan, Henry County, Tennessee, by Ewing Jackson. He contributed his recollections of "Calendar Customs and Folk Beliefs" to the Folklore Archive, Murray State College, Kentucky, while a student there in 1948.

* * *

April Fool Letters

[April Fool] letters were composites of prankishness, deception, absurdity, folk verses, and, I suspect, love.

The letters were never signed, but girls, apparently, made a game of trying to guess who sent them. To receive an April Fool letter during April, for they could be sent anytime during the month, was deemed a most flattering honor and the contents were shared among envious acquaintances, who, in this case, could hardly be called friends....

Letter #1

Sugarville Tenn
Apr 40 / 08

Miss Susie Wilson

Dear Sweetheart.

I seat myself on a stool. to write you an April fool. You know I love you without me telling you that But I must tell you what love is it is inward inwardness, outward, outwardness, all over, everlastedness, a durn Piece of foolishness Ha! Ha! Ha! Ha! hee! I heard that you was at meeting a Sunday Well Darling I wish I had been there so I could have seen You maybe you would have went home with me for this is leep Year you Know

say Honey you Dont know how well I love you but I can tell You I love once I love you twice I love You better than cats love mice But that dont make much difference Come down and we will H A V E. 1 of the Longest talks. U. Ever did see

Listen now. This fact is truth or truth belied no woman yet was ever tongue tied so I know you can talk

Lime stone water and cedar wood

A kiss from you would do me good
  so good by

Honey

Be good at home And Better abroad Love your sweetheart And serve the Lord Ans. soon As I do not live in town Just Back your letters to a hole in the ground Wait a minute I liked to forgot will You Marry me Or will you Not

Letter #2

April 20th 1908
Remember Me Always

Hello Miss Susie

How are you today all o.k. I hope, I thought I would write you an April fool Now Miss Susie you must ans this for it is going to be a good one. My aim is to come to see you never I get able I fell in love with you and it broke both of my arms off. Oh My Susie I sure love you. it nearly breaks my heart to think that you dont care for me. You are so pretty I think of you all the day and dream of you at night. ha Ha. and Miss Susie I am pritty too you ought to see me. You would fall in love with me sure my eyes are like the stars in heaven and they stand out like pipe stems. and if you see any boy of this Description passing by. you must hail him in. for he loves you.

You I love and will ever
You may change but I will never.
And here is another verse you see I am very sharp.

> You can go with J. T. F.
> But if you do you will be Deft
> And if you live by his side
> You will sure be Tongue-tide

Think of me early
think of me late
When you see me coming
meet me at the gate

Source

Tennessee Folklore Society Bulletin, XXVII (March 1961), 5-7. Published by Kelsie Harder to whom they were given "by an elderly woman in Perry County," Tennessee. He kept the "original punctuation and spelling" but changed the name of the addressee.

* * *

The first day of April, in our community [Buchanan, Tennessee] as in every other community, is the day to pull your tricks and get by with them. Anything goes around Buchanan. One of the nice tricks is to write a letter backwards. It can be read in a mirror. You see a lot of these at home on April Fool's Day.

Source

Tennessee Folklore Society Bulletin, XIX (September 1953), 61. As remembered from childhood in Henry County, Tennessee, by Ewing Jackson, a student at Murray State College, Kentucky, in 1948.

* * *

Adult April Fool

Yeah, they play April Fool tricks in the office. I remember a couple that were pretty bad. One, the guys all park out on the street and run up a lot of parking tickets. Mostly, this is ignored. I mean the city's lax about it and some of the guys know the cops. They even come up and get coffee from the girls. But still those tickets are there. One guy had run up a real lot, maybe $500-600. So April Fool we got this cop to come up to the office and pretend to be looking for him. When he found him, he said that there'd been a big crackdown on traffic tickets and he'd have to come along to the Police Station. The guy nearly died, turned white as a sheet, and nobody let on it was a trick till just as they were going out the door. Then we all yelled "April Fool."

But the worst one . . . I don't know if it ever happened. I just heard about it. I wasn't in on it. One of the salesmen had been fooling around with a secretary. He was married and everyone in the office knew about it, though I guess his wife didn't. The girl was a bit crazy, a real screwball, and one of the other salesmen persuaded her to tell her boy friend she was pregnant as an April Fool joke. I guess she went in his office and left the door open so everyone could hear. Finally, it got bad enough she had to tell him it was a joke. You know, most guys would have really been pissed off, but I guess this guy was a little crazy too. He thought it was a big joke. Maybe he was just happy it was an April Fool joke. But he just laughed and kept right on going around with her.

Source and Comment

University of Pennsylvania Folklore Archives, undated. These anecdotes were recorded by T.P.C. during an interview with an insurance salesman in the Providence, Rhode Island, office of Aetna Life and Casualty in the summer of 1984. The informant wished to remain anonymous. The pranks, in his words, "were played a while back."

April Fool tricks are not, it seems, confined to children. Catherine Harris Ainsworth published a number of accounts of pranks played by adult factory and office workers in the Buffalo area of New York in her book *American Calendar Customs,* Buffalo, New York, 1979, I, 3-5, 7-8. One involved bakery employees in collusion with the manager telling a girl who had just finished her shift that she was to substitute for the next shift as well. One involved putting red pepper in a worker's coffee thermos. He took the prank seriously and thought the boss had done it. The trick resulted in an argument. The man quit, and ultimately he ran off with the boss's secretary. Such childish tricks as taping down telephone hooks so the phone will continue to ring after being answered, taping filing cabinets closed, and stapling folders together seem to have been common, as were more elaborate pranks such as faking phone calls, issuing tickets for nonexistent parties, and creating bomb scares.

Radio April Fool

Let us . . . flash back to Sunday evening, March 31, 1940, when radio station KYW included the following telegram on its 8 o'clock newscast:

Your worst fears that the world will end are confirmed by astronomers of Franklin Institute, Philadelphia. Scientists predict that the world will end at 3 P.M. Eastern Standard Time tomorrow.

This is no April Fool joke. Confirmation can be obtained from Wagner Schlesinger, director of the Fels Planetarium of this city.

(signed) William A. A. Castellini
Franklin Institute

Within minutes, other available sources of public information—including the old Electrical Bureau at City Hall—were swamped by telephone calls from people seeking further word. Only 17 months earlier, Orson Welles had brought off his fake Martian invasion, which subsequently had been thoroughly debunked. But it became obvious now that the public still was willing to be fooled.

It turned out that Castellini, the Franklin Institute's press agent, trading on the institute's reputation for scientific authenticity, had sent the telegram to hype an illustrated lecture titled "How Will the World End?" scheduled for April 1 at the Fels Planetarium. Shortly—*very* shortly—after the hoax, the Franklin Institute and the press agent parted company.

Source

Philadelphia Inquirer, April 1, 1989. From "The Scene," a column by Edgar Williams.

April Fool Computerized

An especially destructive computer virus set to "go off" on April 1 was recently discovered in West Germany. This virus attaches itself to ".com" files on IBM and IBM-compatible micro-computers. The only way currently known to detect it is by using any popular utility program (such as Norton Utilities and PC Tools) to search for the virus's "signature" in the first 7 bytes of a ".com" file: EB 07 0A 03 59 00.

Anyone can call the Computing Resource Center, Ext. 8-9085, and make an appointment to bring in copies of their ".com" files on diskette (or bring in their hard drives) to be checked for the virus.

The virus destroys all data on hard drives and diskettes inserted into the computer. A precaution for users of microcomputers is to backup their data files.

Although no current information has surfaced on the worldwide virus alert list about Macintosh or UNIX-based computers, all users should be aware that April 1 may bring out the worst in virus terrorists. Be alert for any unusual system behavior.

Source and Comment

An official notice by the University of Pennsylvania Computing Resource Center published in the *Almanac,* the university's internal newsletter, of March 27, 1990. This proved to be an "April Fool." Such warnings were widely circulated but the virus did not materialize.

Founding of the Church of Latter-Day Saints
April 6

Joseph Smith, religious leader, announced his discovery of inscribed golden tablets which he translated in 1827. These and further revelations provided the basis for the *Book of Mormon* and the establishment of the Church of Jesus Christ of the Latter-Day Saints which he organized as a church on April 6, 1830, in Fayette, New York. Hostility caused him to move with his followers to Kirtland, Ohio, and then to found the settlement of Nauvoo, Illinois. In 1844 Smith was killed while in jail by a mob and the Mormons, under the leadership of Brigham Young, moved west, reaching the valley of the Great Salt Lake, Utah, in 1847.

Birthday of the Mormons

It is not surprising ... that the Mormons, who shared with other Christians such anniversaries and festivals as Christmas and Easter, formed their own calendar of annual celebrations. . . .

Almost immediately the date of April 6, the day in 1830 when the church was officially organized, was given special recognition. Apparently no particular notice was given to the date in 1831 or 1832, but in 1833 a meeting of about eighty persons took place on the Big Blue River near the western limits of Jackson County, Missouri. According to Joseph Smith's history,

> It was an early spring, and the leaves and blossoms enlivened and gratified the soul of man like a glimpse of Paradise. The day was spent in a very agreeable manner, in giving and receiving knowledge which appertained to this last kingdom—it being just 1800 years since the Savior laid down His life that man might have everlasting life, and only three since the Church had come out of the wilderness, preparatory for the last dispensation. . . .This was the first attempt made by the Church to celebrate the anniversary of her birthday, and those who professed not our faith talked about it as a strange thing.

There was no such "birthday" celebration in 1834, 1835, or 1836, apparently, but in 1837 a solemn assembly was held in the Kirtland Temple over several days, including April 6, when special instructions were given. In 1838, April 6 saw the beginning of a "general conference" at Far West, Missouri, to transact church business and "to celebrate the anniversary" of the church.

The following year the prophet [Joseph Smith] was in jail, but in 1840 at Nauvoo, Illinois, another General Conference was held. The pattern was now established, and from then until the present the annual conference has almost always been scheduled so as to include April 6 as one of its days. Thus a need for a regular annual conference was met while at the same time commemorating the founding day.

Source and Comment

Utah Historical Quarterly, XLIII (1975), 68-69. From an essay by Davis Bitton on "The Ritualization of Mormon History." For another celebration combining church business and the commemoration of its foundation, see "Big August Quarterly," p. 317.

Tater Day

First Monday in April

Originally a market fair where sweet potato slips for spring planting could be bought, Tater Day has been revived as a country carnival, with the usual games of chance, side shows and rides.

Sweet Potato Day

Tater Day, held in Benton [Kentucky] on the first Monday in April, was organized in 1843 and has been revitalized. Originally Tater Day was the time when farmers came to Benton to sell or buy "sweet tater" slips for planting and to visit with friends and relatives and maybe do a little mule swapping or knife trading. Nowadays you might have difficulty in finding a sweet tater but the crowds come—an estimated 15,000 in 1974. In honor of the day you might want to try one of our sweet potato recipes.

Glazed Sweet Potatoes

9 large sweet potatoes
1 tbsp. water
1 tbsp. sugar
4 tbsp. butter

Boil potatoes 50 minutes. Pare them, cut in halves lengthwise, and sprinkle both sides with salt. Place them cut side down in a dripping pan. Put sugar and water in a small pan; stir until sugar is dissolved. Add butter and stir over low heat until it melts. Baste the potatoes with this liquid and bake in a 400⁰ oven 20 minutes. The potatoes should be glossy brown when they come from the oven. Serves 12.

Sweet Potato Pudding

1 egg
½ cup sugar
¼ cup melted butter
1 cup grated sweet potatoes
1⅓ cups milk
¼ tsp. allspice
¼ tsp. nutmeg
   pinch of salt

Beat egg and add remaining ingredients. Pour into a greased baking dish. Bake at 400⁰ for 30 minutes or until thick, stirring occasionally. Serves 4.

Source

Kentucky Hospitality (Kentucky Federation of Women's Clubs), 1976, 176. The information and recipes obtained from members of the Kentucky Federation of Women's Clubs, which sponsored this periodical. The glazed sweet potatoes recipe is from Lummie Taylor of Beaver Dam; the potato pudding recipe from Mrs. Carl Jones of Clinton.

Birthday of the Buddha

April 8

The founder of Buddhism had the given name, Siddhartha; the family name, Gautama; the clan name, Shaka; and he is commonly called the Buddha, which in Sanskrit means "the enlightened one." He is thought to have lived in India from ca. 563 B.C. to 483 B.C. His birthday is celebrated by millions of Buddhists in Sri Lanka, Tibet, Nepal, Burma, Vietnam, Korea, China, Japan, and elsewhere in the Orient, and by Buddhists in the United States.

Buddha's Birthday in California

Among the Buddhist holidays [the] celebration on April 8th, the day of the birth of Shaka [a name for the Buddha] ... is the most important celebration of them all....To commemorate the birthday anniversary of Shaka, ... the Buddhist temples in Japan and America alike construct [in 1934] a temporary platform, the roof of which is covered with flowers, in keeping with the traditional story that flowers rained at the birth of Shaka. On this platform is placed an image of the infant Buddha in a tub filled with licorice tea. The members of the church then take part in the ritual of pouring licorice tea over the figure of Buddha with bamboo ladles to signify the act of bathing him. They then drink some of the sweet tea themselves, an act which is supposed to effect the purification of their souls, and cause them to become Buddha-like in thought, word, and deed.

Source

Southwestern Journal of Anthropology, II (1946), 177. From material collected by "Miss N. I." in 1934 on beliefs of Oriental minorities in the San Francisco Bay area. The research director and editor of this material was Paul Radin. Informants were "older residents of Oakland and Berkeley" and the interviews upon which this description is based were conducted in Japanese.

Blessing the Sun

Every 28 Years on a Wednesday

Jewish tradition affirms that God made the sun, moon and stars on the fourth day of Creation. This, according to the ancient reckoning, took place on a Wednesday evening some 6,000 years ago. Since then, once every 28 years, the sun completes a cycle which returns it to the same astronomical position that it held at the time of Creation. The most recent beginning of a new cycle of the sun occurred on April 8, 1981, or, by the Jewish lunar calendar, on the first Wednesday in Nisan, the seventh lunar month. The ritual celebrating this occasion is called Birchat Hahamah, or the Blessing of the Sun. In modern times it has been observed with morning prayers on Wednesday proper. There is a parallel ceremony for the moon.

A Creation Tradition

A pint-sized Shmuli Greenwald, age 4, looked bewildered as he stood on a grassy hillside in Northeast Philadelphia early yesterday [April 8, 1981], squinting in the bright sunlight...

According to Genesis, the sun was placed in the heavens on the fourth day of Creation and yesterday it was supposed to return to that original position. The event occurs every 28 years, and by Jewish reckoning the sun is beginning its 206th cycle.

Saluting the rare religious observance, Jews here and around the world gathered on hills and rooftops and in synagogues, anywhere they might catch a glimpse of the sun's first rays.

And so it happened that bright-eyed Shmuli Greenwald, along with 460 other children at Beth Jacob Jewish day school in Elkins Park, gathered to pay special homage to the sun early yesterday. At 8:15 a.m., the young worshippers bundled in warm jackets stood erect, facing the sun and reciting a blessing and psalms.

Similar ceremonies took place elsewhere in the Philadelphia area—including a noon rally and "discussion on solar energy" at Kennedy Plaza, 16th and JFK Boulevard.

About 50,000 Jews gathered before dawn at the Wailing Wall in Jerusalem, Judaism's holiest shrine, while in Tel Aviv they packed the top floor of the 36-story Shalom Tower, Israel's highest building.

Several hundred celebrants were on hand at the Empire State Building [New York] as the sun rose at 5:28 a.m. Rabbi Zalaman Schachter of Temple University led that service, in which 70 balloons were released to symbolize the hope that "there should be light and peace for all."

Jeffery Dekro, director of the Jewish Energy Project, one of the sponsors of yesterday's rally at JFK Plaza, said, "It's not a highly significant holiday in a religious sense, and yet, despite its infrequent occurrence, it has been remembered and observed repeatedly since the second century.

"It is little known, but this year, largely because of the energy crisis and people's concern for safe, renewable energy, there's been a reconsideration of the relevance of the sun to our normal lives."

There were no such deep thoughts among the toddler set, the 4- and 5-year-olds who gathered in chilly early morning temperatures at Burholme Park in the Greater Northeast [Philadelphia]. Their main preoccupation was just keeping warm.

"I don't know if he's old enough to understand today," said Yochanan Greenwald, Shmuli's father, who is a rabbi and teacher at Beth Jacob. "But I wanted him to be part of it. Maybe he'll remember."

After all, Jews who missed yesterday's sun rite will not have another chance until 2009... "By the next time, everyone here will probably be a parent, and some of us will be grandparents," said Rabbi Nochem Kaplan, 35, who led the service and recalled that the last time he celebrated the occasion, as a 7-year-old, "the day was glorious like today."

"It's remained with me," said Rabbi Kaplan, a bearded man in a black hat, who is one of Beth Jacob school's two principals.

"Part of the ceremony and prayer includes a wish that all may live to see the next such occurrence," the rabbi said.

Not *everyone,* though, is eagerly anticipating the next time the Blessing of the Sun rolls around, 28 years from now.

"I'll be 41," gasped Juda Rosenstein, 13, groaning audibly. "It's not a nice thought. That's *old*."

Source

Philadelphia Inquirer, April 9, 1981. From a feature article by staff writer Linda Loyd.

Shad Planking
Third Wednesday in April

Outdoor political rallies at a time conveniently preceding elections were common when America was more rural and less under the sway of the mass media. They were highlighted by flamboyant oratory, hard liquor, and regional food prepared out-of-doors, such as barbecue, fish stew, and chicken bog, usually cooked according to a traditional recipe by a local specialist. Their number and political importance have diminished, but they are still much enjoyed for their food, drink, and good fellowship. For more than thirty years, when the shad and the politicians are running, the Wakefield, Virginia, Ruritan Club has served them up in its own distinctive way. The shad are cooked as much by the hot sauce in which they are basted as the bed of wood coals over which they remain for many hours. The festivities begin with informal drinking, followed by political oratory, usually supplied by a senator or governor, or at least a congressman. Then comes the eating.

The Wakefield Shad-planking

Getting Ready

The work will get under way at the [Wakefield] Sportsmen's Club on Tuesday, April 19, [1977] at 3:00 P.M. when a truck arrives with over a ton and a half of shad and rock fish. The rock are mainly eaten by the workers and the shad are planked for the guests.

Men from Wakefield farms, business establishments and offices will meet there,and, according to the usual schedule, the entire lot of fish will be scaled, dressed and iced by 6:00 P.M. Then a supper of shad roe and fried rock will be served the workers.

At 5:00 A.M. the following morning, a 150-foot long fire will be lighted and coaxed into a slow bank of coals. At this state the "nailing committee" will take over and tack the shad to planks which will be lined up on each side of the fire. The cooking process is underway by 9:00 A.M. and will continue throughout the day. The fish will be basted no less than 15 times with a special "secret" sauce prepared by Dr. E. C. Nettles of Wakefield. The cooking will end shortly before the address by the Honorable Robert W. Daniel, Jr., at 4:30 P.M. There will be approximately 100 workers assisting in the preparation and serving of a ton and a half of shad, a half ton of slaw, and many hundreds of pounds of cornbread cooked by Lyle Pond and his crew of expert cookers.

The Shad Planking

The gentlemen of Virginia, with politics on their minds and whiskey in their hands, assembled here [Wakefield, Virginia April 16, 1980] this afternoon in the piney woods for the 32nd annual shad planking, a one-day festival of boney fish, speech-making and the search for ice.

The barriers that for years kept women, blacks and Republicans away from the picnic supposedly have fallen. But women today were as scarce as abolitionists: blacks mostly tended the fish, and the Republicans, according to many longtime shad plankers, now sound so much like old-time Virginia Democrats that they are indistinguishable from the regular.

A shad planker is a man, a member of the local Ruritan Club in this town of 1,000 located about 60 miles southeast of Richmond, who got up early this morning, took a galvanized, sheet-metal nail and a hammer, and stuck a cleaned shad to an oak board. The shad then was smoked for nearly six hours over an oak fire.

The salty taste of that bony fish—along with the appeal of Virginia's top elected officials and a sunny afternoon—drew nearly 4,300 people, almost all white males.

The record crowd that paid $7.50 per person for a ticket to the picnic, impatiently listened to the traditional patriotic speech that briefly interferes with the drinking here. Virginia Lt. Gov. Charles S. (Chuck) Robb of McLean, considered the likely Democratic nominee for governor next year, even prefaced his speech by saying, "Nobody comes to shad planking to hear speeches. We come here to quench our thirst.". . .

When the shad-planking picnics began more than three decades ago, political control of Virginia was in the hands of Sen. Harry F. Byrd, Sr., and his political machine. Conservative political power in the state, for the most part, is now held by the Republican Party.

Gov. John N. Dalton, who spoke briefly at today's picnic, didn't let the opportunity of promoting his party's strength slip away.

"When I first came here in 1969," said Dalton, as the afternoon sun filtered through the pine trees, "I bet more than 100 people told me I was the first elected Republican figure ever seen at the shad planking."

Up until this year attendance at the picnic was by invitation only. But 4,000 tickets went up for sale to the general public late this winter, and they were all purchased within a month.

Despite changes in the political labels of the politicians who run Virginia, one thing that has remained constant at the shad planking is the sauce.

Dr. E. C. Nettle, a 78-year-old Wakefield physician who stands 6 feet 5 and today wore a bright red sweater, plaid slacks and a tan wool coat, is in charge of the sauce. It is said here that the best way to know the sauce—which is poured over the shad several times—is to stick your finger in it, that is, if "you got a finger you don't much care about."

Dr. Nettle, who knows the sauce better than any Virginian, enumerated the potent ingredients:

"We got eight gallons of Worchestershire sauce, 45 pounds of butter, 18 quarts of lemon juice, 13 pounds of black pepper and four pounds of red pepper." Nettle said there was also about 18 pounds of salt in the sauce. When the sauce is poured on an open fire it bursts into flame.

Before most of the men had a chance to taste Dr. Nettle's sauce on the 700 pounds of flounder, 400 pounds of rockfish and 2,900 pounds of shad, they sampled some of their own—mostly out of the tailgates and trunks of their cars.

Spencer Perkins, 72, an optometrist from Petersburg, parked his green 1972 Dodge in the pasture parking lot about one-half mile from where the speech-making took place. He and three of his friends broke out a fifth of Jim Beam bourbon, opened an ice chest and gathered around the rear of the car for some conversation. "When you come out here and have two or three drinks, you love everybody, everybody is your friend," said Perkins. "Of course," he said, "you'll find a few blacks and ladies here now, too."

But their numbers today were few. Lyle Pond, 62, a peanut, hog and soybean farmer, said he wouldn't want his wife to come to the shad planking because of the lack of "facilities."

Pond, a member of the Wakefield Ruritan Club who was in charge of cooking 500 pounds of cornbread, said men had a much easier time at the woodsy party because they "can go out behind a tree."

Source and Comment

Washington Post, April 17, 1980. From an article by staff writer Blaine Harden datelined Wakefield, Virginia, April 16. The description of "Getting Ready" is from a news release supplied by James W. Renney, a Wakefield attorney, master of ceremonies for the shad planking since 1959. He also provided background information. Cf. "Labor Day Politicking," p. 327 and "Return Day in Delaware," p. 390.

Arbor Day
Usually Fourth Friday in April

Arbor Day is celebrated in various states across the nation, in various ways and at various times. Although the planting of trees for memorial and ritualistic reasons is an ancient custom, J. Sterling Morton, a Nebraska newspaper publisher, is sometimes given credit for starting formal Arbor Days in the United States in 1872. Recently, with media reports on deforestation and global warming from the greenhouse effect, tree-planting has assumed greater importance.

While city workers passed out 1,500 honey locust seedlings today in small plastic bags, schoolchildren, politicians and officials gathered downtown in fog and drizzle for Chicago's annual celebration of trees.

A bake sale and poster contest, speeches and poetry all marked Arbor Day, celebrated in most states on the fourth Friday of April....

In Wisconsin, Gov. Tommy G. Thompson urged planting a million trees this week to replace those lost in the drought and forest fires last year. In one project, 130 seventh grade students from Shawano, Wisc., planted 5,000 seedlings in an area burned out by a forest fire last summer.

In New Jersey, there were tree-planting ceremonies in 37 communities marking Arbor Day, and in New York trees were planted on the grounds of the Governor's Mansion and in a park at Binghamton....

A volunteer group in Chicago, Neighborwoods, has planted more than 800 trees on vacant lots and empty city land since it began two years ago.

On Friday, in a ceremony at a Roman Catholic high school, Neighborwoods planted a 6-foot sapling that is a direct descendant of the Stelmuze, a 2,000-year-old, 30-foot-wide English Oak in Lithuania that is revered as a national monument.

Source

New York Times, April 29, 1989. By William E. Schmidt. See "Tu B'Shevat," p. 63.

Memorial Trees for Children

Spindly, yet graceful, the trees stood only a few feet apart in Upper Southampton [Pennsylvania], wrapped in ribbons of pink and blue.

A warm breeze slightly tipped the branches of the Tall Red Maples, rustling the 8-inch-by-11-inch signs attached to each of them.

Dianilou. Tierra. Aubrey. Jamil. Celise. One name was written on each of the signs. One name was for each of five sick children who had died—of AIDs, sudden infant death syndrome or other maladies—while in foster care.

The children were remembered yesterday [April 28, 1989] at a special Arbor Day memorial ceremony at Bethanna, a social-service agency in Bucks County that helps children who are abused, neglected or who suffer medical problems.

Before 80 guests and staffers, members of the nonprofit Christian organization planted a tree for each of the five "medically needy" children who died between December 1987 and December 1988.

"There is a fear that these children will die forgotten ... and that would be a second tragedy," said Scott Eldredge, a foster care supervisor at the agency. "We had to do something to remind the community of their responsibility to take care of these children."

Planting the trees was a gesture that the Bethanna staff hopes will spread beyond their 40-acre grounds to places where people want to commemorate the lives of sick children who have died. It is a gesture they hope will become as synonymous with Arbor Day as planting a tree.

Source

Philadelphia Inquirer, April 29, 1989. By staff writer Kristin E. Holmes.

Walpurgis Eve
April 30

Walburga (also spelled Walpurga and Walpurgis), an English nun born early in the 8th century, was a missionary to Germany. Her day coincided with an earlier pagan festival marking the beginning of summer. On Walpurgis Eve devils and witches were said to hold their orgies at Sabbats on mountain tops like the Brocken in Germany. Walpurgis Eve revels are memorably portrayed in Goethe's *Faust*. Walpurgis is regarded as a protector against black magic.

Walpurgisnacht

Norwegians everywhere celebrate their Constitution Day on the 17th of May. In Minneapolis the Norwegians also celebrate a great Norway day in July, while the Swedes hold Swedish Day in June. We have similar festivals on the Coast, where additionally, Leif Erickson Day in October has nowadays become important as a folk festival. A strictly modern creation, it has been celebrated in Los Angeles for decades, and from Los Angeles, too, proceeded much of the organization and energy which led recently to official recognition of Leif Erickson Day by our national government. The celebration of the 30th of April—*Valborgsmässoafton, Walpurgisnacht*—is no such great folk festival among us. In this country it seems to be a pious gesture, small celebrations among Swedes and Finns of the college-educated class, who don their student caps and sing the old Scandinavian and Latin academic songs on such occasions. Potables are consumed, and the dancing goes on all night, with a fervor that is *sui generis* among such activities on the larger scene.

Source

Northwest Folklore, III (1968), 9. From a description of "Scandinavian Folklore and Folk Culture in the Trans-Mississippi West" by Erik Wahlgren of Los Angeles, California. See "Planting on May Day," p. 191.

Beltane

April 30

The Celtic name for the first day of May, Beltane in Scotland was one of the quarter-days or term days when rents were due and debts were settled, along with Lammas (August 1), Hallowmas (November 1) and Candlemas (February 2). Among the Druids of Britain, Beltane divided the year in half and was observed by kindling hilltop "beltane fires" to honor the sun god. In Scotland two fires were built close together and cattle driven between them to ward off disease before putting them out to pasture for the new season. The fires were lit on May Day Eve in keeping with the belief that each day begins with the setting of the sun the night before.

A Beltane Fire

There are few, or no, examples of midsummer or Beltane fire festivals in the folklore of East Tennessee. However, it was recently reported by an informant who lives in Marion County that it was once customary for people in her neighborhood to pile up all brush and undergrowth cleared from new ground and to leave this in stacks until May Day Eve, at which time it was set on fire. May Day Eve was, of course, the date on which one of the more important of the fire-festivals was held, but my informant had never heard any explanation given for the custom.

Source and Comment

Tennessee Folklore Society Bulletin, III (February 1937), 7. Collected by Urban Anderson of Knoxville, Tennessee, as part of a study of survivals of "older beliefs," this one associated with the hilltop bonfires lit during the Druid festival of Beltane, which marked the beginning of summer. Cf. "Puerto Rican Fire Festival," p. 33; "Halloween Bonfires," p. 381; and "Fire and Water on St. John's Day," p. 250. Cf. "Persian New Year," p. 137.

May Day
May 1

A spring festival common in Europe and North America, May Day is celebrated by the gathering of knots, branches, and flowers on May Eve or early on May Day morning; by the crowning of a May Queen; by choral performances at daybreak; by dancing around a May bush, pole or tree; and by mumming from house to house carrying blossoms and soliciting gifts and food. The sports of May Day symbolize spring, relating human fertility to crop fertility and rebirth. Once it was common for young couples to pair up, often by lot, and "may together" in the woods all May Eve night. Similar celebrations occur on Whitsunday and Midsummer's Day. Such goings on, to say nothing of the phallic symbolism of the May Pole, horrified British Puritans. In his history of the Plymouth colony William Bradford reports that in 1628, when the nearby Anglican colony at Mount Merry "set up a maypole, drinking and dancing about it ... inviting Indian women for their consorts," the Pilgrim Fathers sent a military party to cut it down and punish the offenders. Since then in America maypole dancing has been, on the whole, a tame affair. In some countries, particularly Socialist countries, May Day is a labor festival honoring industrial and military might.

May Day at Bryn Mawr

In early 1900 a group of [Bryn Mawr College] students came to the door of Evangeline Walker Andrews of the class of '93, who lived on campus, and proposed some sort of outdoor entertainment that would raise money for a badly needed Students' Building. They left unable to decide on anything that held true to the spirit of Bryn Mawr, but as Mrs. Andrews saw the girls in their long skirts heading across the green to Pembroke and Merion, it occurred to her to hold an Elizabethan festival. Mrs. Andrews became the founder of the Alumnae Association, and her Elizabethan festival became May Day.

The first of Bryn Mawr's extravagant Elizabethan revelries, Grand May Day, was held in 1900, two months after the band of students decided they needed a building. Three years later exam-weary students instituted Little May Day, and for 36 years quadrennial Grand May Days and Little May Days gave Bryn Mawr its image. Today, 42 years later, Traditions Mistress Skye Brainard '79 is working to re-establish the tradition of Grand May Day.

"Grand May Day used to be so enormous that there's no way we can make it as good as it was," says Miss Brainard, and indeed the Grand May Day of yore was a festival of magnificent proportions. Work for each May Day started the summer before, and tumbling was taught all year in the gym in preparation for that one day. Designers came from New York to do the costumes. The programs were printed in Boston, and special trains ran from Pittsburgh and New York to bring spectators to the event. Extra sleeping cars were added to the trains from Boston and Chicago, which also made special stops at Bryn Mawr. "In the event of rain notices will be posted in the station before the departure of special trains," announcements in the major terminals read.

The day itself held so much that no one could possibly see all of it. The traditional breakfast was strawberries and cream, and chipped beef, which the seniors ate in Rockefeller, the dorm sacred to the May. (The Rockefellers gave a large part of the $256,000 finally collected after the first Grand May Day, and the dorm that served the May was named in their honor. In May Day chapel, 1915, M. Carey Thomas said, "Indeed, in a sense the tower of Rockefeller was planned so that the college students could follow the custom of Magdalen College, Oxford, and sing to the sun on the first of May.")

The pageant began at noon, with four oxen—not always white, though the horses often were—pulling the Maypole before a bewildering procession of Maypole dancers, Morris dancers, milkmaids, musicians, floats, players, "boys and girls, two by two, hand in hand," and the lucky one who was to be crowned Queen Elizabeth. The Nine Worthies—Hector, Alexander, David, Joshua, Judas Maccabeus, King Arthur, Charlemagne, and Godfrey de Bouillon—perpetrated various antics on donkeys; pickpockets sold wares and stole wares, auctioning them back to their owners at intervals. As many as five plays were produced every half-hour, from genuine Elizabethan works, mostly

Shakespeare and Ben Jonson, to the Masque of the Flowers, in which various flowingly-clad maidens fluttered around the Cloisters, to more down-to-earth dramas like "The Deanery Murder Case." Milkmaids, Morris dancers and chimney sweeps alternated dances every 15 minutes. Overwhelmed, the farmer who'd brought his oxen from Lancaster to pull the Maypole exclaimed, "Never again will I allow my oxen to see such a sight as this."

The events went on all day. Katharine Hepburn was the star of "The Woman in the Moon" in 1928 and Cornelia Otis Skinner was Queen Bess in 1933. In the gymnasium, banners flying from the battlements, lunch and dinner were catered by the Ritz-Carlton. Five hundred girls, the entire population of the College, danced around the Maypole. And the color to wear, of course, was white.

May Day isn't so grand any more—yet. In 1940, said Philadelphia's *Evening Bulletin,* "the shadows over Europe were spreading too darkly for a bright Elizabethan festival," and Grand May Day was abandoned. Interest dwindled in the 50s and 60s till even Little May Day could scarcely muster an ox. In 1954 classes resumed at noon, in 1955, at 10:00. Many of the hoops for the Senior Hoop Race were lost or disintegrating, and films of the old processions were destroyed in a fire in Taylor Hall.

The costumes,scripts, plans and pageants for May Day were not retrieved until last year and the clothes, in Radnor Attic, are still being cleaned and catalogued. The revival of Grand May Day is actually a practical measure as well as a festive one—instead of depleting the Student Government treasury it will swell it. Grand May Day will charge, as in the past, an admission fee, helping to maintain other traditions foundering for lack of funds. In 1900 Grand May Day cost $5000 to produce, in 1914 Bryn Mawr profited so much that $1000 of the proceeds was donated to the "Wellesley College Fire Loss Fund." Everything, down to the pick-pocket auctions, the Robin Hood plays, and the ballad-mongers, is steadily being revived: costumes, processions, dances; and competition is thick for the sewing machines. Skye Brainard is looking for some oxen and, once again, as always, the Haverfordians will be after the Maypole.

Source and Comment

Bryn Mawr News, April 1978, 6-8. Martha Bayless of Bryn Mawr College, Pennsylvania, gives an account of the origin, history, and prospects of the "traditional" May Day festivities at her institution for its alumnae magazine. She omits Julius Caesar from the Nine Worthies of late medieval literature.

Though it obviously did not emerge from the folk and its future seems to depend upon a "Traditions Mistress," nevertheless, genuine traditions of a folkloristic kind have grown up at Bryn Mawr such as the pattern of a "Grand May Day" every four years with "Little May Days" in between, the use of oxen, and the raid on the Maypoles by the male students from nearby Haverford College.

May Day at Bryn Mawr
Order of the Pageant and Revels

5:45 [Bryn Mawr] Sophomores fill May baskets for seniors and proceed to wake them with "The Hunt Is Up" written by King Henry VIII

6:30 Sophomores and Seniors have champagne together in the halls. Doughnuts will also be provided

7:00 Seniors gather in Goodhart and go on to wake Miss [President Mary Patterson] McPherson. Taylor bell rings until 7:05 to welcome in the May

7:15 Seniors sing the Magdalen Hymn to the Sun from Rockefeller Tower

7:30 Breakfast, including strawberries and cream. Classes eat together—freshman in Erdman—sophomores in Haffner—juniors in Denbigh—seniors in Rhoads

8:45 College Assembly in Goodhart. Chorale will sing and academic awards will be announced

9:30 Procession of heralds, dancers, casts of the plays, the band, the Nine Worthies, the President of the College and the May Queen, beginning at Rockefeller Arch and continuing from Pembroke Arch to Merion Greene and the Maypoles

10:00 Maypole dancing by the four classes and the graduate students The MAY QUEEN is crowned, Miss McPherson and the May Queen respond with humorous speeches and a gift is presented to the May Queen

10:30 Morris dancing on the Greene

11:00 Pembroke East presents Saint George and the Dragon on the steps of Thomas Great Hall A Circus of acrobats and tumblers in front of the gym

11:30– Picnic lunch on Merion Greene—Wandering minstrels, jugglers, fencers and divers entertainment
1:00

1:00 AS YOU LIKE IT, a most excellent play by William Shakespeare, in front of the balcony behind Goodhart, presented by ye Drama Clube Indian Dancing in Thomas Great Hall

1:30 Pembroke West presents THE LADY OF THE MAY in the Deanery Garden behind ye Canaday Library

2:00 Rockefeller presents THE SHOEMAKER'S HOLIDAY on Rockefeller Greene. An exhibition of artwork and Olde May Day pictures and material in the Great Hall

2:30 Barbershop Quartet performs in the Cloisters Senior Tree Planting. Seniors meet at Pembroke Arch: bring ribbons, coins and trinkets to hang on the tree

3:00 GODSPELL, ye moderne miracle play, on Radnor Greene by the students of Radnor Denbigh presents THE SECOND SHEPHERD'S PLAY on Denbigh Greene

3:30 ROBIN HOODE by Denbigh and divers players, in Robin Hood's Dell, behind Rhoads (Follow ye Merry Men)

4:00 Merion presents PYRAMUS AND THISBY from "A Midsummer Night's Dream" featuring a harpist and Miss McPherson's dog on the steps of Merion Archery exhibition and contest, the prize to be awarded by Maide Marian, as of olde. All are invited to enter. In front of gym.

4:40 The Second Annual May Day Croquet Match, Denbigh vs. Miss McPherson and the Deans on Denbigh Greene

5:30 Mediaeval banquet in all dining halls

7:00 Renaissance Choir concert in Thomas Great Hall

8:00 Last Step-Sing of the year on Taylor Steps

9:00 (Or as soon as Step-Sing ends) English dancing in the Great Hall.

All are invited and no experience is necessary The Bryn Mawr Film Series presents ROBIN HOOD with Errol Flynn. Physics Lecture Room, Science Building

GIVEN by the SCHOLLERS of BRYN MAWR COLLEGE
May 1, 1980

Source and Comment

A broadside for May Day, Bryn Mawr College, 1980. Supplied by Susan Davis, Office of Public Information, Bryn Mawr College, who, with Wilma Beaty Cox, provided background material.

The 1980 May Day at Bryn Mawr was a "little" May Day. It began at dawn, included a mounted procession (horses courtesy First Troop, Philadelphia City Cavalry) to the maypoles, and ended with a traditional "Step Sing," a songfest illuminated by the light of hundreds of the lanterns given to each new student on Lantern Night at the beginning of her first year. For Lantern Night, see p. 361.

* * *

Maypole Dance and Woman Power

Elizabethan pageantry and chivalry were the heralds of spring yesterday as Bryn Mawr College held its annual ... May Day celebration.

"I proclaimed, against all odds, that this would be a perfect day. And it is," said Mary Patterson McPherson, college president.

Spirits were high as students cavorted across the sun-splashed campus, many wearing the customary white dresses and May Day crowns of fresh flowers....

After the maypole dancing, the crowd of about 2,000 quieted to listen to McPherson make brief remarks.

About 100 women then took part in what organizer Deborah Rowan, a graduating student and wandering minstrel for the day, called the "mayhole dance." The antithetical event began in 1984, said alumna and participant Denise Tuggle, one of the founders.

The dancers' arms were bound to their bodies with tissue paper, symbolic of the bonds of oppression which they believe bind women, Tuggle said.

Rowan and fellow organizer Cheryl Kim freed one woman from her bonds to begin the 1990 dance. When all 100 women were free, the women shook a lavender parachute in the air, freeing a cascade of colorful flower petals.

"This is about women getting together and empowering themselves through sisterhood," Kim said.

Source

By Stella M. Eisele, special to the *Philadelphia Inquirer,* May 7, 1990.

* * *

Maypole Song

I saw in southern Georgia a number of ring-games which I believe are peculiar to the colored children of that region. One of the prettiest is "The May-Pole Song." One girl skips about inside the ring, and at the singing of the fourth line bows to the one she chooses. Then both "jump for joy," a peculiar step rather like a clog, which outsiders find very difficult to learn. Then the song is repeated, the second girl choosing; and so on.

All around the May-pole,
The May-pole, the May-pole,
All around the May-pole,
Now, Miss Sallie, won't you bow?
Now, Miss Sallie won't you jump for joy,
Jump for joy, jump for joy?
Now, Miss Sallie, won't you jump for joy?
Now, Miss Sallie, won't you bow?

Source

Journal of American Folklore, XXX (1917), 218. Collected by Loraine Darby.

* * *

Planting on May Day

It seems quite a step from the Dionysaic revels to relatively modern East Tennessee, but the experienced folklorist will not have to be convinced that in folklore remoteness is, more often than not, a rare thing. A survival of these ancient rites—or, again, if not a survival, at least a custom based on similar philosophy—existed in Tennessee only about sixty years ago [1877] near a little settlement, then called Phebe, on Powell's River, some twenty or thirty miles above the government dam at Norris. It has been reported to me by four or five informants who lived in the region, that at one time the farmers of the neighborhood thought it necessary in planting turnips to hang a long-necked gourd between their legs to symbolize the male organ of generation. They would march through the plowed fields sowing the seed and chanting as they went an admonition to the turnips-to-be to equal in size the gourds they wore—and employing an obscene term to designate the gourds which they actually identified with their own organs. Two walnuts were sometimes placed inside the gourd, adds one informant.

Apparently, the masculine element of sex was thought necessarily predominant in the planting of turnips. This may be inferred from the fact that a woman was thought completely incapable of having any success at all in raising turnips unless she wore an unusually large gourd-phallus.

And yet woman, because of her position with reference to birth and care of the child, is usually thought to be able to impart fertility to the field and orchard. It was partly due to this feeling that the Indian squaws were permitted to take care of the agricultural interests of the tribe, states Sir J. G. Fraser in *The Golden Bough*. This belief, too, is found at Phebe. Mrs. V. V. (I was asked to withhold the name) was once taken to task for having walked through a neighbor's field, whereat she replied with some heat, "Don't you know corn grows best where I walk?"

Cucumbers were supposed to grow much better when planted by women than when men planted them, and there is some reason for thinking that they were to be planted on May Day in a manner similar to that in which turnips were planted. You will remember that it was supposed to be very unusual for a woman to have luck in raising turnips. Perhaps, the very shape of the two vegetables may explain this belief.

In one community near Phebe, Blue Springs Hollow, it is said that when turnips were sown it was the custom to tie weights, such as bullets and nails, to the male organ before entering the field. My informant tells me it was believed that the more weights the sower could support the greater would be the crop of turnips. In this case, as well as that of the gourd-phallus, tremendous size and weight of the phallic symbol is sought in order that the crops will be quickened. We shall note below other instances of weights used in fertility rites.

The first day of May, Walpurgis Day,or Beltane, as it has been variously called, is ostensibly in recent conception, a date on which languishing young maidens may augur the coming of their princes charming, but its past history is at times unprintable. It was, of old, a vernal festival intended to promote the growth of vegetation and attended by such obscene rites as we have mentioned above in connection with the early history of the phallus. In the course of the ages, it has been purified by asceticism, Platonism and what-not, but just the same, survivals of the old pre-Christian beliefs cling with the tenacity that characterizes folklore in certain parts of the Old World.

In East Tennessee, there was a custom observed rather recently which seems to be a survival of the old spring festivals, although it is just as likely to deserve another interpretation. Many farmers thought it necessary when planting watermelons to go to the fields before sun-up on the morning of May Day, usually without speaking, and, after removing trousers, plant the watermelon seeds in shirt-tails. This may very conceivably be a vestige of an older and more obscene usage in which it was perhaps necessary that the male organ be uncovered. My mother tells me that farmers of yesteryear had a habit of doffing underclothes on May Day,and if we may legitimately add one usage to the other we may infer that removal of the trousers entailed appearance "in the nude" from waist down.

Source and Comment

Tennessee Folklore Society Bulletin, III (February 1937), 3-4. From an essay by Urban Anderson of Knoxville, Tennessee, which he titled, blandly, "A Comparative Study of Some of the Older Beliefs and Usages of East Tennessee." Cf. "To Grow Cabbage," p. 127. For an example from Missouri, see *Folklore in America,* 137-39; and *Journal of American Folklore* LXVI (1953), 333-37.

* * *

It Takes a Man to Plant Cucumbers

Most farmers believe that cucumbers should be planted "when the sign's in the arms," which means that the moon is in Gemini. But many old-timers think that the main thing is to get the seed covered before daylight on May 1, by a naked man in the prime of life. It is believed that the quality of a cucumber depends upon the virility of the planter. Cucumbers grown by women, children, or old men never amount to much. There are several vulgar jokes and stories about this. To say that a girl "ought to be raising cucumbers" means that she needs a vigorous young husband.

Source

Journal of American Folklore, LXVI (1953), 34. Reported by Vance Randolph from "people who live in the Ozark country" Missouri. Printed in *Folklore in America,* p. 139. Plant watermelons on May 1 before sunup. (The informant knew an old Negro Man in Union or Pontotoc County [Mississippi] who always did this even when May 1 was on Sunday. She herself said that the ground had not warmed up sufficiently for such things as melons and cucumbers until about this time.)

Source

Mississippi Folklore Register, I (1967), 29. Collected by Clara Moore Moody.

* * *

In Lehigh County, the first day of May was set apart for planting corn [by the Pennsylvania Dutch].

Source

Journal of American Folklore, I (1888), 130. Collected by W. J. Hoffman.

Barefoot Day

The first day of May is the time to go barefooted. (The informant's mother said regardless of the weather, they always waited for that date).

Source

Mississippi Folklore Register, I (1967), 27. Reported by Clara Moore Moody as a Mississippi "folk belief." Her informant was her mother, Mrs. J. D. Moore. Known from childhood in South Carolina in the 1920s by H.C. cf. "Barefoot Day for Freshmen," p. 141.

* * *

Bees and May 1

There is a certain day of the year, either the 22nd [sic] of February or the 1st of May, when, if you want your bees to stay near home when they swarm, you must not leave the house alone.

Move your bees on the first of May.

Source

Memoirs of the American Folklore Society, XVIII (1925), 120. "Folk-Lore from Maryland," collected by Annie W. Whitney and Caroline C. Bullock. Data on informants incomplete. The date, February 22, should surely be February 2. Cf. "Candlemas or Groundhog Day," p. 65.

* * *

To Remove Freckles on May Day

On the first day of May before the sun is up, go out and wash your face with dew and then place your hands somewhere else on your body. The freckles will leave your face and go to the place on your body that you placed your hands.

Source

Kentucky Folklore Record, X (1964), 17. Collected by Betty Craft of Morehead, Kentucky, from Mrs. Dot Mack of Frenchburg, Kentucky.

* * *

If you wash your face on the first of May in stump water, your freckles will go away.

The first day of May, go to the rye field, and as soon as the sun strikes the rye, rub your face in the rye three times and your freckles will leave.

Source

Memoirs of the American Folklore Society, XVIII (1925), 120. From "Folk-Lore from Maryland," collected by Annie W. Whitney and Caroline C. Bullock, who did not give informants.

To Cure Thrush on May Day

A child may be cured of the thrush [sore throat] by holding it up on May morning so that a ray of light from a crack may enter its mouth.

Source

Journal of American Folklore, II (1889), 98. From "Folklore of the Carolina Mountains, " collected by James Mooney. Informant not given.

* * *

May Day Predictions

Death

Everyone of the Negro race looks forward to May Day, May first. This is the day on which you can tell what will happen to you for the rest of the year.

At exactly twelve o'clock on the first day of May, they (I have actually seen this happen [in Tennessee]) go to a big well, take a mirror and reflect the rays of the sun down into the water. The well must be big, so you can guide the rays to the water. You can see an object on the water that tells or suggests what is going to happen to you. If you see a coffin, you are surely going to die before the year is over. If you see a carriage, it suggests a hearse, and you will surely ride in one before the year is finished.

Source

Tennessee Folklore Society Bulletin, XIX (September 1953), 61. Reported by Ewing Jackson of Henry County, Tennessee, in 1948 when he was a student at Murray State College, Kentucky. He states: "This county has a large number of Negroes . . . I played with Negroes on our farm all my life."

* * *

Marriage

If a young girl will pluck a white dogwood blossom and wear it in her bosom on May morning, the first man met wearing a white hat will have the Christian name of her future husband. Her handkerchief left out on the grass the previous eve will have his name written upon it in the morning, and from analogous beliefs in Ireland and elsewhere it is presumable that the writing is done by a snail crawling over it. If she will take a looking-glass to the spring on May morning, and, turning her back to the spring, look into the mirror, she will see the figure of her lover rise out of the water behind her.

Source

Journal of American Folklore, II (1889), 98. From "Folklore of the Carolina Mountains," collected by James Mooney. Informants not given.

If you take a mirror on the first day of May and hold it over a well, you will see your future husband reflected in the mirror.

If you find a snail real early on the first day of May and lay it on a board, it will make your future husband's initials when it crawls.

Source

Kentucky Folklore Record, X (1964), 13. Collected by Betty Craft of Morehead, Kentucky: the first from Mrs. Mazella Rhodes and the second from Mrs. Dot Mack, both of Frenchburg, Kentucky.

* * *

On the last day of April put a handkerchief where dew will form on it. Get up early and you will find the initial of your future mate on it.

On the night before May 1 a girl should place a snail on a plate of meal under her bed. The initial of her future mate will be on the plate.

On May 1 at 12:00 o'clock hold a mirror over a well to see your future mate.

On the morning of May 1 look out of the window and count the number of live things you can see. That will be the number of years before you marry.

On May 1 look for birds' nests. The number of eggs you find will be the number of years you will be single.

Source

Journal of American Folklore, LXIII (1950), 314-15. Collected by Lelah Allison in the "Wabash region of southeastern Illinois." Informants not given.

* * *

Get up on the first morning of May and before speaking to any one, look out of the window. The number of chickens you see will represent the number of years before you marry.

On the first morning of May a girl should rise without speaking and turn around under a cedar tree three times and listen for noises. If she hears singing, she will be happily married. If she hears knocking, it is the driving of nails in her coffin and she will die before she marries. If she hears no sound at all, she will never marry.

If a handkerchief has been left outside over night before the first day of May, the next morning the initials of your future mate will be written on the handkerchief.

If you walk around a wheat field on the first day of May, you will meet your mate.

If on the first day of May at sunrise, you look into an open well, you will see the reflection of your future husband or wife.

On the first morning in May, place a glass of water in the sun at sunrise and let it remain all day. At sunset, look into the water. If you are to die an old maid or bachelor, a coffin will appear in the water.

Source and Comment

Southern Folklore Quarterly, II (1938), 165-74. Collected by T. J. Farr from " the Cumberland section of middle Tennessee." Informants not given. For more marriage predictions, see " New Year's Beliefs," p.20; " St. John's Day and the Summer Solstice," p. 249; "To See Your Future Husband on Halloween," p. 379; and "St. Andrew's Eve," p. 395.

* * *

Fishing

Also, you must go fishing on May Day. The fish will bite almost a bare hook. This is the day to get your biggest catch. All the Negroes and most of the whites go fishing on May Day. It is believed that if you get a good catch on this day, you will catch fish every day in May and fishing will not be too bad every first day of the month through the year. If you do not catch any fish on May Day, do not go fishing any more that year. You are just wasting your time—unless you love fishing.

Source

Tennessee Folklore Society Bulletin, XIX (September 1953), 61. Collected by Ewing Jackson of Henry County, Tennessee, in 1948 when he was a student at Murray State College, Kentucky.

* * *

May Day Maybe Rhyme

I collected the following folk item pertaining to the first day of May from a resident of Cedar Creek Community, Perry County, Tennessee [who] stated that formerly girls were supposed to receive a Maybe Day Letter on the first day of May from boy friends. She dictated from memory one of the letters she received around 1900:

> Grape vine wrap
> Pine top fillin'
> Me and you'll marry
> If pap and mam's willin'
> Maybe we will
> Maybe we won't
> Maybe we can't
> Maybe we'll have a home
> Maybe we won't
> Maybe we'll have children
>
> Maybe we won't
> Maybe I'll make a home
> Maybe I won't.

My informant could not remember more lines than those given above. I was told, however, that a "maybe" was a "great long letter, all lines except the first ones beginning with 'maybe.' "

Source

Tennessee Folklore Society Bulletin, Murfreesboro, Tennessee, 1955-56, XXI, 105. Collected by Kelsie B. Harder, who does not specify the name of the informant or the date of the interview. Printed in *Folklore from the Working Folk of America,* 180-81.

* * *

May Day Maybe Letter

Maybe letters were written for May 1 [and] were given or sent to the person you liked best. Sue McDonald furnished the following example obtained from her parents:

> Maybe we'll date and maybe we won't.
> Maybe we'll go steady and maybe we won't.
> Maybe we'll marry and maybe we won't.
> Maybe we'll be happy and maybe we won't.
> Maybe we'll have quarrels and maybe we won't.
> Maybe we'll love each other and maybe we won't.
> Maybe we'll have children and maybe we won't.
> Maybe we'll get together sometimes and maybe we won't.
> Maybe we'll meet in Heaven and maybe we won't.

Source

"Folklore in White County, Tennessee," Ph.D. Dissertation, George Peabody College for Teachers, 1969, 194. Collected in 1967-68 by Edwina B. Doran. Her informants were residents or former residents of White County and included public school students.

* * *

May Morning Love Charms

The sparseness of population and the roughness of the country [western North Carolina] prevent frequent gatherings for social enjoyment, and the result is seen in the scarcity of holiday customs and observances. The few which survive from earlier days are mainly love charms pertaining to May morning....

If a young girl will pluck a white dogwood blossom and wear it in her bosom on May morning, the first man met wearing a white hat will have the Christian name of her future husband. Her handkerchief left out on the grass the previous eve will have his name written upon it in the morning, and from analogous beliefs in Ireland and elsewhere it is presumable that the writing is done by a snail crawling over it. If she will take a looking-glass to the spring on May morning, and, turning her back to the spring, look into the mirror, she will see the figure of her lover rise out of the water behind her. A child may be cured of the thrush by holding it up on May morning so that a ray of light from a crack may enter its mouth....

The girls have a number of love charms in addition to those already mentioned, most of them being practiced also in Europe on Hallow Eve, a celebration which appears to have dropped out from the mountain calendar. If an egg, placed in front of the fire by a young woman, be seen to *sweat blood,* it is a sign that she will succeed in winning the sweetheart she desires. By giving to a number of mistletoe leaves the names of her several suitors, and ranging them in line before the fire, she can test the affection of each sweetheart. The leaf which the heat causes to pop over nearest to where she is standing will indicate which lover is most sincere in his professions, and in the same way will be shown the relative ardor of the others. If a girl will take out the yolk from a hard-boiled egg, fill the cavity with salt, then eat the egg and go to bed, her destined husband will appear in the night and offer her a drink. Another way is to eat a mixture of a thimbleful of meal and another of salt, and then, being careful always to observe a strict silence, walk backwards to bed with the hands clasped behind the back, take off the clothing backwards, and get into bed. The apparition of the future husband will come as before and give her a drink of water.

Liverwort is known by the appropriate name of "heart leaf," and the peculiar shape of its leaves has suggested their use as a love philter. A girl can infallibly win the love of any sweetheart she may desire by secretly throwing over his clothing some of the powder made by rubbing together a few heart leaves which have been dried before the fire. She may, if she wish, have a score of lovers by simply carrying the leaves in her bosom. It is to be presumed that the recipe would be equally efficacious if used by one of the opposite sex.

Source

Journal of American Folklore, II (1889), 98-9. Collected by James Mooney from mountaineers in western North Carolina who were farmers. The name of the informant, the place of collection, and the date are not given. Printed in *Folklore from the Working Folk of America,* 179-80.

* * *

St. Tamina's Day

In and around Annapolis [May Day] was long known as St. Tamina's Day, for it was the date set apart by the St. Tamina Society to celebrate the memory of the ancient Delaware Chief, Taminend, "whose equal was never known." Both Pennsylvania and Maryland selected this day on which to honor the Chief. In the Journal of a southern girl visiting in Philadelphia, is the following item under date of May 1, 1771.

"This morning was ushered in by the ringing of bells in memory of King Tammany as he used to be called; but now I think they have got him canonized, for he is now celebrated as St. Tammany."

[William] Eddis, in his *Letters [from America]* writing from Annapolis, in 1771 says,

"The Americans on this part of the continent have likewise a saint whose history is lost in fable and uncertainty. The first of May is however set apart to the memory of St. Tamina, on which occasion the natives wear a piece of buck's tail, etc." The St. Tamina Society seems to have been founded first in Maryland and to have been in existence there until 1841. In Pennsylvania it practically died out during the revolution, with spasmodic resurrections from time to time afterwards.

Why Taminend should have been honored first in Maryland, it is difficult to say, for he is associated with the people of Pennsylvania, and is said to have been under the elm tree with William Penn. His signature to a deed giving property to the latter is still in existence and is "a snake not tightly coiled."

Various legends are told of this great "chief of many days"; he had a hand-to-hand encounter with the devil; had personal intercourse with good spirits; performed miracles, and when his time came to die, set fire to his wigwam, but being too pure and good to perish in the flames, was translated.

The May pole was a feature in the celebration of St. Tamina's Day in Annapolis. It was erected in a public place and garlanded with flowers, the members of the St. Tamina Society forming a ring round it, danced the Indian war dance "with many other customs which they had seen exhibited by the children of the forest." All citizens who chose to take part in this wore a piece of buck's tail in their hats. There was an evening entertainment to which general invitations were issued. In the midst of the dancing, the members of the Society, dressed like Indians, rushed into the assembly with a war whoop which was followed by war songs and dances of the Indians.

Before the evening was over, a collection was taken up.

The celebration of the day in Philadelphia differed from this, a wigwam outside the city taking the place of the May pole. To the Indian dances and war songs, was added the calumet of peace.

Source and Comment

Memoirs of the American Folklore Society, XVIII (1925), 119-20. "Folk-Lore from Maryland," collected by Annie W. Whitney and Caroline C. Bullock. Data on sources incomplete.

Taminend, a Delaware Indian chief who figures in American legend and literature, is said to have befriended William Penn with whom he signed a treaty. During the pre-Revolutionary strife, groups of American patriots took the name "St. Tammany" to ridicule and counter the traditional British patriotic societies honoring St. George and St. Andrew and celebrating their days. They adopted what their members believed to be Indian titles, rites and ceremonies. Tammany Societies, notably in New York, have lingered on as political clubs of a Jeffersonian, and later Jacksonian, persuasion.

Cross Day

May 3

St. Helena, mother of Constantine the Great, undertook a pilgrimage to Jerusalem, visiting shrines and founding churches. She is said to have found three crosses near the site of the Holy Sepulcher buried beneath the debris of heathen temples, one of which, by its miraculous healing properties, was proved the True Cross. In Armenian churches today, it is customary to bury or place a cross beneath an evergreen spray. After this ceremony, worshipers may carry home a twig as a blessing. The festival is known in the Western Church as the Invention (finding) of the Cross and sometimes as St. Cross Day. Cf. "Recovery of the Cross," p. 337; a Greek Orthodox celebration.

Santacruzan

[Filipino community organizations in California] participate in the social events of the larger American community, like the July Fourth parade in Stockton and Seaside, where Filipinos are represented with a float. The social clubs also host cultural revivals, like the May festival in honor of the Blessed Virgin (*Santacruzan*), which is held with a queen contest (the winner becomes *Reyna Elena* or St. [Queen] Helena who went in search of the Holy Cross).... The main feature of the celebration is the religious procession during which the *Reyna Elena,* escorted by her son Constantino (Constantine) marches to the accompaniment of a band, followed by her "court" of ladies known as "*sagalas*" and their escorts. All the participants wear Filipino costumes. In California, the *Santacruzan* takes place in a large indoor dance hall instead of the town or village streets as in the Philippines.

Source and Comment

"Folkloric Communication among Filipinos in California," Ph.D. Dissertation, University of Pennsylvania, 1973, 29. Hermenia Q. Menez, in her dissertation, "used an immigrant ethnic group ... to show how a change in the social situation affects folkloric performance." Her fieldwork took place "in the Filipino communities in Delano, Kern County and in Monterey County, California" in 1969 and 1970. She is a native of the Philippines and speaks Aklan, Ilongo and Tagalog.

The Story of Cross Day

The [Armenian] story of the Cross Day is told as follows: The cross on which Christ was crucified was left on Mount Calvary, where in time it became covered up with dirt and rubbish. A queen who desired to rescue it from eternal entombment came to Calvary in search of it. She threw money on the ground, and the people scrambled to pick it up. This action she performed over and over again, looking each time that the people arose from their scrambling to see if the cross was in sight. After a while, together with the money, there had been picked away so much dirt, that the cross came to view. The day upon which it was found was called "Cross Day." Henceforth, the anniversary of that day has been observed. Religious services are held in the church, and ceremonies are performed. The crosses which are in the church are removed from their places and put in water, where they remain for three days. After this they are taken out and restored to their former positions.

Source and Comment

Journal of American Folklore, XII (1899), 105-06. Collected by G. D. Edwards in Boston, Massachusetts, from an unnamed informant of Armenian origin as an example "of the folklore of Armenians in America."

Cinco De Mayo

May 5

The Fifth of May is the day on which the Mexicans and Mexican-Americans commemorate the defeat of the French by General Ignacio Zaragoza at the Battle of Pueblo in 1862. His defense of this city was an important blow to Napoleon III's attempt to establish a permanent French colony in Central America and led toward their eventual expulsion from Mexico by Benito Juarez five years later. It is a national holiday second in importance only to September 16, Independence Day. Even as early as 1863, the day was celebrated by Mexicans living in American cities such as San Francisco, and it has been considered "*la gloriosa fecha*" (the glorious date) in the Bay Area ever since.

In San Francisco, *Cinco de Mayo* has developed into a festival to perpetuate Mexican nationalism in a foreign land. The language of the associated events (the pageants, speeches, songs, parades) is Spanish, and while the American flag is flown alongside the Mexican flag and while both national anthems may be sung, the celebration is thoroughly Mexican.

For Chicanos today, *Cinco de Mayo* is symbolic of a bold stand against outside forces, against oppression, and against interventions into their lives by the United States and its culture. The celebrations stress such terms as "*La Raza*"; (the Race); the "Mestizo Nation"; "Bronze Culture"; and the homeland of Aztlán (a mythical Aztec domain covering northern Mexico and the southwestern United States). Recently, and perhaps surprisingly, other Latin groups such as Puerto Ricans and Nicaraguans have joined with the Chicanos in celebrating *Cinco de Mayo*. Still, the Chicanos jealously believe that the Fifth of May is their day, and, though joining with other Hispanic peoples when Latin-Americans feel threatened by the host culture, they resent intrusions on their celebrations.

Cinco de Mayo: The Celebration in Aztlán

To be clearly understood, the Chicano celebration of "Cinco de Mayo" must be viewed in the context of a struggle for social justice.

In the last decade, the Chicano movement has shattered the false mirror that was blinding the Chicanos' clear vision into his soul. The term Mexican American died and was replaced by Chicano. The solitude was broken. The Chicano was born from the suffering of the people that had come before. As he looked into his own mirror, he began to retrace the footprints left on the road that his ancestors had traversed. La Raza students have made "Cinco de Mayo" a very important celebration in all the schools. Chicano celebrations of "Cinco de Mayo" have been culturally heavily adorned experiences accompanied by mariachi music and speeches relating the important lessons of the French Intervention. The Chicano yell, "Viva La Raza!" is very significant in that it affirms his faith in the people. The Chicano finds his face in his heritage. He does not deny the past but embraces it. He utilizes these celebrations like a shield to guard against the forces that would erase his roots. The celebration communicates this message to the hearts of La Raza: "We know where we come from. We know where we are going."

In 1969, Chicanos proclaimed "El Plan Espiritual de Aztlán" in all Cinco de Mayo celebrations. The following is the original text of this important document:

> In the spirit of a new people that is conscious not only of its proud historical heritage, but also of the brutal gringo invasion of our territories—we the Chicano inhabitants and civilizers of the northern land of Aztlán, from whence came our forefathers, reclaiming the land of their birth and consecrating the determination of our people of the sun—declare that the call of our blood is our power, our responsibility and our inevitable destiny.

We are free and sovereign to determine those tasks which are justly called for by our house, our land, the sweat of our brows and our hearts. Aztlán belongs to those that plant the seeds, water the fields and gather the crops—and not to the foreign Europeans. We do not recognize capricious frontiers on the Bronze Continent.

Brotherhood unites us, and love for our brothers makes us a people whose time has come, and who struggles against the foreigner gabacho who exploits our riches and destroys our culture. With our heart in our hands and our hands in the soil, we declare the independence of our Mestizo Nation. We are a Bronze People with a Bronze Culture. Before the world, before all of North America, before all our brothers in the Bronze Continent—we are a Nation, we are a Union of Free Pueblos, we are

Aztlán.

Por la Raza Todo—Fuera de la Raza Nada

(All for the Race—Without the Race Nothing).

The Chicanos have added a new dimension to their celebration of this Mexican holiday. Chicano theatre does not reenact the Battle of Puebla on Cinco de Mayo but rather places on stage all of the contradictions of the cultural life of La Raza in its struggle for survival within the political boundaries of the United States. The theatres have demonstrated a strong inclination to present the lives and struggles of the Indigenous Gods. A return to our religious roots to become strong in our struggle is the Chicano's celebration of Cinco de Mayo. This new perspective signifies a return to our past to understand our present to determine our future.

Source

Cinco de Mayo, a booklet printed by the Oakland, California, Unified School District, Educational Department Services, Office of Communications, n.d., 26-7. The material was obtained through Ilene Linssen, Program Manager, Office of Bilingual Education in November, 1988.

* * *

Cinco de Mayo

Children's Pageant for *Cinco de Mayo*

En esta presentación participarán sólo niños. Un niño o una niña empezará la narración explicando el significado de esta fecha.

PARTE I

NARRADOR: BUENAS NOCHES QUERIDO PÚBLICO. ES PARA MÍ UN PLACER DARLES LA BIENVENIDA A ÉSTA, SU ESCUELA. ANTES DE EMPEZAR LA NARRACIÓN ACERCA DE LO QUE ACONTECIÓ EN ESTA FECHA, 5 DE MAYO, VAMOS A RENDIR HOMENAJE A NUESTRA BANDERA Y A NUESTRA NACIÓN. SALUDEMOS A LA BANDERA DE LOS EE.UU.. Y LUEGO CANTAREMOS EL HIMNO NACIONAL EN INGLÉS.

El público participa en saludar la bandera americana y luego cantan el himno nacional.

PARTE II

NARRADOR: OTRA BANDERA, BAJO LA CUAL UN TIEMPO ESTUVIMOS, ES AÚN DIGNA DE NUESTRO HOMENAJE YA QUE ES ELLA LA QUE NOS GUARDA EL TESORO DE NUESTRA HERENCIA. UN NIÑO DECLAMARÁ LA POESÍA "HOMENAJE A TI, BANDERA MEXICANA," ESCRITA POR LA SRA. VALENTINA ESCAMILLA.

NIÑO: MUCHAS GRACIAS. ES UN GRAN HONOR QUE ME HAYAN ESCOGIDO MARA RENDIR HOMENAJE A LA BANDERA MEXICANA.

HOMENAJE A TI, BANDERA MEXICANA EN ESTA FECHA TAN GRANDE VENGO HASTA TI, BANDERA MEXICANA A RENDIRTE HOMENAJE EN ESTA TIERRA AMERICANA.

PARTE III

NARRADOR: AHORA SE PRESENTARÁ UN GRUPO DE NIÑOS CANTANDO UNA ESTROFA DEL HIMNO NACIONAL MEXICANO. VAMOS A PONERNOS DE PIE.

LOS NIÑOS CANTAN: MEXICANOS AL GRITO DE GUERRA AL ACERO APRESTAD EL BRIDÓN Y RETIEMBLA EN SU CENTRO LA TIERRA AL SONORO RUGIR DEL CAÑÓN.

CIÑA, ¡OH PATRIA! TUS CIENES DE OLIVA DE LA PAZ EL ARCÁNGEL DIVINO QUE EN EL CIELO TU ETERNO DESTINO POR EL DEDO DE DIOS SE ESCRIBIÓ.

PARTE IV

NARRADOR: EL DÍA 5 DE MAYO DE 1862 ES UNA FECHA DE GLORIA. EN ESE DÍA LAS FUERZAS MEXICANAS, AL MANDO DEL GENERAL IGNACIO ZARAGOZA, DERROTARON A LOS INVASORES FRANCESES, APODADOS LOS SOLDADOS NÚMERO 1 DEL MUNDO. HABIENDO OCURRIDO LA BATALLA DEL 5 DE MAYO EN PUEBLA, ESTADO DE MÉXICO, Y SIENDO EL VESTIDO DE CHINA POBLANA EL

VESTIDO REGIONAL DE ESTE ESTA-
DO, UN GRUPO DE NIÑOS PRESEN-
TRÁ EL BAILABLE "EL JARABE TA-
PATÍO."

PARTE V

NARRADOR: EN MEMORIA DEL GENERAL IGNA-
CIO ZARAGOZA, A QUIEN ESTA VIC-
TORIA SE LE ATRIBUYE, PRESEN-
TAREMOS A UN NIÑO QUIEN LES
RECITARÁ UN VERSO.

NIÑO:

A DON IGNACIO ZARAGOZA

DEJASTE PARA TU PATRIA TU NOMBRE
CUBIERTO DE GLORIA QUE TE HA HECHO
INMORTAL PARA SIEMPRE EN LA
HISTORIA.

PARTE VI

NARRADOR: PARA NOSOTROS ES UN ORGULLO
QUE UN HÉROE TAN GRANDE
HAYA NACIDO AQUÍ EN NUESTRA
TIERRA. UN NIÑO NOS DIRÁ UNAS
PALABRAS QUE NOS LLENARAN DE
ORGULLO DE SER TEJANOS.

NIÑO:

A DON IGNACIO ZARAGOZA

ES ORGULLO DE LOS TEJANOS QUE
HAYAS NACIDO EN GOLIAD Y
DEFENDISTE A LOS MEXICANOS PARA
DARLES SU LIBERTAD.

PARTE VII

NARRADOR: DON IGNACIO ZARAGOZA EN LA
CARTA DIRIGIDA AL MINISTRO DE
GUERRA NOS PRESENTA UN RESU-
MEN DE LOS ACONTECIMIENTOS
DE ESTA GRAN BATALLA. ES PARA
LOS NIÑOS UN HONOR TENER LA
OPORTUNIDAD DE LEER LAS PALA-
BRAS DE ESTE ILUSTRE HOMBRE A
UDS., UN PÚBLICO QUE SIN DUDA
SE ENORGULLENCE EN ESTA FE-
CHA. UN GRUPO DE NIÑOS SIMU-
LARÁ LOS ACONTECIMIENTOS.

NARRADOR: DESPUÉS
DEL MOVIMIENTO QUE EMPRENDÍ
DESDE LAS CUMBRES DE ACULT-
ZINGO, LLEGUÉ A PUEBLA EL DÍA 3
DEL PRESENTE; . . . .

*Mientras que ésto se está leyendo, un niño, haciendo el papel
de Don Ignacio Zaragoza, llega a un pueblo (el foro vestido
para esto) y se ve como perdido.*

NARRADOR: . . . AL AMANECER DEL DÍA 4 OR-
DENÉ AL GENERAL NEGRETE QUE
OCUPARA LOS CERROS DE LORETO
Y GUADALUPE.

*Llega con un grupo de niños al otro lado y se da a saber por medio
de luces que ha amanecido. De repente se oye una voz que dice:*

NIÑO 1: ¡GENERAL NEGRETE!
¡GENERAL NEGRETE!

NIÑO 2: A SUS ÓRDENES, MI GENERAL.

NIÑO 1: HAY QUE OCUPAR LOS CERROS DE
LORETO Y GUADALUPE.

TODOS GRITAN: ARRIBA ZARAGOZA,
ARRIBA NEGRETE,
ARRIBA LORETO Y
GUADALUPE.

NARRADOR:
. . . A LAS CINCO DE LA MAÑANA
DEL DÍA 5, LAS FUERZAS MARCHA-
BAN A LA LÍNEA DE BATALLA.

*Se ven columnas de niños marchando y en el fondo se oyen
los clarines.*

NARRADOR: . . . A LAS DIEZ DE LA MAÑANA SE
AVISTÓ EL ENEMIGO, Y DESPREN-
DIÓ SUS COLUMNAS DE ATAQUE,
UNA HACIA EL CERRO DE GUADAL-
UPE, Y OTRA PEQUEÑA AMAGAN-
DO NUESTRO FRENTE.

SE VEN LOS CERROS Y AMBOS LADOS
AVANZANDO. EL ENEMIGO, LOS
FRANCESES, EMPIEZAN EL ATAQUE HACIA
EL CERRO DONDE ESTÁ LA GENTE DE
ZARAGOZA Y OTRA HACIA OTRO GRUPO
DE SOLDADOS DE ZARAGOZA.

SE VEN AMBAS FUERZAS EN BATALLA
FEROZ. CON EFECTOS DE LUZ SE VE QUE
OSCURENCE Y YA AL ATARDECER SE
PARA EL FUEGO. LOS MEXICANOS
EMPIEZAN A LEVANTAR Y CURAR LOS
HERIDOS.

AMBAS FUERZAS BELIGERANTES
ESTUVIERON A LA VISTA HASTA LAS SIETE
DE LA NOCHE. LA NOCHE SE PASÓ EN
LEVANTAR EL CAMPO, DEL CUAL SE
RECOGIERON MUCHOS MUERTOS Y
HERIDOS DEL ENEMIGO QUE PASARON DE
MIL HOMBRES.

LAS ARMAS NACIONALES SE HAN
CUBIERTO DE GLORIA Y POR ELLO
FELICITO AL PRI- MER MAGISTRADO DE
LA REPUBLICA. PUEDE AFIRMAR CON
ORGULLO QUE EL EJERCITO MEXICANO
NI UN SÓLO MOMENTO VOLVIÓ LA
ESPALDA AL ENEMIGO DURANTE LA
LARGA LUCHA QUE SOSTUVO.

*TODOS LOS MEXICANOS MARCHAN
EN DESFILE Y EN EL FONDO SE OYE EL
HIMNO NACIONAL MEXICANO.*

PARTE VIII

En coro, un grupo de niños del primer año cantan "Soy Puro Mexicano."

"SOY PURO MEXICANO"

SOY PURO MEXICANO
NACIDO EN ESTE SUELO
EN ESTA HERMOSA TIERRA
QUE ES MI LINDA NACIÓN

MI MÉXICO QUERIDO
QUE LINDA ES LA BANDERA
SI ALGUNO LA MANCILLA
LE PARTO EL CORAZÓN
TODOS: ¡VIVA MÉXICO!
　　　　¡VIVA!
　　　　¡VIVA AMÉRICA!
TODOS: ¡VIVA!
　　　　OH SUELO BENDITO DE DIOS
　　　　¡VIVA MÉXICO!
TODOS: ¡VIVA!
　　　　¡VIVA AMÉRICA!

MI SANGRE POR TI DARÉ YO
SOY PURO MEXICANO
Y NUNCA ME HE RAJADO
SI QUIEREN INFORMARSE
LA HISTORIA LES DIRÁ

QUE MÉXICO ES VALIENTE
QUE NUNCA SE HA RAJADO
VIVA LA DEMOCRACIA
Y TAMBIÉN LA LIBERTAD
TODOS: ¡VIVA!

　　　¡VIVA MÉXICO!
TODOS: ¡VIVA!
　　　OH SUELO BENDITO DE DIOS
　　　¡VIVA MÉXICO!
TODOS: ¡VIVA!
　　　　¡VIVA AMÉRICA!
TODOS: ¡VIVA! MI SANGRE POR TI DARÉ YO.

* * *

Children's Pageant for *Cinco de Mayo*

Only children participate in this play. A little boy and a little girl begin the narration by explaining the significance of this date.

Part I

Narrator　Good evening, dear people. It is my pleasure to offer a welcome to this your school. Before beginning the story of what occurred on this date, the Fifth of May, let us pay homage to our flag and to our nation. Let us salute the flag of the United States and then we will sing the national anthem.
The audience take part in the saluting of the American flag and then sing the national anthem.

Part II

Second Narrator:　Another flag, under which we once lived, is also worthy of our homage, since it is this [flag] which preserves for us the treasure of our heritage. A child will recite the poem "Homage to Thee, Mexican Flag", written by Señora Valentina Escamilla.

Child:　Many thanks. It is a great honor that I have been chosen to pay homage to the Mexican Flag.

Homage to thee, Mexican flag.
On this date of such importance
I come to thee, Mexican flag,
To pay thee homage
In this American land.

Part III

Second Narrator:　Now a group of children will sing a stanza of the national anthem of Mexico. Let us rise.
The children sing.

Mexicans, at the cry of war
The horseman seizes his sword
And the earth is made to tremble to its core
With the sonorous roar of the cannon
Oh fatherland, the divine archangel
Crown thy temples with the olive branch of peace
That your eternal destiny will be written
In the sky by the hand of God.

Part IV

Second Narrator:　The day—May 5, 1862—is a glorious date. On this day the Mexican forces, under the command of General Ignacio Zaragoza, defeated the French invaders, said to be the best soldiers in the world. Because the battle of the Fifth of May took place at Puebla, Mexico and "china poblana" being the regional garb of this area, a group of children will present the dance, *"El Jarabe Tapatio." The children dance.*

Part V

Second Narrator:　In memory of General Ignacio Zaragoza, to whom this victory is attributed, let us listen to a child who will recite a verse.

Child:　To Don Ignacio Zaragoza

You left, for your fatherland,
Your name covered with glory
Which has made you immortal
For always in history.

Part VI

Second Narrator:　For us, it is a matter of pride that so great a hero was born here in our country. A child will recite for us some words which will make us proud of being Texans.

To Don Ignacio Zaragoza

It is a matter of pride for Texans
That you were born in Goliad [Texas]
And defended the Mexicans
In order to give them their freedom.

Part VII

Second Narrator: Don Ignacio Zaragoza, in the letter to the Minister of War, presents a summary of the events in this great battle. It is an honor for children to have the opportunity to read the words of this illustrious man to you, an audience no doubt filled with pride on this holiday. A group of children will enact the events.

Narrator: After the troop movement which I began from the heights of Acultzingo, I arrived at Puebla on the third....
While this is being read, a child, playing the part of Don Ignacio Zaragoza, arrives at a town (the back of the stage decorated for this) and appears to be lost.

Narrator: ...At dawn on the fourth I ordered General Negrete to occupy the hills of Loreto and Guadelupe.

He arrives with a group of children on the other side, and it is clear from the stage-lights that it is dawn. Suddenly, a voice says:

Child 1: General Negrete, General Negrete.

Child 2: At your command, my General.

Child 1: We must occupy the hills of Loreto and Guadelupe.

All cry out: That's the way, Zaragoza,

Arriba, Negrete,
Arriba Loreto and Guadelupe.

Narrator: ...At five o'clock on the morning of the fifth, the forces were marching in battle formation.

Columns of children are seen marching and in the background trumpets are heard.

Narrator: ...At ten o'clock in the morning the enemy are seen and their columns are dispersed for attack, one towards the hill of Guadelupe and the other, small, threatening our front.

One sees the hills and both sides advancing. The enemy, the French, undertake the attack towards the hill where the troops of Zaragoza are, and a second [French force moves] towards another group of Zaragoza's soldiers.

One sees both forces involved in a ferocious battle. The stage-lighting shows that it is getting dark, and then at dusk the firing ceases. The Mexicans begin to collect and to care for the wounded.

Both combating forces are visible until seven at night. The night is passed in abandoning the battlefield, from which many dead and wounded of the enemy are gathered, numbering more than one thousand men.

The national forces have been covered with glory and for this have been congratulated by the leader of the Republic. One can affirm with pride that the Mexican army never for one moment turned its backs to the enemy during the long struggle.

All the Mexicans march in single file and in the background the Mexican national anthem is heard.

Part VIII

In chorus, a group of children from the first grade sing: "I am a true Mexican."

I am True Mexican

I am true Mexican
Born on this soil
In this beautiful land
Which is my lovely country.

My beloved Mexico
How beautiful is the flag.
If anyone dishonors it
It would break my heart.

Long live Mexico!
¡Viva!
Long live America!
¡Viva!
Oh land blesséd by God
Long live Mexico!
¡Viva!

Long live America!
I will give my blood for you!
I am a true Mexican.
And I have never deceived.
If you wish to find out for yourself
History will tell you:
That Mexico is valiant.
That it has never deceived.
Long live the democracy!
And also liberty!
¡Viva!
Long live Mexico!
¡Viva!
Oh land blesséd by God!
Long live Mexico!
¡Viva!
Long live America!
¡Viva!
I will give my blood for you.

Source

5 de Mayo,/from a booklet printed by the Oakland, California, Unified School District, Educational Department Services, Office of Communications, n.d., 65-72. The material was obtained through Ilene Linssen, Program Manager, Office of Bilingual Education in November 1988. Translation by T.P.C. and Albert Harkness,Jr.

Boys' Festival

May 5

Like the Japanese Dolls' or Girls' Festival on March 3 (see p. 117), this is a family-centered holiday. It, too, instills a sense of tradition and a respect for traditional roles. Dolls are displayed, but they are costumed as samurai, a symbol of manliness. Red and black banners in the shape of carp, likewise associated with masculine virtues, are flown from a bamboo pole, one for each boy in the family.

Japanese Boys' Festival

Corresponding to [the] Dolls' Festival, the happiest day of the year for Japanese girls, there is a Boys' Festival—often called the Festival of Flags or Banners—which takes place on May 5th, in honor of male children. On this day, dolls are again displayed, but this time they are images representing soldiers, warriors, and heroes; swords and bows and arrows are also carefully laid out on exhibit. Outside the house, in addition to variegated colored flags and banners, there is the special feature of a long bamboo cane, representing a fishing rod, from which are suspended one or more paper carp. These vary according to the number of little boys in the family. Instead of being occupied in the effeminate pastime of caressing dolls and sipping tea, the boys, on the contrary, spend the day in great glee, fighting mock battles in imitation of the warriors of the glorious feudal days.

The history of the observance of the Dolls' and Boys' Festivals by the Japanese in America has undergone an interesting series of fluctuations. Before the year 1910 or so, there were, strictly speaking as stated before, not many Japanese families in America. This, added to the already mentioned circumstances of the lack of proper equipment, explains the relatively late beginning here of the celebration of these children's holidays. Since the increase in the number of families and therefore of children, and the appearance of large Japanese stores, however, both March 3rd and May 5th have become gala days for Japanese youngsters in America.

Source and Comment

Southwestern Journal of Anthropology, II (1946), 169-70. Based on a research report by "Miss N. I." who studied the holiday customs of persons of Japanese descent living in the San Francisco Bay area in 1934 under the direction of Paul Radin. Her interviews were conducted in Japanese.

Double Five Day

May 5

Ch'u Yuan (328-298 B.C), a patriotic Chinese official during the Chou Dynasty, sought to reform certain policies of the court and when the king treated his suggestions with indifference drowned himself. The festival commemorates the search in boats for his body, and features dragon-boat races. The special food prepared for this holiday was originally an offering to his spirit.

The Dragon Boat Festival

This festival, occurring on the Fifth Day of the Fifth Moon, and one of the most colorful in China, is observed here [California] more in the spirit than in the letter. In China this day is properly celebrated by gala "dragon-boat" races, but these are not held here, for lack of the proper native boats and water facilities. However, the other custom traditionally connected with the feast is scrupulously observed here year after year. This is the eating of *tsungs,* a sort of dumpling or Chinese tamale made of glutinous rice and wrapped in dried plantain leaves. Tsungs are made in both sweet and salty varieties and are very filling.

This festival has a historical origin. A brilliant scholar and official of the third century B.C., Ch'u Yuan, despairing of his monarch's lack of statesmanship, drowned himself in the Milo River [Yunnan Province], in protest against the evils of the court and the moral degeneration of the time. The common people, revering his memory, established boat races symbolizing the search for his body. The *tsungs* originated as food offerings to Ch'u Yuan in his watery tomb; hence they were wrapped in waterproof leaves.

On this festive day people used frequently to eat more of the *tsungs* than was good for them, and the following day the local herb doctors would be kept busy prescribing specifics for many stomachs suffering from indigestion!

Source

Western Folklore, VII (1948), 247. William Hoy describes this and other Chinese festivals which he observed in several California cities and in mainland China.

* * *

The Story of Double Five Day

Long ago there lived a man named Wat Yu who was Chief Minister of a country in the South. At that time China was divided into seven big countries. Wat Yu was very devoted to his country.

The King of this country was indifferent to politics and lived in luxurious splendor, indulging his every whim. The Tun Dynasty of a western country was trying to exploit the King's weakness by sending dancing girls over to him. Wat Yu, seeing what was happening, was alarmed and tried to advise the King to take care, but the King became angry. He would no longer trust Wat Yu and sought to surround himself with flatterers.

Soon the King of the Tun Dynasty extended an invitation to Wat Yu's King. Again Wat Yu tried to warn him and advised him not to go for he was certain the King would be captured as part of a plot to gain control of the country. The King did not listen to Wat Yu but instead exiled him to an isolated land.

For seven years Wat Yu lived in exile writing many books about man and the universe.

Then on the fifth day of the fifth month the Tun Dynasty completely took over his whole country just as Wat Yu had feared. On that day, grieving for his country, Wat Yu went down to a river and committed suicide. Some fishermen saw him leap into the river and they ran to announce it and get help. The women rushed home and cooked rice. Wrapping it in banana leaves and beating drums to frighten the fish they threw the rice into the river so that the fish would not eat Wat Yu's body. The fishermen searched for the body but it was never found.

And so for thousands of years people have continued to do these things on May 5th except that the rice now goes into their own mouths rather than the fish's mouths. Dragon races are held and fishermen beat drums as they search for the body of Wat Yu, who is a symbol of all patriots.

Source and Comment

New York Folklore Quarterly, XXVIII (1972), 237-38. Collected by Rosemary Agonito. Her informant was Marjorie Kam, in 1968 a student at Syracuse University, but a native of mainland China. She recounts a traditional version of the origin of the holiday, celebrated by her family. Cf. William Hoy's description, p. 46. Motifs present include: J 1705.4; Z 71.5.5; and P 711.

Kentucky Derby

First Saturday in May

America's most famous horse race, the Kentucky Derby, is modeled on England's Epsom Derby. It is for three-year-old thoroughbreds, was originally run at one mile and a half (now at a mile and a quarter), and has been held continuously since 1875 at Louisville, Kentucky. Colonel Meriwether Lewis Clark, who organized the first race, wanted it to be a festive occasion, and he gave a Derby breakfast for his friends before the first running—a custom which he continued through his life and which many others have followed. Parties, dances and carnival-like gaiety have long been a feature of Derby Week. The Derby's emergence as an event of national note is due largely to Colonel Matt Winn, a shrewd promoter who cultivated wealthy eastern horse owners and such sports writers as Damon Runyon and Grantland Rice. He had seen his first Derby as a lad, and he directed it from 1902 until his death in 1949.

The One Hundredth Derby: Its Mint Juleps

Sometime around five o'clock on the afternoon of the first Saturday in May, a dozen or so horses will charge around the track at Louisville's Churchill Downs in the 100th running of the Kentucky Derby, a mad but mellow mixture of horses, hysteria and hoopla. A band will play "My Old Kentucky Home," tears will flow like mint juleps, people will scream and jump about. And in the process, a three-year-old Thoroughbred will win the first leg of the Triple Crown, horsedom's biggest biggie. . . .

Considering that it lasts only two minutes, give or take a couple of seconds or fractions thereof, it is a tribute to the race that it has become the country's premier sports spectacle. The Indianapolis 500 may draw more on-the-site spectators: the Super Bowl may engage a larger television audience. But those events last for long and often tedious hours. The Derby boils it down to one frantic burst, and for its brief life-span it pulls them in as does no other event. This year [1974], 125,000 ticket buyers are expected to cram themselves into the Churchill Downs enclosure, built to accommodate half that number, while 75 million others watch it more comfortably on television.

Of course, the Derby is not just a horse race, any more than Mardi Gras is a parade. It is more a kind of fit that seizes the Bluegrass state each May, a fine spring madness with betting windows. The festivities, which last the better part of a week, include a Pegasus parade in honor of the mythical winged horse (who did not win a Derby and therefore is not highly regarded by Kentuckians), a steamboat race on the Ohio River between two surviving stern-wheelers, a massive dance thrown by ladies calling them-

selves Colonettes, and a dinner given for, by and at the expense of Kentucky Colonels. . . .

Why does the Derby arouse emotions and excitement unique in horse racing? It is not the oldest race in the country. The Travers Handicap (begun in 1864) and the Belmont Stakes (1867) have years on the Derby, which was not begun until 1875. Even older is Keeneland's Phoenix Handicap, first run in 1831. Neither is the Derby, a $125,000-added contest, the richest race. Several pay more. . . .

Then, too, the other races have lapsed from time to time. Neither war nor flood nor gasoline rationing has kept the three-year-olds from their appointed round of the Downs since Aristides won the first Derby on May 17, 1875, loping the mile and a half (Derby distance is now a mile and a quarter) in the respectable time of 2:37 ¾. And while the prize money is not the biggest in the business, it is not hay. More importantly, winning it usually leads on to greater things. A Derby winner may command handsome fees as a stud after his racing days are done. And while few Derby winners go on to capture the Triple Crown (Derby, Preakness, Belmont), the fact remains that a horse must win the Derby first to become a Triple Crowner and take his place alongside the likes of Secretariat, Citation, Whirlaway and Gallant Fox.

Still, some owners prefer not to risk burning out their hayburners with a premature race, and some of the great stakes winners of the American turf never touched hoof to Downs on Derby Day. For example, Man o' War, probably the greatest American Thoroughbred, not only did not run in the Derby but also never raced in Kentucky, a fact

Kentuckians prefer not to discuss. And there was Bubbling Over, who never raced again after taking the 1926 Derby.

What sets the Derby apart is that it is, as someone once said (or should have), the right race in the right place at the right time. Kentucky is, after all, the home and heart of the horse industry. Its weather in winter and summer can be foul, but in the first weeks of spring nature blesses it with magic. It is a place of blooming tulips and dogwood, soft-greening trees, warm sun and colts prancing across white-fenced bluegrass acres. Louisville, basically an industrial Midwestern town, takes on an aura of Southern charm. Colonels sprout like mint twigs, and residents only recently arrived from Schenectady or Pittsburgh develop Southern accents and serve mint juleps to their Yankee guests.

"The whole thing," said Wathen Knebelkamp, late president of Churchill Downs, "is corny as hell in some ways. But it's hard to beat.". . .

As a social event, the Derby is something of a mixed bag. Proper hostesses insist that the whole thing is a bore and just a bit tacky, but they compete tensely for distinguished guests, especially for the traditional Derby-eve parties and Derby-morning breakfasts. The customary Derby party begins graciously with mint juleps in frosted glasses and every man a colonel, and winds up, shortly before daybreak, with bourbon and water and every man for himself. Derby breakfast is a strict ritual at which eggs and other staples must be accompanied by country ham and beaten biscuits which look and often taste like the center cut from a cueball. And, of course, mint juleps.

It is also considered good form to take one's guests to breakfast or lunch in the clubhouse dining room at the Downs, where one can view the preliminary races with casual disinterest while downing the same fare and the inevitable juleps. The great majority of spectators, however, could care less about good form. By the thousands they sprawl on the grass of the infield, eating from picnic hampers and getting sozzled on beer, while others swarm through the stands hoping to catch a glimpse of the rich and/or famous. . . .

The first Derby was different only in degree. There were three races then, instead of today's nine, and there were 10,000 people on hand rather than 100,000. They drove out from Louisville in hacks and surreys, or rode the horsedrawn trolley. They could enjoy the whole thing for a dollar, and for some the tab was even less. What is now called the infield was then the "free gate area," and several hundred viewers drove their wagons in, ate a home-packed lunch and watched standing up in wagon beds. . . .

Kentucky, though, was still small potatoes in the horse world, and when the Jockey Club of New York was formed in 1891, its members tended to view Churchill Downs, like all other Southern tracks, with disdain—not the place, really, where a gentleman wanted to race his horses. Horse racing, they decided, belonged in the East, where gentlemen could afford it. After all, it had started in New York where, in 1668, the governor, Col. Richard Nicolls, had presented the winner of the first organized race with a silver porringer.

Matt Winn [President of Churchill Downs] turned the thing around. Until he took over, the Derby had attracted scant notice from the national press. The Downs had a good plant, but its finances depended heavily on the one big event—the Derby. And while crowds were good, they weren't good enough to pay the bills the rest of the year. A natural and tireless promoter, Winn spruced the place up, planted the grounds with banks of tulips and other spring flowers, timed to bloom around Derby week, pioneered the $2 pari-mutuel bet, and began a dogged courtship of the two groups he needed to turn the Derby into a national event—horse owners and newspapermen.

Early on, he got two big breaks. In 1913 a long shot named Donerail came in and paid $184.90 for a $2 ticket in the Derby. This price—and the Derby—got a lot of national attention. Then, in 1915, Harry Payne Whitney, among the bluest of Eastern bloods, agreed to enter his filly, Regret, in the Derby. Regret won, the only filly ever to take the race [until 1980], and again reaped a golden crop of news headlines.

Winn saw to it that Whitney was treated royally during his stay in Kentucky, and the hospitality paid off. "I don't care whether she ever wins another race," boomed Whitney, patting his victorious Regret after the Derby. "She's already won the greatest race in the world." Winn made sure this statement got wide circulation.

Mint Juleps and the Derby

Exactly when the mint julep and the Derby got together is not clear. The julep has been a Bluegrass tradition since before the Civil War, and few Kentuckians of any prominence have gone to their graves without having, at one time or another, produced their personal recipe. Henry Clay, John Campbell Breckinridge, and Irvin S. Cobb went into ecstasies describing the delights of a julep and instructing the uninitiated in the mysteries of its concoction. On the other hand, Marse Henry Watterson, famed Louisville editor, offered this recipe:

"Pluck the mint gently from its bed just as the dew of evening is about to form on it. Select the choicer sprigs only, but do not rinse them. Prepare the simple syrup and measure out half a tumbler of whisky. Pour the whisky into a well-frosted silver cup, throw the other ingredients out the window and drink the whisky straight."

But Winn managed to weave the julep into the richening legend of the Derby, along with bluegrass, colonels and Southern hospitality. The effect of all this was to make

Louisville sound as though it were nestled on the banks of the Suwannee River rather than on the Ohio....

Thousands of bad mint juleps will be consumed by drinkers who would not know a good one if they got one. Visitors will complain about room and meal prices and cab fares. Most of them will eventually get to the Derby, and they will eat and drink and gawk and bet, and squeal at each other and make sure that they are seen. And they will find that, as the afternoon goes on, they are getting very excited, for reasons hard to explain, as slowly the legend and myth and glamour and ballyhoo that surround the Derby build to the awaited climax.

Suddenly a bugle will blow, and out onto the track will come the horses, sleek, beautifully shaped animals, their jockeys crisp in their bright silks. And as they prance by the stands the band will begin the soft strains of "My Old Kentucky Home," and there will be tears in the eyes of people who couldn't tell Kentucky from a corncake. Then the music will die and the horses will be led, one by one, into the starting gate. A hush will fall over the throng until it is swept by the magic shout, "They're off!"

Hokum? Perhaps. Corny? Probably. Manufactured glamour? Maybe. But still the Kentucky Derby, the greatest race of them all.

Source

Louisville *Courier-Journal & Times Magazine,* April 28, 1974. By John Ed Pearce, staff writer, who tells "how a two-minute horse race, abetted by colorful people and odd events, grew into a legend in only one century." The 1974 Derby was won in an upset by Cannonade.

* * *

Chancy Gambling and Surefire Fun

"Lady, don't you know there ain't no telephones at a race track?" an incredulous New Yorker asked me as we stood among bettors at Churchill Down's pari-mutuel windows. New to horse racing, I had never considered that public telephones could be used to spirit race results to off-track bettors in time to wager on the winner before official postings.

I was baptized in the sport—and the chancy gambling and surefire fun that attends it—at the world's greatest thoroughbred horse race last May [1987] in Louisville, Kentucky.

To be sure, the Run for the Roses (as the Kentucky Derby is commonly called) is more than just a great race. Since the first Kentucky Derby in 1875, the race—which some sports writers say constitutes the greatest two minutes in sports—and its preliminaries have evolved into perhaps the world's biggest adult game.

Throughout the 10-day Derby Festival that begins a week before the Derby, movie stars, great athletes, Wall Street tycoons, politicians and con artists descend on Louisville, which becomes an international city during its brief season in the spotlight.

Along streets that converge on Churchill Downs, I passed vendors selling home-cooked meals, fuchsia-colored stuffed giraffes, raincoats, sunglasses and lawn chairs to racegoers—all jammed into parking lots and front yards. I was on my way to see the Kentucky Oaks, a race for thoroughbred fillies held the day before the main event.

Entering Churchill Downs—that mecca of thoroughbred horsedom whose white turreted walls resemble those of Bavarian castles—the first thing I saw were tipsters hawking tip sheets predicting the day's winners. Vendors sold souvenirs and official programs with each day's lineup of races. Inside the clubhouse or amid the clubhouse garden's 10,000 imported Holland tulips, the general-admission patrons had set up folding chairs. Both groups had to be content watching races on TV monitors since the track was not visible from there.

Sophisticated bettors buy the *Daily Racing Form* with its section entitled "Past Performances" that includes a listing of each horse's bloodline, trainer and past race results. Two tote boards—each 15 by 200 feet—serve as scorecards in Churchill Downs' infield, posting the results of each race: win, place, show and fourth place, race times and mutuel payoffs on $2 bets.

Between races, nine to 10 a day during Derby week, patrons have 30 to 50 minutes to place bets, collect wins, buy refreshments, and see and be seen. Dressed to the nines on Millionaires' Row on the clubhouse's top floors, celebrities and near-celebrities looked down on the more casual crowd of 75,000 along the track's infield, many in T-shirts and jeans. Socialites flaunting extravagant, broad-brimmed hats and designer clothes paraded in aisles between reserved boxes along the track. Vendors shouting "mint julep" hawked that legendary southern drink of Kentucky bourbon with a little mint, crushed ice and sugar thrown in.

While Kentucky bourbon and betting are a potentially volatile mixture, the mint juleps (sold in elegant souvenir Derby glasses) are a tame Derby tradition.

Another is the sewing of the roses, a tradition since 1932. On Derby eve, a crowd at Louisville's Kroger Company grocery store watched three women sew 600 rosebuds into a blanket of roses that adorns the Derby winner. From eight o'clock that night to eight o'clock the next morning, the women stitched together the red Kentucky rosebuds timed to open just before the blanket's presentation.

Newer Derby-related events number more than 80, scheduled as part of the Kentucky Derby Festival that began simply as the Pegasus Parade in 1956. The festival has mushroomed into civic celebrations of balls, barbecues, concerts and parades, a sort of Louisville Mardi Gras. Among last year's activities were stern-wheeler and hot-air balloon races, a mini-marathon and the Run for the Rosé, in which local waiters and waitresses carrying trays of wine-filled glasses raced over an obstacle course....

Estimates put Derby-weekend parties as high as 10,000, of which some of the most glamorous (including the winner's party) are catered by Steve Clements at the adjacent Kentucky Derby Museum. But the biggest party happens at the track's front rails. On the day of the Derby, I had a great box seat, but wanting to get closer to the horses, as do many spectators, I moved to a spot across from the tote board near the track's finish line. In one hour, I met an Atlanta, Georgia, investment banker; a Buffalo, New York, couple who attend annually; a Tennessee native who drives up each May; and a former disc jockey from Cleveland whose scientific study of thoroughbreds didn't seem to beat the odds in this year's running.

Rumor has it that bets that pay off are often the result of hunches, superstition or beginner's luck. I had one omen: Only an hour before the Derby I got the autograph of trainer Jack Van Berg, whose colt, Alysheba, soon won the race.

Experienced bettors scrutinize the field for Kentucky-bred entries. Since 1875, when Aristides won the first Derby, three-fourths of all the race's winners have been bred in Kentucky.

In the final analysis, the real Derby pull is the horses. The three-year-olds that race in the Derby are the choicest of the choice, thoroughbreds bred and trained almost from birth to finish first in the Run for the Roses. They are the most spirited, determined, high-strung, beautiful horses in the world—as well as the fastest.

Source

Travel-Holiday, March, 1988, 62-65. Edited from an article by Colleen Ballard Hayes.

* * *

Kentucky Derby Carnival

A few yards beyond the pedestrian tunnel to the Churchill Downs infield, a young man standing on a cooler held up a handlettered sign: "Don't you love smut?" Propped up at his feet was a more elaborate message. "Girls," it read, in red block letters, "get naked here. Expert assistance. Ask for Joe."

He was finding no takers, but it wasn't yet noon. He remained at his stand, confident that as the summery day wore on toward post time for the 106th [1980] Kentucky Derby, the true carnival spirit would take over.

More and more noticeably in recent years, the Derby's center-field picnic has become a "happening" for the college crowd. Seats in the grandstand and clubhouse and the bleachers outside the clubhouse turn are always sold out, so the only area where attendance varies from year to year is the grassy plain enclosed by the bridle path. That crowd swells or shrinks according to the weather, which has never been more promising than it was this morning.

So they came swarming in by the tens of thousands, toting coolers and ice buckets and hampers and blankets and folding chairs. They set up pup tents and hammocks, laid out their goodies and stretched out at ease until the whole broad meadow, seen from above, heaved and pulsated.

Here came a girl in halter and shorts pulling a red wagon loaded with comestibles. There ambled a bearded young man bare to the waist except for red galluses supporting blue jeans, which were rolled up to the knees.

By comparison with his fellows, he was overdressed. Standard attire for males was blue shorts, with or without shoes; for females, a few additional threads. The sun's rays, dazzling in the morning, were strained through a filmy overcast by 1 P.M., but by that time acres and acres of skin had turned a painful pink.

Strollers had to pick their way among bodies. Hour by hour as the throng grew, less and less grass remained visible until there was more to smoke than to walk on. The unmistakable bouquet of burning pot, rather like the scent given off by an overheated electric motor, hung on the still air like incense.

It was a merry crowd, relaxed and friendly and mostly young. There seemed to be no shortage of potables, though management discourages carrying stimulants through the gates. At the clubhouse entrance about 11 A.M., security guards were seen to relieve a customer of assorted bottles which they pitched into a trash can.

"That was a pretty good haul," a bystander said.

Frisbees sailed about the infield scene. Inside the clubhouse turn a volleyball game went on without pause. For the third year in a row, a young entrepreneur worked his basketball grift. He had a basket set up on a standard and charged 50 cents for two shots from the free-throw distance, paying $1 if both throws went in. Maybe one player in 20 hit twice and collected. For its proprietor, the game was a surer thing than any horse.

Admission to the infield is $10 and anyone who has heard that you can't see horses from there has been misinformed. The second race started from the six-furlong gate in the backstretch. Crowds pressed against the tall cyclone fence surrounding the infield could see the field leave the gate and proceed 40 or 50 yards before disappearing beyond the multitude.

State troopers patrolled outside the fence, lending a touch of Dannemora to the happy scene.

"Nuke Iran," a bedsheet banner urged. "Welcome to the rodeo," another sign read, and this could have been editorial comment on the Derby's informal riding tactics. In 105 runnings of this cavalry charge, there has never been a disqualification for rough riding, making the Derby easily the most cleanly contested sports event in America.

Source

New York Times, May 4, 1980. From the sports column by Red Smith, dated Louisville, Kentucky, May 3, 1980. The 1980 Derby was won by Genuine Risk, the first filly to win the race since Regret (see p. 206) in 1915.

Icemänner Days
May 12-14

St. Boniface was an English missionary to Germany in the eighth century; St. Pancratius was a fourth-century boy martyr; and St. Ignatius, consecrated Bishop of Antioch by St. Peter, was thrown into a den of wild beasts in the first century upon the orders of the emperor Trajan. That a folk belief about the weather should attach itself to a series of saints' days is a curious but by no means unique reversal: at first the saints' days were a convenient reminder of weather change, but later the weather change helped to keep the memory of those feast days alive.

Warm Weather Saints

A rather popular saying [in Ellis County, Kansas, among persons of Volga German descent] is that the coldest days of May are the 12th, 13th, and 14th. These are called by the German-Russians the *Icemänner* days of Bonfatz, Pancratz, and Ignatz, named after the three saints, Boniface, Pancratius, and Ignatius, whose feast days fell on these days. They firmly believed that there would never be a frost after these days.

Source

Western Folklore, XXII (1963), 88. Collected by Fr. John B. Terbovich, O.F.M., in Ellis County, Kansas, from descendants of German-Russian Catholics who emigrated from the Volga German colonies established by Catherine II to Kansas in 1876. Informant not cited. Cf. Motif D 1812.0.15.

Mother's Day

Second Sunday in May

On the second Sunday in May, children pay tribute to their mothers. The celebration was conceived by Anne M. Jarvis of Philadelphia in 1907. By 1911 it was nationally observed, and in 1912 a Mother's Day International Association was incorporated to promote it. Originally it was marked by a special church service at which members of the congregation wore white carnations. The day is now characterized by gift-giving and sending greeting cards. The idea is not new, however. Many ancient peoples honored the Earth Mother and motherhood. On Mothering Sunday or Mid-Lent Sunday in England, young people who have moved away return to visit their parents and present their mothers with "mothering cakes," rich plum cakes.

Mother's Day Defined

Question: What is Mother's Day?

Answer: Nine days [months] after father's night.

Source and Comment

Journal of American Folklore, LXXV (1962), 224. Collected in 1960 from "a 44-year-old machinist ... from Altoona, Pennsylvania." Scholars call this a "depraved definition," a "minor genre of obscene folklore" in the form of question and answer.

* * *

Mother's Day Card

Hilton Head [South Carolina] has a number of small cemeteries. Because there is no stone on the island, graves are usually marked with crude headstones fashioned from cement or with wooden stakes. Frequently the name of the deceased is incised in the wet cement and the depressions filled in with black paint....On the graves is to be found an assortment of eating utensils, medicine bottles, wash basins, crockery and the like, a practice, perhaps of African origin, that is common in Negro cemeteries throughout the South. This writer visited a Negro graveyard at Hilton Head on May 8, 1955, and saw on the resting place of a woman who had died within the year an ornate Mother's Day card complete with the signature of her dutiful children.

Source and Comment

Southern Folklore Quarterly, XXII (1958), 94-95. From a paper on burial customs among Gullah Negroes by H.C. Hilton Head is a sea island two miles off the southern coast of South Carolina. It is now a resort, connected to the mainland by a causeway, but in 1955 it had an isolated population of about 1,200 blacks and six white families.

* * *

Uses of a Finnish Proverb

Some [Finnish-American] proverbs, however, show modifications in their use, and there are some variations in phrasing also. For an example of variation in use, there is the common, amusing proverb, "Frost brings the pigs home." Mothers use it when children come in hungry from play, but it is applied also, with slightly acid humor, to relatives who come to visit in hard times, or to grown children coming home on Mother's Day.

Source

Minnesota History, XXIV (1943), 226. From a discussion of "Finnish Proverbs" current in Minnesota by Marjorie Edgar.

Florida Seminole Green Corn Dance

May, When Corn Ripens

Ceremonies involving the planting, ripening and harvest of corn were particularly widespread, practiced by the Indians of the Prairies and Southwest as well as by those of the Eastern Woodlands. The Green Corn Dance or busk, as it was usually called by early white observers, took place when the corn had ripened. It was a first fruits ceremony, marking the beginning of a new year. Thus William Bartram in his *Travels* (1791) among the southern Indians in the 1770s notes that "every town celebrates the busk separately, when their own harvest is ready." He adds: "When a town celebrates the busk, having previously provided themselves with new clothes, new pots and other household utensils and furniture, they collect all their worn-out clothes and other despicable things, sweep and cleanse their houses, squares and the whole town of their filth, which with all the remaining grain and other provisions, they cast together into one common heap, and consume it with fire." Quoting from Bartram's account in *Walden,* Thoreau remarks approvingly, "I have scarcely heard of a truer sacrament, that is, as the dictionary defines it, 'outward and visible sign of an inward and spiritual grace'...."

The Corn Dance

The Green Corn Dance is the principal ceremony among the Florida Seminoles and affords them recreational diversion once a year. Although many of the customs are of recent origin, the Green Corn Dance by way of contrast, is a very old observance. It is not confined to the Seminoles and has constituted an intimate part of the ceremonial life of the Creek Indians, the Alabama tribe, as well as the Cherokee and Natchez, who took on the dance late in their existence. The Seminole dance is derived from the Creek busk ceremony. The word busk is derived from *boskita* meaning to fast, and is an integral part of the ceremony which marked the old Creek new year. Variations of the Green Corn Dance have been given year in and year out among the Florida Seminoles as well as among the Timuquans, who preceded them on the Florida peninsula.

The separate rites which compose the dance are both old and widespread among the original peoples of the Southeast. One such practice is the taking of an emetic. The well-known cassine or *ilex vomitoria* is employed as emetic at the Green Corn Dance. This shrub, which is none other than the familiar holly, is found along the sea coast of the two Carolinas, Georgia, and northern Florida. The French writer Bossu speaks of the use of cassine among the Alabama tribe, who roasted the leaves to make a tea and drank the infusion in the ritual of many ceremonies. The Creeks, also, were inveterate cassine drinkers. They referred to it as *asi* instead of the usual popular expression "black drink." The Creeks likewise had a religious belief that the *asi* used at the busk had the following properties: It

purified them from all sin and left them in a state of perfect innocence. It exalted them with invincible daring in war and was a means of cementing friendship.

Another important feature of the Green Corn Dance is the ceremonial scratching which occurs just before the Feather Dance on the second day of the ceremony. Scratching of this sort was known among the Cherokees, Creeks, Seminoles, Yuchi, and Catawba tribes in particular. In the Cherokee instance ball players are scratched on their naked bodies with a bamboo brier having stout thorns. This left broad gashes on the backs of the victims. Among the Seminoles snake fangs are inserted into a wooden holder and is used to scratch the assembled members. Different purposes for the scratching are as punishment of children, relief of fatigue, and the cleansing of the body from impurities as in the case of the Green Corn Dance ceremony.

Aside from its purely ceremonial purpose the Green Corn Dance is a time for council meetings. All the troubles of the old year, with the exception of murder and any serious infraction of the marriage rules are forgiven. One rule, that of marrying into the clan of one's mother, since the Seminole count descent not from both sides of the family as with us but only on the mother's side, is particularly guarded against. Any infraction here cannot be simply wiped away by the repentance at the Green Corn Dance.

An additional function of the meeting is the naming of youths who have come of age. Remember that an Indian name is more than a label, it is a distinct part of his personality just as much so as are his eyes or his teeth. He believes that injury will result from the wrong handling of his name just as readily as a wound inflicted on some part of his body. Thus the small rites accompanying the dances which occur on the last night of the Corn Dance serve to give the young members of the tribe their ceremonial names. This clan name they then bear for the remainder of their lives. Only medicine men or other important personages receive further honorary names.

The ball game at the Corn Dance which I witnessed in the Big Cypress swamp in May, 1939, had little definite form. It was played in the quiet periods between the ceremonies of more serious import. The object was to send the ball hitting against an indented mark cut some six feet up on a twenty-foot pole. Making a charcoal mark on the pole for each hit registered constituted the method of scoring. Most of the time the boys and girls just played in a formless and desultory fashion—tossing the buckskin ball around aimlessly. On several occasions when the game assumed a more serious character the boys played with small gut-thonged racquets while the girls used their bare hands.

In the evening the so-called stomp dances took place. They had little form and were mere survivals of dances which probably had much significance earlier in Seminole history. The first dance was the Catfish Dance, which was soon followed by the Hair Dance. The latter is probably a survival of the scalp dance which was given earlier in the Southeast when Indians referred to the scalp as "hair." The Alligator Dance and the Buffalo Dance were also given. Other dances often rendered at the Green Corn Dance are Rattlesnake Dance (*cinti chobi talellwi*), Switchgrass Dance (*pahi loci talellwi*), Redbug Dance (*waski talellwi*), and Rabbit Dance (*cokfi talellwi*).

While dancing the women wear rattles made out of tin cans punctured and filled with pebbles. The rattles are tied to the leg just above the ankle. The men carry palmetto fronds in their hands and a few merely held sprigs of bush which they carried in a similar manner.

During the evening dances one Indian acted as fire tender and announcer. He stood within the bough-decked ceremonial lodge on the east end of the ceremonial grounds and called out the names of the dancers who were to participate in a coming event.

Of all the dances the Feather Dance is the only one which merits special notice. It is danced in the morning and immediately after lunch on the last day of the ceremony. Each participant held white egret feathers attached to a

long thin pole. The pole thus adorned was carried over the left shoulder. No women were allowed to take part in the Feather Dance.

The Men went around the ceremonial grounds making four steps, one at each corner. They stopped at the corner, shook their rattles and then let out a short piercing whoop. The ceremonial ground was occupied in the following manner to give this dance:

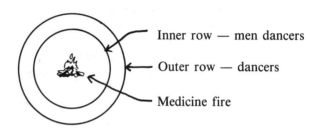

Inner row — men dancers

Outer row — dancers

Medicine fire

At three o'clock the same afternoon the men retired to the same ceremonial grounds near the ball game pole to take the "black drink." This emetic is now composed of six ingredients. Without warning the ceremonial scratching with snake fangs set in a scratching instrument resembling a pocket comb began. First the men pulled up their trousers to the knees and rubbed medicine on their legs. After this they hastily went into the nearby sawgrass to inflict another series of scratches upon their legs just below the thigh and in the shin region as well. Boys received scratches on their fore and upper arm. After the scratching the men went further into the sawgrass. Vomiting ensued for such was the instantaneous effect of the emetic they had taken so soon before.

The Green Corn Dance had little else to recommend it to the visitor. There was a feast, participated in by all, in which large slabs of beef were eaten. Another event was the eating of *kumpti,* a food made from a root resembling cassava. It was also rather interesting to see the women grind the new corn meal in the old stump grinders which the Seminoles and other Southeastern Indians used for so many years.

Source and Comment

Southern Folklore Quarterly, IX (1945), 147-50. Observed by Robert F. Greenlee in May 1939. Cf. "Seneca Green Corn Dance," p. 406. For a discussion of the "black drink" (an effusion of *ilex vomitoria*) as a beverage and as used on ritual occasions by southeastern Indians, see *Black Drink: A Native American Tea,* edited by Charles M. Hudson, Athens, Georgia, 1979.

Memorial Day
May 30

By federal law, Memorial Day is now celebrated the last Monday in May.

The origins of Memorial Day, or Decoration Day as it was first known, are remote and mixed. In rural America, the custom of cleaning the cemeteries and decorating graves, usually in the late summer, was an occasion for reunions, revivals, and picnics (see, for example, "Memorial Day in Northeast Texas," p. 301). But more ancient and widespread are the festivals of the Dead, such as the Japanese Obon or Festival of Lanterns (p. 273) or the Zuñi Indian All Souls' Day (p. 383), which occur at the end of a season or before a new year begins, a time when the boundaries between the living and the dead were believed to thin out. Historically speaking, the immediate origin of the American legal holiday is confused by a number of claimants to priority, as the discussion below shows, and the fact that several states, especially those of the former Confederacy, observe the holiday on different dates. What this seems to indicate is that Memorial Day grew up almost spontaneously from ancient tradition; American folklife; American history; and, as sociologists suggest, from the American need for a secular, patriotic ceremony honoring its military dead. Memorial Day, at the beginning of the summer, like Labor Day at its end, is a convenient open space on the calendar for less somber events, and has become a traditional time for family cookouts in the backyard or sporting events like the Indianapolis Speedway automobile race.

Origin of Memorial Day

For more than ten years, I have been researching the origin of Memorial Day. It began as a hobby when I was a pastor in Boalsburg, Penn., where it was claimed that the decoration of some graves July 4, 1864, made that village the "Birthplace of Memorial Day." As a matter of record, a total of 25 places have been named in connection with the origin of Memorial Day. One of the oldest claims is that of Jackson, Miss., where Sue Landon Vaughan, a descendent of President John Adams, put out a call to decorate Confederate graves on April 26, 1865. Her act is commemorated in stone on a monument erected 1888 on the old State Capital grounds at Jackson, now known as Confederate Park.

Perhaps the most beautiful "claim" is the event at Columbus, Miss., where four women in Friendship Cemetery on April 25, 1866, decorated the graves of their fallen soldiers. It was here that the additional act of decorating the graves of 40 Federal soldiers buried there brought about the writing of the poem, "The Blue and Gray" by Francis Miles Finch. Mr. Finch, an attorney in Ithaca, N.Y., had read of the act in a New York newspaper and included a historical note with his poem, which was published in the *Atlantic Monthly* in 1867. This poem, no doubt, did much to make the Columbus event the best known of all celebrations of Memorial Day.

Hopkinton (Delaware County), Iowa, dedicated a monument on Nov. 7, 1865, to the 44 soldiers from Lenox College who served in the Civil War. Although believed to be the first monument to Civil War soldiers, and thus establishing the basis of Hopkinton's claim to have been the first town in the nation to celebrate Memorial Day, earlier monuments were erected at Kensington, Conn., and Stones River National Battlefield, Murfreesboro, Tenn.

An even earlier event is the decoration of graves by Mrs. George H. Evans (maiden name, Sarah J. Nichols) in a cemetery in Arlington Heights which is near Washington, D.C. Arlington National Cemetery received its first Union soldier for burial in May, 1864. When Mrs. Evans' husband, from Hudson, Mich., enlisted in the Union Army, Mrs. Evans served as a nurse. On April 13, 1862, with the wife of Chaplain May of the Second Michigan Volunteers and two other women, Mrs. Evans decorated 17 graves of soldiers who died in the defense of the capitol. The decoration was repeated in 1863 and 1864. Mrs. Evans was recognized in 1873 by the G.A.R. Post 12, Des Moines, as "Originator of Memorial Day."

Richmond, Va., has several variations; one is that Cassandra Oliver Moncure decorated, or had a part in decorating, graves in the Hollywood Cemetery. Another is that early services were held on Belle Isle in James River near Richmond. Winchester, Va., had a Women's Memorial Society and observed June 6, 1866, the anniversary of the death of Gen. Turner Ashby. But, many southern women established Memorial Societies to organize the return of their dead soldiers to a burial place near home. Petersburg, Va., observed June 9, 1866, the anniversary of the assault of 1864. In Blandford Cemetery, the stone of the grave of Nora Fontaine Maury Davidson credits her as "originator of Memorial Day which was inspiration for the National Decoration Day."

Mrs. John A. Logan, wife of the commander-in-chief of the Grand Army of the Republic recounted more than once of her trip in March, 1868, to see the battle fields around Richmond and Petersburg. Because the General, who was serving in Congress at the time, was busy with his legislative duties and thus unable to make the trip, Mrs. Logan described the trip to him, giving him the details about the decorated graves and tiny flags. According to Mrs. Logan, General Order Eleven was written at that time.

Another version credits Mrs. Henry S. Kimball of W. Philadelphia, Penn., for suggesting the custom to Gen. Logan in a letter she wrote after her return from a southern tour. Yet a third version is given by Logan's Adj. Gen. of the G.A.R., N.P. Chipman, who claims that a comrade of German background, from Cincinnati, suggested the custom of decorating the graves with flowers. According to this version, Chipman wrote most of General Order Eleven.

Carbondale, Ill., the home area of Gen. Logan, held a service on April 29, 1866, in which returned veterans planned and participated in decorating graves of their buddies who had fallen in battle. Significant is the fact that the speaker was Gen. Logan, who so heartily sponsored Memorial Day services throughout the nation. It was reported by several of Gen. Logan's friends, and repeated in his funeral sermon, that he considered General Order Eleven the "proudest act of his life." One historian writes that no one act did more to remove public prejudice against the G.A.R. than did the inauguration of Memorial Day.

Lloyd Lewis, a newspaperman and friend of Carl Sandburg, suggested that Memorial Day was established in the wild delirium following the funeral of Abraham Lincoln. Another newspaper reporter, James Redpath of Charleston, S.C., told of the decorating of 257 graves of Union soldiers by the families of former slaves on May 1, 1865. However, this was, properly speaking, a cemetery dedication.

As a result of the meeting of some women in Columbus, Ga., Mrs. Mary Williams wrote a letter in the local newspaper there on March 12, 1866, which was reprinted throughout the south. She appealed to the women to cover the graves of their soldiers with flowers. April 26 was chosen as the date for the event because that was the anniversary of the surrender of Gen. Joseph E. Johnston, the last of the forces of the Confederate Army. In Linwood cemetery, a tombstone marks the grave of Lizzie Rutherford Ellis, crediting her with the suggestions for originating Memorial Day.

In Waterloo, N. Y., Henry C. Welles and Gen. John B. Murray are given credit as the originators of the day. Their first observance was May 5, 1866. Their claim is qualified as the "first formal village-wide observance of the day." By a Joint Resolution of Congress, Waterloo has been recognized "The Birthplace of Memorial Day."

Source and Comment

Annuals of Iowa, XXXIX (1968), 311-14. Ernest C. Klein provides the historical data and summarizes the priority of claims regarding the origin of Memorial Day. The General Order No. 11 from General Logan, dated May 5, 1868, begins: "The 30th of May, 1868, is designated for the purpose of strewing with flowers, or otherwise decorating the graves of comrades who died in defense of their country during the late rebellion, whose bodies now lie in almost every city, village and hamlet churchyard in the land. . . ." In 1966 by Congressional resolution and presidential proclamation Waterloo, New York, was designated the "birthplace" of Memorial Day.

* * *

General Order No. 11, Grand Army of the Republic

I. The 30th day of May, 1868, is designated for the purpose of strewing with flowers, or otherwise decorating the graves of comrades who died in defense of their country during the late rebellion, and whose bodies now lie in almost every city, village and hamlet churchyard in the land. In this observance no form or ceremony is prescribed, but Posts and comrades will, in their own way, arrange such fitting services and testimonials of respect as circumstances may permit.

We are organized, Comrades, as our regulations tell us, for the purpose among other things, "of preserving and strengthening those kind and fraternal feelings which have bound together the soldiers, sailors and marines, who united to suppress the late rebellion." What can aid more to assure this result than by cherishing tenderly the memory of our heroic dead? We should guard their graves with sacred vigilance. All that the consecrated wealth and taste of the nation can add to their adornment and security is but a fitting tribute to the memory of her slain defenders. Let pleasant paths invite the coming and going of reverent visitors and fond mourners. Let no neglect, no ravages of time, testify to the present or to the coming generations that we have forgotten as a people the cost of a free and undivided republic.

If other eyes grow dull and other hands slack, and other hearts cold in the solemn trust, ours shall keep it well as long as the light and warmth of life remain in us.

Let us, then, at the time appointed, gather around their sacred remains, and garland the passionless mounds above them with choicest flowers of springtime; let us raise above them the dear old flag they saved; let us in this solemn presence renew our pledge to aid and to assist those whom they have left among us a sacred charge upon the Nation's gratitude—the soldier's and sailor's widow and orphan.

II. It is the purpose of the Commander-in-Chief to inaugurate this observance with the hope that it will be kept up from year to year, while a survivor of the war remains to honor the memory of his departed comrades. He earnestly desires the public press to call attention to this Order, and lend its friendly aid in bringing it to the notice of comrades in all parts of the country in time for simultaneous compliance therewith.

III. Department Commanders will use every effort to make this Order effective.

By Command of:

N. P. CHIPMAN,
Adjutant-General.

JOHN A. LOGAN,
Commander-in-Chief.

Source

Reprinted from *Program 1989,* published by the Grand Army of the Republic Memorial Corporation, a consortium of veterans' organizations formed in 1928 "to hold fitting memorial services on Decoration Day." The General Order was dated Washington, D.C., May 5, 1868.

* * *

Memorial Day Service, Arlington National Cemetery

Arlington Memorial Amphitheater

MUSICAL PRELUDE ...."The President's Own," The United States Marine Band Colonel John R. Bourgeois, Director

MOMENT OF SILENCE .... Eleven O'Clock While the President's Wreath is placed at the Tomb of the Unknown Soldier

CALL TO ORDER AND PRESENTATION OF COLORS .... Robert F. Sutphin, President of the G.A.R. Memorial Day Corporation

PLEDGE OF ALLEGIANCE .... Lt. Col. Matt Urban, Congressional Medal of Honor, fr. MI

THE NATIONAL ANTHEM .. The United States Marine Band

INVOCATION .. Chaplain, Lt. Col. F. Walter Montondon, Staff Chaplain, Military District of Washington

WELCOME .... Robert F. Sutphin

OFFICIAL WELCOME .... Major General Donald C. Hilbert, Commanding General, Military District of Washington

MUSICAL SELECTION .. America The Beautiful, Arr. by Thomas Knox MGYUSGT Michael S. Ryan, Baritone United States Marine Band

READING OF GENERAL LOGAN'S ORDER ESTABLISHING MEMORIAL DAY .... Roena Bayes, Department Commander, American Legion

INTRODUCTION OF DISTINGUISHED GUESTS .... Robert F. Sutphin

MUSICAL SELECTION .... Battle Hymn of the Republic, Arr. by Ringwald MGYSGT Michael S. Ryan, Baritone United States Marine Band

INTRODUCTION OF THE SPEAKER .... Robert F. Sutphin

MEMORIAL DAY ADDRESS .. Hon. J. Danforth Quayle, Vice President of the United States

TAPS .... GYSGT. Raymond H. Dryburgh United States Marine Band

BENEDICTION .Chaplain, Lt. Col. F. Walter Montondon

RETIRING OF THE COLORS .... Combined Veteran's Honor Guard

POSTLUDE .... United States Marine Band

Source

Reprinted from *Program 1989,* published by the Grand Army of the Republic Memorial Corporation.

* * *

Flags In

Each year for the past 40 years, the 3d U.S. Infantry (The Old Guard) has honored America's fallen heroes by placing American flags before the gravestones and niches of servicemembers buried at both Arlington National Cemetery and the U.S. Soldier's and Airmen's Home National Cemetery on the Friday morning prior to Memorial Day.

This tradition, known as "flags in," has been conducted annually since The Old Guard was designated as the Army's official ceremonial unit in 1948.

Every available soldier in the 3d U.S. Infantry participates in the traditional flag placement. Soldiers take to the burial grounds at 5 a.m. and place small American flags approximately one foot in front and centered on the tombstones. In Arlington National Cemetery, the mission of placing the flags must be completed prior to the cemetery's 8 a.m. opening. During that three hour period, the soldiers will place flags in front of nearly 175,000 gravestones and about 7,300 niches at the cemetery's columbarium.

Another 13,500 flags are placed at the Soldier's and Airmen's Cemetery.

Additionally, Old Guard soldiers remain in the cemetery throughout the weekend, ensuring that a flag remains in front of each gravestone.

Flags are also placed at the graves of the four unknown servicemen interred at the Tomb of the Unknowns by the Tomb Sentinels.

All flags are removed after Memorial Day before each cemetery is opened to the public.

Source and Comment

Fact Sheet 1988, published by the Public Affairs Office, Military District of Washington, Fort McNair. The Third United States Infantry is the oldest active duty infantry unit in the Army, in service since 1784. It is a ceremonial unit but it also provides security for the national capital. For its history, see "Army Unit Organization Day," p. 346.

* * *

Sacred and Secular

Boalsburg, a town of approximately eight hundred people in central Pennsylvania, proudly announces from its billboards its claim to historical significance:

Boalsburg
An American Village
Birthplace of Memorial Day

In the spring of every year, when American patriots gather at cemeteries, town halls, shrines and churches to celebrate Memorial Day, the citizens of Boalsburg and vicinity remind themselves that their ancestors brought forth an event that has become a national holiday. Memorial Day is, as W. Lloyd Warner has observed, "both sacred and secular, it is a holy day as well as a holiday and is accordingly celebrated." Along with Thanksgiving Day and the perhaps less explicitly religious observances of the Fourth of July and the birthdays of Washington and Lincoln, Memorial Day is part of an American ceremonial calendar. To be sure, it is a day of pleasure, relaxation or outings for most Americans. It is also, particularly for the towns and small cities of the northeastern United States, a sacred day when the war dead are mourned, the spirit of redemptive sacrifice is extolled and pledges to American ideals are renewed.

In Boalsburg and the surrounding communities elaborate preparations precede the day itself. During the week or two prior to May 30th, students in the public elementary schools construct flag displays, many of which are pictured on the pages of the local newspapers. Graves of the war dead are decorated by families and patriotic organizations. The Veterans of Foreign Wars and the American Legion of the area hold meetings to plan for the holy day and services to commemorate their dead. As the day nears, merchants and residents put up American flags, and editorials appear in the newspapers encouraging patriotic observance and sometimes lamenting flagging patriotic zeal in the community. On the Sunday before Memorial Day churches feature sermons on the redemptive power of human sacrifice for God and country, and veterans and their families gather at the Twenty-Eighth Division Memorial Shrine in Boalsburg to hear messages on the same theme. The climax of the celebration occurs, however, at the end of Memorial Day when all the patriotic groups and celebrants converge at the cemeteries to bring their ceremonies to a collective conclusion.

At six o'clock P.M. on May 30th, 1967, a crowd gathered on Church Street in Boalsburg to watch a brief parade made up of a high school band, color guards of the VFW and Legion, fire trucks, and Girl Scouts and Brownies carrying wreaths of flowers. The crowd followed the march two blocks to the cemetery behind Zion Lutheran Church. As the people found their places in front of the speakers' platform, the Girl Scouts placed their flowers on the soldiers' graves and a rifle salute was fired by a drill team. For over a hundred yards behind the crowd stretched the cemetery containing many stones marking those fallen in American wars. The grave of Amos Meyers was there, the private who was killed on the last day of the Battle of Gettysburg at the age of 23 and whose mother decorated his grave on that first Memorial Day in 1864. The minister of Zion Lutheran Church offered an invocation, and the district representative to the State Legislature in Harrisburg rose to give the address.

It was a typical Memorial Day message that lifted up images the people anticipated on the basis of the occasion. The nation's and community's war dead were honored as the speaker symbolically united most of the ethnic and religious groups. He called upon his hearers to remember on this day the sacrificed dead—the Smiths and Steins killed in Vietnam, the Maloneys and Rossis who fell in the Pacific islands, the Heidlers and Lozoskis who made the "supreme sacrifice" in the battle of Meuse-Argonne. These blood sacrifices will not have been in vain only if the living of the community pledge themselves to the principles for which these men died: democratic freedom and the defense of freedom against tyranny and oppression around the world. The sacrifices are the sanctification of America's "destiny under God," the destiny of preserving and dispensing freedom.

Since the spirit of protest against United States involvement in Vietnam was very much in the air in the spring of 1967, a number of Memorial Day speakers attempted to draw a line between democratic freedom and certain types of dissent. "Those who practice civil disobedience," said a Legionnaire at a town a few miles from Boalsburg, "must expect to suffer the penalties provided for violating our laws. It is not an exercise of free expression to burn a draft card, nor to desecrate the flag of the United States."

The Memorial Day celebration is an American sacred ceremony, a religious ritual, a modern cult of the dead. Although it shares the theme of redemptive sacrifice with Christianity and other religions, and although its devotees would insist that the God invoked is the God of Judaism and Christianity, the Memorial Day rite is a national service that unites Protestants, Catholics and Jews beyond their differences.

Source and Comment

American Quarterly, XXI (1969), 739-41. Conrad Cherry describes the Memorial Day observance in Boalsburg, Pennsylvania, as a "case study" of an "American Sacred Ceremony," a rite which validates that "America is the nation destined to act as a missionary and defender of democratic principles around the world." For another view see John F. Wilson, *Public Religion in American Culture,* Philadelphia, 1979.

* * *

Memorial Day Carnival at the Indy Speedway

Seven drunken, bare-chested teenage boys drape themselves across the windshield of my car as I wait for the light to change. Squirming, they relayer themselves like slabs of bacon, and their mirrored sunglasses send blinding jets of light in a dozen directions. The stoplight probably changed some minutes ago, but all I can see is flesh tanned to the color of walnut oil, cans of beer, hairless chests, and lascivious leers. A rhythmic pounding on the car roof tells me that at least one young man is trying to get in feet first. Out of the back window, I watch six more trying to lift the car by its bumpers and cart it away. Another, with a video camera perched like a falcon on his shoulder, zooms in for a close-up of my chest. Just as I begin wondering if this can possibly be for real, I decipher what they have been chanting maniacally for the past few minutes: "Show us your tits! Show us your tits!"

When the light changes, they melt off the car and surge around a young woman reckless enough to take a stroll in a bikini through what appears to be the largest fraternity party on earth, which begins miles from the Speedway in all directions and now, the day before the race, is building to a crescendo that only tomorrow's auto-eroticism will satisfy.

Sixteenth Street, the main drag that leads to the Speedway, looks like a war zone. At the doorway to one trailer, a large papier-mâché sculpture of a woman, naked from the waist up, wears a sign that says OFFICIAL INSPECTION STATION. Unhinged by the sight of females of all ages and body types, the men chant until they're hoarse and then make breast-juggling motions with their hands. At odd moments a girl will leap atop a trailer and pose with her blouse held open, turn, then button up and disappear into the rowdy mob.

Radios blare, people caterwaul, engines rev, and the combined smear of low drama and teeth-rattling noise becomes fiercer the closer you get to the Speedway itself, that sacred arena, the still center of the carnival. Carnival, from the Latin *carne,* "flesh," and *levare,* "to take away." A tub-thumping, earthy, hell-for-leather orgy before life's fun has to stop.

By 6 A.M., when the gates open on race day, people are already in line to find the seats they purchased last year the morning after the race. Next to them stand fans from all over the country and all over the world: shoe salesmen from Switzerland tired of the Grand Prix circuit, bartenders from Phoenix and autobody workers from Detroit who will leave with their first sunburns, carloads of young men, families with small children, women dressed in brightly colored flame suits that hug the body tightly and suggest that they might, at any moment, be called upon to leap into the pits and take charge.

Souvenir stands are already hawking Indy 500 air fresheners, place mats, Frisbees, coffee mugs, miniature cars, black-and-white checkered victory flags, pot holders, and T-shirts. I can't resist buying a turquoise-and-pink T-shirt with an Indy car zooming off the chest, which vows LIFE BEGINS AT 220 MPH. As I slip it on over my sundress to check the size, and then off again, a platoon of men yell from their girl-watching spot. By now this is old news, and I've learned that the men don't touch you; their assaults (or compliments, depending on your point of view) are strictly verbal.

Inside Gasoline Alley, where the cars are stabled, wide boulevards of combed cement separate rows of garages, and life is as serious as a bank balance. The winner will zoom off with half a million dollars, and just being in the race guarantees about $90,000. Companies donate dozens of miscellaneous awards from $5,000 to $75,000 to the oldest driver, fastest qualifier, leader of the first ten laps, best chief mechanic, driver with the least pit time, and so on.

Bustling around the tense streets of Gasoline Alley, young men dressed in Flash Gordon jumpsuits make sure their cars are fit. A high-wing Cessna airplane flies overhead, towing a banner that reads OLD INDIANA FUN PARK—ZOW! It recalls the Kenneth Fearing poem in which he describes a man's brief, highspeed cartoon life with "Zowie did he live and zowie did he die."

The cars emerge from their garages, some towed by long blue canvas ribbons that look like the long lines trainers use when exercising Thoroughbreds. Parts of the cars are often wearing black blankets to keep their flanks covered. A low-slung sulfur yellow car belongs to Al Unser, whose son will be racing against him today; it contains the power of over seven hundred horses, though it's only fifteen feet long and weighs only about fifteen hundred pounds. Unser climbs inside the car, which has been molded to the eccentricities of his bottom and back, and stretches his legs far into the nose. He will race practically lying down.

Enclosed entirely in armor, with only a narrow visor open across their eyes, the drivers are all modern knights, riding horsepower. Speed is their lance. Despite the crews, this is not a team sport. Everyone else out on the track will be an opponent. Medieval knights had allegorical names, like Sir Goodheart or Lancelot; these latter-day knights walk around the grounds and drive cars plastered with slogans. Some call them the fastest billboards on earth. But how eerie it is to see a man with "Living Well" emblazoned on his helmet and "Die Hard" stamped on his back. On his shoulder may be the words "Goodyear" or "Champion" or "Sound Design" or "True Value."

What are you to make of a glossy red car driving toward you with "Sleep Cheap" (the slogan of the Red Roof Inns) on both sides of its nose?

Cars, drivers, and pit crews all push through the crowds and take their places on the racetrack. At some point the crews and officials withdraw a little, and the men are alone with their machines. The steering wheels often have been put in *after* them. Sealed up in their narrow cockpits, they adjust the knitted Ninja masks over their faces, fix the rub of the helmet strap, and check the buckles that hold helmet and flame suit together so that their necks won't sprain in the terrible g forces of the turns. You can see the loneliness in their eyes, the squinting concentration with which they erase every one of the half million people from the raceway. They hear nothing, see nothing, but track....

The national anthem is followed by a Memorial Day invocation by clergy, and it's no coincidence that the race takes place on Sunday at 11 A.M., church-service time, with a somewhat previous prayer for the dead and injured, and then "Taps" while the stands fall silent. Jim Nabors sings about going back home to Indiana. Thousands of multicolored balloons spiral like DNA into the blue. "Gentlemen," the frail voice of the Speedway's chairperson ritualistically intones, "start your engines." "The magnificent machines," the announcer cries, "are ready!"

A heaving and coughing of engines. Pace cars roll away to lead a warmup lap, then there's a pace lap that reaches a speed of one hundred miles per hour as the crews sprint back to their pits to get ready for action. On the electronic scoreboard, silhouetted fans leap and cheer. The crowd stretching thickly around the two-and-a-half-mile oval twitches and yells, rising like the prerace balloons as the cars roar around the far turn and into sight again. The pace car peels off and the drivers take flight....

Three cars collide, metal parts arcing high into the air, and the race stops for a short while. The cars pause at speed and aren't allowed to change position relative to one another until the debris is cleared from the track and the yellow flag is lifted. Suddenly the race restarts....

The speed at which the cars pass is sense-bludgeoning. Whining, they catapult around a corner into the straightaway while their engines growl and gnaw in a thirty-megaton buzz. You need peripheral vision to see the cars arrive, flash past, vanish around the next turn. They move so fast that unless you fix on one car and track it, a loud blur of color whizzes past. Fans shake their heads no, no, no, no, thirty-three times as the field rushes by. People dropping empty beer cans into the scaffolding underneath the bleachers make a constant drizzle of tin. When cars pull into the pits, the crews come alive, changing treadless tires ("skins"), filling the forty-gallon tanks with methanol, tinkering, adjusting, putting out small fires, handing the driver a drink, then shoving him back—all within ten or twenty seconds.

Not only mechanics and engineers but also aerodynamic specialists work with each driver. As the orange wind sock atop the tower reminds you, this is really an air race. How do you keep a light piece of metal going over two hundred miles per hour on the ground? Though the men and occasionally women inside are called drivers, they sit in a *cockpit,* they worry about the car's *wings,* and they are obsessed with *wake turbulence.* Small canard fins at the *nose cone* up front pay homage to Burt Rutan's *Voyager* and all the other canard designs he's made famous over the years. The rear wing functions like an upside-down airplane wing, producing *down force.* An airplane wing is rounded on top, but car wings are rounded on the bottom. Air whooshes all around the wing, but it has farther to travel along the bottom, becomes thinner, and produces a low-pressure area. On top, the higher pressure bears down and keeps the car on the ground. The car's underside holds the ground, too. But these effects combine to churn up small tornadoes, and the swirling whirlpools of wind that each car trails behind it put the next car in peril....

Beating, banging, fighting the steering wheel, pulling g's, the furious cars slide in and out of corners. Drivers need to be aggressive but at a controlled pace. They must be mentally relaxed, but there is constant battering to their neck and muscles. Few sports stay right on the edge of life from start to finish. Exhaust pours from the cars, and, from the drivers, exhaustion. A passion for the extreme must be what fuels drivers and fans alike: a dizzying, all-out, pedalto-the-metal, death-defying effort for as long as life allows. . . .

I don't believe most race fans come to see crashes. They come to see their gods parading at speed before them. Accidents happen, but they are described as "spectacular," and the spectators just confirm how gripping the element of sheer spectacle is. You can't really love cars without disowning the preindustrial world. But the scorpion of progress has a wicked sting in its tail. Nature may thwart us at every turn, but the machines we've created and endowed with superhuman power sometimes terrify and thwart us even more. When men are injured in crashes, the fans sound truly aggrieved. When men walk away from devastating smashups, the fans shriek with joy. They have come partly to see Man vs. Machine, urgently hoping that man will prevail.

Source and Comment

Traveler, May, 1988. From an article in "The Traveling Spectator" by Diane Ackerman. Cf. "The Southern 500 Stock Car Race," p. 330. Car races, like horse races in earlier times, have become a feature of various holidays in America. The "Indy 500" is the major Memorial Day event for a large number of Americans who gather in Indianapolis or around television sets to see it. First run at 500 miles on May 30, 1911, the event has become the premier automobile race in the world with a purse of more than four and one half million dollars, $500,000 of which goes to the winner. The grandstand, which is unique, holds a quarter of a million spectators.

Plebe Recognition Day
Friday of Commissioning Week

"Plebes," first-year midshipmen at the United States Naval Academy, are considered by upper classmen "the lowest of the low." During graduation week, usually at the end of May, a very brief "recognition" ceremony takes place at which they are divested of this ignominious designation, and for the few remaining days are known as "fourth classmen." The recognition ceremony is followed immediately by an attempt to climb the Herndon Monument, a tumultuous event. The monument, erected in 1859, honors Commander William Louis Herndon, a naval scientist who died heroically when his ship went down in a storm. Climbing Herndon Monument parallels spring rites on other campuses. A retired history professor recalls: "When I was an undergraduate at Illinois Wesleyan University, 1933-36, freshman hazing ended in the Spring with a tug-of-war over Sugar Creek and freshman climbing a greased poll to pull down a 'rat' cap that was nailed on top."

The Recognition Ceremony

During the traditional plebe recognition ceremony, plebes (freshmen) strive to climb to the top of a greased Herndon Monument. It is said that the midshipman who removes the plebe hat and places an upperclassman's hat atop Herndon will be the first admiral of the class.

The end of plebe (freshman) year was the occasion for one of the academy's most exuberant celebrations. It began with the last parade at the close of which the upperclassmen shook hands with the new third classmen. Thereupon, the latter turned their caps and coats backwards and did a snake dance through the yard, chanting "'Tain't no mo plebes." Around 1915, the upperclassmen placed a cap atop the granite shaft of Herndon Monument, to be retrieved by the plebes as a final rite of passage. In time, the snake dance was abandoned, and the Plebe Recognition Ceremony, as it is called today, at Herndon Monument became the climax of plebe year.

Each spring, the new midshipmen smear Herndon Monument with grease.... Then hundreds of them try to shinny up that slick obelisk, which rises 20 feet above a courtyard at the U.S. Naval Academy. It's an Annapolis tradition: ... In any event, women first joined the climbing ritual two years ago [in 1977]—much to the consternation of male classmates. On the day of the women's first climb, only one managed to inch part-way up the granite column. Within seconds, she had lost her precarious grip—some eyewitnesses said that she was grabbed, others that she slipped—and down she fell, into the wriggling mass of midshipmen below.... More than three years have elapsed since women were first admitted, by congressional order, to the nation's three service academies: ... For the most part, the women's progress has resembled that slow, slippery climb up Herndon Monument.

Source and Comment

News Release no. 0034-80, United States Naval Academy; San Francisco *Chronicle*, December 29, 1979. News release and background supplied by Captain Clark M. Gammell and Janet T. Steward of the Public Affairs Office, United States Naval Academy. The historical information is quoted from Jack Sweetman, *The U.S. Naval Academy, An Illustrated History*, Annapolis, 1979, 160. The news item on women climbing Herndon Monument is by John Hildebrand and originally appeared in *Newsday*. The retired historian who climbed the greased poll is Robert David Ochs of the University of South Carolina.

Ascension Day and Associated Days
Moveable: Thursday in May-June

Ascension Day (Holy Thursday) is the fortieth day after Easter. It commemorates Christ's Ascension after His Resurrection. Reflecting both Christian and pagan custom, it once featured a religious procession to symbolize Christ's entry into heaven. In many lands, a devil was either chased through the streets and ducked in a pond or pummeled or burned in effigy. This devil seems to have filled the role of the biblical scapegoat who was visited with and punished for the sins of the community on the Jewish Day of Atonement. Young boys were sometimes switched as they were driven along parish boundaries, not only to purify them of evil through flagellation but to teach them the limits of their parish. Other customs attached to the day range from the Roman Catholic removal of the paschal candle from the altar to show Christ's departure from the Apostles to the decoration of doorways with flowers and branches to ward off malignant spirits.

Farm Rites for Rogation Days

The custom of praying for relief from afflictions and for a bountiful harvest on Rogation Days—the Monday, Tuesday, and Wednesday before the Feast of the Ascension—is universal in the Roman Catholic Church. But in the Czech farming communities of Iowa and Minnesota, the importance of these days has always been especially stressed. Until recently, a procession of the entire congregation was organized after Mass on these days to follow the pastor into the fields for the purpose of reciting the prescribed Litany of the Saints and praying for good crops. In New Prague [Minnesota], on the east and south ends of the town crucifixes were erected, and after visiting the fields, the procession made its way to each of these to pray to St. Wenceslaus before returning to church for the benediction and conclusion of the ceremony.

Source and Comment

Journal of American Folklore, LXIX (1956), 284. From Lawrence V. Ryan's essay, "Some Czech-American Forms of Divination and Supplication." For Ryan's sources, see note on "St. Barbara's Day Prediction," p. 425. Rogation is a day of prayer particularly for the harvest during the three days of supplication before Ascension Day. The word also refers to chanting the litany for these days during the Ascension procession.

* * *

Working on Ascension Day

It is unlucky to do any work on Ascension Day.

A man living at Emmittsburg [Maryland] disregarded the prevalent idea that one must not work on Ascension Day. He went into the mountain to cut a fine tree to use in his mill. The tree split when it was cut about halfway through.

This had never happened to him before. It was too long for his wagon, and wanting an augur, he had to send two miles to get it. Going home, his wagon upset, and just as he was about to start again a large rattle-snake nearly bit his horse. He never worked again on Ascension Day.

At the Bethesda state quarries miners refused to work on Ascension Day. Managers tried to break up this superstition and for two years succeeded. The men again refused; there had been fatal accidents both years.

Source

Memoirs of the American Folklore Society, XVIII (1925), 117-18. "Folk-Lore from Maryland," collected by Annie W. Whitney and Caroline C. Bullock. Informants not given.

* * *

Sewing on Ascension Day

Explanations of the reason for bad luck add much to the interest and value of the superstition. A teacher at the [Maryland] Normal School mentioned, as one of the strongest impressions of her childhood, her mother's objection to sewing on Ascension Day. Several of the papers tell us that the sin lies in the fact that "every stitch pierces the Saviour's side." If you sew on Sunday, the stitches pierce his heart, and the devil will make you rip them out with your nose.

Source

Journal of American Folklore, XI (1898), 9. Recorded by Mrs. Waller R. Bullock of Baltimore, Maryland. Cf. "New Year's Beliefs," p. 20.

Anything sewed on Ascension Day will be struck by lightning. "A little company of persons were caught in a storm. One asked: 'Has any one anything on that was made on Ascension Day?' 'I have an apron,' a girl responded. She removed it and placed it on a stump near by, and the lightning struck it immediately."

Source

Journal of American Folklore, IV (1891), 122. Recorded by J. G. Owens in Buffalo Valley, central Pennsylvania.

* * *

Bird-shooting on Ascension Day

One will frequently observe [in the Pennsylvania Dutch country], even at this day, the bodies of birds of prey, with outstretched wings, nailed against the gable ends of barns. Birds of this kind, shot upon the farm, were thus exposed to keep away others. A quarter of a century ago it was the custom for the young men to organize a party and shoot all obnoxious birds, and frequently those beneficial to the farmer, on Ascension Day. The origin of this custom, and the reason why that particular day should be selected, is not known.

Source and Comment

Journal of American Folklore, I (1888), 131. From "Folk-Lore of the Pennsylvania Germans," observed by W. J. Hoffman.

The birds are pests but they also seem to be serving a scapegoat role like the wrens which were stoned in England on St. Stephen's Day. For another community effort at pest control that became a festive event, see the description of rattlesnake hunts, p. 112.

* * *

Customs and Beliefs for Ascension Day

On Ascension Day and on the days of Simon, Judas, and the Apostle St. Andrews, there should be no letting of blood.

Source

Journal of American Folklore, IV (1891), 128. Collected by J. G. Owens from Buffalo Valley, central Pennsylvania, largely settled by German Lutherans. His source was "A 'German Centennial Almanac'" which prescribed "many of their beliefs and practices."

* * *

If it rains on Ascension Day, it will rain for forty days.

Source

Journal of American Folklore, XXXVI (1923), 17. Collected in Dutchess County, New York, by Gertrude Barnes from "old residents" of partially Dutch descent. Cf. "Whitsuntide Beliefs," p. 227, "St. Médard's Day," p. 233; St. Swithin's Day, p. 277; and "Pennsylvania Dutch on St. Patrick's Day," p. 127.

* * *

When a child is very backward in learning to talk, rise very early on Ascension Day, do not speak a word to anyone, lay the child, nude, face down on the dewy lawn or on any clean grass, and silently repeat the three Highest Names, and the child will soon learn to talk.

Source

Memoirs of the American Folklore Society, XVIII (1925), 118. From "Folk-Lore from Maryland," collected by Annie W. Whitney and Caroline C. Bullock, who do not supply informants.

* * *

Warr windla wescht uff der Himmel fawr dawg, don doot's bubble way un beissich warra, un die frau doot seilaiva kne kinner may greega.

Whoever washes diapers on Ascension Day, the baby will be in pain and become itchy, and the woman will never have any more children.

Source

Pennsylvania Folklife, XVII (1967), 30. Collected by Victor C. Dieffenbach. See note on "Pennsylvania Dutch on St. Patrick's Day," p. 127.

Shavout

May-June

Originally Shavout, which is the sixth day of Sivan, the ninth month of the lunar year, was a Canaanite festival honoring the barley harvest. By coincidence it was observed at about the same time as the anniversary of the giving of the Ten Commandments or Torah on Mount Sinai. So as often happens in such cases, the two came to be celebrated as one. This was considered fitting, for the Torah or "law" was believed to embody a covenant between God and Israel, and the grain harvest was evidence of a covenant between man and Nature, an exemplification of God. Shavout is known as the Feast of Weeks because it occurs six weeks after Passover and is looked upon as a continuation of this holiday. It is also known as Pentecost, from the Greek meaning "fifty" because it follows Passover by fifty days, paralleling Whitsunday, the Christian Pentecost, which is fifty days after Easter.

Dairy products, especially cheese dishes, are served during Shavout, often with honey. One explanation is that this combination reminds people that the Torah should be compared to milk and honey because it is nourishing and sweet. A more practical though equally imaginative one is that the Jews, tired and hungry when they returned from Mount Sinai after receiving the Torah, did not want to wait for a cooked meal and ate cheese, the first thing at hand.

Torah Emet

God has given the Torah of Truth
To his people through his faithful Prophet.
God will not change His law
Or alter it ever.

Source

YIVO Institute for Jewish Research Archives, New York. From *Shavout,* p. 35, an undated pamphlet issued by the Labor Zionist Organization of America, New York, and affiliated organizations.

* * *

Cheese Dishes

Cheese Kreplech

½ pt. heavy sour cream
2 eggs

½ lb. melted butter
1 teaspoon salt
3 cups flour
2 teaspoons baking powder
½ lb. cream cheese
½ lb. cottage cheese
1 egg
⅛ lb. butter (melted)

Mix ingredients of first six lines and knead well. In another bowl, mix the ingredients of the last four lines, blending the materials carefully. Roll out the dough in a sheet ¼ inch thick. With a knife mark off 4 inch squares. On each square place a tablespoonful of cheese mixture. Fold dough over cheese in triangles, pinching edges firmly. Place in buttered pan, baking in moderate oven three-quarters of an hour until brown.

Noodle and Cheese Pudding

1 cup sour cream
½ lb. cottage cheese
1 cup milk
½ teaspoon salt
⅛ teaspoon cinnamon
3 eggs beaten
2 cups broad noodles, cooked and drained
2 tbsp. melted butter

1   heaping tbsp. sugar

Mix all ingredients together and pour into a buttered pudding dish. Bake in a hot oven (400⁰) for about three-quarters of an hour or more until a brown crust forms on top.

Easy Cheese
Blintz Casserole

Batter:
4   large eggs
1¼   cs. milk
2   tbsps. sour cream (or plain yogurt)
¼   c. butter, melted
¾   tsp. vanilla
1⅓   cs. flour
1 to 2 tbsps. sugar
1¼   tsps. baking powder

Filling:
2   7½-to 8-oz. pkgs. farmer cheese (about 1 lb.)
1   15- to 16-oz. container ricotta cheese
2   large eggs
2 to 3 tbsps. sugar
1½ or 2 tbsps. fresh lemon juice

With a blender or mixer, combine all batter ingredients until batter is very smooth. Measure out 1 ½ cups of batter and pour it into a buttered 9x13-inch baking dish. Bake at 350⁰ for about 10 minutes or until set.

Meanwhile, combine all filling ingredients in a large bowl and mix well.

When bottom layer of batter has set, remove baking dish from oven and spread cheese filling over it, smoothing the top. Briefly mix remaining batter and slowly pour it into casserole so that cheese filling is covered.

Return casserole to oven and continue to bake for 35 to 40 minutes or until top is puffed and set. Allow casserole to rest 10 to 15 minutes before cutting into squares.

Serve with sour cream, applesauce, or plain or vanilla yogurt. Serves 8 as a main course or more as an accompaniment.

Not-So-Rich
Cheese Cake

½   c. butter or margarine
1   c. flour
¼   tsp. salt
¾   c. confectioners' sugar, divided
3   eggs, separated, divided

Cottage Cheese Strudel

Pastry:
½   lb. cottage cheese
¼   lb. margarine
¼   lb. butter
2   cs. flour
     dash salt

Filling:
     cinnamon
1   c. preserves, any flavor
1   c. coconut
1   c. raisins
½   c. chopped nuts

Source

The first two cheese dishes are collected in *Shavout: A Workbook and Guide,* Jewish Community Center of Detroit, 1953, 10. From traditional holiday recipes "assembled and compiled" in a mimeographed booklet by Max Chomsky, in the archives of YIVO Institute for Jewish Research, New York. Chomsky does not give his informant for the *kreplech* but cites Betty D. Greenberg and Althea A. Silverman, National Women's League, United Synagogue of America, as his source for the noodle and cheese pudding. Additional recipes are from the *Jewish Exponent,* May 20, 1988, from the column "Fannie's Favorites" by Fannie Fertik.

Whitsunday and Whitsuntide
Moveable: Sunday in May-June

Whitsunday, also called Pentecost, occurs on the seventh Sunday or fifty days after Easter and ten days after the Ascension Day, and Whitsuntide is the week beginning with Whitsunday, though often only the first two days are celebrated. For Christians it commemorates the descent of the Holy Ghost as a Pentecostal flame upon the disciples that took place on the Jewish Shavout or Pentecost which honors God's covenant with Israel. The miraculous descent of the Holy Ghost heightened the powers of the disciples to such a degree that they are said to have soon afterward baptized thousands. Because it subsequently became a traditional time for baptism, the English called the day White Sunday for the white garments of the baptismal candidates. The German word for Pentecost is *Pfingsten,* and in Pennsylvania Dutch celebrants were known as *pfingsters* and New York Dutch as *pinksters.*

The holiday is linked to pagan spring rites, such as the English customs of morris dancing and dressing a boy called Green George or Jack-in-the-Green or Whitsunday Lout in green boughs and leaves and marching him through the village. Throughout Europe Whitsunday has long been a spring holiday, a time for picnics, outings into the country, serenading, drinking and merrymaking.

Pinkster

[In Albany, New York, ca. 1800] on Capitol, or "Pinkster," Hill the festival was religiously celebrated each May in a week-long carnival which attracted Negroes and whites alike from the city and the surrounding countryside. For many years the festivities on the hill were presided over by a colorful black, known locally as "King Charley" or "Charley of the Pinkster Hill," occasionally with the aid of Adam Blake, the body servant of the patroon, who acted as master of ceremonies. Gay booths were erected where ginger-bread, cider, and apple-toddy were freely dispensed to all comers. There was lively native dancing, accompanied by the syncopated rhythm of crude drums made by stretching sheepskin over wooden eel-pots or hollow logs, and days and evenings given over to drinking, sporting, love-making, and a variety of other associated activities. Circus acts were often imported for the occasion; and as Albanian James Eights, looking back some sixty years, recalled:

> Here might be seen for a moderate pittance, the royal tiger of Bengal, and the lordly lion from Africa, with a monkey perched over the entrance door, profusely provided for by the youth and children of the white population....

The festival of Pinkster continued to be celebrated in Albany until 1811 when the Common Council passed an ordinance prohibiting the erection of any tent, booth, or stall, and any gambling, dancing, or parading within the city limits during "the days commonly called Pinxter." The town fathers apparently thought the annual revelries of "Pinkster Hill" unbefitting the dignity of a modern city.

Source and Comment

New York Folklore Quarterly, XXII (1966), 18-19. James H. Pickering describes the Pinkster festivities in an article on James Fenimore Cooper's recollections of this holiday in his novel, *Satanstoe* (1845). King Charley, the master of ceremonies at the carnival and a famous drummer, died in 1824. He is said to have been one hundred and twenty-five years old. The festival was banned for "boisterous rioting and drunkeness," but from time to time so were Mardi Gras and masking and mumming at New Year's.

* * *

Pinkster

Pinkster Ode to King Charley

When leaves the fig tree putteth out,
When calves and lambs for mothers cry,
When toads begin to hop about,
We know of truth that summer's nigh.

So after *Pos* [Pasch, Easter] when hens do cluck,
When gawky goblins peep and feed,
And boys get fewer eggs to suck,
We know that *Pinkster* comes indeed.

226

At Pinkster, flow'rs will deck the field,
And pleasures sweet will banish pain;
Love-broken-hearts shall all be heal'd,
Although they may be crack'd again.

Ay, hearts, tho' hard as blistered steel
And tough as nerves of turkey's thigh;
Must break, or melt, whene'er they feel
Bright Pinkster-sparks from Goonna's [Guinea's?] eye.

Of Pinkster, who presumes to sing,
Must homage pay to Charles the King: ...

Tho' for a sceptre he was born,
Tho' from his father's kingdom torn,
And doom'd to be a slave; still he
Retains his native majesty.

O could I loud as thunder sing,
Thy fame should sound, great Charles, the king,
From Hudson's stream to Niger's wave,
And rouse the friend of every slave.
But, cease to clank my hero's chain,
'Twill give his royal bosom pain—
Good Pinkster comes with merry glee,
And brings a gladsome Jubilee.

Rise then, each son of Pinkster, rise,
Snatch fleeting pleasure as it flies.
See Nature spreads her carpet gay,
For you to dance your care away.
"Care! what have we with care to do?
"Masters! Care was made for you.
"Behold rich free-men—see *dull care*
"Oft make their bodies lean and spare.
"How many weave the web of life,
"With woof of care, and warp of strife.
"With care of state and statesman groans,
"As if its weight would break his bones.
"But what have we with care to do,
"My Pinkster boys? 'tis not for you."
Thus spake the genius of the day,
As up the hill she led the way.

Now hark! the Banjo, rub a dub,
Like a washer-woman's tub;
And hear the drum, 'tis rolling now,
Row de dow, row de dow.
The pipe and tabor, flute and fife,
Shall wake the dullest soul to life.
All beneath the shady tree
There they hold the jubilee.
Charles, the king, will then advance,
Leading on the Guinea dance,
Moving o'er the flow'ry green,
You'll know him by his graceful mien;
You'll know him on the dancing ground,
For where he is folks gather round;
You'll know him by his royal nose,
You'll know him by his Pinkster clothes,
You'll know him by his pleasant face,
And by his hat of yellow lace;

You'll know him by his princely air,
And his politeness to the fair;
And when you know him, then you'll see
A slave whose soul was always free.
Look till the visual nerves do pain,
You'll "never see his like again." ...

Source

Pinkster Ode ... Dedicated to Carolus Africanus Rex, Albany, New York, 1803. See "Pinkster," p. 226, and the note.

Transcribed from a pamphlet by the pseudonymous "Absalom Aimwell" cited there.

* * *

Whitsuntide Beliefs

If you desire good luck in a special enterprise, wear all new clothes on Whitsun-day.

It is bad luck to cut your finger nails on Whit-Monday.

Source

Memoirs of the American Folklore Society, XVIII (1925), 118. From "Folk-Lore from Maryland" collected by Annie W. Whitney and Caroline C. Bullock, who did not give informants.

* * *

If it rains on Pfingster [Pfingsten] or (Whitsunday), it rains every Sunday for seven weeks.

Source

Journal of American Folklore, XXXVI (1923), 17. Collected by Gertrude Barnes in Dutchess County, New York, from "old residents of Dutch extraction." Cf. "Pennsylvania Dutch on St. Patrick's Day," p. 127; "Customs and Beliefs for Ascension Day," p. 223; "St. Médard's Day," p. 233; and "St. Swithin's Day," p. 277.

* * *

Whitmonday: Pingsht-Moondawg

Up until a generation or two ago Whit-Monday (*Pingsht-Moondawg*) was considered one of the main holidays of the year in the Pennsylvania Dutch country. Almost 175 years ago, on Whit-Monday, May 15, 1780, to be exact, Christopher Marshall, who was sojourning in Lancaster at the time, entered in his now famous diary: "I went nowhere from home this day although it's a very high holiday in this place, and as it was a most pleasant, agreeable, fine day, numbers were diverting themselves abroad, some riding, some walking, others playing long bullets, &c."

Today only the Amish and a mere handful of our older "worldly" Pennsylvania Dutch any longer celebrate this holiday.

How did our early Pennsylvania Dutch folk spend *Pingsht-Moondawg*? By going to the races, at Rothsville (Hawsa Barrick) and in Hanover, for instance; by taking in battalion day [militia drill] at Hamburg; or by coming to town—to York, Lancaster, Reading, or Easton.

The reason that these market towns were so well frequented on Whit-Monday is that this holiday became the substitute for the two-day June fairs which, having fallen into ill repute, were voted out of existence by borough councils around the 1830s.

In the period from about 1835 to the time of the Civil War and even some years later, Whit-Monday in Lancaster was the greatest gala day of the year. It was called the "Dutch Fourth of July." Great crowds of people from all the rural districts streamed into the city; long excursion trains brought thousands more from as far away as Reading and York. The York Democrat of June 7, 1870, wrote: "Quite a number of our young folks visited Lancaster, where Whit-Monday is kept as a universal gala day." The Columbia Spy of May 26, 1866, reported: "The faithful turned out on Monday to celebrate their dear *Pfingsten*. It took an extra train to carry this motley crowd into Lancaster."

People came to town on Whit-Monday not only to eat and drink: they wanted to be amused, too. So around Center Square one found the booths of the itinerant vendors of patent medicines, showmen with snakes and fat women, persuasive individuals with everything from "Shoe Blackening" to "Razor Powder." But alas, about the time of the Civil War the city fathers refused to license these vendors any longer, and with their passing from the scene Whit-Monday in Lancaster lost much of its drawing power....

There were horse races, rope walkers, bands, balloon ascensions, velocipede races, trained mice and monkeys, stereoscopic views and dancing. Even implement dealers set up exhibits on the Square in Lancaster as early as 1866 to show the newest in farm machinery: "Self-Rakers attached to a reaper."

Then there were the flying horses. "Large numbers of persons visited these revolving horses, most of them, however, simply to see them in operation. All such stopped only a moment to look on, or 'passed by on the other side.' A great many 'went in,' and took a seat on a 'horse' or in a 'coach,' paying five cents each for the privilege, and were whirled round at a rapid rate for a few minutes," reported the Lancaster Daily Express of June 11, 1867.

In the early 1880s the Italian balloon men began to appear on the scene. And there were toy vendors, too, of course. One of the most entertaining of these curb salesmen in 1876 was a glib-tongued fellow who sold a toy by which he was able to make successful imitations of a mockingbird, a poodle dog, a pig, and other animals. He gathered quite a little audience wherever he went, selling his whistles for ten cents each, or:

> *Three for a quarter,*
> *One for yourself, your wife, and daughter.*

Source

Pennsylvania Dutchman, V (May 1953), 5, 12. Recalled by Alfred L. Shoemaker. His sources are his own recollections and nineteenth-century newspapers and informants cited in the text.

* * *

Battalion Day

Whitmonday was the day for the "Battalion." This was a day looked forward to by both young and old. The whole family would go. Whitmonday came in late May or early June. Lenhartsville [Pennsylvania] was a small town, but had a Battalion every year.

There were two hotels in town and each one got a band to play. Each hotel also got a few fiddlers to play for the hoedown dances. Early in the morning the people started to come. Some came by train, some by horse and buggy, and some walked so as not to be bothered by the horse. The hotels would do a big business all day and until the wee hours of the next morning.

Dancing would go on at both hotels all afternoon, all evening, and until the small hours of the next morning. The men would pay so much a set for themselves and their lady partners. In this way the fiddlers were paid. The man also set it up for his partner, either for a drink or for something to eat.

The bands had an outdoor stand at each hotel, a nice platform with seats and in the evening it was lit up by crude lamps, which used to burn gasoline.

The big event of the day was the parade at about two o'clock in the afternoon. That gave the people time for an early dinner at home and sufficient time to get to the Battalion before the parade started.

The first in the parade was a fellow riding a white horse. They used to say: "*Er hut der wise garidda* [He rode the white horse]." Then the first brass band would come along playing a march, then clowns and dressed-up children in old clothing, also grown-ups. There was a big wagon-bed with straw in it and full of children having the time of their life, all this drawn by a pair of high-stepping horses. The horses were not used to band music and the driver had his hands full to drive them. There were decorated floats, not elaborate ones, but they looked good to everyone. Then came the second brass band, which played when the first one stopped; more dressed-up kids followed and then came the "Blue Mountain Fire Company," the latter being in existence merely for that day.

The "Blue Mountain Fire Company" was a wagon with a big barrel of water on the wagon, a hose and a hand pump to force the water out to squirt the pretty girls, standing on the pavement, watching the parade. How they yelled when the water got them, but the day was warm and their thin cotton dresses soon dried and no one was hurt.

The end of the parade was more kids falling in line from the pavement from which they were watching the parade, maybe a couple of stray dogs following, and a drunk or two weaving down the street from one side to the other. The street was now very dusty from so many people walking, but no one minded the dust.

There were stands where one could buy candy, a big piece for a penny, pretzels and peanuts. The upper hotel had a big water trough in front under a big willow tree. This was to water the horses and the water was nice and cold, it coming from a spring near by. It sure tasted good on a hot day. The lower hotel had a well with a big wooden pump. The old pump had an iron handle with a ball at the lower end to weigh the handle down. It also looked nice.

At this old pump a bunch of small boys were standing and planning something. An old drunk came along. His name was "Old Pit." He never passed up a drink or "set up," as it was called at that time. One of the boys said, "Pit, are you thirsty?" Old Pit said, "Yes." So the boy said, "Go to the pump and drink your fill." To this Old Pit said, "Ochs" (ox). This was his usual retort when one got the best of him. Old Pit now weaved up to the other hotel to see if anyone was buying a drink for the people in the barroom. He never liked to miss a "set up." He was a poor old fellow and always so thirsty.

So the day passed into evening, some going home to feed their stock, but they were sure to return for an evening of fun. The bands now lit their lights so they could see the music. The old lamp-lighter made the rounds of his coal oil lamps on posts. He started in the old covered wooden bridge crossing the Ontelaunee. There was a coal oil lamp at each end. Then on up the street he went with a bunch of boys following to watch and ask questions. The huckster stands now also lit up, and the old town looked like fairy land to the kids who were used to dark streets. These old street lights did not make much light as they were small and burned coal oil.

Now the people went from one end of town to the other, afraid if they stood still too long that they might miss something.

One band played while the other rested. Then the other one played while the first one rested. So the people went to the band that was playing. A Battalion was more fun than a picnic. It lasted from early morn to the next morn and there was more to do and see.

In the evening the young folks would pair off and go for walks, up and down the pavement, visiting one dance floor, then up to the other hotel to visit that dance floor. Beer flowed freely and the barroom smelled sour like a swillbarrel.

At about midnight the bands packed up and went home. So did most of the people. The dancers and the drunks, however, stayed on. The dancers danced till too tired to keep it up; the drunks so drunk, but still afraid if they went home they might miss a "set up." Some of the drunks were put in the sheds with the horses to sleep it off in the hay, the hostlers seeing to it that they were far enough away from the horses so they could sleep it off and not run the risk of getting hurt. Sometimes it took till the next afternoon till the old drunks had slept it off and went home.

Source and Comment

Pennsylvania Folklife (Spring 1959), 46. Remembered and described by Elsie Smith, who grew up on a Pennsylvania farm and was an informant for the Pennsylvania Folklife Center at Franklin and Marshall College.

The "Battalion" (in Pennsylvania Dutch the *Badalya*) was a military muster. The military exercises, if not omitted altogether, were followed by dancing, feasting, and carousing at the tavern. As to the drinking at the Whitmonday "Battalions," according to the *Pennsylvania Dutchman* (May 1953), 5, a Lancaster, Pennsylvania newspaper suggested in 1883 that the name "Whitsuntide" be changed to "Whiskeytide."

* * *

Portuguese Fishermen's Whitsunday

At Point Loma [California], where almost all Portuguese are fishermen, every year one of the fishing boats is selected and its captain is made President of the Feast of the Holy Ghost, and he has the usual duties that fall upon such office. A prominent role in the festivities is played by a silver crown and scepter. The crown represents both the supreme power of the Holy Ghost and the royalty of Saint Isabel. The scepter is surmounted by a dove, symbolic of the Holy Spirit. During the seven weeks preceding Pentecost—symbolic of the seven gifts of the Holy Ghost—each Sunday the crown is taken to church and placed on the altar. For each of these seven weeks a family and their friends recite the Rosary. The Sunday before Pentecost the crown is taken to the house of the President of the Feast, and it is offered there for seven nights. Finally Pentecost Sunday arrives. The tuna clippers in the harbor are decorated with bunting. A young girl selected by the President and representing Queen Isabel carries the crown from Portuguese Hall to Saint Agnes' Church. She is accompanied by her regal attendants, by various groups of children and adults, dressed in the clothes or uniforms typical of their religious or patriotic societies. There are also bands and drill teams. Upon the arrival of the procession in church, Holy Mass is celebrated. Before the beginning of Mass, the crown is placed upon the high altar, where it remains until the end of the service. After the last Gospel, the Queen and her maids of honor ascend the altar steps and kneel. Then the celebrant of the Mass blesses the crown and places it upon the head of the Queen, while, accompanied by the choir, he intones the hymn "Veni, Creator Spiritus."

At the conclusion of the religious ceremony the procession forms again and escorts the Queen to Portuguese Hall, where a banquet is served. Fireworks and dancing follow the banquet, and an ample supply of food is brought to the poor of the neighborhood and to those who were unable to be present at the feast.

Source

Western Folklore, XIV (1955), 79-91. Edited from an essay by Charles Speroni. The material above is included in *Folklore from the Working Folk of America,* 339-40. See "Sicilian Fishermen's Festivals," p. 348; "Portuguese Labor Day Festa"; p. 328; and "Festa da Serrata," p. 332.

The Feast of Corpus Christi
Moveable: a Thursday in May-June

In the Roman Catholic Church, the festival of the Body of Christ honors the institution of the Eucharist or Sacrament of the Lord's Supper. It is celebrated on the Thursday after Trinity Sunday, which falls one week after Whitsunday. In the thirteenth century, after the doctrine of transubstantiation was defined, devotion to the Blessed Sacrament became popular, and the festival was established as obligatory, with a new office or service written for it by Thomas Aquinas. By the next century it had become the most splendid feast of the religious calendar. It was characterized by magnificent processions, which showed the Host and paraded the power of church and state, and by religious plays enacted by the craft guilds. The rejection of the doctrine of transubstantiation by Protestant churches led to a marked decline in its celebration though it enhanced its importance for the orthodox.

Corpus Christi in Colorado

Let me tell you something about the customs of this place which may perhaps delight and edify those who do not know it.

First of all, we celebrated [in 1874], in due time, the feast of Corpus Christi, a day of great solemnity for the Mexicans. It is so solemn, in fact, that some of them refuse to confess for Easter saying that they confess only on major feasts, like Corpus Christi.

They prepare for this solemnity with fervor and await it with anxiety. The concourse of the faithful at church is extraordinary.

Even though the procession marches only in the chief town of the mission, all the surrounding villages must co-operate in decorating the path of the procession. Hence, early in the morning, men and women can be seen arriving in wagons. Every village must prepare an altar. The people bring with them poles, covers, sheets and other objects for the adornment of the altar. In a twinkling, they make a room-frame with the poles, in the middle of the field, and cover it with blankets, sheets, and so forth. They even bring along a table; and in less time than it takes me to write about it, they have the repository completed. Once finished, they go around examining which village has the best altar in the procession. Each one judges according to his taste, but no one dares to criticize the other's altar. After the altars are set up, Mass is celebrated and the procession emerges. Everyone, men and women, must march. The cross heads the procession and indicates the course. Behind the cross come the little boys and girls bearing different-colored flags in their hands. Then follow the men and women, and finally, the numerous clergy which consisted of two, because the third—myself—was busy directing the procession. In the procession a young ladies' choir follows along singing songs. The procession stops at each altar where the customary ceremonies take place. After the procession, your Reverence would see these good people happy and joyful singing out: "¡Que cosa tan bonita!" How lovely! "¡que será la gloria!" What must heaven be! Then they chat about each incident in the procession. After dinner, there is exposition of the Blessed Sacrament. That night, when permitted, a *Velorio* is held. The pious faithful has to keep vigil all night until dawn, and when the sun comes up, they watch it from within the church. This watch or vigil begins at sunset. Each one brings a candle. When the people are all gathered together, an old gentleman of the crowd cries out: "*Ave Maria purisima*" and all reply: "*Sin pecado concebida*." Then they begin the rosary which they sing. I assure you, dear Father, that their way of singing the rosary is beautiful indeed. They begin with the "*Aperi Domine*" in Spanish. There follows an invocation to the Holy Spirit. Then begins the chanting of the following: "Virgin, divine tabernacle, we sing thy praises, and in them we shall contemplate the mysteries of the rosary. Powerful Queen, consolation of mortals, Open to us heaven, with a happy death." The song finished, they begin the Our Father, and so on. After the Gloria, the song is repeated. At the end of the rosary, they recite some very beautiful prayers. They conclude asking Mary's blessing and by bidding her good night. Then all yell: "Blessing, the blessing!" and all are astir asking the blessing of the elders. Wives ask the blessing of their husbands; and fathers are asked by children; little ones ask adults. And you can see especially the older people, giving their blessings with great seriousness, and extending their hand to be kissed. This last ceremony is not performed when the rosary is recited before the Blessed Sacrament. This recitation may last forty-five minutes. After it is finished, another old man shouts: "*Ave Maria purisima.*" All answer: "*Sin pecado concebida.*" And then the old man begins a little song to which the people make response, repeating the same refrain. Most of the Mexican wisdom can be reduced to these songs.

Source

Colorado Magazine, XXXI (1954), 173-75. Taken from a report of a Jesuit missionary, Father Salvatore Persone, at Conejos, Colorado, written in Italian and dated August 1874. It was printed in the *Lettere Edificanti* of the Neopolitan Province of the Society of Jesus, as Letter 15, 1874-1917. The editor and translator is E. R. Vollmar, S. J.

* * *

Corpus Christi in Pennsylvania

Christmas and Easter are duly observed, but the great day of the year is the Festival of Corpus Christi, in honor of Christ's triumphant entry into Jerusalem, and the institution of the Sacrament of the Lord's Supper which followed. The festival was observed this year on Sunday, June 19, with great pomp and ceremony, and we were so fortunate as to see it. Preparations for it began in St. Mary's and the outlying farms a week before. The large and beautiful German Catholic Church, where the procession was to form, was decorated with evergreens and flowers more profusely than at Christmas or Easter. On the Saturday before, the farmers brought green saplings and boughs from the woods and stuck them in the earth along the route of the procession. Baskets of cut flowers, green leaves, fresh ferns, and grasses were provided for strewing in the road before the Host, and in all German homes great preparations were made for the feast which was to follow at the close of the ceremonies, the day having as great significance in this respect as Thanksgiving in New England. The route of the procession was to be from the German church to the pretty hilltop cemetery a half mile distant, and return by another road. At intervals along the way, wayside altars were erected—bowers of greenery bedecked with flowers and bearing a Christ on the cross, pictures of the Virgin and saints, and other emblems of the Catholic faith. Lighted candles burned before these shrines during the ceremonies.

The day began with the celebration of Low Mass at eight o'clock. Long before this, the streets were filled with happy groups wending their way toward the church, all attired in gala dress—girls in white, with long white veils floating behind, and bearing bouquets of flowers in their hands; boys each with a boutonniere in his coat lapel; mothers with babes in arms, and fathers escorting them. Great farm wagons, drawn by horses or mules, came lumbering in from the farms, their seats filled with farmer folk having the rugged German features, clad in the garb of the German peasant, and addressing one another in the language of the fatherland.

When the celebration of High Mass began, at nine o'clock, the church was crowded to suffocation, and the worshipers filled the portico and esplanade. At ten, at the conclusion of the service, the procession was formed, the Father Prior acting as master of ceremonies. First came three acolytes in altar vestments, bearing emblems of the Catholic faith; then a standard-bearer with the banner of the Holy Childhood Society of the parish. The members of the society followed—the boys first, and then the girls, the latter, some five hundred in number, clad in white dresses and veils, and bearing baskets of flowers, which they strewed along the road; after them the St. Mary's Silver Cornet Band, then one each of the men's and women's societies of the parish, bearing banners; after them, under a rich canopy borne by four men, came three Benedictine fathers in full canonicals, the central one, a monk of imposing presence, bearing the Sacred Host. Next came more parish societies of both sexes bearing banners; then the St. Mary's Citizen Band; then devotees in general, the whole procession numbering fully two thousand persons, and stretching from the church to the cemetery. As the head of the procession approached the first of the wayside altars, the boys uncovered their heads, and all chanted hymns in praise of the Christ and of the Sacrament. As the priests with the Sacred Host arrived before the altar, the procession halted, and the priests, kneeling before it, performed the appropriate service for Corpus Christi, and bestowed the Benedictus, the whole body of people kneeling during the ceremony. The procession then continued on to the German cemetery, with its quaint Old World tombs and crosses, past the little chapel in its midst, where prayers and masses for the dead are said, and out by another entrance. As the priests arrived at the door of the chapel the people again halted, the celebrants entered and performed the same service as at the altar. The march was again resumed, and the procession returned to the church by another road, passing a second wayside altar, before which the solemn service was again performed. At the church, the procession was disbanded, the members returning to their homes to enjoy the feast which had been prepared for the occasion, perhaps to meet long-sundered members of the family around the board.

Source

Journal of American Folklore, XI (1898), 126-28. This festival which was described by Charles Burr Todd took place at St. Mary's, Pennsylvania, in the Appalachians. The village, founded by Catholics from Alsace, Bavaria, and Belgium in the 1840s, is one of the few places that retains the medieval emphasis on the holiday. In *Folklore in America,* pp. 217-20.

St. Médard's Day

June 8

St. Médardus, who lived from about 456 to 545, was Bishop of Noyon and Tournai in France. He was the patron of farmers, wine harvesting, and good weather. The French and Belgian equivalent of the English St. Swithin, this saint likewise has his rhyme: "*Quand il pleut a la Saint-Médard / Il pleut quarante jours plus tard.*"

Rain on St. Médard's Day

If it rains on St. Médard's Day, it will rain for forty days.

Source

Journal of American Folklore, XL (1927), 186. Collected by Hilda Roberts in Iberia Parish, the southwestern Louisiana bayou country, which has a large French-speaking population. Cf. "Pennsylvania Dutch on St. Patrick's Day," p. 127; "Customs and Beliefs for Ascension Day," p. 223; and "Whitsuntide Beliefs," p. 227; as well as "St. Swithin's Day," p. 277.

St. Anthony's Day
June 13

St. Anthony of Padua, who lived in the thirteenth century, has become the patron saint of careless people, especially those who have lost an animal, a child, or a valuable article. He, like his friend St. Francis of Assisi, was a patron of animals, and once, legend has it, preached to an attentive fish when the congregation failed to listen to his sermon. In Rome, horses and mules and their trappings are blessed on his day, and in Lisbon his eve is celebrated with bonfires, street dancing, and altars set up outdoors by children.

The Feast of St. Anthony of Padua in New York

St. Anthony's Shrine Church, West Houston and Sullivan streets in New York City, has sponsored an annual *festa* honoring St. Anthony of Padua since 1971. In 1978 the celebration, which combines religious observance and evening street carnival gaiety, was held from June 1 through June 13, reaching its high point on the last day, St. Anthony's Day. Father Felician Napoli, pastor of St. Anthony's, describes the 1978 celebration, emphasizing its religious nature:

On June 13 masses are held all day, followed by a procession at seven o'clock in the evening. The statue of St. Anthony is carried through the streets on the shoulders of four men. This year more than a thousand people took part in the procession. The procession was led by a very colorful and talented Italian band. It consisted of eight musicians, and their outfits were made of material containing the Italian colors: green, white, and red. During the procession they played sacred and march music. Another band, called the "Keystone Cops," led by Bill Lesko, made a big hit with the people, playing American, Italian, and Irish music. The streets were decorated and lighted up, and the people marched to band music. They marched up Sullivan Street, crossed West Third, down Thompson, and then back to the Shrine Church.

The festival is organized by the Shrine Church and is the principal religious festival in New York City and the biggest still affiliated with a church. The funds raised go to the church, for the use of the parish. It is not like the Festival of San Gennaro, the patron Saint of Naples, which is sponsored by a lay organization.

The parish is one of the first Italian parishes in the United States, maybe the first. The festival was established twenty-seven years ago by Father Arthur Latanzi, so that people would be attracted to the Shrine. There were a few little stands with games and where people could buy food, so that people could enjoy themselves. Now the festival attracts thousands of people from all over. It has carnival rides, games of chance, gift and craft booths, and all kinds of food. It has gone international. This year not just Italian food, but food from maybe fifteen nations—Thailand, China, the Philippines, India, Korea, Greece, Ireland, France, Portugal, and the Hispanic countries.

The festival has a nice psychological influence on people, since it takes you back to the old days. It's historical, it's what New York used to be like.

Source and Comment

University of Pennsylvania Folklore Archive, undated. This description was obtained by H. C. on July 7, 1978 through a telephone interview with Father Felician Napoli, pastor of the Shrine Church of St. Anthony in New York City. He is a native of Brooklyn, New York, age 55, and had been pastor of St. Anthony's Parish for two years. Cf. "Feast of San Gennaro," p. 345.

* * *

Church Carnival and Much More

My first contact with Wilmington's [Delaware] Italian Festival—this year's began Sunday [June 11, 1989] and runs through this Sunday—was as an eighth-grader at St. Anthony of Padua School, dutifully stuffing festival raffle tickets into envelope after envelope. Even then, in its early days, the festival was much more than your run-of-the-mill church carnival.

Your common carnival does have a certain appeal—with its brightly lit midway, its duck pond, its baseball throw and its requisite cotton candy, snow cones and french fries.

But the Italian Festival was, and is, so much more than that. On the surface, it was rides and games and music and food and death-defying acts and free-flowing wine and beer. It was leathery old men—at times a bit teary-eyed—crooning in their native tongue as the Italian bands played on. It was heaping mounds of spaghetti and ravioli dished out to hungry crowds in a school lunchroom, while accordionists strolled among the tables.

It was a father aiming a dart at a balloon, valiantly—but, as often as not, vainly—attempting to win a stuffed tiger for his daughter. It was the Old World pageantry of the Procession of the Saints, as longtime parishioners trundled out the church's holy statues—St. Rocco, St. Michael the Archangel, St. Gabriel and, of course, St. Anthony—and paraded them through Little Italy to the accompaniment of a modest marching band that moseyed up the streets.

But that's just scratching the surface of what the Italian Festival was all about. To the parishioners at St. Anthony of Padua, it was to a large extent the glue that kept the church and the surrounding community close-knit. As the only "Mc" in that eighth-grade classroom of DiSabatinos and DiMaios and Gioffres, I envied the solidarity that seemed to be the birthright of these sons and daughters of Italy. They were one big, boisterous brood. And during festival week, the rest of Wilmington was able to bask in the warmth of that family.

I've been back to the festival every year since my grade-school days, always for at least one night, often for two or three. Now in its 15th year, the Italian Festival is still everything it used to be; these days it's just played out before a much larger crowd. It's now the biggest Italian festival on the East Coast, its organizers boast. Considering that the crowds are estimated for this year at 250,000 during the festival's eight-day run—with 70,000 on closing night—I'm not one to question their claim. . . .

The secret to this wildly successful fete? Ask John DalGesso, the loquacious festival chairman, and he'll tell you this: "We try to make it like an Italian family visiting. . . . When I grew up in an Italian household we treated people a certain way, and that's the way we treat them at the festival."

One sign of that personal touch is the time and effort spent preparing the food. In a traditional Italian home, one wouldn't dream of serving pasta and "gravy" that came from a box or a bottle. Likewise, the thousands of spaghetti and ravioli dinners dished up at the festival are home-cooked—usually by older women who brought Mama's recipe with them from Sicily or Salerno.

Source

Philadelphia Inquirer, June 16, 1989. Edited from a special article by Margo McDonough.

* * *

St. Anthony's Day, a Family Affair

There was a stiff breeze blowing Sunday evening [June 11, 1989] but that didn't stop the Guerrero Family. They

tipped and tottered on a thin wire about 20 feet above the crowd at St. Anthony's Italian Festival [in Wilmington, Delaware].

One almost slipped off the wire, but they shrugged that off as part of their day's work.

"It's my life," said Jenny Guerrero, 31, who has been performing with her family for 20 years.

Standing in the crowd watching the tightrope walkers were a scarecrow, a tin man, a lion and a girl in braids named Dorothy. They were taking a break from their performances of part of "The Wizard of Oz" during the festival.

"We started with jugglers, mimes and musicians and since everyone else has gone on with that theme, we thought we'd try something new," said John DalGesso, festival chairman.

The Quaker City [Philadelphia Mummers] String Band brought a taste of New Year's Day to the first day of the festival at St. Anthony of Padua Catholic Church at Ninth and Du Pont streets Sunday.

The weeklong festival also features rides, games, music and Italian food.

DalGesso said Sunday's crowd could be the biggest opening-day crowd to date. But Betty Sharp who is working at a fudge stand at the festival said the crowd was "OK."

Sharp and her cousin, Jeanne Lewis Capaldi said they have worked at the festival as volunteers for 15 years.

"When you come here, people you haven't seen in years you see here," Sharp said.

Source

The (Wilmington, Delaware) *News Journal,* June 12, 1989. By staff reporter Jennifer Baldino.

* * *

A Tale for St. Anthony's Day

Many years ago, as it is told, a man and his wife, devotees of Saint Anthony, commenced preparations to celebrate this feast day. While his wife made cookies and *dolci* [sweets], the husband prepared, as was the custom, a humble altar where they would pray with the friends who called specially on that day.

Everything was progressing in good spirit when quite unexpectedly the elder son of this couple fell ill. Within minutes they saw their son was dying.

"What a terrible thing to happen, to lose a son—and on the feast of Saint Anthony!" everyone began to whisper at the same time.

As the months passed, that certain sadness that death brings lingered strongly in this once happy household. And when the feast of Saint Anthony came again, the tragedy of that day a year ago was too well recalled.

Yet, as in years before, the humble altar was prepared and *dolci* were made again for the feast day. That evening, as friends called, suddenly and without warning the second son was stricken ill, and he died as his brother had the year before, in his father's arms.

"How strange that this boy is gone, too, on the feast of Saint Anthony!" everyone thought.

Too deep did the arrow of sorrow pierce the hearts of this man and his wife, a wound that would never heal.

The months passed swiftly and once again the feast of Saint Anthony came near. One day when the wife mentioned the coming feast her husband raged, "There will be no feast here this year or ever! Have you forgotten the compliments paid us last year and the one before?"

"*Peccato*!" (It is a sin!) his wife half whispered, holding her hands to her lips. "You should not talk like that!"

The bitterness he had long concealed in his heart had grown so intense that to reason with him was an impossible feat for the wife.

"No! There shall be no feast in my house!" he stormed vehemently as he made his way to the forest where he found himself walking every evening—alone.

As the figure with head bent low moved along the narrow path in the forest, it became quite startled at the sound of a strange little voice as it sang, "*Buona sera*!" (Good evening!)

The little old man speaking was no taller than an elbow and the pointed white beard he wore was just as long. Observing the young man's amazement at seeing him, the little old man asked (although he planned to anyway), "May I walk with you?"

"Uh? *Si*, of course," he answered as if he were speaking to no one.

"You seem quite disturbed," the old man began.

But from his embittered partner came not a word.

"You would rather not talk about it, eh?" the bearded one tried again.

"*Si*!" at last came a reply.

For a long distance they walked in silence. Only the rustling of the leaves in the cool breeze was heard and an occasional song of a reclining bird.

Quite suddenly the young man stopped still. "Look!" he pointed in horror at a large tree ahead.

"What is it?" the old man calmly inquired.

But his companion could not speak a word. He only shook from head to foot at the horrible sight before him. There from a high branch in the large crooked tree hung a boy.

"Let us go!" the old man advised. And they hurried on down the path.

A little farther along the way they paused briefly to drink from the creek which ran briskly alongside the path. Just as the shaken man was about to sip, he gave a weird cry, "Eeeooooo! What a terrible thing!" [He had seen a second boy in the water.]

"*Si*, terrible indeed," came the whimpering reply.

"Listen, now, to what I shall tell you," began the strange little man. "The vision you beheld in the crooked tree was the death your first son may have well suffered. The boy you saw drowned in the creek, your second son. But, because of your love of Saint Anthony these awful things were spared you, and your sons spent their last moments at home in your arms."

At these words, the young man was bitter no more and his eyes filled with tears. He heard the little man say, "Sometimes tragedy occurs, then a certain mark is visible. Weep, and the tears will erase the stain."

Clearing his eyes the young man searched about for the little old man who had befriended him, but he was nowhere in sight.

The next day when the feast of Saint Anthony came about, the feast was celebrated in the household as before. And the little old fellow with the long pointed beard, who was very much anticipated by this man and his wife, was not seen—nor was he ever seen again!

Source and Comment

New York Folklore Quarterly, XIX (1963), 292-94. Collected by Lydia Q. Pietropaoli from Theresa Nofri and Mary Corridori of Whitesboro, New York, in 1958, first told to Corridori by her mother-in-law. The text is somewhat confused. The informant heard it from "her eighty-year-old grandmother-in-law who visited America." Thus it is an example of the ongoing introduction of Old-World lore into an environment in which lore from abroad tends to disappear. The result of such periodic infusions is that Old-World tradition in the United States is given renewed vitality. According to legend, St. Anthony sometimes, as here, visits the earth in disguise. See Motif K 1811. For this reason, it is well to be hospitable to strangers on St. Anthony's Day (see p. 206 below). Mark Twain has a similar episode in his novel *The Mysterious Stranger*.

* * *

Feed Strangers on St. Anthony's Day

On St. Anthony's Day and also on St. Joseph's Day [March 19], one must always give strangers to eat [sic], since such strangers may be the saints themselves.

Source

Journal of American Folklore, XXIII (1910), 418. Collected by Aurelio M. Espinosa from an unnamed Mexican-American informant in New Mexico. Motif K 1811.

* * *

Matachines Dance for St. Anthony

A ritual folk dance, as I use the term, is a dance connected with a ceremonial observance of a group of people who are united by geographical propinquity, religion, language, customs, or other ties.

There is a great variety of indigenous ritual dances, as well as Spanish-American ritual dances, that are still danced on special occasions in the American Southwest and Old Mexico. I speak from personal experience, as I have witnessed and have myself recorded over a hundred tunes played as accompaniment to several types of ritual dances that I believe to be of European origin. The matachines [clowns] dance is one of these.

Though ritual dances have a social aspect, they differ from social dances whose purpose is mere entertainment or courtship. Ritual dances, as I shall show, often have a religious, group significance. The men often dance by themselves. Occasionally the women join them but they do not dance in contact as is often the case in the social dances. Some of the ritual dances, as informants have told me, have special meanings. There are dances for rain, crops, progeny, victory in battle (war dances), good hunting (buffalo dances), or a good year (some Zuñi dances).

Many of the ritual dances of the area are, as I have said, of American origin. Others would seem to be of European origin. Of these, probably the most important is the matachines dance. In Old Mexico it is also sometimes known as the matlachines dance....

In my opinion ... the matachines dance (and certain similar dances of Old and New Mexico which seem to be merely variants of the matachines dances) are descended from ... European dances....

One reason these dances have been preserved so well for so long is that many people dance them together. There has been less room for error than there might have been had only one individual performed the music or learned the dances at a time. The older people taught and corrected the younger so that year after year these dances have tended to be preserved with great fidelity.

Furthermore, for ritual dances to achieve the magical or curative effect with which they are credited it is thought essential to give them faithful performances.

Another reason for the preservation of these dances is that many of them have religious connotations. The matachines dance, for instance, is danced in honor of the patron saints of the Catholic villages of New Mexico. Still another reason for their preservation is the common practice of swearing oaths to preserve them.... A young man, a war veteran from San Antonio, Bernalillo County, New Mexico, told me that his mother had sworn during the Second World War that if he were spared she would see that he danced the matachines dance every year in honor of the patron saint of the village, Saint Anthony.

A charming legend of this same village of San Antonio relates that many years ago during a battle between the villagers and Indian raiders a little boy in blue was seen fighting beside the villagers. They knew at once that this was Saint Anthony, come in this form to help them and they then and there swore that if he brought them victory they would dance the matachines dance every year on his name day, June 13. This promise was carried out year after year. During the performance the villagers dance all the way to the village spring on the mountainside and back. One year, however, the dance was omitted and shortly thereafter the spring dried up, a calamity in that dry country. The dance, it is said, has been performed faithfully on June 13 each year since then.

Another reason for the preservation of the matachines dances is ... that membership in the matachines group is an honor. The regard in which a member of the group from San Antonio was held is attested by the following poem written in praise of José Apodaca, a local dancer.

> Señores voy a cantar
> Lo que traigo en mi memoria
> De un hombre que fué notable.
> Voy a cantarles la historia.
>
> Del pueblo de San Antonio
> Nacio un hombre muy brillante,
> Y con el tiempo llegó
> A ser el mejor danzante.
>
> Esta dichosa carrera
> Circunstancia mucho abarca,
> Y con el tiempo llegó
> A ser el mejor Monarca.
>
> José Apodaca era el hombre
> De tan grande corazón.
> Siempre lleva en su mente
> De servirle a su patrón.
>
> Con su guajito y su palma
> Y aquel cupil de diamantes
> Se enfrentava de San Antonio
> Con un grupo de danzantes.
>
> Con aquel cupil dorado
> Le nació del corazón
> Y la Malinche a su lado
> Bailándole a su patrón.
>
> Vestido de mil colores
> En nuestra iglesia se alegrabe,

Y el pueblo lleno de gusto
Cuando Apodaca bailaba.

. . .

Quedó triste San Antonio
Con grande luto se vía;
Tan palido y tan sereno
Como un surora del día.

En su tumba está grabado
Con letras interesantes
Con un letrero que dice:
Viva el rey de los danzantes.

Nos despedimos, señores
Aqui termina la historia.
Y Apodaca está en el cielo
Gozando de Dios y gloria.

Gentlemen, I am going to sing you
That which I carry in my memory
Of a man who was notable.
I am going to sing the story.

In the village of San Antonio
Was born a very brilliant man,
And with the passage of time
He came to be the best dancer.

This distinguished career
Was favored by circumstances,
And with the passage of time
He came to be the best *Monarca* [leader of
dancers].

José Apodaca was a man
With a very great heart.
Always he carried in his mind
The thought of service to his Lord.

With his *guajito* [rattle] and his *palma* [forked stick]
And his headdress of diamonds
He presented himself before San Antonio
With a group of dancers.

With this gilded headdress
He touched his heart
And with the *Malinche* [little girl in white] at his
side
He danced before his patron.

In vestments of a thousand colors
In our church he danced,
And the entire village rejoiced
When Apodaca danced.

. . .

San Antonio was left sad
And appeared in deep mourning;
Pale and so serene
Like the dawn of the day.

On his tomb is engraved
In interesting letters

An inscription which says:
"Long live the king of the dancers."

Now farewell, gentlemen.
This is the end of the story.
And Apodaca is in heaven
Rejoicing with God in his glory.

The matachines and related ritual dances, as I have observed them, are a composite art combining many elements—music, costuming, drama, and other elements. Not only are they a composite but they are themselves often part of a larger unit, the fiesta, an annual gathering of people comprising such elements as home-coming, feasting, visiting with relatives, revelry, fireworks, racing and other contests, and religious services.

Many skills enter into a ritual dance. The making of costumes, often by the mothers of the dancers, is one of these. Another is the making of masks (a kind of folk sculpture) or of a fringe or other face covering for the matachines. The purpose of the masks or coverings is to conceal the face and to portray, for example, the devil, or a pig, or a bull. In every case, the aim is to provoke awe, to give the effect of something supernatural. That is the obvious intent, for, as I have said, the ritual dances are associated with magic or religion.

Source and Comment

Western Folklore, XX (1961), 87, 91-92. From "The Matachines Dances—A Ritual Folk Dance" by J. D. Robb, a fully documented study reflecting this investigator's field work and the previous scholarship. See "Matachines Dance for Our Lady of Guadalupe." p. 431. A "matachin" is a grotesque, clownish figure, a buffoon.

* * *

St. Anthony's Dance

We were in Hot Springs [New Mexico] when a rider on a fine horse galloped up, and shouted an invitation to the village to attend a dance at Lojito. He swung his hat, wheeled around, and galloped off again. It was a fine brisk day, and we all decided to go to the dance. Antonio and Amalia went on ahead, by foot. We went in Fidel's car that, after it left the road, bumped with equal briskness over the fields. We had started at about seven, it was growing dusk as we neared the dance, and we passed on the way boys and women on foot, and two boys on one horse who were coming all the way from Hermit's Peak. It was to be a big dance.

Lojito proved to be no town, but a house of ten rooms built at various times since 1881 and extending in ragged single file over the brow of a hill. Here lived the owner, his ten sons and three daughters, their husbands and wives and children, and a few aunts and uncles. The owner was a rich man. His father had come there with nothing but his bare hands, he now owned more than three hundred goats and two hundred kids. He had cows and horses enough for his domestic needs, and drove into town daily to sell goat milk, skins and meat.

The dance was held in the left-hand end room, raftered and whitewashed, about twenty-five feet long and ten wide. It had two small deep-set windows, its plank floor slanted with the hill. A kerosene lamp stood at each window through which you could see the peering eyes of boys and men, one face shoving the next away. Long benches were placed against the walls, and here sat the women, some suckling their babies, all anxious for partners. They kept the same seats throughout the dance, and were brought back by their partner after each number. In the corner were three musicians, our friend Pasquale and two guitarists. There were at least a hundred people jammed into that little room and overflowing at the doors.

Pasquale deserves a paragraph to himself. He was the one fat man of Hot Springs. He had a smooth brown face, sleepy black eyes, and straggling black hair. He was the poorest man in town, for his house had no floor to it while his wife could not go to dances because she had no dress. Yet Pasquale was in demand everywhere because of his talent as a musician. He could play anything, and he loved to play. He could not read a note of music, but when he heard something once he could play it, and he shut his eyes and smiled, and told the guitarists what chords to strike. Pasquale's secret, not too well kept, was that he was a great drinker. If you had no money, he would play for whiskey, and if you did not have that, he would play for nothing, but not without pain. He became quieter and quieter as he drank, smiled the more, and the deep inward look of contentment shone on every feature. One time (not the night of this dance) Pasquale played for us all night, so that we might dance. His good friend Manuel had played the guitar, and now they went out in the dawn to get some fresh air. Pasquale held his fiddle, and Manuel his guitar. As they walked in the dim morning light, with the birds just beginning to chirp, Pasquale started to play. "What for you play?" said Manuel, "no one here to listen." "What kind of man you are?" said Pasquale smiling, "you only play when people listen. I play to the toads and frogs." And he went down to the river and played to the toads and frogs.

Our friend Fidel had been appointed "police" of this dance. He took his duties seriously, inquiring before every dance what was to be played, encouraging the boys to dance with a loud "Hey, *Muchachos!*" and being polite to everyone.

There were all sorts of dances, Pasquale deciding which was to be next—schottische, Barcelona, quadrille, cowboy dance, cotillion, and "lady's choice," where the women chose their partners.

The quadrille was danced in groups of four, and ended up with a general swing around the room when every woman and then every man danced a few steps with every one in the dance. The older people liked this dance and danced it best, and were chosen as partners for it.

The Barcelona was danced to only one tune, a special one. Two partners face the same way, and the steps are formal. The schottische was very active and springy, requiring skillful dancing, and the cowboy dance had much twirling under the partner's arm.

We were told that in old times the gentleman asked his partner for a dance by reciting a tag of complimentary verse, but that is no longer done. It was also said that before a dance the partners used to parade around the room together. We did not see this, but at a later dance an old man who felt particularly happy took two girls on his arm and paraded around the room, beaming, because a young woman had asked him to dance.

All our friends were in Lojito that night, and everyone danced. There were five minute intervals, but no long pauses. The air became hotter, the lamps reeked. As we stamped, clouds of dust rose from the floor. We went into a back room and were given cooling whiskey, and came back refreshed for new labors. Pasquale played on, all "Old Mexican" songs, no American ones. At two o'clock we left, and were the first to go. We were told that the company stayed till dawn and had breakfast, and sang songs in honor of San Antonio. It was a fine dance.

Source

Journal of American Folklore, XLVIII (1935), 148-49. From a description of folklife in "A New Mexican Village" by Helen Zunser.

* * *

St. Anthony Nameday Celebration

St. Anthony's day is on June 13th. The day before, a celebration was held for a baby named after the saint. We were told that name days were celebrated for Anthony, Juan, Anna, and Guadalupe. Romancita said that her brother Manuel had celebrated one on New Year's day, and that was the only one she had ever seen, but that they were not uncommon.

Florippa had decided to name her little baby Antonio, and it was in his honor that the celebration was held. She gave the Americanos personal invitations, but invitations do not seem to be used. Most of the women did not attend. Only Minna and Pasquale's wife came, although the other women came out of their houses and stood watching. Of grown men there were Fernán, Minna's husband Giatano, Rosa's husband, and Pasquale and another man with violins. There was a crowd of children and of adolescent boys. They arranged themselves loosely in procession, the violinists first, the grown men next, and then the boys, hand in hand and by two's. The women straggled behind. Florippa, very nervous, and dressed in her best, stood waiting in the unwalled room that joined the divisions of her grandmother's home. A table near her covered with a napkin held raspberry wine, whiskey, colored candy, and a cake.

The violins played and the three men sang the same melody in a thin artificial falsetto. Some of the words were improvised for the occasion and elicited smiles and laughs, but the men sang very seriously. Giatano led the singing, and substituted the word godfather for father. While he sang, Pasquale's wife pointed out a little dog that stood near Florippa and said "Florippa's husband" in a loud whisper.

The baby was held by its grandmother and was not much in evidence. After the singing, it was put out of sight, and we all went into the house and took refreshments. Some presents, mostly money, were given to the baby.

Something is always promised the serenaders. Florippa promised a dance on the following Saturday. After about fifteen minutes we left, saying thanks, and proceeded to another home, where a grown man by the name of Antonio lived. He was surprised to see the group, and rather grudgingly, after we stayed two or three minutes, promised a quart of whiskey for Saturday's dance.

This is the main verse of the song that was sung as it was written out for us; the others were improvisations:

> *Antonio tienes por nombre*
> *Lovato por mas grandessa*
> *Que te conoscan por povre*
> *Pero con delicadesa.*
>
> [Anthony, you are called
> "Wolf-cub" by way of compliment,
> So people will know that though you are poor,
> Yet you merit respect.]

Source

Journal of American Folklore, XLVIII (1935), 150-51. From a description of folklife in "A New Mexican Village" by Helen Zunser.

Miners' Union Day

June 13

Miners' Union Day was the annual rally and celebration of Local #1 of the Western Federation of Miners which had its headquarters in Butte, Montana, where the local was founded on June 13, 1878. The militant Western Federation of Miners considered itself the toughest union in America. The International Workers of the World, better known as the Wobblies, an equally tough and violent union, was attempting to gain control of the federation, and the flames of the dispute were reportedly being fanned by the bosses who were glad to pit the two unions against each other. On June 13, 1914, during a strike by the federation, a parade of 10,000 miners was broken up by Wobblie agitators and the Union Hall was blown up by dynamite. This act brought about the declaration of martial law in the town, broke the strike, and forced the miners' union to leave Butte. Miners' Union Day was revived in 1934 during the time of the NRA. Cf. "Labor Day," p. 325.

Copper Camp: Stories of the World's Greatest Mining Town, Butte, Montana (New York, 1943), compiled by the Writers' Program of the Works Projects Administration, states that "according to the old time miner's calendar there are three regular legal holidays and four *Butte* holidays—St. Patrick's Day, St. George's Day, Miners' Union Day and Election Day...." The importance of St. Patrick's Day and St. George's Day reflect the preponderance of Irish and Cornish miners in Butte at that time.

Butte Miners' Union Day

Of all the entertainments and holidays in a miner's life in Butte [Montana] in the old days nothing bulked as large as Miners' Union Day, celebrated annually on June 13 from 1878 until 1914 and resumed again in 1934. More was made of the holiday in the days now almost beyond recall than at any time since the first World War, when a whole day's entertainment, including speechmaking, contests of various sorts, picnicking, and all the other things that go with an outing at an amusement park, was held at Columbia Gardens in a canyon east of Butte at the foot of the Continental Divide. The ballad "One Miners' Union Day," by Joe Duffy, gives an unforgettable picture of what happened at Columbia Gardens on one such gala occasion:

The old Butte Miners' Union, one 13th day of June,
  Held a picnic at the "Gardens," where nature was in tune.
The sun was shining brightly and a happy crowd was there;
  The Gardens used to advertise: "Fun, Flowers and Fresh Air."

Each street-car stopping at the gate, had passengers galore
  And when a car was empty, it went back to town for more.
The miners took their families, each mucker took a "frill"—
  The 10-day men took bottled goods to help ward off a chill.

The babies played upon the grass, the girls played on the swings,
  The hobby-horses galloped 'round, their riders grabbing rings.
The young folks all were dancing, the old folks watched the games;
  To mention each feat by itself, would take too many names.

The Sullivans and Harringtons, the Murphys and Malones,
  Richards, Williams, Thomases, Trevithick and Treglowns—
Take-a-hitch and Six-year-itch, Olson, Johnson, Thor
  Were the names of some contestants when they had the tug-o'-war.

The next four stanzas treat the speech of the orator of the day who tells of a baby boy in Dublin who grew to manhood, emigrated to Butte City, joined the union, and, starting from outside guard, "wint thro' all th' chairs—" at which "The audience applauded like they do at County Fairs."

He waved them down to silence—of water took a drink—
  "That ould couple back in Ireland—little did they think
That on this 13th day of June, nineteen an' ought, ought,
  An educated audience would be upon this spot."

"We have a dhrillin' contest an' a thry at muckin' rock
  An' th' street-cars will be runnin' afther 12 o'clock;

There's a lot here to amuse ye, for this is a day av joy—
An' in closing let me mintion, that I was that baby bhoy."

Written much in the same vein, and once more featuring an Irish hero, Bill Burke's "Miners' Union Day in Butte," with a descriptive subtitle, "In the Good Old Days," takes one to a typical parade held in the city proper, with five bands playing, and all the rest.

Call me early in the mornin'
And press me other suit,
For tomorrow is the greatest day
Of all the days in Butte.
Pluck a posy for me frock coat,
Put some lard upon me shoes,
Look in me union stamp book
To be sure I've paid me dues.

'Tis Miners' Union Day, dear,
I'm to wear a white cockade.
I'm fourth assistant marshal
In the Miners' Day parade.
I'm to ride a fine big bay horse;
Sure your heart will burst with pride
Whin you see me ridin' down on Park Street
Like a mounted Lord asthride.

I'll be marchin' with the mayor;
The cops 'll all be there.
Lay out me brightest necktie,
Me new, green shirt I'll wear.
Six thousand miners will be marchin'
While I ride in stately ease,
Just like a Celtic warrior
As handsome as you please.

Five bands will all be playin'
Sammy Treloar at their lead,
While I ride in time to music
Asthride me prancin' steed.
I'll arise at dawn tomorrow
Long afore the whistles toot,
Sure, I wouldn't miss a minute
When 'tis Miners' Day in Butte.

There'll be shots and scoops and Shawn O's,
And big cigars galore;
There'll be dancers, fights, and frolics,
And then we'll drink some more.
There'll be arguments a-plenty,
And perhaps a broken snoot;
For anything can happen
When 'tis Miners' Day in Butte.

The pièce de résistance of any Miners' Union Day was the drilling contest, and this more than anything kept alive memories of working conditions in the mines in the early days of the camp. Mike McNichols and Walter Bradshaw were Butte's greatest drilling team, Bradshaw alone winning $13,000 over the years in prize and wager money at contests all over the West. Joe Freethy, another Butte hammersmith and a Cousin Jack, teamed with Bradshaw at Spokane in 1901 to drill fifty-five inches in fifteen minutes for a world's record. The contests were held not only in Columbia Gardens but at other places in town and at the mines themselves; and granite boulders around town, notably one in Mrs. Globich's yard in the McQueen addition, provided training grounds for aspiring hammersmen. *Copper Camp,* from which I take much of my material, lists the names of other famous teams, including those of a couple of blind men, Harry Rodda and Mike Davey, and gives an excellent description of how short steel is replaced by longer rods without the loss of rhythm in the blows of the double jacker. I am informed that a variety of granite found in Silver Plume, Colorado, was much in demand throughout the West for drilling contests because of its unusual hardness, but all that is changed now that the sport has almost died out. Although drilling contests are occasionally still held in a few camps in the West, no one seems to recall any in Butte for a decade or more. On Labor Day, 1941, I witnessed an exciting drilling contest in Virginia City, Nevada, with three or four crack teams performing. Machine drilling contests are sometimes held, as for example on Miners' Union Day in Park City, Utah, but these have never gained wide favor.

Because of the fact that no special skill was needed, mucking contests were very popular also, and prodigious amounts of rock were mucked from metal "turn sheets," or slabs of iron, brought to the Gardens from the mines in trucks. As in mucking, strength and weight, rather than skill, counted in the tug of war and provided a good means of stimulating group rivalries. Duffy relates one such contest in which Serbians were pitted against the Irish, and after a see-saw battle appeared to be winning, when the wives and sweethearts of the Sons of Erin grabbed the end of the rope and saved the day for their team. What happened after that belongs to the apocryphal lore of the camp. The bull and bear fight, a favorite divertisement of miners in California and elsewhere during the gold-rush period, was revived as late as July 4, 1895, in Butte; and rat baiting, which never was especially associated with the mines, enjoyed a perilous illegal existence, along with cock fighting, dog fighting, and the like.

Source and Comment

California Folklore Quarterly, V (1946), 169-72. In an article on the folklore of the Butte, Montana, hardrock miners, Wayland D. Hand assembles information on holiday observances. Here he draws both from the popular verses of Joseph H. Duffy who evokes the color and tradition of this miners' celebration and from Duffy's Book, *Butte Was Like That* (Butte, Montana, 1941), which contains a prose account of the same celebration. He also cites the Federal Writers' Project memoir of the period: *Copper Camp: Stories of the World's Greatest Mining Town* (New York, 1943).

Juneteenth
June 19

January 1, 1863, the date of President Lincoln's Emancipation Proclamation, is solemnly commemorated in many American black communities. It is, however, only one of a number of "freedom day" celebrations held on various dates, for the end of slavery was a gradual process and often a local one which evoked local observances. Thus the date on which General Gordon Granger arrived in Texas—June 19, 1863—with the avowed intention of enforcing Lincoln's proclamation, is commemorated as "Juneteenth" in eastern Texas and beyond, and a considerable body of tradition and lore has grown up about it. Why is it called "Juneteenth"? Mrs. E. B. Tollette, who lives in a rural black community of Tollette, Arkansas, has this to say: " I was talking with a friend about it today and he said, jokingly, 'You know how we name things,' and said 'was the nineteenth' and says, 'then we began to call it "Juneteenth,"' said, 'we nickname these things.'"

Juneteenth in the South and West

June 19, 1865, was freedom day for slaves in east Texas and portions of the surrounding states. It was on this day that General Gordon Granger landed with federal troops in Galveston, Texas, with the expressed mission of forcing the slave owners to release their slaves. Many of these slaves had been brought to east Texas from other southern states, such as Tennessee, Georgia, Virginia and "all over the south" by slave owners "because the abolitionist had talked freedom for the Negroes and they were afraid that their slaves would be freed and all that investment that they had [made]...." [Legends of three types] soon arose explaining the date of the celebration ... : (1) the news withheld to make one last crop, (2) the news delayed by mule travel, and (3) the news delayed by the murder of the messenger. The most frequently collected legend was the one which explains the date in light of the master's need to make one more crop. Versions of it were used to explain the observance in east Texas and southwestern Arkansas.

Although none of the informants told the legend of the slain messenger, there were several versions of the mule legend collected. The most stylized account was included in a letter sent by Haywood Hygh, Jr., a high school teacher in Compton, California, who attended Juneteenth celebrations as a lad in Karnack, Texas. He wrote:

One [story] is of paramount importance to us. How Juneteenth got started. The story is legendary in nature. However, my eighty-six year old father swears that it is the truth; that an ex-Union soldier (Negro) rode a mule from Washington, with a message given him by Abe Lincoln, Yessuh, all the way to this section of the country. And when he

got to Oklahoma, he informed the slaves that they were free. From there he went to Arkansas [sic] and Texas. It was the nineteenth of June when he arrived in Oklahoma. My father swears it, and he says if his father was still alive, he would do the same swearing without batting his eyes. Many of the old-timers are with him one hundred percent.

Only two informants indicated that they knew the mule legend. Artis Lovelady said he had heard it, but confessed that "I don't know the whole story."

Juneteenth was also originally celebrated in Louisiana. Rupert Secrett, retired barber and former sponsor of the celebration in Brenham, Texas, mentioned friendly "hur-rahing" among blacks of Louisiana and Texas as to which state was the first to celebrate emancipation. Louisiana blacks often said: "The people in Texas didn't know they was free until the people from Louisiana came over and told 'em." David Johnson, Dean of Students at Texas College, Tyler, Texas, and a native of Louisiana, recalls the celebration being observed "... all over the state of Louisiana." He specifically recalled the celebration being strong around the New Orleans area, the city from which General Granger began his historic voyage to Galveston. And U. T. D. Williams, Steward in the Ebenzer AME church, Tyler, Texas, attended Juneteenth celebrations in the northwestern town of Grand Bayou, Louisiana, where "the white folks" furnished all the food.

Southwestern Arkansas was another area of an adjoining state into which the Juneteenth celebration spilled over. This southwestern area of Arkansas, like the adjoining east Texas, is heavily populated with blacks. Mrs. E. B. Tollette lived in the all-Negro town of Tollette in this rural southwestern section of the state. Tollette, Arkansas, "was a large community" of "farmers" and "home owners." She also recalled, with pride, that it also had its own post office. The black farmers in Blevins, Paraloma, Nashville, Tollette, etc. "had great big picnics on the 19th of June." . . .

In the late 1800's many ex-slaves began to migrate out of the tri-state area into the territory which was soon to become Oklahoma . . . and took their precious freedom festival with them. Like the blacks who would take part in the great northern migration of the early 1900's, the ex-slaves who took part in this westward movement of the 1880's were close enough to the end of physical slavery to still have a deep appreciation for the day which signaled its end. Therefore, throughout Oklahoma, especially the newly formed all-black communities, they transplanted their Juneteenth celebrations. Mrs. Lillian Crisp, a public school teacher in Ardmore, Oklahoma, taught in the all-black Oklahoma town of Tatums and recalled Juneteenth being an all-day celebration of picnics, baseball games, occasional political speeches, square dancing and general socializing.

There was a second migration of blacks from the southwestern states of Louisiana, Arkansas, Texas and Oklahoma in the late 1930's and early 1940's. This time the move was further west to California, with the major attraction being good paying jobs in the war industries of the Golden State. So many blacks left the peonage of east Texas sharecropping, the unfulfilled promise of Oklahoma's all-black communities, and the rigid segregation patterns of Arkansas and Louisiana and headed west to California in search of a better life. However, the Juneteenth celebration was one of the cultural casualties of this migration. The generation of blacks who made this trip were some seventy odd years removed from June 19, 1865, that day of days when their ancestors became free men.

These west coast offspring still honored Juneteenth, but not in a manner that would rival their forefathers. In California there were attempts to transplant the tradition once again, but the celebration had dwindled in scope to Juneteenth picnics sponsored by blacks from the same state. For example, an "Oklahoma Picnic" is held in Los Angeles' Lincoln Heights Park every June 19th. However, the biggest change in Juneteenth observances by blacks on the west coast has been homecoming. Like the swallows of Capistrano, each year many of them migrate back home on the weekend nearest the 19th of June. At the 1972

celebration in the all-black community of Branchville, Texas, blacks came back from Kansas, Missouri and California.

Juneteenth has also been celebrated in isolated areas of Alabama and Florida. Mrs. Minnie Lee Riley, an old member of Miles Chapel AME church, Little Rock, Arkansas, told, after church services, how Juneteenth was celebrated in her native home of Clark County, Alabama. And the 19th of June has been observed in the southern Florida town of Boynton Beach. . . .

The most common type of Juneteenth celebrations was an all-day secular affair which began around 10 o'clock in the morning with a parade and ended around 1 o'clock the next morning with the breakup of the dance or "suppers." In the afternoon there were various activities, the biggest being the baseball game, "tie downs" [calf roping], individual games and eating. One of the biggest parades was annually held in Brenham, Texas. . . . Brenham's parades were routed through the heart of the downtown area and witnessed by very large mixed crowds. Holsey Johnson, a sixty year old farmer, regularly attended these celebrations in Brenham and recalled that it was so crowded "you couldn't walk on the streets."

The parade was composed of blacks from the surrounding communities who would prepare their own floats. Mrs. Eloise Holmes, a retired school teacher who grew up in Brenham, Texas, recalled that ". . . each community would decorate floats and they would select children from that community to ride on these floats." Accompanying these ten or twelve floats were men on horseback and a brass band.

The parade had a king and queen. The queen wore the title, "The Goddess of Liberty," and was selected by a money raising contest, in which several "nice looking girls" would solicit donations. Each one carried shoeboxes for this purpose and raised sums which ranged from $600.00 to $1,000.00. The king was selected by the queen.

Source and Comment

" 'Free at Last!': A Study of Afro-American Emancipation Day Celebrations," Ph.D. Dissertation, Indiana University, 1974, 82-85, 88-91. From an authoritative study by William H. Wiggins, Jr. based largely on the "oral records and lifestyles of the many members of the black masses," supplemented with "written records." The quotations, unless otherwise indicated, are from interviews, tape recordings, and correspondence which appear in an appendix to the dissertation. Cf. "Emancipation Day," p. 24.

St. John's or Midsummer's Day

June 24

The Feast of St. John the Baptist is unusual in that it is celebrated on the day of his death rather than on the day of his birth. John was sanctified before he was born. He has been called the saint of the summer solstice because his feast has long been associated with Midsummer's Day and solstitial rites. Thus round dances, men and women bathing nude together, predictions of death, and bonfires are common to the St. John's festival. Fire, a symbol of the sun's power, is central to Midsummer rites, and hilltop blazes through which people leap, drive their animals, and hurl objects cleanse evil from the community and renew reproductive powers. Torches from such fires are carried through fields and even applied to them. On Midsummer's Eve witches, fairies, and ghosts range abroad, evidence of its association with ancient beliefs about the dead. The day is also sacred to lovers. The mingling of these themes, pagan and Christian, are nowhere better seen than in Shakespeare's *A Midsummer Night's Dream*. They are also echoed in the phrase John is supposed to have uttered while preaching in rivalry with Jesus: "He must increase while I decrease"—after St. John's Day the days shorten; after Christmas they lengthen again.

St. John's Eve Voodoo

In Africa the voodoo ritual dance climaxed the ceremony of devil-worship which centered in the god Zombi, symbolized in the sacred snake, which the dance emulated. The voodoo cult entered the western hemisphere about 1724 when slaves were first brought to the Caribbean, and as early as 1782 Louisiana authorities considered the snake-worshipping slaves dangerous enough to prohibit their importation. These restrictions were relaxed after the Louisiana Purchase in 1803, and at the outbreak in 1807 of the revolution in Santo Domingo (now Haiti) many island planters fled to Louisiana and brought their slaves who were voodooes. Within a few years voodoo was firmly established in New Orleans, which remained the center of the cult. In subsequent adaptations, priestesses, called queens, became the focus and power of the cult, and priests were relegated to minor positions. Queens were free women of color who, because of greater freedom, officiated at ceremonies and sold charms and counter-charms, called *gris-gris*.

The first powerful voodoo queen in New Orleans was Sanité Dédé, a quadroon from Santo Domingo, who in the 1820's fixed St. John's Eve, June 23, as the major celebration of the year. Dédé presided at the ceremony described in the first eye-witness account. This description is of extreme importance because it shows that the ritual was well established in a form with which subsequent accounts agree. That early ceremony included about sixty Negroes and a few whites, assembled at night in an abandoned building. At one end of the torch-lighted hall, a table served as an altar on which stood a large black doll decorated with snake and alligator bones. The ceremonial snake was confined in a box beneath the doll, and stuffed cats, one black, one white, stood on each end of the altar.

The ceremony began with a ruffle of drums, a large one made of a cypress cask, the open end covered with animal skin, and a smaller one of similar construction. The large drum was beaten with the thigh bone of a steer, the small one with smaller animal bones. A gourd filled with pebbles maintained another rhythm. As the crescendo ended, the voodooists formed a half circle before Dédé, who stood before the altar. She called forth four priests, sprinkled them with liquid from a gourd as she made ritual signs and intoned magic words. At her signal a priest took the snake from the box, coaxed it to rise to full height, and passed it over the assembly while he repeated the name of the god and the sect. After the meal, a regular part of the ceremony, the snake was again brought forth by the priest, again displayed, and finally thrown into the fire. Immediately the drums increased the tempo, the singers chanted the ritual song, and a woman dancer stepped into the circle and began the ritual dance in imitation of the movements of the snake. The observer recalled:

> Confining herself to a spot no more than two feet in space, she began to sway on one side and the other side. Gradually the undulating motion was imparted to her body from the ankles to the hips. Then she tore the white handkerchief from her forehead. This was a signal, for the whole assembly sprang forward and entered the dance.

In the frenzied group dance which followed, the dancers tore off their clothing and danced nude until the ritual ended, as it always did, in a sexual orgy.

The solo dance mimicking the writhing of the snake is of extreme importance to the evolution of social dancing in the United States. Significantly the dancer confined herself to a small area, and the flat-footed movement with the slow shifting of weight from one foot to the other caused undulations from the ankles to the knees to the thighs to the hips, action now most familiar in the basic step of the Cuban rhumba. The result was a sensual dance specifically designed to arouse sexual excitement. This movement remained in the voodoo dances afterwards, and this ritual dance came to be called the Calinda because of the ritual song of that name.

Though voodoo ceremonials remained secret and were held surreptitiously, the ritual dance came out into the open in 1817, when New Orleans authorities, alarmed that the clandestine meetings might breed uprisings, set aside Congo Square on Sunday afternoons for the slaves so that they might dance under surveillance. There the music was made by the large congo drum, the smaller drum, the calabash, to which was added the jawbone of a horse scraped with a key. The costumes were suitably modified; instead of the red loin cloth for the men and the white chemise for the women, slaves in Congo Square wore the cast-off finery of their masters. Also, the songs accompanying the dances were changed; sung in degenerate patois of French called "Gumbo," these songs sometimes satirized the whites. When the voodoo ritual dance was moved to the light of day of Congo Square, it was considerably modified by omission of the orgy climax and by combination with an African war dance. The result was a showy, secular dance in which the men leaped and mimicked battle in a circle around another circle of women who performed the constricted ankle-thigh-hip steps of the original voodoo ritual dance. George Washington Cable, citing Alexander Dimitry, Creole scholar who had seen the Calinda many times, said: "The Calinda was a dance of multitude, a sort of vehement cotillion. The contortions of the encircling crowd were strange and terrible, the din was hideous." Despite the changes for public performance, the Calinda remained so sensual that the authorities banned it as obscene in 1843, just before voodoo attained its greatest popularity in the 1850's under the leadership of the first Marie Laveau.

A quadroon free-woman-of-color, Marie Laveau presided over the Congo Square gatherings as well as the secret ceremonies. She introduced Catholic motifs into voodoo and turned the St. John's Eve celebration into a show to which she invited some whites, particularly newspaper reporters. She owned a house on Lake Pontchartrain which was used for both the secret rituals and as a place of assignation for white men to meet quadroon girls. Her most profitable business, however, was selling *gris-gris* and blackmailing both whites and blacks. Her reign extended through the Civil War.

About 1869 Marie Laveau II became queen. The daughter of the first Marie and said to have Negro, Indian, and white blood, she substituted for her mother at ceremonies and mastered the role so well that many thought that the first Marie had been rejuvenated. More powerful and ruthless than her mother, Marie II became queen of queens and sometimes permitted less powerful queens to preside at the annual festival. By 1880 her power had waned and she lapsed into obscurity, though her burial place, much disputed, is supposed to have peculiar power even today.

Source and Comment

Southern Folklore Quarterly, XXIV (1960), 135-39. John Q. Anderson studied nineteenth-century descriptions of the St. John's Eve voodoo rituals in order to establish the African origin and survival of the dances which were part of the ceremony. He also summarizes the history of voodoo and its chief practitioners.

* * *

St. John's Eve

Calinda

The true Calinda was bad enough. In Louisiana, at least, its song was always a grossly personal satirical ballad, and it was the favorite dance all the way to Trinidad. To dance it publicly is not allowed this side of the West Indies. All this Congo Square business was suppressed at one time; 1843, says tradition.... One Calinda is still familiar to all Creole ears. It has long been a vehicle for the white Creole's satire; for generations the man of municipal politics was fortunate who escaped entirely a lampooning set to its air.

In my childhood I used, at one time, to hear, every morning, a certain black *marchande des calas*—peddler-woman selling rice croquettes—chanting the song as she moved from street to street at the sunrise hour with her broad, shallow, laden basket balanced on her head.

Mi - chié Pre - val li don - né youn bal, Li fé naig payé trois pi - ass pou ren - tré.
Dan - cé Ca - lin - da, Bon - djoum! Bon - djoum!
Dan - cé Ca - lin - da, Bon - djoum! Bon - djoum!

In other words, a certain Judge Preval gave a ball—not an outdoor Congo dance—and made such Cuffees as could pay three dollars a ticket. It doesn't rhyme, but it was probably true. "Dance, dance the Calindá! Boujoum! Boujoum!"

The number of stanzas has never been counted; here are a few of them.

Dans l'equirie la 'y' avé grand gala;
Mo cré choual la yé t b'en étonné.

Miché Preval, li té capitaine bal;
So cocher Louis, té maite cérémonie.

Y avé des négresses belle passé maitresses,
Qui volé bel-bel dans l'ormoire momselle.

....

Ala maite la geô li trouvé si drôle,
Li dit, "moin aussi, mo fé bal ici."

Ouatchman la yé yé tombé la dans;
Yé fé gran' déga dans léguirie la. (etc.)

"It was in a stable that they had this gala night," says the song; "the horses there were greatly astonished. Preval was captain; his coachman, Louis, was master of ceremonies. There were negresses made prettier than their mistresses by adornments stolen from the ladies' wardrobes (*armoires*). But the jailer found it all so funny that he proposed to himself to take an unexpected part; the watchmen came down...."

No official exaltation bought immunity from the jeer of the Calinda. Preval was a magistrate. Stephen Mazureau, in his attorney-general's office, the song likened to a bull-frog in a bucket of water. A page might be covered by the roll of victims. The masters winked at these gross but harmless liberties and, as often as any others, added stanzas of their own invention.

The Calinda ended these dissipations of the summer Sabbath afternoons. They could not run far into the night, for all the fascinations of all the dances could not excuse the slave's tarrying in public places after a certain other *bon-djoum*! (that was not of the Calinda, but of the regular nine-o'clock evening gun) had rolled down Orleans Street from the Place d'Armes; and the black man or woman who wanted to keep a whole skin on the back had to keep out of the Calaboose. Times have changed, and there is nothing to be regretted in the change that has come over Congo Square. Still a glamour hangs over its dark past. There is the pathos of slavery, the poetry of the weak oppressed by the strong, and of limbs that danced after toil, and of barbaric love-making. The rags and semi-nakedness, the bamboula drum, the dance, and almost the banjo, are gone; but the *bizarre* melodies and dark lovers' apostrophes live on....

Source and Comment

Century Magazine, IX (February 1886), 527-28. From "The Dance in Place Congo" by George Washington Cable, the New Orleans local colorist.

The "kalinda" were the songs of braggadocio sung by the stick-fighters of Trinidad. The stick-fighters, who represented various black "yards" or districts, were so quarrelsome that their stick-fights and bragging bouts often ended in riots. When stick-fighting was banned in 1881, the kalinda was also banned. In its place, a new kind of song emerged based on the "cariso," lyric songs which the women had sung in the intervals or recesses between kalinda singing. These the men transformed into erotic and politically satiric songs, which in turn developed into the modern calypso.

* * *

St. John's Eve

The Decline of Marie Laveau

... I once saw, in her extreme old age, the famed Marie Laveau. Her dwelling was in the quadroon quarter of New Orleans, but a step or two from Congo Square, a small adobe cabin just off the sidewalk, scarcely higher than its close board fence, whose batten gate yielded to the touch and revealed the crazy doors and windows, spread wide to the warm air, and one or two tawny faces within, whose expression was divided between a pretense of contemptuous inattention and a frowning resentment of the intrusion. In the center of a small room whose ancient cypress floor was worn with scrubbing and sprinkled with crumbs of soft brick—a Creole affectation of superior cleanliness—sat, quaking with feebleness in an ill-looking old rocking-chair, her body bowed, and her wild, gray witch's tresses hanging about her shriveled, yellow neck, the queen of the Voodoos. Three generations of her children were within the faint beckon of her helpless, waggling wrist and fingers. They said she was over a hundred years old, and there was nothing to cast doubt upon the statement. She had shrunken away from her skin; it was like a turtle's. Yet withal one could hardly help but see that the face, now so withered, had once been handsome and commanding. There was still a faint shadow of departed beauty on the forehead, the spark of an old fire in the sunken, glistening eyes, and a vestige of imperiousness in the fine, slightly aquiline nose, and even about her silent, woe-begone mouth. Her grandson stood by, an uninteresting quadroon between forty and fifty years old, looking strong, empty-minded, and trivial enough; but his mother, her daughter, was also present, a woman of some seventy years, and a most striking and majestic figure. In features, stature, and bearing she was regal. One had but to look on her, impute her brilliancies—too untamable and severe to be called charms or graces—to her mother, and remember what New Orleans was long years ago, to understand how the name of Marie Laveau should have driven itself inextricably into the traditions of the town and the times. Had this visit been postponed a few months it would have been too late. Marie Laveau is dead; Malvina Latour is queen. As she appeared presiding over a Voodoo ceremony on the night of the 23d of June, 1884, she is described as a bright mulattress of about forty-eight, of "extremely handsome figure," dignified bearing, and a face indicative of a comparatively high order of intelligence. She wore a neat blue, white-dotted calico gown, and a "brilliant *tignon* (turban) gracefully tied."

It is pleasant to say that this worship, in Louisiana, at least, and in comparison with what it once was, has grown to be a rather trivial affair. The practice of its midnight forest rites seemed to sink into inanition along with Marie Laveau. It long ago diminished in frequency to once a year, the chosen night always being the Eve of St. John. For several years past even these annual celebrations have been suspended; but in the summer of 1884 they were—let it be hoped, only for the once—resumed....

... The affair of June, 1884, as described by Messrs. Augustin and Whitney, eye-witnesses, was an orgy already grown horrid enough when they turned their backs upon it. It took place at a wild and lonely spot where the dismal cypress swamp behind New Orleans meets the waters of Lake Pontchartrain in a wilderness of cypress stumps and rushes. It would be hard to find in nature a more painfully desolate region. Here in a fisherman's cabin sat the Voodoo worshipers cross-legged on the floor about an Indian basket of herbs and some beans, some bits of bone, some oddly wrought bunches of feathers, and some saucers of small cakes. The queen presided, sitting on the only chair in the room. There was no king, no snake—at least none visible to the onlookers. Two drummers beat with their thumbs on gourds covered with sheepskin, and a white-wooled old man scraped that hideous combination of banjo and violin, whose head is covered with rattlesnake skin, and of which the Chinese are the makers and masters. There was singing—"*M' allé couri dans déser*" ("I am going into the wilderness"), a chant and refrain not worth the room they would take—and there was frenzy and a circling march, wild shouts, delirious gesticulations and posturings, drinking, and amongst other frightful nonsense the old trick of making fire blaze from the mouth by spraying alcohol from it upon the flame of a candle.

Source

Century Magazine, IX (April 1886), 817-18, 820. George Washington Cable describes his visit to Marie Laveau in her declining years for a local color article, "Creole Slave Songs," in an influential magazine that specialized in literature and the arts.

*   *   *

Seeing the Future on Midsummer Eve

My mother used to tell tales handed down to her mother, whose forebears came from England, about fascinating pagan rites connected with Midsummer Eve (June 23). She also described divination rites which she and her friends practiced on Midsummer Eve. Some of these I have practiced with my friends.

Mamma said that in England young maidens gathered flowers and wove garlands to be worn around the neck on Midsummer Eve and Midsummer Day. In the villages great bonfires were built for Midsummer Eve. These fires were lighted with need fire, kindled by friction. The bonfires were votive fires. Into them the people threw herbs, gathered by moonlight, as charms against witchcraft.

Salt, thrown in, warded off bad luck. The people ate Midsummer cake, drank wine, and danced around the bonfires, calling forth good spirits to render assistance in love. They also practiced all sorts of divinations.

When Mamma was a young girl, living in Morehead City [North Carolina], at Midsummer Eve she and her friends practiced a few divinations. I will describe them as they were told to me.

On Midsummer Eve, at 12 o'clock noon, you put a glass of water in the sun, leaving it there for one hour. During this hour you must not speak a word. If you speak, the spell is broken. If you have not spoken when the hour has passed, you take the white of an egg and pour it in the glass. In a few minutes the egg white has formed a figure indicating the occupation of your husband-to-be. I practiced this divination during my teens. One time the egg white formed a tree trunk; at another, a tent; and at a third, the spars and rigging of a ship.

If you pare an apple round and round without a break in the peeling and throw the peel over the left shoulder, it will form the initial or initials of your future husband.

When girl friends are spending the night together, let each one be given a bowl of water. Write all the letters of the alphabet on bits of cardboard and place the cards, letters down, in the water. Next morning the initials of the beloved will be face up.

If you have a well, take a mirror at noon of Midsummer Eve and reflect the sun's rays into the water. (Remember, the spell is broken if you speak.) In a few minutes you will see the reflected image of your husband-to-be.

Mrs. Mamie Murdock Tolson (Mrs. Cornelius Tolson), whose daughter, Mrs. Jesse Bell, lives in Morehead City, told me she saw her future husband in this way. She and some friends were flashing their mirrors in the well at Wildwood, where they lived as young girls. It was Miss Mamie's turn. The others knew whom she was to marry— she was engaged. They were a little frightened when the water began to boil, but no one said a word. The ripples spread out, wider and wider. Then a man's face appeared. But it wasn't the face of her betrothed. It was the face of a neighbor, Mr. Cornelius Tolson, a man forty-four years older than Miss Mamie.

Another interesting tale was one that Mamma's grandmother told her children. When she was a girl my greatgrandmother lived in Beaufort. One Midsummer Eve Night she and girl friends spending the night with her were performing their magic rites by roasting eggs in the shell in the fireplace. At midnight the husbands-to-be were supposed to walk into the room through the unlatched door. It was a calm moonlight night. All of the girls were silent and shaking with excitement. Suddenly, a roaring, rushing wind was heard, and a mighty gust shook the house. Smoke billowed forth from the fireplace, stinging the eyes of the girls and making them cough as they sat in a semicircle around the fireplace. The door blew open, and two men entered. They carried a pine coffin. One of the girls screamed and fainted. She died before the year was out.

Source and Comment

North Carolina Folklore, VIII (1960), 29-30. Reported from family tradition by Ruth Howland Deyo, "a housewife living in Morehead City," North Carolina. For similar divination, cf. "To See Your Future Husband on Halloween," p. 379.

* * *

Parada San Juan Bautista

There was dancing in the street outside Rosa Santiago's house in South Camden [New Jersey] last week. Everyone was memorizing steps.

Yesterday, Santiago paced in front of a trailer packed full of children, some wearing oversize straw hats and flouncy skirts. No one was sitting still and the trailer heaved back and forth.

"We want to teach the children about the culture," Santiago said, shouting directions to the children. Moments later, Camden's 37th Annual St. John the Baptist Day Parade (Parade San Juan Bautista) began and a chain of beauty queens, salsa dancers and jazzed-up Toyotas headed down Cooper Street.

Aby Bonilla, 9, and Randy Medina, 10,—among the children in Santiago's float—captured the spirit of the day as they danced *La Plana* from Cooper and Second Streets to Ulysses S. Wiggins Park along the waterfront.

"The Spanish like to have one day to be recognized," said Santiago, who moved to Camden from Puerto Rico 33 years ago and has participated in the yearly parade ever since. The event is billed as the only organized parade in Camden and is cherished by many of the city's 15,000 Hispanic residents.

More than 600 people lined the parade route and then gathered in Wiggins Park to eat ice cream, sip cold drinks and watch as awards were given to the top floats. Folk dancers performed the *tuna* and *cumbia* in the hot sun.

The parade culminated a week of festivities—including a banquet, art exhibits and a flag-raising ceremony—recognizing Hispanics in the city.

For some, yesterday's parade was an occasion for nostalgia. Felix E. Montes, president of this year's event and a city administrator, was born in Mayguez, Puerto Rico, and came to Camden in 1944 at age 7. He pointed to the Campbell Soup Co. factory where his father got his first job in this country.

Elena Morales, 17, emigrated just 10 years ago. Yesterday, Morales, wearing a bright red floral skirt, danced *La Plana* in the parade. "It's nice to show people what our country has," she said. "It's not a rich country, but it has it's own [culture]."

The parade is named after the patron saint of Puerto Rico—St. John the Baptist. Christopher Columbus, who historians say discovered the Caribbean island in 1493, christened it St. John the Baptist, which was later changed to Rich Port, or Puerto Rico.

Puerto Ricans first migrated to Camden in the 1940s, many taking jobs at Campbell Soup. By the 1970s, about 7,500 Puerto Ricans were living in Camden, and the number had doubled by this decade....

One purpose of the parade, said Santiago, is to keep Puerto Rican traditions alive among the city's young. In her neighborhood, she is the official guardian of these traditions. "We want to teach the children about the culture," she said. "It's very important."

Santiago was up at 6 a.m. yesterday preparing the float, festooned with red, white and blue crepe paper. "It's very important for me to get involved with the kids," she said, moments before her dancers—a few barely old enough to walk—headed down Cooper Street.

Source

The Philadelphia Inquirer, June 26, 1989. By Laura Quinn, staff writer.

St. John's Day and the Summer Solstice

[In Puerto Rico, saints'] days are observed at least by not working, and often by large attendance at church services. On Corpus Christi the sacred image is carried to slow music through the streets, but in the capital, as in Spain, the greatest celebration is on St. John's Day. This is of interest, because really reminding of the primitive celebration at the Summer Solstice. The Church has appropriated the season, but some customs point back of church usages. On that morning throwing salt on the palm flowers will ensure a crop of cocoas, and a relic of sympathetic magic is seen in the custom of planting a bit of hair at the root of a banana tree—hair and bush growing and helping each other. In Spain, but less often in Puerto Rico, one can see his or her future fate the midnight before St. John's by ceremonies similar to those [poet John] Keats has associated for us with St. Agnes' Eve.

Source

Folk-Lore, XXXVIII (1927), 64. Collected by Peter J. Hamilton of San Juan, Puerto Rico. Informant not supplied.

Fire and Water on St. John's Day

Many Buffalo [New York] children are not permitted to swim until St. John's Day (June 24) when the saint blesses the water....There is one interesting fragment remaining of the old midsummer fire ceremonies associated with St. John's Eve in Europe; Ukrainian girls at summer camp make little boats, decorate them with candles and flowers and launch them on a lake or stream.

Source and Comment

Indiana Folklore, XI (1976), 167. Collected by Lydia Marie Fish for a study of folkloristic elements in the Roman Catholic community of Buffalo, New York. Her sources were students, colleagues and friends in Buffalo, c. 1968-76. She notes that some 60 percent of the Buffalo population is Roman Catholic of various ethnic origins, including several Uniate Rite churches in communion with Rome whose members are largely of Ukrainian descent. Robert Maziarz recalls a similar prohibition against swimming in a New York Polish family, *New York Folklore Quarterly*, XXIV (1968), 304. Cf. "Puerto Rican Fire Festival," p. 33 and "A Beltane Fire," p. 188.

Running the Rooster on St. John's Day

Chicken fighting is freely indulged in by the Mexicans, as it was by the Arabs, but it was probably played by Romans and Carthaginians in Spain long before the Arabs landed; therefore not much stress need be laid upon its existence. The Romans caused to fight both chickens and quails.

There is another form of diversion with fowl which must, however, be mentioned, although it too, in one shape or another, has spread over much of the surface of the earth, and that is the great sport of *correr el gallo,* or "running the rooster," which strictly speaking is more frequently an old hen. The victim selected is buried up to its neck in sand, and then horsemen dash at full speed up to the chicken, lean out from the saddle and try to grasp it. There are many failures, involving ludicrous mishaps and perilous tumbles, but finally some rider, bolder or more dextrous than his comrades, seizes the hen by the neck and gallops down the valley, followed by all the other contestants. The hen is usually torn to pieces in the struggle. This was the method observed at the Indian pueblo of Santo Domingo, New Mexico, in the month of August, after harvest, in 1881.

In the lower Rio Grande, on St. John's Day (June), the young men engage in *correr el gallo,* but instead of a living bird make use of an image of paper, ribbon, and feathers. In both cases the riding is superb, and there are not a few accidents.

Source

Journal of American Folklore, IX (1896), 101-02. Collected in the "Rio Grande Valley" by Captain John G. Bourke.

Throwing Presents on San Juan's Day

In 1894

It being San Juan's Day [at Cochití Pueblo, New Mexico], every one by the name of Juan was obliged to contribute something to be given to the people. Accordingly all articles were carried to the roof of one of the houses near by, and thrown down, one by one, into the crowd assembled below. Juan, possessing the name of the day, was told he must make a contribution as the others of that name did. Accordingly he took some birds he had previously shot for our supper, and carried them to the house-top. All stood with upturned faces and outstretched hands as one article after another fell into some grasping palm. The collection consisted of pieces of leather, bright bits of calico, birds, and tortillas. No one became the actual owner of anything until he reached home with it, and any one who could get an article away from another before he arrived at that place of safety was privileged to do so. This ended the celebration, and at sundown San Juan's Day was over.

In 1947

The 1947 Cochití San Juan's Day celebration differed very little from that witnessed by the Eickemeyers in 1894. The evening of June 23 was marked by fireworks, gunfire, and bonfires in front of the celebrating homes, and the ringing, or clanging, of the church bell. Mass was held in the morning, the time determined by the arrival of the priest from his residence in neighboring Peña Blanca....

The greatest change between 1894 and 1947 was noted in the subsequent throwing of presents, also referred to as *gallo.* In the Eickemeyers' time, gifts were contributed by all Juans and Juanitas to a centralized pool; presents were then thrown from one house-top to the assembled crowd. This practice is followed at present only at the times of Koshari or Kwirena society initiations when families of the initiates contribute to a common pool, which is then thrown from the roof of the society house to the crowd.

In 1947, each household of a Juan or Juanita took presents to their own roof, or, in a few cases, to the roof of a close neighbor in whose yard there was more room for the scrambling that occurred as each present was thrown. The crowd moved around the village from home to home until all had been visited. At what time this change occurred could not be learned, although Goldfrank, who lived at Cochití in the early 1920's, noted, "They [the saint's days, C.L.] are marked by foot races and the throwing of food from the house tops, the villagers going from house to house."

Still another change was noted from the Eickemeyers' observation that the person who succeeded in catching some article did not actually possess it until he had reached the shelter of his own home. Several of my informants recalled that in their earlier years, about the turn of the century, a person who caught something had to run quickly home. If anyone touched him en route, he had to give up the article to this person who was, in turn, chased. The Eickemeyers' account suggested more of a struggle than this version, but in either case, the older pattern appears to have been similar to the struggling and chasing involved in the rooster pulls. This similarity may well be the source of the use of the term *gallo* for the present throwing.

Source and Comment

El Palacio, LIX (1952), 178, 180. Charles H. Lange reprints an 1894 description of the San Juan's Day celebration at Cochití Pueblo, New Mexico, by Carl and Lilian Eickemeyer so that he can compare it with the practices he witnessed in 1947. He concludes that throwing presents, like most of the festivities, "appears to be an Indian adaptation" of a Spanish custom. Cf. *"Carnival throw"* and *"Mister, throw me something"* in "Mardi Gras Words," p. 86.

* * *

St. John's Day Beliefs

On the eve of St. John's Day the white of an egg is placed in a glass of clear water, and the next morning what is to happen in the future is written on the egg.

On St. John's Day women cut the tip of their hair with an axe, or simply wash it, so that it may grow.

Source

Journal of American Folklore, XXIII (1910), 416. From a collection of "New-Mexican Spanish Folk-Lore" by Aurelio M. Espinosa.

Every Mexican, big or little, will take a bath on St. John's Day, and, if possible, in the Rio Grande, and then new, or at least clean, raiment is donned from head to foot. Hair and nails are also cut on this day.

Source

Journal of American Folklore, VII (1894), 130. From a collection of "Customs and Superstitions of the Rio Grande" by Captain John G. Bourke then stationed at Fort Ringgold, Texas.

Fern seed gathered on St. John's Eve has the power to make its possessor invisible.

The fern was said to bloom and seed only at midnight on Mid-summer night.

Source

Memoirs of the American Folklore Society, XVIII (1925), 121. From "Folk-Lore from Maryland," collected by Annie W. Whitney and Caroline C. Bullock. Informants not given.

* * *

Bouquets for St. John and St. Peter

There's an age-old custom which reveals that the communion of saints and the communion of friends generally go hand-in-hand with the Italian people.

Each year on the Feast of St. John, the 24th day in June, many folks gather, or buy, flowers to present the colorful bouquet to a friend. Five days later, on the Feast of St. Peter, the recipient of the bouquet returns to the friend's home with a lovely array of flowers. From that day forward the participating women call each other *comare* (co-ma-ray) and their respective husbands are called *compare* (com-pa-ray).

Many of the *comares* [godmothers] and *compares* [godfathers] renew their friendships by exchanging bouquets or small gifts each year when the feasts of St. John and St. Peter arrive.

This custom originated in the belief that friendships derived of Christian motive last and bring happiness to the *comares* and *compares* and their families.

Source

New York Folklore Quarterly, XIX (1963), 175. Collected by Lydia C. Pietropaoli, from her mother, Maria Trenca Pietropaoli, born in Whiteville, New York, in 1911. She lived in Rome as a child.

Stonewall

June 27-29

The story goes that New York City police surveillance reports described the Stonewall Inn, a gay bar in Greenwich Village, as "notorious" and often harassed its clientele and made arrests for various violations, including state liquor regulations. Such seems to have been the origin of a weekend uprising June 27-29, 1969, in which gay people put up a stormy and unprecedented resistance. This event is now celebrated as crucial in the history of an element in American society which has its own defining customs, stories, slang, and folkways. It may not yet have established itself as an American holiday in the folk tradition, but it appears to be on its way toward doing so. Historically, Stonewall should be seen in the context of the liberation movements, anti-war protests, and student turmoil of the late 1960s.

The Stonewall Raid

At the time of the Stonewall raid, a handful of gay bars, mostly in Greenwich Village, were among the few places where gay men and women could socialize. "We'd carved out a small little world for us, populated by young gay people, which was a happy place, very hip," said Martin Robinson, a co-founder of the Gay Liberation Front in 1969 and of Act-Up in 1987.

The Stonewall Inn was a black-walled bar owned by organized crime. Like a Depression-era speakeasy, it had a peephole in the door and a bouncer who was not afraid to turn people away.

"This was not the polite professional middle-class clientele that worries about making a scene," [historian John] D'Emilio said. "Many of them were drag queens, maybe even runaways, so they had less to lose by fighting back." . . . .

"When the police came in," said Mr. Robinson, who was there, "quite to their surprise, we were no longer self-effacing, we were no longer guilt-ridden. We were offended at their bullying. We didn't put up with it. As soon as the police got inside the bar, we surrounded the bar, made it difficult for them to get out."

Michael Scherker, who is writing a history of the events that night, says . . . :

"It wasn't a rebellion; it was a plain old spontaneous combustion riot. They weren't thinking of gay rights; they just wanted to get back in the bar. It wasn't until the next day or the day after that or the week after that that a lot of people realized what it was really about was gay rights."

Source and Comment

New York Times, June 25, 1989. Excerpted from a front page feature "Homosexuals See 2 Decades of Gains, but Fear Setbacks," by James Barron. To mark the anniversary, the United States Postal Service authorized a special cancellation with a postmark which read: "Stonewall Sta./20 Years, 1969-1989/Lesbian and Gay Pride."

Stonewall Remembered

Sheridan Square [Greenwich Village] this weekend looked like something from a William Burroughs novel as the sudden specter of "gay power" erected its brazen head and spat out a fairy tale the likes of which the area has never seen.

The forces of faggotry, spurred by a Friday night raid on one of the city's largest, most popular, and longest lived gay bars, the Stonewall Inn, rallied Saturday night in an unprecedented protest against the raid and continued Sunday night to assert presence, possibility, and pride until the early hours of Monday morning. "I'm a faggot, and I'm proud of it!" "Gay power!" "I like boys!"—these and many other slogans were heard all three nights as the show of force by the city's finery met the force of the city's finest. The result was a kind of liberation, as the gay brigade emerged from the bars, back rooms, and bedrooms of the Village and became street people.

It began as a small raid—only two patrolmen, two detectives, and two policewomen were involved. But as the patrons trapped inside were released one by one, a crowd started to gather on the street. It was initially a festive gathering, composed mostly of Stonewall boys who were waiting around for friends still inside. Cheers went up as favorites emerged from the door, striking a pose and swishing by the detective with a "Hello there, fella." Wrists

252

were limp and hair was primped. The stars were in their element.

Suddenly a paddywagon arrived and the mood of the crowd changed. Three of the more blatant queens—in full drag—were loaded inside, along with the bartender and doorman, to a chorus of catcalls and boos from the crowd. A cry went up to push the paddywagon over, but it drove away before anything could happen. The next person to come out was a dyke, and she put up a struggle. At that moment, the scene became explosive. Limp wrists were forgotten. Beer cans and bottles were heaved at the windows, and a rain of coins descended on the cops. At the height of the action, a bearded figure was plucked from the crowd and dragged inside. It was Dave Van Ronk, who had come from the Lion's Head to see what was going on. He was charged with throwing an object at the police.

Almost by signal the crowd erupted into cobblestone and bottle heaving. The trashcan I was standing on was nearly yanked out from under me as a kid tried to grab it for use in the window smashing melee. From nowhere came an uprooted parking meter—used as a battering ram on the Stonewall door. I heard several cries of "Let's get some gas," and a blaze soon appeared in the window of the Stonewall. As the wood barrier behind the glass was beaten open, the cops inside turned a firehose on the crowd. By the time the fags were able to regroup, several carloads of police reinforcements had arrived and the streets were cleared.

Source and Comment

Village Voice, June 19, 1989. Edited from the recollections of an eyewitness, Lucian K. Truscott IV. The *Village Voice* was one of the few newspapers that gave full coverage to the three-day uprising, as its editors explained on the twentieth anniversary, "if only because our office at the time was adjacent to the bar." [Reprinted by permission of the author and the *Village Voice.*]

A Gay Tradition

By the hundreds, gays, lesbians and their supporters marched through the streets of Center City [Philadelphia] yesterday, holding hands and carrying signs that proclaimed them proud.

"We are everywhere, and we will be free," the crowd chanted, after marching from 10th and Spruce Streets to JFK Plaza. "We are everywhere, and we will be free." Under blue skies and a brilliant sun, they reveled in each other's company and denounced their detractors as intolerant. . . .

"Only we can affirm our beings," said Rita Addessa, executive director of the Philadelphia Lesbian and Gay Task Force, speaking to a crowd of more than 1,000 from a podium festooned with lavender, pink and blue streamers. . . .

The rally was the first public assembly of gays and lesbians in Philadelphia in 10 years, organizers said. It marked the 20th anniversary of a June 1969 incident at Stonewall, the Greenwich Village bar where a police raid escalated into a riot. The confrontation between police and patrons of the bar—many of them gays—lasted several days. Some activists say the incident marked the beginning of the country's gay-rights movement.

"It's become traditional for the community to celebrate itself in June," said Larry Gross, a professor of communications at the University of Pennsylvania and co-chairman of the local lesbian and gay task force.

Source

Philadelphia Inquirer, June 19, 1989. Edited from an article by staff writer Nancy Phillips.

From Greenwich Village to Central Park

Hundreds of people marched from Greenwich Village to Central Park [New York City] for a rally yesterday [June 24, 1989] that kicked off Lesbian and Gay Pride Weekend, marking the 20th anniversary of a riot that is credited with starting the modern gay-rights movement.

The weekend's biggest event is today's parade, which organizers predicted would attract more than 200,000 participants and at least as many spectators. . . .

The march from Greenwich Village was sponsored by the AIDS Coalition to Unleash Power, or Act-Up, which has complained that the larger parade planned for today is simply celebratory and does not protest militantly enough against government AIDS research, and about the status of gay rights in the United States.

About 600 Act-Up members and supporters marched from Sheridan Square in the Village, up the Avenue of the Americas to the park for the rally. At 34th Street, they paused for a "kiss–in," briefly halting auto and pedestrian traffic.

About a thousand people took part in the rally when it began at 2 P.M., and organizers expected several thousand more as it continued until dusk.

The weekend's events wind up a month of activities marking the 20th anniversary of the Stonewall Rebellion of June 27, 1969, when homosexual patrons fought back during a police raid on the Stonewall Inn, on Christopher Street, in Greenwich Village.

Today's march will start at Columbus Circle and proceed down Fifth Avenue and past Stonewall, which has long since closed.

At 2:30 P.M., marchers will observe a period of silence in memory of those who have died of AIDS. Skywriting planes will trace the words "We Remember."

A dance is scheduled for 4 P.M. today on the Christopher Street pier, followed by fireworks from barges at 10:30 P.M.

Source

New York Times, June 25, 1989. Edited from a news item by the Associated Press.

Footwashing Day

Usually a Sunday in Early Summer

The biblical sanction for the rite of footwashing is to be found in John 13:4-20 which records that Jesus, after the Passover supper, washed the feet of his disciples as an act of love and humility and instructed them to follow his example. Although controversial, this practice became as important in some churches as the celebration of the Eucharist. Originally the rite was performed on Holy Thursday, but among American Protestant sects it may take place at other times and more frequently.

Footwashing in Kentucky

In Floyd County [Kentucky], the devout—some of my own relatives among them—still [c. 1950] cling to a traditional mode of worship. They follow the Biblical custom of foot washing.

Gathering in the church house, the men are seated on highback benches in one side, the women folk on the other. To the right of the home-made wooden pulpit two benches are arranged facing each other. Here are seated the men. On the opposite side two benches are similarly placed. The women are seated there.

At the appointed time, one "sister," having removed her shoes and stockings, sits piously with folded hands while another sister washes her feet and dries them with a towel which has been girthed about her waist. The two then exchange places and the custom of footwashing is repeated. The men on the opposite side of the pulpit do likewise.

For the mountain people, footwashing is a combination of Fourth of July and Thanksgiving. It comes only once a year, but the people spend weeks in preparation for it. Men begin building refreshment stands all up and down the creek while the women folk keep busy cleaning house and getting stuff in for the big dinner.

The Sunday of the footwashing, people come in from miles around. The older people gather in the church house while the youngsters gather around the refreshment stands to eat ice-cold watermelon and soda pop. Every one gets a new outfit for the occasion, and the young beaux can be seen strolling along with their best girls on their arms.

The meeting is dismissed at noon, and the people who live around the vicinity of the church invite the church-goers in for a bite to eat. This bite usually consists of fried chicken, ham, beef, and perhaps some turkey with mashed potatoes, boiled potatoes, green beans, peas, beets, and other garden vegetables thrown in. For dessert there are a variety of pies and cakes as well as cookies for the children, and a churn of lemonade is always kept filled. Every family tries to see which one can feed the most people the most things, and an air of good-natured fun prevails throughout the entire day.

In the evening everyone packs up and takes off for home with the invitation to their hosts to "come and see us real soon." The funny thing about these people is that they mean it.

Source

Kentucky Folklore Record, II (1956), 40-41. From a collection of "Floyd County Folklore" edited by Leonard W. Roberts. His informants were for the first selection Blanche E. Dingus of Martin, Kentucky, a student at Western Kentucky State College, and for the second selection Verna Louis Baldridge, a student at the University of Kentucky. Floyd County, eastern Kentucky, is in the Big Sandy Valley, a region also noted for the Hatfield-McCoy feud.

Independence Day

July 4

The most important American national holiday commemorates the signing of the Declaration of Independence by John Hancock, president of the Continental Congress, on July 4, 1776, at Philadelphia and its adoption by the delegates from the thirteen colonies. Its observance increased in popularity as a sense of national pride and accomplishment increased, and by the 1880s had become a major patriotic occasion. It is a political holiday and a community enterprise traditionally observed with fireworks, parades, band concerts, oratory, picnics, block parties, public entertainment, and especially sporting events. Like Memorial Day, its celebration has always been affected by national crises, such as the sectional conflicts of the 1850s, the Civil War, and later wars.

Boonville Plans to Celebrate the Fourth

On June 7, 1861, the [Boonville, New York] *Black River Herald* announced a "Meeting of the Citizens":

The Citizens of this village and its surroundings, interested in a proper and patriotic observance of the next annual Anniversary of American Independence, are requested to meet in Bamber Hall on Monday Eve. next, at 8 o'clock to take proper steps to that end. A punctual attendance is requested.

The statement was signed, "Many Citizens."

Those who attended drew up an "Order of the Day." The activities were scheduled to commence at sunrise with a "Federal Salute of 34 Guns." At ten A.M. the procession would form in front of Hulbert's Hall and in the following order:
1. Boonville Brass Band
2. The President and Vice Presidents of the Day
3. Orator and Reader of the Day
4. The Clergy
5. The President and Trustees of the Village
6. Soldiers of the War of 1812
7. The Boonville Zouave "Infantry"
8. Jackson's Marshall Band
9. Hawkinsville Union Guards
10. Thirteen Young Ladies, on horse, representing the 13 original states, costumed in Red, White, and Blue
11. Cataract Fire Co. No. 1
12. Mounted Zouaves of Hawkinsville
13. Thirty-four Gentlemen, on horse, representing 34 States of the Union, wearing sashes of Red, White, and Blue
14. Visitors, Citizens and Strangers

The procession when formed would march to the grove of Aaron Willard, Esq., where the following "Order of Exercises" were to be observed: Invocation, Music by the Band, Reading of the Declaration, Singing of Holmes' Army Hymn by the 13 Ladies, Oration, Music and Closing Prayer.

The *Black River Herald* in its columns before July 4, gave this further prospectus:

> At the close of the exercises at the grove, the Procession will reform in the same order as before, repair to the hotel of Joel T. Comstock, where a sumptuous Dinner will be served. After Dinner, Toasts and Speeches.

> Immediately after Dinner, upon grounds near, will be enacted in all the paraphernalia of war, the Battle of Yorktown, in which all the principal characters in that memorable battle will be represented....This is expected to be one of the grandest features of the day.

Source and Comment

New York Folklore Quarterly, XII (1956), 106-07. Using a contemporary newspaper as her source, Martha B. Snow described the celebration of Independence Day in Boonville, New York, from the advance planning, excerpted here, until its conclusion in the evening when "the thirteen ladies who rode in the procession serenaded various prominent citizens."

* * *

The Fourth at Butter Creek

The Fourth was celebrated [in 1877] at Butter Creek post office [near Pendleton, Oregon], and a general good time was had. The Declaration was read by Mr. John Vinson. L. W. Darling delivered the oration and received many tokens of appreciation of the effort from the audience. "God Save the State" was sung by the choir. Toasts were offered and responded to, after which all partook of a lunch, and then the afternoon was taken up with a variety of races and other sports. The foot race, 100 yards, was won by Aaron French. The horse race, 300 yards, six entered, best two in three, was won by Charlie Cates' cream horse, Poindexter. The sack race was won by Johnny Vinson, Darling coming through with a broken nose. The best of feeling prevailed and all voted the entertainment a success. About 50 persons engaged in the celebration.

Source

Western Folklore XXII (1963), 201. Transcribed by C. Grant Loomis from the Pendleton, Oregon *East Oregonian* of July 7, 1877.

The Fourth in Kansas, 1854-1857
1854

Following the passing of the Kansas-Nebraska bill, May 30, 1854, the wave of protest that rolled across the North spent its first force upon the Fourth of July, 1854. People everywhere were indignant. In word and act and symbol they demonstrated their feeling generally. Over a signature of three stars (***) one writer recommended devoting the day to the formation of an anti-Nebraska organization, the sole object of which should be resistance to the extension of slave territory. At Lawrenceville, Pa., from fifteen hundred to two thousand persons, assembled in an orchard, actually took such a pledge. At the end of a three-hour oration by David Wilmot the audience resolved to vote for no one except "a tried and well known friend of Freedom, who had a heart and a conscience, legs of his own to stand on, and a backbone to resist" the Nebraska outrage.

From Ontario, Ind., came the proposal to hoist the American flag at half mast, draped in black, and under it make "the firm, determined, unutterable resolve to battle manfully for Freedom." In Providence, R. I., the common council directed that the bells of the churches be tolled "one hour in the morning, one hour at noon, and one hour at sundown, on account of the passage of the Nebraska bill and the recent proceedings under the Fugitive Slave act." At Painesville, Ohio, a committee of sixteen, that being the number of the nominally free states, proclaimed their determined opposition to the enemies of liberty. Henry Ward Beecher was the orator.

In New York City where the common council appropriated $3,800 for fire-works, powder, band music, and bell chiming, Horace Greeley reminded his readers that the Revolutionary contest was still in progress when he wrote: "Alas that we could not all, on an occasion as fit as this, unite in tracing out the essential principles of our fathers' Revolutionary struggle, the fundamental ideas which led ... to the magnificent destiny we have inherited." At Pierrepont the citizens resolved "that the bells be tolled and crepe be worn on the left arm" and that the people

"concert measures to drive the dark spirit of Slavery back to the infernal regions from whence it came." In Warsaw the bells were tolled "for one hour in solemn and sad *remembrance* of the *spirit of freedom*." The citizens then "*gave this banner to the breeze*: No more Slave Territory! No more Slave States!! No more Slavery!!!"

Chicago also observed the Fourth as a day of mourning, public sentiment against [Stephen] Douglas being so extreme that he canceled his proposed visit to the city. Other Western communities also condemned the Nebraska iniquity. One was at Decorah, Iowa. Another was at St. Anthony, Minnesota territory, where the people felt the principle of the bill exposed them also to incursions of slavery, and they urged the formation of a "Holy League of Freedom."

In Massachusetts Antislavery feeling and concern for the newly opened West colored most Independence day events. Boston considered humiliation and fasting with minute guns on the Common and the tolling of bells; but when the day came, people marked it, "not with humiliation for the past," but with joyful hope for the actual equality of men. Said the orator, the Rev. A. L. Stone, before the city authorities: "Our sons and daughters must settle these new territories; there must be no laggards in the race for freedom; we must admit no more slave states." At Salem, Anson Burlingame answered his own question, "Can we remove the evil?" by quoting Col. James Miller at Lundy's Lane, "'*We can try.*'" Worcester would have every true son of America sign the Declaration anew. North Woburn erected a new liberty pole and inaugurated it at 6 a. m. In Pepperell the people burned effigies of President [Franklin] Pierce and Judge E. G. Loring. Montague burned four effigies and had a mock slave hunt. William Lloyd Garrison, the Abolitionist, won decided approbation at Framingham for burning Judge Loring's decision and the Fugitive Slave act itself, but his consigning of the Constitution to a similar fate met with disgust, indignation, and some hisses. In the same meeting Henry David Thoreau took the people of Massachusetts ironically to task for their too manifest concern over Kansas and Nebraska.

I had thought that the house was on fire, and not the prairie; ... though several of the citizens of Massachusetts are now in prison for attempting to rescue a slave from her own clutches, not one ... expressed regret for it. ...It was only the disposition of some wild lands a thousand miles off which appeared to concern them. ...There is not one slave in Nebraska; there are perhaps a million slaves in Massachusetts. ...What should concern Massachusetts is not the Nebraska bill nor the Fugitive Slave bill, but her own slaveholding and servility. ...

In the much discussed, newly organized territories themselves several happenings marked the arrival or passing of July 4, 1854. Only three of the events, however, were in the nature of social celebrations, and two of those were in what is now Nebraska. The one in Kansas, moreover, was under the auspices of the anti-Abolitionists of Missouri. Only the plans for it survive.

Announced as a general territorial convention at Salt creek valley, near the trading post of Mr. Kivaly, the gathering was to hear the reading of the Declaration of Independence and an address by Charles Grover. An ample public dinner would follow. Although the preliminary meeting at White-head's on June 24 had referred to the people as "settlers of Kansas Territory," the resolutions they adopted were Southern in spirit, favoring squatter sovereignty and refusing protection to any Abolitionist settler, and the persons invited were "citizens of Missouri generally." Afterward one Missouri editor wrote, "The Fourth appears to have been celebrated with much spirit in all directions," but he did not mention specifically the Salt creek valley observance. Business as well as politics and pleasure no doubt marked the day, for the books of the Doniphan county commissioners show that entry number 18 for a claim near Whitehead bears the date of July 4, the claimant, Andrew J. Branson, having begun his residence there March 28, 1854. July 4, 1854, was also the day on which Sen. David R. Atchison and a few of his Platte county friends chose the site of Atchison and dedicated the new town.

For a second time on a Fourth Wm. H. Goode, who was at Shawnee mission in 1843, rode into Kansas [City, Mo.] on horseback and crossed to the Kansas side in a skiff, this year to visit the Wyandots. Kansas [City] was "now a thriving town driving a heavy trade with the plains." At the Wyandot settlement the visitor was satisfied to find the Rev. John M. Chivington, regularly appointed missionary, in possession of the Methodist mission farm. He, therefore, had no leisure to speculate upon the seemingly ominous coincidence of his arriving twice successively in Kansas City "on the day consecrated to freedom, in connection with the struggle for freedom then commencing in that region."

Jotham Meeker, who had been in Kansas for every Fourth of July since 1834, set out in his wagon July 3, 1854, for Westport, in company with J. Miller. He encamped on the prairie for the night of July 3 and arrived at his son-in-law's on July 4, to visit his daughters and his grandchildren.

On this same Fourth of July eve a much larger expedition of the military encamped on Grasshopper creek, Kansas territory, en route from Fort Leavenworth to New Mexico. Under command of Col. F. Fauntleroy the party consisted of "regimental headquarters, the band, and companies B and D 1st Dragoons," with 79 civilians employed as teamsters, drovers, and overseers to care for the "400 upwards public horses" of the quartermaster department. For so large an expedition both the soldiers and band must have made some due recognition of the Independence day

to dawn on the morrow, but both Colonel Fauntleroy and Sgt. P. G. Lowe were too concerned over their extensive charge and their inadequate provision for its care to note the patriotic significance of the day. Sergeant Lowe enumerated besides the troops, many officers, some families, a huge supply train, and "600 extra horses led on strings of about forty horses each."

Nebraska territory had more conventional Independence day observances. At Belleview a delightful repast at Mr. Robinson's marked the first Fourth kept in the new settlement. Native and cultivated products of Nebraska constituted the meal; among them were fresh meat, new potatoes, peas, various kinds of garden sauce, wild gooseberries and raspberries, with a "good cup of coffee" and "plenty of pure ice-water." Toasts followed the food.

On the site of what is now Omaha a party of Iowans celebrated the Fourth with a bountiful picnic. They requisitioned a wagon to convey their supplies to and from the ferry. The wagon also served as speaker's stand for the program. Two blacksmith's anvils were used to fire the salute. Just as H. D. Johnson had begun his oration, Indians appeared and broke up the gathering, lunch baskets and anvils being piled into the wagon and the audience fleeing toward the ferry.

Many events within Kansas territory itself marked July 4, 1855. . . .

When the people of Lawrence first proposed to celebrate this Fourth of July, 1855, in gala way, George W. Brown wrote in an editorial, "About Face," that they were already "an enslaved people, perfectly subjugated." Rather than *celebrate* he thought they had better "re-adopt the principles of the declaration of independence and . . . extend those principles over Kansas at the sacrifice of 'our lives, our fortunes, and our sacred honor.'" The next week when his paper carried notice of the committee's plans and cordially invited all persons to attend the picnic dinner and exercises, he urged the people to come, armed in defense, to give the expedition from Missouri, rumored as on the way, a warm reception. "Our motto is: If we cannot have an honorable peace, let us have an honorable war." Seven days later he wrote, under the caption "Independence":

Independence! If thy name belong to us, let us wear it honorably; . . . And if Kansas is today the political focus of our country, what is expected of us . . . at such a post?

The celebration itself, however, stirred even editorial enthusiasm. "A year ago and Lawrence was not." Now, on the morning of the Fourth, her streets looked like those of a thronged city. "Congratulatory musketry" announced the dawn. Visitors who had begun to arrive the night before gathered in "knots" along Massachusetts street. Families came in from their claims near by. Delaware and Shawnee Indians drove in in wagon loads. The Topeka band rode down by night to be at the levee for the parade at nine o'clock. Franklin sent its representatives in a large covered wagon, from the top of which floated the national flag, with the figures '76 among the Stars and Stripes. The Blue Mound and Wakarusa neighborhoods formed a procession of their own, consisting of men and women equestrians in double column, seven double wagons driven by seven two-horse teams, and three large ox-wagons fastened together and drawn by eleven yoke of oxen. The grouping of the oxen demonstrated the proverb, "In Union is strength." The wagons were all crowded with seats, chairs, and people who waved aloft flags and colored handkerchiefs. Branches of rose trees and flowers ornamented the horses and the carriages.

From the Governor Robinson home on Mt. Oread, Mrs. Robinson watched the groups moving in from all directions. The garlands of leaves and flowers, she wrote, hid the roughness of the vehicles. Dress, distinctive of the place whence they had emigrated, characterized the different groups. Some were from the East; some, from the far West; others were from Missouri.

An assembly of 1,500 to 2,000 participated in the festivities of the day. Two organized military companies in uniform led the procession through the chief city streets. At eleven o'clock near the Union Hotel the ladies of Lawrence presented a rich silk flag to the militia. As the procession moved toward the platform and seats in Clinton park, Indians in fantastic array fell in line. A trio of them had posts of honor on the speaker's stand. The exercises consisted of music, prayer, reading of the Declaration of Independence, speeches, and oration. One of the speeches was an address by William Hutchinson on "The Dignity of Labor."

In the oration Dr. Charles Robinson alluded to the peculiar circumstances surrounding the settlers in this new and strange country. They had come there to plant anew the institutions of the United States; but the citizens of Missouri were imposing laws upon them to force slavery upon the territory.

It is for us to choose ... what institutions shall bless or curse our beautiful Kansas....Every pulsation in Kansas vibrates to the remotest artery of the body politic, and I seem to hear the millions of freemen and the millions of bondmen in our own land ... saying to the people of Kansas: "Do your duty!"

The audience cheered Dr. Robinson heartily. He had made "a most excellent oration,... adapted to the times."

When the audience called loudly for Indian speakers, Mr. Fish of the Shawnees and Mr. Pechalka of the Delawares responded amid "thunders of applause." Chief Pechalka of the Delawares hoped that the settlers would make Kansas a free state, for he believed that "a set of men who would crush and enslave one class ... would crush and enslave another if they had the power." They were both glad to see the Northerners coming into the territory, "not with the

hatchet and sounds of war," but with the "sweet fruits of peace and civilization."

Following the exercises the guests and the officers of the day marched between two lines of military and citizen soldiery to a sumptuous public dinner in the grove. Among the toasts and sentiments pronounced afterward from the speaker's stand, those on territorial themes are of chief interest today.

Young Kansas—The rights of her citizens trodden down for a brief period, have but aroused her to an appreciation of freedom, and inspired her sons with a spirit and vigor which shall bid defiance to her enemies.

The Day We Celebrate—An epoch in the history of the world, which shall be commemorated as long as the spirit of freedom animates the heart of man.

Lawrence—Its course is onward, and its progress as *the* city of Kansas a fixed fact.

The Pioneers of Kansas—May they reap the rewards of their toil and privations, by rearing a state which shall be an honor in the galaxy of the American confederacy.

Our Aboriginal Neighbors— ... May we ever "smoke the pipe of peace" together.

The Laborers of Kansas—The basis of all we are or hope to be.

Of the volunteer toasts one was on the legislature and three were on the territory itself.

The Kansas Legislature—A body alien to our soil, elected by fraud: we are not responsible for their acts, and ask no favors at their hands.

Kansas—[1]. The home of our adoption.... [2]. An *infant* whose growth would astonish Barnum. [3]. Its prosperity and progress are dear to all the friends of freedom. May its fertile soil never be cursed with slavery.

The day passed quickly, Mrs. Robinson said, but to strengthen more the bonds of social feeling, a party of one hundred or thereabouts gathered in the largest hall in town at night and enjoyed refreshments of cake and ice cream together.

Quiet and harmony had been the proud characteristics of the first Fourth of July in Lawrence. Although toward evening there was some evidence "a distillery could send its foul streams thitherward," the day closed without accident or harm....

Two events marked the first Fourth of July in Topeka. E. C. K. Garvey and company began publishing the city's first newspaper, *The Kansas Freeman*, on this day. "The generality of the citizens" observed the holiday by wholesale destruction of the products of the distillery. Having a great antipathy to "whisky," its sale, its use, its existence, they met in the evening on the open prairie and went as a "committee of the whole," to demand of the one liquor dealer in town his entire stock. He would not give it up, but he would and did sell it to them at a stated price. They rolled out the barrels, knocked in the heads, and set fire to the fluid. It " 'went up,' not in a 'blaze of glory,' ... but in an inglorious blaze of *red, fiery rum*." The newspaper commented thus:

Without one dissenting voice let the decree go forth from our midst that the demon intemperance shall be forever banished from among us, and ... our city will ... be *the* place of wealth and influence in Kansas Territory—founded on a basis firm as the Hill of Hills, old "Bunker Hill," and free as the winds that sweep our own beautiful prairies—using for our motto the words of the immortal Adams: "Liberty and Union, now and forever, one and inseparable."

Across the river in Indianola, Samuel J. Reader referred to the event as a "Whisky Riot." Spending most of his holiday in hauling stone and walling up a well, he went in the late afternoon in a wagon to take a neighbor's dog home, shot at a wolf, and saw "Delawares & Potts at Frenchman's drunk." The Indians, returning from a hunt, had patronized the liquor dealer freely. The next day, Columbra, the dealer, told Reader that the crowd had spilled three-fourths of a barrel of whisky for him. "They damn rasks." ...

1856

Unrest characterized the spirit of the American people at the approach of July 4, 1856, and Kansas was the immediate occasion of the widespread concern. For two years the North and the South had been pouring their emigrants into the territory, each in hope of establishing its favored form of government there. In each group were willing leaders and loyal followers who welcomed the publicity attendant upon the cause they represented. Many emigrants, however, more interested in the homes they were founding than in the political destiny of the region, found themselves, literally, victims of circumstance. Caught on the chosen battlefield of the national issue, they not only had to bear indignities of local border strife but they also had to endure public sympathy and public censure. Kansans and the Kansas cause were now the common theme of the common tongue. The press pictured their hardships; editors dwelt on every new injustice; sympathetic friends gave personal letters publication; philanthropists and church societies tried to replace material losses with material gifts; and ever politicians brooded over—and talked of—the ultimate political fate.

The eightieth anniversary of American Independence, therefore, dawned amid circumstances of peculiar solemnity. "It is the crisis of our country's existence, the turning point in her history." Indorsement by the federal administration of Missourians' invasion of the Kansas ballot boxes and election of a Kansas legislature from their own number had at last stirred the nation. In the North orators and clergymen doubled their efforts in serious defense of freedom. In the South toastmasters and after-dinner speakers treated their views more lightly and briefly, but with feeling that was not all jest....

Within Kansas territory itself the citizens awaited the arrival of July 4, 1856, with even greater concern than had the sympathetic nation. Topeka was the center of interest, for there, at noon, was to reassemble the Free-State legislature adjourned March 1. Or wasn't it to reassemble? Thereby hung the tale; therein lay the common anxiety.

New border warfare threatened. Proslavery men had arranged muster and review drills for Lecompton, Tecumseh, and Atchison on July 4. Rumor to the effect that James H. Lane was bringing in a large force from the north had agitated the Missouri border to try "to march 400 Missourians of baser sort to Topeka." Lieutenant McIntosh of Company E, First cavalry, intercepted this plan on July 4. Meantime, federal troops from Fort Riley and Fort Leavenworth, under command of Col. E. V. Sumner, concentrated around Topeka, presumably to maintain "Law and Order" there. When Acting Governor Woodson had first conferred with Colonel Sumner about the proposed assembly of the legislature, the colonel had advised the presence in Topeka of a justice of the peace and a marshal to join Major Sedgwick in drawing writs on all the members of the legislature the minute they assembled. Woodson, however, asked Sumner to come with two troops. Accordingly he concentrated five companies and two pieces of artillery there on July 3.

Preliminary to the legislative assembly the Free-State party met in convention in Topeka July 2-4, with headquarters in the new hotel. On July 2 the delegates met by districts; on July 3-4 they held a mass convention. Some 800 persons were in attendance, among them many members of the legislature. Only from the settlements near by, however, had people ventured to come in numbers. Fear of border depredation in their own communities had detained many at home.

The Free-State legislators had come to Topeka resolved to hold their legislative meeting in spite of any Border-Ruffian interference. Many of them brought in arms privately, though they did not mean to appear with them unless necessary. Some laid double floors in wagon bottoms and packed weapons between; others hid them under loads of wood, hauled in "for sale." Both the legislature and the assembled people, however, now resolved to offer no resistance to the government troops. Gov. Charles Robinson, in prison near Lecompton, sent instructions to make no opposition unless the troops wantonly fired on the legislature or the people; and, if ordered to disperse, they should disperse.

July 3 and 4 the mass convention carried on its business. It passed resolutions indorsing the state movement and the

Topeka constitution. It elected the Kansas State Central Committee to determine, among other things, upon the management and control of the Free-State party. It memorialized congress to admit Kansas into the Union.

On the afternoon of July 3 people learned that the military force about the town was itself to forbid the assembly of the legislature. Both branches of the legislature met on July 3 and resolved to assemble in regular session, agreeable to adjournment, at noon on July 4. The business transacted here secretly, by authority of Acting Gov. John Curtis, was to be security for the perpetuation of their power lest they be prevented from meeting the next day.

Topeka was full of people both indoors and out. To one young man it "look[ed] lively, animated with the tents of volunteers, the covered wagons and camp fires scattered all about, and the scores of horses picketed in every vacant space near them." Holiday celebration began on the evening of July 3 when the "ladies of Topeka" presented a banner of white silk, lettered in blue, to a military company of the city. The men wore uniforms of white pants, blue shirts, and Kossuth hats.

The morning of the Fourth broke cloudily, but fresh prairie breezes soon blew the clouds away. "Naturally a more beautiful, politically a more important day, never rose in Kansas," wrote James Redpath. At sunrise the army artillery fired a cannon thirteen times in salute. Flags floated from every public building. "Franklin Pierce was found hung in effigy at the back of one of the outhouses." Armed, determined men filled the streets. Martial music and gruff commands mingled with the tramp of drill and the roar of firearms. Half a dozen military companies paraded about. Women promenaded with little banners flying from their parasols. Ladies from Lawrence waved on the tops of their sunshades the United States flag embroidered for the occasion and trimmed in mourning.

Gaiety and assumed indifference ill concealed the suppressed excitement with which people awaited the crucial noon hour. The convention, gathered around the hotel, however, continued the semblance of business. About nine o'clock messengers from "the Northern States" arrived with word that "the people of the North were not prepared to stand by us in resisting the federal government." At ten o'clock Marshal I. B. Donalson and Judge Rush Elmore, mistaking the assembly for the legislature, interrupted proceedings to read proclamations of the President and the governor for dismissal. Learning their error, they retired in chagrin, the lanky, jean-clad figure of Donalson with "iron-grey whiskers and imbecile-looking eyes" leading the way back to his Proslavery accomplices—S. D. Lecompte, Judge Sterling G. Cato, and Sec. Daniel Woodson—now in the camp of Colonel Sumner. The convention meantime resumed its business.

The day and the temperature advanced together. Toward twelve o'clock the thermometer stood at 100⁰. Crowds milled through the streets. The band played. Companies F and G of Topeka marched to the legislative hall where the ladies were now to present Company G with a banner bearing the inscription, "Our lives for our rights."

Then word came that Colonel Sumner was approaching in full military array, with the battle flag flying. Beside him, at the head of the procession, was the military band; and close behind were three squadrons of dragoons and two loaded brass cannon," with their muzzles pointing down the street, the gunners at their stations, and the slow matches lighted and burning." The army surgeon had his case of instruments open, ready for use. A committee from the convention at once waited upon Colonel Sumner to inquire whether he meant to disperse the convention or disband the local military companies. He replied that he would disperse only the legislature. Some one then gave three cheers for Colonel Sumner; James Redpath proposed three cheers for Governor Robinson; and some one else, three cheers for Liberty. Since the camp was only 200 yards out of town, the dragoons debouched rapidly into Kansas avenue, formed into position, and pressed upon the Topeka companies at once, the latter stepping out of rank only far enough not to be trampled on. The band played; the drummers drummed until the drumsticks nearly touched the noses of the advancing horses. One little boy beating the kettledrum, rattled it manfully without even turning to look at the dragoons. As Colonel Sumner dismounted and walked toward the legislative hall, Mrs. Gates, of Lawrence, said to him, "We have met to present a banner to one of these Topeka companies on the day of our would-be-independence"; and he replied, 'Madame, I hope you will be independent."

When he entered the hall to dismiss the house, "the rooms were crowded by the citizens ... and some ladies, ... to witness the spectacle." To secure a quorum for roll call the sergeant-at-arms had to summon absentees. Then Colonel Sumner read his order for dismissal.

Gentlemen: I am called upon this day to perform the most painful duty of my whole life. Under the authority of the President's proclamation I am here to disperse this Legislature, and therefore inform you that you cannot meet. I, therefore, order you to disperse. God knows that I have no party feeling in this matter, and will hold none so long as I occupy my present position in Kansas. I have just returned from the Borders, where I have been sending home companies of Missourians, and now I am ordered here to disperse you. Such are my orders, and you *must disperse*. I now command you to disperse. I repeat that this is the most painful duty of my whole life.

All contemporary reports of the occasion indicate that Colonel Sumner did his duty in a gentlemanly way. He and members of the house exchanged civilities. Judge Philip C. Schuyler asked whether they were to understand the legislature was "driven out at the point of the bayonet." Colonel Sumner replied, "I shall use all the forces in my command to carry out my orders." Then he left the hall, mounted his horse, and was about to ride away when some one reminded him that he had not dismissed the senate.

Entering the senate chamber, he found the members had not assembled; therefore, when he read the order for dispersion, the president, T. G. Thornton, informed him that since they had not convened they could not conform. Colonel Sumner replied that his orders were to prevent their meeting. Then Marshal Donalson brought more ignominy upon himself by threatening every member with arrest, should they try again to assemble. Ignoring this "outrageous demand," several senators let Colonel Sumner know they would respect his order. J. H. Pillsbury said that since they were in no condition to resist United States troops, they would of course have to disperse.

As Colonel Sumner came down stairs, he recognized W. A. Phillips and nodded to him.

"Colonel," said Phillips, "you have robbed Oliver Cromwell of his laurels."

Sumner did not speak, but the expression of his eye clearly indicated what he thought.

He looked startled at first, then serious, angry, and agitated.

He ... saw at once the full enormity of the orders he had been compelled to obey....

Outside some one cheered for Sumner to let him know the people did not hold him responsible for the order he had just executed. A new American flag, with an extra star in the corner but not in the Union, was hoisted over Constitution Hall. Three cheers were then given for the flag, three for the orphan star—Kansas coming into the Union—three for Frémont, followed by three groans for Pierce and the present government. The three groans for Pierce, wrote Dr. John H. Gihon, "fairly shook the building and startled the horses of the soldiers," making them break out of line.

The crisis in an historically eventful day had passed....

1857

National interest in independence for Kansas had spent its strength in 1856. In 1857 while the territory itself bided its time, the solicitude of the nation slept. The New York *Tribune,* to be sure, recommended the use of the approaching Fourth of July by the friends of Freedom in the free states and territories "to renew their fealty to old principles, and trace out anew the old landmarks. The attempts ... to nationalize Slavery, and sectionalize Freedom ... call loudly for a reassertion of the doctrines....The claims of Freedom ... should everywhere be ... held up in contrast with Slavery, its bitter antagonist." The editorial evoked little response.

Only at Berea, Ky., does there seem to have been any Fourth of July consideration of Freedom in 1857 as it might affect Kansas. Here Cassius M. Clay "enchained the

attention of the audience for 2½ hours" by an address upon the practical superiorities of freedom over slavery. To show the tyranny of slavery, he cited the rule of the slave power in Kansas; to prove the advantage of free labor over slave labor, he used figures of the United States census. As a final result of human progress he prophesied universal freedom to all men. At the end, he and his audience of 2,000-3,000, "*Resolved,* that the principles of 1776 are again in jeopardy and whether attacked by a foreign or *home foe,* will be again defended by all constitutional means to the death." Down in South Carolina, however, the militia, after toasting P. S. Brooks who "Though dead, yet liveth in the hearts of the sons of Carolina," and slavery which the "wants of society keep in existence" with negroes in the South and white slaves in the North, declared "*the hemp crops of Kansas*—ought to be applied in a domestic way, to hang Free-State agitators in the Territory."

In the territory itself in 1857, the Fourth of July had wide observance. Twenty-two communities are known to have kept the day more or less formally. The territorial press recommended local festivals. Kindly recollections of times gone by, thought one editor, might not be without benefit to the people of Kansas. The roar of cannon, soul-stirring music, and an oration would "refresh and invigorate the inner man," said a second; or a good dinner, the dance, or any other convivial party would strengthen feelings of fellowship. Another liked to hear spoken words of gratitude to the old veterans to whom we owe our liberty. To him, moreover, "the bright and beautiful shades of Kansas" seemed especially suitable for social gatherings. With "unprejudiced hearts" the people should assemble to rejoice over the glorious change that had come over the territory within the last twelve months. "From a disturbed and almost ruined land," Kansas now seemed to them all prosperous and at peace. In that spirit the people of Kansas met on July 4, 1857, to enjoy themselves and their blessings....

Source and Comment

Kansas Historical Quarterly X (February 1941), 34-78. Edited from the second of three carefully footnoted articles by Cora Dolbee on Fourth of July celebrations and politicking in the Kansas Territory.

In the years before the Civil War, Kansas became a major battleground for the pro- and anti-slavery supporters. This struggle, triggered by the passage of the Kansas-Nebraska Bill of 1854 repealing the Missouri Compromise which had attempted to settle the slavery question in the Louisiana Purchase territories, led to guerilla warfare. It also brought about the formation of the anti-slavery Republican Party, John Brown's famous raid near Pottawatomie Creek, and the Lecompton Constitution. The nation's tension during the years 1854-1857 was reflected in contemporary Independence Day observances.

July Fourth Housewarming in Mexican San Francisco

In the early years of the nineteenth century few ships visited [San Francisco Bay], but the ever-increasing number during the third decade (vessels coming for hides and whalers for provisions) determined Governor Figueroa to establish a trading post on Yerba Buena cove, as it had been found that here was a much better anchorage than near the Presidio. Though Figueroa died before his project was carried out he is entitled to be considered the founder of Yerba Buena, the village which in 1847 was re-christened San Francisco, and which in its expansion under American rule soon embraced the earlier settlements at the Presidio and the Mission Dolores.

Figueroa had appointed as Harbormaster of the new port Captain William A. Richardson, an Englishman who owned a ranch at Sausalito and operated two small schooners on the bay, collecting hides and tallow from Dolores, Santa Clara and San José Missions and from the near-by ranches. He was directed to draw a plan for the town, which he did, laying out a single street, *La Calle de la Fundacion* (Foundation Street), running northwest from a point near what is now the intersection of Kearny and Pine Streets. On the north side of this street he chose a hundred vara lot, upon which in 1835 he built of ship's canvas on redwood posts a shelter for himself and family, who thus became the first inhabitants of Yerba Buena. A lonely spot it must have been, between two and three blocks from the water of the cove, surrounded only by sand dunes and chaparral.

The next year Jacob P. Leese built the first frame house on a lot adjoining Richardson's on the south. If you walk today [c. 1923] from Portsmouth Square up Clay Street to Grant Avenue and stand facing west, you can visualize Richardson's tent on your right hand and Leese's house on your left. You can imagine this house just completed on the Fourth of July, 1836, and the great company which Leese gathered together for the double celebration, Independence Day and his housewarming. Richardson had delivered the invitations while Leese had hastened the completion of his home. All the Spanish families around the bay responded as well as officers and families from the Presidio, officers from ships in the harbor and families from the Mission—about sixty in all. Over the long table a canvas was raised for protection from the sun and tents were provided for the comfort of the guests. They came by boat and on horseback, there being as yet no wagon road to the cove. The entertainment began by a grand feast at five o'clock followed by toasts and responses, then music and dancing kept up until nearly morning; a few hours sleep and more feasting and dancing. As a grand finale a picnic on Rincon Hill. Livelier times had begun for the little town. This first Fourth-of-July celebration was a patriotic demonstration as well as a social function. It was the occasion of the first raising of the American flag on the site of the future San Francisco, ten years before the official flag-raising in Portsmouth Square, Leese's house being adorned by all the bunting the ships in the harbor could spare, American and Mexican flags floating amicably together. A few days after his house-warming Leese opened a $12,000 stock of general merchandise in a part of his house. He married a sister of General Vallejo and in this house, in 1838, was born their daughter, Rosalie, the first white child born in Yerba Buena. Here we have by April, 1838, within a stone's throw of the square, the first two dwellings, the first mercantile establishment, the first social affair, the first Independence Day celebration, the first raising of the American flag and the birth of the first white child ....

Source

California Historical Quarterly, III (April 1924), 30-1. Edited from a paper read before the California Historical Society on March 25, 1924 by Helen Throop Purdy and entitled "Portsmouth Square". Portsmouth Square was the area about which the town Yerba Buena (later San Francisco) clustered. California was ceded to the United States in 1848.

* * *

How to Organize a Fourth of July Celebration

A very appropriate day for a general celebration, in the United States, is the Fourth of July.

In preparing for such a celebration, it is first necessary to appoint suitable committees to carry out the details of the work incident to such an occasion. This is done by calling a meeting of the citizens at some public place, *"for the purpose of making arrangements for celebrating the forthcoming anniversary of American Independence!"* which meeting should organize in the usual form, by the appointment of president and secretary.

The meeting should consider the feasibility of such celebration, and, if it is deemed advisable to celebrate this anniversary, should appoint an executive committee of three, to have general supervision of the whole affair, to be assisted by:

1. A finance committee, who will solicit the necessary funds.
2. A committee on grounds, to select a suitable place for holding the celebration, furnishing speakers' stand, seats for people, etc.
3. Committee on orator, who will provide speakers, reader of Declaration of Independence, etc.
4. Committee on music, to provide band, singing by the glee club, etc.
5. Committee on procession, who will induce the various societies, and a representation from the different trades, to appear in street procession, along with a representation of the different states in the Union.

6. Committee on military display, who will organize any military exhibition that may be thought advisable, take charge of firing guns, etc.

7. Committee on fireworks, who will attend to the arrangements for such exhibition in the evening.

8. Committee on amusements, whose especial duty it shall be to organize such street display of burlesque, etc., as will entertain and amuse the people.

The executive committee may appoint the president of the day, the necessary marshals, and arrange for additional attractions and novelties calculated to secure the success of the celebration.

Let these arrangements be made three or four weeks before the "Fourth." Now, let the executive committee thoroughly advertise the list of committees, and what it is proposed to accomplish. In the meantime, the finance committee should report to the executive what amount of money may be relied upon, and the committee on orator should report the names of their speakers, while the various other committees will report what the attractions are to be in their several departments.

Then the executive committee should prepare their posters and programmes, descriptive of what strangers from abroad will see who attend the celebration, and crowds of people will come from near and far.

Source and Comment

Hill's Manual of Social and Business Forms, 1880, 253-54. Thomas E. Hill, in his frequently reprinted handbook on social forms, customs, and etiquette, includes a section on the "celebration of public holidays" in which he provides plans for a Fourth of July celebration that can serve as a guide for "other public entertainments." The edition used here is the one copyrighted by Moses Warren & Company, Chicago, 1878. The first edition is dated 1873.

* * *

July Fourth and the Rodeo

In 1880 he would have been a hardy soul indeed who predicted that in the first half of the next century the cowboy would become the leading American folk hero. For at that time he was known, if known at all outside the region he frequented, at best as a provincial rustic and at worst as a ruffian and a thief and a murderer. How he attained his present status is a complicated story, only a single chapter of which will be attempted here.

One of the most effective means by which the cowboy established a favorable image of himself was by the public exhibitions of his occupational skills, skills hitherto unknown to Europeans and Eastern Americans. The range cattle industry, out of which these skills developed, had been established in the southern tip of Texas by Mexican rancheros, from whom the Anglo Texans borrowed the equipment and techniques for handling wild longhorn cattle by men on horseback. Basic to this equipment was the rope (*lasso, lariat, reata*), and a strong saddle with a horn to serve as a snubbing post. A highly skilled roper, who could catch an animal by the horns, neck, forefeet, hindfeet or any single foot named, was much admired. Admired too was his horse, which knew exactly what to do when he found a steer or a bull on the other end of the rope.

These horses had not been brought up as pets. Whether they were captured mustangs or horses raised on the ranch, they had been allowed to run on the range until mature. When first ridden they invariably tried to unseat their riders by a series of violent movements called pitching (bucking in the Northwest). Since pitching was peculiar to the range horse of the Americas, the contest between horse and rider had a novel fascination for those unaccustomed to range life. It has an equal (though not novel) fascination for the range men themselves, for whenever broncs were to be ridden cowboys and *vaqueros* gathered to see the show and to shout derision or encouragement....

... In a bronc riding contest held in Deer Trail, Colorado, on July 4, 1869, a cowboy named Gardenshire, lately from England, by riding a famous outlaw horse known as Montana Blizzard, won first prize and the praise of a newspaper reporter, who described the performance in some detail and called it "a magnificent piece of horsemanship."

Perhaps earlier than the Deer Trail competition was a more elaborate one held in San Antonio, and reported by John Duval in a book of which he says all the events happened, though not necessarily to the persons or in the sequence represented. Participating were "Comanche warriors, decked out in their savage finery," Texas "rangers" and "a few Mexican rancheros, dressed in their steeple crown, broad brim sombreros, showy scarfs and 'slashed' trousers, holding gracefully in check the fiery mustangs on which they were mounted.

Some of the events, such as picking up objects from the ground, shooting at targets from horses running at full speed, riding hanging by one leg from the saddle and firing under the horse's neck, were related to border warfare and the protection of herds. But it was the bronc riding that Duval found the most "interesting and exciting of them." Each contestant saddled his own horse in the ring without assistance. The winner was a ranger named McMullen, whose mount, "snorting and absolutely screaming with rage and terror, gave one tremendous bound, and then darted off at headlong speed across the prairie."...

In view of the enthusiastic admiration they elicited, as well as the business they brought to town, it was to be expected that roping and riding contests would be staged throughout the cattle country. Those held before 1890 include the following: Austin, Texas, 1883; Pecos, Texas, 1883; San

Antonio, 1883; Galveston, 1883; Mobeetie, Texas, 1884; Miles City, Montana, 1885; Albuquerque, 1886; Denver, 1887; Montrose, Colorado, 1887; San Antonio, 1888; Prescott, Arizona, 1888; Canadian, Texas, 1888; San Angelo, Texas, 1889.

The Pecos contest, held on July 4, 1883, was staged to settle a long dispute among the ranch hands about which outfit had the best ropers. The news spread rapidly, and soon the town was overcrowded with people.

> Cash prizes were posted, and the leading ropers from each ranch were selected. Morgan Livingston of the NA ranch took first money, and Trav Windham second. There was a barbecue, and the town was crowded with people. Business was booming, especially around the saloons.

Exactly one year before the Pecos contest a celebration had been held at North Platte, Nebraska, that initiated a series of events that was to bring the cowboy and his skills before millions in America and Europe. The ranchmen of that region decided to celebrate the Fourth of July with an "Old Glory Blowout" and appointed William Cody to get it up. Under the name of Buffalo Bill, Cody was already famous as a scout and stage actor whose role was to play himself in a melodrama of variant forms, but always involving Indians, cowboys, scouts and frontiersmen, a lost maiden and comic relief. As he had long felt the need of a larger stage, he welcomed the opportunity. "I got out some handbills," he said later, "and sent them to all the ranches around for hundreds of miles and advertised in the papers that prizes would be given for some fancy cowboy stunts." He expected about a hundred cowboys and a thousand responded. To the cowboy events he added the attack on the Deadwood stagecoach by Indians (he had used real Indians on the stage), horse races, shooting contests and a drive of a small herd of buffalo. The attendance was gratifying. "North Platte had the biggest crowd it has ever had before or since." "I tried it out on my neighbors," Cody said "and they lived through it and liked it. I made up my mind I'd take the show East."

For three decades Buffalo Bill's Wild West Show was to tour America and Europe and to bring the cowboy before millions and to win approval of the ranking military brass of both continents, the sporting plutocracy and the peerage and royalty of Europe, that is, of the taste makers of the era.

Source and Comment

American Quarterly, XVI (1964), 195-98. Mody Boatright documents his history of "The American Rodeo" fully with contemporary descriptions and newspaper accounts. He does not emphasize its association with Independence Day, being mainly concerned with the rodeo as "a professional sport ... that grew out of the daily labor of the cowboy" and contributed toward making him a "popular symbol of the American frontier."

Bull Fight at Dodge City

The first and with perhaps one exception the only real bull fight ever held in the United States was staged at Dodge City on the fourth and fifth of July, 1884. It was a genuine Spanish importation, via Mexico, featuring expert Mexican bull fighters and actual swording of the bulls. In defiance of the nation-wide protest which arose against this "barbarous celebration of our national holiday" the Cowboy Capital, as was its habit in those days, presented the spectacle as advertised and thumbed its nose at the clamor.

To A. B. Webster, a former mayor of Dodge City, goes credit for the town's unique sporting venture. It was while struggling on the horns of a dilemma presented by the necessity for concocting something new in the way of Fourth of July entertainment, that Webster was prodded by his inspiration. After a moment's consideration of the feasibility of the idea, he made a hasty calculation of the expense involved and with characteristic frontier promptitude set out to sell his proposition to the town. Within an hour Dodge's business men had subscribed and paid in over $3,000. By the end of the following day the estimated budget of $10,000 had been raised.

Webster and his associates in the project of course had no motive other than a desire to make money. Certainly they would have scouted the imputation that any Spanish innovation was necessary to maintain Dodge City's notoriety as a two-gun metropolis. Yet, whether they realized it or not, Dodge in 1884 stood in need of just the sort of lurid publicity it immediately received when the bull fight was announced. The days of its lusty youth were slipping away, and the town was drifting perilously close to the shores of respectability. True, it was still the home of Bat Masterson, then advertised as the killer of thirty-two men, but the outside world was gaining the impression that it had turned pacifistic. In spite of its past reputation and the fact that it was still only a fringe on the outskirts of civilization men were hinting openly that Dodge wasn't as bad as it once had been. . . .

In order to handle the business affairs of the venture [Webster and friends] organized the Dodge City Driving Park and Fair Association. H. B. (Ham) Bell was elected president; D. M. Cockey, vice president; J. S. Welch, secretary; and A. J. Anthony, treasurer. Webster was made general manager. The first and most important job of the association was to engage "the genuine Spanish bull-fighters" who were to be the main feature and principal drawing card. This Webster was fortunate enough to do through a Scottish lawyer of Paso del Norte, one W. K. Moore, of the firm of Moore & Sierra. Moore not only engaged the troupe, but he came with them as their manager. Also he served as press agent. In this capacity he apparently came in immediate contact with the antagonism the fight had engendered, and one of his first tasks was to pour oil on the troubled waters. . . .

In Dodge City itself there were many who did not relish this new accession to the town's already lurid reputation. The minister of one of the churches publicly prayed that Dodge City might be relieved from this "stench in the nostrils of civilization." Nor was criticism confined within the church; some business men, even, while expecting to make money from the crowds, deplored the notoriety which they felt would hinder the future growth of the city.

However, neither Eastern sensibilities nor local delicacy weighed heavily upon the conscience of the Cowboy Capital. For the most part Dodge was enjoying the limelight without qualm or misgiving. It gloried in its sanguine past and was in no hurry to succumb to the soft amenities of civilization. It was getting a lot of fun out of this bull fight. It talked much and loudly about what was going to transpire, even though certain of its remarks were made with tongue in cheek. In the matter of the bulls, especially, Dodge injected a spirit of levity into the proceedings that would have been incomprehensible to any Spanish community on the eve of a serious bull fight.

These bulls the management had decided to secure locally. D. W. (Doc) Barton, said to be the first man to drive a herd of cattle from Texas to Dodge City, was given the contract. The grazing grounds were full of Texas herds containing bulls about whose fighting abilities and proclivities there was no question, and Barton's instructions were to choose them for their ferocity without fear or favor. Accordingly he combed the ranges with but one idea in mind, and that was to round up the most agile and pugnacious bovines the cattle country could produce. In the last week in June he delivered the twelve of his selection at the arena corral.

The public excitement aroused by the arrival of the bulls was exceeded only when the matadors put in their appearance a few days later. The citizens of Dodge were livestock connoisseurs, and after due inspection they were of unanimous opinion that these bulls were decidedly ugly customers. "By nature," stated one observer, "a Texas bull is all the time as mad as he can get." The mere presence of onlookers "was enough to bring them pawing and plunging against the corral fence till the boards bent like paper and the braces creaked with the strain."

Describing these bulls the *Ford County Globe* [of July 1, 1884] said: "As some of them are liable to be numbered with the dead before our next issue, we deem it proper to give a short sketch of these noted animals, together with their pedigrees. These pedigrees are kindly furnished by the famous bull raiser and breeder, Brother Barton, of the great Arkansas river."

Number 1 on the *Globe's* list was "Ringtailed Snorter, the oldest and most noted of the twelve. He has been in twenty-seven different fights, and always came off victor. Pedigree: Calved February 29, 1883; sire, Long-Horns; dam, All Fire, first of Great Fire, who won big money in a freeze-out at Supply in 1882."

Iron Gall, Number 3, was "a famous catch-as-catch-can fighter, and very bad when stirred up." Pedigree: Calved March 25, 1880; sire, Too-Much Gall; dam, Gall, by Gally.

Of Klu Klux, Number 7, the *Globe* said, "He is a four year old, and next to Ringtail Snorter is the oldest noted fighter that will come to the front on next Friday. It is this animal that the bull fighters most fear, having laid out his man in Old Mexico, while playing 'four you see and one you don't.' Pedigree: Got by Frank, out of Healy-Boy, who was given a commission in 1878 in the Neutral Strip."

Number 8 was "Sheriff, an animal that was never tamed or branded but showed good points in his past go-as-you-please fights on the plains, and since then has captured several prizes in different parts of the country."

Numbers 10, 11 and 12, were Rustler, Loco Jim, and Eat-Em-Up-Richard, all two-year olds. "Boyce has been training Loco Jim for the past month," the *Globe* reported, "and he will likely get away with his man. These animals are all sired by Ringtail Snorter and are the coming heroes of the day." The other entries were Cowboy Killer, Lone Star, Long Branch, Opera, and Doc. It was said of the latter, owned by and named for Doc Barton, that he was "a splendid formed gentleman, with well-developed muscles, and there is no doubt but that he will do good work."

This published list of the names and pedigrees of the bulls, containing allusions to persons and incidents familiar to everyone in the range country, was typical of the cow town's semihumorous attitude toward its Spanish-Mexican entertainment. The cow hands had respect for their bulls, and it tickled their fancy thus to dignify them with proper names. There was considerable betting as to the havoc the bulls would make among the matadors. Public sympathy was not wholly on the side of the bullfighters. While the cattlemen had a certain admiration for anyone with the nerve to engage a maddened bull on foot, they felt that their four-footed entries were about to do battle for the honor of the cattle country and were entitled to proper recognition and support.

On the Sunday preceding the Fourth Manager Moore and the matadors arrived in Dodge. Their appearance raised the town's interest and excitement to a fever pitch. The skeptics were silenced; the promoters redoubled their optimistic preparations.

There were five of these bullfighters, all native Mexicans. The chief matador was Capt. Gregorio Gallardo, a merchant tailor of Chihuahua. Gallardo was billed as the most noted of all the noted bullfighters of Old Mexico. Several Dodge City citizens remembered his having killed bulls in a ring at Paso del Norte some years before. He carried two swords, "used for dispatching purposes," with straight two-edged blades three feet in length. These, so Moore said, were made at Toledo, Spain. One of them, he claimed, was 150 years old and had been owned and used by Captain Gallardo's great-grandfather, once a professional matador of high degree in Spain.

The other members of the band were Evaristo A. Rivas, picador, inspector of public works in the state of Chihuahua; his son, Rodrigo Rivas, an artist by profession; Marco Moya, a professional musician from Huejuequillo; and Juan Herrerra, a musician from Aldama.

The newspapers, especially, waxed enthusiastic over the arrival of the matadors. They were described in phrases worthy the ingenuity of the most up-to-date sports propagandist. "They are a fierce lot," exclaimed one writer, "and fear is an unknown sensation to them. They have followed this avocation from boyhood. They have had many narrow escapes from death and have been seriously wounded at times. They understand that the people want an exciting and dangerous fight, and they are ready to satisfy them. Some day, they all feel, they will come to their death in the bull pit, but they like the life and would not be satisfied to leave it. Yet they are as intelligent a party of men as any person would wish to meet. Their all-redeeming trait is that they cannot be forced to drink a drop of strong liquor."

This last touch may have been inspired by Manager Moore. In his efforts to give a tone of respectability to an affair which its critics stigmatized as a return to barbarism, Moore continued to lay as much emphasis on the reputations his charges bore as exemplary citizens as he did on their records in the bull ring. Possibly he still questioned the reception Dodge would accord after so much talk of gore.

On the morning of the Fourth, however, any fears Moore may have had were set at rest. Before ten o'clock it was evident that the fight would be a financial success. As the town filled up it made a bizarre and colorful spectacle. Cowboys from every section of the Southwest were on hand, armed and spurred, and tanned by the prairie sun and wind, prepared to crowd enough excitement into the two days to last through the next six months of monotony. They had money to spend, and they had no difficulty in finding places to spend it. Dance halls filled with girls and gaming places sprinkled with gamblers were running full blast. The saloons were doing a capacity business. In the Opera House, the Congress Hall, the Long Branch, the Lone Star, and the Oasis, milling throngs of cowmen rubbed elbows with the hundreds of visitors brought in by the Santa Fe from the East. Correspondents for metropolitan newspapers in search of atmosphere made the rounds and, if one may judge from their stories, found no lack of copy.

By noon Dodge was jammed by eager crowds awaiting the appearance of the grand parade which was to mark the beginning of festivities. Cow ponies lined the hitching racks along the streets and were picketed in every available vacant lot. Shortly before two o'clock Former Mayor and Manager Webster, with Manager Moore of the matadors, led the procession to the fair grounds. Behind them came the town dignitaries, followed by the famous cowboy band. Then, to the delight of the spectators, the bullfighters passed in review. In their red jackets, blue tunics, white stockings and small dainty slippers, they seemed, in the words of a contemporary writer, "the perfection of litheness and quickness, and were heartily applauded as their dark handsome faces looked on the crowd gathered along the streets."

The arena, toward which all faces were turned after the parade, lay on a tract of forty acres between the town and the Arkansas river, which had been purchased and fenced by the association. Facing a half-mile track, an amphitheater with a seating capacity of four thousand had been erected. In front of the grandstand an eight-foot fence enclosed the arena proper, which was one hundred feet in diameter. At intervals along the fence eight light board screens, or escapes, were provided, where the bullfighters could take refuge when too closely pressed. West of the arena was the bull corral, connected with the main enclosure by a chute. Parallel with this chute was a wider passage through which the bodies of the victims would make their exit.

Before two o'clock the spectators began filing into the amphitheater. At least a third of the crowd, estimated at 4,000, were women and children. Since some of the ladies of the town were not remarkable for their sanctity a deputy sheriff had been detailed to draw a dividing line which should separate the *demi monde* from their more respectable sisters. The name of the frontier St. Peter assigned to this delicate task is lost to posterity, as are the social reverberations which must have accompanied some of his decisions. Immediately over the entrance gate the reporters and the band were seated, and at both sides sections were reserved for Dodge's leading citizens and their families. Opposite sat the cowboys and their ladies. The ambition of every cowpuncher, one writer reported, seemed to be to get a big fat girl and a high seat at the same time. "The wait before the appearance of the first bull," he wrote, "was filled with chaffing and calling of the usual kind, variegated with music by the cowboy band."

At half past two the work of driving the bulls from the corral into the pens opening on the arena was begun by Mr. Chappell, track horseman and tournament rider. He was assisted by bullfighter Juan Herrerra, who wielded a red mantle when the animals proved unusually refractory. When the bulls were safely penned the tips of their horns were sawed off and the ends rasped smooth.

At 3:40 a bugle sounded the signal for the grand entry. Amid the enthusiastic cheers of the multitude the matadors and picadors, four afoot and one mounted, came into the arena. They had changed into their fighting costumes and their parade had all the color of a pageant. Gallardo was magnificent in a scarlet tunic and knee breeches, with a green sash and sable trimmings. Rivas was attired in a yellow tunic trimmed with red, yellow knee breeches, and a white cap surmounted by a pair of horns. The other two matadors were dressed in red and blue. The picador wore ordinary cowboy clothes. They circled the arena, made their obeisance to the officials, and awaited the appearance of the first bull. The bugle sounded again and the first bull bounded into view of the crowd. He was a red, fierce-looking brute, and full of fight. As he passed through the door two decorated barbs were thrown into his neck, just below each horn. Infuriated by the darts, he charged madly at his tormentors. Gallardo attracted his attention and began to play him. Again and again, encouraged by the roars of the crowd, he drew the charges of the bull and deftly swerved him from his course with his mantle, escaping the rake of the horns by inches. After several of these preliminary passes Gallardo took refuge behind one of the escapes. The bull made a complete circle of the enclosure, then halted defiantly in the center of the ring and pawed the ground, covering himself with clouds of dust.

The other fighters now approached to display their skill. As they closed in the bull rushed, but the savage thrust of his horns met only thin air, and another festooned dart hung from his shoulders. Time and again he wheeled and charged, until his back and sides were decorated with a floating sea of colored streamers that reached from his horns to the end of his tail. The cow punchers forgot their girls and even the best citizens stood and applauded. The matadors were in their glory. Here was an animal worthy of their mettle; one that gave them an opportunity to exhibit all the tricks of their profession.

This bull was played for thirty minutes before he tired. Then Mr. Chappell was called on to lasso the bull and take him out. When the animal had been roped, the cow hands, anxious for a display of their own technique, set up a cry for Chappell to throw the brute. This he attempted to do, but the bull was too strong for him, and it was all he could do to pull the maddened animal into the chute. Here the bull made a desperate rush at Chappell, grazing his horse, and broke loose. Finally he was tied and restored to the pen, furious but unharmed.

When the second bull was released the spectators anticipated another display of brute ferocity and human agility. But they were disappointed; this bull proved to be a coward and ran from his assailants, and was soon driven out. The third was little better, merely providing some exercise for the fighters after they had covered his sides

with darts. The fourth also had to be dismissed. The fifth had even fewer fighting qualities than his predecessors. He became entangled in one of the escapes and was whipped out by a cowboy who sat in the first row of seats, to the derisive laughter of the onlookers.

By this time the crowd wanted more action and began demanding that the first bull be returned. It had been announced that the last bull of the day would be put to the sword by Gallardo, and the cowboys wanted to see this highly advertised maneuver executed on an animal worthy of the swordsman's skill. Accordingly, the fighting red bull was lassoed and pulled back into the arena.

When Gallardo reentered the enclosure and the spectators saw him take the Toledo sword which was passed down by Manager Moore they understood that the most exciting episode of the drama was at hand. They were aware that Gallardo must repeatedly attract the rushes of the bull until the precise opening for the death thrust presented itself. This lightning thrust, as they knew, must be accomplished by one stroke made from directly in front of the animal as it charged, and must result in a clean-cut and instant death.

When the bull caught sight of the matador, therefore, a hush of anticipation fell upon the noisy crowd. As if it appreciated its perilous situation the brute charged at once and with redoubled fury. With a graceful sweep of his cape Gallardo deflected the animal's first rush safely past his side. The bull wheeled and flung himself again at the matador. Once more his horns found nothing more substantial than the elusive cape. Repeatedly he returned to the attack and Gallardo's escapes grew narrower and narrower. Then, suddenly, the crowd gasped in dismay and jumped to its feet. Gallardo was down. For an instant it seemed the fight was about to end in tragedy. But fortunately the accident had occurred at the entrance to one of the established escapes. At the moment when it appeared to the crowd that Gallardo was caught between the bull's horns and the high board fence he threw himself lengthwise on the ground at the animal's feet and crawled to safety behind the guard. The bull charged on the light boarding of the screen and almost tore it down; then, meeting no active resistance, backed angrily away.

Although Gallardo had received a slight bruise on his left thigh he immediately stepped into the open to renew the encounter. Bowing gracefully to acknowledge the plaudits of the spectators he signaled the band to resume the music for the swording. Then, with a pardonable touch of bravado, he slowly began walking directly toward the bull. Through bloodshot eyes and with lowered head the brute watched him approach. When the matador was almost upon him the bull charged. Poised, and with sword balanced for the thrust, Gallardo waited, but at the last possible instant, not finding the opening he desired, was forced to deflect the bull's rush with his sweeping cape.

Twice more he parried the furious onslaughts. But at the fourth attack came the opportunity he sought. Swiftly the blade struck home, bent, and then penetrated to the vital spot. The bull staggered a pace or two, stumbled to his knees, and then sank to the ground.

"Thus," reported the *Ford County Globe,* "ended the first day's bull fight in Dodge City, and for all we know the first fight on American soil. The second day's fighting, with the exception of the killing of the last animal in the ring, was more interesting than the first .... The matadors showed to the people of America what bull fighting really was. No one could see it and go away saying that it was not a genuine bull fight. It was not that tortuous or inhuman punishment inflicted upon wild animals as the term 'bull fighting' would seem to imply, save and except the single animal that was killed. The punishment, tortures or cruelty was even less than that inflicted upon animals in the branding pen."

In the face of strictures by an unsympathetic press, both in Kansas and the East, the *Globe's* statement expresses the reaction of Dodge City's citizens to their first and only bull fight. What the more inarticulate cowboys thought of this Spanish entertainment can only be a matter of conjecture. That they enjoyed themselves may be surmised from a news item which appeared in the Larned *Optic* [July 11, 1884.] a few days after the fight:

"Quite a number of our boys visited Dodge last week to see the bull fight. Some of them returned looking as though they had had a personal encounter with the animals."

Source and Comment

The Kansas Historical Quarterly, II (1933), 294-308. Edited from an article by Kirke Mechem.

Bullfights were frequent in the American Southwest when it was under Spanish rule, and there are rumors of fights held in Texas and Louisiana later. Mechem discusses other attempts to introduce bullfighting and bullbaiting into this country in a long footnote. He lists Cripple Creek, Colorado, as the only other town where bulls were "actually sworded" while fighting, however.

* * *

Homemade Fireworks

Well after the turn of the century the village of Gilbertsville, New York, was still celebrating the Fourth of July in an unusual way.

During the night of July 3rd there was a pandemonium of drums, bells, and every variety of noise. Rising above the tumult was the indescribable sound of a "horse fiddle." This was made by stretching a rope tightly across the top of an open barrel. A plank, serving as a bow and drawn vigorously over the rope, produced a screech that could be heard for miles.

More unusual were the "fireballs." A day in advance a few older girls, instructed by a very old man, would gather to make them. Candlewicking was twisted into loose balls about the size of a small grapefruit. With a long needle and string they were stitched through and through to hold the wicking together. The finished balls were left to soak overnight in pails of turpentine.

On the evening of the Fourth, as soon as it was dark, the balls were taken out and lighted with matches. They were then thrown up and down the main street of the village. Arching overhead with a blaze of two or three feet, they made an impressive display. Competition to throw them was keen, and there was a scrimmage over each ball as it fell.

Strange to say, the flaming balls did not burn the hands. Turpentine burns at a moderate temperature. The motion of snatching the ball from the ground carried the flame away from the hand. In the split second of throwing the only damage was to singe the hair on the back of the hand.

Source

New York Folklore Quarterly, XV (1959), 112. Katharine G. Ecob remembers homemade fireworks and noisemakers before "prudence, law, or inertia finally ended these unique demonstrations."

* * *

July Fourth at the Front

The great and glorious Fourth [in 1918] has come and gone. The weather here was perfect. It was a gala day everywhere. It would have done your heart good to see the crowds of Englishmen, Frenchmen, Scotchmen, Irishmen, Australians, and Canadians mixing with our lads in a perfect realization of what July Fourth meant to America and what it means to the world today ....

And now, folks, let me tell you about the day's program in our own little camp. We had an afternoon of sports, track and field events and boxing contests that would be hard to beat anywhere. Two hundred English Tommies and their officers were with us. It was an afternoon of fun. The lads surely enjoyed the contests as it was a fight for supremacy between platoons. And they gave their guests some good, wholesome ideas of the strength, speed, and alertness of real Americans....

As I have often written to you, the English officers at this place have made it their duty to do for us everything in their power to make our camp better and more pleasant. We have appreciated their kindness and resolved to do something for them on the Fourth. So I asked them for the privilege of their officers' mess that evening that we might give them a regular dinner. We have not as yet the facilities in our camp for staging such affairs. But they agreed with pleasure and with the aid of their English cooks and their school adjutant we went to work and staged a dinner, which for its completeness, its good fellowship, and its patriotism was the peer of any I have ever attended, and I would wager it had no equal in France.

The circumstances made it such. There we were, nine Americans and ten British officers, dining together in an English school, celebrating the day that gave America liberty from Britain, celebrating the fact that America and Britain are now allies in a common cause and all of us on foreign soil! It was a cosmopolitan gathering. We ranged in rank from second lieutenant to major. The major commandant of the British school is a famous athlete from Cambridge University. One of his instructor captains is from Oxford University, where he played on the football, cricket, and track teams. Other English officers attended the University of London-West. Among the Americans the following universities were represented: Yale, Vanderbilt, Tennessee, Washington and Lee, Richmond College, Michigan, Georgetown, Marquette, and Wisconsin. Could you ask for a representation more varied among such a number of men?

The table was gorgeous in American and British flags, red, white, and blue flowers. I had the honor of being at the head of the table, with the major commandant on my right. At the other end of the table, acting as vice-master, was a Scotch captain. At the conclusion of the "oats" I said a very few words apropos the occasion and proposed a toast to His Majesty, the King of England. The major responded by lauding America's efforts, reading the official communique of the day, wherein it told of America's million soldiers in France, and of the launching that day of a hundred American ships. He praised President Wilson as the greatest statesman of the day and then asked a toast to "His Excellency, Woodrow Wilson, president of the United States." Toasts were then proposed to the English navy, which has performed one of the miracles of the war in keeping the English channel open, and in helping in the transport of America's army across the seas with the loss of less than three hundred lives. Then came words of praise for General Pershing, General Haig, and General Foch, and finally a toast to the English staff, who prepared the dinner. The bombardier, a quick-witted Irishman, McCarthy by name, said that while in his opinion the dinner with its fixings was the best they had ever staged at the school, yet it was the easiest to prepare, "because your toastmaster came to me with a fistful of money, told me that the sky was the limit, not to bother about expenses, and that if I needed more money to come to him." It was the truth. We spared no effort to make the affair one which the guests would never forget, one which the hosts would always cherish as one of the most glorious "Fourth" celebrations ever.

When we went into the anteroom we sang "America" and "God Save the King," gave about a dozen yells for each university represented and a lot that were not represented. Then the party broke up. My throat is still sore.

Source

Wisconsin Magazine of History, II (1918-19), 298-301. Letter of Lieutenant Harry Kessenich, in France, to his parents, dated July 7, 1918, and first published in the Madison, Wisconsin, *Democrat* of August 6, 1918.

* * *

July Fourth Block Party

For the last 12 years, the residents of the dead-end section of Dickinson Avenue in Swarthmore [PA] have held an annual block party in the turnaround at the end of the street. This year's event is scheduled for Sunday [July 3, 1988] at 4:30 in the afternoon.

If things run true to form, the weather will be hot and sticky, and the party will start slow. The big plastic garbage cans often show up first. They're followed by a grill of coals for the hot dogs and hamburgers, a cooler of ice and soda, another of ice and beer. Watermelons float in another tub of ice water.

Other equipment arrives—a few long tables to hold the food, a volleyball net in the meadow down by the creek.

Some kids wander down with a dog, who doesn't even bother to sniff the watermelons. "Hey," the kids say to each other. "Where is everybody?"

But by 5 or 5:15 or 5:30, just about everybody will have turned up with their lawn chairs, plates and utensils. The neighbors will hope to see Jim and Edna Hornaday, who remember when theirs was almost the only house on the block and the whole area was treeless fields. They'll hope to meet Rachel Merz and Brian Clark, who just bought the Jacobs' house. But of course some people won't be able to make the party and some will be out of town.

Each household pays 50 cents per person and brings a main dish, salad or dessert. Once in a while someone gets carried away and makes a seafood mousse, but mostly it's macaroni, cole slaw and good old three-bean salad. Plenty for seconds and thirds. There are always brownies among the desserts and sometimes homemade vanilla ice cream.

Lots of greetings—" Hi, how are you, seems like I haven't seen you since the last block party!" Lots of talk—Iraq, Noriega, babies, aging parents, and of course, the local schools.

In recent years the egg-catching contest has been replaced by a water-filled balloon catching contest. The eggs were too hard to clean up. Later on, the vigorous play some volleyball and the sloths have another beer. At dusk, there might be sparklers for the kids.

When it gets dark, the moon may appear, and a mosquito or two. The children are gone, and the talk gets quieter and more personal. One person is grieving for a friend who just died of AIDS. Another describes a teenage daughter's resourcefulness in thwarting a would-be rapist.

Eventually, the diehards collect their gear and straggle home. They leave behind an orphan lawn chair and the big plastic garbage cans.

They like knowing that the chairman for next year's party has already been chosen.

Source

Philadelphia Inquirer, July 1, 1988. By Margaret Robinson, an author and teacher at Widener University who lives on Dickinson Avenue, Swarthmore.

* * *

July Fourth Block Party
Block Party Again

On Sunday, July 2, at 4:30 p.m., the neighbors of the dead-end section of Dickinson Avenue will hold their 14th annual Independence Day block party in the turnaround area at the end of the street. In case of rain, the festivities will be moved up to July 4, same time and place.

The block party is an informal get-together to which all comers bring their own lawn chairs, plates, and utensils. Tables to hold the food are provided by those living closest to the end of the street. Laurel Otte is this year's party coordinator.

The bill of fare, as in other years, will be grilled hamburgers and hot dogs plus casseroles, salads, and desserts contributed by those attending. Kimberly Smith has promised to crank up some vanilla ice cream, a homemade favorite at previous block parties, and Carol Smith will make hot fudge sauce to go on it.

In past years the entertainment has included volleyball, playing catch with water balloons, sparklers, watching small children run in large circles, and conversation. This year should be pretty much the same.

Source

The Swarthmorean (Swarthmore, Pennsylvania), June 30, 1989. By Margaret A. Robinson, an update of a traditional July 4 neighborhood event.

Folksay

Before we moved to Vermont, we were told that there were two seasons—winter and the Fourth of July. Just the other day I repeated that to a native Vermonter. He corrected me and said, "Vermont weather consists of winter and then four months of hard sleighing."

Source

Vermont Historical Society, Proceeding, N.S., XXI (1953), 315. From Alice Windnagle of Bennington, Vermont.

* * *

As hot as a firecracker on the Fourth of July....

Source

Tennessee Folklore Society Bulletin, XVII (September, 1951), 58. Heard by Herbert Halpert from a western Tennessee student at Murray State College, Kentucky.

* * *

Farming and the Fourth
Corn

Corn had to be hoed by hand [on New York farms], and good corn weather was that when the sweat dropped off your nose at every hill as you hoed along. Those long hours of work under a summer sun led to the saying, "You never see too many hoes in a cornfield."

Knee high
By the Fourth of July

was the rule. In fact, "Corn that will not grow in three full moons will never feed you in the cold."

Source

New York Folklore Quarterly, VII (1951), 45. The corn lore was collected by Edith E. Cutting who provides a list of informants, "Yorkers," mostly her students and those of Louis C. Jones. She does not supply information about them.

* * *

Wheat

Wheat [in Maryland] that does not ripen before the Fourth of July will die.

Source

Memoirs of the American Folklore Society, XVIII (1925), 121. In "Folk-Lore from Maryland." Annie W. Whitney and Caroline C. Bullock collected the belief, but they do not name the informant.

* * *

Grapes

If there is thunder [in Tennessee] on the Fourth of July the grapes will drop off.

Source

Tennessee Folklore Society Bulletin, XXIV (June 1958), 67. Mary E. Miller collected farm folk beliefs in Dickson County, Tennessee, and lists the persons she interviewed.

* * *

Going to See the Elephant

I paid fifty cents
To see the elephant jump the fence.

He jumped so high
He touched the sky
And didn't come back till the Fourth of July.

Source

Journal of American Folklore, XLIV (1931), 434. From a collection of "Negro Songs" from the Peedee River region of South Carolina made by Robert Duncan Bass. See Roger Abrahams, *Jump Rope Rhymes: A Dictionary* (Austin, 1969), 72-73, for a bibliography to other texts.

Obon, Festival of the Dead
July 12-16

This festival may be compared with All-Hallows or All Souls' Day in the Roman Catholic calendar. In Japan it is commonly believed that the spirits of the dead return to the earth during *Obon* (cf. Halloween), and so preparations are made to receive and honor them. Family shrines are cleaned and special meals cooked for these spirits. Because lanterns are lighted in the cemeteries, and in some cases bonfires made at doorways to welcome ghostly visitants, the holiday is also called the Festival of Lanterns.

Obon festivals are often sponsored by Buddhist religious congregations. Although the dates of *Obon* are fixed, in many American cities public celebrations are held from July to early September. For instance, in Hawaii, with almost 100 Buddhist churches, there is an *Obon* festival almost every weekend during the summer.

Festival for the Spirits of the Dead

July 12th to 16th are the dates of the Festival of the Dead. Among the Japanese, the belief is held that the dead return once a year to visit their living relatives, and elaborate plans are made for the reception of these returning spirits. Fruit and other delectable foods, as well as gifts, are placed upon altars in all the temples and private shrines. From time to time tea is poured out for the refreshment of the unseen visitor, while many prayers are recited. When night sets in, innumerable lanterns are hung along the streets and in the cemeteries to guide the footsteps of the souls, and everyone takes part in the large group dances conducted in the streets, in which, it is supposed, the spirits of the dead participate. On the 16th of July, the final day of the celebration, a picturesque ceremony is held. A few of the various things offered at the altars are placed on a lotus leaf, and with a lighted candle in the center, this is sent sailing into a nearby body of water. As each little "boat" bursts into flames, the spirit contained in it is supposed to rise and be on its way back to its heavenly abode.

In connection with this festival a curious evolution has taken place. Originally a religious celebration, specifically Buddhist, it became secularized and developed into a popular national holiday and an occasion for much merriment and exchange of gifts.

In America, the Festival of the Dead, or *obon* as it is called by the Japanese, has remained a religious holiday, observed for the most part only by the Buddhists. It has almost come to correspond to Memorial Day in America, with the services being held in church and the organization of groups to clean up and freshly decorate the graves in the various cemeteries where Japanese are buried. Even in America, the custom of offering food and gifts at private family altars to deceased members of the family has been preserved. About three years ago [1931], the feature of the group dances was, for the first time in America, added to the celebration of the Festival of the Dead. All indications point to the increasing popularity of these bon-odoni or bon dances, which are today held along one or two city blocks, temporarily roped off and illuminated by Japanese lanterns. These dances are participated in by groups numbering anywhere from one hundred upwards, composed of men, women, boys, and girls, all dressed in simple yet colorful one-piece Japanese garments.

Source and Comment

Southwestern Journal of Anthropology, II (1946), 173-74. Based on the research of "Miss N.I." She investigated holidays observed by Japanese-Americans living in the San Francisco Bay area in 1934 under the direction of Paul Radin who edited this report. Informants were "older" persons and were interviewed in Japanese.

* * *

Obon in Rural New Jersey

"It's a joyful remembrance of the lifetimes of our mothers and fathers and all of our ancestors, their contributions to our existence today," said Ellen Nakamura in explaining why Japanese-Americans gathered at the Buddhist Church in Seabrook, N.J., this weekend to celebrate the *Obon* Festival, a traditional ceremony honoring the dead.

The *Obon* Memorial Service, a Buddhist ritual honoring the dead—said in English and Japanese—was conducted yesterday [July 11, 1982] morning to conclude the annual festival held in the farming community.

273

The night before, more than 100 dancers—from toddlers to the elderly, all dressed in colorful kimonos—participated in traditional folk dances at the *Obon* Festival, held each summer on the seven-acre grounds of the Seabrook Buddhist Church.

Mrs. Nakamura, a church member who served as a master of ceremonies for the Saturday night activities, said the *Obon* rituals are "a nurturing of our own joy in faith."

The dancers, who had been rehearsing the popular Japanese folk dances for several weeks, moved to the beat of the *Soh Daiko* drum unit of the New York Buddhist Church, whose members participated in the Seabrook festival.

The resident priest, the Rev. Shingetsu Akahoshi, led the dancers and audience in silent meditation of thanksgiving.

The evening's entertainment, which was open to the public, culminated with the Japanese circle dance, called "*Tanko Bushi*" the Coal Miner's Dance. Everyone joined in to depict, through hand movements, the miner's work—digging, heaving coal, wiping sweat from their brows.

Source

Philadelphia Inquirer, July 12, 1982. News item by staff writer Suzanne Gordon. Seabrook is a small rural town in southern New Jersey.

* * *

The Obon Legend

According to the legend of Moggallana and his mother, Moggallana with his super-human insight, was able to visualize his mother in the realm of the *Preta* (world of hungry devils), emaciated as the result of her being so selfish in her earthly life. It was not that the mother did not have the desire to be loving and kind, but that desire was concentrated all in the direction of her only son, at the expense of other people. At any rate, Moggallana, seeing his mother in this pitiful state, and with a great sense of pity and compassion for her, took some food to her. The moment mother touched the food, it turned into fire. The reason for it was that the mother had nothing but selfish thoughts within her to try to eat the food by herself with no thoughts of sharing it with the other hungry and emaciated devils, and also the feelings of compassion that Moggallana had was strictly limited to his mother. Feeling unbearable

sadness for his mother's plight, Moggallana went to the Buddha for guidance on how he could help to get his mother out of this pitiful situation.

The Buddha said, "The evil deeds that your mother committed are so grave that it is beyond your own power to extricate her from this state. Fortunately, however, tomorrow is the last day of *Vassa*. Gather all of the monks around you and give offerings to them. They shall appreciate it greatly and sincerely. By the merit of their appreciation, your mother may be relieved from the pains of "*Preta*." Moggallana followed the Buddha's instructions, and lo and behold, he found that his mother was reborn into Buddha's beautiful land living peacefully and happily. Seeing this, Moggallana danced with joy, and all the monks joined him in rejoicing this most happy event. This is said to be the origin of the *Obon* dance.

The above legend reminds us of the importance of *dana* (charity). It was because of Moggallana's unselfish and undiscriminating *dana* or giving to the disciples that his mother was released from the state of greed and the resulting hunger and thirst.

The term *bon* or *urabon* is a transliteration of the term *ullambana* which means "being hung upside down," symbolizing the pains of evil and suffering fundamentally caused by the delusions of inverted views. The deeds of pure *dana* perform a double purpose of helping others while simultaneously purging oneself of egoism.

The tradition of the *Obon* Festival had its origin, according to history, in China in 538 A.D. where services were conducted to alleviate the suffering of the dead. According to this tradition, the spirit of the ancestors returned home on July 13, welcomed by paper lanterns hung in the doorway to guide them home to spend a couple of days, and depending upon the efforts of the earthly relatives through chantings and offerings, on July 16 the spirits returned to the world from whence they came, or perhaps to a better world, once again guided by the send-off lights of the relatives. This festival is called the festival of the spirits.

Source

Betsuin Jiho, No. 213, June 17, 1978. From the newsletter of the Hongwanji Buddhist Church of Los Angeles, supplied by the Rev. H. Seki, New York Buddhist Church, 332 Riverside Drive, which sponsors an *Obon* festival.

Bastille Day
July 14

A patriotic holiday in France comparable with July 4 in the United States, it commemorates the seizure of the Bastille, a state fortress in Paris, in a popular uprising on July 14, 1789. The Bastille (the word simply means a building) had been used to house political prisoners such as Voltaire and the mysterious "Man in the Iron Mask," and, as a symbol of royal absolutism, was hated by the French revolutionists. Its demolition on the first anniversary of its capture was a revolutionary gesture, and the date was made a national holiday of the French Republic. In the United States, Bastille Day has been observed especially by the descendants of French Canadians in Louisiana and New England.

Cajun Bastille Day

This weekend [1989] the Bastille will be stormed once again, but this time it will be made of crayon and cardboard and glue and its bars will be the inner tubes of paper towel rolls covered with aluminum foil.

And its destruction will be the highlight of the year in this Cajun town [Kaplan, Louisiana] of 5,000 people about 75 miles southwest of Baton Rouge.

"The Bastille Day Festival is such a big part of what Kaplan stands for," said Janet Merritt, this year's festival chairman. "It's a very big deal."

As in many other towns in southern Louisiana, many of the people here are descendants of Acadians (Cajuns), French colonists who migrated from Canada to this area, which was settled by Germans. Those of French heritage still speak a unique dialect of French; their English is often accented with Brooklynese.

There is no party in Kaplan on the Fourth of July. Here they celebrate Bastille Day.

* * *

Kaplan was named for a Jewish merchant, Abram Kaplan, whose great-great-nephew, Connie Kaplan, runs the local newspaper, The Kaplan Herald. Abram Kaplan never lived here; the town was officially founded in 1902. He did arrange to route the Southern Pacific Railroad through this area, then a collection of rice farms owned by Cajun and German farmers. Railroad officials named the depot after him.

In 1888 a young Frenchman, Eugene Eleazar, migrated to Louisiana. He was saddened that the Cajuns did not observe his favorite holiday, July 14.

He tried to arouse interest, first in New Orleans, then in a country town, but the residents were not enthusiastic. He moved to Kaplan in 1906, to find that farmers would travel for miles to attend an observance. It became a town ritual. . . .

Preparations were under way this week at the Kaplan Recreation Center, down the block from Abshire's Welding and across the street from LeMaire's Slaughterhouse.

Members of the Key Club and the Keyettes were draping the stage in purple and blue crepe paper and building a runway for the Bastille Baby Contest.

The club members were under the eye of Luddie Herpin, who has helped organize the event since 1976. Considering, he said, that "13 years is a long time," this year he brought with him the Broussard twins, Jerry and Terry, and is training them to take over his role.

"There are about 100 members of the Jaycees," said Kathy Touchet, director of advertising for the festival. She said those members might be happy to attend, but not always happy to work. "Maybe 20 of the hundred are active members and maybe 10 show up to help," she said. "It's a heavy load for us committed ones."

The committed ones coordinate the egg toss and the watermelon-eating and the beer-drinking contests. They must get the automotive grease and spread it over the entire length of a telephone pole for the greasy pole-climbing contest. They must place a flag atop the pole (American, not French, and that is the subject of a heated debate) and make sure $60 is available for anyone who reaches the top.

And they must set up the table outside Cher's Cajun Gifts where volunteers who work for the post office will give letters a special Bastille Day postmark.

And the committed ones must book the bands for the outdoor dancing. This year Echouffe, or Cajun National Orchestra, will play Saturday night; Mrs. Merritt says she is lucky to get the band. "The president of the Jaycees, her brother is in the group," she said, "so that helped."

There will be no band for the 10-block parade. "All the bands, they're playing at other festivals," said Mrs. Touchet.

Outside the recreation center, the grass is newly mowed. Mrs. Merritt's husband brought over the family rider-mower. Mrs. Merritt feared that a thick growth would bring mosquitoes. The field, used for softball practice, is the temporary home of a Ferris wheel, bumper cars and a small merry-go-round.

Standing near a patch of mud she hopes will dry in time, Mrs. Merritt said she wanted to make it clear that her town was not unpatriotic.

She likes the Fourth of July, she said, but she sees no reason to celebrate it in Kaplan. "If we want fireworks," she said, "we just drive over to Erath," another tiny town about 20 miles away.

"We don't cut into their festival and they don't cut into ours," she said.

"This is what we have that makes Kaplan special."

Source

The dateline is Kaplan, Louisiana, September 13. By special correspondent Lisa Belkin, to the *New York Times,* July 14, 1989. Thus, publication took place on the two hundredth anniversary of the storming of the Bastille. Copyright © 1989 by The New York Times Company. Reprinted by permission.

* * *

Bastille Day Wine Glass Race

It was a race in the best tradition of the bon vivant: shattered champagne glasses, spilled wine and a winner who sauntered into the red-ribbon finish with the élan of a Maurice Chevalier.

J.P. Smith from Clarke Cooke House in Newport sailed around the orange cones in Kennedy Plaza [Providence, Rhode Island] yesterday, outmaneuvering 40 competitors from 20 area restaurants to win the eighth annual Bastille Day Waiters and Waitresses Race.

The contestants had each paid $15 to race the sloped walkway while balancing trays of wine-filled glasses with one hand.

The Omni Biltmore hotel sponsored the event and directed all proceeds to the Journal-Bulletin Summertime Fund.

Smith finished far ahead of the six other waiters who had won their qualifying heats, and was rewarded with an awed "wow" from the sidelines.

After dealing with a barrage of accolades, he flopped down in shady seclusion to "rest my feet."

Representatives of Pot au Feu on Custom House Street turned out handsomely for the fete in tricolored bow ties. The standard-bearer carried the red, white and blue French flag.

Unfortunately, on the day before the 200th anniversary of the storming of the Bastille, the "French" representatives were shackled. Neither competitor from Pot au Feu qualified for the final heat.

Were they disappointed? "A little bit," but why cry over spilled wine, said Pot au Feu's Kevin McGavock, 26, last year's first-place winner.

"I have to stop coming back and beating these 21-year-old kids," said a laughing Smith, who won in 1987. Smith is 33.

Smith left the competition with a large bottle of Moët & Chandon and a trip for two to Lake George, N.Y.

Paul Dubuc, a waiter from the Sheraton-Islander Inn in Newport finished second and won a trip to Boston.

Rene Saulnier, a waiter at Cafè in the Barn in Seekonk, Mass., won a dinner for two at Stanford's American Bar and Grille for his third-place finish.

Source

Providence Journal–Bulletin, July 14, 1989. By staff writer Sue-Sun Yom. Cf. "International Pancake Race," p. 98.

St. Swithin's Day

July 15

St. Swithin, Bishop of Winchester, died in 862. He is said to have requested burial not within but outside the church because of, according to one story, his humility or, according to another, his wish that "the sweet rain of heaven might fall on his grave." According to legend, when he was canonized centuries later, clerical authorities decided to move his remains to a site within the church. The date set was July 15. As the disinterment began, the saint showed his displeasure by sending down a torrential rain which lasted for forty days, thus making removal of his body impossible. Hence the English rhyme:

> St. Swithin's Day if thou dost rain,
> For forty days it will remain.
> St. Swithin's Day if thou be fair,
> For forty days 'twill rain na mair.

Rain on St. Swithin's Day

Wons rayert uff St. Swithin's Dawg no rayert's fer 40 dawg; wons net rayert, no doot's 40 dawg net rayera.

When it rains on St. Swithin's Day, it will rain for 40 days; when it doesn't, it won't rain for 40 days.

Source and Comment

Pennsylvania Folklife, XVII (Autumn, 1967), 29. From the collection of Victor C. Dieffenbach. See note on "Pennsylvania Dutch on St. Patrick's Day," p. 127, and cf. "Rain on St. Médard's Day," p. 233, "Customs and Beliefs for Ascension Day," p. 233, and "Whitsuntide Beliefs," p. 227.

Turtle Days
Mid-July

Snapping turtles commonly weigh ten or twelve pounds. Those in the mud-bottomed lakes near Churubusco, Indiana, a town of about 1,500 people in a prosperous farming region, are said to grow larger. Soon after he took the place, Gale Harris, a farmer with a reputation for integrity and seriousness of purpose, heard that an unusual turtle lived in the seven-acre lake on his farm. In the fall of 1948, while patching his roof with the help of his Nazarene minister, he sighted the turtle at a distance, and within a few days they and others saw it often and at close range. It was agreed that the turtle was as big as the top of a dining-room table—maybe four or five feet wide and six feet long, in short a monster. With notable persistence and help from his neighbors, Harris sought to capture the turtle, which he hoped to exhibit. He tried nets, grapples, homemade traps and pens, professional divers, and a female turtle as a decoy. Finally, he began to pump out the lake. The story was reported in the press, and high-spirited crowds came to watch the various efforts. Some of the attempts were almost successful, but the turtle, by now known as Oscar, always broke away. Efforts continued until January 1950 when the dam retaining the pumped-out water collapsed, and the lake filled up again. At that point, Harris gave up. That spring the town needed to raise funds for a community meeting hall, and almost spontaneously decided to have a local festival on the order of a county fair that would exploit the fame of Oscar, the so-called "Beast of 'Busco." Among its attractions would be a parade featuring a turtle float and booths selling turtle soup. Socially and financially successful, it set the pattern for the Turtle Days that have been held ever since.

Interview with a Turtle Hunter

Question: Were you there?

  Answer: There was eight of us the first day. The next day about sixty-five were out there.

Question: Did you see the turtle?

  Answer: I seen it. I went out in the boat and I can't swim. The turtle was out about ten feet from the shore. He was sunnin' himself. I wanted to put an oar along side of him to see how long he was. But Harris, he didn't want to; he thought I'd scare him away. Hell, we coulda lifted him outta there with hooks and pulleys, but he was afraid to. A ten-year-old kid could of got it. He always had it in his head we were gonna hurt that turtle.

Question: How big was the turtle?

  Answer: I'd say about three and a half, four feet across, but don't know how long, if I coulda got that oar in there, oh, maybe six feet, six and a half. It was an awful big turtle. Big as anyone ever seen. He's down there now probably dead covered with mud and tree limbs. That guy could have been a millionaire on that turtle if he played his cards right but he lost everything.

Source and Comment

"American Folklore and the Modern American Community Festival: A Case Study of Turtle Days in Churubusco, Indiana," Ph.D. Dissertation, Indiana University, 1977, 134-35. John Anthony Gutowski, author of the dissertation, interviewed Dick Zolman, a retired farm worker at Churubusco on June 15, 1971. Using interviews and newspaper files, Gutowski establishes the history of the turtle hunt, the folklore that emerged from it, and its germinal place in the evolution of a community folk festival which, he argues cogently, grew out of traditional lore and life as influenced by the mass media. This combination, he believes, is typical of the modern American folk festival.

*   *   *

Turtle Hunter

The Turtle Ballad

Churubusco's on the map now
  With a monster in Fulk Lake
And if he stays too lively
  All the traps and nets will break.
The business men of our town
  Spent much time for their sake,
To get that enormous turtle
  Out and above the lake.
He got into their trap one day;
  They pulled him to the shore.
All at once he jerked and splashed

And then was seen no more.
Some worked from morn to night for days
  To prove their story true
For they had seen him in the trap
  That broke and had gone through.
The papers spread the news around,
  And cars there came in number.
Telephones began to ring
  But Oscar slept in slumber.
Our hopes are high and will power strong
  To see him out some day,
So that is all that it will take
  To make things come our way.

Source and Comment

"American Folklore and the Modern American Community Festival: A Case Study of Turtle Days in Churubusco, Indiana," Ph.D. Dissertation, Indiana University, 1977, 116. Gutowski quotes the ballad, which was printed in the local newspaper, *Churubusco Truth,* of April 21, 1949. The author was Hannah H. Hyndman. It should be compared with American newspaper verse, which like the traditional broadside ballad popular in England and America in the seventeenth and eighteenth centuries often recounted events of local interest and provided the basis for many ballads that went into oral tradition.

* * *

Turtle Hunter

Tall Tales about the Turtle

Frank Flowers Jr. declares that when the turtle was frozen in the ice this winter, it tried to walk to the bank and in doing so moved the whole lake twenty feet.

Ralph Shanabarger says the turtle, when he swims in the lake, pushes so much water ahead of him that he kicks up dust from the bottom with his hind legs.

Others say that Jake Jones, who formerly owned the farm, now knows what happened to the black Angus cattle that used to turn up missing and why a fence erected between the cattle and the lake stopped the loss.

Charlie Horner, the butcher, says that when a mule was used in an attempt to pull the "Fulk Lake monster" from the water, the turtle pulled the mule into the lake—ate him—and came out of the water picking his teeth with a singletree.

When two ministers from Kalamazoo stopped at the Harris farm for a turtle chat, Gale Harris told them he was surprised that they, as preachers, would be interested in the turtle, since so many lies had circulated about old Oscar. The ministers replied that they figured Churubusco, because of the number of liars, would be a pretty good spot in which to set up business.

Source and Comment

"American Folklore and the Modern American Festival: A Case Study of Turtle Days in Churubusco, Indiana," Ph.D. Dissertation, Indiana University, 1977, 113-14. These windies (typical American tall tales) were first published in special "Turtle Editions" of the *Churubusco Truth* dated March 10, 1949; March 17, 1949; and March 24, 1949. See Thompson Types X 1890-1909 and Baughman, X 1322* ff.

* * *

Turtle Hunter

The Beast of 'Busco

The Beast of 'Busco is supposedly in a lake in Churubusco, Ind. This town is 20 miles NE of Fort Wayne, Ind. This animal is a turtle 19 feet in diameter. The story goes that a small boy was out playing on the lake and the turtle came up on the shore. When people came looking for the boy all that could be found were his shoes and a few pieces of clothing. There were turtle footprints about 6 to 8 inches. Residents nearby say they hear weird noises when the moon is out. No one has ever seen this animal. Some claim they have seen him or something that resembles him.

Source and Comment

"American Folklore and the Modern American Community Festival: A Case Study of Turtle Days in Churubusco, Indiana," Ph.D. Dissertation, Indiana University, 1977, 151. Quoted from the Legend Collection, Indiana University Folklore Archive No. 910. Reported from Indianapolis in 1961. This is an example of a legend in the process of development. It is no longer simply a locally told story, but, probably due to the mass media, told at a distance from its place of origin.

* * *

Turtle Hunter

Churubusco Turtle Story

There was once a couple of turtle hunters in a boat snaring turtles in a north central Indiana lake. It seems as though they spotted an extremely large turtle, snared it, and as the turtle was swimming into the depths one of the hunters got his leg caught in the snare rope and was dragged overboard into the depths also. Today, over thirty years later, it is frequently reported that a large turtle was seen swimming along the bottom of this lake dragging a snare rope and human skeleton along behind.

Source and Comment

"American Folklore and the Modern American Community Festival: A Case Study of Turtle Days in Churubusco, Indiana," Ph.D. Dissertation, Indiana University, 1977, 151. Quoted from the Legend Collection, Indiana University Folklore Archive No. 759. Reported from Kokomo, Indiana. Gutowski states that it was "widely believed in the 1930s and '40s in Indiana."

The Feast of Our Lady of Mount Carmel and St. Paulinus
Two successive Sundays in July

Primarily a celebration by descendants of Italians from the vicinity of Naples that has been observed in the Greenpoint section of Brooklyn, New York, for more than a century, and elsewhere, it in fact combines the feast days of Our Lady of Mount Carmel on July 16 and St. Paulinus of Nola, a town near Naples, whose day is June 22 and who is the primary patron. St. Paulinus is said to have been an architect who built aqueducts and churches. When Vandals raided Nola and carried off a number of the townspeople into slavery, he offered himself as a substitute for the only son of a widow. Somehow he miraculously managed to obtain the freedom of all of his fellow citizens. St. Paulinus was canonized in 431. The festival includes a mass, street fair, and reunions but its main feature is a procession that ends at the Church of Our Lady of Carmel in which bearers carry a "giglio," a tower some six stories high weighing two tons, which is surmounted by a statue of the patron saint. Because June 22 is the summer solstice and because of the shape of the "giglio," there is speculation that a pagan fertility rite lies behind the holiday.

The Giglio

A Traditional Celebration in Brooklyn

At the feast of Our Lady of Mount Carmel and St. Paulinus yesterday in the Williamsburg section of Brooklyn, feast workers, above and below, carried the giglio, a tower honoring St. Paulinus's exchange of himself for a widow's son captured in a raid in the fifth century.

Source

Caption accompanying two photographs in the *New York Times,* July 9, 1989. A *giglio* is Italian for "lily."

* * *

Carrying the Giglio

Each year, in Greenpoint, there are a hundred and twenty-eight lifters under the command of three capos [heads, chiefs]. There is the capo paranza [head of the company], the head capo. Under him are Capos No. 2 and No. 3. There is often an honorary capo from a previous year, and a godfather of the giglio [tower]: they do nothing more laborious than represent the past. There is also a singer, who, along with a ten-man brass-and-drum band, sits in front of the giglio on a giant platform and serenades the capos and their lifters. Each successive capo paranza has his trademark tune, his style of conducting the lift, and his favorite kind of lift. The repertoire is limited by the bulk of the object being carried. Mostly, the lifts are a matter of heaving the giglio aloft, then walking it forward and dropping it without anyone's getting hurt. The giglio rarely moves more than thirty yards in a given lift. Some capos

ask the paranza [group, company] to bounce the giglio. Some like to see the giglio rotated through three hundred and sixty degrees. The lifters never know what a capo plans until he raises his cane of office in the air. The capo paranza deploys the cane much as a conductor does his baton. Certain capos carry the cane solemnly, projecting heartbreaking dolor. Certain capos pump the cane like a Giants cheerleader at the halftime break. Certain capos grunt and shout at the cane as if it were something alive. And certain capos invent a technique as they go along, drawing on the whim of the moment, the temperament of the music, the emotion they absorb from the paranza and the crowd.

Source and Comment

New Yorker, June 4, 1990, 81-82. From an article on the festival titled "Our Local Correspondents" by Guy Trebay. The group of lifters, or "paranza" in Italian, are an organized society with an elected membership. They wear uniforms—shorts perhaps, tee shirts decorated with the club emblem, and seamen's caps, when they are carrying the giglio. Because of its height and weight, the paranza seldom carries the giglio more than thirty yards at a time. The lifters must work together or there is danger of injury, and they do this as much through intuition as from the signals of the capo. In fact, carrying the giglio is an expression of ethnic and neighborhood solidarity, and though the feast has secular qualities, the performance of the paranza has a touch of the penitential and transcendent.

* * *

The Grand Marshall

More than 100 men, huffing and grunting, hoisted 5,000 pounds of shrine onto their shoulders yesterday and marched through a sweltering Bronx street to commemorate a feast that dates to fifth-century Italy. At the base of the 63-foot shrine, beneath figurines representing Saints Anthony and Joseph, the Blessed Mother, Christ and six cherubs, stood a tearful real-life figure: the grand marshal, Mario Biaggi.

It was three days after he was convicted of racketeering and extortion in the Wedtech trial, and two days after he resigned his seat in Congress, and Mr. Biaggi said he has been waking in the night, looking at a jail term and asking himself: "What am I doing here? How did all this happen?"

Despite his criminal conviction, the organizers of the Feast of the Giglio and others in the crowd, largely emblematic of his core constituency, said they were there to support the 70-year-old former Congressman....

"The man is like Adam Clayton Powell," said Dominick Rocco, a court clerk and shrine-bearer from Queens. "The authorities came after him, but his people are still behind him."

Source

New York Times, August 8, 1988. Edited from an article by Sam Howe Verhovek. Copyright © 1988 by The New York Times Company. Reprinted by permission.

Mormon Pioneer Day

July 24

In 1844, after the murder of their founder, Joseph Smith, the Mormons, under the leadership of Brigham Young, moved from their settlement at Nauvoo, Illinois, to the valley of the Great Salt Lake, where they established Salt Lake City. According to Mormon tradition, the site was chosen by Young on July 24, 1847. He is supposed to have risen from his sick bed as the party emerged from Immigrant Canyon and proclaimed, "This is the place." Within a year, more than 4,000 Mormon pioneers had made the difficult journey, following the Oregon Trail to Fort Bridger and then south into what was then Mexican territory. Some of them, without other means of transportation, were organized into "handcart companies" and walked, pushing their carts before them.

Pioneer Day Celebration

For festive purposes the day that came to be the annual Mormon celebration par excellence was July 24, the official day of entry into the Salt Lake Valley in 1847. Long enough after July 4, Pioneer Day was still in the summer and seemed to be a time after sowing and before harvest when a day of celebration could be afforded. The day was not celebrated in 1848 due to the harsh conditions, but in 1849 an elaborate celebration was held. Included in the procession, for example, were:

> Twelve bishops, bearing banners of their wards.

> Twenty-four young ladies, dressed in white, with white scarfs on their right shoulders, and a wreath of white roses on their heads, each carrying the Bible and Book of Mormon; and one bearing a banner, "Hail to our Chieftain."

> Twelve more bishops, carrying flags of their wards.

> Twenty-four silver greys [older men], each having a staff, painted red on the upper part, and a branch of white ribbons fastened at the top, one of them carrying the flag.

After parading to the tune of band music, the people settled down to a round of addresses, poems, toasts, and more speeches. It was quite an extravaganza for a young, precariously established frontier community.

Besides the annual celebration, longer intervals seem to have lent themselves to commemorative purposes. On July 24, 1874, for example, a jubilee was held celebrating the twenty-seventh anniversary of the arrival of the Saints in the valley. The Sunday School prepared a program held in the Tabernacle, featuring bands, a special hymn entitled "O Lord Accept Our Jubilee," prayers, and sermons.

Participating in the "grand Sunday School jubilee" were some eight or ten thousand children.

Celebrations were also held in the individual settlements throughout Mormon country. In 1874, for example, there was a celebration in Bloomington, Idaho:

> At sunrise this morning silence was broken by a volley of twenty-four guns.

> The people assembled at the schoolhouse at nine o'clock A.M., formed a procession and marched to martial music through the principal streets then back to the schoolhouse in the following manner—twelve fathers of Israel, twelve mothers of Israel, twelve daughters of Zion dressed in white, and twelve sons of Zion, the citizens and Sunday School children following in line.

> The services consisted of an oration by James H. Hart, George Osmond read an address in behalf of the daughters of Zion, John Walker spoke in behalf of the fathers of Israel, Christian Madsen in behalf of the sons of Zion, Sister Jarvis in behalf of the mothers of Israel. A number of toasts were given.

> At two o'clock all were seated at table, spread with viands, including strawberries, sugar, and cream.

> At four o'clock the dance opened for the small children, and in the evening for larger children and parents.

> All was joy, peace, and unity. The whole was gotten up under the auspices of the Relief Society.

Even more than the usual annual celebration or that of the twenty-fifth anniversary, the fiftieth anniversary was emphasized. There was then a sense of historical distance. While a few of the original members and leaders remained, a new generation had come to the fore. Besides, the celebration of fifty years had Old Testament precedent as a time of jubilee. Such an opportunity presented itself in 1880, fifty years from the organization of the church. Coinciding with General Conference, this date was mentioned by many of the speakers, including especially church historian Franklin D. Richards, who reviewed the history of the church during the preceding decades. He mentioned Stephen A. Douglas, Sen. Thomas Hart Benton and the Mormon Battalion [recruited to serve in the Mexican War], the coming of [Colonel Albert Sidney] Johnston's Army [which enforced federal control, 1857-58], and the fate of government officials. "In all these things we recognized the hand of the Lord," he said, "and we should reflect on His providences and be stirred up to individual righteousness, and to battle against the drunkenness and whoredoms and various forms of evil now being introduced by our enemies for our overthrow." Other sermons followed the same theme, as did the great prayer of Apostle Orson Pratt.

In July 1880 the jubilee was continued in a mammoth celebration. In the parade or procession were the following:

> The surviving Pioneers of 1847 in five wagons. Portrait of Brigham Young on both sides of the first wagon with the inscriptions "Gone Before Us" and "Absent But Not Forgotten." Above them was the "old pioneer banner," on which were the names of all the pioneers and a picture of Joseph Smith blowing a trumpet. Also the U.S. flag.
>
> Surviving members of Zion's Camp.

> Surviving members of the Mormon Battalion and wagon with "Women of the Mormon Battalion."
>
> The "minute Men."
>
> Wagon with representatives of the various countries of the earth. On the side were various mottoes.
>
> 24 couples. "The ladies looked lovely in cream-colored riding habits, with white silk caps and white feathers, and the young men presented a fine appearance in black dress suits, white neckties, and white gloves."
>
> Education was represented by a car containing five ladies, personifying Religion, History, Geography, Science, and Art.

The parade continued with representation of different church auxiliaries, school children, and industry of Utah. The whole procession extended over three miles. During part of this 1880 celebration Wilford Woodruff told of Brigham Young's "this-is-the-place" statement that has since become a standard feature of pioneer celebrations.

Source and Comment

Utah Historical Quarterly, XLIII (1975), 70-72. David Bitton describes the celebrations commemorating episodes in Mormon history as "ritualization" of the past, quoting Emile Durkheim on a society's use of such rituals for "upholding and reaffirming at regular intervals collective sentiments and collective ideas which makes its unity and personality." Bitton's main source for the descriptions of Pioneer Day in 1849, 1874 and 1880 is the *Deseret News,* the Salt Lake City newspaper.

Cheyenne Frontier Days
July—last full week

The first rodeos were held by the forerunners of the American cowboy, the Mexican *vaqueros*. They developed out of the normal tasks of the cattle ranch: roping, lassoing, bulldogging, and bronco riding. Contests between individual cowboys, outfits that ran into each other, and rival ranches served as entertainment and offered ample opportunities for betting and bragging. Known in the American Southwest shortly after the Civil War and flourishing in Texas by the 1880s, they were nationally popularized by touring, circus-like extravaganzas such as Buffalo Bill Cody's "Wild West Show" and formalized in celebrations such as Cheyenne Frontier Days, the Pendleton (Oregon) Round-up, and the Calgary Stampede. Before long they developed large followings and commercial possibilities. Today, aided by the long tradition of the cowboy novel, movie, and television show, the rodeo has a full "circuit" of events, corporate sponsorship, and professional performers who may earn large incomes.

Cheyenne Frontier Days, which originated in 1897, before the novels and the movies, is an elaborated folk event. It has, however, developed a tradition of its own.

First Frontier Days Celebration

The idea of the Frontier Days Celebration originated in the brain of Col. E. A. Slack, owner and editor of the *Cheyenne Sun-Leader*, now the *Wyoming Tribune*.

The towns in northern Colorado were celebrating every fall with a fair, calling attention to their particular farm products, such as "Potato Day" in one town, "Pickle Day," "Pumpkin Pie Day," etc., etc. On the occasion of a visit to Greeley with my mother and Col. Slack and his wife, we were discussing the idea of some kind of a fall festival in Cheyenne [Wyoming]. Cheyenne and vicinity did not produce much in an agricultural way at that time, so Col. Slack suggested an old time display of riding bucking horses, roping cattle, branding cattle, stage holdups, and anything else that suggested the early days. "We will call it Frontier Days," said the Colonel. The next day he had a long article in the *Cheyenne Sun-Leader*, developing the idea and calling for a public meeting at the City Hall, which meeting was held and attended by the Mayor, W. R. Schnitger, the city councilmen and citizens. At that meeting the Mayor appointed the following committee to plan the first Celebration of Frontier Days....

These committees worked diligently, and in twenty days developed a programme for the first show, which was held on September 23, 1897. We advertised the show all over the United States, and had people from the East, West, North and South. Special trains with sleeping cars were used to take care of visitors who could not get accommodations.

The Union Pacific sent a special man, Mr. F. W. Angiers, General Traveling Passenger Agent, to assist us in every way, and Mr. Angiers was a very enthusiastic booster at many of the early shows. The attendance at this first show was estimated at 15,000. No admission to the grounds was charged, the bleacher seats were fifteen cents and grandstand seats were thirty-five cents. The entire space around the half-mile race track was packed five to ten deep with people.

In 1897, there were many wild horses in the vicinity of Cheyenne. Twenty or thirty miles east and northeast was open country, with very few fences. Stallions, closely herding their bunches of mares, sometimes met at watering places, and fights frequently resulted which were really vicious biting affairs, the stallions rearing up on their hind legs and striking with their front feet like tigers. The horses used at these first shows had never been roped, or even herded, and the cowboys who brought a bunch of about fifty to the corral at the park had a real job.

Of course, everything about the first show was unique, but I think the wild horse race and the bucking contest were the most outstanding features.

The horses were roped in the corral and snaked to the track in front of the grandstand—the judges' stand being opposite. When ten had been so snaked in for the wild horse race, the bridling and saddling began. This first wild horse race has never been excelled. Pictures were taken that are still being sold today; and no pictures of any rodeo performance have had as large a sale as the postal card showing this first event of that kind, with the caption "Wild Horse Race at Cheyenne Frontier Days Celebration."

The bucking contest, where the horses were all bridled and saddled on the track, each man having a helper, was an event to be remembered for a life time by all who witnessed it.

The stage coach holdup was one of the thrilling events. One event was the hanging, by vigilantes, of a horse thief. Bill Root of Laramie, a humorist and newspaper associate of Bill Nye, and a close friend of mine, was in the grandstand, and I persuaded him to let himself be taken out of the grandstand by masked vigilantes to be apparently hanged on a cross arm erected for that purpose. Bill was game up to the point where the hangman's noose was dangling over his head, when he said: "This is carrying a joke too far, boys;" so they substituted a dummy, which was conveniently near, and hanged it instead of Bill.

One alarming incident happened during the afternoon of this first show. The wild horses had been milling around, having become nervous and excited when some of them had been roped by the cowboys, and finally they broke out of the corral and all stampeded up the race track. When opposite the middle of the bleachers, they suddenly turned and drove straight through them. People yelled and screamed and scrambled madly about, trying to get out of the way. The bleachers, six tiers high, and made of 2 x 12 planks, were knocked down and an opening made for the horses to get through. I wonder to this day how every one escaped. They did, and no one was seriously hurt.

As a result of our advertising our programme in the Denver papers, some neurotic members of the Colorado Humane Society thought the show was going to be too rough—and even cruel. Denver has always been a little jealous of Cheyenne—and more so fifty years ago than now. They sent a fellow up to Cheyenne to see just how rough the show was. The first steer that was thrown resulted in his getting a small group together and giving a free lecture to the effect that the performance should not be permitted to go on. After he had kept this up for a short time, two cowboys gently slipped a rope over him and took him to the buffalo corral, where they tied him up with the buffalo for the afternoon, releasing him just in time to take the excursion train back to Denver....

The bulls which were driven at the show were oldtimers taken out of a good bull train, and they were certainly wise to "gee", "whoa", "haw", "buck", and could be driven to within an inch of any opening.

In one of the early shows, the committee ran into a bitter cold spell in September and the result was $6,000.00 in the red.

At the following show, which was advertised as "bigger and better," etc., the stands were all filled and a large crowd was waiting for the show to start when suddenly the heavens opened and the rain came down in torrents. The storm lasted an hour, and water was running six inches deep down the race track in front of the grandstand. Some of the boys thought it was too dangerous to ride in the mud, and that the show should be postponed until the next day. This, of course, was impossible, as an attempt to refund money to a crowd, many of whom were in free, would have resulted in complete failure. There was a girl, Miss Bertha Kaepernick, who had entered the bucking contest, also the wild horse race; and my brother Clarence, who was in charge of the programme, conceived the brilliant idea of getting this girl to ride a wild horse in front of the grandstand. This she did—one of the worst buckers I have ever seen—and she stayed on him all the time. Part of the time he was up in the air on his hind feet; once he fell backward, and the girl deftly slid to one side only to mount him again as he got up. She rode him in the mud to a finish, and the crowd went wild with enthusiasm. Result— the cowboys thought if a girl can ride in the mud, we can too, and the show was pulled off. The real active idea of Woman Suffrage was thus demonstrated in Wyoming at a Frontier Days show—the idea that has gone around the world. Hurrah for the Wyoming gals! They lead in everything!....

These early shows lasted six or seven hours, starting at one o'clock in the afternoon; but the enthusiasm of the crowds waned not a whit. They lustily cheered every single event and stayed until the very end. Dr. Jeremiah Mieger of Toledo, Ohio, after seeing the first Frontier Days Celebration said: "I am a surgeon in a State Insane Asylum, and I am used to excitement, but Cheyenne takes the cake." George Eastman, of Kodak fame, enthusiastically remarked: "If we only had a moving picture of that show!"

Source

Annals of Wyoming, XIX (January 1947), 39-44. Edited from an article by Warren Richardson, "History of First Frontier Days Celebrations." Richardson was chairman of the first Frontier Days Committee in 1897. Cf. "July Fourth and the Rodeo," p. 264.

* * *

Frontier Days Breakfast

Over 30,000 people were treated to a free breakfast of pancakes, ham and coffee or milk at the three free Cheyenne Frontier Days breakfasts last year [1987].

That, folks, is a bunch of flapjacks! More than 100,000 to be nearly exact. Mixed in a cement truck (you heard it right), the pancakes are the focus of a breakfast which also includes ham, syrup, butter, coffee and/or milk—and no one waits in line more than 20 minutes.

Good food and good fun are served up with blue denim hospitality on Monday, Wednesday and Friday from 7 to 9 a.m. at the City Center Parking Mall in downtown Cheyenne.

In true Cheyenne Frontier Days fashion, the free pancake breakfasts are a cooperative venture. The Frontier Committee provides the food with the help of donors and sponsors and the City of Cheyenne provides the facility and cleanup.

Food is prepared in traditional open-range style by the 390-member Cheyenne Kiwanis Club, who put in an estimated 2,300 man-hours getting breakfast prepared and served.

Planning to serve 30,000 for breakfast? A "typical" recipe calls for 3,600 pounds of pancake mix, 1,130 pounds of butter, 300 gallons of syrup, 2,800 pounds of ham, 9,000 pints of milk, 520 gallons of coffee, 125 pounds of sugar and 12 gallons of cooking oil.

People from all 50 states and more than 20 foreign countries enjoyed breakfast Frontier Days style last year.

Take a deep seat on a hay bale, enjoy your flapjacks and be entertained by various bands, the Southern Plains Indians, local talent and the Frontier Days royalty.

The Frontier Days pancake breakfast. It's fun ... it's tasty ... it's Western ... it's free!!!

Source

Program for the 1988 Cheyenne Frontier Days, advertisement for Old Timer Meat Products, n.p.

* * *

Cowgirls and Frontier Days

The world of the rodeo is generally believed to be ... the rough, tough, rigorous competition of the western cowboy, a masculine domain of thrills, excitement and danger. Developed out of day-to-day ranch tasks, informal contests for entertainment at the close of the work day or for the social gatherings hosted by the ranch owners, these contests eventually became the major entertainment at county fairs. From these simple beginnings, the rodeo developed into highly organized and vigorous competition among men, "but, as in every other activity in the West, females quickly invaded their ranks as participants."...

The early pioneer ranch women of necessity became accomplished equestrians. Horses provided their primary mode of transportation, and the far reaches of the sprawling ranches or the nearest neighbors were most easily accessible by horseback. Prior to the twentieth century, almost every woman rode "sidesaddle like a lady," but skilled horsemanship even in the "modest sidesaddle positions which twisted their spines askew" was a desirable asset to ranch life. By the late 1800s, however, some women were beginning to adopt the more practical attitude about riding of ranchwoman Agnes Morley [who wrote, in *No Life for a Lady*:]

> My own great concession to a new age was to abandon the sidesaddle ... I recall the steps that led to emancipation. First, I discarded, or rather refused to adopt, the sunbonnet, conventional head gear of my female neighbors. When I went unashamedly about under a five-gallon (not ten-gallon) Stetson, many an eyebrow was raised; then followed a double-breasted blue flannel shirt In time came blue denim knickers worn *under* a short blue denim skirt. Slow evolution (or was it decadence) toward a costume suited for immediate needs. Decadence having set in, the descent from existing standards of female modesty to purely human comfort and convenience was swift. A man's saddle and a divided skirt (awful monstrosity that was) were inevitable.

Many ranchwomen followed the example of Agnes Morley, and for some of them the transition from sidesaddle to rodeo was but a single step.

Long before the end of the nineteenth century women were giving public exhibitions of their equestrian skills. During the 1850s "one Mary Ann Whitaker made a career of her skill ... under the title of 'First Female Equestrian Artist in America.'" Other women joined the ranks of the circus to display their skilled horsemanship. With the introduction of rodeo to the West, however, a new arena opened up for the skilled horsewoman. When the citizens of Cheyenne, Wyoming, set aside a festival day in 1897 to commemorate early life on the Western frontier, it is doubtful that the planning committee considered the possibility of female entrants in the male world of cowpony races, roping contests, or pitching and bucking events. They failed to reckon with the interest and persistence of the Wyoming horsewoman, and within a short time, she, too, was a participant in Cheyenne's Frontier Days, the oldest continuous rodeo in existence.

The first scheduled event for women appeared in 1899 when "The Committee decided to have a half-mile ladies' race and will give as a prize a $45.00 saddle." The official program of events listed the race as the Ladies' Cow Pony Race, one-half-mile, prize, a ladies' sidesaddle to the winner. The sidesaddle prize was perhaps indicative of the masculine view of the female contestants; the sidesaddle was still more appropriate for women even though they were racing astride in a regular Western saddle. Although news reports described the race as unsatisfactory in regard to the starting, it was considered an interesting event and apparently paved the way for the continued inclusion of women's events in future years.

During the next four years of Frontier Days the Ladies' Cow Pony Race was the only competition open to women participants. No entry fee was required, but regulations were as strictly enforced as those for men contestants. No thoroughbred horses were allowed; only Wyoming cowponies could be ridden; and cowgirls' saddles, the conventional Western saddle for riding astride, were required. Beginning in 1900, prize money rather than a saddle was awarded to the first, second, and third place winners in the race. The amounts of $25, $15, and $10 were less than those for comparable men's races; however, a small "purse" in no way dampened the enthusiasm of the women riders nor that of their cheering supporters in the stands. [*Cheyenne Leader* of August 21, 1901 described the action:]

> The Ladies' Cow Pony Race was one of the most enjoyable features of the program and was as exciting as the most exacting could desire. Nowhere else in the world do women display the fearless horsemanship to be found on the prairies of Wyoming, and as the ladies came under the wire at break neck speed they were wildly cheered. There were eleven entries and the race was hotly contested owing to the great rivalry as to who is the best girl rider in the state. Those who have never seen Wyoming girls ride were amazed at the remarkable exhibition they witnessed. As the ladies started around the track the grandstand and bleachers went wild with excitement, and the interest taken in the race was greater than any of the running events of the afternoon.

In 1902 the Ladies' Cow Pony Races were scheduled on each of three days of the celebration. Prize money had increased to $75 a race ($40, $20, and $15) and the title "champion of the world" was bestowed on the winner of a final heat in which winners of two previous contests had qualified. The ladies had established themselves as bona fide rodeo participants in at least one event and the cowpony race was popular with both participants and spectators throughout the years in which women competed in Cheyenne's Frontier Days.

One of the most unlikely rodeo events in which women might have been expected to participate at the turn of the century was bronco riding. But as early as 1902 "several lady riders ... expressed a desire to enter the bucking and pitching contests during frontier days ... "

Since no rough riding events were scheduled for women, one enterprising young woman, Bertha Kaepernick, entered the men's events in 1904. She was headlined in the [*Wyoming Tribune* of September 1, 1904] as

> the only (woman) rider to ever enter the championship bucking and pitching contest ... (she) drew a vicious mount and within a few seconds the girl was compelled to pull leather disqualifying her from the contest. After the

animal had apparently been subdued, the crazy brute again seemed possessed of an evil spirit and began bucking in so wild and erratic a manner that Miss Kaepernick was thrown completely over the animal's head.

Even though disqualified from a chance to win the contest, the fearless Miss Kaepernick climbed back on the horse and rode him to submission amid the roaring cheers of the crowd. Though few women had either the interest or the inclination to risk life and limb astride a bucking bronco, the excitement generated by those who did led to the inclusion of the event as an annual exhibition. No prize money was awarded, but each year the ladies' bronco riding drew enthusiastic applause from the spectators. As numbers of entrants increased in the exhibitions, the Frontier Days Committee became convinced that a World Champion Ladies Bronco Riding contest would be a success, and in 1914 the event was initiated as a regular part of the scheduled program. Rules governing the event were the same as those for men. Riders had to stay on their mount for eight seconds; spur the horse at the start of the contest; and could not grab the saddle or horn to assist in staying on the horse. Women, however, had the option of riding with or without hobbled stirrups—stirrups hooked together by a cinch under the horse to avoid the wild flapping that occurred when the horse bucked. Ladies' bronco riding was extremely popular in Cheyenne for several years, but interest waned in the 1920s. The number of contestants was too small to provide a fair or interesting competition, and the judges found it increasingly difficult to determine a winner fairly. She was often either the person riding the most spectacular horse, or one who could tolerate the most punishment in the time allotted. Thus in 1928 bronco riding for women was discontinued at Cheyenne's Frontier Days.

Other events for women which began only as exhibitions in Cheyenne's Frontier Days were steer roping and trick and fancy riding; but these, too, became regularly scheduled contests as horsewomen became more daring and proficient. Steer roping was conducted under essentially the same rules as those for men. While riding at full speed the contestant had to rope the running steer, dismount and tie three of his flailing legs, as her horse held the rope taut. The winner was the person completing the tie in the shortest time. As numbers of entrants increased and times improved, the steer ropers were required to perform on three consecutive days with first place awarded to the "best average time for the three steers." Results were sometimes disappointing, however, when the ladies had difficulty in performing the various skills required in the event. On one occasion three of the four contestants were unsuccessful in catching their steers and the fourth caught hers, but could not "bust" him (throw him to the ground) and complete the tie. Even with such set-backs, steer roping continued to be one of the prize money events for women for a number of years.

In trick and fancy riding "the girls ride upside down, jumping on and off, at the horse's side, under it, and go through all manner of exciting stunts while the horse is on a tearing run." The event was essentially one of the showmanship and many women became adept at a large repertoire of tricks that displayed their riding abilities and their courage to greatest advantage. One championship rider of the 1920s, Lorena Trickey, was noted as "the only girl who can go entirely around under her horse's neck and back up to the saddle on the other side while the horse is on the run."

Perhaps the most spectacular of all the women's events in Frontier Days was the Ladies' Relay Race. Initiated in 1906 the relay drew a large number of contestants during most of its forty years' existence. The prize money was the largest purse of any of the women's events, and the winner also was awarded a large silver loving cup donated by *The Denver Post,* sponsor of the race [described in the *Wyoming Tribune* of July 21, 1906 as follows,]:

> In this event each contestant is provided with three horses. When the word is given she mounts one of the animals, dashes around the half mile track, dismounts, leaps onto another cowpony and is off again. The race is one and one-half miles long, so that each lady must dismount and remount twice. As much time is either lost or gained according to the dexterity of the fair competitor to leap from a horse, often with the animal in full gallop, and spring on to her next mount, it can well be imagined that the contest is such as to excite the greatest possible enthusiasm and excitement in the spectators. The committee has decided that the riders need not use the same saddle for all three horses as in their great haste to be off again saddles are often put on in a careless manner and by using a separate saddle for each horse a great element of danger to the ladies will be eliminated and the race lose nothing of its exciting nature.

The relay race became one of the most popular rodeo events, and various rules changes through the years were indicative of the skill attained by the riders. At one time the riders used only one saddle; one assistant held the waiting horse, but the rider had to saddle, unsaddle, mount and remount with no help from the assistant. Clearly, dexterity in handling the saddle became as important as riding skill and a fast horse in determining a winner. At other times when saddled horses were again used, regulations stated that the rider's feet must touch the ground in changing mounts. Prior to that rule, the fastest riders merely crossed under the half-mile wire, leaped out of one saddle and flew through the air on to another. There were obvious advantages for those riders skilled enough to change mounts in this manner, but the possibilities for accidents were surely decreased with the rule change barring such acrobatics....

Roman riding or racing two horses in a standing position with one foot on the back of each mount enjoyed some popularity with both men and women riders for a time. Since it seemed more appropriate for the circus ring as a spectacle than the rodeo circuit, where the most popular activities were outgrowths of ranch chores, Roman riding never held the interest of spectators as did some of the other events.

The stake race for women, introduced in Cheyenne in 1916, was probably the forerunner of the modern women's barrel race. Unlike the barrel race in which the riders weave around a barrel course in a cloverleaf pattern, the early stake riders raced down a straightaway, turned sharply around a stake at the end of the stretch, then sped back to the finish line. The race was a short sprint, and the speed of the horses and deftness in the turn generated great excitement among the spectators.

Trick and fancy roping also appeared as one of the women's exhibitions in the early 1900s. Though roping was not scheduled as a contest, some women developed the skill to a high degree. "A particularly difficult trick was to twirl the rope into a large loop catching several mounted men as they rode by."

During the early years of the twentieth century women entered rodeo contests across the country in increasing numbers. Some riders, like Lorena Trickey, developed rodeo skills out of necessity when ranch responsibilities were thrust upon them. Upon the death of their father, Lorena and her two brothers were left to run their ranch. She weighed barely a hundred pounds, yet she was known as one of the best "cowboys" on her home range and could handle a lariat and branding iron as efficiently as her two brothers. Bertha Kaepernick owned and operated her own ranch and developed riding skills comparable to those of any man in the day-to-day operation of the ranch....

Unlike Miss Kaepernick and Miss Trickey, many women never had to assume the full responsibility of the ranch owner, but they grew up on Western ranches and, in carrying their share of ranch chores, became proficient riders at an early age. The experiences that catapulted Mrs. Goldie St. Clair to the title of "Champion Woman Bronco Buster of the World" were probably typical of most early women champions. [The *Cheyenne State Leader* of August 21, 1909 notes,]

> Her parents were riders, her mother being a noted relay rider, and the children were given the run of the range. Mrs. St. Clair and one of her brothers herded cattle on barebacked horses as soon as they were able to toddle. As they grew older the children rode the horses to and from school and

were such daring little experts that they nearly wore them out. At last the father restricted the children to some mules. They were small mules but could match with Steamboat or Rocking Chair (well known bucking horses) when it came to bucking ... As time went by they began to have bucking contests every Sunday afternoon. The exhibition ground was a wheat field, and the spectators were neighbors ... It was in this wheat field that Mrs. St. Clair got the training which was afterward to make her the champion of the world.

Cheyenne's Frontier Days had offered the first opportunities for women to participate in the colorful world of the rodeo, and it was perhaps fitting that the first state giving women the legal right to vote in 1869 and hold public office should also pave the way for their entry into other activities generally considered the exclusive domain of men. As rodeo developed and expanded in other parts of the country, additional opportunities for women were made available, and they did not hesitate to take advantage of them. Two of the best known rodeos, other than Frontier Days, the Pendleton, Oregon, Round-up, originating in 1909, and the Calgary, Alberta, Stampede in 1912 both scheduled events for women in their early stages of development. Many smaller communities offered their own versions of the larger celebrations, and women along with men became "circuit riders," moving from one rodeo to another to test their skill and finesse in handling a horse, a rope, or a steer. On occasion the best women riders challenged each other to special contests to claim such titles as "champion rough rider of the world."

Lucille Mulhall, a champion steer roper who could rope eight horses with one throw of a lariat made a million dollars in silent westerns. [Such] women also had a profound effect on rodeo costuming. They soon tired of their tailored shirtwaists and long divided skirts of drab colors and exchanged them for shorter split skirts of red velvet and fancy silk shirts of equally brilliant hues. With this kind of colorful competition, men, too, discarded their denim jeans and work shirts and adopted the bright colored attire which women had made popular.

Women were involved in rodeo for almost half a century, and in the early years, "they attempted to do everything their male counterparts excelled at." The number of contestants decreased markedly in the 1940s, and women's events began to disappear not only from Cheyenne's Frontier Days, but from other rodeos as well. A number of factors probably contributed to the paucity of women contestants, but the prominent seemed to be these: (1) Prize money for women was relatively small and was always less than that for men competing in the same events. (2) The danger inherent in bronco riding and steer roping kept many women from competing. (3) Maintaining and transporting specially trained horses, particularly the three to six needed for the relay races, was very expensive. (4) Fewer rodeos were scheduling a wide range of events for women, and it was difficult for a rider to stay in top form with fewer contests. "With the demise of the ladies' relay race in 1946 female participation in (Frontier Days) ceased." Although all girl rodeos were initiated at about this same time, and the barrel race was introduced as the only event in men's rodeo in which women could compete, the conclusion of women's participation in Frontier Days signalled the end of an era. Women had competed in almost every rodeo event and had tested their skills in the same arena as the best men contestants. For almost fifty years they had shared the limelight and "old timers remembered with regret the intense competition among the cowgirls and the excitement provided by them..."

Source

Journal of the West, XVII (July 1978), 44-52. Edited from a carefully documented article by Mary L. Remley entitled "From Sidesaddle to Rodeo." The book by Alice Morley Cleaveland, *No Life for a Lady,* was published in Boston, 1941.

St. James's Day
July 25

The Apostle James the Great (Santiago) is the patron saint of Spain. Supposedly, after he was beheaded in Palestine, his body was placed in a boat without a rudder or crew and guided to Compostela, Spain, by angels. Buried there, James's body was ignored for 800 years until a hermit, attracted by heavenly lights playing over the gravesite, found it. His feast day is celebrated on the anniversary of this event, and a church, built on the site, became the center of the town of Santiago. St. James, in the manner of the English St. George, is reported to have been seen on a white charger leading Spanish troops in their battles against the infidel Moors.

Fiesta of St. James the Apostle

The population of Loíza [Puerto Rico] and its neighboring *barrios* totaled in the 1950 census 7,740 inhabitants. More than eighty-seven per cent of these belong to the Negro race, and the great majority of them are descendants of the Negro slaves concentrated in the region. There is a remarkable stability of population in the village. Many families can easily trace their ancestry for several generations back, and the names of some of the early and powerful *hacendados* are still found in the descendants of their slaves, who, according to the custom, adopted their master's name. This stability in the population, together with the relative isolation in which the village has lived, are in part responsible for the greater purity of old customs and beliefs in Loíza than in other regions of the island.

The economy of the region is still dependent on the sugar plantations, which today are mostly owned by the government. More than ninety per cent of the people derive their income by working in the sugar fields. Since the work in these is limited to less than six months of the year, the economic condition of the people is very poor. Some complement their earnings by fishing or working on the coconut plantations. In general, the people lead very poor and drab lives.

The slow and monotonous life of the inhabitants of Loíza and its environs undergoes a violent change during one week of each year when the people, with an indescribable overflowing of spontaneous joy and popular enthusiasm, celebrate their traditional festival, the Fiesta of Santiago Apostol (St. James the Apostle). This fiesta traces its origin to Spain, where the cult of Santiago Apostol became tremendously popular during the war against the Moors. The Spanish conquerors brought the cult with them to America. Santiago was considered by the Spaniards as a divine warrior who helped them on earth to fight the infidels. In America "*Santiago!*" became the cry of the conquistadores when they led a charge against the Indians, just as it had been the battle cry against the Moors.

Origin of the Fiesta in Loíza

The origin of the Fiesta of Santiago in Loíza is uncertain. The celebration is so old that its beginnings have been forgotten. Some of the elderly residents, in their desire to express the antiquity of the festival, place its beginnings in "the days when God walked on earth." Since Loíza was one of the early settlements which most frequently suffered the attacks of the Carib Indians and European corsairs, we may surmise that the devotion to the warrior Saint of the Spaniards took root among the villagers, who continually found themselves obliged to take arms to defend themselves against these attacks. The faith which the inhabitants placed in the Saint and in his divine aid may have made it possible for them to remain in the district and to resist the continuous attacks of Indians and corsairs.

In Loíza, Santiago found his most faithful devotees among the Negro population, which was concentrated in the sugar plantations of the district. This makes it natural to consider the possibility that in Loíza, and about the figure of Santiago, a fusion of Hispano-Christian and African beliefs took place....

Of the African cultures represented among the Negroes who were brought to Puerto Rico, the Yoruba culture appears to have predominated. In the Yoruba religion, Shangó, a god whose attributes are very similar to those of *Santiago Matamoros* (killer of Moors) is an important figure. Shangó is the god of war and thunderbolt. In Yoruba sculpture he is represented as a warrior on horseback. *Santiago Matamoras* was not only the warrior Saint who protected the Spaniards in battle, but was also the Saint possessed of the power to call down the fire of heaven to annihilate the infidel. The similarity between the attributes of the African god and the Christian Saint is such that it could well have led to a fusion of the two conceptions among the Negro population of Loíza.

But if such a process of syncretism took place in Loíza about the figure of Santiago, the only affirmative evidence which remains is the devotion of the present Negro population to the Saint and the fact that he is sometimes referred to by the residents as "the god of wars."

The Fiesta of Santiago in Loíza has several well-marked characteristics of its own. The Apostle is represented in three images, each one of which is associated with a different division of the population. Thus we find three distinct Santiagos, one for the men, one for the women, and one for the children. During the festival each of the three versions of the Saint is shown special honor on a day of his own.

The three images are each the property of a different person. The three proprietors are known as the *mantenedoras* (maintainers) of the Saint. Each of the images remains in the house of his *mantenedora* throughout the year, being removed only during the festival. The persons who keep these images are usually women, although many men have been *mantenedores*. If the proprietor of an image finds himself unable to continue to take active part in the celebration, he surrenders the image to someone else who has distinguished himself for his devotion to the Saint and who has actively participated in the planning of the Fiesta.

The oral tradition of the people of the town preserves interesting accounts of the origin of the three images. Although this tradition is sometimes self-contradictory, all versions agree that one of the images, that of *Santiago de los Muchachos* (St. James of the Children), or *Santiaguito,* as he is commonly called, appeared miraculously many years ago.

The festival was celebrated with the miraculous image alone until, according to the tradition, two families of the town ordered two new images from Spain, one, that of *Santiago de los Hombres* (St. James of the Men), and the other, that of *Santiago de las Mujeres* (St. James of the Women)....

Preparing for the Fiesta

Beginning at the end of June, evening meetings of devout residents are held in each of the houses where an image is kept. In these meetings ways of obtaining funds to meet the expenses of the festival and plans aimed at making it as successful a celebration as possible are discussed.

The meetings, which are frequent affairs and subsidiarily a social activity, are conducted very informally. The *mantenedora* of the Saint and persons who have especially distinguished themselves in previous celebrations draw up the plans to be followed to make the festival as brilliant as possible. In general the men keep away from these meet-

ings, although they congregate near the houses where they are being carried on to await the exit of the women. Two groups are distinguishable among those who take part, one made up of women well along in life and another of young girls. The chief theme is the collection of funds. There are, in general, three ways of collecting the money required: raffles, benefit performances in the theater of the town, and donations. Of the three, the first two are the most effective. The sum spent by each of these *Hermandades* (Sodalities) varies between one hundred and fifty and two hundred dollars, almost half of it being used for the purchase of rockets and other fireworks. The expenditure which follows this in importance is the sum paid to the musicians who take part in the procession of each Saint on his day. Another expense is that of the masses which are said by the priest on the days dedicated to each of the Saints.

It is plain that there has long existed a rivalry among the three *Hermandades.* This rivalry manifests itself in a desire on the part of the members of each that the day dedicated to their Saint be the most successful of the whole festival, and in the belief that their image is the one that has performed the most miracles.

Early in the morning of the first of July the inhabitants of Loíza and the surrounding district awaken to the report of a rocket which is fired to remind them that the month in which the Fiesta of Santiago is to be celebrated has begun. It is at this point that the direct preparations for the celebration begin, and from this time on the celebration is the favorite topic of conversation.

The Fiesta

On the twenty-fifth of July, the day on which the Roman Catholic Church celebrates the miraculous discovery of the remains of St. James the Apostle, the fiesta begins in Loíza Aldea and environs. The town has taken on suitable gala dress for the occasion. At the entrance to the town signs are placed announcing the celebration and welcoming the strangers who always visit it during the festival. The Plaza is decorated with wreaths and small red and yellow cloth or paper flags. In the center of the Plaza platforms are constructed for the dances and spectacles which are to be celebrated during the evenings.

Early in the morning the image of *Santiago de los Hombres* is carried from the house of the woman who has it in her keeping to the town Church. In the afternoon hours there is great activity in the streets of the village and its environs, and in the evening of the same day a dance is held to the music of a small local orchestra.

On the next day, which is dedicated to the image of *Santiago de los Hombres,* the gay and showy masks so characteristic of the festival are seen for the first time. In the morning mass is celebrated in honor of the Saint, whose image has remained in the church since the preceding day. At five in the afternoon several rockets are fired to announce to the inhabitants that the procession, which is to terminate in a place called Las Carreras (where, according to tradition, the image of *Santiago de los Muchachos* was miraculously discovered), has begun.

The privilege of carrying the litter is granted to a number of the devout by the *mantenedora* of the image. The procession begins amid the pealing of bells and is led by the *mantenedora,* who carries a flag which is the Saint's emblem. She is followed by four of the faithful carrying the litter and by the rest of the devout. Later on the masqueraders, who by order of the parish priest are forbidden to enter the church, have joined the procession outside. They pass along the principal streets of the town before turning off toward Las Carreras, the rear drawn up by a group of musicians who ride in a truck and play on the way.

Before reaching its destination the procession passes by the house in which the image of *Santiago de los Muchachos* is kept. The encounter is marked by the firing of several rockets by the devotees of both images. Sometimes there is a contest to see which of the *Hermandades* can fire the greatest number.

When the procession passes in front of the house where another Saint is kept, it is the custom that the other Saint come forth accompanied by several faithful to salute the Saint of the day. The bearers of the litters of the two Saints, following the instructions of a person who acts as master of ceremonies, lower the litters three times in sign of salutation. After this, the Saint of the day moves on in procession with the second Saint, in this case *Santiago de los Muchachos,* following.

Shortly before turning off the highway onto the sandy road which leads to Las Carreras, the Saint of the day passes before a small chapel where the image of *Santiago de las Mujeres* is kept during the festival. Once more several rockets are fired and the same ritual of salutation is performed with the three images taking part. The image of *Santiago de las Mujeres* accompanied by his devotees joins the procession, which now continues toward Las Carreras.

At Las Carreras, which is near the seashore, the procession halts near a rubber tree where, according to one of the legends, the image of *Santiago de los Muchachos* was discovered many years ago. The traditional ceremony of racing with the flags of the Saints is performed. Masqueraders mounted on horseback and dressed as caballeros request of the *mantenedora* of their favorite image the privilege of racing with his banner. Each rider, upon reaching the end of the eight hundred meter course, returns with the banner to the *mantenedora,* who then delivers it to another rider who has requested the same privilege.

In the meantime there are dances in which some of the masqueraders take part, while others celebrate the occasion at the stands where food and drink are sold.

After remaining at Las Carreras for approximately half an hour, the procession returns to the town. On the following days similar processions are held in honor of the other images.

The Masqueraders

During the Fiesta of Santiago, laborers who during the year have been engaged in hard and dangerous work in the sugar cane fields, on the coconut plantations, and in the fishing industry, forget their tasks and daily cares to participate in the various phases of the celebration. Hundreds of these laborers dress in traditional costumes and sing and dance in the streets of the village and its environs, asking for gifts of money. The numerous and striking costumes constitute one of the most colorful aspects of the Fiesta.

These costumes are made by the women but worn only by the men. There is a connection between the kind of costume worn and the social position of the wearer. The masqueraders begin to appear on the streets of the town on the twenty-sixth of July, the day on which the first of the three processions is held. Among the many different varieties of costumes four types can be distinguished, which, being of traditional design, at the same time impose upon the wearers a particular part in the celebration.

One of these four types is the *caballero,* who attempts to imitate the dress of the old-time Spanish gentleman seen in the images. The *caballeros* represent the Saint. They stand for good in conflict with evil, for Christianity in conflict with paganism. Their costume includes a jacket and trousers made of lustrous materials such as cheap satins and rayons. Each piece is particolored: red, yellow, and green are the common colors. *Caballeros* wear masks made of screen wire and painted to represent what are taken to be the features of a typical Spanish gentleman. In addition, a hat is worn which is generally decorated with small mirrors, bells, ribbons of various colors, and sometimes with paper flowers and birds. Owing to the expense of this costume and to the custom that the *caballero* appear at the festival upon horseback, those who adopt this dress are always townsmen of superior means. The behavior of the *caballeros* is always more grave and circumspect than that of the other masqueraders.

It would appear that formerly the *cabelleros* were the Saint's escorts and performed certain pantomimes representing battles between themselves and Santiago Apostol on the one hand and the Moors on the other.

The *vejigantes* are the counterpart of the *caballeros* and represent evil, the devil, the Moors whom the Santiago Apostol and the *caballeros* combat. The traditional costume of the *vejigante* is a kind of jumper, the broad sleeves of which are connected with the body of the garment in such a way that when the wearer raises his arms a bat or devil effect is produced. The costume is made of a showy, brilliantly colored but cheap fabric which in some cases bears printed patterns. The characteristic feature of a *vejigante* is his mask, which is a grotesque horned face made of pasteboard, coconut, gourd, or tin plate. The coconut masks are the most popular and showy of the whole celebration. Several weeks before the beginning of the festival, the fishermen who have decided to make these masks select a number of dry coconuts, halve them lengthwise, and extract the nut. Upon the outer surface, and as the form of each specimen permits, they carve a grotesque face the nose and lips of which are always prominent. The mouth is generally provided with teeth carved of wood and covered with silver or gilt paper. In the upper part of the mask holes are bored for the horns, which are made of coconut shell or wood and are sometimes simple and sometimes compound like the horns of a stag. The masks usually bear two or three horns and are painted several colors with ordinary paints. The colors most used are red, black, blue, and gray. Sometimes a moustache and beard made of horsehair are added. . . .

The *vejigantes* have a special affected way of speaking and frequently emit howls or screams. They roam the streets of the town on foot and are generally accompanied by a group of small children who serve as chorus to their traditional chants. The air-filled bladder (*vejiga*) tied to the end of a slender rod, which the *vejigante* formerly carried to strike passers-by, has disappeared. A paper bag has replaced the bladder. Some of this class have the custom of carrying certain small manikins which they show to the public when soliciting gifts.

In third place come the so-called *viejos* (old men). The part of *viejo* is chosen by those of the inhabitants who for lack of money or time have not prepared a costume of one of the other kinds. The *viejos* dress in torn and frayed castoff garments and wear masks made of shoe-boxes or pasteboard. This is the role most closely connected with the music of the festival, during which groups of *viejos* are commonly seen playing in the streets and soliciting gifts.

The music and dances which the masqueraders perform are of African origin. Important among the musical instruments used are the *bombas,* wooden drums about three feet high with a goatskin parchment. The *bongó,* pairs of small drums likewise made of wood and provided with a goatskin parchment, are also used, as well as tambourines (*Panderetas,* simple iron hoops covered with goatskin), the *guiro* or *guícharo* [dried gourd cut with grooves and scraped], the *palillos,* (wooden sticks), the *maracas* or rattle, and the guitar. The dances which are performed to the music of these instruments are versions of the *bomba* and the *plena.*

The *viejos* are associated with a fourth traditional type of mask, that of the *locas* (mad women). These are men who dress as women and pretend to be mad. The *locas* pass along the streets of the town with brooms and cans, sweeping and cleaning the streets and porches of the houses and asking a recompense for their "work." They wear costumes of clashing colors and fit themselves with artificial busts. They do not customarily wear masks, but usually paint their faces black. In the lively street-dancing characteristic of the celebration, the *locas* and the *viejos* take the principal part.

In recent years outside influences have led to the introduction of several new kinds of costumes. One of these represents the role of the "Mexican." Here the influence of Mexican films is seen. Some appear in reasonably accurate copies of typical Mexican dress, while others wear adaptations. The war, too, has led to an innovation. Some of the former soldiers have made certain changes in their uniforms and use them as costumes. Others wear old police uniforms and take the part of policemen, directing traffic and levying fines upon the passers-by. Still others appear as photographers, physicians, fishermen, and in similar roles.

Function and Significance of the Fiesta

Although there is more than one aspect to the Fiesta of Santiago in Loíza, it is clear that the religious side is still the most important. The devout find the festival the most satisfactory way of expressing their devotion and respect for the Saint. The festival is also the occasion when those who have asked favors of the Saint fulfil their vows. The vows which are made to the Saint are of many different kinds and there are two ways of fulfilling them: by giving gifts to the image or by performing "services" (*servicios*) to the Saint. Gifts may consist of donations of money to be used in the festival, candles which are lighted before the Saint, colored ribbons to adorn the image, or of *ex-votos* which give testimony of miracles. The *ex-votos,* which are usually called *mandas,* are gold, silver, or tin plate. They are small representations of the organ or part of the body which has been healed by the Saint's intercession. The *mandas* are made by popular artists and are bought from wandering vendors or in the market-places of the neighboring towns. The services which are promised to the Saint are of several different kinds. Sometimes the service consists of accompanying the image of the Saint in the long and frequent processions. Frequently, too, a devotee promises to assist in the carrying of the litter which supports the image of the Saint or to race on horseback with the Saint's banner in the ceremony which takes place at Las Carreras.

The religious function of the festival is also seen in the numerous activities of a more conventionally sacred character. There are prayers and singing for nine nights before each of the images of the Saint, and four masses are celebrated during the festival which are undoubtedly the best-attended of all those said in the old church of the town. In addition, St. James Day is considered in the district to be the time for the performance of certain other religious acts: baptisms and marriages are frequent on this day. In sum, the festival is the time and the cause of the most important manifestation of religious activity of the year.

It is also very evident that the festival has its social function. Many of the inhabitants look upon the festival only as an opportunity for diversion. The celebration undoubtedly offers the inhabitants of the district the best chance of the year to meet and enjoy themselves. A man is able to meet old friends from other parts of the district, recollect old times, and compare the present festival with those of the past. Not a few of the inhabitants abandon their work and employment during the days of the festival to be able to enjoy the entertainments with more freedom. Members of the younger generation who have found employment in other towns return to Loíza to visit their friends and enjoy themselves....

Apart from its religious and social aspects, the festival also has an economic function. Months before the celebration, the *mantenedoras* of the three images begin to give thought to the obtaining of the necessary funds. Delegations representing the three *Hermandades* visit business estab-lishments and the houses of the more prosperous to ask for donations and to sell lottery tickets and tickets for the benefit performances which are to be given in the theater of the town. The business people cooperate with the organizers of the festivities in the knowledge that they will bring greater profits. The custom of wearing new clothes during the festival is the cause of brisker business in the small shops of the town....

The Fiesta of Santiago in Loíza is today an isolated phenomenon in the dynamic media in which the social structure of the Puerto Rican communities is developing. The reason for its survival is explained by the great ethnic and social homogeneity of the vicinity and the relative isolation in which it has lived. This situation, together with the antiquity of the village, explains the presence of old customs and beliefs of Hispano-Catholic origin, as well as African, which are not present in any other village of the island.

Source and Comment

Journal of American Folklore, LXIX (1956), 125-33. Richardo E. Alegría studied the fiesta of St. James at Loíza, Puerto Rico, as an example of "the survival of old Hispano-Catholic practices as well as the persistence of African beliefs and customs, which have already disappeared from other communities of the island."

St. Christopher's Day
July 25

His name literally means Christ-bearer, and according to his legend he was a giant who was converted to Christianity and wished to perform acts of charity. One day he was carrying a child across a river which had no bridge and found that his burden became increasingly heavy. When he complained that he seemed to be bearing the weight of the world on his shoulders, he was told by the child, "Marvel not, for you have carried on your back the world and him who created it." This legend made Christopher a popular saint, especially revered by ferrymen and travellers, but because so little authentic is known about him, he has been removed from the canon.

Blessing Cars on St. Christopher's Day

Fifty years ago [in 1928] a young Roman Catholic priest named Agnello J. Angelini had his third serious car accident, no mean feat in the days when cars were even rarer than roads in these parts.

"I was a little shaky on the wheel," he admits now. He did two things about it. For one thing, he stopped driving.

"I decided you could be the best driver and your life is at stake anyway. Nothing more than supernatural intervention is going to protect you."

The second step waited until he became pastor of Our Lady of Mount Carmel Church here [Nesquehoning, Pennsylvania] in 1933—he started blessing automobiles on the commemorative day of St. Christopher, the patron saint of travelers.

"I felt at first I could pass on my regard for safety and carefulness, and give people the nerve to continue to drive," he said.

The custom has flourished here in this out-of-the-way village in the coal region. There are 3,000 souls here, where the whitewashed houses are cut into two facing hillsides, and the numerous church spires are set off by the greenery of the skyline. ("We have lots of churches," he noted. "We keep people holy here.")

The years have brought changes—the priest is now a monsignor—and they have brought 11,000 cars by his estimates, cars of "every shape, size, color, make and imported or domestic." These days, he and his assistant bless cars for an entire week, ending this Saturday.

Business was somewhat slow on Tuesday, St. Christopher's day itself, but Monsignor Angelini considers that merely a sign of his success.

Once upon a time, people were bringing their cars from all over the country to Nesquehoning, but they seem to have spread the word and many other Catholic churches have taken up blessing their own parishioners' cars. As a result, Monsignor Angelini has mostly a local trade, "but we still get them from New York, New Jersey and Pennsylvania."...

The actual blessing of the cars, performed either by the monsignor in his lavender sash or his assistant, the Rev. James M. T. Connolly, in a multicolored Guatemalan stole, is done by dipping a silver aspergillum into a brass Holy Water bucket and sprinkling the car's windshield. (Or, as in the case of 11-year-old Jimmy McLean, of New Columbus, Pa., the handlebars of the bicycle.)

Source and Comment

Philadelphia Inquirer, July 27, 1978. From a feature article by Rod Nordland, staff writer. Lydia Marie Fish, *Indiana Folklore,* IX (1976), 167, reports that the Bishop of Buffalo annually blesses the motorcycle fleets of the Buffalo Police Department and the Sheriff's Department, though not on St. Christopher's Day.

Hurricane Supplication Day
July 28

The custom of "rogations" seems to have begun in England in the fifth century following a frightening series of storms, earthquakes and other natural disasters. The word "rogation" comes from a Latin root meaning to beg or supplicate. Rogation or supplication ceremonies usually include litanies, responsive prayer, and petition. They take place on special occasions or annually: on the Rogation Days that precede the Feast of the Ascension, or at the beginning of the hurricane season in the Virgin Islands and other islands of the West Indies which have been ravaged by hurricanes.

Hurricane Prayers

Residents of all three United States Virgin Islands attend church services to pray that they are spared the ravages of hurricanes.... October 20 [is] Hurricane Thanksgiving Day. Services are held on all three islands giving thanks for being spared hurricanes during the past season.

Source and Comment

United States Virgin Islands 1980 Calendar of Events, 2-3. Bulletin issued by the Division of Tourism, Virgin Islands Department of Commerce, where the date July 28 is given. For another example of religious supplication, see "Ascension Day," p. 222. See also "Hurricane Thanksgiving Day," p. 369. According to a news item in the *Philadelphia Inquirer,* July 27, 1988, in the Virgin Islands "most of the 11,000 public employees took the day off . . . to pray the rains and winds away."

Kentucky Horse Sale

Monday and Tuesday in Late July

The annual auction of selected yearling horses by the Keeneland Association, Incorporated, is the premier thoroughbred sale in America. Normally about 325-350 carefully chosen yearlings are sold with prices rising each year. In 1985 a colt by the famous sire Nijinsky II went for $13,100,000, a price that would have bought all the thoroughbred yearlings offered for sale in North America in 1962. Horse sales have been held for centuries, and among the most celebrated is the October Horse Fair at Ballinasloe, County Galway, Ireland, where during Napoleonic times army quartermasters from all over Europe came to purchase mounts. Legend has it that as many as six thousand horses might change hands in a day. In nineteenth-century America, horse sales were a vivid part of folklife. E. F. "Pop" Geers who was born in 1851 recalls in his autobiography that in Tennessee several thousand people assembled on "Jockey Day" and "everyone who has a horse he desires to sell or trade will bring him in and put him in a yard known as Jockey Yard and it is not uncommon to see several hundred horses of all kinds and descriptions in one of these yards, and before night they will generally be disposed of."

Keeneland Select Yearling Sales

In keeping with ancient Bluegrass custom, the Sunday before the [1978] Keeneland Summer Sales of selected yearlings, the most prestigious horse sale in the world, is set aside for a lot of serious wining, dining, and selling. For sure, the day is gone when a slick-talking Kentucky breeder could find himself a "live one," load him to the gills with Kentucky's finest bourbon and sell him some expensive horseflesh before he sobered up. Buyers today are more sophisticated and knowledgeable. Even if they do not know much about horses, they bring along trainers and agents who do. "This is a business," says John Williams, manager of lordly Spendthrift Farm. "It's nobody's plaything anymore."...

The most flamboyant entertainer in the Bluegrass is Anita Madden. She is blond, statuesque and uninhibited. Her Kentucky Derby parties, with their blatantly sexual themes, always are attended by a bizarre mix of socialites, horsemen, entertainers, celebrities and voyeurs. She drinks only imported champagne, wears all sorts of see-through, peek-a-boo clothes, designed exclusively by Suzy Creamcheese of Las Vegas, and is apt to turn up anywhere, doing just about anything with anybody. The wire services carried a picture of her dancing with Billy Carter at a Super Bowl party in New Orleans last winter.

But there is method to her boldness. She has become so much an object of curiosity and speculation that many prospective buyers are thrilled by the idea of being invited to her parties. She knows precisely how to exploit her reputation to help her husband sell horses. If feminists disapprove, so be it. In the horse business, as in most businesses, you use whatever works, and, at heart, Anita Madden is a business person more than a socialite, a pragmatist more than a playgirl. Her rivals speak of how she likes to stand in front of a picture window in a diaphanous gown while guests are supposed to be gazing out the window at yearlings brought up from the barns. There is a note of jealousy here, of course. Anita Madden's gowns probably have sold a lot of horses for Hamburg Place, and that is what it is all about....

The Keeneland Summer Sales is excellent theater, full of drama, mystery, romance and excitement. A typical evening session begins at precisely 8 p.m., when auctioneer Tom Caldwell pounds his gavel and the first yearling is led into the ring. Caldwell wears a black tuxedo. So do the bidtakers who roam the aisles, heads bobbing crazily as they frisk the audience for bids. The auctioneer sits high above the crowd, behind what can only be described as a pulpit. Indeed, the scene is invested with a certain kind of religious mysticism. As Caldwell, the high priest, chants his mysterious incantations ("Who'll gimme 50 now, will-ya ...") the congregation sits mesmerized, clutching its hymnals—the thick sales catalogues.

The audience looks like a *People* magazine convention. Liz Taylor asked for seats but was a no-show. But over here is Texas oilman Nelson Bunker Hunt, reputed to be the world's richest man. And over there is David Cassidy, the erstwhile teeny-bopper rock star. And there is A. J. Foyt, the race-car driver, and [Robert] Sangster, the soccer-pool king. And so on and so forth.

In the bars at the back of the pavilion, the children of high society play their own games. Handsome young men in polo shirts and khakis hold their drinks and cigarettes just so as they chatter away at sweet young things with tans, flashing eyes and dazzling smiles. Through the hum of conversation and the layer of blue cigarette smoke come the tinkle of ice cubes and the champagne bubbling of laughter. Romance is in the air. Those with harder hearts can look up and watch the sales on closed-circuit TV.

Outside, under the stars, grooms lead the yearlings from the barns to their appointments with destiny. The yearlings are the equine equivalents of the buyers, all sons and daughters of such well-bred, aristocratic sires as Sir Ivor, Nijinsky, Northern Dancer and Secretariat. Identified only by a number pasted on the hip, each yearling is led into the pavilion by a groom in green coveralls. Sometimes the glare of the bright lights and dull roar of conversation can frighten a yearling, causing it to pace nervously on the tanbark floor of the sales ring.

The actual bidding is a special kind of game, sort of a cross between Monopoly and high-stakes poker. The competition often is so fierce that buyers hire agents to do their bidding, all the better to keep their moves and plans secret. If word got out that Bunker Hunt was interested in a particular horse, for example, the price might be driven out of sight. Trying to figure out who is bidding for whom takes a sharp eye. A bid of $50,000 can be as subtle as a slight nod of the head. In the next row of seats, a man can scratch his nose and up the ante to $100,000. Auctioneer Caldwell and the bid-takers must be careful not to mistake a yawn for a $25,000 bid.

Around Keeneland, they still talk about the night in 1968 that Charles Engelhard, then the world's richest man, lost a bidding war to Wendell P. Rosso of Newport News, Va., the owner of a chain of open-air supermarkets.

Everyone, of course, knew Engelhard, the platinum king. He and his American, Irish and English advisers were assigned choice seats near the front of the pavilion. Somewhere during the course of the evening, Engelhard decided to bid on a filly by Sea Bird II, out of Libra, who already had dropped Ribocco, winner of the Irish Sweeps Derby and the St. Leger Stakes.

As the bidding progressed, Engelhard found himself in a duel with Rosso. Nobody knew Rosso. He had no assigned seat, nor did he see fit to wear a coat and tie. As the bids increased, Keeneland president Bassett began to get nervous. Who was this fellow with the audacity to challenge the mighty Engelhard?

"Every time Engelhard made a bid, he was countered in the back by Rosso," said Bassett. "When it reached $300,000, Engelhard's advisers told him to drop out, but he kept going. He finally bid $400,000, a record, and the pavilion erupted. But as soon as the noise died down, Rosso bid $405,000. Engelhard stopped. Then the place really buzzed."

His heart full of trepidation, Bassett approached Rosso. "Have you established your credit?" asked Bassett.

Rosso cooly pulled out four $100,000 certified checks and handed them over. "Is that sufficient?" he asked....

Soon as the last yearling is sold, the sales pavilion empties quickly. The rich and the beautiful jump into their Cadillacs and Continentals and roar off to the next party or the next state or the next continent, wherever it is that rich people hang out between horse sales. Back at the barns, the grooms sip beer and cheap wine and let some of the tension seep out. The quiet is broken only by their laughter, and by the nickering of the most expensive horseflesh in the world.

Source and Comment

Classic, No. 5, (August/September 1978), 94, 96-99. The description of the traditions, customs, and colorful personalities associated with the internationally famous auction of yearling horses was edited from an article written by Billy Reed for a magazine no longer published which specialized in materials of interest to people who breed, race, show, and train horses. The statements of E. F. Geers in the "History" are from Bob Womack, *The Echo of Hoofbeats*, Shelbyville, Tennessee, 8.

Captain Brady Day

July—August

Brady Lake in Ohio is named for Captain Samuel Brady (1758-95), an American frontiersman who fought in the Revolutionary War and served as a scout in the Northwest Territory under General Anthony Wayne. His legendary exploits include an escape from Indians by submerging himself beneath the surface of the lake and breathing through a reed. The celebration, first held in 1973 and since then on a date not yet firmly fixed, is an example of a folk festival in the process of evolving since it reflects a profound sense of local tradition and at the same time shows parallels with practices of distant cultures.

Captain Brady and the Muskrats of Brady Lake

Anthropological literature is replete with descriptions of people who consider themselves related to one or another species of plant or animal. Often, members of a social group call themselves by the name of such a species, surround that species with an aura of respect or sanctity, and share a prohibition against killing or eating members of that species. This phenomenon is commonly called "totemism." ...

Brady Lake is a small community located in Ohio's Portage County, about midway between the city of Kent (home of Kent State University) and the county seat of Ravenna. Attention was first called to the lake during the late eighteenth century when Captain Samuel Brady of the Continental Army is said to have escaped a group of Wyandotte Indians by breathing through a hollow reed while hiding underwater. This event serves as a sort of origin myth for the community and focuses attention on the lake from a very early date.

For about a century following Brady's escape the area immediately surrounding the lake was mostly woods and farmland. In the 1890's the lake was made into a feeder reservoir for the Ohio-Pennsylvania Canal. In the waning years of the last century, a major tourist resort was developed around the lake, complete with waterfront cottages, a dancing pavilion, boating, swimming, and assorted other forms of entertainment. In 1927, the east side of the lake was incorporated as a village....

Beginning in 1976 the level of Lake Brady began to drop precipitously. In a two-year period the surface area declined from 99 to 75 acres. Informants say the growth of algae, weeds, and the appearance of unsightly mud flats has impaired the lake's aesthetic quality. The appearance has deteriorated and it has lost much of its appeal to swimmers, fishermen, and boaters. Simultaneous with the recession of the lake has been a decline in the water level of many local wells. Some wells have gone dry, and most have been to some degree affected.

Residents of Brady Lake were asked to identify the most important problems facing the community. They were unanimous in selecting the water crisis as one of the most pressing problems. Much time and effort has been expended in the search for a solution. Innumerable hours have been spent at meetings, conferences, and informal conversations. Studies have been conducted, plans drawn up, revised, and scrapped, and water is a constant topic of discussion.

Undoubtedly, the falling water table has created problems for the people of Brady Lake. Lack of water has affected activities ranging from cooking to washing clothes and flushing toilets, transforming everyday pursuits into tests of ingenuity and will. And people are concerned about the possible impact of the crisis on the value of their land and homes. Yet, the fact remains that people are getting along. Informants indicate that property values have kept pace with inflation.... As far as we could tell no one has moved out of Brady Lake because of the water problem, nor would anyone admit to contemplating such a move. And many residents assert the crisis has helped to bring them closer together, making them into more of a community. From a distance, the lake still looks almost idyllic, and from personal experience I can attest that it is still a pleasant spot to swim, while fishing is as good as that in any of the local lakes. Why is it, then, that everyone is so preoccupied with water and the falling level of the lake?

Evidently, water has more than a practical significance to people of the area. The lake is a shared symbol. People identify with the lake and are conscious of the lake as something that they hold in common, differentiating them from outsiders....

The importance of the lake is evident in the very fact that the community is named for it. The "origin myth" involves the founding "ancestor" escaping death by hiding in the lake which offered him protection, and every year at Captain Brady Day this event is re-enacted. Physically as well as conceptually the community is centered around the lake, and the events of Captain Brady Day take place at the water's edge. Residents of Brady Lake describe themselves collectively as "Lakers" as opposed to nonresidents who are not designated by this term. Alternatively, they identify themselves as "Muskrats." The muskrat is a water animal, associated with the lake, and it appears to be symbolically isomorphic with the lake itself. The muskrat is an emblem of the community. In preparation for Captain Brady Day in August, 1978, signs were posted at close intervals within about a three-mile radius of Brady Lake. The signs encouraged people to join the celebration, and in the middle of each sign was printed a large picture of a muskrat. A wide variety of objects were on sale at the festivities, but the most popular appeared to be T-shirts made especially for the event, printed with a picture of a muskrat on the front and the inscription, "Muskrats do it better," on the back. By mid-morning the entire stock already had been sold.

The term, muskrat, first appeared in conjunction with Brady Lake during the early 1950's, when a group of area youths formed a club and began trapping muskrats to sell the pelts for spending money. Eventually, they took the name, "The Muskrats," for the club.

The club quickly gained a reputation as a group of young toughs and were viewed with disapproval by the other residents. As they got older, however, the original Muskrats either moved away or settled down to become respected members of the community, and gradually the name came to be adopted by all residents of Brady Lake. As acceptance of the name spread through the population a sense of identification with the animal increased. During the study, when one informant complained of muskrats destroying her vegetable garden the interviewer suggested that she kill the pests. The informant's horrified response was that "We couldn't do that! Not now!" The sanctification was now underway....

The community consists of dwelling houses distributed in a rough circle surrounding the sacred lake which constitutes the center. It is the lake upon which attention has always been focused. The lake symbolizes the unity and solidarity of the community. And it is at the lake shore that the sacred ceremony of renewal takes place annually. Beyond the periphery exists the outside world, seen as dangerous and often hostile, fraught with forces bent upon destruction of the way of life established by the Lakers and jealously guarded by them.

Brady Lake's concentric structure is cross-cut by a diametric one. The east side of the lake constitutes a formally incorporated village; the people on the west side reside in Franklin township. Although both sides see themselves as making up a joint community and there are many activities in which these boundaries are overridden, a sense of differentiation and competition between the sides remains. The township residents often disparage the village government and make such statements as, "They're too busy playing village to get anything done." The two bars of the area are frequented by members of the "moieties" in which they are located. The Club House, in the township, is the larger of the two, has fewer amenities, and has a down-to-earth appearance. The Chaparell Lounge, in the village, creates an image of a more refined, genteel establishment, with clientele to match. People in the village see the other side as poorer, and I was warned by several village residents that if I should go swimming in the lake I ought not to approach the western shore because of sewage seeping down into the water. The village shore, I was assured, remained pollution-free and safe for swimming.

The moiety division is given ritual enactment each year at Captain Brady Day. A major event each year appears to be a tug-of-war between the patrons of the two bars, each team representing its moiety. Water mediates between the two opposing sides as it is sprayed between them with a hose. The first team to be pulled through the mud puddle in the center loses. True to cultural proprieties, for the past several years the Club House has emerged victorious from this test of muscle power.

Source and Comment

"Muskrats of Brady Lake: A Case of American Totemism," Research Report of a Field School in Cultural Anthropology, Kent State University, Ohio, 1978, unpublished. Excerpted from a field report by Richard Feinberg, director of the field school. Based upon data collected by his students, particularly Martin Bramlett. Their main interests are in the lake and the totemic muskrat as "collective representations" of the community, and in suggesting that Americans, as instanced by the residents of Brady Lake, may have more in common with nonwestern peoples than is generally recognized. A shorter version of Feinberg's report, with the same title, was published in *The Gamut*, No. 5 (1982), 20-26. The escape from Indians by hiding underwater and breathing through a reed is also told about other frontiersmen such as Tim Murphy and Daniel Boone.

Graveyard Cleaning and Decoration Day
Summer, Especially July

The Romans held a state funeral, Parentalia, during the last month of their calendar, and one of the rites they performed was to repair and decorate ancestral graves. In the South, quite apart from the national observance of Memorial Day (see p.214), local memorial holidays came into being from the folklife of a rural people. They are often held in July but any time from late May until early September is considered appropriate. Their purpose is to honor the dead and to maintain the cemeteries, but they are significant social, religious, and patriotic occasions as well. They feature picnics, "dinner-on-the-ground," preaching and speech making, and the homecoming of former neighbors and family who had moved away. The times chosen are for local convenience, without regard for the official Decoration Day and Memorial Day observances: for instance, the whitewashing of tombs in New Orleans on All Saints' Day. The indigenous origin of these local decoration days is suggested by the fact that the term "Decoration Day," according to the *Dictionary of Americanisms,* was first used in the United States.

Memorial Day in Northeast Texas

In rural northeast Texas during the 1930s the annual memorial services conducted at each community church revealed some interesting traits of the society. For example, since each community depended on the funds raised each Memorial Day to pay for the maintenance of the cemetery grounds for the following year, there was open competition among the individual Memorial Day committees. Each community tried to attract a larger crowd than its neighbors had attracted the previous year. These observances were never scheduled on 30 May; there was no community observance associated with the nation's observance of Memorial Day. Instead, the individual committees selected a weekday in July that did not conflict with a day chosen by another community in the county or in a neighboring county. The committees did not select a Sunday because the communities depended primarily on the profits derived from the sale of soft drinks, ice cream, and candies to pay for the maintenance of the cemetery grounds. The belief was that the carnival atmosphere created by the presence of refreshment booths was inappropriate for a Sabbath.

Early in the morning of the scheduled Memorial Day program a few men would take their shotguns and go to the woods in search of six or eight squirrels to be used as the main ingredient in a stew. By 7 A.M. the men had shot the squirrels, skinned them and prepared them for the stewpot, an old-fashioned black washpot borrowed from one of the local families. Then the men opened cans of corn, tomatoes, and peeled fresh potatoes and onions, which they dumped into the pot. They often added a few chickens to

complement the "wild" flavor of the squirrels. Certain men in each community took pride in the quality of the stew produced annually just as their wives took pride in making mashed-potato salad flavored with beet-colored vinegar and decorated with carved pieces of boiled eggs shaped as flower buds.

At 11 A.M., before the food was served, the women, children, and many of the men gathered inside the church where the women fanned themselves with cardboard fans distributed by the local undertaker or candidates for various local offices. Some of the men preferred to remain outside under the huge oak trees, squatting on the ground or leaning against the fenders of trucks and cars, talking of the crops or local politics. There was competition among the various communities to see who could attract the most popular minister, "dedicated layman," or local public official as the featured speaker. An important part of the eleven o'clock service was the reading of the names of the people whose bodies had been buried in the cemetery since the previous Memorial Day. Usually a young girl from the congregation lighted a candle for each name.

After the lavish noon meal, the women, children, and a few of the men would gather inside the poorly ventilated church for an afternoon of singing. The group sang hymns traditional in Protestantism, though many were gospel songs in paperbound books that had been cheaply printed for mass distribution by commercial publishers. Usually by three or four o'clock in the afternoon the number of the people in the church and on the grounds had diminished considerably. One community, however, had a reputation for a lively evening song service. Many of the people who had spent the entire day at the church went to their homes for a couple of hours to tend their livestock and change their clothes; then they returned for the evening service. Since this particular community was one fortunate enough to have been served by the Rural Electrification Administration before World War II, its committee was able to plan activities for the evening. Besides being able to illuminate the church itself, the committee was able to string light bulbs around the top of the outdoor concession stand, adding to the carnival atmosphere. One problem created by illumination was the horde of moths and other insects that often dropped into the ice cream containers when the lids were opened.

Though the mass migration to the cities, prompted initially by the defense buildup prior to World War II, helped to eliminate some of these annual observances, several communities in Hopkins and Franklin Counties still sponsor these annual events. Instead of depending on the profits derived from the sale of refreshments, however, many of the community cemeteries have incorporated themselves and assess dues to those people whose relatives are buried in the cemetery.

Source and Comment

Western Folklore, XXXI (1972), 120-21. Described by Robert Cowser. Cf. "Graveyard Cleaning and Dinner-on-the-Ground," below, and note. According to Guy Kirtley "Graveyard-workings and dinner-on-the-ground are still held annually in many settlements of East Texas. During August or September a day will be set aside . . . and the whole community will turn out with full baskets, each person bringing a hoe, rake, or shovel." See *Publications of the Texas Folk-Lore Society,* XXVI (1954), 202.

* * *

Graveyard Cleaning and Dinner-on-the-Ground

"Fourth Saturday in July" is the great day at the Shady Grove Baptist church close to my home [Tennessee]. This is the day the members have graveyard cleaning and afternoon preaching, with dinner-on-the-ground between these two occasions. The reason for this gathering is to clean off the graveyard and to get the revival meeting off to a big start.

Everyone comes and brings food. Each lady in the community fixes the things she likes and her family likes. Everything you can imagine for one to eat is brought to these gala affairs. Almost every kind of meat and meat substitute can be seen on the table somewhere. When I use the word "table," I mean on the cloths that are spread out on the ground. However, most of the people that go to this affair depend on fried chicken and boiled or fried ham for the meat for the meal. That is what they have in their homes, and not having to buy it is the first thing they take into consideration. The meat is all sliced; none is unsliced. Not only meat, but all the meal is served cold.

Almost any vegetable conceivable can be enjoyed at this dinner. The vegetables are home grown: beans, peas, okra, greens, turnips, tomatoes, lettuce—any vegetable adaptable to this part of the country.

Almost all the food that you eat at this gathering is home grown except the dessert. Most of the ladies buy the material to make the dessert. Common among desserts are: banana pudding, jello and fruit cocktail, and all kinds of pies and cakes. Occasionally you will find cookies.

The only beverages are ice water, coffee, and iced tea. Occasionally some bright brother will slip and have beer. This is a rare case.

Each lady takes a cloth and spreads it on the ground. She then sets the food she has brought on the cloth in a group. This enables her to find again the unmarked dishes, forks, and knives that she has brought to the dinner.

After the food is all on the table, someone is asked to say grace. It is usually the same memorized words year after year. Then all line up and go around the table, each taking what he wants. Anyone can eat anything he desires. He can also go back as many times as he chooses, and in the fashion he likes. You eat either sitting on the ground or standing, whichever you want to do. Each mother usually gets her young ones something and this eliminates a lot of worry for her while she is eating.

After all have eaten until they can hardly walk, the women clean up the remains while the men enjoy a cigarette or cigar. Each woman attends to her own dishes and takes home what is left of the food to have at dinner that night. When all this is done, the people go inside and enjoy a good-old Baptist sermon.

Source and Comment

Tennessee Folklore Society Bulletin, XIX (September 1953), 63-64. Described by Ewing Jackson of Buchanan, Henry County, Tennessee in 1948, then a student at Murray State College, Kentucky. He states that "church denominations in our neighborhood are Baptist, Methodist, and Church of Christ. All of them are becoming more broadminded and do not turn people out of church for dancing as some of them used to do." Cf. "Washing the Tombs on All Saints' Day," p. 383.

* * *

Grave Day at Pleasant Grove

The latter part of August is tobacco-cutting time in Kentucky—perhaps the busiest time of year for farmers. However, on the fourth Saturday of August [before 1959] nearly everyone visits Pleasant Grove, a small community in western Hardin county, to attend Decoration Day services. The weather never influences the services; at least they are never postponed. Large crowds, representing a complete cross-section of our county, attend the services regularly. Not only is the community well represented, but many people visit from Louisville; others "come home" from as far as Chicago and Birmingham.

Perhaps the most interesting point about the crowd is their different modes of transportation to the services. People arrive not only in automobiles, ranging from model "A" Fords to shiny new Buicks, but in roadwagons, buggies, and on horseback. Some of these people have planned the trip for months—it is the most important social event of the year to them. One of the first acts of a family after arrival is the placing of wreaths on the graves of their respected loved ones.

Although the church is Methodist the services, beginning at ten o'clock, are interdenominational, and guest speakers are frequently used. Most of the crowd, however, remain outside the church, since it is too small to hold all of the people. About two hours are taken for lunch; then services are resumed. A different minister conducts the afternoon services. These services traditionally begin the annual "protracted meeting" at the church.

But the great majority of the people consider this a homecoming. For many people this is an occasion to meet their friends, particularly old acquaintances, and talk over old times. Young people tend to pair off—many lasting romances were begun on "Grave Day."

One of the highlights of the day is the noon meal. "Dinner on the ground" is served for the ministers and various distinguished visitors, but most families serve their lunches picnic style. Every person who did not bring his lunch receives numerous invitations to dine with his friends. Since the women go "all-out" in their preparation of this meal, it is a feast. Suitable picnic spots are easily found, as the church grounds consist of almost an acre and are well shaded by numerous large, stately oaks. Nature, seemingly determined to cooperate as much as possible, has provided a large spring of excellent drinking water.

One of the older customs that still persist is the consumption of large quantities of watermelons during the day. Two or three truckloads of melons are sold and eaten, or are carried home, each year. With all these pleasantries, it is surprising that the afternoon services are well attended. The services are concluded about four o'clock and the crowd begins to straggle homeward.

Grave Day has a colorful past. It was originated about 1875 by various community leaders who believed that the church, being the center of community activities, should be the leader in maintaining a friendly, peaceful atmosphere. War issues had split the county into two factions. Some people had supported the Union, others the Confederacy. The younger men had fought under both banners, and they were still bitter at one another, as old wounds heal slowly. The community leaders believed that bringing everyone together would, as it did, heal old animosities. In addition,

the community could honor all their boys as the heroes they were.

The ceremonies were colorful, although humorous situations frequently developed. The "old soldiers," accompanied by a military band playing martial music marched to the cemetery. They marched under "Old Glory," but each man wore his personal uniform, the Union blue or the Confederate gray. At the cemetery a selected speaker made a short speech eulogizing the various veterans present. He praised each man individually, indirectly resulting in one of the funniest episodes in the history of the services. In 1915 the orator, unaware of the customs of the ceremony, made a patriotic speech. Finally an old gentleman could stand the pressure no longer. He interrupted the speaker to say, "When are you going to say something about me? Why don't you talk about me? I'm here."

Even the church has a colorful name—"The Old Spiggot." No one seems to remember how the church received its nickname. The present church building was constructed in 1885, and Old Spiggot became a schoolhouse. It was finally razed in 1923, after a long, useful history.

The custom of setting dinner on the ground was begun early and still persists. All food was set on benches placed together. In earlier years old soldiers brought watermelons and, after slicing them open, placed them on the benches as their contribution to the feast. This custom was discontinued about 1910.

Ceremonies became less elaborate as the old soldiers died. By 1915 the singing of hymns had replaced the band. During World War I the rites at the cemetery were drastically changed. Marching to the ceremony ended about 1930. Few people who attend the services now know anything about the historical background of the day's activities.

Source and Comment

Kentucky Folklore Record, V (1959), 117-19. From the recollection of Philip E. Hoskinson on file in Western Kentucky Folklore Archive at Western Kentucky University, Bowling Green, Kentucky. Informant and the date not supplied. For a description of grave decoration today in Spring Hill, Kentucky, see *Folklore from the Working Folk of America,* 341-44.

* * *

Memory Day in Michigan

It was on December 6, 1903, that the dread angel Death visited the home of the writer [John T. Daniells] and took from earth to Heaven the spirit of a precious wife, leaving a once happy home lonely and desolate. An only child, our baby boy, died many years ago. In the spring following my wife's death, after placing the sacred earth in the rural cemetery four miles distant from our home in becoming condition, and removing thither the remains of our child from the grave by the home where flowers had bloomed upon it each summer time, I stood by the graves of my dead in loneliness and sorrow, and thought of the deep interest which my dear wife ever felt in the highest welfare of all who came within her influence. It was then and there that the desire came to me, almost irresistibly, to do all within my power, in memory of this precious woman, to better the condition of the graves of our dead.

With this purpose in view, I offered a resolution at the annual meeting of the State Association of Farmers' Clubs held at the State Capitol in December, 1904, which was adopted and endorsed by the State Grange in annual session also at the same time and place. The resolution asked that September 30 be designated "Memory Day," and be devoted to appropriately caring for our cemeteries on that autumn day, and making beautiful with flowers and loving care the graves of our dead. Taking up this matter with the Legislature at the following session an Act was passed in accord with the spirit of this resolution. My request soon afterward to the Governor of the State, Hon. Fred M. Warner, asking that he issue his proclamation inviting the people to observe "Memory Day," was complied with, and the proclamation was issued.

Proclamation by Governor [Woodbridge N.] Ferris:

MEMORY DAY

A Proclamation by the Governor:

Once upon a time a Michigan school teacher traveled two-hundred forty-seven miles for the sole purpose of hearing Adelina Patti sing "Home Sweet Home." This dear old song brought to the consciousness of four or five thousand listeners the precious memories of childhood's days. In large measure human personality is the aggregate of one's memory. At the grave of father, mother, wife, husband, son, daughter, baby, neighbor, friend, the joys and sorrows of the past, through memory, are revived and retouched with the benediction of love. Our cemeteries are cities of the dead, made beautiful through the magic touch of loving hands. It is hoped that on "Memory Day" every cemetery in Michigan will command the special attention of our citizens. If, by chance, a neglected grave is found, put it in order and place upon it a handful of flowers. If there is a corner called the potter's field, clear away the weeds and rubbish. Here strew and plant flowers. The condition of this particular spot is the real test of community love and loyalty. In remembering the dead, we serve the living.

I, Woodbridge N. Ferris, governor of Michigan, invite her people to convene in the cemeteries at 2:00 o'clock, p.m., on September 30, designated by the Legislature as "Memory Day," and there scatter flowers and hold appropriate exercises in memory of the dead.

Source and Comment

Michigan History Magazine, II (April 1918), 491-93. John T. Daniells was born in 1840 of pioneer stock. During his life he was active in farmers' organizations, in advocating rural free delivery, and in local historical societies. A poem by Will Carleton and a hymn, both entitled "Memory Day," were composed for this occasion. Daniells hoped the day would become a "fall Decoration Day" but it never became popular. Cf. "Obon, Festival for the Dead," p. 273.

The Crow Fair
First Weekend in August

The Crow Indians were a Siouan tribe, originally part of the Hidatsa. Legend has it that two equally powerful Hidatsa chiefs had a dispute late in the 18th century which resulted in one chief and his followers separating and moving west from the banks of the Missouri River to the vicinity of the Rocky Mountains. There they became a tribe of wandering hunters, superior in horsemanship, and extremely warlike. The modern Crow Reservation in eastern Montana covers about 2400 square miles of their original range, and the Crow Fair is held on the banks of the Little Bighorn River.

The Crow Fair seems to echo the Sun Dance ceremonies that were originally celebrated in late summer or early fall by almost all the Plains tribes. Probably a summer solstice rite at the start, it developed into a mixture of secret rites and public performances designed to unite the tribe and verify its traditions. Dancing, drama, parading, elaborate costuming, both fasting and feasting, sacrifices, self-torture, politics, and socializing were all part of this major event. Opposed by missionaries and the United States government, the Sun Dance was stamped out or greatly modified. The Crow Fair, embracing all Native Americans and open to tourist viewing, is a tribal and an ethnic spectacle, more suitable for the 20th century.

A Native American Fair

Crow Fair, which always begins on the [first weekend] in August, attracts Native Americans from all over North America. They come to compete in the All-Indian Rodeo, to sell beadwork, jewelry and T-shirts, to fry bread and Indian tacos, to dance and drum at the powwow and to greet friends they haven't seen for a year.

Tawny children race their ponies through the grass and swim in river shallows. Young men and women buckle on their chaps and spurs beside the rodeo stalls. Parents raise camps, throwing leafy cottonwood boughs over arbor frames, and exercise Thoroughbreds and quarter horses for the races. Elders paint the faces of their clan children, carefully outfitting them in traditional Crow dress for the parades.

Medicine man John Pretty On Top, never without the deerskin-wrapped medicine bundle on a thong around his neck, has participated in every aspect of Crow Fair. He says those morning parades are the vital center of the five-day celebration; they keep alive Crow arts, giving clan members a chance to use the precious artifacts held in their families for generations. "The parade is a good way to show young people the use, the value of these things," says Pretty On Top.

In tribute to their modern warriors, the Crows choose veterans from World War II, Korea and Vietnam to lead the morning parades. In uniform and medals, they carry the flags of the Crow Nation, of Montana and of the United States. Crows of all ages follow, dressed in the finest regalia of their ancestors. Young mothers cradling their babies ride on original high-backed Indian saddles; children wrapped up like teddy bears in buckskin and beads sit on the hoods of cars spread with buffalo robes and Pendleton blankets; clan members dance and drum on flatbed trailer floats. Montana politicians, the Christian Cowboys, local celebrities and Indian princesses from a dozen other tribes are scattered through the procession.

It is a breathtaking sight, as it must have been 150 years ago when Crow bands streamed across mountains and prairies to their summer celebration. The fleet Crow horses, manes and tails woven with eagle feathers, wore ornate saddles, breast collars and bridles. Their long-haired riders wore buckskins quilled and tasseled with ermine tails and scalplocks; their eagle-feather head-dresses sailed on the wind.

"No part of the human race could present a more picturesque and thrilling appearance on horseback," wrote painter George Catlin in 1832, "than a party of Crows rigged out in all their plumes and trappings—galloping about and yelping in what they call a war parade." Catlin said that he and fur traders of the era thought the Crows ("beautifully clad, handsome and gentlemanly") surpassed all other Plains tribes for their high sense of honor and fearless pride.

Each August that graceful, bold Crow world of the buffalo days is resurrected—not for tourists, though they are welcome to witness the spectacle, but for the reunion of family and clan, and for the celebration of a culture still nurtured by the 7,000 Crow people.

Source

Travel and Leisure, Volume 19, #3, 127-28. From an article entitled "Powwow!" by Constance Poten. [Reprinted with permission from *Travel and Leisure,* March, 1989. Copyright © 1989 American Express Publishing Corporation. All rights reserved.]

La Percíngula

August 2

Francis of Assisi (1182?-1226), one of the greatest of the Christian saints, was distinguished for his joyous piety, ascetism, and compassion. The son of a prosperous merchant, his extravagant generosity to the poor caused his father so much concern that he had him legally disinherited. Soon thereafter, he began to minister to lepers near Assisi and to frequent a ruined chapel known as *Porciúncola* which he rebuilt and is said to have punningly called his "portion" or "little inheritance." It was here that he sensed his vocation and though a layman began to preach and gather disciples. In 1209, he received papal permission that led to the establishment of the Franciscan order. He died on October 3, 1226. His feast day is October 4 (see p. 359).

A Feast of St. Francis

Among the traditions and customs [in northern New Mexico and southern Colorado] that are on the verge of disappearing is a feast dating back to the 13th century that is particularly interesting because of the manner in which it has evolved. This feast is usually known as *La Percíngula,* but it is also called *La Precíngula*; the two forms are New Mexican variants of the Spanish *Porciúncula* (from Italian).

Porciúncula, Italian diminutive from of *Porción,* was the name given to a small portion of the land in the neighborhood of Assisi, Italy, which the monks of St. Benedict gave to St. Francis. It was also the name given to the little chapel in ruins on that piece of land, the place where St. Francis experienced his religious vocation. It was in this chapel, which the saint restored from a dilapidated state to a habitable dwelling, that he received revelations and supernatural grace from God. For this reason he always spoke of it with the greatest of reverence, advising his followers never to abandon it and declaring that whosoever should pray in it with fervor would be heard.

The name *Porciúncula* was also given to the plenary indulgence that could be gained by visiting this sanctuary on August 2d. This grace, according to tradition, was granted to St. Francis by Christ in 1221. Shortly afterward it was recognized canonically by Pope Honorius III, who set August 2d of each year as the date on which the visit to the temple should be made. Later, the time was extended so that the visit could be made at any time between the afternoon of August 1st and sunset of the following day. The indulgence could be gained at first only in the *Porciúncula,* but in 1480 Pope Sixtus IV extended it to all the churches of the First and Second Orders of St. Francis, and in 1622 Pope Gregory XV granted the same privilege to all the churches of the Capuchins. The act of devotion that was to be performed consisted of confession, the receiving of Holy Communion, and the visitation of one of the churches designated. Later in the same century the privilege was extended not only to all the churches of the Third Order, but also to all churches with which the Franciscans were connected in any way, including non-Franciscan churches in which the Third Order held its meetings. It must have been through this channel that the observance of the feast was brought to New Mexico by the early Spanish settlers, for the *penitentes* or flagellant brothers, the sponsors of the feast in New Mexico, appear to be an outgrowth of the Third Order of St. Francis. The strange thing about the existence of the feast in New Mexico is that it is not general. In fact, I know of only one place where it is observed either in southern Colorado or in New Mexico, and that is in the little town of Arroyo Hondo, about eighty miles north of Santa Fe and about forty miles south of the Colorado-New Mexico boundary.

The feast is observed under the auspices of the flagellant brothers, who take full charge of all the ceremonies, though anyone may partake in it. Formerly, according to one of my informers, the preparations were in the hands of some kind of lay sisters—apparently female members of the flagellant organization, but my informer was vague about them. At present, the preparations are under the direct care of several *mayordomos* or sponsors selected from among the *Penitente* brotherhood.

In the village of Arroyo Hondo a double observance of the feast is held. In this place there are two plazas, both of which are hemmed in by flat-roofed adobe houses, as is usual in most New Mexican villages. The two plazas are about a mile apart from each other and each has its own *morada,* or chapter house. Since their origin, there has always been a certain amount of rivalry between the two branches, and on religious feast days each one celebrates the particular feast independently of the other. With regard to *La Prorciúncula,* this was not always the case. Previous to 1902, the feast was observed only in the place where the main church is situated, and under the auspices of the *morada* near the church; but in that year the double celebration of the feast came into being.

The feast is observed on the eve of August 2d and the ceremonies consist of a *velorio* or wake. The wake begins after it grows dark. Prayers are recited and *alabados* or hymns are sung in alternation. Formerly, the chief ceremony used to take place about nine o'clock. An outdoor procession started from the church's main entrance and was led by several of the faithful, who carried the images of St. Francis of Assisi and other saints. The people, each person carrying a lighted candle, lined up in two single files, one on each side of the street. At intervals of fifteen or twenty yards along the way there would be *luminarias* or bonfires, which were lighted just as the procession started.

Shortly before the church procession began, another procession from the *morada,* a quarter of a mile away, got under way. In this procession, only the members of the flagellant brotherhood took part. In it there were usually eight or ten barefooted *penitentes,* naked above the waist. The only clothing they wore was a pair of homemade drawers, and a handkerchief with which they covered their faces. These flagellants scourged themselves, as the procession progressed, with disciplines made from the palmlike leaves of the *amole* or soap plant. Seldom did they ever carry the *moraderos,* or heavy wooden crosses, used in their other religious ceremonies. The flagellants were accompanied by other members of the fraternity dressed in their usual street clothes. The accompanying brothers sang an *alabado,* or a member of the organization played an *alabado* melody on a homemade flute. This group joined the end of the main procession, which advanced slowly around the church. During the procession, the rosary was recited out loud by the faithful, a leader reciting the first part of the "Our Father" and the "Hail Mary" and the rest of the people reciting the second part. Before the beginning of each decade, the appropriate mystery [Mass] was sung, during which the procession stopped. When the singing of the mystery ended, the recitation of the rosary continued and the procession advanced slowly. The progress of the procession around the church was timed so that the recitation of the rosary should end just as the head of the procession reached the main entrance to the church once

more. The people entered the church and the flagellant brothers returned to the *morada* in the same manner in which they had come. Thereafter, the singing of *alabados* continued throughout the night. Toward midnight, dinner was served in a neighboring house. The dinner was prepared under the direction of the sponsors and at the expense of all the members of the fraternity. Everybody, whether a member of the community or a stranger, was invited to partake of the repast.

About one o'clock in the morning a second procession of flagellant brothers would visit the wake, in the same way as before, but this time they would enter the church and stay there for some time, returning then to the *morada.* The self-flagellation went on in the church as well as during the procession. As to what took place in the *morada,* no one knows, for only the members of the society are permitted to enter on such occasions and they keep absolute secrecy about their indoor ceremonies. At the wake the singing of *alabados* went on till dawn, at which time everybody went home.

Such was the practice thirty years ago, and at that time hundreds of persons attended the ceremonies, many of whom traveled from villages seventy miles away, a remarkable thing when one realizes that it meant a two days' journey over mountain roads. But things have changed a great deal since then. In the summer of 1940, when I attended the feast, I was surprised to find that it had almost completely disappeared. Instead of the hundreds of persons who used to partake in the ceremonies, there were fewer than thirty. Some religious hymns were sung, and the rosary was recited out loud, but the colorful procession of former years was omitted entirely and, of course, there were no flagellants. The wake did not last all night, as it used to do, and on the whole there was very little of the old enthusiasm. The participants were men and women of the older generations.

Source and Comment

California Folklore Quarterly, I (1942), 83-86. Juan B. Rael investigated "popular Spanish traditions and customs which up to 1910 enjoyed undisputed sway among New Mexicans," among them the feast honoring St. Francis of Assisi surviving in the New Mexican village of Arroyo Hondo. This village "has almost always been without a priest" and hence its religious practices have drifted from official Catholic tradition. Cf. *velorio* in "Birthday Party for the Virgin of Guadalupe," p. 430. For Easter observances of the *penitentes,* see "The Penitentes," p. 169. See also "St. Francis of the Pets," p. 359.

Assumption Day

August 15

Assumption Day, which commemorates the bodily ascent of the Virgin Mary into Heaven after her death, dates from the fourth century, but the Assumption was not dogma until Pius XII ruled it so in 1950. Nonetheless, as early as the ninth century the festival was a major one, and it is now considered the prime feast day of the Virgin Mother. It is a Christianization of an earlier Artemis harvest feast, and in much of Europe the celebration is called the Feast of Our Lady of the Harvest.

Harvest Festival for Our Lady of the Flowers

In Poland, whence came the vigorous, hard-working, black dirt farmers of Florida and Pine Island in Orange County [New York], the people made merry at harvest time in the *Dozynki Pod Debami,* the Festival Under the Oaks. The joys of that festival never faded from the memories of these sturdy folk, and in 1939 and 1940 they held their beloved Dozynki again. Only this time the wheat fields of Poland became the black dirt meadows of Orange County, and choice Orange County onions took the place of golden sheaves of wheat. And this time it was their American-born children and grandchildren who trod the measures of its lively dances.

August fifteenth, which Catholics in the United States observe as the Feast of the Assumption, is a day set aside by Americans of Polish ancestry for honoring the Blessed Mother under the title of Our Lady of the Flowers. It is the fiesta of the wheat harvest in Poland, a holiday as well as a holy day. August fifteenth had always been a holiday for the Polish black dirt growers of Orange County, though they had never held a formal celebration before.

August fifteenth, 1939, then, was a holiday of holidays, and the spirit of fiesta and celebration burst into life the instant dawn came to the little Polish communities. Out of sight went the blue overalls, kerchiefs, and big straw hats, and every member of the family dressed in his or her best for *Dozynki* day.

Though work was temporarily forgotten and merrymaking the order of the day, these humble Polish folk did not forget that it was also a day of thanksgiving, and entire families attended morning Mass, bringing with them bouquets of flowers and bags of seed for next year's harvest. These were blessed by the priest who prayed that next year's harvest would be as fruitful.

Then—on to the village of Florida, near where the giant motorcade was to start. Excitedly, people poured into Florida's streets, which were literally banked with piles of ten-pound bags of onions donated by the growers and purchased by visitors as souvenirs as they awaited the arrival of the parade.

At last, it hove into sight—some fifty spectacular floats in a dazzling line. One saw historical floats, depicting the arrival of the Polish immigrants in America, the clearing and draining of the lands, the old and modern methods of production, fleeting pictures of the progress of Orange County's onion industry. There was the float of the Auxiliary of the Polish Legion of American Veterans showing an American flag made of onions, and that of the Florida Board of Education—a ship with a swivel gun on its afterdeck which actually shot onions along the parade route. Then the longbearded "Ex-Onion King" (bowing out to the Harvest Queen) who sat mournfully on his throne of onions, and the pageant dancers themselves aboard a huge truck. There were all kinds of commercial floats, and floats bearing a 16-piece Polish-American orchestra from New York and the Florida Firemen's Band. And, of course, Queen Martha, with yards of white tulle flowing to her feet and gay flowers in her hair, seated on a pale blue chair on a platform of snowy white, surrounded by her fair courtiers who were gowned in yellow. Selected from among many contenders, Martha was, according to the contest rules, a member of an onion grower's family and had herself worked in the onion fields.

Passing first before the reviewing stand at Florida, the procession wended its way on a gala 40-mile tour of the countryside.

Late that afternoon, the thousands already gathered at the pageant site heard the sound of music and singing, and soon the motorcade swung through the gates (made of onions, of course!). One by one, each car entered the field, making way finally for Queen Martha. Smiling and waving, she rode up to the platform, bowed to the audience, and with her court in attendance, descended to take her seat to review the harvest festival.

Then suddenly, breaking the eager silence that had fallen over the multitudes in the field, came a fanfare of trumpets blown by four red- and white-coated men on horseback, heralding the arrival of the harvest procession. A bit of old Poland sprang to life—the *Dozynki Pod Debami* had begun!

The gay, hearty music of accordions rang out as a colorful Polish orchestra followed the couriers onto the field atop a load of hay, the men dressed in gay peppermint-stick trousers, shiny black boots, vivid tunics, and jaunty hats. Then, in gala array, the pageant characters appeared—the *Szlachcic* and the *Szlachcianka*—the Lord and Lady of the Manor, resplendent figures in rich blue satin trimmed with imitation ermine; the *Staroscina* (the pageant queen) and her escort, the *Starosta* (the outstanding male worker) carrying a Maypole of onions bedecked with colored streamers; a peasant maiden selected as the *Przodownica* or harvest wreath-bearer; four gaily dressed little girls bearing harvest offerings and, with them, all the pageant dancers, representing the inhabitants of the Polish village.

The pageant characters paused to hear the choral group of 200 young children whose clear, well-blended voices rose first in America's national anthem and then in "*Jeszcze Polska Nie Zginela*," the national anthem of Poland, with one of the talented young women of the community as soloist. Wrinkled women, their hair tied back with scarves, rose from the seats they had found in the field and stood by their aged husbands, many of whom had seen fifty years of varying fortune in the onion business. Together their lips gave forth the familiar words which as youths they sang in Poland. Tears came to their eyes to be hastily brushed away—for were they not sturdy people and had they not much to be thankful for?

Following a welcome by Father Felczak, chairman of the pageant committee, the pageant proceeded. The harvesters, having presented themselves at the Manor House, stood proudly by as the *Przodownica* presented the mammoth wreath of onions, flowers, and colored ribbon to the Lord and Lady. The *Starosta* and the *Staroscina* bowed to the Lord and Lady, and the four little girls carrying baskets of choice onions (symbolic of the harvest gifts made in Poland) also made their presentation to the Lord and Lady. The priest stepped forth to bless the harvest gifts and led the villagers in prayers of thanksgiving.

Then the spirit of merriment and celebration broke out anew as the villagers, accepting the invitation of the Lord and Lady to take part in the harvest festival in the courtyard, performed the traditional Polish dances....

Also included on the program was the *Trojak Cebulowy*, or Onion Dance, created especially for the festival. Little girls

in white with Kelly green skirts and matching bonnets, and little boys in blue overalls and straw hats depicted the activities of the onion grower. To a jaunty rhythm, they interpreted the sowing of the seeds, weeding and cultivating, picking and preparing onions for market, selling and returning from market with full pockets.

It was sunset before the dances were finished, making a striking background for the lithe young dancers, their faces aglow, stamping their booted feet in gay abandon or moving lightly in more stately tempo. The Polish parents in the audience, beating their feet and nodding to the lilt of the accordions, were justly proud of the vivid picture their sons and daughters made against the sky of coming evening.

Then suddenly it was over and the blonde young narrator who had been explaining the movements of the dances told the listeners, "That is all," and made way for Lieutenant Governor Poletti and State Senator Desmond to speak. After the addresses, the crowning of Queen Martha, and the final chorus of "God Bless America," the crowd departed....

Source and Comment

New York Folklore Quarterly, II (1946), 197, 199-204. Betty Jane Wright reports on the revival of "the Polish *Dozynki* in an American setting," among farm families of Polish background in "one of the richest onion-producing areas in the United States." The elaborate American celebration, according to Wright, may have originated with a local newspaper editor or one of the parish priests but more likely "it just came about as a result of a mutual wish of all the farm folk to celebrate the successful development of their rich black lands...." The continuity of folk tradition is evident in the choice of the Feast of the Assumption for the harvest celebration which, she notes, "had always been a holiday for the Polish black dirt farmers of Orange County."

* * *

Blessing Herbs and Spices on Assumption Day

On the morning of the Feast of the Assumption (15 August), housewives [in Czech-American farming communities of Iowa and Minnesota] bring their kitchen herbs and spices to church to be blessed by the priest. It is hoped that the blessing will protect the home from evils and add to the well-being of the family. The origin of this rite is obscure, but the appropriateness of this day for blessing herbs and spices is suggested in the Lesson for the Assumption: "I gave a sweet smell like cinnamon and aromatic balm: I yielded a sweet odor like the best myrrh" (Ecclesiasticus 24:15).

Source and Comment

Journal of American Folklore, LXIX (1956), 284. From Lawrence V. Ryan's "Some Czech-American Forms of Divination and Supplication." For his sources, see note on "St. Barbara's Day Prediction," p. 425. This custom is also common to the Polish.

Rites for the Feast of the Assumption

The Feast of the Assumption of the Virgin is a very popular one in Buffalo [New York] and is especially associated with the Church of Our Lady, Help of Christians. This church was built as fulfillment of a vow by a nineteenth century immigrant who was almost shipwrecked on the way to America and is a well-known local healing shrine. Many people still walk to the shrine from their homes on this day, often a distance of ten miles or more. Services are held outdoors at a grotto built by members of the parish. Behind the altar in the grotto there is a double flight of rough stone steps lined with the Stations of the Cross. Most worshipers go around the Stations, occasionally on their knees or barefoot. At the top of the steps are several rather crude statues, two of which appear to represent the Virgin. Petitioners leave rosaries, holy pictures, articles of costume jewelry and scarves around the statues, as well as little pieces of paper with their requests written on them. During the day several masses are celebrated, unction is administered, a relic of St. Anne is displayed, and Benediction is performed, after a Sacrament procession around the extensive grounds of the church.

Source and Comment

Indiana Folklore, IX (1976), 167. Collected by Lydia Marie Fish. For her sources, see note on "St. Joseph's Day Feast," p. 132. Her main interest is "traditional religion." The parishioners are of various ethnic origins including Irish, Puerto Rican, Italian, Polish and German.

* * *

Flowers to Prevent Lightning

On August fifteenth [Polish-American] children would take bouquets of flowers, an apple and a carrot were included, to the church to be blessed. The bouquets were then dried and placed in the attic to prevent lightning from striking the house. (My grandmother used to place the flowers in the attic, but today after being blessed, the flowers are placed about the house.)

Source

New York Folklore Quarterly, XXIV (1968), 304. Reported by Robert Maziarz. See "Polish Christmas Eve Supper," p. 440 and note, p. 441, for background and informants.

* * *

Awaiting a Miracle on Mary's Day

More than 5,000 pilgrims braved temperatures in the 90s [at Lubbock, Texas] and camped under beach umbrellas Monday to recite the rosary in hopes of a miracle.

Thousands of worshipers began arriving during the morning with lawn chairs, coolers and blankets to stake out a spot for an evening outdoor mass of the Feast of the Assumption. Monday was the Catholic feast of the ascension of the Virgin Mary into heaven.

By early afternoon, police Col. Ray Huffman estimated the crowd at St. John Neumann Catholic Church at more than 5,000 and growing.

The charismatic parish in West Texas attracted national attention after three parishioners said they received messages from the Virgin Mary last spring.

Mike Slate, Mary Constancion and Theresa Werner said Mary promised miracles on her holy day. Later, however, they said Mary would send no messages Monday.

"She said this is her day and she will be with us and there won't be any messages," Msgr. Joseph James said.

Phones rang almost constantly in the church office, where volunteers fielded questions from people planning to attend the service. Hundreds of callers requested prayers of healing, said parishioner Ron Trimmel.

On the grounds, parish members and priests laid hands on the pilgrims and prayed.

Hundreds of people using wheelchairs or walkers settled on the grassy hillside beneath a 60-foot-long altar built atop the church office.

"I heard that Mary's crown was spinning on the statue inside the church last night, so I believe anything can happen," Marilyn Oliver said as she stepped off a bus with 43 other Catholics from East Texas.

Parish officials did not confirm the rumor about the crown.

The reported messages at the church came after James and several parishioners returned from Medugorje, Yugoslavia, where six youths have claimed to see apparitions of Mary since 1981.

One group skeptical of the reports said the trip and the beginning of the messages were too coincidental to be believable.

"While we are certainly open to any verifiable paranormal events, so far the only amazing thing that has happened here is the fact that thousands of people would flock here from all over," said Harvey Madison, spokesman for West Texans to Promote Rational Thought.

Source

Charlotte Observer, August 18, 1988.

Anniversary of Elvis Presley's Death
August 16

Elvis Aaron (he often spelled it "Aron") Presley was born to a truck driver and a sewing-machine operator in Tupelo, Mississippi, on January 8, 1935. By his late teens he was locally successful as a country singer, appearing at the Grand Ole Opry and on Louisiana Hayride. He got his big break in the mid-1950s with appearances on the Jackie Gleason and Ed Sullivan television shows, and with an RCA recording contract. Using a variety of styles based on black and white gospel singing, on black blues, and even on light opera, he had one smash record after another, defining a rock-and-roll style which became the symbol of teen-age rebellion and culture. A gifted performer with a versatile voice, and suggestively good-looking, he would, as one critic described it, "make love to the mike", gyrating and "un-huh-ing." In Bob Hope's words, he was "wearing his trousers out from the inside." Songs like "Don't Be Cruel," "Teddy Bear," "Love Me Tender," and "I'm All Shook Up"—along with a host of movies—made him a fortune.

Unfortunately his private life was a confusion of drinking, dope, indulgence, and unsuccessful love affairs. In 1977 at the age of 42 Presley died on a bathroom floor of heart failure. However, his commercial appeal and following were so great that a host of imitators, his old managers and associates, his wife Priscilla, and his old girl friends have continued to make money from his name. His lavish home at Graceland in Memphis has become a shrine. Each year a tribute week honoring his death brings thousands of tourists, fans, and other curiosity seekers to the town. Whether the week and the Presley cult will continue into generations who did not see him is moot. Elvis' followers and the people who make money from his name have given him the trappings of a true folk hero. Guarding his memory, they have created what one might call a modern, pseudo-religious festival.

Taking Care of Elvis

There is the woman from Paris who goes every morning to the Meditation Garden behind Elvis Presley's home to sit by his grave and cry.

There is the 7-year-old boy from Boone, Iowa, who wears a gold suit and walks among the boozey hard trade of a bottom-line barroom to sing "Blue Suede Shoes" and throw scarves to screaming ladies, just as Elvis did.

There is Sunny Burke, the man from New Orleans who paints cars for a living and admits he's broke because he's spent $17,000 turning his pickup truck into a rolling tribute to Elvis. The grill says "Elvis1" and the bug screen says "The King Lives On Forever" in quarter-inch steel.

And there are tens of thousands more who have come here, turned pilgrims and sometimes poets by a man who in his pathetic, lonely death gave them a warm and comfortable way to make a mean, crazy world stand. still.

The people who have jammed Memphis for Elvis Presley Tribute Week—which climaxes today, the 10th anniversary of his death—are almost exclusively white and far from wealthy.

They do little else outside home, work and family but honor Elvis. He and Graceland, his home, are their Rotary Club, their trip to the Bahamas. They care not so much for the music as the man, who they believe handled fame and wealth as it should be handled and never got uppity.

As they wait in often-bored obligation to board the tours buses for yet another look at Graceland; as they move through the souvenir shops to consider Elvis beach towels, baby clothes, Love Me Tender Moisturizing Cream and clocks that feature pink Cadillac second hands; as they participate in the attendant rituals of trivia and impersonator contests, they seem united in an almost defiant willingness to forgive and, in many cases, forget.

They forgive Elvis his flabby death-by-excess on a bathroom floor. They forgive or refuse to acknowledge his slide from raw, greasy rocker to a paunchy self-parody who sang "My Way" in American Eagle jumpsuits.

But they do not forgive the transgressors. They do not forgive his wife, Priscilla, for leaving him. They do not forgive Lucy de Barbin, the Louisiana lady who claims to have been Elvis's lover for 24 years and wrote a book about it. "Lucy Lied" pins were big sellers in Memphis this week.

They say crude, nasty things about Albert Goldman who wrote a scathing Elvis biography that details bizarre sexual habits. Peggy Sue Sosebee of Atlanta, who teaches her grandchildren to say "Elvis" before they say anything else, says she wrote to Goldman to ask how many whorehouses he visited in order to be able to compare Graceland to one. He didn't write back.

Sosebee, who wears a jumpsuit covered in Elvis patches, owns some burned-out wires from Elvis's stove, a piece of carpet and a dimmer switch from Graceland, and the needle and thread used to sew up Elvis's pants when they split during a concert in Alabama.

"If you're not an Elvis fan, you can't understand," she said, reciting what has become a fairly typical response to the prevailing question, "What does it all mean?"

There is a reassuring "us against them" feeling in the blind love of Elvis that in some ways reflects the singer's own flamboyant rejection of how a rich man in America should live.

And the people who run the great money mill that Graceland has become do nothing to dispel it. Todd Morgan, Graceland's communications director and its bubbling, forever-up answer to Pat Sajak, told fans to be polite to reporters who ask them what it all means.

He told them reporters often just don't understand and end up spreading foul thoughts about The King.

As with anything that approaches a religion—and the worship of Elvis surely does—there is an accepted gospel and articles of faith.

The devoted know that Elvis was a good man who gave away Cadillacs and houses, loved his mother, had perfect Southern manners, contributed to charity, didn't go to orgies and didn't like liquor.

"And he brought together more people in love than anyone else in the world, including Jesus," said Grace Bledsoe of Adel, Ga., whose Elvis fan club won the first Elvis window-decorating contest, in 1981."

But the fans, the true fans and not the tourists, know, too, that Elvis was vulnerable, that he was badly used, that he didn't have good people around him when he needed good people most.

"He was very vulnerable," says Prof. Charles Wilson of the Center for the Study of Southern Culture at the University of Mississippi. "His talent was an intuitive talent, not intellectual. There was great feeling, sentiment, passion. But he was not a particularly shrewd or clever person who could have coped with the pressure."

It is in the vulnerability, in the real or imagined betrayal by those closest to him, that many who come to the Memphis shrine seem to forge their strongest link with Elvis.

There is the feeling that if only they could have been there to help, to undo the wrong done by others, one of rock 'n' roll's most bizarre tragedies might not have occurred.

So they wear bracelets, pendants and pins that say "TCE" for "Taking Care of Elvis." It is a loving, post-mortem variation on the "TCB," or "Taking Care of Business," motto that Elvis plastered on just about everything, including his two private jets, the Lisa Marie and Teddy Bear.

They take care of Elvis by pouring their money into Graceland to assure that it will always be there for them to come back to. They raise money for many of the same charities to which Elvis generously contributed. They fashion their hair into jet-black helmets with sideburns down to the jawline. Some even indulge in a bit of morbid resurrection.

"You'll probably think I'm crazy, but I don't think he's dead," said Sonny Burke, the car painter from New Orleans who has blown his savings on his pickup truck. "That could have been a dummy they put in that coffin."

Not too many agree with Sonny, but some do.

Artie Mentz, who comes from Dubuque, Iowa, and has been called "Dubuque's Own Elvis" because of his alleged striking resemblance to Presley, does not believe that Elvis is alive.

He also thinks some people put Elvis a little too close to Jesus. After all, says Mentz, those problems with the prescription drugs have been pretty well verified.

But Mentz, who works as a professional Elvis impersonator, believes he has a mission, and the mission is Elvis.

"An Elvis impersonator is like a priest to a church," he said. "He gives that performance Elvis can't give anymore."

Mentz was standing in the haze of Bad Bob's-Vapors nightclub, where he is appearing nightly and competing in a week-long impersonator contest. On stage was 7-year-old Jamie Kelley of Boone, Iowa. Jamie, in the gold suit, made the finals.

His father, who opted for black leather, got knocked out in the preliminaries. His mother wore a low-cut dress and handed him the scarves that he, in turn, handed to the dutifully frenzied women near the stage.

It was a week to flaunt it, to sneer the way Elvis sneered, to be an Elvis fan in the protective circle of other Elvis fans. They left behind the derision they admit they sometimes suffer at the hands of the heretics back home.

"To fans, Elvis is a martyr," said Michael Stern who co-wrote the book *Elvis World* with his wife, Jane. "That's one of the central themes to Elvis. When [television host] Steve Allen made him put on a tux and sing to a basset hound, the fans hated it.

"That was one of the first attempts to put him down. The blinders the fans put on is a reaction to that. They feel an obligation and a duty to blindly defend him for all they got from him. When they say 'taking care of Elvis,' that's what they really do."

The Sterns, who have made careers out of writing about roadside food in America, think they know why Elvis lives on.

"He lived a life every poor boy dreams of," said Michael Stern. "He didn't get into a stock portfolio; he gave away Cadillacs. And fans love that house. It is to interior decoration what "Hound Dog" and "Jailhouse Rock" were to the popular music of the '50s."

At Humes High School, on Manassas Street, where Elvis graduated in 1953, black students dressed in blue shirts and ties are conducting tours of the rooms where Elvis sort of studied and of the auditorium that bears his name and where he sang "Old Shep" in a school talent show.

Still, Humes students know they belong to a different musical era.

Stephanie Tate, who will be a ninth-grader this fall, said that Elvis means a lot to the students at Humes because he went to the same school they do. But she said she likes [singer] Whitney Houston a lot more.

Source and Comment

Providence Journal Bulletin, August 16, 1987. Edited from an article by Bob Kerr, staff writer. This article and the following one reveal that Presley's fans have treated his life and career in much the same way that they treat their heroes. The ideas that he may still be alive, that his end was a sort of martyrdom, that his mission was religious, distinguish him from other cult figures of the entertainment world such as Marilyn Monroe, James Dean, and John Lennon. The tribute week in Memphis has attained festival status within only a decade.

* * *

Did Elvis Fake His Death?

Elvis Presley is alive, if the King faked his own funeral and has been hiding out somewhere for the last 11 years. Ann Dinsik figures he could do a lot worse than Vicksburg.

"He'd need a place like this, kind of out of the way and quiet where he wouldn't be bothered much," said Mrs. Dinsik, talking from behind the counter at the Malt Shoppe, an ice cream parlor in this town of 2,800 people in southwestern Michigan. "I mean, look at the way people are. They wouldn't even let the man be dead."

There has been a lot of talk like that over the last year in Vicksburg, ever since a local woman, Louise Welling, began telling people that she saw Elvis Presley—she says she is absolutely certain it was he—standing in checkout line No. 2 one Sunday at Felpausch's Supermarket.

He was wearing a white jumpsuit, she said, and paying for an electrical fuse. "I was so dumbfounded I couldn't speak," she said. She remembers that he seemed nervous, as someone might who had something to hide.

She went straight to the editors at The Commercial Express, the weekly newspaper in town, but they didn't believe her. Neither did reporters at The Kalamazoo Gazette. But she found an ear at The Weekly World News, a supermarket tabloid published from Lantana, Fla.

"Elvis is Alive!" the newspaper bannered last May. "The King admits his funeral was faked and tells of secret life in Michigan!"

They printed it all, not only that Elvis shopped at Felpausch's, but was seen eating at a nearby Burger King and was probably living in an old hotel in downtown Kalamazoo, about 10 miles away. . . .

Radio stations and disk jockeys from California to New York called Felpausch's, demanding interviews with clerks. In Kalamazoo, someone filed petitions nominating Elvis Presley as a Republican candidate for precinct delegate, and Mayor Ed Annen fielded telephone calls from reporters around the country.

Mr. Annen said, "I told them that everyone knows this is where he lives and that they should send their residents here to spend tourist dollars to find him."

With the news that Elvis had patronized Felpausch's, a rival supermarket put out its own sign: "Jimmy Hoffa Shops Here." The Main Street restaurant introduced "Don't Be Cruel" bean soup on its menu. Next door, a dentist advertised: "The King gets regular check-ups here."

As it turns out, what happened here was only an early symptom of a much wider mania that in recent months has resulted in a barrage of other sightings and dubious reports, circulated in the tabloid press: grainy telephoto pictures of a man said to be Elvis standing in a Las Vegas parking lot; the purported discovery by astronomers of a statue of Elvis on Mars.

Then there was the book published earlier this year by an Atlanta woman offering evidence that Elvis, exhausted and overwhelmed by his fans, staged his own death and funeral in 1977 and went into hiding.

Mrs. Welling says the book certainly persuaded her; she believes he still lives in the area, but has now adopted a beard as a disguise.

Source

New York Times, October 17, 1988. From a column, "Vicksburg Journal," by William E. Schmidt. Copyright 1988 by The New York Times Company. Reprinted by permission.

*   *   *

Elvis and an NFL Exhibition Game

Forget about winning one for The Gipper.

The [New England] Patriots wanted to win this one for The King.

As the Pats kicked off here last night in the Liberty Bowl against the [Houston] Oilers, Elvis International Tribute Week did, too.

Tuesday marks the 11th anniversary of the death of Elvis Presley, who is buried here at his mansion, Graceland. And, in memory of the King of Rock and Roll, a week-long series of events has been planned.

If you want to talk excitement, well, there is far more to be found during Elvis International Tribute Week than you ever could hope to see in an NFL [National Football League] preseason game.

You could attend the Aloha From Graceland Luau, inspired by Elvis' 1961 movie, Blue Hawaii, on Wednesday.

You could go see a "Visions of Elvis" art exhibit—don't you just loooove that velvet texture, Jim Bob—? or stop in at the Elvis Fan Festival being hosted by the Elvis Presley Burning Love Fan Club from Streamwood, Ill.

Not to be outdone, the Then, Now and Forever Elvis Presley Fan Club of Memphis is sponsoring an open house for Elvis fans at the Pizza Hut at 429 Elvis Presley Boulevard, which used to be plain, old Bellevue Ave., Route 51.

You could tour Humes Junior High School, which was a high school when Elvis graduated in 1953, or attend the Elvis Memorial Service being conducted Tuesday at the Memphis State University Theater, or even take part in the fifth annual Elvis Presley Memorial Karate Tournament.

Then there's the "Elvis: Legacy in Light" laser light show at the Pink Palace Planetarium, or you could tap your blue

suede shoes while watching the Memphis State Pompon Squad dance to the music from Jailhouse Rock.

Last night's halftime show was a bowl-game type extravaganza, featuring Andy Childs, an Elvis impersonator—oops, ahem, an Elvis *stylist*.

The emotional highlight of the week, of course, is the candlelight vigil, which begins at 10 tomorrow night at Graceland and lasts until the last fan in the procession has walked up the mansion drive to Elvis grave in Meditation Garden. Last year, that wasn't until after sunrise.

Such devotion is understandable to Patriots guard Ron Wooten.

"I've been to Graceland," said Wooten, who grew up in North Carolina. "It was one of the high points of my life."

Asked if he was an Elvis fan, Wooten replied: "Elvis doesn't have fans. They're more like worshippers. He has an unusual, god-like status. That's part of the package when you're one of the chosen few, one of the immortals."

Does Wooten believe The King lives still?

"He's alive in my heart," said Wooten. "He'll never die."

There are many who believe Elvis isn't dead.

"I was on a radio show in San Diego," Oilers coach Jerry Glanville said one day last week, "and there were people who called up who said they'd seen him. They said he's trimmed his sideburns and doesn't look as heavy as he used to."

Just in case Elvis might still be around, Glanville left a ticket for him last night at the "Will Call" window.

"There'll be a pass for him, left under the name of The King," Glanville said. "I hear Elvis is living now in Michigan or Minnesota. Well, we'd like him to come and be on our bench. I don't care how much weight he's gained. We still love him."

So do Patriots coach Raymond Berry and his wife, Sally.

"Some of the first money I ever spent was on Elvis records," Berry said last week at training camp at Bryant [College]. "I really dug Elvis.

"He started his rise to fame traveling through East Texas in the '50s. My wife saw him then. We were in on his rhythm wavelength."

Source

Providence Sunday Journal, August 14, 1988. From a sports column by Jim Donaldson. The final score was Houston, 27; New England, 13.

St. Bartholomew's Day

August 24

The apostle Bartholomew is believed to have been flayed alive in 44 A.D. for his faith. On his day a trade fair was held at Smithfield near London from 1133 until well into the nineteenth century. It soon became famous for riotous dissipations as well as the merchandise it offered. Ben Jonson's play *Bartholomew Fair* (1614) vividly depicts the folklife of the occasion during Jacobean times. In France, the date is memorable for the massacre of the Huguenots in 1572.

St. Bartholomew's Beliefs

If the 24th of August be bright and clear,
Then hope for a prosperous autumn that year.

All thunderstorms after St. Bartholomew's Day (Aug. 24th) are more or less violent.

Source

Memoirs of the American Folklore Society, XVIII (1925), 121. "Folk-Lore from Maryland," collected by Annie W. Whitney and Caroline C. Bullock. Informants not supplied.

African Methodist Quarterly Meeting

Last Sunday in August

The African Union Methodist Protestant Church was founded in Wilmington, Delaware, early in the nineteenth century as a black congregation and is the "Mother Church" for some eighty-seven congregations presently active. The idea for a "Big August Quarterly" was borrowed from the Quakers whose quarterly meetings combined religious observance, church business, and socializing.

Big August Quarterly

The Big August Quarterly has come back to downtown Wilmington [Delaware].

Once a rousing religious festival that drew tens of thousands of blacks from Delaware and surrounding states, the Big August Quarterly in recent years had dwindled to a gathering of a few dozen people.

But on Sunday [August 31, 1980], the once-a-year revival meeting returned in a big way to the spot where it began 167 years ago.

The Big August Quarterly celebrates the founding of the Mother African Union Methodist Protestant (A.U.M.P.) Church, incorporated in 1813 as the Union Church of Africans. It was the first independent black congregation in Wilmington.

The church was razed in 1966 to make way for Wilmington's new government complex, but the church's founder, Peter Spencer, is still buried beneath the plaza of the complex.

Sunday's activities began with a ceremony at the statue placed on his grave.

The crowd did not approach the size of some Big August Quarterlies—during its heyday in the years before World War II, it is said to have drawn as many as 30,000 people. But for old-timers and young folks alike, the 500 people who gathered on French Street were proof that the Big August Quarterly has survived the lean years of the last few decades.

"It was people from everywhere—Maryland, Virginia, all states," recalled Juanita Starling, 58, who said she had been coming to the Big August Quarterly all her life.

"After they moved the church, it really died out," she said. "But we've been trying to revive it, and I believe this is about the best crowd we've had. Some of these people I haven't seen for years. It's really nice."

Mrs. Starling and some friends were munching on fried chicken, collard greens and sweet potato pie dispensed by members of church and community groups in red and white striped tents that dotted the two blocks roped off for the celebration.

In 1805, Spencer, an influential black religious leader, led a group of 41 followers out of Wilmington's Asbury Methodist Church because the white members did not allow them full participation in the services. Under his guidance, some members of that group later formed the Union Church of Africans....

Spencer's meeting served both as a celebration for his own church and as a religious revival and social event for blacks throughout the region. Before the Civil War, slaves in the surrounding areas were given time off and safe-conduct passes to come to Wilmington for a weekend of nonstop revival preaching, gospel singing and reunions with friends and family.

The flavor of those early gatherings returned Sunday with the smell of soul food, the sounds of musical groups entertaining the crowd with a history of black music and the reminiscences of old-timers talking about Big August Quarterlies of earlier days.

Source

Philadelphia Inquirer, September 2, 1980. Special feature article by Sara Engram.

Jousting Tournaments

Usually Late Summer

The "tournament," a display of horsemanship and an expression of what was thought to be chivalric gallantry, flourished in the South after the publication of Sir Walter Scott's romantic novel, *Ivanhoe* (1819). Its direct ancestor was the Elizabethan tournament in which famous knights, such as Sir Philip Sidney, paraded their equestrian skill in tilting contests. Elaborate ceremony and flowery courtesy rather than serious military combat characterized both the Elizabethan and the Southern revivals of a feudal practice.

A Confederate Ring Tournament

The following letter, written by Emmet D. Cavett to his sister, Emma C. Cavett, and his plump cousin, Sallie Sale, both of whom had recently enrolled in Judson Female Institute at Marion, Alabama, describes the tournament. Its detail was inspired by the hope that it would amuse the young ladies, gloomy over their schoolwork, scornful of the food—there was too much corn bread and "rotten" bacon—and resentful of the elaborate restrictions imposed by the Alabama Baptists administering the seminary."

Head Quarters 3rd Corps A.N.Va. [Army of Northern Virginia]

Thursday April 14th 1864

Dear Sister & Cousin

Your very kind and long-looked for letters of the 27th ult. arrived here last evening and I hasten to answer, for I prize your and "Cousin Sally's" letters more than any others (always excepting those from home) that I receive.

I hardly know how to commence your letter but I believe I will describe as well as I can the grand Tournament and Coronation Ball given by the Officers of the third Corps and which excelled by far anything of the kind ever given by the A.N.Va.

The Tournament was to have taken place on the 5th of this month and then the Ball was to have been given on the evening of the 6th at 7 oclock in honor of the Queen of Love & Beauty and her Maids of Honor (of whom there were four).

Owing to the rain and bad weather it had to be postponed until last Monday and the Ball until last Tuesday evening.

Each Knight had to put in $30.00 apiece (and there was 50 Knights) and 50 Gentlemen subscribed $30.00 apiece for the privilege of attending the ball. The whole sum subscribed with $3000.00 (three thousand dollars), we sent the money to Richmond and foraged around in the surround-ing country and got up a most splendid Supper, Cake of all sorts and kinds, Icecream, Lemonade, Champagne, Candy, Chicken Salad, meats of all kinds and served in every style, Oysters in the greatest abundance, and every thing else that we could possibly get.

We had a large Ball room built and covered with tentflys. It was 50 feet long and 18 feet wide and capable of having three double sets dancing at once. It is needless to tell you I was one of the Knights. Monday came and by eleven (11) oclock a vast crowd of Citizens and Soldiers and about one hundred Ladys had assembled on the ground. . . .

All the Knights having assembled we proceeded to Register our names alphabetically and out of the 50 there were only 5 privates, (myself among the number), we were to ride 5 times apiece (and all had sabres) we had first to cut off a head on a post, next take a ring then cut a head on the ground and last take off a bag of straw (about the size of a man's head) from a pole, on the point of your Sabre. The Knights having registered they were formed in a line and addressed by Gen. Davis. [Joseph R. Davis, Jefferson Davis' nephew]. That being over we commenced riding Gen [A.R.] Wright calling out their names alphabetically and we starting at the Sounding of a bugle. Each Knight had told who (what young lady) he was riding for and she would send him a Rosette to designate her Knight. I was riding for Miss Kate Willis an elegant and accomplished young Lady of Orange, and I send you the rosette she sent me and which I wore at the Tournament and at the Ball (pinned over my heart).

By some means (that I have not been able to account for whether on account of looking so young or some other reason) I had gained the Sympathy of all the young Ladies and in fact of the whole crowd. They rode around until they got to me Gen. Wright called out my name. I mounted my Charger, the bugle sounded and I was off like the wind, (for recollect we all had to ride at full speed) I took the first one, took the ring cut off the lower head and took the last

318

one making a clean through (and by far the best ride that had been made) amid the cheers of the whole crowd and waving of the Lady's handkerchiefs.

Every time I rode through it was the signal for them to commence cheering and they did not stop until I regained my place in the line.

After the third ride I was ahead of all the Knights Gen. Davis (who you know is a Mississippian) stepped up to me and told me to go ahead and sustain Mississippi's bright reputation. We rode the five times and upon counting up found that a Georgia Captain and myself had tied for the first honors and consequently had to ride over. They cleared the track and we commenced. We rode three times and tied each time until riding through the fourth time I had taken everything up to the last Head and as I went to take that my horse slipped and I missed it. Capt Lucket came through and took it and consequently was proclaimed first Successful Knight. Gen. Wright then called out 12 names (myself and Lucket among the number) to ride for horsemanship.

Having built a high fence we made our horses jump it and whoever kept his saddle best was proclaimed best rider. We jumped twice and Lucket and 8 others were ruled out leaving Capt John Cage, Capt Heth (aidecamp and Brother of Gen. Heth) and myself were the ones left and we commenced riding for it. We rode about 6 times still it was so even that they could not come to any decision, at last the bugle sounded and we rode up to the stand and they announced Capt Cage the first best Horseman. Capt Heth as second, myself as third having written down the names of the Successfull Knights and who they wished to crown, we all formed and rode up in front of the audience, and Gen Wright read them out, and said the coronation would take place at the coronation Ball tomorrow night at 7 oclock Out of 50 Knights chosen from the whole corps I was very well satisfied to be put down as second successfull Knight and third for horsemanship.

As we were about to disperse, everybody commenced hallooing out, give the Courier another trial and to do Captain Lucket justice he expressed himself perfectly willing to do it, but of course I would not accept it. After I started on home Officers both that I was acquainted with and those that I was unacquainted with told me I ought to have been the first Successfull Knight and also first for Horsemanship. on the road Mrs A.P. Hill and about a dozen young ladies sent me word that in their estimation I deserved the place of first Successfull Knight as well as of best horsemanship. I thanked them and told them that I appreciated it a great deal more highly coming from the source it did than if it had been awarded me by the judges themselfs. And at the ball as soon as I was introduced to the Ladies they would commence complimenting me on my good riding and excellent horsemanship. We had two splendid Brass bands that discoursed sweet music to the ear. We had no Coronation as my Maid of Honor was unfortunately delayed on the road.

Each Successfull Knight danced the first set with the Lady he crowned and was allowed to carry her to supper.

As soon as they announced supper We all walked into the dining room of Mr Mavye house for the ball room was built in Mavye's yard and the Ladys reception room and the refreshment room was in his house.

No Gentlemen but the Successfull Knights and two or three committees (consisting each of 3 men) and the three or four General Officers that were present were allowed to come in the supper room Gen. Wright has two of the most intellectual and accomplished Daughters that I have ever had the pleasure of being acquainted with.

I got Miss Kate & the Misses Wright to-gather and waited on all of them. I told Gen. Wright just to step out of the way as I must have the pleasure of waiting on them.

Mrs Hill is one of the most pleasant Ladys that I have ever seen. I told her that if I had known that only the Successfull Knights were admitted in the dining room and to the first table it would have added renewed vigor to my efforts, and that next to Woman's Smiles it was the highest incentive a Soldier could have. Gen. A. P. Hill told me if he had been one of the judges I should have been awarded the prize of best horsemanship.

After supper we again resumed the dance and did not cease until broad daylight in the morning. I danced every set. I asked a Miss Bailey to dance with me the 5th set and she told me she was engaged and handed me her card. I took it off to the light and rubbed off Gen. Perry's name and put mine down. The 5th set came and we took our places and Gen. Perry stepped up and said that he was engaged for that set with Miss Bailey. I referred him to her card and before he could remonstrate the music struck up and they sung out all balance, and we left the old General standing there.

I carried on quite a flirtation with Miss Sallie Wright and think I would have lost my heart if it had not been lost before. . . .

Emmet D. Cavett.

To Cousin Sallie & Sister Emma
[Endorsed on back of last sheet]
You must take care of my Rosette for I appreciate it very much send it home.

E.D. Cavett.

Source and Comment

The Journal of Mississippi History, III (January, 1941), 289-96. In the original, a number of paragraphs of the letter were omitted. The present editors have dropped a few more lines. This tournament took place a month before the Army of Northern Virginia left winter quarters to take part in the battle of the Wilderness and was held April 11, 1864. Cavett, who was but 18, was nevertheless a veteran of two and one-half years service. A native of Noxubee County, Mississippi, he was enrolled in Company A of the 19th Regiment. Cavett survived the war and lived till 1910, active in Mississippi politics.

* * *

Old St. Joseph's Tournament

Records show the first tournament was held August 26, 1868, in connection with a festival arranged by the ladies of several churches in Talbot County [Maryland] at St. Joseph's and St. Peter's Catholic Church, Chapel District. Winner of the first tournament was S. W. Hopkins of Wye Mills. Colonel Sam Hambleton of Easton made the address at the crowning of the Queen.... The festival concluded with a second tournament on August 28, won by Charles C. Wilson of Warrington ... over 22 other contestants.

True to Southern tradition, the food served in connection with the tournaments is a much-enjoyed part of the event. Barbecues and picnics have been the most popular forms, and demonstrate the strong community spirit that still exists. Even today, this Southern tradition is being carried on with dinner served on the grounds by the Ladies of the Parish....

St. Joseph's tournament was held each year from 1868 to 1917 when Knights tried spearing the rings riding on the running board of automobiles rather than mounted on horses. The practice apparently did not prove popular because it, and the fact that quite a few riders were in the Armed Services, were cited as reasons for not holding the tournament in 1918. The tournament was revived in 1927 and has been held continuously since that time. It was in 1934 that Miss Betty Moore and Miss Frances Sullivant became the first women in the St. Joseph's Tournament.

Source and Comment

Horse Show and Tournament, August 1, 1979, 52-54. Extract from official program, published by St. Joseph's Roman Catholic Church of Cordova, Maryland, which sponsors it. The church, on the Eastern Shore, was founded in 1765.

Maryland officially calls itself "The Tournament State" and schedules its tournaments often in combination with horse shows, parades, and barbecues during August. Among them are the Dutch Picnic Jousting Tournament at Joppa; the Mechanicsville Jousting Tournament and Horse Pulling Contest; the Calvert County Jousting Tournament; and the St. Joseph's Tournament above.

Sacred Harp Singing
Summer, Weekends

Just before the American Revolution, a half-blind tanner and music-master, William Billings, invented a simple method which showed musically naive Americans how to sing what he called "fugues" (psalm-tunes) and anthems in harmony. He was very successful and his system, though scorned by the musical establishment, spread widely. The ultimate result of Billings' work was the "shape-note" songbook, in which the notes were distinguished by their shape as well as by their position on the staff. "Shape-note" singing quickly swept through rural America in the late 18th and early 19th centuries, hundreds of old hymns and folk tunes being arranged in this fashion by travelling and often musically naive preachers. The result has been a tradition of unconventional harmony and deep religious expression which has survived until today.

The "Original Sacred Harp" as published in Cullman, Alabama, 1966, is typical of the old songbooks, and "Sacred Harp" singers can be found in the area that spreads from northern Georgia across the Deep South to East Texas. A characteristic session is held on a church ground, features a picnic, and lasts pretty much all day. Appropriately, one of the hymns still sung is Billings' "Chester" which, with different lyrics, was a popular song during the American Revolution.

A Singing Convention

When we arrived at ten o'clock on Saturday morning, the singing had been in progress for an hour. It went on until lunchtime, when all adjourned to a fifty-yard long table set under the post oak trees, laden with chicken, ham, hot rolls and biscuits, corn pone and every kind of cake and pie known to the cooks of northern Alabama. I think the congregation enjoyed watching us stuff ourselves almost as much as they did seeing us run our stereo recording machine. They were a kindly, hospitable group of farmers, small town merchants, school teachers and their wives and children. Singing from the Sacred Harp book is the cultural center of their lives.

Promptly at two o'clock, the chairman called the meeting to order. The "school" assembled in the nave of the church—about forty people ranged around four sides of a hollow square—trebles, sopranos, tenors and basses—both sexes and all ages in each group. The committee had already drawn up a list of song leaders containing the names of every experienced singer present, and the chairman now called someone forward. Everyone had his "Original Sacred Harp" song book in hand and turned to the page number announced by the leader. In a matter of seconds, everyone had found his place and the older heads in the group had established the pitch. The leader launched immediately into a sol-fa interpretation of the song with the whole group joining in. Thus, every song is rehearsed once with its notes and then one or two verses are sung; another song is announced, found, pitched sol-faed and performed, and another leader is called. Matters proceed so briskly and efficiently that perhaps a hundred songs are sung in one day, and before the week-end singing is over, most of the favorites in the book have been sung.

Every well-practiced Sacred Harper knows all the parts of all the songs in the book and can move from side to side of the hollow square as he wishes. All can conduct capably but when one of the old-timers steps into the leader's place, he is likely to set a more appropriate tempo and to carry his chorus with more swing.

That the harmonies are unconventional at times is due to three causes. First, the influence of the Billings school; second the blessed ignorance of some of the early composers who had more feeling for folk music than knowledge of the "rules of harmony;" and third, the powerful character of some of the old tunes, themselves, which demanded a really fresh treatment. Further, the Sacred Harpers sing in the folk style of the South, adding many interesting embellishments, using tremolo, glissando and attack in traditional folk style and pitching their voices in the old manner of their folk ancestors. This style of vocalizing lends a thrilling quality to their harmony, reminding one faintly of a Ukranian country chorus. Indeed, if the Sacred

Harp music is performed by a city choir it loses half of its punch, and one hopes that, when the "Original Sacred Harp" becomes one of the Bibles of the folk song movement, as it certainly will, the singers will take the trouble to learn *how* to sing as well as what to sing.

These singing meetings are intensely emotional. The Sacred Harp folk are deeply religious. When I asked one old gentleman what lay back of his beautiful singing, he slapped his big, country palm down on his book and said, "Every word in that book is true—true as Gospel." One feels this emotion when individuals rise to speak, for their voices often tremble with feeling and tears sometimes course down their cheeks.

The Sacred Harpers feel themselves members of a family, or rather a clan, that will someday be singing in harmony with the angels. Meantime they deeply mourn the passing of each beloved member and they part from one another at the close of the meeting with keen regret. This musical community is also deeply democratic. All chairmen and officers are elected by an open show of hands and these officials run their meetings in accordance with the parliamentary rules of order. Everyone who wishes has an opportunity to lead and every person is treated with a tender respect in regard for his or her feelings.

Source

Description edited with permission from an essay by Alan Lomax on the back cover of the record "All Day Singing from 'The Sacred Harp' " in *Southern Journey*, Prestige/International 25007; as quoted in Tristram Potter Coffin, *Uncertain Glory, Folklore and the American Revolution* (Detroit, 1971), 145-47.

Feast of the Hermit

September 1

Though such a thing would not surprise us if it were to have occurred in an East Mediterranean village centuries ago or were to occur in India today, we do not expect to find a saint complete with legend, relics, and a feast day manifesting himself in America. Yet within recent memory, the Hispanic culture of New Mexican hamlets has produced its own venerated holy man. A locally celebrated feast day honors his memory and is an occasion for miraculous cures, objects associated with him are held in awe for the supernatural qualities they are believed to possess, and legends of his remarkable feats are current. Like Moses, he produced water from a rock, and like Jesus satisfied the hunger of multitudes. The folklorist who describes him reports that in the 1930s these legends were called "true stories."

Tales of the Hermit

There were two Catholic societies in Hot Springs [New Mexico], to which most of the natives belonged. Everyone, men and women, belonged to the Association de Santa Maria de Guadalupe. This association had meetings twice yearly on Hermit's Peak, and people came from great distances to attend, our friends said. The first meeting of the year was usually held on May first, or the nearest fine day; the second and more important meeting was always on September first. Everyone went up then with food and clothing, there was a picnic, and some families had built little huts where they could stay overnight. Huge bonfires were built that could be seen for miles around "so everyone know we praying for the holy man." Though the fires were so big we were told that they would not ignite the pine needles. People came up at this time to be cured, and trails, fences and crosses were repaired, everyone contributing if money was needed. The meetings were not secret, and we were invited to attend. All the male members of this society had large rosaries with metal medals, which they kept at home, and which were supposed to be returned on the owner's death.

The Holy Man around whom all this centers was a hermit by the name of Juan Maria de Castellano. He lived on the mountain, and died before any of our friends were born, though we were told that there were some old men living who had seen him. We were shown, with great veneration, a photograph of him. This seemed to be a photograph of another photo, or of a painting. It showed a tall bearded man with a staff and cape. Juan himself gave this to Fernán's grandfather, José. We were told many stories about him, for he was "a saint, not the same as other men."

Juan Maria de Castellano lived on the peak for three years, in a cave whose entrance had in-pointing nails, so that he cut himself going out. He knew everything. He slept on a rag on the ground. He had a chest full of religious things, so heavy that no one could lift it. No animal touched him, and wild animals would come up to be stroked. He wore out a trail walking backwards and forward. He built a cross too heavy for anyone to carry. He left the peak because he knew that a man wanted to kill him. When he met this man he said, "I know you will kill me." He walked to France and died there.

Once twelve men came up to Hermit's Peak to make the fourteen crosses for the stages. They worked all day very hard. For dinner he cooked only a little bit of mush, as big as a fist, and put it on a plate. The men felt bad, and thought they would be hungry, but the little piece made them full and they worked all day.

This happened to an old man, still living, whose name is Jesus, and lives nearby. He is now very old. The hermit used to haul water in a five-pound lard pail. He had to walk down all the way to town, then up to the top again, because there was no water. One day all the people in Gaillnas [New Mexico] decided to go up and get him some water. He was very glad to see them and said to this man Jesus, then a young man, "Jesus, go, and near a certain rock you find three does and a young buck. Take your gun and go there." Jesus went and found the animals. He got down on his knee to shoot, but saw in front of him water shooting out. He ran to call all the people to see, and the does went away.

This water is very cold. Good to drink, but if fifteen or twenty cans of it are poured slowly on your face and neck, it will burn. But it is good for curing. A boy they knew was led barefoot up the mountain by his mother. He was blind. They all prayed rosaries. Twenty cans of water were trickled on the boy, who was cured of blindness.

A girl took a picture of all the people praying there. When it was developed, Maria de Guadalupe, the angels and hell were visible. It's in Gaillnas now.

Source and Comment

Journal of American Folklore, XLVIII (1935), 155-56, 174. Helen Zunser's account of the folklife of the New Mexican village of Hot Springs, twelve miles from Las Vegas, includes a description of a holy man and the annual festival and the tales told about him. She discusses her informants, *ibid.*, 145. See her "St. Anthony's Dance," p. 238. The other Catholic religious society to which "most of the natives belonged" was the Penitentes. Thompson has no exact parallels to the feats of the hermit, but see Motifs B 530f and F 639.1.2 and F 1005.

Labor Day

First Monday in September

Peter J. Maguire, a labor union leader, was the originator of Labor Day. He suggested to the Central Labor Union of New York a celebration honoring the American working man. Acting on this idea, some 10,000 workers paraded in Union Square, New York, reviewed by officials of their fraternal society, the Knights of Labor. Afterwards there were political speeches, fireworks, and a picnic. The celebration became an annual event, made official by state proclamations. The date has no traditional or historic significance. It was simply convenient, chosen, according to Maguire, because it was "nearly midway between the Fourth of July and Thanksgiving, and would fill a gap in the chronology of legal holidays." In time, the significance of Labor Day as a trade union holiday declined, but it remains important because it marks the end of the vacation season and provides a good time for family picnics, sporting events, political rallies, reunions of various kinds, and festivals not necessarily tied to a fixed date. See "Miners' Union Day," p. 241.

Holiday for the Workers?

To many of the people marching in the parade up Fifth Avenue yesterday [September 5, 1988], the point of having a Labor Day holiday was clear.

"This is for the honor of the working class of this country," said Bob Zuzzolo, a member of Local 28 of the Sheet Metal Workers Union International. "This is our day."

True enough. Just as on Memorial Day Americans are supposed to pause and remember the nation's fallen soldiers, so Americans were supposed to pause yesterday to praise working men and women and contemplate the role of labor unions in the nation's history.

Many did, and perhaps rumors of the holiday's metamorphosis are a bit premature. But just as Memorial Day has largely become a time to gather 'round the barbecue and welcome the beginning of summer, so Labor Day has largely become a day to give the season a good send-off.

"The idea should be, 'Let's go out and march,'" said Francis Rodriquez, a cafeteria worker at Public School 31 in the Bronx. "Instead for a lot of people it's, 'Let's go to the beach one last time.'"

Indeed, just a few blocks away from the parade route yesterday, there was plenty of evidence, 106 years after the holiday's inauguration, that Labor was not the operative word in Labor Day.

"Independence Day, right?" was one response in Central Park to a question about what, exactly, was being celebrated.

"Somebody got killed or something," was another.

"The idea is to take a rest from your labor," ran a third.

"Let's face it," said Cynthia Salmons who was walking with a friend. "A lot of our holidays have lost their original meaning. I actually remember, when I was a kid, we'd go to the cemetery on Memorial Day. Sure we'd have a picnic afterward, but we'd always go to the cemetery to remember what the day was all about."

Are holidays not what they used to be? Or have they never been what they were intended to be?

Professors of leisure studies are taking a look at these questions. "I think you'd have to say that Labor Day is essentially celebrated as a three-day weekend rather than as a meaning-laden holiday," said Dr. John R. Kelly, a professor of leisure studies at the University of Illinois in Champaign-Urbana.

Dr. Kelly noted Americans' voracious pursuit of leisure has altered the traditional dividing lines between the week, the weekend and holidays. For the convenience of the three-day weekend, for example, Americans gladly take Washington and Lincoln's birthdays, put them together and celebrate them on a date that usually corresponds to the birth date of neither.

Source

New York Times, September 6, 1988. Edited from an article by Sam Howe Verhovek. Copyright© 1988 by The New York Times Company. Reprinted by permission.

Labor Day and the Labor Movement

The labor songs and speeches had nearly ended when Jim Moran took a final look at the departing crowd. He stood on a platform overlooking the Judge Lewis Quadrangle in Center City, his hands tapping his thighs to the catchy rhythms of the East Logan Drill Team.

A satisfied smile broke through his grizzled white beard.

"We feel we hit a grand-slam home run," said Moran, 50, a key organizer of the Philadelphia area's tri-state Labor Day march and rally. He faced another labor leader and said, "It looks like there's some movement back in the movement."

About 2,000 people paraded yesterday through nearly barren city streets and rallied at the quadrangle in what organizers said was the first such march in Philadelphia in 107 years, since a parade pressing for an eight-hour workday was held.

Morgan and others predicted that the strong turnout would herald a revitalized labor movement.

"Putting people on their feet one day of the whole year doesn't necessarily change the labor movement," said Morgan, director of the nonprofit Philadelphia Area Project on Occupational Safety and Health. "But it's one piece of what we have to do to bring back that spirit." ...

Veteran organizers and rank-and-file workers gathered under cool, crystalline skies. It was the first rally for 2-month-old Reed Frye, who bounced contentedly in a shoulder sling worn by his father, Chris, a Camden printer and member of the Graphic Communications International Union Local 14M. And it was one of many rallies for white-haired Sophia Jackson, a retired Philadelphia schoolteacher who remembered when May 1—now called national Law Day—was a day for labor, not lawyers.

"I'm proud to be a member of the union," said Chris Frye. "I think there's an all-out war against organized labor in this country. I'm afraid there's a plan to do away with unions in this country, and we're not going to let that happen.

"I want there to be good jobs for him when he grows up," he said.

Marches yesterday had villains aplenty. There was the Pittstown Coal Group Inc., whose Virginia and West Virginia mines have been the scene of a bitter, five-month-old strike. There was Amtrak president W. Graham Claytor Jr., depicted on one sign as presiding over colliding toy trains and buses. One union official accused Claytor of attempting to cut wages 30 percent in contract talks.

There was, as always, former President Ronald Reagan, under whom labor "certainly took a beating," said Andrew Douglas of Mount Laurel, another member of Local 14M of the Graphic Communications Union.

There were the unnamed profit-driven "corporate pirates" and the foreign investors behind "the buying of America," said Edward J. Keller, executive director of Council 13 of the American Federation of State, County and Municipal Employees.

But the most often reviled corporate manager yesterday had to be Frank Lorenzo, chairman of Eastern Airlines' parent company, who appeared on buttons ("Weenie!") and on a sign as a vampire (held at bay by the Statue of Liberty's torch).

In the last year, Labor Day "sure took on a lot more significance than picnics and ballgames," said Phil Harris, 41, one of four area strike coordinators for the International Association of Machinists and Aerospace Workers, which along with the pilots is striking Eastern.

"I think all the members now realize what unscrupulous managers like Lorenzo are trying to take away from us," he said.

Keller of the AFSCME said labor today was seeking a different social agenda that includes raising the minimum wage, securing health benefits, and providing day care.

Moran's wife, Aggie, paraded in a red, white and blue Uncle Sam suit, with her 6-year-old grandson Jimmy, in a matching costume, as that "real-live nephew of my Uncle Sam."

"I think the labor movement's been on its knees too long, and it just stood up for the first time today," she said in a light Scottish brogue.

Source

Philadelphia Inquirer, September 5, 1989. By Michael L. Rozansky, staff writer.

* * *

Joe Hill on Labor Day, 1971

On Labor Day, 1971, while several AFL-CIO unions joined to present a colorful songfest on the National Mall in Washington, Jonathan Eberhardt performed the "Will" ["My Last Will" by Joe Hill], accompanying himself with a complicated guitar arrangement.

> My Will is easy to decide
> For there is nothing to divide
> My kin don't need to fuss and mourn
> "Moss does not cling to rolling stone."
> My body?—Oh!—If I could choose
> I would to ashes it reduce
> And let the merry breezes blow
> My dust to where some flowers grow—
> Perhaps some fading flower then
> Would come to life and bloom again.

This is my Last and Final Will.—
Good Luck to All of you.

Joe Hill

Present at this songfest facing the Washington Monument, I was drawn to the moody rock treatment of Hill's poetry. In my mind I contrasted Eberhardt's "uptown" guitar with a faraway second instrument—the gospel mission piano in San Pedro where Joe Hill had picked out the tunes of his parodies. Despite my long interest in Joe Hill, as a figure in history and folklore, the meaning of his "Will's" proverbial imagery did not really come alive for me until this past Labor Day. When a "folk revival" guitarist used Hill's simple poem to bring together staid labor unionists and counterculture youngsters, new flowers did indeed take root and bloom.

Source and Comment

From the section on Joe Hill in *Folklore from the Working Folk of America,* 408-09. The description of the Labor Day rally in Washington is by Archie Green, an authority on labor history and its lore. The "Will" was actually written just before his death by Joe Hillstrom (Joe Hill), a labor organizer and poet-songwriter who was executed on November 19, 1915, for the murder of a Salt Lake City grocer. Convicted on shaky evidence, Hill emerged as a hero of the labor movement and sent a famous telegram from his death cell to IWW headquarters reading "Don't mourn for me: organize!" The "Will" was printed in the ninth edition of the IWW "little red songbook," *Songs of the Workers,* and has been famous ever since.

* * *

Labor Day Politicking

TUSCUMBIA, Ala.—Jimmy Carter returned to his native South yesterday [September 1, 1980] to open his 1980 re-election campaign beneath a towering weeping willow tree.

Speaking near the edge of this picturesque small town, the President struck two major themes that his aides said he would repeat throughout the campaign—increased employment and strong national security.

Carter traveled from the White House to attend the Tuscumbia Springs Park Labor Day picnic, an annual event featuring barbecue, balloons and music—high school bands playing "Dixie" and the Charlie Daniels Band, a favorite of Carter's, playing bluegrass....

The Labor Day trip was deliberately fashioned as a reaffirmation of his roots and a reminder to the crowd of 25,000 that they are the base on which he built his successful campaign in 1976.

"I have seen a lot of places and a lot of people the past four years," he told the crowd. "But I just want to say how great it is to be with folks who don't talk with an accent." ...

Carter returned to Washington after the speech here to host a more traditional Labor Day picnic on the White House lawn with labor union leaders, who constitute another cornerstone of his re-election effort.

Source and Comment

Philadelphia Inquirer, September 2, 1980. Extracts from a news story on the 1980 presidential political campaign by Tom Fiedler of the *Inquirer* Washington bureau. Cf. "Shad Planking," p. 184 and "Return Day in Delaware," p. 390.

* * *

Portuguese Labor Day Festa

More than 500 years ago, Queen Isabella of Portugal ... honored the peasant poor with a feast in a rural village. The festival was climaxed when the Queen removed her crown and placed it on the head of one of the villagers.

This weekend [Labor Day weekend, 1975] the descendant of that feast of charity will be celebrated in West Warwick [Rhode Island], as the Portuguese Holy Ghost Society launches the 3-day festa it has sponsored for the past 64 years.

From early Saturday morning until late Monday night the Ventura Street neighborhood where the society is located in Lippitt, will fill with the sights, smells, and sounds of brass bands, rides, games, auctioneers and Portuguese food. Lots of it.

While the original feast was a strictly secular affair, this weekend's Feast of the Holy Ghost has a definite religious background.

According to Holy Ghost Society Treasurer Peter Furtado the religious element was introduced by Portuguese inhabitants of the Azore Islands. They worshipped the third member of the Trinity—the Holy Ghost, symbol of charity—and incorporated their belief into the celebration of the feast.

Thus the symbol of the feast is no longer simply a crown, in remembrance of the queen, but a crown placed under charity's representative, a dove. That's the way that society secretary Steve Salois tells the story.

While the Feast of the Holy Ghost is central to the celebration it is by no means all of it.

Festivities begin Saturday morning, when Msgr. Hyacinth Moniz of St. Anthony's Church will bless the *oferta*—food to be given out to society members in recognition of payment of their *pensoa*—club dues. Society members will deliver that food all day.

At about 6:30 Saturday evening, one of the festa's many parades will proceed from Granfield Square along East Main and Main Street to Ventura Street. At the head of the parade will be society president Manny Ferreira.

When the parade reaches the society grounds, the festival begins. The rides will run, members of the women's auxiliary will sell the *casouila*—barbequed beef sandwiches seasoned with Portuguese spices—they have prepared, and two bands will battle for the crowd's attention.

Sunday morning features the big event. An eight division parade will leave Ventura Street around 10:00 A.M., headed for St. Anthony's Church on Sunset Avenue. A Coronation Mass will be celebrated at 11:00 A.M. Then the parade, to be composed of representatives of the Portuguese Citizens Club, the Portuguese Sports Club, the West Warwick Police, the Coventry Fire Department and various veterans' organizations, will head back towards Ventura Street, to the accompaniment of the Tiverton, Bristol, and Washington Independent bands.

Then comes the Feast of Charity. To everyone present, members of the Holy Ghost Society will distribute portions of a specially prepared dish. In Portuguese it is called *Soupas do Espirito Santo*. In English it means the soup of the Holy Ghost. Rides, games and bands are to follow.

Monday—Labor Day—will be occupied by the *migalha,* the collection of food and livestock for the auction Monday night. Funds from the auction go to defray the costs of the festa, treasurer Furtado explains.

Finally, on Monday night, a special ceremony is held. At the conclusion of the festa, lots will be drawn to see which six families will have custody of the Crown of the Holy Ghost during the coming year.

Source and Comment

Pawtuxet Valley (Rhode Island) *Daily Times,* August 29, 1975. News article on the festa sponsored by the *Sociedade Portuguesa do Spirito Santo* with the byline of Bob Stewart, a staff reporter. For another holiday involving a Holy Ghost Society and Queen Isabella, see "Festa da Serreta," p. 332 and "Portuguese Fishermen's Whitsunday," p. 229.

The Feast of the Holy Ghost, a Portuguese-American ethnic festival held on Labor Day, evolved from several sources: a dinner for the poor given by a Portuguese queen centuries ago, a religious devotion to the Holy Ghost as a symbol of charity, a desire to recall Old World customs in a new and changing environment, and perhaps most of all a reunion with family and friends of like background. Labor Day itself merely provides a suitable space in the calendar. One local authority, Mary Pacheco, suggests that the festa first appeared in Gloucester, Massachusetts, among fishermen who wished to express their gratitude after a voyage in particularly stormy seas. By 1911, it had spread to the Portuguese in West Warwick, Rhode Island. Charity and gratitude remain important elements of the festa. For example, children who have recovered from a serious illness are carried or walk in the festa parade, and a person who had regained the use of an injured leg might give a loaf of bread baked in the shape of a leg to be sold at the charity auction held in connection with the festa. Farmers who have prospered during the year likewise show thanks by donating produce for sale at the auction.

Other Portuguese communities have similar festivals which originated in the Old World. The St. Paio celebration in Naugatuck, Connecticut, is forty years old. It honors the patron saint of Torreira, a Portuguese seacoast town. For residents of Naugatuck of Portuguese descent, it is the most important social event of the year. It occurs annually on or near Labor Day.

Portuguese Labor Day Festa
The Festa Crown

When the sterling silver crown topped with a golden dove is carried through the streets of West Warwick this weekend [Labor Day weekend, 1978], close to 500 years of Portuguese tradition and symbolism will be carried with it.

The annual week-long Festa of the Holy Ghost began centuries ago as a social event, gradually took on a spiritual meaning, and now ranks as the largest ethnic religious celebration of its kind in the state of Rhode Island.

The festa traces its roots back to 15th-century Portugal, during the reign of Queen Isabella, who was known for her generosity toward the poor. Each year she threw a lavish feast for the village peasants. During the feast, the Queen would place her crown on the head of a peasant child.

In the modern-day festa, the Queen's gesture is re-enacted with the crowning of a local child. This year's choice is Gina Andrade of West Warwick, who will be crowned after each of the processions and parades during the festa.

The sterling silver filigree crown she will wear is not just a reminder of Queen Isabella and a symbol of charity. It has religious meaning as well. The small golden dove on top of the crown symbolizes the protection and guidance of the Holy Ghost.... This religious aspect of the festival was incorporated by the Portuguese residents of the Azores, who worshipped the Holy Ghost as a symbol of charity....

The crown used in the festival is developing a history of its own. It was originally brought here from the Azores in 1911 by the Holy Ghost Society. But over the years, as it was carried through the streets and placed on the heads of dozens of awed children, the crown began to show its age. About 12 years ago, the Society ordered a new replica of the crown from the motherland and retired the old one from active duty. The original crown now rests in permanent display in the Society's hall on Ventura Street, surrounded by fresh flowers.

The new crown leads a more active life. In addition to being carried through the streets of West Warwick each year, the crown rests with several local families.... At the end of the festa each year, there is the *sortes,* or drawing of lots among the members of the Holy Ghost Society. Six families are chosen. One is selected to keep the crown for the next 46 weeks. The five other *domingas* [designated crown keepers] each host the crown for one week.

Source and Comment

Pawtuxet Valley (Rhode Island) *Daily Times,* September 1, 1978. Unsigned feature article which was part of the extensive newspaper coverage of the Festa of the Holy Ghost. The word *domingas,* hosts of the crown, is apparently derived from the verb *domingar,* meaning to dress up for a special occasion such as for church on Sunday. *Domingo* means Sunday.

Childhood Memories of the Festa

I can remember the aroma of *Masa,* Portuguese sweet-bread, that was escaping from almost every home in Roverpoint village on Thursday and Friday of that week. I can remember the chickens cackling before they became that holiday meal. And the never failing "Sweetrice with cinnamon" a sure treat.

Most of all I recall the shiny window panes framed in starched curtains and the young lassies with rag curls so they'd be real curly-tops for the big Sunday parade.

With a chuckle I can recollect how many slept on the wood or linoleum floors so that the master bedroom had a guest-like appearance. The snow-white dust ruffle and counterpane of heavy embossed cotton with matching pillow shams were kept perfect until the relatives came. We were poor but for this occasion it almost always meant a new dress. The village seamstress would purchase a pattern or make one up and come Sunday afternoon, after the big parade, 20 to 25 youngsters from our area would all have the same design but in different fabric patterns.

It was really a great time as we followed the Crown for the six weeks of transfer. Every night we would go to the host's house and sing the rosary. The lady who was our leader had a high loud voice and the din was something as the young boys and girls tried to out-do her. Actually many of us would try to hurry it along because it meant a thick slice of *masa* and some homemade rootbeer afterwards.

Source

Pawtuxet Valley (Rhode Island) *Daily Times,* August 29, 1975. A newspaper interview with Mary Pacheco of West Warwick, Rhode Island. She was born Mary Mello in West Warwick of parents who came to America from the Azores in 1900. She is known locally as an authority on the festa.

* * *

Labor Day Mass for the Unemployed

There will be a Mass as usual at 9 A.M. Monday [September 5, 1984] at the new St. John the Evangelist Roman Catholic Church in Lower Makefield Township, Bucks County [Pennsylvania]. But it will not be a usual Mass.

The church, dedicated Aug. 1, will be the scene of a special Mass for the unemployed on Labor Day—a Mass the pastor and a spokesman for the Archdiocese of Philadelphia said would be the first of its kind ever in the archdiocese.

"It is very unusual," said the archdiocesan spokesman. "I have never heard of one like it before. We've had special Masses in the area for disasters, but not for the unemployed."

The Rev. Francis P. O'Reilly, the church pastor and a priest for 42 years, said it was also new to him. "I've never heard tell of one before, but because something never happened before is no reason it can't happen now," he said yesterday in an interview.

Father O'Reilly, pastor at St. John's since 1969 and a native of Bucks County, said he decided to offer the special Mass "because unemployment is a critical stress on our society."

He said that on previous Labor Days worshipers had asked for God's blessings on workers. But he said that after reading about unemployment nearing 10 percent in the area, he decided on a special Mass for all the jobless in Lower Bucks County.

"I have found that many times when we have a need we turn to God. The Lord has said, 'Ask and ye shall receive' and 'Knock and ye shall find.' It seemed an ideal situation with a brand new church because a lot of people would like to see it," he said.

"We will celebrate Labor Day and ask God's help to find work. Mass is the perfect prayer, and we will adopt it for something very important."

Source and Comment

Philadelphia Inquirer, September 4, 1982. News item by Lacy McCrary. The principal employer in the Lower Bucks area of Bucks County, Pennsylvania, is the U.S. Steel Fairless Works where, at the time of the "unusual" Labor Day Mass, twenty-three hundred of the plant force of eight thousand had been laid off.

The Southern 500 Stock Car Race
Labor Day

In 1949 a local group, headed by Harold Brasington, a sometime racing driver, decided to organize a corporation to build a major speedway for stock cars, a sport that had hitherto been pretty much left in the hands of amateurs and confined to the hinterlands. The site chosen was a farm on the outskirts of Darlington, South Carolina, the county seat of a largely agricultural region, and Brasington's home town. The first race was on Labor Day, 1950. Stock cars had never before been raced at a distance of 500 miles and only a third of the seventy-five starters were there at the end. The winner was a Yankee, Johnny Mantz, driving a new Plymouth at an average speed of 76.26 miles per hour. The stock-car race is an important proving ground for manufacturers, and it is accompanied by a fair amount of festivity, including a parade that displays politicians and television personalities and a beauty pageant.

Southern 500

Until 30 years ago it was the prettiest little patch of farm land in Darlington County [South Carolina], the older folks say.

It had a white rail fence around it, and corn and cotton grew peacefully. Now, it is the most hallowed but most battered ground in stock car racing. It is Darlington Raceway. It changed the face of an entire sport forever. And events here are more like pilgrimages than races.

On this very morning [September 2, 1979], on the eve of the 30th Southern 500, the already-tipsy fans are sticking their noses through its chain-link fences, sniffing for memories.

This is where a child named William Caleb Yarborough sneaked in under the fence to see his first stock car race, and where the man Cale Yarborough flew off the track in a stock car like a fighter plane taking off.

This is the track that gave Fireball Roberts and Little Joe Weatherly room to become legends.

It was the first of the Southern super speedways. The third, fourth and fifth—Daytona, Charlotte and Atlanta—came a decade later.

Before Darlington, stock car racing had been confined to short dirt tracks.

But then Harold Brasington, a soldier of fortune of the construction industry, changed it all.

Long ago, "Lady in Black" became a sports writer's cliché for Darlington.

She is an ancient woman now, a hag, compared with her prettier peers. She is misshapen—more like a pear than a smooth oval—because the farmer who owned the land made them build around his minnow pond.

Still she's Harold Brasington's darling daughter, and though they've been apart these many years, he can remember when she was his little girl.

"I'd been going to races in the South since 1920," says Brasington, who at age 70 still lives in Darlington. "Mostly they were run on high-banked board tracks and dirt tracks."

And they were short tracks—quarter-miles and half-miles, mostly.

"Then in 1930, I went to Indianapolis—a paved, 2 ½-mile track. I'd never seen crowds of 200,000 before. I was amazed. From then on, it became a fever with me."

He felt that if Indianapolis could draw big crowds for the little open-wheeled cars, which weren't like passenger cars, then "if we could build a big track in the South and race stock cars on it for 500 miles, every butcher, baker and candlestick maker would turn out to see it." As an adult, Brasington got into the earthmoving business, and his fever for a big track—"combining the high banks of our short Southern dirt tracks with the length of the Northern paved tracks"—continued.

In 1949 he made a deal with S. J. Ramsey, the farmer who owned the land, and work began.

In 1950 the first Southern 500 was held, and the South seceded from the Indianapolis 500. Southerners had never really liked those little open-wheel doodle bugs anyway, and now they could see good, honest stock cars run in the South's first 500-mile race. And it was on a big, paved track—the spanking new, 1.33-mile Darlington.

There was no particular reason to build such a track in a little South Carolina town of 7,000, except that "this was home" to Brasington....

Bill France Sr., founder of NASCAR (National Association for Stock Car Auto Racing) shaped the sport. But Harold Brasington shaped its style and its speed.

With some bulldozers and workmen he scraped a cotton field into the world's first giant, high-banked oval. He is not ashamed of the track's odd design, because in his day, engineers didn't have computers to help them design tracks. And they didn't have to be careful about S. J. Ramsey's minnow pond.

"The reason the first and second turn have a shorter radius than the third and fourth," explained Brasington, "is that Mr. Ramsey had a fish pond and a minnow pond. He said, 'You can build that track, but you've got to make it miss that minnow pond.' Well, I was just anxious to go ahead and build, so I said 'Okay, sure.'"

And that little agreement gave Darlington its most famous characteristic.

As the track grew near completion Brasington reached an agreement with a sanctioning body called the Central States Racing Association, based in Indiana, to sanction the race—that is provide the cars and drivers.

"But only four months before the race date (Labor Day, which now in the South belongs solely to the Southern 500), he had only had eight or ten entries. So he made an agreement with Bill France that NASCAR would co-sanction the race."

The marriage of NASCAR and Darlington in those talks was, perhaps, the most significant event in the history of American automobile racing, other than the opening of Indianapolis Motor Speedway.

Source

Atlanta Journal, September 2, 1979. From a feature article by Ed Hinton, staff writer. For another example of an automobile race that is now traditionally linked to a legal holiday, see "Memorial Day Carnival at the Indy Speedway," p. 218.

* * *

Southern 500

Beliefs about the Lady in Black

The raceway is called "the Lady in Black" because she acts like a strange woman; she's so fickle.

Sherman Ramsey had a minnow pond. Told Harold Brasington [said] it was all right to build a track but not to mess up his minnow pond. So Paul Psillos, a Darlington engineer and contractor just shaped the track like an egg to get around the pond. He hadn't ever seen a raceway when he laid out the Darlington track, so the curves and banks were not much like the Indianapolis Speedway.

Stock car drivers won't eat peanuts when they drive. Why? Well, back in the early days a guy got killed. They found peanut shells in his car. I think this happened in North Carolina. In Midland, near Charlotte.

We never had a car numbered thirteen. There's no car running with that number. When we came to the thirteenth year of the Darlington 500, we just numbered it 12-A. This was in 1962. Then we went on to fourteen.

Superstitions change. Green was a bad color. Nobody wore green or had a green car. But this got knocked in about 1977 when Darrell Waltrip started running for Gatorade [his sponsor], and their colors are green and orange. His car was green with orange lettering. He won. That broke the superstition.

David Pearson won first place in eleven races in Darlington and is still [1980] running. He's the largest money winner. He's famous for close finishes. The Lady in Black always smiled on David.

Source

The background and superstitions about "The Lady in Black" are from an interview in 1980 by H. C. with Bill Kiser, public relations director for the Darlington Raceway. He was born in Lincoln, North Carolina, in 1921.

Festa da Serreta

September 8-15

The village of Serreta, on the island of Terceira in the Portuguese Azores, is on a high cliff overlooking the sea. In the sixteenth century a priest built here a small chapel in which he placed an image of *Nossa Senhora,* Our Lady. The image came to be esteemed for its miraculous powers and was moved to a larger church. A religious society was founded to serve and pay homage to it, and particularly to restore it to its original site. This was finally achieved in 1842. The sponsors of the Festa de Serreta in Gustine, California, emigrated mainly from Terceira and São Jorge, both important for cattle-raising, and Gustine is a dairying town. This is appropriate, for the festa begins with a *Bodo do Leite,* or Banquet of Milk, from festively decorated cows, following the practice in the Azores.

The Festa da Serreta in California

The Azorean Portuguese colonies in California honor holy personages and saints with a series of religious celebrations during the summer months. Although the greatest number of these are festivals of the *Divino Espírito Santo* and *Rainha Santa Isabel* (the Holy Ghost and Saint Isabel), one of the most popular and unique is that devoted to *Nossa Senhora dos Milagres* (Our Lady of Miracles) as celebrated at Gustine. It is known as the "Festa da Serreta" because it is closely patterned on the festival honoring *Nossa Senhora dos Milagres* in the village of Serreta, Terceira Island....

The first president of the [sponsoring] brotherhood dictated the following statement to his daughter for my use.

ORGANIZATION OF "LADY OF MIRACLES," GUSTINE, 1932

Started by a small organization called the Portuguese-American Club to help the Portuguese to become good American citizens. The Portuguese nation is a Catholic nation. These Portuguese wanted to form an organization that would unite all the Portuguese people of California in a big and beautiful festival. A member, M. B. Souza, proposed to name their beautiful festival "Lady of Miracles" after the beautiful festival he saw in Terceira, Azores, in the village of Serreta. Then they chose a good popular man with experience in the Portuguese festivals, John T. Mattos, who then became the festival's first president, to organize the events to start this festival. First, he had to go to the priest and tell him what the people wanted and to obtain the orders from the Catholic Church to obtain an image of the Blessed Virgin, "The Lady of Miracles." The priest gave him all the power to do all that he felt was right and was under the rules of the Catholic Church. Second, the first year of this

festival about four thousand people attended; it was a success. Third, the third year the Catholic Church took the whole festival over. This annual celebration always starts September 8 and ends on the fifteenth. It starts with a novena to Our Lady of Miracles, all in Portuguese, like it was in the Azores, Portugal, with twenty to thirty young girls singing in Portuguese beautiful melodies to our Blessed Virgin. All this lasts a week. Before the week of the novena the images of sixteen different saints are decorated with satins, flowers, and laces. After the week of the novena, on the Sunday, all the images of the saints are taken in a beautiful procession all over the town and back to the church, leaving the Blessed Virgin in a little chapel all day until Monday morning, receiving promises and veneration. Then Monday morning the Blessed Virgin is taken back to the church, closing the religious Catholic celebration.

The procession consists of sixteen decorated statues, eight or more bands, twenty to twenty-five queens from all Portuguese towns, all Catholic societies from all over California. This Sunday there were twenty-five to thirty thousand people. Starting Sunday morning there is served the most favored and delicious meal, in Portuguese called *sopas e carne.*

A traditional bullfight on Monday afternoon and night is a popular sport. Beautiful fireworks, and a band concert, and a tug o' war end this beautiful festival.

I, John Mattos, the organizer of this festival, have been with the festival from the beginning, 1932 to 1947. This year I spoke to a couple from Hawaii. They said they will bring their friends next year when they come. I am sure that a lot of people from out of state would come here to enjoy themselves at this festival if they knew about it.

During the week Gustine seems to be "Little Portugal," where friends that haven't met from twenty to thirty years meet in the festival of the Blessed Virgin.

Active preparations begin far in advance, and, since the date is set permanently for the week between the second and third Sundays in September, rooms, too, are reserved weeks ahead of time each year. The focal centers of the festival are the Roman Catholic church, the city park, and a near-by fraternal hall. The *Igreja do Divino Espírito Santo* stands on a street parallel to the main street. About seven blocks to the north, on the same street, is a spacious park, half of which is an open lawn, dotted with flowers, shrubs and trees, all well kept. A line of tall trees separates this section from the other, less well kept and clear ground for the most part, where a commercial carnival was in operation.

On the garden side, and with back against the tree barrier, was placed a portable *capela* (chapel) at the head of a broad path leading diagonally to the main corner entrance of the park. Thus, when processions leave the church they proceed eastward to the main street, thence northward until opposite the park, and then turn west to it. At the corner, the section of the parade pertaining to the chapel diverges into the park, while the remaining sections return southward to the church. The long rectangular parade route probably covers about a mile.

The hall across from the park is the *Salão do Divino Espírito Santo* or "Gustine Pentecostal Hall" and is unusually capacious. The basement contains all the furnishings for serving food to hundreds of people, while the main floor is for dancing, assemblies, and so on.

Unlike the usual *festa,* which lasts barely two days (Saturday evening through Sunday), the Festa de Serreta lasts a week. The religious program of the novena is an important part. But, in 1947, secular pleasure was centered in a series of *cantorías ao desafio* (extemporaneous song contests). Some of the singers were visitors from the Azores: two named to perform there were Francisco Rodrigues de Lima and Francisco Ferreira Santos. Other participants, *cantares* and *tocadores,* were gathered from all over California. This competitive singing, in which first one, then the other continues to invent *quadras* on a selected topic until one resigns, is especially popular in the islands of Terceira and São Jorge, from which come most of the Gustine residents.

On Saturday the major events begin. The first of these is the *Bodo do Leite* (Banquet of Milk) at noon. This consists of freshly drawn milk and *bolos doces* (round rolls of sweet dough) given to all persons present. In former years the cows were driven down to the park, where they stood in the street facing the sidewalk, and beside each was a milking girl with stool and bucket. Photographs showed the girls in white "dairymaid" uniforms of English or American style;

the pails were of the usual galvanized-iron sort. After being blessed by a priest, the milk and *pão doce* were distributed by young men.

The cows were decorated with crêpe paper rosettes and streamers. This ornamentation is used in the islands; a photograph from another source showed cows with identical trimmings at a *Bodo do Leite* in Terceira. There pitch, rather than glue, is used as the adhesive. An added decoration this year, described to me, was the arc of paper on wire between the horns.

This year (1947) the cows were not driven to the park, for practical reasons: they soil the streets where the evening procession will walk in a few hours. Instead, they were milked at the owner's place, although decorated as usual. The milk was taken to the park "in a great boat-shaped tub" and handed out with the rolls of sweet dough. (Unfortunately I arrived just too late to witness this.)

By 1:00 P.M. the park was well filled with visitors, sitting or walking about and taking advantage of the shade, for the September weather was intensely hot. Many were patronizing the booths set up outside the hall across the street, where soft drinks, ice cream, *linguiça* sandwiches, *tremoça,* and so forth, were vended. The carnival, running continuously, seemed not to attract many adult Portuguese, though some children were on the simpler mechanisms such as a merry-go-round.

The *capela* [stood on] a rectangular platform ... raised about four feet above ground, [and] had a porchlike extension in front, whereon a piano was placed. Broad, firm plank steps led from the walk up to the platform. Approximately 10 feet by 12, this little portable structure is but a light framework; when not in use it is stored outdoors on property adjacent to the church.

The front was covered with *aqua*-blue crêpe paper; the little cross was red, wound with silver tinsel. Clusters of paper flowers, some with paper ribbon streamers, ornamented the front. Within, the curved ceiling was of smooth cerulean blue paper on which scattered silver stars were pasted. Just above the altar was a similarly decorated space, with a crescent moon in the center. The plain blue center panel (which was directly back of the image when in place) had bunches of white paper carnations fastened at the edges.... The remaining interior was covered with a paper of bold design on a white background—great red roses climbing on a dark-green lattice. This may have been selected because of fondness for roses as a symbol of Queen Saint Isabel; it greatly added to the flowery, bower effect.

The next major event was in the early evening at the church, where the final rosary and benediction of the novena were said. Within the church all the images for the next day's procession were already prepared, standing upon their *andores* (litters), lavishly ornamented with lace-trimmed satin hangings and paper flowers. The flowers, far from being garish, were of dainty types, arranged in airy bouquets giving a light, springlike effect. The images were divided; all the male statues were on the left, facing the door, all the female on the right. They were placed on the extreme outer ends of the pew backs, the handles of the *andores* overlapping. These life-size statues on their litters considerably limited the seating space. Nevertheless, the arrangement of the figures in elevated lines down each side of the church, in all their finery and appearing to be but waiting to move out in procession, made an impressive, almost gay array.

In spite of stifling heat, the church was packed with people; they overflowed into the vestibule, down the steps, and all around the front of the church. A loud-speaker system carried announcements of parish affairs to the people outside. These were made by the local, non-Portuguese pastor, and one of immediate concern[s] was an order by the visiting Portuguese priest that no "majorettes" should appear in the processions, even if they had come with their bands.

Soon the queen of the festival and her attendants, all in light dresses, entered the church, singing in antiphony with the choir of girls aloft, and made their way to the places reserved for them near the altar rail. All the religious songs, like the service, were in Portuguese.

The Portuguese priest who had been invited to officiate throughout the week was immensely popular. A visitor from Lisbon, he had been much in demand all summer for the *Espírito Santo festas*. As an evangelist for the "Miracle of Fátima," he emphasized, though not continuously, what we may call the "Fátima aspect" of Our Lady of Miracles.

At the close of the service the evening procession to carry *Nossa Senhora dos Milagres* from church to chapel took place. About 8:45 P.M., while participants were lining up in the street before the church, occasional aerial bombs and a few skyrockets were exploded at a safe distance. The order of the procession was as follows:

First came large American and Portuguese flags, one each in front to the right and left (respectively) of a thirty-piece band. Next, alone in the center, was carried the religious banner of the *Irmandade do Nossa Senhora dos Milagres*. Then the image itself, its *andor* borne on the shoulders of four young men. These men wore light-blue satin *opas* (tunics) over their normal clothing. Behind the image walked a middle-aged, plainly dressed, woman devotee carrying two lighted tapers. A woman companion walked with her.

Then came the girl choir and attendants to the queen, paired in graduated sizes, the smallest first. The queen, wearing a small, simple crown in her hair and flanked by two aids, was dressed in white, the aids in blue. Their long dresses were cut to the same pattern, and all carried small, stiff bouquets. Following them were four male accordionists, who, like the band, played the hymn of *Nossa Senhora dos Milagres* continuously. On either side of the band and the line of young girls walked boys holding flares. And, following the procession in the street, came crowds of men, women, and children, some alone, some in family groups. Other people who were not participating so directly strolled along the sidewalks in the same tempo. Hundreds of onlookers lined the streets. On entering the park the band parted in two lines, while the image was borne up to its altar and the chorus of girls sang continuously.

The religious service was not yet over, for there at the *capela,* the priest, via microphone, gave an exhortative sermon, the general tenor of which was: Gustine as a Catholic Portuguese center must continue its good example of religious devotion.

Thereafter the entertainment commenced. In the hall dancing started and continued until midnight. The evening was still hot and vendors' business in cold drinks and ice cream was continuously lively. In the park, at the *capela,* a casual announcer took over the microphone; he introduced the priest as the first performer. In cassock and with cigarette dangling from lips, the padre played various popular compositions such as the Portuguese song, "Cantiga da Rua," his own foxtrot with the jocular title, "The Slow Fox," "Maria Elena," and so on, to the crowd's intense delight. Finally, the oppressive heat being unbearable, he impatiently tore off his heavy cassock and played in sport shirt. At this the crowd both gasped and clapped in shock and pleasure.

Much of the evening was given over to Portuguese folk songs, sung by men and women who unaffectedly went up to the microphone; some remained seated near the piano, conversing and taking turns. The priest-pianist accompanied them "by ear" successfully; neither guitars nor violas were in evidence at this time.

All this while, from the time the image had been placed in the *capela,* a group of women whose duty it was to remain there, sat on folding chairs ranged along the inner wall. They received or watched over the donations of money (*esmolas*) left at the feet of the image and for which a dish was provided. The receptacle was flanked by large glass-encased votive candles; at each side were the churchly brass candelabra. During lulls in the entertainment many persons of all types went up to leave offerings and receive souvenir ribbon badges. Some knelt for a few moments of devotion.

By midnight the tiring entertainers and audience began to depart, though hundreds still remained in the park. Many slept there or in their cars. *Nossa Senhora* remained in the *capela* with a few watchers; the next morning at 10 A.M. she was taken back to the church for the Mass and procession. . . .

The bullfighting came next, on Monday, beginning about noon and continuing into the evening. A dollar entrance fee was charged. The bullfight is the kind called *tourada á corda,* most popular in Terceira; there it is played at in the street by the common folk, although there is a professional bull ring in Angra. A long rope is attached to the animal: in the islands it is fastened to the horns; here, around the neck. Both there and here the horns are padded. . . .

The construction of the arena shows in the pictures; it is a long narrow rectangle, approximately 100 by 200 feet. The entry chutes and corrals are at the east end, another corral at the west end, and exit gates at both ends. The side walls are so constructed that the men can easily clamber up them to safety. Every timber is solid, the whole structure being of plain but absolute stability. The "bleachers". . . are unshaded, on the north side, and on this hot day were used only by men, hardy youngsters, or undeterred latecomers. On the south side . . . a wooden framework runs overhead the entire length. Beneath this the women sat. To shade themselves they fastened colored blankets and bedspreads on the top and back of the framework. The general effect of this array was both gaudy and old-worldly. The seats are but planks, without risers, and hence are open from below. Older women were excessively cautious about leg exposure, bringing with them other light spreads or shawls to wrap sarong-like around their skirts when moving over the high entry way (a sort of cat walk) or open plank seats. There, upon sitting down, the spreads were opened wide so several persons could sit on them, and the interstices of the planking were thus covered. Many women, especially those in the front row, kept spreads over their knees. Younger women wore slacks, though these are exceptional garments for Portuguese ladies and are rarely seen elsewhere or under other circumstances. A few men sat in these shaded seats among the women, but most stood or clung to various parts of the bleachers and corrals.

No "cowboy" or other costume-like dress was noted, the men's clothing being the workaday type. . . . There was no artificiality or attempt at a spectacular atmosphere: the affair was seemingly a satisfying reality—fun without frills. Chatter, banter, and laughter were continuous among the spectators or between them and the men in the arena. At no time did anyone, even when most intensely interested and vocal, rise up in the "grandstand," yell, scream, or gesticulate wildly. At one time the Brahma bull fell while running, tripped by the rope; the crowd groaned and sighed, then clapped, seemingly with relief and approval, as he rose to his feet and galloped on.

Bullfighting is not a suitable term for this affair which is rather "play with a bull." The rope, some seventy-five feet long, is grasped near its free end by a few men who attempt to hold back the animal when he is running. If he is headed for any of the several men confronting him in the arena, those on the rope cling harder and try to dig in their heels. Others may jump to their aid. But usually the men on the rope were dragged along, running fast, willy-nilly, to keep from falling on their faces, much to the great amusement of all. Most men in the arena were cautious, scrambling hastily up the walls while still not in immediate danger, at which action everyone laughed even more heartily.

Men trying to interest or bait the bull did so most casually—approaching slowly and waving their arms; two men grasping a gunnysack between them waved that. An improvised "bait" made of a large carton, propped up on a pole rammed through it, drew a forceful charge from the animal, though some minutes later he came upon the demolished object, gingerly stretched out his neck to give it a sniff, and with an air of indifference walked off. Neither of the bulls we saw was very active; and no vicious attempt was made to goad them into anger. Perhaps more lively and aggressive animals were saved for later in the day. Each stayed in the arena about an hour, until fairly tired out.

Getting a bull out and corralled safely before letting in the next takes some time, as does also the preparation of an animal for entrance. He must be forced into a chute, and there, while he is kicking and struggling and "sticking his horns around," one or two men try to tie the great rope about his neck. The noose must, of course, be just right— neither too tight nor too loose, and with a knot that will not slip.

The program for the evening announced more bulls, fireworks, and music by a band. Outside the arena, but visible from the seats, were the standards on which the *fogos da presa* (set pieces) were already fastened. The patterns were recognizable by their frames, and these all seemed to be of the same kinds offered at other *festas*. *Fogos do artificio* (fireworks) are part of almost every *festa* program but are usually set off on a Saturday evening. Here they are saved for the finale of the secular entertainment on Monday. . . .

Source and Comment

Western Folklore, VII (1948), 251-54, 257-59, 262-64. A. H. Gayton witnessed this festa from September 13 to 15, 1947, at Gustine, California, and supplemented her observations with information obtained from Mr. and Mrs. John T. Mattos, Mrs. Ida V. Azvedo, and Mr. and Mrs. M. T. Cunha. Her account is part of a larger study of Portuguese festivals in California. Cf. "Portuguese Labor Day Festa," p. 327, "Portuguese Fishermen's Whitsunday," p. 229, and "Sicilian Fishermen's Festivals," p. 348.

Double Nine Day

September 9

According to a Chinese story, Sun Go was warned by a witch to seek refuge on a mountaintop in order to escape a disaster that would take place on the ninth day of the ninth moon. (In another version, Fei Ch'ang-fang dreams of impending destruction and escapes to the hills.) The anniversary of this miraculous escape is observed by family outings to hilly places and by kite flying, since kites were believed to carry misfortune off into the skies. The custom of kite flying was once common among Chinese-Americans, but the holiday is now often marked by offerings to ancestral spirits and family dinners. In China the holiday is also known as the "Festival of High Places."

The Legend of Double Nine Day

Sun Go was a [Chinese] villager, a common man. He had a happy family and a small farm with animals and fowl. Sun Go knew a witch who paid him a visit at his farm one day. As they spoke together the witch gazed at the color of Sun Go's face and could see the circulation of his blood. Based on this the witch made a prophecy that there would be a killing at Sun Go's farm on the ninth day of the ninth month. Sun Go was alarmed and asked the witch's advice. He advised Sun Go to take his whole family and leave the house on that day of coming death. He convinced them to go up to the mountains on that day, away from the tragedy.

So, on September 9th, the entire family fled to the mountains and waited in fear. When they returned the next day all the animals and fowl on the farm were dead. The family had escaped death.

From that day on people used the day of September 9th to hike up to the mountains, to repair the graves of their dead ancestors, and to prune away dead branches from the trees.

Source

New York Folklore Quarterly, XXVIII (1972), 238-39. Collected by Rosemary Agonito in 1968 from Majorie Kam, a native of mainland China. See note on "The Story of Double Five Day," p. 204, and "Graveyard Cleaning and Decoration Day," p. 301.

Recovery of the Cross

September 14

St. Helena, the mother of Constantine the Great, found the True Cross in 326 near the site of the Holy Sepulcher. Her search was particularly difficult because, according to her legend, the site had been built over with pagan temples. The comparable festival in the Eastern Church is the Invention of the Cross (Latin, *invenire,* to discover) on May 3, known as Holy Cross Day in the Armenian church.

Recovery of the True Cross

Throughout the Orthodox church year, on a number of special occasions, offerings of various types are provided by the faithful for use in religious services. On the fourteenth of September, the feast of the Recovery of the True Cross, for example, church members bring sprigs of basil to church in commemoration of the role the herb played in designating the site where the Cross was to be found. The basil is arrayed around a crucifix on a tray which is carried around the interior of the church following the liturgy. When the special service is completed, the sprigs of basil are distributed to the members of the congregation and taken home to grace the family *eikonostasi* [altar, icon stand]. A similar procedure is followed with respect to the flowers offered—or at least paid for—by community members for decoration of the *epitaphion,* or "bier of Christ," employed in the Good Friday service. Once the entombment has been ritually commemorated with a procession outside of the church, the bier is replaced in the sanctuary and the flowers are distributed to members of the congregation.

Source and Comment

"Votive Offerings Among Greek-Philadelphians," Ph.D. Dissertation, University of Pennsylvania, 1974, 276-77. Described by Robert Thomas Teske who observed Greek Orthodox rituals in Philadelphia area churches. Cf. Armenian "Cross Day," p. 197, and note, and Filipino "Santacruzan," also p. 197. Basil may, as legend has it, have grown at the site of the True Cross, but it has been used ceremoniously by the Greeks since ancient times. In some areas, it is also associated with poverty, which would relate it to St. Helena.

* * *

Retrieving the Cross: Combining Church Festivals

For a moment it seemed as if Aegean waves were lapping against the Jersey shore today [September 21, 1980] as hierarchs of the Greek Orthodox Church, clad in gilded white vestments and glittering crowns, threw a white wooden cross into the greenish blue waters of the Atlantic.

It was part of the blessing of the waters, a celebration held each year here [Asbury Park, New Jersey], in which Greek-American youths dive into the ocean in a competition to retrieve the cross.

The celebration recalls the discovery of the true cross by St. Helen in A.D. 325 and honors the historic importance of the sea to the Greek people.

Ten thousand people from throughout the metropolitan area crammed onto the Asbury Park Boardwalk to watch a procession of church officials, led by Metropolitan Silas of New Jersey, Metropolitan Iakovos of Mytiline, Greece, and Bishop Timotheos of Detroit.

In embroidered liturgical vestments of gold, silver and orange silk the clergymen made their way to a platform overlooking the ocean on the side of the city's convention hall, accompanied by the music of a church chorus.

Fifteen New Jersey teen-agers stood at the shoreline, each listening to the blessing and tensely waiting to compete for his parish.

As Metropolitan Silas turned toward the water and tossed the cross seaward, the water churned white with the kicks and strokes of the swimmers, guided in part by shouts from the crowded boardwalk.

The winner emerged from the water with cross in hand, on the shoulders of the other swimmers.

"I saw it, but I couldn't believe that my hand was on it," said 17-year-old Chris Kokkinakis of Wyckoff, N.J., who received a blessing of good luck and a gold cross for his victory.

The Blessing of the Waters is usually celebrated by members of the Greek Orthodox Church around the world on Jan. 6, the Feast of the Epiphany. However, because of the temperature of the water in the metropolitan area in January, the Archdiocese, which has been conducting the celebration in New Jersey since 1947, changed the date here to September, combining it with another celebration, the exaltation of the cross.

Source and Comment

New York Times, September 22, 1980. Unattributed article "Special to the New York Times," datelined Asbury Park, New Jersey, September 21. For other examples of blessing the waters, see "Epiphany Celebration of the Sponge Fishermen," p. 35 and "Blessing the Waters on Epiphany," p. 36, the latter an instance of a celebration commemorating more than one religious event concurrently. See also "Feast of Lights," p. 36, for another modification of diving for a cross due to weather conditions.

Blessing the water, a rite important for seagoing peoples such as the Greeks, usually takes place at the Festival of the Epiphany on January 6 and often includes the retrieval of a cross that has been cast into the waves by a priest. This is the practice among the sponge divers of Tarpon Springs, Florida. But if the weather of a northern clime is difficult, the rite may take place during a more clement season especially if there is a suitable church festival or festivals with which it may be combined. At Asbury Park, New Jersey, the cross is retrieved and the waters blessed in September, shortly after the dates for celebrating Recovery of the True Cross by St. Helena and the Exaltation of the Cross, which marks the restoration of the cross by the Emperor Heraclitus after he recaptured it from the Persians.

The Laguna Indian San José Day Festival
September 18-19

In the areas of early Spanish influence in the Southwestern part of the United States, fiestas featuring Catholic masses and processions, carnival atmosphere, markets, dancing, and entertainments honor various patron saints. These are village ceremonials and are not sponsored by commercial organizations. They are traditional, with histories going far back to the time of the Spanish conquest. The Laguna festival honoring St. Joseph is a fine example.

The pueblo of Laguna, some 45 miles west of Albuquerque, New Mexico, was established about 1697. A Catholic mission was built there soon after and the official name of the village became "San José de la Laguna." The fiesta, the origins of which are lost in the last two and one-half centuries, was originally celebrated on St. Joseph's Day, March 19. However, the date was eventually shifted to September 18-19 because of better weather conditions and because the plentiful late summer harvest encouraged the exchanges of food and goods.

The Laguna Fiesta

An observer's first impression of the fiesta is that thousands of people move rather aimlessly through a welter of activities during the two days of festivities. But after continued observation and systematic interviewing over three or four successive seasons, the initial impression gives way to an understanding of the fiesta situation as a highly structured series of events. The fiesta is at one and the same time: (*a*) a religious ceremonial which combines Catholic vespers, masses, and processions honoring St. Joseph, with a Laguna Harvest Dance in the plaza; (*b*) an enormous "native" market for the exchange of economic goods; and (*c*) a carnival with merry-go-rounds, tent dances, bingo and other games of chance, hot dog and hamburger stands, etc.

At present [c. 1950] it is estimated that over 5,000 people participate in the fiesta. The main cultural groups represented, in order of numbers attending, are as follows: Navahos (predominantly from parts of the Eastern Navaho area); Lagunas; Acomas; Spanish-Americans; Anglos; Zunis; Eastern Pueblos....

Most Laguna families move in from the farming villages in the week preceding San José's Day. As "hosts," they prepare for the fiesta by whitewashing the inside and plastering the outside of the church, cleaning the floor and repairing and plastering the walls of the plaza, and cleaning and plastering their houses. There is singing and dancing practice for the Harvest Dance, and food preparation which includes baking bread in great quantities, roasting corn, and butchering sheep and cattle.

Meanwhile, the "guests" are also making preparations. The Navahos butcher sheep, weave rugs, and make jewelry to trade at the fiesta.... [The] Navahos are cognizant of Pueblo ceremonial calendars and use this knowledge to full advantage in planning trading expeditions. Traditionally, Navahos also engaged in trading ritual consisting of prayers and songs; today they still think of the dangers of being bewitched and carry "gall medicine" as a protection against witchcraft at the fiesta. Some Navahos also visit a "curer" in Acomita for witchcraft cures at this time. The Zunis make jewelry to sell, and the more devout say prayers and sing sacred songs the night before they leave for Laguna. The Spanish-Americans from the Rio Grande Valley pick fruit to sell; a few from the nearby villages make plans for selling liquor to the Indians who attend the fiesta. Precautions against possible witchcraft are also taken by Spanish-Americans, who wear crosses and "rosarios" (containing the image of the Virgin Mary and Infant Jesus) to ward off witches. Families in the Eastern Pueblos prepare turquoise (especially in Santo Domingo), chile and melons (especially in Isleta), and other goods to sell or trade.

For weeks in advance, Anglo ranchers, farmers, and traders in western New Mexico are under increasing pressure from their Navaho employees for "time off" for and transportation to the fiesta. Many prepare to haul truckloads of

Navahos to Laguna in order to insure their return to the job.

The Anglo and Spanish-American concessionaires who bring the merry-go-rounds, bingo games, etc., to Laguna operate on fixed annual schedules, moving from one fiesta to another throughout New Mexico, and they plan their arrival at Laguna for the afternoon of September 18.

For all cultural groups, travel to the fiesta is now almost entirely by automobile. On the way to the main pueblo of Laguna the incoming "guests" stop in the farming villages at the homes of their Laguna or Acoma "host-friends," leave gifts (Navahos leave mutton, rugs, or jewelry; Zunis leave jewelry; Spanish-Americans leave yard-goods, soap, or towels; and Isletas leave chile, melons, or other foods) and often spend the night of the 17th with them before proceeding on to the fiesta grounds....

By late afternoon on the 18th, the market and carnival aspects of the fiesta have been set in motion.... It is significant that a *definite pattern* emerges which has important relationships to (*a*) the location of the religious structures, i.e., the Catholic church and the Laguna Plaza, which are linked ceremonially with the processions on the following day; (*b*) the geography of Laguna Pueblo, and particularly the fact that roads leading into the center of the pueblo are convenient locations for the lines of concession and peddlers' stands; and (*c*) the economic and social position of various cultural groups: the Anglo, Spanish-American, and Pueblo concessionaires purchase permits and are assigned locations near the centers of religious activity while the peddlers in the market do not buy licenses but move into location (with their products and camps) more informally along the roads leading out to the highway. The Navahos occupy the most peripheral position with their camps ranging at some distance from the roads both to the northeast and northwest of the center of the pueblo. The Pueblos and Spanish-Americans invariably set up tents or sleep in the back of tarp-covered pickups or trucks; the Navahos camp out in the open.

Trading activities begin as soon as families from different groups arrive. Action is always initiated by the Spanish-Americans and Pueblos, who make the rounds of the Navaho camps, selling or trading their products. The Navahos, for the most part, stay close to their camps and wait passively for the various peddlers to arrive. There is an understandable urgency on the part of the more enterprising Spanish-American and Pueblo traders to dispose of their products (particularly the perishable items) as early as possible, for the Navahos have more cash and more goods when they first arrive at the fiesta and are willing to pay more on the first afternoon than later on. Bread or melons, for example, which sell for 25 cents on the first afternoon, can be purchased in the market for 10 cents at the end of the fiesta. Later in the afternoon the peddlers extend their activities into the concessions area, which is not as lucrative for them, however, since they are competing with hamburger stands, bingo games, and a multitude of other items.

Before sundown many of the wandering Pueblo and Spanish-American peddlers have established their combination camps and stands along the roads leading from the highway into the pueblo. By sundown the Navahos, who during the afternoon have waited passively in their camps for the parade of peddlers, begin to take more initiative in the trading process. They move more cautiously into the fiesta situation but by dark are wandering slowly in either family or peer groups through the concession area. In the family groups it is typical for the father to carry over his left shoulder a Navaho blanket he wishes to sell and to wear the jewelry he expects to trade or sell; his wife will also wear jewelry she expects to sell. The young peer groups are not interested in trading, but ... are looking for a good time, including sex partners, as the night wears on....

While the market and carnival continue almost without interruption for two days, the religious aspects of the fiesta are divided into a series of definitely spaced events. The first of these is the evening vesper service which begins with the ringing of the Catholic church bells at 7:30 P.M. on the 18th. In 1951 and 1952 only some 50 persons attended the service, including 12-15 Spanish-Americans, 5-8 Eastern Pueblos, and 30 Lagunas. The Navahos and Zunis were conspicuously absent; the only Anglo-Americans present were the priest and several nuns. Special prayers are said for St. Joseph, and after the service the priest announces that it is time for confession. In each of these years (I did not attend the service in 1947 or 1949) only a few Lagunas went forward to confess.

During the evening, the market and carnival continue along much the same lines as in the afternoon, but there is a noticeable increase in the size of the crowd and a number of new emphases are apparent. Additional Spanish-American families arrive for the evening dance. The younger unmarried members dance in the meeting house while their parents (who inevitably accompany the girls as "chaperones") sit on benches outside and visit with one another and with passing Indian friends. Navahos who have been working during the day in the nearby Bluewater carrot fields begin to arrive in large trucks provided by the farming companies, who send along one or more Anglo foremen to "look after" their labor force.

After dark the opportunities for acquiring liquor are markedly increased and Navahos begin to drink heavily. The ultimate sources of the liquor are the bars in Spanish-American villages along the highway, but most liquor which actually changes hands at the fiesta is brought in by Navahos who purchase a supply from Spanish-Americans and resell it to other Navahos at Laguna.

As Navaho drinking increases, the Indian police force, supervised by a special officer from the Indian Service, begins to make arrests. Intoxicated Navahos are locked up in the "Navaho jail," a small room next to the meeting house. During the 1951 fiesta a group of Navaho prisoners happily sang Enemy Way songs inside the jail, pounding on the door of the jail as a drum. It is significant that this is defined by every cultural group as a "Navaho jail," for everyone expects the Navahos to get drunk, be put in jail for the night, and to be tried and fined ten to twenty dollars by the Laguna Tribal Council the following day. I have observed many young Spanish-Americans, Lagunas, Acomas, and Zunis who were as drunk as the Navahos, but in actual practice only Navahos are arrested. The only exception was in 1952 when a Sandia Indian was arrested for bootlegging. When questioned, the Indian Service special officer reported that the Indian police have the authority to arrest anyone who becomes drunk and disorderly. However, *in fact* only Navahos are arrested. It should be emphasized that this procedure is not so much a matter of discrimination as it is a matter of expectations. Everyone expects the Navahos to get drunk, the police watch for Navaho intoxication more than for other disorder....

As the evening progresses, the younger Navahos begin to seek sex partners. This procedure is also highly patterned. A group of two or more Navaho girls will walk up and down the road by the concession stands until they attract the attention of two or more young Navaho men. Then the girls walk slowly—with the boys following at a discreet distance behind—down the road toward the highway and turn off into the darkness of the bushes west of the pueblo. Other cultural groups also seek sex partners on fiesta nights, but the procedures are not as highly patterned. There is evidence of philandering by the Pueblo men, both with women from their own cultures and with Navaho women. Since Spanish-American girls are strictly chaperoned, young Spanish-American males also seek partners in the Pueblo and Navaho groups. The most common practice at present for philandering Pueblo and Spanish-American men is to take girls for rides in cars out to the edge of the pueblo.

After the carnival closes at midnight, a group of Navahos usually gathers either near the stands or out in the camp area to sing Enemy Way songs and hold what is traditionally called a "squaw dance." Recently there has been no dancing, but the traditional singing still takes place from about 2 A.M. until daybreak....

The activities of St. Joseph's Day are initiated by a sparsely attended mass at 7 A.M. At 9 A.M. there is Solemn High Mass in the church, attended by approximately 300 people. In 1951 and 1952 the congregation consisted of 60-75 Spanish-Americans; the rest were Lagunas and Acomas, with a sprinkling of Eastern Pueblos—especially Isletas

and Santo Domingos (the parish of Laguna includes Acoma and several neighboring Spanish-American villages and has a total membership of about 4,000). There were no Navahos in either year, and no Zunis in 1951, but in 1952 one Zuni couple attended. Each year two Anglo-American tourist families stood at the rear of the church for a few minutes.

The choir is composed of Laguna women led by an Anglo-American nun. Anglo-American priests (four in 1951, three in 1952) officiate during the service, which includes prayers, communion (administered to Lagunas, Acomas, and Spanish-Americans), and a sermon on St. Joseph, delivered in English. The virtues of St. Joseph (respect, kindliness, and justice) are stressed, as well as the fact that St. Joseph is the universal patron of the church "and our own patron here at Laguna." After an offertory, the formal church service ends, and the priest asks the governor and his lieutenants to come forward and "talk to the people." The priests then leave while speeches are made in the Laguna language by the governor and by seven other members of the Tribal Council who also stress the fact that this is the fiesta for St. Joseph and ask the people to prepare to carry the wooden image of the saint in the procession out to the plaza....

After the speeches, the priests return and sprinkle holy water on the wooden image of St. Joseph. The image is then lifted from its niche by the parish priest and handed to two Laguna women who take turns carrying it in the procession which, after leaving the church, passes south of the plaza and enters the plaza on the east. The governor and his staff lead the way, making symbolic "trails" with their staffs of office; next comes an acolyte bearing a gold cross, followed by the women carrying the wooden image; the choir, which sings hymns about St. Joseph; the main body of the procession, composed of a total of 150-200 Lagunas, Acomas, and Spanish-Americans with a few Santo Domingos and Isletas; and, finally, the priests. A few Navahos, Zunis, and Anglo tourists watch the procession, but do not join in.

Upon arrival in the plaza, the image of St. Joseph is placed on a table at the north side in a bower constructed of poles, covered with cornstalks. The front of the bower is left open and on either side of the entrance is a poplar tree. After a prayer the priests leave, the crowd disperses, and Laguna officials are left sitting with the saint during the rest of the day....

Dancing in the plaza begins shortly after the procession (about 11 A.M.) and continues until almost sundown. The Darawee—the so-called "corn dancers" or "harvest dancers"—alternate with a team of younger men who perform a more secular dance. The 20 Darawee dancers (10 men and 10 women) are accompanied by a chorus of 10-12 men with drums. The chorus comes in first, singing, gesturing with their hands, and beating time with their feet. The dancers follow in two long lines, two men abreast, followed by two women abreast.... In 1952 the women in the dance formation were still dressed in traditional Pueblo dress, but the men were all in white-style trousers and shirts. The two leading men wore kilts, sashes, fox skins, and bells over their trousers and shirts. Four other men had bells on their legs, and all except two held gourd rattles. Only one man wore a headband, and three wore white-style ties. In the chorus only three men wore headbands; all others had large cowboy hats and all were dressed in white-style trousers and shirts.

The more secular dance was formerly a Comanche dance..., but is now either a Hoop Dance (in 1949), an Eagle Dance (in 1952), or is even omitted altogether (in 1951). The Hoop Dance, performed by a team of six younger Lagunas dressed in red, green, and blue feathers, mirrors, and bells (Oklahoma-Indian-style), was very popular with the Indians in the audience and received loud applause at the end of each performance. There was only scattered applause after the 1952 performances of the two Eagle dancers, who were dressed in U. S. Navy enlisted men's blue uniforms with cotton headpieces, wings of eagle feathers, bells, and moccasins.

During the dancing, gifts of food (principally corn, bread, and green chile) are brought into the plaza by Lagunas and Spanish-Americans and placed in front of Saint Joseph. Later in the afternoon this food is distributed to the crowd by the Laguna officials.

Throughout the afternoon an audience composed of several hundred persons surrounds the plaza. All groups are represented in approximately the same proportion as the totals attending the fiesta, except that there are relatively *fewer* Spanish-Americans and relatively *more* Anglo-American tourists. The Spanish-Americans who participated in the Catholic Mass and procession have drifted away to other activities. Anglo tourist participation reaches a height at this point with as many as 10 groups of tourists present at one time, but they do not stay long. The typical Anglo tourist watches the dancing for a time, wanders through the concessions to buy cokes and ice cream, and through the market to make a few purchases of pottery or jewelry before leaving. Disappointment is almost always expressed because the Laguna dancers do not wear more of their native costumes.

During the last period of dancing, the Darawee and the more secular dance team perform simultaneously in the plaza. Shortly before sundown the dancers leave, the priest reappears and St. Joseph is returned directly to the church by a very small procession consisting of the priest, the governor and his lieutenants, the women who carry the image, and about forty others—all Lagunas and Acomas. Inside the church, St. Joseph is returned to his niche, and

the religious phase of the fiesta ends when the priest leads those present in the Lord's Prayer....

The market and carnival activities, which have continued throughout the day as an adjunct to the religious phases of the fiesta, are again stressed on the evening of the 19th, and there are no changes from the evening before. Many people leave the fiesta on the night of the 19th, but the main exodus takes place on the morning of the 20th. The visiting Navahos, Pueblos, and Spanish-Americans finish their trading activities and break camp. Final stops are made at the homes of Laguna or Acoma friends in the farming villages on the way out, and at this time the visitors are fed and given gifts (usually corn, melons, bread or other foods) in exchange for the gifts left at these houses at the beginning of the fiesta. Mutual expectations are expressed to the effect that "we'll see you again next year at the fiesta." This gift exchange pattern takes place within the framework of an institutionalized "friend" relationship.... The friendships are initiated in various ways. In some cases, especially those involving other Pueblos, members of the two families may have met years ago at an Indian Service boarding school. In the cases involving Navahos, the original contacts were often made two or three generations ago and the "friend" relationship is maintained by the younger generation through the years. No bargaining is involved in the exchange of gifts; no questions are raised as to amount or quality of the gifts. But controls are present in the pattern, especially in the case of visiting Pueblos, by the fact that the visits will be returned and goods exchanged again when the Lagunas go to fiestas in other pueblos. In the case of the Navaho-Laguna relationship, the Navahos may decide to go to a different house the following year at fiesta time if they do not receive gifts in return that compensate them adequately for the goods they brought. On the other hand, if the Navaho visitors are "stingy" with their gifts, the Laguna hosts will provide less in exchange. In brief, a continuing process of adjustive reciprocity makes the system workable.... For the Lagunas, the fiesta for St. Joseph is the high point in the annual calendar of events. The important religious meanings centered in both the Catholic church and the ancient Harvest Dance are combined with the economic meanings centered in the market place and the recreational values in the carnival. All phases are now important in the Laguna definition of a good fiesta. The Lagunas also feel strongly their responsibilities as hosts to hundreds of visitors. The Spanish-American and Eastern Pueblo visitors are regarded as having many of the same interests in the fiesta, especially since these groups are also Catholic and have similar celebrations in their own villages. There is likewise a strong feeling of solidarity with Zunis, whose customs are similar and whose visits will be returned at Shalako time when Laguna families go to Zuni. The Navahos, on the other hand, are regarded as peripheral participants. There is no expectation that they will attend the church services or that their visits will be reciprocated by Laguna attendance at Navaho ceremonials. On the whole, Navahos are viewed as still being "wild Indians" who live back in the woods and whose presence at the fiesta is valued mainly as a source of economic profit.

The image of the fiesta held by the Acomas and the Eastern Pueblos is similar to that of the Lagunas, since these Pueblos also have fiestas which the Lagunas attend. The Acoma definition is closest to that of Laguna, for the Acomas play the role of host for incoming visitors in the farming villages and are members of the same Catholic parish.

The Zuni image of the fiesta is somewhat different. The fiesta is called either "Dance for the Saint" or "Corn Dance." There is recognition of the fact that a Catholic saint (they do not know which one) is involved, but the stress comes upon witnessing the "Corn Dance" (rather than upon the total religious ceremonial linking the Catholic Church with the dance in the plaza) and upon trading. The Zunis expect to "trade and watch the Lagunas dance," in the words of a Zuni informant. Younger Zunis describe the fiesta as "a peddling fiesta, where you can get more for your jewelry and make a little profit." The Zuni interpretation of the presence of other groups is that "the other Pueblos come to trade and watch the Lagunas dance, the Spanish to worship the saint and to jitterbug in the dance hall, and the Navahos to court the girls and eat."

In the Spanish-American image the stress is upon the Catholic aspects of the situation (vespers, mass, and procession) combined with a lesser stress on the trade and the recreational aspects, especially the evening dance in the dance hall or tent. In the words of one of the Spanish-American informants:

It's according to old custom. The saints' days. It has been practiced by the Spanish people as a custom for ages. Always united with each other in the celebration for the saint. I can remember it since I was a boy. I have been at this fiesta every year since I was five years old. This is one of the oldest gatherings and is taken in by all the Spanish villages in western Valencia County. We come to see old friends, to do a little trading, and we always go to vespers and mass. After the procession, the Indians take over and dance in the plaza. Sometimes we watch them, but we are just spectators there. That's their own ritual.

The Spanish-American definition of the presence of other groups in the situation is that other Pueblos come primarily to trade, that the Navahos come to do some trading but also to "roam around, drink and have fun." The Spanish-American response is to joke about the "fun-loving" Navahos whose employers "have to bring them over here in big trucks to be sure they get them back to work again."

The Navahos call the fiesta "Corn Brush Hogan," referring to the bower in the plaza in which the saint remains during the Harvest Dance. The use of this name for the fiesta indicates a recognition that something important to the

Lagunas is kept in the bower, but none of the Navahos interviewed knew that a Catholic saint was involved or that it was a saint's day in the Catholic calendar. One informant reported:

The Navahos call this "Corn Brush Hogan." It means they have a big feast. We say this time of year all these Lagunas have their crops in. All these people got corn, oats, peaches, apples. They all get ripe this time of year. That's why they have a big feast.

For the Navahos, the stress is on the market and carnival aspects of the fiesta—defined as a traditional harvest festival, the date of which was set by the Lagunas long ago to insure success for the crops. As a large trading center, the fiesta is a place at which they can obtain goods not ordinarily available to them; there is an abundance of food of choice varieties (each Navaho informant made a point of providing a detailed list of all the foods he obtained or expected to obtain), and there are objects for personal adornment and for the representation of wealth (e.g., turquoise beads). As a carnival, the fiesta becomes a place in which to find liquor to drink and girls to sleep with, along with games to play and many and varied novel activities to observe.

Anglo-American images of the fiesta vary according to the five different roles the Anglos play in the situation: (a) The Anglo-American Catholic priest views the fiesta as a religious celebration for St. Joseph, but recognizes the persistence of Indian religious elements. He expresses less concern about this than he does about the commercialization and the carnival aspects of the fiesta. He expressed relief when the merry-go-round did not appear in 1951 and 1952. (b) The Anglo concessionaires define the fiesta almost entirely in terms of economic gains, with no interest expressed in Indian or Catholic rituals or customs. (c) The Anglo-American police view the fiesta as a problem situation in which bootlegging must be controlled and law and order preserved. (d) The traders and ranchers who bring Navaho employees express some interest in the Indian rituals and customs, but it is clear that they would not attend at all if they were not concerned about getting their employees back on the job. (e) The Anglo tourists define the fiesta as an "interesting" situation, a place to observe the curious rituals and customs of the American Indian.

There are three important common elements in these images of the fiesta: (a) it is a large and important trading and market center; (b) it is a place to "meet friends" in all the various cultural groups; (c) but it is viewed (except by the Anglo group) as a dangerous situation in which there are likely to be witches present in the large crowds. This fear of witchcraft is most marked in Navahos, but is also present in the Pueblo and Spanish-American participants.

There is clearly no consensus among the seven cultural groups attending the fiesta as to the religious meaning of the celebration and no common set of sacred values.

Rather, the fiesta is articulated as a multicultural system in terms of varying definitions and varying roles played by cultural groups in such a way that the critical functions of trade and of feeding and entertaining a large, diverse crowd are carried out. These mutual role-expectations for fiesta behavior have shown remarkable stability and continuity over a long time span.

Some significant acculturative changes, however, are evident in the comparisons with the earlier accounts of the fiesta. The most impressive economic changes are in transportation and in the logistics of feeding the large fiesta crowds. These two changes are interrelated in that the shift from horse and wagon to automobile transportation has resulted in less dependence of visitors upon hosts for several days of feeding and housing during the fiesta. As adherence to the older reciprocal hospitality patterns between cultural groups declines, there is an increasing tendency for Laguna and Acoma hosts to set up hamburger stands and feed the visitors commercially.

The additional recent change in men's costumes for the Harvest Dance, and the shift from Spanish to English in the sermon during the Solemn High Mass, are traceable to further direct acculturation to Anglo-American ways of life. On the other hand, it is clear that acculturation to Spanish-American customs is important in the secular dance patterns found at the fiesta. In these dances, young Acomas and Lagunas dance with steps and to music that are indistinguishable from those found in the *bailes* [dances] held in neighboring Spanish-American villages....

Source

American Anthropologist, LVII (1955), 820-39. Edited from a scholarly article, fully referenced, by Evon Z. Vogt. His findings are based on visits to the Laguna Fiesta in 1947, 1949, 1951, and 1952. The study was part of the Comparative Study of Values in Five Cultures, a project of the Laboratory of Social Relations at Harvard University. Vogt indicates in footnotes where other pueblo saint's days fiestas have been described. Cf. "St. Joseph's Day," p. 129. ff.

Feast of San Gennaro

September 19

San Gennaro or St. Januarius, patron saint of Naples, died for his faith during the persecutions of the Emperor Diocletian. According to the legend, he was killed with a sword but only after miraculously surviving a fiery furnace and a den of wild beasts into which he was cast, and after converting many of his persecutors. Two vials believed to contain his congealed blood are preserved in the Cathedral of San Gennaro in Naples. They liquefy on the anniversary of his death. In New York, the festival is sponsored by a lay organization consisting mainly of Italian-Americans of Neapolitan origin, the Society of San Gennaro. Its setting is a half-mile stretch of Mulberry Street in the heart of Little Italy. Their first festival took place in 1925, and the celebration runs from the thirteenth to the twenty-first.

Feast of San Gennaro in Little Italy

In Little Italy tomorrow [September 13, 1980], the Feast of San Gennaro will offer the pageantry befitting *"A festa 'e tutte 'e ffeste"*—"the festival of all festivals," in the translation of the Society of San Gennaro.

As a marching band plays, the silver-and-brass bust of San Gennaro, the patron saint of Naples, will be borne along Mulberry Street, under the 42 arches with a million lights and past the 300 food and game booths.

Today and through Sept. 21, the half-mile stretch of Mulberry Street will be awash with laughter, music and all varieties of Italian food, including sausages, peppers, clams, calzone, *zeppole* and *sfogliatelli*.

In an age when street festivals have become as much a part of New York as open fire hydrants on a summer day, San Gennaro remains something special, the granddaddy of street affairs.

"People keep asking what's new about the festival," said Arthur Tisi, president of the Society of San Gennaro. "The answer is nothing is new about the festival. It is the same thing, the same tradition, the same cultural and religious activity."

And when all the other street festivals fade, Mr. Tisi insists, San Gennaro will remain.

"This is our 54th year," he said. "And we'll be here for another 54 years."

The fair stretches along Mulberry Street for 10 blocks, from Worth to Houston Streets, and continues from 9 A.M. to midnight each day. Last year, the 11-day event attracted three million people, who, the organizers say, consumed two million sausage heros alone. This year organizers expect nothing more and nothing less....

At last night's official opening, the bust of the saint was carried from the storefront headquarters of the society at 140 Mulberry Street to the corner of Hester and Mulberry Streets, where it was placed in a temporary shrine. The parade tomorrow takes place at 3 P.M. and is the first of several to come.

A week from today, Sept. 19, on the traditional anniversary of San Gennaro's martyrdom in the year 305, there will be a parade with the relic of the saint. Bishop Lorenzo Graziano will participate.

The following day, Saturday, Sept. 20, there will be a celebration with more of a Mardi Gras flavor, presided over by this year's queen of the festival, 17-year-old Kim Ianniello.

According to Mr. Tisi, each one of the queens has married within two years of her festival reign. Matrimony, in fact, is one of the goals of the event, said Mr. Tisi, who keeps a thick book of all the couples who met at San Gennaro festivals. Among those in the book is Mr. Tisi himself, who met his wife Marie at the 1966 festival.

Source

New York Times, September 12, 1980. From a news story by Ari L. Goldman. Cf. "Feast of St. Anthony of Padua in New York," p. 234, another New York street festival.

Army Unit Organization Day

Certain units of the United States Army set aside a day honoring their military history, usually on the anniversary of a battle in which they served with distinction. These occasions were made official by the War Department in 1920, but prior to that time older regiments, the Third Infantry for example, had such holidays. The Third Infantry (The Old Guard), the senior infantry regiment on active service, observes the anniversary of the Battle of Monterey, September 21-23 during the Mexican War. Another example is the 82nd Airborne Division which has its Organization Day on June 6, the date of the D-Day Landing at Normandy.

Army Unit Organization Day

The Official Origin

GEN. ORDERS NO. 8, SEC. 2. WAR DEPT., JAN. 31, 1920.
(Extract)

The commanding officer of each regiment, or other separate unit similarly organized, will select a day in the calendar year, which will be designated as regimental or unit Organization Day. This should be preferably a day noteworthy on account of some event in the history of the organization. It will be observed as a holiday by that regiment or organization for the purpose of commemorating the history and traditions of the organization and engaging in such suitable ceremonies as the organization commanders may prescribe. Addresses on selected day will be reported officially to the Adjutant General of the Army. As far as practicable on that day all military duty for the organization concerned will be suspended. If it falls on Saturday, Sunday, or a holiday, the day after or the day preceding will be designated as the official day.

The following are suggested as a basis of a program for observing Organization Day:

a. General assembly of the organization.

b. Reading of citations and official commendatory orders or other commendations.

c. An address embodying a brief history of the organization and noting conspicuous events participated in by the organization.

d. Address by the commanding officer on the spirit of the organization and its future actions.

e. Addresses on the accomplishments of the men and officers of the organization.

f. Presentation of recruits to the colors.

g. Music and other forms of entertainment.

Following this a brief program of celebration may be held by companies in their mess halls or assembly rooms.

By order of the

SECRETARY OF WAR:
PEYTON C. MARCH,
General, Chief of Staff.

Source

General Orders, cited above.

* * *

Official Origin of Third Infantry Organization Day

HEADQUARTERS THIRD INFANTRY

G. O. No. 2.   Camp Eagle Pass, Texas, March 8, 1920.

1. During the Mexican War the Third United States Infantry participated in the assault, siege and capture of Monterey, on the 21st, 22nd, and 23rd of September, 1846. On the 21st, the regiment formed part of the assaulting column upon the eastern defenses of the city, which was gallantly carried, with a loss, however, to the regiment, of six of its most gallant and valuable officers and sixteen enlisted men killed or mortally wounded, and one officer and twenty-nine men wounded. A total loss of fifty-two out of an effective strength of fourteen officers and two hundred and forty-eight enlisted men.

2. Some years ago the anniversary of the above date was chosen from among the many on which the regiment had distinguished itself upon which its officers should assemble for its proper observance. This occasion has been for years one upon which the officers have gotten together in so far as exigencies of the service permitted for its appropriate observance.

3. The 21st day of September each year is hereby selected and set aside and designated as "Organization Day" for this regiment. This day, or, should it fall upon a Sunday, the day following will be observed as a holiday thruout the

Regiment and will be celebrated with appropriate military ceremony and such further features as will impress upon all the glorious part the Third United States Infantry has played in the Military history of our country.

By order of COLONEL GIDDINGS:
HOMER C. BROWN, Capt. 3d. Inf., Adjutant.

Source

General Orders, cited above. See "Flags In," pp. 000-000, for the Third Infantry Memorial Day ceremony.

* * *

Third Infantry Organization Day, 1925

Organization Day Program

SEPTEMBER 21, 1925

Commemorating the 79th Anniversary of the Participation of the Third Infantry in the Capture of Monterey, Mexico.

7:30 A. M.—Reveille Marches by the Third Infantry Band.

10:00 A. M.—Review of the Third Infantry by its Former Members.

COMMEMORATIVE CEREMONY ON THE MAIN PARADE

March—"The Rifle Regiment" ....*Sousa*
(Dedicated to the Officers and Men of the Third Infantry)
Third Infantry Band

Invocation—*Chaplain Frank C. Rideout or Visiting Clergyman*

Greetings—*Colonel W. E. Welsh, Commanding Officer Third Infantry*

Historical Sketch of the Third Infantry—
Lieutenant Colonel E. M. Norton, Third Infantry

Song—"The Old Guard" .... *Dillon*
Third Infantry Band and Assembly

Greetings from the Third Infantry Veterans' Association—
Mr. John C. Young, (Ex-Sergeant Major, Third Infantry), President Veterans' Association

Overture—"Soldiers and Sweethearts" ....*Bergenholtz*
Third Infantry Band

Presentation of Troops to the Colors—
Colonel W. E. Welsh, Commanding Officer, Third Infantry

"Star Spangled Banner".................................. *Key*
Third Infantry Band

Benediction ....*Chaplain*

12:00 A. M.—Inspection of Post by the Veterans.

12:30—Barbecue Dinner, Third Infantry Veterans, Honorary Guests.

2:00 P. M.—Athletic Events for All.

4:00 P. M.—Exhibition Stunts, Novelty Jumping; Lieutenant Hazelrigg on "Whiskey."

4:45 P. M.—Retreat.

7:00 P. M.—Veterans' Meeting at the Service Club.

8:00 P. M.—Third Infantry Pavement Dance.

Source and Comment

Regimental Organization Day Program, Fort Snelling, Minnesota, September 21, 1925, made available through the courtesy of the Third United States Infantry (The Old Guard) Museum. The printed program is elaborate. It includes a photograph of the commanding officer and a roster of the regiment, considerable historical information, and a photograph of the oldest surviving veteran of the Third Infantry, Amasa Clark of Bandera, Texas, born in 1825, who served in the Mexican War. Staff Sergeant Brian E. Jagielo, U. S. Army, Public Affairs Supervisor, writes: "The current [1989] Organization Day consists of a Regimental Run, sports competition between different Old Guard companies and a cookout. Family members of soldiers also participate in these activities." [Letter to HC, August 24, 1989].

Sicilian Fishermen's Festivals
Late September

A number of fishermen's festivals are held in California by Italian, Slavonian, and Portuguese communities. In spite of differences in the national origin of those who sponsor them, these celebrations have much in common, being patterned on world-wide customs. A festival in San Francisco honors Our Lady of Light, the protector of Porticello, a Sicilian fishing village, and Monterey Sicilians honor St. Rosalia, patron saint of Palermo, an anchoress who lived in a nearby grotto and is said to have died in 1160. Her day is September 4. Although essentially religious in nature, a fiesta spirit dominates and the Chamber of Commerce is supportive.

Maria Santissima del Lume in San Francisco

Although there have been a few irregularities—for instance, in 1947, when the festival was observed on Sunday, September 28—San Francisco's Italians gather to pay homage to their protectress, Maria Santissima del Lume (Our Lady Mary of Light), on the first Sunday in October. Festivities are well attended and impressive but are not on the same grandiose scale as at San Pedro, and in recent years at Monterey. This more modest display is undoubtedly assignable to two reasons: in San Pedro and in Monterey the chambers of commerce and other civic and religious organizations have taken a keen interest in the promotion of the festival, whereas in San Francisco this ancient observance has remained strictly a traditional fishermen's affair; also, in San Francisco the fishermen's festival comes at the same time of year when San Francisco is busy staging the colossal, nationally known Columbus Day celebration.

The preparation of the *festa* is in the hands of the Society of Maria Santissima del Lume. This religious society was founded in 1937 to do honor to Mary, Mother of Light, protectress of the fishermen of Porticello, a village near Palermo in Sicily. According to a legend, untold years ago, some Porticello fishermen found washed ashore a white marble statue with the inscription, *Maria Santissima del Lume.* The statue, of incredible beauty, was taken to the church and placed upon the altar, only to be found again the next day on the beach. When this happened twice more, the fishermen brought the church to the statue. Thus, Our Lady of Light became their patroness. In San Francisco the Sicilian fishermen have a large painting of Maria Santissima del Lume, which is kept in the Church of SS. Peter and Paul at North Beach, the heart of the Italian colony.

Ceremonies have varied slightly from year to year, but basically they are as follows: A Solemn Mass in the Church of SS. Peter and Paul; procession of a few hundred people, with the clergy, members of the Madonna del Lume Society dressed in white gowns and blue satin capes (the colors of Our Lady of Light), pupils of SS. Peter and Paul parochial school, a flower-decorated float carrying the image of Our Lady of Light, a few children dressed like angels, and a band. Although in a couple of "election" years there has been a "Queen" of the *festa,* it is not customary to have one, for *the* Queen is Maria Santissima del Lume. The procession goes from Washington Square, where the church is located, to the famous Fishermen's Wharf. Here, in the presence of several thousands of people, after a few appropriate speeches by religious dignitaries and civic leaders, the pastor of the Church of SS. Peter and Paul blesses the sea, and also the fishing boats which, on several occasions, have been colorfully decorated. Then the procession forms again and returns to Washington Square, where additional speeches are made and prayers recited. The religious rites are concluded with a Rosary and solemn benediction. Later a bazaar is held for the rest of the day and evening, but the spirit of the *festa* is evident in all parts of North Beach, down to the cafes on the pier....

Santa Rosalia in Monterey

In Monterey the two-day fishermen's festival is celebrated in September, and at present the date is set to coincide with the full moon, for, at full moon, sardine fishing is poor, and the fishing folk are in port and can participate in the ceremonies.

Although at Monterey there are fishermen of many nationalities, it is the large and religious Sicilian group that is responsible for the colorful festival. Since 1934, it seems, the Sicilians of Monterey have carried the statue of Santa

Rosalia, their patron saint, through the streets of Monterey to the side of the bay, where churchmen have asked in her name that all fishermen be protected while at sea, and that their catch of fish be abundant....

At Monterey the statue of the saint is kept in the right wing of the transept of San Carlos Church. The early processions with the statute to fishermen's wharf were not recorded by the local newspapers, but they were identical with those held right after World War II. There were no festivities during the war years. The traditional festival of Santa Rosalia was resumed on September 8, 1946, and that year there was a Mass at San Carlos Church, a breakfast, and at 2:00 P.M. the procession from the church to the wharf, followed by the blessing of the fleet. At the conclusion of the religious ceremonies (sermon, Rosary, and blessing), the statue of Santa Rosalia was carried back to the church, where the closing religious services were conducted. In the evening there was a dance at the parochial hall. Similar celebrations were observed annually between 1947 and 1950.

In 1951 the Monterey fishermen's festival was celebrated on a much larger scale. Whereas—as it is also customary in Sicily—the Santa Rosalia festival was observed either on September 4th, if it fell on a Sunday, or on the Sunday following that date, in 1951 it was decided to hold the festival on a Sunday of full moon. In September 1951 the moon was full about the middle of the month, and so on September 2nd and 3rd (Sunday and Monday, respectively), a combination Labor Day and Santa Rosalia Fishermen's Festival variety show was held to raise funds for the big event of September 15-16. There was also a "Queen Contest," and more than two thousand people participated in the double holiday. On the week-end of the 15th and 16th brilliantly colored fish enmeshed in nets were strung across the downtown streets of Monterey. There were parades, water events, fireworks, etc.—a lighthearted spectacle of fun that contrasted with the solemn religious rites of the Santa Rosalia feast. Sicilian fishermen's stocking caps were the official costume of the fiesta and they were distributed gratis by the Chamber of Commerce. In order to give the reader a better idea of the entire spectacle I shall list here some of the numerous events: on Saturday there was an exhibition of the works of the Monterey Peninsula artists, the crowning of the Queen of the Wharf, a parade, skiff races, greased pole climbing contests over water and on land, tugs-of-war, pie and watermelon eating contests, sack races, Sicilian dances in costume, an illuminated boat parade held at night, fireworks, and street dancing. On Sunday festivities began with an open-air Mass. Then there was the traditional procession to the wharf, the blessing of the fishing fleet in the name of Santa Rosalia, and band music. In the afternoon there was dancing, and then the parade of decorated boats over the course from Pacific Grove to Monterey. In the evening at a grand ball, prizes were awarded to the best decorated boats.

Source

Western Folklore, XIV (1955), 79-91. Edited from an essay by Charles Speroni. Included in *Folklore from the Working Folk of America*, 335-39. Similar celebrations are held by fishermen of Portuguese origin in Rhode Island and Massachusetts. Cf. "Portuguese Fishermen's Whitsunday," p. 229 and "Portuguese Labor (Day) Festa," p. 327.

Rosh Hashanah
September—October

The Jewish New Year is referred to in the Bible as "a memorial proclaimed with the blast of horns." The earliest Jewish calendar had four "new" years, corresponding to important periods in the agricultural cycle, but the autumn new year gained priority probably because of its proximity to two other important holidays, the harvest festival, Succoth, and Yom Kippur, the solemn Day of Atonement, and the fact that as a time of "memorial," it was the occasion when God judged the deeds of all men during the preceding year. Thus Rosh Hashanah, the first day of Tishri, the first month of the lunar year, came to rank with Yom Kippur as one of the most sacred celebrations of the year, and begins the High Holiday season. The most conspicuous feature of its observance is the ritual of sounding the *shofar* or ram's horn, a stirring signal that was believed to have the power to drive away evil spirits and cause the walls of enemy fortresses to come tumbling down. On Rosh Hashanah it signals the sovereignty of Jehovah.

The Sounds of the *ib Shofar

Tekiah

Shevarim

Teruah

Source and Comment

Traditional. Remembered by H. C. from religious services attended, 1930 to present. For further notations and comment see Abraham Z. Idelsohn, *The Ceremonies of Judaism* New York, 1930, 14-16, and *The Jewish Encyclopedia* New York, 1901-6, XI, 305.

On the morning of Rosh Hashanah the *shofar* is blown by a "master" in a prescribed order which consists of sequences of three elements (which may vary somewhat). They are known as the *tekiah,* a sustained blast ending abruptly on a fourth or fifth note above the sustained note; the *shevarim,* three groups of two notes, each quavering to a fourth or fifth note above; and the *teruah,* nine very short staccato notes, or a variant, tremolo on one tone ending abruptly with a fourth or fifth note above. The *shofar* has a limited range, and though the sage Maimonides said its sound could penetrate the soul and cause the heart to tremble, it has never been praised for its musical qualities.

Begin the Year with Sweetness

A [Rosh Hashanah] holiday dinner begins (*rosh*) the year (*hashanah*). Women ceremonially light the candles for this dinner and recite the *kiddush* [prayer]. Then bits of *challah,* the sweet holiday bread, or sliced apples are customarily dipped in honey as a symbol of sweetness and health for the new year. And in keeping with the joyous spirit, no bitter or sour foods are used during the holiday.

There follow two days of synagogue services that include the blowing of the *shofar*—the ram's horn trumpet. On the second night, a "new" fruit, generally one just coming into season, is served. As one of the "first fruits" of the New Year, apples are used in a number of recipes. Other symbolic foods include fish (fertility), the round *challah* bread (life without end), honey (sweetness) and carrots (prosperity).

Honey and fish are combined in this recipe for Sweet Fish.

2	fresh water fish, trout or other, 1 pound each
½	teaspoon salt
¼	teaspoon pepper
3	tablespoons flour
½	cup oil
1½	teaspoons rosemary leaves
⅓	cup water
¼	cup honey
3	tablespoons pine nuts
3	tablespoons raisins
3	tablespoons lemon juice
1	clove garlic crushed

Clean fish; sprinkle inside with salt and pepper. Coat fish with flour. Heat oil in large skillet. Add rosemary. Saute fish about 10 minutes on each side or until cooked and golden. Remove to a 2-inch-deep, heat-proof dish. Combine water, honey, pine nuts, raisins, lemon juice and garlic in saucepan; bring to boiling. Pour over fish and simmer gently five minutes. Makes two servings.

Source

Philadelphia Inquirer, October 4, 1977. By Marilynn Marter, staff food writer.

*   *   *

Shaking Sin into the Water

Another custom which is slowly dying out in this country [c.1916] is known as *Tashlik* ["thou wilt cast"]. This is the ceremony of shaking one's sins into the water. It is based on a verse in the prophet Micah: "Thou wilt cast all their sins into the depths of the sea." On the afternoon of the Jewish New Year the more extreme of the orthodox Jews repair to some stream, where they recite prayers and shake the ends of their garments as though they were casting their sins from them. It is not known where or when this custom originated. Many very pious Jews have ridiculed it, since there is not religious sanction for the practice. It is gradually becoming extinct in this country, although one can still see on Manhattan and Brooklyn bridges in New York earnest old men and women who sincerely believe that their transgressions are being hurled, Satan-like, into the abyss below. Eads Bridge in St. Louis, too, is the witness of a like scene, and the waters of the Missouri at Kansas City undoubtedly suffer a similar pollution.

Source

Journal of American Folklore, XXIX (1916), 415-16. Leah R. C. Yoffie describes "Survivals of Ancient Jewish Customs" mainly within the St. Louis, Missouri, "community of orthodox Jews who have emigrated from Russia, Poland, and Galicia."

*   *   *

Table Cloth Cure during Rosh Hashanah

[A ritual among Greek Sephardic Jews in Seattle] called *mantel a la mar* [tablecloth to the sea] ... is performed during Rosh Hashanah (one of the High Holy Days) for the curing of someone who might be sick of any ailment at that time. Two tablecloths are placed on the dining table, one over the other, and sugar is sprinkled, in the name of the sick person, on the four corners of the bottom tablecloth. The sugar is said to absorb the blessings which are said during the evening meal. Both cloths are then folded under the pillow of the patient that night. The next morning the cloths are taken to a body of water and shaken out, and after invoking God and the Patriarchs in the name of the patient all the evil is "told" to go into the depths of the sea.

The tablecloth is again placed behind the patient's pillow that night, and taken to the body of water the next day, the same ritual being then repeated. During the course of the ritual the patient observes all the isolation and dietary restrictions that pertain to *cerradura* [literally, "closing"; a period of rigid isolation].

Source

Journal of American Folklore, LXXV (1962), 308. From an article by Melvin Firestone on the curing rituals of a community of Sephardic or culturally Spanish Jews who came to Seattle about 1903.

Yom Kippur

September—October

Yom Kippur, which is the most important of Jewish holidays, is the tenth Day of Tishri, the first lunar month, and the last of the Ten Days of Penitence. It means "Day of Atonement" and is marked by twenty-four hours of fasting (neither food nor drink) and prayer. During this time, each Jew asks for forgiveness for all the sins of mankind, particularly pride, vanity, greed, jealousy, and lust. "Father," the prayer begins, "we have sinned before Thee...." Normally, the family assembles for a festive meal the evening before Yom Kippur (in keeping with the old idea that each day commences at sunset). Candles are lit, members of the family ask each other for forgiveness for whatever wrongs they have committed, and then they go to the synagogue to pray. White, the traditional color of purity, is used for altar clothes, the cover of the Torah, the synagogue officials' robes, and usually for the skull caps of the congregation as well. Yom Kippur is a solemn day, but dedicated to joyfulness in the belief that God will forgive old sins and a fresh start will be made by all.

Sin Offering

One of the oldest and most important of the religious observances of the Jews was the sacrificial offerings of animals in the Temple. This practice has almost entirely been abandoned [1916]. The only survival of it is the killing of a fowl before the Day of Atonement as a sin-offering. The bird is later eaten to break the fast which is required of all Jews on that day. But it is not absolutely essential to shed blood for the remission of sin, for a sum of money may be offered instead. This money does not go to the synagogue, but to the poor.

Source

Journal of American Folklore, XXIX (1916), 416. A vestige of an ancient rite surviving among orthodox Jews in St. Louis is reported by Leah R. C. Yoffie. It is observed by "late comers" from Russia, Poland, and Galicia, many of whom "brought with them century-old traditions."

Succoth

September—October

Succoth is the seven days, beginning on the fifteenth of Tishri, the first month of the lunar year. The word means "booths" or "tabernacles" and the holiday is known as the Feast of Booths and the Ingathering. It is the last festival in the fall sequence beginning with Rosh Hashanah (see p. 350). Originally it celebrated the harvest and later also the wanderings of the Israelites in the desert. Observant Jewish families build *succah* or temporary dwellings and deck them with greenery and fruit. Here they sing, read suitable religious texts, and enjoy themselves. Ceremonial objects associated with this holiday include the "Four Species" of plants: *ethrog* or citron, *lulav* or the shoot of a palm tree, *hadassah* or twigs of myrtle, and *aravah* or willow branches. These are carried in a daily procession around the synagogue, often in containers artistically worked in precious metals, to the accompaniment of chants. Rabbis attach ethical meaning to this rite and these objects, but they have agricultural significance as well—thanksgiving for a harvest and invocation to fertility. In fact, on the day immediately following is a solemn occasion for praise and supplication, *Atzeret,* meaning "restraint." It features a prayer for rain. The rainy season begins in Palestine in the fall.

Yom Tov

yom tov la - nu chag sa - me ach ye - la - dim na - gi - la na

lesu - ka - te - nu va o - re - ach av - ra - ham a - vi - nu ba - ruch ha - ba

ya - chad et ha - chag na - chog be - lu - lav ha - dass et - rog

hoi he - ach nis - mach me - od u - va ma - gal nir - kod

Holiday

Holiday, happy festival:
    Children, let us rejoice.
To our succah, a guest has come:
    Father Abraham, we welcome you.
Let us rejoice together
    With palm, myrtle, and citron.
Hey, come, join in and be merry,
    And dance around in a circle.

Source

YIVO Institute for Jewish Research Archives, New York. From *Sukkot,* 28, an undated pamphlet issued by the Zionist Organization of America, New York, and affiliated organizations.

Simhath Torah

September—October

Simhath Torah is the twenty-fourth day of Tishri, the first month of the lunar year. Associated with the harvest season and the beginning of the Jewish New Year, this occasion marks the completion of the cyclical ritual of reading the Torah (Hebrew for "law"), the first five books of the Old Testament, and the beginning of another annual cycle of ritualistic reading. To be chosen as readers of the last chapter of the Torah and the first chapter of Genesis is considered a signal honor. The festival features the removal of the scrolls of the Torah from their shrine and parading them around the synagogue and sometimes out into the streets.

Rejoicing in the Law

Jews danced in the streets of Brooklyn [New York] until the early morning hours yesterday [October 12, 1971] in numbers that the police estimated at "the multiplied thousands."

They sang hymns of joy, filled synagogues to overflowing, stood atop chairs and perched precariously on window sills to celebrate Simhath Torah, the "Rejoicing in the Law," the happiest day on the Hebrew religious calendar.

The holiday marks the completion of the year-long reading of the Torah cycle: the chanting of the last chapter and the immediate reading again, starting with Genesis.

"There is no real beginning and no end to the Torah and its commandments and that is why we read and reread," said a rabbi.

And in scores of houses of worship from the smallest to the largest in the Crown Heights, Borough Park and Williamsburg sections Simhath Torah had particular meaning for the Hasidim.

With unbridled gaiety, garbed in their traditional long coats, wide-brimmed hats and yarmulkes [skullcaps], they carried the Torahs aloft, the covers glistening with richly adorned ornaments. They danced and sang with love and reverence for the Torah as they circled the *bima* (the center platform of the synagogue).

For the followers of Rabbi Menachem M. Schneerson, spiritual leader of the worldwide Lubavitcher Movement, the intellectual and religious Orthodox body, the focal point was 770 Eastern Parkway.

For some six hours, 1,500 persons with little space to move, listened to their *rebbe*—the affectionate expression for the spiritual leader of the movement. Only at rare intervals would the 69-year-old blue-eyed Rabbi Schneerson, a graduate of the Sorbonne and the University of Berlin, pause.

Then, it was a signal for his followers to sing, to lift paper cups and toast Rabbi Schneerson with a "L'Chayyim" (to your health).

Seated atop a platform in the walnut-paneled auditorium-synagogue with its crystal chandeliers, Rabbi Schneerson, speaking in Yiddish, repeatedly emphasized that the Torah was the very core of all Jewish experience and that "it gave life meaning, that complete adherence to its commandments meant for the enrichment of every phase of Jewish religious life.". . .

The silence that permeated the synagogue-auditorium gave way to a resounding joyous din as some 25 Torahs were removed from the Ark shortly after midnight. The worshippers carried the Torahs outside and danced and sang for more than an hour.

Source

New York Times, October 13, 1971. By Irving Spiegel, with the headline, "Joyful Jews in Brooklyn Celebrate Simhath Torah."

Ramadan

Retrograde in regard to the Gregorian Calendar

Ramadan or Ramazan is the ninth month, the most sacred of the Moslem year. It is a time of fasting, sometimes for as long as forty days, a time of the expiation. It might be compared with the Jewish Yom Kippur or Day of Atonement and the Christian period of Lent. Islamic belief holds that God revealed the Qur'ān to the prophet Mohammed during the month of Ramadan. During Ramadan, one does not eat or drink while "the white thread can be distinguished from the black:" that is from dawn till sunset. Thus, the nights are often given over to feasting. Nevertheless, this is a time of patience and suffering, especially if the weather is hot.

On the 27th day of Ramadan, the day the Qur'ān was sent down from Heaven, the tree of Paradise is shaken and the names of those to die can be read in the fallen leaves.

The Holy Month of Ramadan

Try working or going to school without eating or drinking anything from sunrise to sunset. Try having breakfast before the sun comes up, your next meal only after the sun goes down.

All day. Every day. For four weeks.

That's what observant Muslims are doing these days, around the world and even in the Philadelphia region.

For Muslims, the annual holy month of Ramadan—the equivalent of the Christian season of Lent—began early last week.

It is a holy time.

It might seem a difficult time.

Especially difficult in a non-Muslim society like the United States, where sizzling smells from vendors' carts and sidewalk sights of snacking strollers are all too common.

Is it difficult to observe a religious fast in the midst of a secular society?

Ask an American-born Muslim.

"This is the first Ramadan ... without my family, and that's kind of hard because you don't have the support" of other people fasting, said Bashera Abdul-Hadi, a West Philadelphian who is a freshman at Ursinus College in Collegeville [Pennsylvania].

"Here I'm alone," she said, "and there aren't any other [observant] Muslims I can share Ramadan with."

Ask a foreign-born American who is Muslim.

"It is easier when everyone is observing Ramadan and fasting," said Manzoor Chaudhry, a chemical laboratory manager in Northeast Philadelphia who was born in Pakistan.

But fasting is "self-discipline," Chaudhry said. "You could discipline yourself, regardless of the circumstances where you are."

On Saturday evening, Chaudhry gathered with almost 100 other foreign-born Muslims at a storefront mosque in Kensington, to break the fast at sundown and to offer the sundown prayer.

Each week during Ramadan, the mosque is the scene of a sunset prayer, a community meal and then a final prayer at 9:30 p.m.—not only on the holy day of Friday but on Saturday and Sunday as well.

The fast was on the minds of these members of the eight-year-old Muslim Society of the Delaware Valley. Chaudhry is its president.

At precisely 7:42 p.m., the moment of sunset, their religious leader—their *imam*—gave the word and the men went to tables at the back of the main room, each to take a handful of dates or shelled nuts and a cupful of orange juice or grapefruit juice.

Later, they would have a tasty multinational meal—ground beef rolls known as *kunafa,* meat turnovers known as *somosa,* grape-speckled rice, lots more.

But now, after breaking their fast, they went to the front of the room, formed themselves into four lines and waited for the *imam* to begin the 10-minute prayer. They were facing east, facing toward the Muslim holy city in Saudi Arabia, toward Mecca.

A Saudi was the only one there to wear the head scarf common to desert nations. A few wore the knitted skull cap usually worn under such headdress. A few others wore the hip-length tunics common in some Middle East countries. Most wore suits and jackets.

There were worshipers who had been born in Egypt and Kuwait, India and Pakistan, Indonesia and Malaysia, Syria and the Sudan.

In Collegeville, there is no such gathering, no such mosque for Abdul-Hadi, the Ursinus freshman. There is isolation.

Now 18, she has been fasting each year since she was 11. So she knows what it feels like.

"Sometimes you think to yourself, 'I'm going to eat a lot [at pre-dawn breakfast] so I won't be hungry during the day.' It doesn't work," she said with a laugh.

"When I think, 'O, God, I'm so hungry,'" Abdul-Hadi said, "I tend to think, 'There's a reason I'm doing it.'"

Thinking that, she said, was easier among other Muslims, back home near 52d and Chestnut Streets.

"On campus, when I'm around everyone else ... I feel like I have no support. That's why," she said, laughing again, "my phone bill is so high, because I call my Mom all the time."

It is a physical strain, even on those who have been fasting during Ramadan for decades.

"The last couple of hours [each day], you feel tired and weak," said Dr. Abdul Safi, a Manayunk physician who came from Syria in 1974.

But the tiredness is worth the effort.

"Ramadan puts you in the experience of those who don't have something to eat," said Safi, chatting at the Kensington mosque Saturday.

That's important, he said, because "Ramadan is also the month of giving, the month of sharing—to give to others, to give to the needy."

Fazal Rehman of Bensalem is a salesman for a pharmaceutical firm who came from Pakistan in 1974.

Do non-Muslim colleagues ever unthinkingly offer him a coffee during the day?

"No, my God, no," he said. "During fasting, whenever I go to meetings, they have respect for me."

It's the American way, he said.

"This is an open country," he said. "You have the freedom to believe. People respect your belief and that's the greatness of this country."

Source

Philadelphia Inquirer, April 25, 1988. By staff writer Walter F. Naedele. See "Islamic New Year," p. 23, for information on the retrograde cycle of the Muslim calendar.

* * *

Food for Ramadan

When Azmi Takiedine was growing up in Damascus, Syria, the month of Ramadan—during which devout Muslims fast from dawn to sunset—was an exciting time.

He remembers with deep fondness the sounds of the *mussaher,* the men who broke the pre-dawn silence to let people know it was time for *sohour*—one of two meals permitted each day.

"A man in each neighborhood would carry the *durbaka* [small drum] and make noise to wake the people up, hollering, 'I'm here to wake you up,'" Takiedine recalled. "I used to look forward to him. I always thought he was invisible, because by the time we got up, he was gone."

Takiedine, 37, left Syria with his wife, Dina, 30, in 1973 to attend the University of Florida, where he majored in economics. The couple now live in Pine Valley [Pennsylvania], where they observe Ramadan with their children, Maya, 6, and Omar, 3.

Though some of the traditions—like the pre-dawn drumming of the *mussaher,* or the firing of cannons to signal the setting of the sun and the end of the daily fast—are difficult to duplicate in the Philadelphia area, the special foods associated with breaking each day's fast are not....

When each day's fasting is done, Dina Takiedine said, *tskia* is one course that most Muslims will have on their table. It is made mostly of pita bread soaked in a chickpea sauce, then covered with chickpeas, plain yogurt, sesame sauce and pure Arabic butter (homemade from raw milk and then clarified).

"Kibbe is also popular," said her husband. His family's version is ground meat filled with pine nuts and wheat germ and seasoned with allspice. It is formed into small football shapes and fried.

Lentil soup is another Ramadan staple and often joins the kibbe and babaghanouj (eggplant-sesame dip) along with yogurt. Stuffed grape leaves are also eaten during Ramadan.

"We also make a dish of lima beans together with rice. We call it *ruz* and *foul,*" he said. "And lamb shanks covered with pine nuts." ...

Here are recipes for some of the dishes prepared by the Takiedines:

Rice and Bean Pilaf

1 cup uncooked rice
½ cup oil
1 medium onion, chopped
1 bunch fresh coriander, chopped
4 cloves garlic, crushed
1 teaspoon salt
½ teaspoon allspice
½ teaspoon cinnamon
2 pounds fresh broad beans or fava beans, removed from pods and soaked overnight
1½ cups water

Wash and soak the rice for 10 minutes; drain and set aside. Heat the oil, and saute the onion until transparent, about five minutes. Add the coriander, garlic, salt, allspice, cinnamon and beans. Combine by stirring for another five minutes. Cover with water, and cook until the beans are tender, about one hour.

Add the rice to the bean mixture. Cover with the 1 ½ cups water. Bring to a boil, cover, reduce heat, and simmer until the water is absorbed to the point where the surface appears perforated. Remove from heat, and allow to stand for 10 minutes. Serve with plain yogurt. Makes four to six servings.

Lentil Soup

1½ tablespoons butter
1 cup ground lamb
2 small onions, coarsely chopped
1½ cups lentils
10 cups water
    Salt and freshly ground black pepper to taste
    Juice of 1 lemon

Melt the butter in a Dutch oven, and saute the meat and onions. When the meat is browned and the onion tender, add the lentils. Cover with the water, and season with salt and pepper. Bring to a boil, cover, reduce to a simmer, and cook until the lentils are tender, about 45 to 60 minutes. Squeeze the lemon juice on top, and serve. Makes four to six servings.

Babaghanouj

1 large eggplant
¼ cup tahini (sesame paste)
2 cloves garlic, crushed
1 teaspoon salt
2 tablespoons water
¼ cup lemon juice
    Lemon wedges, for garnish
    Chopped parsley, for garnish
    Olive oil, for garnish

Preheat the oven to 375 degrees. Wash the eggplant, and remove the stem. Pierce the eggplant with a fork in six to eight places. Place it in a baking dish and bake until tender, about 45 minutes. Remove the eggplant from the oven, and let it cool. When it is cool enough to handle, peel and then mash the eggplant. Set it aside.

In a bowl, combine tahini with the garlic and salt. Gradually add the water and lemon juice while beating well. Fold in the mashed eggplant. Garnish with the lemon wedges, chopped parsley and a drizzle of olive oil. Serve as a dip with pita bread. Makes about four servings.

Source

Philadelphia Inquirer, April 26, 1989. By Gerald Etter, staff food writer.

Id al-Fitr

Retrograde in regard to the Gregorian Calendar

In translation from the Arabic, this is called "The Festival of Fast Breaking." It follows immediately after the month of Ramadan when fasting ends and feasting begins upon seeing the new moon that in the lunar calendar indicates the first day of the tenth month, Shawwal. A three-day festival, it is a time of thanksgiving, visits to friends, the exchange of gifts and good wishes, official receptions, the putting on of new clothes (cf. Easter), and visits to the graves of deceased relatives (cf. All Saints' Day and Obon). It is, with Id al–adha one of the two principal festivals of Islam.

An Ecumenical Festival of Fast Breaking

You are invited to a celebration. Food and friendship will be in abundance. Please join us, the Muslim community at Penn/Drexel [University of Pennsylvania, and Drexel University, Philadelphia], as we break fast during the Islamic month of Ramadan.

For a month each year, Muslims observe a fast—not a fast of penance, but o[f] renewal. This period, *Ramadan,* is considered by Muslims to be one of the most important expressions of their faith.

During t[he] daylight hours of Ramadan, Muslims neither eat nor drink while conducting their normal affairs. Evenings and nights can be given to prayer and meditation, but they begin with a meal which is often taken communally—*Ifar,* the breaking of the day's fast.

To widen the circle of companionship and celebration, the Muslim Students Association has set aside several evenings to introduce to the Penn community the customary activities of Ramandan, as well as the diversity of the Muslim population.

Source

Daily Pennsylvanian, April 2, 1990. The invitation to celebrate the end of the fast of Ramadan was issued by the Muslim Student Association through an advertisement in the campus newspaper. See "Islamic New Year," p. 23, for a note on the Muslim calendar.

Feast of St. Francis of Assisi

October 4

St. Francis (1182?-1226), founder of the Franciscan order, is notable for his love of nature and his humility. One legend relates how he preached a sermon to sparrows and another that he saved bees from freezing to death. More detailed information on St. Francis appears in the headnote to La Percíngula (August 2), p. 307.

St. Francis of the Pets

[Today] is the Feast of St. Francis. At Holy Cross School in Springfield, Delaware County [Pennsylvania], students brought their pets—dogs, cats, rabbits, hamsters, even hermit crabs—to be blessed yesterday by the Rev. Frank Truger of the school. [Caption for newspaper photograph.]

Source

Philadelphia Inquirer, October 4, 1978. Cf. "Blessing the Animals," p. 158.

Blessing the Animals in New York City

Animals are not normally part of the cityscape. There are "no dogs" signs in store windows and "no pet" clauses in city leases. Yesterday, however, animals were given center stage at the Cathedral of St. John the Divine, a church that often draws its inspiration from the Middle Ages.

For its annual celebration of the Feast of St. Francis, the cathedral opened its doors to an 8,000-pound elephant, a dromedary, a macaw with a 30-word vocabulary, other birds, dogs, cats and a skunk named Respect. One by one, the animals were blessed at the altar in the cathedral, which is the length of two football fields, at Amsterdam Avenue and 112th Street.

The procession of animals came at the end of a joyous two-hour religious service of dance, communion, jazz, preaching—and occasional barking.

For some, it was just another side show at an Episcopal cathedral that celebrated its centennial with a performance by an aerialist and that one Easter displayed a sculpture of a female Christ named Christa.

But to the Rev. James Parks Morton, the innovative dean of St. John the Divine, the blessing of the animals was a serious, if not exactly solemn, occasion, and one particularly appropriate for New York. "Animals are like vest-pocket parks," he said.

"They help get the urban dweller rooted in reality. Life has to be more than a series of trips on the subway to the office and back again. Animals give us a fundamental link to creation." . . .

Among the 4,000 worshipers at the service were Blanca Guzman and her daughter, Felisa, who brought their dog, Luna, from their home in the Bronx for a blessing. "We want her to be with us for a long, long time," said the younger Ms. Guzman, tugging at the leash of their 4-year-old Siberian husky. "She's a good companion," said her mother, who stays home with Luna when her daughter is at work. "I only wish she would be a better guard dog. Luna looks tough, but she doesn't bark."

As Robert Gilmor of Huntington, L.I., took his cat, Tom, for a blessing, he said his wish was that the cat "would become a vegetarian."

"He brings home chipmunks, mice, squirrels and birds," said Mr. Gilmor, whose raincoat was covered with white hairs from Tom's coat. . . .

The festival took in not just animals but everything God created, as was evident from the service for the day, known as "Missa Gaia/Earth Mass." The piece was performed by the Paul Winter Consort, the Omega Liturgical Dancers and the cathedral's choristers, chorus and singers, with the added sounds of wolf, whale and loon. The mass was commissioned by the cathedral and first performed there in 1981.

The work has the essentials of the mass—the Kyrie, Sanctus, Benedictus, Agnus Dei—as well as the text of the "Canticle of Brother Sun," a prayer written by St. Francis.

Still, as was appropriate, the animals had the final word. Pete Brandon of Manhattan took his macaw, Captain Casanova, to Dean Morton for a blessing. In the silence of the church, the dean put his hand over the beak of the red, green and blue bird and whispered a prayer. Captain Casanova, digging into his own vocabulary for a response, announced: "Come on! Let's go!"

Source and Comment

New York Times, October 5, 1987. From an article by Ari L. Goldman. Copyright © 1987 by The New York Times Company. Reprinted by permission. The blessing of the animals has become quite a spectacle in New York City and has featured a good bit of humor and whimsy in the last few years. In 1988, for instance, 10 billion algae in a flask, a turtle rescued from a Chinese restaurant where it was to have been made into soup, and a 14-foot tall ginkho tree were blessed.

Lantern Night at Bryn Mawr College

First Friday in October

In the late 1880s, women at Bryn Mawr College near Philadelphia became piqued because townies teased them with a satiric song, "The Only Lantern at Bryn Mawr," about a "lantern man" who met their train at night and escorted them to their dormitories. Determined to prove that there was ample illumination on their campus, sophomores, at a campus quiz show in 1896, awarded lanterns as prizes to bright freshmen. By 1901 Lantern Night was separated from the sophomore show, and since then has been held in the evening in the Cloisters of the College Library.

The Tradition of Lantern Night

Tradition is alive and well on the campus of Bryn Mawr, the elite Main Line women's college.

One tradition, which has continued uninterrupted since 1889, is Lantern Night.

On a recent [1978] chilly Friday night, almost the entire freshman and sophomore classes—acting without prompting from the administration—donned black academic robes for a haunting but impressive ceremony in which the freshmen are inducted into Bryn Mawr.

As juniors, seniors, parents and alumnae watched from turrets, the freshmen marched single file into the pitch-black courtyard of the Cloisters, an intimate, Gothic-style quadrangle with a small lily pond at its center.

Once the freshmen were assembled, there was stillness. Then a lilting chorus of soft female voices broke the air, and the sophomores, carrying the lanterns with lighted candles, filed into the courtyard, placing a lantern behind each first-year student. All the while, the sophomores were singing an ancient song—in classical Greek.

The song invokes Athena, the goddess of wisdom and the symbol of Bryn Mawr.

When all the freshmen had received their lanterns, they sang in response a solemn Greek funeral oration. "Lovers of wisdom let us gather together" is the translation of one line.

"Oh, it was so moving," freshman Elizabeth Schmitt said after the ceremony. "It makes me feel accepted. It makes me feel like I'm finally a Bryn Mawr student."

Senior Lisa Gaston asked her parents to travel all the way from California to share the ceremony.

"I think it means even more to a senior," she said. "This is my last one."

Afterwards, all four classes retreated to the steps of Taylor Hall, the main administration building, for a traditional "step sing," in which the classes sing songs and parodies—some more than just a bit bawdy.

Source

Philadelphia Inquirer, November 6, 1978. From a feature story on college traditions by staff writer Edward Schumacher. There was once a belief that the ghost of M. Carey Thomas, long president of the college, joined the procession as it passed through the courtyard in which she is buried.

* * *

Lantern Night

The Lantern Night Procession

When the ceremony begins, the initiates walk into the courtyard and range themselves facing the diminutive duckpond. Each class has a songmistress who stands on the wall of the duckpond. Together the songmistresses lead the singing, keeping time by lowering and raising their lanterns.

A junior will stand in each arch swinging her lantern while the sophomores file in with lighted lanterns. Each sophomore places a lantern behind a freshwoman, while from the arches seniors sing an ancient Greek song which implores the goddess of strength and wisdom, Pallas Athena, to:

> Give us wisdom
> be with us always
> blessed goddess, hear!
> Sanctify our lanterns now,
> to shine clearly forever,
> lighting the way
> making bright the dark.

The freshwomen are then supposed to answer with "Sophias," whose lyrics are taken from the funeral oration of the Athenian politician Pericles. Much to the pain of the songmistresses, the freshwomen and transfers generally sing discordantly and weakly, but a courageous few carry the song:

> Friends of wisdom, let us be present,
> We love beauty, but without display,
> We love learning, but we must be strong,
> We use our means and power
> To find a way
> To help the world where we belong.
>
> The goal is noble, worth our pain and risk ...
> The task is hard. Our hopes are high.

After the presentation of the lanterns, everyone assembles on the steps of Taylor Hall for a step-sing.... During the step-sing freshwomen eagerly peer at the tea invitations [from upperclasswomen] tied to each lantern. According to Traditions Mistress Martha Bayless, the Mawrter whose lantern goes out first will be the first to marry and the lucky Mawrter whose candle flickers out last will finish her Ph.D. first. In addition, tradition has it that if a freshwoman spills wax on her bat robe [campus slang for academic gown], she will become a hall president for sure....

The original lanterns were only four inches high and made of isinglass. Each year sophomores designed different panels for the lantern. Eventually, the lantern pattern was standardized to save money, but each class has different colored lantern panels.

"Lantern Night is symbolic of the cycle of things at Bryn Mawr," commented Bayless, explaining that last year's senior class [1979] color, green, would be given to this year's entering class [1983].

Part of the beauty of Lantern Night is the near total darkness, illuminated only by the lanterns. To preserve the atmosphere, Bayless requests that no pictures be taken.

Source

Bryn Mawr-Haverford College News, October 5, 1979. From a news story for the college paper by Bryn Mawr student Susan Davis.

Leif Ericson Day

October 9

About the year 1000, Leif Ericson, a Norwegian convert to Christianity, was commissioned by King Olaf I to convert the Vikings of Greenland. One account in a collection of sagas states that he was blown off course and as a result reached the coast of North America. Another has him setting out from Greenland and spending the winter at Vinland, a point somewhere between Virginia and Nova Scotia. Because the date and place of his "discovery" of America are uncertain, in 1964 the originators of this celebration arbitrarily selected October 9 to commemorate it. This seemed appropriate because the first organized body of Norwegian emigrants landed in America on October 9, 1825. Also, it is near Columbus Day.

Leif Erikson, Norseperson

Proclamation 4524
Leif Erikson Day, 1977

By the President of the United States of America

A Proclamation

Once again it is appropriate for Americans to honor the intrepid Norse explorers who overcame hardship and adversity to reach our shores so long ago.

The United States is a young Nation, but our debt to that courageous Norseperson, Leif Erikson, predates 1776 and recalls a distant age when brave adventurers sailed forth into the unknown. As a people we continue to embody this spirit of bold discovery, and we take pride in his historical exploits.

As a mark of respect for Leif Erikson and the Norse explorers, the Congress of the United States, by joint resolution approved September 2, 1964 (78 Stat. 849, 36 U.S.C. 169c), authorized the President to proclaim October 9 in each year as Leif Erikson Day.

NOW THEREFORE, I, JIMMY CARTER, President of the United States of America, do hereby designate Sunday, October 9, 1977, as Leif Erikson Day and I direct the appropriate Government officials to display the flag of the United States on all Government buildings that day.

I also invite the people of the United States to honor the memory of Leif Erikson on that day by holding appropriate exercises and ceremonies in suitable places throughout our land.

IN WITNESS WHEREOF, I have hereunto set my hand this twenty-third day of September, in the year of our Lord nineteen hundred seventy-seven, and of the Independence of the United States of America the two hundred and second.

Jimmy Carter

From the *Congressional Record*

(Mr. MICHEL asked and was given permission to address the House for 1 minute and to revise and extend his remarks.)

Mr. MICHEL. Mr. Speaker,... How ... can you account for President Carter's proclamation, quoted in the Washington Post the other day, which decrees that Leif Ericson was not in fact a Norseman. The President has declared that Ericson and all his countrymen, excuse me, country-persons, were Norsepersons.

If this is indeed a sign that history is being rewritten, I must express grave concerns. What is it going to cost to rewrite all those history books and reprogram those of us already educated in the old-fashioned way of doing things?

I think our President ought to explain this new application of his power. He is ultimately responsible. One of his first actions as President was to proudly display on his desk a reminder that "the buck stops here," a reminder first made famous by that great leader and great President, Harry S. Truperson.

Source

Federal Register, September 27, 1977, 38-39. The remarks of Robert H. Michel, Eighteenth District of Illinois, the House of Representatives, were first published in the *Congressional Record* of September 30, 1977.

* * *

Leif Ericson and Columbus

Here we go again. Who really discovered America?

Supporters of two main contenders celebrate their conflicting claims on the same day, Oct. 9.

Officially, though not legally, it's Leif Ericson Day.

Legally, though not officially, it's Columbus Day—pushed forward from the formal Oct. 12 by Congress to make a long weekend possible.

Ivar Christensen, president of the Leif Ericson Society, which claims the Viking hero landed in North America in 1004 (488 years before Columbus sailed into the New World), has scheduled a gala dinner-dance near his headquarters office in Media [Pennsylvania] "and we have invited various Italian organizations and also will have our Viking ship 'Raven' parked outside," he said.

"It's an inspiring ship and some of the non-Vikings might walk a big circle around it because those dragonheads mounted on it are intimidating," he said. "But we've encouraged the Sons of Italy to bring a replica of the Santa Maria (the Columbus flagship) to see which looks best."

The party will wind up a three-day Scandinavian Festival, sponsored jointly by the Danish, Finnish, Icelandic, Norwegian and Swedish societies to mark Ericson's historic voyage to America, not yet recognized in most history books.

"It's really a friendly thing because there is no dispute any longer over who discovered America—is there?" Christensen said.

Source and Comment

Philadelphia Inquirer, October 11, 1978. By Lee Linder, Associated Press staff writer. His informant, Ivar Christensen of Media, Pennsylvania, is of Norwegian birth and is president and founder of the Leif Ericson Society which promotes this celebration. For Leif Ericson Day, see also "Walpurgisnacht," p. 187.

Columbus Day

October 12

By sailing westward, Christopher Columbus reached the New World, landing on a small island in the Bahamas which he named San Salvador on October 12, 1492. The anniversary of his landing was formally celebrated for the first time by the Society of St. Tammany, also known as the Columbian Order, in New York City in 1792 and was made a legal holiday by presidential proclamation a century later at the opening of the Columbian Exposition in Chicago. Now by federal law it is celebrated on the first Monday in October.

Although Columbus to his dying day believed he had reached the East Indies, and although other sailors and explorers may have preceded him to America, and although America is named for a navigator, Amerigo Vespucci, who followed after him and extended his discoveries, Columbus Day serves as a tribute to the revelation of a New World. A native of Genoa, Italy, Columbus is the particular hero of Italian-Americans, and Columbus Day has become for them a patriotic occasion of importance.

Columbus Day Pageant

Although the celebration [of Columbus Day in San Francisco] takes place on a Sunday, the festivities actually begin on the preceding Saturday night when, at a Grand Ball, the young woman who is to play the role of Queen Isabella in the pageant is chosen by popular vote, and crowned. This past year [1947] October 12 fell on a Sunday. On the evening of October 11, the Columbus Day Ball and the Coronation of the Queen were held at the Aquatic Park Building. On Sunday the ceremonies began with Solemn High Mass, which was—and always is—celebrated in the Church of SS. Peter and Paul, in the North Beach district, where most of San Francisco's Italians reside. The civic festivities, however, did not begin until the afternoon, when, at one o'clock, a parade assembled at the Civic Center and then proceeded down Market Street to Kearny Street, Columbus Avenue, Stockton Street, Filbert Street, and Powell Street. No fewer than five thousand marchers passed before the reviewing stand opposite the Church of SS. Peter and Paul. Thousands of people watched the impressive procession of more than eighty units.

This first float was the Queen Float, with the Queen, Rose Amodio, and her ladies-in-waiting. Then followed the official cars, the band of the 2d Infantry Division, the San Francisco Naval Base band and marching sailors, the Coast Guard band, and many other bands, hundreds of horses and riders in their dazzling trappings, the Irish Freedom League float, howling Red Men improvising war dances, the blue-clad Vallejo Rainbow Girls patrol, colorful drill teams of the Native Daughters of the Golden West, the Italian Catholic Federation's drum and bugle corps, the showy red-and-orange clad drum corps of the Chinese girls of Old St. Mary's Church, hundreds of marching young men from the Salesian Boys Club and the San Francisco Boys Club. The parade lasted more than two hours.

Even before the parade ended, throngs of people had gathered at Aquatic Park where, since half-past one, other festivities had been in progress: a symphony orchestra played several selections; the San Francisco Fire Department gave an exhibition of water-front fire fighting, and so on. By the time the parade was over, a large percentage of the spectators had arrived at Aquatic Park. The bleachers set up for the occasion were filled to capacity, and the rest of the crowd moved about restlessly, trying to secure a place from which to get a glimpse of the beach where Columbus was soon to land.

While the spectators were waiting for the Queen and her retinue to arrive, one of the officials of the day gave the address of welcome. A soprano sang "God Bless America," the audience joined in the Pledge of Allegiance, and a group of dancers performed some Spanish dances. Meanwhile, on the beach, only a short distance from the blue waters of the bay, several tepees had been erected, and squatting and walking among them, in colorful Indian costume, were numerous members of the Improved Order of Red Men, and of the Degree of Pocahontas. A few of them participated in typical Indian dances.

Finally, with some delay, the Queen arrived on her float with her attendants. They alighted and went to take their places on a platform which had been set up not far from the Indian tepees. Everything was now ready for the "landing" of Columbus. Thus, a few minutes later, three boats, provided by the Italian fishermen of the city and rigged up to resemble the famous *Santa Maria, Pinta* and *Niña,* entered the cove and cast anchor a short distance from the shore. Columbus and a few of his men descended into a rowboat, came ashore, and proceeded to the Indian village. The Admiral uttered a few words of thanks to God for having guided him to the Indies, and smoked the pipe of peace with the Indian chief. Then, accompanied by some of his men and a few Indians, he walked over to the platform representing Queen Isabella's court in Barcelona, and there was met by Cardinal Mendoza, beautifully clad in bright red. The Cardinal escorted Columbus into the presence of the Queen, who was surrounded by three ladies-in-waiting and three children, all dressed in appropriate costumes. She graciously listened to the great navigator's account of his voyage, while looking with interest at the gifts and the Indians he had brought back; and when he finished his report, she thanked him for all he had accomplished.

Thus ended the colorful pageant. Later in the afternoon, prizes were awarded to the winning organizations that had participated in the parade, and in the evening the entire celebration closed with the annual Columbus Day dinner, at which the principal speakers were General Mark Clark and Dr. Herbert C. Clish, Superintendent of Schools, City of San Francisco....

[By] 1892 the Italians of New York, San Francisco, and a few other American cities had been celebrating Columbus Day for several years. As far as I was able to ascertain, the Italian population of New York City began to celebrate the discovery of America on October 12, 1866. The honor of having begun these Columbian festivities goes to the *Compagnia del Tiro al Bersaglio di New York* ([Italian] Sharpshooters' Association of New York). Their example was soon followed by other Italian associations in other parts of our country, so that by 1869 very elaborate festivities—in New York, a parade, sharpshooting contests, dancing, a banquet, and Italian ships in the harbor gaily decorated with flags—were held not only in New York, but also in Philadelphia, St. Louis, Boston, Cincinnati, and New Orleans.

As far as can be learned, it was in 1869 that Columbus Day was first celebrated in San Francisco. This city, however, observed Discovery Day on Sunday, October 17. On that day flags were displayed from various armories of the city. At noon the procession formed and started from the corner of Post and Montgomery streets in this order: A. D. Grimwood, Grand Marshal, assisted by his aids; a band of music; the Swiss Guards; a triumphal carriage, drawn by

four horses and decorated with a half hemisphere on which was the "eagle, bird of freedom," as if it had just alighted on the newly discovered continent to claim it as its own. In the center of the car was a statue of the great Discoverer, and in the rear of the platform was a raised dais on which were seated two young ladies, one dressed to represent Isabella of Spain, the other, America. The whole was decorated and surmounted by Italian, American, and Spanish flags. Then came the Lafayette Guard with a brass band; the California Jaeger corps; the Car of State with thirty-two young ladies dressed in white and bearing in their hands the colors of the United States and of the other republics of America. Then, in barouches, came the President of the Day, the Orator of the Day, the Italian and Spanish consuls; a band; the Garibaldi Guard; the *Santa Maria,* a large boat rigged in imitation of the caravel which bore Columbus to our shores. The boat carried Columbus with an escort of several sailors in red shirts and dark pantaloons. Then came the decorated wagon of the Italian gardeners, bearing a young lady surrounded by the implements of agriculture. Then another float with a pyramid of punch bottles (it advertised an Italian liquor store), decorated with flowers, ribbons, and so forth. The procession moved through the main streets, and on to the City Gardens, where an oration was delivered on the exploits of Columbus. The festivities ended with a dinner provided by the Garibaldi Guard (hence the red shirts and dark pantaloons of the sailors on the *Santa Maria.*)

Source

Western Folklore, VII (1948), 326-29. From "The Development of the Columbus Day Pageant of San Francisco" by Charles Speroni. His sources, in addition to personal observation, included John J. Mazza of San Francisco, "who since 1941 has been playing the role of Columbus in the pageant," and San Francisco newspaper files.

* * *

Italian-American Columbus Day

For much of the nineteenth century, the celebration of Columbus in literature, the arts, and ritual remained in Yankee hands. But while the "Italianization" of Columbus began in eastern cities such as New York and Philadelphia, Italian-Americans in the West made significant contributions to this process....

One of the interesting questions about the Columbus Day complex is the extent to which it combined Italian and Anglo-American elements. The landing pageant and the costuming of Columbus impersonators, for example, may owe much to the John Vanderlyn painting, *The Landing of Columbus,* commissioned for the U.S. Capitol rotunda in 1839 and reproduced widely on U.S. postage stamps in 1869 and 1892. The Columbus Day parades (generally not a feature of the Anglo-American Columbus Day before 1892) may owe much to Italian religious processions, especially if we consider the importance of Columbus statues in the Columbus Day complex. The Italian-American community of Walla Walla, Washington, erected its Columbus statue in 1910 and, according to local historians, the annual Columbus Day festival dates from that year. Meanwhile, in 1907 Colorado became the first state to make Columbus Day a legal holiday, thanks to a drive led by local *prominenti* aided by the Italian consul in Denver. The holiday and its associated practices and artifacts remain an important cultural landmark for Italians. For example, when during the recent restoration of California's Gold Rush era capitol in Sacramento architects proposed eliminating an anachronistic Columbus statue that had been installed in the capitol rotunda under Anglo-American auspices in 1882, Italian-American politicians and organizations raised a storm of protest, forcing the reinstallation of the statue.

Source and Comment

Folklife Center News, XI (Summer 1989), 11-12. From "Italian Regionalism and Pan-Italian Traditions" by John Alexander Williams. His emphasis is on the "transformation of Italian-Americans from immigrants to ethnics," and he identifies Columbus "as an ethnic hero" and Columbus Day as an amalgam of a traditional Italian saint's day festival and an Anglo-American patriotic ceremony.

* * *

Columbus Lands in San Francisco

On September 30, the 1989 Columbus Landing Ceremony was held at Aquatic Park, in San Francisco, with the U.S. Navy Band providing music and a local T.V. personality serving as master-of-ceremonies. Christopher Columbus was played by Joseph Cervetto, Jr., a member of the Columbus Day Celebration's Board of Directors. Cervetto's father had also taken the role.

Source

Folklife Center News, XI (Fall 1989), 8.

* * *

Dialect Story for Columbus Day

Columbus Day is still observed in the northern [Upper Peninsula] by Italian fraternal groups. In schools the teachers give special attention to the day, read again of the discovery, have the students recite poems, write themes. In my grade this theme was given. Tony had come from Italy the summer before and learned English as we taught it to him but writing the theme was beyond him. So at the suggestion of some of the kids, he told the story.

"Christopho Colombo was greata man. Dis time wen he was small kid, he live Genoa, Italy. An he sailed de liddle boat on de big ocean. One days he getta big idea. An he say, 'I tink I gonna fin' America.' So whad you tink? He'll gone see de queen, because de queen you know was a good fren' for him. An he's say, 'Queen old kid, you pretty good fren' to me ain't you? Howsa chance you catch for me tree boat, I gonna find America?' And de queen is say, 'Don't you maka so much noise; de king is playa de check, he no wanta so much noise.' So whad you tink, de queen is sell his broach, his earring, his wristwatch, and is buy tree new boat, Nina, Pinta, Santa Maria. An' one days he sail on de big ocean. An' he's a saila for tree, four months. An' one day de big osh is getta pretty rough. Everybody was getta sick. He's a comin' one boy from up de hole, an' he say, 'Chris I tink de whole idea is cockeye. Is better we turn around an' go home.' An' Chris was getta pretty mad. An' he say, 'No sirree. Don't you give uppa da ship till you see his whita eye.' So he's sail again for two, tree months. An' is come one udder boy. An' he's say, 'Chris, I tink I see de tree.' An' Colombo is say, 'Never min' de tree, is land we wanta see.' So he's a saila tree or four monts some more. An' ona day is come annudder boy from de hole, an' he's a-say, 'Colombo, I tink I see de land.' An' Colombo's a-say, 'Dat's a good boy, old kid, datsa whad we wanta see.' So whad you tink, he's put his foot on land, An' he's come one Indian chief. An' Indian chief he's say, 'Hollo, Mister Colombo, it's you, ain't it?' An' Colombo say, 'Hollo, hollo, you Indian fella too, ain't you?' And Indian chief is turn around say to his pals, 'Boys, jig is hup, now we're discover.' "

Source and Comment

Journal of American Folklore, LXI (1948), 145-46. Richard M. Dorson collected dialect stories from the North Peninsula of Michigan, which is particularly rich in such material due to its ethnic diversity. He makes the point that the dialect story "fits the definitions of the folk narrative." It is meant to be told, not read: "print tends to resist dialect." He collected the Columbus Day story from Walter F. Gries of Ishpeming, Michigan, on May 15, 1946.

* * *

Columbus Day Turkey Shoot

Keith Geiges squinted down the barrel of his .22-caliber rifle yesterday [October 11, 1981] afternoon, trying desperately just to sight his target.

It wasn't much to shoot at—just a tiny white head with a minute speck of red blending into a dense autumn background of crimson and gold woods.

So tough was the shot that Geiges was about to make at 2:30 P.M. yesterday that 21 contestants before him, each paying $1 a shot for the same chance, had come up empty. But finally, on the 57th shot of the afternoon, Geiges, 22, of Newfoundland, Pa., got lucky.

And the crowd cheered when he finally blew the turkey's head off.

Welcome to the 30th Annual Turkey Shoot, an event that has become something of a legend to the folks in this rural Pocono Mountains township in Pike County.

Every Columbus Day weekend since 1951, thousands have come from miles around to the little hamlet called Bohemia, about 150 miles north of Philadelphia near the New York border, to watch contestants take their best shots at the head of a caged turkey 75 yards away.

The event is the featured attraction in the Central Valley Fire Department's annual fund-raising event, which comes complete with food, plenty of beer and a room featuring bingo, wheels of fortune and other games of chance....

It was well after noon yesterday when fire company member Walter Frisbie drove his battered blue pickup truck into the wooded enclave. Ten live white turkey hens, worth a total of $105, were caged in the back of the truck.

Frisbie, who runs the booth at the live turkey shoot, drove 75 yards back into the woods to what folks around here call the "Turkey Bunker." It's a simple, 5-foot-high cinderblock wall with steel plating on its face.

Just behind the wall is a weathered and cracked orange plywood crate with a hinged door. On the top of the crate, just above the wall, are two hinged slats, each with a semicircle cut out. The crate holds the turkey in place; the slats hold its neck.

And at 2 P.M., just before the first contestant loaded his .22-caliber short-barreled rifle (long barrels are prohibited), the two "spotters" crouching behind the wall slipped the first turkey into the crate and went to work. One spotter is called the watcher. He looks for the first sign of blood on the turkey's head after each shot is fired. The other is called the gooser. He prods the caged turkey's rear end with a stick to make sure the turkey keeps its head above the wall.

"All set?" Frisbie shouted to the spotters when the turkey's head appeared above the wall. Then Frisbie turned to the large crowd that had gathered and called out: "OK, who's going to kill the first turkey?"...

"Oooh, oooh, oooh; yep, yep, yesiree, you've got 'em," Frisbie finally shouted when Keith Geiges' bullet hit the turkey between the eyes.

Seconds later, a big red flag flew up behind the turkey bunker. One of the two spotters immediately grabbed the wounded turkey from the crate, raised his hatchet and finished the job. ("It's more humane that way," Tussel had said earlier. "The turkey doesn't suffer one bit.")

Source and Comment

Philadelphia Inquirer, October 12, 1981. The dateline is Lackawaxen, Pennsylvania, and the article is by staff writer Mark Fineman. He notes that live turkey shoots were a colonial sport and that today most sportsmen shoot at paper targets in competitions for frozen turkeys, and he quotes the condemnation of officials of humane societies.

* * *

1492

In 1492
Columbus sailed the ocean blue.

Source and Comment

University of Pennsylvania Folklore Archive, undated. This well-known rhyme was collected by H.C. in South Carolina, c. 1935, from primary school children, but known from his own childhood, c. 1925. For other "Columbus" rhymes, see Mary and Herbert Knapp, *One Potato, Two Potato,* New York, 1976, 129.

Hurricane Thanksgiving Day

October 17

Originally days of thanksgiving were Religious expressions of appreciation for being spared a particular disaster or of thanks for an unusual blessing received. In this instance a recurring threat, the annual hurricane season, gave rise to an annual thanksgiving.

Hurricane Supplication Day [c. July 28] marks the traditional start of the hurricane season for the group of three Caribbean islands of St. Croix, St. Thomas and St. John's [The Virgin Islands of the United States].

The islanders also celebrate Hurricane Thanksgiving Day, on Oct. 17. That's traditionally the last day of the hurricane season, and a day set aside for giving thanks for sparing the U.S. territory from the storms.

Source and Comment

Philadelphia Inquirer, July 27, 1988. See also "Hurricane Supplication Day," p. 296 and headnote for "Thanksgiving," p. 396. The date of the observance varies slightly because of the custom of celebrating holidays on the Monday following, regardless of when they fall.

St. Jude's Day

October 28

The disciples St. Jude and St. Simon, according to western tradition, were martyred together in Persia and so their feast is celebrated jointly. St. Jude, so-called in English to distinguish him from Judas Iscariot, was supposedly the brother of Jesus and, following the family trade, a carpenter. He is the saint of hopeless causes.

Saint of the Impossible

St. Jude and St. Joseph are the most important local saints; Buffalo [New York] religious supply stores still [in 1976] do a flourishing business in St. Jude medals.... St. Jude, patron of lost causes and those who attempt the impossible, is especially popular with students, who often ask for his help on exams.

Source

Indiana Folklore, IX (1976), 166. Collected by Lydia Marie Fish who was investigating Roman Catholicism "as a Folk Religion." Her sources included "students, colleagues, and lay and clerical friends."

Dewali, Hindu Festival of Lights
October—November

The word *dewali* means cluster of lights, and illumination by lamps, fireworks, and bonfires are an important feature of the week-long festivities which mark the beginning of the Hindu New Year. It is a particularly holy day for devotees of Vishnu, the Preserver. One story relates how Vishnu killed a filthy and obnoxious demon on this day, but the most widely held belief is that Dewali honors the coronation of Rama, a manifestation of Vishnu, following his conquest of the demon ruler of Sri Lanka, Ravana, who had stolen his beloved wife. During Dewali, effigies of Narakasura or of Ravana are burned, Hindu merchants settle their accounts, presents are given, fairs are held, and games of chance are played.

Dewali in New Jersey

Nearly 1,000 Hindu families in the Philadelphia area will gather tomorrow [November 15, 1981] for their annual Dewali celebration at the Osage School, opposite the Echelon Mall in Voorhees, N.J.

Dewali is the most important Hindu festival, similar to Christmas in the Western world.

The world's 500 million Hindus celebrate this day with festivities, worship, gift exchanges, good wishes, fireworks and the decoration of homes with lights.

On this day, Hindus believe, Shri Ram (God incarnate) returned to his kingdom after 14 years of self-imposed jungle residence and after having defeated the fierce 10-headed demon Ravana.

The day signifies victory of light (knowledge) over darkness (ignorance), truth over falsehood and spirituality over immorality.

The celebrations in New Jersey will include folk and classical dancing, devotional music, religious discourses, the *Arati* (ceremony of lights) and a dinner. The programs are free, sponsored by the India Temple Association, a nonprofit organization that serves the cultural and religious needs of Hindu families in the area.

Source

Philadelphia Inquirer, November 14, 1981. Unsigned news item for a regular Saturday column of religious news titled "In the Churches and Synagogues."

Food for Dewali

[The] festive meals prepared during Dewali, the Indian Festival of Lights, which begins today [November 1, 1978] and peaks Tuesday night [November 7] with a family feast similar to Christmas dinner, are typically vegetarian.

The vegetarian meal is natural on this pure and auspicious day when families get together to say prayers and friends and relatives visit and exchange gifts of sweets, dried fruits and nuts.

As described by Amar Bhalla [of Philadelphia], owner of the Indian restaurant Siva's and an excellent cook himself, the holiday is celebrated not only with sweets but also with new clothes, firecrackers and family entertainment such as card games, which are most common in northern India. Homes are lit by earthen pots with wicks set in wax or oil. Natural materials prevail.

In earlier times the poor served dinner on cleaned banana leaves and in little "cups" made from the leaves. The modern meal, however, is presented in individual *thalis,* which are round serving trays, typically of stainless steel, though sometimes of silver or brass. Each *thali* holds four or five little cups, called *katoris,* for the separate foods being served.

Bhalla prepared a typical *thali* for us, including vegetable balls called *Sabji Kofta* and *Dahl* (cooked lentils), for which his recipes appear [below]. Also on the menu was *Began Bhurta,* eggplant roasted, mashed and cooked with tomatoes, herbs and spices. These were accompanied by a yogurt-cucumber-tomato mixture called *Raita,* a rice pilaf and *Samosa,* a pastry filled with peas, potatoes, raisins, herbs and spices. The traditional puffed bread, *puri,* and tortilla-like *papadum* were the bread selections.

Sabji Kofta
(Vegetable Balls)

1½ pounds mixed, diced vegetables of your choice, cleaned and peeled as needed
4 cloves garlic
¼ ounce fresh ginger root, grated
¾ teaspoon salt
¼ teaspoon *garam masala* (commercial or homemade spice mixture)
2 ounces dry bread crumbs

Gravy:
4 ounces butter
4 ounces chopped onion
4 ounces grated onions
½ teaspoon red (cayenne) pepper
½ ounce ginger
8 cloves garlic
1 rounded teaspoon ground coriander
1½ teaspoons salt
½ teaspoon *garam masala*
8 ounces sliced tomatoes
2 green chili peppers, optional
1 cup water
1 teaspoon chopped fresh coriander leaves

Steam-cook diced vegetables, adding garlic, ginger and salt. When tender, mash the mixture. Add *garam masala* and bread crumbs. Mix thoroughly and divide mixture into 10 to 12 equal parts, shaping into balls 1 ½ to two inches in diameter. In a skillet, fry the vegetable balls in oil until golden brown. Serve hot with gravy. Makes four to six servings.

To prepare the gravy, heat butter, add onions and fry until golden. Remove from heat; add red pepper and stir until the color of the pepper is infused into the butter. Add ginger, garlic, coriander, salt, *garam masala* and tomatoes; cook until *masala* (spice mixture) is fried and "ghee" (clarified butter) separates from it. Add green chilies and water; simmer until raw flavor of garlic disappears and sauce thickens. Serve hot over vegetable balls and sprinkle with fresh coriander leaves. . . .

Dahl
(Cooked Lentils)

Dahls or cooked lentils are the most popular of Indian foods. About 60 different varieties of lentils are used for thick, soup-like mixtures also called *dahls*. This *dahl* recipe from Bhalla also contains kidney beans, which, when cooked and mashed along with the lentils, result in tiny, chewy bits that resemble ground meat. Once again, the feeling or impression of meat is found in a purely vegetable recipe.

8 ounces whole black beans (*urad dahl*), available in Indian or Oriental groceries
2 ounces kidney beans
4 cups water
2 ounces fresh ginger root, grated, divided
2½ teaspoons salt
12 cloves garlic, finely chopped
5 tablespoons clarified butter, divided
3 green chilies, chopped fine
½ teaspoon *garam masala*

Wash beans several times, removing grit. Boil water; add beans. Cover and return to a boil, cooking about five minutes. Add one ounce ginger, salt, garlic and one tablespoon butter. Simmer three to four hours. (Alternatively, you may pressure cook the beans at 15 pounds pressure for 30 minutes, allowing the pressure to drop by itself. Uncover and cook the beans further in the same pot or another pan over low heat for 30 minutes more.) Stir and mash beans occasionally during cooking (except in pressure cooker) until reduced to a creamy thick consistency.

Heat remaining four tablespoons butter with remaining one ounce ginger. Add green chilies and *garam masala*. Mix with the cooked *dahl* and serve. Makes four or more servings.

Source

Philadelphia Inquirer, November 1, 1978. From a feature article by Marilynn Marter, staff "Food Writer."

Halloween, All Saints', and All Souls' Days
October 31—November 2

All Saints' or All-Hallows' Day is November 1, which according to pagan custom begins as the sun sets the evening before. A festival of the dead, it was made into a celebration of all the known and unknown saints and martyrs of the Catholic Church by Pope Boniface IV in the seventh century. Originally, it was celebrated on May 13, but was shifted to its present date by Gregory III in the eighth century. All Saints' Day is followed by All Souls' Day, November 2, another Christian adaptation of pagan festivals for the dead. This is a day of intercession for dead souls that have not yet been sufficiently purified, in the belief that the prayers of the living will help. It originated as a memorial in the tenth century. Unlike All Saints', All Souls' Day was abolished by the church of England, although it is recognized informally by many Protestants. Thus the two days have become combined in modern secular tradition. Mumming, pranks, bonfires, decoration of graves, belief in the return of ghosts or dead souls, fortune-telling and ritualistic games are associated with the eves and days of both November 1 and 2 in America.

"Trick or treat," the Halloween threat of little children, is apparently a recent American phenomenon, as distinct from pranks and mischief long customary on this holiday. It seems to be related to the Gaelic practice of giving cakes to the poor at Samhuinn or "summer-end," a seasonal festival that coincides with All Souls' Day. They came to be called "soul-cakes," and in return recipients were obligated to pray for a good harvest. Somewhat closer is an English Plough Day custom. Ploughmen went about begging for gifts, and if they did not receive anything, threatened damage to the grounds with their ploughs. One sociologist observing the trick or treat custom in a southern college town saw little traditional in it. He explained it as "a rehearsal for consumership" in a mass society.

What We Did on Halloween

About 7:00 [P.M., in 1972] we would all meet at the back of the store. I think they was seven of us. We all had our soap, toilet paper, maybe some wax, firecrackers, and a couple of stuffed dummies. To start the night rolling we would soap a few windows and rap on them when the people would be watching television. Next we found a tree limb that grew over the road. A couple of us would climb up and tie a dummy on a rope. As soon as a car was almost under the tree, they swung the dummy right down in front of it. They would either stop and get out and start cussing or just slow down and then keep going. Or just as a car was coming down the road one of us would throw a dummy in the road. You could smell the rubber two miles away. This was really stupid but we got our kicks out of it. We'd make our way down the road, soap some more windows. Then the big trick of the night. At the trailer court at the power switches. There was two of us at each board. The first group would light a firecracker flick ... flick. Twelve trailers lose their lights. Did we get the hell out of there. I think we were chased for two days.

Source

New York Folklore Quarterly, XXIX (1973), 180-81. By Jack Jindra, one of a series of accounts "written by a group of eighteen and nineteen year old youngsters from the area of Niagara Falls, New York" for Catherine Harris Ainsworth.

* * *

Halloween

Trick or Treat

Hallowe'en, when I was a child in the 1920's in the state of North Carolina, was noticed and celebrated, but not always; and when it was, with a marked degree of caution and frugality. There was some candy but not big brown paper bags full of it as there was for my younger daughter in Michigan in the 1950's. I do not recall the custom or phrase of "trick or treat" in North Carolina or in Florida when my older daughter was in her childhood in the 1940's. In fact, I first heard the expression when I was in Holly, Michigan, in 1955. An acquaintance, born in 1911, who grew up in Philadelphia, Pa., said he did not hear the expression there. The young people, did, he recounts, indulge in "mischief night," when they did destructive, mischievous acts on the night before Hallowe'en....

> Trick or treat,
> Smell our feet.
> We want something
> Good to eat.

Source and Comment

New York Folklore Quarterly, XXIX (1973), 164, 176. Collected by Catherine Harris Ainsworth who was interested in identifying vestiges of Celtic influence in recent American Halloween practices. The rhyme was obtained from Jonny Davis, who chanted it as a ten-year-old in Niagara Falls, New York, c. 1972. Cf. "More on All Souls' Day," p. 384, especially the rhyme of Indian children in which they threaten to break windows if they are not given presents.

* * *

Halloween Junkpile

The very small village of Danbury, N.H. has long had an unusual way of celebrating Halloween. Junk (old cars, bathtubs, broken bicycles, lumber, barrels, and other trash) mysteriously appears in the center of the common during the night, and no one seems to have had a hand in it. Although such littering, even by supernatural beings, is illegal, the town constable doesn't bother to interfere. In fact, the one time a lawman did try to investigate and stop proceedings, he was burned in effigy. Most of the residents figure that no one gets hurt, property isn't damaged, and the stuff is cleared away the next day, so why not? But there are those who feel that the whole thing is childish and lowers the town's image. Whatever, the tradition seems as well established as "trick or treat" and will undoubtedly continue as long as spirits do mischief at All Hallows.

Source

Reported orally to T.P.C. by a graduate student at the University of Pennsylvania whose name is now forgotten. Recalled upon seeing the custom written up by Dave Zilavy in the October, 1988, issue of *Yankee* magazine.

* * *

Halloween Egg-Throwing

It's Halloween. It's egg time.

It's time for young people to buy them by the dozen and for grown-ups to worry about the impact of eggs on their neighborhoods.

And these last few days, the grocery store managers of New York have been the actors in a small, annual morality play: Is it mischief or is it mayhem? To sell or not to sell?

To many, holiday egg-buying is simply a phase of growing up.

"I used to throw eggs myself when I was younger," said Mohammed Marini, the manager of a Key Food grocery store on Court Street in South Brooklyn. Mr. Marini said he doubled his egg order last week, to 8,216 eggs, to satisfy both shoppers with legitimate egg needs as well as the seasonal surge in demand.

But Won Kyu Lee, manager of Frank's Big Apple Deli on Smith Street, frowns on such antics.

"We don't sell eggs to kids," said Mr. Lee, who added that he was hit by an egg Saturday night. "This is not play," he said. "This is almost bad."

Still, what remains a seasonal mystery is why the egg—a self-contained food that sells for 6 to 9 cents each and is carefully decorated on other holidays—makes such an attractive weapon. Is it the size? The hard shell? The ghoulish pleasure of seeing, post-collision, the slimy, yellowish mess that results when the yolk, the white and the shell shatter against someone's shirt, car or house?

"It's cheaper than tomatoes," said Robert Vallo, a 14-year-old from South Brooklyn. He and two of his friends, Joseph Hajaistron, 14, and Anthony Sanzone, 13, were riding their bicycles around their neighborhood yesterday afternoon, but, having purchased five dozen eggs, were prepared for a night of egg warfare.

They wore long pants with big pockets on the legs, and several sweaters and jackets, all with lots of pockets. And they wore the indispensable hooded sweatshirt—Anthony had his hood strings pulled tight, almost covering his face—that is necessary to protect the adolescent head from eggs filled with chemical hair remover.

"Last year, a couple of my friends came into school the next day with bald spots," Joseph said.

Why throw that kind of egg? "To be mean," he said, adding, somewhat sanctimoniously: "We're in it for the fun. We stay in open areas, where there are no houses." Homeowners, he discovered after an angry one punched him last year, do not appreciate having to remove dried egg.

Tricia Joyce, a social worker who works at a mental-health clinic in Flushing, Queens, said mothers in the area were worrying about the impact of eggs on their neighborhoods. In recent days, she said, "kids were throwing so many eggs that they couldn't really walk into their apartment buildings without slipping and sliding."

Eggs were selling briskly yesterday at the Key Food in South Brooklyn. "There's some kids buying eggs now," Mr. Marini said, sprinting to a checkout aisle to prove his point. Two small boys, both wearing hooded sweatshirts, were purchasing a dozen eggs. Grade A. Large.

"What are you buying the eggs for?" Mr. Marini asked them.

The boys blushed. "It's for my mother," one whispered.

Once outside the store, the boys fled down the street, in the direction of a local Chinese restaurant called Me and My Egg Roll, clutching their sack of eggs.

Kaz Zahrieh, the manager of another Key Food store, on Nostrand Avenue in the Bedford-Stuyvesant section, said egg sales soared over the weekend, coinciding with eggs meeting tragic fates on the exterior walls of his store.

"They come in with their masks on and everything," Mr. Zahrieh said. "It's a mission."

Source

New York Times, October 31, 1988. An article by Constance L. Hays. Copyright© 1988 by The New York Times Company. Reprinted by permission.

*   *   *

Halloween

Halloween Apple Games

In Elkin, North Carolina, which is in the Piedmont area of Southern United States, bobbing for apples was standard fare at all private Hallowe'en parties and at public Hallowe'en festivals given at the school or at a church to raise money for the institution. At any fall carnival, as well as at Hallowe'en, bobbing for apples was considered great amusement and entirely appropriate. A dozen or more apples were put into a large galvanized tub of water and contestants, for a prize, attempted to capture an apple with their teeth without the assistance of their hands. I have experienced, also, a variation of the bobbing-for-apples in which an apple was suspended in a doorway by a string tied to its stem, and contestants were to snag it with their teeth, again without the help of their hands. It is interesting to note also, that when my cousins moved into my community from a more remote and mountainous one and gave a Hallowe'en party, they had bobbing for apples as one of the games at their party. Since they had hardly had time to become acquainted with our community customs, I believe that they, too, acquired this custom from our common Scottish ancestors. Perhaps bobbing for apples is the modern expression of the role of the mystic apple in the old Celtic ceremonies and fairy tales.

Source and Comment

New York Folklore Quarterly, XXIX (1973), 167-68. Remembered from her childhood in North Carolina by Catherine Harris Andrew," p. 395, and "To See Your Future Husband on Halloween, " p. 379.

Catching or dipping for apples was a means of divination among the Druids and survives in the folklife of countries influenced by Celtic culture. Since the apple is also a common love charm, the practice seems to be associated with the selection of a lover. It is, as well, a Christmas game, originally a fertility rite, during a season when other fertility rites were regularly performed. There appears to be no reason to play this game on Halloween except that apples are plentiful at this time.

Halloween

Halloween for Grown-Ups

Halloween isn't just for kiddies any more.

Hundreds of grown-ups, more or less, roamed the main drags of Georgetown [District of Columbia] Wednesday night, wearing a glittering variety of Halloween garb. Costumes dotted the landscape around 19th and M streets, too, and at a number of bars and private parties around town.

San Francisco may not have been impressed; Halloween is a longstanding tradition for adults there. But even there changes are taking place, says an observer of the Bay Area social scene. Its Halloween scene used to be dominated by gays; now straights are dressing up and indulging themselves, too.

The Washington Halloween scene Wednesday night was an event for people of many ages and races and sexual orientations.

Though many of the revelers were young adults, some were not so young. As a carload of older folks wearing masks inched through the traffic, they were asked if they were going to a party. An old woman lifted her mask and shouted out that no, she was going to the Miss America pageant.

It was that kind of night.

A trio of George Washington University students—dressed rather conservatively as a Roman, a witch and a pirate—confessed that they had actually been trick-or-treating among the posh homes of Georgetown. At their ages? "If you ate dorm food, you'd go trick-or-treating too," replied the pirate.

A group assembled for dinner at the Foundry included a duck, a "priest," a Great White Hunter, a bat and an assortment of other creatures. In real life they were workers on the Hill, at the Brookings Institution, the Pan American Union and at other formidably starchy institutions,but tonight they were expressing their "real, inner selves," they said.

Except for one woman: "I didn't have the breasts for Dolly Parton so I decided to come as a little old man instead," she explained.

At the corner of Wisconsin and P streets, the windows of Avant-Garde, a new boutique, seemed to be shaking. A closer look through the fog on the windowpane revealed the wiggling bodies inside, dancing the night away. Owner Alain Chetrit had moved out all the clothes and installed a disco for Halloween, open without charge to anyone who was strolling by, and the place was packed with gyrating dancers wearing elegant and exotic costumes.

Outside the store was a campaign worker for Republican mayoral candidate Arthur Fletcher, passing out brochures to the disco crowd. She applauded Chetrit's opening of his doors to the public and said Fletcher would do the same thing if elected.

Down the street, at La Serre, was a group that might have disagreed. "Trick or treat with Marion Barry," said the invitations, and inside, the Democratic mayoral candidate was dispensing conversation and handshakes while surrounded by pumpkins and orange and black crepe paper. Discreet little masks were available at the door, but not many people were wearing them.

On the sidewalk outside La Serre practically everyone was wearing a mask of some sort, and few of them were discreet.

The Potatoheads were holding court at the corner of Wisconsin and M. These were little figures with enormous heads who liked to silently surround individual strollers. Rugged interrogation by the press finally exposed them as normal-sized pals from Cheverly who occasionally had to dart behind buildings to take off their heavy heads and give their bodies a break. Such are the burdens of Halloween.

The Potatoheads said they had been called everything from homosexuals "to Devos to cute little honeys."

Two young bottles of Tanqueray and Michelob, walking down Wisconsin en route to Sarsfield's, were asked why so many people were doing this sort of thing this year. One of them ventured the opinion that a whole new school of whacko comedy has become popular lately—what with the Coneheads, Steve Martin, "Animal House"—and everyone wants to join the fun.

Source

Washington Post, November 2, 1978. By Don Shirley, staff writer.

* * *

The Greenwich Village Parade

Over the last couple of years the Halloween Parade through the West Village and the late-evening masquerade party at the Theatre for the New City have been enjoyed with ever-increasing attention by me and my family. The parade starts from Westbeth in the early evening, and I can stand at my living-room window while the crowds begin to gather and Ralph Lee's fantastic and beautiful creations take their places, and then, when things seem ready to start, the kids and I can run down the fire stairs and slip right in. The watching has to be integrated, of course, with steady runs to the door for the hordes of trick-or-treaters availing themselves of Westbeth's soft touches. This year I got dressed a bit myself (tailcoat, top hat, Swiss army all-leather motorcycle jodhpurs, Adidas, rubber glove in handkerchief pocket, wristwatch on bicycle chain draped across chest), to the amusement of my adult neighbors, the scorn of the teenagers, the bemusement of the four- to 10-year olds, and the complete disinterest of the younger-than-fours, all of whom just said "Hewwo Joel," as if I looked like that every day.

Ralph Lee's creations are of course masks and figures; this year we walked in company with a four-humped camel and a tall Medusa, while some sort of gigantic general strutted, chest covered with medals. Before, behind, and around us, a huge, sectioned snake, supported by bamboo poles in the hands of 15 or so volunteers, wove its way on a route that ended at Washington Square Park. We were led by a hay wagon for the very little ones and an honest-to-God marching band, which I never saw but kept hearing loud and clear. Along the way we were greeted by ghosts on a Bleecker Street fire escape, the traditional scarecrow riding up and down the flagpole at Seventh Avenue, pumpkin-headed goblins on a low roof on Twelfth Street, windowsful of Victorian grotesques in the brownstone on Charles where two years ago a lifesize Punch and Judy was acted out as we paraded by, and then, predictably, a hail of eggs from one of those lovely high-rises that make the Village what it is today.

Traffic on Seventh Avenue was agreeably stalled; my neighbor said, "God, do they have to wait until the whole parade goes by?" and I answered "I hope so." Once a year it's nice to be able to cross Seventh Avenue in safety. I suppose it's corny, but the parade is the one time all year that the Village feels like we all keep saying it does year 'round: warm and pleasant and small-towny. People yelled hellos all along the route, joined in, dropped out, and generally were there for fun and not hassles. Of course, fame has begun to take its toll—I'd estimate that fully 42 per cent of the marchers this year were dressed as photographers or videotapers or filmmakers, but for once they seemed part of the thing, rather than interlopers and disrupters. They tended to converge on a marvelous Dracula, who brought along his own upright rolling coffin, and who later showed up at the Theatre for the New City's party selling the opportunity to be photographed with him as a benefit for this chronically under-funded artistic endeavor.

The Theatre for the New City is the work of Crystal Field and George Bartenieff, with lots of dedicated help, and it goes on, somehow, year to year. Its productions, to my taste, have been spotty—some great, some awful, and some in between; whatever else, it always provides its actors and playwrights and the whole theatre with enthusiasm and élan. I suspect that a million-dollar endowment would ruin it forever, but someone ought to be able to give it something less than that just to keep it with us. The Halloween Ball started a year or two ago as a fundraiser, and this year it was just splendid. There was a giant swing band and a reggae-band and a loud rock band and a quiet jazz trio, and there were singles acts, including that great lady of everything, Rosalyn Drexler, singing. There were jugglers, and small plays, and a graphologist, and a sign for a phrenologist, although I never saw one in action. And there was a parade of costumes with prizes of a year's pass to the theatre and a lottery ticket. I had the honor to be one of the judges, for which I received no remuneration, no bribes, and a great deal of calumny because I picked a woman with terrific breasts as the Most Poetical. Why not?

All in all, the evening seemed a suitable way to say good-bye to the streets for the next six months, and when we hit them again, it'll be in the individual outbursts of spring. This was a huge and good and happy gathering of all of us, grown-ups and children, men and women, straights and gays, blacks and whites, all the dualities out there, holding off the darkness and the ghosts, and saying Goodbye, Sun, see you next year.

Source

Village Voice, November 14, 1977. From the column "Mix and Mask" by Joel Oppenheimer. Greenwich Village is situated in lower Manhattan, New York City. It was designated an historic district in 1969. It was once a separate village and has become noted as a literary and artistic district.

* * *

The Greenwich Village Parade

A Policeman's Lot

Time was when the Greenwich Village Halloween Parade was a small-town affair, a procession of kids and attendant parents straggling down streets where half the houses still had boot scrapers on the front steps. That time is no more. With floats on flatbed trucks, and with steel-drum, Dixieland, and conga bands, and crowds of revellers, the marchers barely distinguishable from the gawkers, the parade has gone big time. It requires major arteries on which to disport itself. It also requires police, to keep the revellers moving and happy. We know a sergeant of the Auxiliary Police Force in the Sixth Precinct, and when we learned that he was going to be on duty at the parade we decided to spend the evening in his company.

On the way to the precinct house, the sergeant told us about crowds. The passersby in the early darkness still seemed normal enough, with the exception of the odd demon. Sixth Avenue, up which the parade would flow, was lined with blue sawhorses. "Sixth Avenue will be the worst," the sergeant said. "It's where all the people will go as soon as they get off the subways at Sheridan Square or West Fourth Street. When the parade used to end in Washington Square, that was bad for crowd control, because it was harder to leave. Union Square, where the parade ends now, is better—people can take the subway right there. One problem with the Halloween parade is that it's at night. Halloween isn't like Thanksgiving or St. Patrick's Day, when you can see what's happening. The

other problem is that people think, It's the Village, I'm gonna have a good time."

The Auxiliaries of the Sixth Precinct—there were seven of them that night—rendezvoused in a room on the second floor of the precinct house on West Tenth Street. The commanding officer, a trim, white-haired man, who had supplied himself with a bullhorn for the evening, gave them their posting—a pedestrian passage across Sixth Avenue, at Fourth Street. This represented an innovation. The year before, Sixth Avenue had been a sealed column—you couldn't cross. This year, there would be a human sluice. "Remember, folks," the C.O. said. "Be firm but gentle."

Back on the streets, the crowds had become thicker, and distinctly odder. We passed a flamenco dancer, a headless woman, a bearded Aunt Jemima. Geishas were out in force. We took up a position between a hot-dog cart and a sawhorse just west of the crossing place. The crossing had two lanes, and it was the job of the Auxiliaries, and also of some regular officers, to keep people, or whatever, moving in the right direction. There were ninja, wizards, pharaohs, droogs, cows, lobsters, sandwiches, mice, a dinosaur squiring a belle. A young man in normal clothes came along shouting, "I'm a full marching band! You didn't notice the disguise, right?" The spectators included lots of out-of-towners. Two men in bow ties and with earnest faces stopped near us, and one asked, speaking precisely, with European vowels, "Could you explain where we go to see something?" Others—from closer to home, apparently—spoke of catching the eleven-thirty train to Hoboken. Every tenth person, it seemed, wanted to take a shortcut through the crossing's sawhorses; these jaywalkers were firmly but gently rebuffed. "My favorites are the people who say they *live* here," the sergeant told us. "Like, they don't know what October 31st is?"

At about seven-thirty, the real parade appeared, heading north on Sixth Avenue, and caused a surge along the already dense sidewalks. From where we stood, the individual marchers were invisible, and even the more elaborate displays—the plant from "Little Shop of Horrors," the Brooklyn Bridge, bagpipers—reached us in fragments: bars of music, glimpses of superstructure. We did get a good view of a green-and-white paper snake about twenty feet long. The only sign we saw of a politician was a placard that said "Al Gore."

The Auxiliaries waved three men off a windowsill; a fourth man grabbed the bottom rung of a fire escape but gave up trying to climb it before he had to be restrained. At one point, Death, carrying a scythe, decided to cross Sixth Avenue, and slipped under a sawhorse. The sergeant waved him back. "How do I get in the parade?" a bat-winged lizard carrying a sceptre crowned with a skull wanted to know. The sergeant told her (for the lizard was a woman) to go down Cornelia Street and left on Bleecker. "Ah, come on," she said, in unghoulish disappointment. We bought two hot dogs for a corpse who couldn't reach the pushcart.

After about an hour and a half—when the cold was beginning to spread from fingers and toes into the thighs—a sanitation truck came up the avenue. It was so bright and shining that we took it for a prop, but it was followed immediately by five sanitation trucks that were unmistakably real, and by a squad car with its cherry flashing. The commanding officer called through his bullhorn "Dismissed!" In no time, the streets filled with people. We lost our sergeant.

Source

New Yorker, November 11, 1988, 32-3. From "The Talk of the Town."

* * *

Gay Halloween Parade

With his broad shoulders, rose-red lipstick, white chiffon dress and runs in his stockings, William Shultz looked like Joan Crawford on a bad night.

"The shoes!" Mr. Shultz, a 40-year-old Atlanta businessman, said Saturday night as he grimaced in pain at his high heels. Then he took them off to walk down the middle of Duval Street, dangling the white pumps over his shoulder.

He was barely noticed, swallowed by a sea of cave men, dinosaurs, Frankenstein monsters, jesters, cheerleaders, bridesmaids and phantoms of the opera, the rank and file of the 10th Halloween parade here [Key West, Florida]. Some costumes were elaborate: two cockatoos, for example, painstakingly made out of white plastic. Others were more statements than costumes, like a string of pearls worn with a black T-shirt.

For thousands of homosexuals here and in New York, San Francisco, Los Angeles and elsewhere, Halloween has become the big holiday of the year. It is to gay people what St. Patrick's Day is to the Irish, a time to celebrate who they are and flaunt it, too.

What started out as parades have over the last decade evolved into something akin to Mardi Gras, drinking and dancing and carrying on in the streets, be it Duval Street here, Christopher Street in New York, Castro Street in San Francisco or Santa Monica Boulevard in West Hollywood.

That is not to say that all paraders and spectators are homosexual; most are heterosexual, and many are parents with their children. And that is not to say that all homosexuals dress up in costume on Halloween. But their participation in the parades and especially in the street festivals is strong.

"There's no question that for many gay people Halloween has become the major holiday," said Thomas B. Stoddard, executive director of the Lambda Legal Defense and Education Fund, a New York-based advocacy group for gay rights.

Bob Oppenheimer, associate editor of the Los Angeles-based Advocate, a gay publication, said: "People start planning their costumes for the next year the day after Halloween. It's absolutely a major event."

No one can say just why that is so. Bruce Mailman, an organizer of gay events whose Halloween party in Manhattan drew 3,000 people Saturday night at $30 each, said Halloween offered gay people, who in the workaday world must often hide their sexuality, a chance to let go and be themselves. "Somehow they feel they don't have to hide on that holiday," he said.

Mr. Stoddard said the public partying on Halloween fit into gay liberation in general, part of what he sees as a greater demand by homosexuals to be heard.

The columnist who uses the pen name Dee Sushi in The New York Native, a gay newspaper, said he believed that because of the AIDS epidemic, Halloween, a nonreligious holiday with a long tradition of being a party night, provided the perfect escape valve.

In addition, some gay activists say that eight years of the Reagan Administration, which has fought any broadening of gay rights, has caused frustration among homosexuals and that Halloween offers a way to vent it.

"Everyone wants to dress up as Barbara Bush this year [1988]" Dee Sushi said, referring to the wife of Vice President Bush. . . .

Source

New York Times, October 31, 1988. Edited from an article by Jeffrey Schmalz. Copyright © 1988 by The New York Times Company. Reprinted by permission.

* * *

Halloween

Needle in a Halloween Haystack

What an experience. I gave a lady a bale of hay for decoration at Halloween. Out of kindness she brought the bale back to feed to my horses. My first instinct was not to feed the hay. I already fed my horses at 5:30 P.M., but I thought I'd give them an extra treat for the night which turned out to be a nightmare. It was 8:30. I was sitting in my house painting and something told me to go and check on my horses. I went down to the barn and noticed my bay mare was making funny faces. Right away I knew there was something wrong, so I stuck my hand way in the back of her mouth and on the back of her tongue there was a point of a pin sticking from her tongue. I reached in her mouth and tried three or four times, but I couldn't get it. My fingers were so full of saliva that I couldn't grab it. I tried again and finally got it. It was two inches long. How the needle stuck in her tongue without going down her throat, I'll never know. It was a blessing from God. I found out later the pin came from the scarecrow pants.

Source and Comment

The Horse Digest, II, #9 (April 1984), 55. From the "Letter" section, this anecdote has all the earmarks of becoming a family legend, a common, if minor, form of folklore. It was submitted by Roxanne Armatti of Gwinn, Michigan. No further detail given.

* * *

The Halloween Sadist

Although Halloween itself dates back over several centuries, the myth of the Halloween sadist is a relatively new invention. It was created during the early 1970s when some of the nation's most prestigious periodicals began reporting the discovery of the Halloween sadist as a dangerous new type of killer.

Newsweek magazine, for example, warned that "several children have died and hundreds have narrowly escaped injury" from dangerous objects concealed inside Halloween goodies. And the New York Times cautioned that the plump red apple that junior gets from the kindly old woman down the block ". . . may have a razor blade hidden inside."

Legislators in California and New Jersey responded to the alleged threat by passing tough new laws. A few communities even tried to ban trick-or-treating altogether. Schools started training children to inspect their goodies for tampering.

Soon everyone from Dear Abby to the local police chief began giving advice on how to protect children from Halloween sadists. But those of us who study crime for a living have long been skeptical about the actual existence of Halloween sadists. For it seems implausible that a homicidal maniac would limit his attacks to one night a year. And it sounds too much like the Halloween legend itself.

At long last, the record has been set straight. In 1985 two California State University professors, Joe Best and Gerald Horiuchi, published a study which concluded that the Halloween sadist was essentially a myth. After an exhaustive examination of the nation's newspapers, covering a 15-year period (1959-1984), they managed to locate only 76 cases of tampering with Halloween candy.

Most reports turned out to be either mistaken or fraudulent: Only 20 cases resulted in injuries, and all of them were minor. There were two deaths, but one involved a child who ate heroin hidden in candy he found at his uncle's house; the other child was poisoned by his father, who put cyanide in his candy to make it look like he was killed by Halloween sadist. . . .

The truth is that unless you're a nutrition buff, you really don't have to worry about your child's Halloween candy. What you need to worry about is flammable costumes, masks that obscure a child's vision; and your kid getting hit by a car in the dark. Take some precautions here, but forget about the candy. Let your child be a child, at least one night a year.

Source and Comment

Philadelphia Inquirer, October 29, 1987. From a feature by Richard Moran.

The idea that the Halloween sadist was "created during the early 1970s" is certainly not correct. One of the editors of the present volume recalls being warned against such persons in the 1930s.

* * *

To See Your Future Husband on Halloween

Maryland

If you are born on Hallowe'en, you can see and read things in dreams.

On Hallowe'en melt some lead and pour it from an iron spoon into cold water. The form that it assumes will be prophetic of your future life. One girl who tried it saw the lead take the shape of a coffin, and her husband took up the trade of an undertaker after her marriage.

On Hallowe'en, run around the square with your mouth full of pins and needles. Come home and look in the glass, and you will see your future husband, if you are to be married; but if not, you will see a coffin.

If you drop two needles into a bowl of water, you can tell by the way they move in the water whether you and your lover will come together.

On Hallowe'en, put some apples in a tub of water, and name them with a label. Let a girl kneel over the tub, shut her eyes, put her hands behind her, and try to catch an apple with her teeth. The one she succeeds in catching will be her future husband.

Suspend some apples, labeled with names over a doorway, blind-fold a girl with her hands behind her, and let her try to bite an apple. The one she bites, will be her future husband.

Walk around your house three times or around the town, with a mouthful of water in your mouth, and you will marry the first man you meet.

Walk into a room backward at twelve o'clock at night on Hallowe'en, looking over your left shoulder, and you will see your future husband.

Put three chestnuts on a hot stove. Name one for yourself and the others for two men. If one jumps and bursts, that lover will be unfaithful; if one blazes or burns, that one has some regard for the one making the test. If the girl's nut burns with one of the lovers, they will marry before the next Hallowe'en.

On Hallowe'en go chestnutting with a party. The one finding the first burr will be the first to marry. If the burr opens easily, the love will not last long, if it is hard to open the love will last.

Bake small cakes, and put in one a piece of money, in another a ring, in a third a rag, and in a fourth a thimble. You can tell who will be rich, who will be married, who will be poor, and who will earn her own living.

Take three dishes, and in one put clear water, in another milky water, and have the third one empty. Blindfold a girl, and if she touches the clear water, she will marry a bachelor; the milk water, a widower; the empty one, she will not marry at all. This must be tried three times.

If you eat a salt cake and go to bed backwards without speaking, you will dream that your future husband will bring you a drink of water. If the cup be of silver or gold, you will be wealthy; if of glass moderately rich, and if of tin, you will be poor. If you help yourself to a drink, you will never be married, and if the vessel out of which you drink is a gourd, you will be a pauper.

A salt cake was eaten by a girl in Emmittsburg [Maryland] on Hallowe'en. She went to bed without speaking, and dreamed that she was sitting in a certain house looking out of a window and longing for someone to bring her a drink of water, and getting weary of waiting, she went into the kitchen and helped herself from a tin bucket with a tin cup. Returning to the window, she was just in time to see a dark-haired man ride away. She was never married, and is terribly poor.

Source

Memoirs of the American Folklore Society, XVIII (1925), 123-35. "Folk-Lore from Maryland," collected by Annie W. Whitney and Caroline C. Bullock. Informants not given.

Divination is commonly associated with Halloween in Britain because at the time, according to old beliefs, the veil between the living and the dead is partially lifted, and clairvoyants, witches, diviners, and ghosts are about. A child born on Halloween is supposed to have second sight, and if a young woman wishes to catch a glimpse of her future husband, her chances are good provided she performs certain rites and is lucky. For other days and ways of divining a future mate, see "New Year's Beliefs," p. 20; "Seeing the Future on Midsummer Eve," p. 248; "St. John's Day and the Summer Solstice," p. 249; "May Day Predictions," p. 193; "St. Andrew's Eve," p. 395; and the following selections.

* * *

Take your undergarment off at Halloween, wash it backwards, dry it backwards, then sit down before the stove backwards without speaking; and if you are to marry, you will see your future husband come down the steps. If you are not to marry, you will see a black cat come down the steps, followed by four men carrying a coffin.

Or, walk *downstairs* backwards, carrying a mirror, and counting each step. At the thirteenth you will see a reflection of your future husband.

Source

Journal of American Folklore, XI (1898), 9-10. Collected by Mrs. Waller R. Bullock. No informant given.

* * *

North Carolina

If you stand in front of a mirror at twelve o'clock on Halloween, the man you are to marry will look over your left shoulder.

If on Halloween you take a mirror and walk down the stairs backward, you will see in the mirror the person you will marry.

On Halloween night, if one holds up a candle and looks in a mirror, the face of one's future husband or wife will be seen.

Look into a spring with a lightwood torch at midnight on Halloween and see the face of your future husband (or wife).

Look into the well at eleven o'clock on Halloween Day and your future will be disclosed.

On Hallow Eve, if an egg placed in front of the fire by a young woman in love is seen to sweat blood, it is a sign that she will succeed in getting the man she loves.

On Halloween, children used to put corn meal by the side of their beds, and then ghosts would write with it the name of the man each was to marry.

Source

North Carolina Folklore Journal, XX (1972), 135. As cited in a general article in on Halloween by Joseph D. Clark.

* * *

Tennessee

On Hallowe'en night, peel an apple and toss the peeling over the left shoulder. The letter formed is the initial of the girl's future husband.

Source

Tennessee Folklore Society Bulletin, II (October 1936), 10. Collected in middle Tennessee by Neal Frazier, who did not list the informant.

Halloween Projects

I wind, I wind, my true love to find,
The color of his hair, the clothes he will wear,
The day he is married to me.

Throw a ball of yarn into barn, old house, or cellar, and wind, repeating the above lines, and the true love will appear, and wind with you. To be tried at twelve o'clock at night, October 31.

An old lady of eighty told me that in her youth this was tested by a girl. Some one knowing she was going to make the test hid himself in the barn, and when the proper time came called out, "Timothy B."—the name of a man very much disliked by the girl, who was in love with her. She, thinking he had really appeared, and believing from the sign or project that she would have to marry him, became very ill, and only began to recover when they assured her he was not really there.

Cut up two alphabets, put them face down in water at night; then those that are turned over in the morning are the initials of the one you will marry. [Also, to be tried at midnight] October 31.

Source

Journal of American Folklore, V (1892), 318. Reported by Gertrude Decrow as current in Maine, but she does not give the exact date, place, or name of the informant. Included in *Folklore in America,* 115-16.

* * *

Halloween Bonfires

Michigan

In Bloomfield Township, Michigan, in the Upper Long Lake's Estate subdivision from 1955 to 1961, I attended yearly with my younger daughter a huge bonfire built on the shore of the lake for the celebration of Hallowe'en. All of the children of the subdivision came to the bonfire for apple cider and doughnuts and stood around in their various costumes.

Source and Comment

New York Folklore Quarterly, XXIX (1973), 169. Reported by Catherine Harris Ainsworth in a study of Celtic influences on American Halloween practices. Informant not given.

Halloween bonfires are a survival of the Druid practice of building hilltop fires to celebrate important festivals. November 1 was the Druid New Year and marked the return of winter. The Scottish custom of fire-jumping is another Druid survival. It took place on May Day or Beltane and was believed to bring good luck. Cf. "No Rooz," p. 137.

Maryland

In East Market, on the Eastern Shore [of Maryland before 1935], on Hallowe'en night boys jump over bonfires or ride over them, as was done in Scotland.

Source

Memoirs of the American Folklore Society, XVIII (1925), 6. "Folk-Lore from Maryland," collected by Annie W. Whitney and Caroline C. Bullock. Informants are not given. Cf. "A Beltane Fire," p.188.

* * *

Devil's Night Fires

The eve of Halloween has been called Devil's Night for decades in Detroit, but for years it was a time for soaping windows, ringing doorbells and other harmless pranks.

False fire alarms and broken windows were generally the worst Devil's Night problems until the early 1980s, when fires began breaking out after dark on and around Devil's Night. Mass arson erupted in 1983, when 650 fires were reported on Devil's Night alone.

There was a similar outbreak the next year.

By 1985, reports of Detroit's bizarre ritual had spread around the globe. News crews from Europe and Japan roamed city streets capturing the blazes, while fire buffs—people fascinated with fire-fighting lore and technology—gathered in the city each year for what the nationally circulated trade journal Firehouse called "the Super Bowl of fire fighting."

According to city officials, fires have declined each year since 1984, when there were 810 fires on Oct. 29-31.

Source

Detroit Free Press, October 31, 1989. By Bill McGraw, staff writer.

* * *

Fighting Fire on Devil's Night

On a warm and moonless Monday night, more than 30,000 volunteers, police, fire fighters and other city employees tried to take the devil out of Devil's Night, but he still got his licks in.

In parts of the city, fire crews were kept constantly busy through the traditionally busiest mid-evening hours. It was not clear, however, whether the number of Devil's Night fires had declined for the fifth straight year.

"They're kicking our a— compared to last year," said a fire lieutenant who spoke on condition of anonymity.

But mayoral spokesman Bob Berg said it was too early to tell whether this year's fire totals would exceed last year's tally of 229 fires over three days including Halloween.

City officials won't report the number of Devil's Night fires until after Halloween, when the uniquely Detroit custom of seasonal arson has run its course.

By 10 p.m., there had been fires in at least a half dozen abandoned houses, including several that spread flames to neighboring occupied dwellings.

There were numerous trash bin fires, a mid-afternoon fire at Alonzo Bates Academy, and an afternoon fire that caused a backup on I-75.

There were more fires than in an average 24-hour period, when about 65 are reported. There were no immediate reports of serious injuries.

Youths under the age of 18 were required to be indoors from 6 p.m. to 6 a.m. Sunday, Monday and today, unless accompanied by an adult.

Through 10 p.m. Monday, police had detained 294 youths for curfew violation, and four people—two adults and two juveniles—were arrested on suspicion of arson.

Last year, 452 youths were charged with violating curfew over the three-day period.

Vacant houses have been a prime target of Devil's Night arsonists. The Free Press counted more than 15,200 vacant buildings in Detroit earlier this year, including more than 11,000 residences....

In the 1100 block of Junction, neighbors reported seeing young children running from an abandoned house seconds after flames began shooting from the two-story wooden structure. The fire spread to the occupied home next door.

"When we got here it was really going. The whole sky was orange. I can't believe someone didn't call to report it" earlier, said a fire chief who spoke on condition of anonymity.

Oscar Saldivar, 19, who lives at the home with his parents, Juan and Beatrice Saldivar, complained that "people have asked that this house be knocked down for years and years and nothing has been done about it...."

Another fire that began in a vacant house on Cabot in southwest Detroit damaged occupied homes on either side of it.

Jesse Perez said, "They were supposed to knock it down many times. I've reported it and reported it."

Someone suggested the city might knock down the abandoned house now....

Later, a two-story vacant house burned across from the Detroit Fire Extinguisher Co. in the 6300 block of 14th Street, south of Grand Boulevard.

Neighbors said it took fire fighters 30 minutes to arrive, and that television crews arrived before fire trucks.

Source

Detroit Free Press, October, 31, 1989. By staff writers Michael Betzold, Roger Chesley, Darryl Fears, Bill McGraw, and Jim Schaefer.

As the article indicates, derelict houses invite Halloween arsonists. But the Halloween custom should be compared with "Halloween Bonfires," p. 381.

* * *

To Make Your Wish Come True on All Saints' Day

The Creole Negroes of New Orleans have a grewsome fashion of invoking a consummation of their wishes that I believe is entirely indigenous to the soil of that quaint cosmopolitan semi-foreign old city. Among the numerous fête days, high days, and holidays that are scattered so liberally among the too sober pathway of the twelve months of the year, none is more beautifully observed by the New Orleanaise than the first of November. This is by legal statute a state holiday, and in the Catholic and Episcopal church calendars All Saints' Day, but in Louisiana, and particularly in the Crescent City, it is a day for the remembrance of the dead.

That tomb is, indeed, neglected, and its occupant forgotten, that does not bear a memento. From the simple conch shell, or perhaps only a little mass of white, glistening sand, with a paper rose stuck in its midst, to the elaborate, expensive floral tribute that crowns the lofty marble of the rich man's resting-place, not one is left without decoration. A general pilgrimage to the many cemeteries in and around the city takes place, and its observance is universal to a surprising degree.

It is on that day the old cradle superstition tells you to pursue the following method if you want to have your wish, the dearest desire of your heart, fulfilled.

You must purchase beforehand a handkerchief, and it must not be used, but kept clean and white for this occasion.

On the eventful morning you must leave home as early as possible and also as quietly, and not a word or a sound must escape your lips from the time you close the door behind you until you return. You must go to a cemetery, enter the main gate, walk from there to the opposite wall, on the main avenue, and somewhere on its length you must pick up a piece of dirt; tie this in one corner of the new handkerchief, naturally expressing your most heartfelt wish.

Leave the cemetery by the same gate you entered, and make your way to a second; enter this and pursue the same course, tying a bit of dirt from the main walk into a second corner of the handkerchief with a second wish. Visit a third cemetery, and tie a third bit of dirt into a third corner of that blessed handkerchief, with a third and last wish. Return home, roll the handkerchief into a compact little ball, and toss it upon the top of an armoire, or on the cornice of a high window, or, perhaps, on the tester of the bed. Any high place that is likely to be undisturbed, save by spiders, will answer.

Then, and not until then, must you speak. The charm is broken if a single audible sound escapes during this rite. When it is remembered that you are most likely to meet your dearest friend and foe among the crowds that pass to and from the cemeteries, attending their own and viewing others' decorations, it will be seen that it is not an easy matter to keep absolutely quiet; but those wishes will come true before twelve moons have shed their rays upon you. . . .

Source

Journal of American Folklore, V (1892), 331-32. Reprinted from "a collection of cuttings relating to folk-lore." The cutting was from an unnamed "Northern journal of June 6, 1891" which attributed it to "The *St. Louis Republic.*"

* * *

All Saints' Day

Washing the Tombs on All Saints' Day

Cemeteries in New Orleans are all made of vaults above the ground. This is necessary because of the swampy condition of the land.

On All Saints' Day the vaults or tombs are washed, whitewashed and profusely decorated with flowers and wreaths. The favorite flower for this occasion is the chrysanthemum.

In New Orleans the downtown cemeteries are particularly festive. The women weep and gossip, men discuss local politics, and children run in and out of the crisscrossing aisles. The street vendors do a lively business selling gumbo, snowballs, pralines, peanuts, balloons, mechanical birds and toy skeletons.

The outlying districts have a custom not practiced in New Orleans. At night on All Saints' Day candles are lighted in the cemeteries giving an eerie aspect to the surroundings.

Schools and some business establishments are closed in New Orleans on this day.

Source

Wayne State University Folklore Archive, 1961. Collected by Marvy Evelyn Hill, a student of folklore at Wayne State University, in 1961. Her source was Mrs. Hazel Heine, age 55, of New Orleans, Louisiana. Cf. "Graveyard Cleaning and Dinner-on-the-Ground," p. 302.

* * *

All Saints' Day Chickens

The 2nd of November was All Saints Day [sic] and all the people of the village [Mesilla, New Mexico] would get together at the little church. On this day every family would take a plate of food and put it on the altar with a candle, some pastry, or any sort of food. This was for the priest. Some would bring chickens, tie their legs with a string and lay them there on the altar for the priest. Sometimes in the middle of the mass, the chickens would become restless and flap their wings and blow out the candles on the altar. The little children in the church would start giggling and the mothers would pinch them angrily. It was a ceremony which was supposed to be serious but it always ended up that way.

Source

New Mexico Folklore Record, V (1950-1951), 25. From "Recollections of Early New Mexico" of Teresita Garcia-Fountain, age 88, of Mesilla, New Mexico. Recorded on October 15, 1950, by J. D. Robb. Translated from the Spanish by Joe Salazar. In fact, November 2 is All Souls' Day, not All Saints'.

* * *

Prayers for the Dead

Prayers for the dead are an integral part of traditional All Saints' Day services which are scheduled at churches around the state today [November 1, 1980] and Sunday.

The feast day on Nov. 1 follows the folk celebration of Halloween.

In the church, All Hallow's Eve (earlier known as All Holies Eve) was the time of preparation for the feast day which dates from the ninth century.

The Mass of All Saints, or All Martyrs, however, has been celebrated since very early in Christian history, possibly around A.D. 600.

Traditionally, all Saints' Day has been a time to remember all the known and unknown saints and martyrs of the church not specifically given their own Saint's Day on the ecclesiastical calendar.

Since in the New Testament all Christians are referred to as "saints," it is the time when many modern congregations name in their prayers those members who have died during the previous year.

At Trinity Episcopal Cathedral, celebration of the Holy Eucharist will be held at 10 A.M. today, followed by a special litany in the churchyard at the grave of Bishop Louis Melcher.

The schedule for masses for All Saints' Day at St. Joseph's Roman Catholic Church began Friday night with a Vigil Mass at 5:30 P.M. and includes Masses today at 7:45 A.M., noon, and 6 and 7:30 P.M.

Source

The State (Columbia, South Carolina), November 1, 1980. Leading item from an unsigned newspaper listing of religious news published regularly on Saturdays.

The Day of the Dead and All Souls' Day

Elsie Clews Parson's Description

Towards the end of October the Zuñi celebrate *ahoppa awan tewa* ("the dead their day"). It is announced four days in advance from the house-top by *santu weachona'we,* the saint's crier. He also calls out that it is time to bring in wood. A portion of whatever is cooked on *ahoppa awan tewa* is thrown on the house-fire by the women, or carried by the men to the "wide ditch" on the river-side, where possessions of the dead are habitually buried.

At nightfall boys go about town in groups, calling out, "*Tsale'mo, tsale'mo!*" and paying domiciliary visits. At the threshold they make the sign of the cross, saying the "Mexican" prayer, *polasenya*; and the inmates give the boys presents of food—bread or meat. In spite of the "Mexican" features of *ahoppa awan tewa,* the Zuñi assert that the day has always been observed by the people, and that it is in no wise a Catholic ceremonial.

In Catholic Acoma the Catholic character of the day is of course recognized. It is known as a church celebration to fall on a calendar day, Nov. 1 or 2, guessed my informant. At Acoma, too, parties of boys, as many as ten perhaps, will go around town, calling "*Tsale'mo, tsale'mo!*" They also ring a bell. Their "Mexican" prayer is, "Padre spirito santo amen." They are given food. Food is also taken to the cemetery and placed around the foot of the wooden cross which stands there in the centre. The war-chiefs stand on guard. By morning, however, the food has disappeared. What becomes of it my informant did not know.

At Laguna, food is also taken to the cemetery. The day is called *shuma sashti* ("skeleton day"); and to give to the dead on *shuma sashti,* the fattest sheep and the best pumpkins and melons are saved. A story goes that once a young man was told by his mother to bring in for the occasion the fattest two lambs of their flock. The young man objected. Soon thereafter he fell sick, and he lay in a trance for two or three days, until the medicine-man restored him. On coming to, he reported he had been with the dead. The church was full of them. Happy were they who had been well-provided for by their families. The unprovided were befriended by the provided.

On *shuma sashti,* candles are set out on the graves. A little ball of food made up of a bit of everything served to eat is also put on the fire. The boys who go about getting food call out, "*Sare'mo, sare'mo!*" Their "Mexican" prayer is called *porasinia.*

More on All Souls' Day

[Concerning All Souls' Day at Zuñi, Acoma, and Laguna ...] I beg to make here a few additional suggestions and some corrections to the notes of Mrs. Parsons....Even where the church exists and the Catholic curate is present, as is the case in pueblos like San Juan and Isleta, I have reasons for believing that the Catholicity of the Indians is not genuine. In spite of this, however, it is too much to assume that the religion of the Spaniards has not left its influence among them; and, in fact, many of their old ceremonials and festivals seem to have been more definitely established through the introduction of the new Catholic doctrines and ceremonies.

The All-Souls-Day festival of Zuñi, Acoma, and Laguna, is certainly a continuation of the Catholic festival. The Zuñi festival, which comes late in October, comes sufficiently close to the date of the church calendar to prove this. Furthermore, the whole ceremonial seems to be a direct continuation of the Catholic church feast, the assertions of the Zuñi Indians notwithstanding.

The leaving of food for the dead is not alone an Indian custom. Ethnologists and folk-lorists are familiar with this institution, which is found among many peoples, even in modern times.

The words which accompany the ceremony of the making of the sign of the cross are all Spanish. They are all perfectly clear. This shows how Catholic and how Spanish the ceremony still remains. There is no such thing as a Mexican prayer, *polasenya* (Zuñi) or *porasinia* (Laguna). These Indian vocables are regular phonetic developments of the first three words of the Catholic ceremony in question: *Por la señal,* [By the sign]. In New-Mexican Spanish, and also in Andalusian Spanish, the current familiar pronunciation of these three words is *po la señal* or *po la señá.* This is exactly the Zuñi *polasenyá.* Mrs. Parsons does not write it with *a* final accented, but I presume that is the correct accentuation. The Laguna form, *porasiniá,* is also a perfectly normal Spanish dialectal development....

Mrs. Parsons finds it difficult to explain the Indian words *Tsalemo* (Acoma and Zuñi), *Saremo* (Laguna), which the Indian children repeat from house to house as they go forth begging for food on All-Souls Day. This also is a purely Spanish custom.... The complete version of the New-Mexican Spanish invocation is,

> *Oremos, oremos,*
> *angelitos semos,*
> *del cielo venemos.*
> *Si no nos dan*
> *puertas y ventanas*
> *quebraremos.*
>
> Let's pray, let's pray,
> We are little angels,
> From heaven we come.
> If you don't give to us
> Your doors and windows
> We will break.

The Zuñi and Acoma form *Tsalemo,* and the Laguna form *Salemo,* are Indian developments of the first word of the invocation. Curiously enough, these Pueblo Indians have preserved only the first word of the Catholic invocation, evidently taught to them by the old *padres*. In the current familiar Spanish pronunciation the first two words of the invocation are thus divided into syllables:

> *Oremo, soremo.*

The initial verse is frequently repeated before passing to the second; and hence,

> *Oremo, soremo,*
> *soremo, soremo.*

Soremo is the Spanish word that is now pronounced *Tsalemo* and *Saremo* by the Zuñi, Acoma, and Laguna Indians.

Source and Comment

Journal of American Folklore, XXX (1917), 495-96 and XXXI (1918), 550-52. Elsie Clews Parsons describes the Day of the Dead among the Pueblo Indians of Zuñi, Acoma, and Laguna, New Mexico. The original date of this ceremony was reckoned by the moon and fell in October. Her description is supplemented by Aurelio M. Espinosa, who emphasizes linguistic evidence to support his view of the importance of Spanish and Roman Catholic influences in the celebration of this holiday. Cf. The "trick or treat" Halloween custom with the verse of the little angels.

Guy Fawkes' Day
November 5

Guy Fawkes was one of a small group of conspirators involved in the "Gunpowder Plot," an attempt to kill King James I when he convened Parliament on November 5, 1605. The discontent was caused by the government's refusal to modify its policy of repression directed against Roman Catholics. Fawkes and his associates planned to set off thirty-six barrels of powder hidden under wood and coal in the cellar of the House of Lords. A Catholic peer advised not to attend reported this information to the authorities and the plot was foiled. November 5 was proclaimed a day of thanksgiving. It came to be known as Guy Fawkes' Day or Pope's Day and is still observed in England (though no longer in the United States) with bonfires and mumming. An effigy, called "the guy," is carried through the streets before being burned. It is reminiscent of the dolls and figurines that are borne from house to house in Europe by Christmas, Boxing Day, and Midsummer mummers.

Pope's Night

The celebration of the anniversary of Guy Fawkes' night on Saturday by the young people of this city was not so extensive as in former years, no doubt owing to the condition of the streets, but nevertheless small bands paraded the streets and made the early part of the evening hideous with music(?) from the tin horns they carried for the occasion. Some carried the usual pumpkin lanterns. The ringing of door-bells was also extensively indulged in. Very few of the paraders knew that the celebration was in keeping of the old English custom of observing the anniversary of the discovery of the famous gunpowder plot to blow up the House of Commons.—*From the Portsmouth Republican News, November 7, 1892.*

Chaps in this city had their annual blow-out on Guy Fawkes' night, and in parts of the city the toot of the horns was something terrific. Some grotesque pumpkin lanterns were seen, and altogether the "celebration" was evidently enjoyed by the boys.

Portsmouth is not alone in this peculiar observance, for down at Marblehead the night of the 5th of November is remembered by a huge bonfire on the Neck, around which the chaps with horns dance in fantastic glee. The blaze Saturday night on the M[arblehead] N[eck] was a bigger one than usual.

It's a queer custom the youths of Portsmouth and Marblehead have.—*From the Portsmouth Daily Evening Times, November 7, 1892.*

It is said there are only three places left in New England in which Pope Night continues to be celebrated. These are Newburyport, in Massachusetts, and Portsmouth and New Castle, in New Hampshire. In regard to Newburyport I can only speak from common report; but of Portsmouth and New Castle I can bear eye-witness, or rather ear-witness, for it is a celebration in which noise is the main element. It is boys, however, and rather young boys who maintain a custom once pretty general in the cities and larger towns of New England, and the small boy's enjoyment and way of manifesting himself is and ever has been by making a noise, helping himself thereto by every sort of instrument that will produce the loudest sound with the least music. It has been said that human beings in the various stages of growth, from infancy to manhood, pass through and typify the progressive stages in the development of races. The so-called music of the barbarian and half-civilized man corresponds to the strange and rude sounds which seem to delight the ears of boyhood.

Pope Night, in Portsmouth and New Castle, which is a seaside village below and very near to Portsmouth, is at present celebrated by boys from six to fourteen years of age by the blowing of horns and the carrying of lights of all kinds. They march through the streets in procession, or in small bands, gathering in, as they march, single groups, or dividing again and sending off detachments, so as to leave no street unvisited. The horns are of all sorts, from the penny whistle to those of two and three feet in length. Whence the origin of the custom of blowing horns on Pope Night I am uncertain. But the lanterns and other devices for lighting the darkness of the November night have evidently something to do with the discovery of Guy Fawkes under the chambers of Parliament in the act of blowing them up with gunpowder. In childhood I remember well looking at pictures of the scene which represented armed men with lanterns searching about in a subterranean place while the dwarfish Guy crouched among great casks of supposed gunpowder. Formerly the lights used by the boys in their observance of Pope Night were candles set in hollowed-out pumpkins, the light showing through holes in the shells of the pumpkins, cut to represent a very squat human face. To the lighted pumpkin-heads have now been added all sorts of illuminations, chiefly lanterns and torches.

There is no doubt that in Portsmouth at least Pope Night has been observed from the earliest times, and formerly by older boys than at present; those indeed who knew what they were celebrating and in which they took a serious interest. It is doubtful if the children who now take a part in it know what their own act signifies or commemorates. I shall presently produce a curious proof of this in the case of the boys of New Castle. It is a very singular fact that in Portsmouth, which long since outgrew its early local boundaries, the observance of Pope Night is entirely confined to the ancient portion of the town. This portion has remained substantially unchanged since the colonial period; and along with its antique houses, streets, alleys and docks, there remain the remnants of old families, many local names and traditions, and this historic survivor of the observance of the Gunpowder Plot. But it will not apparently survive much longer in Portsmouth. Every year the interest grows less and less and the boys who take part in it fewer and of a younger age.

The same may be said of New Castle, where even the name, Pope Night, has become confounded and the whole meaning of the celebration obliterated. It sufficiently attests the easy loss of the primitive significance of customs and observances and the complete transformation of their names, to note that in this obscure village the name Pope Night has undergone the absurd change to *Pork* Night.

Source and Comment

Journal of American Folklore, V (1892), 335-36 and VI (1893), 68-69. Two newspaper cuttings and the "eye-witness or rather ear-witness" accounts were contributed by John Albee of New Castle, New Hampshire.

Most colonial Americans on the eve of the Revolution considered themselves British and cherished British customs, though they sometimes adapted them to American circumstances. Guy Fawkes' Day, which commemorated tumultuous political events with street parades climaxed by burning effigies, lent itself readily to American political protest, as examples from colonial Charleston and Boston newspapers indicate. Nathaniel Hawthorne makes notable use of such pre-Revolutionary demonstrations in his tale, "My Cousin, Major Molineux." The Devil's "large Lantern, in the shape of a Tea Cannister," served a propaganda purpose in 1774. By 1892, when Guy Fawkes mumming in America had been generally supplanted by Halloween, the few schoolboys who celebrated it "carried the usual pumpkin lanterns."

Guy Fawkes and the American Revolution

Charleston

Saturday last, being the Anniversary of the Nation's happy Deliverance from the infernal Popish POWDER-PLOT in 1605, and also of the glorious REVOLUTION by the Landing of King William in 1688, two Events which our Brethren in England seem of late to have too much overlooked, the Morning was ushered in with Ringing of Bells, and a "Magnificent Exhibition" of Effigies, designed to represent Lord North, Gov. Hutchinson, the Pope, and the DEVIL, which were placed on a rolling stage, about eight feet high and fifteen feet long, near Mr. Ramadge's Tavern in Broadstreet, being the most frequented place in town. The *Pope* was exhibited in a Chair of State, superbly drest in all his priestly Canonicals; Lord North (with his Star, Garter, & showing the Quebec Bill) on his right hand; and Governor Hutchinson on his left, both chained to stakes; the Devil, with extended Arms, behind the Three, and elevated above them, holding in one Hand a Javelin directed at the Head of Lord North, and in the other a scroll, inscribed "Rivington's New York Gazetteer;" on his arm was suspended a large Lanthorn, in the shape of a Tea Cannister, on the side of which was writ in Capitals, "Hyson, Green, Congo and Bohea Teas." The Exhibition was constantly viewed by an incredible Number of Spectators, among whom were most of the Ladies and Gentlemen of First Fortune and Fashion. The *Pope* and the *Devil,* were observed frequently to bow, in the most complaisant manner, to sundry Individuals, as if in grateful Acknowledgement of their past services. About 8 o'clock, A.M. the whole was moved to the square before the State-House, and back again to Mr. Ramadge's, when Divine services began in St. Michael's Church; in which situation it remained throughout the Day, without the least Appearance of Opposition, Tumult, or Disorder. The figure Representing Lord North, was reckoned a tolerable Likeness, and that of Governor Hutchinson a very striking one; both their heads having been carved from very good Designs. In the Evening the whole Machinery was carried thro' the principle [sic] streets, to the Parade, without the Town Gate, when a pole 50 feet high was erected, strung with and surrounded by a great number of Tar Barrels. The tea collected by young Gentlemen the Tuesday before, being placed between the Devil and Lord North, was set on fire, and brought on our Enemies in Effigy, that Ruin they had designed to bring on us in Reality. The whole was consumed in a short time, in the Presence of some Thousands; who rejoiced to see the Abbetors of American Taxation consumed, By that very Engine of Oppression. It is remarkable, that during the whole Transaction, *not* the least Disorder happened; and by 8 o'clock at Night, the Town was in as great a Quiet as on a Sabbath Evening....

Besides the above exhibition, the young Gentlemen from the schools, prepared another Pope and Devil, which they also burnt in the Evening, after parading all the Streets with them throughout the Day. Their Devil was a most grotesque figure, curiously tarred and feathered. Their Pope was also in a fitting Posture, which a large Lanthorn before him, on Front of which was writ—Liberty, Property, and Carolina Forever—on one side was drawn, a large Cannister of Tea in Flames—on the other the Figure of America hurling a Spear at the Lord N——th, Kneeling upon a chest of tea, and bound with a cord, held by a hand representing Magna-Charta. . . .

Source and Comment

South Carolina Gazette, November 21, 1774. Transcription supplied by Andy Cohen of Charleston, South Carolina. Lord North, the British prime minister, responded to the Boston Tea Party of December 1773, with the so-called "Intolerable Acts" which closed the port and strengthened the hand of the Tory Governor of Massachusetts, Thomas Hutchinson. The "Quebec Act" of 1774, which granted extensive lands to the Province of Quebec at the expense of New England and Virginia and toleration to Catholics, proved even more provocative. These events led to the First Continental Congress in September 1774. The editor of the *South Carolina Gazette,* Peter Timothy, was a staunch patriot. James Rivington, editor of *Rivington's New York Gazetteer,* was a Tory.

* * *

Boston

In a series of articles called Reminiscences, printed in a Boston newspaper late in the year 1821, the author, alluding to the celebrations which took place on Pope Day, said:

> A man used to ride on an ass, with immense jack boots, and his face covered with a horrible mask, and was called Joyce, Jr. His office was to assemble men and boys in mob style, and ride in the middle of them, and in such company to terrify adherents to Royal Government, before the Revolution. The tumults which resulted in the Massacre, 1770, was excited by that means.—*Joyce Junior* was said to have a particular whistle which brought his adherents, &c. whenever they were wanted.

Source

Publications of the Colonial Society of Massachusetts, VIII (1903), 90-91. Quoted by Albert Matthews in a speech published in the above periodical. The "reminiscences" appeared in the Boston *Daily Advertiser,* November 9, 1821.

* * *

Guy Fawkes Mumming

[The] observance of the day at Newburyport [Massachusetts, before 1775] was probably typical of those in other large New England towns. . .:

> In the day time, companies of little boys might be seen, in various parts of the town, with their little popes, dressed up in the most grotesque and fantastic manner, which they carried about, some on boards, and some on little carriages, for their own and others' amusement. But the great exhibition was reserved for the night, in which young men, as well as boys, participated. They first constructed a huge vehicle, varying at times, from twenty to forty feet long, eight or ten wide, and five or six high, from the lower to the upper platform, on the front of which, they erected a paper lantern, capacious enough to hold, in addition to the lights, five or six persons. Behind that, as large as life, sat the mimic pope, and several other personages, monks, friars and so forth. Last, but not least, stood an image of what was designed to be a representation of old Nick himself, furnished with a pair of huge horns, holding in his hand a pitchfork, and otherwise accoutred, with all the frightful ugliness that their ingenuity could desire. Their next step, after they had mounted their ponderous vehicle on four wheels, chosen their officers, captain, first and second lieutenant, purser and so forth, placed a boy under the platform, to elevate and move round, at proper intervals, the moveable head of the pope, and attached ropes to the front part of the machine, was, to take up their line of march through the principal streets of the town. Sometimes in addition to the images of the pope and his company, there might be found, on the same platform, half a dozen dancers and a fiddler, whose

> Hornpipes, jigs, strathspeys, and reels
> Put life and mettle in their heels,

> together with a large crowd who made up a long procession. Their custom was, to call at the principal houses in various parts of the town, ring their bell, cause the pope to elevate his head, and look round upon the audience, and repeat the following lines.

> The fifth of November,
> As you well remember,
> Was gunpowder treason and plot;
> I know of no reason
> Why the gunpowder treason
> Should ever be forgot.
> When the first King James the sceptre swayed,
> This hellish powder plot was laid.
> Thirty-six barrels of powder placed down below
> All for old England's overthrow:
> Happy the man, and happy the day
> That caught Guy Fawkes in the middle of his play.
> You'll hear our bell go jink, jink, jink;
> Pray madam, sirs, if you'll something give,
> We'll burn the dog and never let him live.
> We'll burn the dog without his head,
> *And then you'll say the dog is dead.*
> From Rome, from Rome, the pope is come,
> All in ten thousand fears;
> The fiery serpent's to be seen,

All head, mouth, nose and ears.
The treacherous knave had so contrived,
To blow king parliament all up alive.
God by his grace he did prevent
To save both king and parliament.
Happy the man, and happy the day,
That catched Guy Fawkes in the middle of his play.
Match touch, catch prime,
In the good nick of time.
Here is the pope that we have got,
The whole promoter of the plot.
We'll stick a pitchfork in his back
And throw him in the fire.

After the verses were repeated, the purser stepped forward and took up his collection. Nearly all on whom they called, gave something. Esquire Atkins and Esquire Dalton, always gave a dollar apiece. After perambulating the town, and finishing their collections, they concluded their evening's entertainment with a splendid supper; after making with the exception of the wheels and the heads of the effigies, a bonfire of the whole concern, to which were added, all the wash tubs, tar barrels, and stray lumber, that they could lay their hands on. With them the custom was, to steal all the stuff. But those days have long since passed away.

Source and Comment

Publications of the Colonial Society of Massachusetts, XII (1909), 293-94. From an article by Henry W. Cunningham on the contents of a colonial diary. He quotes from Joshua Coffin's *History of Newbury . . . 1635-1845,* Boston, 1845, 249-516. Coffin says that Guy Fawkes' Day was not celebrated in Newbury after 1775, in deference to the French "whose assistance was deemed so advantageous at that time."

* * *

Colonial Almanac Verse for November 5

Gun Powder Plot
We ha'nt forgot.

———————

Powder-plot is not forgot.
'T will be observed by many a Sot.

Source

Publications of the Colonial Society of Massachusetts, XII (1909), 289. Quoted from Ames's *Almanacs* for 1735 and 1746.

Return Day in Delaware

Thursday after the Presidential Election Day

For some 150 years, it has been the custom at Georgetown, the seat of Sussex County, Delaware, to announce formally and festively the returns of the presidential election (which since 1845 falls on the first Tuesday following the first Monday in November) two days after the voting is over. This ritual came about as a result of an election reform in 1828 that allowed Delaware residents to vote in the "hundreds," as political subdivisions of the county were called. The tabulations would then be rushed by couriers to the county seat. Two days later, the tally sheets would be officially inspected and the totals posted. In more recent years the official announcement of two-day-old election returns isn't particularly exciting, but the colorful parades, picnics, military displays, songfests, and politicking that grew up around the announcement of the returns continue to attract festive crowds. Governors and members of the state congressional delegation, current and past, usually are present, along with a hoard of lesser politicos. Office seekers recently in contention shake hands in a display of unity, ride in the parade together, and begin preparing for the next political contest with a ceremonial "Burial of the Tomahawk." Since 1965, Return Day has been legally a "half-holiday" in Sussex County.

Early Return Days: Politicking and Parading

Early Days

In January, 1791, the General Assembly [of Delaware] directed that a commission choose a central site for a new county seat. This was done by May and the new town, named Georgetown after George Mitchell, one of the commissioners, was ready for the election of 1792.

Was the first "Return Day" held that year? One may assume that it was, but if that is true it was much different than the "Return Days" of the present era. Voters had to drive into Georgetown to cast their ballots and it is unlikely that they would return two days later for the results. Undoubtedly the results of the election were known that night or the next day and the voters would stay over to learn the results.

As early as 1803 complaints about having to go to Georgetown over rough roads in bad weather, leaving their families at home unprotected, were made by large groups of men in the outer districts.

It took a long time in those days for the people to change customs, especially in Sussex County, so it was not until 1828 that the General Assembly adopted new election laws providing that the Presidential electors should be chosen by the people rather than by the Legislature and that the polling places should be in the hundreds [political subdivisions] rather than at the county seat. This meant that the election officers had to bring the results from each of the

hundreds into Georgetown where they were turned over to the sheriff and tabulated and the results announced from the courthouse at noon on Thursday.

Thus the voters did not have to go very far from home to vote, but since there were no county newspapers in those days there was no way of knowing who had won the election. So many of the farmers decided to take a day off, load their whole families into wagons and go to Georgetown on Thursday to get the results.

It would seem that "Return Day" as we now know it probably started with the election of 1830 or the Presidential election of 1832. Certainly by the 1840s the custom was well established.

Several thousand persons would pour into Georgetown that morning coming on foot, in wagons drawn by mules, horses, or oxen, in carriages of all types and on horseback.

While waiting for the results the crowd listened to band concerts, wagered on cockfights, and engaged in other pastimes. Soon merchants saw an opportunity for gain and stalls and booths selling all kinds of food, clothing, and other articles were set up.

The results were read from the door of the courthouse at noon and were printed on a white sheet hoisted over the courthouse door. The winning candidates were placed on to the shoulders of their adherents and paraded around the Green. A large pole was erected in the Green and the emblem of the winning party was run up it. Generally an ox roast was provided by the winners.

However, the spirit of good feeling and reconciliation which marks the "Return Day" of the present was not always there in the old days. The losers quite often did not take their defeat with good grace and in one fight in 1844 a Dagsboro man was killed....

One of the best descriptions of "Return Day" was that published in the *Wilmington Every Evening* which sent a city slicker down to Georgetown to cover the event in 1872 just one hundred years ago. Excerpts from his story follow:

"Strolling from the Brick Hotel kept by a New Castle man, J. H. Wood, I found in front of the courthouse and on either side of the main street leading to the jail work benches, tables, and temporary stands, numbering 30 or 40 and called stalls and many were the boxes of confections on them.

"By 10 o'clock people of both sexes and all colors dressed in every manner and style, in wagons drawn by one, two and four horses with mule teams as well poured in from all directions. The ladies especially were gotten up well and I doubt not *Harper's* would have sent one of the best artists of the fashion world had they known of the day.

"By noon at least 2,000 persons had been added to the town's population for every avenue, lane, alley and street were lined with wagons in which old fashioned settees and chairs, some going back to Revolutionary times, had been installed as seats.

"Many dined at the hotels, others fared sumptuously in their wagons and carriages while others enjoyed roast beef, turkey, chicken, fish, coon, rabbits and possum at will, all of which could be had among the stalls cooked to order. Many ladies who had not visited the "Capitol" since the last "Return Day" could be seen in the crowd buying nicknacks for 'the little ones.'

"A part of the programme of the day is to see that young girls are treated. A pretty young lady, whether acquainted or not, is licensed to receive a box of candy and be it said for the young gentlemen of Sussex that no pretty damsel goes away empty."

Politicking and Parading

Return Day, of course, is much more than the announcing of the election results. The celebration that has grown up around the occasion has elements to please everyone. The main aspect of the celebration is still political, and in this regard Return Day offers those who come to Georgetown an opportunity to meet the candidates. The politicos themselves also made use of the occasion to mend fences and to garner support. As one member of the 1974 Return Day Committee noted, "More politicking goes on on Return Day than any other day of the year.... I guess they figure it's as good a time as any to get started for the next election."

Today the "politicking" generally gets started at a luncheon held for the candidates, where winners and losers circulate amidst supporters, accepting congratulations or condolences as the case may be. In earlier days, however, candidates, townspeople and all others assembled in Georgetown shared a repast in the streets of the town. In the town's public square, booths, stalls and stands were erected, complete with cooking stoves. From these booths "all kinds of edibles were for sale, such as Delaware biscuit, hot corn pone, with black molasses to pour over it, sweet potato biscuit, opossum, rabbit roasted upon a spit, white and sweet potatoes baked in hot ashes, fish, oysters, maninose (clams), fried chicken and hominy made in mortars chopped from a sturdy gum.... Always a large steer would be roasted in the open air and eaten. Hogsheads of beer, fresh cider, and vast quantities of Sussex County apple jack were consumed."

This tradition has also endured, only today, the street vendors offer a slightly different menu. Roast oxen is the principle food for modern revelers. The oxen, cooked on a spit in a lot just off the Georgetown Circle, is put to the fire on the day before Return Day so that it may be slowly turned and roasted, ready to be served to the waiting crowd at the next day's festivities....

The well fed crowds are also treated to various forms of entertainment. The highlight of the day is the parade down Market Street. This tradition probably began at one of the early Return Days, growing out of the practice of some celebrants who would arrive at Georgetown "in carts drawn by oxen, or in wagons drawn by six and eight horses gaily decorated with flags, ribbons and sleigh bells." No doubt these revelers would have used their decorated wagons to parade the winning candidates through the streets of Georgetown to receive the congratulations of the crowd.

Perhaps the most colorful of the Return Day parades took place in 1882, when Charles Stockley was elected Governor of Delaware. The Wilmington *Sunday Star* of November 12, 1882, described the parade as follows: "A procession moved through the town while the people cheered and guns boomed. A boat in bright new paint was mounted on wheels, rigged like a ship, and labeled the 'Old Constitution.' The craft was profusely decorated with a blue hen draped in ribbon and a dried coon skin was suspended from the mast. Six men on horseback moved in front and one hundred and twenty mounted men in the rear, all decorated and giving back to the crowd cheer for cheer. Standing on the quarter deck of the mimic ship, bowing to the multitude who enthusiastically applauded and saluted him, was the Governor Elect Charles Stockley. When the ship was drawn into the Square the people flocked from all sides to shake hands with the new Governor and at length he was lifted on brawny shoulders and carried into the Court House above the heads of the crowd, which cheered louder and louder." ...

Georgetown's own Senator Willard Saulsbury ably demonstrated that politics and liquor can be mixed and the spirit of Return Day celebrations was often enlivened by this potent brew. Partisan political feelings, when mixed with alcohol, would occasionally lead to brawls when members of one party would rejoice too much over their defeated and crestfallen opponents. In general the high spirits of Return Day were not conducive to good order in the earlier days and, as William P. Frank noted in the 1970 Return Day Program, "The newspapers of the past century always commented on whether there was any trouble. For example, the *Morning News* in 1884 noted: 'Everything considered, the crowd was remarkably orderly and seemed jubilant over the county victory and the prospect for the inauguration of a Democratic president on the 4th of March next.'" ...

While the parade has been the highlight of Return Day, the celebrants have often added gaiety and entertainment to the fete by attiring themselves in ludicrous costumes and riding or roaming through the streets of town. In the evening, by torch or by moonlight, there would be folk dancing on the green, where "fiddlers scraped the Virginia Reel and the Schottische and joy ran unconfined."

Source and Comment

Return Day Programs, Sussex County, Georgetown, Delaware, for November 9, 1972, 2, 5-6; and for November 6, 1980, 5-6. The 1974 program selection is from "History of Sussex County Return Day" written by W. Emerson Wilson and the 1980 selection is from "Return Day" by William J. Wade. Cf. "Shad Planking," p. 184, and "Labor Day Politicking," p. 327. For references to comic antics as part of parades, see "Fantasticals," p. 8.

St. Michael's Day

November 8

The Hebraic tradition of Michael as a prince and the greatest of the angels carries over into the celebration of Michaelmas, the festival of Michael and all the Angels, on September 29 in the Western Church, and on November 8 in the Greek Orthodox Church. Greek sponge fishermen, when they came to Tarpon Springs, Florida, from the Dodecanese Islands, brought with them a reverence for St. Michael. It was enhanced and transformed into a significant local religious festival with the miraculous cure of a Greek-American boy which is believed to have taken place through the intercession of St. Michael. A votive shrine built by his family commemorates the event.

St. Michael's Day Miracle

All three generations of Greek-Americans in Tarpon Springs, Florida, have a strong faith in the power of prayer for intercession, and in the miraculous and supernatural. . . . This belief is strongly reinforced by a miracle which was experienced by one of the local men in the city.

About forty years ago [c. 1926], when this man was a young child, he became ill with what appeared to be a brain tumor, or a disease of the brain. He was near death in a hospital in Tampa, and all hope had been given up for his life, when he had a sudden vision. The informant related the story as follows:

> I got to the point where I could not recognize people and I felt I was going to die. I wasn't afraid at all and couldn't figure out why I wasn't. My family gathered around my bed and brought near to me an ikon from St. Michael's church in Symi in the Dodecanese Islands of Greece. They told me I was in a coma and "out of my mind." Suddenly I saw my home in an intense light, and a voice which I recognized somehow as that of St. Michael who said, "I want you to build me a shrine in your home." Then I said, "I can't do it; I'm going to die." The voice then said, "Don't worry, tomorrow by ten o'clock you will be well." I felt that we couldn't afford it. The voice assured me that this would be accomplished. I dreamt, or saw in my vision, that I went for a walk where the shrine should be built. Then I ran back to my mother and told her about this. She said she would do it.

All of this was related by the man who had experienced the vision. Immediately after the vision, he woke up and his mother was talking to him. The next day, as promised in the vision, he felt "brand new" and left the hospital in two days. This was the first and last time that he ever had a vision. As promised by his mother, a beautiful small shrine and chapel were built on the grounds of his home in honor of St. Michael. On St. Michael's day in November, church services are held in the small chapel which accommodates about thirty people. Chairs are placed on the lawn for several hundred more. This is an important day for the Greek-Americans in Tarpon Springs. Long services are held in the chapel, and during most of the morning, the streets leading to the shrine are crowded with worshipers going to the services.

Source and Comment

"The Greek-American Group of Tarpon Springs, Florida," Ph.D. Dissertation, University of Pennsylvania, 1967, 324-26. Described by Edwin Clarence Buxbaum. He does not name his informant, but states that the miracle is widely known and accepted by "Greeks *and* Americans."

St. Cecilia's Day

November 22

A third-century Roman martyr, St. Cecilia, is said to have invented the organ and as a result of her musical ability to have caused an angel to fall in love with her. She is the patron saint of musicians apparently because her legend states that she praised God by instrumental as well as vocal music. She inspired a famous ode by John Dryden which George Frederick Handel set to music in 1736, the year before colonial Americans observed her day with a concert.

St. Cecilia Concerts

At the new Theatre in Queen Street [Charleston, South Carolina], on Tuesday the 22d Instant being St. *Cecilia's* Day, will be performed a Concert of Vocal and Instrumental Musick, for the Benefit of Mr. *Theodore Pachelbel*, beginning precisely at 6 o'clock in the Evening. Tickets to be had at the House of the said Mr. Pachelbel, or at Mr. Shepheard's, Vintner.

N.B. As this is the first time the said Mr. Pachelbel has attempted anything of this kind in a publick manner in this Province, he thinks it proper to give Notice that there will be sung a Cantata suitable to the Occasion.

— *South Carolina Gazette,* November 5, 1737

Monday, the 22nd Day of this present Instant, November, being St. Cecilia Day, all the Members of the St. Cecilia Society, are desired to meet at Eleven o'clock in the Forenoon of the said day, at Mrs. Frances Swallow's [a public house] in order to celebrate the Anniversary of the said Society.... N.B. A Concert will be performed in the Evening, to begin precisely at Half an Hour past six.

— *South Carolina Gazette,* November 8, 1773

Source and Comment

South Carolina Gazette, November 5, 1737, and November 8, 1773. Transcription supplied by Andy Cohen of Charleston, South Carolina. Charles Theodore Pachelbel, a German-born organist and composer, worked in Boston, Newport, and New York, as well as Charleston, in the 1730s. The St. Cecilia Society, which still exists, was distinguished in its early history for the quality of its musical performances and in later years its debutante balls.

St. Andrew's Eve

November 30

St. Andrew was the brother of Simon (Peter) and one of the twelve disciples. Tradition says that he was crucified in Patras about 70 A.D. He is the patron saint of both Russia and Scotland. His name means "manly or courageous"; thus it is appropriate that young girls seeking lovers appeal to him. St. Katherine, whose day is November 25, was born in Alexandria of noble family. She was beheaded when it was learned that she had made a Christian of a pagan sent to reason with her. Her cult became popular in the tenth century, and even today she is the patroness of old maids and so unmarried women.

Andrzejki: Eve of St. Andrew

Winter is the season of courting and arrangements for marriages [among Polish-Americans in Ohio]. Two holidays in November are devoted to divination by which young people try to discover whether, whom, and when they will marry.

Boys try to read their future on St. Katherine's Eve (November [25]), while the girls, still more elaborately, make their divinations on the Eve of St. Andrew.

In the course of the gaieties of the evening, the girls make auguries from the shapes formed by pouring spoonfuls of melted wax on cold water.

Another method used by the girls is to place their boots in order in a line leading from the stove to the door. The girl whose boot is the first to come outside the door will be the first to marry from those present.

Peeling apples is still another practice used. The apple must be peeled round and round and the peeling must be unbroken. The peeling then is thrown over the peeler's left shoulder, and whatever letter it forms will begin the name of the future husband—or wife, if the young men are included in the game.

One more method is popular, and that is for girls to write names of boys on slips of paper, which are then folded and placed in a basket or other large receptacle. After mixing them well, each girl picks a slip of paper; the name on the slip will be that of her future husband.

If boys and girls are taking part in the "game," the boys use girls' names on the slips of paper, and their papers are kept separate, so that boys will only choose from their basket.

There is one more idea, but, of course, it should be used with care, and only in a small and well supervised group.

Paste a small slip of paper bearing the name of one of the opposite sex into an empty walnut shell; then insert a lighted candle, fastening it with a little of the hot wax. The walnut shells then sail on water in a large basin or tub of water. The names which sail toward each other, and the shells which touch each other, predict the "drifting of the two people together on the Sea of Matrimony."

Source and Comment

Cooperative Recreational Services, Delaware, Ohio, 1953, 14-15. Natalie Stefanski-Budzikowski has recorded these Polish beliefs about how to foresee one's future spouse but does not supply her sources. Her main concern was traditional Polish holiday recreation. For other ways to foretell a future mate, on other holidays, see note on "To See Your Future Husband on Halloween," p. 379.

Thanksgiving

Moveable: Fourth Thursday in November

American Thanksgiving Day began in Plymouth Colony in 1621, when the Pilgrims who had migrated to Massachusetts gave thanks that the new land had been good to them and that they had been able to harvest a good crop their first year. The first officially designated day of thanksgiving was in 1631 in Massachusetts. Abraham Lincoln was the president to proclaim the day a national celebration, and he set the date as the last Thursday in November. This moveable date was changed by Franklin D. Roosevelt in 1939 to the fourth Thursday in November, although some states have been reluctant to shift. In Canada, the second Monday in October is Thanksgiving.

Actually, days of thanksgiving with their prayers and feasting are far older than Pilgrim times. The American celebration is an adaptation of Lammas (Loaf Mass) Day, August 1, which was celebrated in Britain if there was an abundant crop of wheat but not otherwise. On Lammas Day the farmers brought loaves of bread made from the successful crop to mass (thus Loaf Mass Day) as a token of thanksgiving. Moreover, thanksgivings for successful crops are common enough to all agricultural peoples, as the selections that follow testify, though usually the dates are later than August 1 when the yield of crops in addition to wheat is known. Harvest Home observances mark the end of seasonal tasks involving the work community and at the same time express gratitude for the bounty of nature.

Origins of Thanksgiving

Our modern Thanksgiving is a combination of two very different and very old holidays: 1) the harvest home feast celebrated when the main crops were harvested and 2) the formal day of thanksgiving proclaimed by a community's authorities to focus on a particular event, such as a military victory, or the need for rain....

For almost the next two hundred and fifty years, these two kinds of "thanksgiving" remained quite distinct. Very few formal "days of thanksgiving" coincided with harvest. They were proclaimed at various times in all regions of the English colonies and were popular. No special foods became associated with them. During the same period (1620-1870) harvest home feasts also flourished. The menus of these feasts differed along regional and ethnic lines. The harvest supper of the Germans in Pennsylvania, the Dutch in New York, the Scotch-Irish in Appalachia, the African Americans in the South, and the English in New England: all were unique. Because these regional ethnic cultures remained isolated and autonomous, their harvest home and thanksgiving day feasts continued to be local and provincial in character.

During and after the Revolutionary War (1775-83), a desire for national rather than local holidays developed and an attempt was made to combine harvest home with the formal day of thanksgiving. George Washington noted in his orderly book on October 31, 1777, "Tomorrow being the day set apart by the honorable Congress for Public Thanksgiving and praise, and duty calling us devoutly to express our grateful acknowledgements to God for the manifold blessings he has granted us...." Later in 1789 as President, he appointed the last Thursday in November as a national thanksgiving day. Regional feeling was, however, still too strong for the feast to be accepted nationally. But regionalism began to crumble in the nineteenth century as mass communications and transportation evolved. Hard surfaced highways, canals, and railways helped a national market develop. An industrial revolution began, cities expanded, and tens of millions of immigrants flooded in from Europe. A nationalistic spirit developed and pressure was put on both regional and immigrant ethnic cultures to adopt the new national, popular culture. Compulsory education in public schools insured a measure of common enculturation. The story of the Pilgrims became an ideal medium for fostering "Americanism." Regionalism's last attempt to thwart this nationalism came in 1861 when the southern slave owning states seceded, setting off Civil War. During the worst of the fighting, President Lincoln in an attempt to bolster unionist spirit, appointed the last Thursday in November as an annual national Thanksgiving holiday. Soon afterwards, the northern regions won the war and the union was preserved. As regionalism quickly faded, the tradition of a combined harvest home and thanksgiving day feast celebrated nationally was accepted. The "new" holiday featured all the characteristics common today: a church service in the morning, followed by an afternoon's feast and a weekend of sports. The menu centered around roast turkey, stuffing, cranberry sauce, numerous vegetables, and pumpkin pie—the main dishes of the New England harvest home feast. Many of these foods had gained popularity because of their supposed connection to the Pilgrims. Thanksgiving as a national cultural event is now just about a century old and still relatively unchanged. In a nation of continual and rapid change, it remains surprisingly vital.

Source

...satieteellinen Arkisto 26, Suomen Muinaismuistoyhdistys, 1975, ...1. From a paper by Jay Allan Anderson presented at a conference ...thnological food research and published in the *Journal of the ...ish Society of Antiquities* of Helsinki. The first part "describes the ...as it is commonly celebrated today and traces its history." For ...rt of Anderson's emphasis on officially proclaimed days of ...sgiving and the Pilgrim Fathers tradition, see "First Thanksgiv-...Illinois," p. 411.

* * *

Harvest Home

Harvest Home was once—in the farming valleys west of the Delaware—more important to Pennsylvania farmers of Dutch tongue than the November Thanksgiving Day, which was looked upon as a dubious and unnecessary, almost resented, Yankee gift. Lutherans and Reformed celebrated Christmas and gave their private and public thanks to God for their summer's harvest at the summer Harvest Home. Hence for many years they felt no need of celebrating the Yankee Thanksgiving.

Let us look at the history of this Pennsylvania festival which was long the rival of Thanksgiving Day, and even after the absorption of Thanksgiving into Pennsylvania's calendar, is still celebrated in Lutheran and Reformed churches, even in the cities, and has been borrowed by Mennonites, Methodists, and other church groups in Pennsylvania and areas where Pennsylvanians settled in North, South, and West.

The comparative study of folklore and primitive religion has shown the universality of harvest festivals throughout the world. To show his gratitude to the gods the farmer celebrated harvest variously with a harvest supper, a blessing of the fields and the produce of the fields, harvest dances and merry-making, harvest songs, harvest fertility rites, harvest services in temple and meetinghouse. The Palestinian harvest festivals described in the Old Testament are only one example of primitive harvest festivals

with a religious motivation. Roman Catholicism, with its multitude of holy days, had no special harvest thanksgiving festival, but in Germany the Autumn Ember Days (*Quatemberfasten*) and the beating of the bounds (*Flurprozessionen* or *Bittgänge*) served the purpose. In the Protestant Churches of Germany, as witnessed by the oldest church liturgies from the Reformation period, there were special Protestant services (Lutheran and Reformed) for harvest thanksgiving. Many of these, we are told, were held in September, on the Sunday nearest to St. Michael's Day (September 29). This was known as the *Erntedankfest* or *Erntefest,* and the sermon preached on the day was the *Erntepredigt* or *Ernterede.*

In the British Isles ancient Celtic and Saxon rituals united to give us the time of summer or autumn merrymaking known as "Harvest Home." Brand's charming chapter on "Harvest Home, alias Mell Supper, Kern, or Churn Supper, or Feast of Ingathering" [in *Observations on Popular Antiquities*] tells us of the British customs in their variations from Cornwall to Scotland, with the Harvest Doll or Kern (Corn) Baby, or as the Scots called it, the "Maiden" (the last sheaf dressed and paraded through the fields), Harvest Dinners, Harvest Suppers, Harvest Dances. These rites were part of the "Merry England" tradition and for the most part were pagan survivals. The Church gave its blessing on Lammas Day (August 1) to the first loaves made from the harvest wheat, which were offered at mass. In more recent times in Protestant England the "harvest thanksgiving" has become an official religious festival, on a Sunday in September or October. In both the Church of England and the Free Churches it has become customary to "decorate the church with fruit, flowers, and vegetables which are later devoted to charity; special hymns are sung; and there is frequently a visiting preacher. There seems to have been no provision for such a service in the Book of Common Prayer, as there was in the continental German liturgies, but special forms do exist from the end of the 18th century.

The Pennsylvania "Harvest Home" as celebrated by Lutherans and Reformed, consisted originally of a service, with harvest sermon, in the church, usually during the week, either in the midst of harvest or at the close of harvest. It could be held anywhere from the first week of July till mid-October, depending upon the decision of pastor or congregation. Sometimes the Harvest Home service was combined with the Fall Communion and the ingathering of Fall catechumens. In the period after the Civil War we begin to read of churches decorated with the fruits and vegetables and grains of harvest, and the gradual centering of the festival on a Sunday rather than on a weekday. The service had its hymns and its liturgy and was one of the joyous festivals of the church year as conceived by rural Pennsylvanians.

A special feature of Pennsylvania's Harvest Home was the special collections—"harvest thank offerings"—which were usually a part of it. The early editorials on Harvest Home in the Lutheran and Reformed press begin to mention this offering in the 1830's and are happy to report that while a few congregations devoted it to parish needs (the earlier custom?), generally it was shared by the church boards and given to missions, education, and other benevolent causes.

As the churches came to be decorated with the fruits of the harvest, it became customary to give the display either to the minister and his family, or to the church orphanages or homes for the aged. The custom of giving the fruits and vegetables to the minister is related, of course, to the old American custom of the "Donation" or "Pound Party" which in most cases came to be centered in the Advent and New Year Season. . . .

By 1820 we find Harvest Home in full operation in Pennsylvania as a church festival.

Since it was not a general American custom, references by travelers through the Dutch Country tell us something of the practice in the early 19th century. The earliest of these is a blast from the eccentric Methodist circuit-rider, Jacob Gruber (1778-1850), who lost no opportunities to point up what he considered the lack of "religion" among Pennsylvania's Lutheran and Reformed people. Describing his travels on Dauphin Circuit in German Pennsylvania about 1820, he writes: "I found they had an old custom. On Sunday after harvest their parson preached a harvest sermon, as it was called; but this year there were very few to hear it; most of the congregation were gone to the mountain to gather whortleberries. It would be hard if the poor parson should have to preach another thanksgiving sermon when the berries are all gathered; then when all is safe take a weekday for it. That would hinder any from visiting on Sunday, and having their play and amusements."

This early reference by an outsider—if the Pennsylvanian Jacob Gruber can be called an "outsider"—can be paired with the reference made by John W. Richards, grandson of Henry Melchoir Muhlenberg, in 1825, when pastor of the New Holland Lutheran charge in Lancaster County, to preaching "harvest sermons."

The nation learned of the custom in August, 1847, when the *Union Magazine* commented on Pennsylvania's distinctive harvest festival. "In Pennsylvania, where perhaps a preponderance of settlers from the continent of Europe—a less absorbingly ambitious people than the Yankees—has infused a more genial spirit; they hold what they call a harvest service—a general meeting for thanksgiving and prayer. This is a graceful and interesting custom, and one which might be adopted wherever the plough opens the soil."

Source

Pennsylvania Folklife, IX (Fall 1958), 3-5. From an article by Don Yoder on this harvest thanksgiving observance and its German and British background.

* * *

Harvest Home on St. Wenceslaus' Day

Czech-Americans [in Iowa and Minnesota] used to celebrate the harvest-home with a thanksgiving supper on the feast of their national patron saint, Duke Wenceslaus of Bohemia (28 September). This celebration was called *pout* 'a pilgrimage' because it was customary for people from the surrounding countryside to make the journey into town on foot like pilgrims. In Bohemia the *pout* really was a sort of pilgrimage, for groups of peasants sang hymns as they walked to the festival and stopped at wayside shrines to offer prayers of thanksgiving for a successful harvest. That Czech-Americans held this celebration on the day of their national patron saint was doubly fitting, for Wenceslaus is said to have been in one respect a farmer himself. According to tradition, "good King Wenceslaus" with his own hands sowed the wheat and pressed the grapes to be used for the Mass in his own household.

Source and Comment

Journal of American Folklore, LXIX (1956), 284. Reported by Lawrence V. Ryan in a study of "rites of divination and supplication" among rural Czech-Americans in Iowa and Minnesota. Duke Wenceslaus was prominent in the conversion of what is now Czechoslovakia to Christianity in the early tenth century. He was murdered in 929 by his brother as part of a power struggle. He was popularized as "the good King Wenceslaus" in the nineteenth-century carol by John M. Neale.

* * *

Harvest Customs

Harvesters were in some places [in Maryland before 1925] liberally supplied with a drink of cold water, ginger and molasses, and they always had an extra dinner given them. In other places ginger bread and egg-nog was the standard treat, and sometimes beer was substituted, this being in most cases home made, and made from hops.

The last day of the harvest was celebrated as a "Harvest Home," and the evening was given over to merriment, the neighbors coming from miles around to take part.

There were also husking parties; and a feature of this in some places was a chicken potpie baked in a Dutch oven, sweet potatoes and preserves being its necessary accessories. The favorite games at these husking parties were "sock-a-bout," "foul and fair," and "watch the candle."

It was customary during corn husking for the finder of the "red ear" to throw it to the prettiest girl, and then chase her until he had caught and kissed her. Then they danced together.

Source

Memoirs of the American Folklore Society, XVIII (1925), 122. "Folk-Lore from Maryland," collected by Annie W. Whitney and Caroline C. Bullock. Data on informants incomplete. For another belief about the "red ear," see "Corn Husking Song," below.

* * *

Plantation Corn-shucking

Recently I obtained a letter, written in 1852 from Laurens, South Carolina, describing a Negro corn-shucking on a plantation....This letter, with the account of the corn-husking, was written by Mrs. R. H. Marshall, a relative of President Millard Fillmore, to her two grandchildren. The portion of the letter describing this activity is as follows:

> Would you not like to be here next fall at their corn shuckings? It would be fine sport for you. I believe I promised you a description of one in this letter. When the overseer has a quantity of corn to husk, he allows his Negroes to invite those on the neighboring plantations to come and help them in the evening. When all things are ready, they light the torches of pitch pine, (their [*sic*] being an abundance of it about here) and march while singing one of their corn songs to the spot. Then the captain mounts the heap of corn, and all sing a *call song* for the others to come, which is immediately answered from the other plantations, in a song that "they are coming." You can hear them distinctly more than a mile. They sing as they march all the way, and when they arrive at the spot, they all join in one *grand chorus*—and make the forest ring with their music. Then they appoint captains to succeed each other from the different companies—who mount the heap in turn and play their *monkey pranks*—while they take the lead in singing as those around them shuck and toss their corn into the crib—seemingly the happiest beings that live. I was never more amused than while watching their movements and listening to their songs. Some of them have very fine voices. We waited until twelve o'clock and left them to enjoy their supper, prepared for them by their overseer.

Source and Comment

Journal of American Folklore LXXXVI (1973), 61-62. Contributed by David J. Winslow. For a later though longer description, see David C. Barrow, Jr., "A Georgia Corn-Shucking," *Century Magazine,* XXIV (1882), 873-78.

Corn-husking bees are still fairly common among white farmers, but they are much rarer among blacks. Combining work and play, feasting and frolicking, they are, at least informally, harvest celebrations.

* * *

Corn Husking Song

A correspondent sent to the Baltimore *Sun,* several years ago [c. 1925], an old Maryland corn husking song...

The Jack Snipe said unto the Crane,
>   Whisky Johnny,
I wish de Lord there would come rain.
>   Oh, Hilo!
The Wild Goose said unto the Swan,
>   Whisky Johnny,
The coming winter will be sharp and long,
>   Oh, Hilo!
They say old master's sick again,
>   Whisky Johnny,
He suffers many an ache and pain,
>   Oh, Hilo!
When my old master's dead and gone,
>   Whisky Johnny,
This old nigger will stop husking corn,
>   Oh, Hilo!
Oh, my old master's good to me,
>   Whisky Johnny,
And when he dies he'll set me free,
>   Oh, Hilo!
We've possum fat and taters, too,
>   Whisky Johnny,
Good enough fir me and you,
>   Oh, Hilo!
If you have cider good and strong,
>   Whisky Johnny,
I'll be to see you before very long,
>   Oh, Hilo!
The watermillons now in their height,
>   Whisky Johnny,
I stol'd two out de patch last night,
>   Oh, Hilo!
The nigger who finds the most red corn,
>   Whisky Johnny,
Will be de next leader 'sho as he's born,
>   Oh, Hilo!
The corn is husked, the supper is o'er,
>   Whisky Johnny,
And now we'll pull for the other shore
>   Oh, Hilo!
And all you niggers start tonight,
>   Whisky Johnny,
So you'll get home before daylight,
>   Oh, Hilo!
And now my friends I'll bid you all adieu,
>   Whisky Johnny,
I've done the best I could for you,
>   Oh, Hilo!
And remember that we niggers all,
>   Whisky Johnny,
Will be on hand next fall,
>   Oh, Hilo!
And now, my friend, again good night,
>   Whisky Johnny,
We husked that corn good and all right,
>   Oh, Hilo!
We stripped the husk off like a shirt,
>   Whisky Johnny,
And left no silk that would ever hurt,
>   Oh, Hilo!

Source and Comment

Memoirs of the American Folklore Society, XVIII (1925), 164-65. "Folk-Lore from Maryland," collected by Annie W. Whitney and Caroline C. Bullock. Data on sources incomplete.

The corn husking song is an adaptation of a widely known sailors' work song, "Whisky Johnny," a halyard chanty, or chant used to synchronize the rhythm of men pulling a rope to raise sail. It has been used on British and American ships since the days of Queen Bess. The black version contains stereotypes reminiscent of the minstrel stage.

* * *

Cotton Picking

Mary Ann Dodson [of White County, Tennessee], age ninety, remembered joint cornhuskings for men and quiltings for women. Just before her recent demise [c. 1967] she recalled that candy and cookies were prizes at cotton pickings [removing fiber from seed by hand] and that people sometimes "took off their shoes and put the cotton in them as they picked it." The following December 22, 1925, entry in the diary of Paul E. Doran describes a picking he attended.

> I went tonight to a cotton picking at Joe Sparks, the first one I ever attended. Many people here raise a small cotton patch for home use. Since there is no gin near they pick it by hand, frequently by having a picking such as this tonight. Cakes are baked, homemade candy is prepared, and the cotton is thoroughly dried in sacks by the fire. The old folks in one room, the youngsters in another, the picking begins. A prize is offered to the one who picks the most, a big slice of cake and some candy. All work feverishly until around 10 o'clock; then each one's cotton is weighed and the prize is awarded. Then candy and cake are passed, a song is sung, and all go home. It is a fine social affair for both young and old. The old folks tell tales of their young days and the young laugh and enjoy themselves. I am told that in the old days an affair of this kind would wind up with everybody drunk.

Source

"Folklore from White County, Tennessee," Ph.D. Dissertation, George Peabody College for Teachers, 1969. Collected in 1967-68 by Edwina B. Doran.

* * *

Papago Harvest Festival Songs

The [*Vigita* or harvest] festival is held the last of November, supposedly every four years [by the Papago Indians]. But it depends largely upon the success of the harvest of the crops and it has now (1919) been six years since it was held. It may be held this year or may never be celebrated again, as the establishment of a government school, public power plant, and trader's store at Santa Rosa will naturally result in a speedy loss of conservatism.

The celebration of the *Vigita* is vested in the five principal villages of the Santa Rosa valley, though celebrants attend from all villages of the Indian Oasis and ally themselves with one or other of the five....The festival is always held at Achi, which is considered the foremost Papago village....

The following eight songs were taken down as typical *Vigita* songs. They were sung by Achi at the last celebration.

1. geNhu ηe tcevaηi cahkali wucanyi
   Over there the   clouds   in a row   come out.

   gaмhuη itoinaηe dam ane muvitci
   Over there   our field   above,   there with corners

   ane wucanyi tuahi djuhku
   there   come out. Thunders,   rains.

2. atci itoinaη mehk osekaitaη iuηidjeh
   Achi   our field   far off   is heard   to shake.

   dama itonenami tcevahaηi wucanyeh
   Above   shining   clouds   come out.

   ioh toinaη djuhku hunyi wucaNYE
   Here   our field   rains,   corn   springs up.

3. vavahki eda vadjuhku'
   Big house   within   it rains.

   daмhana tcevahaηi wucanyeh
   Up above   clouds   come out.

   sapowekaki namenoahi djuhku'
   Well hear   that thundering,   rains.

4. winyim itoinaηe winyim itoinaηe
   Winyim   our fields,   Winyim   our fields,

   damaiηe huNya pewuwahkime
   on them   corn   springs up.

   yatci toinaηe yatci toinaηe
   Achi   our fields,   Achi   our fields,

   tamaiηe hunya pewuahkime
   on them   corn   comes out.

   ak'tcin it.oinaηe ak'tcin it.oinaηe
   Akchin   our fields,   Akchin   our fields,

   yanegam it.oinaηe anegam oinaηe
   Anekam   our fields,   Anekam   fields,

5. yahtci t.oinaηe damain cuda'ki merikuhte mamasemel
   Achi   our fields   on   water   ran   ran.

   iakonyehite iotam vahcaN nawitcu huhunyi
   Here look   people!   Yonder   clown   ears of corn

   behkeme behkeme
   bears away,   bears away.

6. wewesi u'si wehtceh wewesi u'si wehtceh
   All   sticks   are there.   All   sticks   are there.

   we's ametcutca kakai pevaupanyime
   All   we stand up   lay across.

   wes amatcutca vaupah
   All   we stand up   lay across.

7. muhkisi tcewana kahtce
   Dying   world   here lay.
   muhkisi tcewana kahtce
   Dying   world   here lay.

   daмhanai hunyi wuca
   Above it   corn   comes out.

   mudatatci kiohta
   Bend   stalks.

   damhana wuca djuhku
   Above   comes out.   Rains.

8. yalisi tcetceto'ki litoɪ   vavu·ca
   Little   green   Montezuma is coming out.

  yalisi dodo haiyu hunyi vuca
   Little   white   corn is coming out.

  mumui tcewaŋ akenyapenyukena
   Many   clouds   rain on me.

  mumui tcewaŋ akenyapenyukena
   Many   clouds   rain on me.

  tcewaŋ iwucanye kenyapenyukua
   Clouds   come out,   rain on me.

Source and Comment

American Anthropologist, XXII (1920), 14, 24-25. J. Alden Mason obtained a full description of a *Vigita* in 1919 from José Juan, "one of the singers at the festival of 1913." At the time Mason was studying the Papago language, and his texts and translation conclude his account.

The Papago were an agricultural people who once occupied most of southern Arizona and northern Sonora, Mexico. They raised corn, beans, and cotton and their harvest songs invoked the rains, which brought a bountiful corn crop. Eight new songs were composed by each of the five participating villages whenever a harvest celebration was held, and the heart of the ritual consisted of the village groups, in sequence, masked and carrying rattles, performing their songs.

* * *

Chinese Harvest Moon Festival

Chief symbol of [the Chinese Harvest Moon] festival is the "moon cake," a small cake made in the shape of the moon, about one inch thick, stuffed with sweetened and pulverized soya beans of several varieties, mixed with shelled melon seeds and whole egg yolks, and baked to a golden brown.

Accompanying the moon cakes is the *pomelo,* a fruit similar to our grapefruit except that it is twice as large and the meat is sweet. However, the *pomelos* grown in California are usually fairly sour, as the climate is not very favorable for the growth of this tropical fruit. As substitutes, apples, oranges, and other California citrus fruits are used.

Also part of the Moon Festival are little figures of rabbits and other animals made from candied sugar, and cookies shaped into miniature pigs enclosed in Chinese-style reed cages. The use of rabbits has special significance: Chinese mythology has it that there is a rabbit in the moon who is forever busy pounding out the elixir of life.

No traditional ceremonies are connected with this festival other than taking the day off from toil and gathering family members together for a good dinner and the enjoyment of moon cakes afterward. In former days, however, some California Chinese families performed the ceremony of honoring the moon by placing moon cakes, fruits, and lighted incense sticks on a table up on the roof or on a balcony. Then, at the stroke of midnight, when the moon becomes full, the ceremony of "capturing the moon" is observed. This is done simply by catching the moon's reflection in a basin full of water. This ceremony, however, is more or less forgotten today [in 1948].

Source and Comment

Western Folklore, VII (1948), 248. From a description of "Native Festivals of the California Chinese" by William Hoy. He observed festivals in "sizable Chinese colonies," mainly of Cantonese origin, in San Francisco, Oakland, Los Angeles, Sacramento, Marysville, Bakersfield, Fresno, San Diego, Visalia, and other cities.

According to Chinese belief, the moon influences crops and therefore is an object of happy veneration at harvest time when it becomes full. Originally an agricultural festival, this holiday is celebrated on the fifteenth day of the eighth moon, said to be the time when the moon is brightest. Bakeries and candy shops display moon-shaped confections.

* * *

Chinese Harvest Moon Festival
Chinese Festival Changes with the Times

In an effort to revive business from visitors and tourists, the businessmen [in San Francisco's Chinatown] have expanded the Moon Festival, or Mid-Autumn Festival, which celebrates the year's harvest.

The celebrations began Monday [September 26, 1977], 22 days after three masked men invaded the Golden Dragon restaurant here and shot five customers to death in what the police are sure was an act of retaliation between Chinese gangs here. The festival is to end on Oct. 11.

On Tuesday a procession of several hundred children, representing four schools, marched four blocks to Portsmouth Square in Chinatown, followed by others carrying the papier-mache effigy of a dragon. Ceremoniously, onlookers poked the dragon with sticks of burning incense, but for this celebration, there were no firecrackers.

"Business has been off 50 per cent," Stephen Fong, president of the Chinese Chamber of Commerce, said at a news conference at which the Mid-Autumn Festival was announced, speaking of what has happened to Chinatown since the Golden Dragon killings. He said that the purpose of the festival, which has not been observed here as often as it has in other Chinese-American communities, was to wipe out memories of the Golden Dragon restaurant killings of Sept. 4.

A week after those killings, a 20-year-old Chinese was shot in an apartment house foyer and his 18-year-old companion wounded. On Sept. 18, the operator of a mah jongg game was killed by holdup men. So far, the city's offer of a $100,000 reward for information in the killings has gone begging. . . .

The festival, conveniently, will continue through the dates of two important Chinese political anniversaries. Today marks the 28th anniversary of the Chinese Communist takeover of mainland China, which some here in San Francisco's Chinese community celebrate; others, who are in sympathy with the Chinese Nationalist Government on Taiwan, will be celebrating the 66th anniversary of Sun Yat-sen's declaration of the Republic of China, on Oct. 10.

"That way everybody will be happy," said a woman clerk at the Chinese Chamber of Commerce.

Source and Comment

New York Times, October 2, 1978. From a news report, "Chinatown on Coast Seeks to Quiet Fears," by Wallace Turner, datelined "San Francisco, October 1."

This news report demonstrates how a waning folk celebration was revived, extended, and adapted to the contemporary realities of gang warfare (no firecrackers), commerce (business decline due to "fears of violence"), and politics (rivalry between supporters of the Chinese Nationalists and Chinese Communists).

* * *

Chinese Harvest Moon Festival
Day of the Moon Cake

Today is the Day of the Moon Cake.

Actually, it is the Autumn Moon observance, celebrated by the Chinese on the 15th day of the eighth month of the Chinese lunar calendar, which this year [1980] falls on Sept. 23. It is not only the day of the full moon, but the time each year when the full moon is most intense. In Chinese mythology the moon is a traditional female element, and because of that the *yin,* the feast of the autumn moon, is, according to Chinese belief, essentially gentle and quiet.

Unlike most Chinese festivals, which are preceded by days of preparation and often followed by days of recovery, the Autumn Moon observance lasts but one day, and on this day families eat a good deal of fruit, particularly fruit with many seeds, to symbolize fertility. And they eat lots of moon cakes, since this is the one day in the year that the cakes, because of their composition, become symbolic as well as enjoyable.

Moon cakes are simple affairs. At their heart is a thickened paste of lotus seeds, to which nuts might be added. The paste is rolled into balls and these are covered with dough. The paste-filled balls are then pressed into carved wooden molds of various shapes and out come round or squarish cakes with calligraphic designs celebrating the holiday. These are brushed with egg yolk for glaze before baking.

Though moon cakes are available throughout the year in [New York] Chinatown bakeries, it is on Autumn Moon Day that they become special, as well as symbolic. Preserved duck egg yolks, representing the moon, are often placed in the middle of the lotus seed centers. The cakes are marked with one, two, three or four red dots to indicate the number of duck eggs inside.

For a couple of weeks the Chinatown bakeries have been trying feverishly to keep up with the demand for moon cakes, as people have been buying them and storing them, waiting for today.

One day last week, almost a hundred people were lined up in front of the Lung Fong Bakery at 41 Mott Street, waiting to buy moon cakes.

Choon Wah Lee, the owner, showed a visitor a rear storehouse packed to the ceiling with cartons of preserved duck egg yolks from Taiwan. Two huge Hobart mixers were working the dough. In the bakery's basement, other mixers were combining lotus seeds, sugar, oil and water into the paste.

"It's really not all lotus seeds," Mr. Lee confided, "because they are too expensive. We add some crushed lima beans to make the paste thick." All around were pails of paste waiting to be taken upstairs to the production line.

Does anyone mind that there are lima beans in the lotus seed paste, Mr. Lee was asked. "No," he said. "They cannot be tasted. The cakes are still very, very good."

Source

New York Times, September 23, 1980. Article by Fred Ferretti, a staff writer.

* * *

Czech Harvest Festival

The house of the gymnastic society "Sokol" (Falcon) in Detroit was built in the eighties. Since then, the Bohemian and Moravian Czechs have been carried away by the continuous waves of residential mobility which shift the ethnic groups one after the other, according to their economic progress, across the Detroit plain; and today, the black Americans who inhabit what was once the Czech quarter, observe with curiosity the reading and discussing, the athletic training, the celebrating, dancing, and singing Slavs. There is hardly a Czech in the town who does not belong to the "Sokol," and the society itself is a member of the American Sokol Federation, which in turn is a branch of the parent society in the home country. Their slogan "Neither profit nor glory" speaks for its ethos. "A man, perfect physically, spiritually and morally, of a firm and noble character, whose word is irrevocable, like the law," is the formula with which new members are sworn in. Documents stored in the library are witness to past activities and endeavors of the members, aiming towards the reconstruction of political freedom in the native country, the welfare of the common people, liberal and social idealism. The motto of the society's theater defines its function: "To bring before the eyes of our people the glorious heritage of our gallant ancestors, their glory and martyrdom, their perseverance in conviction and their humiliation." The titles of the plays on the yellowing programs show that the task was carried out: "Jan Hus," "Jan Hus a Jeroným," "Jan Žižka," "Psohlavci," "Jan Výrava," "Karel Havlíček Borovský," and other names of Czech historical heroes. But dramas and comedies from village life are not missing: "... about young people, when he is rich and she is poor, and the father does not allow him to marry, or disinherits him. We know these things from our lives there, but it also happens here. You can laugh and cry in it....About the son who gets rich and does not acknowledge his father any more. That happens more often at home than here." On different festive occasions the society shows pictures borrowed from the Film Library. "People love to come, especially if it is something from the Fatherland and they can see their old country." For twenty-five years they have been making their own films and have recorded all the national Czechoslovak and American celebrations and manifestations in which they have taken part—festivals, weddings, and funerals, life in Czech communities and families, on farms and in Detroit.

Martin Kovařík is an outstanding example of a Sokol. Both he and his wife by virtue of their wisdom, life experience, and achievements, as well as by genuine kindness, are the recognized spiritual leaders of the group. They came to America as teenagers from Moravian villages and married here. "We had nothing when we came; first our people wanted to have a wife and a house, but the first thing one had was a car. Now they have big, beautiful farms and I have a house with all the modern equipment and gadgets." Cultural activities within both the American and Czech societies, conscious allegiance to their new country, as well as awareness of civic responsibilities, distinguish them. "Our people began to settle here a century ago. We have a share in the growth of the city. On the 250th Anniversary of Detroit, we marched right behind the American Indians."

Both of the Kovaříks remember clearly their holidays in the old country. "At carnival time masked men used to go around the village, straw wrapped all over their bodies, boys disguised as women, each taking what he could. There were no theatrical outfitting companies where one could rent a costume as there are here; they blackened their faces, went around on wooden goats, or led a bear; in short, they used anything which was at hand." When the Kovaříks' son was getting married not long ago, his wedding was celebrated in the Sokol Hall, "the way it always is whenever at least one of the newlyweds is a Moravian." At midnight the older women take the wreath—one should say veil—from the bride's head and, singing the usual songs of parting with girlhood and parents, they bind her head with a scarf. Then everyone buys a dance with her. Sometimes over three hundred dollars is collected. Then they seat the bride on a chair in the middle of the hall and the boys lead the bridegroom away. In a hurry they put in her place an ugly man, ridiculous and small, and cover him with a white bed sheet. They call the bridegroom and tell him that he cannot get the bride as easily as he thought. "How much do you give?" "I don't have any money." If he understands what is going on, he refuses to pay and makes

as many jokes and jests as possible. Eventually, he gives his whole purse and is supposed to embrace the bride. At the last moment they pull away the bed sheet and he kisses the ugly man. If the bridegroom is an American, he gets scared. Afterwards one shaves the groom with a special wooden blade and then puts a horseshoe on the bride's shoe. "You want to know what it means? It simply means that we want to collect some money for the bride."

Kovařík was obliging enough to show me moving pictures of their life, among which there was a complete record in color of a harvest celebration of the year before. It was organized by the Western Czech Brethren Unity, to which all of them belonged, at the Ryzners' farm in Owosso, where the Detroit Sokol has its summer camp. Kovařík arranged the program.

In his native village, Žeravice, there were two kinds of harvest celebration. One of these was on the Berchtold Estate, where half of the village was employed. The crop was brought home with two sheaves; the first was the "bride," the second was the "old woman." They were carried by the two most popular boys among the reapers, and two girls carried the two wreaths. After the ceremony at the landowner's house, they got a barrel of beer and danced in the yard. The other celebration, for the rest of the community, was given by the mayor. Kovařík got some other ideas from a booklet printed in Prague, "*Harvest Celebration,* an ancient Moravian custom from the time of serfdom, to be performed at harvest and on other occasions." The characters in the program of the Owosso celebration were "the landowner and his wife, the grandfather, old and young maid, two boys, a night-watchman, older people, young laborers and servants, children. All, including the people, in national costume."

The procession seemed endless. In front went the band, then two boys with bouquets of grain-ears and field-flowers, two girls with wreaths, children, women, and men. "The nicest thing about it is that all the children were born in America," said Mrs. Kovařík. Some rakes were seen, which had been brought from among the stage properties of the theater, as well as a few scythes, whose blades were covered with paper. "More of them would mean trouble; who would transport them here from the theater? Our farmers have hundreds of acres, they must use machines. We always used to go on wagons with sickles and scythes, but since one of the women fell down and the sickle almost pierced her body, we march. The majority of people you see are our farmers. Look at those from Bannister, how worn out, how bent they are. They settled there because the farms there were in a bad state and cheap. Now they have excellent ground, a National Hall, and a Czech school, where their children learn how to read and write in Czech." They came in various native costumes, from Detroit and from the farms around the Lakes and in Canada.

In the yard there was a platform with a microphone, before which stood the landowner and his wife. "There were so many people that I had to use it so that everyone could hear well." Behind them sat the grandfather in the old-fashioned outfit of a Czech peasant—Kovařík himself. The two boys and girls step onto the platform, approach the landowner and his wife with bouquets and wreaths, and recite some verses of good will. A night-watchman appears and, running here and there, he blows his horn towards the crowds and complains that he does not get any credit for watching the village every night. A young man and woman replace the landowner couple at the microphone and begin to quarrel, when the grandfather, supporting himself on his cane, gets up and says, "But children, children, don't argue..." and with a few more admonishing words he reconciles them. The young people dance around the landowner and his wife, the crowd applauds and slowly leaves the yard to dance on the meadow. Kovařík turned on the lights in the room.

"After our celebration a few years ago, two young Americans came and wanted to know what it was, what our beginnings in this country were and whether there was a book written about it. So we sent an article to the American newspapers with the explanation that it was a harvest festival which means thanks given to God for a good crop. A year later an American society organized a similar harvest festival. They liked the idea, the meaning. You see how easy it is to spread our customs in America? But something should be done with the play. It should be Americanized. Or—you are educated and you know us from here and from the old country—why wouldn't you modernize it? Why wouldn't you write a play for us?" I asked him for suggestions.

"Something should be added so that our children would *believe* it. Talk about the old Czech history, but as if it would be here, not there. They all should know about our past. Here they read about the cowboys and Indians and horseback riding, but that is American history. They don't know anything about the cultivation of the soil, how their ancestors worked there and we here. The modernization of this city has happened during our lifetime. We lived in huts with no water or electricity, many of us together. These were our beginnings, our lives. Tell them how we bought a cottage, a small farm, worked and paid for it. How much easier it is today with tractors and everything. It is pleasure, not work. We came here to provide a better life for our children. They have gadgets, but gadgets will not save them if bad times come. It would be a pity if they forgot their origins."

Kovařík introduced new figures into the Harvest celebration. They extend the scene at the landowner's house by repeating its symbolic action on a new level: the bouquet of grain ears and the wreath are to transfer fertility from the grain to the landowner and his wife, while the speech of the grandfather is to convey his wisdom to the young couple. The sheaf is absent, and it is the old man who carries off the climax. Commenting upon the play, Kovařík preserves the attitude of this old man and interprets the scene in terms of a cultural conflict between the two generations of Czechs in Detroit, the old one which immigrated from abroad and the younger one born in America. Protagonist of the moral values inherited from his tradition and contained in his life experience, Kovařík sees an unbridgeable gap between the material ideals of his sons and himself. Having attained, at the expense of hard work, material security for those who will follow, he feels unable to transmit to the new generation his spiritual legacy. The play is therefore intended by him to make the past an integral part of the present ("speak about the Czech history but as if it were here") and to reveal moral values as the only basis of personal and communal well-being and as the ultimate safeguard for the continuity of life. In trying to create an actually efficient, "modern" play out of the conventional harvest ritual, Kovařík was on the way to making a human drama out of the very core of this ritual, the principle of death and resurrection. Such work was accomplished by Sophocles, when he wrote his *Oedipus Rex* for the Dionysos Festival in Athens.

Source and Comment

Journal of American Folklore, LXIX (1956), 276-79. Svatava Pirkova-Jakobson describes and analyzes the harvest festivals of American Czechs and Slovaks. She notes that in the process of Americanization they have lost their "symbolism of the vegetable and animal world in the ritual," and have become more dramatic and humanized. Her "informants in America were of peasant origin." She provides full information about them and her sources, which include a color film of the Czech-American harvest play. The play was performed at Owosso, central Michigan, but she does not give the exact date. Nor does she supply dates of its European prototype.

* * *

Hungarian Harvest Festival

Vintage, the harvest of grapes in October, was generally celebrated with a customary ritual procession all over Hungary in regions where wine was grown, on the land of the masters or on the small plots of villagers. The pickers, dressed in festive costumes and carrying bunches of grapes were led by horseback riders and followed by mummers on wagons or afoot and by a band of Gypsy musicians. The group marched through the vineyards and the main thoroughfares of the community, magically-symbolically "closing" and protecting the next harvest and the land from the perils of winter. Finishing the parade, the villagers joined in a feast of roast calf, pig or lamb stew, and new wine. The bunches of grapes were suspended to decorate the dance floor where the young engaged in play party games and dancing after the meal. A forfeit game included the stealing of grapes by young men before the watchful eyes of the girl-rangers who reported to a "judge," expecting to penalize their sweethearts by playful humiliation ending up with reconciliatory kissing.

This custom, marking the end of the harvesting season, is still popular in Hungary. It is not altogether clear when and how it was carried over to America, why it had spread to all Hungarian-American settlements, whether grapes were planted or not, and why it had become one among the very few ethnic rituals which defied acculturative processes. The early generations of peasant immigrants evidently tried to transplant their local customs connected with wine making, the provision of the beverage without which Hungarian cooking was unimaginable. What actually happened was, that they did not plant grapes but bought them from farmers. As was reported from Delray, the Hungarian section of Detroit, "the railroad ran special cars . . . loaded with grapes from California," and the households were busy with making wine. Although the processing of the grapes did not call for a community *szüreti mulatság* (grape harvest feast), "this was usually the best dance of the year" and the hall was decorated with bunches of grapes hanging from the ceiling. In the course of time, while the home pattern remained highly variable, this American version became standardized and formularized just like other symbols of ethnicity, following immediate socioeconomic needs.

The Hungarian-American vintage festival is an arranged dance, usually set up in a community hall, and sponsored by an ethnic association with admission tickets, food and drinks for sale, to benefit some charity. The ceiling of the hall is decorated with red, white and green paper ribbons (the colors of the Hungarian flag) and store-bought, select bunches of grapes, apples, and oranges are suspended on wire from the ceiling. Guards watch carefully for fruit-thieves and make them pay a fine to increase the income. A band plays standard Hungarian dance music and a group of young people, dressed in the standard Hungarian dance costume open the dance with a conventional *csárdás*. After the performance of the well-rehearsed, carefully choreographed, staged dance, the dancers mingle with the crowd and the floor is opened for general informal entertainment, singing, and improvised dancing.

The Árpádhon [Louisiana] Harvest Festival, no doubt, originates in this homogenized Hungarian-American custom and genetically might be traceable to the import of one or several of the early settlers. But it has nothing of the more or less spontaneous festive pair dances so common in ethnic neighborhoods. On an October Sunday, following an ethnic luncheon, consisting of *húsleves* (meat noodle soup), *töltött káposzta* (stuffed cabbage) and *kalács* (walnut roll), the afternoon is opened by the dance program of a group of eight to fourteen couples. The single dances and their combination into a whole sequence has a clear cut choreography taught and coached regularly (twice a week for two months preceding the performance) by the current teach-

ers, committed to the observation of ancestral tradition from which deviation is not permitted. There are four dance teachers, one of whom being French. Everyone agrees that the Harvest Dance was brought directly from Hungary to America and must be maintained in its original form to enhance national distinctiveness. Loyalty to heritage, however, is more theoretical than practical because different leaders trace the custom to different ancestors and suggest various intermediary stages in its evolvement. Some say that the Harvest Dance was initiated by the parents of the Reverend Bartus, others refer to a settler from Detroit, and some mention a certain Tony Nagy from South Bend. Four different participants insisted that their parents were the first to dance it in 1902, 1908, 1912 and 1921. Inevitable modifications must have occurred according to generational change over more than a half century, conscious innovations must have been carried out by talented dancers and inspired musicians, even if current performers—children, grandchildren and great-grandchildren of the initiators—are convinced that both the dance and its accompanying music were preserved in their original form, that in all its parts it is a genuine archaic Hungarian folk custom. Be that as it may, the dance has been performed over a period of more than seventy years. Today, as in the past, the Harvest Dance remains a common property of Árpádhon settlers; everyone, young and old, knows the steps and the tunes, even if they do not participate actively in the performance.

Árpádhon families preserve photographs of earlier Harvest Dance performances which show a remarkable consistency in the style of the costumes if compared to those worn today. Slight changes by individual seamstresses are limited to the width of the skirt or drawers, the elaboration of women's headdress, the embroidery of the bodice, but any radical change needs community consent. Mr. M. D., a leading dancer who was among the performers since his early teens, mentioned a controversy over the questions if the girls should wear boots as recently suggested instead of the customary laced black patent leather shoes. Mrs. M. K. said that when she first danced with her husband in 1920 the drawers were gathered differently and it was she who made them wider. From then on, she made the *gatyas* (drawers) for the boys and Mrs. E. K. sewed the girl's dresses.

The costumes do not copy any of the regional Hungarian folk styles but rather represent an abstract, imaginary Hungarian national tradition. The men wear white *gatya* drawers cut out of rectangles with matching white wide sleeved shirts, trimmed with the red-white and green ribbons, a black bow-tie, black boots, a black vest with the tricolor ribbon running diagonally across the front and back and a black English derby hat (available in New Orleans) with the tricolor ribbon. The women's costumes consist of a full-pleated white skirt and a tiny white apron trimmed with the national colors, a red velvet tight bodice embroidered with gold beads and ribbons, and a blouse with short puffed sleeves and ruffled round collar. The accessories are the *párta* (beaded velvet headdress) worn only by unmarried young women in Hungary, a *keszkenő* (a red kerchief) and black shoes (or more recently, boots). Traditionally members of the band did not have formal wear. Recently however, they adapted the costume of Hungarian Gypsy music bands playing in restaurants all over the world; white shirt, red vest, black bow tie and black trousers.

As far as people can remember, the Harvest Dances were set for two October Sunday evenings. They were planned well in advance, not to conflict with football games in New Orleans or Baton Rouge. One was held in the Presbyterian Hall, and the other in the Catholic Hall with the participation of the same dancers, band, and audience. A three course Hungarian dinner preceded the program. After a pause, while tables and chairs were pushed aside, the floor was ready for the dance. The dancers, boys and girls, marched in from opposite sides and joined in the middle to perform. Following the dance, the band played on till the early hours. Hungarian *csárdás* tunes alternated with modern American jazz and the audience joined in the general entertainment. Since high winds had destroyed the Presbyterian Hall in 1959, the Catholic Hall became the sole place for the event. There were changes. People complained about too much smoking and drunkenness and fist fights out in the church yard under the cover of darkness so that the Catholics moved the feast to daytime. Following the services in both churches people gathered in the Catholic Hall for a Hungarian luncheon and the Harvest Dance was performed immediately thereafter. By five o'clock the whole program was over.

Source and Comment

Ethnologia Europaea, X (1977/78), 120-23. Linda Dégh describes the harvest festival and dance of a rural community in Livingstone Parish, Louisiana, founded in 1896 and the "largest Hungarian settlement in the U.S." Her concern is how, in a community not notable for its ethnic cohesiveness, a traditional Hungarian vintage festival continued to exist and the transformations it underwent. On the one hand it might be termed a "disfiguration of folk art"; but at the same its history reveals vitality, adaptation, and a powerful dedication to the celebration from which it evolved through the years. This was especially notable after "the beginning of the ethnic revival movement" that was a part of the Bicentennial celebrations of 1976. Dégh concludes "that in the light of the Árpádhon example the criteria for genuineness need revision."

* * *

Lithuanian Harvest Dances

By their very nature, the Lithuanian folk dances are of the agricultural-ceremonial type. The social dances were for everyone's participation, but the folk dances were demonstrations in which only those versed in the dances partici-

pated. The dances described chores in the fields and other related subjects. . . . *Kubilas,* the Tub, was a fast-moving dance that demonstrated the joy at a bountiful harvest. Choice vegetables were placed in a tub while the dancers spun round it. *Rugučiai* demonstrates the harvesting, gleaning, scythe honing, and so forth. There is a multitude of figures for *Malūnas,* the dance of the Mill which produces the flour for the daily bread. *Blezdingėlė* originally was danced in the fields—as the swallows left the countryside in the autumn to return next spring; so did the field workers bid their farewell. This dance, by the way, won great acclaim from about 120,000 spectators at a *Tribune* sponsored Festival [in Chicago] in 1944, when the everchanging "V" formation of the dance was interpreted as being "V" for Victory sign during those war years.

Source and Comment

Sixth Lithuanian Folk Dance Festival, July 6, 1980, 75. From an article on "The Changing Scene of the Lithuanian Folk Dance in the U.S." by Vytautas Beliajus from the program of the dance festival. He is a native of the Lithuanian agricultural village of Pakumprys and emigrated to the United States in 1923 where he taught Lithuanian dances and founded the folklore magazine, *Viltis.* The dance festivals are international. They are held every five years in Chicago.

It is widely believed that Lithuanian harvest dances originated in pagan ceremonies designed to propitiate the forces of nature. For instance, *Blezdingėlė* has been explained as a fertility dance suggesting death as the swallows fly southward in the winter and regeneration as they return in the spring; and the *Malūnas* and *Rugučiai,* with movements imitating the harvesting and grinding of grain, are magical rites to express thanks for a plentiful crop.

* * *

Seneca Green Corn Dance

Among the festivals of the Iroquois Indians, one of the most important is the *Ah-dake-wa-o,* or Green Corn Festival, commonly called the Green Corn Dance. This dance continues for three days, and, though varied in proceedings, the ceremonies of each day terminate with a feast. Like all the religious ceremonies of the red man, "thanksgivings" predominate in this, the *Ah-dake-wa-o.* The "Great Feather Dance," included in this festival, is also religious, and, that guests from each nation may unite in the universal thanksgivings, and join in this dance, these festivals are never "called" the same day of the month on the separate reservations.

In the distribution of the various offices and duties pertaining to the ceremonies, the matrons, as well as the men, take share. They are denominated *Ho-non-de-ont,* or "Keepers of the Faith," and to their care is entrusted the "preparations" for the feast. As the festival-time draws near, these matrons are also appointed to visit the cornfields at sunrise every day, and bring to the council-house several ears of corn, there to be examined by one of the "head men," who decides, when it is in fit condition for eating, the date when the feast shall be called.

This year [1890] the "summons," or invitations, from the chiefs at the Cattaraugus Reservation were sent to those who were to be the active participants and guests from Tonawanda and Allegany reservations that, on September 10th, at sunrise, the introductory ceremony of the *Ah-dake-wa-o* would begin at the council-house on the Cattaraugus Reserve. This council-house, located one mile from Lawton Station on the Erie Railroad, and standing on a prominent elevation in the centre of an open space of eight acres of undulating grassy ground, was erected on the spot where the Seneca Indians, withdrawing from the Buffalo Reservation, felled the trees of the dense forest, and made the settlement they called "The New Town." This little Indian village, retaining its old name through having lost its significant "The," is now known as Newtown. The council-house, a one-storied wooden structure about eighty feet long and fifty feet wide, constructed in accordance with the cardinal points of the compass—north, south, east, and west—has two entrances, one at the northeastern end of the building, designed for the women, and the other at the opposite southwest end for the men only; and although the council-house has no inner division, the women always sit apart from the men during a council or a dance. At the east end of the building, within a brick chimney that juts out about four feet from the wall, yawns a huge fireplace, in which still remained the ashes of the last feast (in the old times these ashes were not removed save at the New Year festival); the long crane that hung within its smoke-begrimed depths suggested the swinging of the great kettles of the corn soup and succotash of the winter-time feasts. On the three sides of the chimney above the fire-place are projecting shelves, on which were deposited the various donations to the feast which had been presented by the "foreign" guests and friends. At the west end of the building stands an old-fashioned iron stove, rusty and fireless during the summer time, but in which great logs can be thrust to the comfort of the participants in the winter festivals. On the south and west sides of the council-house, and extending lengthwise, are three rows of undivided seats, not unlike the pews in very old churches, arranged step-like, one above the other; and for further accommodation ordinary wooden benches are provided in the east end of the house, that all may be seated during the ceremonies. In the centre of the room two benches were apportioned to the singers and musicians. One of these benches was well worn in deep ridges, the result of the vigorous strokes of the turtle-shell rattles in the hands of the musicians.

It is the custom for the *Ho-non-di-ont,* or men keepers of the faith, to build at sunrise, on the morning of the feast, the "first fire," and to place upon it tobacco and some ears of corn as a special offering to the Great Spirit, and, while the offering was burning, to ask his blessing, after which the fire is extinguished and a new one built in its place by the women who have charge of the public feast. Although

the "summons" called for a convening of the people at sunrise, yet at eight o'clock the councillors had not assembled, which delay, however, was afterwards explained. The great variety of vehicles that had brought the guests to the festival were ranged around the outer edges of the grounds; groups of young men playing ball; young women and girls sauntering about, evidently intent in the "chat of pleasant conversation;" old men with tottering steps, elderly women with pathetic gaiety slowly making their way to the council-house; matrons hurriedly busy preparing the soup and succotash boiling vigorously in large iron kettles suspended over the great logs that burned with a glow suggestive of comfort and warmth in the chill mist that veiled the far-away hills,—all added to the picturesqueness of a scene that was striking in its effectiveness.

It was not long before a general movement in the assemblage gave notice that the ceremonies were about to begin. The women slowly entered the building by the northeast door, the men passing in at the southwest entrance and arranging themselves with order in the seats; the musicians, with their turtle-shell rattles, had already taken their places on the benches appropriated for them; and when quiet prevailed—and there is no congregation of people who remain so perfectly quiet as an assemblage of Indians at a religious "gathering"—the "head speaker" began the feast ceremonies with an invocation to the Great Spirit. The men, with uncovered heads, bent in reverent attention (Indians never kneel), and the women looked solemn and earnestly serious as the speaker, in low voice, rendered his prayer. After a pause, lifting his voice, he proceeded with the following address (I give the *literal* translation):

"My friends, we are here to worship the Great Spirit. As by our old custom we give the Great Spirit his dance, the Great Feather Dance. We must have it before noon. The Great Spirit sees to everything in the morning; afterwards he rests. He gives us land and things to live on, so we must thank Him for his ground and for the things it brought forth. He gave us the thunder to wet the land, so we must thank the thunder. We must thank Ga-ne-o-di-o [Handsome Lake, the prophet of the "new religion"] that we know he is in the happy land. It is the wish of the Great Spirit that we express our thanks in dances as well as prayer. The cousin clans are here from Tonawanda; we are thankful to the Great Spirit to have them here, and to greet them with the rattles and singing. We have appointed one of them to lead the dances."

During this speech the men remained with their heads uncovered. At its conclusion, and following a slight pause, a shout from outside the council-house gave notice that the "Great Feather" dancers were approaching.

The "Great Feather Dance," one of the most imposing dances of the Iroquois, is consecrated to the worship of the

Great Spirit, and is performed by a carefully selected band of costumed dancers, every member of which being distinguished for his remarkable powers of endurance, suppleness, and gracefulness of carriage. As they drew near to the council-house the swaying crowd gave way, permitting the leader and his followers to pass through the west door, where, taking their places at the head of the room, they remained stationary a moment as the speaker introduced the leader to the people and proceeded, in a voice keyed to a high pitch, to offer the ceremonial "thanks," the dancers, meanwhile, walking around the room, keeping step to the slow beating of the rattles. Each "thanks" was followed by a moderately quick dance once around the room, and terminating at the halt into a slow walk, which was continued during the recital of each "thanks" until all were rendered.

THE THANKSGIVINGS.

We who are here present thank the Great Spirit that we are here to praise Him.

We thank Him that He has created men and women, and ordered that these beings shall always be living to multiply the earth.

We thank Him for making the earth and giving these beings its products to live on.

We thank Him for the water that comes out of the earth and runs for our lands.

We thank Him for all the animals on the earth.

We thank Him for certain timbers that grow and have fluids coming from them [referring to the maple] for us all.

We thank Him for the branches of the trees that grow shadows for our shelter.

We thank Him for the beings that come from the west, the thunder and lightning that water the earth.

We thank him for the light which we call our oldest brother, the sun that works for our good.

We thank Him for all the fruits that grow on the trees and vines.

We thank Him for his goodness in making the forests, and thank all its trees.

We thank Him for the darkness that gives us rest, and for the kind Being of the darkness that gives us light, the moon.

We thank Him for the bright spots in the skies that give us signs, the stars.

We give Him thanks for our supporters, who have charge of our harvests. [In the mythology of the Iroquois Indians there is a most beautiful conception of these "Our Supporters." They are three sisters of great beauty, who delight to dwell in the companionship of each other as the spiritual guardians of the corn, the beans, and the squash. These vegetables, the staple food of the red man, are supposed to be in the special care of the Great Spirit, who, in the growing season, sends these "supporters" to abide in the fields and protect them from the ravages of blight or frost. These guardians are clothed in the leaves of their respective plants, and, though invisible, are faithful and vigilant.]

We give thanks that the voice of the Great Spirit can still be heard through the words of Ga-ne-o-di-o (by his religion).

We thank the Great Spirit that we have the privilege of this pleasant occasion. [Vigorous dancing followed this, all shouting in gladness, in which the speaker joined.]

We give thanks for the persons who can sing the Great Spirit's music, and hope they will be privileged to continue in his faith.

We thank the Great Spirit for all the persons who perform the ceremonies on this occasion.

With this the thanksgiving ended. There is an Iroquois harvest festival in which is included thanksgivings for all the harvest, when each grain and fruit-producing tree, vine, or bush is separately recognized.

The speaker then ordered the dance to begin, and the dancers, who in single file had walked slowly around the room during the recital, save at the interludes of the "thanks," began a movement of a more animated character.

In all its features and characteristics the Feather Dance is quite unlike the War Dance. In its performance the dancer remains erect, not assuming those warlike attitudes of rage or vengeance which so plainly distinguish the two dances. All the movements of the Feather Dance are of a graceful character, its undulating and gentle motions designed to be expressive of pleasure, gladness, and mildness. Each foot is alternately raised from two to eight inches from the floor, and the heel brought down with great force in rhythm to the beat of the rattles. At times there was an indescribable syncopated movement of wondrous quickness, one heel being brought down three times before it alternated with the other, the musicians beating the rattles three times in a second, every muscle of the dancer strung to its highest tension, the concussion of the foot-stroke on the floor shaking the legging bells; the lithesome, sinuous twistings and bendings of the body momentarily accelerated by the dancers' shouts of rivalry mingled with the plaudits and encouraging cries of the excited spectators, as they filed swiftly round and round the council-house, were thrilling to a degree of intenseness! The dancers accompanied themselves by joining the singers in a weird syllabic chant consisting of but two notes—a minor third—which was strongly accented as they sang the *Ha-ho—Ha-ho—Ha-ho;*

then with quicker time all joined in the refrain, *Way-ha-ah, Way-ha-ha, Way-ha-ah,* and terminating in the strong guttural shout, *Ha-i, ha-i,* as the dancers bowed their heads in accent.

In this dance there were fifty men in costume, for whom, at the "rest" intervals, a refreshing drink, made from the juce of the wild blackberry, added to sweetened water, was provided. In the slower movements many of the women, at the exhortation of the speaker urging all to unite in the Great Spirit's dance, joined the dancers at the foot of the column, finally forming an inside circle.

At noon the costumed dancers went to their homes, returning again in ordinary citizen's dress. During their absence an opportunity was offered to any person who might desire to have children named, or names changed. A child three months old was "presented" for a name, the babe having been the realization of a dream. Before its birth its "grandfather" had dreamed that a boy would be born who would be a great hunter, and as the older Indians have strong faith in dreams, this child was particularly mentioned as a proof of the infallibility of the dreamer. The name given was "The Swift Runner."

The speaker of the day then made a short address, inviting all to partake of the feast. This was the signal for the young men, who then came in, bearing two great kettles, of the capacity of eight gallons each, and containing, one the beef soup, and the other the succotash. One of the *Ho-non-di-ont,* in a prolonged exclamation, said grace, in which he was joined by a swelling chorus from the multitude in acknowledgement of their gratitude to the Great Giver of the feast. As the red men do not sit down together at a common repast, except at religious councils of unusual interest, the succotash and soup were distributed in vessels brought by the women for the purpose, and all the guests carried equal portions to their respective homes, there to be enjoyed at their own fireside.

It was near sunset when the feast was over, and the people slowly dispersed, making way to their homes, a few, however, remaining for the social dances not included in the religious feast. Previous to their departure a faith-keeper announced that, according to the ancient ways, the feast games between the rival clans would be played on the next day. He also cautioned them that they "must not be dejected if they lost, as they had heard by the Great Spirit that what they lost on earth would be returned to them in heaven. If they won they must not boast, nor hurt the feelings of their opponents, but assume their victory with dignified silence."

The second day opened with the *Gus-ka-eh,* the peachstone or Indian dice game. This was played in a dish a foot in diameter, and four articles were contributed as a donation to a "pool." A good deal of excitement prevailed during the betting, which was a privilege extended to any of the members of the contending clans. The Wolf, the Bear, Beaver, and Turtle clans played against the Deer, Snipe, Heron, and Hawk. The game was won by the latter clans. There were no other events of particular interest that day. It was expected that the game would continue all day (the festival cannot go on until this game is finished, and it sometimes lasts two or three days), but on this occasion it proved of short duration. At the end of the contest a feast was offered, as on the previous day, and there were more social dances in the evening to "entertain the visiting guests from Tonawanda and Allegany."

The third day was "Women's Day"—the women opening the ceremonies with a dance, for which there were special singers, and songs accompanied by a small drum and rattles made of horns, about four inches in length, and not unmusical in effect. The women dance entirely unlike the men. They move sideways, raising themselves alternately upon each foot, from heel to toe, and then bringing down the heel upon the floor at each beat of the rattle and drum, and keeping pace with the slowly increasing column that moved around the council-house with a quiet and not ungraceful movement. After some urging by the faith-keeper, two thirds of the women present joined in the circle, also many young girls, and children from four years upwards.

There was no pairing or taking of partners in any of the dances, as each individual danced alone. Following this "women's" dance came another, in which both men and women joined, called the "Thank Dance for the Crops." After that another women's dance, the "Shuffling Dance," followed by the men's dance, "Shaking of the Rattle." For each of these dances there were different steps and songs. Next came the "Snake Dance," beginning with four men clasping hands, the leader shaking a rattle and singing; others, including the women and children, gradually joining the dance line until there was not room enough in the council-house for the circle within circle of dancers. This dance, which includes in its movements the "hunting" for the snake, and represents the action of its body in swift gliding and in the convulsions of death, lasted about three quarters of an hour.

There had been a misty rainfall all the day, but as the dancers were exulting in enthusiasm the sun separated the clouds, and, as an Indian expressed it, "looked in" upon them through the west window, filling the room with its cheery glowing. The nodding plumes, the tinkling bells, the noisy rattles, the beats of the high-strung drums, the shuffling feet and weird cries of the dancers, and the approving shouts of the spectators, all added to the spell of a strangeness that seemed to invest the quaint old council-house with the supernaturalness of a dream!

As the sun neared its setting the dancers stopped in a quiet order, and the "speaker of the day" bade farewell to the

409

clans, "active officers," and guests, wishing them a safe journey homeward under the guidance of the Great Spirit; and admonishing them all to lead good lives for another year, and hoping they might be privileged to meet again to thank the Great Spirit for his goodness, he dismissed the "gathering," and, after invoking the blessing of the Great Spirit, declared the Green Corn Festival of 1890 ended.

A final and bountiful feast was then served, after which the people peacefully separated, and in an orderly way departed for their homes.

Source and Comment

Journal of American Folklore, IV (1891), 72-77. This account was written by Mrs. Harriet Maxwell Converse, by adoption a member of the Snipe Clan of the Seneca nation. It is reprinted from the *Buffalo Express* of October 12, 1890. The festival took place in the Cattaraugus Reservation, Newtown, New York. It was attended by "between 500 and 600 Indians. . . and during the three days there was no irreverence, vulgarity, nor any unseemly conduct." Cf. "Florida Seminole Green Corn Dance," p. 212 and "Games at the White Dog Feast," p. 44.

The Green Corn Festival or Busk was part of the elaborate harvest ceremony of the southwestern and northeastern Indians. After the corn ripened, it was not to be eaten until the Great Spirit was properly thanked. Often a sacred arbor was built and a large fire lighted under it, and dances and other rites were performed about this fire. Among the Iroquois, of whom the Senecas were part, the thanksgiving observance, with which the ritual began, took place in the council house. The entire celebration, with its prayers, dances, feasting, and games, sometimes lasted for a week or more. In fact, in his description of Onondaga festivals, Joshua Clark states that "when the green corn becomes fit to use . . . the first ears are broken off to be roasted or boiled" at "the most joyous and merry-making festival in the Indian calendar," and a second or extension of the corn festival (*Onondaga*, 1849, I, 54) takes place "after the corn harvest; usually about the first of November." Differences in growing season affected the timing of this widespread ritual.

* * *

Bread and Apple-butter Thanksgiving

Bread, butter and apple-butter play an unusual role in Schwenkfelder culture. For the past 226 years, the Schwenkfelders have observed, on September 24, a thanksgiving service (*Gedaechtnisz Tag*) which is unique in several aspects. The only fare provided at the traditional meal consists of water, bread, butter and apple-butter. This service of thanksgiving was instituted on September 24, 1734, by the Schwenkfelder immigrants, two days after their arrival in Pennsylvania. It has been observed annually thereafter in remembrance of the safe voyage and the rescue from intolerance; as a measure of gratitude for the blessing of freedom; as a reminder of the responsibility for the preservation and extension of freedom to others; and as an expression of gratitude to God for his grace and guidance. . . .

The Schwenkfelders did not construct meeting-houses until the 1790's, so the annual services were held in individual homes. The difficulties attendant to serving one or two hundred people a full course meal from the "kitchen" of a log or plank house are evident. In all probability, the traditional meal was served on long plank tables set up near the house, crocks of apple-butter were brought up from the cellar or spring-house, and loaves of bread were gingerly removed from the warm bake oven.

With the construction of meeting-houses, the scene for the annual *Gedaechtnisz Tag* services shifted, and so did the method of serving. Phebe Earle Gibbons has provided us with a vivid description of one of these "yearly meetings.". . .

[The Rev. C. Z. Weiser] tells us, that whoever is not providentially prevented is bound to attend their yearly reunion. Nor has it been found necessary thus far to enter an urging statute to secure the presence of the fraternity. The "seeding" is done, the corn stands in shocks, and the farmwork of September is timely put aside, in order that all may participate in the memorial ceremonies of the 24th with a light, gay, and thankful heart. It is on the day and day before that you may feast your eyes on many a well-laden carriage, the horses all in good condition, moving on towards one of the Schwenkfelder meeting-houses, selected in rotation, and one whole year in advance. The aged and infirm of both sexes stay not behind. The young men and women are similarly enough clad to be considered uniformed. So too are the mothers arrayed in a manner very like to one another, with snow-white caps and bonnets that never vary. The sons and daughters do indeed not love the habits of their elders any the less, yet only the wicked world's a little more.

The morning service opens at nine o'clock, and is filled out with singing, praying, and recitals of portions of their ancestral history. All is gone through with in the Pennsylvania German dialect, but withal reverentially, solemnly, and earnestly, just as though it were newly and for the first time done.

At twelve o'clock, the noonday feast is set. This is the feature of the day. It consists of light and newly-baked rye bread, sweet and handsomely printed butter, and the choicest apple-butter. Wheat bread is now used. (At a Schwenkfelder house I ate apple-butter, sweet, because made from sweet apples, and seasoned with fennel, of which the taste resembles anise.) Nothing beyond these is set, but these are of the first water. The bare benches, but lately occupied by devout worshippers, serve as tables, along which the guests are lined out. Not in silence, nor in sullenness, do they eat their simple meal, but spicing it with cheerful talk, they dine with hearts full of joy. Still, you need fear no profane utterance or silly jest. They are mindful of the spirit of the occasion, of the place in which they congregate, and of the feast itself, which the singing of some familiar hymn has consecrated. If any one thirst, let him drink cold water.

And now think not that they feign simply to eat and drink—that the meal from first to last is but a poor pretense. A full and hearty dinner is "made out" there. It is a bona fide eating and drinking that is done in the meeting-house of the Schwenkfelders on their *Gedächtniss Tag* (anniversary). They are all hard-working men and women—farmers and farmers' wives and farmers' children. They are sunburnt, healthy, and hungry besides. And why should they not relish the sweet bread, with their sweet butter and apple-butter, then? Even strangers who attend and are hospitably entertained by the society show that one can make a full hand, even at such a table.

At two o'clock the tables become pews again, and the afternoon exercises are conducted according to the programme of the morning. These concluded, a general invitation is again extended to partake of the baskets of fragments gathered up and stored away in the rear of the meetinghouse. A fraternal hand-shaking closes the anniversary for the year. The reflection that many part now who may never meet again on earth causes tears to trickle down some furrowed cheek, which generally proves more or less contagious, as is always the case in a company of hearts, when those tears flow in sincere channels. Hence, though all were happy all day long, they now feel sad.

To appreciate the meaning and spirit of this apparently homely scene, it is necessary to know that it is a memorial service all through. It was on this very 24th of September, 1734, that some seventy (forty) families of Schwenkfelders, who had landed on the 22d, and declared their allegiance on the 23d, held their thanksgiving service, in gratitude to God for a safe deliverance to the colony of Pennsylvania. They had arrived in the ship St. Andrew, at Philadelphia, as fugitives from Silesia.

Poor, but feeling rich in view of their long-sought liberty, they blessed God in an open assembly. We may judge their store and fare to have been scant and lean indeed; and to perpetuate the original service of their fore-fathers from generation to generation, they statedly celebrate their *Gedächtniss Tag.*

The poor fare before them is finely designed to impress the sore fact of their ancestors' poverty indelibly upon their minds, memories, and hearts. They eat and drink in remembrance of former days—the days of small things. They join thereto at the same time a gladsome worship, in thankfulness for the asylum opened up for them from their former house of bondage, and which proved so fair a heritage to their people ever since.

This description by Phebe Earle Gibbons presents a fairly accurate picture of the *Gedächtnisz Tag* scene throughout the 19th Century. The setting for "bread and apple-butter day" changed to its present form in the early years of the present century when the Schwenkfelders closed the old meeting-houses and moved into larger church structures, equipped with kitchens.

The traditional meal is now served on tables in church social rooms, the plain garb of the 19th Century has been replaced by modern dress, the sermons and hymns are rendered in English in lieu of German, but the fare—bread and apple-butter—remains the same, as it has for the past two and a quarter centuries.

Source and Comment

Pennsylvania Folklife, XII (Fall 1961), 42-43. Andrew S. Berky describes the traditional thanksgiving service of the Schwenkfelder, a persecuted Protestant sect. He quotes extensively from Phebe Earle Gibbons's *Pennsylvania Dutch and Other Essays,* second edition, Philadelphia, 1874; first edition, 1872. Gibbons was a Quaker journalist. How the traditional fare originated is not certain, but Berky points to contemporary records of the Schwenkfelder colonists giving thanks for fresh water, bread, and apples obtained immediately after landing in America in 1734.

* * *

First Thanksgiving in Illinois

As we all know the first-comers into the Sangamo Country [Illinois] were for the most part, Kentucky pioneers, and, since the south and south-central portions of the state were about all that could be considered "settled" at that time, it naturally followed that the customs and traditions of the South predominated. The population turned out to celebrate New Year's, the 8th of January [Battle of New Orleans], Washington's birthday, the Fourth of July and Christmas, with much enthusiasm and in most cases, explosion of gunpowder and ringing of bells. The three purely patriotic holidays were further distinguished in the late [18]30's by the firing of a "*feu de joie*" at sunrise. Thanksgiving was merely a tradition of the "Yankees," whom the Kentuckians lumped carelessly as shrewd itinerants addicted, according to popular report, to the tinkering of clocks and the vending of wooden nutmegs in their natural habitat, and who, being transplanted to western soil, could "dicker" in such a masterly and efficient manner that the party of the second part was considered fortunate if he escaped with his eye teeth intact. . . .

In the late [18]30's there was a small settlement of "Yankees" a few miles west of Springfield, who, according to an old settler with whom I talked, "were left pretty much to themselves and were not much thought of." It is quite possible that these derelicts of the prairie sea may have celebrated a quiet Thanksgiving of their own if they felt that they had any occasion for it, but if so, nobody seems to have noticed, or, at least, commented upon it. But when Simeon Francis, editor of the *Sangamo Journal* from 1831 to 1855, came to Springfield, he, being a native son of Connecticut in good and regular standing, openly deplored the absence of any regular observance of the Yankee holiday in his adopted western home. It was quite to be expected, therefore, when the *Chicago Democrat,* in the autumn of 1838, published what purported to be a Thanksgiving Proclamation issued by Governor Joseph Duncan, that the *Sangamo Journal* promptly copied it, while the editorial columns of the paper reflected the pleasure its editor felt on account of the adoption by Illinois of the Yankee holiday; nor did he fail to remind his readers that a pumpkin was indispensable to a correct observance of the day—and would some subscriber have the kindness to send him one?

Certainly the Proclamation had all the ear-marks of the genuine article, being couched in sounding phrases, and duly signed and sealed. It read as follows:

STATE OF ILLINOIS.
FOR A DAY OF THANKSGIVING, PRAYER AND PRAISE.

Whereas, for many years it has been customary in several states of the Union, to set apart one day in the year near its close, for the ascription of honor and praise to the Almighty Ruler of the Universe, the Maker of Heaven and Earth, for His infinite goodness to the children of men, in giving His only Son to be the Way, the Truth and the Light, and for His watchful providence in the days that are past, I, therefore, as the Executive of the State of Illinois, appoint Thursday, the 29th day of November next, as a Day of Public Thanksgiving, Prayer and Praise; and do earnestly beseech all its citizens to refrain from their usual occupations, and to devote it entirely to religious purposes—to the review of their past life—to the confession of their manifold transgressions—to the amelioration of the poor and distressed—to the furtherance of the Gospel doctrines—to the liberation of those that are in bondage—to the reparation of injuries—to the promotion of friendly intercourse among their kindred and neighbors—to fervent prayer for all classes and conditions of men, and above, all, to the glorifying of their Heavenly Father for life, health and an unusual degree of prosperity among all branches of human industry; and, moreover, for the blessed Gospel of our Lord and Saviour, Jesus Christ, which is the Source of every blessing, and the Rock of all our hopes.

"Upon that day, let the Name of God be praised in the family circle and in the Holy Tabernacle, each one according to the dictates of his own conscience; and let prayers everywhere ascend for success to attend the efforts that are making for the unusual dissemination of the Christian religion, 'that sovereign balm for every wound' which alone, can fit us for an easy transition from this, to a world beyond the grave, 'where the wicked cease from troubling, and the weary are at rest.'

"Given at Vandalia, this 25th day of October, in the year of our Lord 1838, of the Independence of the United States the 63rd, as a true copy for

A.P. FIELD,   JOSEPH DUNCAN,
Secretary of State.   *Governor.*

In the *Sangamo Journal* of December 1st, 1838, the editor made the following statement to the public:

"We are constrained to believe that the Proclamation purporting to have been issued by Governor Duncan for a "Day of Public Thanksgiving, Prayer and Praise," published in last week's paper, is a forgery. We have come to this conclusion with much regret, because, in the first place, a proclamation for the observance of a day for public thanksgiving, prayer and praise we would consider proper and appropriate; and, in the second place, we were loth to believe that any man having access to the columns of a newspaper, would deliberately perpetrate such a forgery. The spurious Proclamation first appeared in that vehicle of loco focoism, the *Chicago Democrat.*"

As wild turkeys and pumpkins were plentiful, to say nothing of other ingredients necessary to a proper culinary observance of the day, it is very probable that the Proclamation was productive of some orthodox Thanksgiving dinners, forgery or no forgery.

Of one of these, at least, we are certain—a "stag party" which took place at the American House in Springfield, a pretentious building just completed by Elijah Iles, to reinforce the hotel accommodations of the new State Capital. It was the most ambitious structure that had, as yet, been provided for public entertainment in Springfield, and while most of the hotel proprietors in the town were Kentuckians or Virginians, the American House opened triumphantly November 24th, 1838, under the auspices of a real, live Bostonian. Thus it happened that, when this adventurous pilgrim from the city of beans entered the arena of public hospitality in Springfield, a few kindred spirits, hungry and thirsty for real Thanksgiving cheer, quietly planned among themselves to hold a rousing little celebration that would, so to speak, "knock the spots" off anything the Battle of New Orleans or Washington's Birthday had ever shown Sangamon county in the line of good cheer.

Mine host, Clifton, was only too pleased to demonstrate, so early in the game, what Boston enterprise could do in the way of banquets, and accordingly on Thanksgiving—at the hour of midnight—a little band of self-convicted Yankees (the late Mr. Edward R. Thayer, who related the story to me, being one of the number) sat down in the dining room of the American House, to such a Thanksgiving dinner as we read about—and the participants probably dream about, afterwards.

As the solid viands disappeared, and the liquid refreshments began to stir the blood of young New England to greater enthusiasm, its expression became more vociferous. Songs and toasts went around the board, and the fun was at its height when the door at the end of the banquet hall swung open and the small, determined figure of the hostess of the American House stood upon the threshold. There was a glint in her eye that boded no good to the hilarious guests. Her voice rang through the suddenly silent room with a finality that was convincing:

"Men"—she said—"I cannot call you *gentlemen,* since you are behaving like anything else—I will not allow this uproar! Do you not know that this house is full of guests who are unable to sleep on account of this disgraceful carousal?"

Like an assemblage of naughty boys detected by the schoolmistress in the act of affixing a bent pin to her chair, the descendants of the Pilgrim Fathers sat in abashed silence. Finally, mine host, Clifton, who had probably had previous experience in dealing with emergencies of a similar character, rallied to the rescue. "Come along, boys," he exclaimed, "let's go down to the wash-room where we can make all the noise we want to." He led the way; each man grasped such portion of the good cheer of the occasion as was nearest to him and followed....

No regular Thanksgiving celebration was held during the following two or three years.... However, by 1841, the northern part of the state had begun to feel the influence of a population that was drifting in from the East and which had, generally speaking, been brought up on Thanksgiving dinners; and the Presbyterian State Synod, at its fall meeting that year, adopted a resolution recommending to the churches under its care, the observance of Thursday, November 25th, as a day of Thanksgiving for the blessings of the past year. [In 1842 Governor Thomas Carlin officially proclaimed] the last Thursday of November next as a Day of Thanksgiving....

Mr. Francis, of the *Sangamo Journal* ... delicately hinted that "since a goodly portion of the community was not thoroughly broken to Thanksgiving observances and might not possess the knowledge of what was required by immemorial usage," he would offer a few suggestions, not as to the spiritual preparations which would be attended to by the "dominies," but on strictly material lines. We trust that his suggestions, which follow, were accepted in the helpful spirit in which they were given:

"A large supply of the good things of life are required, such as turkies, chickens, geese, partridges, and such like. Families give out their invitations to the dinner a week ahead, so that all can go like clock-work. All the eatables, including a large lot of pumpkin pies, are prepared for the oven the night beforehand.

"At 11 o'clock on Thanksgiving Day, all the supernumeraries of the family (leaving only those at home necessary to perform the duties of cooking) proceed to church where the service is of great length, rendered so by the singing of one or two extra hymns. This is done to impress the inner man with due solemnity of the importance of the Day—and also has the effect of sharpening the appetite of the outer man for the things that are about to be set before him. There is no hesitancy that we have ever discovered under such circumstances, in hastening from the church to fulfill their respective engagements. The tables are soon filled and the important business of eating is performed with all due deliberation. The old then retire to talk over the occurrences of younger days, the children romp, and the young men and girls prepare for the interesting duties of the evening—what those are, all can judge. At such times the young ladies are generally at home, and the young men are generally more courageous than usual.

"The remaining part of the week, (Thanksgiving should always be set on Thursday, as Governor Carlin has very properly done in this case), should be spent in visiting, social parties and such, and when Saturday night comes, in reckoning up matters it is usually found that, in neighborhoods, old grudges are healed, new courtships are under progress, and the people are generally better satisfied with their condition and happier by far than before the Thanksgiving holiday. And we trust that Governor Carlin's Thanksgiving will be productive of these good fruits."

In closing his suggestions, Mr. Francis urged everybody to remember the poor, as Thanksgiving is a most fitting time to remember the widow, the orphan and the distressed; also not to forget to "send the '*dominie*' a couple of turkies," which would indicate that the pastor's quiver was well-filled, unless, indeed, the "turkies" of that day were inclined to be skinny.

Source

Journal of Illinois State Historical Society, XI (1918-1919), 370-77. The sources of Isabel Jamison's historical sketch are newspapers and local informants, listed in her text.

Thanksgiving Dinner and What It Means

... Because eating is a total sensory activity, food has extraordinary symbolic potential. Thanksgiving is a good example. The basic menu of roast turkey, stuffing, cranberry sauce, sweet potatoes, mashed white potatoes, and pumpkin pie as a unit is thought by the people who eat it to be very old, very rural, and more "natural" than ordinary fare. It is like Plymouth in 1621, better, simpler, and somehow more American. It elicits strong nostalgic feelings and a yearning for the good "folk" life. Few Americans, of course, would or could put these feelings into words, or even bother to formulate the question "What does this food mean to you?" in the first place. They simply eat and compliment the housewife and tradition for setting such a good table. Still, the attitudes and feelings are there as the advertizing men are well aware. When Thanksgiving food is marketed, primarily in magazines and newspapers, it is usually surrounded by images that suggest the "good old days on the farm—once upon a time." The exceptions reverse the image and sell a particularly convenient way to cook the traditional food. But they, too, reinforce the tradition by suggesting ways traditional proscriptions can be met (the right meal cooked in the right way in the right place at the right time) more easily. They understand that Thanksgiving is a kind of secular, nationalistic "mass" where people eat symbols of their folk history, thereby regaining some of the qualities they believed their ancestors possessed. And they are clever enough not to tamper with this. When changes in the meal are suggested—it is usually the addition of side dishes that also symbolize the past (wholemeal bread, maple syrup, etc.) or more historic recipes.

Source

Kansatieteellinen Arkisto 26, Suomen Muinaismuistoyhdistys, 1975, 12-13. In the second part of his paper presented at a conference on ethnological food research and published in the *Journal of the Finnish Society of Antiquities* of Helsinki, Jay Allan Anderson (see p. 331) analyzes the function of Thanksgiving, stressing its role "in reinforcing basic beliefs and values."

* * *

Thanksgiving Dinner

Pumpkin Pie

... While no mention has been made of the pumpkin being a part of the first Thanksgiving dinner, the Northeastern Indians did raise some, which in all probability they gave to the Pilgrims, and certainly the "pompion" was known to and eaten by the later colonists. Pumpkins, native to the Western Hemisphere, came through the normal trade routes from Central and South America, and were experimented with by the North American Indians centuries before Columbus reached the West Indies. They were boiled, baked in ashes, used in making bread, and dried. In the beginning the Pilgrims stewed "pompion" and mixed it with Indian cornmeal to make bread, but they also filled the pumpkin shell with milk, sugar and spice and baked it in the fireplace. The Indians themselves baked the pumpkin with honey. Today Pumpkin Pie is a part of most traditional Thanksgiving dinners. Recipes for this dish are endless, and methods of serving provide an equal variety. Comparison can be made between a simple New England Pumpkin Pie which can be found in almost any good cookbook, and a recipe found in a hand written cookbook of Martha Washington. The New England pie calls for 1½ cups cooked pumpkin, ⅔ cups brown sugar, 1 teaspoon

cinnamon, ¼ teaspoon each of ginger and nutmeg, ½ teaspoon salt, 2 eggs slightly beaten, 1½ cups milk and ½ cup cream. The recipe of Martha Washington is copied here in its entirety: "Pare and cut into pieces a good pumpkin. Put it into a granite or porcelain kettle with not more than a teacup of water; cover the kettle and steam the pumpkin until tender. While it is hot, add a tablespoonful of butter to each quart. Press the whole through a colander, rejecting every particle of water. Also sprinkle over, while the pumpkin is hot, after it goes through the colander, a tablespoonful of flour to each quart. Now take a quart of this strained pumpkin, add to it six well-beaten eggs, a cup of sugar, a quarter of a teaspoonful of mace, a tablespoonful of ginger, a quarter of a nutmeg, and one gill of brandy. Have the dishes lined with good, rich paste, pour in the mixture, put strips of twisted paste across and bake three-quarters of an hour in a quick oven."

Source

Kansatieteellinen Arkisto 26, Suomen Muinaismuistoyhdistys, 1975, 22-23. From a paper by Margaret Louise Arnott titled "Thanksgiving Dinner: A Study in Cultural Heritage."

* * *

Thanksgiving Dinner

A Family Thanksgiving Custom

The story goes that during the first winter after the Pilgrims landed at Plymouth their food supplies were so badly depleted that they were nearly starving. Don't know why they could not have shot a deer or other game unless they were also out of gunpowder. Anyway, the supply ships from England had been delayed so long that they were down to the equivalent of three kernels of corn per person when the ship was finally sighted. So the custom has always been that when the Thanksgiving table is laid, the plates are turned upside down and when you turn your plate over, there underneath are three corn kernels. Then you are reminded every year to be *truly* thankful.

Source

Letter to H. C. from Sylvia Carroll of Chula Vista, California, November 14, 1989, on deposit in the University of Pennsylvania Folklore Archives. Mrs. Carroll writes further: "I remember Mom doing it a couple of times and it was thru her mother ... she had the story. Her mother was born in Waco, Nebraska." The family is descended from Mayflower colonists.

* * *

Thanksgiving Dinner

Thanksgiving Turkey with Ethnic Dressing

... Today in the United States [Thanksgiving] is celebrated by many Americans whose roots do not stem from Britain and therefore whose taste varies. Generally, it has been found roast turkey remains central to the meal but that the accompanying dishes are those of another cuisine. The Puerto Rican will serve turkey, rice and beans, with *Arroz con Dulce,* a pudding made of rice, sugar, coconut milk, and milk, spiced with cinnamon and ginger in place of pumpkin pie. Among the Armenians, the old country people serve the traditional Armenian foods but do use turkey because it is similar to chicken and will feed a large number of people. Those born in the United States vary in custom but most have turkey with pilaf and the Armenian bread, *Cheorig,* while all the food is seasoned with oriental spices. Pumpkin pie is not generally served by the old country people but the new generation does use it, though there is no hard and fast rule. On the other hand, the Greek community tends to serve the traditional American menu, even in those families which adhere regularly to the Greek cuisine. However, the salad and condiments, namely feta cheese, are Greek, and sweet sauces or candied yams are avoided. Families from India usually depend upon being invited by an American family, but when they are not, since most of them are vegetarians, they tend to keep to their own cuisine. The Italians mix the menu, serving soup, roast turkey, ravioli, macaroni, pumpkin pie, wine and coffee. They cannot tolerate the sweet potato. The Poles use turkey with various vegetables, but serve apple pie and lots of beer and whiskey.

Source

Kansatieteellinen Arkisto 26, Suomen Muinaismuistoyhdistys, 1975, 20-21. From a paper by Margaret Louise Arnott titled "Thanksgiving Dinner: A Study in Cultural Heritage." Dr. Arnott's informants are: Puerto Rican, Elsa Alvarez, Philadelphia, June 28, 1973; Armenian, Ara Der Marderosian, Philadelphia, June 18, 1973; Greek, John Nikelly, Philadelphia, June 22, 1973; Italian, Joanna Palmieri, Philadelphia, June 24, 1973; Polish, John Szlemp, Philadelphia, June 18, 1973.

* * *

Thanksgiving Dinner

A Hare Krishna Thanksgiving

... In a Hare Krishna shelter in North Philadelphia, they ate soybean turkey....

On North Broad Street, families entered a storefront under a rainbow sign that read "Hare Krishna Food for Life." Inside the shelter for homeless women and children was a banquet of soybean turkey, greens, mashed potatoes, green beans, stuffing, cranberries and pumpkin pie.

On long, brown, wooden tables under yellow and orange streamers, women, children and men from another Hare Krishna shelter ate their vegetarian meals under the gaze of the "guest of honor."

He was Hari, a 6-month-old bull from the Krishna farm in Port Royal in central Pennsylvania.

The religion forbids the eating of meat, and at the farm, Hari will live and work until he dies a natural death.

That was fine with Sherlyn Williams, who along with her three children, were staying at the shelter. They don't mind not eating meat, though Williams said of the soybean, "They've got a long way to go to make that taste like turkey."

But she was hardly grumping.

"I'm thankful having a place to stay," she said, wiping pumpkin from her son's chin. "Just having Thanksgiving dinner, I'm thankful we have that."

Source

Philadelphia Inquirer, November 27, 1987. Edited from an article by staff writer Daniel LeDuc.

* * *

Thanksgiving Parade Publicity Handouts

Macy's, New York

The [1979] Parade starts off at 77th Street and Central Park West, promptly at 9:00 A.M. All units proceed south on Central Park West to Columbus Circle, then around to Broadway; down to Times Square and then to 35th Street. The Streets of New York are Macy's stage for this annual event. Between 35th and 34th Streets the Parade elements stop for performances, and then again on 34th Street between Broadway and 7th Avenue. The Finale of the Parade is signaled by the arrival of Santa Claus, a huge Mass Band Finale, and Macy's own choir, plus elves, toy soldiers and more! This choreographed finale truly reaffirms that the Holiday season has officially begun and Macy's continues to be the Miracle on 34th Street.

The Macy's Parade was originated and is completely directed and operated by Macy's employees. As the lead banner proclaims, the event is presented as a "Holiday Treat for Children Everywhere." The first Parade was held in 1924, entertaining an estimated audience of over 10,000. At that time, we started at 145th Street and Convent Avenue and included elephants, camels, and monkeys in the line-up. Today, the Parade delights two million spectators along the line of march. Of course, that figure varies according to weather conditions. However, rain or shine, the show always goes on, and it captivates well over 80 million television viewers on the NBC and CBS television networks.

Macy's huge balloons, a unique trademark for the store, made their first appearance in 1927. They were designed by master puppeteer, Tony Sarg (who also created the Christmas Fantasy windows at the store). Construction is carefully executed by the Goodyear Aerospace Corporation, in Akron, Ohio.

Parade preparations are year round, handled by Special Productions Department Staff and design artists. Operations are at their highest pitch on Thanksgiving Eve. When the balloons arrive by truck at 77th Street and Central Park West, they are removed from their shipping crates and anchored by sandbags and giant nets which secure them during inflation.

Between 6:00 A.M. and 7:30 A.M. on Thanksgiving Day, over 2000 Macy's employees who will march in the Parade, arrive at Herald Square for professional costuming and makeup. These enthusiastic employees come from all over the tri-state area; some as far away as Albany, New York, 150 miles north! When each group is ready, they are bussed to the Starting Line. While these in-store preparations take place, the Goodyear technicians check the weather bureau for barometric pressure, a key element in determining the mix of helium and air that goes into each balloon. Hundreds of employees who have been assigned to their favorite balloon are standing by. Parade divisional marshalls test walkie-talkies so that they can maintain the correct order of elements and keep in contact with the Herald Square staging area.

The Parade floats built and assembled in New Jersey, will be brought through the Lincoln Tunnel and are unfolded to their individual shapes. Twenty-nine Chevrolet Caprices will pull Macy's Parade floats from their home in New Jersey to New York and through the two and a half mile Parade route.... These cars have been specially selected to complement the color scheme of each float, according to the Float's motif and music selections.

The marching bands, selected from all over the country, have arrived and are placed on Central Park West. The celebrities who appear in the Parade cause additional excitement as they are escorted to their respective floats.

The countdown begins 10 seconds of 9:00 A.M. Promptly at 9:00 A.M., the grand marshalls and lead banner, cross the intersection. The show is on. The Holiday has finally arrived!

Source

Macy's 53rd Annual Thanksgiving Day Parade, 1979. News release from a publicity file prepared by Jean McFaddin, Director of Special Productions for Macy's, New York.

* * *

Gimbel's, Philadelphia

Step right up ladies and gentlemen, boys and girls, and feast your eyes on beauty, color, thrills and excitement as Gimbel's presents "The Circus" and our 60th Annual Thanksgiving Day [November 22, 1979] Parade.

It all started on Thanksgiving Day in 1920 when Ellis Gimbel gathered fifteen cars and fifty people and a fireman dressed as Santa Claus and called it a parade. Little did Mr. Gimbel know that he would create such a prestigious tradition. Now the Gimbel's parade has the distinctive honor of being nationally acclaimed as the oldest and largest parade of its kind in America. The parade has grown in size from fifty to over 3,000 participants. Last year it was estimated that close to one million people lined the streets of Philadelphia to watch this fantastic parade while many more viewed it on television....

This year amid a myriad of color, animation and excitement, the Benjamin Franklin Parkway will act as a Midway for "The Circus." Twenty-four floats, each averaging over fifty feet in length, will glide along the parade route on Thanksgiving morning introducing "Two-Two the Clown," ferocious lions, dancing ladies, performing horses, penguins playing merry tunes on horns and balancing nimbly on a colorful ball, "Two-Foot Teddy," talented canines, and a Tom Thumb wedding. Don't be surprised if you see a huge purple elephant—it's only "Eleanor the Elephant." And there is music provided by, what else, but a carousel, holding colorful figures and revolving gayly while the ticket taker looks on. And what circus would be complete without clowns! We'll have clowns that bob, slide and tumble, and laughing and crying clowns. All floats are animated, like the high wire act, or the lions jumping through rings of fire.

And there's more! In a clash of color and excitement, we'll find approximately 2,000 bandsmen from California to New York, and Maine to Florida, forming on the broad steps of the Art Museum. They're mostly high school youngsters, filled with anticipation and proud to strut their stuff for the city and national television....

This year, the real "star of the parade," Santa Claus, will make his appearance on an exciting fifty-five foot float towed by his regal reindeer and surrounded by Santa's six beautiful snow maidens. The festivities reach a climax at the official welcoming of Santa Claus in front of the Gimbel store when he is greeted by the Queen of the Thanksgiving Day Parade. Our queen is picked from thousands of six to twelve year old girls and it is her duty, along with her Court of Honor consisting of four girls, to present the key of the city to Santa.

Let's not forget—in keeping with the spirit of Thanksgiving, each year over 5,000 underprivileged and orphaned children of Greater Philadelphia are invited to be special guests of Gimbel's and sit in reserved reviewing stands at City Hall.

Source

News from Gimbel's, 1979. Press publicity prepared by Christian Mattie, Jr., of Gimbel's, Philadelphia.

* * *

Hudson's, Detroit

Santa's Thanksgiving Day Parade officially marks the beginning of the Christmas season for many Detroiters.

The first parade was staged in 1924. There were interruptions in 1941 and 1942 because of a shortage of materials at the start of World War II.

This year [1979], more than 2,500 people will march in the parade. Another 300 work behind the scenes on repair and preparation of floats and other chores.

Employees begin setting up the parade at Hudson's Fort Street Events Studio at 3:30 A.M. on Thanksgiving Day. At 4 A.M., a Detroit Police escort arrives to take the floats down to the parade starting point at Woodward Avenue and Putnam.

Marchers arrive later in the morning to be costumed, made-up and receive last-minute directions. There is no dress rehearsal. The parade itself is the first and only run through.

The first parade consisted of horse-drawn lumber and milk wagons, covered with papier-mâché and other decorative materials. About 150 employees participated in the event, which boasted 10 to 12 floats.

Because of a runaway horse team during one of the early parades, manpower was used for many years, with some 24 persons pulling a single float. Cold weather caused another problem when metal-rimmed wheels froze to the street surface. This led to the use of mechanical floats. This year's floats are pulled by tractors obtained from the Ford Motor Company.

Source

Hudson's News Bureau Release, November 5, 1979. From "Parade History" in a press kit prepared by Diane Girard Brown and Kathy Pitton of the J. L. Hudson Company of Detroit, Michigan.

* * *

Thanksgiving Toasts

Among the delightful titbits that afford variety and merriment on certain festal occasions, may be toasts and sentiments, thus:

"Our opinion on the Eastern Question: We agree with Russia, that *Turkey* ought to be *gobbled.*"

"The health of our venerable host: Although an American citizen, he is one of the best *Grand Seniors* that ever presided over *Turkey.*"

"Thanksgiving: The magnetic festival that brings back erratic wanderers to the Old Folks at Home."

"The Thanksgiving board: While it *groans* with plenty within, who cares for the whistling of the wind without."

"Thanksgiving: The religious and social festival that converts every family mansion into a Family Meeting House."

Source and Comment

Hill's Manual of Social and Business Forms, 1880, 255. These toasts are from the edition of *Hill's Manual,* copyright by Moses Warren & Co., Chicago, 1878.

Thomas E. Hill was the author of this very popular guide to letter writing, etiquette, and social custom first published in 1873. It reflected and formalized traditional practices such as the toast ritual of holiday dinner tables. Though obviously literary in origin, sentimental, and often topical, their very triteness caused them to be passed along by oral as well as written means. Hill has toasts "For a Christmas Dinner," "For the Fourth of July," and for wedding anniversaries.

* * *

Thanksgiving Grace

Yes ma'm, no ma'm,
Thank you ma'm, please.
Open up the turkey's butt
And fork out the peas.

Source

Known to H. C. from his childhood. Cf. *Journal of American Folklore,* LXXII (1959), 94, in which Ray B. Browne prints the same grace from Alabama using "chicken" instead of "turkey."

* * *

Thanksgiving Prayer

A religious thanksgiving ceremony of [an American Indian] tribe, the Umpqua, in southwestern Oregon, was observed many years ago by a pioneer, Samuel B. Flowers. Invited to attend a religious council on the bank of the Umpqua River, he cautioned his men to approach in a reverent manner. He had always been friendly with his Indian neighbors, and he knew that he was being honored with the invitation.

As he and his company entered the village, everything was quiet. All the men, both old and young, were sitting on the grass in a great circle around a tall pine tree, their heads bowed low. After they had remained in that position for some time, the head man of the village arose and began to walk slowly around the council pine. Then he looked up at the sky and began his prayer of thanksgiving:

> "Oh, bright sun, Oh, noble sun, father of all living!" he said. Then he praised the sun for rising each morning to drive away the darkness and fill the world with light. He eulogized the power of the sun to melt the snow off the mountains, and to send the warm rains. He thanked the sun for making the fruits bloom, the leaves grow and the green grass cover the earth. He lauded the power of the sun over the sea and the river. He thanked the sun for sending the red salmon up the streams so that the Indians might have fish for food.

> Then the chief addressed the earth: "Oh, earth, mother of all living!" He poured out praises to the earth for feeding grass to make the elk and the deer, that the Indian might have meat for food to make them strong and brave. He thanked the earth for the wild fruits and berries which gave the Indians health and gladness. Then the chief

paused. Looking about him he called loudly upon the wild streams to praise the sun and the earth. He commanded the rocks and the trees to praise them. He eloquently commanded his people to honor the sun and the earth as father and mother of all living. He begged the sun and the earth to send good to the Indians and to guard them from harm.

When the chief had ended his prayer, he drew an arrow from the quiver hanging on his back and slashed his bare chest with the sharp point. The blood flowing over his heart was his oath of sincerity, of loyal devotion to the sun and the earth.

Source

Oregon Historical Quarterly, LXI (December 1960), 348-49. From an article on "Indian Thanksgiving in the Pacific Northwest" by Ella E. Clark. Her source was a collection of Indian legends compiled by the U.S. Federal Writers Project, "Oregon Oddities," No. 28, December 15, 1939. Specific date and place not given. Similar thanksgiving ceremonies among tribes in Washington, Idaho, and Montana c. 1900 are described by James A. Teit, *45th Annual Report, 1927-28,* Bureau of American Ethnology.

* * *

Thanksgiving in Massachusetts 360 Years Later

Today's [November 26, 1981] activities in Boston and throughout Massachusetts reflect the mood of the Thanksgiving holiday.

Along with the annual festivities going on in Plymouth and Old Sturbridge Village, one Boston organization is supplying a feast with all the fixings to those who would not normally sit down to a Thanksgiving dinner.

The Little Brothers of the Poor, a Boston organization composed of seven individuals, will provide 150 meals to "older friends" in the Boston area today....

The annual Thanksgiving celebration is being held today at Old Sturbridge Village. It begins with a historical meeting house service on the Common with traditional text and song, according to Lilita Podsiadlo, coordinator of press and media services at the village. The meetings will be held at 1:15 p.m. and 3:45 p.m. A musket-shooting demonstration will be held at 2 p.m., weather permitting.

Cooking demonstrations will be conducted by people dressed in traditional costume and turkeys will be roasted in tin reflector ovens at open hearths in the village houses throughout the day. A public dinner, which has been sold out, will be held four times during the day, with 350 people at each sitting, said Podsiadlo.

In Plymouth, the day's festivities will begin at Plymouth Rock at 10 a.m. when 52 residents will gather for the Pilgrim's Promise march, said Carolyn Kneip, executive director of the Plymouth Area Chamber of Commerce. The group will march to First Church for a Thanksgiving service.

Thanksgiving dinner will be served buffet-style at Memorial Hall on Court Street between 11 a.m. and 4 p.m. Two thousand dinners are expected to be served.

Source

The Boston Globe, November 26, 1981. A newspaper roundup story by a correspondent, Diane Roux, on Thanksgiving activities in Plymouth, Massachusetts, where it all started, and in Boston and Old Sturbridge Village, an historic restoration.

Black Friday

Moveable: Day following Thanksgiving

Since World War II, the Friday after Thanksgiving, festive and frantic, has become the traditional date for the beginning of the Christmas commercial season. Though it evolved from a consumer-oriented society and has been nurtured by the advertising industry, Black Friday has something in common with the seasonal fairs held since the Norman Conquest in England and earlier on the Continent. In fact, trade fairs grew up at such religious festivals as the Olympic games of the Greeks and have continued to be associated with religious holidays.

Philadelphia Black Friday

Lured by big promotions, thousands of shoppers descended on stores [in the Philadelphia area] for the official start of the Christmas [1980] shopping season. But Gary Hopper, president of the merchants' association at the Gallery, wasn't exactly ecstatic.

In fact, Hopper admitted to being downright disappointed by the size of the crowds at the Center City mall.... At John Wanamaker's Center City store, traffic also was reported to be lighter than on past Black Fridays—that is the name given by retailers to the frenetic day of shopping that follows Thanksgiving. Some industry observers viewed the lighter-than-normal traffic in downtown Philadelphia as an ominous sign for retailers, because Black Friday is usually regarded as an indication of what sales volume will be for the entire holiday season.

"This is not the kind of weather we pray for," said Kay Murray, a spokeswoman for Wanamaker's. The weather, however, had no discernible effect on shopping at the suburban malls....

"The merchants here are pleased," John Morales, president of the merchants' association at the Cherry Hill [New Jersey] Mall, said.... "Traffic is up," said David Philippone, general manager of the Neshaminy [Pennsylvania] Mall.

Source

Philadelphia Inquirer, November 29, 1980. Ewart Rouse, "business writer," reports on the prospects for Christmas seasonal sales for the financial section of his newspaper.

Philadelphia Black Friday
Shopping Boom and Wall Street Crash

Forget about the stock market crash. Forget about debts and deficits. No, this wasn't a day to worry. This was a day to do what American consumers do best, to shop.

"We lost money in the stock market. But what are you going to do? Sit home and cry about it? Christmas only comes once a year," said an enthusiastic Mary Irelan of Vineland, N.J., plunking down a credit card at the jewelry counter of Strawbridge & Clothier.

Her mother, Margaret Quinn, agreed wholeheartedly. "Sure, I lost a little bit in the market. But what the heck!"

Yesterday was "Black Friday," the traditional day-after-Thanksgiving kickoff of the Christmas shopping season.

This year, retailers and economists alike have anticipated the event with more than the usual anxiety. With the Oct. 19 [1987] stock market crash fresh behind us, many forecasters fear a slowdown of consumer spending that could drive the U.S. economy into recession.

But shoppers yesterday appeared to be blind to the woes of Wall Street. Right on cue, they were out there doing what they do every year.

Shopping malls and department stores around the Philadelphia area reported heavy traffic.

Brian Ford, a retailing consultant at the accounting firm of Arthur Young & Co. in Philadelphia, conducts an exploratory shopping trip through the New Jersey and Philadelphia malls on the day after Thanksgiving every year. Yesterday, he was bullish on Christmas.

"It was a fabulous shopping day. Just great.... I don't think I ever remember seeing it so crowded in the last three to four years," Ford said.

Retailers were braced for the day. Malls were decked with Christmas glitz. Some stores opened at 8 A.M. Some planned to stay open until 11 P.M.

There were extra sales clerks, extra security guards and even extra Santas. At the Center City John Wanamaker store, there were three Santas on duty, each in a separate chamber so that "each child thinks he or she has seen the *real* Santa Claus," said store publicist Joyce Mantyla.

Still, by 2 P.M., the Santa wait had reached three hours at Wanamakers. There were lines for the escalator, lines for the cafeteria, lines for gift-wrapping. Baby strollers were grid-locked in the aisles of the toy department as parents picked through bins of teddy bears, discounted 40 percent for a clearance sale....

The weeks between Thanksgiving and Christmas are a critical season for many U.S. retailers, who, some say, coined the name "Black Friday" to refer to the day that the red ink on the income statement turns black.

Actually, "Black Friday" is not the biggest shopping day of the year. The heaviest spending usually comes in the week before Christmas.

But the early days are critical because they set the tone. If shoppers do not respond well, retailers are forced to do what they hate most during Christmas: to put merchandise on sale. That is an especially pressing fear this year because last month's stock market crash came too late for retailers to make big changes in their inventory levels.

Source

Philadelphia Inquirer, November 28, 1987. Edited from an article by staff writer Barbara Demick.

Hanukkah

Usually in December

Hanukkah is an eight-day festival. It begins on the twenty-fifth day of Kislev, third month of the lunar year, which usually falls in December. The story of Hanukkah is told in the first book of the Maccabees, in the *Apocrypha*. The Syrian king, Antiochus Epiphanes in 162 B.C. ordered that an altar to the Greek god Zeus be placed in the Temple at Jerusalem. This provoked a successful rebellion led by Judah Maccabee, and the Temple was cleansed and rededicated. According to a Talmudic legend, only a limited amount of consecrated oil was available for relighting the perpetual lamp, but miraculously it lasted for eight days. Thus Hanukkah is known as the Feast of Lights and the Feast of Dedication. A *menorah* or lamp with eight candles is lighted, one on the first evening, and the number increases by one each night of the festival. It is a joyous holiday, celebrated with games, plays, gifts, and meals which feature *latkes* or potato pancakes.

Chanuke, O Chanuke!

This song has been popular among Yiddish-speaking Jews the world over, for several generations. The text is accredited to M. Rivesman (1868-1924) born in Vilna, Lithuania. The tune is Chassidic. The text and tune which I am sending here correspond to the way we used to sing it when I was a little girl in Canada, some thirty-five years ago [c.1920], at the "Feast of Lights" in December.

Cha - nu - ke, O Cha - nu - ke, a yon - tev a shey - ner A
lus - ti - ger, a frey - li - cher, ni - to noch a - zoy - ner!
A - le nacht in drey - dl shpi - ln mir, Zu - dig - hey - se lat - kes
e - sn mir. Ge - shvin - der, tsindt kin - der di kley - nin - ke lich - te - lech on.
Zogt "Al - ha - ni - sim, loybt Got far di ni - sim, un kumt a - le tan - tsn in kon!"

Chanuke, Oh Chanuke, a beautiful holiday,	Hurry then, children and let light
A gay one, a jolly one, there's none like it!	The little candles!
Every night we spin the teetotum,	Intone the "Al-hanisim" and praise the Lord for the miracles,
And we eat red-hot pancakes.	And let us all dance in a ring!
2. Yehuda hot fartribn dem soyne, dem rotse-ach,	Judah routed the cruel enemy,
Un hot in Beys-hamikdosh gezurgen "Lamnatsey-ach",	And sang in the Holy Temple a hymn of joy,
Di shtot Yerusholayim hot vider oyfgelebt	The city of Jerusalem revived
Un tsu a nayem lebn hot yederer geshrebt.	And to a new life, everyone did strive.

Refrain:
Deriber, dem giber,
Yehuda Makabi loybt hoych
Zol yederer bazunder, bazin-gen di vunder,
Un libn dos folk zolt ir oych!

Therefore, the hero
Judah Maccabee, praise high!
Let everyone sing to the miracle,
And may your love for the people never cease!

Source and Comment

New York Folklore Quarterly, X (1954), 308-9. Contributed by Ruth Rubin from "my own memory." But she had forgotten the second stanza, which was supplied by her "former secular Yiddish teacher, born in Warsaw, who was still living in New York in 1948." His name was Hershl Novak. The "*Al-hanisim*" is a special prayer recited during the lighting of the Hanukkah candles.

* * *

Hanukkah Riddles and Problems

The Holiday of Chanukkah is an important week of joy and thanksgiving. During the days of the week, work continues as usual, but in the evenings songs are sung around the table, and puzzles, riddles, arithmetical problems and enigmas are provided for entertainment. Games of cards and "*Dreydl*" (teetotum or trendel) are played.

The following problems in arithmetic and riddles are among those which my mother used to ask [in Yiddish] during the Chanukkah holiday.

Riddles

1. It clothes the entire world, but walks naked. What is it? (*a needle*)

2. It stands in the middle of the square. When you shake its hand, it weeps. What is it? (*the town pump*)

3. It has four legs, but is not an animal? What is it? (*a bed*)

4. It has feathers, but is not a bird. What is it? (*a feather bed*)

5. Seventy fellows in a wooden hut and each and all are bald. What is that? (*a box of matches*)

6. All day it moves about the house and in the evening it stands in a corner. What is it? (*a broom*)

7. A thousand fellows who wear one belt. What's that? (*a bundle of straw*)

8. Two rhymed variants of a riddle about snow:

> Flies without wings,
> Builds without bricks,
> Sits without an arse,
> Departs without feet.
>
> Flies in without wings,
> Builds without bricks,
> Lies down like a lord,
> Rises like a fool.

This refers to the fact that when snow first falls, it is gentle and clean; when it melts and disappears, it is soiled and slushy. (This, of course, was the explanation given me by my mother.)

9. Dressed in seven petticoats and whoever undresses it must weep. What is it? (*an onion*)

10. Your father's son and no brother of thine? Who is it? (*you*)

11. Patch on patch and not a single stitch. What's that? (*a cabbage head*)

12. Looks like a horse, eats like a horse and his tail can see as well as his eyes. What is that? (*a blind horse*)

13. Why does a hare run to the woods during both summer and winter? (*because the woods won't come to him*)

14. When it rains what kind of tree does a hare sit under? (*a wet tree*)

15. A little barrel fell off the roof and there wasn't a barrel-mender in the world who could mend it. What was that? (*an egg*)

16. He climbs up and pokes about and takes it out and shakes it off and climbs down. What is that? (*a chimney sweep*)

Arithmetic Problems

1. A city slicker, walking up a country road, met a herd of geese. "Good morning, ye hundred geese," he greeted them, doffing his hat gallantly. "Ah," said the leading goose at the head of the herd, "but we are not a hundred. Now if you will but double our number, and add to it half of our number, then a quarter of our number and then one of us, only then will we be a hundred!" How many geese were they?

(*Answer: 36*)

2. A farmer, who had been selling eggs at the market, was left with 35 eggs at the end of the day. When his three sons, who had been helping him all day, were gathering up the baskets for their return home, the farmer turned to them with the following problem: He asked his eldest to take *half* of the number of eggs; his middle son to take a *quarter,* and the youngest to take *two-ninths.* The sons started to divide the eggs in the manner their father had indicated, but they simply got nowhere. What should they have done?

(*Answer: Pretend that you have 36 eggs, one more than the actual number left over, and now PROCEED AS THE FARMER HAD INSTRUCTED HIS SONS TO DO. Lo and behold, it works! As to why it works—why does it work this way? Well, that's too deep for me, and Mother didn't have the answer for that one.*)

3. A man had to cross a lake in a rowboat. He had to take with him a lamb, a wolf and a head of cabbage. However, he was permitted to transport only *two* of these at one crossing. Now, if he left the wolf and lamb alone, the wolf would eat the lamb. If he left the lamb and cabbage alone, the lamb would eat the cabbage. The problem is to transport all three in a minimum of crossings. How many crossings did he make and how did he manage the transportation of his three charges?

(*The answer to this problem can be resolved by many in different ways. I have been able to do it in seven trips:*

The man first crosses over with the lamb.

Then he returns and takes the cabbage across.

Then he returns with the lamb, leaves the lamb there and returns with the wolf.)

Source

New York Folklore Quarterly, XII (1956), 257-59. Collected by Ruth Rubin. Biographical data on informant not supplied.

* * *

Hanukkah and Christmas

Billy Apple painted a holiday picture two years ago without any of the traditional signs of the season.

Conspicuously absent from his colorful poster were the decorated trees, falling snowflakes, galloping reindeer and likenesses of old St. Nick present in the artwork of his classmates.

Billy is Jewish, and to him the holiday season meant Hanukkah; therefore, it was only natural for him to draw a *menorah*.

"I just drew the Hanukkah *menorah* because that's what we have at home," Billy, a fifth-grade student at the Burnside

Elementary School in Jeffersonville [Pennsylvania] said yesterday [December 12, 1980].

Little did he suspect that his artwork would be reproduced 50 million to 60 million times and distributed to homes across the nation. But it has—his painting was one of the 50 selected to be used on the traditional Christmas seals produced by the American Lung Association. The seals are used as a fundraising tool by the organization in its battle against tuberculosis and other lung diseases.

"This is the first time a Jewish holiday picture has been used on a Christmas seal in the 73-year history of the Christmas seal program," said Chalmers Stroup, executive director of the American Lung Association of Philadelphia. . . .

Billy, who is 11 years old, drew the picture when he was 9. According to Barbara Forman, his art teacher, Billy had no idea that it would be entered in the lung association's seal contest. Billy's picture competed against the works of 700 other elementary school children in a statewide competition. The association selected one picture from each state for its seals.

Source

Philadelphia Inquirer, December 12, 1980. Written by David Harris, "Special to the Inquirer."

* * *

Potato Latkes for Hanukkah

4 large potatoes, peeled and grated
¼ onion, chopped
2 eggs
¼ cup flour
1 teaspoon salt
¼ teaspoon pepper
¼ teaspoon baking powder
    oil for frying

In a large bowl, place grated potatoes, onions and eggs. Stir to mix. Add flour, salt, pepper and baking powder, and mix well. Heat about one-half cup oil in the skillet. Drop mixture by spoonfuls into hot oil, flattening with a spoon. Cook until browned, about three minutes on each side. Drain on paper towels. Makes about 24 small *latkes* . Serve with Crisp Fresh Applesauce.

To make applesauce, pour one-half cup orange juice in the jar of a blender or the work bowl of a food processor. Add four unpeeled red apples, cored and quartered. Chop coarsely. Turn into small bowl and add sugar or honey to taste. Makes about 1 ¼ cups.

Source

Philadelphia Inquirer, November 27, 1983. From an article in the food section by Ethel G. Hofman on "dishes of Hanukkah." For *latkes* made with *matzo* meal rather than potatoes, see "Matzo Meal Latkes," p. 124.

Hanukkah and Civil Liberties

In an unusual variation on the debate over religious symbols on public property, city officials in Vermont's largest city [Burlington] have allowed a Jewish group to erect a menorah in City Hall Park.

Early this week Sidney Baker, the city's superintendent of parks and recreation, said the Vermont Organization for Jewish Education could display a menorah from Dec. 15 through Dec. 23, the duration of the Jewish festival of Hanukkah. The organization is part of the Lubavitcher movement, a Hasidic sect that seeks to reawaken interest among Jews in Orthodox Judaism.

The decision by city officials came just one week after a Federal magistrate recommended that a cross be ordered removed from the front lawn of a courthouse in nearby Hyde Park because its presence violated the constitutional separation of church and state. That case was brought to court by the American Civil Liberties Union.

Scott Skinner, executive director of the Vermont chapter of the civil liberties organization, said he believed the Burlington menorah posed the same fundamental problem.

"Such religious symbols should not be displayed in front of public buildings because they give the impression of government endorsement of religion," Mr. Skinner said. He said his office had received complaints about the menorah.

The Jewish organization has been raising the menorah in the park for four years, but it attracted little attention the first two years because it was up for only one day, said Rabbi Yitzchok Raskin, who emigrated to Vermont from Brooklyn four years ago. Last year, he said, it was on display for the full eight days of Hanukkah.

But the menorah has become a subject of real controversy only this year, said Joseph McNeil, the Burlington City Attorney, who said "there is a heightened awareness" of religious symbolism because of the dispute over the Hyde Park cross.

Rabbi Raskin insisted the message of the menorah transcended Judaism. He said the nine-pronged candlestick symbolizes "a universal message of freedom of the human spirit, freedom from oppression and the victory of good over evil."

"These principles are shared by a majority of the American people," he said. "The menorah represents this message to the entire world."

He added that the Lubavitcher movement was advocating the display of menorahs all over the country.

Mr. McNeil said at a news conference today that they had a constitutional obligation to allow the menorah to be displayed.

"City Hall Park is a public-forum location where the expression of political and religious viewpoints is not only tolerated but encouraged," Mr. McNeil said. "We are proud of that fact. We have had everything from peace demonstrations to carol singing."

"This has been a true New England town square in the best sense of that tradition," added his colleague, Assistant City Attorney John Franco.

The lawyers noted that in 1984, the Federal Court of Appeals for the second circuit, which includes Vermont, allowed a crèche to be displayed on public property in Scarsdale, N.Y., ruling that it was in a place that had often been a public forum....

Source

New York Sunday Times, December 20, 1987. From an article by Sally Johnson. Copyright © 1987 by The New York Times Company. Reprinted by permission. See "Supreme Court Ruling on a Creche Display," p. 457.

St. Barbara's Day

December 4

St. Barbara was a third-century martyr. Her father kept her in a tower so that the world would not contaminate her purity and beauty, then beheaded her when he learned that she had become a Christian. In some parts of France, on her day, which marks the beginning of the Christmas season, wheat grains are placed in water. If the grains grow rapidly, crops will be good the next year; if the grain rots or withers, crops will be poor.

St. Barbara's Day Prediction

On St. Barbara's Day (4 December), a girl may place a twig from a cherry tree in a glass of water. If the twig blooms by Christmas Eve, she is certain to marry during the following year.

Source and Comment

Journal of American Folklore, LXIX (1956), 282. From an article on Czech-American divination by Lawrence V. Ryan. He collected information in the "countryside around the towns of Spillville and Protivin, in northeast Iowa" and Le Sueur and Rice counties, Minnesota where Czech-Americans form a majority of the population. Ryan notes that there is nothing in the legend of St. Barbara to associate her with divination or marriage, but he adds that "the prayers of the Roman Catholic Mass for her feast (the Common Mass of a Virgin Martyr) are full of allusions to the bride and bridegroom." Cf. "Cutting Lilacs on St. Nicholas' Eve," p. 428.

St. Nicholas' Day

December 6

So little is known about St. Nicholas that in 1969 the Pope made the celebration of the anniversary of his death optional and dropped his day from the calendar. However, many people still exchange gifts on December 6, and Nicholas survives as the patron saint of Christmas giving under the name Sanct Herr 'Claus (Santa Claus). St. Nicholas was born in Patera, in what is now southwestern Turkey, about the end of the third century and probably was Bishop of Myra during the reign of Diocletian. He has been the patron of such diverse groups as sailors, wanderers, college students, and children. He is associated with gift-giving because of the legend that he saved three impoverished girls from becoming prostitutes by throwing money down the smoke-hole into their stockings which were hung by the fire. St. Nicholas has been fused with pagan figures such as Knecht Ruprecht (a Teutonic New Year's gift giver who wore straw or animal skin clothing), Befana (a Roman hag who rewarded good children and punished bad), the Christ Child or the Christkind (Kris Kringle). In Europe St. Nicholas is accompanied by a Satanic figure, Black Pete, who switches the bad children while he rewards the good. Much of his present popularity is due to the influence of nineteenth-century New York magazine and newspaper writers and artists, particularly Washington Irving, James K. Paulding, Thomas Nast, and to the poem popularly called "The Night Before Christmas" that is generally credited to Clement Moore.

St. Nicholas' Day Gifts

Much German-Russian religious folklore [of Ellis County, Kansas] is centered around the principal feasts of the year in the ecclesiastical calendar. It was customary to give dates in terms of these feast days of Our Lord, His Mother, or the Saints, and not in terms of the actual days of the Gregorian Calendar. Months were referred to by the more solemn feast days' names which highlighted the particular month. For example, March was "*Heiliger Josephs Monat*" (St. Joseph's Month), May was "*Mutter Gottes Monat*" (Mother of God Month), December was "*Krist Kindlein Monat*," (Christ Child Month), and so forth.

Since the ecclesiastical year began with the first day in Advent, the first important feast day was Christmas. The German-Russians preserved a number of unusual customs during Christmastide and also preceding it. St. Nicholas' Day on December 6 anticipated the joyful time of gift-giving. In Victoria, Kansas, it was customary to have a rough, mean person dressed as St. Nicholas who would come to the house to check up on the discipline of the children, often reprimanding them for past offenses. At best, he would give out peanuts to the good children, but never candy and cookies. Other German-Russians celebrated St. Nicholas' Day with more joy and gift-giving. One custom practiced by some German-Russians was an arrangement whereby the mother of the family would

choose an evening a few days before Christmas during which the children gathered in one room, and then would rattle the screen on the outside of the window. The purpose of this was to draw the children's attention and then show them different presents, while she was hidden from their sight. The idea was to impress upon the children that good children will receive many gifts at Christmas.

Source

Western Folklore, XXII (1963), 85. Collected by Fr. John B. Terbovich, O.F.M., from German-Russian Catholics who settled in Ellis County, Kansas, in 1876. Their ancestors were Volga Germans. Cf. "A Visit from El Agüelo," and notes, p. 437.

* * *

St. Nicholaus

There is a day set aside in December on which the children [of Ithaca, New York] believe that Saint Nicholaus is sent by the *Weinachtsmann* (Santa Claus) to see if the children are good. He goes from house to house, they believe, looking in the windows to watch the children. The children set their shoes in the window or under the crib and the parents put little candies or apples in them, if they have been good. If they are bad, they get nothing.

Source

New York Folklore Quarterly, XI (1955), 256. Alice P. Whitaker collected this example of "German lore" in Ithaca, New York, during "Christmas holidays of 1941-42." Her informant was Mrs. Elsa Langnickel, age about 65, place of birth not supplied.

* * *

St. Nicholas Visits an Old Dutch House

Suddenly, the white horse and its rider appeared at the entrance to the park and proceeded, amongst the cheers of the children gathered near the old farmhouse, upon his December mission.

His mission was to bring presents and spread goodwill, and yes this was December, but no, it was not Santa Claus. After all, it was only December 3, much too early for a visit from Father Xmas. But it was not too early for the Dutch holiday of Saint Nicholas Day (which actually falls on Dec. 6) to be celebrated at the Pieter Claesen Wyckoff House Museum.

The return of St. Nicholas was enjoyed by a crowd of 150 people who came from all over New York City to see how Brooklyn's earliest Dutch settlers commemorated the holiday that was the forerunner to present day Xmas celebrations.

St. Nick and his assistant Black Piet were greeted at the farmhouse steps by children carrying wooden shoes filled with hay and carrots, which were greatly enjoyed by his horse. Hundreds of years earlier, Wyckoff children had once filled their wooden shoes and left them by the fireplace, hoping to find them full in the morning with treats and candies. If coal or an onion was found instead, this meant they had not been good!

Black Piet, the keeper of the list of good and bad children, was watched anxiously by the children gathered around him as he reached into his bag and pulled out oranges, apples, candies and sometimes, for the more mischievous children, onions and coal!

St. Nick and Piet led the crowd in singing, and after Nicholas recounted the story of his life and how he came to be adopted by the Dutch as their symbol of caring and goodwill, everyone was invited into the kitchen of the Wyckoff House to enjoy some hot cider, cookies, fruit and candies. Children were put to work making holiday decorations to take home with them. Stenciling, a favorite form of colonial and early American decoration, was taught to the children of today. Ornaments made of pine cones and other traditional materials were also created as part of the workshop.

Program

Saturday, December 2, 1989

1:00 pm	Arrival of Saint Nicholas and his assistant Black Piet
1:30 pm	Sing-a-long and storytelling lead by Linda Russell
2:00 pm	Indoors Refreshments: hot cider, cookies and sweets Outdoors Children's games and apple cider pressing
3:00 pm	Farewell 'til next year

Good Saint Nicholas

"Good Saint Nicholas is in Holland once again
With his horse and Pieter from Sunny Spain
And even if he can't stay long,
we hope he'll stop and hear our song.
Dear Saint Nicholas, the door is open wide,
For you and Piet to step inside."

Source and Comment

Newsletter, I, #3 (February 1989), 1, 4-5: the Pieter Claesen Wyckoff House, Brooklyn, N.Y., courtesy of Alan J. Lipsky. Cf. "A Visit from El Agüelo," p. 371. The song accompanying the program is traditional. See "Songs for St. Nicholas Day," below. It is difficult to decide whether the visit of St. Nicholas to a colonial Dutch House, now a museum, is a revival of an old tradition or its continuation. The museum setting and the varied national origins of the children argue for revival, but among American families of colonial and more recent Dutch descent, St. Nicholas Day is still remembered.

* * *

Songs for St. Nicholas' Day

Speaking of songs, I should like to tell you some of the little [Dutch] songs I learned as a child [in the 1920s]. The very earliest I remember is one called

Sint Nikolaas kapoentje,
Gooi wat in myn schoentje.
Gooi wat in myn laarsje,
Dank je Sint Nikolaasje.

Santa Claus, *kapoentje,*
Throw something in my shoes.
Throw something in my boots,
Thank you, Santa Claus.

We also often sang:

Zie de maan schynt door de boomen,
Jongens staakt je wild geraasch.
'T Heerlyk avondje is gekomen,
'T avondje van Sint Nikolaas.

Vol verwachting klopt ons hart,
Wie de koek krygt, wie de gart.
Vol verwachting klopt ons hart,
Wie de koek krygt, wie de gart.

See the moon shining through the trees,
Boys, stop that terrible noise.
The big evening is here,
With expectance beat our hearts,
Who will get the cake, who will get the stick.
With expectance beat our hearts,
Who will get the cake, who will get the stick.

One of the most famous Sint Nikolaas songs is *Sint Nikolaas, Goed Heeligman.*

Sint Nikolaas, goed heeligman,
Trek je beste stappers on.
Ryd daarmee naar Amsterdam.
Amsterdam en Spanje.
Appeltjes van Orangje.
Peertjes van de hooge boom.
Sint Nikolaas dat is myn Oom.

Santa Claus, good holy man,
Put your best shoes on.
Drive with them to Amsterdam.
From Amsterdam to Spain.
Take apples from Orange,
Pears from the high tree.
Santa Claus that is my uncle.

Source and Comment

New York Folklore Quarterly, X (1954), 253-54. Remembered by Louise Van Nederynen Atteridg who learned the first song from her mother, a native of Holland, and the second from Mrs. Carrie Van Altena, both residents of Castleton, New York. The word *kapoentje* has no exact equivalent in English but refers to St. Nicholas affectionately as a little bird.

Cutting Lilacs on St. Nicholas' Eve

Mrs. Hamlin describes a custom followed in the Pruyn family reminiscent of the English one of cutting hawthorne branches to bloom for Christmas. She says, "All of us in Ancient Fort Orange (Albany [New York] was Fort Orange before it was Beverwyck) knew for a fact that if you go out after sundown on St. Nicholas eve and cut white lilac slips they will flower by Christmas. They must be put in a vase of water and kept very warm. The old coal ranges had a shelf, and this was a good place for the slips, as the hot coals gave off heat all night. On Christmas morning, on our library table stood an old Russian silver vase of lovely white lilacs. The leaves were small and very light, and the blooms were fragile; but there they were—white lilacs at Christmas."

Source

New York Folklore Quarterly, XI (1955), 250. Collected by Dorothy V. Bennit from "Mrs. Charles S. Hamlin, born Huybertje Pruyn, a descendent of one of Albany's first Dutch settlers." Cf. "St. Barbara's Day Prediction," p. 425. Also see Motif F971.5f.

* * *

Saint Nicholas in Tarpon Springs

[The sponge fishermen of Tarpon Springs, Florida, are sure] that Saint Nicholas, the patron saint of Greek seamen, has not abandoned them in their new homeland. This saint is the namesake of the religious community and of the church. It is said that Saint Nicholas makes his presence known every year on December 6th—the day set aside in the religious calendar in his honor—by causing a raging tempest at sea. It is also believed that he provides special protection for the town of Tarpon Springs and its inhabitants. Informants aver that the town has never been struck by a hurricane because of Saint Nicholas' omnipresence. Furthermore, severe storms have invariably shifted direction, thus providing positive proof of the saint's intercession. "All the hurricane go by here. They don't bother us," Catherine Vostistanos commented. "We have had weather, like a lot of rain; and trees came down and everything. But not as much as other places. It just cuts in half the hurricane. We never have had weather because Saint Nicholas is with us."

Source

"Greek-American Folk Beliefs and Narratives: Survivals and Living Tradition," Ph.D. Dissertation, 1964, 65. Collected and discussed by Robert A. Georges. His informant, Catherine Vostistanos, was born about 1920 in Tarpon Springs, Florida, of parents born in Greece. At the time of her interview, she ran a coffeehouse frequented by sponge fishermen. See Motif D 2140.1.1.

Id al-adha

Retrograde in regard to the Gregorian Calendar

In English, the Arabic name for this major Islamic holiday is "Festival of Sacrifice" for it celebrates Abraham's sacrifice of a ram as a substitute for his son. It begins on the tenth day of the final month, Dulheggia, of the Muslim calendar and lasts for two or three days. Known also as the "Greater Festival," in comparison with Id al-Fitr which is designated the "Lesser Festival," it is also a joyous time.

A Festival of Sacrifice and Sharing

An Islamic celebration of sharing began yesterday, as Muslims filled mosques in the New York area with prayers and holiday greetings.

At the Al-Faruq Mosque in Brooklyn, where crowds of men greeted each other with backslaps, handshakes and hugs, women and children waited to be given neatly packed bags of meat—a customary holiday gift to the needy.

"Today the mosque gives it to us,' explained Hadijan Ocasio, a Muslim housewife from Brooklyn, lifting a bag of lamb chunks. "This is enough for my family. We are eight people. This is for those who can't afford their own sheep."

A man entering the mosque said, "It is a way of showing that I care for those less lucky."

The distribution of meat, the warm exchange of greetings, the mosque prayers and the exchange of gifts are all part of the Muslim celebration of Id-al-Adha, or the Feast of Sacrifice, one of the most important feasts in the Islamic calendar.

Central to the three-day holiday is an individual family's sacrifice of a sheep, cow, goat or even a camel and the sharing of the meat with the needy and the poor of the community regardless of their religious beliefs.

The feast started with 9 A.M. prayers at mosques throughout the New York area after rain canceled meetings in Prospect Park and Flushing Meadows in Queens. The Al-Faruq Mosque, a six-story Art Deco-style building at 552-554 Atlantic Avenue in downtown Brooklyn, could not accommodate all its congregation at once and held three prayer shifts—each with more than 1,000 people.

Many dressed in traditional garb—men in long flowing white robes or shirt-like tunics and checkered head scarves, and women in bright embroidered ankle-length Palestinian dresses and shawls. Others came in jeans, and several wore tuxedos. . . .

Living in New York City has forced certain changes in the ritual of sacrifice. The sacrifice of the chosen animal—a commemoration of Abraham's sacrifice of a ram as a substitute for his son, Ismael—is traditionally performed by the male head of each household.

But legal and physical hurdles involved in keeping a goat or cow in a city apartment have created a boom for New Jersey's slaughterhouses, said Mohammad Awad, 26 years old, who owns a supermarket. Community groups place wholesale orders, and only one or two people go to the slaughterhouses and preside over the sacrifice—facing Mecca, uttering the appropriate ritual along with the name of the persons on whose account the sacrifice is being made.

The slaughterhouses do well over the Id weekend. Prices range from about $1,200 for a cow to $250 for a lamb and $160 for a sheep depending on weight. Most meat is turned over to the mosques that will redistribute it among the poor, said Abdul Malik, who oversees distribution at the Al-Taqwa Mosque near Prospect Park.

Mr. Awad said he missed the simplicity and ease with which the ceremony was performed in Egypt. "In Egypt, everyone got their own animal and killed it in the backyard," he said.

Source

New York Times, July 14, 1989. By Donatella Lorch. Copyright © 1989 by the New York Times Company. Reprinted by permission.

The Day of Our Lady of Guadalupe
December 12

The famous legend of Guadalupe tells how an Indian, Juan Diego, saw the Virgin Mother on a hill near Mexico City while he was gathering herbs. She told him to go to the bishop and have him build a shrine to her on the site of the vision. The bishop thought the Indian was crazy, but the Virgin again appeared to Juan Diego three days later. This time she told him to pick roses miraculously growing on a stony hillside near-by and take them to the bishop as proof of his story. Juan Diego picked the roses which were flourishing in extremely barren soil at a time when flowers do not normally bloom. When he took them to the bishop and opened his mantle to drop them on the floor, an image of the Virgin appeared among them. The bishop built a sanctuary as instructed. That was 1533. There is a church on the site today, though it dates from 1695.

The image of Our Lady of Guadalupe has been carried all over the Spanish-speaking world. She became the patroness of Mexico City, and by 1746 was the patron saint of all New Spain, and by 1910 of Latin America.

Birthday Party for the Virgin of Guadalupe

It was one of those clear cold nights in December when the stars in the Arizona sky look like small diamonds set in black velvet. My father and I climbed into our coupé and followed Joe Sandoz' old sedan into a narrow unpaved street in the Barrio Anita, one of the poorest Mexican districts in Tucson. Joe stopped in front of an old frame house where he and his wife, Cholita, and their four children got out. We could see a light in the front room, and faintly we heard voices singing. Whispering to us that the *velorio,* or watch service, already was in progress, Joe beckoned us to follow him around the side of the house. We saw him stoop as his bulky figure passed through the side doorway. Then, with Cholita and the children, we tiptoed inside.

I had expected to see a devotional service, but nothing like this. From the bare scrubbed kitchen we looked in on about thirty people, all kneeling toward a corner of the living room hidden from our view. As we watched, they began to sing in Spanish an *alabanza,* or hymn of praise. There was no accompaniment, just the soft chanting of men's and women's voices. After a while they stopped and began to recite prayers. Then, still on their knees, they resumed their chanting. I began to wonder how long this could continue.

During the service I had been conscious of the sound of children's voices coming from behind a bedroom door. Now the door opened and Richey, Joe's five year old boy, ran out. His older sister came in quick pursuit and hustled

him back inside, closing the door. I heard loud giggles, and presently, children singing. There was no mistaking the tune—"London Bridge's Falling Down"—and it was being sung in English. The familiar chorus made a strange counterpoint to the melancholy minor tones of the *alabanzas.*

And now came a new sound—the raucous, deep-throated whistle of a steam locomotive. I had forgotten that the old house was only a few feet from the Southern Pacific tracks. With a roar that drowned all other noises, the train swept past. I knew it was a freight train because after the bellowing rhythm of the engine I could hear the regular clanking beat of the boxcar wheels as they rolled, two by two, over the joints of the rail. The house shook to their clanking and groaning but in the front room the people remained on their knees. By their moving lips I could tell they were still singing.

While the service continued, I had time to look around. Had it not been for the large kerosene range, spotless in its white enamel finish, I would not have known I was in the kitchen. There was a big table in the center of the room but I saw no kitchen sink. Then I remembered that the house, like many of its neighbors, had no inside plumbing. All water had to be carried in buckets from a faucet outside the back door. That, I guessed, was the way they had filled the two big cauldrons and the coffee pot which now stood steaming on the stove. The simmering pots, in turn, explained the mingled aromas of coffee and tamales which for some little time had been distracting my attention from the *alabanzas*.

At last, at midnight, the prayers were halted temporarily, and the weary worshippers rose from their knees. They turned around to find the kitchen almost filled with new arrivals. Besides ourselves, many other visitors had come into the house after the service started. Two couples had come with small children, which they promptly parked in the bedroom, and a young high school girl named Loli, and several boys in Army uniform. There were many cries of joy as these boys now greeted the older people in the house. For many months they had been lost in Europe and the South Pacific, and now, miraculously, they were back again.

Only one boy was a little sad. While he was on Okinawa his wife had died at home. Now all he had left was their two year old, Anna Maria. He put the little girl on top of the kitchen table where she toddled around while everybody held out their arms and tried to play with her.

But now it was time to serve the tamales. Señora Mendoza, Joe's sister, taking charge, whisked off little Anna Maria, covered the table with a fresh white cloth and then began to dish out the still steaming tamales. Graciously, old Mrs. Sandoz, head of the household, invited us to sit at the first table. The other four at the table all were returned soldiers. Among themselves these boys talked American slang, but when they rose to thank their hostess, all spoke Spanish.

While others were being served, my father and I walked into the living room to see the altar. The sight dazzled us. An entire side of the room had been covered with white sheets, and against this background many beautiful flowers had been pinned in orderly rows from floor to ceiling. Frank, Señora Sandoz' oldest son, had brought some of these flowers from Los Angeles. Halfway up the wall was the silver altar decorated with a beautiful image of the Virgin of Guadalupe, the patron saint of Mexico. In the corner of the room were several beautiful water color portraits of her done by one of the returned soldiers. I could see that this shrine was the work of many hours and that no expense had been spared to make it a fitting birthday present to the Virgin.

Joe had told us that his mother held the *velorio* each year on December 11, the eve of the day of the Virgin of Guadalupe, just as his grandmother had done in Mexico many years before. Looking at old Señora Sandoz now, I saw her wrinkled face radiating a quiet peace to all in the room. Although she was stone deaf, she kept track of everyone. I saw her old eyes flash with pleasure as she watched us admire the shrine she and her children had created.

After the last table had been served, the worshippers returned to the living room, while we stole back to the kitchen. Soon again they were down on their knees and the second half of the service began. This we knew would last until well after dawn. For a while we stayed and listened to the prayers and songs, but by 2:30 a.m. we were tired. Looking into the bedroom, we could see that we were not the only ones. The children lay sprawling, some on the bed, and others curled up in blankets on the floor. The last thing we heard as we closed the kitchen door behind us was the soft chanting of an *alabanza*—the one about a white dove that comes only after midnight. They were singing "Happy Birthday" to the Virgin.

Source

New Mexico Folklore Record, V (1950-51), 17-18. George C. Barker of Pacific Palisades, California, recalls attending a *velorio* in Tucson, Arizona, in the mid-1940s. For a *velorio* held by the Penitentes, see "La Percíngula," p. 307.

* * *

Matachines Dance for Our Lady of Guadalupe

There exist a surprising number of firsthand observations of the New World matachines [clowns, buffoons] dances as observed between 1902 and 1955 in various places in Old and New Mexico....While the various accounts reveal local differences, it is possible to see a remarkable degree of uniformity in the dance, even though danced at isolated villages, far removed from one another.

In general, at all these places, the dances share the following characteristics:

I. The matachines dancers are a group dedicated to the service, through dancing, of the Virgin of Guadalupe.

II. There is a leader, known usually as *el Monarca*.

III. There is a girl (or, in Mexico, a boy dressed as a girl) known as *la Malinche*.

IV. There are two lines of dancers, each ranging in number from six to twelve or even larger numbers.

V. There is a character known as *el Toro*.

VI. There is a clownish character, often masked, known as *el Abuelo* ("the grandfather") who speaks in falsetto.

VII. The dancers usually dance on December 12, the feast day of the Virgin of Guadalupe, and on other special occasions.

VIII. They usually dance to the music of fiddle and guitar.

IX. They wear tall, mitre-like, decorative headdresses, have their faces partially covered by fringes or handkerchiefs, and wear bright colored ribbons and aprons.

X. They carry in one hand a gourd rattle with which they keep the rhythm of the dance steps and in the other a wooden trident, often gaily painted.

XI. The dance often terminates with the figurative killing of the bull.

XII. They dance in front of, or inside, the Catholic church of the village....

The musical selections which I have chosen and which are transcribed below... are performed by a solo fiddler. They are of particular interest as the fiddler was intelligent and articulate and was able to ascribe a definite title to, and give some information about, each dance. These twelve dances, he said constitute one complete set of the dances done each year on December 12, the feast day of Our Lady of Guadalupe, at Tortugas [New Mexico].

The fiddler, Pete Maese, himself danced with other dancers from 1928 to 1941 and these are the tunes which he learned from his predecessor, whom he knew as an old man. When the old man died Maese was elected as fiddler. The dancers at Tortugas are known as "matachines" or "*Danzantes.*" The group are of mixed blood—Indian, Spanish, American. Some fifteen of them, including Maese, have been sworn in as slaves of the Virgin and dance in fulfillment of their vows.

The ceremonies commence with *la Entrada* ("the entry"), a danced procession that terminates in front of the main entrance of the Catholic church where the other dances take place. The dancers consist of a leader known as *el Monarca*, six to eight little pre-adolescent girls in white communion dresses who alternate in the part of *la Malinche* (*la Malinche* was the Indian mistress of Hernando Cortes), the matachines dancers (twelve in number), *el Polverero* ("powder man") who carries a shotgun and fires it precisely on the final note of each dance. This is intended as a salute to the Virgin. There are also two additional characters—*el Toro* and *el Abuelo* who act as clowns.

The titles of the dances furnish a clue as to the nature of the dance formations.

"*La Batalla*" ("The Battle") is self-explanatory. In "*la Mudanza*" ("The Cross") dancers exchange places in a crisscross movement. "*La Ese*" (the letter S) is a description of the pattern by which the dancers move from one position to the next. "*Guajes*" ("Gourds") is the name given to a gourd filled with dried beans or other noisemaking particles which is carried by each of the *danzantes*. These add a percussive rhythm to the dance. "*Los Panos*" ("The Handkerchiefs") employs large handkerchiefs. In "*El Son de la Malinche*" several of the little malinches dance, the one in the lead escorted by *el Monarca*. "*La Entre Tejida*" ("The Weaving Entrance") is distinguished by a dance pattern which is supposed to simulate the weaving of cloth. "*La Transa*" ("The Braids") is a Maypole dance. "*La Procesión*" ("The Procession") is what its name indicates. The dance known as "*el Toro*" ("The Bull") is characterized by a simulated combat between *el Monarca*

and *el Toro*, who is dressed to resemble a bull. *El Monarca* eventually kills the bull after the dancers make a circle like a bull ring. This is regarded as a humorous dance, the bull acting as a clown. The bull charges and before being killed is supposed to kill *el Abuelo*. Actually, this is supposed to end the dances but these are not always taken in the proper sequence. In "*la Escondida*" ("The Hidden One") one of the malinches is symbolically hidden by *el Monarca* and the *danzantes,* presumably from pursuit by *el Toro*.

Matachin

La Entrada

La Batalla

La Mudanza

La Ese

Guajes

Los Panos

El Son de la Malinche

La Entre Tejida

La Procesión

El Toro

La Escondida

As the dances are sometimes of interesting and subtle musical form, it seemed appropriate to analyze one of them merely as a sample of what one finds. For this purpose I have chosen "*El Son de la Malinche*."

This piece consists of three two-measure phrases which I have marked A, B, and C, with a fourth which I have marked A' and which consists of the first measure of A combined with the second measure of B. These phrases are used in the following combinations. First, we hear the following: ABC, ABC, A'C, A'C. This appears to represent a sort of introduction. Second, we hear a series of verses all in identically the same pattern as follows: AB, ABC, A'C.

Finally, there is a brief coda. What appears at first hearing of this tune as an elusive but somewhat haphazard throwing together of musical ideas is seen to follow a definite formal scheme. Chaos is foreign to the human mind. Similar formal patterns are to be found in other dances.

The effect of monotony which is often felt in the seemingly endless repetition of a short melody is a part of the tradition of more than one people. The same sort of effect, for instance, is produced by the drone bass of the music of India. In India music is conceived of as one of the pathways to eternity. The use of the drone bass represents a kind of changelessness which is akin to eternity and seems to be its symbol as it underlies the changing and sometimes wildly exciting improvisations of the drummer and soloist, which, it seems, symbolize human life.

I think we should listen attentively for what this monotony can mean to us in the matachines dances as well. It is a symbol not only of changelessness, and hence of eternity, but also unity. I hear in it a kind of godlike depth and profundity which in Hindu music could exist without the alliance of melody and rhythm, but here, because the monotony is based on repetition, is inextricably associated with both as well as with a rudimentary two-voice harmony.

Source and Comment

Western Folklore, XX (1961), 94-101. From "The Matachines Dance—A Ritual Folk Dance" by J.D. Robb. He is concerned mainly with the European sources and ritualistic nature of this ceremonial dance. The study is based upon his own collections and field work, supported by the earlier research of anthropologists and folklorists. See other material drawn from this same essay, "Matachines Dance for St. Anthony," p. 237. Cf. the "clownish character . . . *el abuelo*" and "A Visit from El Agüelo," p. 437.

St. Lucy's Day

December 13

Santa Lucia or St. Lucy was born in the third century of a noble family in Syracuse, Sicily. Because the beauty of her eyes attracted a heathen nobleman, she had herself blinded, supposedly on the shortest (and darkest) day of the year, a tradition that links her to sun worship. She was tortured and stabbed to death for rejecting her heathen suitor and for being a Christian. In Italy, where she remains popular, she became the patroness of sufferers from eye disorders. In Sweden, St. Lucy's Day marks the beginning of the Christmas season. A young woman in the household is designated as "Lucia." Representing the spirit of Christmas and crowned with a headdress of lighted candles, she is often attended by a court of young men and is not unlike the queen who reigns on May Day.

Luciadagen

St. Lucy's Day [is] the 13th of December (*Luciadagen*). Lucia was a Sicilian saint of the 4th century concerning whom legends report, among other things, that she preserved her chastity at the cost of having her eyes put out. As a symbol of the preciousness of light, and of the annual return of the sun at the winter solstice (calendrical displacement gives us the anachronistic date of December 13), and via a route which nobody can now trace, St. Lucy became conspicuous among the customs of the western provinces of Lutheran Sweden. During the 19th century she was introduced to Uppsala and other Swedish cities by Swedish students from those provinces. Symbol of light, clad in white nightgown and red sash with a wreath of green-wrapped burning candles in her hair, and accompanied by one or more so-called star-boy attendants, each bearing a star on a pole and wearing a conical cap adorned with stars, these "Lucy-Brides" spread like wildfire. Not every Lucy survived this ordeal by candle, and the latter have now happily been converted to electricity. From Sweden the Lucy celebrations spread to America, then to Finland, Norway, and to some slight extent finally to Denmark, all of whom now sing *Santa Lucia*—a Sicilian folksong, mind you—serve gingersnaps (*pepparkakor*) and "Lucy cats" (*lussekatter*), a kind of bun, with coffee to the factory or office or club or school or in private families, early in the morning, with a daughter of the house (in public ceremonies, an elected Lucy) serving as Lucy and her brother(s) as star boy(s). For irrational reasons we have followed this custom at home for some years; it is very common in Los Angeles. The Lucy cat is actually a sun symbol, technically a type of swastika, antedating Hitler by several thousand years and quite without political significance. This is an interesting development, for it is not at all apparent from the records that Lucy Day ceremonies were practiced by immigrants to this country before 1900. Most immigrants had not yet heard of Lucy!

Source

Northwest Folklore, III (1968), 9-10. Described by Erik Wahlgren, in part from personal observation, but mainly from many printed sources which he cites.

* * *

Santa Lucia Buns

Custom has it that the youngest daughter of a family is called Lucia for a day. She wakes her family with a tray of saffron buns, perhaps singing the familiar Santa Lucia melody.

1   teaspoon saffron threads
¼   cup boiling water
1¾ cups milk
5   tablespoons butter
1   cup sugar
1   teaspoon salt
½   cup lukewarm water
2   teaspoons sugar
2   packages active dry yeast
1   egg
7   to 7 ½ cups unbleached all-purpose flour
½   cup blanched slivered almonds
½   cup candied orange and lemon peel, diced
⅔   cup golden raisins
1   egg beaten with 1 teaspoon water
     Raisins for decoration

Soak saffron in boiling water and set aside. In saucepan, combine milk and butter over medium heat until very warm. Stir in the one cup of sugar and salt. Cool to lukewarm. Combine warm water and the two teaspoons of sugar, and sprinkle yeast over mixture to dissolve.

In mixer bowl, beat egg. Add milk-butter and yeast mixtures, saffron threads and saffron water.

Gradually add 3 ½ cups sifted flour. Beat for five minutes with electric mixer. Gradually add three more cups of flour, using only as much of the last half-cup as needed to keep dough from being sticky. Turn dough onto lightly floured board, and knead until smooth and elastic, about eight to 10 minutes. Gently work in almonds, fruit peel and raisins, distributing evenly. Place in greased bowl, turning to grease top of dough. Cover with plastic wrap and let rise in warm place until doubled in bulk. Punch dough down.

Divide dough into pieces weighing 2 ½ ounces, or about the size of a lemon. There should be about 27 pieces. Roll each piece of dough into 10-inch-long strip. Form into S-shapes, coiling ends inward. Place on greased baking sheets two inches apart. Cover with kitchen towel and let rise in warm place until doubled in size.

Brush with egg-water mixture. Press a dark raisin into the center of each coil. Bake at 350 degrees for about 15 minutes. Cool buns, lightly wrapped in terrycloth towel, on wire rack. Makes about 27 buns.

Source and Comment

Philadelphia Inquirer, December 7, 1983, from the *Christian Science Monitor* Service. A traditional holiday recipe in Swedish-American homes is popularized, like so many ethnic holiday food-ways, through the weekly food sections of metropolitan newspapers. Thus the mass media and food marketing help to maintain the vitality of holiday food customs. For other examples, see "Fortune Cookies for the Year of the Rooster," p. 60; "Chicken Soup and Matzo Balls," p. 146; and "Food for Dewali," p. 371.

The Posadas
December 16-23

The word *posada* means "lodging," and it commemorates the journey of Mary and Joseph from Nazareth to Bethlehem where they sought lodgings at the inn. In Mexico, *Posadas* is a community festival beginning with a procession bearing images of Joseph and Mary riding a burro. Singing and carrying torches, the procession moves from house to house seeking lodging for Mary.

Room at the Inn

Every Christmas season, the parishioners of St. Bonaventure's Church in North Philadelphia stage a nightly parade through their neighborhood streets. When they do, they are carrying on a centuries-old Hispanic tradition symbolizing the fundamental message of Christmas.

The custom of *posada,* Spanish for "the inn," is in some ways an eight-day-long party. But the festive atmosphere is the outgrowth of a spiritual joy flowing from people who find a place in their homes for a modern representation of the baby Jesus.

Members of the congregation carry a doll, representing the Christ Child, through the streets, re-enacting Joseph's search for a room for the night. The procession stops at a previously selected home, asks for lodging for the night and is invited in to read from the scriptures, sing spontaneously composed Christmas carols called *alguinaldos* and enjoy refreshments provided by the hosts.

The visitors leave the doll overnight at the chosen home and return the next night, when the procession continues to another house to again find a room at "the inn."

This year's *posada* began Dec. 16 [1979] and ended Sunday. Father Donald Farrell, pastor of the church at Ninth and Cambria Streets, the largest Spanish-speaking parish in the Philadelphia Archdiocese, said St. Bonaventure's has been celebrating the *posada* for about eight years.

"The *posada* is a symbolic celebration to say Christ is welcome not only in our homes but in our hearts," he said. "The atmosphere is one of reverence, of anticipated joy in the coming of the Christ Child. It brings hope and joy in our community.

"I don't know when it began, but it is centuries old, as old as the Hispanic culture."

The homes used as stops in the procession are selected at random from the 740 families in the congregation. Parishioners are always eager to open their homes, Father Farrell said.

This year, as many as 100 persons took part in the processions and crowded into the modest rowhouses at each stop, he said.

The *alguinaldos* are one of the most joyful features of the celebration. They are accompanied by guitars and other musical instruments of Spanish origin. One person sings improvised lines that are then repeated by all members of the group.

Source and Comment

Philadelphia Inquirer, December 25, 1979. Reported by Tom Belden, staff writer. His principal source, Father Donald Farrell, who had been pastor of St. Bonaventure's Church for the previous four years, states that "each year he can see more enthusiasm in the *posada*." For another procession dramatizing the search for room at the inn, see "St. Joseph's Day," p. 129, especially "The Play of St. Joseph," p. 130.

Christmas Eve and Christmas Day
December 24-25

For more than three centuries Christ Mass was a moveable feast, and in many places it was celebrated on Epiphany, January 6, the day, according to the biblical account, when Jesus manifested himself to the Magi. Even after the Western church, using a solar calendar, settled on December 25, the Eastern church for almost a century continued to fix Christmas by the moon. The western date of Christmas was made to coincide with the Roman midwinter festival of the Kalends. Kalends was preceded by seven days of tribute to the god of agriculture, Saturn, and for devotees of Mithra by the Birthday of the Unconquered Sun. Many of the pre-Christian rites are still celebrated as part of Christmas: the evergreen decorations, the exchange of gifts or *strenae*, the indulgence in food and drink, the license in kissing and sexually related activities, the mumming.

By 567 the twelve days between December 25 and January 6 (Old Christmas Day) had become days of revelry following the penitence and fasting in Advent. Many of the Christmas customs were common to various thanksgiving days and to New Year rites. Some are extremely old: ivy worship going back to the Dionysian revels of ancient Greece; mistletoe being the golden bough sacred to the Druids. But Christmas has also generated new customs. The Christmas card began in England in the nineteenth century; Santa Claus' reindeer date from about the same time in America. The Christmas tree was introduced in English-speaking lands by Prince Albert of Saxony as late as 1844. It is an adaptation of the *Paradeisbaum* (the decorated tree of life) so popular in German medieval drama and of the pagan *Tannenbaum*.

A Visit from El Agüelo

On Christmas Eve, or on an evening two or three days before Christmas Eve, an old man, called *El Agüelo* (*El Abuelo*) [the grandfather], visits the homes of all people who have children, to see if all have been good and have learned their prayers. Years ago, when this custom was common in New Mexico and southern Colorado, the *Agüelo* was a veritable scarecrow for small children. He was feared more than anything else, and there exist stories of the floggings he gave to bad boys who did not know their prayers or were disobedient to their parents. I do not know the origin of this custom. At all the homes he visited he was given sweets and cookies, which he carried away in a large bag. In this bag he carried away also incorrigible little children. His presence was announced by a hard knock on the door, with the cry, "¡El Agüelo! ¡El Agüelo! ¡Aquí viene el Agüelo! [Here comes the grandfather!]" The children would then appear and recite their prayers to him. After this the children and the *Agüelo* would form a circle; and all would dance from right to left, and again from left to right, singing the following verses:

(a) *Baila, paloma de Juan Turuntún.*
[Dance, dove of Juan Turuntún.]
Turún, tun, tun, Turún, tun, tun.
  Baila, paloma de Juan Turuntún.
Turún, tun, tun, Turún, tun, tun.

(b) *Baila, paloma de Juan Durundún.*
Durún, dun, dun, Duurún, dun, dun.
  Baila, paloma de Juan Durundún.
Durún, dun, dun, Durún, dun, dun.

In case *El Agüelo* was not well satisfied with the prayers or general conduct of some child, he would crack his whip and make the child dance alone, repeating to him the verses in a threatening manner.

Source

Journal of American Folklore, XXIX (1916), 517-18. From a collection of games and diversions "of very young" Mexican-American children "very popular in New Mexico and Colorado" assembled by Aurelio M. Espinosa. Exact date and informants not given. For some visitors during the Christmas season, see "Old Christmas Frights," p.28; "St. Nicholas' Day Gifts," p.426; "Belsnickels among the Pennsylvania Dutch," p. 444; and "The John Kuner Ceremony," p. 445.

Santa Claus Lady

The holidays added zest and interest to the shut-in days of winter [in Dade County, Wisconsin, c. 1855]. No day of all the year is more anticipated and enjoyed by children than is Christmas. We counted the nights that we must sleep before Santa Claus would come. The event began with Christmas Eve when the Santa Claus Lady appeared dressed in a long white robe—for this occasion my grandmother's burial robe was used—carrying a tiny stick in her hand. Touching the smaller children gently with her willow twig, she asked if they had been good children. Since we children were afraid of our own voices, our parents replied in the affirmative which relieved us greatly. The Santa Claus Lady gave us a few nuts and a stick of horehound candy, or a few peppermint balls, saying that she would speak in our behalf to Santa Claus and tell him what good children we had been and that he must try to come to our house and bring us a few things. She told us not to count too much on his coming as he was very busy and might not be able to get to our house as it was rather far in the country. We were filled with uncertainty, but he never failed us, as we found out on Christmas morning.

The Christmas tree, a young tamarack cut from our trees near the marsh, was never wanting. It was festooned with yards of popcorn strung on thread. Gingerbread boys and girls hung all over the tree, and somewhere on the branches there was a small package of candy for each child and an apple too, if it was possible to get them. Mother's relatives, near Rochester [Wisconsin], usually sent us a barrel of Greenings or Baldwins for Christmas. We could look at the Christmas tree all we wanted, but it must not be touched till after breakfast.

Christmas breakfast was a feast of *Stollen,* made in wreaths, braids, or other designs. They were on the table in abundance and vanished without delay. It is much richer than coffee cake, and the dough is filled with nuts, citron, and lemon peel. The top is spread with sugar and nuts and rose water. I make it annually for my children, and they like it.

Breakfast over, we went into the parlor. The table, on which the Christmas tree stood, and the floor beneath were covered with piles of candy, graded in size according to the age of the child, and also a cup cake for each of us. We felt sure that Mrs. Santa Claus had spoken so well of us that Santa Claus had not been able to forget us.

As long as Grandfather lived, we were expected at the log house on Christmas morning, and we went in a body. The white cloth which covered the gifts on the table was removed and revealed as many piles of candy, nuts, and fruit, as there were children. Here were the hazel and hickory nuts, in varying amounts, that had been gathered through the year. We never failed to note that the largest amount went to the oldest child, and the smallest to the

youngest. My grandparents dealt generously with us, and they knew what children liked. It was expected that some of the Christmas candy and other sweets would last over until New Year's Day that Santa might know we were not greedy children.

Source and Comment

Wisconsin Magazine of History, XXIX (1945-1946), 82-3. From Part III of the article "Peter Schuster, Danz County Farmer" by Rose Schuster Taylor.

The German "lady Santa Claus" is probably a derivative of Berchta, who is a disheveled, hook-nose hag who checks on the cleanliness and industry of children during the Twelve Days. By the time she had arrived in Wisconsin, she had been modified into a kindly, saintlike person, evidently married to Santa himself. Another similar female figure is the Roman Befana.

Cf. "Visit from El Agüelo" above.

* * *

Christmas Eve Bonfires

As dusk falls on Christmas Eve, Nolan Oubre gives the signal to light the string of wooden pyres that seems to stretch to infinity along the spine of the Mississippi River levee. Over his car's PA system, he speaks the long-anticipated words: "It is now 7 P.M.; you may light your bonfires." It is ironic that the leathery, walrus-mustached Oubre would be among those charged with the setting of fires, causing a hundred curtains of purple and orange flame to rise into the black velvet night, crackling and popping and sparking showers of gold along the green flank of the man-made ridge. Ordinarily—as chief of the volunteer fire department in Gramercy, Louisiana (pop. maybe 3,500)—he is in charge of putting them out.

But the fire chief's role reversal is symptomatic of the fever that pervades rural St. James Parish each December. Between Halloween and Christmas, a host of locals devote thousands of hours to the construction of intricate log masterpieces. Most are 25-foot-high, tightly wrought pyramids. Some, like those of industrial maintenance worker Ronald St. Pierre, are detailed reproductions of familiar local subjects, such as a log cabin, an oil rig with derrick, a two-story plantation house with double-curved stairway, or a turn-of-the-century locomotive complete with cowcatcher and smokestack (p. 149). A few whimsical constructions—PeeWee's Playhouse or the roughly cut digits of a graduation year—round out the field. But at the fire chief's signal, all of the structures—regardless of artistry or size—are uniformly torched.

Christmas Eve is the only time of year when River Road, once the only highway between New Orleans and Baton Rouge, becomes a curvy, two-lane gridlock from the Mt. Airy town line west to Convent. Nightfall brings thousands of pedestrians, who swarm back and forth among the cars inching along to get a close-up view of the blazing sentinels. The light radiating from within the geometric skeletons makes them look eerily akin to the chemical plants and refineries that dominate the flat landscape.

From the river waft the rollicking soprano notes of calliopes on paddle wheelers up from New Orleans, the hoarse bass of freighter horns and the insistent buzzing of small craft. The bounce of swamp pop and *chank-a-chank* Cajun music mixes with the blare of jam boxes, car horns and firecrackers, while smells of kerosene, sweet smoke, burned powder, beer and gumbo permeate the air.

Lighting bonfires on Christmas Eve in St. James Parish has been a holiday ritual since the 1880s, though its origin is still debated. The most popular explanation is that the bonfires were started to light the way for Papa Noël, the Cajun version of Santa Claus, as he paddled his pirogue to deliver gifts to good Cajun children—but traditionally Papa arrives on New Year's Eve.

Others say the fires were functional, begun as navigational signals to help guide steamboats through the dense December fog; or religious, to light the way to midnight mass. Or the fires may have celebrated Epiphany, the Twelfth Night, when Christmas trees were taken down and burned, and chestnuts and potatoes roasted over the blaze. Most likely, the bonfires were introduced into the area by French Marist priests who, in 1864, took over Jefferson College (now Manresa House of Retreats) in nearby Convent. The Brothers built their fires on the batture next to the river and entertained their students. The practice caught on, but why it was moved from the traditional New Year's Eve to Christmas Eve remains a mystery.

Whatever its origins, the German-Acadian Coast Historical and Genealogical Society attributes the first Christmas Eve levee bonfire to merchant George Bourgeois in the town of Mt. Airy in 1884. He is said to have collected boxes and packing material in which merchandise for his New Camelia Plantation store arrived, massing them into a flaming heap on the levee across from his business. The flames were so large and salutatory that riverboats pulled right up to his landing to join the Christmas Eve celebration. Bourgeois had also built a game room behind his store where local men played poker and ate gumbo. Sometimes, when they arrived with their sons in tow, the entrepreneur gave the boys fireworks and sent them off to the levee to entertain themselves around a bonfire.

By the turn of the century, says Leonce Haydel, the area's acknowledged unofficial historian, scattered, private bonfires were built on Christmas Eve. Trash wood, scrap lumber, old boxes, cardboard, tires and anything else that fathers and sons could scavenge made a good bonfire in those early days.

Whether social pressure eventually demanded a grander style than that of a trash heap, or whether safety demanded more careful construction, the configuration of levee bonfires evolved from amorphous piles into a conical tepee shape. After World War II the bonfire tradition began to strengthen; and the individual bonfires began to reach higher with the introduction of the pyramid shape: the neat, articulated superstructure imposed over a tepee.

Gathering the wood (willow, which is abundant and fast-growing, is the material of choice) is still largely a father-and-son affair. Today a boy's rite of passage is likely to be the first time he uses a chain saw or the day he's allowed to drive the pickup truck, swaying with a bed of ragtag willow poles, back to the levee.

There, on December weekends, the entire community congregates, either to build bonfires or to offer moral support to those who do. The big night itself has evolved into a typical southern Louisiana festival, with souvenir hunters in search of logoed sweatshirts, and long lines of people waiting for a fresh batch of cracklings. But at its heart, Bonfires on the Levee is still a family-style celebration.

Source

Smithsonian, December, 1989, 146-50. By Mary Ann Sternberg, an authority on Louisiana life.

* * *

Moravian Children's Love Feast

The Children's Love Feast held [in the Moravian Church at Bethlehem, Pennsylvania] at three o'clock on December 24th inaugurates the holiday season. The children together with the choir sing many of the old hymns such as, "Softly the Night is Sleeping" and "Silent Night, Holy Night." Eagerly the group listens to the Minister's Christmas message and his prayer. Then the doors open, and ladies in white enter carrying baskets of sweet buns. Each child takes one and places it on a clean handkerchief on his lap. Soon men come in bearing trays of white mugs, containing warm sweetened coffee. When everybody is served the Minister lifts his cup and takes a sip of coffee and a bite of his Love Feast Bun, as a signal for all to participate in the birthday party of the Baby Jesus. The second part of the service is just as impressive when again the men and women enter carrying trays of lighted bees-wax candles. Each candle is decorated with a paper frill (usually red) to make it more convenient to hold as well as to catch the drip of grease. Tiny tots and teen-age children leave the church carrying their lighted bees-wax candle, carefully protected by a tiny hand, to hurry home to place this light in a window as an invitation to the Baby Jesus to come in.

Source

Pennsylvania Dutchman, V (December 1953), 5. Observed and described by Marion Ball Wilson. The Moravian Church, an evangelical communion, established colonies in America in the 1740s. Among them was Bethlehem, Pennsylvania, where the Christmas love feast takes place.

Moravian Christmas

Christmas Putz and Putzing

The Putz

One of the unique customs of the Moravians is the building of what they call a Christmas Putz (*putz* is from the German verb, *Putzen*—meaning to decorate). Building a Putz, then, is creating a scene to depict the birth of Christ. One may make a simple mantle decoration or a very elaborate miniature landscape under the Christmas tree. In preparation for building the Putz, families make trips to the woods to gather moss, pine, stones and even logs to construct the necessary landscape. Moss is always used as a ground covering, and miniature pine trees may be added to make the scene more natural.

On our visit to Bethlehem [Pennsylvania] we were fortunate to see the large Community Putz in the Moravian School Building as well as two individual ones in a private home. At the school the entire stage was used for the Putz. Many pine trees were used to form the background, with a large decorated tree to one side. An effective landscape was produced by moss, stones and logs as a realistic setting for the beautiful hand carved figures. The majority of these figures and animals are very old, many having been brought from Germany years ago and preserved with loving care by the Moravians. As the Narrator described the various events in the Christmas story, lights would illuminate that particular scene. At the conclusion of the story, when the entire Putz was lighted, it was a thrilling sight to behold.

I was intrigued by the host of "Heavenly Wax Angels" and the Bethlehem star, which hung over the manger. This star, better known as the "Herrnhut Star," is made of heavy white paper, consisting of many points. These many-pointed stars are carefully preserved from year to year in Moravian homes, as this lighted star is usually hung in the hall or on the porch to proclaim its message to friend and traveler. My "Herrnhut Star" hangs on a lower branch of the Christmas tree, where it will shed its kindly light on the Babe in the Manger.

Putzing

"Putzing" is what everybody in Bethlehem does during Christmas week, as it signifies neighborliness and hospitality and wherever one stops he will always find refreshment—a plate of Moravian cookies. There are two distinct kinds of Moravian cookies. The brown ones, dark spicy and very thin, are made in the form of men, birds and animals. The traditional white ones, rich crisp and even thinner, are shaped like stars, hearts and angels. Moravian families treasure their heirloom cookie cutters as well as their carved wooden dough, or *springerle,* boards.

Source

Pennsylvania Dutchman, V (December 1953), 5. Observed and described by Marion Ball Wilson.

* * *

Slovak Christmas Eve Supper

On Christmas Eve our table is spread with lots of food, such as all kinds of fruits, dishes of mixed nuts, candy, *kolácki* (cakes—cheese, poppy seed, and nut), and a dish of little tiny rolls (made out of raised dough) which are covered with poppy seeds, sugar, honey, a little hot milk, and butter. We always have a little Christmas Eve service before we begin to eat—we sing Slovak carols with no musical accompaniment, but my parents know all the tunes to the carols. ("We" refers to my mother and dad, my brother and his wife, and my sister and me.) We always sing *cas radosti* ["Time of Joy"]. After singing a few songs, my mother says the long Christmas Eve prayer, thanking God and asking Him to watch over us, and we conclude with the Lord's Prayer. Then my Dad takes the *oplatki* (very thin wafers shaped oblong with inscriptions on them) and on each one he spreads a little honey and gives us one each. We eat this first. Then comes the soup—the traditional soup being cabbage and meat cooked together, but since none of the family is especially fond of this kind, we have either chicken or mushroom soup—it almost always has some meat in it. After the soup we eat the *buchti,* the little rolls covered with poppy seed; then we usually eat a little of everything on the table, some fruit, some nuts, *kolácki,* and candy. We always have a temptation to nibble at something before the meal begins, but my parents have a little saying that goes well at this time: "Nibble now and you will nibble before each meal the rest of your life!" The candle on the table stays lighted through the meal and until the time we go to bed. . . .I enjoy this Christmas tradition very much, and hope that I can continue it when I have a home of my own. (That is, everything but the cabbage soup.)

Source

New York Folklore Quarterly, VIII (1952), 311-12. Mildred Buso describes the traditional Christmas Eve meal of her Slovak-speaking family then living in Mottville, Onondaga County, New York.

* * *

Polish Christmas Eve Supper

When my grandmother came to this country from Poland, she was sixteen. Even at this age she brought with her holiday customs, proverbs, recipes, games, and other folk material typical of life in Poland. In becoming Americanized there was much that she forgot, but there is much that she remembers. In talking with her recently I learned a great deal about the Polish people, and I can see her influence in many things our family does today. I would like to share with you some of her reminiscences; I have added comments where these customs are still followed in our family.

On Christmas Eve the whole family gathers together for the evening meal, called *wilia,* waiting for the first star to appear before beginning the meal. Earlier in the week each family received from the church the communion wafer; it is a large rectangular piece, rather than the small circles, and is called *opatek.* This is passed down the table, each person breaking off a small piece for himself and wishing the person next to him good luck, good health, and a long life. The table is covered with white cloth, over which straw is placed. In the center of the table is a figure of Christ in the crib, and an extra place is set for a stranger. Twelve different types of foods are served, one for each of the apostles. Foods included are fish; *pierogi,* which is a dough filled with cheese, cabbage, potatoes, or fruit; *barszcz,* a soup made with beets or mushrooms; *babka,* a sweet bread with raisins; and *mazurek,* a cookie with raisins, figs, and dates. (We still [in 1968] gather together for the meal, starting with the *opatek* and having the traditional foods, but straw is no longer placed on the table, nor is an extra place set; the meal begins as soon as everyone arrives.)

Source

New York Folklore Quarterly, XXIV (1968), 302. Described by Robert Maziarz, as traditionally observed and remembered by his family. His Polish-born grandparents settled in New York Mills, New York.

* * *

Christmas Cooking, Italian Style

In old southern Italy, it was habitual to retire and rise early during the year. Nevertheless, a few evenings before Christmas meant going to bed late, at least, for the young and older women, who helped one another prepare and bake their traditional *porcellate* [fruit cookies] and *biscotti* [biscuits] which required many hands. There was much rubbing of tired, sleepy eyes, but the pleasure of sharing the festive spirit was immense as goodies were placed one by one on oblong metal trays, then into brick ovens, cleaned of their ashes from burning wood that helped make them white-hot. After inserting the *balata* (a small, iron door) and securing it with wet rags around its edges, to prevent air escaping into those ovens, they chattered about the important day and waited for golden brown delicacies to come from the oven....

The traditions of southern Italian holiday cooking are continued by many in the United States, and the recipes are offerings for rich and delicious holiday eating.

Biscotti Italiani

6 eggs
1 cup sugar
4½ cups flour
4 tsp. baking powder

8 oz. jar of maraschino cherries (chopped)
½ tsp. salt
¼ lb. butter (creamed)
3 oz. finely chopped almonds

Beat eggs with salt. Add sugar and beat thoroughly. Sift flour and baking powder. Add to eggs and sugar mixture. Add cherries, cherry liquid, butter and almonds. Mix well until dough is smooth. Cut dough into 4 even sections. On greased cookie sheets, spoon and shape dough into 4 oblong loaves, 5 inches wide and ¾ inch thick. Bake in 375 degree oven for 25 minutes. Remove from oven and cut into 1 inch slices. Let bake for another 10 minutes.

Porcellate Siciliani

¾ cup of shortening
½ cup of sugar
2 eggs
3½ cups flour
3 tsp. baking powder
⅓ tsp. salt
½ cup lukewarm water
2 tsp. vanilla extract
   confectioner's sugar

FILLING:

1 cup chopped, roasted almonds
3 cups ground dry figs
1½ cups ground raisins
4 tsp. grated orange rind
1¼ cups water
½ cup sugar
1 tsp. cinnamon

Place figs and raisins in casserole with water over low heat. Cook for 5 minutes stirring constantly. Remove from heat. Add almonds, orange rind, sugar and cinnamon. Let cool. Makes 3½ dozen.

Combine all dry ingredients. Add eggs. Blend in shortening with hands until fine. Then add water and vanilla. Knead until smooth. Divide dough. Roll ⅛ inch thick into 3½ inch squares. Fill with fruit. Fold and pinch edges. Make horseshoe shapes. Place on cookie sheets. Bake for 25 minutes in 375 degree oven. Remove from oven. Cool. Sprinkle with confectioner's sugar.

Source

New York Folklore Quarterly, XXI (1965), 189, 191-92. These traditional Christmas recipes are from an article on "Southern Italian Folklore in New York City," by Pauline N. Barrese. Informants not given.

* * *

Slovenian Christmas Customs

On Christmas Eve it was customary for each child to set a plate on the table before going to bed. The next morning young children would find apples, cookies, walnuts, and a switch on the plate. (Incidentally, the switches were hung up in the kitchen, and when a child was punished, he had to get his own switch for his parent to use.) School children would receive, in addition to the fruit and switches, pencils and tablets. Older girls got hose, head kerchiefs, aprons; older boys, bandanas, hose, and knives. In Slovenia this same kind of gift exchange takes place on December 5, the night before St. Nicholas' Day, and there are no presents given on Christmas. Here [in Indianapolis, c. 1946], however, Slovenian children would be too disappointed not to have gifts as their American friends do.

The day before Christmas is a day of fasting. After chores are finished, and everyone is dressed in his Sunday best, all kneel and pray the rosary three times. Then a light supper is served, consisting of coffee, milk, or wine, potica, and English walnuts. After eating, the family prepares the crèche on a shelf which is always built in a corner of the room for that purpose. Moss is laid down first, then the stable with the manger and the figures and animals. Small candles are placed around and lighted. Today virtually every family still has the crèche, but Christmas tree lights are used as a precaution against fire. Some of the people had paper angels that could be folded flat and used from year to year. These angels formed a circle around the candles. Either the way they were made or the heat of the candles made them flutter, much to the children's delight. The crèche took the place of our tree, but today Slovenians usually have both.

On Christmas Eve not even the children go to bed. There is an exchange of neighborly visits. At virtually every house there is a lot of dancing and singing to the music of the harmonica (accordian). It is a gay time. At four A.M. a huge breakfast is served. After a little rest and completion of chores they are ready for a huge noon dinner. There are several kinds of meat, individual loaves of bread, poticas with different fillings, such as nuts and raisins, cottage cheese, cracklings, and poppy seeds. Plates are filled and heaped high with a piece or slice of each kind of food on the table. There is no hurry about eating; in fact, the one who can make his food last the longest is supposed to be the thriftiest. What he can't eat is hidden, and there is fun finding and stealing the food.

In the afternoon there is more dancing and singing. Then a light supper is served, and the glorious holiday is over.

Source

Hoosier Folklore, VI (1947), 122-23. Collected by Margaret Montgomery from a Mrs. Reinhold, a Slovenian-speaking housewife whose mother came to the United States "after World War I." For information on the Indianapolis Slovenian community, see note on "Blessing Food on Holy Saturday," p. 157.

Swedish Pioneers Celebrate Christmas

The Swedes [in Iowa, ca. 1879] appear to have but one holiday during the year; that is Christmas. But they make the most of that. All their energies are directed towards having a good time then, and this year they succeeded admirably. In the family the festivities began Christmas Eve. While all sat carelessly around the fire the door suddenly opened and a bundle was thrown in. The name of the recipient is on each package, but Santa Claus himself is invisible; more or less bundles come as the number of years, friends, or the length of the purse may be. Your wife engages a neighbor boy to throw in a box of cigars with your name on it, while you bespeak another to throw in a silk handkerchief appropriately inscribed, and so on. At 5 o'clock on Christmas morning they hie themselves to the church where they hold services which last until sunrise. With the building brilliantly illuminated with four large twelve-light chandeliers, twenty side lamps and nearly two hundred tapers one is reminded of the customs of the Catholic church. Above the altar, and in front of the pulpit, was a large arch crowned with an illumination and sustaining twenty-three tapers. On the illumination, was inscribed the motto; "*Åra vare Gud i höjden,*" which, translated, means "Glory be to God in the highest." At either side of the altar stood a chandelier with eighteen tapers; in each window an arch with six, and in fact there was a taper in every nook and corner. These morning services were followed in the evening by a Christmas tree. With the house brilliantly lighted as in the morning, the tree loaded with nice presents and the floor beneath thickly strewn with the fruit too heavy for the boughs; of course the children enjoyed themselves.

Source

Swedish Pioneer History Quarterly, XII (1961), 160-61. Reprinted by Walter F. Peterson from a fragment of *The Record,* a weekly newspaper published in Red Oak, southwest Iowa. Peterson estimates the date as 1879 and states about half of the population in the Red Oak section was of Swedish origin.

* * *

A Christmas Wheat Sheaf for the Birds

Hugo Nisbeth, a Swedish traveler who visited Minnesota in 1872, commented: "It is not only the Scandinavians who celebrate Christmas here in America in a true ancient northern fashion, but even the Americans themselves have in late years begun to give more and more attention to this festival of the children and have as nearly as possible taken our method of celebration as a pattern." He drove out onto the prairie near Litchfield, where he spent the Christmas holiday with one of his countrymen who was living in a sod house, built half above and half under ground.

Upon his return to Sweden, Nisbeth published a book about his travels in which he tells about the frontier festivities. The day before Christmas was spent in preparing for the celebration; among other things a "small sheaf of unthreshed wheat was set out for the few birds that at times circled around the house, in accordance with the lovely old Swedish custom." As in the fatherland, the principal celebration took place on Christmas Eve. "There was no Christmas tree, for fir trees are not yet planted in this part of Minnesota," he records, "but two candles stood on the white covered table and round these were placed a multitude of Christmas cakes in various shapes made by the housewife and such small presents as these pioneers were able to afford, to which I added those I had brought." Nisbeth was disappointed because the traditional Swedish Christmas dishes, *lutfisk* [codfish preserved in wood ashes] and rice porridge, were not served, but he observes that the "ham which took the place of honor in their stead banished all doubt that the settler's labor and sacrifice had not received its reward." After the meal the children were given their presents.

Source

Minnesota History, XVI (1935), 388-90. From an article on holiday celebrations by Bertha L. Heilbron who quotes from the travel account of Hugo Nisbeth, published in Stockholm in 1874.

* * *

Danish Christmas Tree

Dancing on Christmas Eve around a Christmas tree placed in the middle of my grandmother's and grandfather's living room was always a highlight of each year when I was a child [in Troy, New York]. My small hand in my grandfather's big one, I helped form a complete family ring around the tree. Then 'round and 'round the tree we moved, gliding and skipping, while we sang songs, "Nu hav ve Jul igen" [Now have we Yuletide again] for my grandparents and "Away in a Manger" for the young folks. The words of the Danish song made no sense to me, but they and the peppy tune to which they were sung were inseparable from the excitement of Christmas Eve....

On farms [in Denmark] before nightfall on Christmas Eve ... cattle are given something extra to eat, and the pets receive tidbits, too. A sheaf of grain for the birds is hung outside. (In our family when the Christmas tree was taken out of the house, it was put in the back yard and hung with bread for the birds.)...

After dinner [in Denmark] the family join hands in a circle and dance around the Christmas tree, which is trimmed gaily with national flags, candies, and bright trimmings. (I recall the paper red and white Danish flags strung along a long string hanging from bough to bough of the tree and the American flag on a lollypop stick fastened to another branch....)

Source

New York Folklore Quarterly, X (1954), 266-68. Mildred R. Larson recalls Christmas customs current in Troy, New York, among families of Danish descent and compares them with customs in Denmark collected from Mrs. Agner Larsen, formerly of Copenhagen.

* * *

Norwegian Pioneer Christmas

The early [Wisconsin] pioneers brought all the old country's customs with them. Two weeks before the day, they commenced making preparations to celebrate the great event. I am afraid it wasn't so much in honor of the Savior born to mankind, as it was the anticipation of a long holiday free from labor, full of gaiety, and with all they could eat and drink of the best that could be produced. For be it known, Jul consisted not of one day as it does with us, but of thirteen days, and some even added one more before the celebration finally ended. No labor of any kind, except feeding the stock, could be done until after New Year, the third of January, there being two New Year holidays. The first three days of Christmas were considered too holy for any gaiety. If anyone could not get to church, a sermon must be read by the head of the family while all other members sat around listening. But when the three days were up, then the real old pagan Yulefest started with parties and dances. A deep rooted respect for the Christian holiday kept everybody within the bounds of decency. There were no wild parties, but all enjoyed themselves to the uttermost while it lasted. As the years went by, this lengthy holiday was shortened, but even today among the older people Christmas lasts till New Year.

In my early days many pagan customs connected with that Jul gaiety were still in vogue. Prominent among them was the custom of what was called 'going Julebuk.' This consisted in dressing up in the most grotesque and fantastic manner that we could invent, put a mask over our faces, and go around from house to house as long as any one was up. It was always done evenings, and nearly always by young people, the greater the number the better. We would sneak up to the house, rap at the door and when it was opened, burst in, often filling the room. We would then parade around the room a few minutes, giving the inmates a chance to identify us if they could, but never daring to talk lest they would recognize our voices. I never knew the origin or meaning of this custom, but I do know that we had lots of fun.

The parties and dances were mostly for the younger set, the older people using these two weeks mostly for visiting each other. Through any other part of the year the steady grind of making a living and opening up a farm did not give any time for visiting, so now through these holidays they made up for it. Those who in the old country had been near neighbors and close friends, but here lived miles apart, would now come in whole sleigh loads and visit for several days. Then likely as not when the visit was over, those who had been hosts would get into their sleighs and follow their friends home for a stay of several days. Invitations for those long visits had perhaps gone out and been accepted months before, so they were seldom surprise visits, otherwise it would often have been well-nigh impossible in those cramped quarters to receive so many guests at a time. The pure friendship and the hospitality of those early settlers are something rarely found today. They may have been sadly lacking in the true Christmas spirit as the incentive, but surely 'Peace on earth, good will toward men' reigned supreme through those well earned holidays.

Giving each other gifts was not so much in vogue in those days. However, gifts were often given and were always of a substantial nature, such as a quarter of beef or pork, or a sack of flour, and always given to those who were in need. If the gifts could be given without revealing the identity of the givers, they were given that way. The Christmas spirit of today is a far cry from what it was in those days.

Source

Wisconsin Magazine of History, XXI (1937-1938), 176-7. From "Some Recollections of Thomas Pederson." Cf. "Greeting the New Year," p. 1; "New Year's Calling," p. 13; and "New Year's Calling in Early Wisconsin," p. 14.

* * *

Cornish Miners and Christmas Underground

In the very early days the headframes over [mining] shafts were bedecked with holly or evergreen branches at Christmas time. Although many old-timers have heard of this custom, I have only talked with one who actually knows it at first hand. Leon Ponce, a venerable and well-informed Chilean at Columbia, remembers having seen, when a boy, a decorated headframe at Murphys. Likewise the custom of taking Christmas trees underground was observed for a time in the Cornish camps in California as well as those in Michigan. In an attempt to revive this old custom, miners at the Argonaut some years ago installed a Christmas tree on the landing of the 5500-foot level.

The custom of singing carols underground on Christmas Eve, which once flourished, is now not widely known. The Grass Valley Carol Choir, conducted by Harold J. George, himself of Cornish extraction, has tried to revive it. On Christmas Eve, 1940, this choir broadcast over a national radio hook-up from the 2000-foot level of the Idaho-Maryland Mine, and the response was gratifying enough to justify making it an annual event. Carol singing on the main streets of Grass Valley by Welsh and Cornish groups goes on today as it has since the 'fifties [1850s].

Source

California Folklore Quarterly, I (1942), 152. From an essay by Wayland D. Hand on California miners' folklore. He notes that the

customs of decorating the headframes over mine shafts and carol singing in the mines are well known in Cornwall.

* * *

Welsh Christmas Greeting

This rhyme is a greeting with which Welsh folk [in the mining camps of East Tennessee and Kentucky] greeted each other on Christmas morning. It was the custom to go from house to house early Christmas morning and recite this greeting. The family in the house thus greeted asked those outside to come in and receive gifts. The custom of obtaining gifts in this manner was not followed when the collector was a child, but it was when her mother, Mrs. A.J. Jones, was young.

> I wish you a merry Christmas and a happy New Year,
> A pocket full of money and a cellar full of beer,
> A big fat hog to last you the year.
> The roads are very muddy, and my shoes are very clean,
> I got a little pocket to put a penny in.

Source

Tennessee Folklore Society Bulletin, IX (December 1943), 1-2. Collected by Wynn Jones, a graduate student at the University of Tennessee, as remembered in her family. Her mother's parents are both Welsh and her father came to the United States from Wales when he was sixteen. For background, see "Eisteddfod on St. David's Day," p. 115.

* * *

Belsnickels among the Pennsylvania Dutch

Christmas Eve, along about 8 o'clock, one would hear a sharp knock on the door and one of the parents would open up. There in the doorway stood some of the weirdest characters that one ever had the occasion to behold. Belsnickels they were, masked and carrying a peeled willow whip or a buggy whip. Then the kids would get a workout. A belsnickel demanded to hear their *grischtdawgs schtick* (a poem memorized for the Sunday school Christmas festival) or the latest poem that was learned in school. After this devilment was indulged in for awhile, there began to appear from the folds of the belsnickel's garments chestnuts, walnuts, peanuts and pretzels. These were tossed in front of the children and when they tried to pick them up, they were whipped around the legs with the willows or buggy whip. After a few moments, however, the kids were allowed to pick up what had been thrown on the floor for them.

Then came the host's time to act. The woman of the house would bring *grischtdawgs kichlin* (Christmas cookies) and apples. The man of the house went to the cellar for a pitcher of *schdeefens schtofft* (hard cider) or a jug of homemade wine, or both. Well, you can imagine what happened to the belsnickel along about the fifth stop. I can pity those kids today that were the victims of one of the later stops. Those lashes of the whip stung. I know.

In my youth in Saegersville, Lehigh County, I do not recall ever seeing an adult belsnickel. Instead, we children would disguise ourselves by putting on a mask and hanging some burlap bags over our shoulders. Then we went from house to house in the village, begging for good things to eat. (I still remember who baked the best cookies in Saegersville.)

Source and Comment

Pennsylvania Dutchman, II (December 15, 1950), 7, 3. The description of belsnickeling on Christmas Eve is from an anonymous reader "who hails from Lancaster County." The recollection from Lehigh County is that of Alfred L. Shoemaker. Cf. "A Visit from El Agüelo," p. 437; and "Belsnickels and Shanghais," p. 444.

Belsnickels or Belsnickles is a corruption of the name of a German folk figure, Pelz Nicholas or Furry Nicholas, whose body was covered with fur or who wore furs. He gave presents to the deserving and chastised the wicked during the Christmas season. The fur trimming on Santa Claus' red suit is a legacy of Pelz Nicholas.

* * *

The John Kuner Ceremony

In antebellum North Carolina, John Kuner was quite a figure at Christmas, especially in the counties bordering Albemarle Sound and in the lower Cape Fear River region. He was not, as has sometimes been thought, confined to Wilmington, where, according to *The Frank C. Brown Collection of North Carolina Folklore* (I, 240), "on Christmas Eve, John Kuners, Negroes, went about singing, dressed in tatters with strips of gay colors sewn to their garments. All were men, but some dressed as women. They wore masks. Some rattled beef ribs; others had cow horns, triangles, Jew's-harps. They collected pennies at each house." This entry, taken from Paul Green's contributions to the collection, acknowledges that the "custom resembles that reported from the Bahamas."

If one may draw conclusions from the few first-hand accounts in North Carolina, the John Kuner ceremony was similar in all areas. Regardless of how the custom arrived in the state—and it seems not to have been practiced in any other section of the country—it flourished as a result of the leniency which slave-owners allowed their charges during the Christmas season. In 1824, Dr. James Norcum of Edenton wrote that at Christmas, slaves had "comparative freedom," that they had "dances & entertainments among themselves," and that drunkenness was only "too common on these occasions."

In 1849, George Higby Throop, a Northern schoolmaster at Scotch Hall plantation in Bertie County across the Chowan River from Edenton, was eyewitness to the John Kooner [sic] antics. It was explained to Throop that

> "... The negroes have a custom here of dressing one of their number at Christmas in as many rags

as he can well carry. He wears a mask, too, and sometimes a stuffed coon-skin above it, so arranged as to give him the appearance of being some seven or eight feet high. He goes through a variety of pranks, which you will have an opportunity to see by and by, and he is accompanied by a crowd of negroes, who make all the noise and music for his worship the John Kooner."...

Breakfast was announced, and we had barely left the table when a loud shout betokened the arrival of the hero of the Christmas frolic. We hastened to the door. As the negroes approached, one of the number was singing a quaint song, the only words of which that I could distinguish were those belonging to the chorus, "Blow dat horn ag'in!" One of them carried a rude deal box, over which a dried sheep-skin had been drawn and nailed, and on this, as if his salvation depended on it, the man was thumping with ear-splitting din. Beside him was another, who kept up a fierce rattle of castanets; another beat a jaw-bone of some horse departed this life; and still another had a clevis, which he beat with an iron bolt, thereby making a very tolerable substitute for a triangle. The chief mummer, or John Kooner, kept up, in the meantime, all conceivable distortions of body and limbs, while his followers pretended to provoke his ire by thrusting sticks between his legs. One of the party seemed to officiate as bear-leader, to direct the motions of the unknown chief mummer. They approached the piazza, knelt on the ground, and continued to sing, one of them improvising the words while the rest sang in chorus, "O! dear maussa! O! dear missus! Wish ye merry Christmas!" The expected dram was given them. A few pieces of silver were thrown from the piazza, and they left us, singing a roisterly song, the chorus of which was "By on de row!"

Another eyewitness wrote of what happened at Somerset Place, the large Josiah Collins plantation on Lake Phelps, across Albemarle Sound from Scotch Hall and Edenton. It was about 1855 that this impressionable young man observed the custom of "John Koonering," followed by the slaves

> notably on Christmas day. The *leading* character is the "ragman," whose "get-up" consists in a costume of rags, so arranged that one end of each hangs loose and dangles; two great ox horns, attached to the skin of a raccoon, which is drawn over the head and face, leaving apertures only for the eyes and mouth; sandals of the skin of some wild "varmint;" several cow or sheep bells or strings of dried goats' horns hanging about their shoulders, and so arranged as to jingle at every movement; and a short stick of seasoned wood, carried in his hands.

The *second* part is taken by the best looking darkey of the place, who wears no disguise, but is simply arrayed in what they call his "Sunday-go-to-meeting suit," and carries in his hand a small bowl or tin cup, while the other parts are appropriated by some half a dozen fellows, each arrayed fantastically in ribbons, rags, and feathers, and bearing between them several so-called musical instruments or "gumba boxes," which consist of wooden frames covered over with tanned sheep-skins. These are usually followed by a motley crowd of all ages, dressed in their ordinary working clothes which seemingly comes as a guard of honor to the performers.

Having thus given an idea of the *characters* I will describe the *performance* as I first saw it at the "Lake." Coming up to the front door of the "great house," the musicians commenced to beat their gumba-boxes violently, while characters No. 1 and No. 2 entered upon a dance of the most extraordinary character—a combination of bodily contortions, flings, kicks, gyrations, and antics of every imaginable description, seemingly acting as partners, and yet each trying to excel the other in the variety and grotesqueness of his movements. At the same time No. 2 led off with a song of a strange, monotonous cadence, which seemed extemporized for the occasion, and to run somewhat in this wise:

"My massa am a white man, juba!
Old missus am a lady, juba!
De children am de honey-pods, juba! juba!
Krismas come but once a year, juba!
Juba! juba! O, ye juba!

"De darkeys lubs de hoe-cake, juba!
Take de 'quarter' for to buy it, juba!
Fetch him long, you white folks, juba! juba!
Krismas come but once a year, juba!
Juba! juba! O, ye juba!

while the whole crowd joined in the chorus, shouting and clapping their hands in the wildest glee. After singing a verse or two No. 2 moved up to the master, with his hat in one hand and a tin cup in the other, to receive the expected "quarter," and, while making the lowest obeisance, shouted: "May de good Lord bless old massa and missus, and all de young massas, juba!" The "rag man" during this part of the performance continued his dancing, singing at the top of his voice the same refrain, and striking vigorously at the crowd, as first one and then another of its members attempted to tear off his "head gear" and to reveal his identity. And then the expected "quarter" having been jingled for some time in the tin cup, the performers moved on to visit in turn the young gentlemen's colony, the tutor's rooms, the parson's study, the overseer's house, and, finally, the quarters, to wind up with a grand jollification, in which all took part until they broke down and gave it up from sheer exhaustion. Except at the "Lake" and in Edenton, where it originated [sic] with the Collins' negroes, I never witnessed this performance in America, and I was convinced from the first that it was of foreign origin, based on some festive ceremony which the negroes had inherited from their African ancestors.

Rebecca Cameron (1844-1936) of Hillsborough wrote of the antebellum Christmas festivities at Buchoi, her grandfather's rice plantation on the Cape Fear River. As the salves ventured into the swamp to fell the Yule log, they "chanted a part of the 'Coonah' song":

> Christmas comes but once a year,
> Ho rang du rango!
> Let everybody have a share,
> Ho rang du rango!

At Buchoi, the second day after Christmas was set aside for the John Coonah ceremony:

Some time in the course of the morning an ebony herald, breathless with excitement, would project the announcement: "De John Coonahs comin'!" and away flew every pair of feet within nursery precincts.

There they come sure enough! A long, grotesque procession, winding slowly over the hill from the quarters; a dense body of men (the women took no part in it, save as spectators) dressed in the oddest, most fantastic garb, representing birds and beasts and men, ragged and tattered, until "ragged as a Coonah" was a common plantation simile; with stripes and tatters of all sorts of cloth, in which white and red flannel had a conspicuous part, sewed all over their clothes in tufts and fringes. They were, indeed, a marvelous spectacle. Rude imitations of animals' heads, with and without horns, hid some faces; pasteboard masks covered some, while streaks and spots of red, white and yellow paint metamorphosed others, and immense beards of horse hair or Spanish moss, were plentiful.

The leader—for there seemed to be some regular organization among them, though I could never persuade any negro to explain it to me—was the most fantastic figure among them all. A gigantic pair of branching deer horns decorated his head; his arms, bare to the elbows, were hung with bracelets thickly set with jingling bells and metal rings; similar bells were fastened to the fringes of rags around his legs.

The banjo, the bones, triangles, castanets, fifes, drums and all manner of plantation musical instruments, accompanied the procession. One of the Coonahs, generally a small and very nimble man, dressed in woman's clothes, and though dancing with frantic zeal, never violated the proprieties supposed to be incumbent upon the wearer of skirts.

Once before the hall-door the leader snapped his whip with a crack like a pistol-shot. Everything stood still for an instant; we dared not draw a breath and could hear the tumultuous beating of our hearts as we pressed close to mammy or grandpa.

The awful stillness is broken by another resonant crack of the whip, and at the instant the whole medley of instruments began to play, and, with their first note, out into the open sprang the dancers. Those weird, grotesque, even hideous creatures embody the very ideal of joyous, harmonious movement. Faster and faster rings out the wild, barbaric melody; faster and faster falls the beat of the flying feet, never missing the time by the space of a midget's breath. One after the other of the dancers fall out of line, until only the woman and the leader are left to exhibit their best steps and movements.

About this time one of the dancers, a hideous travesty of a bear, snatches a hat off the head of the nearest pickaninny, and begins to go around to the "white folks" to gather the harvest of pennies with which every one is provided. All the while the dance was in progress the musical voice of the leader was chanting the Coonah song, the refrain of which was taken up by hundreds of voices.

As the wild chant draws to a close out of the hall door run a bevy of white children with laps and hats full of nuts, raisins, apples, oranges, cakes and candy, and scatter the whole among the crowd. Such a scramble as follows! The last fragment gathered up, all at once the leader cracks his whip, and whirls around with his face from the house, and the crowd marches to the next plantation. . . .

Oddly enough, the custom survived for a while among whites who seem not to have been aware of its Negro origin. In eastern North Carolina villages before the turn of the century, "joncooners" were an established part of the Christmas observance.

Joncooners were young men, usually the beaux of the village, who on Christmas afternoon—never any other time—dressed up in the most outlandish feminine attire they could find, masked, and rode horseback up and down the streets throughout the afternoon. Their masks were not the romantic-looking black ones such as are worn to masquerade balls, but awful-looking "scare-faces." A joncooner was certainly not good to look at. To one who did not know what composed him he was unspeakably terrifying.

In Fayetteville the "Johnny Cooners" were said to be "the rag-tag and bob-tail of the community, and children." They went about the streets singing,

> Oh, poor Cooner Johns
> Farm, farm, my lady;
> Give poor Cooner one more cent,
> Farm, farm, my lady.

The word *farm* was presumably a contraction of *for me*. . . .

But the custom was fading away, even among the whites. When the brash young men no longer paraded the streets, the boys of the town brought on a gentler observance. There remains a reminiscence from Wilmington in 1905:

Do you member when we went "Coonering"? Each year after the exciting festivities of Christmas Day had gone by, and, in an effort perhaps to overcome the let down feeling, the boys of my neighborhood . . . began to think of "Coonering." "Coonering" was engaged in at no other time except between Christmas Day and the New Year.

A group of from five to ten boys ranging in age from nine to sixteen would with great preparation gather together after supper, when the dark had fallen, and each would don whatever costume or garment he had been able to get. There were sashes, and shawls, overcoats, and long pants (most of us being in knee pants at that time). There were red bandannas and shirts and dresses. Everything had to be old and ill fitting. And then there was always the "Cooner Face" or mask to completely cover the features, so that none could tell who we were. We were always a motley crew.

The procedure was to call on selected homes in the neighborhood. We only called upon those we knew and those we liked. We would ring the front door bell. I do not remember ever having been refused admittance, and it was always done with an apparent pleasure coupled with considerable amusement. We did not call on the children, but upon the older folk. Our own particular homes were omitted, and left for others to call upon, which they always did.

When admitted we were ushered into the living room or the parlor and comfortably seated. Then began a conversation mostly led by those we had come to visit. We did not sing and we had no particular program to follow. We did not try to say or do something funny, but just fitted ourselves into the mood of the home we were in. There was plenty of giggling however.

It being the Christmas season there was always plenty of fruit and candy around, and we were generously plied with these, which we put into our pockets, as to eat would mean the removal of "Cooner-faces," and that was just not done. We were glad to get and accepted the candy, but that was not our purpose, as most of us at this season had plenty of that at home. We never stayed long at any house, and seldom overstayed our welcome, and in that manner were able to make several calls in one night, and before time to be in bed around ten as our mothers had demanded.

What was the real purpose? Purpose!? There wasn't any purpose. It was just fun, and we had fun, getting ready, doing, and laughing about it afterwards. Why did we do it? Well, I did it because my older brother had done it. My father had gone "Coonering" before me, and they appeared to have been pleased with it and had fun.

I never knew that there was any other name for a funny face, or mask, as we call them now, but a "Cooner-face." I was astonished to find in my later years that only in Wilmington were they so called. At any time of the year a mask was a "Cooner-face," no matter what it looked like or when. But we never went "Coonering" except at the Christmas season.

During the Christmas of 1905, Edward Ash, Glasgow Hicks, Hart McKoy and I went "Coonering" and called on the Kenlys. They had a visitor from the North who was so intrigued by our local custom (which I then thought universal) that she had us dress up again the next day, and she took our picture, which I still have.

Source and Comment

North Carolina Folklore Journal, XIX (1971), 161-66, 169-71. Richard Walser, author of this description of the John Kuner (variously spelled) Christmas ceremony, began his study after seeing, in 1969, a similar ceremony at Nevis in the West Indies. The printed descriptions that he quotes in chronological order are: *Bertie: or, Life in the Old Field* by "Capt. Gregory Seaworthy," pseudonym of George Higby Throop, Philadelphia, 1851, 217-19; Edward Warren, *A Doctor's Experiences in Three Continents,* Baltimore, 1885, 200-203; Rebecca Cameron, "Christmas at Buchoi, a North Carolina Rice Plantation," *The North Carolina Booklet,* July 1913, 3, 8-10; Frank English Cox, Raleigh *News and Observer,* December 13, 1936; Nell Battle, Raleigh *News and Observer,* December 22, 1935; and Henry Bacon McKoy, *Wilmington, N. C.—Do You Remember When?,* Greenville, S.C., 1957, 141-45.

For the origin of the custom, see Ira DeA. Reid, "The John Canoe Festival: A New World Africanism," *Phylon,* III (1942), 349-70. Reid argues that the prototype was a tribal chief, John Connu, who lived c. 1720 on the Guinea Coast. A festival he originated was brought by slaves to the West Indies and thence to North Carolina, the only place in the United States where it has been found. But see also "St. George's Play," p. 449.

* * *

Christmas Shooters

Groups of shooters once made the rounds of American communities at Christmas, fired guns for their neighbors, and were then invited in for refreshments. These Christ-

mas shooting rounds were celebrated in Indiana in the 1850s: "Bands of young men armed with muskets, horns and conch-shells made the rounds of the neighborhood on Christmas eve, shooting in front of houses and demanding treats of liquor, apples, pies or cakes, according to taste or local custom." Another instance of the Christmas rounds can be found in the autobiography of Gert Göbel (1816-1896), a German settler in Missouri. Presumably his account describes the custom as practiced in Franklin County, on the Missouri River, where he and his parents settled in 1834.

> The celebration of Christmas was a good deal simpler. A religious observance was out of the question, nor were gifts exchanged. Even less known was the fine German custom of decorating a Christmas tree. There was just shooting. On Christmas Eve, a number of young fellows from the neighborhood banded together, and, after they had gathered together not only their hunting rifles but also old muskets and horse pistols from the Revolutionary War and had loaded them almost to the bursting point, they went from house to house. They approached a house as quietly as possible and then fired a mighty volley, to the fright of the women and children, and, if someone did not appear then, another volley no doubt followed. But usually the man of the house opened the door immediately, fired his own gun in greeting and invited the whole company into the house. There the whiskey jug made the rounds, and some pastry was also handed around. After everyone had chatted for a little while, the whole band set out for the next farm, where the same racket started up anew. In this way, this mischief was carried on until morning, and since, as a rule, a number of such bands were out and about one could often hear all night the roaring and rattling of guns from all directions.

A third account of the Christmas shooting rounds concerns Boone County, Iowa, just northwest of Des Moines.

> One of the ways in which the coming of Christmas was celebrated in the early history of the county was for a number of men to get together on Christmas eve, each one having a gun and about an hour after dark set in, they would start on a trip and visit many of the homes in the neighborhood. Before starting they would elect one of their number captain whose commands they must all obey.

> On arriving at a house the captain would call out the name of the owner in a stentorian voice and then order his men to fire. The noise produced shook the house and reverberated among the hills. When the noise subsided the man of the house would open the door and invite the men to come in. His hospitality was accepted with pleasure, and there were hand shakings and congratulations,

joking and laughter. The good woman of the house would then set out pies and cakes and serve warm coffee, which was partaken of with a relish.

The men would then reload their guns and pass on to the next house. These visits were kept up until midnight, when Christmas was ushered in and then they would separate and depart for their homes. At times in making their departure, some devoted person would start a familiar hymn and all of them would join in singing it. It sometimes happened that a party of this kind would call at a house where a number of persons were assembled for devotional purposes. On such occasions the men would tarry for a while, get down on their knees when prayer was offered and join in the singing.

A fourth account of the Christmas shooting rounds comes from the South Carolina "Dutch Fork," an area between the Broad and Saluda rivers settled by Germans and Swiss-Germans in the eighteenth century. The account, by John A. Chapman, describes the rounds in the 1830s:

Sixty years ago, the young men of the Dutch Fork retained many of the wild, frolicksome habits which their forefathers brought with them from the Fatherland. Perhaps the wildest of these customs was, to ramble throughout the night of Christmas Eve, in companies of a dozen persons, from house to house, firing heavily charged guns, and having thus aroused the family they would enter the domicile with stamping scramble to the blazing fire, greedily eat the *praetzilies* and *schneckilies,* imbibe, with many a rugged joke and ringing peal of laughter, heavy draughts of a compound liquor made of rum and sugar, butter and allspice stewed together, and then, "With monie an eldritch screetch an' hollo," rush out into the night to visit the next neighbor.

Source and Comment

Journal of American Folklore, LXXXVI (1973), 48-49. Walter L. Robbins collected and analyzed American and European descriptions of this custom as practiced on Christmas and New Year's. He concludes that it is "German in origin." His quotations are fully documented. Cf. " Greeting the New Year," p. 1. Editor H.C. recalls exuberant Christmas shooters on Indian Branch, Darlington County, South Carolina, in the 1930s occasionally shooting off dynamite to celebrate the holiday.

* * *

Aguinaldos

Aguinaldo: traditional Christmas-carol, frequently, but not always in couplet form; similar to the Mexican *posadas* and the Spanish *villancico*; in Puerto Rico, occasionally referred to as *parranda*: (as in Spain, a revel, or to go reveling). It is customary to offer gifts to singers during the Christmas season. The term *aguinaldo* has come to stand for the gift itself. In Puerto Rico during Christmas season

singers dressed as "The Three Kings" are commonly seen going from house to house asking for *aguinaldos.*

Demen mi aguinaldo	Give me my Christmas gift
Si me lo han de dar	If you are going to give it to me
Que la noche es larga	For the night is long
Y tenemos que andar.	And we have to walk.
A la media noche	At midnight
El gallo cantó	The rooster sang
Y en su canto dijo	And in its song it said
Ya Cristo nació.	Now Christ is born.
Ama de casa salgase	Mistress of the house
Para afuera	Come out, outside
Y con un cuchillo	And with a knife
Partiendo cazuela.	Cutting the tart.
Por allá bajito	Down over there
Me dijo un embustero	A liar told me
Que en esta casita	That in this little house
Había mucho y bueno.	There was plenty and good.
Y no dijo embuste	And he didn't lie
Que dijo verdad	He told the truth
Con esta risita	With his little laugh
De ja-ja-ja.	Of ha-ha-ha.
Dáme mi aguinaldo	Give me my Christmas gift
Que me ofreciste el año pasado	Which you offered me last year
Y no me lo diste.	And did not give to me.
Si tú no conoces	If you do not know
Este que ha llegado, Es un coronado, Rey de la	The one who has arrived, He is the crowned one, King of
Heraquía Que en voz decía	the Hierachy Whose voice is saying
Déme mi aguinaldo.	Give me my Christmas gift.
Llegaron los reyes	The Three Kings arrived
Bendito sea Dios	Blessed be God
Ellos van y vuelven	They do and return
Y nosotros no.	But we do not.
Estas Navidades	This is the Christmas season
Vamos a gozarlas	Let us enjoy it
Pues en dos semanas	Because in two weeks
Vamos a pasarlas.	We will be past them.
Este árbol de Christmas	This Christmas tree
Tiene muchos adornos	Has many ornaments
Y el dueño de casa	And the master of the house
Tiene mucho romo.	Has a lot of rum.

Source

Journal of American Folklore, LXIV (1951), 59-61. Collected by Maxine W. Gordon from "students of the public schools," at Vieques, an island about twelve miles off the coast of Puerto Rico. For another example of singing *alguinaldos,* see "Room at the Inn," p. 436.

* * *

St. George's Play

It seems not to be generally known among students of the popular drama that the St. George Christmas Play was a familiar feature of Boston life in the eighteenth century. The following passage from the "Recollections" of Mr. Samuel Breck will be found of interest:

I forget on what holiday it was that the Anticks, another exploded remnant of colonial manners, used to perambulate the town. They have ceased to do it now, but I remember them as late as 1782. They were a set of the lowest blackguards, who, disguised in filthy clothes and ofttimes with masked faces, went from house to house in large companies; and, *bon gré mal gré,* obtruding themselves everywhere, particularly into the rooms that were occupied by parties of ladies and gentlemen, would demean themselves with great insolence. I have seen them at my father's, when his assembled friends were at cards, take possession of a table, seat themselves on rich furniture, and proceed to handle the cards, to the great annoyance of the company. The only way to get rid of them was to give them money, and listen patiently to a foolish dialogue between two or more of them. One of them would cry out, 'Ladies and gentlemen sitting by the fire, put your hands in your pockets and give us our desire.' When this was done, and they had received some money, a kind of acting took place. One fellow was knocked down and lay sprawling on the carpet, while another bellowed out,

> See, there he lies,
> But ere he dies
> A doctor must be had.

He calls for a doctor, who soon appears, and enacts the part so well that the wounded man revives. In this way they would continue for half an hour, and it happened not unfrequently that the house would be filled by another gang when these had departed. There was no refusing admittance. Custom had licensed these vagabonds to enter even by force any place they chose. What should we say to such intruders now? Our manners would not brook such usage a moment.

Source and Comment

Journal of American Folklore, XXII (1909), 394. Contributed by G. L. Kittredge. His source was *Recollections of Samuel Breck from his Note-Books,* Philadelphia, 1877. Breck, who served in Congress, was born in Boston in 1771 and died in Philadelphia in 1862. For another colonial Boston Christmas play, see *Journal of American Folklore,* IX (1896), 178. The "Anticks" should be compared with the "fantasticals" who paraded on New Year's, Old Christmas, and other holidays (see p. 5 and note, pp. 5-6). Cf. "The John Kuner Ceremony," p.445, and "A Plough Monday Play," p. 39.

The play of St. George was performed during the Christmas season. It featured a struggle between a Turkish Knight and St. George, who is slain but revived by a comic doctor. This mummery, a pagan survival, is said to signify the conflict between winter and summer, and the cyclical rebirth of the year. The cast often included a number of ludicrous characters: Father Christmas, Beelzebub with a frying pan who begged money from and threatened the audience, performers dressed in animal skins, and men called "tommies" and "bessies" wearing women's clothing. According to legend, St. George, the patron saint of England, was torn into twenty-five parts before the Archangel Michael restored him to life. Plays and Christmas jollity were not looked upon with favor in late eighteen-century Boston where the Puritan tradition was still strong.

A New Mexican Nativity Play

The *Pastores* plays of the Southwest are entitled variously....The Chavez MS is entitled *La Pastoría,* an orthodox term for a group of shepherds. Many manuscripts exist which are more or less anonymous, the owners using them for local seasonal festivities, others keeping them only for their documentary or personal value. Edwin C. Munro has made a study of thirteen representative Shepherd's Plays, wherein he concluded that each play has some scenes in common with most of the others, but that no two have identical plots. His careful break-down of plots and characters indicates that the first part of Próspero Baca's *Los Pastores,* which he calls version E, and the Chavez MS which is the basis for the present study, are the only two plays that show the shepherds arriving at the manger in separate groups. The comparison here is in conjunction with Mr. Munro's, since *La Pastoría* was not available to him. Unique also to the Baca MS, as to the Chavez MS, is the episode where Martín wants to tease and play with the babe Jesus (to be included in the excerpt). Because the Chavez MS is so long, consisting of three parts, it will not be possible in this article to reproduce a very large part of it, but in order that the reader may understand the selection in its context, a brief summary of the plot is included.

In *La Pastoría,* contrary to most New Mexican pastoral plays, the shepherds appear in separate groups to make their offerings at the manger in the first act, and the camp scenes which depict the simple life and the carefree manner of the shepherds is given in the second part. The third act is a more allegorical version of the pastoral offerings, preceded by Miguel's defense of the *pastores* against Lucifer and Asmodeo. Although there is a similarity in the action between parts one and three, the lyrical presentation is ingeniously altered to make a doubly strong impression without tiring the audience. There are nine double parts and five single ones, making it possible for the play to give the impression of having a large cast. Thus, in reality, the shepherds in part one take different names for parts two and three. The adoration of the promised Messiah is the underlying moral and religious element most evident throughout the play, but the clowning antics of Bartolo provide the down-to-earth reflection of a simple man—a necessary compromise between religious and secular drama since the Middle Ages.

In this first part of *La Pastoría* the *posada* [inn] theme of the Christmas celebration is the main point of departure. The play opens with a song which exalts the virtues of the Virgin Mary and asks for her protection in the promised birth of the Messiah. The Chorus then relates the difficulties encountered by Mary and Joseph in their search for lodging before they find shelter with the animals at an inn. Here the Christ Child was born and here he received the tributes of the Wise Men. Praises are sung as the Angel announces the glad tidings to the shepherds. Tetuán, caring for the sheep as the others rest, is the first to hear the news, then realizes that as a child he had heard that a Divine Redeemer was to be born. He is thoroughly convinced by the dazzling light of the star that guides him, its brilliance turning the night into day. Jumping in his excitement, he goes to share his joy with his companions. The first one he meets is Tubero, who is consumed with curiosity and wants to go invite Tubal and Rotín to the feast which no doubt will be held to celebrate the event. The latter has a guitar which will make it possible for them to dance for the Child as they offer their personal gifts. They find Tubal asleep and dreaming of pleasant things, but at the unusual prospect of witnessing the Babe, he is quite willing to forego his slumber and walk, despite a sore foot, to Bethlehem.

To facilitate the illusion of passing time in the minds of the audience, the four shepherds sing of their desire to arrive at the inn where the Holy Family is to be worshipped. Once there, they sing the famous New Mexican lullaby which ends with the refrain *a-la-ru a-la-ru a-la-me.* They then proceed to make their offerings to the infant Jesus. Tubero gives a young lamb which to him is a symbol of the gentle shepherd, or God, who must suffer the loss of his own son. Tetuán makes an offering of cheese and bread, saying it is but a small portion of the multiple blessings he has received. Rotín makes a present of a bowl of stew which represents something very special in his life, while Tubal dances, excusing himself for lack of something better. They sing the lullaby once more and exit. Here the story continues as other shepherds hear the news and proceed to the Holy City.

SONG	LETRA
Sleep, wondrous child	*Duérmete, niño lindo*
In the tender arms of love	*En los brazos del amor*
Let your mother lull you	*Que te arrulle tu madre*
By singing this lullaby:	*Cantándote a la ru-ru.*
A la ru-u, a la me, a la ru-u, a la me,	*A la ru, a la me, a la ru, a la me,*
A la ru, a la ru, a la me.	*A la ru, a la ru, a la me.*

OQUIAS	OQUIAS
Last night I saw the shepherds	*Anoche vi a los pastores*
Inviting each other to a feast.	*Que se andaban convidando*
This is more strange than it seems	*Para no sé qué festín.*
I had better be alert,	*Será muy chistosa mano;*
Lest something happen the while.	*No por mucho madrugar*
I shall leave my flock here	*Me amanezca más temprano.*
I am sure it will not stray.	*Dejaré aquí me rebaño*
Or better yet, I'll entrust it	*Que no se me ha de perder,*
To my young friend Tarano.	*Y a más se lo encargaré*
As I now remember things,	*A mi amiguito Tarano.*
I saw a mountain burning	*A según mi parecer*
By night, and as the prophecy says,	*Vi un monte que anoche ardía*
	Y como ya es profecí
The mountains shall give forth	*Los montes destilarán*
Milk and honey in their joy.	*Dulce leche en alegría.*
This is according to Isaiah,	*Esto es según Isallías [Isaías].*
Which is now being fulfilled.	*Se cumple en esta ocasión*
No doubt by now the Messiah	*Sin duda que ya el Mesías*
Has been in glory incarnated,	*Salió de su encarnación.*

Born of man He's to become	*Ha nacido para ser*
The salvation of the world.	*Del mundo la redención.r*
I'll now go to ascertain	*Me voy a desengañar ahora*
The truth of this great event	*Que es buena ocasión*
And to offer the Holy Child	*A ofrece [r] le liberal*
My soul, my life and my heart.	*Alma, vida y corazón.*
I'll approach these shepherds	*Me acercaré a estos pastores*
To find out the truth from them	*A que me den relacón,*
And so that all as one	*Para que juntos todos*
Can sing to Him a la ru-u.	*Le cantemos a la ru-u.*

OQUIAS (Makes Offering)	OQUIAS (Ofrecimiento)
I have nothing more to give	*No tengo maś que ofrecerte*
O wondrous and beauteous child	*Niño lindo de mi amor*
Than this magnificent staff,	*Todo cuanto en casa tengo*
Which is all I have at home.	*Y este lucido bastón.*
Tomorrow I shall return and	*Ay manãna volveré que te*
Promise to bring with me	*prometo el traer*
My wife and my children all	*A mi mujer y a mis hijos*
That they may worship Thee too.	*Que te vengan a adorar.*
Good-bye my beautiful babe,	*Adios, mi niño lindo,*
I take my leave of Thee	*De ti me despido*
And kneel humbly in thy presence.	*A tus plantas rendido.*

SONG	LETRA
When during the cruel winter	*Cuando por el invierno*
Flowers bloom no more	*Hay [ya] no [se] producen flores*
The rough shepherds, much amazed,	*Se quedan admirados*
Marvel at this great wonder.	*Los rudos pastores.*

CERECIAS	CERECIAS
What is that I see	*¿Qué será lo que deviso*
In yon pleasant, green meadows?	*De lejos en aquellos prados?*
My companions are celebrating	*Fiestas de mis compañeros.*
Something they must've stolen.	*Ellos algo habrán robado,*
I am much surprised at this.	*Es cierto admirado estoy.*
I am not going just to stay	*De ver andar en arte voy*
Without trying for my share,	*A que no me quedo sin parte*
So I'll celebrate along	*De festejar en unión,*
With them while I have the chance.	*Pues se me ofrece ocasión*
Therefore I will join the dance	*De intretenerme en el danze*
And take whatever comes.	*A la suerte que relance*
No good thing must be despised	*Le sucede a un desdichado.*
Even if it doesn't please me.	*No hay bien que sea des-preciado*
But this I do not mind,	*Aunque mi genio se canse.*
For I am a reasonable man.	*Mas esto no me atormenta*
I will gladly make believe	*Que también soy de la cuenta*
And dance with great glee.	*Y me haré desemulado [di-simulado].*
Come what may, I'm game.	*Y bailaré alegremente*
I see the shepherds yonder	*Salga lo que saliere.*
Dancing and joined together.	*Bailando andan los pastores*
No doubt they are celebrating	*Y todos encadenados.*
The event of someone's wedding.	*Sin duda son desposorios*
I had better hide myself	*Que en el día se han celebrado.*
Since I have not been invited.	*Me ocultaré por aquí,*
For if I should suddenly appear	*Que en fin no soy convidado*
They would think me simple indeed.	*Porque tan pronto salir*
If they ask me afterwards	*Dirán que soy atontado.*
I'll know something to say,	*Según lo que ellos dijeren,*
For I have a speech in mind	*Yo también podré decir*
Which I've rehearsed for	*Una [a] renga que he estudiado*

awhile.
What's new here amongst you
To make you all so happy?

ALL
Marvels never seen before

And of those but rarely seen,
Don't you see what beauties
Cause us to be so delighted?

CERECIAS
But hold, sirs, let us wait.
For I too am a gentleman.
I'm off to congratulate
Good Joseph the carpenter.

CERECIAS (Makes Offering)
Blessed Joseph, you are
  fortunate
To be worthy of all these gifts,
To have for wife this fine
  woman.
Please accept, with my esteem,
What I humbly come to offer.
Music from heaven itself
Which is but a small part
Of what she truly deserves.
I would like to please you,
Oh lamb without sin
And to you, O blessed Joseph.
(Amen)

HERAS
Last night as I sat by the fire
I heard singing at the top
Of those precipitous peaks,
But I can't tell you now

What it then meant to me.

It may be a certain whim
Which God has made to
  occur.
If you want to investigate
You can come at once with
  me
For I heard once people say
That a child would be born
Of a pure and spotless maid,
Born thus of heaven's bidding
And it is a plausible truth.
So it may possibly be
That the Messiah is born.
For the prophecies foretell
That the mountains shall
  o'erflow,
The deaf shall speak sweetly,
And the blind and old
Shall come forth in joy,
And the event shall be
  propitious
If Lucifer does not win.

Oh, wicked angel,
His end is the sepulchre.
The sepulchre of burning hell
For he tried to make himself
The like of God above.
In his ill-advised attempt

El rato que he estado aquí.
¿Qué hay de nuevo entre
  vosotros,
Que parece que andáis locos?

TODOS
'Villas [Maravillas] que jamás
  se han visto
Y de estas se ofrecen pocas.
¿No ves qué hermosuras,
No ves qué bellezas,
Cosa como esta que nos
  embelesa?

CERECIAS
Pues aguardar, Señores mios
Que yo también soy caballero
Voy a darle el parabién
A José el carpintero.

CERECIAS (Ofrecimento)
Santo José, que a la dicha

Tanto puedes merecer.
Que has de tener por esposa
A tan benedita mujer
Recibe de mi cariño
Lo que te vengo a ofrecer.
Múisicas de los cielos.
No ham llegado a merecer
Tanta dicha como de Angeles.
Te quisiera complacer
A ti cordero sin mancha,
A ti, bendito José. (Amén).

HERAS
Anoche estando sentado
Calentándome en la lumbre,
Oí que estaban contando En

lo alto de aquella cumbre.
Mas no te podré decir
Lo que en ella [ello] pueda ber
  [haber].
Puede ser algun placer
Que Dios haiga [haya] puesto
  allí.
Si quieres desengañarte
Conmigo puedes venir.

Que en un tiempo oí decir
Que nacería un infante
De una mujer pura y limpia
Desde su primer instante,
Pues esto es firme y constante.
Que puede haber sucedido
Que habrá nacido el Mesías,
Porque está en sus profecías.
Nos dicen que en estos dias
Los montes destilarán;
Los callados echarán el resto de
  sus dulzuras,
Y el hombre de oscura luz
En edad podrá salir.

Y el tiempo será feliz
Si no se dejan vencer
De quien llaman Luicer.
O, Angel malo, por figura
Tiene este por sepultura
El infierno que ha de arder
Porque este se quizo hacer
Semejante como Dios.
Y como terrible atroz

He tried to imitate
Our holy and peerless deity.
As punishment for his folly
He is cast into darkening hell.
Have you listened carefully
To what I have said so far?
This is the plan I have chosen
Which we'll carry out entire.
We shall, humble of heart,
Adore him as is his due.
Upon arriving we'll kneel
And humbly offer this bowl
Of succulent food which I vow
Is the best I've ever seen;
For I prepared it with care
In making it for myself,
And thus in such perfect state
I want the child to enjoy it.

AFRÓN
Tell me more, my shepherd
  friend,
Who are sent from heaven
  itself. Your good talk has
  strengthened me
And comforted my poor soul,
Though my heart is very sad.
Wonder of all wonders,
That a poor shepherd could
  have
Such a pleasant conversation.
Would that I were worthy
Of hearing such good news
(For the glory of heaven
  itself).
Fortunate like Tobias
I would gladly count myself.
But come, let us go
Wherever you wish to take
  me,
For I can truly say
You are of the same deity of
  God.

HERAS
Stop! I would be insane
To let you think me a God!
Do not regard me as divine.
Hush, don't let this get about,
I am but the shepherd Heras
And known to all as such.

AFRÓN
Forgive me, dear friend,
I shall not speak again thus.
And we'll both in silent
  reverence
Go to the blessed portal
They call that of Bethlehem.
There we shall sit and talk
Until the dawn appears.

HERAS
Follow me and let us hasten

So that we may there arrive
For if we should now delay
We may something miss, no
  doubt.

AFRÓN
It's a great wonder to see
All the heavens lighted up.
See there, how on our way
The light begins to appear
Announcing a bright new

Se quizo este asemejar
A la deidad sin segunda.
Que [por] castigo se la da
El infierno, que es el peor.
¿Me has oido con atención
Lo que te he estado diciendo?
Pues ahora vengo en acuerdos
Sin que cometamos yerros.
Le daremos adoración.
Y humildes de corazón.
Al llegar nos postraremos,
Y humildes le ofreceremos
Este jarrito de migas,
Que te prometo que están
Lindas, lindas de mi vida;
Que todo el esmero puse
Para hacerlas para mí,
Y te prometo que así
Las ha de comer el niño.

AFRÓN
Dime, pastorcito,

Que eres inbiado [enviado] del
  cielo,
Pues que tu conversación
Me ha llenado de consuelo,
Y me ha herido el corazón.
Válgame, y válgame Dios
Que un pobre pastor tendrá

Tan dulce conversación.
Acase seré yo digno
De oirnos una razón
Para ningo celestial

Dichoso como Tobías
Me pudiera yo llamar
Andar para ninfo andar
Lliévame para donde quisiéreis
Porque puedo decir que eres
De Dios la misma deidad.

HERAS
Calla, que es temeridad
El que por loco me tengas.
No me tengas por deidad.
Calla, esto no se refiera
Que yo soy el pastor Heras
Conocido como tal.

AFRÓN
Perdóname, compañero,
Que no te volveré a hablar,
Y con los brazos cruzados

Nos iremos al portal
Que le llaman de Belén.
Allí nos sentaremos a parlar
Mientras el día es.

HERAS
Sígui[e]me y vamos aprisia
  [aprisa]
Para que lleguemos a él.
Porque si nos dilatamos
Algo puede suceder.

AFRÓN
Admirado estoy de ver
Todo el orbe [i] aluminado.
Mira para donde vamos
Como va resplandeciendo
La aurora de la mañana.

morn.

HERAS

Didn't I tell you that this day
Would be better than the rest?
And since you are guiding me

To yonder elegant portal
I shall too be able to say
That you're a heavenly angel.

AFRÓN

Then too, I see in our time

That man is given his bread
Or of what'er he has need
With bounteous greatness and
joy.

HERAS

You will see that sure, you
fool.
It is quite easy to see
Why they call you the
shepherd
shepherd Afron,
For from Afrón to a fool
There is not far to go.
Follow me and let us hurry,
Ere my heart jumps out within
me.

HERES AND AFRÓN
(Make Offering)

Heras and Afrón worship thee
And give our most humble
thanks.
Together here we make
offering
Of this small bowl of food.

SONG

Let us all dance, oh shepherds,
With great gladness and peace.
We'll make a gay pattern
To express our great joy.

MARTIN

Martinico, my friend,
Let's go for a walk
To the place where the
shepherds
Went in humbly to worship.

MARTINICO

We'll go where you like,
As you know I am your
friend.
And no matter where you die
I shall be there at your side.

MARTIN

All the people seem to say
Festive functions are afoot.
Let us make our hearts more
gay
By attending the affair.

MARTINICO

I would also prize the chance
To go along with the rest
And find myself at the dance
In the company of my friends.

MARTIN

Let us start upon the way
Ere I die of anxiety.
For I want to dance a while
And take a thousand steps.
It is a source of great joy

HERAS

¿Pues no te lo decía yo
Que este día era sinigual?
Conque parque tu me guilles
[guíes]
Para ese rico portal
Yo también podré decir
Que eres ángel celestial.

AFRÓN

También veo que en nuestros
días
Se le puede dar el pan
O el paso natural al hombre
Con grandeza y alegría.

HERAS

Pues esto has de ver, tontón,

Bien se echa de ver
Que te llaman el pastorcito

Afrón.
Que de Afrón a tontón
Poca diferencia hay.
Sígueme y vamos aprisa,
Que me salta el corazón.

OFRECIMIENTO (Los Dos)

Heras y Afrón te adoramos
Y te damos gracias rendidas

Y entre los dos te ofrecemos

Este jarrito de migas. (Amén.)

LETRA

Pastores, bailemos
Con gusto y con paz.
Haremos cuadriolas
Ay nomás, ay nomás.

MARTIN

Martinico, amigo,
Vamos a pasiar
Donde los pastores

Fueron a adorar.

MARTINICO

Vamos donde gustes
Abes [ya ves] soy tu amigo

Donde tu mueras
Muero yo contigo.

MARTIN

Todo dicen que hay
Célebres funciones.
Vamos a que se alegren

Nuestros corazones.

MARTINICO

Yo también quisiera
Con crecido esmero
Andar ya bailando
Con mis compañeros.

MARTIN

Vamos a pasiar [pascar]
Que me muero de ansia.
Que quiero bailar
Y hacer mil mudanza
De que [a] mi me toca

For me to have my turn.
I can cut some capers
Stepping (as high as) my
knees.
But wouldn't you rather
That I tell you more than
this?
Have you ever before
Seen such a beautiful child?
I'm going therefore
To tease him a bit.

MARTINICO

Relax, there, my friend
And take hold of yourself,
For regarding this small child,
You are to leave him alone.

MARTIN

I wish you would stop
nagging.
I shall not steal him away,
And by his own gracious leave
We'll begin at once to play.

MARTINICO

Hold there, and don't touch
him
How can you be so shameless?
Can't you see how tenderly
His parents regard him,
And with what great reverence
His person they worship?

MARTIN

Entertain then his parents
For just a short time.
And while they're busy
Listening to you
I shall sneak him out quietly
And then he can play
With your little kid
Which I have hidden there.

MARTINICO

Oh, what a rude shepherd,
And so utterly uncouth!
Go on, for they'll to your
house
To beat you in truth,
With that length of rope
Which serves as a noose.

MARTIN

E'en tho they beat me,
My good friend Martin
I mean to go through
With this plan of mine

MARTINICO

I'll swear I will send you
To a couple of rogues
To beat you for being
Such a fool and a dolt.

MARTIN

You can be certain
If I do not finish
What I have begun
We shall be quite sorry.

SONG

I will sing rejoicing
The victory of Michael
O'er that great proud dragon,
And the glory of God in the
highest.

LUCIFER

Oh, fateful heavens!

Cosa de alegría.
Echo cuchilladas
Hasta las rodillas.

Quieres que te diga
Esto y algo más?

¿Has viso chiquillo
De tanta hermosura?
Lo voy a echar
A la travesura.

MARTINICO

Sosiégate, amigo
Estáte por ay, [ahí]
Porque este chiquillo
No lo has de agarrar.

MARTIN

No me estés molestando.

No lo he de llevar,
Y con su merced
Hermos de jugar.

MARTINICO

Mira, no lo tientes.

No seas insolente.
¿No ves que sus padres
Que lo están mirando
Y con atención
Lo están adorando?

MARTIN

Debierte [diviertе] a sus padres
Un poco por ay.
Mientras que contigo
Están divertidos
Me lo llevaré
Por aquí escondido
Para dibirtilo con aquel cabrito
Que tengo escondido.

MARTINICO

¡Qué pastor tan rudo
Y tan masorral!
Anda, que ha de ir a tu casa

Y allí te han de pelar
Con acquella reata
Que sirve de pial [e].

MARTIN

Pues aunque me pelen,
Amigo Martín,
Con acquí esta [e] impresa
Yo me he de salir.

MARTINICO

Voy a que te mando
Con dos galafatos [galafates]
A que te manellen [meneen]
Por tonto y tompiato.

MARTIN

Pues si no consigo
El intento que ando,
Abrazo partido
Hemos de ir llorando.

LETRA

Del dragón soberbio
Miguel la victoria.
Contaré la gloria,
La gloria en excelsis Deo.

LUCIFER

¡Cielos!

It must be true
That you reveal many truths
To the humble and meek
Which from me you keep ob-
scure.
So to treat the Proud Master
of earth!
I'll know how to disguise,
But today among these people
I must definitely inquire
If the Messiah's been born
Whom I hold in such great
dread.
I really doubt this event

Will in reality occur.
It's unlikely that the Word
Should be born from this
portent.
How come you make offering
here.
In the presence of a calf?
And how dare you make war
On the dauntless prince of
hell?

ANGEL
If you insist upon making
This opposition to God,
Your effort will be for naught
As my zealous care forbids it.
For who doth consent
To all things of the heart?
And this daring Lucifer
I shall kill without delay.
And as a token of my wrath
I shall make of hell his tomb.
With this shining naked sword
I shall conquer him with ease.
Who can imitate our God?

Woe be to the one that tries.
He shall die for his attempt
As long as God has full sway.
Till when will his power last?
Our God, forever and ever!

We must truly give him
worship
As is meet the sacred being
Of Moses' tablets inscribed.
It is therefore just for all
To obey his every command
And thus to confess our faith
In the expected Messiah.
We shall as one

Offer Him our adoration
Let all the world come!

Angels, men, and skies,
The earth and all waters,
Hills, mountains and fires,
Come all in contrition
To celebrate this great day.
Let us sing with gladness
To God, the Word incarnate.

SONG
I am worthy to be enthroned
above
As manifestation of spirit in
truth.
Let all men in humility invoke

Si es cierto que reveláis
A muchos secretos
A los humildes que ocultas.
Tener al sabio del mundo y so-
berbio,
Yo lo sabré disfazar.

Hoy entre esta gente
Quiero averiguar
Si ha nacido el Mesías
Que tanto tengo [temo]
Y a la verdad.

Dudo muchos se verifica [mucho
se verifique]
Un portento tan extraño.
Me parece un imposible
De que naszea de ella [o] un
verbo
¿Como le das adoración a un
becerro?
¿Como le publicas guerra
Al príncipe del infierno?

ANGEL
Si ha regido algún intento
De oponerse contra Dios,
No [se] le ha de permitir, no;
Ni mi celo lo consiente.
¿Pues quién todo lo consiente
De lo interior?
Porque su muerte violenta
Pronto muerte le daré.
Al infierno lo echaré,
Dándole por sepultura.
Con esta espada desnuda
Mi furor lo ha de vencer.
¿Quien como Dios pueda [e]
ser?

Ni quién diga lo contrario.
El mu [o] rirá sepultado
Mientras Dios deje de ser.
¿Cuándo dejará de ser?
¿Dios, para siempre y para
siempre!
Oh mientras venerado

Como si fuera sagrado
Las tablas de otro Moisés
Aunque justísimo es
Que todos los obedezcamos,
Y así mismo confesemos
Por el Mesías deseado
Y que juntamente implados
[empleados]
Le daremos adoración.
En una aunime [ánima] y
unión.

De ángeles hombres y los cielos,
[De] tierra y agua,
Montes, fuegos y callados
Venir todos obligados
A celebrar este día.
Cantemos con alegría
A Dios "Deum Deo un Verbo."

CANTICO
Digno soy humanado en los
cielos
Sustento del alma que lo
verifica.
Hoy humildes, postrados los
hombres.

Hosannas of gladness and joy.

Cantemos alegres con dulce
armonía.

CHORUS
Oh bread of life
Oh bread of life
Oh, blessed lamb of God,
Stainless and pure.

— — —

You are come down from God
To Mary's virgin womb,

And today in glad acceptance
She's let this wonder take
place.

— — —

On the night of the last
supper
Ere the ascension of Thy
spirit,
Thou gave us thy blood and
thy body
As a eucharistic sacrament.

— — —

Though I see not with man's
eyes
In this host I think it's given,

And by saying the five words,

Your conversion is complete.

CORO
Oh, pan de vida!
Oh, pan de vida!
Oh cordero de Dios sin mancha.
Oh cordero de Dios sin mancha.

— — —

Hoy del seno del Padre bajastes
Al vientre virginio del Ave
María.

Y ella dando su consentimiento
Hizo que el misterio se abrase
[abrazárase] en un día.

— — —

En la noche de la última cena

Estando dispuesto para su
partida
Nos dejaste tu cuerpo y tu
sangre
En el sacramento de la Eu-
caristía.

— — —

Aunque no con los ojos os miro,

Yo creo que en esta hostia está
concedido,
Que en virtud de las cinco
palabras
Luego que están dichas que-
dáis convertido.

—END OF PART 1—

Source and Comment

New Mexico Folklore Record, II (1947-48), 47-57. Fred Meza Brewer
has edited the folk drama, *La Pastoría*, from the manuscript notebook
of Felipe A. Chavez of Albuquerque, New Mexico. The manuscript
"though written in prose form, is apparently in the octosyllabic
romance pattern" and is "translated into a four-stress line, roughly
equivalent to the Spanish ballad form." The sometimes archaic
language is corrected in brackets.

Coloquios are dramatizations of biblical stories and saints' legends
derived from the medieval mystery plays of Spain which were brought
to the New World by friars in the sixteenth century and were used in
the religious instruction of Christianized Indians and peasants. *Los
Pastores*, literally "The Shepherds," concentrates on the Christmas
story of the shepherds who hear of Christ's birth while tending their
flocks and who take gifts to the Child in the manger. Such dramas
might also include elements from the Christian legend of the battles
between the Archangel Michael and Lucifer, and episodes and songs
from professional writers of the period such as Luis de Gongara. They
feature slapstick humor, dances, and stock characters—for example, a
hermit, a coquettish country girl, a lazy glutton, and a simple-minded
shepherd. Their ultimate ancestor is the "Office of the Shepherds"
introduced into the Christmas mass in the eleventh century, one seed
of the revival of drama in Western Europe. Some one hundred and
twenty-five *Pastores* have been found in the American Southwest and
Mexico. These Spanish language plays are the most important
examples of folk drama in unbroken tradition to be found in the
United States.

Nativity Play

The Origin of a *Los Pastores* Script

Now about the play, *Los Pastores*—I remember what was told to me by him [Candelario Barreras, father of the informant, who transcribed the script in 1895] and by my grandmother. This script was passed on from one generation to another; he did not compose it, although being one of the few persons who could read or write in those days, some of the older men would depend on him to teach the shepherds and other actors, who couldn't read or write, how to memorize their parts. He also acted in the play, as one of the shepherds. Then as I grew old enough and they would scout for actors (which was almost every Christmas) he'd lend me out to any group or person who was going to promote the play, and it was then that he'd tell me of what he did as a boy in reference to this play.

I remember very clearly about the part where the Infant Jesus is stolen and taken to some home. Some family, in anticipation, has prepared a feast as an offering of religious faith as well as to arouse the spirit of the season. Then all the actors and some invited people made a procession to search for the Child pretending they don't know where he was. They would end at this home, but before the Child was returned, they would sing and pray. As a rule it ended in a *velorio* or "wake," and they would sing and pray all night. When the Child was returned, they were asked to stay for a big dinner. This was the only part I liked!

Source and Comment

New Mexico Folklore Record, IX (1954-55), 22. T.M. Pearce traced the history of a handwritten copy of a nativity play carefully transcribed into a ledger book in the Library of the University of New Mexico. Eventually he located the son of the transcriber, Henry Barreras, in California, who informed him by letter, dated February 24, 1954, of the role of his father, Candelario Barreras, as a folk play producer, and his own as an actor in the play. The Barreras version "is the best copy and probably source of plays since being produced in Socorro, Albuquerque, Los Griegos, Corrales and Sante Fe, New Mexico."

Nativity Play

A Synthesis of *Los Pastores* Plays

The traditional materials [in the *Los Pastores* plays] may be shown by synthesizing them into twelve main episodes. Not all of these episodes appear in each of the texts, but most of them do....

I

Las Posadas (The Inns). The visit of Joseph and of Mary to various inns at Bethlehem is enacted at a number of homes in the village; Lucifer conceals himself in each home and rejects the wayfarers; then he finally welcomes them at one house where a *nacimiento* or crèche has been prepared for the Christ Child. Some copies of the play summarize these events in an opening song by the choir.

II

The Song of the Star. Several of the plays open with a hymn describing the Star of Bethlehem and the event it symbolized. The role of the Star, usually nonspeaking, is described in two texts as played by either a young man or a young woman. A silver-tinsel star is placed on the forehead of an actor, who speaks a quatrain identifying his part. In the Salomon Apodaca text, from Socorro, New Mexico, the Star walks at the front of two processionals and sits beside the manager during the play. A small flashlight on the forehead of the actor is used to illuminate the orb. The title *Estrella* is given to one New Mexican play.

III

The Processional. The great majority of the texts I have examined bring the entire cast on the stage with the singing of hymns, such as *La Gloria, De la Real Jerusalén* and others. Leading this procession are Joseph and Mary, who move down the hall to the *nacimiento* (manger), a kind of altar holding a cradle. Mary takes the image of the infant Jesus from the cradle on the *nacimiento* and puts the figure in a larger cradle placed before the chairs where she and Joseph are to sit. The shepherds march around the hall until they arrive at a spot in the center marked by a campfire.

IV

The Camp Scene. *Los Pastores,* from the point of view of entertainment, begins here, because the vivid human personalities appear in this scene and the elements of profane subplot begin. Men are assigned to protect the flock from wolves. The shepherdess Gila quarrels with her husband or with several of the shepherds as she calls for wood to prepare her fire. The Hermit joins the shepherds. Finally, the guards return to report hearing heavenly music and the song of the angel Gabriel. In some texts *El Primer Paseo* or The First Promenade occurs here; in this *paseo* the shepherds march around the hall indicating the passage of time.

V

The First Appearance of Lucifer (*Luzbel, Dragón*). The Devil enters the play in some texts immediately after the Processional. This gets the play off to a vigorous start. He leaps on the stage with an explosion of firecrackers. His costume usually consists of red tights, tunic, cape, mask, horns, and tail. Lucifer denounces Heaven and its powers; he decries the reports he has heard of the Messiah and proclaims his determination to make war on mankind. "*Viva el Infierno!*" he cries. "Hurrah for Hell, and war against Heaven!" In other texts, Lucifer enters the play after the first Camp Scene. Encountering the shepherds, he provokes one or more of the comic interludes. Additional devils are sometimes introduced to reinforce the comedy.

VI

Entremes **or Interlude of Cucharón.** In the Rio Grande City play, a young shepherd named Cucharón (meaning "Big Spoon," or as María Lopez de Lowther translates it, "Ladle Mouth") encounters the Devil while the other shepherds are sleeping. He is so slow-witted that when the Devil asks about what *patria* (country) he comes from, Cucharón says his *padre* (father) is dead, and when Lucifer questions him about the *Mesías* (Messiah), Cucharón thinks the Devil is asking about his cousin *Matías* (Mathias), who was banished for killing a man. Cucharón then goes on to trace the ancestry of Matías back to *Matusalém* (Methuselah). Lucifer finally is so exasperated by the simpleton that he seizes him; then Cucharón cries out in the name of God and is saved. Cucharón runs to the other shepherds telling what he has experienced. I have found no manuscripts in New Mexico employing this character or this episode.

VII

Entremes **or Interlude of the Hermit.** In the Rio Grande City play the character of the Hermit is a serious one. He leaves his desert retreat to help the shepherds in their search for the Messiah, and he challenges Lucifer, helping to ward him off. In the New Mexican versions, the Hermit becomes a figure of comedy. He steals mutton and a coat from the shepherds and (at the suggestion of the Devil) he tries to kidnap Gila. He is beaten by the leader of the shepherds, Bato, and another shepherd gives him a blow on the head. As Sister Joseph Marie remarks, in her study of the religious drama in New Mexico: "The missionaries would not have included a scene in which a hermit is held up to even a mild derision, nor would they have stressed scenes in which a person, dedicated to giving a good example to others, would be accused by Lucifer of stealing, or of desiring to run off with Gila. This ironic scene is obviously a folk addition."

VIII

The Second Appearance of Lucifer. Lucifer usually tries to join the main body of the shepherds, after previous encounters with one or more of them outside the camp. He appears as a lost wayfarer, seeking food and fellowship. When he is confronted by the Archangel Michael, he cries, "The shepherds whom you defend will not escape me." "Yield thy neck to the power of Heaven," recites Michael, whose role is always played by a young boy. After a rhythmic touching of swords Lucifer falls down vanquished. Because of his antics, Lucifer is obviously a favorite with audiences and in some versions he makes a final appearance before the shepherds complete their offerings at Bethlehem.

IX

Entremes **or Interlude of Bartolo.** From the first discovered text to the last, Bartolo is the chief clown in the "Shepherds' Play." Whether he is portrayed as the husband of Gila, an uncle of a shepherd, or just one of their number, all join in berating him for his laziness and insatiable desire for food. He talks to his bedroll with loving affection and lies down at every opportunity. In one or more scenes when he dominates the stage, Bartolo puns on the phrases with which his brother shepherds encourage him to "get up and go." Exhorted to use the *caminos* (roads), Bartolo answers, "*Comemos*," (Let's eat); to *llegar* (arrive) at Bethlehem, he replies *cenar* (supper); to hurry to see San José, he answers drowsily, *café* (coffee). When, at last, Bartolo reaches the *portal* of Bethlehem, Tebano makes his final persuasion:

En Belén está la gloria	In Bethlehem there is glory
Bartolo, vamos allá.	Bartolo, let us go there.
Bartolo replies:	
Si quiere la Gloria verme	If Glory wishes to see me
Que venga la Gloria acá.	Then let Glory come here.

Bartolo cannot see why he should go to a baptism in Bethlehem unless he is to be the godfather, and he is afraid to view the ox warming the Infant Jesus for fear it will gore him with its horns. In the Mexican border versions, such as those at Rio Grande City and San Antonio, and also in the recently discovered California text, Bartolo is a lazy old fellow, shirking work and always hungry, but he is addressed with some marks of humorous respect and with some condescension to his age. In the New Mexican presentations, he has degenerated to a shiftless sheepherder, whom the shepherds put up with and laugh at, who even has the irreverence to ask the Child Jesus to give him all the presents the other shepherds have offered to their Savior. He also asks the Holy Child to find him a bite to eat and to cure him of his laziness.

X

Las Caminatas **(The Walkings, Promenades).** There are a number of *paseos* or promenades about the hall, indicating travel and the passing of time. The last of these *paseos* I choose to call *Las Caminatas,* because here the shepherds go individually or in pairs to make their offerings. They sing individually and in chorus, and as they walk forward they tap with their ornamented crooks or staves in rhythm to the music. In every "Shepherds' Play" I have seen, this effective tapping device is used, along with the *caminata* step, which is one step forward and one back on alternate feet, with a final step forward. The pattern of the *caminata* confirms lines which the shepherds speak about "dancing" their way to Bethlehem.

XI

The Adorations and Offerings. The climax of design in all the "Shepherds' Plays" is the adoration of the Infant Jesus and the bringing of gifts. One might say that the emotional climax occurs in the battle between Michael and Lucifer, but the spiritual climax occurs when each of the shepherds goes to the manager to present his personal gift. There is considerable contrast between the gifts offered by shepherds in some of the Mexican versions and those in the New Mexican texts. In the Rio Grande City play, the Hermit offers a necklace, a rosary, his prayer book, his discipline or scourge, and a "richly wrought" silver relicary made by a craftsman of Mexico. Finally, he presents an herb, rosemary, which Mary is enjoined to rub on the infant's navel for healing. Only the herbs remain as his gift in one New Mexican text, and white lilies in another. Where the Mexican shepherds give a chain with a cross, a baby spoon, a lute, and a whistle, the New Mexican shepherds commonly give gourd cups, little charms, a fleece of wool or a lamb, a dish of stew and tamales, even a bowl of bread crumbs. Humble gifts they are, but a shepherd called The Cripple, appearing in one New Mexican variant, offers a loaf of bread as a symbol of Jesus in the Blessed Sacrament. This gift is paralleled by the offering of the Hermit in the Ibañez-California text. Tubal in the Chavez manuscript of Albuquerque has nothing to offer but a dance which he does before the manger to entertain the Holy Family.

XII

The Lullaby and *Las Despedidas* (The Farewells). Before *los pastores* say farewell, they sing a lullaby to the *Niño Dios*. These lullabies are an interesting study in themselves, with the refrain they all have in common: "*a la ru, a la me, a la ru.*" The shepherds sometimes dance after this song, singing to the Christ Child in the manger at Bethlehem a stanza that repeats the line, "*Me gusta y me gusta, y me gusta bien*" (I love and I love and I love very much). The Farewells usually consist of addresses to each of the members of the Holy Family (in some of which the parents are called Aunt Mary and Uncle Joseph); of calls to the flocks to turn homeward; occasionally, with greetings to the audience at the Christmas season. Two of the New Mexican plays allow Joseph and Mary to respond, thanking the shepherds for their gifts and offering the blessing of the Infant Jesus in return. Joseph assures them he is their true friend and obedient servant.

This, then, is the traditional "Shepherds' Play" in which there are opportunities for innovations in the clowning of the Hermit and Bartolo and in the acting and extemporaneous "thunder" of Lucifer and his assistants. But greater innovations can occur when a separate episode or part is introduced, such as the kidnaping of Jesus episode or the Navajo Indian interlude. The latter is found as a kind of epilogue to the Agua Fria play, but it appears independently in a text *Pastores Chiquitos*, identified as the manuscript of Juan Climaco Lucero. In the Lucero script, the Indian greets the shepherds as they prepare to leave the manger. He slautes them with an "Ave, Maria," adding, "Listen to what I have to say." Then he turns out to be an entertainer, for he sings a comic song about a Comanche man and a Comanche woman who went to war; the man howled and an Apache grabbed the woman.

Source and Comment

Western Folklore, XV (1956), 83-87, T.M. Pearce synthesized the published texts of the nativity plays in order to see how New Mexican texts are related "to the general pattern of other published texts," especially "their adaptation to local audiences." He notes that some 125 copies of the play" have been discovered in the American Southwest and in Mexico."

* * *

Nativity Play

Songs from *Los Pastores*

Lullaby

> *Duermete niño lindo*
> *En los brazos del amor*
> *Que te atolla tu madre,*
> *Cantándote a la ro*
> *A la ro, a la me, etc.*

> Sleep beautiful boy
> In the arms of love
> While your mother rocks your cradle,
> Singing hushabye
> Hushabye, hushabye, etc.

Farewell

> *Adiós Jose, Adiós Maria*
> *Adiós Niño chiquitito*
> *Que ya se van los pastores*
> *Para los campos de Egipto.*

> Farewell, Joseph, farewell Mary.
> Farewell tiny babe.
> For the shepherds now are leaving
> For the fields of Egypt.

Source and Comment

Western Folklore, XVI (1957), 277, 280. J.D. Robb recorded and transcribed the songs from a performance of *Los Pastores* in

Albuquerque, New Mexico in 1946. The performers were from Socorro, New Mexico. Their "text and music . . . can be regarded as typical." The "Lullaby" is almost identical to that of the Chavez manuscript, p. 382, where the shepherds sing and dance before the Christ child. The "Farewell" *(despedida)*, is sung by the shepherds at the end of the folk play.

* * *

Supreme Court Ruling on a Crèche Display

From The "Opinion"

We granted certiorari to decide whether the Establishment Clause of the First Amendment prohibits a municipality from including a crèche, or Nativity scene, in its annual Christmas display.

Each year, in cooperation with the downtown retail merchants' association, the City of Pawtucket, R.I., erects a Christmas display. The display is situated in a park owned by a nonprofit organization and located in the heart of the shopping district.

The display is essentially like those to be found in hundreds of towns or cities across the nation, often on public grounds, during the Christmas season. The Pawtucket display comprises many of the figures and decorations traditionally associated with Christmas, including, among other things, a Santa Claus house, reindeer pulling Santa's sleigh, candy-striped poles, a Christmas tree, carolers, cut-out figures representing such characters as a clown, an elephant, and a teddy bear, hundreds of colored lights, a large banner that reads "Seasons Greetings," and the crèche at issue here. All components of this display are owned by the city.

The crèche, which has been included in the display for 40 or more years, consists of the traditional figures, including the Infant Jesus, Mary and Joseph, angels, shepherds, kings and animals, all ranging in height from five inches to five feet. . . .

There is an unbroken history of official acknowledgment by all three branches of government of the role of religion in American life from at least 1789.

Our history is replete with official references to the value and invocation of divine guidance in deliberations and pronouncements of the Founding Fathers and contemporary leaders. Beginning in the early colonial period long before Independence, a day of Thanksgiving was celebrated as a religious holiday to give thanks for the bounties of nature as gifts from God. President Washington and his successors proclaimed Thanksgiving, with all its religious overtones, a day of national celebration and Congress made it a national holiday more than a century ago.

Executive orders and other official announcements of Presidents and of the Congress have proclaimed both Christmas and Thanksgiving national holidays in religious terms. And, by acts of Congress, it has long been the practice that Federal employees are released from duties on these national holidays, while being paid from the same public revenues that provide the compensation of the Chaplains of the Senate and the House and the military services.

Art galleries supported by public revenues display religious paintings of the 15th and 16th centuries predominantly inspired by one religious faith. . . .

Justice Brennan describes the crèche as a "re-creation of an event that lies at the heart of Christian faith." The crèche, like a painting, is passive: admittedly it is a reminder of the origins of Christmas. Even the traditional, purely secular displays extant at Christmas, with or without a crèche, would inevitably recall the religious nature of the holiday. The display engenders a friendly community spirit of good will in keeping with the season. . . .

To forbid the use of this one passive symbol, the crèche, at the very time people are taking note of the season with Christmas hymns and carols in public schools and other public places, and while the Congress and legislatures open sessions with prayers by paid chaplains would be a stilted overreaction contrary to our history and to our holdings.

The Court has acknowledged that the "fears and political problems" that gave rise to the Religion Clauses of the 18th century are of far less concern today. We are unable to perceive the Archbishop of Canterbury, the Vicar of Rome, or other powerful religious leaders behind every public acknowledgement of the religious heritage long officially recognized by the three constitutional branches of government. Any notion that these symbols pose a real danger of establishment of a state church is far-fetched indeed.

We hold that, notwithstanding the religious significance of the crèche, the City of Pawtucket has not violated the Establishment Clause of the First Amendment. Accordingly, the judgment of the Court of Appeals is reversed.

It is so ordered.

From the "Dissent"

. . . First, all of Pawtucket's "valid secular objectives can be readily accomplished by other means." Plainly, the city's interest in celebrating the holiday and in promoting both retail sales and good will are fully served by the elaborate display of Santa Claus, reindeer and wishing wells that are already a part of Pawtucket's annual Christmas display. More importantly, the Nativity scene, unlike every other element of the Hodgson Park display, reflects a sectarian exclusivity that the avowed purposes of celebrating the holiday season and promoting retail commerce simply do not encompass. To be found constitutional, Pawtucket's seasonal celebration must at least be nondenominational and not serve to promote religion. The inclusion of a distinctively religious element like the crèche, however, demonstrates that a narrower sectarian purpose lay behind the decision to include a Nativity scene.

The "primary effect" of including a Nativity scene in the city's display is, as the district court found, to place the government's imprimatur of approval on the particular religious beliefs exemplified by the crèche. Those who believe in the message of the Nativity receive the unique and exclusive benefit of public recognition and approval of their views. The effect on minority religious groups, as well as on those who may reject all religion, is to convey the message that their views are not similarly worthy of public recognition nor entitled to public support. It was precisely this sort of religious chauvinism that the Establishment Clause was intended forever to prohibit.

Finally, and most importantly, even in the context of Pawtucket's seasonal celebration, the crèche retains a specifically Christian religious meaning. I refuse to accept the notion implicit in today's decision that non-Christians would find that the religious content of the crèche is eliminated by the fact that it appears as part of the city's otherwise secular celebration of the Christmas holiday.

The Court also attempts to justify the crèche by entertaining a beguilingly simple, yet faulty syllogism. The Court begins by noting that government may recognize Christmas Day as a public holiday; the Court then asserts that the crèche is nothing more than a traditional element of Christmas celebrations; and it concludes that the inclusion of a crèche as part of a government's annual Christmas celebration is constitutionally permissible. The Court apparently believe that once it finds that the designation of Christmas as a public holiday is constitutionally acceptable, it is then free to conclude that virtually every form of governmental association with the celebration of the holiday is also constitutional.

The vice of this dangerously superficial argument is that it overlooks the fact that the Christmas holiday in our national culture contains both secular and sectarian elements. To say that government may recognize the holiday's traditional, secular elements of gift-giving, public festivities and community spirit, does not mean that government may indiscriminately embrace the distinctively sectarian aspects of the holiday.

Contrary to the Court's suggestion, the crèche is far from a mere representation of a "particular historic religious event." It is, instead, best understood as a mystical re–creation of an event that lies at the heart of Christian faith. To suggest, as the Court does, that such a symbol is merely "traditional" and therefore no different from Santa's house or reindeer is not only offensive to those for whom the crèche has profound significance, but insulting to those who insist for religious or personal reasons that the story of Christ is in no sense a part of "history" nor an unavoidable element of our national "heritage."

Source and Comment

The United States Law Week: "Supreme Court Opinions," LII, #34 (March 6, 1984), Bureau of National Affairs, Washington, D.C. Excerpted from the March 5, 1984, Supreme Court decision on the action brought by Pawtucket, Rhode Island residents, individual members of the Rhode Island affiliate of the American Civil Liberties Union, and the Union itself challenging the city's right to include a crèche in its annual Christmas display. The action eventually came before the United States District Court for Rhode Island, which found that the city had "tried to endorse and promulgate religious beliefs" by the inclusion of the crèche in its display. The action was then referred to the Supreme Court. The "Opinion" in the 5-4 ruling that overturned the District Court finding was written by Chief Justice Warren E. Burger, the "Dissent" was written by Justice William J. Brennan. See also "Hanukkah and Civil Liberties," p. 423.

* * *

A New York City Version of an Old Carol

A few years ago [ca. 1885], Catholic children, in the streets of New York, were in the habit of singing a peculiar version of an old carol.

> I wash my face in a golden vase,
>   Golden vase, golden vase,
> I wash my face in a golden vase,
>   Upon a Christmas morning.
>
> I wipe my face on a lily-white towel,
>   Lily-white towel, lily-white towel,
> I wipe my face on a lily-white towel,
>   Upon a Christmas morning.
>
> I comb my hair with an ivory comb,
>   Ivory comb, ivory comb,
> I comb my hair with an ivory comb,
>   Upon a Christmas morning.
>
> Two little ships were sailing by,
>   Were sailing by, were sailing by,
> Two little ships were sailing by,
>   Upon a Christmas morning.
>
> Guess who was in one of them,
>   One of them, one of them,
> Guess who was in one of them,
>   Upon a Christmas morning.
>
> The Blessed Virgin and her son,
>   And her son, and her son,
> The Blessed Virgin and her son,
>   Upon a Christmas morning.

So far the carol may be a late importation; but the following stanza, chanted in perfect good faith, and without intentional irreverence, is a curious evidence of the manner in which ancient religion is affected by newly acquired patriotism, among children accustomed to too little literary culture to perceive the incongruity:

> Guess who was in the other of them,
>   Other of them, other of them,
> George Washington and his son,
>   Upon a Christmas morning.

459

Source

Journal of American Folklore, V (1892), 326. Collected by William Wells Newell. The tune is the familiar "Christmas Day in the Morning."

* * *

Christmas Eve on the East Side

My heart it is breaking, it's Christmas eve night.
I'm in the slums on the East Side without any light.
I've no gas or electric to make myself a cup of tea.
Oh tell me, fellow workers, how can this be?

Tell me, fellow workers, how can this be?
A home of the brave and the land of the free.
Starvation and misery is all that is free
For poor hard-working masses like you and like me.

While the poor hard-working masses lives in rat-infested
    slums
Those rich & mighty grafters they all have nice homes.
Yes, the rich & mighty grafters, they all have nice homes,
While hard-working masses live in old rat-infested slums.

The rich they have robbed us of our food and our
    homes.
Now they all live in luxury while we breathe on their
    crumbs.
Yes, the rich, they have robbed us of our food and our
    homes;
Now they all live in luxury while we breathe on their
    crumbs.

So come along, fellow workers, and let us unite
And take all that belongs to the laborers from those rich
    parasites.

United we stand and divided we fall.
Come and join the Workers Alliance while I'm making
    this call.

Come and join the Workers Alliance while I'm making
    this call.
United we stand and divided we fall.

Source and Comment

"Aunt Molly Jackson," Library of Congress Recordings, VII, 4 (1961). Collected by Alan Lomax, issued by Rounder Records of Somerville, Massachusetts. The music was transcribed by Lee Ellen Friedland at the Folklore Archives of the University of Pennsylvania.

Aunt Molly Jackson (1880-1960), born Mary Garland, was a well-known American folksinger and labor activist. Although she had a vast repertoire of traditional songs, and recorded 204 for the Library of Congress, she is best remembered for the songs of protest that she composed and sang after she became a vigorous champion of the rights of the Kentucky miners and other laborers in the 1930s. "Christmas Eve on the East Side" is one of these songs. It was written when a utility company refused to make an installation on Christmas Day in 1936 when she was residing in New York City. The melody is commonly used for "The Cherry-Tree Carol" which is #54 in Francis

J. Child's *The English and Scottish Popular Ballads,* 5 vols., Boston, 1892-98. See p. 26.

* * *

The Carol of the Twelve Numbers

The following fragment, representing family tradition going back at least a century, may be recognized as part of a carol belonging to the Christmas season....

> Twelve, the twelve apostles;
> Eleven, the eleven who went to heaven;
> Ten, the ten commandments;
> Nine, the nine, how bright they shine;
> Eight, the royal martyrs;
> Seven, the seven stars in the sky;
> Six,...
> Five,...
> Four, the gospel preachers;
> Three,...
> Two, the two lily-white babes clothed all in
> green, O!
> One's the one who dwells alone, and ever
> more shall do so.

A more complete version is contained in the "Bizarre Notes and Queries," Manchester, N.H., vol. vi. No. 2, 1889, p. 248, being contributed to that journal by Rev. J.H. Hopkins, from the singing of children in Essex, N.Y., who, during a residence on the southern shore of Lake Superior, had caught it by ear from Cornish miners employed in the copper mines of that region. In reprinting, I venture to make some slight changes of punctuation.

The carol is sung by two voices, alternating with successive lines, the numbers previously given being repeated in chorus:

> *1st voice.* Come and I will sing you!
> *2d voice.* What will you sing me?
> *1st voice.* I will sing you One, O!
> *2d voice.* What is your One, O?
> *1st voice.* One of them is God alone, and He ever
>   shall remain so.
>
> Come and I will sing you!
> What will you sing me?
> I will sing you two, O!
> What is your two, O?
> Two of them are lily-white babes, all
>   clothed in green, O!
>
> *Chorus.* One of them is God alone, and He ever
>   shall remain so.

The carol continues in the same manner, and the conclusion and summary being:

> Come and I will sing you!
> What will you sing me?
> I will sing you twelve, O!
> What is your twelve, O?
> Twelve are the twelve apostles,

Chorus. Eleven of them have gone to heaven,

Ten are the ten commandments,
Nine is the moonshine, bright and clear,
Eight is the Great Archangel.
Seven are seven stars in the sky,
Six are the cheerful waiters,
Five is the ferryman in the boat
Four are the gospel preachers,
Three of them are strangers,
Two of them are lily-white babes, all
clothed in green, O!
One of them is God alone, and He ever
shall remain so.

Source

Journal of American Folklore, IV (1891), 215-16. Collected by William Wells Newell from Mrs. R.B. Storer, formerly of Concord, Massachusetts. Newell also gives English examples of Christmas counting songs and cites many European examples, including a German carol "sung as part of the Jewish Passover service." See "A Passover Song and a Christmas Carol," p. 149, and "The Twelve Days of Christmas," p. 474.

* * *

The Joys of Mary

While collecting games of children, some years ago, I came upon several examples of old English songs, preserved in America in versions independent of print....

The first joy that Mary had, it was the joy of one,
To see her son Jesus into the world to come.
Into the world to come, good man, and blessed
may he be,
With Father, Son, and Holy Ghost, and Christ
eternally.

The second joy that Mary had, it was the joy of
two,
To see her son Jesus go through the world, go
through.

The third joy that Mary had, it was the joy of
three,
To see her son Jesus upon the cursed tree.

The fourth joy that Mary had, it was the joy of
four,
To see her son Jesus open wide the door.

The fifth joy that Mary had, it was the joy of five,
To see her son Jesus make the dead alive.

The sixth joy that Mary had, it was the joy of six,
To see her son Jesus bear the crucifix.

The seventh joy that Mary had, it was the joy of
seven,
To see her son Jesus wear the keys of heaven.

The eighth joy that Mary had, it was the joy of
eight,
To see her son Jesus make the crooked straight.

The ninth joy that Mary had, it was the joy of
nine,
To see her son Jesus make the water wine.
....

The twelfth joy that Mary had, it was the joy of
twelve,
To see her son Jesus (burst the gates) of hell.

The reciter could not give the tenth and eleventh verses, nor the whole of the last line.

From English children in Philadelphia the following version of the first verse is obtained:

The first good joy that Mary had, it was the joy of
one,
To bring into this sinful world her dear and only
son.

The next good joy that Mary had, it was the joy of
two,
To teach her dear son Jesus to read the Bible
through.

Source

Journal of American Folklore, V (1892), 325-26. Collected by William Wells Newell. His first example "comes from Connecticut, whence ultimately derived I could not discover."

* * *

Go Where I Send Thee

[Joe Townsend's] tunes are a curious blending of the elements of Negro spirituals, "blues," and idiom of Negro "soul" music—a style which has been popularized in recent years by Negro performers....

Townsend claimed that he composed the lyrics and the tunes himself, but I suspect that he was not entirely honest with himself in making this claim...."Go Where I Send Thee" is a variation of a centuries old folk song which has gone by the various titles of "Green Grow the Rushes," the English "Dilly Song," and "Carol of the 12 Numbers." The exact origin of the song is unknown, but we do know that it has been in existence in English-speaking lands since the 16th century. Versions of the song are popular throughout the southern United States today, and it is for this reason that I maintain that Townsend must have heard the song performed and learned it, instead of composing it himself.

Go Where I Send Thee

Well, chil-dren go where I send thee. Well, they're gon-na send thee one by one; one gon-na be the old-est ba-by, born by the birth of li'l ole Ma-ry. They wrapped it all up in a li'l swine-a clothes, and they

laid it in the ox of a manger, and it was born
born in Bethlehem. Now children want you to go where I send thee, well,
they're gonna send thee twelve by twelve; Twelve's gonna be the twelve disciples,
Lebn, etc. (through two)

Well, children, go on ware I sen' de,
Well, dere is gonna sen' de one by one,
One gonna be da oldes' baby
Bawn by the verje of little ole Mary,
Dey rapt it all up in a little swīn'n clōth
'N tha laid it in tha ox of a manger
'N it was bawn, bawn in Bethlehem.

A now chile a wan' ya go whar I sen' de,
Well, dare gonna sen' de twelve by twelve,
Twelve gonna be da twelve disciples,
'Lebn gonna be the one nevah get ta heaven,
Ten gonna be tha' ten commanment,
Nine gonna be da one dat dress so fine,
Eight gonna be da one stan'in on da gate,
Seven gonna be the one go'n on ta heaven,
Six gonna be the one never get fix,
Five gonna be tha' gospel writah,
Fō gonna be, chile, knockin on ya dō.
Three gonna be the Hebrew children,
Two gonna be tha Paul 'n Silan,
They stayed in jail, chile, all night long,
'N one gonna be tha' olest baby
born by the verge of little ole Mary,
Tha wrap't it all up in a little swīn'n clōth
'N they laid it in the ox of a manger
'N it was bawn, bawn in Bethlehem

Now children I want ya ta go where I sen' de,
Well, there gonna send one by one,
One gonna be tha oldes' baby.
Two gonna be 'n Paul 'n Silan,
Three gonna be tha Hebrew chil-un,
Fo gonna be knockin' on ya do,
Fi gonna be the gospel writah,
Six gonna be the one never get fix,
Seven gonna be the one gon'onna heaven,
Eight gonna be chile stannin' on ya gate,
'N nine gonna be the one dres' so fine,
Ten gonna be the Ten commanment,
'Leven gonna be the one nevah get ta heaven,
Twelve gonna be tha' twel' disciple.

'N fo-ah gonna be chile knockin' on ya door,
Three gonna be tha' Hebrew child-un,
'N two gonna be tha' Paul 'n Silan,
Who stayed in jail, chile, all night long,
'N one gonna be the ol-les baby
Born by tha verge a little ole Mary,
They wrapt it all up in a little swīnin clōth
'N they laid it in the ox of a manger
'N it wuz born, born in Bethlehem.

The number symbolism of the version of the song is unique. I suspect that some of the phrases (for instance, those concerning the numbers "six" and "nine" especially) have no real religious significance to the singer, but are used chiefly for their rhymes. Many other versions of this song, though, also employ lyrics which are not necessarily meaningful in a symbolic sense, but which are sung merely for the sound of the words.

Source

Mississippi Folklore Register, III (1969), 89, 92-94. Performed by a black singer and composer, Joe Townsend, age 74, of Independence, Mississippi, in 1968 and recorded by Charles Neale, a folklore student at the University of Mississippi. The transcription of the words and tune and the comment are by Larry Gunn.

* * *

Negro Christmas Carol

The Christmas songs of Negroes, given below, are examples of the true carols, or *noëls,* still sung in that State. Unhappily we cannot add the melody:

I.

De leetle cradle rocks to-night in glory,
    In glory, in glory,
De leetle cradle rocks to-night in glory,
    De Christ-chile born.
    Peace on earth,
        Mary rock de cradle,
    Peace on earth,
        Mary rock de cradle,
    Peace on earth,
        Mary rock de cradle,

De Christ-chile born in glory,
    In glory, in glory,
De Christ-chile born in glory,

II.

De Christ-chile am passin',
    Sing softly,
De Christ-chile am passin',
    Sing low.
Don' yo' hear he foot on de treetop,
    Sof' like de south win' blow?
        Glory hallelu!
    Glory, glory, glory,
        Glory hallelu!

Source

Journal of American Folklore, XII (1899), 272. Communicated by Emma M. Backus. Informant not given.

* * *

Parodies of Christmas Carols

We three Kings of Orient are,
Trying to smoke a rubber cigar;

It was loaded; it exploded—
We two Kings of Orient are.

We two kings of Orient are,
Trying to smoke a rubber cigar,
   etc., etc.

Deck the halls with poison ivy.
Deck the halls with Balls of Charley,
Fa-la-la la-la, la-la la-la.
Deck the Balls of Uncle Charley,
Fa-la-la la-la, la-la la-la.

God rest ye merry gentlemen,
And rest ye merry heart.
Feen-a-mints are just the thing,
They'll surely make you fart.
When you're sick and when you're dry
And when you need some booze,
Feen-a-mints are just the thing,
They're full of juicy chewz.

(O tidings of comfort and joy,
Comfort and joy,
O tidings of comfort and joy.)

God rest ye merry gentlemen,
And rest ye merry heart.
When you wake up at night
And to your funny foolish fright
And find you have a feeling
Classified as constipation,
You open up the Feen-a-mints
And then run to the station.
(O tidings of comfort and joy,
Comfort and joy,
O tidings of comfort and joy.)

Now that you are on the throne
And now you're feeling good
Remember always do
As Mother McCreedy would.
Open up some Feen-a-mints
And then run to the station.
Now you surely are relieved
Of constipation.
(O tidings of comfort and joy,
Comfort and joy,
O tidings of comfort and joy.)

Source

Journal of American Folklore, LXXVII (1964), 50. Collected in Rhode Island by George Monteiro, the first from an unnamed adult, and the others from "children." He observes that religious parody, having "virtually disappeared as a literary form, nevertheless maintains an active folk life."

* * *

Children's Taunts

Can't catch a flea on a Christmas tree.

    I see Christmas,
    I see stars.

    I see somebody's
    Underdrawers.

Source

Western Folklore, XIV (1955), 207. Collected by Ray B. Browne from Mrs. Robert T. Burns of Wehadkee, Alabama in 1955.

* * *

Yuletide Rhyme

This rhyme . . . was usually recited in Yuletide [by Welsh in Kentucky and Tennessee] because of the first line.

    Christmas comes but once a year,
    There's not much strength in table beer.
    What's far off cannot be near,
    Nor Irish is not Latin.
    A hackney coach is not a truck,
    A billy goat is not a duck,
    A cockatoo is not a rook,
    Nor a boot-jack's not a barrel.
    These are honest truths I vow,
    Pay attention to me now,
    And in the end you will allow
    That this is truthful knowledge.

Source

Tennessee Folklore Society Bulletin, IX (December 1953), 2. Collected by Wynn Jones, a graduate student at the University of Tennessee, from family tradition. It was known by her parents, of Welsh origin, in Kentucky and Tennessee mining communities where they lived. See "Eisteddfod on St. David's Day," p. 115, for background.

* * *

Christmas Similes

Slow as Christmas.

Waiting for him is like waiting for Christmas.

Source

Mississippi Folklore Register, V (1971), 126. Collected by Bonnie Bringar from "speakers black and white" in Adams County, Mississippi.

* * *

[A house] lit up like a Christmas tree.

Source

Keystone Folklore Quarterly, X (1965), 9. Collected by Mac E. Barrick in Carlisle, Pennsylvania from Mrs. Ella Barrick and Mrs. Elsie Snyder.

* * *

Fat as a Christmas turkey.

Full [of crap] as a Christmas turkey.

Source

Southern Folklore Quarterly, IV (1940), 128. From an article by Joseph D. Clark on "Similes from the Folk Speech of the South."

Colder than Christmas.

I wouldn't have it on a Christmas tree.

Source

"Folklore in White County, Tennessee," Ph.D. Dissertation, George Peabody College for Teachers, 1979, 122. Collected by Edwina B. Doran from residents or former residents of White County, Tennessee.

* * *

Christmas Riddles

The joking question "What's black and white and red all over?" with the answer "A newspaper" is perhaps the most common example of a folk riddle collected in the United States in the twentieth century. . . . A number of riddles and riddle jokes, running throughout almost all types of riddles, at least in American collections, have several possible answers. These multiple-answer riddles are found in the repartee of minstrel shows ("What has four legs and flies?" "—A dead horse." "Wrong, two pairs of pants."), in folk conundrums of the early twentieth-century ("What goes around a button [a-buttin']?" "—A button-hole." "No, a billy-goat."), and in the semisophisticated elephant jokes of the 1960's. Unlike ancient riddles of impossibility ("How many fish in the sea?"; "What am I thinking?"), whose purpose was to show the cleverness of the person answering the riddle as in the tale of the King and the Abbot, the purpose of these modern riddle jokes seems to be to make the person answering look ridiculous because he is unable to guess which answer the riddler has in mind. Of course, no matter which answer is given, the riddler insists that the other is the correct one. Thus with the [multiple answer riddle] new answers continue to proliferate, such as the following collected in Shippensburg, Pa., in October, 1973: "What is black and white and red all over?" "—Santa Claus coming down the chimney on Christmas Eve." Although here more logically the progression of colors should be "red and white and black all over," the order of the original . . . is preserved to mislead the victim into thinking that the answer is the same.

Source

Journal of American Folklore, LXXXVII (1974), 253, 257. Collected and commented on by Mac E. Barrick.

* * *

"How is Santa Claus like a beatnik?"

Answer: "Because he doesn't shave and just works one day a year."

Source

"Folklore in White County, Tennessee," Ph.D. Dissertation, George Peabody College for Teachers, 1979, 287. Collected in 1967-68 by Edwina B. Doran. She lists informants, residents or former residents of White County, but does not always specify their contribution.

A Christmas Spell for Making a Divining Rod

I will add a few more spells of interest. One for making a divining rod is as follows: In the first night of Christmas, between eleven and twelve o'clock, break off from any tree a young twig of one year's growth, in the three highest names, facing toward sunrise. Whenever you apply this wand in searching for iron, ore, or water, apply it three times. The twig must be forked, and each end of the fork must be held in each hand, so the third and thickest end must stand up, but don't hold it up too tight. Strike the ground with the thickest end, and that which you desire will appear immediately, if there is any in the ground where you strike. The words to be spoken are as follows: "Archangel Gabriel, I conjure thee in the name of God the Almighty to tell me if there is any water here or not. Do tell me." If you wish iron or ore, use either word in place of water. Other words to be spoken, when breaking the twig, are: "Divining wand, do thou keep that power that God gave thee in the very first hour."

Source

Journal of American Folklore, XV (1902), 271. Collected by Letitia Humphreys Wrenshall. Her source was a "gentle witch, who was pretty, rosy, and plump." This witch learned "how to use the words, how to speak them, how to move her hands" from a "German man" who married her aunt and adoptive mother. She had a "book of spells translated from the German in 1820," apparently a manuscript.

* * *

Christmas Weather Rhyme

When Christmas does no winter bring,

Look for winter in the spring.

Source

New York Folklore Quarterly, VII (1951), 41. Collected by Edith Cutting, who provides a list of informants, "Yorkers," mostly her students and those of Louis C. Jones. She does not supply information about them.

* * *

Graveyards at Christmas

White Christmas, poor graveyard.

Green Christmas, fat graveyard.

Source

Tennessee Folklore Society Bulletin, XXIII (September 1957), 86. Collected by Kelsie B. Harder in Perry County, Tennessee.

* * *

Dirty Linen on Christmas

No bed clothes should be washed between Christmas and Old Christmas.

If you wash clothes within three weeks after Christmas, you will wash someone out of your family.

Bad luck to hang clothes on the line between new Christmas and old Christmas.

Source

Southern Folklore Quarterly, XXVI (1962), 212. Collected by Joseph D. Clark from students at North Carolina State College at Raleigh in 1955-56 and 1960-61.

* * *

Born at the Same Time as Christ

In the traditional Italian culture, no one is supposed to be born on the same day (December 25) and at the same time of night (12:00 o'clock A.M.) as Christ. Females born at this time will become witches, while males will turn into werewolves every Christmas eve for a few hours. During this time he will have no control over his actions nor will he remember what he did as a werewolf. A werewolf will run and howl wildly, unearthing and throwing large rocks. He will kill anyone he sees, by ripping out their throat. The only way to cure him is to cut him when he is a werewolf, so that he bleeds.

Mrs. Nappi told me a story about a man who was born at 12:00 on Christmas eve. When this man got married he told his wife that when he went out on Christmas eve, she was not to let him back in the house until he had come to the door and knocked for the third time. On one Christmas eve his wife fell asleep. When the man, still a werewolf, banged on the door for the second time, his wife awoke. Thinking it was the third time her husband had come to the door, she let him in and was killed.

Source

New York Folklore Quarterly, XXVIII (1972), 259-60. Collected from Mrs. Stephanie Nappi by Michael Brunetti. She was born in Italy and came to the United States to get married in 1914. Thereafter she lived in Schenectady, New York, where she worked as a dishwasher and in a baseball bat factory.

* * *

Christmas Baby

A baby born on Christmas day can understand the speech of animals.

Source

Journal of American Folklore, LII (1939), 116. From a collection of "Tennessee Folk Beliefs Concerning Children" by T. J. Farr. Farr collected in "the remote mountain sections" and included material given him by "at least five different informants."

* * *

You will have good luck if you were born on Christmas Day.

Source

Journal of American Folklore, XL (1927), 190. From "superstitions" collected by Hilda Roberts in Iberia Parish, Louisiana. Her informants included "three races . . . the white, the black, and the red, and . . . three nationalities . . . the French, the Spanish, and the Anglo-Saxon."

* * *

Christmas Names

[A study of] "Child Naming in Tennessee during the Depression Years" [reveals that the] calendar date of birth accounted among our students for two Noels . . . [and] one Eva (Christmas Eve). . . .

Source

Southern Folklore Quarterly, XXIII (1959), 150, 153. Seven hundred children's names were studied by George C. Grise. His subjects were white freshmen at Austin Peay State College born in Tennessee and adjoining counties in Kentucky, 1935-40.

* * *

Christmas Eve Dance

Dances and balls were frequently given on Christmas night and many gay young folks could be found in attendance. In 1857 some of the younger set in Hamilton County [Iowa] drove a four-horse sleigh from Saratoga to Rose Grove for a Christmas Eve dance. Near Kamrar they were set on by a pack of a hundred prairie wolves but reached Rose Grove in safety. The perils of the wintry prairie were soon forgotten in the whirls of the dance. "At twelve o'clock," one of the merrymakers related, "our landlord called us to supper. The meal consisted of deer, elk and buffalo meat, corn bread baked on an iron griddle, fried cakes and pumpkin pie. After doing it ample justice we danced on till morning. . . . The wind did blow and the snow drifted and filled our tracks, and it was bitter cold the next day when we ate our breakfast and started for home. Our bill for the fun we had, was one dollar per couple."

Source

Iowa Journal of History and Politics, XLIII (1945), 176-77. Collected by William J. Peterson. His source was an Iowa newspaper, the *Webster City Freeman-Tribune,* July 23, 1913.

* * *

Playing Snap during the Holidays

The country dance and the play-party have existed in Mills County [Texas] since settlement, but they have never been so popular as the Snap party, partly because many Mills County boys and girls have been brought up to believe that dancing is wrong. For this reason only the "rougher elements" of society attend the dances and play-parties. Then the town of Goldthwaite has never sponsored a public dancing place of any sort, and since the rural dances have always been the rendezvous of the county's bootleggers and the scene of its most sensational murders, it is easy to see why most Mills County boys and girls do not go to dances until they go to college.

The play-party has never been very popular in this locality, partly because of its similarity to dancing, but primarily because of the great popularity of Snap. For Snap is a game that everybody can play at the same time and that a group can keep on playing together for hours on end.

Most boys and girls do not begin going to Snap parties until they are thirteen or fourteen years old. But if there are older sisters in the family and no big brothers to take them to parties, the parents go and take the smaller children along. Since I was one of the smaller children in such a family, I started going to Snap parties many years before I was old enough to play, and I started playing the game years before I began going with an escort or "date" of my own. Thus I grew up going to a Snap party almost every Saturday night, often on Friday night, the year around, and every night during the Christmas holidays....

It takes four people to play a game of Snap, the two who "hold up," the one who snaps, and the one who is snapped. During a game, the player passes through four stages: namely, being snapped, snapping someone, holding up with the person who has snapped him, and holding up with the person he has snapped.

The original way to choose a partner was to snap one's fingers at the desired person, and from that custom the game received its name. This method of snapping, however, has been discarded in Mills County. When one person snaps another at our parties, he usually says, "Will you come catch me?" or simply "Come catch me," but often such expressions as "Let's run a race," "Get started," and "Lady, take after me," are heard. Little variation from these forms of address is permitted. One night at a party, a visiting boy from Wichita Falls went over to one of the girls and, following the coaching he had received from some local joker, said, "Come catch me, chicken. I'm full of corn." The girl answered him with a brisk slap in the face, and the boy from Wichita Falls played no more Snap that night.

The game starts with a boy and girl "holding up;" that is, they stand facing each other holding hands. Let us call them John and Mary. Another boy, say Tom, snaps a girl, Jane. Tom then walks or runs around the couple standing, and Jane chases him. When she catches him, John leaves the game; Tom holds up with Mary; and Jane snaps another boy, Henry. When Henry catches Jane, Mary leaves the game, and Tom and Jane hold up. Henry now snaps a girl, and the game continues. Thus the game goes on in an endless procession of entering, holding up with two different people, and leaving the game.

The chief action of the game comes when the couple runs around the couple holding up. The movement differs according to individual players. Some couples walk calmly and sedately through a game, but in my home community we usually played very hilariously. I have often seen the players holding up almost thrown to the floor by a runner's "swinging around the corner."

Assuming that the young folk are playing outside the house, any girl who participates is definitely associated with four different boys in the cycle of one Snap game. Let us take a girl named Jane through a game. She walks out with Tom, the boy who snapped her. She catches him and returns to the house with John, the boy who is leaving the game. She then snaps Henry and returns to the game. After he catches her, Jane remains outside holding up with Tom while Henry and the girl leaving the game go into the house together. Henry returns with another girl, and after he is caught, Jane holds up with him while Tom goes into the house with the girl Henry snapped. This girl returns with a new boy, and after he catches her, Jane, who is leaving the game, walks into the house with the new boy. During the game, then, she has been associated with both Tom, who snapped her, and Henry, whom she snapped, two different times, and with two other boys once each.

Snap may sound like a dull and uninteresting game, but it is far from that. It keeps the crowd constantly changing and moving about, and after several hours of play, each boy has had ample opportunity to talk to every girl present. The game moves with such automatic regularity that one is scarcely conscious of anything except that life is moving about him and that he is a part of it. In my heyday of Snap parties, which extended from about 1928 to 1934, they were always gay and colorful, with much laughter, talking, and noise....

About 1932 a new type of Snap became common in Mills County. It was called "Swap-out," or "Car" Snap. It is played exactly like ordinary Snap except that the players sit in a car instead of standing up in the yard. And instead of running around the car and catching each other, the players merely get in or out of the car. The advent of this fad caused a great deal of indignation among the older people. Many mothers thought that "Swap-out" was improper and refused to permit it at their parties. But time cures all things. Today Swap-out is the most common form of outdoor Snap in Mills County. A few enemies of Car Snap still exist, however, and their daughters are not allowed to play that form of the game.

In recent years [c. 1950] the rural dance has become more popular and the Snap party is beginning to disintegrate. Play-party games are played in the house, and Snap is played outside at the same time, and the combination works very nicely. But not so with dancing. The crowd either snaps or dances. The two simply will not mix.

Snap parties in Mills County are still gay and colorful, but they are not what they used to be. In appearance they are about the same. Dress among the boys ranges from blue overalls and cowboy chaps and boots to tailor-made suits and lettered football sweaters. A sprinkling of John Tarleton and A. and M. uniforms appears at them during the Christmas holidays. Girls always dress up for a party, and to the casual observer they at first all look alike. But the colors and cut of their clothes and their hair styles mark the difference between the stay-at-homes and those who are at home only for the holidays or vacation.

Source and Comment

Publications of the Texas Folk-Lore Society, XXVI (1954), 190-92, 194-95. Described by Mae Featherstone of Mills County "in the hills of Central Texas." The play party was a substitute for dancing to music in communities with religious scruples. Partners held hands or clapped hands and sang as they moved through their "games" or "plays," avoiding the term "dance." But snap, in the Ozark region at least, could be "a rough and rowdy game often characterized by a great display of lingerie or the lack of it." See, for example, *Folklore in America,* 186-87.

* * *

Christmas Parties in the Factory

The office Christmas party is a cliché in which blue collarites participate with gusto. The formal parties at local restaurants or country clubs are attended by both management and workers. The in-plant parties involve only the workers, for the foremen, who pretend not to notice, are not officially allowed to sanction drinking at work. These parties are small group affairs, seldom numbering more than a dozen participants. A few weeks prior to the party, a collection of $3-$4 per person is taken, and, on party day, a convenient workbench is spread with cold cuts, hot Italian food, turkeys, and booze. One recent Christmas [c. 1973], for some reason, even the foremen were drinking, and there was not a sober person in the shop. Thanksgiving parties are less frequent, and, unlike Christmas parties, occur almost exclusively on the second or third shift, although the form is similar. One Thanksgiving party involved the commandeering of a heat-treat oven to roast turkeys.

Source

Journal of American Folklore, LXXXVII (1974), 137. While employed in a "large industrial plant as a machinist," Bruce E. Nickerson observed traditional behavior and customs of blue collar workers.

* * *

Christmas Office Parties

Quietly, without fanfare, a great corporate tradition is dying. The office Christmas party, which dates back more than 50 years, has grown up to become a big business risk.

As a result, the institution that simultaneously provided the ambitious with a proving ground and the lonely with fertile ground for romance, may be headed the way of the dinosaur, business consultants say.

Traditional holiday office parties, where people primarily came at night to socialize and drink, are on the way out, often replaced by brunches, alcohol-free breakfasts and year-end afternoon meetings to recap corporate goals.

The changing times, which reflect public concern about drinking and the widening scope of legal liabilities for alcohol-related behavior, have encouraged many employers to put the traditional party on the shelf, said Andrew Sherwood, chairman of The Goodrich & Sherwood Co. in New York, a management-consulting firm that deals with how people relate to one another....

Sherwood said yesterday, "I think there is greater liability in terms of the employee who goes to the office party and kills a bunch of people on the way home or falls under a train ... A number of things could happen that the company could be liable for."

Then, too, office parties do not serve the purpose they once did, Sherwood said.

"They started right after the Depression when there was a lot of bad news going on. People didn't have money, so I think companies got together and said, 'Why don't we put on a Christmas party for people who are struggling?'"

Another purpose was to boost employee morale and productivity.

"Today, there is very little productively to be gained [by] the traditional office party," Sherwood said. "What companies are doing is having year-end parties ... they recap the year ... maybe hand out some service awards, and then people go home or go shopping."

Source

Philadelphia Inquirer, December 24, 1987. Edited from an article by staff writer Linda S. Wallace.

* * *

Christmas Tree Ornament

[The] sweetgum tree has afforded a particularly good Christmas tree ornament. In more recent years [c. 1970] some rural children have been taught to gather the foil from chewing gum wrappers and use it to wrap the globose sweetgum balls that are composed of many woody carpels. The sharp end protrusions of the carpels hold the foil quite well, and the stem on the ball is used to hang the ornament on the tree.

Sweetgum ball tree ornament

Source

Mississippi Folklore Register, IV (1970), 75. From "Folk Toys and Amusements of Rural Mississippi Children" by Rosalie B. S. Daniels.

* * *

Bladder Busting on Christmas Morning

Christmas [in rural Tennessee c. 1925] was a season more for games and fun. And again the special things with which to celebrate had to be improvised. A unique method for providing some inexpensive "guns" (the noise) was by the use of hog bladders. We always killed five or six hogs at home. The bladders were carefully saved by us children. After these had been well stretched by inflating and deflating and pulling, they were then "blowed" up and the ends tied and then hung up in some safe place to keep for Christmas. A quill made from the joint of a wild cane, inserted in the neck of the bladder with plenty of breath to blow, did the trick of blowing up. If we forgot which end of the quill went in the mouth, little damage was done. Anyway, all of the blowing was probably unconsciously developing our lungs. On Christmas morning the bladders were taken down and "busted." This "busting" was accomplished by using the back of an ax or by the use of a plank. The noise was really surprisingly loud. So we were well paid for all our trouble. And I'm still wondering why someone did not write a song on "When It's Bladder Busting Time in the Country" and become famous.

Source

Tennessee Folklore Society Bulletin, XII (March 1946), 19-20. From a paper by Robert Lassiter on "games we played as children" in Tennessee.

* * *

Bringing in the Yule Log

In preparation for this Christmas celebration [in medieval England] a tree had been felled, the log cut, marked, and hidden away in the nearby forest. At a given time the people hurried out in search of it. When it was found, it was carried and dragged joyously to the manor house where it was cut in half and carried into the great hall.

There one half was placed on the fire and the other half was set aside for use in kindling the fire the following year.

While the log was never used as a religious symbol, it came to be held in respect verging on reverence. Many superstitions grew up around it. Even the ashes were carried away to protect the homes in which they were kept from evil. They were diluted in water and swallowed as cure for internal disorders. They were made into a paste and applied externally for infections.

Our Yule Log [at the Williamsburg Inn, Williamsburg, Virginia] is now hidden somewhere on the grounds. We will all go out to hunt the log, and when it is found it will be dragged to the Lounge. The finder of the log must try to ride it and all others will help with the rope. After it is brought in, it will be cut in two, with one section being set aside for the burning of the Yule Log and the other used for kindling wood for the fire next year....

Each part of the ceremony has an allegorical meaning based on ancient superstitions. Thus the sprig of green, symbolizing the woes of last year, is cast on the fire to banish those woes forever; to protect the house from "ghosties and ghaisties and things that go boomp in the night," wine is poured into the fire during the traditional blessing of the log. It is hoped that everyone will join in the ceremonies and in the carol singing.

Source and Comment

Ceremony of Bringing in the Yule Log, Colonial Williamsburg Foundation, 1980. Information from programs issued by the Williamsburg Inn for its guests during the Christmas season. Though such Yule log ceremonies are within British tradition and probably took place in the American colonies, Ruth L. Watkins, research assistant for the Colonial Williamsburg Foundation, states that no mention of them has been found in "colonial Virginia records" and "because we cannot substantiate the beautiful old custom of a Yule log we do not have this officially observed within the Historic Area" of Williamsburg but in "our hotels."

* * *

Yule Log

Burning Yule Logs

If you have a fireplace and are in the habit of burning a Yule log at Christmas, be sure to save a part of the log during the year because it is the best insurance you can get against lightning and fire for the next 365 days.

Source

Richwood (West Virginia) *News Leader,* December 25, 1957. This is a local belief, which was published in a weekly newspaper in Hancock County, West Virginia.

* * *

Christmas wood is the red oak split from a large tree.

The All-Day [Christmas] fire is made from green sycamore. It's a slow burner.

Source

North Carolina Folklore, XIX (1971), 150. From an article on "Survivals of Old Christmas" by F. Roy Johnson. The belief about red oak is from Colin Parker of Murfreesboro, North Carolina; the one about sycamore from Tommy Piland, a native of Hertford County, North Carolina.

* * *

Christmas is tradition and wassail and Yule logs and songs dating back to pagan customs and sharing, with a whole lot of love.

Nowhere is that exemplified better each year than at the Publick House [in Sturbridge, Massachusetts] where the Yule Log Celebration on two weekends in December brings a very special spirit to more than 2,600 persons.

"The Yule Log Celebration is a feeling, a pageant of sorts that replaces, for all of us involved in presenting it, a little bit of the love that's gone out of the world," as the Producer David Hyatt describes it.

Somehow it's even more than that.

For those who saw and were a part of this year's [1980] celebration, it brought to mind the dreams of childhood that made this holiday the brightest part of the year. There are huge gingerbread houses brightly decorated with icing and gumdrops, ice sculptures almost as large, a boar's head, wassail bowl, Yule logs, ivy and holly, and processions of minstrels, the inn's waiters and waitresses more properly called "Beefeaters and Wenches" and the grand master of it all, Innkeeper Buddy Adler....

There was the ceremony of adding the Yule log to the fire, with three glasses of brandy to heighten the blaze as Adler toasted the "health, wealth and happiness" of each and everyone; gifts of holly and ivy, to be placed on the blouse or lapel, even a special-for-this-year but appropriate-to-the-season singing of John Lennon's "In My Life."

Hyatt, a native of Monson who now lives in Springfield with his family and travels weekly to his acting roles in New York City, conceived The Yule Log Celebration eight years ago in conjunction with Innkeeper Adler who saw it as a "chance to give something back to the community at the most beautiful time of the year."

Source

Springfield (Massachusetts) *Daily News,* December 23, 1980. From a newspaper feature by Elsie Osterman who describes a holiday banquet at a Massachusetts inn established in 1771. The inn provides a professionally produced entertainment based on the revival of what are claimed to be old Christmas customs.

* * *

Barring Out the Schoolmaster at Christmas

Barring out the schoolmaster—either on Christmas or Shrove Tuesday—used to be an annual occurrence throughout the width and breadth of the Pennsylvania Dutch Country.... In the western area—Lancaster, Lebanon and west—the date was almost invariably Christmas. The motivation at Christmas is clear: to exact a gift, edibles, from the teacher....

The custom of barring out the teacher seems to have been practiced widely in the day when there were predominantly men teachers. When women teachers began to take over, the "sport" became less interesting and began to disappear. Many an old-timer in the Dutch Country recalls participating in this custom. One old grandfather from Reamstown told the author that his teacher used to give the pupils who were well-behaved *en gonser tsoocker-schtengel* (a whole stick of candy). The bad boys and girls he said, *hen als yoosht en halb schtick grickt.* I have evidence of the custom being practiced as late as the early 1930's in Lehigh County.

There follow now the published accounts of barring out the teacher which we have on file in our Folklore Center archive.

Two Examples

Bareville had no special services on Christmas; but was disgraced by the revival of an old custom—the barring out of the teacher of the primary and grammar schools. It is a disgrace for the community that would-be young men are yet to be found who have no common sense and are ignorant of the simplest forms of politeness. It may, however, be said to the credit of the seventy pupils of these schools that only one was found who was willing to do such work and he had to accomplish it by entering the school building at midnight.

It was the common practice for the larger "scholars" to assemble and get possession of the school-house in advance of the "master's" arrival, very early on the morning of the day preceding Christmas, and "bar" him out and keep him out until he subscribed his name to a paper something like the following, (which I gave from memory founded on my own observation, having, like many others of my age, more than once participated in the popular and exciting game of barring out the master:)

Three dozen Ginger-Cakes; Six dozen Sugar-Cakes; Six dozen Molasses-Crackers; Four dozen Ginger-horses; do, Ginger-Rabbits; Six dozen Mintsticks; Three dozen Belly-guts; one hundred Loveletters; 2 Galls of Beer; one half bushel of some kind of Nuts, and one weeks Holidays."

Source

Pennsylvania Dutchman, VII (Winter 1956), 14-15. Introduced by Alfred L. Shoemaker, the two examples are credited to *"The Lancaster New Era"* of December 28, 1878 and "H. L. Fisher's *Olden Times,*" York, 1888.

"Christmas Gift": Southern Greeting

The origin of the Southern term ["Christmas Gift!"] is uncertain.... "Few of us who own slaves," writes Joseph B. Cobb of Mississippi in 1841, "ever refuse to grant this innocent and appropriate indulgence to these creatures of our will; and I remember well paying the penalty to old Nanny and her little Joe on the morning in question."

The gift, however, is incidental to the greeting and in most instances is not really expected, since in the old days most plantation families, including the servants, exchanged gifts on Christmas morning in a ceremony presided over by master and mistress. The general use of the term among all ranks of society is another bit of evidence (along with the shooting of fireworks, for example) of the traditional exuberance of Southerners, both black and white, at the Christmas season. The attitude was different in New England....

The correct time for the use of the Southern greeting was on Christmas morning before the general presentation of gifts. The stir began, says Thomas Nelson Page, before daylight when "small white-clad figures would steal through the dim light of dusky rooms and cold passages, opening doors with sudden bursts, and shouting 'Christmas Gift!' into darkened chambers, at still sleeping elders." A young school teacher from Michigan describes the custom as he first experienced it in the 1850's when he spent a year on a plantation in the Mississippi Delta. The servant who came to build a fire in his room on Christmas morning called out "Christmas Gift!" when he first opened the door. Then the room, and apparently the whole house, was filled with young Negroes, all shouting the same thing. The Northern visitor returned with a "Merry Christmas!" but eventually gave way and adopted the local manner. "We had a chat, at table, about the Southern custom of greeting one with a 'Christmas Gift!' instead of wishing you a 'Merry Christmas!' as we of the North did. They knew nothing about the origin of their custom, it had been with them time immemorial."

Today, "Merry Christmas!" is the usual form of greeting in most parts of the South, particularly in urban areas. "Christmas Gift!" is associated with old-fashioned manners, not particularly desirable any longer. Usage among the Negroes has also declined, though the term lives on in such local folk stories as the one in Mississippi about why there are so many Negroes in the Delta. Once on Christmas morning a Negro saw the "Lawd" coming down the road. He hid in a pine thicket and at the right moment jumped out and surprised the "Lawd" with "Christmas Gift!" Finding Himself caught, the "Lawd" said: "Take the Delta. Hit ain't fitten for nothin but Hell and highwater nohow."

Source

Kentucky Folklore Record, XIII (1967), 38-39. Elmo Howell provides a discussion of the southern Christmas greeting as background to an explication of its use in William Faulkner's *The Sound and the Fury* to indicate loss of old traditions. He provides references for his quotations in the footnotes. The dialect joke at the end was collected by the WPA Historical Research Project of Mississippi, 1936-1939.

* * *

"Christmas Gift": Southern Greeting
More "Christmas Gift" Greetings

Notes are written to Santa Claus, or the children call up the chimney what they most desire; or cry "Christmas gift!" "Caught the other Christmas gift."

Some Baltimore children always put a pillow in the chimney place that Santa Claus might alight in comfort.

Source

Memoirs of the American Folklore Society, XVIII (1925), 128. Contributed by Mrs. C. C. Marden. Her source was a questionnaire on Christmas customs sent to "different sections of the State" by the Maryland Folk-Lore Society.

* * *

Christmas day was devoted largely to family reunions. In our family during my early childhood [c. 1875] the Christmas dinner was served at grandfather's house. Everybody, uncles, aunts and cousins came piling out of sleds, shouting "Merry Christmas" and "Christmas Gift." There seemed to be an idea that if you could say that before the other fellow did, he owed you the gift. But I never saw the gift delivered.

Source

Annals of Iowa, XXXII (1955), 501. Christmas reminiscences of Mrs. R. A. Poage, "a grown girl" in 1890, who was born and lived in a rural Iowa community.

* * *

On Christmas Eve morning [in White County, Tennessee] if you say "Christmas Eve Gift" to someone before he says it to you, he owes you a gift. The same for "Christmas Gift" on Christmas morning.

Source

"Folklore in White County, Tennessee," Ph.D. Dissertation, George Peabody College for Teachers, 1969, 208. Collected in 1967-68 by Edwina B. Doran. She lists informants, residents or former residents of White County, but does not always specify their contribution.

* * *

The "Just Right" Christmas Present

There was a fellow gave a colored man a quart of whiskey for Christmas. It goes along about a week or ten days, he finally met up with the old colored man, and he asked him how his whiskey was. "Oh," he says, "it's just right, just right!" "Why," he says, "what do you mean by 'just right'?" "Well now," he says, "if it had been any better you'd have kept it for yourself," he said, "if it had been any worse, it'd have killed me!"

Source

Kentucky Folklore Record, VI (1960), 73. Collected by Jan Harold Brunvand from tapes made by Pleas C. Wilson of Bond, Kentucky in 1959. The editor of the journal adds a parallel told "in the medical department at Capadachino Air Base, Naples, Italy, in 1945. The jest was often related as an opinion on the available ladies of the town— D. K. W. [Wilgus]."

* * *

"We didn' get anything that Christmas ..."

I've cut three a four sets a barn logs f'r diff'rent men, an'-uh we use t' split a lot a rails, I wuz quite a rail-splitter, I went ... to the woods on Chris'mas Day in eighteen eighty three when I wuz jus' twelve years ol' an' made a hunnerd rails by myself ... I had a good smite, at it 'course I didn' have th' strength of a man but I, I had a small maul, my father made me, and-uh my father's in bed sick 'n' couldn' to t' town, we didn' get anything that Chris'mas 'tall, I b'lieve I did too get a ... there wuz a neighbor woman gave ... me a, a little black duck-legged hen, f'r gettin' her a, goin' t'th', some branch somewhere 'n' gettin' her about a gallon of sand. They use sand t' scrub th' floors with, they sprinkle 'at sand on th' floor 'n' take a mop, big mop made out a shucks, and-uh scrub, scour, the, th' floor wi' that sand, 'at 'd get it white y'know ... an' get ev'thing off, all 'e grease 'n' ev'thing like 'at come up. An' she gave me that little ol' duck-legged hen, an' I walked t' ... Erlington a town not very far away, 'bout, prob'ly three-four miles, an' sol' at' hen f'r twenty cents, an' bought me a harmonica, a we called 'em French harps then, an' 'at's all I had f' Chris'mas. An' I went to the woods on Chris'mas Day, took my axe an'-uh a wedge an'-uh a maul an' went to the woods an'made a hunnerd rails 'at day, split a hunnerd rails ... eighty-fo' years ago.

Source

Tennessee Folklore Society Bulletin, XXXIV (September 1968), 79. From an interview with George W. Mitchell, age 96, of Thomaston, Georgia, conducted by Kay L. Cothran in 1967. For details see the note on "A Pound Supper on Valentine's Day," p. 77.

* * *

Long Lasting Christmas Trees

Keeping Christmas Alive

A month after Christmas, it *still* looks a lot like Christmas on some country roads in Bucks County [Pennsylvania.]

Drive along River Road north of New Hope and, in the early evening, the occasional bush or small tree still stands lit, bright and white, in the occasional front yard.

Drive along Point Pleasant Pike, north of Doylestown, and a single lighted Christmas tree can be seen through a darkened living-room window.

Drive up Route 413 toward Pipersville and, even on a sunny afternoon, candles sit lit in every window of an old stone home.

The lights, in bush and tree and home, mark no religious moment.

The Christian religious season ended on Jan. 6—Epiphany, the last of the 12 days of Christmas.

Instead, some see the lights as the last lingering embers of December's secular celebrations.

"It's so dreadful" on those death-gray days that dominate January, Susan Pfeiffer said earlier this week, standing outside her home.

Until January dies each year, she keeps electric candles lit in all her windows in her home near Pipersville, where the woods and fields are the barren brown of winter.

"I think I've done it ever since I got married and moved here, 10 years ago," she said.

For far longer, Hazel Castree has let the sense of Christmas linger.

Castree lives on Groveland Road in Plumstead Township, 40 miles north of Center City and about a mile from Pfeiffer. And there, tradition stretches all the way back to 1944.

"We've gotten into the habit of leaving it up until the first of February," Castree said the other day, standing in her living room, admiring her still-green Christmas tree.

This year, she won't take it down until a week later than usual.

A friend is in Australia and has asked to see this year's tree, even though she won't be back until Feb. 7. So, Castree said, "I'll leave it up till she gets home."

It is no ordinary Christmas tree.

It is filled with birds' nests from Pennsylvania and Mississippi and Arizona, with glass and metal birds from Germany and Czechoslovakia, from Mexico and India.

It has a few lights, too.

"I got 150 new ones this year," she said.

And why the birds?

"This is an almost-70 acre farm," she said, where "we had horses and used to go out riding.

"And, in the wintertime after the birds had left the nests, we would collect them, from trees on our place."

"We had a doctor who did a lot of riding, and he would collect them for me. Children at school would collect them."

But why, each year, let it last so long?

"It takes at least 16 hours to set it up," a day or two before Christmas each year, she said. "There are over 300 birds in there . . .

"That's why I don't take it down—lots of effort to get it up."

And like the landscape painter that she once was, she considers the tree an effort that she wants her friends to enjoy— even her friends on the other side of the world.

In the village of Point Pleasant, on the Delaware River north of New Hope, the small tree outside the home of Nora and Jim Kelly is still strung with white pin lights.

"My husband has been ill, so he just hasn't gotten around to taking them down," Nora Kelly told a visitor the other evening.

"Because my wife likes them up," Jim Kelly called down, from his sickbed upstairs.

Jim Kelly is a retired artist, Nora Kelly owns a New Hope gift shop known as the Jacaranda Tree and so, she suggested, they have a taste for decoration.

But the outside tree isn't the only one that gets to stay bright long after Christmas.

The indoor tree came down only a little while ago, Nora Kelly said, and if her husband had his way, "the tree would be up until next Christmas."

She said it as if she wouldn't mind if it did.

Source

Philadelphia Inquirer, January 28, 1989. By staff writer Walter F. Naedele.

* * *

Christmas and Non-Christians

In the Cobble Hill section of Brooklyn, a Christmas tree may help light Santa's way to the house of Kaid and Fatima Almontaser. The Almontasers are Moslems.

In Mount Vernon, N.Y., St. Nick may admire the origami on the tree prepared by Satomi Higashi, with a little help from her husband, Nobuyoshi. The Higashis are Buddhists.

In Los Angeles, Santa Claus is expected at the home of Alan Rachins and his wife, Joanna Frank, who play Douglas and Sheila Brackman on "L.A. Law," the NBC-TV series. Mr. Rachins and Ms. Frank are Jewish.

None of these parents celebrate Christmas as a religious holiday, yet all want their children to enjoy the romance of the season and to feel in step with much of the rest of the country.

Not everyone agrees with their approach, however. In Tacoma, Wash., for example, Rabbi Richard Rosenthal tells his 300-member Reform congregation that "Christmas is not for Jews." In Brooklyn, a Jehovah's Witness from Crown Heights teaches her sons to accept being different, even at Christmas, which is just another day for Witnesses.

Such varied strategies highlight this generation of parents' conflicting attitudes about coping with Christmas. In many neighborhoods, the holiday takes center stage for a month and is almost unavoidable. It also poses a particular dilemma for parents who remember the pain of being different when they were children but take comfort in their own adult religious beliefs.

Mr. Rachins, 45 years old, recalled feeling isolated from his friends at Christmas. Today, although his 5-year-old son, Robbie Rachins, is still too young to feel such discomfort, he and his parents will greet the holiday with a ceiling-high tree and a gathering of friends. Carols will be sung, and Mr. Rachins and Ms. Frank may read "A Visit From St. Nicholas" to their son.

As in the Rachins-Frank household, Mrs. Higashi, 33, a homemaker, and her husband, 50, a martial-arts instructor, celebrate Christmas as much for themselves as for their children, Shintaro, 3, and Mie, 2. The family attends a Buddhist temple on Sundays, and there the children learn about their culture and meet other Japanese youngsters. But Mrs. Higashi said that they were also Americans and that Christmas was more than a religious holiday. "It's a custom of the United States," she said, adding that she did not want her children to feel "left out at such a fun time."

That attitude is criticized by the Jehovah's Witness, a 31-year-old hair stylist who, to protect her family's privacy, asked that her name not be used. She said her children must live without Christmas, in keeping with her church's beliefs. "We don't try to hide the fact that we're different," she explained. "We are trying to be different, and we have to be up front about that."

In the hair stylist's case, her 11-year-old son is forbidden to participate in Christmas-related activities, including parties at school. When these occur, he sits apart from his classmates. The isolation, he said, did not upset him, since God would reward his steadfastness with a life after death. "I keep it up, and I won't die," he said.

Mr. Almontaser, 47, came to the United States from Yemen in 1965. A co-owner of the Near East Restaurant in Cobble Hill, he said that despite the traditional Moslem aspects of their lives, the five of his six children who live in the United seemed comfortable with themselves and with American society.

Still, Mrs. Almontaser, 43, wears a robe and veil, and Mr. Almontaser and his brother Abdullah pray daily at the nearby Islamic Mission of America mosque. The Almontaser children, who range in age from 5 to 17, study the Koran, attend mosque weekly and visit Yemen each summer. But they also exchange gifts among themselves and with Christian friends, and Ali, 13, recently decorated his own two-foot vinyl tree. "As an American, I have feelings for Christmas," he said. . . .

Mensah Wali, 45, of Brooklyn observes Kwanza, an African-American holiday that extends from Dec. 26 to Jan. 1 and honors blacks of African-American ancestry. The name, Kwanza, is Swahili for "the first fruits of the harvest."

Mr. Wali has been teaching his children about Kwanza. "It reflects important principles, such as unity among blacks, self-determination, sharing workloads and responsibilities and creativity," he said.

Many blacks, he said, have replaced Christmas with Kwanza: "It has become an alternative for black parents who don't know what to say to their kids."

A transportation coordinator for the New York City Board of Education, Mr. Wali is the father of JaJa, 10, and Namyamka, 9. He said that if his children insist on celebrating Christmas, "it won't be a problem—when they say they want to be more like other kids, they'll be paying their own rent."

Paula McNabb, 42, a psychotherapist who is the mother of Michael, 7, and Katie, 3, said that while it can be comforting for a child to understand who he is, a sense of being different and separate can cause dangerous feelings. "They can last into adulthood and cause low self-esteem," she said.

Ms. McNabb, and her 43-year-old husband, Dennis, also a psychotherapist, are Catholics who live and work in a predominantly Jewish neighborhood in Great Neck, L.I. Two years ago, Mrs. McNabb said, Michael wanted to celebrate Hanukkah. She encouraged him to learn about the holiday and to participate in some Hanukkah customs, such as making the toy tops called dreidles.

Source

New York Times, December 16, 1987. By Brenda Lane Richardson. Copyright © 1987 by The New York Times Company. Reprinted by permission.

The Twelve Days of Christmas
December 25-January 6

Christmastide extends from the anniversary of the birth of Christ, officially established as December 25 by the Western church, to the Feast of the Epiphany twelve days later, which celebrates the manifestation of Christ to the gentiles in the persons of the Magi. This joyous period was popularly called the Twelve Days. It includes New Year's Day, traditionally a time when midwinter fertility rites were performed as the season moved from barren winter toward burgeoning spring. The Romans, for instance, who began their year on January 1, introduced it with the notorious Saturnalia in honor of Saturn, the god of agriculture. During this week-long festival license prevailed. The Twelve Days also embraced more somber religious occasions such as the anniversary of the martyrdom of St. Stephen and the Massacre of the Innocents. But even these are overlaid with festivity, and generally speaking the time is one of revelry, mumming, the exchange of gifts, and feasting, with vestiges of pre-Christian fertility magic such as decoration with evergreens, kisses under the mistletoe, and lighting new fires. In short, the events and customs usually associated with Christmas are spread across the Twelve Days. Epiphany, January 6, was the first day on which Christmas was observed for centuries by many Christians, and hence is sometimes called "Old Christmas" to distinguish it from the holiday that falls on December 25.

"The Twelve Days of Christmas": A Rhyme

This rhyme, once in use as a carol, has been very popular in New England, where it circulated in numerous variants [before it became nationally known as a Christmas song]. The following version was obtained from Miss Nichols (Salem, Mass., about 1800):

Twelve Days of Christmas

The first day of Christmas my true love sent
  to me
A parteridge [sic] upon a pear tree.
The second day of Christmas my true love
  sent to me
Two Turtle doves and a parteridge upon a
  pear tree.
The third day of Christmas my true love sent
  to me
Three French hens, two Turtle doves, and a
  parteridge upon a pear tree.
The fourth day of Christmas my true love
  sent to me
Four Colly birds, three French hens, two
  Turtle doves, and a parteridge upon a pear
  tree.
The fifth day of Christmas my true love sent
  to me
Five gold rings, four Colly birds, three
  French hens, two Turtle doves, and a par-
  teridge upon a pear tree.

The sixth day of Christmas my true love sent
  to me
Six geese a laying, five gold rings, four Colly
  birds, three French hens, two Turtle doves,
  and a parteridge upon a pear tree.
The seventh day of Christmas my true love
  sent to me
Seven squabs a swimming, six geese a laying,
  five gold rings, four Colly birds, three
  French hens, two Turtle doves, and a parteridge upon a pear tree.
The eighth day of Christmas my true love
  sent to me
Eight hounds a running, seven squabs a
  swimming, six geese a laying, five gold
  rings, four Colly birds, three French hens,
  two Turtle doves, and a parteridge upon a
  pear tree.
The ninth day of Christmas my true love sent
  to me
Nine bears a beating, eight hounds a running, seven squabs a swimming, six geese a
  laying, five gold rings, four Colly birds,
  three French hens, two Turtle doves, and a
  parteridge upon a pear tree.
The tenth day of Christmas my true love
  sent to me
Ten cocks a crowing, nine bears a beating,
  eight hounds a running, seven squabs a
  swimming, six geese a laying, five gold

rings, four Colly birds, three French hens, two Turtle doves, and a parteridge upon a pear tree.

The eleventh day of Christmas my true love sent to me

Eleven lords a leaping, ten cocks a crowing, nine bears a beating, eight hounds a running, seven squabs a swimming, six geese a laying, five gold rings, four Colly birds, three French hens, two Turtle doves, and a parteridge upon a pear tree.

The twelfth day of Christmas my true love sent to me

Twelve ladies a dancing, eleven lords a leaping, ten cocks a crowing, nine bears a beating, eight hounds a running, seven squabs a swimming, six geese a laying, five gold rings, four Colly birds, three French hens, two Turtle doves, and a parteridge upon a pear tree.

Source

Journal of American Folklore, XIII (1900), 229-30. Contributed by Pamela McArthur Cole of East Bridgewater, Massachusetts. Her source was "Miss Lydia R. Nichols of Salem, Massachusetts (now deceased)" and is from "the earliest memory of the reciter, about 1800." The word "Colly" probably means "coal-black." Colly is British dialect for grime or soot. For Christmas season counting songs, see p. 460.

* * *

"The Twelve Days of Christmas"

Numerology in the "Twelve Days" Carol

The recently popular carol, "The Twelve Days of Christmas," which is presumably of medieval origin, contains a charming example of medieval numerological wit. In our day numerological fancies are so out of style that it is perhaps necessary to point out in wholly prosaic terms the exact nature of the witticism.

It is to be noted that on the first day the true love gave one gift (a partridge in a pear tree), on the second day he gave three gifts (two turtle doves and a partridge in a pear tree), etc., so that on the twelfth day he gave seventy-eight fanciful gifts. Since on each xth day, he gave the sum of the first x natural numbers, a convenient formula for the sum of these superficially senseless gifts is:

$$S = \sum_{i=1}^{n} \left(\frac{x_i(x_i+1)}{2} \right)$$

where "S" denotes the sum of the gifts, where the large sigma denotes the operation of summation over 1, 2,..., n cases, where "x+7i" denotes the number of the day and where "n" denotes the total number of days.

When this formula is applied to the case of n equals 12, as in the carol, it turns out that the giving is far from senseless for the lady has received exactly 364 gifts—enough to last until next Christmas. A modern might ask, "What about the 365th day?"; but I am sure that to the medieval mind there was no need for a gift from a mortal giver on Christmas Day itself.

Source

Journal of American Folklore, LXXII (1959), 348. The calculation is that of William H. Riker, Lawrence College, Appleton, Wisconsin.

* * *

"The Twelve Days of Christmas"

"Twelve Days" in a Hospital Emergency Room

On the twelfth day of Christmas
Central sent to M.E.H.
Twelve 'terns a 'flailing
Eleven blades a 'cutting
Ten grumes a 'scratching
Nine turkeys seizing
Eight pelvics waiting
Seven psychs a 'screaming
Six stabs a 'swearing
Five P.I.D.s
Four D.O.A.s
Three flail chests
Two "H" O.D.s
and a gomer in the D.T.s

For the benefit of readers unfamiliar with medical argot, Central Emergency [in San Francisco] has sent the following to Mission Emergency Hospital: Twelve interns are flailing about, that is, acting in a frantic way to no useful purpose. Eleven surgeons are performing with scalpels. Ten grumes (extra filthy gomers) are scratching to relieve their itching. Nine turkeys are having or are pretending to have seizures. Eight women are waiting to have pelvic examinations. Seven psychotic patients are screaming. Six victims of stabbing are cursing. Five women have pelvic inflammatory disease. Four individuals are brought in "Dead on Arrival." Three individuals are brought in with flail chests, that is, with crushed rib cages. Two drug users who overdosed with heroin are admitted. A gomer suffering from delerium tremens is the first to enter the emergency room, a fact which signals the importance of the gomer in hospital life. [It is explained that " 'gomer' appears to be the most common term in hospital argot for an unkempt, unsavory, chronic problem patient."]

Source

Journal of American Folklore, XCI (1978), 572-73. This parody was collected in 1977 by Victoria George, a licensed vocational nurse, from staff personnel of the San Francisco General Hospital Emergency Room. It is known to have been written by two nurses. She and her collaborator, Alan Dundes, cite it because "it contains a number of examples of hospital folk speech," their main concern.

The Goblins of the Twelve Days

... They [expatriated Greeks in Massachusetts] will tell about the *Callicandjari,* the goblins who appear during the Twelve Days, between Christmas and Epiphany. They will tell about the woman who neglected to strew ashes about the foundations of the house and so the *Callicandjaros* came and sat on the chimney when she was preparing her fried cakes; how he called down a little doggerel to her—full of Turkish jabber and Greek phrases—threatening to break her frying pan if she did not give him a cake. They tell of how another woman carelessly spoke out loud her plans for kneading bread; how a *Callicandjaros* heard her, and jumped on to her wooden bread-trough as she was carrying it to the village bakery; how he led her a dance about the village all night, till the cock crowed and freed her.

Source

Folk-Lore, XLVII (1936), 300. Collected by Dorothy Demetracopoulou Lee in 1934-35 from persons of Greek origin in Boston, Massachusetts, and its environs. Her purpose was "to evaluate the influence of emigration and immigrants on the folklore itself and on the attitudes of the expatriated Greeks toward it."

* * *

Twelve Days Weather

Call Christmas January, and the next eleven days will foretell the weather of each month of the new year.

Source

Journal of American Folklore, XXXI (1918), 208. From a collection of "present-day superstitions" by Ethel Todd Norlin. Her informant was Mr. Robinson, age 58, of Scottish descent, of La Harpe, Hancock County, western Illinois, where he was born.

* * *

Belsnickles and Shanghais

I wish to record a folk custom of the Christmas and New Year season, now extinct, which formerly existed in the Shenandoah Valley of Virginia. During the period between Christmas and New Year, bands of young people, about fifteen to twenty years of age, went about in disguise visiting neighbors. Those going about in the evening, dressed in various kinds of makeshift disguise, were known as "belsnickles" and those going about in the daytime, frequently dressed like clowns, were called "shanghais." I am of the opinion that the activities of shanghais were limited to New Year's day and the day before New Year's, but of this I am not sure.

At the time I was acquainted with these sports (during the first quarter of the present century), the shanghais did nothing much except ride about on horseback sometimes shouting or attracting attention to themselves by foolish antics. Belsnickles, travelling about in the evening, on

approaching a house they wished to visit usually called out in falsetto voices until they attracted the attention of the inmates. There was no set pattern of behavior, but usually some of the mummers represented a family group of husband, wife (made very buxom by means of padding), and child. Some time was spent in trying to discover who the persons disguised were, the attempt resulting in a struggle to remove the false face of the mummer. After the visitors had removed their masks, they would ordinarily be served cider and cake.

This custom appears to have had a more definite form in the nineteenth century. An uncle of mine, who left Virginia about 1900, told me that he remembered nothing about belsnickling, but did remember riding around with others on horseback on New Year's day wearing a clown's cap or something of the kind, and doing foolish things outside the houses such as jumping on and off their horses. They were given cider and cake at the houses where they stopped, though they did not enter. He also remembered that a man of about eighty years who lived nearby shot off a gun a number of times at midnight on New Year's eve.

Source

Journal of American Folklore, LXXI (1958), 164. Reported by Ruth H. Cline. The specific area is Weyer's Cave, Augusta County, Virginia. Cf. "Belsnickels among the Pennsylvania Dutch," p. 444. For shooting guns New Year's Day, see "Philadelphia Mummers Parade," p. 4, and on Christmas, "Christmas Shooters," p. 448.

* * *

Holiday Riddles and Rhymes

Another favorite pastime at the ranch, especially among the elders, was the telling of riddles. Within the riddles was a certain wisdom which the ranchers understood. According to my mother, these riddles, or *adividanzas,* always popped out at any gathering, large or small; but especially were they recited on Christmas and New Year's Day when the families would gather to eat tamales and other dishes. "Anyone could say them if they were smart enough to learn them from books that had them," she said. Grandfather said that the riddles were just handed down through the years, and that they could also be found in books. Recently I found a small booklet of riddles published in Mexico City. It seems that the Mexican people still enjoy themselves with them as did the people at the ranch long ago. The riddle about the ring, which is related later, was the only one familiar to me. But my mother had heard some of them said in other ways.

The following are some of the riddles that my grandfather has related to me:

Soy de cutise blanco	I am of white skin
De corazón negro	Of black heart
Que retorciones me hacen	Twistings are made on me
Que a veces me matan.	Sometimes they kill me.
	Answer: A cigarette.

Barbas coloradoas	Red beard
Rodillas para atras	Back-sided knees
Cara de cuerno	Face of horn
Tú lo seras.	Is what you are.
	Answer: A rooster.

Blanco fué mi nacimiento	White was my birth
Me pintaron de colores.	I was painted with colors.
He causado muchas muertes	I have caused many deaths
Y he enpobrecido senores.	And I have made men poor.
	Answer: A deck of cards.

Soy quien me miran nomas	I'm what you only see
Que todo lo mío doy	That everything of mine I give
Pero sin rascarme atras	But without scratching my back
Porque entonces nada soy.	Because then I'll be nothing.
	Answer: A mirror.

Tres pajaros en un palo	Three birds on a branch
Y tres hombres tirando	And three men shooting
Cada uno mató el suyo	Each one killed his
Y dos se fueron volando.	And two flew away.
	Answer: "Cada uno" was the name of one man. He got his bird and the other two flew away.

From a niece of my grandfather came this one:

Retorción, retorción	A turn, a turn
Cuida la casa como un león.	Guards the house like a lion.
	Answer: Key to a house.

From my mother came these two:

Redondito, redondón	Round—very large or small
Que no tiene tapa ni tapón.	Has no cover or stopper.
	Answer: A ring.

Patio barrido, patio regado	Swept patio, watered patio
Sale un viejito muy empinado.	Comes out an old, bent man.
	Answer: The *metate*.

The last riddle needs a little explanation. The *metate* is the kitchen utensil used by the Mexican people for grinding and rolling corn into corn meal for tortillas. As the women gather the corn meal or *masa*, they sweep it across the surface of the *metate* and as they sweep it across they carry along whatever milk has come out of the fresh corn, thus watering the *metate* as they sweep it with the meal. A *metate* does not have a level surface. One end is low while the other is tilted upward, making it look like an old, bent man.

A favorite *adividanza* of mine is the one about the hawk and the doves. I first heard it from my grandfather as a young child. It was one of the hardest riddles he ever gave us young children. He always ended up by giving us the answer—thirty-six; even recently, when he again related it to us, he had to supply the answer. I resorted to the modern way of calculation—algebra—to get the answer; but my grandfather's method is generally the same in theory. In Spanish the riddle goes like this:

> *Pasa un gavilán volando*
> *Y viendo unas palomas en un ramo dice:*
> *"Adiós, palomar de cien palomas!"*

> *Oyéndolo le contesta el dueño:*
> *"Con estas, y otros tantas como estas,*
> *Y la mitad de estas, y cuarta parte de*
> *Estas, y usted, Señor Gavilán, se completan*
> *las cien palomas. Dime, ¿cuántas palomas*
> *son?"*

Translated:

> A hawk flies by
> And seeing some doves on a branch he says:
> "Goodbye, brood of one hundred doves!"
> Hearing him, the owner answers:
> "With these, and another as many as these, and one-half of these, and one-fourth of these, and you, Mister Hawk, make up the one hundred doves. Tell me, how many doves are there?"

Source

Publications of the Texas Folk-Lore Society, XXXI (1962), 151-53. Collected by Rosalind Gonzalez who learned them from members of her family when she was a child living at La Esperanza Ranch from about 1910 to 1920. The ranch was in the Lower Rio Grande Valley. Most of them she heard from her grandfather, born near Donna, Texas. They were in oral tradition at least from the late nineteenth century until the 1940s.

* * *

Another Holiday Riddle

A calf was born in the Christmas,
Died in the Spring,
An' didn't live to see New Year.

Answer: Died in a spring of water befo' New Year.

Source

Journal of American Folklore, XXXIV (1921), 35. Riddle number 73 collected by Elsie Clews Parsons in 1920 from black school children in Aiken, South Carolina. She reports that it was also recorded from a white woman in South County, Rhode Island.

* * *

Under the Mistletoe

It is proper to kiss a girl:

Under the mistletoe, from December 25 to January 1.

Source and Comment

Journal of American Folklore, XXXVI (1923), 13. This prim New England version of an English custom, dating from the early seventeenth century, was collected by Martha Warren Beckwith from "college girls," discreetly unnamed, at Vassar. A parasitic evergreen, mistletoe (the golden bough) was sacred to the Druids and in Scandinavia considered an emblem of peace. Because of its pagan associations, it was not a permissible decoration in English churches. It was once believed to be a cure for sterility.

St. Stephen's Day

December 26

St. Stephen, the first Christian martyr, was stoned to death for blasphemy. Little is known about him, but he was probably a Greek Jew who converted to Christianity. He is the patron saint of Hungary and of stonecutters. In England, St. Stephen's Day is also Boxing Day. Boxes placed in churches for donations to charity are opened, gratuities for services rendered during the year are distributed, and children go from house to house asking for contributions much in the way they do on Halloween in America. Boxing Day is not observed in the United States.

Saint Stephen and Herod

St. Stephen and Herod

St. Stephen was a serving man
In Herod's royal hall.
He serv-ed him with meat and wine
That doth to kings befall.

He was serving him with meat one day,
With a boar's head in his hand,
When he saw a star come from the East
And over Bethlehem stand.

St. Stephen was a righteous man
And in his faith was bold.
He was waiting for the birth of Christ
As by the prophets told.

He cast the Boar's head on the floor
And let the server fall.
He said, "Behold a child is born
That is better than we all."

Then quickly he went to Herod's room
And unto him did say.
"I am leaving thee, King Herod,
And will proclaim thy wicked ways."

Mr. Edwards [*the informant*] added October 16, 1934, "The song tells that Herod became excited with doubt and said that if such a thing were possible, even the capon on the platter before him would rise up and crow. When the capon thereupon *did* rise up and crow, Herod had Stephen stoned to death." A few weeks later Mr. Edwards recalled the following fragment:

"What aileth thee, Stephen?
What aileth thee?
Do you not like the meat and drink
As served in Herod's hall?"

(He knew that the cock crew the moment Christ was born. It was in the dish before the king when it crew.)

"The men took Stephen and led him away
        ... ere the end of the day."

Source and Comment

First cited in *Vermont Historical Society Proceedings,* VII (1939), 74; later printed in Helen H. Flanders' *Ancient Ballads Traditionally Sung in New England,* Philadelphia, 1960-65, I, 240-41. Collected by Helen H. Flanders from George Edwards who claims to have learned this song from his father. However, it is so rare in the United States that his variant may come from a printed source. Edwards's version is much like the text in Francis J. Child's *English and Scottish Popular Ballads,* 5 vols., Boston, 1882-98, #22, which dates from the fifteenth century. Originally in this pseudo-biblical legend, Herod tells the Wise Men that it is as impossible for the Messiah to have been born as it would be for the roast capon on a plate before him to crow, whereupon the roast capon rises from the plate and crows "*Christus natus est*" ("Christ is born"). In later versions, Stephen displaces the Wise Men.

Kwanza

December 26-January 1

Meaning "first fruits" in Swahili, Kwanza is a traditional African celebration which has been adopted by many American blacks. In characteristic thanksgiving fashion, many Africans celebrate the first harvest of their crops with singing, dancing, and feasting. African-Americans find in Kwanza not only the opportunity to re-establish community ties, but also the chance to re-establish their links to an African past.

A Celebration of Blackness

TRADITIONAL SYMBOLS OF KWANZA

MKEKE = straw mat to represent a foundation

MAHINDE = corn plant to symbolize growth

KINARA = candleholder with seven candles

(one for each Kwanza principle)

MATUNDA = first fruits of the harvest

KIKOMBE = unity cup used to toast and praise the ancestors

ZAWADI = gifts of love for the children (watoto)

COLORS OF KWANZA

RED
...represents the struggle of the black people.

BLACK
...represents the beauty of the black people.

GREEN
...represents growth, the symbol for new life.

PRINCIPLES OF KWANZA

(expressed with African proverbs)

UMOJA (oo-MOH-jah) = unity

(When spider webs join together, they can tie up a lion)
—*Ethiopian proverb*

KUJICHAGULIA (koo-gee-CHAH-goo-lee-ah) = self determination

(No matter how full the river, it still wants to grow)
—*Zairean proverb*

UJIMA (OO-GEE-mah) = to work together

(When two elephants fight, only the grass will suffer)
—*Nigerian proverb*

UJAMAA (oo-jah-MAH-ah) = to share with others

(A brother is like one's shoulder)
—*Somalian proverb*

NIA (NEE-ah) = purpose

(He who learns, teaches)
—*Ethiopian proverb*

UUMBA (koo-OOM-bah) = creating beauty

(A tall tree is the pride of the forest)
—*Nigerian proverb*

IMANI (ee-MAH-nee) = faith in yourself and in the beauty of blackness

(He who cannot dance says the drum is all bad)
—*Ashanti proverb*

Source and Comment

Information provided by Cora Burns Forcell, Librarian-in-Charge, Black Resource Center, Los Angeles. Letter dated August 24, 1988, and leaflet published by the Afro-American Resource Center in Compton, California.

Kwanza is celebrated for seven consecutive days. A candle is lit each day and the traditional symbols are displayed on the mat or Mkek. Discussions of the meanings behind each principle of Kwanza are held and blackness is celebrated through storytelling, drama, and poetry. On the final day a thanksgiving feast at which children receive gifts and elders are honored is held. This is called Karamu. See also "Christmas and Non-Christians," p. 472 and cf. "Thanksgiving," p. 396.

Kwanzaa in Detroit

Lee Thomas lit a green candle, then turned to face his family.

"The principle of today is *nia*," he said. "*Nia* is purpose. The purpose of my life is to do the best I can for my fellow man."

Nia, he explained, is from the East African language of KiSwahilia. It also represents one of the seven principles of the African-American holiday known as Kwanzaa (first fruits).

Kwanzaa, which started about 20 years ago in Los Angeles, is beginning to spread throughout Metro Detroit, Thomas said.

This year the seven-day Kwanzaa tradition began Dec. 26 and will end tonight [January 1]. Each day focused on a principle or basic value. In addition to *nia*, Kwanzaa celebrates *umoja*, unity; *kujichagulia*, self-determination; *ujima*, collective work and responsibility; *ujaama*, cooperative economics; *kuumba*, creativity; and *imani*, faith.

During the weekend, the Thomases—Lee, his wife, Sheryl, and their daughters Khalia, 12, and Shaura, 9—dressed in flowing African garments and gathered around the dining room table in their Detroit home. One by one, they recited their intentions for the new year and lit several of the seven candles.

The seventh candle will be lit tonight, signifying the end of Kwanzaa. Also, a special ceremony is planned that often includes storytelling, poetry recitals and gift exchanges.

"It is not an African holiday. It's American, but it is based on African tradition," Sheryl Thomas said. "It's a relatively new holiday that has become more socially accepted in the last 10 years.

"We started observing it because we like the principles. In Kwanzaa, you are perpetuating a positive self-image and our children need that."

One of the first principles is unity, *umoja*. "When you think about our race, we need unity. We've never had a tradition that is both historical and contemporary, something we can pass on to our children," she said.

But, for most, Kwanzaa hasn't replaced Christmas.

"We sent Kwanzaa cards and we sent Christmas cards" she said. "We're Christian so we celebrate both."

Source

Detroit News, January 1, 1990. By Denise Crittendon, staff writer. For a family celebration of Kwanza, see "Christmas and Non-Christians," p. 472. Reprinted with the permission of the *Detroit News*, a Gannett newspaper, copyright 1990.

Childermas or Holy Innocents' Day

December 28

Childermas or Holy Innocents' Day commemorates the anniversary of Herod's slaughter of the infants in his efforts to kill the Infant Jesus. In many parts of Western Europe it has become a day when children are allowed to play tricks on their parents. In Mexico it is the equivalent of April Fool's Day.

Chilmer's Day

The [Maryland] Negroes have seized upon many European superstitions, which, now changed, exist as survivals; as that of "Chilmer's Day," or Holy Innocents'. No work can be begun that day. They will work late the night before to begin a new piece, rather than start it the next day. Their "Animal Christmas," when the cattle kneel in their stalls at midnight, on Old Christmas Eve, is a survival of an ancient belief.

Source

Journal of American Folklore, XI (1898), 12. Reported by Mrs. Waller R. Bullock of Baltimore, Maryland. Chilmer's Day is Childermas. For the Old Christmas belief about kneeling cattle, see p. 34.

Playing Tricks on Holy Innocents' Day

Around Christmas time, especially on December 28, the Day of the Holy Innocents, which is Mexico's April Fool's Day, the people at the ranch [on the Mexican border] diverted themselves by playing tricks and saying the following little verse to the one who was fooled:

Inocente palomita,	Innocent little dove,
Que te dejaste engañar,	That let yourself be fooled
Sabiendo que en este día	Knowing that on this day
Nada se debe prestar.	Nothing should be lent.

Source and Comment

Publications of the Texas Folk-Lore Society, XXXI (1962), 150. Reported from childhood memory by Rosalinda Gonzalez in her article, "Work and Play on a Border Ranch." She lived on a family ranch near Edinburgh, Texas, until about 1920.

On the *Dia de los Inocentes,* Mexican children attempt to trick or play on the innocence of others by borrowing money or small objects from them and giving in exchange some worthless trifle. Sometimes they taunt their victims with the jingle above.

The Candlewalk

Eve of January 1

The custom of watching the old year out and the new year in on the night of December 31 is English, and John Wesley, the founder of Methodism, encouraged its religious observance. In America, watch-night services were first held in 1770 at St. George's Methodist Church in Philadelphia. The custom has continued, though it is now called a "candlelight" service.

The Candlewalk

A strange and fascinating remnant of the ancient midwinter fire-festival appears today, celebrated regularly on Christmas Eve and New Year's Eve by the black people of rural Bladen County [North Carolina]. I first heard of this celebration, known as the Candlewalk, or the Watch, several years ago around Christmas time. A great deal of what I heard, I am sure, had been embellished with gossip and speculation. But the fact remains that the Candlewalk does exist in 1971 and that it is a genuine local legend, as well as an actual happening in many Negro churches. I have not witnessed a Candlewalk as it is celebrated in the rural black churches, nor a Watch as it is celebrated in the African Methodist Episcopal Zion Church of Elizabethtown.

I have been told that in some cases the Candlewalk is a highly exclusive ritual, closed to white people and nonbelievers. In other cases, this is not so. It depends on the tradition and the mood of the particular congregation involved....

One type of the Candlewalk occurs on Christmas Eve at a small rural church in the northeast part of Bladen County, in the general vicinity of Highway 242. This is the Bladen Lakes State Forest area, dotted with numerous bays and shallow marshes, thickly forested in oak, pine, and much scrub vegetation. There are several good-sized lakes, some of them state-owned: Salter's Lake, Little Singletary, Sugg's Mill Pond, and Jones Lake. The bleached-white sand contrasts sharply with the dark waters of the lakes and swamps. Many clumps of trees are festooned with grey Spanish moss. And many trees bear huge growths of mistletoe in their top branches.

... It is a place to which people withdraw in order to learn something of the mysteries of nature and life.

This symbolic withdrawal is seen in the Candlewalk. The women of the church, including young girls and children, congregate in a band and go deep into the forest surrounding the church. The men and boys of the church are forbidden to follow. If they do so, they are in peril of a death-curse. Local legend says that this period of withdrawal into the forest is a period of sexual indoctrination, a fertility rite, and is also wrapped up with the adoration of the Holy Virgin Mary, mother of Jesus.

After some time in the swamp-forest, the women, all bearing lighted torches or candles in uplifted hands, return in a single-file procession. They sing or chant ancient hymns. Local legend insists these songs and chants are done in Swahili, or a kind of pidgin English understandable only to the congregation. The men and boys gather inside the church to await them. And as each woman enters the church, she extinguishes her torch or candle.

A similar walk or Watch is celebrated in the African Methodist Episcopal Zion Church of Elizabethtown. According to Mrs. Sallie Powell, a mathematics instructor in the Elizabethtown High School and member of the A.M.E.Z. Church, the Watch generally takes place on New Year's Eve. The people then gather at the church for a traditional "watching the old year out" and "waiting the new year in" vigil. The chief participants dress in white or wrap white sheets around themselves, carry one lighted candle, and march around the church sanctuary twice, singing as they go. The Watch ritual can be accompanied by other religious ceremonies, such as a sermon, prayers, and hymn-singing; but the most important part takes place in the hour before midnight: the hour of the death and rebirth of the year. Joy and gratitude are expressed at the rebirth of the year. It is considered a gift of heaven to be allowed a new year of life.

Source

North Carolina Folklore Journal, XIX (1971), 153-54. Described by Heather R. Miller of Elizabethtown, North Carolina. Her sources are an informant cited in the text and "both black and white people, all natives of the Bladen Lakes area" of whom she "asked many questions."

Indexes

Subject Index

Holiday entries are indicated by boldface type

Ethnic and Geographic Index

Collectors, Informants, and Translators Index

Song Titles and First Significant Lines Index

Indicates musical score in text

Song Titles and First Significant Lines Index

507

Motifs and Tale Types Index

Motifs

References are to the motifs listed by Stith Thompson in his *Motif-Index to Folk Literature,* 6 vols., Bloomington, Ind.: Indiana University Press, 1955

Tale Types

See Aarne, Antti, and Stith Thompson, *The Types of the Folktale,* 2d. ed., Folklore Fellows Communications, No. 184, Helsinki: Academia Scientiarum Fennica, 1961